MW01244810

# BK ENGLISH

COMMUNICATION SKILLS IN THE NEW MILLENNIUM

LEVEL IV

J.A. Senn
Carol Ann Skinner



BK

PROJECT MANAGER
**Sandra Stucker Blevins**

EDITORIAL DIRECTOR
**Sandra Mangurian**

EDITORIAL STAFF
**Marianne Murphy**
**Marlene Greil**
**Donna Laughlin**
**Susan Sandoval**
**Vicki Tyler**
**Catherine Foy**
**Michelle Quijano**
**Elizabeth Wenning**
**Cheryl Duksta**
**Margaret Rickard**

PRODUCTION DIRECTORS
**Gene Allen**
**Pun Nio**

PHOTO RESEARCH AND PERMISSIONS
**Laurie O'Meara**

ART AND DESIGN
**Pun Nio**
**Leslie Kell**
**Rhonda Warwick**

PRODUCTION
**Bethany Powell**
**Isabel Garza**
**Rhonda Warwick**

COVER
**Leslie Kell Designs**
**Pun Nio**
**Images © Photodiscs, Inc.**

EDITORIAL AND PRODUCTION SERVICES
**Book Builders, Inc.**
**Gryphon Graphics**
**Inkwell Publishing Solutions, Inc.**
**NETS**



Printed in the United States of America.

ISBN 1-58079-113-1 2 3 4 5 6 7 RRD 06 05 04 03 02 01

# Senior Consultants

**Tommy Boley, Ph.D.**
Director of English Education
The University of Texas at El Paso
El Paso, TX

**Deborah Cooper, M.Ed.**
Coordinating Director of PK-12 Curriculum
Charlotte-Mecklenburg Public Schools
Charlotte, NC

**Susan Marie Harrington, Ph.D.**
Associate Professor of English, Director of Writing, Director of Placement and Assessment, and Adjunct Assistant Professor of Women's Studies
Indiana University-Purdue University, Indianapolis
Indianapolis, IN

**Carol Pope, Ed.D.**
Associate Professor of Curriculum and Instruction
North Carolina State University
Raleigh, NC

**Rebecca Rickly, Ph.D.**
Department of English
Texas Tech University
Lubbock, TX

**John Simmons, Ph.D.**
Professor of English Education and Reading
Florida State University
Tallahassee, FL

**John Trimble, Ph.D.**
University Distinguished Teaching Professor of English
The University of Texas
Austin, TX

# Contributing Writers

**Jeannie Ball**

**Grace Bultman**

**Richard Cohen**

**Elizabeth Egan-Rivera**

**Laurie Hopkins Etzel**

**Bobbi Fagone**

**Lesli Favor**

**Nancy-Jo Hereford**

**Susan Maxey**

**Linda Mazumdar**

**Elizabeth McGuire**

**Shannon Murphy**

**Carole Osterink**

**Michael Raymond**

**Duncan Searl**

**Jocelyn Sigue**

**Lorraine Sintetos**

**James Strickler**

**Diane Zahler**

**Kathy Zahler**

# Critical Readers

**Alan Altimont**
St. Edwards University, Austin, TX

**Larry Arnhold**
Deer Park High School, Houston, TX

**Kerry Benson**
Santa Fe Public School, Santa Fe, NM

**Elaine Blanco**
Gaither High School, Lutz, FL

**Peter Bond**
Randolph School, Huntsville, AL

**Christina M. Brandenburg**
Rancho Cotate High School, Rohnert Park, CA

**Paulette Cwidak**
John Adams High School, South Bend, IN

**Jean Ann Davis**
Miami Trace High School, Washington Courthouse, OH

**Terri Dobbins**
Churchill High School, San Antonio, TX

**Susan Drury**
Springwood High School, Houston, TX

**David Dunbar**
Masters School Dobbs Ferry, NY

**Chuck Fanara**
Brebeuf Preparatory, Indianapolis, IN

**Jason Farr**
Anderson High School, Austin, TX

**Marilyn Gail**
Judson High School, San Antonio, TX

**Gary Gorsuch**
Berea High School, Berea, OH

**Monica Gorsuch**
MidPark Sr. High School, Cleveland, OH

**Donna Harrington**
Churchill High School, San Antonio, TX

**Janis Hoffman**
John Adams High School, South Bend, IN

**Norma Hoffman**
John Adams High School, South Bend, IN

**David Kidd**
Norfolk Academy, Norfolk, VA

**Kate Knopp**
Masters School, Dobbs Ferry, NY

**Suzanne Kuehl**
Lewis-Palmer High School, Monument, CO

**Michelle Lindner**
Milken Community High School, Los Angeles, CA

**Stephanie Lipkowitzs**
Albuquerque Academy, Albuquerque, NM

**Sarah Mannon**
Hubbard High School, Chicago, IL

**Linda Martin**
Valley Torah, North Hollywood, CA

**Lisa Meyer**
Lincoln High School, Tallahassee, FL

**Karla Miller**
Durango High School, Durango, CO

**Stacy Miller**
Santa Fe High School, Santa Fe, NM

**Eddie Norton**
Oviedo High School, Oviedo, FL

**Diana Perrin**
Johnson High School, Huntsville, AL

**William Petroff**
R. Nelson Snider High School, Ft. Wayne, IN

**Linda Polk**
Deer Park High School, Houston, TX

**Lila Rissman**
Suwanne Middle School, Live Oak, FL

**Carmen Stallard**
Twin Springs High School, Nickelsville, VA

**Jeanette Taylor**
Rye Cove High School, Duffield, VA

**Eric Temple**
Crystal Springs Uplands School, Hillsborough, CA

**Sherry Weatherly**
Denton High School, Denton, TX

# Exploring Writer's Craft

## CHAPTER 1 Using Your Writing Process



## CHAPTER 2 Developing Your Writing Style

## Chapter 3 Writing Different Kinds of Paragraphs

## Chapter 4 Writing Effective Compositions

# D Achieving Writer's Purpose

## Chapter 5 Personal Writing: Self-Expression and Reflection

## Chapter 6 Using Description: Observation

## Chapter 7 Writing Stories, Plays, and Poems

## Chapter 8 Writing to Inform and Explain

## CHAPTER 9 Writing to Persuade

## Chapter 10 Writing About Literature

# Applying Communication Skills

## Chapter 11 Summaries and Abstracts

## Chapter 12 Research Reports

## Chapter 13 Communication for Careers and College

## Chapter 14 Communication in the World of Work

# Chapter 15 Speeches, Presentations, and Discussions

# Communication Resource

## Chapter 16 Vocabulary

## Chapter 17 Reference Skills

# Grammar

## Chapter 1 The Parts of Speech

## CHAPTER 2 The Sentence Base

## CHAPTER 3 Phrases

## Chapter 4 Clauses



# Usage

## Chapter 5 Using Verbs

## CHAPTER 6 Using Pronouns

## CHAPTER 7 Subject and Verb Agreement

## CHAPTER 8 Using Adjectives and Adverbs

# Mechanics

## Chapter 9 Capital Letters



## Chapter 10 End Marks and Commas

## CHAPTER 11 Other Punctuation

# Spelling

## CHAPTER 12 Spelling Correctly

# Study and Test-Taking Skills Resource



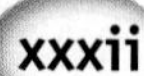

# COMPOSITION

CHAPTER 1

# Using Your Writing Process

**E**very writing project creates challenges—even for experienced writers. Inspiration may help get you started, but rarely is it reliable. A writing process itself, though, usually is. As a strategy for generating ideas, your writing process can help you get started and keep you on target through drafting, revising, editing, and publishing.

You have probably experienced how this writing process does not always proceed in a straight line. Writers usually have to return to some earlier stages in order to address a particular concern. As a writer, your progress through these stages will vary. Sometimes you will move slowly at the beginning as you explore various topics. At other times you will begin with a clear topic and barely pause at the early stages. Later, though, in the revising stage, you may go back to explore the topic further. The passage from idea to finished essay is rarely a direct, straightforward journey.

## *Reading with a Writer's Eye*

Eudora Welty began learning about the power of words as a child, literally at her mother's knee. In *One Writer's Beginnings* she describes how she learned to love the sound and feel of words as she spoke, how she connected the sounds with printed text, and how, together, they produced meaning for her. As you read Welty's memoir, think about your own first attempts to interpret the written word.

FROM

# One Writer's Beginnings

*Eudora Welty*

Learning stamps you with its moments. Childhood's learning is made up of moments. It isn't steady. It's a pulse.

In a children's art class, we sat in a ring on kindergarten chairs and drew three daffodils that had just been picked out of the yard; and while I was drawing, my sharpened yellow pencil and the cup of the yellow daffodil gave off whiffs just alike. That the pencil doing the drawing should give off the same smell as the flower it drew seemed part of the art lesson—as shouldn't it be? Children, like animals, use all their senses to discover the world. Then artists come along and discover it the same way, all over again. Here and there, it's the same world. Or now and then we'll hear from an artist who's never lost it.

In my sensory education I include my physical awareness of the *word.* Of a certain word, that is; the connection it has with what it stands for. At around age six, perhaps, I was standing by myself in our front yard waiting for supper, just at that hour in a late summer day when the sun is already below the horizon and the risen full moon in the visible sky stops being chalky and begins to take on light. There comes the moment, and I saw it then, when the moon goes from flat to round. For the first time it met my eyes as a globe. The word "moon" came into my mouth as though fed to me out of a silver spoon. Held in my mouth the moon became a word. It had the roundness of a Concord grape Grandpa took off his vine and gave me to suck out of its skin and swallow whole, in Ohio.

This love did not prevent me from living for years in foolish error about the moon. The new moon just appearing in the west was the rising moon to me. The new should be rising. And in early childhood the sun and moon, those opposite reigning powers, I just as easily assumed rose in east and west respectively in their opposite sides of the sky, and like partners in a reel they advanced, sun from the east, moon from the west, crossed over (when I wasn't looking) and went down on the other side. My father couldn't have known I believed that when, bending behind me and guiding my shoulder, he positioned me at our telescope in the front yard and, with careful adjustment of the focus, brought the moon close to me.

The night sky over my childhood Jackson was velvety black. I could see the full constellations in it and call their names; when I could read, I knew their myths. Though I was always waked for eclipses, and indeed carried to the window as an infant in arms and shown Halley's Comet in my sleep, and though I'd been taught at our diningroom table about the solar system and knew the earth revolved around the sun, and our moon around us, I never found out the moon didn't come up in the west until I was a writer and Herschel Brickell, the literary critic, told me after I misplaced it in a story. He said valuable words to me about my new profession: "Always be sure you get your moon in the right part of the sky."

**M**y mother always sang to her children. Her voice came out just a little bit in the minor key. "Wee Willie Winkie's" song was wonderfully sad when she sang the lullabies.

"Oh, but now there's a record. She could have her own record to listen to," my father would have said. For there came a Victrola record of "Bobby Shafftoe" and "Rock-a-Bye Baby," all of Mother's lullabies, which could be played to take her place. Soon I was able to play her my own lullabies all day long.

Our Victrola stood in the diningroom. I was allowed to climb onto the seat of a diningroom chair to wind it, start the record turning, and set the needle playing. In a second I'd jumped to the floor, to spin or march around the table as the music called for—now there were all the other records I could play too. I skinned back onto the chair just in time to lift the needle at the end, stop the record and turn it over, then change the needle. That brass receptacle with a hole in the lid gave off a metallic smell like human sweat, from all the hot needles that were fed it. Winding up, dancing, being cocked to start and stop the record, was of course all in one the act of *listening*—to "Overture to *Daughter of the Regiment*," "Selections from *The Fortune Teller*," "Kiss Me Again," "Gypsy Dance from *Carmen*," "Stars and Stripes Forever," "When the Midnight Choo-Choo Leaves for Alabam," or whatever came next. Movement must be at the very heart of listening.

Ever since I was first read to, then started reading to myself, there has never been a line read that I didn't *hear*. As my eyes followed the sentence, a voice was saying it silently to me. It isn't my mother's voice, or the voice of any person I can identify, certainly not my own. It is human, but inward, and it is inwardly that I listen to it. It is to me the voice of the story or the poem itself. The cadence, whatever it is that asks you to believe, the feeling that resides in the printed word, reaches me through the reader-voice. I have supposed, but never found out, that this is the case with all readers—to read as listeners—and with all writers, to write as listeners. It may be part of the desire to write. The sound of what falls on the page begins the process of testing it for truth, for me. Whether I am right to trust so far I don't know. By now I don't know whether I could do either one, reading or writing, without the other.

My own words, when I am at work on a story, I hear too as they go, in the same voice that I hear when I read in books. When I write and the sound of it comes back to my ears, then I act to make my changes. I have always trusted this voice.

# Thinking as a Writer

## Analyzing the Process of Becoming a Writer

Eudora Welty talks about how children use all of their senses to discover and learn about the world that surrounds them.

- Think about how Welty makes you, the reader, understand her experience of learning as a young child by connecting sensory details with specific memories and experiences. What kind of language does she use to accomplish this? How did these experiences help her to develop her inner voice and shape her to become a writer?

## Connecting Sound to Memory

Oral Expression

Welty remembers back to her mother singing and the family Victrola. These sounds influenced Welty's inner voice.

- Form a group with two or three other students. Take a few minutes to think collectively of well-known childhood songs, or even theme songs from popular television shows that you watched as a child. Recite the lyrics or sing the songs aloud. Then take turns talking about what memories each of these songs conjures up for you.

## Creating from Visual Cues

Viewing

The close association Welty made between the daffodil and pencil and paper was essential to her creative writing process.

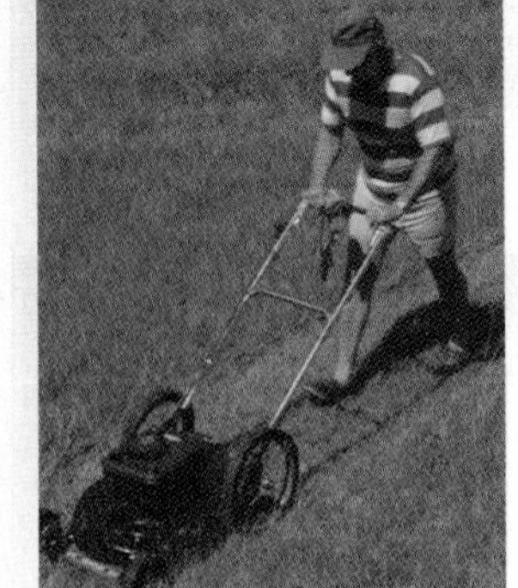

- With a partner, look at the photograph of grass being cut. What kinds of associations can you make with this image? Which of your senses does this image stimulate?
- Write your answers, and then compare them to those of your partner. How are your responses similar? How are they different?

# Refining Your Writing Process

"It is a great thing to write," declared French novelist Gustave Flaubert. "To be no longer yourself, but to move in an entire universe of your own creation." As a writer, you too can fashion and inhabit the world of the written word. The writing process is what makes it possible.

Your **writing process** is the recursive series of stages that you proceed through when developing your ideas and discovering the best way to express them.

As a writer, you will plan, draft, revise, and polish your writing. These stages of the writing process remain the same no matter what the writing task. However, the path you take will vary from writing project to project. You will take detours, travel back and forth, and linger on certain steps. As a writer, you are also a mapmaker, creating your route from idea to finished piece.

In this chapter you will learn a number of strategies that are helpful at different stages of the writing process. Each stage of the process has its own distinct characteristics. The diagram on the following page illustrates and describes these stages and shows the relationship between them. As you review the diagram, think about the stages you go through when you create a piece of writing. Keep the various strategies in your repertoire so that you can call on them when you need them.

You will notice this icon throughout this book as you work through the stages of different kinds of writing. It will remind you to save your work in a convenient place so you can return to it and continue to work on it, or simply use it later for inspiration. You may wish to use a manila folder or a pocket in your binder to store your work. If you work on a computer, you may want to create a folder on your hard drive, along with a backup copy.

## Process of Writing

The following diagram illustrates the elements, or processes, writers use as they create. Notice that the diagram loops back and forth. This looping shows how you often move back and forth among various stages of writing instead of going step-by-step from beginning to end. You can go back to any stage at any point until you are satisfied with the quality of your writing.

**Prewriting** includes the invention you do before writing your first draft. During prewriting you find and develop a subject, purpose, and audience, collect ideas and details, and make a basic plan for presenting them.

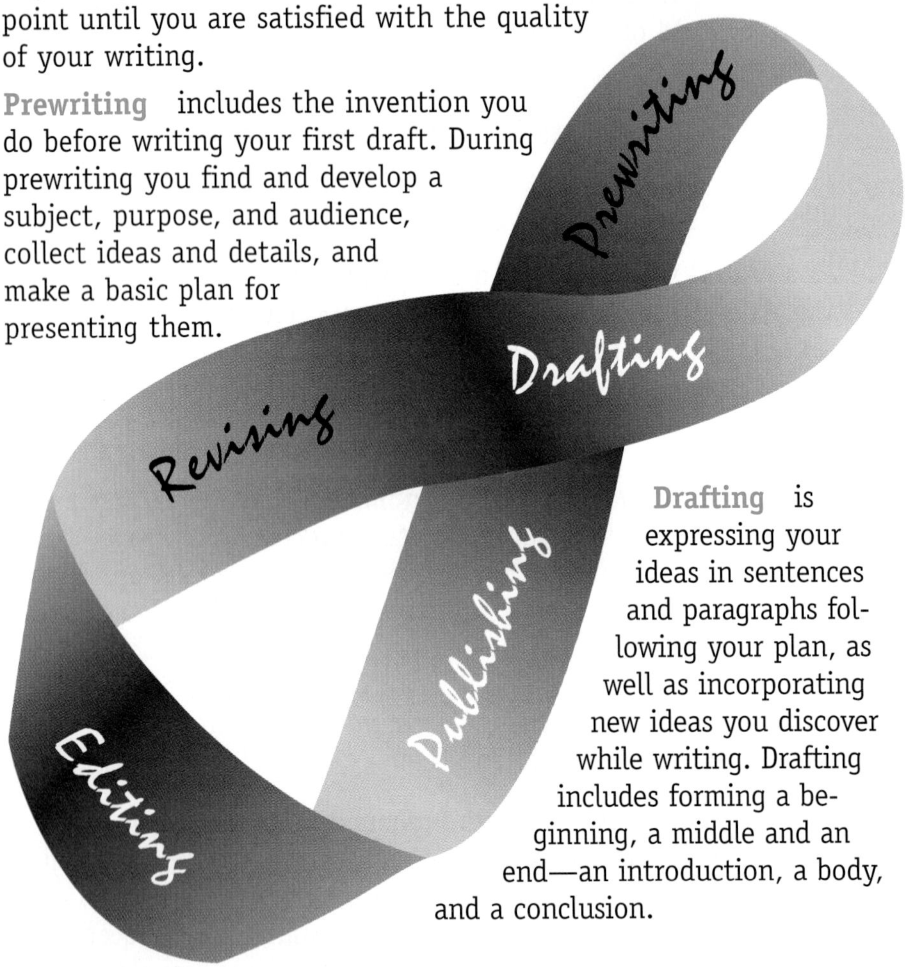

**Drafting** is expressing your ideas in sentences and paragraphs following your plan, as well as incorporating new ideas you discover while writing. Drafting includes forming a beginning, a middle and an end—an introduction, a body, and a conclusion.

**Revising** means rethinking what you have written and reworking it to increase its clarity, smoothness, and power.

**Editing** involves checking and reworking sentences and sentence structure. It also includes looking for, and correcting, errors in grammar, usage, mechanics, and spelling, and then proofreading your final version before making it public.

**Publishing** is sharing your work with others in an appropriate way.

## Your Writer's Portfolio

As you begin your writing this term, think of yourself as an apprentice learning a craft. Ideally, with each new essay you write, you come a step closer to developing your own composing processes. A good way to track your progress is to keep a **portfolio**—a collection of your work that represents various types of writing and your progress in them.

PORTFOLIO

This icon represents a reminder throughout the book to place your work in your writing portfolio. When you add a piece to your portfolio, be sure to date it so you will later have an accurate chronological record of your work. You will also be reminded in the chapter-closing checklists to consider including the essay you have been working on in your portfolio, but the choice is always yours, possibly with guidelines from your teacher.

As you work through the writing assignments in your class, you will be asked to do many kinds of writing—sharing a story from your own life, writing a poem, urging a solution to some social problem, describing the loveliest scene you have ever observed, researching a complex topic, writing a letter, and much more. No single assignment could show all your skill as a writer, but collecting various essays along the way can demonstrate the range of your growing skills.

You may be asked to write evaluations of your progress as a writer throughout the year. You should include these evaluations in your portfolio along with your various writings. This activity will help you examine both your successes as a writer and the areas of your work that could be stronger still. At the term's end, you may be asked to write a "cover letter" for your portfolio in which you summarize its contents, explain why you included each piece, and evaluate your overall progress, strengths, and weaknesses.

Throughout the writing activities, you will be asked to take "Time Out to Reflect." Reflecting on your experience as a writer will give you an opportunity to develop your process even further. Use these reflections to think about what you have learned, what you want to learn, and how you can continue to grow as a writer. Your written reflections are suitable additions to your portfolio.

On the following page are a few guidelines for including work in your portfolio.

### Guidelines for Including Work in Your Portfolio

- Date each piece of writing so you can see where it fits into your progress.
- Write a brief note to yourself about why you have chosen to include each piece—what you believe it shows about you as a writer.
- Include unfinished works if they demonstrate something meaningful about you as a writer.

## Prewriting

Writing Process

The process of putting words on paper begins long before those words are actually written. By the time you take pen in hand for your first draft, you should know what you want to say and how you want to say it. **Prewriting** includes all of the thinking, imagining, and planning that precedes the writing of the first draft. Much of your prewriting may occur only in your mind. Prewriting can also mean creating lists, notes, outlines, and graphic organizers as you (1) clarify your subject; (2) consider your occasion, audience, and purpose; and (3) organize your material.

Keep a writing folder as you work through the following prewriting strategies. At some later time you may be able to use many of the ideas.

## Strategies for Finding a Subject

Writing ideas lurk everywhere—in a memory, a friendship, a conversation, an ocean wave. Following are strategies that will help you tap this vast store of writing subjects. As you become acquainted with the many different techniques, you will be able to determine which will work best for you.

**Taking an Inventory of Your Interests** You write more effectively when you write about a subject you personally find interesting. As a result, you should begin your search for ideas with your own interests. The following activity will help you explore those interests.

## Practice Your Skills

### *Exploring Your Interests*

**Complete each statement thoughtfully and completely.**

1. The most interesting projects I have completed are . . .
2. In the next five years of my life, I would like to . . .
3. Courses that I would like to take are . . .
4. As President the issues that I would deal with are . . .
5. I disagree with my friends about . . .
6. My favorite places are . . .
7. I would like to know more about . . .

**Freewriting** The search for subjects involves uncovering some of the countless ideas that lie buried in your mind. Freewriting is one way to dig deeply into your mind. **Freewriting** means writing down anything and everything without pausing to reflect. You can begin writing about anything, or you can do **focused freewriting,** in which you use a word, a topic, or a question to start your mind moving. Write sentences, fragments, unconnected words—whatever encourages your thoughts. Following is an example of how freewriting led one student writer to the subject of performing before audiences.

**Model: Freewriting from Scratch**

Here I go again—writing, writing to find something to write about. My cat? The importance of recycling? What I'd do if I were president? I've written about that stuff a million times—lots of other stuff too. Any topics left? Sure doesn't feel like it. Think I'm all written out by now. But—got to come up with something. My teacher says any word, any object, any anything can make you think of a subject. All right. Try some words . . . plant—light bulb—glue—enemy—stormy—crowd—audience. Audience. Well, there are all the plays I've been in. But I've written about those many times. Audience. Audiences still make me nervous. Stage fright is a horror. But I've learned to deal with it. How?

By freewriting on the subject of movies, this student found himself writing about films based on works of literature.

**MODEL: Focused Freewriting**

*Movies. What can I write about movies? What do I know about movies? Well, movies are a huge part of our culture. Who writes movie scripts? Now that would be a great job. How do they think of all of the plots? A lot of films are based on historical events or periods. A surprising number of films are based on novels or other works of literature. How many film versions of Shakespeare's plays, for example, have been made? Or Jane Austen's novels? Many. I know that there are lots of movies made from modern literature, too. I can write a lot on this subject.*

## PRACTICE YOUR SKILLS

### *Freewriting*

**Timing yourself, freewrite for five full minutes. Let your thoughts pour out onto the page. Do not even lift your pen or pencil from the paper. If you find your thoughts drying up, then just note that fact. Write anything, as long as you keep writing. When your time is up, place your notes in your writing folder for possible later use.**

### *Freewriting with a Focus*

**Freewrite for five minutes on one of the following subjects about the future. Focus on that subject in the beginning, but let your thoughts take you in whatever direction they want to go. When you finish, be sure to place your notes in your writing folder for possible later use.**

**1.** transportation

**2.** different means of communication

**3.** fashions and hairstyles

**4.** scientific discoveries

**5.** occupations

## Across the Media: Breaking Stories

When two writers begin to write, even if they're writing on the same subject, there is little chance that they'll go about their task in the same way. This is also true of camera operators, recording artists, or video editors. Each person puts his or her own stamp on the project, and the result is a complete work—each done in a slightly different way.

Compare the accounts of a news story across different media. As a class, choose an important story that is certain to be covered across several media. Then form groups of about five students to study the treatment of the story as it appears in one of these media: radio, television, newspapers and newsmagazines, magazines such as *People* or *Life*, and the Internet. Use these questions to guide the inquiry.

**Questions for Analyzing News Coverage**

- What medium are you studying?
- How much coverage is provided? Is it a comprehensive or a sketchy treatment? If the treatment is sketchy, what might be the reason?
- To what extent does the medium provide pictures or video of the event?
- Is there an interview with a central figure? If so, who? What information might not have been available otherwise?
- What kind of impact does the story have?
- How did your version of the story affect the individuals in your group?

When the analysis is complete, have spokespersons from each group report their findings to the rest of the class. To close the study, hold an informal class discussion comparing the quantity and quality of the coverage offered by each medium.

**Keeping a Journal** A **journal** is a notebook in which you make daily entries about your experiences, observations, and reflections. When you write in your journal, you should date each entry. In doing so, you will be chronicling certain stages of your life or, in the case of your writer's journal, of your progress as a writer. You will find this record of your personal feelings and observations to be a rich source for writing ideas. Like the writers quoted below who kept such daily records, you'll find a journal an excellent repository for all sorts of opinions, feelings, and comments. In fact, there can be nearly as many uses for a writer's journal as there are writers.

A journal can recount daily events:

March 13, 1728
In the afternoon our hunters went forth, and returned triumphantly with three brace of wild turkeys.

—*William Byrd, Virginia colonist*

It can be a place to express feelings:

October 16, 1660
After that I went by water home, where I was angry with my wife for her things lying about, and in my passion kicked the little fine basket, which I bought her in Holland, and broke it, which troubled me after I had done it.

—*Samuel Pepys, British diarist and historian*

It can be a place to reflect on life:

May 1, 1943
If I just think of how we live here, I usually come to the conclusion that it is a paradise compared with how other Jews who are not in hiding must be living.

—*Anne Frank, student and Holocaust victim*

A journal can even be a place to make a joke:

July 6, 1762
[about a comment made earlier to a Scottish guest] "But Sir, [I said] I believe the noblest prospect that a Scotsman ever sees is the road which leads him to England!"

—*James Boswell, British writer and biographer*

A journal is a safe place to ask questions and look for answers:

> September 28, 1942
> Why do grownups quarrel so easily, so much, and over the most idiotic things? Up till now I thought that only children squabbled and that that wore off as you grew up.
> —*Anne Frank, student and Holocaust victim*

It's also a personal travelogue:

> October 2, 1704
> About three o'clock in the afternoon, I begun [sic] my Journey from Boston to New-Haven; being about two Hundred Mile. My kinsman, Capt. Robert Luist, waited on me as far as Dedham, where I was to meet the Western post.
> —*Sarah Kemble Knight, Boston colonist*

Finally, it's even a great place for complaints about the weather:

> September 21, 1732
> I was sorry this morning to find myself stopped in my career (journey) by bad weather brought upon by a northeast wind. This drives a world of raw unkindly vapors upon us from Newfoundland, laden with blight, coughs, and pleurisies.
> —*William Byrd, Virginia colonist*

## Practice Your Skills

### *Writing in Your Journal*

Every day of your life you are bombarded with other people's words. You hear and read comments from teachers, friends, family, people standing next to you on the bus. You get messages from books and magazines, radio and television, and even popular songs. Of the countless statements that come your way, some undoubtedly will start you thinking. They may excite you or puzzle you, move you or irritate you. Beginning today, write in your **journal** whatever you hear or read that makes an impression. Then write your thoughts about it.

**Keeping a Response Log** Your **journal** is also a good place to write your responses and reactions to literature. Recording what you are learning helps you to clarify what you read and reflect on what you've learned. Try setting aside part of your **journal** for these comments on literature.

### Exploring Literature in a Response Log

**Fiction, Drama, and Poetry**

- Write about a piece of literature, or a script for television or film, exploring the character, the action, the setting, or some other aspect of the medium.

  *You can learn more about literary analysis in Chapter 10, pages C432–C483.*

- Write about the theme, or central message, of a story, poem, or play. If a story addresses peer conflict, for example, you may choose to address this issue in your writing.
- Write about some aspect of a character, such as the character's personality. If a character is often jealous, you may decide to write about the issue of jealousy.
- Write about an aspect of the work that you really enjoyed.

**Nonfiction**

- Decide whether you agree with an editorial in a newspaper, or with an expression of opinion in some other medium, such as a magazine, the radio, or television.
- Comb newspapers and magazines and surf the Internet to find issues or subjects that you could explore and write about.
- Think about biographies and autobiographies you have read. Write about the subject of any of them: What does that person mean to you?

## Practice Your Skills

*Responding to Reading*

**Create a section called *Response Log* about halfway through your journal by attaching a tab onto the side of a page. Then scan the front page of a newspaper. Use the Response Log to list five subjects you could write about.**

**Keeping a Learning Log** A **Learning Log** is another section of your **journal** in which you can jot ideas and material from science, history, math, a foreign language, or any other subject that interests you. One very important function of a Learning Log is to help you identify what you already know about a subject and what you still need to learn about it. Suppose, for example, your class is studying the literature of medieval England. Your entry might look like this:

**MODEL: Learning Log Entry**

A lot of my classmates are moaning and groaning about having to read Beowulf, "The Wanderer," and "The Seafarer." But I love the stuff! Beowulf reminds me of a Superman in leather and fur, grappling with an enemy given to fits of rage. (And I'm someone who can't stand horror movies because they scare me.) How can I get my hands on more medieval literature? I guess the Internet is out—it's not exactly a hot topic. But both St. Louis U. and Washington U. have great medieval collections! Maybe I can get some limited access through school.

## PRACTICE YOUR SKILLS

### *Learning More About a Subject*

**Create another section in your journal, this one called *Learning Log*. (Once again, attach a tab about three fourths of the way through your journal, a little lower than you did when you set up the Response Log.) Then mention a school subject that you enjoy but would like to know more about. Write an entry that summarizes your existing knowledge and mentions what else you'd like to learn. Note where you might be able to find more material on the subject.**

**Creating a Personalized Editing Checklist** A **Personalized Editing Checklist** is a section of your **journal** in which you keep a list of errors that recur in your writing. These may include words you frequently misspell; usage mistakes, such as forgetting to use the possessive case before a gerund; and mechanical errors, such as overusing commas. When you edit an essay, you should read your work against this checklist as well as the standard list in your text.

## Practice Your Skills

*Keeping Track of Errors*

**Create another section at the back of your journal and label it "Personalized Editing Checklist." List some of the errors you routinely make when you write. Later, as you think of them, add others that come to mind. Add to your checklist as you work on the writing assignments in this book.**

## Choosing and Limiting a Subject

Writing gives you the opportunity to know yourself better and to present your ideas and interests to others. You should make the most of this opportunity by writing about subjects you find personally stimulating and challenging. The following guidelines will help you choose such subjects.

### Guidelines for Choosing a Subject

- Choose a subject that genuinely interests you.
- Choose a subject that will interest your readers.
- Choose a subject you can cover thoroughly through your own knowledge or a reasonable amount of research.

**Limiting a Subject** Once you have chosen a subject, you may have to limit it, or narrow it so that it is more manageable. To limit a broad subject, use the following strategies.

### Guidelines for Limiting a Subject

- Limit your subject to one person or one example that represents the subject.
- Limit your subject to a specific time or place.
- Limit your subject to a specific event.
- Limit your subject to a specific condition, purpose, process, or procedure.

The student writer who came up with the broad subject, *performing before audiences,* narrowed that subject in the following way.

**Model: Limiting a Subject**

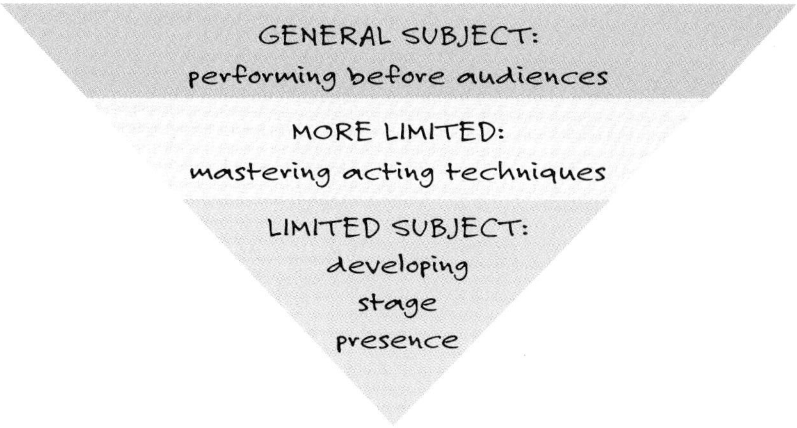

GENERAL SUBJECT:
performing before audiences

MORE LIMITED:
mastering acting techniques

LIMITED SUBJECT:
developing
stage
presence

## Practice Your Skills

### *Limiting a Subject*

**Following the example above for limiting a subject, choose three of the following subjects and limit them.**

**1.** football
**2.** college
**3.** environment
**4.** computers
**5.** contemporary music
**6.** immigration
**7.** Mexico
**8.** movies

## Considering Your Occasion, Audience, and Purpose

Often your writing has a specific purpose, such as completing a school assignment or writing a letter to the editor of a newspaper. At the same time, every piece of writing has a general purpose. **Purpose** is your reason for writing or speaking. For example, the purpose of your school assignment may be to explain something; the purpose of your letter to the editor may be to persuade readers. Whatever your purpose may be for a particular piece of writing, it is important to define it clearly before you begin writing. In successful communication, the purpose of your message is appropriate to both the occasion that prompts it and the audience who will receive it. The following chart lists the most common purposes and forms, although writing purpose can take almost any form in the hands of a creative writer.

| WRITING PURPOSES | POSSIBLE FORMS |
|---|---|
| **Informative**<br>to **explain** or **inform**; to focus on your subject matter and audience | **Factual writing**<br>scientific essay, research paper, business letter, summary, descriptive essay, historical narrative, news story |
| **Creative (literary)**<br>to **create**; to focus on making imaginative use of language and ideas | **Entertaining writing**<br>short story, novel, play, poem, dialogue |
| **Persuasive**<br>to **persuade**; to focus on changing your readers' minds or getting them to act in a certain way | **Convincing writing**<br>letter to the editor, persuasive essay, movie or book review, critical essay (literary analysis), advertisement |
| **Self-expressive**<br>to **express** and **reflect** on your thoughts and feelings | **Personal writing**<br>journal entry, personal narrative, reflective essay, personal letter |

Sometimes writing purposes overlap. For example, you can give people information *and* express your thoughts at the same time. You can write informatively about a place you have visited *and* persuade your audience to visit that place. Being clear about your purpose is important because it will affect many of the writing decisions you make.

**Occasion** is your motivation for composing—the factor that prompts or forces you, as a writer, to decide on your process for communicating. In other words, do you put a message in writing, or do you prepare a speech? Suppose you are applying for a job, which requires responding to questions on an application. In this case, filling out the application is the occasion for writing.

Occasion usually can be stated well using one of the following sentences.

- I feel a need to write for my own satisfaction.
- I have been asked to write this by [name a person].
- I want to write an entry for [name a publication].
- I want to enter a writing contest.

As you plan your writing, you also need to remember the **audience** you will be addressing, or who will be reading your work. What are their interests and concerns? How can you best communicate to this particular audience? For example, if you were writing an explanation of how to make a robot, you would present the steps in a different way and with different language for an eight-year-old than for someone your own age.

### Audience Profile Questions

- Who will be reading my work?
- How old are they? Are they adults? teenagers? children?
- What do I want the audience to know about my subject?
- What background do they have in the subject?
- What interests and opinions are they apt to have? Are there any words or terms I should define for them?

## Practice Your Skills

*Writing for Different Audiences*

**Write two paragraphs that describe an important event of the last 50 years, such as the invention of the Internet. Address your first paragraph to a third-grade student. Address the second paragraph to an adult.**

**Writing Tip**

Make sure the **purpose** of your message is appropriate to the **occasion** that prompts it and the **audience** who will receive it.

## Developing Your Voice

Part of a writer's growth involves the discovery of his or her own distinctive voice and the ability to adapt that individual voice appropriately to different situations. **Voice** in writing is the particular sound and rhythm of the language the writer uses. Voice is an important part of your writing style that has to do with word choice. There may be times when you create or imitate someone else's voice. One example of this is writing dialogue; another is writing from the point of view of a particular narrator. A great writer's voice can and should vary, depending on the subject, audience, occasion, and purpose. In speaking, you probably use a different voice when asking your teacher to clarify an assignment than when rejoicing with a friend about an accomplishment. Similar differences in voice would be appropriate if you were approaching those same tasks on paper. In your journal, you might use one voice when you are in a good mood and another when you are feeling irritable, one voice when recording a personal goal and another when responding to a poem.

## Practice Your Skills

### *Recognizing Writers' Voices*

**Read the following statements, and match each statement to one of the descriptions below. Be prepared to give reasons for your answers. (If you have difficulty deciding which voice is which, read each statement aloud, matching your expression to the feeling created by the words.)**

1. Woman must not accept; she must challenge. She must not be awed by that which has been built up around her; she must reverence that woman in her which struggles for expression. (Margaret Sanger)
2. I think that I shall never see
   A billboard as lovely as a tree.
   Perhaps, unless the billboards fall,
   I'll never see a tree at all. (Ogden Nash)
3. It was involuntary. They sank my boat. (John F. Kennedy in a reply when asked how he became a war hero.)
4. The trouble with being in the rat race is that even if you win, you're still a rat. (Lily Tomlin)

**a.** facetious **c.** sarcastic
**b.** compelling **d.** ruefully humorous

### *Comparing Speaking and Writing Voice*

**Join a classmate and take turns explaining something that interests you or about which you care deeply. Then put in writing what you said. Use the same words and sentence structure you used in conversation. How are your speaking and writing voice similar?**

### *Developing Different Voices*

**Freewrite for three minutes on each of the following scenarios.**

- A co-worker at your after-school job constantly and deliberately tries to get you in trouble with your supervisor. What would you say to him or her to change the situation?

- A new student from another country has just joined your class. He speaks little English, but you understand how hard he is trying to learn. What would you say to encourage him?
- You're usually responsible about returning from after-school or evening dates on time. This evening, however, you deliberately stay out later than you should. What do you say to your parents to explain why you did so?

Reading your work aloud will help you hear whether your writing voice sounds the way you want it to sound. The work becomes a slightly different piece, and you will detect features that you missed in a silent reading.

To evaluate your written **voice**, read your work aloud.

## Strategies for Developing a Subject

Once you have chosen a subject, limited it, and determined your occasion, audience, and purpose, you can move on to fleshing out your ideas with supporting details. **Supporting details** are the facts, examples, incidents, reasons, procedures, or other specific points that back up your main idea and give life and meaning to your subject. The following strategies will help you gather supporting details to develop your subject.

**Observing** **Observing** is one of the best ways to collect information and develop your own view and interpretation of a subject. When you observe, you open all your senses, focusing on one sense at a time and on one detail at a time to describe the sights, sounds, smells, tastes, and feelings associated with your subject. Following are some techniques that will help you use your powers of observation.

### Techniques for Observing

- Be aware of the reason why you are observing. Keep your purpose in mind as you decide what and how to observe.
- Use all your senses. Look, listen, smell, touch, taste.
- Use your mind. Think about what your observations mean or what the details have in common.
- Observe from different viewpoints: near and far, above and below, inside and out, and even upside down.
- Sketch your subject. Make a drawing of what you observe.

Knowing how to collect and organize the information you get in a way that is easy to draw from when drafting is an important part of observing. Taking notes on note cards or in computer files is a convenient way to keep a record of your observations. Following is an example of a note card showing how a student took notes on Eudora Welty's *One Writer's Beginnings*.

*Eudora Welty*

*American*

*Eudora Welty talks about her childhood experiences, including watching the moon rise, listening to music, and listening to her mother singing. She also talks about reading and her beginnings as a writer.*

**SUMMARIES OF MAIN IDEA:**

YOUR NOTES RECORD THE WRITER'S MAIN MESSAGE AND FACTS.

**COMPUTER TIP**

Using the Note Pad feature of your computer, rather than word-processing software, can help you avoid the temptation to format or organize your words. The ideas should then come to you more freely. When you are ready to expand these ideas, any material you keep can be copied and pasted directly into a word-processing program.

## Practice Your Skills

### *Observing*

**Use the preceding guidelines to observe the scene in the picture below. Place yourself in the scene so that you can use all your senses. Then record ten or more details that you could use to describe the scene, including ones that may not be obvious at first. Save your notes in your folder for possible later use.**

### *Gathering Information from Observations*

**Review your journal entries and writing folder for subjects that you can observe in person for the purpose of gathering descriptive details. You may want to do some additional focused freewriting, starting with *When I think about sitting and observing, I think about . . .* Then observe that subject, making notes as you observe. Try to write down at least 25 details.**

**Brainstorming for Details** Brainstorming is another effective way to discover details for an essay, once you have chosen and limited your subject. In **brainstorming**, your goal is to work with a partner or a group of classmates and freely list all ideas related to your subject as they occur to you. Just let them flow from one to another until you have unearthed a large store of ideas.

### Guidelines for Brainstorming

- Set a time limit, such as 15 minutes.
- Write the subject on a piece of paper and ask someone to be the recorder. If your group meets frequently, take turns recording ideas.
- Start brainstorming for details—facts, examples, incidents, reasons, connections, and associations. Since you can eliminate irrelevant ideas later, contribute and record any and all ideas.
- Build on the ideas of other group members. Add to those ideas or modify them to make them better.
- Avoid criticizing the ideas of other group members.

*You can learn more about group discussions on pages C691–C693.*

When you have finished brainstorming, you should get a copy of all the supporting details from the group recorder. Then, from the group list, select the details that are best for your own essay.

Following is part of a brainstorming list made by a small group on the subject of performing.

**Model: Brainstorming List**

Developing Stage Presence

—thrill of being in front of an audience
—awful stage fright sometimes
—need to turn nervous energy into performing energy
—exercise can help
—study the character
—audience's eyes always on actors
—project confidence
—rehearse, rehearse, rehearse
—know lines perfectly
—always need to be "on" when onstage

## Practice Your Skills

### *Brainstorming for Ideas*

**Get together with one or more classmates to brainstorm ideas for a new television series based on a book. Following the guidelines on the previous page, come up with the details of how the show will work, as well as a good name for it.**

**Clustering** A good way to develop a subject while you discover details is to use clustering. **Clustering** is a visual form of brainstorming that is a good technique to use for developing supporting details. Instead of just listing ideas, however, you connect them. Begin with a single word or phrase and then arrange associated ideas around that nucleus, linking the ideas back to the original word or phrase. Continue this process by linking each of the surrounding words, in turn, to other words as they occur to you. In the end you have a diagram that provides you not only with details but also with the paths that connect them. As a result, you can see groups, or clusters, of related details.

### COMPUTER TIP

You can use the drawing tools of your word-processing program to create a customized clustering diagram. Choose the shapes that appeal to you—such as circles, ovals and rectangles—and connect them with the arrows or lines. You can print out the diagram and fill it in by hand, or you can create text-boxes and type text in the figures on your screen.

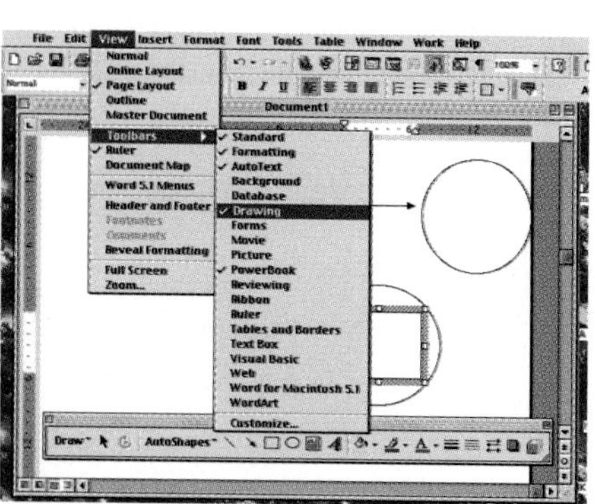


The following is a portion of the cluster developed by the student planning an essay about developing stage presence. Notice how various ideas are clustered together.

**MODEL: Cluster**

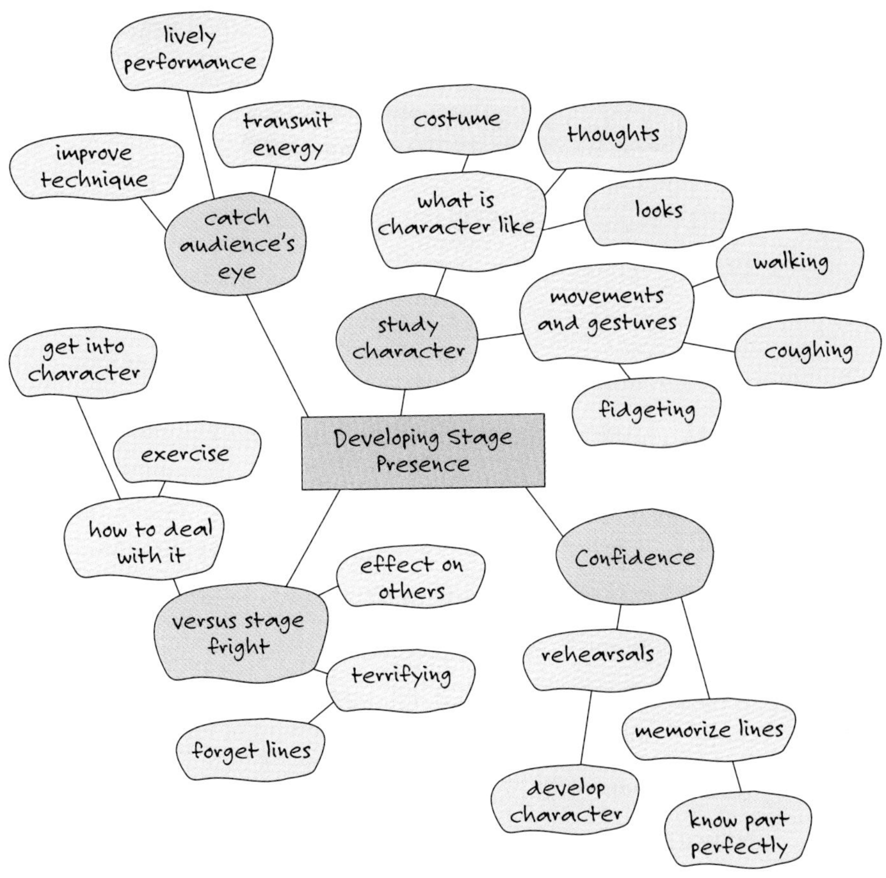


## PRACTICE YOUR SKILLS

### *Using a Cluster Diagram*

**Create a cluster about what you think you will be doing a year from now.**

**Inquiring** To explore a writing topic, you can also use the technique of inquiring—a method that journalists use to gather information. Ask questions that begin with *who, what, where, when, why,* and *how*. For certain kinds of writing, such as narratives and informative pieces, finding the answers to such questions can provide many of your supporting details.

This model shows some questions one writer used as a guide in finding details about early musical instruments. Notice that the writer developed more than one question using *who, what, when,* and *how*.

**MODEL: Inquiring to Develop Supporting Details**

**EARLY MUSICAL INSTRUMENTS**

| | |
|---|---|
| **Who** | played musical instruments in ancient times? |
| **Who** | invented first musical instruments? |
| **What** | are the oldest instruments known? |
| **What** | sounds did the instruments make? |
| **What** | did they look like? |
| **Where** | have ancient instruments been discovered? |
| **When** | were they discovered? |
| **When** | were they created? |
| **Why** | did different instruments develop in different places? |
| **How** | were the instruments made? |
| **How** | were they played? |
| **How** | did ancient instruments evolve into modern ones? |

## PRACTICE YOUR SKILLS

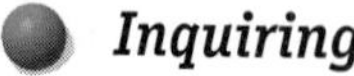

*Inquiring*

**Write a series of questions that would help you develop supporting details on the subject of how viewers can influence television programming. Write at least one question that begins with each of the six question words: *who, what, where, when, why,* and *how*.**

## Recalling

Your own experiences often furnish you with some of the most interesting subjects to write about. As you explore such subjects, you will use the skill of **recalling**. You probably will be surprised to find out how many past experiences, events, and reactions have left lasting impressions in your mind.

Suppose that one of your most vivid memories is your first trip to New York City and that you now want to develop the subject for a class assignment. Focus your thoughts on the subject and think about who was with you. When did you go there? What happened? What sensory details do you recall? A chart like the following might help you focus and recall the details.

MEMORY: FIRST TRIP TO NEW YORK CITY

| | |
|---|---|
| **Who?** | parents, sister, and I visited cousins |
| **When?** | one week last July, hottest days of summer |
| **Where?** | New York City |
| **Events** | toured city, saw Statue of Liberty, Empire State Building, Central Park, Metropolitan Museum, Chinatown |
| **Sights** | tall buildings, crowded streets, theater marquees |
| **Sounds** | car horns, street vendors, sirens |
| **Smells** | pretzels, ethnic foods, raindrops on hot pavement |
| **Reactions** | amazement, curiosity, excitement, sore feet |

### THINKING PRACTICE

**Choose one of the following topics or a topic of your own. Then make a chart like the one above to help you recall your memories.**

- first dance
- first date
- first part-time job after school

## Strategies for Organizing Details

When you are searching for and exploring subjects, you unlock your thoughts and set them free. After you have collected your ideas, however, it is time to give your thoughts focus and structure—to examine the details you have gathered in an organized, logical way so that you can make sense of them.

**Focusing Your Subject** To determine how best to organize your details, you first need to determine your focus. Exactly what do you want to say about your subject? Your answer to this question will become your focus, or main idea.

### Guidelines for Deciding on a Focus

- Look over your supporting details. Think of meaningful generalizations, or general statements, that you can draw from some or all of the details.
- Choose a main idea that holds great interest for you.
- Choose a main idea that suits your purpose and audience.

Think back to the student who wants to write on the subject of performing. After reviewing his prewriting notes, he decided to focus on the best ways to develop stage presence. As a performer in school plays, he is interested in the subject and can say something meaningful about it. His purpose is to write an essay that informs his classmates about something. His main idea suits this purpose, and since all students have participated in performances in some way, his audience is likely to find the subject appealing.

## Practice Your Skills

*Focusing a Subject*

**Review the questions you wrote on page C30 about how viewers can influence television programming. Circle the three questions you think might have the most possibility for expansion into an essay. Choose the one you prefer, and state it as a main idea.**

**Classifying Your Details** The supporting details you collect for an essay are likely to fall into certain categories. As you study your details, some of these categories will become obvious. If you are explaining weather forecasting, for example, some of the details may deal with kinds of weather, some with forecasting methods, and some with forecasting successes and failures. If you are comparing and contrasting the U.S. Congress and the British Parliament, your details will fall into the categories of similarities and differences.

When you classify, be sure to use categories that fit your purpose and main idea. If some details do not fit into any category, discard them. The student writing about stage presence classified his details into two groups: *during rehearsals* and *before performance.*

**Ordering Your Details** Your next step is to order your details so that they progress logically from one to the other. A clear method of organization helps your reader follow and understand the details you present.

**WAYS TO ORGANIZE DETAILS**

| Type of Order | Definition | Examples |
|---|---|---|
| **Chronological** | The order in which events occur | story, explanation, history, biography, drama |
| **Spatial** | Location or physical arrangement | description (top to bottom, near to far, left to right, etc.) |
| **Order of Importance** | Degree of importance, size, or interest | persuasive writing, description, evaluations, explanations |
| **Logical** | Logical progression, one detail growing out of another | classifications, definitions, comparison and contrast |

The order you choose will depend on your writing purpose and your supporting details. For example, for a narrative you would probably choose chronological order, while for a description you might choose spatial order. The writer of the essay on stage presence, whose purpose was to inform, chose a combination of chronological order and order of importance, going from most to least important. The following is the list he made.

**MODEL: Ordering Details**

**During rehearsals**
—develop confidence
—know your part perfectly
—practice movements, gestures as well as script
—study your character
—practice staying in character
—practice reacting to what's happening onstage

**Before performance**
—rechannel nervous energy
—exercise; stretch, shake
—do not practice lines
—get into character

## PRACTICE YOUR SKILLS

*Organizing Details*

**Decide which organizing method would be most suitable for each of the writing subjects listed below. Then write *chronological, spatial, order of importance or degree, logical order,* or *comparison/contrast* after the proper number.**

**1.** differences between European and American schools
**2.** description of night sky on a particular date
**3.** accomplishments of your current United States senator
**4.** the history of the automobile
**5.** thoughts on academic freedom

When you write a draft, you draw together your ideas on paper, pulling your prewriting notes into complete sentences and forming an introduction, a body, and a conclusion. You write more than one draft to assure a worthwhile essay. In your additional drafts, you will be able to look for more ideas, rethink your ideas, or even find a more workable subject. However, even though your first draft is just a preliminary version, it should be in a form that a reader can understand. The following strategies will help you prepare a draft.

### Strategies for Drafting

- Write an introduction that will capture the reader's interest and express your main idea clearly. You may want to return to your introduction at a later stage to evaluate its effectiveness in reaching your audience and addressing your purpose.
- After you write your introduction, use your organized prewriting notes as a guide, but depart from those notes when a good idea occurs to you.
- Write fairly quickly. Do not worry about spelling or phrasing. You will have the opportunity to go back and fix such problems when you revise.
- Stop frequently and read what you have written. This practice will help you move logically from one thought to the next.
- Do not be afraid to return to the prewriting stage if you find that you need some more ideas or need to clarify your thinking. You can always stop and freewrite, brainstorm, or cluster to collect ideas.
- Write a conclusion that drives home your main idea.

The model on the following page shows the first draft of the student's essay about stage presence.

## MODEL: First Draft

~~There are certain perfo Do you~~ Have you ever felt yourself watching a minor character in a play instead of the star? Some actors always ~~hold~~ catch and hold the audience's eye, ~~even if they have~~ no matter how small a part they play. These performers have stage presence. This is a certain something that is transmitted and sent to the audience. Stage presence is not magic. You too can have it. Just work on your technique during rehearsals. Also learn to ~~control~~ channel your emotions at performance time.

~~Be conf~~ Stage presence is based on confidence. Your first and most important step then is to learn your part. Know it as if it was really part of you. Try different deliveries, moves, and gestures until you find just the right ones. Then rehearse them until they come naturally. Another important thing is to ~~work on your movements~~ develop your character ~~you are playing~~ as you rehearse. Think about what the person is like. Practice staying in character every moment. Listen and react to everything that happens onstage. Do that even when you have no lines. Finally, consentrate onthe way you move. Avoid halfway movements. If you grin grin from ear to ear. if you do turn your head, really turn it. Transform yourself into the character so that you behave like the character. When performance time arrives you ~~will~~ can expect to be nervous. Expereinced actors do not try to calm themselves. They draw on their nervous energy instead. That way they can increase their energy level. By the way, avoid the temtation to practice you're lines, especially trouble some ones. Misteaks only will end up making you nervouser. The best way to rechanel your nervus energy is to get into character. Chat with others as your character would walk around as your character would. Another importent strategy is Exercise. Even just a healthy stretch and shake of your limbs, head and body will help.

~~What is Achieving stage presence~~ Stagepresence depends on ~~wer~~ concsciousnes—of your character, of your emotions, and of your audience above all. According to Ms Keller Drama Teacher "There are no small parts, only small actors. When you use the techniques above, you can always be a big actor.

## Practice Your Skills

### *Studying a Draft*

**Write answers to these questions about the student's first draft.**

1. Which part did the writer seem to have the most trouble with? Why do you think that was so?
2. Where did the writer change the order of the details in his prewriting notes? Why, do you think, did he make the change?

### COMPUTER TIP

When using a word-processing program, remember to save your work regularly. Power outages, computer glitches, and human errors do happen, often resulting in lost data. Usually material that has been saved is not lost. Make a habit of clicking on the Save icon whenever you pause in your writing or selecting Save from the pull-down file menu. You can also let your computer do the remembering for you. Just program it to save your work every fifteen minutes.

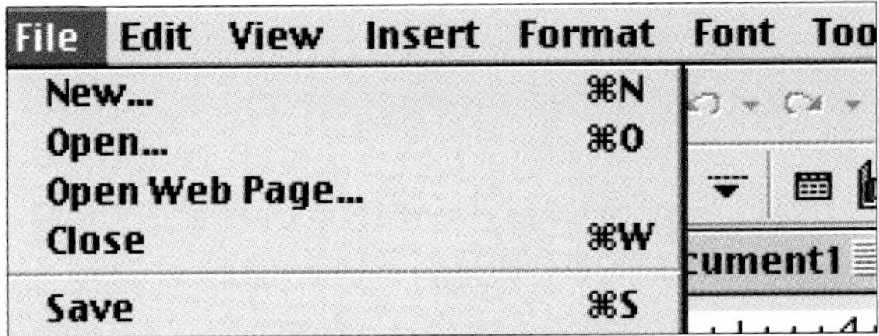


**Drafting a Title** The final step in writing the first draft is to think of a suitable title. A good title will express the main idea of the essay and at the same time catch the reader's attention. Many times words or phrases found within the essay can be used as titles.

## Practice Your Skills

### *Drafting a Title*

**Review the first draft of the essay about stage presence. Then brainstorm a list of five possible titles for the essay.**

Although you can and should be making revisions at every stage of the writing process, your major revising job comes after your first draft. In the revising stage, your purpose is to evaluate and improve your first draft. A helpful technique when revising is to put yourself in your reader's place and ask yourself, "Will my reader understand exactly what I mean?"

Keep in mind that revising is not a one-time procedure—you may feel a need to write a second, third, or even a fourth draft. Of course, if you are able to use a word processor, you will find the task of revising easier and more efficient.

## Revising on Your Own

Your first approach to revising your draft will be self-evaluation. Think about the overall organization and effect and zero in on the smallest details. Put your draft away for a time and then review it once more. Next look at it objectively, as if you were seeing it for the first time. Do you need to refine your subject? Do you need to generate more details? After you have evaluated your draft, you are ready to make whatever changes are needed. Following are some general revision strategies used by experienced writers.

**Adding Ideas** Look over your essay. Have you covered every aspect of your limited subject? Do your ideas seem lively? Are they ideas that will spark people's interest? Are the ideas sound—or do you need to explore the subject in greater depth? If so, you may need to think of new ideas. Try freewriting about the subject or talking it over with someone more knowledgeable than you.

**Adding Details and Information** Do you have enough details to support your main idea? Do you have enough details to make your ideas clear and interesting? Look for places where additional details and information would be helpful.

**Rearranging** Consider carefully the organization of your ideas and facts. Are any ideas out of place? Does one idea lead logically to another so that the reader can easily follow your train of thought?

Would a different order be more effective? If so, rearrange your ideas so that one flows smoothly and logically into another.

**Deleting Unnecessary Words or Ideas** Irrelevant details cloud your ideas. Are there words that are not needed? Have you repeated yourself unnecessarily? Are there ideas that stray from the main point? Delete what you do not need.

**Substituting Words and Sentences** Once again read over your draft. Will any parts of it confuse the reader? If so, think of a clearer way to express the same idea. If any words or phrases sound dull, think of more original ways to say the same thing. Revise your sentences if they sound sound monotonous.

Using a checklist is an excellent way to determine whether or not your draft includes all the qualities of a good essay. You will find evaluation checklists throughout the book, all of which should help as you attempt to explain, reword, reorganize, or otherwise modify your work, walking you through the revising stage.

### Evaluation Checklist for Revising

✓ Did you clearly state your main idea?
✓ Does your essay have a strong introduction, body, and conclusion?
✓ Did you support your main idea with enough details?
✓ Do your details *show* instead of merely tell what you want to say?
✓ Did you present your ideas in a logical order?
✓ Do any of your sentences stray from the main idea?
✓ Are your ideas clearly explained?
✓ Are your words specific?
✓ Are any words or ideas repeated unnecessarily?
✓ Are your sentences varied and smoothly connected?
✓ Is the purpose of your essay clear?
✓ Is your writing suited to your audience?
✓ Is your title effective?

Stage Presence

Have you ever felt yourself watching a minor character in a play instead of the star? Some actors always catch and hold the audience's eye, no matter how small a part they play. These performers have stage presence. ~~This is~~ a certain ^poise and energy^ ~~something~~ that is transmitted ~~and sent~~ to the audience. Stage presence is not magic. ~~You too can have it. Just work~~ ^By working^ on your technique during rehearsals. ~~Also learn to~~ ^and^ channel^ing^ your emotions at performance time. ^, you too can project that special quality when you step onstage.^

Stage presence is based on confidence. Your first and most important step then is to lern your part. Know it as if it was really part of you. ~~Try~~ ^Practice^ different deliveries, moves, and gestures until you find just the right ones. Then rehearse them until they come naturally. Another important ~~thing~~ ^tactic^ is to develop your character as you rehearse. Think about what the person is like ^—how he or she talks, feels, thinks, moves, eats, and sleeps.^ Practice staying in character every moment. ~~L~~isten^ing^ and react^ing appropriately^ to everything that happens onstage ~~Do that~~ even when you have ~~no lines~~ ^nothing to say^. Finally, consentrate onthe way you move. Avoid halfway movements. If you grin, grin from ear to ear. if you do turn your head, really turn it. ^Learn to^ Transform yourself into the character so that you ~~behave like the character.~~ ^automatically walk as the character walks, cough as the character coughs, even fidget as the character fidgets.^

# Practice Your Skills

## Studying a Revision

**Read this revision of the first part of the essay on stage presence. (Remaining errors in spelling, capitalization, and usage will be corrected later.) After you read it carefully, answer the questions that follow.**

**1.** For what reason were the words *and sent* in the first paragraph deleted?

2. Where were details added? Why?
3. Which idea was shifted? Why?
4. Why was the word *thing* replaced with the word *tactic* in the second paragraph? Where was another change like that made?
5. Where were groups of sentences replaced with a single sentence? Why?

### *Revising a Draft*

**The following paragraphs are from the student's model of a first draft on page C36. Rewrite the paragraphs, using the Evaluation Checklist for Revising, page C39, as a guide for making improvements. Ignore any spelling, punctuation, and usage errors for now, as they will be corrected later on.**

When performance time arrives you can expect to be nervous. Expereinced actors do not try to calm themselves. They draw on their nervous energy instead. That way they can increase their energy level. By the way, avoid the temtation to practice you're lines, especially trouble some ones. Misteaks only will end up making you nervouser. The best way to rechanel your nervus energy is to get into character. Chat with others as your character would walk around as your character would. Another importent strategy is Exercise. Even just a healthy stretch and shake of your limbs, head and body will help.

Stagepresence depends on concsciousness—of your character, of your emotions, and of your audience above all. According to Ms Keller Drama Teacher "There are no small parts, only small actors." When you use the techniques above, you can always be a big actor.

## Revising Through Conferencing

No matter how hard you try to distance yourself from your writing, the words and thoughts remain your own. Therefore, as you revise, you may find it helpful to get an objective reaction from someone else. You may want to ask a classmate, a family member, or a friend to read your essay and tell you what works well and what needs improvement. Don't defend your work; just listen. Then think about the comments to revise your draft further.

**Peer Conferencing** When you use peer conferencing, you form a small group with three or four other students and read one another's essays. You then take turns discussing each person's essay, offering praise for what each writer has done well and providing suggestions to make the essay better. No matter which form of conferencing you choose—one on one or small group—the following guidelines will help you get the most out of this revising technique.

### Guidelines for Conferencing

**Guidelines for the Writer**

- List some questions for your classmate. Which aspects of your essay most concern you?
- Try to be grateful for your critic's candor rather than being upset or defensive. Keep in mind that the criticism you are getting is well intended.

**Guidelines for the Critic**

- Read your partner's work carefully. What does the writer promise to do in this essay?
- Point out strengths as well as weaknesses. Start your comments by saying something positive like, "Your opening really captured my interest."
- Be specific. Refer to a specific word, sentence, or section of the essay when you comment.
- Be sensitive to your partner's feelings. Phrase your criticisms as questions. You might say, "Do you think your details might be stronger if . . . ?"

Prewriting Workshop
Drafting Workshop
**Revising Workshop**
Editing Workshop
Publishing Workshop

# Sentences

Although published authors like Eudora Welty sometimes relax the rules of grammar and mechanics, you should try to follow them as closely as possible. At this point in your writing career, you need a strong background in the elements of essays. Later, when you are more confident of your ability to write, revise, and edit correctly, you will have time to experiment with words.

When you edit, you pull together, or integrate, what you know about usage and mechanics skills. As you review the different language skills in each essay chapter, write them in your Personalized Editing Checklist. Then, at the end of the essay section, you will have covered every major language skill in this book.

## Sentence Fragments

A subject and a verb are the foundation of each sentence you write. In fact, without these two main sentence parts, you have no sentence at all. You have only a **sentence fragment**, a group of words that does not express a complete thought. As a result, when you read through a piece of writing, you should look for any missing subjects and verbs.

| | |
|---|---|
| Sentence Fragment | The first and most important step in building stage presence. (This fragment is missing a verb.) |
| Sentence | The first and most important step in building stage presence **is learning your part.** |

## Subject and Verb Agreement

After correcting any sentence fragments, you should read through your essay again, making sure that the subject and the verb in each sentence agree in number. **Number** refers to whether a subject and verb are singular or plural. If a subject is singular, its verb must also be singular; if a subject is plural, its verb must also be plural.

In the following examples, the subject is underlined once, and the verb is underlined twice.

| | |
|---|---|
| SINGULAR SUBJECT AND VERB | That actor with only a few lines has stage presence. |
| PLURAL SUBJECT AND VERB | The actors wearing masks have stage presence. |

## Run-on Sentences

Before you write a final copy of your essay, check to see if you have included an end mark—a period, a question mark, or an exclamation point—at the end of each sentence. Forgetting to put an end mark will result in a run-on sentence—two sentences mistakenly written as one. One way to correct a run-on sentence during editing, therefore, is to separate the sentences with an end mark and a capital letter.

| | |
|---|---|
| RUN-ON SENTENCE | Stage presence is not magic you can have it just like famous actors have it. |
| CORRECT SENTENCE | Stage presence is not magic. You can have it just like famous actors have it. |

Although editing takes time, think of that time as an investment. When you have edited well, you have unleashed the maximum power of your words, and those words will produce the maximum effect on your readers.

## Revising Checklist

- ✔ Are there any sentence fragments?
- ✔ Do the subject and verb in each sentence agree?
- ✔ Does each sentence begin with a capital letter and end with an end mark?
- ✔ Are there any run-on sentences?

## Practice Your Skills

*Revising and Conferencing*

**Pair up with a partner and use the strategies on the preceding page and the Evaluation Checklist for Revising on page C39 to review the last section of the writer's draft about performing. Errors in spelling, punctuation, capitalization, and usage will be corrected later on. Using the Guidelines for Conferencing on page C42, look at each other's revisions. Check to see if there are any areas in which you could make improvements that either of you may have left uncorrected.**

Throughout prewriting, drafting, and revising stages, you have been concentrating on the form and substance of your work. While you may have noticed—and sometimes corrected—slips in spelling, punctuation, capitalization, grammar, and usage, your focus has been on the more substantive concerns of presenting your ideas clearly and refining your words. **Editing** is the stage in which you locate and correct your mechanical errors.

## Strategies for Editing

Errors in spelling, usage, punctuation, and capitalization can muddle your writing and seriously jeopardize your credibility. So a piece of writing is not finished until you have checked it for these errors. An editing checklist and proofreading symbols will help you find and correct them.

**Using an Editing Checklist** Good writers often use an editing checklist to help them to avoid forgetting things. The best way to use such a list is to go over your work several times, each time looking for a different kind of problem. For instance, you might look for spelling errors in one reading and comma errors in the next. You might also want to read your essay backward, word by word. You will find that you are able to spot many errors that you might have otherwise missed. The following checklist will help you.

### Editing Checklist

- ✓ Are the sentences free of errors in grammar and usage?
- ✓ Did you spell each word correctly?
- ✓ Did you use capital letters where needed?
- ✓ Did you punctuate each sentence correctly?
- ✓ Did you indent paragraphs as needed and leave proper margins on each side of the paper?

**Using a Manual of Style** Writers often consult style guides or handbooks to review rules for grammar, spelling, mechanics, and usage. As you edit, you may wish to consult one of the following:

- *APA Publication Manual of the American Psychological Association.* 4th ed. Washington, DC: American Psychological Association, 1994.
- *The Chicago Manual of Style: The Essential Guide for Writers, Editors, and Publishers.* 14th ed. Chicago: University of Chicago Press, 1993.
- *MLA Handbook for Writers of Research Papers.* 5th ed. New York: Modern Language Association of America, 1999.

**Creating a Personalized Editing Checklist** As you work through the editing stage, you should reserve an eight-page section at the end of your journal as a Personalized Editing Checklist. Write one of these headings on every other page: *Grammar Problems, Usage Problems, Spelling Problems, Mechanics Problems*. Then use these pages to record any mistakes that you commonly make in your writing. Consult the index in this book to find the pages on which each particular problem is addressed. Then write the page numbers in your **journal** next to the error, along with some examples of the corrected problem. Add to this checklist throughout the year and refer to it each time you edit an essay.

**Proofreading** **Proofreading** means "reading and marking corrections." You may become so familiar with your essay while revising that you skip over mistakes. Proofreading during the editing stage will help give you the distance to pick up mistakes that you missed earlier. The following techniques will help.

### Proofreading Techniques

- Focus on one line at a time.
- Exchange your work with a partner and check each other's papers for errors.
- Read your essay backward, word by word. By changing the way you read your work, you will find that you will spot many errors.
- Read your essay aloud, very slowly.
- Use a college dictionary for spelling and a handbook for grammar, usage, and mechanics to double-check anything you are unsure of.

To make the process of proofreading efficient, most writers use shorthand notations, called **proofreading symbols**. The most common symbols are listed below. Use them, for they will save you time when you edit your work.

### Proofreading Symbols

| Symbol | Meaning | Example |
|---|---|---|
| ∧ | insert | Ms. Tey spoke ∧ (about) graduation. |
| ∧, | insert comma | We ate corn, hamburgers∧, and salad. |
| ⊙ | insert period | The party ended at eleven ⊙ |
| delete mark | delete | The fair was a great ~~enormous~~ success. |
| ... | let it stand | Pago Pago is in ~~American~~ (...) Samoa. |
| close-up mark | close up | Each set of finger prints is different. |
| transpose mark | transpose | They only arrived yetserday. |
| ¶ | new paragraph | ¶ Dunn Field resounded with cheers. |
| ≡ | capital letter | Is Ohio in the southwest or Midwest? |
| / | lowercase | To the Southwest lay barren desert. |
| (sp) | spell out | I ate (sp) 2 oranges. |
| ∨" ∨" | insert quotes | ∨" I hope you can join us,∨" said my brother. |
| =∧ | insert hyphen | I attended a school=∧related event. |
| ∨' | insert apostrophe | The ravenous dog ate the cat∨'s food. |
| move mark | move copy | I usually (on Fridays) go to the movies. |

The following model shows how the student edited a section of his essay on developing stage presence.

**Model: Edited Draft**

¶When performance time arrives, you can expect to be nervous. Experienced actors, rather than trying to calm themselves, draw on their nervousness to increase their energy level. The best way to rechannel your nervous energy is to get into character. Chat with others as your character would. walk around as your character would. Another importent strategy is Exercise. Even just a healthy stretch and shake of your limbs, head, and body will help.

## Publishing

Writing Process

Although some of what you write is for your eyes alone—such as your **journal** or diary—most of what you write is for others to read. The final stage of the writing process, then, involves presenting your writing in final form for an audience. That form may be as simple as a letter to a friend or as complex as a Website. This stage is called **publishing**.

Your first step after the editing stage is to copy your work over neatly, incorporating your revisions and corrections. Neat presentation and proper manuscript form are essential for making your work appear inviting to read. Then, if you have not done so already, select an appropriate way to publish the piece, taking into account your purpose and audience. Following are some possible choices.

### Ways to Publish Your Writing

**In School**

- Read your work aloud to a small group in your class.
- Display your final draft on a bulletin board in your classroom or school library.
- Read your work aloud to your class or present it in the form of a radio program or videotape.
- Create a class library and media center to which you submit your work. The library and media center should be a collection of folders or files devoted to different types of student writing and media presentations.
- Create a class anthology to which every student contributes one piece. Use electronic technology to design a small publication. Share your anthology with other classes.
- Submit your work to your school literary magazine, newspaper, or yearbook.

**Outside of School**

- Submit your written work to a newspaper or magazine.
- Share your work with a professional interested in the subject.
- Present your work to an appropriate community group.
- Send a video based on your written work to a local cable television station.
- Enter your work in a local, state, or national writing contest.

**Using Standard Manuscript Form** The appearance of your essay may be almost as important as its content. A marked-up paper with inconsistent margins is difficult to read. A neat, legible paper, however, makes a positive impression on your reader. When using a word-processing program to prepare your final draft, it is important to know how to lay out the page, and how to choose a typeface and typesize. Use the following guidelines for standard manuscript form to help you prepare your final draft. The model on pages C51–C52 shows how the writer used these guidelines to prepare his final draft on performing.

### Standard Manuscript Form

- Use standard-sized $8\frac{1}{2}$ by 11-inch white paper. Use one side of the paper only.
- If handwriting, use black or blue ink. If using a word-processing program or typing, use a black ink cartridge or black typewriter ribbon and double-space the lines.
- Leave a 1.25-inch margin at the left and right. The left margin must be even. The right margin should be as even as possible.
- Put your name, the course title, the name of your teacher, and the date in the upper right-hand corner of the first page. Where applicable, follow your teacher's specific guidelines for headings and margins.
- Center the title of your essay two lines below the date. Do not underline or put quotation marks around your title.
- If using a word-processing program or typing, skip four lines between the title and the first paragraph. If writing by hand, skip two lines.
- If using a word-processing program or typing, indent the first line of each paragraph five spaces. If handwriting, indent the first line of each paragraph 1 inch.
- Leave a 1-inch margin at the bottom of all pages.
- Starting on page two, number each page in the upper right-hand corner. Begin the first line 1 inch from the top. Word-processing programs give you the option of inserting page numbers.

**Time Out to Reflect**

You have now traveled through the five stages of the writing process. At the beginning of this chapter (page C8), you saw a diagram illustrating the stages of the writing process. Look at this diagram again. Take a moment to write down your understanding of the writing process. How closely does this process match your previous experiences as a writer? What might account for any differences between the writing process as described in this chapter and the writing process as you have previously experienced it?

1 INCH

Andrew Dunn
English: Ms. Jones
September 14, 2000

2 LINES

Stage Presence

4 LINES

1.25 INCHES

Have you ever felt yourself watching a minor character in a play instead of the star? Some actors always catch and hold the audience's eye, no matter how small a part they play.

These performers have stage presence—a certain poise and energy that is transmitted to the audience. Stage presence is not magic. By working on your techniques during rehearsals and channeling your emotions at performance time, you too can project that special quality when you step onstage.

1.25 INCHES

Stage presence is based on confidence. Your first and most important step, then, is to learn your part. Know it as if it was really part of you. Practice different deliveries, moves, and gestures until you find just the right ones. Then rehearse them until they come naturally. Another important tactic is to develop your character as you rehearse. Think about what the person is like—how he or she talks, feels, thinks, moves, and sleeps. Learn to transform yourself into the character so that you automatically walk as the character

1 INCH

walks, cough as the character coughs, even fidget as the character fidgets. Practice staying in character every moment, listening and reacting appropriately to everything that happens onstage—even when you have nothing to say. Finally, concentrate on the way you move. Avoid halfway movement. If you grin, grin from ear to ear. If you turn your head, really turn it.



When performance time arrives, you can expect to be nervous. Experienced actors, rather than trying to calm themselves, draw on their nervousness to increase their energy level. The best way to rechannel your nervous energy is to get into character. Chat with others as your character would. Walk around as your character would. Another important strategy is exercise. Even just a healthy stretch and shake of your limbs, head, and body will help. Finally, avoid the temptation to practice your lines, especially troublesome lines. Mistakes will only end up making you more nervous.

Stage presence depends on consciousness—of your character, of your emotions, and of your audience above all. According to Ms. Keller, drama teacher, "There are no small parts, only small actors." Using the techniques sketched above, you can always be a big actor.

## Writing Process Checklist

Remember that a writing process is recursive—you can move among the stages of the process to achieve your purpose. The numbers in parentheses refer to pages where you can get help with your writing.

### PREWRITING

- Find a subject to write about by taking an inventory of your interests, freewriting, exploring the Internet, keeping a journal, and reading and thinking about literature. *(pages C10–C17)*
- Choose and limit a subject. *(pages C18–C19)*
- Consider your purpose, audience, and occasion. Be aware of the voice you choose. *(pages C20–C24)*
- Develop your subject by observing, brainstorming for details, clustering, and inquiring. *(pages C24–C30)*
- Organize your material by focusing your subject, classifying your details, and ordering your details. *(pages C32–C34)*

### DRAFTING

- Write a first draft and choose a title, using the strategies on pages C35–C37.

### REVISING

- Revise your draft by adding ideas, adding details and information, rearranging, deleting needless words or ideas, and substituting words and sentences. *(pages C38–C40)*
- Use the Evaluation Checklist for Revising and Revising Checklist as reminders and guides. *(pages C39 and C44)*
- Use conferencing to help you revise your draft. *(page C42)*
- Revise your draft as often as needed. Repeat some of the prewriting and drafting strategies if necessary.

### EDITING

- Use the Editing Checklists to look for errors in grammar, usage, spelling, capitalization, and punctuation. *(page C46)*
- Use proofreading symbols to correct errors. *(page 47)*

### PUBLISHING

- Follow standard manuscript form and make a neat final copy of your work. Then find an appropriate way to share your work with others. *(pages C49–C52)*

CHAPTER 2

# Developing Your Writing Style

In expressing thoughts about any subject, writers use unique styles. That is, they choose words and shape sentences to make their writing powerful and concise. Although good writers always use well-crafted sentences to express their thoughts, they also have a talent for choosing the right word at just the right time.

As you develop your writing style, you will realize that your choice of words has everything to do with your clarity of expression and that a creative simile or metaphor can often help you and your readers to see familiar things in new ways. In this chapter, you will learn ways of developing your own writing style. The end result will be written works that say what you want them to say—in a style that your audience will want to read.

## *Reading with a Writer's Eye*

In the following short story, the author, Russell Baker, uses language to create a satire of the children's classic tale of Little Red Riding Hood. As you read Baker's "revisiting" of the tale, notice how he humorously changes the story by his use of language. On a second reading, look for examples of words and expressions that are especially effective in creating the satiric twist on this familiar story.

# Little Red Riding Hood Revisited

*Russell Baker*

Once upon a point in time, a small person named Little Red Riding Hood initiated plans for the preparation, delivery and transportation of foodstuffs to her grandmother, a senior citizen residing at a place of residence in a forest of indeterminate dimension.

In the process of implementing this program, her incursion[1] into the forest was in midtransportation process when it attained interface[2] with an alleged perpetrator. This individual, a wolf, made inquiry as to the whereabouts of Little Red Riding Hood's goal as well as inferring that he was desirous of ascertaining the contents of Little Red Riding Hood's foodstuffs basket, and all that.

"It would be inappropriate to lie to me," the wolf said, displaying his huge jaw capability. Sensing that he was a mass of repressed hostility intertwined with acute alienation, she indicated.

"I see you indicating," the wolf said, "but what I don't see is whatever it is you're indicating at, you dig?"

Little Red Riding Hood indicated more fully, making one thing perfectly clear—to wit, that it was to her grandmother's residence and with a consignment[3] of foodstuffs that her mission consisted of taking her to and with.

---

[1] **incursion:** An entering in or into.

[2] **interface** *n.*: Meeting.

[3] **consignment** (kən sīn′mənt) n.: Delivery.

At this point in time the wolf moderated his rhetoric[4] and proceeded to grandmother's residence. The elderly person was then subjected to the disadvantages of total consumption and transferred to residence in the perpetrator's stomach.

"That will raise the old woman's consciousness," the wolf said to himself. He was not a bad wolf, but only a victim of an oppressive society, a society that not only denied wolves' rights, but actually boasted of its capacity for keeping the wolf from the door. An interior malaise[5] made itself manifest[6] inside the wolf.

"Is that the national malaise I sense within my digestive tract?" wondered the wolf. "Or is it the old person seeking to retaliate for her consumption by telling wolf jokes to my duodenum[7]?" It was time to make a judgment. The time was now, the hour had struck, the body lupine[8] cried out for decision. The wolf was up to the challenge. He took two stomach powders right away and got into bed.

The wolf had adopted the abdominal-distress recovery posture when Little Red Riding Hood achieved his presence.

"Grandmother," she said, "your ocular[9] implements are of an extraordinary order of magnitude."

"The purpose of this enlarged viewing capability," said the wolf, "is to enable your image to register a more precise impression upon my sight systems."

"In reference to your ears," said Little Red Riding Hood, "it is noted with the deepest respect that far from being underprivileged, their elongation and enlargement appear to qualify you for unparalleled distinction."

"I hear you loud and clear, kid," said the wolf, "but what about these new choppers?"

---

[4] **rhetoric** (rĕt′ər ĭk) *n.*: Verbal communication.

[5] **malaise** (mă lāz′, -lĕz′) *n.*: A vague sense of mental or moral ill-being.

[6] **manifest** *adj.*: Easily understood or recognized by the mind.

[7] **duodenum** (doo′ə de′nəm) n.: Part of the small intestine.

[8] **lupine** (loo′ pīn′) adj.: Wolfish.

[9] **ocular** (ok′yə lər) adj.: Of or relating to the eye.

"If it is not inappropriate," said Little Red Riding Hood, "it might be observed that with your new miracle masticating[10] products you may even be able to chew taffy again."

This observation was followed by the adoption of an aggressive posture on the part of the wolf and the assertion that it was also possible for him, due to the high efficiency ratio of his jaw, to consume little persons, plus, as he stated, his firm determination to do so at once without delay and with all due process and propriety, notwithstanding the fact that the ingestion of one entire grandmother had already provided twice his daily recommended cholesterol intake.

There ensued flight by Little Red Riding Hood accompanied by pursuit in respect to the wolf and a subsequent intervention on the part of a third party, heretofore unnoted in the record.

Due to the firmness of the intervention, the wolf's stomach underwent ax-assisted aperture[11] with the result that Red Riding Hood's grandmother was enabled to be removed with only minor discomfort.

The wolf's indigestion was immediately alleviated with such effectiveness that he signed a contract with the intervening third party to perform with grandmother in a television commercial demonstrating the swiftness of this dramatic relief for stomach discontent.

"I'm going to be on television," cried grandmother.

And they all joined her happily in crying, "What a phenomena!"

---

[10] **masticating:** Chewing.

[11] **aperture** (ăp′ər chər) *n.*: Opening.

# Thinking as a Writer

## Analyzing Writing Style

- How has Russell Baker used language to put a unique stamp on his retelling of a familiar tale? Cite examples from Baker's version of the story. What words and expressions might you use to retell the story in your own way?

## Conveying Author's Style

Oral Expression Choose a section from Russell Baker's version of "Little Red Riding Hood."

- Read the section aloud, choosing the mannerisms and voice that you think are appropriate to each character. How does the style of the piece affect your delivery?

## Analyzing Art Style

Viewing Elements of art—line, color, shape, texture—are to a visual artist what words are to a writer. Both the artist and the writer use these means to express their thoughts, feelings, and imagination. Principles of design—pattern, variety, rhythm, unity—are to an artist what sentences and paragraphs are to a writer. They govern the way the elements are used to convey ideas and feelings.

- What ideas and feelings does this photograph suggest to you? How does the artist's style—that is, his unique way of expressing his ideas—influence your interpretation of the work?

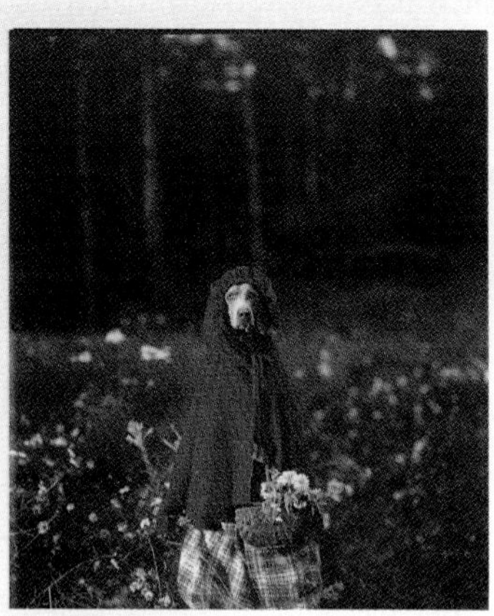

William Wegman. *Little Red Riding Hood,* 1992. Color Polaroid, 20x24. ©William Wegman

# Developing Your Stylistic Skills

"How do I know what I think until I see what I say?" pondered E. M. Forster. As a writer Forster realized that putting words on paper is a way of exploring ideas as well as expressing them. Writers who start out with a general notion of what they want to say often find their own words and sentences leading them to better formulated and sometimes unexpected ideas.

Whether you are writing a letter, a research report, a poem, or a story, a well-chosen word can reveal new avenues of thought. A single detail like Russell Baker's description of the wolf—"In reference to your ears, . . . their elongation and enlargement appear to qualify you for unparalleled distinction"—can open the eye of the imagination. A creative use of language can help you see things in new ways, as do Russell's words on page C57: "The wolf's indigestion was immediately alleviated with such effectiveness that he signed a contract with the intervening third party to perform with grandmother in a television commercial demonstrating the swiftness of this dramatic relief for stomach discontent."

In this chapter you will discover ways to select that well-chosen word, be more expressive, and write more concisely. In the process you will develop an effective writing style of your own.

Your writing **style** is the distinctive way you express yourself through the words you choose and the way you shape your sentences.

### Your Writer's Journal

In your journal, jot down your thoughts about Russell Baker's version of Little Red Riding Hood. How has he used word choice for comic effects? Freewrite about how you might apply similar verbal techniques to create a comic version of another folk tale with which you are familiar. Think about how you would use language to give each character a unique way of speaking. Write as many specific examples as you can.

## Choosing Vivid Words

Words with rich, precise meanings give life to your thoughts and your writing. Look for vivid words in this scene, which describes a famous moment in horror-story history.

**Model: Vivid Words**

It was on a dreary night of November that I beheld the accomplishment of my toils. With an anxiety that almost amounted to agony, I collected the instruments of life around me, that I might infuse a spark of being into the lifeless thing that lay at my feet. It was already one in the morning. The rain pattered dismally against the panes, and my candle was nearly burnt out. Then, by the glimmer of the half-extinguished light, I saw the dull yellow eye of the creature open. It breathed hard, and convulsive motion agitated its limbs.

—*Mary Shelley,* Frankenstein

Just as Dr. Frankenstein sparks life into his creature, Shelley sparks life into her writing with carefully chosen words. Indeed, her own words may have helped her to visualize the scene as she wrote—just as they have helped readers ever since.

When you write, search for words that paint vivid mental pictures which will help you develop an effective writing style.

## Specific Words

Use specific words to convey clear messages and create clear images. In each example below, a general word is replaced by one of the specific words Mary Shelley uses in the preceding passage. The specific word may be a more precise synonym or a word with a different, richer sense.

| | |
|---|---|
| General Verb | The rain **fell** against the window. |
| Specific Verb | The rain **pattered** against the window. |
| General Adjective | The **big** blast shook the house. |
| Specific Adjective | The **convulsive** blast shook the house. |

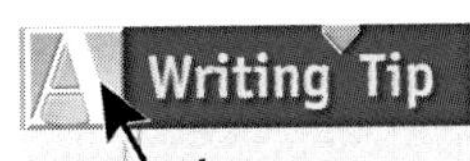

Choose **specific words** over general words.

## Practice Your Skills

### *Choosing Specific Words*

**Write two specific words for each of the following underlined general words.**

**1.** Nothing ever stopped Lou and Henry from talking.

**2.** The book kept Andrew reading late into the night.

**3.** As the rocket blasted off, the earth moved.

**4.** It was an awful defeat, but the season had just begun.

**5.** Whenever Anna came into a room, everyone knew it.

**6.** The new state champions marched happily around the field.

**7.** That summer was a great time for the entire Diaz family.

**8.** Prince never behaved like an ordinary dog.

**9.** Surprisingly all three beginners skated well.

**10.** The nice breeze carried the scent of lilacs.

## Figurative Language

A good writer knows how to use language figuratively as well as literally—to stretch the literal meaning of words so that they appeal to the imaginations of readers. **Literal language** uses words for their exact, direct meaning. **Figurative language** is usually composed of **figures of speech**—expressions that use words in inventive ways. Compared to literal language, figurative language is a more powerful tool for creating strong images, as shown in the following example.

| | |
|---|---|
| Literal Language | The moon appeared in the cloudy sky. |
| Figurative Language | The moon was a ghostly galleon tossed upon cloudy seas. |
| | –*Alfred Noyes,* "The Highwayman" |

Here the poet appeals to the reader's imagination with his choice of imagery. Rather than simply stating that the night sky was cloudy, the poet compares the moon to a galleon, or ship, being tossed upon a sea of clouds.

Use **figurative language** to appeal to your reader's imagination.

**Similes and Metaphors** Similes and metaphors fire the imagination by making unusual comparisons. **Similes** use *like* or *as* to make a comparison. **Metaphors,** on the other hand, imply a comparison without using *like* or *as*, or they simply state that one thing *is* another. Such figures of speech can enrich your writing and help your reader view ideas or things in new ways.

| | |
|---|---|
| SIMILE | Here he stopped again, and glanced suspiciously to right and left, **like a rabbit that is going to bolt into its hole.**<br>—*E. M. Forster* |
| METAPHOR | The days ahead **unroll in the mind, a scroll** of blessed events in the garden and the barn.<br>—*E. B. White* |

Forster uses *like* to compare a suspicious man to a rabbit. White implies a comparison between the days ahead and a scroll.

When you use figurative language, beware of two hazards—the mixed metaphor and the cliché. In a **mixed metaphor**, two different comparisons are illogically combined.

| | |
|---|---|
| MIXED METAPHOR | His car was a spoiled child, drowning him in the waves of its demands. |
| IMPROVED | His car was a spoiled child, eternally whining for his attention. |

A spoiled child cannot drown someone in its waves, but a spoiled child can certainly whine for attention.

## Comparing

When you **compare**, you think of similarities or differences between people, places, things, or even ideas. One effective way to compare is to create a simile or metaphor. For example, if you compared the human brain to a computer, you would find several similarities. Both a brain and a computer process large amounts of information quickly. They both have extensive memories, and they both can classify related pieces of information into groups.

Effective similes and metaphors use creative comparisons that allow people to see things in new and different ways. Following is an example.

> Angered by events, the crowd of people flew down the street **like a swarm of bees.**

Making a chart like the following one will help you write your own powerful comparisons.

COMPARISON CHART

| Person, Place, Thing, or Idea | Similar Qualities | Comparison |
|---|---|---|
| Subject 1<br>CROWD OF PEOPLE | angry, threatening | CROWD OF PEOPLE<br>= |
| Subject 2<br>SWARM OF BEES | angry, threatening | SWARM OF BEES |

### THINKING PRACTICE

**Make a comparison chart for one of the following phrases. Then write a resulting simile.**

1. The truck was like . . .
2. A friendship is like . . .
3. The bridge spanned the bay like . . .

**Clichés** A **cliché** is an overused comparison that has lost its power to evoke a strong mental image. If you find clichés in your writing, replace them with new similes. The following are some examples.

CLICHÉS

Andrea was **happy as a lark** with her examination score.

Dad used to be **stubborn as a mule** about my allowance.

On the subject of classroom hours, her word was as **good as gold**.

Jim could always be relied on to know **what's up.**

**Personification** When you attribute human qualities to objects or ideas, you are using **personification**. Here are examples.

PERSONIFICATION

The book **beckoned** to me from the shelf.

The trees **danced** to the rhythm of the wind.

Darkness **crept** silently into the house.

The mountain **dared** me to try its slopes.

Of course, books cannot beckon, trees cannot dance, darkness cannot creep, and mountains cannot dare. Yet the meaning of each sentence is clear, since the actions described are understandable human actions. Through personification, objects and ideas take on fresh, new identities.

**Onomatopoeia** Some figures of speech rely on the sounds of words to create vivid impressions. **Onomatopoeia,** for example, is a figure of speech in which the word's sound matches its meaning. The following are examples of onomatopoeia.

| ONOMATOPOEIA | | | |
|---|---|---|---|
| | crash | slither | ooze |
| | thump | hiss | quiver |
| | boom | whistle | jangle |
| | purr | swoop | sizzle |

Onomatopoeia is a figure of speech that is more widely used in poetry than in prose. Used sparingly, however, it can enrich prose writing by calling on the reader's sense of hearing to bring a passage to life.

## Practice Your Skills

### *Experimenting with Onomatopoeia*

**Write one sentence about each subject. Use onomatopoeia to add sound effects appropriate to the subject.**

**1.** doorbell
**2.** surf
**3.** traffic
**4.** busy office
**5.** cat
**6.** fireworks

### *Identifying Figures of Speech*

**The following sentences are from a novel by Stephen Crane. Identify the underlined figure of speech in each case by writing *personification, simile, metaphor,* or *onomatopoeia*.**

**1.** The trees began softly to sing a hymn of twilight.
**2.** The regiment was like a firework . . .
**3.** There was a little flower of confidence growing within him.
**4.** The red sun was pasted in the sky like a wafer.
**5.** The regiment was a machine run down.
**6.** War, the red animal, war, the blood-swollen god . . .
**7.** The voices of the cannon were clamoring in interminable chorus.
**8.** The guns belched and howled . . .
**9.** The black weight of his woe returned to him.
**10.** Thus, many men of courage, he considered, would be obligated to desert the colors and scurry like chickens.

### *Using Figurative Language*

**Write a paragraph about something that moves, such as the ocean, clouds, or a car. Include literal language, a simile or a metaphor, and personification.**

## Writing Concise Sentences

Just as a hiker carries only the essentials in order to move easily, a writer should use only the words needed to communicate clearly. Lighten your reader's load by avoiding needless words.

**Writing Tip**

Keep your sentences **concise** by eliminating needless words and phrases.

### Redundancy

**Redundancy** means unnecessary repetition of words or phrases. Find the redundancy in the first sentence of each pair below. Then notice how it is eliminated without any loss of meaning.

| | |
|---|---|
| REDUNDANT | Our memorable trip to London was unforgettable. |
| CONCISE | Our trip to London was unforgettable. |
| REDUNDANT | Animals who are members of the mammal family are warm-blooded. |
| CONCISE | Mammals are warm-blooded. |

### Empty Expressions

Fillers—words that contribute no meaning to a sentence—are called **empty expressions.** Reduce empty expressions to a single meaningful word or eliminate them entirely, as shown below.

| | |
|---|---|
| EMPTY | The thing of it is that I cannot turn in my paper due to the fact that I forgot it. |
| CONCISE | I cannot turn in my paper because I forgot it. |
| EMPTY | It seems there were 20 people at the party. |
| CONCISE | Twenty people attended the party. |
| EMPTY | Due to the fact that there was a power failure, my television went off. |
| CONCISE | My television went off because there was a power failure. |

**COMMON EMPTY EXPRESSIONS**

| | |
|---|---|
| on account of | so as you can see |
| what I want/believe/think is | the reason that |
| it seems as if | the thing of it is that |
| due to the fact that | there is/are/was/were |
| in my opinion | I believe/feel/think that |

## Practice Your Skills

### *Eliminating Redundancy and Empty Expressions*

**Revise the following sentences to eliminate redundancies and empty expressions. Some sentences may need more than one revision.**

1. Many of the popular sports that many people enjoy in Japan are contests of strength and power.
2. There is *sumo* wrestling, for example, which pits two huge, giant men against each other.
3. The first wrestler to touch the floor before the other with anything but his feet loses the match.
4. Preceding the match the contestants enact a traditional ritual that they perform before the wrestling begins.
5. After clapping their hands, they extend their arms out with open hands to show the fact that they carry no weapons.
6. Finally they stamp their feet on the ground at the end to symbolize driving away evil.
7. It seems that *kyudo*, a centuries-old form of archery, dates back hundreds of years.
8. Also, fencing with swords, or *kendo*, is centuries old too.
9. *Kendo* is well known due to the fact that it is taught in Japan's schools where students can learn it.
10. The thing of it is Japanese law enforcement officers are experts in karate and judo, and they carry no firearms.

## Wordiness

The expression "less is more" may sound illogical, but it makes good sense for writing. In general your writing style will be sharper if you use as few words as possible to express your point.

**Wordy Phrases and Clauses** Constructions that use more words than necessary are referred to as **wordy**. Because wordiness detracts from your writing style, try to reduce each wordy construction to a shorter phrase or a single word.

**Phrase to Word**

WORDY Winds on Greenland's ice cap howl **in a fierce way.** (prepositional phrase)

CONCISE Winds on Greenland's ice cap howl **fiercely**. (adverb)

WORDY Dry snow, **having the quality of sand**, covers the ice. (participial phrase)

CONCISE Dry, **sandlike** snow covers the ice. (adjective)

**Clause to Phrase**

WORDY Because of the winds, scientists **who work in Greenland** do not venture far from their stations. (adjective clause)

CONCISE Because of the winds, scientists **working in Greenland** do not venture far from their stations. (participial phrase) or Because of the winds, scientists **in Greenland** do not venture far from their stations. (prepositional phrase)

WORDY The ice cap, **which is a perilous wilderness**, appears serene from the air. (adjective clause)

CONCISE The ice cap, **a perilous wilderness**, appears serene from the air. (appositive phrase)

**Clause to Word**

WORDY A glare **that is blinding** rises from the ice cap on a sunny day. (adjective clause)

CONCISE A **blinding** glare rises from the ice cap on a sunny day. (adjective)

**Inflated Language** Some writers tend to use inflated language—words with many syllables that sound impressive but do not communicate as effectively or concisely as simple, direct words. Avoid using long or pretentious words merely to impress your reader.

INFLATED In the process of implementing this program, her incursion into the forest was in midtransportation process when it attained interface with an alleged perpetrator.

—*Russell Baker*

CONCISE On her way into the forest, she met a wolf.

## PRACTICE YOUR SKILLS

### *Eliminating Wordiness*

**Revise the sentences below by reducing wordy phrases and clauses or by translating inflated language into simpler words.**

1. Kampsville, which is a center for archaeological research and training, is located in west central Illinois.
2. Every year young students who are interested in archaeology go to Kampsville in order to dig up the past.
3. The remains of 2,000 communities of prehistoric times are being uncovered.
4. Students are taught to dig in a very careful way.
5. The site is divided into areas measuring six feet square.
6. Items that are excavated are identified by the number of the square in which they are found.
7. On unearthed bones and shells, students look for points, notches, and grooves which are signs of human handiwork.
8. A student who is at Kampsville learns much about the life that ancient people led every day.
9. Bones that come from animals can be revealing.
10. Zoo archaeologists, who are experts in animal bones, surmise that early Native Americans kept dogs as pets.

IN THE MEDIA

## Advertising Campaign

You receive a catalog in the mail from an outdoor clothing company. Flipping through the pages you see a rugged-looking jacket on a model with wind-blown hair. You stop and read the "copy," the written blurb that goes with it:

> *You thought about turning back, but something in the wind kept you moving. And then, in the hush of nightfall, you heard the whimpers. A quick flash of white fur, and a mother wolf grabbed her pup by the scruff and trotted off into the darkness. The coat kept you warm through that starry night, and so did the memory of that rare glimpse into wolf motherhood.*

The copywriters have used evocative language to create an appealing scene that you now associate with that jacket. Chances are you'll never wear it on a starry night in the wilderness with a mother wolf and pup as companions, but the imaginative association may make you want the coat even more than ever. The message behind the ad: *This coat will put you in harmony with nature, you rugged individual, and in it you will experience both unsurpassed coziness and a glimpse into nature's secrets.* In reality, a jacket can keep you warm, but all the rest of the implied benefits of that jacket are things the jacket itself simply cannot deliver.

The success of any ad campaign depends on the ability of the advertising team to combine creative, exciting language with compelling visuals to deliver a carefully chosen message to a targeted audience.

### Media Activity

In order to explore these challenges, imagine you work for an advertising agency that has won contracts to advertise the following products.

- a new line of cross-training shoes
- an unusual new Internet search engine

- a public interest group exposing dangers in the water supply
- a state-of-the-art planetarium funded by the state and local government

Divide into four teams, each of which will develop an advertising campaign for one of these products. Use the following questions to help you design your strategy.

## Questions for Developing an Advertising Strategy

- How will you create interest in the product?
- Who will be your audience?
- What characteristics of the product will you highlight?
- Will the tone of your campaign be amusing, dramatic, intelligent, emotional? Why?
- Which two media will be most effective?
- What slogan will you use?
- What kinds of text, visuals, and music will you use?
- What will be the roles of the team members?
- What equipment will you need? How will you get it?

Summarize your answers in a one-page strategy statement. Then prepare a detailed proposal to present to the client. In the proposal lay out your strategy as clearly as possible, including sketches and approaches for each of the two media you identified.

Create one ad for each of the media. (If you are creating a video ad, refer to *A Writer's Guide to Electronic Publishing,* pages C788–C813, for help in creating the video.) Make a schedule showing what each team member will do by what target dates. You may want to refer back to your strategy statement frequently.

Develop a questionnaire to distribute to your class after they have had a chance to see your work. Take time to think of questions that will provide you with constructive responses. After showing your ads and receiving the completed questionnaires, write a summary of what you learned about your ad from the questionnaires.

## Creating Sentence Variety

Clothing with an appealing style flatters the human form. Similarly an appealing writing style shows ideas to their best advantage. One important feature of writing style is sentence construction. An interesting pattern of sentences appeals to the reader's ear and gives a graceful shape to ideas.

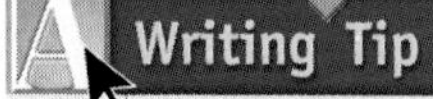


Vary the length and structure of your sentences.

### Sentence-Combining Strategies

Short, choppy sentences suffer from two serious weaknesses. First, their rhythm soon becomes tiresome to the reader. Second, they obscure the relationships among ideas.

Compare the following two examples. The first presents a series of short, choppy sentences, while the second combines the short sentences into one. Notice how the relationships among the ideas become clearer when the sentences are combined.

| | |
|---|---|
| SHORT SENTENCES | Alfonso beat John in the mile race. John was Alfonso's best friend. John was also Alfonso's chief rival in track. Alfonso felt proud of his victory. He also felt sorry about John's defeat. |
| COMBINED | After Alfonso beat John in the mile race, Alfonso felt proud of his victory but sorry about the defeat of his best friend and chief rival in track. |

The techniques of sentence combining on the following pages will help you link related ideas and vary the lengths of your sentences.

**Combining Sentences with Phrases** Two sentences can be combined by turning one sentence into a phrase that modifies the main idea expressed in the other sentence.

**A.** Police departments today use computers. Computers store important information about suspects.

Police departments today use computers to store important information about suspects. (infinitive phrase)

**B.** In 1967, the first computer system used to fight crime was developed. The FBI developed it.

In 1967, the first computer system used to fight crime was developed by the FBI. (prepositional phrase)

**C.** The National Crime Information Center provides information by computer. It aids police nationally.

The National Crime Information Center provides information by computer, aiding police nationally. (participial phrase)

**D.** CATCH can call up a picture of a suspect on a computer screen. It is a highly advanced system.

CATCH, a highly advanced system, can call up a picture of a suspect on a computer screen. (appositive phrase)

## Practice Your Skills

### *Combining Sentences with Phrases*

**Combine each of the following sets of sentences, using one or more of the preceding techniques. Add commas where needed.**

**1.** Birds navigate the long distances of their migration routes. They use innate compasses and clocks.

**2.** The arctic tern holds the distance record. It is an amazing bird. It flies a round-trip distance of 23,000 miles. It goes from the Arctic to the Antarctic every year.

**3.** Many birds use the sun. It helps them navigate.

**4.** Tens of millions of shearwaters land on islands off Australia. The time they will arrive is one November day.

**5.** The shearwaters land within a 20-minute period. They have come from many different places. These include Japan and Canada.

**Combining Sentences by Coordinating** Ideas of equal importance can be joined with a coordinating conjunction (*and, but, or, for, nor, yet,* and *so*). Following are some examples of sentences that were combined by coordination.

**A.** In many science fiction novels, robots grow too powerful. They try to take over the world.
In many science fiction novels, robots **grow** too powerful **and try** to take over the world. (compound verb)

**B.** Robots in most early works were dangerous. In *Star Wars*, C3PO and R2D2 are friendly.
Robots in most early works were dangerous, **but** in *Star Wars*, C3PO and R2D2 are friendly. (compound sentence)

**C.** One famous movie robot is Gort in *The Day the Earth Stood Still*. Another is Robbie the Robot in *Forbidden Planet*.
Two famous movie robots are **Gort** in *The Day the Earth Stood Still* and **Robbie the Robot** in *Forbidden Planet*. (compound predicate nominative)

## Practice Your Skills

### *Combining Sentences by Coordinating*

**Combine each of the following pairs of sentences, using the conjunction shown in parentheses.**

1. Animals' tails are used for communication. They are also used for locomotion. (and)
2. The position in which an animal holds its tail may indicate aggression. The position may also be an indicator of the animal's social rank. (or)
3. Running cheetahs bend their tails in the direction they want to turn. Running wolves bend their tails in the direction they want to turn. (and)
4. For many animals, tails are rudders. For many animals, tails are balances. (both/and)

# Nouns

In this chapter you have learned that the most memorable words are ones that are specific. Specific words make a greater impact on readers than general words because they create clear images in the minds of readers. However, to ensure the clarity of your words, you need to edit your writing for correct capitalization, punctuation, and spelling. Russell Baker deliberately wrote his spoof of Little Red Riding Hood in jargon, but the grammar and mechanics are standard.

## Capitalization of Proper Nouns

One way to make some nouns specific is to substitute proper nouns for common nouns. A **common noun** is *any* person, place, or thing; a **proper noun** names a *specific* person, place, or thing. All proper nouns, of course, begin with capital letters.

| | |
|---|---|
| Common Nouns | The **poet** wrote a sonnet about a **pharaoh** who once ruled that **country**. |
| Proper Nouns | **Shelley** wrote a sonnet about **Rameses II** who once ruled **Egypt**. |

## Punctuation with Possessive Nouns

To form the possessive of a singular noun, simply add *'s*. To form the possessive of a plural noun, you need to do one of two things: Add only an apostrophe to a plural noun that ends in *s* or add *'s* to a plural noun that does not end in *s*.

| | |
|---|---|
| Singular Possessive | This is the **traveler's** report about his trip to Egypt. |
| Plural Possessive | These are the **travelers'** reports about their trip to Egypt. |

## Punctuation with a Series

A **series** is three or more similar items listed in consecutive order. A series of nouns—or any other series of words, phrases, or clauses—would be confusing to read if the words in the series were not separated by commas.

| | |
|---|---|
| INCORRECT | The time was now the hour had struck and the body lupine cried out for decision. |
| CORRECT | The time was now**,** the hour had struck**,** and the body lupine cried out for decision. |
| INCORRECT | Jan wanted to be with Frank every moment hear his every word and even watch him sleep. |
| CORRECT | Jan wanted to be with Frank every moment**,** hear his every word**,** and even watch him sleep. |

## Spelling the Plurals of Nouns

Simply add *s* to form the plural of most nouns. The endings of a few nouns must be changed, however, before you add *s*. For instance, if a word ends in a consonant and *y*, you must change the *y* to *i* and add *es*. *Jury*, for example, becomes *juries*.

| | |
|---|---|
| SINGULAR NOUNS | My **memory** of the **statue** is vague. |
| PLURAL NOUNS | My **memories** of the **statues** are vague. |
| SINGULAR NOUNS | The **dinghy** was on the **beach**. |
| PLURAL NOUNS | The **dinghies** were on the **beaches.** |

### Editing Checklist

- ✓ Are all proper nouns capitalized?
- ✓ Is an apostrophe used correctly with possessive nouns?
- ✓ Do commas separate any series of words?
- ✓ Are plural nouns spelled correctly?

**Combining Sentences by Subordinating** Ideas of unequal importance can be combined by **subordination**—by turning the less important idea into a subordinate clause. Following are some words that introduce subordinate clauses.

| RELATIVE PRONOUNS | | SUBORDINATING CONJUNCTIONS | |
|---|---|---|---|
| who | that | after | because |
| whom | which | until | whenever |
| whose | whoever | unless | although |

**A.** Capitol pages have a chance to see government in action. They are aides to lawmakers.
Capitol pages, **who are aides to lawmakers,** have a chance to see government in action. (adjective clause)

**B.** The Supreme Court uses only three students as pages. The chances of becoming a Supreme Court page are slim.
**Because the Supreme Court uses only three students as pages,** the chances of becoming a Supreme Court page are slim. (adverb clause)

**C.** A person may want to become a Capitol page. That person should write to his or her senator and representative for information.
**Whoever wants to become a Capitol page** should write to his or her senator and representative for information. (noun clause)

## PRACTICE YOUR SKILLS

### *Combining Sentences by Subordinating*

**Combine each of the following sentences, using the joining word given in parentheses. Add commas where needed.**

1. Senate pages may be between fourteen and seventeen years old. Pages in the House must be high school juniors or seniors. (while)

2. The *Capitol Page School Handbook* tells pages about their jobs. It is issued by the House of Representatives. (which)
3. The tasks of Capitol pages are varied. They include running errands and handling phone calls. (which)
4. Parliamentary rules must be followed strictly. Pages sound bells to call House members to a vote. (because)
5. Capitol pages serve out the terms to which they are appointed. They must still attend school. (while)
6. The school is part of the Washington, D.C., public school system. The schedule is adjusted for the pages. (although)
7. Regular classes begin in the morning. Capitol pages have already finished their special early classes. (when)
8. Pages attend school. They rush to Capitol Hill for a day's work. (after)
9. Someone may come from outside Washington, D.C., to be a page. He or she must arrange for room and board. (whoever)
10. Pages are well paid. Living expenses are high. (although)

## Varying Sentence Structure

By combining sentences, you can create sentences that have different lengths and different structures. Using a mix of the four basic sentence types will improve your writing style.

| | |
|---|---|
| SIMPLE | Rita read the letter. (one independent clause) |
| COMPOUND | Rita read the letter, and Sam waited. (two or more independent clauses) |
| COMPLEX | While Rita read the letter, Sam waited. (one independent clause and one or more subordinate clauses) |
| COMPOUND-COMPLEX | While Rita read the letter, Sam waited, but she never uttered a word. (one or more independent clauses and one or more subordinate clauses) |

## Varying Sentence Beginnings

Beginning every sentence with a subject can become monotonous. Use the following sentence starters for a change of pace.

| | |
|---|---|
| ADVERB | **Probably** the largest meteor to fall within recorded history landed in Siberia in 1947. |
| ADJECTIVE | **Brittle** as glass, the meteor broke into thousands of pieces on its way to Earth. |
| PREPOSITIONAL PHRASE | **In its original form,** it probably weighed 200 tons. |
| INFINITIVE PHRASE | **To trace the source of the meteor,** scientists studied the debris at the site. |
| PARTICIPIAL PHRASE | **Landing with great destructive force,** the meteor felled all trees within 40 miles. |
| ADVERB CLAUSE | **If the meteor had fallen two hours later,** it would have hit Leningrad. |

## PRACTICE YOUR SKILLS

 *Varying Sentence Beginnings*

**Write a sentence for each type of sentence starter listed above. Then challenge yourself by selecting a topic and writing a paragraph in which you use several different types of sentence beginnings.**

##  Correcting Faulty Sentences

Most writers, when writing their first drafts, concentrate on just the content and organization. Only later do they go back to polish their sentences and correct any errors. In this section, you will find ways to revise your sentences to eliminate some common sentence faults.

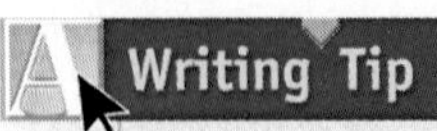

Revise your sentences to eliminate **faulty coordination, faulty subordination, rambling sentences,** and overuse of the **passive voice**.

## Faulty Coordination

You can prevent problems in faulty coordination in three ways. First, avoid using the wrong coordinator, which will blur the meaning of your sentence. Notice in the following example how the writer sharpens the meaning by supplying the appropriate coordinator.

| | |
|---|---|
| FAULTY COORDINATION | I want to learn more about photography, **and** I am going to take lessons. |
| CORRECT | I want to learn more about photography, **so** I am going to take lessons. |

The following lists some common coordinators according to their use.

| SOME COMMON COORDINATORS | | | |
|---|---|---|---|
| **To Show Similarity** | **To Show Contrast** | **To Show Alternative** | **To Show Result** |
| and | but | either/or | so |
| both/and | still | neither/nor | therefore |
| furthermore | nevertheless | or, nor | as a result |

Second, coordinate only those ideas that are related to each other. If the ideas are not related, express them in separate sentences.

| | |
|---|---|
| FAULTY COORDINATION | Planes fly over our house every hour, and flying is really a safe way to travel. |
| CORRECT | Planes fly over our house every hour. Flying is really a safe way to travel. |

Finally, coordinate only those ideas that are equally important. If the ideas are not equal, subordinate one of them by putting it in a phrase or a subordinate clause.

| | |
|---|---|
| FAULTY COORDINATION | Inez forgot our phone number, and she did not call us. |
| CORRECT | **Forgetting our phone number,** Inez did not call us. (phrase) |
| CORRECT | **Since Inez forgot our phone number,** she did not call us. (subordinate clause) |

## Faulty Subordination

Subordination is used to show the relationship between ideas of unequal importance. Subordination can lead to two types of problems: (1) using the wrong subordinator and (2) subordinating the wrong idea.

To avoid the first problem use a word that shows exactly how the ideas are related.

| | |
|---|---|
| FAULTY SUBORDINATION | Yuki trained for months **even though** he would be ready for the Olympic trials. |
| CORRECT | Yuki trained for months **so that** he would be ready for the Olympic trials. |

To avoid the second problem, use a subordinator and turn the less important idea into a subordinate clause. Then express the more important idea as an independent clause.

| | |
|---|---|
| FAULTY SUBORDINATION | Although they took a walk in the park, it was snowing. |
| CORRECT | Although it was snowing, they took a walk in the park. |

The chart on the following page shows common subordinators, listed according to their use.

| SOME COMMON SUBORDINATORS | | | |
|---|---|---|---|
| **To Show Time** | **To Show Cause** | **To Show Purpose** | **To Show Condition** |
| after | because | that | if |
| before | since | so that | even though |
| whenever | as | in order that | unless |

The following guidelines will help you correct faulty coordination and faulty subordination as you revise your writing.

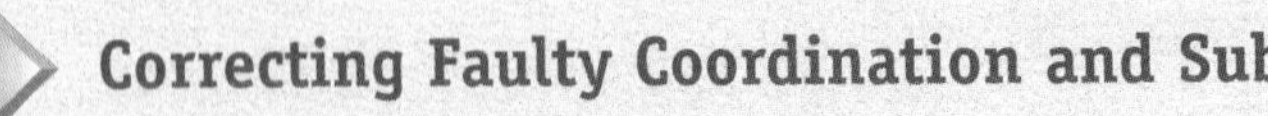

### Correcting Faulty Coordination and Subordination

- Use the connecting word that best expresses how the ideas are related.
- Express unrelated ideas in separate sentences.
- If related ideas are equally important, use a coordinating word to combine them.
- If related ideas are not equally important, turn the less important idea into a phrase or a subordinate clause.

## Practice Your Skills

### *Correcting Faulty Coordination and Subordination*

**Use the guidelines in the box above to revise each of the following sentences.**

1. Tales of western cowhands depict adventurous heroes, and actually their lives were exhausting and dangerous.
2. On the range water was scarce and raiders were common; furthermore, cowhands on the open range endured many hardships.
3. The cowhands' most precious possessions were their horses; also horses were their only means of transportation.

4. A cowhand might give the last drop of water in his canteen to his horse since he himself was thirsty.
5. A western saddle was designed for support; because a cowhand could even nap in the saddle without falling.
6. A cowhand had to be skilled with a rope, and it was his most important tool.
7. Cowhands in different regions had different names for the rope, for in the Southwest it was a lariat, while along the Pacific Coast it was a lasso.
8. The cattle roundup was an important part of the cowhand's work, so it was also a type of social gathering.
9. They finished their work, and they competed in contests of skill called rodeos.
10. Because rodeos are still popular today, they have become more commercialized.

## Rambling Sentences

Sentences that ramble on and on are usually the result of excessive coordination. To break up rambling sentences, separate ideas into concise sentences of their own.

RAMBLING Some lions live in groups, which are called prides, and the lions who live this way can be said to be more fortunate than solitary lions, because the members of a pride of lions share all of the important tasks—for example, tasks such as hunting and protecting their turf—while solitary lions must feed themselves and must protect themselves on their own.

IMPROVED Lions who live in groups, called prides, are more fortunate than solitary lions. Members of a pride share important tasks such as hunting and protecting their turf, while solitary lions must feed and protect themselves.

## Practice Your Skills

### *Revising Rambling Sentences*

**Revise the following rambling sentences into shorter sentences. Capitalize and punctuate the new sentences correctly.**

1. The Beatles were an immensely popular singing group in the years during the 1960s and 1970s, and they expressed in their words and in their music the feelings of the young people of those times, but even though they were controversial and their records and their appearances were banned in some places, still their popularity held steady for many years.
2. People who are interested in a research career in the field of chemistry must choose between basic research and applied research, and the choice is an important one because there are significant differences between the two types of research, since in basic research the main goal of chemists is to expand knowledge about nature, while in applied research, chemists refine or develop products and services, and there are more jobs available in applied research.
3. Denim is a durable fabric used for making jeans, and the name *denim* evolved from the French, who called the fabric *serge de Nímes,* because it was originally woven in Nímes, France, but Levi Strauss was the first to popularize denim, and he used it to make pants for gold miners in the San Francisco area in the mid-1800s.
4. "What's in a name?" asked Shakespeare 400 years ago, and some psychologists are still asking the very same question today, for they maintain that people's names can have an effect that is profound on their attitudes and behavior, and so these psychologists make a plea for parents' devoting considerably more thought to what they name their children than to what they name their pets.
5. The sign language that is used by many deaf people can be very descriptive, and the signs for animals are especially so, since *elephant*, for example, is signed with the hand extending from the nose, like an elephant's trunk, and the sign for *monkey* is the famous chest-scratching motion.

## Faulty Parallelism

A parallel structure is one in which two or more ideas linked with coordinate or correlative conjunctions are expressed in the same grammatical form. Ideas being contrasted should also be parallel. **Parallelism** helps readers understand related ideas. **Faulty parallelism**, on the other hand, adds a jarring effect to a sentence.

| | |
|---|---|
| FAULTY | The committee members were **enthusiastic, energetic**, and **of great diplomacy**. (two adjectives and one prepositional phrase) |
| PARALLEL | The committee members were **enthusiastic, energetic**, and **diplomatic**. (three adjectives) |
| FAULTY | Neither soft **words** nor **offering treats** could coax the kitten down from the tree. (noun, gerund) |
| PARALLEL | Neither **soft words** nor **treats** could coax the kitten down from the tree. (both nouns) |
| FAULTY | **Doing** your best is more important than **to win**. (gerund, infinitive) |
| PARALLEL | **Doing** your best is more important than **winning**. (both gerunds) |
| PARALLEL | **To do** your best is more important than **to win**. (both infinitives) |

### *Correcting Faulty Parallelism*

**Revise the faulty parallelism in the following sentences.**

1. Vernetta's goals are to study law and saving money.
2. Some toys are neither of any educational value nor safe.
3. After the audition, Tom felt both disappointed and relief.
4. Roberto proved himself trustworthy and a hardworking person.
5. The sense of smell is more powerful in evoking memories than how things sound.

6. Police dogs must be both good retrievers and good at barking.
7. Neither raking nor to sweep can remove all the leaves.
8. The club members discussed how to recruit new members, where to go for the club outing, and the pros and cons of raising dues.
9. The acting in the movie was better than the people who wrote the script.
10. As we watched the sailboat race from the shore, we saw billowing sails, rippling waves, and that the gulls swept by.

## Active Voice and Passive Voice

Writers always have a choice between the active and passive voice. The **active voice** stresses the doer of an action. The **passive voice** stresses the receiver of an action. In fact, the doer is sometimes left out of a sentence written in the passive voice.

| | |
|---|---|
| ACTIVE | The plumber just fixed the kitchen sink. |
| PASSIVE | The kitchen sink was just fixed by the plumber. |
| PASSIVE | The kitchen sink was just fixed. |

The passive voice not only requires more words, but it can also rob a sentence of its feeling of action. In general, choose the active voice over the passive except when the doer of the action is either obvious or unimportant, as in these examples.

| | |
|---|---|
| PASSIVE | Jimmy Carter was elected President in 1976. |
| PASSIVE | The old library has been completely remodeled. |
| ACTIVE | José and Tina prepared the chicken and beef tacos. |
| PASSIVE | The chicken and beef tacos were prepared by José and Tina. |

When you wish to place emphasis on the receiver of the action, the passive voice is proper and useful.

Martin Luther King, Jr. is honored on his birthday by people throughout the nation.

## Practice Your Skills

### *Changing Passive Voice to Active Voice*

**Rewrite each of the following sentences in the active voice.**

EXAMPLE The car was driven by me while my sister followed the map.

ANSWER I drove the car while my sister followed the map.

1. A yard full of holes was dug by the persistent husky.
2. A decision was made by the company president to present employees with year-end bonuses.
3. A foul ball was called by the first-base umpire.
4. The plan for a new shopping mall was vetoed by the mayor.
5. Cinco de Mayo is celebrated by thousands of people.
6. The telephone bill was handed to me by my mother with a stern look in her eyes.
7. A donation was made by our graduating class to the school library.
8. Survival techniques were learned from the Native Americans by the Pilgrims.
9. A cool midsummer's evening was ushered in by the passing thundershower.
10. An enormous amount of money was being spent by executives on business travel and entertainment.

### *Writing Effective Sentences*

**Rewrite each of the following sentences to correct the problem indicated in parentheses.**

1. Stan repeated the phrase in his mind over and over again. (redundancy)
2. The book that is sitting on my desk is about people who work as archaeologists. (wordiness)
3. Becky wanted the job more than anything else in her life, but she knew she could do it well. (faulty coordination)

**4.** Rhoda has always had an easy time making conversation with strangers and to bring out the best in people. (faulty parallelism)

**5.** The gymnasium was emptied by the spectators after the disappointing defeat. (misuse of the passive voice)

### *Correcting Faulty Sentences*

**Revise the paragraph below to correct faulty coordination and subordination, rambling sentences, and overuse of the passive voice.**

Patterns in the way in which we use our language have been traced by language researchers who work in the field called statistical linguistics, and interesting statistical regularities have been found by them. For example, the 50 most common words in the language account for almost half of what is written by us. Furthermore, about 60 percent of what we say is composed of consonants, so the other 40 percent is composed of vowels. In addition to which certain letters occur more frequently than others. You may know that the most commonly occurring letter in English is *e*, and do you know the letters that come next? You guessed correctly unless you chose *t* and *a*, which are second and third in frequency.

**Time Out to Reflect**

Now that you have gained some expertise in using words and sentences effectively, take a moment to think about your overall writing style. How do readers tend to respond to your written work? Do they suggest deleting words or phrasing ideas differently? Is your vocabulary adequate to your need for vivid, specific words? Spending a bit of time thinking about *how* you write whenever you write will help your writing style dramatically.

## Writing Style Checklist

Style is like a writer's unique fingerprint; it is created through the careful drafting of sentences and words. Use the following checklist to review some of the many ways you can develop your writing style. The page numbers in parentheses refer to pages where you can get help with your writing.

### CHOOSING VIVID WORDS

- Use specific rather than general nouns, verbs, adjectives, and adverbs to make your writing clear and vivid. *(page C60)*
- Use figurative language, such as similes, metaphors, personification, and onomatopoeia to appeal to your reader's imagination. *(pages C61–C65)*
- Avoid clichés. *(page C64)*

### WRITING CONCISE SENTENCES

- Keep your sentences concise by eliminating redundancy, empty expressions, wordy phrases and clauses, and inflated language. *(pages C66–C69)*

### CREATING SENTENCE VARIETY

- Vary the length and structure of your sentences by combining short, choppy sentences into longer ones by means of phrases, coordination, or subordination. *(pages C72–C74, C77)*
- Vary your sentence structure by using a combination of the four sentence types: simple, compound, complex, and compound-complex to guarantee sentence variety. *(page C78)*
- To avoid monotony, vary your sentence beginnings by using words and phrases other than the subject to start a sentence. *(page C79)*

### CORRECTING FAULTY SENTENCES

- Revise your sentences to correct faulty coordination and subordination. *(pages C79–C82)*
- Break up rambling sentences by expressing separate ideas in separate sentences. *(page C83)*
- Avoid faulty parallelism by using the same grammatical constructions to express similar ideas. *(page C85)*
- Avoid using the passive voice except when the performer of the action is obvious or unimportant. *(page C86)*

# Connection Collection

## Representing in Different Ways

***From Print . . .***

The sound of rain and watery weather draws long faces on some, making them sad and gloomy. The clouds in the sky seem to block the sun that shines inside these people who do not like the rain. However, the patter of raindrops in puddles and on the street invigorates me. The first plip-plop of a rainstorm makes my heart rush and makes my limbs want to wiggle. The rain makes me want to click my heels and clip-clop down the soaked streets and dance!

***. . . to Visuals***

Draw a picture or take a photograph that closely represents the tone of the journal entry above. You may also find a photo in a book, a magazine, or on the Internet.

## From Visuals . . .

Charles Burchfield. *November Sun Emerging*, 1956–1959.
Watercolor on paper, 37 1/2 by 31 3/4 inches.
Courtesy of SBC Communications Inc.

## . . . to Print

Write a journal entry that represents the tone and style of the painting above. Use figurative language, such as similes and metaphors, to appeal to your reader's imagination.

- **Which strategies can be used for creating both written and visual representations? Which strategies apply to one, not both? Which type of representation is more effective?**
- **Draw a conclusion, and write briefly about the differences between written ideas and visual representations.**

## Writing in Academic Areas

### *Poster for a Math Bee*

As Issy Isosceles, head math instructor at Brown High School, it is your duty to promote student support of academic activities. Since the school hallways are often filled with posters for upcoming football games, you believe it is time to use this method to promote an upcoming statewide math bee—a contest you feel Brown has a good chance of winning.

**Design a poster for the hallways of Brown, and write a short paragraph describing the math bee to students. Be sure to include language with vivid words and descriptions that will make the contest sound appealing. Keep your tone lively, convincing your student audience that the contest will be beneficial and fun to attend.**

**What descriptive strategies did you use to interest the students in the math contest?**

## Writing for Oral Communication

### *Speech to Campers*

You are a counselor at Camp Sunburn. This summer, there has been a terrible problem with mosquitoes in the area. Susan Chang, the head counselor, has asked you to prepare a speech to the campers—who range in age from 10 to 12—about ways to avoid the mosquitoes.

**Prepare the speech about how to avoid mosquitoes for the camp children. Make your speech lively by using vivid words and figurative language. Vary your sentence structures and sentence beginnings, and avoid rambling or faulty sentences. In addition, consider methods of making the introduction and conclusion of your speech lively and enjoyable. Practice your speech by giving it to your classmates.**

**What strategies did you use to inform the camp children about avoiding the mosquitoes?**

*You can find information on preparing speeches on pages C672–C681.*

# Assess Your Learning

Once upon a point in time, a small person named Little Red Riding Hood initiated plans for the preparation, delivery and transportation of foodstuffs to her grandmother, a senior citizen residing at a place of residence in a forest of indeterminate dimension.

In the process of implementing this program, her incursion into the forest was in midtransportation process when it attained interface with an alleged perpetrator. This individual, a wolf, made inquiry as to the whereabouts of Little Red Riding Hood's goal as well as inferring that he was desirous of ascertaining the contents of Little Red Riding Hood's foodstuffs basket, and all that.

—*Russell Baker,* from Little Red Riding Hood Revisited

- **Rewrite Russell Baker's satirical passage. Change the jargon-filled sentences into simple, direct language. Use an informal and playful tone as if you were telling the story to a group of your close friends.**
- **Use specific words to create clear images and to avoid using jargon. Use figurative language such as similes and metaphors to appeal to your reader's imagination. However, be sure to avoid clichés and mixed metaphors.**

*Before You Write* **Consider the following questions:**
What is the ***subject?***
What is the ***occasion?***
Who is the ***audience?***
What is the ***purpose?***

*After You Write* **Evaluate your work using the following criteria:**

- Have you used specific words to create clear, vivid images?
- Have you avoided using jargon?
- Have you used figurative language, such as similes and metaphors, to appeal to your reader's imagination?
- Have you checked your writing for clichés and mixed metaphors?
- Have you revised by elaborating, deleting, combining, and rearranging text?
- Have you proofread your writing for appropriateness of style and conventions?

**Write briefly on how well you did. Point out your strengths and areas for improvement.**

CHAPTER 3

# Writing Different Kinds of Paragraphs

You have analyzed the structure of sentences and how to build effective ones. Now is the time to focus on ways in which to make these sentences work together to form the four basic types of paragraphs: narrative, descriptive, informative, and persuasive.

Narrative writing tells stories in which the events usually take place in chronological order. Descriptive writing paints pictures with words, portraying a person or depicting a scene so well that readers feel they are seeing what is being described. Informative writing explains or provides information. Persuasive writing supports an opinion by offering facts and examples to convince the reader to agree with the author's opinion.

In "Tuxedo Junction," author P. Dee Boersma uses a combination of these paragraph types to achieve her writing purpose. You will learn firsthand how each type of paragraph is constructed and have opportunities to polish your skills in writing different kinds of paragraphs.

## *Reading with a Writer's Eye*

In "Tuxedo Junction" P. Dee Boersma writes an animated account of visiting a colony of Galápagos penguins on tiny Fernandina Island. The birds live and breed in the Galápagos Islands on a scorched bit of lava rock surrounded by frigid Pacific waters. As you read, try to imagine living in such an inhospitable climate. Notice, too, the author's graceful intertwining of paragraph types, all of which work together to produce an effective piece of writing.

# TUXEDO JUNCTION

*P. Dee Boersma*

That first day on Fernandina I didn't even glimpse a penguin. At night I lay awake, hoping that the creature that had eluded my eyes would reveal itself to my ears. Penguins are noisy. Each species has its trademark call. The emperor trills, the Adélie cackles, the king trumpets, and members of the *Sphenicus* genus sound like donkeys. Early explorers in South Africa, hearing braying at night, feared they were surrounded by wild donkeys; at sunrise they discovered not donkeys, but a nearby penguin colony. Like its African cousin, the Galápagos penguin makes a braying sound that has earned both species the sobriquet[1] jackass penguins.

There were no brays the first night on Fernandina but the next day, after climbing over what appeared to be an endless coastline of lava, there it was—a Galápagos penguin standing nonchalantly on the shore, a tiny shape against the horizon. Weighing nearly five pounds and standing about a foot tall, the Galápagos is one of the smallest penguins.

My best rendition of a lonesome Galápagos penguin cry, a long plaintive *Haaaa*, brought one curious customer in from the ocean. Momentarily, it stood just below my feet, perhaps wondering what this big object was that didn't seem much like a penguin. But the scorching sun makes the land a difficult place to stay for long, and the penguin soon headed back to sea. Penguins frequently jump into the water to cool off or stand with their flippers extended, like a runner cooling down. When penguins lay eggs,

---

[1] **sobriquet** (sō bri kā´): Nickname.

they must be incubated and protected. Since this would be impossible to do on the exposed barren lava, Galápagos penguins lay their eggs in lava tubes, crevices, or in holes where brooding[2] adults are shaded.

Whenever the cold Cromwell Current provides sufficient food for the penguins to breed, the birds lay two white eggs—ordinarily twice a year. Penguins pay more attention to food availability than to season or month. The Cromwell Current is variable and penguin life is governed by the nutrients that feed the plankton,[3] which in turn are consumed by the small schooling fish that penguins eat. When white mullet and other schooling fish aren't available, indicating that the Cromwell Current is not providing sufficient nutrients, Galápagos penguins turn to colorful reef fish.

Although they are monogamous[4]—Galápagos penguins are not always faithful. "Divorces" sometimes occur among pairs from one breeding attempt to the next. The second egg is laid four days after the first, permitting the female to leave the nest to forage for food and water between laying the first and second egg. Both male and female take turns incubating. After about 40 days the eggs hatch into gray, fluffy chicks resembling little bean bags with tiny beaks and big stomachs. In about 60 days, the chicks are ready to leave the nest and begin life on their own.

Days in the Galápagos are divided into 12 hours of light and 12 hours of dark. Because seasons are not well-defined, breeding doesn't commence on a set schedule. This distinguishes Galápagos penguins from other species of penguins that live in sub-antarctic and antarctic regions, where breeding is so regular you could use the birds' schedule as a calendar. Magellanic penguins which breed in Argentina, arrive at their nesting grounds on nearly the same day, year after year after year.

Since my first visit in the early 1970s, the population of Galápagos penguins has been reduced by 50 percent, to its current

---

[2] **brooding:** Sitting on the eggs.

[3] **plankton:** Tiny animal and plant life found in bodies of water.

[4] **monogamous:** Having only one mate.

estimate of from 4,000 to 8,500 birds, all believed to be living on Fernandina and Isabela islands. There are a number of probable causes. Following the 1982–83 El Niño, the penguin population declined to about a quarter of the numbers present in the early 1970s. Then, prior to the El Niño of 1997–98, the penguins appeared to be recovering. The effects of the recent El Niño, along with the risk to the penguins posed by warming temperatures resulting from global climate change, have yet to be determined. Other factors to consider: For more than a century, the Galápagos Islands were lost in time, remaining much as they had been when Charles Darwin weighed anchor in 1835. In the early 1970s, when I started my field research, I had Fernandina all to myself. I saw no people. Just a wilderness of land and sea. But the past 25 years have brought sweeping changes. Hundreds of tourists visit Fernandina daily. Fishing boats harvest fish and other sea life, sometimes illegally. The remoteness, the isolation, and the wildness are disappearing. Today, cruise boats anchor offshore. What protects the islands are the park service and the government's desire to continue bringing tourists to see the natural wonders.

Don't misunderstand me. The Galápagos Islands are still spectacular. The penguins still contend with vagaries[5] of the Cromwell Current. Marine iguanas still sneeze salt from their noses, and sea lions still snooze in the sun. What is different reflects the demands of the world's rapidly expanding human population. In Darwin's day, there were one billion people on Earth. Now, we number nearly six billion, using more resources and taking more from wildlife than ever before. As transport among the islands grows heavier, pollution is likely to increase. In addition, boat traffic can bring in unwanted insects, plants, rats, and even domestic cats to Fernandina, as has happened on other Galápagos Islands. Geologically the newest and least hospitable of the islands, Fernandina has so far escaped this fate.

---

[5] **vagaries:** Unpredictable situations.

## Thinking as a Writer

### NARRATION Analyzing Print for Visual Representation

- Imagine you are going to make a short documentary based on the scientific investigation described by P. Dee Boersma in "Tuxedo Junction." Which parts of Boersma's trip to and experiences on Fernandina Island would you want to capture on film? Why do you think those are important for a viewer? In what sequence would you order Boersma's experiences on film? Why?

### DESCRIPTION Observing Like a Scientist

Viewing

- Imagine you are a scientist writing an article on Galápagos penguins. You need to describe them in as much detail as possible for your article and you have only the photograph to the right with which to work. From the photograph, how much descriptive information can you derive for your article? What details about the penguins would you like to know for your article but are unable to determine only from the photograph?

## INFORMATION Evaluating Presentation of Information

- Think about the main pieces of information the writer includes in the article. Then brainstorm on several other titles the author might have used that would reflect that information. Which of your new titles do you think works best? Why?
- In the article Boersma discusses several categories of information, such as the appearance of the adult penguins and chicks and the characteristics of their environment. Has the information been clearly presented so that readers can understand it easily? Explain, giving examples.
- Part of the article involves the effect of visitors and other arrivals on the island. How do these intrusions affect the penguins and their environment? How does the writer make the danger clear to you?
- After reading the article, do you think something might be done to help protect the Galápagos penguins? How has the writer's presentation of information led you to this conclusion?

## PERSUASION Evaluating the Soundness of an Argument

A writer's **argument** is a statement of opinion supported by facts, examples, and reasons.

- What opinion does the writer of "Tuxedo Junction" give about the probability of the Galápagos penguins' survival? Which ideas support this opinion? Is the argument sound, or faulty and illogical?
- What does Boersma say might protect the penguins and ensure their continued presence on Fernandina Island? Do you feel that such an action would be effective?

# Developing Your Skills of Writing Paragraphs

Whenever and whatever you write, your purpose is to convey a message to your reader. As a writer you must bear the responsibility for providing a message with substance and an easy-to-follow structure. Paragraphs contribute to the logical structure of your writings.

A **paragraph** is a group of related sentences that present and develop one main idea.

## Paragraph Structure

Paragraphs help the reader by breaking up a series of continuous thoughts into smaller pieces. Each paragraph is an entity all its own, with its own specific facts and ideas. Notice how the following well-written paragraph is easy to read and understand.

**TOPIC SENTENCE:** STATES MAIN IDEA

**BODY OF SUPPORTING SENTENCES:** DEVELOPS MAIN IDEA WITH SPECIFICS

### *Stellar Compromises*

Director George Lucas considers his original *Star Wars* a "real low-budget movie." He had to pare down his original budget estimate of $18 million, and, as a result, the film is full of compromises. He cut out over a hundred special effects shots. New sets were made from old sets. Space weapons were made out of cut-down machine guns. On such a low budget, the robots didn't work right at first. The original R2-D2 couldn't go more than three feet without running into something. (Extra footage had to be shot later for some scenes in the beginning.) Even the cantina scene, in which Luke and Ben Kenobi hire Han Solo and Chewbacca from among a roomful of bizarre, otherworldly creatures, is only a shadow of what was in Lucas' imagination. The designer fell sick, and the studio wouldn't give Lucas enough money

**Concluding Sentence:** REINFORCES MAIN IDEA

to have someone fully complete it. "The film is about 25 percent of what I wanted it to be," he has said.

—*Dian G. Smith,* American Filmmakers Today

This paragraph succeeds in delivering its message. Its clear structure is relatively easy to follow. The main idea of the paragraph is stated in the topic sentence and is amply supported with specific details. The sentences in the body of the paragraph relate to the main idea and are presented in a smooth, logical order. In short, this model includes the basic features needed for an effective paragraph.

A paragraph that stands alone should include the three main parts noted in the previous example: (1) a topic sentence, (2) a body of supporting sentences, and (3) a concluding sentence. The following chart summarizes the function of each of these elements.

## Elements of a Paragraph

The **topic sentence**

- states the main idea.
- limits the main idea to one aspect of the subject that can be covered in one paragraph.
- controls all the other sentences in the paragraph.
- is more general than the sentences that develop it.

The **supporting sentences**

- explain, develop, or prove the topic sentence.
- provide details, events, facts, examples, or reasons.

The **concluding sentence,** or clincher,

- provides a strong ending.
- restates, summarizes, evaluates, or adds an insight to the main idea.

The topic sentence can appear at the beginning, in the middle, or at the end of a paragraph. The main idea may also be stated in two sentences or not stated at all, but merely implied. All of these alternatives are available to help you—the writer—express your main idea clearly, as in the examples that follow.

**MODEL: Topic Sentence in the Middle**

Japan is a collection of large islands, strung along the eastern shore of the mainland of Asia. The islands are very rugged and very mountainous. High over all the other peaks rises the one supreme peak—the perfect cone of snowclad Fuji. Like most of the high mountains of Japan, Fuji is a volcano, sleeping, but far from dead. Compared to the Alps and the Himalayas, Fuji is not especially high. It seems high, however, because it rises in one superb sweeping curve right from the shore to the sky, a curve that can be seen for a hundred miles on every side.

–*Richard Halliburton,* Complete Book of Marvels

**MODEL: Implied Main Idea**

When the newborn seal pup slips from the warmth of his mother's body onto the ice, crystals form on his wet little body and his skin temperature falls to 70°F. He shivers so vigorously that in about 45 minutes he has produced enough heat to bring his skin temperature to 93.4° F. Only a light coat of baby fur, the lanugo, protects him from the zero temperatures of the Antarctic spring. His metabolism, however, is exceedingly high during his early life, and he can take in great quantities of milk. Seal mothers' milk is richer than heavy cream; it is half butterfat. On this creamy diet the pup gains about 250 pounds in six weeks and has a good coating of fat.

–*Lucy Kavaler,* Life Battles Cold

*Implied main idea:* Seal pups have natural mechanisms to help them survive frigid temperatures.

## Practice Your Skills

### *Identifying the Main Idea*

**Find and write the topic sentence of each paragraph. If the main idea is implied, write a sentence expressing that idea.**

**1. Forest Rangers**

Park rangers' work includes planning and carrying out conservation efforts to protect plant and animal life in the parks from fire, disease, and heavy visitor traffic. Rangers plan and conduct programs of public safety, including law enforcement and rescue work. They set up and direct interpretive programs such as slide shows, guided tours, displays, and occasionally even dramatic presentations. These programs are designed to help visitors become aware of the natural and historic significance of the areas they visit.

—*Walter Oleksy,* Careers in the Animal Kingdom

**2. Starry Neighbors**

Easter Island is the loneliest inhabited place in the world. The nearest solid land the islanders can see is above in the firmament, the moon and the planets. They have to travel farther than any other people to see that there really is land closer. Therefore, living nearest the stars, they know more names of stars than of towns and countries in our own world.

—*Thor Heyerdahl,* Aku-Aku

**COMPUTER TIP**

When you write a draft of a paragraph, you can keep the paragraph in your standard folder, perhaps labeled "My Works in Progress."

## Generalizing

**Generalizing** is the process of developing a general principle based on specific facts. Many topic sentences are generalizations supported by ideas and details, but generalizations must avoid exaggeration. Therefore, avoid using words like *all, always,* or *never.*

**All** teenagers like loud music. (broad generalization)

This generalization is not valid because it could never prove that *all* teenagers like loud music. *All* should be replaced with *some, many, most,* or *few.*

**Some** teenagers like loud music. (valid generalization)

The chart below is based on the topic sentence *All students litter the school campus.*

GENERALIZATION CHART

| Supporting Facts | Nonsupporting Facts |
|---|---|
| The campus has accumulated litter. | The wind blows some papers onto the campus. |
| You saw some students littering on the lawn. | Many students throw trash in trash cans. |
| You noticed that some cans were knocked over. | Some animals knock over trash cans. |
| **Revised: Some** students litter the school campus. | |

### THINKING PRACTICE

**Test one of the following topic sentences or your own generalization by making a chart like the one above.**

1. Students cheat due to a variety of pressures.
2. All teenagers are influenced by what they see on television.
3. All video games are harmful to teenagers.

## Features of a Good Paragraph

Not every paragraph with a topic sentence, supporting sentences, and a concluding sentence is an effective paragraph. What the sentences say is as important as how they are put together. Features of a good paragraph are adequate development, unity, and coherence.

### Adequate Development

The supporting sentences in a paragraph have the job of developing the main idea with specific details. These details explain, illustrate, describe, or argue for the main idea. They may take one or more of the forms listed below.

| TYPES OF SUPPORTING DETAILS | | |
|---|---|---|
| facts | reasons | descriptive details |
| examples | events | comparisons and contrasts |

Whatever their form, supporting details must be numerous enough and specific enough to do their job—that is, to develop the main idea. If the main idea is not strongly supported, the reader may not understand it or believe it.

In the following model, the writer has used enough specific details to support the full weight of the main idea. In this paragraph the details take the form of facts and examples.

**Model: Adequate Paragraph Development**

Around the turn of the last century child-labor practices led to a grueling life for many American children. In 1900 at least 1.7 million children under the age of sixteen worked for wages. Children working at night were kept awake by having cold water splashed in their faces. Some girls under sixteen worked sixteen hours a day in canning factories, capping forty cans per minute. Ten-year-old boys crouched over dusty coal chutes for ten hours a day to pick slate out of the coal sliding past. In city tenements many children seven years and younger made artificial flowers at night to be sold the next day at street stands. Some states began passing laws protecting child laborers after 1905. Not until 1938 was a federal law passed that prevented employers in most industries from hiring children under the age of sixteen.

—*Clarence L. Ver Steeg,* American Spirit

Use sufficient **specific details** to develop your main idea adequately.

## Practice Your Skills

*Improving Development*

**Using the facts in the following table, revise the paragraph below so that the main idea is adequately developed. Retain the first sentence and the last sentence, which is the topic sentence.**

### Cities Take Over

Between the years 1860 and 1910 the nation's population increased enormously. The new population moved to both rural and urban areas, but more people moved to cities. The number of cities increased dramatically. Since the early 1900s, the United States has been a nation of cities.

| Facts | 1860 | 1910 | Percent of Growth |
|---|---|---|---|
| overall population | 31 million | 92 million | 200 |
| rural population | 25 million | 50 million | 100 |
| urban population | 6 million | 42 million | 600 |
| number of cities | 400 | 2200 | 450 |

number of immigrants from Europe (1865–1910): 19 million

## Unity

In a paragraph that has **unity**, all the sentences support and develop the main idea. A unified paragraph is easy to follow, for the reader is not distracted by ideas or details that stray from the primary thought.

**Writing Tip**

Achieve **unity** in a paragraph by making sure that all the supporting sentences relate directly to the main idea.

In the following paragraph, the crossed-out sentences stray from the main idea. If you read the paragraph without those sentences, you will notice how much easier it is to follow.

**Model: Paragraph Unity**

### *Sammy Lee*

Sammy Lee, a second-generation Korean American, has devoted his life to athletic excellence and physical fitness. In 1948 he won the Olympic medal for high diving. When he repeated his feat at the Olympics four years later, he became the first male diver to win two consecutive times. ~~Another Korean American, Richard You, was an Olympic weight lifting coach.~~ Lee also won the James E. Sullivan award for outstanding sports achievement in 1958. He now practices medicine and has served on the President's Council on Physical Fitness. ~~Richard You is also a doctor at present.~~

At first the crossed-out sentences may seem related to the topic. The topic sentence, however, limits the main idea of the paragraph to Sammy Lee. When you write and revise, ask yourself whether each sentence in a paragraph really is related to the main idea.

## Practice Your Skills

### *Achieving Unity*

**Each of the following paragraphs contains sentences that stray from the main idea and weaken the paragraph's unity. Find and write the sentences in each paragraph that do not belong.**

**1. Science or Magic?**

Although the alchemists of long ago are often regarded as superstitious magicians, they did help pave the way for some important discoveries. In their vain search for an elixir of life and a way to turn metals into gold, they discovered chemicals that are now common in such products as dye, varnish, medicine, glass, and steel. Alchemists also developed waterproofing, smelling salts, and some painkillers. Some alchemists, nonetheless, were undoubtedly frauds. One early alchemist developed a theory of gas, and others led the way to an understanding of blood circulation and enzymes and hormones. One famous alchemist, Merlin, may have existed only in legend. Although their work was limited by a lack of scientific knowledge, many alchemists were serious scientists whose discoveries opened new doors.

**2. Director of Volunteer Services**

Because volunteers are so important in the smooth running of a hospital, the director of volunteer services is usually a well-paid professional. The requirements for this position often include a college education, normally in sociology, psychology, or management. In fact, many of the jobs available in a hospital require advanced training of some kind. The salary of the director of volunteers varies according to the person's previous experience and the size and resources of the hospital. Most doctors, of course, earn more money than the volunteer director. Still the job is so important that most directors do earn a good wage.

## Coherence

The details in a paragraph must relate not only to the main idea but also to one another. A **coherent** paragraph is one in which the ideas are smoothly and logically related. The keys to a coherent paragraph are (1) logical organization and (2) appropriate connecting devices.

Achieve **coherence** in a paragraph by ordering the ideas logically and using suitable connectives.

The following chart shows the most common ways to organize paragraphs and longer pieces of writing as well.

| WAYS TO ORGANIZE IDEAS | |
|---|---|
| **Chronological Order** | Arrange details in the order in which they occurred (time order). |
| **Spatial Order** | Arrange details according to their location—near to far, top to bottom. |
| **Order of Importance** | Arrange details from most to least or from least to most important. |
| **Developmental Order** | Arrange details in a logical progression, in which one idea grows out of another. |
| **Comparison/Contrast** | Arrange details to show how two items are similar or different. Describe one item and then the other or compare and contrast by feature. |

A writer can use various devices, as shown in the chart on the next page, to help the reader understand how the ideas in a paragraph are related.

### WAYS TO CONNECT IDEAS

- Repeat key words occasionally to link ideas.

  **Ten years ago** the tree was a sapling, barely able to stand alone. **Ten years ago** I was a child, leaning on my parents.

- Use synonyms to connect back to key words.

  My **parents** guided me through that long period of growth. **Mother and father** sustained me with their love.

- Use pronouns to relate back to key nouns.

  My **father** believed in being strict with his only **child**, and **his** training served **me** well in later years.

- Use *transitions*—words and phrases that show how ideas are related to one another.

  **Finally** I felt ready to set out on my own.

  The tree, **furthermore**, had grown tall and sturdy.

The following chart lists some common transitions and the types of order with which they are most often used. Most transitions may actually be used with more than one kind of organization.

### COMMON TRANSITIONS

| | |
|---|---|
| **Chronological Order** | first, second, then, by evening, in the beginning, soon, immediately, finally, years ago, tomorrow |
| **Spatial Order** | above, below, right, next to, beyond, inside, behind |
| **Order of Importance** | first, second, more, most important, the largest, above all, furthermore, also, another |
| **Developmental Order** | furthermore, besides, however, despite, another, as a result, therefore |
| **Comparison/Contrast** | similarly, like, just, as, but, on the other hand, in contrast to, however |

## PRACTICE YOUR SKILLS

### *Identifying Paragraph Organization*

**Write *chronological, spatial, order of importance, developmental,* or *comparison/contrast* to describe the organization of each of the following paragraphs.**

**1. Zookeepers Then and Now**

The job of animal keeper in a zoo once required no advanced education. The primary responsibilities of the keeper were to feed the animals and keep their cages clean, and working with wild animals was not considered a particularly desirable activity. Recently, however, more and more zoos have begun to hire college graduates to fill the role of keeper. In contrast to earlier times, the job of animal keeper now includes more challenging activities, such as presenting educational programs to the public and studying the animals' habitats. Furthermore, unlike years ago, zoos are deluged with applications from college graduates interested in working with animals.

**2. Tail Snaring**

"Catch and release" has become a popular slogan for those who fish for sport rather than for food. As a result the search is on for ways to land fish without harming them. One such device is the tail snare, which catches fish by lassoing their tails. Besides being useful to people who fish, tail snares help conservationists in tagging fish. Furthermore, they can prevent damage to the meat of big game fish. In short, tail snares hold advantages for people who enjoy fishing.

**3. The Distant Past**

Throughout most of the Mesozoic era, sometimes called the Age of Reptiles, primitive mammals scurried about, lost in the shadows of the mighty dinosaurs who lumbered through the gloomy swamps and giant softwood forests. In the beginning of the Cretaceous, the period which marks the last chapter in the reign of the giant reptiles, the earth cooled. Inland seas receded, marshes dried up, and the monster dinosaurs clambered out onto the trembling uplands and began to live on open ground. Great hardwood forests soon covered the land.

Life for the small, ancestral mammals was perilous, and while the terrible dinosaurs ruled, the little animals scurried about in the deep green shade of the forests or took refuge in the branches of bushes and trees, often venturing forth only at night. They waited, unaware of the kingdom they were soon to inherit, and used their wits and mammalian advantages to survive.

*—Judith Grosch,* You and Your Brain

**4. A Man of Many Talents**

Benjamin Franklin accomplished many things in his eighty-four years. He was a recognized inventor. Franklin gave to the world the stove, bifocals, and the lightning rod. He invented a draft for fireplaces and a combination chair and stepladder for the kitchen. He was also a city planner. Franklin reorganized the British Post Office, established a city police system in Philadelphia, and a fire-control organization. Furthermore, Franklin was a military strategist. He organized a successful defense of his colony when it was threatened by attack by the French. He led a force of men into the wilderness near Bethlehem and supervised the building of three important forts in that area. Finally Franklin was an active statesman. He was a member of the committee which drew up the Declaration of Independence, a delegate to the Constitutional Convention, and an ambassador to England and France for over twenty-five years.

*—P. Joseph Canavan*

**5. Whose Desk Is It?**

There was no name on the office door, but I recognized the desk immediately. Its surface was hidden beneath tall, precarious mounds of paper. Just visible behind a pile of folders stood a framed photo of my parents and me, smiling out over the rubble. On the wall above hung a painting I had done in second grade. "For Dad!" it proclaimed in shaky but bold green letters. Undoubtedly this was my father's desk.

### *Recognizing Transitions*

**Find and write the transitional words and phrases used in each of the paragraphs in the previous practice activity.**

## Process of Writing Paragraphs

Remember that you use different types of writing for a variety of purposes. Most paragraphs serve one of four main functions: (1) to tell a story (narrative), (2) to describe (descriptive), (3) to explain or inform (informative), or (4) to persuade (persuasive). Although each of these four types of writing calls for special techniques, the main stages in the writing process remain the same.

### PREWRITING

- Tap your interests, knowledge, and experience for ideas. *(page C10)*
- Make a list of subjects. *(pages C10–C15)*
- Determine the purpose and audience of your paragraph. *(pages C20–C21)*
- Choose a subject and limit it. *(pages C18–C19)*
- Brainstorm a list of supporting details. *(pages C26–C27)*
- Arrange your details in a logical order. *(pages C109–C110)*

### DRAFTING

- Write a topic sentence that states the main idea. *(pages C100–C102)*
- Use your prewriting notes to write supporting sentences. *(pages C105–C106)*
- Add a concluding sentence. *(page C101)*

### REVISING

- Check your paragraph structure. Is your topic sentence strong? Are your supporting sentences appropriate and adequate? Is your concluding sentence strong? *(pages C100–C102)*
- Check your paragraph for unity and for coherence. *(pages C107–C110)*
- Check your sentences. Are they varied? Have you combined sentences that go together? Are they concise? Have you avoided faulty parallelism and overuse of the passive? *(pages C66–C88)*
- Check your words. Did you use specific words? Did you use figurative language? *(pages C60–C65)*

### EDITING

- Use the **Editing Checklists** on pages C46 and C126 and the Writing Style Checklist on page C89 to check your grammar, usage, spelling, and mechanics.

### PUBLISHING

- Find an appropriate way to publish your paragraph. You might want to share your work with a classmate, with friends, or with family members. *(pages C48–C52)*

# Developing the Skills of Narration

Whenever you tell a joke, relate what you did over the weekend, or note the progress of a storm approaching your town, you are narrating. Learning to write a single narrative paragraph will give you the skills you need to write longer pieces as well—including history reports, short stories, and even comic strips.

**Narrative writing** tells a real or imaginary story with a clear beginning, middle, and end.

### Your Writer's Journal

Keep your eyes and ears open—there are stories happening all around you. In your journal, record events at home, at school, in the news, and in what you read that capture your attention. You may find that one or more of them will serve as a powerful narrative writing topic.

## Narrative Paragraph Structure

The following chart shows the function of each part of a narrative paragraph.

### Structure of a Narrative Paragraph

- The **topic sentence** makes a general statement about the story, captures attention, or sets the scene.
- The **supporting sentences** tell the story, event by event, of how the problem or situation developed, what happened at its height, and how it was resolved.
- The **concluding sentence** summarizes the story or makes a point about its meaning.

Most narratives involve a **conflict**, or problem, at their core. In the following narrative paragraph, the conflict is between a polar bear and the crew of a coast-guard vessel. As you read the paragraph, be aware of its main elements and transitional words and phrases.

**MODEL: Narrative Paragraph**

## A Curious Clown

**TOPIC SENTENCE:** MAKES A GENERAL STATEMENT

**SUPPORTING SENTENCES:** TELL THE STORY EVENT BY EVENT

**CONCLUDING SENTENCE:** GIVES THE OUTCOME

The polar bear has an insatiable curiosity, and sometimes he can be quite a clown. **In 1969**, a coast-guard vessel in the Canadian Arctic received a visit from an adult male polar bear traveling atop a drifting ice-floe. The animal was obviously bent on a shopping expedition, and the crew obliged by throwing it a carton full of black molasses which the bear **soon** spread all over itself and the ice. This was **followed by** some jam, salt pork, two salami sausages, an apple which it spat out in disgust, and a jar of peanut butter which disappeared in about two seconds flat. It refused to touch bread or potatoes but loved chocolate bars. **Eventually** the food supply ran out, but the 363 kg (800 lb.) bear, its appetite now thoroughly whetted, decided to investigate further. It stuck its head through one of the port-holes in search of further nourishment. **When** nothing turned up, it decided to climb aboard, much to the alarm of the crew, who decided to open up the hoses on it. This was a big mistake, however, because the bear absolutely loved the drenching and raised its paws in the air to get the jet of water under its armpits. **In the end** the coastguards were forced to fire a distress rocket rather close to the interloper **before** it reluctantly moved away.

—*Gerald L. Wood,* Animal Facts and Feats

## Point of View

The person who tells the story is called the **narrator**. Who the narrator is determines the **point of view** of the story. With a **first person point of view**, the narrator is involved and uses first person pronouns. With a **third person point of view**, the narrator tells what happens to others, using third person pronouns. When you write a narrative, choose a point of view and then use it consistently.

| | |
|---|---|
| FIRST PERSON | In **my** disappointment, **I** wanted only to sleep, but **my** mind kept wandering back to the rally.<br>—*Ralph Ellison,* Invisible Man |
| THIRD PERSON | In **his** disappointment, **he** wanted only to sleep, but **his** mind kept wandering back to the rally. |

## PRACTICE YOUR SKILLS

### *Identifying Points of View*

**Indicate the point of view in each of the following narrative sentences from "Tuxedo Junction" by writing *first person* or *third person.***

**1.** That first night on Fernandina I didn't even glimpse a penguin.

**2.** Penguins frequently jump into the water to cool off or stand with their flippers extended, like a runner cooling down.

**3.** After about 40 days the eggs hatch into gray, fluffy chicks resembling little bean bags with tiny beaks and big stomachs.

**4.** In the early 1970s, when I started my field research, I had Fernandina all to myself.

**5.** If the little Galápagos penguin is to have a future, we must protect the wild where it lives.

# Process of Writing a Narrative Paragraph

"You can't wait for inspiration," said the novelist Jack London. "You have to go after it with a club." Whenever you begin a narrative, remember that even if ideas don't seem to come to you immediately, you can use prewriting strategies such as freewriting and brainstorming to generate ideas and subjects for your narrative paragraph.

## Writing a First-Person Narrative

### Prewriting

As a senior you will soon be closing many chapters in your life. "Last times" are not new to you, however. Over the years you have said good-bye to friends, to places, to activities, and even to some hopes and dreams. Think back to moments when you experienced something or saw someone for the last time.

- Brainstorm a list of "last times" in your life. Check your **journal** for ideas.
- Choose the experience on your list that would make the best narrative paragraph.
- Relive the experience in your mind. How did the "last time" start? If there was a conflict, what was it? What was the outcome?
- Develop a list of details and events by brainstorming answers to the questions *Who? What? Where? Why? When?* and *How?*
- Arrange the events in chronological order.
- Join a small group of classmates and tell your narrative as you envision it, without notes. When you finish, ask for feedback on the coherence of your account.

### Drafting

Making use of your oral story and the listeners' comments, draft your paragraph.

### Revising

Review your draft carefully. Then use the guidelines on pages C113 and C119 to revise your paragraph.

### Editing

Refer to the writing style Checklist on page C89 to edit your draft.

### Publishing

Copy your edited draft neatly to share with your classmates.

**PORTFOLIO**

## Writing a Third-Person Narrative

Often an embarrassing moment becomes a humorous story. Write a third-person narrative based on such an incident. Follow the process on the following page. Keep a copy of this and all other completed pieces in your portfolio.

**PORTFOLIO**

## Process of Writing a Narrative Paragraph

Remember that when writing your paragraph, you can move back and forth to suit your needs as a writer. In other words, the writing process is recursive. After you finish drafting, for example, you may decide to take another look at your prewriting notes to see if there is another detail or idea that you might want to add to your paragraph.

### PREWRITING

- Using various strategies for thinking of subjects, scan your memory for experiences and events that would make a good story. Then choose one and limit it. *(page C19)*
- Consider your purpose and audience. *(page C21)*
- Think back to the first incident that sets the story in motion. Then list all the events in the story, including details of time and place. *(pages C24–C27)*
- After arranging your notes in chronological order, delete any details that you decide not to use. *(pages C32–C35)*

### DRAFTING

- Write a topic sentence that captures attention, sets the scene, or makes a general statement about the events. *(page C101)*
- Write supporting sentences that relate the events of the story. *(page C101)*
- Organize the details in chronological order and use transitions that show when the events occurred. *(pages C109–C110)*
- Write a concluding sentence that tells the outcome of the story or makes a point about its meaning. *(page C101)*

### REVISING

- Should you add anything to strengthen development? *(page C105)*
- Should you delete anything to strengthen unity? *(page C107)*
- Should you rearrange anything to strengthen coherence? *(pages C109–C110)*
- Do your sentences have variety? *(pages C72–C79)*
- Did you avoid rambling sentences? *(pages C83–C84)*
- Can you substitute any vivid, specific words for general ones? *(page C60)*

### EDITING

- Using the Editing Checklists, check your grammar, usage, spelling, and mechanics. *(pages C46 and C126)*

### PUBLISHING

- Is your handwriting clear and your typing clean? *(pages C49–C50)*
- Prepare a neat final copy and publish it in one of the ways suggested on page C49.

# Developing the Skills of Description

Whenever you bring a subject to life using sensory details, you are writing description. If you can write a single descriptive paragraph, you have the seeds of skills with which you can write anything—from poetry to science fiction.

**Descriptive writing** paints a vivid picture in words of a person, object, or scene by using sensory details.

**Your Writer's Journal**

Wake up your senses and really see, hear, feel, taste, and touch the world around you. Record your sensory impressions past and present in your journal. Among them you may find rich ideas for writing description.

## Descriptive Paragraph Structure

Like a narrative paragraph, a descriptive paragraph has three main parts. The following chart shows the function of each part of a descriptive paragraph.

### Structure of a Descriptive Paragraph

- The **topic sentence** introduces the subject, often suggesting an overall impression of the subject.
- The **supporting sentences** supply details that bring the subject to life.
- The **concluding sentence** summarizes the overall impression of the subject.

When you write a description, focus on the aspects of your subject that convey one strong overall impression. In describing a city street, for example, you might choose features that convey an exciting hustle and bustle, or you might focus on different features to convey a tense, chaotic scene. Once you have your focus, state the overall impression in a topic sentence, as in the following examples.

> The aged tree brooded over the pond like a father over an ill child. (overall impression: concern, gloom)
>
> From his twinkling green eyes to his ever-present smile, he was a picture of good cheer. (overall impression: cheerfulness)

In your supporting sentences, specific and sensory details should bear out the overall impression. For example, the man described above might have a lilting voice, a roaring laugh, and high, round eyebrows. Rather than telling what the impression is, show your reader through sensory details, specific words, and figurative language.

Use **sensory details, specific words,** and **figurative language** to paint a vivid picture.

**COMPUTER TIP**

If the thesaurus that came with your software does not provide you with the word you need, you can find help online. Use the digital version of *Roget's Thesaurus* at this web address:

http://humanities.uchicago.edu/forms_unrest/ROGET.html.

## Spatial Order and Transitions

Spatial order is the most common method of organizing descriptive details. You may, for example, present the details from top to bottom, right to left, outside to inside, or near to far. Alternatively, you may record the details in the order in which they strike you. Then use appropriate transitions to help the reader piece the details together. The transitions appear in **bold** in the following model.

## MODEL: Details Ordered as Observed by the Writer

The memories of Beach Haven run all to smells and sounds and sights; they are physical, of the blood and appetite, as is natural to summertime. At the **west end** of Coral Street the marshes began, turning soft with color at sunset, pink and lilac and golden green. The ocean beach at low tide lay hard **underfoot,** wet sand dark **below the waterline. On the dunes**—we called them sandhills—we played King of the Castle or slid down on our bloomer seats, yelling with triumph and pure joy. The floors of Curlew Cottage, the chairs, even the beds were sandy. Always a lone sneaker sat **beneath the hall sofa;** by August our city shoes were mildewed in the closets, and towels were forever damp.

—*Catherine Drinker Bowen,* Beach Haven

## PRACTICE YOUR SKILLS

### *Analyzing Details in Spatial Order*

**Reread the second and third paragraphs of "Tuxedo Junction" on pages C95–C96. Copy and complete the spatial order chart below based on that passage. Then decide if the details contribute to a clear and logical order.**

| Details | Order |
|---|---|
| endless coastline of lava | far from the observer |
| | |
| | |
| | right next to the observer |

# Process of Writing a Descriptive Paragraph

If a writer fails to create a vivid impression of what she or he feels about the subject, the description will not touch or move the reader. When you write a descriptive paragraph, make your reader see and feel what you are describing. Readers enjoy having a writer engage their imagination, thus awakening their senses.

## Writing a Paragraph That Describes a Scene

### Prewriting

Ordinary settings can take on extraordinary qualities when conditions change. A normally crowded playground or theater can turn tranquil or eerie, inspiring or haunting, when it is deserted. Prepare to describe a place under unusual conditions—a rural area teeming with people, a house before or after you move in, a street decked out for a festival, or your high school during summer vacation.

- Begin by listing places familiar to you—classrooms, outdoor sites, homes, rooms, stores. For each one, jot down an unusual condition—one you have seen or imagined.
- Choose a scene that is particularly vivid to you, one that conveys a strong overall impression.
- Brainstorm or use a cluster diagram to compile sensory details about the scene that also support the overall impression.
- Decide which type of spatial order suits your details best. Experiment with a spatial order chart.

### Drafting

Use the guidelines on page C113 and your notes to write a draft of your paragraph. Picture the scene as you write.

## Revising Conferencing

Share papers and reactions with a classmate. Then, if your partner's comments are helpful, use them and the **Process of Writing a Descriptive Paragraph** on page C127 to revise your draft. Be sure to save your work.

## Editing

Edit your paragraph for grammar, mechanics, usage, and spelling. Use the following Editing Workshop to check for correct use of adjectives. Then ask a classmate to read it and comment on your use of adjectives. Make changes if you feel that you can strengthen your writing.

## Publishing

Print out a clean copy or neatly copy your paragraph and share it with your classmates.

**PORTFOLIO**

# Writing a Paragraph That Describes a Character

Put a person in the scene you described above. Give the person a personality and a reason for being there. Write a descriptive paragraph that conveys a strong overall impression. Use the chart on page C120 and the checklist on page C127. Revise and edit your work and save it in your portfolio for later use.

**PORTFOLIO**

# Writing a Paragraph That Describes a Place

A traditional place to hold a graduation ceremony is the school auditorium. Write a paragraph that describes the school auditorium—or some other place where graduation could be held—an hour after graduation is over. Save your work.

**PORTFOLIO**

# Adjectives

As you read "Tuxedo Junction," you may have begun to "feel" the heat of the sun on the rocks where the penguins lived. And you may have imagined the birds finding temporary relief by plunging into the cold waters of the Pacific.

> Although the water is cool, often 65 degrees Fahrenheit, the black lava of Fernandina is warmed by a fierce sun that distorts its outline in undulating heat waves.

The underlined words in the description are **adjectives**, words that describe nouns and pronouns. Without the adjectives you would have no mental picture at all of Fernandina.

## Regular Comparison of Adjectives

All one-syllable adjectives and most two-syllable adjectives add *-er* to form the comparative degree. All adjectives with three or more syllables use *more*.

| | |
|---|---|
| ONE OR TWO SYLLABLES | The water is always **cooler** than the land. |
| THREE OR MORE SYLLABLES | The black lava appears **more undulating** than usual when the sun is high above. |

When you use adjectives to compare three or more people or things, you use the superlative degree. To form the superlative degree, you add *-est* to all adjectives with one syllable and to most adjectives with two syllables. Adjectives with three or more syllables use *most*.

| | |
|---|---|
| ONE OR TWO SYLLABLES | The water is always **coolest** in the evening. |
| THREE OR MORE SYLLABLES | The black lava appears **most undulating** when the sun's rays are directly overhead. |

## Irregular Comparison of Adjectives

The following adjectives change form completely when used to make comparisons.

| | | | | |
|---|---|---|---|---|
| Adjective | bad | good | little | many |
| Comparing Two, | worse | better | less | more |
| Three, or More | worst | best | least | most |

## Capitalization of Proper Adjectives

Proper adjectives, formed from proper nouns, begin with a capital letter. For example, *Colombian* coffee is more specific than simply *coffee*.

## Punctuation of Adjectives

When a conjunction does not connect two adjectives before a noun, a comma is sometimes used. To decide if you should use a comma, read the sentence with *and* between the adjectives. If the sentence sounds natural, a comma is needed.

| | |
|---|---|
| Comma Needed | The bleak, barren landscape is home to the Galápagos penguin. (*Bleak and barren* sounds natural.) |
| Comma Not Needed | Whenever their usual food is unavailable, the penguins turn to colorful reef fish. (*Colorful and reef* does not sound natural.) |

### Editing Checklist

✔ Have you used the correct form when writing the regular and irregular comparison of adjectives?

✔ Are proper adjectives capitalized?

✔ Have you correctly punctuated adjectives?

## Process of Writing a Descriptive Paragraph

Remember that the writing process is recursive—you can move back and forth among the stages to accomplish your writing goal.

### PREWRITING

- Scan your memory of persons, subjects, or scenes to describe. Then choose one and limit it. *(pages C10–C19)*
- Determine your audience by asking yourself questions about your readers. *(pages C20–C21)*
- Form an overall impression of your subject. Then list all the specific details and sensory impressions you could include to convey that overall feeling. *(pages C24–C27)*
- After you arrange your details in spatial order, delete any that do not support the overall impression. *(page C32–C35)*

### DRAFTING

- Suggest an overall impression in a topic sentence. *(page C120)*
- Write supporting sentences that include specific and sensory details that communicate the overall impression. *(page C120)*
- Organize the supporting details in spatial order, adding transitions to guide the reader through the description. *(pages C121–C122)*
- Add a concluding sentence that reinforces the overall impression conveyed in the paragraph. *(page C120)*

### REVISING

- Should you add anything to strengthen development? *(page C105)*
- Should you delete anything to strengthen unity? *(page C107)*
- Should you rearrange anything to strengthen coherence? *(page C109)*
- Do your sentences have variety? *(pages C72–C79)*
- Did you avoid rambling sentences? *(pages C83–C84)*
- Can you substitute any vivid, specific words for general ones? *(page C60)*

### EDITING

- Using the Editing Checklists, check your grammar, usage, spelling, and mechanics. *(pages C46 and C126)*

### PUBLISHING

- Prepare a neat final copy and publish it in one of the ways suggested on page C49.

# Developing the Skills of Informative Writing

Informative, or explanatory, writing is the most common and practical of the four types of writing. Writing that *explains* gives a set of directions for doing something or relates how something works. Writing that *informs* offers information or presents facts on a topic.

**Informative writing** explains or informs.

**Your Writer's Journal**

Explore different topics for an informative paragraph by writing in your journal about subjects that interest you. You might want to note the things you are good at doing, which you can explain to others.

## Methods of Development

Depending on whether you are writing to explain or to inform, you will need to decide on a method for developing your ideas. Often the main idea expressed in your topic sentence will suggest the most suitable way to explain how to do something or to inform your readers about your topic.

| METHODS OF DEVELOPING INFORMATIVE PARAGRAPHS | |
|---|---|
| facts and examples | comparison and contrast |
| steps in a process | analogy |
| set of directions | analysis of parts |
| incident | cause and effect |
| definition | grouping into types |

## Classifying Supporting Details

In order to select the best method for developing your subject, **classify** or group your details into categories. Notice how the ideas expressed in the following topic sentences lead to the most appropriate way to classify supporting details.

*You can learn more about classifying on page C33.*

**1.** MAIN IDEA Many areas of the country have their own colorful traditions for celebrating Fourth of July.
DETAILS **Classify** information according to facts about Fourth of July traditions and examples of cities or areas that follow such traditions.
METHOD OF DEVELOPMENT Facts and examples

**2.** MAIN IDEA The process by which the Declaration of Independence was prepared and approved demonstrated democracy in action.
DETAILS **Classify** information according to the steps followed in the preparation and approval of the Declaration of Independence.
METHOD OF DEVELOPMENT Steps in a process

**3.** MAIN IDEA After the flag is lowered, it must be folded properly.
DETAILS **Classify** information about folding the flag in a set of directions.
METHOD OF DEVELOPMENT Set of directions

**4.** MAIN IDEA I did not realize the depth of my patriotism until I visited a foreign country for the first time.
DETAILS **Classify** information about what patriotism means to you in relation to your first visit to a foreign country.
METHOD OF DEVELOPMENT Incident

**5.** MAIN IDEA Patriotism involves both emotions and actions.
DETAILS **Classify** information according to the characteristics of patriotism.
METHOD OF DEVELOPMENT Definition

**6.** MAIN IDEA The British government of today, while deeply rooted in tradition, differs significantly from the British government of colonial times.
DETAILS **Classify** information according to similarities and differences.
METHOD OF DEVELOPMENT Comparison and contrast

**7.** MAIN IDEA Britain treated its colonies as a parent treats a child.
DETAILS **Classify** information according to similarities and differences.
METHOD OF DEVELOPMENT Analogy

**8.** MAIN IDEA The Constitution of the United States created a government with three distinct branches.
DETAILS **Classify** information according to the three distinct branches.
METHOD OF DEVELOPMENT Analysis of parts

**9.** MAIN IDEA A long series of grievances against the British Crown led to the final break and the creation of a new nation.
DETAILS **Classify** information into cause (grievances) and effect (creation of new nation).
METHOD OF DEVELOPMENT Cause and effect

**10.** MAIN IDEA The grievances against the British Crown can be classified as economic, political, and idealistic concerns.
DETAILS **Classify** grievances according to three concerns.
METHOD OF DEVELOPMENT Grouping into types

*You can learn more about methods of development in A Writer's Guide to Presenting Information, pages C152–C169.*

Two techniques you can use to classify information are charting and outlining. The following model shows how one student used the technique of charting to classify information from example 8 above.

*You can learn more about outlining on pages C348–C354.*

## **Model:** Charting to Classify Details

Main Idea: The Constitution of the United States created a government with three distinct branches.

| **Branches** | **Legislative** | **Executive** | **Judicial** |
|---|---|---|---|
| **Members** | Congress | President and the Cabinet Members | Supreme Court and other Federal Courts |
| **Functions** | Makes laws | Approves or vetoes laws | Decides whether laws are constitutional |
| | Approves or vetoes Presidential appointments | Appoints Supreme Court Justices | Reviews rulings of lower Courts |

Notice how the writer developed the following informative paragraph based on the preceding chart.

## **Model:** Informative Paragraph

### *Three Branches of Government*

**TOPIC SENTENCE:** STATES MAIN IDEA

**SUPPORTING SENTENCES:** EXPLAIN THE THREE BRANCHES OF GOVERNMENT

**CONCLUDING SENTENCE:** ADDS A STRONG ENDING

The Constitution of the United States created a national government with three distinct branches. They are the legislative branch (Congress), the executive branch (the President/Cabinet), and the judicial branch (the federal court system). No one branch has absolute power; each one has its own duties and limitations. For example, the President is the one to appoint Supreme Court justices, but those appointees must be approved by Congress. When Congress, on the other hand, makes a law, the president has the right to veto it, and the Supreme Court may determine whether it is constitutional or not. This separation of powers prevents any one branch or person from becoming too powerful.

## Practice Your Skills

### *Analyzing Classification of Details*

In "Tuxedo Junction" the author informs you that the environment of the Galápagos penguin has changed since she first visited the island. Reread the paragraph that begins "Since my first visit in the early 1970s" *(pages C96–C97).* Then copy and complete the comparison/contrast chart below based on that passage.

**Main Idea:** The environment of the Galápagos penguin has changed since the 1970s.

| Human Involvement | Cause | Effect |
|---|---|---|
| Tourists | | |
| Government | | |

### *Analyzing Methods of Development*

**Identify the method of development used in each of the following paragraphs. Refer to page C128 for a list of the methods.**

**1. Police Officer with the K-9 Unit**

Dogs and the officers who handle them are carefully trained from the start. Dogs are obtained from the public, preferably between the ages of 6 months and 16 months. They are, in the first instance, kept at the Dog Training Establishment for a period varying from one week to three weeks in order to assess their health, physique, and working abilities. On completion of this period, if found satisfactory, they are given to a handler, who takes a five days' course of instruction. The dog is then taken to the home of the handler to begin a period of familiarization, which is very important, as it is essential to build trust and understanding between dog and handler before serious training is undertaken.

—*Scotland Yard of London,* Metropolitan Police Dogs

**2. Qualities of a Good Broadcaster**

To help broadcasters decide which candidates to hire for a position in radio or television, the National Association of Broadcasters drew up a list of qualities to look for in job applicants. The most successful broadcasters have most, if not all, of these qualities. One important trait is enthusiasm. Another is a sense of public relations, since broadcasters must anticipate the needs and interests of viewers and listeners. Creativity is also a desired trait; developing entertaining programming amidst fierce competition requires a lively imagination. A balanced temperament and reliability are two other important qualities that go hand in hand. The pressures in the field of broadcasting can be very strong, and a person who can get the job done and work well with others is very valuable. While cooperation is important, so is initiative, since employees in responsible positions are expected to monitor their own work schedules and progress. Finally, a good broadcaster has a good business sense. Without the ability to manage budgets and handle other financial matters, a broadcaster is not likely to rise very high in the professional ranks.

##  Organization and Transitions

The way you order details in an informative paragraph is determined in large part by your method of explanation. If the supporting details are steps in a process or a set of directions, chronological order is usually the most appropriate. In some paragraphs of analysis, in which the parts of an object are explained in relation to the whole, spatial order may be the most useful. Most informative paragraphs, however, use order of importance or developmental order, with transitions clearly showing the relationship of ideas. Notice how the details are ordered in the following models. The transitions are shown in **bold** type.

*You may wish to refer to page C110 for a list of common transitions.*

## Model: Facts and Examples—Order of Importance

The Tennessee Valley Authority (TVA), a federal agency set up in 1935, brought significant progress to the people of its region. **First,** before 1935, flood damage in the area averaged two million dollars a year. The TVA dams were successful in controlling floodwaters and putting them to good use. **Another** accomplishment was educating the region's farmers in methods of soil conservation. Through techniques **such as** contour plowing, strip-cropping, and tree planting, the region's soil was restored. **Probably the most important** benefit of the TVA, **however**, was the generating of electric power. Without electricity the once-depressed region could not have kept pace with the rest of the country. **Now** people from all over the world visit the region to learn how to improve river valleys in their own countries.

## Model: Definition—Developmental Order

Artificial Intelligence is the study of ideas that enable computers to be intelligent. Note that wanting to make computers *be* intelligent is not the same as wanting to make computers *simulate* intelligence. Artificial Intelligence seeks to uncover principles that all intelligent information processors use, not just those made of wet neural tissue (human brains) instead of dry electronics (computers). **Consequently** there is neither an obsession with mimicking human intelligence nor a prejudice against using methods that seem involved in human intelligence. **Instead,** there is a new point of view that brings along a new methodology and leads to new theories.

*–Patrick Henry Winston,* Artificial Intelligence

*You can find additional models for showing methods of development in A Writer's Guide to Presenting Information, pages C153–C167.*

## Practice Your Skills

### *Identifying Organization and Transitions*

**Identify the type of order used in each of the following paragraphs by writing *order of importance, comparison and contrast, steps in a process,* or *facts and examples.* Then write the transitions used by the writer.**

**1.** Whenever the cold Cromwell Current provides sufficient food for the penguins to breed, the birds lay two white eggs—ordinarily twice a year. Penguins pay more attention to food availability than to season or month. The Cromwell Current is variable and penguin life is governed by the nutrients that feed the plankton, which in turn are consumed by the small schooling fish that penguins eat. When white mullet and other schooling fish aren't available, indicating that the Cromwell Current is not providing sufficient nutrients, Galápagos penguins turn to colorful reef fish.

**2.** The Galápagos Islands are still spectacular. The penguins still contend with vagaries of the Cromwell Current. Marine iguanas still sneeze salt from their noses, and sea lions still snooze in the sun. What is different reflects the demands of the world's rapidly expanding human population. In Darwin's day, there were one billion people on Earth. Now, we number nearly six billion, using more resources and taking more from wildlife than ever before.

# Process of Writing an Informative Paragraph

Science fiction writer H. G. Wells once wrote, "I write as straight as I can, just as I walk as straight as I can, because that is the best way to get there." Explanation requires a straightness, a sense of order, to develop an idea from start to finish. Although following the writing process will not *totally* ensure clarity, it will at least give you a chance to go back at any point and "straighten out" your ideas.

##  Writing a Paragraph to Explain a Process

### Prewriting

Recent years have witnessed a surge of interest in physical fitness and health. Suppose you are working on a newsletter for and by students on fitness and health. It offers the reader explanations of processes, not how-to directions. Subjects range from the process of tooth decay and how exercise builds muscles to how the heart works. What health-related process could you write about? What process would you like to learn more about?

- Use brainstorming or clustering to think of subjects.
- Choose a process that will interest you and your audience. It can be one that you know or one that requires research.
- Do any necessary research. Then list the steps in the process in chronological order.
- Read the steps aloud to a partner. Do they make sense? Then listen carefully to your partner's steps and share comments.

### Drafting

Use your notes and the guidelines on page C113 to write a paragraph that explains the process.

### Revising

Review your paper carefully. Has each step in the process been included? Is each step clearly described? Does each lead logically to the next? Are the steps in the correct order? Revise your draft following the guidelines on page C113.

### Editing

Refer to the checklists on pages C46 and C126 to edit your draft.

### Publishing

Copy your paper neatly for inclusion in the newsletter.

PORTFOLIO

## Writing a Paragraph of Cause and Effect

When things happen to you by accident or chance, they can become either opportunities or disasters depending on the way you handle them. Write an informative paragraph about an accidental or chance incident that affected your life in some important way. Develop the paragraph using cause and effect. Keep a copy of your work in a portfolio in case you decide to revise and polish it at a later time.

PORTFOLIO

## Writing a Paragraph of Definition

Write an informative paragraph that explains the value or importance of school traditions like graduation ceremonies. Use the checklists on pages C113 and C138. Save your final draft in your portfolio.

PORTFOLIO

## Process of Writing an Informative Paragraph

Remember that the writing process is recursive—you can move back and forth among the stages of the process to achieve your purpose. For example, during editing you may wish to return to the revising stage to add details that have occurred to you while editing. The numbers in parentheses refer to pages where you can get help with your writing.

### PREWRITING

- Use the **Guidelines for Choosing a Subject** to think of possible subjects for a paragraph that explains or informs. *(page C18)*
- Determine your audience and analyze their knowledge, attitudes, needs, and interests. *(pages C20–C21)*
- Determine what you know about the subjects or can learn to explain accurately, and then choose a subject that interests you and will interest your audience. *(pages C24–C31)*
- Limit and focus your subject. *(page C19)*
- List and classify your supporting details to determine the best way to develop your paragraph. *(pages C33* and *C128–C131)*
- Arrange your details in logical order. *(pages C33* and *C109)*

### DRAFTING

- Write a topic sentence that makes clear your purpose. *(page C101)*
- Draft the supporting sentences in the body of your paragraph. Include all the information your reader needs to know. *(page C101)*
- Add a concluding sentence that summarizes the main idea, adds an insight, or evaluates the details in the paragraph. *(page C101)*
- Check paragraph structure, development, unity, coherence, sentences, and word choice. *(pages C105–C110)*

### EDITING

- Using the **Editing Checklists**, check your grammar, usage, mechanics, and spelling. *(pages C46 and C126)*

### PUBLISHING

- Prepare a neat final copy and present it to an interested reader. *(page C49)*

# Developing the Skills of Persuasion

When you use persuasive writing, you are trying to convince others that they should share your opinion or take a certain course of action. Advertisers use persuasive techniques to sell products, and book reviewers use the art of persuasion to defend their opinions. Whenever your purpose for writing is to state and support an opinion, you are using persuasive writing.

**Persuasive writing** states an opinion, develops an argument, and uses facts, examples, reasons, and the testimony of experts to persuade readers to accept that opinion and/or take a specific action.

### Your Writer's Journal

What ideas or situations do you feel strongly about? What arguments or debates have you heard at school or on television that stir up deep feelings in you and make you want to speak your mind? Record your opinions about anything and everything in your journal. These opinions may serve to inspire topics for persuasive writing you will do at a later time.

## Persuasive Paragraph Structure

Like narrative, descriptive, and informative paragraphs, persuasive paragraphs have three main parts. The chart on the next page shows the function of each part. Use the parts any time you write a persuasive paragraph.

### Structure of a Persuasive Paragraph

- The **topic sentence** states an opinion on a subject.
- The **supporting sentences** use facts, examples, and reasons to back up the opinion.
- The **concluding sentence** makes a final appeal to readers.

In contrast to an informative paragraph, the topic sentence of a persuasive paragraph states an opinion, not a fact. Propositions that can be argued make good subjects for persuasive paragraphs; simple preferences do not. The test of an appropriate opinion for a persuasive topic sentence is the availability of reliable facts, examples, and expert judgments to back it up.

## Order of Importance and Transitions

Order of importance is probably the most effective way to organize your arguments. Usually you will build from least to most important, although sometimes the reverse order is more effective. Then make sure you use transitions to show how the ideas are related.

## Tools of Persuasion

The persuasiveness of your writing will depend in large part on how well you use the tools of persuasion summarized in the following chart.

### Tools of Persuasion

- Use logical arguments that are free of fallacies.
- Use reliable facts, examples, and statistics that support, instead of using more opinions.
- Use the testimony of experts in the field.
- Use polite and reasonable language. Avoid charged, emotional words.
- Anticipate arguments on the other side of the issue. Concede the opposition's valid points but show why they do not change your opinion.

## Conceding a Point

As you write, always keep in mind the fifth tool of persuasion. If you ignore opposing viewpoints, you will weaken your appeal. By admitting that your opponent has a good point, you help to establish your credibility and forestall objections. Of course, you must then go on to show why that good point is not convincing enough to tip the argument in your opponent's favor. Following are some transitions to use when conceding a point.

| TRANSITIONS FOR CONCEDING A POINT | | | |
|---|---|---|---|
| while it is true that | nevertheless | however | despite |
| notwithstanding | granted that | although | |

The following paragraph demonstrates the use of the tools of persuasion. The transitions are shown in **bold** type.

**Model: Persuasive Paragraph**

### *The Fall of Rome*

**TOPIC SENTENCE:** STATES AN OPINION

**SUPPORTING SENTENCES:** FACTS, EXAMPLES, TESTIMONY OF EXPERTS

Historians have long been fascinated by the fall of the Roman Empire and the causes of that fall. **Although** at one time most historians blamed Rome's collapse on the invasion of barbarians, a more careful study shows that Rome contained the seeds of its own destruction. **For one thing,** the economy of Rome was in serious disorder. The historian Max Weber argues that the decline of slavery and cities, coupled with the development of self-sufficient manors, left the city-based governments in poverty. **At the same time,** wealthy Romans indulged in lavish luxuries, widening the gap between the social classes. **Another** historian, Mikail Rostovtzeff, adds an intellectual crisis to the causes of Rome's collapse. He claims that the influx of conquered nationalities "barbarized"

CONCEDING A POINT

CONCLUDING SENTENCE

Rome, sapping it of its intellectual vigor. **Perhaps most important,** Rome's political structure was in disarray. Uncertainty over who held the ruling power, the people or the Senate nobles, led to revolutions and massacres. **Although** no single one of these forces would have been sufficient to topple the great empire, the combination of internal weaknesses ultimately left it unable to defend itself against the barbarian invaders.

## PRACTICE YOUR SKILLS

### *Analyzing a Persuasive Paragraph*

**Read the following paragraph and identify the writer's opinion and method of development. Use phrases to list the evidence that supports the opinion. Finally, identify the conclusion.**

All cats and dogs, except those which an owner might want to breed, should be neutered unless good homes can be found for the offspring. Each year, millions of pets are abandoned and become strays. Most of them die alone of starvation, disease, or injury. Even those taken to shelters often have short and hopeless lives, since only a small percentage are ever adopted. Neutering pets, however, assures that they will not produce more kittens and puppies to die unwanted and abandoned in the streets. Do not add to the numbers of sick and homeless pets by failing to have your cat or dog neutered. Make this a priority in your home, and urge your neighbors and friends to do the same.

# Across the Media: Visuals

The visual media, like the written media, can be used for many different purposes. Three of the most common are to inform, to entertain, and to persuade.

The graphic below is a good example of an informational visual. If you imagine how much space it would take to convey in writing all of the information this graphic contains, you can see why it is a good, economical way to present facts.

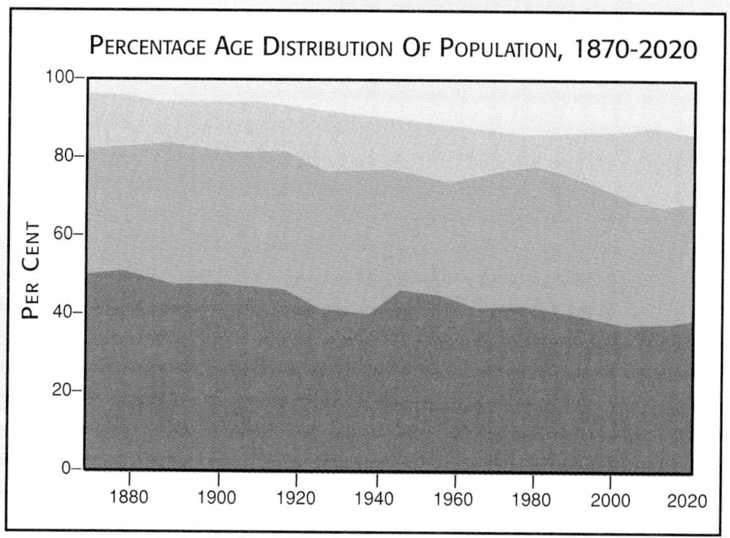


## Media Activities

For practice in making an **informational visual,** turn the material in the model informative paragraph on page C131 on the three branches of government into a graphic.

When you go to the movies or watch a sitcom on television, you experience media whose purpose is to entertain. For practice in creating an **entertaining visual**, draw a picture or cartoon (by hand or on the computer) that represents an entertaining aspect of the paragraph on page C115 about the clowning polar bear.

Any time a media presentation tries to get viewers to make a choice or take sides on an issue, its purpose is persuasive. Advertising and editorials are two common forms of media texts that seek to persuade. For practice in creating a **persuasive visual**, create an original newspaper ad for a movie you have recently seen.

# Process of Writing a Persuasive Paragraph

"How vain it is to sit down to write when you have not stood up to live." These are the words of the philosopher Henry David Thoreau. Just as one cannot imagine Thoreau writing *Walden* without having lived there, it seems equally impossible for one to write persuasively without having a deep conviction about something and the need to persuade others that it is right.

As you write, remember that the objective is to convince your audience. Therefore, take time to state your conviction clearly and with authority. Also take time to find reasons that will persuade them.

## Writing a Persuasive Paragraph to Convince

### Prewriting

Seniors are being polled for their opinions on the recruitment of athletes by colleges. Should athletes be recruited? Should they be held to the same standards as other students?

- Explore your ideas by brainstorming or freewriting.
- Choose one opinion that you feel strongly about, one that you think you can defend.
- Gather whatever information you need to defend your opinion. You may want to speak to college students, coaches, and athletes. Listen carefully to opposing as well as supporting arguments.
- Arrange your arguments from least to most important. Discard any that are mere opinions.

### Drafting

Use your notes to write a first draft of your persuasive paragraph, beginning with a topic sentence that states your opinion.

## Revising

Read your draft. Are your arguments persuasive? Why or why not? Use a partner's comments and the relevant steps on pages C113 and C146 to revise your draft.

## Editing

Refer to the guidelines on page C113 to edit your draft.

## Publishing

Copy your paragraph neatly. Share your paragraph with classmates.

PORTFOLIO

##  Writing a Persuasive Paragraph That Sells

The writing that goes into advertisements on the radio and on television can be among the most persuasive. Companies announce the virtues of their products or stores declare their prices to be the best with the hope that consumers will go out and buy. Prepare to "sell" something of yours on television. Write a paragraph that will persuade the audience to buy something you own or have made. Use the checklists on page C113 and on the following page. Save your work in your portfolio.

PORTFOLIO

##  Writing a Persuasive Paragraph to Express a Conviction

Write a persuasive paragraph about a strong idea or conviction that you have. Check your **journal** for possible topics. Follow the process outlined on page C113 and on the following page.

PORTFOLIO

**Time Out to Reflect**

You've now written four different types of paragraphs—narrative, descriptive, informative, and persuasive. Which of the four types did you find easiest to write? Why? Which did you find the most difficult? Why? Now think back over the instruction you were given for each type of writing. Which parts of the instruction do you think were the most helpful or valuable to you as a writer? Why?

## Process of Writing a Persuasive Paragraph

Keep in mind that the writing process is recursive—you can move back and forth among the stages of the process to achieve your purpose. For example, after revising, you may wish to return to the drafting stage and try a different approach to your subject.

### PREWRITING

- Using various strategies for thinking of subjects, explore your opinions on a variety of subjects. Then choose one opinion you feel strongly about and limit it. *(page C18)*
- Determine your audience by asking yourself questions about your readers' opinions. *(page C21)*
- Gather whatever information you need to persuade people that your opinion is worthwhile. As you gather evidence, also note opposing views. *(pages C24–C30 and C140–C141)*
- Arrange your details in order of importance. *(page C109)*

### DRAFTING

- Write a topic sentence that states an opinion. *(page C140)*
- Use your prewriting notes to write supporting sentences that provide facts, examples, and reasons that support your opinion. *(page C140)*
- Add a concluding sentence that makes a final appeal to your audience. *(page C140)*

### REVISING

- Should you add anything to strengthen development? *(page C105)*
- Should you delete anything to strengthen unity? *(page C107)*
- Should you rearrange anything to strengthen coherence? *(pages C109–C110)*
- Do your sentences have variety? *(pages C72–C79)*
- Do you use precise, reasonable language? *(pages C66–C69)*

### EDITING

- Using the **Editing Checklists**, check your grammar, usage, mechanics, and spelling. *(pages C46 and C126)*

### PUBLISHING

- Prepare a neat final copy and present it to an interested reader. *(page C49)*

# A Writer Writes

## A Letter About a Family Tradition

**Purpose:** **to inform and persuade, using narration and description**

**Audience:** **future children**

### Prewriting

Because traditions should be passed on to younger generations, write a letter to your children. (Since they will probably not be born for many years, keep your letter in a safe place for them.)

Prepare to write each of the following paragraphs—one after another in your letter. (1) The first paragraph, a narrative paragraph, should reenact a family tradition. For example, tell what happens—as if it were happening. (2) The second paragraph should describe where the tradition takes place and any objects used to perform the tradition. (3) The next paragraph should be informative, explaining the reasons why this tradition means so much to you. (4) The last paragraph should persuade your children to continue that tradition.

Use brainstorming or freewriting to think of and explore ideas for all of your paragraphs. Choose the most interesting and the most important ideas to include. Then, after developing a list of appropriate details for each one, arrange the details in a logical order.

### Drafting

Write a topic sentence that captures the main idea of each of your paragraphs. Then write your letter, including your lists of details within each paragraph. Finally, add a concluding sentence to each one to sum up what you have said in that paragraph.

## Revising

Before revising your letter, take it home and read it to a member of your family. Ask that person if each paragraph was clear, interesting, and helpful. Why or why not? Then review the letter yourself. Are there enough supporting details in each paragraph? Are the details covered by each main idea? Have you used connecting, devices to lead your readers from one idea to another? Does each paragraph fulfill its purpose? Keeping in mind the comments of your family member, revise your letter.

## Editing

Use the **Editing Checklists** on pages C46 and C126 as guides to correcting any mistakes in usage and mechanics.

## Publishing

As you write your final letter, follow the form of a friendly letter. Before putting your letter away for safekeeping for your children, read it to another member of your family—a younger brother or sister if possible. Afterward ask that family member if the tradition is more meaningful to him or her now that you have written about it.

# Connection Collection

## Representing in Different Ways

### *From Print . . .*

#### Can You Bill Me?

As the hygienist cleans her teeth, Delia recalls the day's events. She woke up early and brushed her teeth twice, both before and after breakfast. She was about to leave to pick up the dry cleaning when Dad gave her the check for the dentist. On her way home the cellular phone rang. It was Mom calling to ask her to pick up Josh from soccer practice. After she took Josh home, Delia had only ten minutes to get to the dentist's office.

Now the cleaning is done, and she sits up in the chair. Suddenly she realizes she does not have her purse with the check in it! She frantically tries to remember where she left it. Then she hears Mom's voice in the waiting room. "Looking for this?" Mom smiles and holds up the purse and the check. What a day!

### *. . . to Visuals*

Use the story to create a sequence chart showing the order of events that took place in the course of Delia's day. Be sure to include every event from the moment she woke up to the moment she sat up in the dentist chair.

### *From Visuals . . .*

1. **Woke up on wrong side of bed**
2. **Searched kitchen for cereal**
3. **Walked to convenience store in bathrobe**
4. **Bought cereal**
5. **Walked back home in bathrobe**
6. **Locked out of house**
7. **Maria drives me to school**

### *. . . to Print*

Use the sequence chart above to write a story. Be sure to connect the events into a cohesive paragraph. Although you should use all the events, they need not be chronologically ordered in your story.

- **Which strategies can be used for creating both written and visual representations? Which strategies apply to one, not both? Which type of representation is most effective?**
- **Draw a conclusion and write briefly about the differences between written ideas and visual representations.**

## Writing in Everyday Life

### *Descriptive E-mail*

After months of planning, you finally ascended to the summit of Mount Everest. Back in the United States, you find yourself besieged by friends who want to hear about your experience. To satisfy all the questions you received, you have decided to write an E-mail and send it to everyone in your address book.

**Write an E-mail to your friends describing your journey to the top of the world's tallest mountain. Include your feelings of triumph upon reaching the pinnacle and any fears you experienced along the way. Remember to use techniques like brainstorming and envisioning before you begin writing.**

**What strategies did you use to describe your experience to your friends?**

*You can find information on writing descriptive essays on pages C249–C275.*

## Writing in Academic Areas

### *Instructions for Using the Library*

As head librarian at Coolidge College you have been asked to contribute to the orientation guide for incoming college freshmen. Your job is to inform students about the library on campus and the process for checking out books. You realize that most students have learned how to check out books from the library earlier in their lives, but you think it is a good idea to remind them anyway.

**Write instructions that will inform students how to check out books from the library. Be sure to include the hours when the library is open. Use the second person point of view to write your instructions. Classify your details in order of importance.**

**What strategies did you use to instruct the incoming students?**

*You can find information on writing instructions on pages C153–C154.*

# Assess Your Learning

Your favorite professional sports team is considering a move to another state. Fan loyalty is fading and the city refuses to fund the construction of a new sports arena that the team needs in order to generate more revenue. The state says it can only afford to raise capital for the construction of the arena if they cut the education budget. You don't want your team to leave the area, but you believe that sports are not more important than the funding of the public schools. You also believe the sports team is responsible for funding its own projects, but that the city owes it to the team and other business to offer support and prevent them from moving to other cities or states.

- **Write a persuasive letter to the editor of a local newspaper explaining why you think the city government should or should not support the building of a new sports arena.**
- **Use a compare and contrast technique and be sure to avoid emotionally charged language. Also make sure to check for spelling, punctuation, and grammatical errors before sending your piece to the newspaper.**

*Before You Write* **Consider the following questions:**
What is the ***subject?***
What is the ***occasion?***
Who is the ***audience?***
What is the ***purpose?***

*After You Write* **Evaluate your work using the following criteria:**

- Have you identified your audience and geared your argument in order to influence them?
- Are pros and cons included?
- Have you acknowledged opposing viewpoints and conceded a point, if appropriate?
- Are facts and opinions presented clearly?
- Have you developed your arguments in a coherent manner so as to support your ideas?
- Have you used connecting devices so that your thinking moves in a logical progression?

**Write briefly on how well you did. Point out your strengths and areas for improvement.**

# A Writer's Guide to Presenting Information

The world is bursting with information. There is so much to absorb that you may at times find yourself overwhelmed just by the amount of it. Whether it is nutrition information on a cereal box, directions to your school, or an article in a magazine about your favorite band, information comes at you in a barrage from all directions.

The most basic function of writing is to convey information. In fact, when you have information you want to convey to others, often writing is the best means to organize and present it clearly. It is helpful to choose the organizational model and method of development best suited to what you want to write.

Information can be categorized in several ways, depending on its type. If, for example, you need to explain how to assemble a piece of furniture, you would write a how-to paragraph. A how-it-works paragraph might explain how data is sent over the Internet, while a cause-and-effect paragraph might explain what makes your heart beat faster when you exercise. If you want to categorize the various kinds of music in your collection, a classification paragraph would be the best model to follow. You could write a compare-and-contrast paragraph to compare one kind of tree to another, but a definitions paragraph to tell what a cyborg is. If you need to describe the organization of your student council, an analysis paragraph would most likely be the best model to follow. A problem-solution paragraph is a good model to follow if you want to tell how a dispute with your neighbor over cutting down trees was resolved. This guide offers you information that will help you decide how best to gather and present the information you want to convey.

# How-to Paragraphs

A process is a sequence of steps by which something is made or done. There are several kinds of processes; one common type is the how-to process. Use this kind of paragraph to describe the sequence of steps in the process of making or doing something.

A **how-to paragraph** gives step-by-step instructions for making or doing something.

Generally these paragraphs describe simple tasks or processes that almost anyone could do. No matter what process you write about, your goal is to provide a clear and simple explanation for your readers. The following is an example of a how-to paragraph.

**Model: How-to Paragraph**

### *Changing the Oil*

Changing the oil every 3,000 miles can add years of life to your car. To change the oil, you will need oil, a new oil filter, a basin, an oil filter wrench, and a wrench sized to fit your car's oil drain plug. First check your owner's manual to find out the amount of oil and type of oil filter that your car needs. Then place the basin under the oil drain plug and remove the plug with a wrench. When all the oil has drained—it will take about 20 minutes—replace the drain plug and tighten it with the wrench. Next, locate the oil filter at the side or bottom of the engine and remove it with the oil filter wrench. Before you insert the new filter, use your finger to apply a layer of oil on the rubber gasket around the filter. Now screw the new filter onto the engine by hand until tight. (Using the filter wrench to tighten the oil filter can cause damage.) Locate and remove the oil filter cap on top of the engine and add the required number of quarts of oil. Replace the cap and check for leaks around the drain plug and oil filter. Tighten them if needed. Finally, use the dipstick to check the oil level and add more oil if necessary.

## Writing a How-to Paragraph

The following activities will help you write a paragraph that explains how to do something.

### Prewriting

Take a few minutes to list some things you know how to make or do and would be able to teach to someone else. Be sure that each is an activity that you can explain in a single paragraph, such as making pancakes or fashioning a child's kite. Then make a list of ingredients or materials you would need, and a second list of the steps to follow, written in the correct order.

### Drafting

Begin by writing a topic sentence that identifies the end product. In the next sentence, mention the ingredients or materials needed. Then explain each of the steps in order as simply and clearly as possible, using transitional words and expressions to connect them. Finally, end your paragraph in some suitable way, such as reminding readers to admire or use the finished item.

### Revising

Read your paragraph carefully, making sure that you have included all the steps in the correct order. Check for little things you may have omitted—things you take for granted yourself but that might not occur to beginners, such as sifting the flour or using a special kind of kite string. To check the thoroughness of your explanation, ask someone else to read it and provide feedback. Add any items or steps that your partner identified, and then check your work against the Evaluation Checklist for Revising on page C39. Save the paragraph in your folder in case you want to polish it to share with someone later.

## How-It-Works Paragraphs

When you are describing how something forms, happens, or is put together, you are explaining the stages in a process or an operation. The information is usually arranged in chronological order.

A **how-it-works paragraph** describes how something happens, forms, works, or is put together.

This type of paragraph usually explains a technical or abstract process, rather than something readers could do themselves, as in a how-to paragraph. A how-it-works paragraph often resembles narrative writing. The following is an example of a how-it-works paragraph.

### MODEL: How-It-Works Paragraph

#### How Springs Arise and Form

Springs get their start when rain and melting snow seep into the ground. For a time the water remains there, filtering through the soil into layers and layers of rock, being purified naturally as it flows. Eventually, because this *groundwater* is lighter in weight than the rock around it, it rises until it finds a way out of the earth, where it becomes a *spring*. The water that forms the largest springs first collects in underground caves and caverns. When it finally reaches the surface, the spring often gushes forth like a miniature waterfall. In other places, trickles of groundwater seep in a leisurely way through their natural filters. When they rise to the surface they form small, deep pools of fresh, clear water.

## Writing a How-It-Works Paragraph

The following activities will help you write a paragraph that explains how something happens or works.

### Prewriting

Choose a topic by brainstorming or freewriting about a natural phenomenon or a manufactured item that interests you. Read an encyclopedia article or part of a book that deals with the subject. Once you understand how your subject forms or works, make a short outline or other graphic organizer that breaks down the process into simple steps.

### Drafting

Draft your how-it-works paragraph by following the steps listed in your outline or organizer, describing the process clearly in your own words. Adopt a light narrative tone that will hold the interest of your readers.

### Revising

Like the how-to paragraph, the how-it-works paragraph involves a process, with a beginning, middle, and end. As you revise, be sure the steps progress logically. Note your vocabulary and check for evenness of tone. As before, you may want to have a classmate read your work and offer feedback. Then check it once more against the Evaluation Checklist for Revising on page C39 and save it in your folder in case you want to polish it to share with someone later.

# Compare-and-Contrast Paragraphs

To understand a concept, you might find it helpful to compare it to another that is similar or contrast it with one that is dissimilar. A compare-and-contrast paragraph is a good way to do that.

A **compare-and-contrast paragraph** examines the similarities and differences between two subjects.

This type of paragraph will help you interpret, understand, and explain two related subjects or events (such as a film and a book on the same topic). One way to do this is to explain all the characteristics of Subject A and then, in the same order, all the characteristics of Subject B. Another way is to take the characteristics one at a time, describing them alternately as they appear in Subject A and then in Subject B until all the characteristics are covered. The following paragraph is an example of the second approach.

## Model: Compare-and-Contrast Paragraph

### Boxers and St. Bernards

Dog breeds are often classified by the way people use them. The boxer and the St. Bernard, for example, are both working dogs; both are medium-to-large animals, and both are trained to help people. Yet there are interesting differences between them. The boxer was bred in Germany and was crossed with the bulldog during the 1800s. The St. Bernard, however, was developed during the 1600s by monks at the abbey of Saint Bernard in the Swiss Alps. Boxers normally weigh 60 to 75 pounds and stand 21 to 24 inches tall at the shoulder. In contrast, St. Bernards weigh from 165 to 200 pounds and stand 26 to 30 inches tall at the shoulder. Boxers make excellent companions for children and are often used as seeing-eye or hearing-ear dogs. St. Bernards, on the other hand, are best known as rescue dogs for people lost in the mountains; they also make excellent watchdogs.

## Writing a Compare-and-Contrast Paragraph

The following activities will help you write a paragraph that compares an object or concept to another that is similar and/or contrasts it with one that is dissimilar.

### Prewriting

Choose two subjects that are alike in some ways but different in others. Make a list of their similarities and differences. You may want to use a graphic organizer such as a Venn Diagram or a chart to keep track of these characteristics. In the paragraph on the previous page, for example, the writer identifies similarities and differences between two breeds of dog. The similarities are handled together, but the differences are examined one by one, alternating between the two breeds. Keep this order in mind as you diagram or chart the similarities and differences of your subjects.

### Drafting

Begin with a topic sentence that identifies the two subjects you are writing about. Since you will be discussing their differences in detail, it may be best to identify the similarities first. Do this in one or two sentences, and then move on to the differences. For this part of the paragraph, it does not matter which subject you mention first and which second, but it *is* important that you always discuss them in the same order. For example, mention a characteristic for Subject A and then the contrasting characteristic for Subject B. Do the same for the other differences, first addressing Subject A and then Subject B. You may wish to write a concluding sentence, but in a compare-and-contrast paragraph it may not be necessary.

### Revising

For this paragraph the revising process is fairly straightforward. As always, check to be sure that the topic sentence clearly identifies your subjects and explains in a simple but interesting way what you are going to do. For the rest of the paragraph, be sure the similarities are grouped together and that you alternate between subjects for the differences. You may wish to have a classmate read your work for inconsistencies. Finally, check the paragraph against the Evaluation Checklist for Revising on page C39 and keep a copy in your folder in case you want to polish it to share with someone later.

# Cause-and-Effect Paragraphs

When your informative subject requires you to explain *why* something happened, very often the best type of writing to use is a cause-and-effect paragraph.

A **cause-and-effect** paragraph explains why actions or situations (causes) produce certain results (effects).

A simple cause-and-effect paragraph deals with a single cause, such as an icy sidewalk, and a single effect, such as a fall. A more complex paragraph describes a *series* of causes and effects, each one dependent on the one before, called appropriately a *chain of events*. The following is an example of a paragraph which describes a chain of events.

### Model: Cause-and-Effect Paragraph

## How the Seas Become Polluted

When waste material is dumped into the sea, natural bacteria regularly break it down into substances that will not harm the fish or plants. But what happens when too much waste matter accumulates? The natural bacteria in the sea attempt to cope with the influx, but they cannot keep up with the amount of waste. As a result, the water grows dirtier and dirtier. Fighting the increased load, the bacteria work as hard as they can, but in the process they use up too much oxygen. In consequence, little of the precious gas is left for the fish and plants, and eventually they die. Their remains add even more waste matter to the water. Finally, the oxygen is used up. That is when, in the waste area, the sea itself "dies," choked by pollution.

# Writing a Cause-and-Effect Paragraph

The following activities will help you explain a "chain-of-events" using a cause-and-effect paragraph.

## Prewriting

Use a science textbook to study a situation that depends on a chain of events, such as an earthquake or a forest fire. On your paper, break the chain down into a series in which each event causes the next. Be sure that the incidents are all in the correct order, or the chain will be broken. Make the last event a sort of conclusion—the result of the chain.

## Drafting

With your list or diagram, draft the paragraph. As you write, use transitional expressions to move from event to event. (Be sure that each event actually *causes* the next; simply occurring afterward is not enough.) Adopt a serious tone appropriate to a scientific study. Conclude the paragraph with your last result.

## Revising

Read your draft, checking the position and interaction of each cause and effect. If necessary, change or add transitions to smooth the reading. (Note that you do not always have to begin with *Then* or *As a result.* Experiment with transitions that adapt themselves naturally to the events you record.) As with other paragraphs, you may want to enlist the services of a classmate who will be more able than you to spot inconsistencies or errors. If you wish, check your work against the Evaluation Checklist for Revising on page C39. When the revision is complete, save a copy of the paragraph in your folder in case you want to polish it to share with someone later.

# Definition Paragraphs

One of the most basic functions of informative writing is to explain what something means. If you suspect your audience may be unfamiliar with a term you will be using, or if a concept you are discussing might be misinterpreted, use a definition paragraph.

A **definition paragraph** explains the nature and characteristics of a word, an object, a concept, or a phenomenon.

These paragraphs are an excellent way to provide background information on a topic that is central to your main idea.

**Model: Definition Paragraph**

### *What Is a Quasar?*

The word *quasar* is short for "quasi-stellar radio source." Quasars are celestial objects that look like stars to Earth-based telescopes. Actually, however, they are radio objects —phenomena in the universe powered by radiant energy. Situated within "host galaxies," quasars develop "black holes," objects thought to be created by the collapse of massive stars. These black holes have gravitational fields so strong that nothing—not even light itself—can escape their pull. The black holes of quasars devour dust, gas, and stars from the host, and in the process produce enormous amounts of energy—more than their host galaxies. This energy accounts for their star-like brightness. Little else is known about quasars. It is hoped that Cygnus A, a new quasar discovered only 600 million light-years from Earth, virtually in Earth's backyard, will increase our knowledge of these mysterious entities.

## Writing a Definition Paragraph

The following activities will help you compose a paragraph that explains or defines a word, concept, object or phenomenon.

### Prewriting

Join a group to brainstorm some suitable topics. If nothing the group suggests appeals to you, your family heritage might suggest something: a special dish, a custom, or an article of clothing worn for holiday celebrations. Once you have a topic, narrow it to something you can cover in a paragraph; for example, the festival of Hanukkah or the practices of Ramadan would be too long. However, you may be able to focus on a single aspect of the subject. Then make a brief outline or other graphic organizer to guide your writing.

### Drafting

Write an introductory sentence that tells what your topic is. The definition may occur either in the first sentence or within the sentence or two that follows. However, *do* place it near the beginning of the paragraph so your readers will know what you are going to define. After the definition, explain the parts, or components of the subject. A holiday, for example, might involve a ceremony or a special meal; an object such as the *Bayeux Tapestry* will have historical elements that need explanation. Conclude your work with a sentence that summarizes what you have written or that completes the paragraph in some other suitable way.

### Revising

Checking facts is especially important in a paragraph of definition. A good dictionary, a history book, or—if you are writing about a custom, a well-versed family member—will be good resources. Examine your topic and concluding sentences for clarity and interest, and be sure that both your vocabulary and your tone are appropriate to the subject matter. To analyze the flow of your work, check for suitable transitions. Last, check the paragraph as a whole using the Evaluation Checklist for Revising on page C39. Then save a copy of your work in your folder in case you want to polish it to share with someone later.

# Classification Paragraphs

There may be times when the supporting details of your informative subject are too numerous for your readers to keep track of easily. A classification paragraph is one way to organize such details.

A **classification paragraph** groups similar types of items of information into separate categories or classes.

These kinds of paragraphs are common in writing about natural phenomena. Although each class is treated separately, the parts become a paragraph when they are recognized as elements of the larger work. The following is an example of a classification paragraph.

### Model: Classification Paragraph

## *Common Birds*

Hundreds of birds form the class *aves*, or true birds. Five groups, however, are the most familiar. Pigeons are equally at home in the suburbs and the city. About 12 inches long, pigeons are a soft, sandy buff and sing a mellow "kooo-krooo." Cuckoos nest in pastures and orchards, grow to 12 inches, and are a soft buff or gray. Cuckoos are named for their song, a clear "cu-cu-cu-cu." Hummingbirds live in suburban parks and gardens. They are only $3\frac{1}{2}$ inches long but sport exquisite shades of red, orange, and green. Their song is a mere twitter, but their name comes from the humming of their wings. Woodpeckers nest in tree holes. From 7 to $9\frac{1}{2}$ inches long, they have black-and-white barred backs, and some wear black, red, or white caps. Their call is a loud "churr" or "chuck-chuck." Perching birds are a group of 60 common types of birds, such as sparrows and robins. They live in city parks, grasslands, and forests, and each has its own colors, markings, and call. Although each group is distinct, all enrich our lives with the sight of fluttering wings and the sound of birdsong.

## Writing a Classification Paragraph

The following activities will help you write a paragraph that groups information into classes or categories.

### Prewriting

Brainstorm or freewrite to compile a list of groups to which familiar objects or creatures belong. Select one group, note what all the classes in the group have in common, and choose three or four qualities to explore. Then identify the specific characteristics of each class.

In the paragraph on birds, for example, the writer chose five familiar bird groups living in a certain area. The qualities chosen to explore were *habitat, size, colors,* and *song*. In the paragraph the writer explains how the members of each class exhibit these qualities.

Once you choose the group to write about and the qualities to explore, make a chart of the specific characteristics of each class. Be sure that all the characteristics are in the same order.

### Drafting

Begin with a topic sentence that identifies the group to which all your classes belong, such as birds of the northern Western Hemisphere, and make a general statement about the group as a whole. Then, as you mention each class, use your prewriting chart to describe its specific characteristics. For the sake of clarity, follow the same order in each explanation. Use transitions to move smoothly from each class to the next. End your paragraph with a statement that applies to all the classes in the group.

### Revising

Since the classification paragraph involves so many details, strive to make it easy for readers to understand while at the same time including full information on each class. Check your topic and concluding sentences for appropriateness and interest. Be sure that each part of the paragraph follows the order you established in your chart of specific characteristics. Add or change transitions to smooth the progress from each class to the next. Then revise for consistent tone and an interesting vocabulary. If it helps, use the Evaluation Checklist for Revising on page C39. Save the paragraph in your folder in case you want to polish it to share with someone later.

# Analysis Paragraphs

Good informative writing requires a number of critical thinking skills, such as observation or interpretation. For example, when you want to explore the relationship of your subject's parts to its whole, use an analysis paragraph.

An **analysis paragraph** examines a person, place, thing, or idea by breaking it into parts and showing how, together, they make a whole.

One common use of the analysis paragraph is artistic or literary analysis, in which a work of art is examined in detail. The following is an example of an analysis paragraph.

**Model: Analysis Paragraph**

### A Pointillist Masterpiece

The painting *Sunday Afternoon on the Island of La Grande Jatte* by French painter Georges Seurat is an example of the technique of *pointillism.* Unlike the Impressionist painters who strove to capture what the eye sees at a glance, Seurat, a Postimpressionist, used a more controlled, scientific approach. Instead of brushstrokes, he composed the painting using tiny dots of color side by side. The color of each dot contrasts sharply with that of the one next to it. Yet when the painting is seen from a distance, the colors seem to blend into one another. Painting with dots, however, also forces the artist to simplify his figures. As a result, the couples on their Sunday outing look more like robots than real people. The shadowed and sunlit grass, the leaves on the trees, and even the water all resemble elements of a newspaper photo under high magnification. Despite these drawbacks, Seurat's canvas remains a triumph of color and light—and a joy to the eye.

# Writing an Analysis Paragraph

The following activities will help you compose a paragraph that analyzes a person, place, thing, or idea.

## Prewriting

Look around at some of the sights you see every day. How are familiar things (such as flowers, shrubs, trees) or inanimate objects (such as fabrics, wall paint, and table lamps) made? Who are some of the people you see every day? What does it take to become an engineer, a musician, a pilot? Choose an object, an idea, or a profession to write about, and freewrite to capture some of its elements. You may want to consult references as well, just to be sure you haven't left anything out. Once you know the parts or the characteristics of your topic, make a graphic organizer to guide your writing.

## Drafting

Begin with an interesting topic sentence that identifies your subject. (A question might make a good opener for an analysis paragraph.) Then explain how your subject becomes what it is, and name the parts or procedures that help it develop. In some cases the order of the detail sentences might be important. In every paragraph, however, be sure they all fit together logically. Finish the draft with a creative conclusion.

## Revising

Reread your paragraph with a critical eye. Do the topic and concluding sentences make a good beginning and end? Are the middle sentences developed in a logical way? Do effective transitions guide readers comfortably through your explanation? Now look at your work even more critically. Are any of your word groups clumsy or unnecessary? Will a single specific word do the job better than a trite or overused phrase? Might a simile or other comparison help readers see your subject more clearly and better understand its importance? When most of the flaws are corrected, check your paragraph once more using the Evaluation Checklist for Revising on page C39. Keep a copy of the revision in your folder in case you want to polish it to share with someone later.

## Problem-and-Solution Paragraphs

In a sense, all informative writing presents the writer with a problem: that of communicating clearly and effectively with the reader. The solution of course is the piece of writing the writer eventually produces. When your subject is a challenge that was or will be faced and resolved, use a problem-and-solution paragraph.

A **problem-and-solution paragraph** presents a problem and offers a way to solve it.

This type of paragraph presents the details of a problem and outlines the steps that were followed or are proposed to be followed in finding a solution. The following is an example of a problem-and-solution paragraph.

### Model: Problem-and-Solution Paragraph

#### *Engineering the Wetlands*

We've all heard it before. A developer wants to destroy a wetland area to build another shopping center. Should this be allowed to happen? Wetlands are nature's way of preventing floods and recharging the aquifers that hold groundwater. Microorganisms in the wetlands break down organic pollutants, while the roots of wetland plants hold the soil and slow erosion. Although environmentalists would immediately lobby against the shopping center, there may be a way to placate both parties in the dispute. The solution? Engineer an artificial wetland. Suppose the shopping center is approved and building begins. When it is completed, engineers survey an adjacent area and prepare the soil. Environmental experts then plant typical wetland greenery. Water may be added until the new plants take hold. Finally, after the next big rain, runoff will flow into the artificial wetland, and nature can take over from there.

## Writing a Problem-and-Solution Paragraph

The following activities will help you write a paragraph that presents a problem and offers a way to solve it.

### Prewriting

Freewrite or talk with a small group to identify problems in several areas (at home, at school, or in your town, state, nation, or the world). Choose a topic that appeals to you, and brainstorm or research a solution. Be sure that both the problem and the solution can be handled in a single paragraph. Then make a graphic organizer to lay out the ideas in your work and put them into a logical order. You may wish to share your organizer with a classmate so he or she can catch any details that you may have omitted.

### Drafting

Follow your organizer as you work through the paragraph. Your topic sentence should clearly identify the problem, and the detail sentences expand upon it and eventually offer a solution. Help your readers to understand the process with specific words and expressions, appropriate transitions, and an objective tone. End with a concluding sentence that sends the message *This problem has been solved!*

### Revising

Since your readers will be trying to understand the problem you present as well as weigh the solution, it is important that you guide them through the process. Be sure you have defined any terms they may not know. Check that you have not unjustly placed the blame for the problem and that you have maintained an evenhanded tone. Then read over your solution to assure yourself that it is equitable. Next, go back and assess the aptness of transitions and the strength and usefulness of your concluding sentence. Finally, check the paragraph as a whole with the Evaluation Checklist for Revising on page C39. Keep a copy of the revision in your folder in case you want to polish it to share with someone later.

## Checklist for Presenting Information

When you are writing to inform, you will probably find that the information you want to express falls into one of the categories below. Use the following checklist to review some of the guidelines for each category. The numbers in parentheses refer to pages where you can get additional help with your writing.

### HOW TO

- The process should be clear. *(page C153)*
- Give step-by-step instructions. *(page C153)*

### HOW IT WORKS

- Your paragraph should have a clear beginning, middle, and end. *(page C155)*
- Always describe a process clearly. *(page C155)*

### COMPARE AND CONTRAST

- Clearly identify two subjects. *(page C157)*
- Discuss the two subjects in the same order in which they were presented. *(page C157)*

### CAUSE AND EFFECT

- Place your causes and effects in the correct order. *(page C159)*
- Your tone should be appropriate to the subject. *(page C159)*

### DEFINITION

- Your topic should be sufficiently narrow. *(page C161)*
- Make sure your facts are correct and accurate. *(page C161)*

### CLASSIFICATION

- Choose a subject that can be broken down into categories. *(page C163)*
- Order your information in a way that makes sense. *(page C163)*

### ANALYSIS

- Begin your paragraph with a topic sentence that clearly identifies your subject. *(page C165)*
- Your detail sentences should fit together logically. *(page C165)*

### PROBLEM AND SOLUTION

- Clearly present your problem with a solution. *(page C167)*
- Maintain an evenhanded tone. *(page C167)*

CHAPTER 4

# Writing Effective Compositions

An author's passion for an issue can often determine the success or failure of a written composition. Whatever the subject matter—the social life of bees or new zoning laws in a growing city—a composition written with feeling will invariably engage readers. Conversely, no matter how well constructed it is, a composition written *without* feeling will fail to connect with its audience.

As you work through this chapter, keep in mind that one of the most important ingredients in an effective composition is the writer's genuine interest in, and feelings for, a subject.

## *Reading with a Writer's Eye*

In the following lecture, the author Virginia Woolf challenged the idea that a woman in the distant past was not capable of achieving the same literary goals as a man. The obstacles women faced, she argued, were not due to a lack of ability, but to a lack of opportunity. As you read, you may be thinking about how much life and opportunities have changed since then. As a writer, think about the way that Woolf effectively presents her argument.

# Shakespeare's Sister

*Virginia Woolf*

*In 1928, Virginia Woolf addressed the women students of Cambridge University, England. There she gave two lectures focusing on the position of women in society. Later on, these lectures were published as one work entitled* A Room of One's Own.

*In the following excerpt from* A Room of One's Own, *Virginia Woolf narrowed her focus to the role of women in Elizabethan society. Her search for information about the Elizabethan woman, however, produced very little. She did, though, find that a contradiction existed between the woman portrayed in the literature of that day and the woman in real life. In developing her essay, she imagined what would have happened if Shakespeare had had a sister who was as gifted as he. Would his sister have had the same opportunities?*

Here am I asking why women did not write poetry in the Elizabethan age, and I am not sure how they were educated; whether they were taught to write; whether they had sitting-rooms to themselves; how many women had children before they were twenty-one; what, in short, they did from eight in the morning 'till eight at night. They had no money evidently; according to Professor Trevelyan they were married whether they liked it or not before they were out of the nursery, at fifteen or sixteen very likely. It would have been extremely odd, even upon this showing, had one of them suddenly written the plays of Shakespeare, I concluded, and I thought of that old gentleman, who is dead now, but was a bishop, I think, who declared that it was impossible for any woman, past, present, or to come, to have the genius of

Shakespeare. He wrote to the papers about it. He also told a lady who applied to him for information that cats do not as a matter of fact go to heaven, though they have, he added, souls of a sort. How much thinking those old gentlemen used to save one! How the borders of ignorance shrank back at their approach! Cats do not go to heaven. Women cannot write the plays of Shakespeare.

Be that as it may, I could not help thinking, as I looked at the works of Shakespeare on the shelf, that the bishop was right at least in this; it would have been impossible, completely and entirely, for any woman to have written the plays of Shakespeare in the age of Shakespeare. Let me imagine, since facts are so hard to come by, what would have happened had Shakespeare had a wonderfully gifted sister, called Judith, let us say. Shakespeare himself went, very probably—his mother was an heiress—to the grammar school, where he may have learnt Latin—Ovid, Virgil and Horace—and the elements of grammar and logic. He was, it is well known, a wild boy who poached rabbits, perhaps shot a deer, and had, rather sooner than he should have done, to marry a woman in the neighborhood, who bore him a child rather quicker than was right. That escapade sent him to seek his fortune in London. He had, it seemed, a taste for the theatre; he began by holding horses at the stage door. Very soon he got work in the theatre, became a successful actor, and lived at the hub of the universe, meeting everybody, knowing everybody, practicing his art on the boards, exercising his wits in the streets, and even getting access to the palace of the queen.

Meanwhile his extraordinarily gifted sister, let us suppose, remained at home. She was as adventurous, as imaginative, as agog to see the world as he was. But she was not sent to school. She had no chance of learning grammar and logic, let alone of reading Horace and Virgil. She picked up a book now and then, one of her brother's perhaps, and read a few pages. But then her parents came in and told her to mend the stockings or mind the stew and not moon about with books and papers. They would have spoken sharply but kindly, for they were substantial people who knew the conditions of life for a woman and loved their daughter—indeed, more likely than not she was the apple of her father's eye. Perhaps she scribbled some pages up in an apple loft on the sly, but was careful to hide them or set fire to them. Soon, however, before she was out of her teens, she was to be betrothed to the son of a neighboring wool-stapler. She cried out that marriage was hateful to her, and for that she was severely beaten by her father. Then he ceased to scold her. He begged her instead not to hurt him, not to shame him in this matter of her marriage. He would give her a chain of beads or a fine petticoat, he said; and there were tears in his eyes. How could she disobey him? How could she break his heart?

The force of her own gift alone drove her to it. She made up a small parcel of her belongings, let herself down by a rope one summer's night and took the road to London. She was not seventeen. The birds that sang in the hedge were not more musical than she was. She had the quickest fancy, a gift like her brother's, for the tune of words. Like him, she had a taste for the theatre. She stood at the stage door; she wanted to act, she said. Men laughed in her face. The manager—a fat, loose-lipped man—guffawed. He bellowed something about poodles dancing and women acting—no woman, he said, could possibly be an actress. He hinted—you can imagine what. She could get no training in her craft. Could she even seek her dinner in a tavern or roam the streets at midnight?

Yet her genius was for fiction and lusted to feed abundantly upon the lives of men and women and the study of their ways. At last—for she was very young, oddly like Shakespeare the poet in her face, with the same grey eyes and rounded brows—at last Nick Greene the actor-manager took pity on her; she found herself with child by that gentleman and so—who shall measure the heat and violence of the poet's heart when caught and tangled in a woman's body?—killed herself one winter's night and lies buried at some crossroads where the omnibuses[1] now stop outside the Elephant and Castle.[2]

That, more or less, is how the story would run, I think, if a woman in Shakespeare's day had had Shakespeare's genius. But for my part, I agree with the deceased bishop, if such he was—it is unthinkable that any woman in Shakespeare's day should have had Shakespeare's genius. For genius like Shakespeare's is not born among laboring, uneducated, servile people. It was not born in England among the Saxons and the Britons. It is not born today among the working classes. How, then, could it have been born among women whose work began, according to Professor Trevelyan, almost before they were out of the nursery, who were forced to it by their parents and held to it by all the power of law and custom? Yet genius of a sort must have existed among women as it must have existed among the working classes. Now and again an Emily Brontë or a Robert Burns blazes out and proves its presence. But certainly it never got itself on to paper.

When, however, one reads of a witch being ducked, of a woman possessed by devils, of a wise woman selling herbs, or even of a very remarkable man who had a mother, then I think we are on the track of a lost novelist, a suppressed poet, of some mute and inglorious Jane Austen, some Emily Brontë who dashed her brains out on the moor or mopped and mowed about the highways crazed with the torture that her gift had put her to. Indeed, I would venture to guess that Anon, who wrote so many poems without signing them, was often a woman. It was a woman Edward Fitzgerald, I think, suggested who made the ballads and the folksongs, crooning them to her children, beguiling her spinning with them, or the length of the winter's night.

---

[1] **omnibuses** *n. pl.*: Buses.

[2] **Elephant and Castle:** The name of a British inn.

# Thinking as a Writer

## Analyzing Evidence

As she explores the conditions under which women lived in the past, Virginia Woolf skillfully takes the listener on an intellectual journey through her thought process.

- Read the piece again to see how she does this. How does she acknowledge and deal with the ideas of the other scholar, the Bishop?
- What details does she include as evidence? What conclusion does she reach? Is it the same as the Bishop's? If not, how does it change?

## Speaking Versus Writing

Oral Expression

Look over the selection by Virginia Woolf. It was written to be presented as a lecture to an audience of college students. Much of it is written in a conversational tone. With the phrases *I think, I concluded, let me imagine*, and *let us suppose*, Woolf makes specific references to herself and her thought process. With the words, *here am I*, she even acknowledges that she is speaking to an audience. If she had written it to be published as an article in a magazine, she might have written it differently.

- Compare this piece to a newspaper article on a related subject about women in the workforce. Read both out loud and pay attention to the differences in language and tone. If you were going to rewrite Woolf's lecture as a newspaper article, what changes in wording and tone would you make?
- If you were going to present the newspaper article as a lecture at a school, what changes would you make to suit the audience and occasion?

## Interpreting Nonverbal Messages

Viewing When you compare these two photos, what do you notice? What time periods are these photos are from? How can you tell? What messages do the images convey about the changing world of work for women?

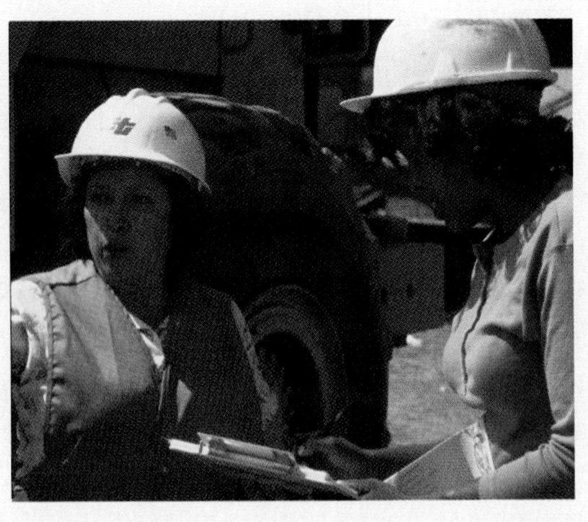

# The Power of Composing

Woolf's essay is a good example of one of the most valuable uses of writing compositions: to explore an interesting idea and uncover insights and understandings along the way. Much of the writing you do in school will have the same value—and power. When you can write about the world you inhabit, you take a step toward understanding that world. Writing a composition about something you have read or studied can help give you increased insight into a subject. That is why you are asked to write compositions in school, both as assignments for various classes and on essay tests.

## Uses of Composition Writing

**Compositions are also practical life tools. Think of the power in each of the following situations.**

- **You and another applicant are equally qualified** to attend the college of your choice. The admissions board looks to the compositions in your applications to help them choose one of you.
- **The city council is poised to vote** on a tax increase. A community leader writes a letter to the local newspaper supporting the tax, and the citizens rally behind her.
- **You want to buy a used car** but lack the information to decide which one to get. A concise article on what to look for when buying a used car helps you evaluate all the evidence and you end up finding a reliable car at a fair price.
- **During a difficult time in your life,** you read a personal essay about how someone made some important decisions. The composition helps you understand your own feelings better.

# Developing Your Composition Writing Skills

"Without feeling," said Leo Tolstoy, author of *War and Peace*, "one cannot write anything decent." This quote from the Russian writer explains why it is important to write about subjects you already know about or want to explore. Developing a feeling for your subject is the first step toward writing a composition that convinces and connects with your readers. A passion for the subject of your composition is the soundest foundation for all of your other writing skills.

A **composition** presents and develops one main idea in three or more paragraphs.

**Your Writer's Journal**

As you prepare for life after high school, you may be wondering what opportunities and obstacles you will face in the future. It may be helpful to think about the opportunities you have had so far and what you did with them. Did they all just present themselves to you, or do you think you played a part in shaping or creating some of them? Also think about any missed opportunities, and why you may have allowed them to pass by. You may also realize that you have some opportunities today that people your age did not have in the past. In your journal, make some notes exploring your thoughts about the theme of opportunities—where they come from and what you do with them.

## Structure of a Composition

In professional writing, compositions show a wide range of structures and styles—some tightly knit, some proceeding more casually. Whether they are three paragraphs or many pages long, virtually all compositions have the same basic parts: an introduction (which includes the thesis statement), a body, and a conclusion. Notice how the parts of a composition work toward the whole effect in the selection that follows.

**Model: Composition Structure**

## But Did They Floss?

INTRODUCTION

As anthropologists imagine it, early humans sat by the fire after a hard day at the hunt, chewing on roasted mammoth and picking their teeth with sticks cut to sharp points. At other times, they just picked their teeth idly, while contemplating what a daub of paint might do for drab cave walls. The simple toothpick, recent discoveries reveal, may have been one of the first "tools" of human design.

THESIS STATEMENT

BODY

Evidence of Stone-Age toothpicks is indirect but compelling, anthropologists say. Fossil teeth, the most durable relics of early life, seem to tell the tale. Analysis of grooves on ancient teeth has led to a consensus that these are the marks of heavy toothpick use by early humans. The journal *Nature* has reported that the earliest known example of the grooved-teeth phenomenon was found in 1.8–million-year-old fossils. The grooves were especially common in the teeth of Neanderthals and other archaic *Homo sapiens* of Europe and Asia between 130,000 and 35,000 years ago. Researchers considered whether the grooves could have been the result of tooth decay, dietary grit or stripping and processing fibers in making domestic goods. "None of these, however, really fits the evidence," *Nature* reported. The similarity of the prehistoric grooves to toothpick-caused abrasions in historical and modern populations of American Indians and Australian Aborigines argued for the toothpick interpretation of the data.

CONCLUSION

In a recent article in *Current Anthropology*, Christy G. Turner II, professor of anthropology at Arizona State University, concluded, "As far as can be empirically documented, the oldest human habit is picking one's teeth."

*—John Noble Wilford,* The New York Times

## PRACTICE YOUR SKILLS

### *Analyzing a Composition*

**Write answers to these questions about what you have just read.**

1. What is the main idea of the composition?
2. What is its purpose?
3. What audience might this be addressing? Is it effective in addressing that audience?
4. How do the body paragraphs support the main idea?
5. Evaluate the conclusion. Is it effective? Why or why not?

## Communicate Your Ideas

PREWRITING *Ideas for Composition Subject*

Look over your **journal** notes exploring your attitudes about opportunities in your life. Is there an idea there that can be developed into a topic for a composition? Use freewriting or any other strategy to develop an idea that you feel would make a good subject for a composition. Save your work for later use.

SAVE YOUR WORK

## Introduction of a Composition

Just as you want to make a good impression when you make a presentation or go on a job interview, you need to make a strong first impression on a reader in the introduction of your composition. The introductory paragraphs of a composition should accomplish all of the following purposes.

### Functions of the Introduction

- It introduces the subject.
- It captures the reader's attention and prepares the reader for what is to follow.
- It establishes the tone—the writer's attitude toward both the subject and the audience.
- It presents the main idea in a thesis statement.
- It states or implies the purpose for writing.

## Capturing the Reader's Attention

"Always grab the reader by the throat in the first paragraph, sink your thumbs into his windpipe in the second, and hold him against the wall until the tag line," advised the American writer Paul O'Neil. Here are some less aggressive, but equally effective, ways to begin your composition so that your reader will be motivated to keep reading.

- Start with a story or anecdote.
- Tell how you became interested in your subject.
- Offer vivid and/or startling background information.
- Ask a hard-to-answer question.
- Describe in vivid detail something that relates to your main idea.
- Begin with a humorous or satirical statement.
- Take a stand on an issue that is important to you.

## Tone

Despite the apparent silent nature of the written word, everything you read has a tone of voice.

**Tone** is the writer's attitude toward his or her subject and audience.

**MODEL: Comic Tone**

The other day when a commercial came on, I automatically pressed "Muting" on the TV remote control and realized what a great modern development muting is.

Essentially I've remained a 1950s guy, but I do recognize a good invention when I see it. "Seek and Scan" on my car radio you can have. I have never mastered seek and scan. I just don't know what they're for. I thought it was perfect when you had your on/off knob and a tuner to find the station. Period. That's it. Fine. Now you can seek or scan and lock in stations. What?

–*Charles Grodin,* "Modern Times"

**MODEL: Reflective Tone**

The best teachers have showed me that things have to be done bit by bit. Nothing that means anything happens quickly—we only think it does. The motion of drawing back a bow and sending an arrow straight into a target takes only a split second, but it is a skill many years in the making. So it is with a life, anyone's life. I may list things that might be described as my accomplishments in these few pages, but they are only shadows of the larger truth, fragments separated from the whole cycle of becoming. And if I can tell an old-time story now about a man who is walking about, *waudjoset ndatlokugan,* a forest lodge man, *alesakamigwi udlagwedewugan,* it is because I spent many years walking about myself, listening to voices that came not just from the people but from animals and trees and stones.

–*Joseph Bruchac,* "Notes of a Translator's Son"

## Practice Your Skills

### *Identifying Tone*

**Read each introduction below. Then write an adjective—such as *lighthearted, reflective,* or *bitter*—to describe the tone of each one.**

**1.** A proper holiday, coming from the medieval "holy day," is supposed to be a time of reflection on great men, great deeds, great people. Things like that. Somehow in America this didn't quite catch on. Take Labor Day. On Labor Day you take the day off, then go to the Labor Day sales and spend your devalued money with a clerk who is working. And organized labor doesn't understand why it suffers declining membership? Pshaw. Who wants to join an organization that makes you work on the day it designates as a day off? Plus, no matter how hidden the agenda, who wants a day off if they make you march in a parade and listen to some politicians talk on and on about nothing.

—*Nikki Giovanni,* "On Holidays and How to Make Them Work"

**2.** Vietnam is a black-and-white photograph of my grandparents sitting in bamboo chairs in their front courtyard. They are sitting tall and proud, surrounded by chickens and roosters. Their feet are separated from the dirt by thin sandals. My grandfather's broad forehead is shining. So too are my grandmother's famed sad eyes. The animals are obliviously pecking at the ground. This looks like a wedding portrait, though it is actually a photograph my grandparents had taken late in life, for their children, especially for my mother. When I think of this portrait of my grandparents in the last years of their life, I always envision a beginning. To what or where, I don't know, but always a beginning.

—*Le Thi Diem Thuy,* "The Gangster We Are All Looking For"

**3.** Before you even get the cone, you have to do a lot of planning about it. We'll assume that you lost the argument in the car and that the family has decided to break the automobile journey and stop at an ice-cream stand for cones. Get things straight with them right from the start. Tell them that there will be an imaginary circle six feet away from the car, and that no one—man, woman, or especially child—will be allowed to cross the line and reenter the car until his ice-cream cone has been entirely consumed and he has cleaned himself up. Emphasize: Automobiles and ice-cream cones don't mix. Explain: Melted ice cream, children, is a fluid that is eternally sticky. One drop of it on a car-door handle spreads to the seat covers, to trousers, and thence to hands, and then to the steering wheel, the gear shift, the rear-view mirror, all the knobs of the dashboard—spreads everywhere and lasts forever, spreads from a nice old car like this, which might have to be abandoned because of stickiness, right into a nasty new car, in secret ways that even scientists don't understand.

–*L. Rust Hills,* "How to Eat an Ice-Cream Cone"

## Communicate Your Ideas

**PREWRITING** *Subject, Tone*

Review your earlier writing on the subject of opportunity. Choose one of your ideas as a subject for a composition. Limit your subject to a manageable size. See pages C18–C19 for more help with this, if necessary. Then think about your purpose for writing and clarify your audience. With those two considerations in mind, decide on a tone that is appropriate for your composition. In one word, or one phrase, describe the tone and your reason for choosing it. Save your work for later use.

## Thesis Statement

In compositions written for school, a strong thesis statement that directs the rest of the paper is an important ingredient.

The **thesis statement** states the main idea and makes the purpose of the composition clear.

The following model thesis statements both limit the subject and convey the purpose of the composition.

**MODEL: Thesis Statements**

Considering the overall performance of the stock market in the past three years, I see three possible trends in the year ahead. (The purpose is to present several possible directions that the stock market will take in the near future.)

To be better prepared for work in the international economy of the future, all students should be able to speak more than one language by the time they graduate from college. (The purpose is to persuade educators to change the requirements for a college degree.)

The time I spent with my family hiking and camping in the mountains was not the most pleasant summer vacation I ever had, but it taught me a lot about my own abilities and strengths. (The purpose is to relate personal experiences and draw meaning from them.)

The first thesis statement you come up with in your prewriting notes—your working thesis statement—will no doubt need to be revised as you flesh out your composition. Be sure your final thesis statement is broad enough to cover all your supporting points but narrow enough to keep the composition focused on your main idea.

In some compositions, especially essays written by professionals, the thesis statement may not be stated directly in the introduction—or anywhere for that matter. Nonetheless, it will be implied in the composition so that the reader will never feel adrift.

## Practice Your Skills

### *Identifying Thesis Statements*

**Write the thesis statement in each of the following introductory passages. If the thesis statement is not expressed in any one sentence, compose a sentence that expresses it. Then write a sentence telling what you would expect from the rest of the composition.**

**1.** The voice I assume for children's bad behavior is like a winter coat, dark and heavy. I put it on the other night when my eldest child appeared in the kitchen doorway, an hour after he had gone to bed. "What are you doing here?" I began to say, when he interrupted: "I finished it!"

The [domineering] tone went out the window and we settled down for an old-fashioned dish about the fine points of *The Phantom Tollbooth.* It is the wonderful tale of a bored and discontented boy named Milo and the journey he makes one day in his toy car with the Humbug and the Spelling Bee and a slew of other fantastical characters who change his life. I read it first when I was ten. I still have the book report I wrote, which began "This is the best book ever." That was long before I read *The Sound and the Fury* or *Little Dorrit,* the Lord Peter Wimsey mysteries or Elmore Leonard. I was still pretty close to the mark.

All of us have similar hopes for our children: good health, happiness, interesting and fulfilling work, financial stability. But like a model home that's different depending on who picks out the cabinets and the shutters, the fine points often vary. Some people go nuts when their children learn to walk, to throw a baseball, to pick out the "Moonlight Sonata" on the piano. The day I realized my eldest child could read was one of the happiest days of my life.

—*Anna Quindlen,* "Enough Bookshelves"

**2.** You can make computers that are almost human. In some respects they are superhuman; they can beat most of us at chess, memorize whole telephone books at a glance, compose music of a certain kind and write obscure poetry, diagnose heart ailments, send personal invitations to vast parties, even go transiently crazy. No one has yet programmed a computer to be of two minds about a hard problem, or to burst out laughing, but that may come. Sooner or later, there will be real human hardware, great whirring, clicking cabinets intelligent enough to read magazines and vote, able to think rings around the rest of us.

Well, maybe, but not for a while anyway. Before we begin organizing sanctuaries and reservations for our software selves, lest we vanish like the whales, here is a thought to relax with.

Even when technology succeeds in manufacturing a machine as big as Texas to do everything we recognize as human, it will still be, at best, a single individual. This amounts to nothing, practically speaking. To match what we can do, there would have to be 3 billion of them with more coming down the assembly line, and I doubt that anyone will put up the money, much less make room. And even so, they would all have to be wired together, intricately and delicately, as we are, communicating with each other, talking incessantly, listening. If they weren't *at* each other this way, all their waking hours, they wouldn't be anything like human, after all. I think we're safe, for a long time ahead.

—*Lewis Thomas,* "Computers"

### *Writing Thesis Statements*

**Use the list of details accompanying each of the following subjects to formulate a possible thesis statement for each one.**

**1. Subject:** Mother's Day

**Details:**
- Mother's Day had been celebrated on June 2.
- Idea for June celebration came from Julia Ward Howe, who wrote the words to "Battle Hymn of the Republic."

- Howe wanted a day when mothers could step forward into the public arena and work for peace.
- Anna Jarvis had a different idea.
- Jarvis wanted Mother's Day celebrated in May, to commemorate the anniversary of her mother's death.
- She wanted it to be a day to honor mothers, not to work for peace.
- Congress approved Jarvis's idea in 1913.

**2. Subject:** Training Dolphins

**Details:**

- Positive reinforcement is a key ingredient.
- Each successfully performed act is rewarded, usually with a whistle or a fish.
- Applause is also a reward.
- Breaking down a trick into its parts is another key ingredient.
- The dolphin learns each small part before putting it all together in a trick.
- The dolphin learns each new part by trial and error, and any movement toward the desired behavior is rewarded.
- It's like playing "hot and cold," when a person comes into a room and is supposed to do something that the rest of the group has agreed on, but the person has no idea what the action is. The person tries various things and if she or he is close, the rest of the group says "hot," and if she or he is headed off in the wrong direction, the group says "cold." Eventually the person learns the expected behavior.

## Communicate Your Ideas

PREWRITING, DRAFTING *Introduction*

Review your prewriting notes on the subject of opportunity. Then develop a working thesis statement that is broad enough to cover the points you want to make, but narrow enough to keep your focus clear. Draft several different introductory paragraphs using the strategies on page C181 to capture attention. Experiment with the best place to position your thesis statement. Also experiment with the tone of your composition—did your earlier choice continue to make sense as you began drafting, or did a different tone emerge? Stick with the tone that works best for your subject. When your introduction (including the thesis statement) is to your liking, save your work for later use.

# Body of a Composition

When you have your reader's attention and have charted the course, you can lead your reader to a deeper understanding of your ideas in the body of your composition.

## Supporting Paragraphs

In one way or another, all of the supporting paragraphs in the body of a composition relate to the main idea. Ideally, they *develop* the idea—extend it, take it a step further, add new meaning or insight, and fortify it with examples.

The **supporting paragraphs** in the body of a composition develop the thesis statement.

Notice how the five supporting paragraphs in the following composition develop the main idea expressed in the thesis statement.

## *Running the Whole Show*

Starting a business while going to school and leading an active social life takes time! So why do young entrepreneurs do what they do? Besides the obvious—earning money—learning to operate a business is a very broadening experience.

"The experience you gain as an entrepreneur can provide tremendous insights," says Lon Goforth, an official with Entrepreneur America and host of the video, *How to Become a Teenage Entrepreneur*. "You learn more than just one specific job skill. Instead of flipping hamburgers, for example, you might learn about selling, managing, accounting, and other functions."

Taking the path of an entrepreneur can be a great confidence booster, too. "Starting a business is an excellent way to discover self-worth at an early age," says Sarah Riehm, author of *50 Great Businesses for Teens*. "In work, kids learn how to strive for important goals and cope with real problems."

Another plus is that you discover more about your future job interests. "You might find that you enjoy selling, but hate accounting," Goforth says. "If you learn this while in high school, it can help you in choosing the right major in college."

In fact, running a small business can provide great preparation for both college and careers. Some teen entrepreneurs use their experience as a basis for studying business in college, going to work in the corporate sector, or starting new companies later in life.

Others experiment with business, but then go into entirely different fields. Whatever the case, the process teaches skills in areas such as planning, time management, and communication. Perhaps most important, when you're an entrepreneur you become accustomed to thinking and acting independently.

In the following outline of this composition, you can clearly see how the supporting paragraphs develop the thesis statement. Each Roman numeral corresponds to a paragraph in the body.

**Thesis Statement:** Besides the obvious—earning money—learning to operate a business is a very broadening experience.

I. Teaches more than just one skill
II. Boosts confidence
III. Helps point to future job interests
IV. Prepares for college and work
V. Teaches independence

## Practice Your Skills

### *Analyzing Supporting Paragraphs*

**Reread "But Did They Floss?" on pages C179–C180. Write the thesis statement. Then develop an outline like the one above. In your outline, use Roman numerals to show the main ideas of each supporting paragraph and the way each idea supports the thesis statement.**

### *Developing Supporting Ideas*

**Under each of the following thesis statements, write five ideas that could be developed into five supporting paragraphs for the body of a composition. Write them in the form of the preceding outline.**

1. Going away to college has advantages and disadvantages.
2. If I were to follow in my family's footsteps, my career path could lead in several directions.
3. As Arnold Toynbee wrote, "The supreme accomplishment is to blur the line between work and play."
4. Health care is one of the fastest growing fields, offering jobs in a variety of areas and at several skill levels.
5. Local businesses should collaborate with the high schools to create work-study programs that provide good preparation for a profession.

## Communicate Your Ideas

**PREWRITING** *Organization of Ideas*

Review your work so far on the subject of opportunities. From all of the ideas you have developed, select the ones that support your thesis statement and arrange them into meaningful categories for your composition. You may need to try several different categories to find the best ones. Then arrange your categories into the most logical order for your composition, and write a simple outline that you will be able to use to draft the body of your composition. Save your work for later use.

## Adequate Development

In a composition with **adequate development**, the main idea is enriched and elaborated upon with facts, examples, incidents, reasoning, and other specifics. Readers feel they have gotten their money's worth, so to speak, out of their experience. The writer has delivered on promises made in the introduction and thesis statement.

**Writing Tip**

Check your compositions for **adequate development** and, if necessary, add more information to clarify and enrich your main idea with strong, lively examples, illustrations, and other supporting details.

Look back at the composition "But Did They Floss?" on pages C179–C180. The examples and other supporting details in the body of the composition are clear and strong. In addition to the specific research findings, the author includes ideas that are still being debated among scholars. These details add flesh to the outline and help create a complete whole.

## Theorizing

**O**ne purpose of the composition is to organize and present new ideas about a subject in a compelling and interesting way. When you present an original idea in a composition, and you want your readers to know how you came to your conclusion, you need to present your ideas in a logical and organized way.

Due to a lack of factual evidence about women's lives in Elizabethan society, Woolf **theorizes,** or speculates, that if women were unable to pursue literary careers in the past, it was due to social constraints, not intellectual ones. Her evidence is presented in a chronology of causes and effects in which one situation leads to another. Based on these conditions, Woolf reaches a conclusion about what might have happened in the past.

The chart below shows the evidence that Woolf cites to support her claim, and her conclusion.

| CAUSE | | EFFECT |
|---|---|---|
| young women did not go to school | → | no formal education |
| had many chores at home | → | no time to read books |
| obligations to family | → | pressured to marry young |
| no professional training | → | no chance to be independent |

### THINKING PRACTICE

**Use a cause-and-effect chart like the one above to analyze the composition "Running the Whole Show" on page C190. What claims is the author making about the relationship between work and education for teenagers? How does this evidence support the author's theory that students who start businesses do so in order to gain a broader experience?**

## Practice Your Skills

*Checking for Adequate Development*

**Reread the introduction and body of the composition about teen entrepreneurs *(page 190)*. Make a paragraph-by-paragraph listing of all the supporting details used. Then write a sentence or two evaluating the development of this composition. Is it adequate? Are enough specific details offered? Is anything missing?**

## Unity, Coherence, and Emphasis

In a composition with **unity**, all the supporting paragraphs relate directly to the main idea in the thesis statement. If a composition lacks unity, readers will be led to detours and dead-ends that take away from the impact of the main idea.

In a composition with **coherence**, one idea flows logically to the next. A well-planned, logical structure is the most important element of coherence. Within that structure, transitional words and phrases should help readers follow the logical progression of ideas. Writers also repeat key words and phrases from one paragraph to the next and use pronouns in place of key words to make the flow of their writing smooth and coherent.

In a composition with **emphasis**, readers know which ideas are most important to you. They know where you place emphasis by such key transitional words such as *most important,* by how much space you give each idea, and by the order in which you present your ideas.

Check your compositions for the qualities of **unity, coherence,** and **emphasis.**

The composition "But Did They Floss?" on pages C179–C180 shows all of these qualities. It has unity because the supporting paragraph describes evidence of Stone-Age toothpicks. It has coherence because the key word *toothpick* is repeated appropriately. Finally, the writer reveals his emphasis by discussing his most important idea at the beginning of the supporting paragraph.

## Practice Your Skills

### *Testing Coherence with a Flow Chart*

Since every interesting idea takes twists and turns, one way to test the coherence of your composition is to picture the paragraphs within it as a series of connected boxes. Doing so will remind you that readers need to know clearly why one idea follows another. The lines connecting the boxes will remind you to use appropriate transitions.

**Complete the flow chart below for the composition *(page C190).* Use each box to show connected ideas in the supporting paragraphs.**

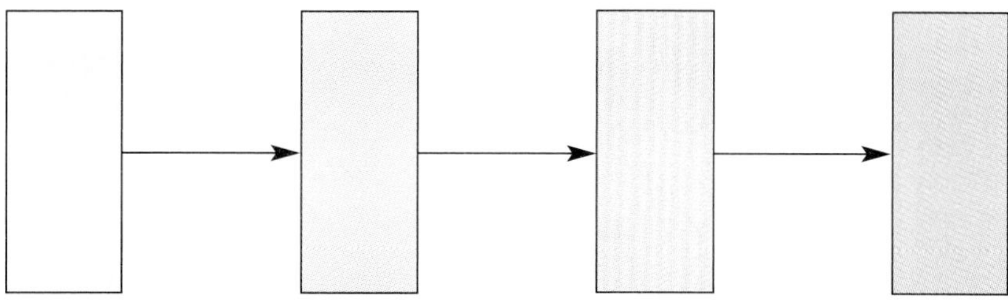

### *Analyzing Unity, Coherence, and Emphasis*

**Reread the introduction and the body of the composition on young entrepreneurs. Then write answers to the following questions.**

**1.** How do the body paragraphs help the composition achieve unity?

**2.** What transitions in the body paragraphs link each paragraph to the previous one?

**3.** What key term is repeated in the fourth body paragraph to help link it back to the previous one?

**4.** What phrase in the final body paragraph helps both the coherence and the emphasis of this composition?

**5.** How would you evaluate the unity, coherence, and emphasis of this composition? Evaluate each quality in a separate sentence.

## Visual Compositions

Like a written composition, a visual composition contains elements that contribute to the whole. Also like a written composition, visual compositions convey meanings, attitudes, and tones. "Read" this photograph.

Write a paragraph answering these questions about the photograph.

**Questions for Analyzing a Photograph**

- What feeling does this photograph give you about people working with computers?
- How do line, shape, color, and texture in the photograph contribute to its meaning?
- What is the tone of this photo? What visual elements convey the tone?
- What attitude does this photograph convey about our contemporary culture?

## Media Activity

Bring in pictures from magazines that convey a message about our culture. Explain how the elements of design contribute to the message the pictures convey.

Communicate Your Ideas

**DRAFTING** *Body*

 Review the outline you created for the topic of opportunities. Use it to help you draft the body of your composition. As you write, follow the organizational pattern in your outline or graphic organizer. Be sure to work on adequate development, unity, coherence, and emphasis as you create your draft. Save your work for later use. 

## Conclusion of a Composition

You have grabbed your readers' attention with your introduction and held their interest with the body of your composition. In your conclusion you add the tag line—a memorable phrase or statement that leaves a deep impression—before letting your readers go. The conclusion completes the composition and reinforces the thesis statement.

Earlier you read the introduction to a composition—a newspaper column by Anna Quindlen about her happiness at her son's reading *(page C186)*. This is how she concludes that work.

**MODEL: Conclusion of a Composition**

You had only to see this boy's face when he said "I finished it!" to know that something had made an indelible mark upon him. I walked him back upstairs with a fresh book, my copy of *A Wrinkle in Time,* Madeleine L'Engle's unforgettable story of children who travel through time and space to save their father from the forces of evil. Now when I leave the room, he is reading by the pinpoint of his little reading light, the ship of his mind moving through high seas with the help of my compass. Just before I close the door, I catch a glimpse of the making of myself and the making of him, sharing some of the same timber. And I am a happy woman.

–*Anna Quindlen,* "Enough Bookshelves"

Like many good conclusions, Quindlen's conclusion returns to an image or idea from the introduction. Referring back to the introduction helps a reader feel the experience has been completed.

## Communicate Your Ideas

**DRAFTING, REVISING** *Conclusion*

Read over your composition about opportunities. Add a strong conclusion, possibly one that refers back to ideas in the introduction. Then read the whole composition again, testing it against the qualities of strong compositions: adequate development, unity, coherence, and emphasis.

- If your composition seems skimpy, brainstorm other possible supporting points and details to flesh it out.
- If an idea does not directly support your thesis statement, eliminate it, or rework it until it fits better with your main idea.
- If your composition seems disconnected or choppy, check your organization, and look for places to add transitions to smooth out rough edges.
- If your main idea is not clear, or supporting points come across without strength, rework your composition to improve its emphasis.

Share your work with a classmate and ask for feedback on how well you achieved these qualities. Revise your work until you are satisfied that it reflects the qualities of good compositions. Save your work.

**Time Out to Reflect**

What have you learned in this chapter about writing longer compositions? When reviewing the qualities of good compositions, did you recognize your problem areas? What are your strengths as a writer? What would you like to improve? In the Learning Log section of your **journal,** write answers to these questions. Then set a goal for improving in one or more areas you identify.

# Run-on Sentences

In *But Did They Floss?*, the authors carefully examine a variety of evidence to show the reasoning leading to their conclusion. They are careful not to make the mistake of relying on invalid or inaccurate evidence. Before you present your composition, you need to take equal care checking the grammar and punctuation of your work.

One of the most serious mistakes is the **run-on sentence**—the incorrect joining of two complete sentences. When this mistake is made with a comma between the sentences, it is called a **comma splice**.

| | |
|---|---|
| RUN-ON SENTENCE | Researchers considered whether the grooves could have been the result of tooth decay, dietary grit or stripping and processing fibers in making domestic goods "none of these, however, really fits the evidence," *Nature* reported. |
| COMMA SPLICE | Researchers considered whether the grooves could have been the result of tooth decay, dietary grit or stripping and processing fibers in making domestic goods**,** "none of these, however, really fits the evidence," *Nature* reported. |

*Researchers considered whether the grooves could have been the result of tooth decay, dietary grit or stripping and processing fibers in making domestic goods* is a complete thought, an independent clause. It can stand alone as a sentence. The same is true for *"none of these, however, really fits the evidence,"* Nature *reported*. One way, then, to correct the problem is to rewrite the ideas as separate sentences. Notice the way the sentences appear in the original composition.

CORRECTED Researchers considered whether the grooves could have been the result of tooth decay, dietary grit or stripping and processing fibers in making domestic goods**.** "**N**one of these, however, really fits the evidence," *Nature* reported.

In some cases, a more complete and flowing correction would be to combine the sentences by making one clause dependent on the other.

CORRECTED Although researchers considered whether the grooves could have been the result of tooth decay, dietary grit or stripping and processing fibers in making domestic goods, "none of these, however, really fits the evidence," *Nature* reported.

Another way to correct run-on sentences is with a comma and a conjunction. In this case, both sentences are rewritten as independent clauses before the conjunction is added. The word *although* is omitted.

CORRECTED Researchers considered whether the grooves could have been the result of tooth decay, dietary grit or stripping and processing fibers in making domestic goods, **but** "none of these, however, really fits the evidence," *Nature* reported.

As you finish each piece of writing in the editing stage, remember to watch for and correct serious grammatical errors.

### Editing Checklist

✔ Are there any run-on sentences or comma splices?

✔ Could these run-on sentences be broken into multiple sentences or combined with proper punctuation?

## Communicate Your Ideas

### EDITING, PUBLISHING

Check your composition, looking with special care for any run-on sentences. Then edit your draft using the guidelines in the **Editing Checklist** on page C200 and your Personalized Editing Checklist. Make a final copy reflecting all your corrections. As you prepare your final copy, consider ways you can use typefaces and other typographical elements to enhance the readability of your composition. Are there places where you can effectively use *italics?* Are there places where a bulleted list would clarify details? What about **boldface**? Try adding boldfaced headings before each of the main points in the body of your composition. Do they help clarify your organization? As a writer, you need to use all the tools available to you to present your work as effectively as possible.

**PORTFOLIO**

### COMPUTER TIP

Most word-processing programs have a toolbar at the top of the screen that lets you choose different typefaces and type alignment. Many look like this: **B** *I* U ≡ ≡ ≡
The **B** stands for **boldface,** the *I* for *italics,* the U for underlining. The remaining three buttons give you options for placing your text on the page, either flush against the left margin, centered, or flush right.

If your school has a Website, plan a Web presentation of the compositions your class has completed. Design a top page with links that lead to the individual compositions. Decide whether you want the compositions to be linked to one another when they explore related ideas. Decide whether to include links to other writings on the subject of work that are available on the Internet. Following your school's guidelines, publish your work online.

*You can find information on creating Web pages in* A Writer's Guide to Electronic Publishing, *pages C809–C813.*

## Process of Writing Effective Compositions

As you continue your work, remember that the writing process is recursive—you can move freely among the stages to achieve your writing purpose. The numbers in parentheses refer to pages where you can get help with your writing.

### PREWRITING

- Find subjects by drawing on your personal experiences and insights, and choose one to develop into a composition. *(pages C10–C18)*
- Limit your subject. *(pages C18–C19)*
- Focus your ideas by choosing a purpose and identifying your audience *(pages C21–C22)*
- Determine the appropriate tone for your subject and audience. *(page C182)*
- Brainstorm, freewrite, or use a cluster diagram to develop supporting ideas. *(pages C24–C31)*
- Sort through your ideas and classify them into meaningful groups. Organize your groups into a simple outline. *(pages C32–C34)*

### DRAFTING

- Write a working thesis statement that expresses your main idea and states or implies your writing purpose. *(page C185)*
- Write an introduction that catches the attention of your audience, establishes your tones and includes your thesis statement. *(page C181)*
- Write the supporting paragraphs of the body. *(pages C189–C195)*
- Use transitional words and phrases to link your supporting paragraphs. *(page C194)*
- Add a concluding paragraph with a summary statement. *(pages C197–C198)*
- Add a title. *(page C37)*

### REVISING

- Revise your composition for structure and well-developed paragraphs. *(page C192)*
- Check for unity, coherence, and adequate development. *(pages C192– C194)*
- Review for emphasis and varied, lively sentences and words. *(pages C60, C72–C79 and C194)*

### EDITING

- Use your **Editing Checklists** to check your grammar, usage, mechanics, and spelling. *(pages C46 and C200)*

### PUBLISHING

- Present your finished composition to a reader in standard manuscript form. *(pages C49–C52 and C201)*

# A Writer Writes

## A Composition Pointing Out Individual Qualities

**Purpose: to convince prospective employers that you are an ideal employee for a job in their company**

**Audience: prospective employer**

### Prewriting

You're looking ahead now. You have finished this year in school, and you want a summer job, but you want the job to be in a field in which you would eventually like to work full time. Freewrite to come up with three or four good possibilities for your perfect job. After reviewing them, decide which you would like the most and which would best suit your plans for your future.

Then think about the qualities you would bring to that job that would make you a perfect choice as an employee. Freewrite, brainstorm, or use any other prewriting strategy to come up with at least six reasons why you would be a good choice for the job. After looking them over, try to generalize from them—what do they all have in common, if anything? Formulate a working thesis statement that would cover all of your major points.

Next choose the three or four strongest reasons why you should get the job of your dreams and arrange them in an order that makes sense to you. This simple plan is the working outline of your composition.

Flesh out your outline, filling out each reason with supporting details. For example, if one of your reasons is that you are a hard worker, be prepared to show how you worked hard on specific, tangible projects.

Finally, give some thought to how you might get your composition started. Review the strategies for capturing

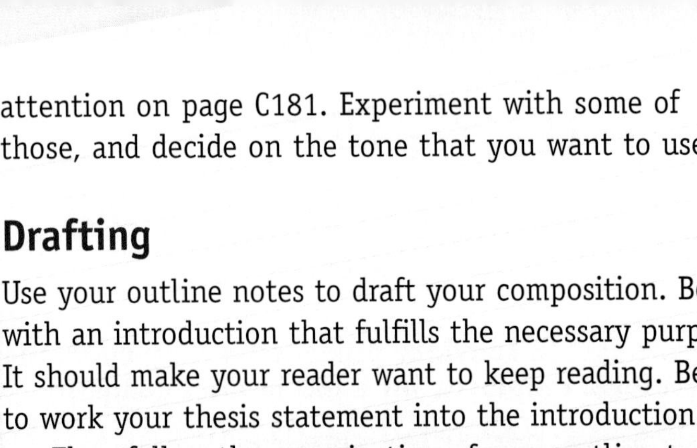

attention on page C181. Experiment with some of those, and decide on the tone that you want to use.

## Drafting

Use your outline notes to draft your composition. Begin with an introduction that fulfills the necessary purposes. It should make your reader want to keep reading. Be sure to work your thesis statement into the introduction.

Then follow the organization of your outline to flesh out the body of your composition. Use your liveliest examples. Add a conclusion that rounds off your points with a memorable finish.

## Revising

Let your draft sit for a while, if possible. Then read it over, checking it against the points in the **Evaluation Checklist for Revising** on page C39. Pay special attention to the qualities of a good composition: adequate development, unity, coherence, and emphasis. When you are satisfied with it, share it with another reader to get another perspective. Make further revisions if you feel they are warranted.

## Editing

Use the checklists on pages C200 and C46 to edit your work. Be especially careful to eliminate run-on sentences, which diminish your qualifications in the eyes of potential employers.

## Publishing

If possible, share your finished composition with someone who works in your dream job field. Take his or her comments seriously. You can use this composition as the basis of a cover letter to accompany your résumé.

# Connection Collection

## Representing in Different Ways

### From Print . . .

3332 Poll Lane
Hoover, AL 35226
December 21, 2000

Mr. Stan O'Leary
Heaven Scent Potpourri
546 Odiferous Avenue
Plainfield, MA 01070

Dear Mr. O'Leary:

The two weeks of testing are over, and I have finished the poll concerning the use of your potpourri samples in our offices. Our employees' opinions are as follows: 14% liked the vanilla scent best; 12% liked rose; 9% liked sandalwood; 9% liked cinnamon; 5% liked cucumber; 5% were undecided; and 56% preferred no potpourri at all.

Thank you for your interest in scenting our company offices. We do not wish to purchase your products.

Sincerely,
*Mason J. Miller, Esq.*
Mason J. Miller, Esq.

### . . . to Visuals

Create a pie chart based on the results of the potpourri testing in Mason J. Miller's offices.

### From Visuals . . .

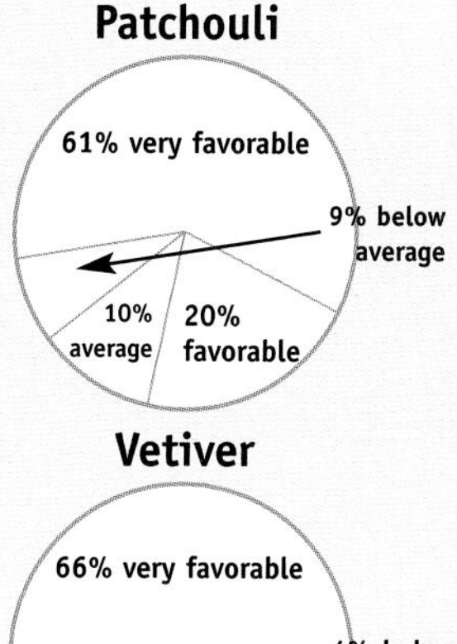


**Vetiver**

66% very favorable
4% below average
11% average
19% favorable

### . . . to Print

The above pie charts represent a separate study done by you, Stan O'Leary, of Heaven Scent. You have tested your two new potpourri scents on another group of employees. Now write another letter to Mason J. Miller, convincing him to buy these scents for his offices. Be sure to prewrite, and maintain a tone suitable for appealing to Mr. Miller.

- **Which strategies can be used for creating both written and visual representations? Which strategies apply to one, not both? Which type of representation is more effective?**
- **Draw a conclusion, and write briefly about the differences between written ideas and visual representations.**

## Writing in Everyday Life

### *Essay for the School Newspaper*

The administration of the university where you teach library science has decided that maintaining the library is too costly. Furthermore, the administration announces that they plan to close down the library and sell all the books. Once the library has closed, students will be expected to get all necessary academic materials from resources on the World Wide Web.

**Write an essay for the school newspaper arguing why you believe the library should not be closed. Include reasons why books are preferable to information on computer screens. Your essay should also include other positive attributes of having a library on campus. Make sure the thesis statement states the main idea and makes the purpose of the essay clear.**

**What strategies did you use to convince the administration?**

*You can find information on writing persuasive essays on pages C386–C431.*

## Writing in the Workplace

### *Letter to the Owner*

Coffee is provided free of charge at your workplace, The Conundrum Coffee Company. During an average workday, you drink two cups of coffee. Just yesterday, on the company bulletin board, a memo was posted, stating that employees will have to start paying for each cup of coffee they consume. You are devastated. This means a good portion of your paycheck will now go toward the purchase of your daily coffee.

**Write a business memo to the owner of the company, describing how free coffee is essential to a well-functioning workplace. Be sure your letter has a main idea and that you develop your main idea by using specific details.**

**What strategies did you use to describe the importance of coffee to the owner of the company?**

*You can find information on writing business letters on pages C645–C646.*

# Assess Your Learning

The mayor of your city, Tom Katz, hates dogs because, in his words, "All dogs are stupid." In order to rid your city of dogs, Mayor Katz has introduced a piece of legislation would criminalize owning dogs within the city limits. You own three dogs, your father is a veterinarian, and your mother grooms dogs for a living. Quite naturally, you are vehemently opposed to the mayor's proposed legislation. You have decided to write a composition extolling the virtues of dogs and then post it on lampposts and fire hydrants all over town.

- **Write a composition to the citizens of your city in which you explain why you are opposed to the mayor's plan to criminalize owning dogs. You may focus either on the financial implications of this plan for your family or your personal feelings about your canine friends.**
- **In trying to convince others of your ideas, be sure to identify your audience. Use the difference between fact and opinion to support your ideas about the topic. Present pros and cons, and be sure your argument is organized to ensure coherence, logical progression, and support for your ideas.**

*Before You Write* **Consider the following questions:**
What is the ***situation?***
What is the ***occasion?***
Who is the ***audience?***
What is the ***purpose?***

*After You Write* **Evaluate your work using the following criteria:**

- Does your composition have an introduction, a body, and a conclusion?
- Does your introduction capture the reader's attention? Has it used a strong quotation, a thought-provoking fact, or an example from your own life?
- Have you established a strong tone and kept it consistent throughout the composition?
- Have you distinguished between fact and opinion in a way that strengthens your argument?
- Have you organized your ideas in the composition to ensure coherence, logical progression, and support for these ideas?

**Write briefly on how well you did. Point out your strengths and areas for improvement.**

CHAPTER 5

# Personal Writing: Self-Expression and Reflection

Have you ever found yourself in a situation where, for just a moment, you had a sudden flash of insight? You may have been at home and for a single second, seen your mother or another relative not as Mom or Uncle Jack but as a person, in many ways like you. You may have seen the ocean or the Grand Canyon for the first time and were suddenly struck by your own smallness in the vastness of nature.

These moments of insight are excellent subjects for essays of expression and reflection. By recounting the circumstances that led you to the moment, and by thinking about them as you write, you arrive again at that same awareness, this time to share it with others.

## *Reading with a Writer's Eye*

In the following selection, Gary Soto recounts a moment of awareness he and his wife experienced on holiday in Oaxaca, Mexico. As you read this personal narrative, notice how the events that precede their insight seem like a story, with characters, a setting, and a series of incidents. Note too how Soto describes his sudden awareness and the changes in the couple's thinking when the concert is over.

# The Concert

*Gary Soto*

Once in Mexico City and tired of its noise and rushed people, my wife and I flew to Oaxaca, a city known for its pottery, weavings, and the nearby ruins of Monte Alban and Mitla. We stayed in a hotel whose courtyard was sheltered by a huge skylight that let in a hazy, almost silver light. For two days we took buses to the ruins, bought Mexican toys, and walked from one end of the town to the other in search of out-of-the-way shops.

On our last night we went to hear the National Symphony. I bought low-priced tickets but when we tried to sit on the ground floor, a portly usher pointed us to the stairwell. We climbed to the next landing where another usher told us to keep climbing by rolling his eyes toward *el paraiso*[1]—the gallery of cheap seats. We climbed two more flights, laughing that we were going to end up on the roof with the pigeons. An unsmiling usher handed us programs as we stepped to the door. We looked around, amazed at the gray, well-painted boxes that were our seats. There were no crushed velvet chairs with ornate wooden arms, no elegant men and women with perfect teeth. Most were Indians and *campesinos*[2] and a few university students holding hands, heads pressed together in love.

I led Carolyn to the boxes in the front row against the rail and together we looked far down where the others sat. Their rumblings rose like heat. They fanned themselves and smiled wide enough for us to see their teeth. We watched them until an old man touched my shoulder, said *con permiso*[3] and took small steps to get past me to the box on our left. When he sat

---

[1] ***el paraiso*** (êl pä rä ē′sō): Top gallery of a theatre.

[2] ***campesino*** (käm pā sē′nō): Peasant.

[3] ***con permiso*** (kōn păr mē′sō): Excuse me.

down I smiled at him as I wanted to be friendly. But he didn't look at me. He took out a pair of glasses from his breast pocket. They were broken, taped together at the bridge. I looked away, embarrassed to see that he was poor, but stole a glance when the program began: I saw his coat, slack and full from wear, and his pants with oily spots. His shoes were rope sandals. His tie was short, like a withered arm. I watched his face in profile that showed a knot of tape protruding from his glasses, a profile that went unchanged as it looked down at the symphony.

I listened but felt little as the violins tugged and pulled and scratched through an hour of performance. When the music stopped and the conductor turned around, moon-faced and trying to hide his happiness by holding back a grin, I craned my neck over the rail and watched the *elegantes*[4] applaud and smile at one another. We applauded, too, and looked around, smiling. We were busy with an excitement that lit our eyes. But while the *elegantes* got up to take drinks and stand in the foyer under torches, those around us leaned against the wall to smoke and talk in whispers. A group of young men played cards and, in a sudden win, laughed so hard that the usher came over to quiet them down.

We stayed for the second half—something by Haydn—but no matter how hard I tried to study the movements of musicians and conductor on his carpeted box, I couldn't help but look around the room at the Indians and *campesinos* whose faces, turned in profile in the half-lit shadows, held an instinctive awareness of the music. They would scratch a cheek or an elbow, speak quietly to one another, and sometimes squirm on the boxes. But most were attentive. It amazed me. I had never known the poor to appreciate such music, and I had lived among the poor since I was a child. These field laborers and rug weavers listened to music that was not part of their

---

[4] ***elegantes*** (ā lā gän′tās): Elegant or stylish people.

lives, music written to titillate the aristocrats who wanted so much to rise above the dirty faces of the poor. The poor sat on the fifth tier on painted boxes, bodies leaning in the direction of the music that couldn't arrive fast enough to meet their lives.

When the concert ended, the old man next to me stood up and asked for permission to pass. I pinched my knees together, and Carolyn stood up. She sat back down and together, heads touching like lovers, we looked down to the first floor where the *elegantes* chatted with drinks and fluttery fans, and shook each other's hands as if celebrating their wealth.

After a while we got up and, with *campesinos* who were talking about a recently read book, descended the four flights to the ground.

## Thinking as a Writer

### Summarizing the Narrator's Reflections

In Gary Soto's personal narrative, he expresses himself by telling about an event that happened to his wife and himself, and he subtly reflects on the meaning the event had for him.

- In one sentence, summarize the event.
- Summarize the meaning the event seems to have had for Gary Soto.

### Recalling Visual Details

Viewing

- Study the photograph on the preceding page carefully for a minute or two; then cover it. Which elements are the most important or central in the photograph as you remember it? What words would you use to describe the scene captured on film? Which details or elements of the photograph make those words come to mind?
- Uncover the photograph and ask yourself the same questions. Are your answers the same? If not, why do you think they are different?

### Describing the Narrator

Oral Expression

- With a partner, discuss what you can tell about Gary Soto's personality based on his personal narrative. How does his first-person point of view in recounting his experience of going to the concert help us, the readers, see his personality? How does he get us to see his wife's personality?

# The Power of Personal Writing

Gary Soto's "The Concert" is a narrative of expression and reflection. In the context of narrating a real-life event, he tells the reader how it changed him. Turning points—of whatever kind—are ideal subjects for this kind of writing.

## Uses of Personal Writing

**The power of narration is the story it tells and the effect it has on listeners and readers. Here are some examples of personal writing.**

- **Prospective college students write brief autobiographies** that tell about their personal and academic achievements and hopes for the future.
- **Writers use a single real or imagined event** as the seed of an entire novel.
- **Friends exchange tales** of upsetting, frightening, or thrilling events that really happened to them.
- **Artists, performers, and politicians write their memoirs** as a way to keep their names and deeds alive.
- **Parents write or recount family stories** so that children become familiar with the family's heritage and history.
- **People of all walks of life keep journals** to remind themselves of what they have done with their lives–and often of what they still want to do.

# Process of Writing a Personal Narrative

"The end of all our exploring," wrote T. S. Eliot, "will be to arrive where we started, and know the place for the first time." In a sense, that is what happens when a writer narrates a personal experience. The writer relives an experience and comes to understand it better. In a well-written personal narrative, the reader, too, may come to new understandings and insights.

A **personal narrative** expresses the writer's personal point of view on a subject drawn from the writer's own experience.

### Your Writer's Journal

In your journal, write about times and experiences that changed you, even a little. Note how a certain event occurred and how it changed your outlook or your life in some way. You may want to make a chart, perhaps grouped by years, such as *childhood, elementary school, middle school,* and *high school years.* In each column, jot down at least one event that affected or changed you somehow. Then expand one or more of the items into a journal entry. Any one of them could be the seed of an exceptional essay.

## Prewriting

Writing Process

A personal narrative may grow out of one of life's big events, such as a graduation, or out of a seemingly minor event, such as a camping trip or a rock concert. In the following excerpt from a personal narrative, Hal Borland wrote about a simple, common experience—yet one that had a great deal of significance for him.

I suspect that a midsummer dawn is so special because so few people are up and trying to manage or improve it. It is a tremendous happening in which man has no part except as an occasional fortunate witness. And it happens with neither haste nor confusion. The stars aren't hooked to a switch that turns them all off at once. The birds don't bounce out of bed and immediately start singing in unison. Darkness doesn't rise like a theatrical curtain and reveal the sun crouched like a sprinter ready to race across the sky.

I was up at four o'clock the other morning to go fishing before breakfast. First streaks of light were in the sky and the lesser stars had begun to dim when I got up, but I brewed a pot of coffee, had a first cup, filled a vacuum bottle, gathered bait and gear, and still had only half-light when I cast off my boat. By then the first birds were wakening and uttering first sleepy calls. But I went almost half a mile up the river before they really began to sing.

I had boated three fish before the full light of dawn, and even then the sun hadn't risen. Time was so deliberate that when I looked at my watch I thought it had stopped. I had been caught up in a different rhythm, one that seemed to have no relation to clocks. So I sat and watched and listened, and it was like seeing the earth emerge from the ancient mists. I was alone with creation; I and the birds who were in full voice now, a vast chorus of sheer celebration.

—*Hal Borland,* "Summer and Belief"

The preceding excerpt has three important characteristics of a personal narrative. First, the writer draws on a personal experience that was important to him—watching a midsummer dawn. Second, he uses the pronoun *I,* which makes the telling more vivid and personal. Finally, he uses conversational style, as if he were sitting in your living room, talking personally to you. The overall effect is to make the narrative more compelling and immediate.

## Drawing on Personal Experience

Hal Borland's essay may have grown out of random observations that he had made in his journal. Like many writers of personal narratives, you will find your **journal** to be a rich source of possible subjects. Look for a subject by going through your journal and circling any experiences you have written about repeatedly, as well as the feelings that you expressed about those experiences. Also circle your observations of people, accounts of places, or reflections about objects that are promising subjects. In addition to using your journal, try clustering and freewriting. Then explore the following sources.

| SOURCES OF SUBJECTS FOR PERSONAL NARRATIVES | |
|---|---|
| photograph albums | school newspapers |
| letters from friends | souvenirs from vacations |
| family stories | school yearbooks |
| scrapbooks | items in your desk |

*Communicate Your Ideas*

**PREWRITING** *Subjects for a Personal Narrative*

Look through your **journal** and the sources listed above for subjects that might make an interesting personal narrative and list five possibilities. Then examine your list and select one that prompted a special moment of awareness or insight. Save this subject for later use.

SAVE YOUR WORK

## Exploring the Meaning of an Experience

A personal narrative should express a main idea to readers. Sometimes you will state this main idea directly, but other times you may simply imply that idea, giving clues to it in your descriptions and the incidents you narrate. Either way, the main idea of the personal narrative will evolve from the meaning, or significance, that the experience had for you. Suppose, for example, that you have decided to write a personal narrative about a time you helped to renovate a state park in your region. That experience probably would have been important to you for several reasons, any one of which could become the main idea.

- The experience taught you about the ecology of your region.
- Because the experience deepened your interest in the outdoors, you may seek a career in a related field.
- Because you worked with other students, you learned the value of cooperation in accomplishing a goal.

In the continuation of Hal Borland's essay about a summer dawn, notice how he explores the meaning of his experience.

**MODEL: Personal Narrative**

And at last came the silence, the hush—not a birdsong, not a rustled leaf. It was a kind of reverence, as though everything was awaiting the daily miracle. It lasted until the first ray of sunlight lit the treetops. Then the silence ended. The birds began to sing again, a vast jubilation. The sun had risen. A new day had begun. But it would be still another hour or two, until diurnal human beings were up and stirring, before the . . . haste would start all over again. Meanwhile, I had witnessed the deliberation of the dawn.

That is what I mean by perfection. Everything is right, at dawn. Nothing is hurried. Everything necessary to the day's beginning is in order and happening on its own schedule. Time is reduced to its true, eternal dimensions.

–*Hal Borland,* "Summer and Belief"

As Borland makes clear, dawn is significant to him because it reveals the perfection that he sees in the natural world. He expresses this meaning directly in sentences like "That is what I mean by perfection. Everything is right, at dawn." However, he also expresses the meaning indirectly through details such as "The birds began to sing again . . . The sun had risen." The simplicity of such details work through the reader's senses to convey meaning.

## PRACTICE YOUR SKILLS

### *Finding the Main Idea*

**Look back at "The Concert." In your own words, write the main idea of Soto's personal narrative.**

### *Comparing Processes*

Oral Expression

Determining the main idea of an essay with a view toward writing one of your own is not always a simple matter. It can become an easier task, however, if you talk it over with a classmate or a group. Explain how you deduced the main idea of "The Concert" and compare it with the process the others used. Then mention the subject and the possible main idea of your own personal narrative—and ask for input from the group.

## *Communicate Your Ideas*

**PREWRITING** *Main Idea*

Think about the experience you have chosen for your personal narrative. Then, in a sentence or two, express the main idea you wish to convey. To keep yourself on target, briefly mention your immediate feelings and impressions about the experience. The feature on the next page may offer you some help. Save your main idea statement for later use.

**Time Out to Reflect**

Now you have thought about and determined the subject and main idea you wish to convey in your personal narrative. What was it about this experience that made you decide on this subject and main idea? Record your answer in the Learning Log section of your **journal.**

## Interpreting

When you select an experience for a personal narrative, you may know that the experience was important, but you may not know why. To figure out why, you need to interpret that experience. **Interpreting** first involves recalling your feelings and impressions at the time, then asking yourself questions like the following.

### CHECKLIST FOR INTERPRETING EXPERIENCE

**Experience:** I was reprimanded by my new boss, which angered me until I realized she was right.

This experience is important to me now because it
- ☐ helped me see something in a new way.
- ☑ changed the way I felt about someone.
- ☐ changed the way I felt about myself.

I will always remember this experience because it
- ☐ strongly affected my emotions.
- ☐ gave me new knowledge or understanding.
- ☑ had important consequences.

This experience is worth writing about because
- ☐ it will be familiar to many readers.
- ☐ it is unique or extraordinary.
- ☑ writing will help me to understand it better.

**Interpretation:** This experience helped me learn to delay judgments about people until I have learned more about them.

### THINKING PRACTICE

**Select one of the following experiences or one of your own choice and interpret that experience, by answering the questions above. Then write a statement that interprets the experience.**

**1.** an incident in which your opinion of a person changed
**2.** an incident that taught you about leadership

## Determining Purpose and Audience

After you have thought through the significance of an experience, you need to decide on an appropriate purpose and audience for your narrative. Usually your overall purpose in a personal narrative is to express your thoughts and feelings in a way that entertains readers. To achieve this purpose, you may use narrative, descriptive, or informative writing. For example, if you were writing a personal narrative about helping to renovate a state park, you might use paragraphs having the specific aims shown in the following box.

*You may wish to consult pages C94–C169 on writing different kinds of paragraphs.*

**PURPOSE IN PERSONAL NARRATIVES**

**Overall Purpose:** to express how the experience of renovating a state park teaches the value of teamwork

| Specific Aims | Kinds of Paragraphs |
| --- | --- |
| to describe the conditions of the park before work was started | descriptive |
| to explain the process of renovating a campsite and the reasons why this effort requires cooperation | informative |
| to tell an anecdote about how teamwork achieved a goal | narrative |

**Considering Your Audience** Give special consideration to your audience when writing a personal narrative. Because you are writing from your personal experience, you need to relate your subject to your readers' experiences. For instance, suppose that you have planned to write about several funny and interesting individuals you observed at your family reunion. However, introducing the members of your family to your readers and establishing the relationships among them could be a problem. To overcome this problem, you might develop the narrative by using anecdotes. For instance, do not simply tell readers that Uncle Bob is hilarious. Instead, include a story or two that shows his sense of humor and tells readers some of the funny things he has said and done. In using this strategy, you will have considered your audience and shaped your writing to suit that audience.

## PRACTICE YOUR SKILLS

### *Determining Purpose and Audience*

**Select four of the following subjects for personal narratives and write the overall purpose and audience for each one.**

1. learning to drive a car
2. participating in an activity in which you made a difference or had an effect on other people
3. achieving an important personal goal
4. participating in an activity with friends
5. going on a trip or a vacation
6. creating something new, such as a drawing, an invention, or a computer program
7. learning something new about a place or person you thought you knew very well
8. going to a concert or other live performance that impressed you

## Communicate Your Ideas

**PREWRITING** *Purpose and Audience*

Evaluate the main idea statement for your personal narrative to be sure that it still accurately summarizes the meaning of the experience for you. Then add a statement about the purpose of the narrative and the audience to whom it will be directed. Save your statement about the overall purpose and audience for later use.

## Developing and Selecting Details

Details are the lifeblood of a personal narrative because they make the experience you are writing about seem truly compelling. The following strategies will help you make a list of vivid details.

| STRATEGIES FOR DEVELOPING DETAILS | |
|---|---|
| **EVENTS** | Close your eyes and slowly visualize the experience that you are writing about. Then write down the details as you "see" them. |
| **PEOPLE** | Visualize each person that you are writing about. Start by visualizing the head of each person and slowly move down to the feet. |
| **PLACES** | Visualize the places you are describing. Start at the left side of the setting and visualize slowly to the right. |
| **FEELINGS** | Imagine yourself once again undergoing the experience that you are writing about. Focus on your feelings and thoughts as you move through the experience. |

After making your list of details, make a check mark next to those that you will include when you write the first draft of your personal narrative.

### Guidelines for Selecting Details

- Choose details appropriate for your purpose and audience.
- Use factual details to provide background information.
- Use vivid descriptive and sensory details to bring your experience to life.

In the following excerpt from a personal narrative, writer Annie Dillard describes a creek that has overflowed because of a hurricane. She has carefully selected details to develop her main idea—that the flood has completely transformed what was once a peaceful and quiet setting.

## Model: Details in a Personal Narrative

That morning I'm standing at my kitchen window. Tinker Creek is out of its four-foot banks, way out, and it's still coming. The high creek doesn't look like our creek. Our creek splashes transparently over a jumble of rocks; the high creek obliterates everything in flat opacity. It looks like somebody else's creek that has usurped or eaten our creek and is roving frantically to escape, big and ugly, like a blacksnake caught in a kitchen drawer. The color is foul, a rusty cream. Water that has picked up clay soil looks worse than other muddy waters, because the particles of clay are so fine; they spread out and cloud the water so that you can't see light through even an inch of it in a drinking glass.

—*Annie Dillard,* Pilgrim at Tinker Creek

## Practice Your Skills

### *Identifying Vivid Details*

**Analyze the model paragraph above for details that are so vivid that you can visualize the scene in an instant. Make a list of the writer's carefully selected details and comparisons that make the scene immediate and real.**

## Communicate Your Ideas

**PREWRITING** *Vivid Appropriate Details*

Use the strategies on the previous page to create details you will use in your personal narrative. When you have a list, evaluate the details to be sure that they relate to your main idea, purpose, and audience. Cross out any that are not appropriate or vivid enough for your readers to visualize. Remember that you can add others that occur to you as you write. Keep your list of details for later use.

## Organizing Details

Like all essays, your personal narrative should be logical and easy to follow. The overall organization of personal narratives is often **developmental order**. In this type of order, one idea grows out of the previous idea and leads into the following one. Within this pattern of organization, however, you may also use narrative, descriptive, and informative writing. To organize the details when using these different kinds of writing, use the following methods of organization.

**ORGANIZING DETAILS**

| Kind of Writing | Kind of Details | Type of Order |
|---|---|---|
| Narrative | events in a story, narrated from beginning to end | chronological order |
| Descriptive | details to help readers visualize a person, object, or scene | spatial order (left to right, top to bottom, far to near, etc.) |
| Informative | background details and details explaining the meaning of a particular experience | order of importance (most to least important or least to most important) |

*Communicate Your Ideas*

**PREWRITING** *Organization*

Arrange the details you developed for your personal narrative in groups or categories, each of which will become a paragraph in your personal narrative. Then organize the details within each group in logical order, following the method of development you prefer. Using your groups of details, make an outline that will guide you in drafting your personal narrative. Save your outline for later use.

# Drafting



Personal narratives are more informal in structure than informative or persuasive essays. Nevertheless, a personal narrative should have the three parts of any good essay: an attention-getting introduction, a body that develops the subject in an interesting way, and a striking conclusion.

## Drafting the Introduction

In a personal narrative, you will be writing about a subject that may not be important or relevant to readers at first glance. Therefore, your goal in the introduction is to make an immediate impact on your readers. Following are some strategies for beginning your work.

### Ways to Begin a Personal Narrative

- Begin with a startling statement that catches readers by surprise, as Eudora Welty begins her essay "A Sweet Devouring."

> When I used to ask my mother which we were, rich or poor, she refused to tell me. I was nine years old and of course what I was dying to hear was that we were poor.

- Begin with a statement that promises interesting things to follow, as John Updike introduces his essay "Central Park."

> On the afternoon of the first day of spring, when the gutters were still heaped high with Monday's snow but the sky itself was swept clean, we put on our galoshes and walked up the sunny side of Fifth Avenue to Central Park.

- Begin with an interesting detail related to the setting of your essay, as N. Scott Momaday does in "A Kiowa Grandmother."

> A single knoll rises out of the plain in Oklahoma, north and west of the Wichita Range.

**Creating a Tone** In addition to building interest, your introduction should establish the **tone**, which is your attitude toward the subject. To choose an appropriate tone, think about the effect the subject had on you. If it made you laugh, for example, you would use a humorous tone. Personal narratives have a variety of tones, as the following excerpts show.

**Model: Alarmed Tone**

> There is something uneasy in the Los Angeles air this afternoon, some unnatural stillness, some tension. What it means is that tonight a Santa Ana will begin to blow, a hot wind from the northeast whining down through the Cajon and San Gorgonio Passes, blowing up sandstorms out along Route 66, drying the hills and the nerves to the flash point. For a few days now we will see smoke back in the canyons, and hear sirens in the night. I have neither heard nor read that a Santa Ana is due, but I know it, and almost everyone I have seen today knows it too. We know it because we feel it. The baby frets. The maid sulks. I rekindle a waning argument with the telephone company, then cut my losses and lie down, given over to whatever it is in the air.
>
> –*Joan Didion,* "Los Angeles Notebook"

Joan Didion creates a tone of alarm through phrases like "something uneasy," "hot wind," and "drying the hills and the nerves to the flash point." The detail at the end about the argument and her concluding phrases contribute a dramatic touch and reinforce the tone. Now notice how another writer uses different kinds of phrases to create a different tone.

**MODEL: Reflective Tone**

> The sound of the sea is the most time-effacing sound there is. The centuries roll in a cloud and the earth becomes green again when you listen, with eyes shut, to the sea—a young green time when the water and the land were just getting acquainted and had known each other for only a few billion years and the mollusks were just beginning to dip and creep in the shallows; and now man the invertebrate, under his ribbed umbrella . . . pulls on his Polaroid glasses to stop and glare and stretches out his long brown body at ease upon a towel on the warm sand and listens.
>
> —*E. B. White,* "On a Florida Key"

E. B. White's details like "the earth becomes green again when you listen, with eyes shut, to the sea" create a reflective tone. Like E. B. White and Joan Didion, choose words carefully to create the tone you want to convey.

## PRACTICE YOUR SKILLS

### *Generating Sensory Details*

**Copy and complete the following sensory details chart with specific words and details that Gary Soto used in "The Concert" to create a reflective and affectionate tone.**

| Sense | Reflective | Affectionate |
|---|---|---|
| Sight | | |
| Sound | | |
| Touch | | |
| Smell | | |
| Taste | | |

**For which senses were you unable to find specific words and details? If you were Gary Soto, would you have used words and phrases to appeal to these senses? Why or why not?**

### COMPUTER TIP

You might prefer to make your sensory details chart using the word-processing software on the computer.

Find the Table icon on the toolbar and follow the prompts to create a chart two cells across and five cells down.

Move the cursor to inside the chart and type the names of the five senses and your sensory words and details. Use the Tab key to move from cell to cell in the chart. Each cell will automatically expand to accommodate the space you need. Use the Save feature to save your work.

### Communicate Your Ideas

**DRAFTING** *Introduction and Tone*

Review the outline you wrote for your personal narrative and draft two introductions for it, each in a different tone. If you wish, use a sensory details chart to help you. When you finish, keep both introductions in your writing folder. As you work on the body of your composition, you may have a better sense of the tone you want to establish in the introduction, and at some point you will be able to select one of them.

## Drafting the Body

Once you have written an introduction that piques the interest of your readers, move on to draft the body of your essay. While writing the body, include the details that you selected earlier in your planning.

The following guidelines will help you draft the body of your personal narrative.

### Guidelines for Drafting the Body

- Make sure that each supporting paragraph has a topic sentence that supports the main idea.
- Follow a logical order of ideas and details.
- Use transitions between sentences and paragraphs to give your narrative coherence.
- If you discover new ideas and details as you write, go back and make changes in those sections of the narrative that are affected by the new insights or details.

As you draft the body of your essay, note that you should narrate the experience as if it were a story, with events arranged in chronological order. Remember, however, that descriptive details will be especially important in establishing and maintaining its tone. In the model that follows, writer Agatha Christie uses description to help the reader visualize her first concept of the famous fictional detective, Hercule Poirot.

**MODEL: Description in a Personal Narrative**

> Sure enough, next day, when I was sitting in a tram, I saw just what I wanted: *a man with a black beard, sitting next to an elderly lady who was chatting like a magpie.* I didn't think I'd have *her,* but I thought *he* would do admirably. Sitting a little way beyond them was a large, hearty woman, talking loudly about spring bulbs. I liked the look of her too. Perhaps I could incorporate her? I took them all three off the tram with me to work upon—and walked up Barton Road muttering to myself.
>
> –*Agatha Christie,* Agatha Christie: An Autobiography

Later in her essay, Christie explains the thought process by which she arrived at the name *Hercule Poirot* for her detective.

**Model: Explanation in a Personal Narrative**

How about calling my little man Hercules? He would be a small man—Hercules: a good name. His last name was more difficult. I don't know why I settled on the name Poirot; whether it just came into my head or whether I saw it in some newspaper or written on something—anyway it came. It went well not with Hercules but Hercule—Hercule Poirot. That was all right—settled, thank goodness.

—*Agatha Christie,* Agatha Christie: An Autobiography

**Communicate Your Ideas**

**DRAFTING** *Body*

Look back at the two introductions that you wrote for your personal narrative and choose the one that establishes a fitting tone and will more effectively capture your readers' attention. Then draft the body of your personal narrative. As you write, remember to use narration as your predominant writing mode but to take advantage of other modes as well. Save your draft for later use.

## Drafting the Conclusion

The conclusion of your personal narrative should leave the readers with a memorable impression of the personal experience or insight that serves as your subject. The following strategies will help you write a striking conclusion.

### Ways to End a Personal Narrative

- Summarize the body or restate the main idea in new words.
- Add an insight that shows a new or deeper understanding of the experience.

- Add a striking new detail or memorable image.
- Refer to ideas in the introduction to bring your narrative full circle.
- Appeal to your readers' emotions.

The following paragraph concludes the E. B. White piece from which you read a paragraph on page C227. The conclusion adds a new insight that reveals a further understanding of his subject.

**Model: Conclusion of a Personal Narrative**

> The sea answers all questions, and always in the same way; for when you read in the papers the interminable discussions and the bickering and the prognostications and the turmoil, the disagreements and the fateful decisions and agreements and the plans and the programs and the threats and the counter threats, then you close your eyes and the sea dispatches one more big roller in the unbroken line since the beginning of the world and it combs and breaks and returns foaming and saying: "So soon?"
>
> —*E. B. White,* "On a Florida Key"

In your reading experiences, you may have felt that what makes a strong conclusion was a bit of a mystery, but using the strategies listed above should help you craft your own.

## Communicate Your Ideas

**DRAFTING** *Conclusion*

Review the introduction and the body of your personal narrative. Think about the type of conclusion that would be most appropriate for your work, and then draft two different conclusions. After a day or two, review them and choose the one that seems more effective. Give your work an interesting title, and save it for later use.

## Across the Media: Personal Narratives

Personal narratives are everywhere in the media. They range from celebrity anecdotes to the poignant, sometimes terrifying stories related by victims of war and natural disasters.

In the visual media, narrative resources range from 2- to 3-minute stories on the nightly news to 20-minute segments on newsmagazines and 50-minute documentaries. In the print media, newspapers may have more coverage than a story on the nightly television news but not as much as a newsmagazine. Narratives on the Internet, a mix of visual and print presentations, are often comparable to those in newspapers, although they can be supplemented with related links. Some of the most interesting narratives on the Internet are found in newsgroups where members share their experiences related to the group's interest.

## Media Activity

Choose three media forms to explore for personal narratives. After identifying a good example from each form, prepare an analysis by answering these questions.

**Questions for Analyzing Personal Narratives**

- What are the subjects? In which medium and where in the medium did you find each one?
- What was the writer's or speaker's motive? What do you think was the motive of the producer or publisher?
- How are the narratives alike and different? Does the medium explain some of their differences? If so, how?
- Has the writer shaped the narrative to fit the medium? Why or why not? Has an interviewer or reporter influenced the delivery of the narrative?

After you have drafted your personal narrative, put it aside for a few days so that you will be able to reread it with a fresh eye. When you review it, read it aloud to yourself and ask yourself whether it sounds lively. Do you hear your personality in it? Do your feelings about the subject come through?

Once you have evaluated your draft in this way, revise it with the goal of making it as fresh and natural sounding as possible. The following box shows some common problems with first drafts and ways to fix them.

**STRATEGIES FOR REVISING PERSONAL NARRATIVES**

| Problem | Strategy |
|---|---|
| The essay is too short, general or vague. | Find more details. Visualize again the people, places, things, or experiences you are writing about. |
| The tone is inconsistent. | Revise parts of the personal narrative that stray from the tone set in the introduction. |
| The essay sounds too stiff and formal. | Replace formal or technical words with everyday vocabulary. |

## Communicate Your Ideas

**REVISING** *Development*

Evaluate your personal narrative by asking yourself whether it is adequately developed and natural sounding. Decide whether your feelings will come across to your readers. Then revise your personal narrative using the strategies above and the Evaluation Checklist for Revising on the next page as guides. Save your revised draft for later use.

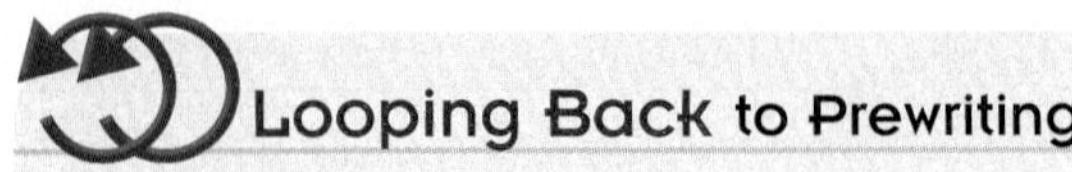


*Vivid Details*

Look at your list of details. Evaluate how successful they are in helping to bring your narrative to life. You may want to replace some details with others from your list to recreate your experience more vividly.

**Evaluation Checklist for Revising**

✓ Does your introduction capture the reader's interest? *(page C225)*

✓ Have you held the reader's interest to the end? *(pages C228–C230)*

✓ Does your feeling about your subject come through? *(page C226)*

✓ Does your ending give the reader a sense of completion? *(pages C230–C231)*

## Editing

Writing Process

Remember to reread your draft carefully, correcting all errors. Put your writing aside for a while and then return to it, in order to help yourself see where you need improvements.

*Communicate Your Ideas*

**EDITING**

Use the Editing Checklist on page C236 to edit your revised personal narrative. Check for errors in usage, mechanics, and spelling. Also check for any fragments or run-on-sentences. After you have finished, you might want to ask a partner to check your work for errors you may have overlooked.

# Phrases

The characters in "The Concert" might have lived in a small town anywhere in the world. Yet they speak to us from Soto's work, and we can understand and appreciate them. Does this happen in your personal narrative? Part of the answer may lie in the skillfulness with which you have used details like **phrases**—groups of words that do not have subjects and verbs.

## Prepositional Phrases

A **prepositional phrase** begins with a preposition and ends with a noun or pronoun and modifies another word in a sentence. Prepositional phrases add information to a sentence.

| | |
|---|---|
| Prepositional Phrases | **For two days** we took buses **to the ruins**, bought Mexican toys, and walked **from one end of the town to the other . . .** |

## Punctuation with Prepositional Phrases

When a prepositional phrase four words or longer begins a sentence, place a comma after it, unless the sentence is very short. Using prepositional phrases at the beginnings of some sentences will help you create sentence variety.

| | |
|---|---|
| Prepositional Phrase | **On our last night,** we went to hear the National Symphony. |

## Appositive Phrases

An **appositive phrase** is a phrase that identifies or explains a noun or a pronoun in a sentence.

| | |
|---|---|
| Appositive Phrase | Another usher told us to keep climbing by rolling his eyes toward *el paraiso*—**the gallery of cheap seats.** |

## Punctuation with Appositive Phrases

If an appositive phrase is not essential in identifying a noun, that phrase should be set off with commas or dashes, as in the following example.

> Once in Mexico City and tired of its noise and rushed people, my wife and I flew to Oaxaca, **a city known for its pottery, weavings, and the nearby ruins of Monte Alban and Mitla.**

Soto might have added the following:

> Once in Mexico City and tired of its noise and rushed people, my wife **Carolyn** and I . . .

Note that since the word *Carolyn* is essential to identifying *my wife,* there are no commas.

## Combining Sentences by Using Phrases

You can use prepositional phrases and appositive phrases to combine short, choppy sentences into fluid, sophisticated ones.

| | |
|---|---|
| Three Sentences | I led Carolyn to the boxes. They were in the front row. They were against the rail. |
| One Sentence | I led Carolyn **to the boxes** **in the front row** **against the rail.** |
| Two Sentences | We stayed for the second half. The music was something by Haydn. |
| One Sentence | We stayed for the second half—**something by Haydn.** |

### Editing Checklist

✔ Have phrases been used to add information and variety?

✔ Are all phrases punctuated correctly?

✔ Could phrases be used to combine any sentences?

You may decide to share your writing with someone who was part of the experience you wrote about, or with someone who may have an interest in it.

## Communicate Your Ideas

### PUBLISHING

Once you are satisfied with your personal narrative, make a clean, neat copy. Share it with the class or with others in your school.

**PORTFOLIO**

**Time Out to Reflect**

How have your narrative skills improved with the completion of your personal narrative? Take out a narrative piece you wrote earlier in the school year, and compare it with your current work. How do the two pieces differ? Have you improved in your use of details and in the structure of your sentences? Is there anything that you did better in the earlier piece? In which areas do you think you have made the most progress? In which areas do you feel that you still need improvement? Record your answers to these questions in the Learning Log section of your **journal.**

## Process of Writing a Personal Narrative

Remember that the writing process is recursive—as a writer, you can move freely among the various stages. For example, while drafting, you may discover that you need to return to prewriting to develop more vivid sensory details to bring your writing alive.

### PREWRITING

- Sift through your memories for experiences, reflections, and observations. *(page C216)*
- Review your list of possible subjects and choose one that interests you most. *(page C216)*
- Decide on the meaning of the experience for you and from that meaning write a main idea. *(pages C216–C217)*
- Focus on the probable audience for this subject and your purpose for writing. *(pages C220–C221)*
- Choose a suitable means of developing your subject: narration, description, exposition, or all three. *(page C224)*
- List the details that best develop your main idea. *(page C222)*

### DRAFTING

- Introduce your subject in a way that catches the reader's interest and sets the tone of your personal narrative. *(pages C225–C227)*
- Build the body from the details you have chosen so that you can make your point. *(pages C228–C229)*
- Add a conclusion that leaves your readers with the idea or feeling that you wish to convey. *(pages C230–C231)*

### REVISING

- Revise your work for adequate development by adding vivid and interesting details where necessary. *(page C234)*
- Revise for unity, coherence, emphasis, and smooth transitions. *(pages C233–C234)*
- Choose a title that is true to the tone of your personal narrative. *(page C37)*

### EDITING

- Use the Editing Checklist to polish your grammar, spelling, and mechanics. *(page C236)*

### PUBLISHING

- Refer to the Ways to Publish Your Writing for ideas on how to present your personal narrative. *(page C49)*

# A Writer Writes

## A Personal Essay About a Memory

**Purpose:** **to inform and entertain by sharing a memory of a teenage experience**

**Audience:** **readers of *Today's Parent* magazine**

### Prewriting

Imagine that *Today's Parent* has invited high school students to submit a personal essay that recalls the best or the most unforgettable memory of their teenage years. Winners will receive a prize.

Sift through the ideas in your **journal** to select your best or most unforgettable memory as a teenager. If you cannot find a good subject in these sources, write freely about teenage memories until you find the one you will most enjoy writing about. Based on the meaning of that memory for you, write the main idea of your essay. After making sure that your subject is suitable for your audience, brainstorm for a list of specific details you will use to develop your main idea. To make your memory come alive on paper, remember to include sensory details as well. When your list is complete, organize your details in a logical arrangement. Since you will be recalling an experience, you probably will want to use chronological order.

### Drafting

As you write the first draft to the introduction and body of your article, you may find it helpful to refer to the guidelines on pages C225 and C229. Keep in mind as you write that your personal essay is for an audience of parents. Therefore, choose an appropriate tone and keep it consistent. Remember there are a variety of tones to choose from for a personal essay, such as reflective, humorous, serious, or even alarmed. As you conclude your essay, follow the strategies listed on pages C230–C231. Be sure to remember to leave your readers with the idea or feeling you wish to convey.

## Revising

If possible, read your essay aloud to yourself or to someone else—preferably an adult. Does the listener find your work interesting and entertaining? Is the listener left with any questions? Are any parts of your memory hazy or hard to visualize? After you respond to your listener's comments, go over your essay a couple of times. Each time, check for different points on the **Evaluation Checklist for Revising** on page C234. Then revise, rearrange, and rewrite until you are proud of your essay and sure that you will win the magazine's prize.

## Editing

Edit your personal essay, using the **Editing Checklists** on pages C46 and C236.

## Publishing

Copy your essay into a final form and give it to your teacher, who will submit it to a panel of judges.

# Connection Collection

## Representing in Different Ways

### From Print . . .

Dear City Travel,

It is hard to believe it is true. I am tanning on a beach in Hawaii! I have not been out of my bathing suit for three days. I can't believe it's February! The gang and I went to a luau last night where we ate poi and roasted pig. The luau was fantastic, but I think I really came to Hawaii for the waves!

Thanks for the good travel advice.

Yours Truly,
Akita Miro

City Travel
123 Cross Dr.
New York, NY 10025

### . . . to Visuals

You work for City Travel designing posters that advertise vacation destinations. Using Akita's postcard, create a travel poster advertising a vacation resort in Hawaii.

### From Visuals . . .

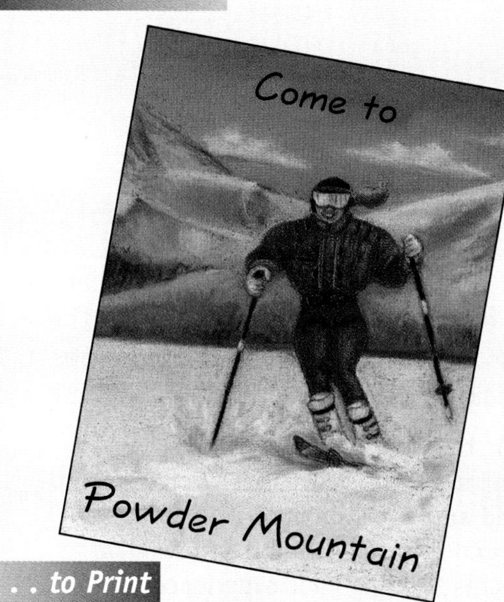
Come to
Powder Mountain

### . . . to Print

Using the poster above, write a postcard to City Travel describing your vacation on Powder Mountain.

- **Which strategies can be used for creating both written and visual representations? Which strategies apply to one, not both? Which type of representation is more effective?**
- **Draw a conclusion and write briefly about the differences between written ideas and visual representations.**

## Writing in Everyday Life

### *Narrative Essay*

The editor of the school newspaper has selected you to write an essay for a special edition of the paper. The purpose of the special edition is to prepare freshmen for the shock of starting high school by including personal narratives by the seasoned seniors.

**Write a narrative essay for the school newspaper describing the experience of your first day of high school. Use a friendly tone for your essay. Interpret your experience by answering the following questions: What do you remember most about the experience? How did the experience affect you at the time? How have your feelings about the experience changed?**

**What strategies did you use to describe your first day of high school for the incoming freshmen?**

## Writing in the Workplace

### *Narrative Report*

You are a policeman who has received a call from a concerned citizen about a man in the park who is dressed in black and wearing white makeup. When you arrive at the scene you immediately recognize that the man in question is a mime. He is miming the following actions for a group of senior citizens: climbing ropes, being trapped inside an invisible box, giving flowers, and looking sad.

**Write a narrative report for the police chief describing what happened when you responded to the call. Choose details appropriate for your purpose and audience. Be sure to use factual details to provide background information and to use vivid descriptive and sensory details to bring your experience to life.**

**What strategies did you use to write the report for the police chief?**

# Assess Your Learning

It is mid-December. You have finished writing 20 college entrance essays and you have only one more to write. So far, your essays have been about people you admire, world problems that concern you, and the contributions you think you can make to society. You anticipate a long night of writing. You are extremely relieved to read the final question: *Look back at your life so far. What have you done that has thrilled you?*

- **Write a personal narrative describing the most exciting experience in your life with such vivid detail that the people on the admissions committee will feel as if they have experienced it too.**
- **Choose details appropriate for your purpose and audience, and be sure to use factual details to provide background information. Use vivid descriptive and sensory details to bring your experience to life. Make sure that supporting paragraphs have a topic sentence that supports the main idea and follow a logical order of ideas and details.**

*Before You Write* **Consider the following questions:**
What is the ***subject?***
What is the ***occasion?***
Who is the ***audience?***
What is the ***purpose?***

*After You Write* **Evaluate your work using the following criteria:**

- Have you chosen a title that is true to the tone of your personal narrative and catches the reader's attention?
- Have you built the body of your personal narrative from the details you have chosen so you make the point you wish to share?
- Is your content organized logically? Have you included appropriate information to support your ideas? Do your ideas hold together throughout the paper?
- Have you refined your style to suit your audience, occasion, and purpose for the personal narrative?

**Write briefly on how well you did. Point out your strengths and areas for improvement.**

CHAPTER 6

# Using Description: Observation

**O**n the most obvious level, description is a matter of reporting physical sensations; for instance, there is an oak tree in the western corner of the garden, and on autumn afternoons the sun slants at a certain angle that illuminates the leaves from underneath as they change color. Other senses could be added to this visual description: the sounds of birds in the tree, the tangy scent of burning leaves in fall, the feel of bark, the remembered taste of herbs growing nearby.

In order for any of these physical details to be activated and communicated, there has to be a human observer, one who is thinking and feeling and choosing which elements of the scene to take notice of. Observation and description are mental processes at least as much as they are physical. For this reason, people in the field of writing believe that accurate, clear description is a sign of vigorous thought and that vague, inaccurate description is a sign of incomplete thought. Strange as it might seem, the habit of observing and describing can sharpen your intelligence.

## Reading with a Writer's Eye

As a young boy, Chang-rae Lee immigrated to the United States from Korea with his family. Eventually he mastered English so well that he became a professional writer whose work has appeared in *The New Yorker* magazine and in books. In the following selection from his memoir, he describes watching his mother cook. As you read, absorb the descriptions with several senses, and notice how Lee inserts bits of characterization amid the physical descriptions.

# Coming Home Again

## *Chang-rae Lee*

When I was six or seven years old, I used to watch my mother as she prepared our favorite meals. It was one of my daily pleasures. She shooed me away in the beginning, telling me that the kitchen wasn't my place, and adding, in her half-proud, half-deprecating way, that her kind of work would only serve to weaken me. "Go out and play with your friends," she'd snap in Korean, "or better yet, do your reading and homework." She knew that I had already done both, and that as the evening approached there was no place to go but her small and tidy kitchen, from which the clatter of her mixing bowls and pans would ring through the house.

I would enter the kitchen quietly and stand beside her, my chin lodging upon the point of her hip. Peering through the crook of her arm, I beheld the movements of her hands. For *kalbi*, she would take up a butchered short rib in her narrow hand, the flinty bone shaped like a section of an airplane wing and deeply embedded in gristle and flesh, and with the point of her knife cut so that the bone fell away, though not completely, leaving it connected to the meat by the barest opaque layer of tendon. Then she methodically butterflied the flesh, cutting and unfolding, repeating the action until the meat lay out on her board, glistening and ready for seasoning. She scored it diagonally, then sifted sugar into the crevices with her pinched fingers, gently rubbing in the crystals. The sugar would tenderize as well as sweeten the meat. She did this with each rib, and then set them all aside in a large shallow bowl. She minced a half-dozen cloves of garlic, a stub of gingerroot, sliced up a few scallions, and spread it all over the meat. She wiped her hands and took out a bottle of sesame oil, and, after pausing for a moment, streamed the dark oil in two swift circles around the bowl. After adding a few splashes of soy sauce, she thrust her hands in and kneaded the flesh, careful not to dislodge the bones. I asked her why it mattered that they remain connected. "The meat needs the bone nearby," she said, "to borrow its richness." She wiped her hands clean of the marinade, except for her little finger, which she would flick with her tongue from time to time, because she knew that the flavor of a good dish developed not at once but in stages.

Whenever I cook, I find myself working just as she would, readying the ingredients—a mash of garlic, a julienne of red peppers, fantails of shrimp—and piling them in little mounds about the cutting surface. My mother never left me any recipes, but this is how I learned to make her food, each dish coming not from a list or a card but from the aromatic spread of a board.

# *Thinking as a Writer*

## Recording Observations

- Reread the second paragraph of the selection and, while doing so, list at least ten descriptive details in it. Then list three details that convey attitudes, thoughts, or feelings rather than mere physical details; for example, they may imply something about his mother's character traits or his attitudes toward her. What impact does the external description have on internal attitudes?
- What does his mother's cooking mean to Chang-rae Lee? How does he express this between the lines of his description?

## Describing from Memory

Oral Expression

- Talk to a partner about a memory of food. Make your oral description rich in detail yet natural in tone. In turn, listen to your partner's description on the same subject. Listen to each other attentively, appreciatively, and critically so that you can evaluate each other's descriptions, providing useful suggestions and asking questions for clarification. Try also to participate in evaluating your own oral presentation, responding constructively to your partner's feedback.
- Discuss what makes a successful spoken description and how successful your attempts have been.

## Comparing and Contrasting Visual and Verbal Descriptions

Viewing

- What does the photograph on page C246 show you about the subject that Lee's words do not? What do Lee's words convey that the picture does not? What is conveyed by both?
- In your opinion, do illustrations usually enhance or detract from verbal descriptions? Explain your thinking.

# The Power of Description

In Chang-rae Lee's writing, you have read rich sensory detail about a subject the author knows intimately. Description is not always found in the obvious places, however, such as in the details of cooking exotic food. Description has a place in many kinds of writing, including narrative, informative, persuasive, and expressive writing.

## Uses of Description

**The following are some places where verbal description and observation can be found.**

- **Scientific papers include observations** of the phenomena studied.
- **Novels, stories, and poems describe settings, characters, and objects** as part of creating a believable fictional world.
- **Orators arguing for solutions to social problems provide specific, vivid, moving descriptions** of those problems' effects.
- **Soldiers in the field must report local conditions** accurately to their commanders.
- **Radio announcers describe sports events** so clearly that a listener can visualize the play-by-play.
- **Students at college describe life in the dorms, classes, and new friends** in letters, E-mail, and phone calls to their families.

# Refining Your Skills of Description

"It is better to think than to do, better to feel than to think, but best of all simply to look," said Goethe. Since the great German poet-philosopher-scientist led an active life of profound thought and powerful feeling, that motto need not be taken at face value. What Goethe was saying is that looking—observing—can be a profound and pleasurable activity in itself and is the basis of more active endeavors. This is certainly true of writing. To learn to write well, you must first learn to observe well.

**Descriptive writing** creates a well-developed verbal picture of a person, object, or scene.

### Your Writer's Journal

Close your eyes and recall one or more sense memories: memories that are triggered by the senses of sight, sound, touch, taste, or smell. They should be memories that remain strongly with you, whether they happened yesterday or ten years ago. Zoom in on the most powerful memory, and freewrite a description of it, including as many specific details as you can. You may want to refer to this as a possible starting point for a descriptive essay later in the chapter.

## Descriptive Essay Structure

As with the descriptive paragraph, a descriptive essay should have three major sections.

### Structure of a Descriptive Essay

- The **introduction** captures the reader's interest, introduces the subject, and suggests or implies an overall impression of the subject that the writer wishes to convey.

- The **body of supporting paragraphs** presents vivid details, especially sensory details.
- The **conclusion** reinforces the overall impression and ties the essay together, possibly leading the reader to further thought.

## Practice Your Skills

### *Analyzing a Descriptive Essay*

**Answer the following questions about "Coming Home Again."**

1. What constitutes the beginning, or introduction, of the essay?
2. What constitutes the body of the essay?
3. What constitutes the conclusion of the essay?
4. What overall impression does the essay convey?
5. List six or more details that convey or imply the overall impression.
6. Find one or more examples in which the writer uses a comparison, either stated or implied, to enrich a description.
7. How would you describe the organizational pattern of this essay? What is the underlying logic connecting one paragraph to the next?
8. By means of a description of food, what is the author saying about human life?

## Specific Details and Sensory Words

You may be familiar with the literary adage "Show, don't tell." This means that you should use strong, specific details and words that appeal to the senses in order to make the reader feel that he or she is actually seeing, hearing, and feeling the things you describe. A description is not merely a list; it is a re-creation of a part of life.

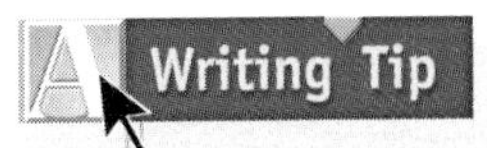

Use **specific details** and **sensory words** to bring your description to life.

One reason "Coming Home Again" is so richly descriptive is that Chang-rae Lee's observations show his attitudes about his subject. The selection is not an impersonal account of someone cutting up meat and vegetables; it is a description of the author's mother preparing meals the author has loved since childhood. Readers can sense how important the subject is to Chang-rae Lee and can participate in Lee's experience because they may have had similar life experiences.

The fundamental reason Lee's descriptive writing succeeds, however, is because its physical details are specific, vivid, accurate, and imaginatively worded. Some of these details are listed on the chart below.

| SPECIFIC SENSORY DETAILS | |
|---|---|
| **Sights** | small, tidy kitchen; the shape of a beef bone; the glisten of meat; dark oil swirling in circles in a bowl; sight of mother's arms moving; mounds of ingredients on cutting board |
| **Sounds** | clatter of mixing bowls and pans |
| **Smells** | "aromatic spread" including garlic, ginger, shrimp |
| **Taste** | sweetness of sugared meat; flavor of marinade |
| **Feelings** | child's chin lodging on mother's hip; her rubbing of sugar into meat |

## Figurative Language

Figurative comparisons can add extra flavor to a description; think of them as seasonings added to a dish of food in just the right proportion. The most familiar types of figurative comparison are imagery, similes, and metaphors. Others include personification, onomatopoeia, oxymorons, hyperbole, and symbolism. Chang-rae Lee uses figurative comparisons sparingly, applying a subtle effect at carefully chosen points. The following are some examples from "Coming Home Again."

| | |
|---|---|
| IMAGERY | "the barest opaque layer of tendon" |
| SIMILE | "the flinty bone shaped like a section of an airplane wing" |
| PERSONIFICATION | "The meat needs the bone nearby . . . to borrow its richness." |
| ONOMATOPOEIA | "snap"; "clatter"; "flick" |
| HYPERBOLE | "There was no place to go but her small and tidy kitchen." |
| SYMBOLISM | Food is often a symbol of love, the warmth of family life, and nostalgia for home. |

*You can learn more about figurative comparisons on pages C61–C62.*

Use **figurative language** and **comparisons** to add color and depth to your description.

### *Composing Figurative Language*

**Recall the conversation about food you had with a partner after first reading "Coming Home Again." Write down three details from the conversation. They may come from your recollections, your partner's, or both. For each detail, write a descriptive sentence containing a figurative comparison.**

### *Finding Similarities Using a Comparison Cluster*

You are already familiar with clustering as a strategy of developing ideas. A special kind of cluster diagram can not only develop figurative comparisons, but also show you how to analyze the things being compared. To make a comparison cluster, follow this procedure:

- In the center of a piece of paper, write the object for which you want to find a comparison. Circle it.
- Surround the circled word or phrase with words or phrases that come to mind as possible comparisons. It is important to be spontaneous at this point; write down anything that comes to mind, whether or not you understand the comparison and no matter how weird it seems.
- Focus on each word or phrase in turn, and try to think of how it is similar to the circled word or phrase. Draw a connecting line, and on that line, write a brief description of the similarity.
- If you have trouble thinking of a point of similarity,

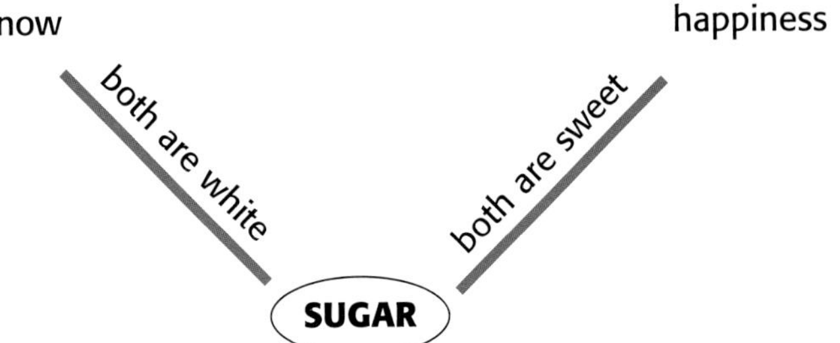


leave the connecting line blank so that you might fill it in later. If you are certain there is no similarity, write an *X* on the connecting line.

**Add at least three possible comparisons for "sugar" on the diagram above. Then make a comparison cluster for a detail from your recollections of food—other than sugar, of course.**

# Process of Writing Description

When you think of descriptive writing, you probably think first of literature: poems, stories, and novels all rely on description for their power to summon up the sights, sounds, and emotions of life. In literature, narration and description go hand in hand. Descriptive writing, however, is also found in informative, creative, and persuasive writing. If you want to explain how to do something, it is helpful to describe the actions and objects involved; if you want to give the reader information, some of that information—whether it is about current hairstyles or current theories of gravity—will undoubtedly be descriptive. If you want to persuade the reader to think or feel a certain way about an issue in order to take action, you will be better able to rouse those responses if your arguments—especially your appeals to emotion—convey the look and feel of your subject.

Prewriting is often the first thinking that a writer does, but bear in mind that prewriting can continue throughout the other stages of the writing process as well. The fact that you have made a plan and begun to draft does not mean that you should stop thinking about your subject or evaluating your approach. In addition, although the prefix *pre–* suggests that prewriting is done *before* putting pen to paper, remember that many aspects of prewriting, such as listing, freewriting, clustering, charting, and outlining, are best done on paper.

## Choosing a Subject

Chang-rae Lee chose to describe a subject that was important to him. His subject was not a major event in world history and perhaps not even in his own life. A mother cutting meat and vegetables in a kitchen is not newsworthy, even though it has had a powerful emotional impact on the author. The scale of the event is not the crucial factor in determining whether a subject is worth describing. What is important is that the author is able to transmit the impact of the subject to the reader.

The following guidelines will help you choose a subject for your descriptive essay.

### Guidelines for Choosing a Subject

- Ask yourself, "How interested am I in this subject?" If you are not very interested in your subject, your reader is probably not going to be, either.
- Ask yourself, "How well do I know this subject?" For your descriptive essay, select a subject that you know thoroughly and in detail.
- Ask yourself, "Does this subject have the potential for rich descriptive detail?"

Of the three questions, the first is the most important. If you know only a little bit about a subject, you can learn more by doing research, provided your interest is strong. If you are at first unaware of how your subject offers potentially rich descriptive detail, a deeper knowledge of the subject will probably make you aware of it.

## Practice Your Skills

### *Evaluating Potential Subjects*

**Return to the sense memory you described in your journal entry at the beginning of this chapter. Ask yourself the three questions listed in the Guidelines for Choosing a Subject. If your answers to all three questions are yes, retain this sense memory as a possible subject for a descriptive essay. If you have not answered yes to all three questions, try one or both of the following strategies.**

1. Keep focusing on the sense-memory in deeper detail until you are able to answer yes.
2. Recall one or more different memories and question yourself about them in the same way.

## Identifying Your Audience

If Lee had been describing his mother's preparation of food for an audience of professional chefs, he probably would have presented details with somewhat different vocabulary. For whom you are writing should to some extent influence how you write. The level of vocabulary you choose should be geared to your intended readership, and so should the length and complexity of your sentences. You should also think about whether your audience already knows a great deal about your subject. This will affect the amount of background material you need to provide. For example, since Lee is writing for a relatively sophisticated general audience, he does not provide any background explanations of what a *marinade* is. If he were writing a cooking textbook for a high school home economics course, he probably would have defined the word marinade and given additional background information about the uses of marinades and possibly their history.

The following questions will help you refine your style so that it suits the occasion and your audience, and purpose.

### Questions for Analyzing an Audience

- How much, if anything, does my audience already know about my subject?
- What background information, if any, must I include if my description is to be clear, concise and meaningful for this particular audience?
- How does my audience feel about my subject? Should I expect to encounter any biases, and if so, how can I organize my essay in order to neutralize or disarm them?
- What tone and what kind of vocabulary would be best in order to bridge any gap between my view of the subject and my audience's view?

## Practice Your Skills

*Identifying Your Audience*

**Identify four possible audiences for each of the following descriptive subjects.**

| | |
|---|---|
| Example | a mountain |
| Audiences | geologists, mountain climbers, artists, flatland dwellers who have never seen a mountain |

**1.** a lamp

**2.** a superhighway

**3.** a beehive

**4.** a family

**5.** a blueprint for a building

### Communicate Your Ideas

**PREWRITING** *Subject, Audience*

Using such techniques as brainstorming, freewriting, and clustering, as well as any other techniques you have found useful, select a subject for a descriptive essay that you can make vivid and interesting. Review your **journal** entries for ideas. Follow the suggestions for thinking of subjects on page C255. Visualize your audience and write answers to the questions on the previous page. Save your work. SAVE YOUR WORK

## Developing an Overall Impression

As rich in detail as "Coming Home Again" is, it is also an excellent example of selective detail. Lee does not describe everything he saw, heard, felt, smelled, and tasted while watching his mother prepare food. If he had, he could have written an entire book about that one scene. Imagine the kinds of things that might have been left out of this published description of a woman cooking: the phone rings, another character enters the room to ask an unrelated question, the cook turns on the stove, the narrator's eyes stray to the refrigerator and he feels hungry for a snack. . . . The list is almost infinite. One of the most important skills of descriptive writing is selecting, or filtering, details: knowing what to put in and what to leave out.

Writers intuitively have personal criteria for filtering details in or out of a given composition. To develop a sense of the relative value of details, it is helpful to have in mind an overall impression you wish to convey to the reader. You can then filter in any material that contributes to the desired impression and filter out any material that does not. Different readers may receive different impressions from the same text, but the writer should always have a clear vision in mind.

## Practice Your Skills

### *Identifying Overall Impressions*

**Reread "Coming Home Again" and answer the following questions.**

1. What is the overall impression Lee was trying to convey in "Coming Home Again"?
2. What phrases or passages introduce this overall impression in the introduction to the essay?
3. What phrases or passages sustain this overall impression in the body of the essay?
4. What phrases or passages carry this overall impression into the conclusion of the essay?
5. Did you derive any different or conflicting impressions from the essay? If so, what were those impressions and how did you get them?

## Communicate Your Ideas

**PREWRITING** *Overall Impression*

Review your prewriting notes and thoughts on a descriptive subject. What overall impression do you want your essay to convey? State that impression as concisely as you can; try to say it in one or two words. Save your work for later use.

## Developing a Description

Bearing in mind your intended audience and the overall impression you want to make, you can begin to work with the details you intend to include in your descriptive essay. Use the strategies below.

### Strategies for Developing a Description

- List sensory images you associate with your subject—as many images as possible. Make a chart like the one on page C251 if you wish.
- Brainstorm figurative comparisons that come to mind in association with your subject and your sensory images.
- If background information would significantly help provide a basis of knowledge for your readers, find the relevant facts and data. Do research if necessary.
- Draw a picture (or a map, if appropriate) as a prewriting tool to clarify your mental image of your subject.
- For each detail, ask yourself whether it fits with the overall impression you wish to make; filter out those details that do not fit.

## PRACTICE YOUR SKILLS

*Filtering Details*

**Look at the following list of details for a descriptive essay about a city. Write the ones that do not seem to fit the overall impression. Explain why you think they do not fit.**

OVERALL IMPRESSION inspiring, active, civilized, beautiful

DETAILS
- skyline lit up at night
- boats in the harbor tooting their horns
- cockroaches running through apartment buildings in the dark
- nannies wheeling babies to a park

- two cabbies who have crashed their taxis, arguing loudly
- women and men in a wide array of clothing, walking briskly to work or other destinations
- the scent of roasting chestnuts from a street vendor's cart wafting toward the museum steps
- steam surging up from an open manhole as a utility crew makes repairs
- a jackhammer drilling into the pavement
- from a playground basketball tournament, the cheers of passersby and the whistle of a referee
- pigeons, picking at a loaf of bread that dropped from a delivery truck, scattering upward at the approach of a bus
- an ambulance stuck in a traffic jam, impatiently sounding its siren
- diners in an elegant restaurant bringing forkfuls of delicious food to their mouths

## Communicate Your Ideas

**PREWRITING** *Development of Details*

Use the strategies on page C251 to help you develop details for your descriptive essay. Check the sensory details and figurative comparisons against the overall impression you hope to convey so that you can delete any details that would counteract that impression. Save your work for later use.

## Observing

If a machine observed a woman preparing a meal, the machine's observations would be **objective**. "Human cuts meat. Smaller human watches. Humans talk." Human beings are not like machines. Our personal responses influence our observations and make them **subjective.**

Although Chang-rae Lee makes few explicit statements of his feelings in the selection, his choices of words are subjective and often enable a reader to infer his attitudes. The following chart shows some objective facts Lee observes about his subject and some of the subjective "spins" he (or the reader) puts on those facts.

| OBJECTIVE DETAILS | SUBJECTIVE DETAILS |
|---|---|
| He watches his mother cook. | Watching her cook "was one of my daily pleasures." |
| His mother tries to shoo him out of the kitchen. | Her tone is "half-proud, half-deprecating." |
| As an adult, he cooks Korean food without recipes. | His Korean cooking is a loving legacy from his mother that comes "from the aromatic spread of a board." |

If you compare the two kinds of details, you can see that the objective ones would be verified by any impartial onlooker. The subjective observations and inferences, in contrast, might vary depending on the attitudes, personality, and outlook of each person. These subjective passages, which interpret the experience rather than merely reporting it, are what make Lee's descriptive essay touching, personal, and revealing.

### THINKING PRACTICE

**Make a chart like the one above to record objective and subjective observations of your school. Compare your work to that of a classmate.**

## Organizing a Description

The organizational plan for a descriptive essay should depend on your aim and on the nature of your details. The following chart shows some possible patterns of organization.

| WRITING AIM | KINDS OF DETAILS | TYPE OF ORDER |
|---|---|---|
| to **describe** a person, place, object, or scene | sensory details | spatial *(pages C109–C110)* |
| to **re-create** an event | sensory details, events | chronological *(pages C109–C110)* |
| to **explain** a process or show how something works | sensory and factual details, steps in a process, how parts work together | sequential *(pages C109–C110)* |
| to **persuade** | sensory and factual details, examples, reasons | order of importance *(pages C109–C110)* |
| to **reflect** | sensory and factual details, interpretations | developmental *(pages C109–C110)* |

## PRACTICE YOUR SKILLS

### *Organizing Descriptive Details*

**Review the list of details describing a city on page C259–C260. Decide on an appropriate organizational pattern for them and make a rough outline showing the order in which you would present them. Exclude any details that would work against your desired overall impression. Conclude by writing a sentence or two explaining your choices.**

## Communicate Your Ideas

**PREWRITING** ***Organization of Details***

Look over your details for your descriptive essay. Then use the chart on page C33 to help you choose an appropriate order in which to present your supporting points. Make an outline to help you as you draft.

# Drafting

**Writing Process**

Some writers feel freest when drafting because they can let their pens flow or their fingers fly over the keyboard, secure in the knowledge that they can cross out, add to, or rephrase things later. This is not to say that you should not have a sense of direction during drafting. By this point you should have a fairly clear, if flexible, idea of what you want to describe. You should also know the light in which you wish to present your description and the general shape it will take. Additionally, keeping your audience in mind will keep you on course toward a finished essay.

### Tips for Drafting a Description

- Find a "hook" to arouse the reader's interest during the introduction; try out several possible beginnings if necessary.
- Suggest or imply your overall impression early on to unify the essay; this impression should be conveyed through your choices of details and words.
- Follow your outline, but be prepared to improvise changes in response to inspiration.
- Use fresh, vivid, descriptive sensory words and images.
- Use appropriate transitions to carry through your organizational plan *(page C110)*.
- Draft a strong conclusion, perhaps referring back to earlier ideas or leaving the reader with an intriguing thought.

# Adverb Phrases and Clauses

Descriptive writing often contains modifiers—adjectives and adverbs. An **adjective** is a word that modifies a noun or pronoun; an **adverb** is a word that modifies a verb, an adjective, or another adverb. Too many modifiers, however, can weigh down a description. Varying the form of your modifiers can alleviate this problem. You can often choose between an adjective, as in, "He spoke in a **loud** voice," or an adverb, as in, "He spoke **loudly.**"

An **adverb phrase,** then, is a phrase that acts as an adverb. It modifies a verb, an adjective, or an adverb. Like other adverbs, adverb phrases answer the questions *Where? When? How? To what extent or degree?* and *Why?* Adverb phrases begin with prepositions—they are a form of **prepositional phrase.**

EXAMPLE
She did this **with each rib,** piling them **in little mounds about the cutting board**.
(two linked adverb phrases)

An **adverb clause** is a clause that functions as an adverb and modifies a verb, an adjective, or an adverb.

EXAMPLES
**When I was six or seven years old,** I used to watch my mother . . .
**Whenever I cook,** I find myself working **just as she would . . .**
(two adverb clauses in one sentence)

When you write descriptively, look for ways to vary your sentence structure by using adverb phrases and adverb clauses.

Communicate Your Ideas

**DRAFTING** *First Draft*

Write a first draft of your descriptive essay, using the details you developed, your outline, and the tips on the chart on page C263. Save your work. 

## Revising

Writing Process

The revising stage is your chance to sift through what you have thought and planned and written, separating the things that work from the things that do not. You should revise for both style and content, and on both the micro-level (the level of individual words and details) and the macro-level (the level of concept and organization). Remember that the drafting stage and the revision stage are often interwoven. While writing your first draft, you might pause to change a few words in a paragraph. While revising, you might draft an entirely new paragraph to be inserted within the essay.

### Evaluation Checklist for Revising

**Checking Your Introduction**

✓ Does your introduction seize the reader's attention? *(page C249)*

✓ Does the introduction give a sense of your subject? *(page C249)*

✓ Does your introduction set a tone that is appropriate for your subject and audience? *(page C256)*

✓ Does your introduction provide necessary background information for your audience? *(page C256)*

**Checking Your Body Paragraphs**

✓ Have you supported your overall impression with suitable supporting details? *(pages C257–C258)*

✓ Did you include specific, well-chosen sensory words and details, and have you avoided generalities? *(pages C250–C251)*

✓ Is each paragraph within the body well-developed, with a clear main idea and adequate supporting details? *(page C259)*

✓ Did you use figurative language effectively? *(pages C251–C252)*

✓ Did you move logically from one paragraph to the next in a clear order and with helpful transitions? *(pages C110, C262)*

**Checking Your Conclusion**

✓ Does the conclusion reinforce the overall impression? *(page C250)*

✓ Do you refer back to an idea in your introduction to give a sense of completion to your essay? *(pages C197, C263)*

✓ Did you end with a memorable phrase or image that might linger in the reader's mind? *(page C263)*

**Checking Your Essay Overall**

✓ Is your essay adequately developed with supporting details, or do parts seem skimpy? *(pages C192, C259)*

✓ Does your essay have unity, coherence, emphasis? *(page C194)*

**Checking Your Words and Sentences**

✓ Are your words specific and lively, and do they appeal to several senses? *(pages C60 and C250–C251)*

✓ Are your sentences varied? *(page C72)*

## Communicate Your Ideas

**REVISING** *Specific Language*
Conferencing

Use the Evaluation Checklist for Revising on pages C265–C266 to revise your descriptive essay. When you feel confident that you can answer *yes* to all the questions on the checklist, form small groups with your classmates to share your papers. Listen open-mindedly to your peers' comments and make any changes with which you agree. Save your work for later use.

# Editing

Writing Process

This is your chance to catch any errors you may have missed during the revising phase. Look for any remaining stylistic flaws, such as weak or excessive use of modifiers. Think about ways to fix any lingering problem sentences by changing the form of your modifiers—for instance, by using adverb phrases or clauses. As always when editing, correct any errors in spelling, grammar, usage, or mechanics.

## Communicate Your Ideas

### EDITING

Spend time polishing your revision when you are happy with it. During the editing stage, carefully go over your essay looking for any errors. Use your Personalized Editing Checklist and the Editing Checklist on page C46 to help you check your description for problems with spelling, grammar, usage, and mechanics. Save your work for later use.

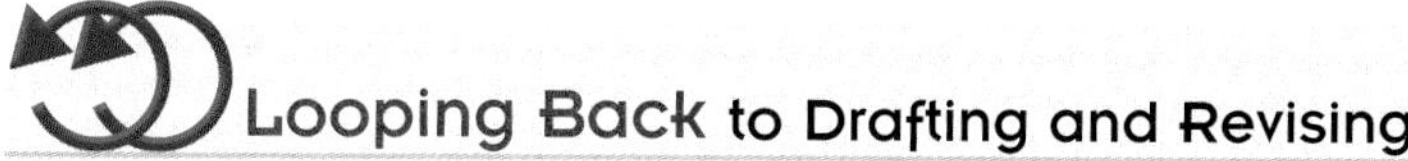

## Looping Back to Drafting and Revising

### *Elaboration*

Entering the editing stage does not mean that it is too late to add a really striking additional detail or two. Professional authors often do this when correcting the proofs of their work that are sent to them by their publishers. If you add some final touches, or if you decide at the last moment to delete a word or phrase or sentence, make sure to subject these last-minute changes to the same process the rest of the essay has gone through. That way, last-minute changes will be as polished as all of your other words.

## Publishing

Writing Process

Make your writing available to interested readers by publishing it in an appropriate format of your choice. Consider the following possible forms of publication for your descriptive essay—and try to think up some others as well, perhaps by collaborating with one or more partners.

- Include your essay in a class anthology.
- Send your descriptive essay as an E-mail to a friend who shares an interest in your subject.
- Create a bulletin board to display the essays from your class. Enhance the essays with illustrations.
- Submit your descriptive piece to a magazine or other periodical that publishes student writing, such as your school literary magazine.
- Conduct an oral reading in your classroom.

### COMPUTER TIP

Before printing your final manuscript, preview it in the Print Preview format, which shows how your pages will appear when printed.

### Time Out to Reflect

As a reader, what are your feelings about descriptive writing? Have your feelings changed as a result of working on this chapter, and if so, how? As a writer, do you like writing descriptions more, less, or the same as before you worked on this chapter? As you go on to college or to the world of work in the near future, what kinds of writing do you expect to do, and how might descriptive writing be part of that?

## Photo Essay

The photo essay is a composition form that combines visual art and text. Though it has existed for more than a century, the form has come into its own only in the past fifty years. The text for a photograph might be as short as one sentence or stretch to a page or more. The essay as a whole covers one subject, and the photographs may be sequenced logically, narratively, or intuitively, even if explaining the sequence would be difficult.

### Media Activity

Look for visually striking subjects in your everyday life. Go to new places in search of photogenic subjects. Take many photographs of your subject, in black and white or color. As you work, investigate such elements as light and shadow, composition, camera angle, focus, and cropping. Include at least six photographs in your finished photo essay. If you do not have access to a camera, make detailed drawings instead.

The text may contain a description of the picture, but the most compelling text will be your responses to the picture. Bind your photographs and texts in a scrapbook, thinking carefully about the visual relation of photo to text. Give your photo essay a title, and present the work in class. Then discuss the following questions.

**Questions for Evaluating Your Photo Essay**

- How do the text and pictures enhance or detract from each other?
- Who is your audience? What ideas might someone get from your work? How might those ideas differ from what you intended?
- What were the problems and pleasures of creating a photo essay? How did your ideas about photography or descriptive writing change?

## Process of Writing Description

Remember that writing is a recursive process—looping back and forth among the stages rather than proceeding in lockstep fashion.

The page numbers in parentheses indicate places where you can get help with your writing.

### PREWRITING

- Use brainstorming, freewriting, or clustering to recall potential subjects from your life or prior knowledge. *(pages C254–C255)*
- Select your strongest subject—one that is important to you. *(page C255)*
- Identify your purpose and audience. *(page C256)*
- Identify and briefly state an overall impression you would like to convey to the reader. *(pages C257–C258)*
- Filter details in or out depending on whether they contribute to the overall impression. *(page C258)*
- Make a plan, possibly including an outline, for your essay. *(page C262)*

### DRAFTING

- Write a catchy introduction that suggests or implies your purpose and your desired overall impression. *(page C263)*
- Use your plan or outline to help you draft the body of your essay. *(page C263)*
- Use transitions and other connecting devices to ensure that your words and ideas are clear and logical. *(pages C110, C263)*
- Write a concluding paragraph that reinforces the overall impression and ties the essay together. *(page C263)*
- Add a title.

### REVISING

- Make sure you have used words in vivid, specific ways, avoiding clichés. *(pages C250–C252)*
- Use peer conferencing to get a new perspective on your essay and on possible means of improvement. *(page C266)*
- Revise for development, unity, coherence, and emphasis. *(pages C194, C265)*

### EDITING

- Use your **Editing Checklist** and Personal Editing Checklist to remove errors in grammar, usage, spelling, and mechanics. *(page C46)*
- Make a neat final copy of your essay in standard manuscript form. *(page C48)*

### PUBLISHING

- Search for suitable ways to find a reading or listening audience for your descriptive essay. *(page C268)*

# A Writer Writes

## A Description of a Future Vision

**Purpose: to visualize and communicate your own goals, dreams, or aspirations through descriptive writing**

**Audience: you and people close to you**

### Prewriting

Many people feel that the first step toward achieving a goal is to visualize it clearly and convincingly. For example, suppose that a child wants to become an astronomer. The child will imagine being an astronomer, working at an observatory and looking through a huge telescope. If the child believes in this goal, he or she will pursue it by reading about the stars, taking astronomy courses, joining an astronomy club, and looking at the stars through actual telescopes.

Your own future is approaching. You have undoubtedly had plans and dreams of your future all your life, and they may have changed a great deal over time. At this point, visualize one thing that you hope or believe is in your future. It may be an object, such as a car or house. It may be an activity, such as a job or a way of life. Or it may be an aspect of yourself, such as a wish to become independent or adventurous.

Take some time to visualize this future development. How does it look to an observer? Use all your accustomed prewriting techniques, such as clustering and freewriting and listing, as you prepare to write a description of this one aspect of your future.

### Drafting

Draft your description either in the form of a journal entry for yourself alone, or in a letter addressed to a specific person

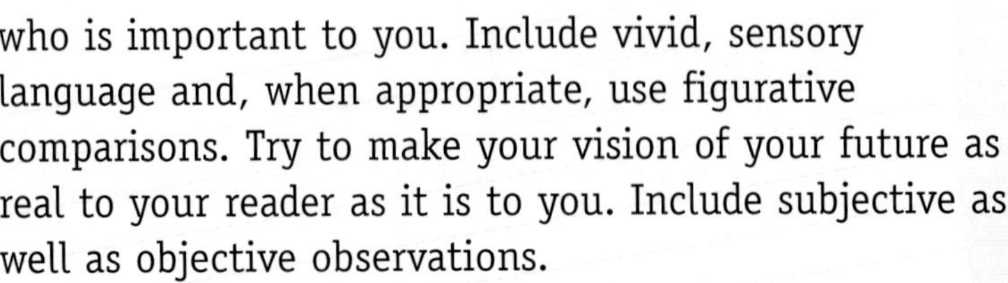

who is important to you. Include vivid, sensory language and, when appropriate, use figurative comparisons. Try to make your vision of your future as real to your reader as it is to you. Include subjective as well as objective observations.

## Revising

Read your description and ask yourself whether it truly captures the essence of the future that you have envisioned. If not, revise for style and content. Also you may want to take more time to visualize your subject. After all, this might be the first step toward achieving your goal!

## Editing

Use the checklist on page C46 to edit your letter or **journal** entry for spelling, grammar, usage, and mechanics.

## Publishing

Prepare a neat copy of your letter or **journal** entry and think about whom you would like to have read it. Perhaps you will be the only audience; that is perfectly acceptable for this particularly private description. If you have addressed your letter to someone, consider whether you would like that person to read it in real life, or whether the salutation is only a matter of form. If you do show your letter or **journal** entry to others, this would be a good opportunity to loop back to revising, asking your readers for constructive comments and acting upon any with which you agree. After arriving at a final version, save your work in your portfolio.

## Representing in Different Ways

### From Print . . .

65 Jump Street
New Braintree, MA 01005
September 6, 2000

Dear Coach,

I am writing to recommend that we change the name of our team from the Buffalo to the Brainstorm. I believe that the name, Brainstorm, better represents our school and the qualities for which our school stands.

I suggest that the logo should consist of a bright green brain backed by two crossed and yellow bolts of lightning. Inside the brain there should be a bright white lightbulb. The lightning represents the speed of our basketball squad and the energy with which we are able to solve problems and overcome adversity. The brain and the lightbulb represent the intelligence and ideas that allow us to succeed both on the court and in the classroom.

Do you think the alumni will accept this idea for a new logo?

Sincerely,
*Alexandra Perez*
Alexandra Perez

### . . . to Visuals

Using the description in the letter to the right, draw the new mascot for the New Braintree Brainstorm.

### From Visuals . . .

### . . . to Print

As editor of the school newspaper, you have been allowed a sneak preview of the design of the new school mascot. Write a brief article for the editorial column describing the logo and your opinions about it.

- **Which strategies can be used for creating both written and visual representations? Which strategies apply to one, not both? Which type of representation is more effective?**
- **Draw a conclusion, and write briefly about the differences between written ideas and visual representations.**

## Writing in Everyday Life

### *Descriptive Friendly Letter*

Bart, your penpal from Cerebellum City, is a genius. He skipped middle school, high school, and college and went right to work for NASA designing rocket boosters for the Space Shuttle. Bart has no idea what a high school is like. He has never been to a school dance, and he has never experienced the last day at school. Most importantly he has never had a high school locker.

**Write a letter to Bart describing what he might observe at the hallway lockers between classes. Be sure to create an overall impression with sensory details and figurative language and to use words in vivid, specific ways, avoiding clichés.**

**What strategies did you use to describe a high school locker to Bart?**

## Writing in the Workplace

### *Descriptive E-mail*

You work for an elevator company installing computer terminals in the elevators of the skyscrapers so that passengers can check their E-mail on their long rides up. You love your job, but the music piped into the elevators drives you crazy.

**Write an E-mail message to your boss describing the elevator music, and describe the type of music you would rather hear while you work. Be sure to use both objective and subjective details in your description.**

**What strategies did you use to describe the elevator music to your boss?**

*You can find information on writing E-mail on pages C828–C831.*

# Assess Your Learning

You have been chosen as a student representative for the Time Capsule Committee. As a member of the committee, you have been asked to write a letter to a teenager living 1000 years in the future describing some aspect of your everyday life. You want to describe something that is representative of your everyday life, so you decide to describe what you observe every day on your way to school.

- **Write a letter to a teenager living 1000 years from now, describing your daily observations on your way to school. Take your reader on a descriptive journey from your home to your school.**
- **Be sure to consider what background information, if any, you must include if your description is to be clear, concise, and meaningful for your particular audience. Use specific details and sensory words to bring your description to life. Use figurative language and comparisons to add color and bring your description to life.**

*Before You Write* **Consider the following questions:**
What is the ***subject?***
What is the ***occasion?***
Who is the ***audience?***
What is the ***purpose?***

*After You Write* **Evaluate your work using the following criteria:**

- Have you considered what background information, if any, you have to include if your description is to be clear, concise, and meaningful for your particular audience?
- Have you written in a voice and style appropriate to audience and purpose?
- Have you used specific details and sensory words to bring your description to life?
- Have you used figurative language and comparisons, such as metaphors and similes, to add color and depth to your description?
- Have you demonstrated control over grammatical elements such as subject-verb agreement, pronoun-antecedent agreement, verb forms, and parallelism?

**Write briefly on how well you did. Point out your strengths and areas for improvement.**

CHAPTER 7

# Writing Stories, Plays, and Poems

If you could look into a writer's mind, there is no limit to what you might experience—it contains the scope of the vast universe. There is almost no limit to how stories can be told. The special quality of a story is created not only by a distinctive writing style, but by a unique, compelling plot. Consider how the uniqueness and impact of your tale will be affected by whether you choose to tell it in a story, in a play, or in a poem. Then, analyze your strengths and weaknesses in writing a story, play, or poem. If you are able to evaluate these factors wisely in choosing a form for your story, then you will be well on your way toward telling a story that is both original and compelling.

## *Reading with a Writer's Eye*

In the following excerpt from *The Writing Life,* author Annie Dillard writes about the influence successful fiction writers have had on one another, and about the importance of loving the work. Read the passage once for pleasure. Then reread it, noting the creative twist she puts into her persuasive comments.

# The Writing Life

*Annie Dillard*

Hemingway studied, as models, the novels of Knut Hamsun and Ivan Turgenev. Issac Bashevis Singer, as it happened, also chose Hamsun and Turgenev as models. Ralph Ellison studied Hemingway and Gertrude Stein. Thoreau loved Homer; Eudora Welty loved Chekhov. Faulkner described his debt to Sherwood Anderson and Joyce; E. M. Forster, his debt to Jane Austen and Proust. By contrast, if you ask a twenty-one-year-old poet whose poetry he likes, he might say, unblushing, "Nobody's." In his youth, he has not yet understood that poets like poetry, and novelists like novels; he himself likes only the role, the thought of himself in a hat. Rembrandt and Shakespeare, Tolstoy and Gauguin, possessed, I believe, powerful hearts, not powerful wills. They loved the range of materials they used. The work's possibilities excited them; the field's complexities fired their imaginations. The caring suggested the tasks; the tasks suggested the schedules. They learned their fields and then loved them. They worked, respectfully, out of their love and knowledge, and they produced complex bodies of work that endure. Then, and only then, the world flapped at them some sort of hat, which, if they were still living, they ignored as well as they could, to keep at their tasks.

# Thinking as a Writer

## Analyzing Creative Arguments

Annie Dillard writes that "poets like poetry, and novelists like novels," as a way of introducing the idea that the love of creating is all the inspiration a great artist needs.

- Look back through the passage for examples of how Dillard creatively makes her point. How effective is her way of presenting her argument?
- What advice do you think Dillard would give her imaginary twenty-one-year-old poet?

## Interpreting Works of Art

Oral Expression

With a small group of classmates, bring in selections from your favorite stories, poems, or plays. Those who have favorite works of visual art may be able to bring in posters or art books showing the works. Arrange viewings and readings of these works.

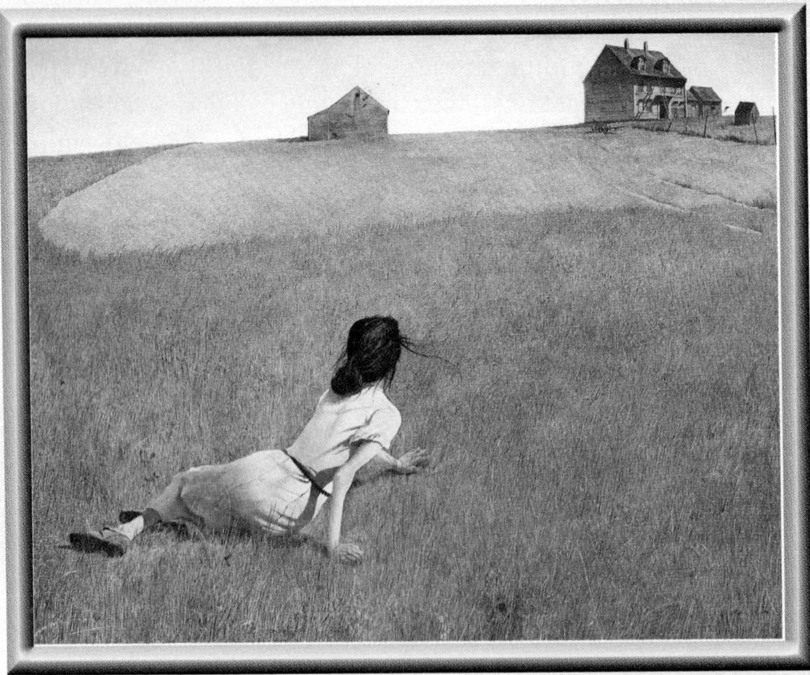

Andrew Wyeth. *Christina's World*, 1998. Tempera on gessoed panel, 32 1/4 by 47 3/4 inches.
The Museum of Modern Art, New York.

- Take turns discussing these works, either literary or visual. For each work, discuss whether you think the artist or writer was inspired through their love of the form or through sheer determination.

## Synthesizing Visual and Literary Forms

Viewing Dillard includes the painters Rembrandt van Rijn and Paul Gauguin in her argument about the sources of creative expression.

- Look at the painting by Andrew Wyeth. What visual elements give clues to how Wyeth felt about his subject? Do you think he had a "powerful heart" to create such a painting? Explain your answer.
- What stories, poems, or plays have you encountered that give you a response similar to the one you have to Wyeth's painting? What was it about the literary works that stirred that response in you?

# The Power of Creating

The power of creating is everywhere, within everyone. Yet the way in which it is expressed by each individual is unique. As Annie Dillard asserts in *The Writing Life,* it is this uniqueness that gives creative writing its power.

## Uses of Creative Writing

**Here are some of the ways in which stories, plays, and poems enrich the world.**

- **People send poems on greeting cards** for almost every conceivable occasion, from birthdays to illnesses, and even for no reason at all.
- **People give books of fiction or poetry as gifts** to those they care about.
- **Workers on breaks,** or waiting for transportation, or sitting in vehicles, read stories in print or online to keep their minds active.
- **People all over the world are familiar with famous fictional characters**—from Hamlet to Luke Skywalker—and allude to them in conversation.
- **Science fiction helps people speculate** about—and thus begin planning for—the future of our society, our species, our planet.
- **Millions of people throughout the world** spend hours per day engrossed in fictional drama on television.

# Writing a Short Story

Think about the stories that you have enjoyed reading. What aroused your curiosity and kept your interest?

Short stories are born in the author's imagination. The characters and events can be realistic or fanciful, ordinary or extraordinary. The events all revolve around a conflict faced by the main character. Just how the character deals with this conflict provides the story with its interest and suspense.

A **short story** is a well-developed fictional account of characters resolving a conflict or problem.

As you read the following short story, written by Vladimir Nabokov, think about the plot. When you read for a second time, think about each character's relation to one another.

## First Love

She would be ten in November, I had been ten in April. Attention was drawn to a jagged bit of violet mussel shell upon which she had stepped with the bare sole of her narrow long-toed foot. No, I was not English. Her greenish eyes seemed flecked with the overflow of the freckles that covered her sharp-featured face. She wore what might now be termed a playsuit consisting of a blue jersey with rolled-up sleeves and blue knitted shorts. I had taken her at first for a boy and then had been puzzled by the bracelet on her thin wrist and the cork-screw brown curls dangling from under her sailor cap.

She spoke in birdlike bursts of rapid twitter, mixing governess English and Parisian French. Two years before, on the same *plage*[1], I had been much attached to Zina, the lovely, sun-tanned, bad-tempered little daughter of a Serbian *naturopath*[2]—she had, I remember (absurdly, for she and I were only eight at the time), a *grain de beauté*[3] on her apricot skin just below the heart, and

---

[1] ***plage*** (plŏj) *n.*: Beach. (French)

[2] ***naturopath*** (nā′ chər • ə - păth) n.: A believer in a system of natural remedies to fight disease.

[3] ***grain de beauté*** (grăn də bō ta′) *n.*: Beauty mark. (French)

there was a horrible collection of chamber pots, full and half-full, and one with surface bubbles, on the floor of the hall in her family's boardinghouse lodgings which I visited early one morning to be given by her, as she was being dressed, a dead hummingbird moth found by the cat. But when I met Colette, I knew at once that this was the real thing. Colette seemed to me so much stranger than all my other chance playmates at Biarritz! I somehow acquired the feeling that she was less happy than I, less loved. A bruise on her delicate, downy forearm gave rise to awful conjectures. "He pinches as bad as my mummy," she said, speaking of a crab. I evolved various schemes to save her from her parents, who were *"des bourgeois de Paris"*[3] as I heard somebody tell my mother with a slight shrug. I interpreted the disdain in my own fashion, as I knew that those people had come all the way from Paris in their blue-and-yellow limousine (a fashionable adventure in those days) but had drably sent Colette with her dog and governess by an ordinary coach-train. The dog was a female fox terrier with bells on her collar and a most waggly behind. From sheer exuberance, she would lap up salt water out of Colette's toy pail. I remembered the sail, the sunset, and the lighthouse pictured on that pail, but I cannot recall the dog's name, and this bothers me.

During the two months of our stay at Biarritz, my passion for Colette all but surpassed my passion for Cleopatra. Since my parents were not keen to meet hers, I saw her only on the beach; but I thought of her constantly. If I noticed she had been crying, I felt a surge of helpless anguish that brought tears to my own eyes. I could not destroy the mosquitoes that had left their bites on her frail neck, but I could, and did, have a successful fistfight with a red-haired boy who had been rude to her. She used to give me warm handfuls of hard candy. One day, as we were bending together over a starfish, and Colette's ringlets were tickling my ear, she suddenly turned toward me and kissed me on the cheek. So great was my emotion that all I could think of saying was, "You little monkey."

I had a gold coin that I assumed would pay for our elopement. Where did I want to take her? Spain? America? The moun-

---

[3] **des bourgeois de Paris** (dā bür jwŏ′ də pŏ rē′) *n.*: Middle-class Parisians. (French)

tains above Pau? *"Là-bas, là-bas, dans la montagne,"*[4] as I had heard Carmen sing at the opera. One strange night, I lay awake, listening to the recurrent thud of the ocean and planning our flight. The ocean seemed to rise and grope in the darkness and then heavily fall on its face.

Of our actual getaway, I have little to report. My memory retains a glimpse of her obediently putting on rope-soled canvas shoes, on the lee side of a flapping tent, while I stuffed a folding butterfly net into a brown-paper bag. The next glimpse is of our evading pursuit by entering a pitch-dark *cinéma* near the Casino (which, of course, was absolutely out of bounds). There we sat, holding hands across the dog, which now and then gently jingled in Colette's lap, and were shown a jerky, drizzly, but highly exciting bullfight at St. Sébastian. My final glimpse is of myself being led along the promenade by Linderovski. His long legs move with a kind of ominous briskness and I can see the muscles of his grimly set jaw working under the tight skin. My bespectacled brother, aged nine, whom he happens to hold with his other hand, keeps trotting out forward to peer at me with awed curiosity, like a little owl.

[4]***La-bas, la-bas, dans la montagne*** (lŏ bŏ lŏ bŏ dŏn lŏ mŏn tŏn′): Far away, far away, on the mountain. (French)

## Your Writer's Journal

In his short story "First Love," Vladimir Nabokov recounts the events of a vacation at the beach where he finds summer love. Nabokov describes many of his memories using great detail. One such memory is that of ". . . her obediently putting on rope-soled canvas shoes, on the lee side of a flapping tent, while I stuffed a folding butterfly net into a brown-paper bag." In your journal, note some memories of a summer past, or of a trip that you once took. Throughout the week, continue noting thoughts and ideas related to these memories, as well as new ones.

At the end of the week, reread your journal entries and think about how you could use your imagination to turn some of your memories into short stories. Next to each memory, add an imaginative twist to lend creative angles to ordinary situations.

The creative process does not occur all by itself. To create an effective short story, painting, song, or poem, you need to encourage and direct your imagination. The prewriting strategies that follow can help move the creative process along as you plan the conflict, theme, characters, point of view, and plot of your story. Treat the strategies as suggestions only, for, as a writer, you will work out your own ways of generating ideas. Feel free to move back and forth among the techniques and to select and add as you work your way through them.

## Choosing a Conflict or Problem

What will your story be about? All short stories are based on a central conflict or problem. Therefore, deciding what your story will be about actually means deciding what the main conflict or problem will be.

A story can revolve around any kind of conflict, as dramatic as a disabled spaceship or as ordinary as a misplaced homework assignment or a trip to the movies. Usually the conflict builds between the main character and some other force in the story. The following chart summarizes and gives examples of the most common kinds of conflicts that are at the center of short stories.

### Types of Conflicts

- **Between the main character and another character:**
  A son objects to his mother's limits on his use of her car.
- **Between the main character and a natural force:**
  An inexperienced surfer faces unusually rough surf.
- **Between forces or feelings inside the main character:**
  A student is torn between her desire to go to college and the need to help support her family.

You might begin your search for story ideas by brainstorming lists of familiar conflicts or problems, such as those relating to friendships, family situations, school activities, and other areas of your life. Also review your **journal,** which—if you record thoughts and observations regularly—can be a rich source of ideas. Discuss story ideas with others. A comment from someone else may ignite your imagination.

As you search for story ideas, remember that dramatic stories do not always require extraordinary conflicts. If the events are well told, a search for a lost book can be as absorbing as a search for a lost planet. Also, hold on to your sense of humor. Problems and their solutions do not always have to be serious.

After you put together a list of possible conflicts, review the list and cross out any conflicts that seem difficult, unfamiliar, or dull. For those that remain, see what ideas come to mind. Put a check next to the conflicts that inspire an interesting character or plot and then choose one you think you would enjoy writing about.

## Practice Your Skills

### *Listing Familiar Conflicts*

**Brainstorm a list in answer to each question below, basing the list on your own experiences or the experiences of those around you. Then save your list in your writing folder.**

1. What personal values of yours are different from those of a friend or a relative? What conflicts has this caused?
2. If you were writing a situation comedy for television called "Senior Year," what situations might you use for some of the episodes?
3. When has humor helped you or someone else deal with a problem?
4. What sorts of problems have been caused by the weather, a power failure, illness, or some other event beyond your control?
5. When have you had to struggle to fulfill a dream?

## Choosing a Theme

The main purpose in writing a story is to entertain the reader. You may also want to leave the reader with some message, idea, or question. The main idea you want to plant in the reader's mind is called the **theme.** Usually you imply the theme, rather than state it directly. You arrange the details so that your reader can infer your message. In the following excerpt from *The Doll's House,* Katherine Mansfield centers the conflict around a young girl's desire to reach out to some poorer children, of whom her family and friends disapprove. Rooted in this conflict is the theme, which is about the cruelties of differences between social classes. Like many writers Mansfield does not state her theme directly but leaves clues for the reader to infer it. In the following excerpt, notice how Mansfield implies the theme.

**MODEL: Implied Theme**

"Hullo," she said to the passing Kelveys.

They were so astounded that they stopped. Lil gave her silly smile. Our Else started.

"You can come see our doll's house if you want to," said Kezia, and she dragged one toe on the ground. But at that Lil turned red and shook her head quickly.

"Why not?" asked Kezia.

Lil gasped, then she said, "Your ma told our ma you wasn't to speak to us."

"Oh, well," said Kezia. She didn't know what to reply.

–*Katherine Mansfield,* The Doll's House

Before you write a story, you should decide on a theme—a comment that you want your story to make, such as a comment about growing up. If you do not have a theme in mind, freewrite to generate possible themes. Keep in mind, however, that the theme should be an idea you care about, as well as one that fits your story.

## Practice Your Skills

*Generating Story Themes*

**Go back to your notes from the previous Practice Your Skills activity and choose three conflicts. First freewrite about each conflict to generate possible story themes and then choose a suitable theme for each one. Write a statement expressing the theme in each case.**

## Sketching Characters

Whether you start with real people or work entirely from your imagination, you can make your characters look and behave just as you please. Your only limits are the boundaries of your imagination and the requirements of your story.

Every story has one or more **main characters**—the characters who deal with the central problem. To develop each character, freewrite, brainstorm, or cluster around a detail or idea. You can begin with the smallest detail, such as the name. However, you must go on to sketch the characters fully if you are to bring them to life. Use the following diagram to help you develop character sketches.

**Model: Character Cluster**

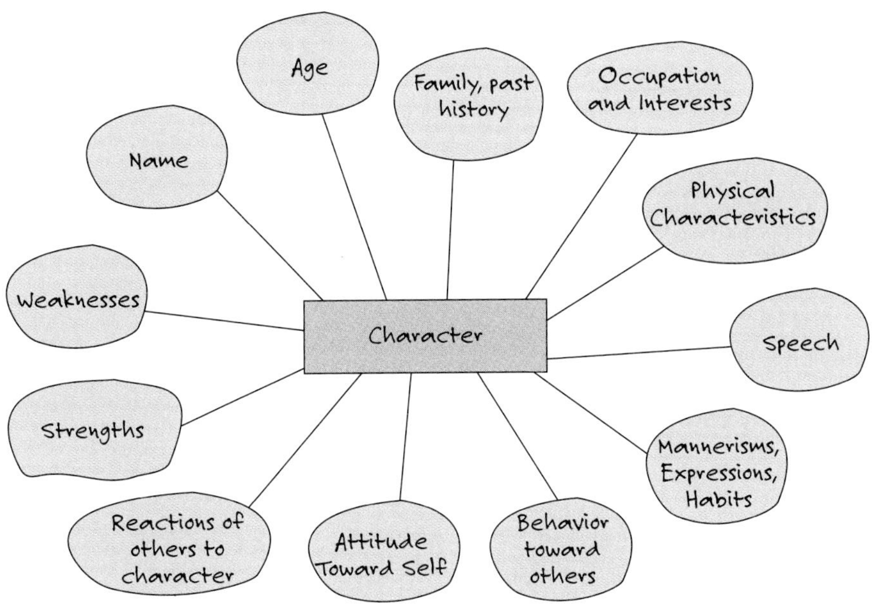

## Practice Your Skills

*Sketching Characters*

**Use three of the details below to sketch three story characters. Freewrite about one detail, brainstorm about the second, and cluster about the third. Then, for each character, complete a character cluster like the one on the previous page. Save your work.**

**1.** a person with a fringed, red-leather jacket

**2.** a person with a high-pitched, squeaky voice

**3.** a person named Ramona DeTromblay

**4.** a person who is an ambitious young musician

**5.** a person who is always late

## Choosing a Point of View

Every story has a **narrator**—the person who tells the story. When you choose the narrator, you decide not only who will relate the events but also through whose eyes, or from whose **point of view,** the reader will see them. Once you choose a point of view, use it consistently throughout the story. Otherwise your story will be confusing. The following chart outlines the choices you have for point of view.

| POINT OF VIEW | NARRATOR |
|---|---|
| **First-Person** | • Observes or participates in the action personally.<br>• Tells personal observations and thoughts.<br>• Uses first-person pronouns. |
| **Third-Person Limited** | • Observes one character who participates in the action.<br>• Tells the words, actions, and feelings of the character and observations about him or her.<br>• Uses third-person pronouns. |

| | |
|---|---|
| **Third-Person Omniscient** | • Observes but does not participate in the action. |
| **"All Knowing"** | • Tells the words, actions, and feelings of all the characters as well as observations about them.<br>• Uses third-person pronouns. |

The **first-person point of view** allows the reader to view the events from inside the mind of one of the characters. This adds a personal tone to the story, as shown in the following example.

| | |
|---|---|
| First-Person | **I** closed the door softly, wondering if anyone had seen **me.** |

When you choose the **third-person limited** point of view, your story has a less personal tone. Yet this point of view allows you to give the reader more information.

| | |
|---|---|
| Third-Person Limited | **Eva** closed the door softly, wondering if anyone had seen **her. She** did not even realize that **she** had held **her** breath all the way down the stairs. |

The **third-person omniscient** point of view, on the other hand, balances the disadvantage of being impersonal with the advantage of letting the reader know the thoughts of all the characters.

| | |
|---|---|
| Third-Person Omniscient | **Eva** closed the door softly, wondering if anyone had seen **her.** A block away **David** waited anxiously, hoping that **she** would come. |

## Practice Your Skills

### *Using Different Points of View*

**The following summary of events can be told in a story of just a few paragraphs. Write three versions of the story, choosing a different point of view each time: (1) the first-person as Leon,**

**(2) the third-person limited as Mr. Gomez, and (3) the third-person omniscient. Be aware of the different effects the stories have as you write the three versions.**

Leon and three other high school seniors have been performing as a rock group since eighth grade. They audition for a local variety show. They perform but lose to another group. Discouraged, they decide to disband after graduation. Then Mr. Gomez, one of the judges, invites them to perform at his club.

## Outlining the Story

Always prepare an outline of the important elements of your story to make sure that the parts fit together. Include the following headings in your outline.

**STORY OUTLINE**

**Title:**
**Setting:**
**Characters:** (List the characters and include brief descriptions.)
**Conflict:**
**Plot:** (List the events, one by one, in order of presentation.)
**Resolution:**

**Title** Although the title naturally appears first in the outline, you may want to choose it last, when you have a clearer sense of your story. Select a title that fits the selection in subject and mood and one that will arouse the reader's interest.

**Setting** The setting is the time and place in which the story occurs. However, it is more than a physical location; it is also an atmosphere and mood that provide a suitable framework for the events. In order to convey these elements to the reader, you need to use description. For example, what are the descriptive details used in the following setting? What sorts of events do you think might occur?

*You can learn more about description on pages C244–C275.*

**MODEL: Setting**

> The room that afternoon was full of such shy creatures, lights and shadows, curtains blowing, petals falling—things that never happen, so it seems, if someone is looking. The quiet old country room, with its rugs and stone chimney pieces, its sunken bookcases and red and gold lacquer cabinets, was full of such nocturnal creatures . . .
>
> But, outside, the looking glass reflected the hall table, the sunflowers, the garden path so accurately and so fixedly that they seemed held there in their reality unescapably. It was a strange contrast—all changing here, all stillness there. One could not help looking from one to the other.
>
> —*Virginia Woolf,* "The Lady in the Looking Glass: A Reflection"

This "strange contrast," as well as the mirror itself, provides an appropriate framework for a story in which the main character herself seems to move into another person—as caught, of course, by the mirror. In the same way, choose a suitable backdrop for the events of your story and describe it briefly in your outline.

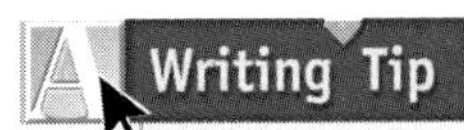


Match the **setting** of your story to the action, mood, and characters' feelings.

**Characters** In your story outline, write a brief description of each character, starting with the main character.

**Conflict** Add a sentence or two telling about the conflict or problem that the main character will have to face.

**Plot** Next in the outline of the story is the series of events, or **plot.** Most plots begin with an incident that triggers the conflict. Then, as the plot progresses, the conflict becomes more and more serious until it reaches a critical point, or **climax.** After that the conflict is resolved.

In your outline, list the events in the order in which you will relate them, such as **chronological order.** Sometimes, to establish the setting or to begin at an exciting point, you may instead use **flashback**—that is, you may interrupt the action to go back to an earlier event and then return to the main action.

**Resolution** To complete your outline, write the **resolution**—the way the conflict or problem is settled. Be sure to tie up the events of the story in a way that will satisfy the reader.

## Practice Your Skills

### *Outlining a Story*

**Choose a story that you have read and outline it, following the form given on page C290.**

## Communicate Your Ideas

**PREWRITING** *Conflict, Point of View, Character, Plot, Outline*

Using your **journal** notes, your responses to Practice Your Skills activities, and the prewriting activities discussed in this section, prepare to write a short story on a theme of your choice. First choose a conflict or problem and a point of view. Then, before you sketch your characters and outline your story, add one unexpected element to your plot.

SAVE YOUR WORK

## Implying

By implying information a writer can captivate and involve readers, forcing them to make inferences and draw conclusions, as Katherine Mansfield does in the following excerpt from "The Singing Lesson."

> This little ritual of the flower . . . was as much part of the lesson as opening the piano. But this morning . . . Miss Meadows totally ignored the chrysanthemum, made no reply to her [Mary's] greeting, but said in a voice of ice, "Page fourteen, please . . ."

Through specific details Katherine Mansfield implies that Miss Meadows is not in a good mood. First, Miss Meadows acknowledges neither the flower nor Mary's kind gesture. Second, she continues to direct her class "in a voice of ice."

A chart like the one below can help you imply unstated facts or conclusions. On the left list events, settings, or character traits for your story, and on the right list details to imply those elements.

| TRAIT | DETAILS |
|---|---|
| considerate | fearful of awakening sister, uses hallway light to guide her, creeps softly into room |
| **EVENT** | **DETAILS** |
| graduation | field of blue and gold ribbons, applause fills the stadium, tasseled caps tossed in the air. |

### THINKING PRACTICE

**Write a passage that implies a setting, event, or character trait from your story or use any of the following suggestions.**

1. **traits:** kindness, dishonesty, perseverance
2. **settings:** an amusement park, a university, a mall
3. **events:** a track meet, a job interview, a car accident

Your goal in drafting a story is to produce a workable narrative, one that can be shaped and polished into a solid story. As you draft your story, you can use a variety of types of writing, including narration, description, and informative writing.

This section will show you how to use these types of writing in different parts of your story—the beginning, the middle, and the end.

*You can learn more about these types of writing on pages C244–C275.*

## Drafting the Beginning

As the following examples demonstrate, you can open a story in many different ways.

| | |
|---|---|
| Dialogue | "They say he's worth a million," Lucia said.<br>*—Graham Greene, "Across the Bridge"* |
| Introduction of the Character | With despair—cold, sharp despair—buried deep in her heart like a wicked knife, Miss Meadows, in cap and gown and carrying a little baton, trod the cold corridors that led to the music hall.<br>*—Katherine Mansfield, "The Singing Lesson"* |
| Descriptive Details | North Richmond Street, being blind [dead end],was a quiet street except at the hour when the Christian Brothers' School set the boys free.<br>*—James Joyce, "Araby"* |

| | |
|---|---|
| NARRATIVE DETAILS | Toward the end of her day in London Mrs. Drover went round to her shut-up house to look for several things she wanted to take away. |
| | *—Elizabeth Bowen, "The Demon Lover"* |
| GENERAL STATEMENT | People should not leave looking glasses hanging in their rooms any more than they should leave open checkbooks or letters confessing to some hideous crime. |
| | *—Virginia Woolf, "The Lady in the Looking Glass: A Reflection"* |

Each of these openings sets up a situation that makes the reader curious. Is the man really worth a million? Why is Miss Meadows full of despair? What does the boys' school have to do with the story? Why is Mrs. Drover's house shut up? Why shouldn't people have looking glasses hanging in their rooms? Use your opening sentences, like these sentences, to hook your reader. Then give further details to keep the reader engaged. The box below lists some ways to begin a story.

### Guidelines for Beginning a Story

- Set the time and place.
- Introduce the main character or characters.
- Provide needed background information.
- Set the plot in motion with a triggering event.
- Establish the conflict or problem.

## Drafting the Middle

As you draft the middle portion of your story, connect the events so that they flow naturally. Transitions—such as *the next day* and *a week later* help tie events together and show the passage of time. Also try to make every event add to the development and extension of the story until the climax of the plot is reached. If you include a flashback, use one of these two methods.

| | |
|---|---|
| SHOWING A FLASHBACK WITH SPACING | As Ben walked along the beach, his eyes followed the gulls, but his thoughts were far away.<br><br>"Ben, wake up! Are you up, Ben?" That day had begun like every other school day, with his mother's voice. |
| SHOWING A FLASHBACK WITH NARRATIVE | As Ben walked along the beach, his eyes followed the gulls, but his thoughts were on that day almost a year ago. It had begun like every other school day, with his mother's voice. |

As you develop your characters, give details that tell how they look, what they think, and how they behave. Notice in the following excerpts how much livelier the version with the dialogue is. Then use the guidelines below to draft the middle section of your story.

| | |
|---|---|
| NARRATIVE | They stopped talking when they heard a noise. |
| DIALOGUE | "Shhh!" hissed Elena. "I just heard something!" |

**Guidelines for Drafting the Middle of a Story**

- Relate the events either chronologically or with flashbacks.
- Use transitions to connect the events smoothly and clearly.
- Use dialogue to make your characters vivid.
- Use descriptive details to bring your story to life.

## Drafting the Ending

A story ending does not need to be positive or happy, nor does it need to solve every problem. It does, however, need to bring the story to a close by tying the events together. In other words it needs to feel like an ending to the reader.

### Guidelines for Ending a Story

- Resolve the conflict and complete the action of the plot.
- Use dialogue, action, or description to show, not just tell, what happens.
- Leave the reader feeling satisfied.

## Practice Your Skills

*Drafting a Story*

**Without looking back at the original version, write your own draft of the story you outlined. Following the guidelines on pages C295 and C296, resolve the conflict in a surprising way. Save your draft in your writing folder.**

*Communicate Your Ideas*

DRAFTING *First Draft*

 Write a draft of your own story, using your outline. Follow the guidelines on pages C295–C297. Be sure to save your work for later use. 

"I have never thought of myself as a good writer . . ." claimed James A. Michener, "but I'm one of the world's great rewriters." For many writers the revising stage can be the most productive of all.

## Improving Plot

Not every sequence of events is a plot. Compare the following two sets of sequences and notice how they are different.

| | |
|---|---|
| EVENTS | Mark got dressed. He went for a walk. He walked to the bank. He returned two hours later. |
| PLOT | Nervously Mark got dressed. He walked to the bank for a job interview. The bank was being robbed. Mark ran for the police. He was a hero. He did not get the job. |

In the first sequence, the events are related only chronologically. In the second sequence, every event relates to Mark's job interview. One event leads naturally to the next in a pattern of rising action. To tighten your plot as you revise, ask yourself the following questions.

### Guidelines for Improving the Plot

- Are events arranged chronologically, except for flashbacks?
- Are flashbacks easily recognizable?
- Are transitions used to help tie events together and to show the passage of time?
- Does every event revolve around the central conflict?
- Is each event clearly linked to the events before and after?
- Does each event add to the tension and build to the climax?
- Does the resolution tie up the events?

## PRACTICE YOUR SKILLS

### *Improving a Plot*

**Think of an event that could be added to the plot of "First Love" that would make sense in relation to what Vladimir Nabokov has already written. Then decide whether you think your proposed plot addition would improve the story, weaken the story, or keep its quality unchanged. Explain your reasoning.**

## Improving Characterization

Bland, predictable characters mean that even the most exciting of plots will be dull. As you revise, look for ways to make your characters real and engaging. Read the following excerpts and try to identify the techniques D. H. Lawrence uses to draw the picture of a woman so bitter and disappointed that she finds it hard to feel love.

**Model: Characterization**

There was a woman who was beautiful, who started with all the advantages, yet she had no luck. She married for love, and the love turned to dust. She had bonny children, yet she felt they had been thrust upon her, and she could not love them. They looked at her coldly, as if they were finding fault with her . . . Everybody else said of her: "She is such a good mother. She adores her children." Only she herself, and her children themselves, knew it was not so. . . .

"Mother," said the boy Paul one day, "why don't we keep a car of our own? Why do we always use uncle's, or else a taxi?"

"Because we're the poor members of the family," said the mother.

"But why *are* we, Mother?"

"Well—I suppose," she said slowly and bitterly, "it's because your father has no luck."

—*D. H. Lawrence,* "The Rocking-Horse Winner"

Following are characterization techniques that Lawrence and other writers use. Look for places to apply them in your own story.

### Guidelines for Improving Characterization

- Add natural-sounding dialogue that fits the personality.
- Add descriptive details about appearance and behavior.
- Show how the character acts and reacts.
- Show how others react to the character.

## Practice Your Skills

*Improving Characterization*

**Write a scene for a story starring one of the characters you sketched on page C288. Then revise the scene to improve the characterization.**

## Improving Style

Style refers to the way you use words and sentences. Your style may be simple and spare or lush and complex or somewhere in between. The choice depends upon your personal preference and the needs of your story. Every style, however, demands skillful use of language—the right word connected to the right word to form the right sentence.

Go over your story for style, reading it aloud and listening to the rhythm and flow of the words. As you do, keep the questions listed below in mind.

### Guidelines for Improving Style

- Does your style fit the theme, events, and characters?
- Is the style appropriate for your audience?
- Do your words and sentences fit the style and the characters?
- Does the language fit the tone, or feeling of the story?
- Have you maintained the style consistently?
- Are your words vivid and precise?
- Have you varied the length and the structure of your sentences?

## Practice Your Skills

*Improving Style*

**Revise again the character sketch you wrote for the previous activity, improving its style using the guidelines above.**

## Using an Evaluation Checklist for Revising

The following checklist will help you remember basic points to look for as you revise a short story.

### Evaluation Checklist for Revising

- ✓ Does your beginning capture attention and present the conflict, setting, and main characters? *(pages C294–C295)*
- ✓ In the middle do you present events chronologically or through flashbacks? Do all events relate to the conflict and build to a climax? Do transitions connect the events and show the passage of time? *(pages C295–C296)*
- ✓ Is your resolution fitting and satisfying? *(page C297)*
- ✓ Do you use dialogue and description? *(page C299)*
- ✓ Is the theme clearly implied? *(page C286)*
- ✓ Is the point of view consistent? *(pages C288–C289)*

## Practice Your Skills

*Revising a Story*

**Use the guidelines on pages C294–C300 and the checklist above to revise a story that you outlined and drafted.**

### Communicate Your Ideas

**REVISING** *Revision of a Draft*

Read your short story to some classmates. Then use their comments and the preceding guidelines to revise it. Save your work for later use.

# Editing

Writing Process

In the editing stage, the writer produces error-free writing that shows accurate spelling and correct use of the conventions of punctuation and capitalization as well as control over grammatical elements such as subject-verb agreements, pronoun-antecedent agreement, verb forms, and parallelism. You may become so familiar with your work that you miss errors. Putting your work aside long enough to give you some distance will help you see these instances. You may want to use the checklist on page C304 as you edit.

## COMPUTER TIP

Take advantage of the Help function of your software whenever you are unsure how to perform a word processing task. This offers you help on a variety of broad subjects, including using the software, using reference information—even how to use the Help function!

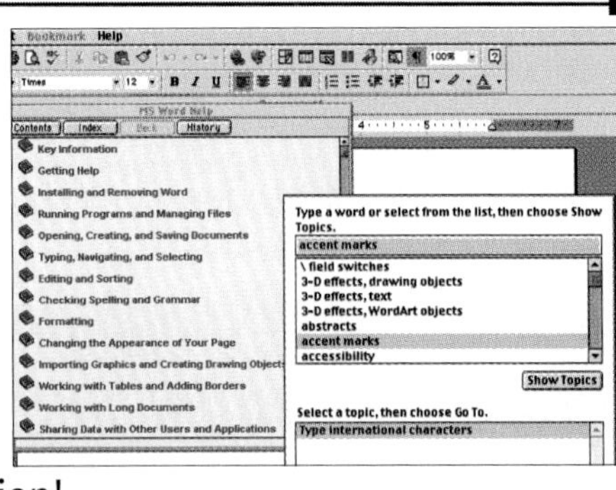


## Communicate Your Ideas

### EDITING

Use the Editing Checklists on pages C46 and C304 to edit your story for accurate spelling, capitalization, and punctuation as well as control over grammatical elements such as subject-verb agreement, pronoun-antecedent agreement, and verb forms.

Prewriting Workshop
Drafting Workshop
Revising Workshop
**Editing Workshop**
Publishing Workshop

# Dialogue

When you read the pronoun *thee* in a poem, you know that it is an old, familiar form of *you*. For Shakespeare, *thee* was a natural word to use. If you used that pronoun in a poem today, it would probably sound false. (There are occasional exceptions when *thee* is still used in song lyrics.) Choosing the right word is crucial in writing poetry—including the right pronoun.

## Cases of Pronouns

A **pronoun** is a word that takes the place of a noun. In English, pronouns have cases, or different forms for different functions. Pronouns in the nominative case are used as subjects or as predicate nominatives; they include *I, you, he, she, it, we,* and *they*. Pronouns in the objective case are used as objects; they include *me, you, him, her, it, us,* and *them*. Pronouns in the possessive case indicate ownership or possession; they include *my, mine, you, yours, he, his, her, hers, its, our, ours, their,* and *theirs.*

| | |
|---|---|
| Nominative Case | When **I** came in, **he** came down the stairs. |
| Objective Case | The young man in the shop told **me** that there had not been enough work for **him.** |
| Possessive Case | **His** boots were better than any of **my** boots. |

Most short stories contain **dialogue** or conversation between characters. To make sure that your readers clearly understand the conversations between your characters, you will need to know how to punctuate dialogue correctly. The examples on the following page from Katherine Mansfield's "The Doll's House" and D. H. Lawrence's "The Rocking Horse Winner" show the effectiveness of clearly written dialogue.

## Capital Letters with Dialogue

Just like a regular sentence, a direct quotation begins with a capital letter. If a speaker tag is placed in the middle of a sentence—as in the following quotation—the part of the quoted sentence that follows the speaker tag does not begin with a capital letter.

## Quotation Marks with Dialogue

Quotation marks enclose only a person's exact words—not a speaker tag, such as *he said* or any other words.

> "Why not?" asked Kezia.
>
> Liler gasped, then she said, "Your ma told our ma you wasn't to speak to us."
>
> "Mother," said the boy Paul one day, "why don't we keep a car of our own? Why do we always use uncle's, or else a taxi?"
>
> "Because we're the poor members of the family," said the mother.

Use a comma to separate the direct quotation from the speaker tag. Place the comma inside the closing quotation mark. Also, you should usually place end marks inside the closing quotation mark when the end of the quotation comes at the end of the sentence.

> "But why *are* we, Mother?"
>
> "Well—I suppose," she said slowly and bitterly, "it's because your father has no luck."

### Editing Checklist

- ✓ Has the correct case of each pronoun been used? *(page C303)*
- ✓ Has all the dialogue been punctuated, capitalized, and indented correctly? *(page C304)*

## Publishing
Writing Process

In the publishing stage, the writer makes a final copy to share with his or her intended audience. You may also decide to read your story aloud to family members or friends. If your school has a literary magazine, consider submitting your story to it.

### Communicate Your Ideas

**PUBLISHING**

Make a neat final copy of your story. Then combine it with your classmates' stories to form a collection of short stories. 

# Writing a Play or Screenplay

Plays and screenplays are forms of writing which are intended to be performed by actors. The story of a play or a screenplay is told through dialogue—the words that the actors say—as well as action.

A **play** is a piece of writing containing action that can be presented live on a stage by actors. A **screenplay** is a piece of writing containing action that can be presented on film.

William Shakespeare's *Romeo and Juliet* is so important in Western culture that you probably know something about it even if you have never read or seen the play. Romeo and Juliet, teens from enemy clans in Verona, Italy, meet at a dance and fall in love at first sight, opposing the wills of their families with tragic results.

The scene that follows is from the movie script *Shakespeare in Love,* a comic portrayal of what twenty-something playwright William Shakespeare may have been like at the time he was writing his great love story. In the movie young Shakespeare is stuck with writer's block as he tries to write *Romeo and Juliet.* Meanwhile, a wealthy young woman named Viola has her heart set on becoming an actor. Shakespeare and Viola fall in love, and theatre and love reflect each other.

In the scene that follows, Viola is presented at the palace and the Queen tartly questions her about their shared interest. To solve a disagreement about whether plays can truly present love, the Queen proposes a wager—which will involve Shakespeare.

*(Angle on The Queen.)*
*(The Lord In Waiting has presented Viola. Viola speaks from a frozen curtsey.)*
**Viola:** Your Majesty.
**Queen:** Stand up straight, girl.
(*Viola straightens. The Queen examines her.*)
**Queen:** I have seen you. You are the one who comes to all the plays—at Whitehall, at Richmond.
**Viola:** *(agreeing)*
Your Majesty.

**Queen:** What do you love so much?

**Viola:** Your Majesty . . .

**Queen:** Speak out! I know who I am. Do you love stories of kings and queens? Feats of arms? Or is it courtly love?

**Viola:** I love theatre. To have stories acted for me by a company of fellows is indeed—

**Queen:** *(interrupting)*

They are not acted for you, they are acted for me.

*(Viola remains silent, in apology. Angle on Will. He is watching and listening. He has never seen the Queen so close. He is fascinated.)*

**Queen:** *(Cont'd.)*

And—?

**Viola:** And I love poetry above all.

**Queen:** Above Lord Wessex?

*(She looks over Viola's shoulder and Viola realizes Wessex has moved up behind her. Wessex bows.)*

**Queen:** *(Cont'd.) (to Wessex)*

My lord—when you cannot find your wife you had better look for her at the playhouse.

*(The courtiers titter at her pleasantry.)*

**Queen:** *(Cont'd.)*

But playwrights teach nothing about love, they make it pretty, they make it comical, or they make it lust. They cannot make it true.

**Viola**: *(blurts)*

Oh, but they can!

*(She has forgotten herself. The courtiers gasp. The Queen considers her. Wessex looks furious. Will is touched.)*

**Viola:** *(Cont'd.)*

I mean . . . Your Majesty, they do not, they have not, but I believe there is one who can—

**Wessex:** Lady Viola is . . . young in the world. Your Majesty is wise in it. Nature and truth are the very enemies of playacting. I'll wager my fortune.

**Queen:** I thought you were here because you had none.

*(Titters again. Wessex could kill somebody.)*

**Queen:** *(Cont'd.)*

*(by way of dismissing him)*

Well, no one will take your wager, it seems.

**Will:** Fifty pounds!

*(Shock and horror. Queen Elizabeth is the only person amused.)*

**Queen:** Fifty pounds! A very worthy sum on a very worthy question. Can a play show us the very truth and nature of love? I bear witness to the wager, and will be the judge of it as occasion arises.

*(which wins a scatter of applause. She gathers her skirts and stands.)*

I have not seen anything to settle it yet.

*(She moves away, everybody bowing and scraping.)*

So—the fireworks will be soothing after the excitements of Lady Viola's audience.

**Your Writer's Journal**

Think back to movies that you have seen. In a journal entry, list a handful of such movies, and write a very brief summary of the idea behind each one. The description should be only one or two sentences long. For example, an entry for *Shakespeare in Love* might read, "Young Will Shakespeare, trying to write *Romeo and Juliet,* falls in love with a beautiful rich girl who wants to be an actor." This practice will help you focus your own screenplay ideas when you have them.

## Finding Ideas for Plays

You will be writing a screenplay scene—a linked series of camera shots that tells a small part of the story of your imaginary movie. As in a stage play or a short story, you should build your screenplay idea out of the building blocks of characters who are involved in a compelling conflict, or problem. Their struggles with the problem take them through a series of connected actions—a plot.

Your scene will capture the characters at one important point in their involvement with the conflict.

To find ideas for a screenplay, use the tried-and-true methods that you have used to generate ideas for short stories, and in earlier grades perhaps for stage scenes. Question yourself about your life, the lives of people around you, and lives you have only heard about or dreamed about. Reread your **journal** notes in search of concepts. Freewrite about events that have seemed dramatic. Make cluster diagrams for characters you know, or imagine, who seem larger than life.

In addition, many successful movie concepts are combinations of previous movie concepts. Return to your journal entry describing movies you have seen, and try to build on it using the following tips.

*To find out more about characterization, conflict, and plot turn to pages C297–C299.*

### Tips for Developing Screenplay Ideas

- Describe each of your ideas in a single sentence, to help you pinpoint the dramatic essence of the concept. Focus on the sentence as a way of tinkering with the concept.
- Take an existing movie concept and add a twist; for example, "Young Will Shakespeare trades places with his rival Christopher Marlowe, and the two geniuses live out each others' lives and deaths."
- Splice together the ideas for two different movies, using the pattern "Movie A Meets Movie B" for example, "Shakespeare in Love Meets Robin Hood" or "Shakespeare in Love Meets The Hunchback of Notre Dame."

## PRACTICE YOUR SKILLS

### *Finding Ideas for a Scene through Freewriting*

**Freewrite a response to each question below. Save your work.**

**1.** Who is the most "larger-than-life" person you know, and why do you characterize this person that way?

**2.** At times, have you said to yourself, "My life is like the movies"? Describe one or more moments that might fit that description.

**3.** What news events during your lifetime have seemed most dramatic? Freewrite your strongest impressions of the events.

**4.** If you could live in another world, or in the future, what would it be like?

*Finding Ideas for a Scene By Building on Previous Ideas*

**Return to the list of movie concepts in your journal entry. Select one of them, and add a twist or variation that would make it an essentially different movie.**

## Characters

In movies, characterizations are fleshed out by actors; the personality of a movie star can drastically affect the nature of a role. The screenplay writer gets "first crack" at the characterization, however, by writing the character's dialogue and giving the character actions to perform. A published screenplay may not contain a capsule sketch or description of the characters; for example, the screenplay of *Shakespeare in Love* does not contain an actual description of Shakespeare, because the physical appearance of the actor is the only description needed. As a writer, however, you might want to compose a brief sketch of each character for your own use.

## Practice Your Skills

*Sketching Characters*

**Complete two of the following exercises:**

1. Write a concise, vivid, one-paragraph sketch of the person you named as the most larger-than-life figure you know.
2. Write a character sketch based on yourself, using the same format.
3. Write a character sketch of a public figure you admire, using the same format.
4. Write a character sketch of a public figure you do not admire, using the same format.

## Setting

In contrast to the settings of traditional plays, which are limited by the need to fit them on a stage, the settings of movies are almost infinite in range, and they can change from shot to shot. A movie may show Mount Everest in one frame, and the quiet midwestern home of an Everest climber in the next frame, one twenty-fourth of a second later. It can even show both settings at the same time in split screen. It can show imaginary settings that are created digitally using computer graphics or by means of special visual effects. The action of a movie may occur on a sound stage in front of artificial scenery, or scenes may be shot on location—in real places such as streets, houses, ranches, or wilderness lands. Many movies use both location shots and studio scenery. While the typical play takes place in one room, it is a rare movie whose setting is so restricted.

Your biggest problem in planning a screenplay setting might be that of limiting your settings to a manageable scope. In real movie productions, money is the major limiting factor: to shoot scenes in too many different locations may cost more than the production company can afford. In addition, an audience may be confused or put off by excessive changes in setting. Although your screenplay scene will not involve planning a budget, try to keep in mind a realistic evaluation of the number of settings the scene can accommodate.

## Practice Your Skills

**Complete one of the following activities:**

1. List five or six places which you have been to that you think would make interesting settings for movies.
2. List five or six places that you have not been to—but have read or heard about or seen pictures of—that you think would make interesting settings for movies.
3. Imagine two or more worlds that do not exist but that you can visualize as movie settings. List them, with brief descriptions.

## Dialogue

Although dialogue is important in movies, the typical movie contains much less dialogue than the typical play. In a stage play, dialogue is by far the single most important vehicle for conveying action, characterization, and even basic information. In a movie, dialogue is just one of many such modes of conveyance. Visuals—camera shots of characters, settings, or actions—are often more important than dialogue. Many screenplay writers (and directors, who often participate in revising screenplays) take pride in keeping dialogue to a minimum, having characters speak only what cannot be said in pictures. Playwrights and fiction writers who attempt screenplays often find that their biggest challenge is to cut the dialogue severely, leaving only what is absolutely needed in order to express a scene. A scene that might contain six or eight or ten lines of dialogue in a play or story might be pared down to one or two or three lines in a screenplay.

## Practice Your Skills

### *Writing Screen Dialogue*

**Follow the steps listed below.**

1. Imagine a conversation between the person you named as larger-than-life and one other character. The second character may be based on yourself, on someone you know, on a public figure, or on imagination. Take a couple of minutes to imagine a substantial discussion.
2. Write down the conversation as completely as you can. Include at least five separate speeches per character.
3. Now cut as much of the talk as you can without losing the essential point of the discussion.

## Camera Directions

In the texts of plays, there are stage directions that describe actions: they are usually found in italics. Screenplays also include directions that tell the reader what the camera shows. The fact that a movie camera can show a scene from a number of possible angles, at various distances, makes camera directions vital. For example, a camera direction in *Shakespeare in Love* specifies, "high angle on audience and stage"—the camera shows the audience and stage from above. Also, because cameras can show closeups, stage directions in screenplays sometimes specify gestures that would be too small for the audience at a stage play to care about.

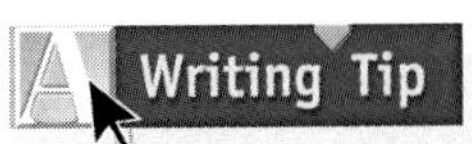

Writing Tip

Remember that in a **screenplay**, each new passage of directions represents a new **camera** shot, not just a gesture by an actor. The change in camera placement is the crucial factor that makes a direction necessary.

Screenplays differ in how specifically they describe camera shots. One screenplay might give each shot a number and describe it in technical terms, such as, "*50. closeup on the Sheriff's face. He looks determined. cut to—51. closeup on the Sheriff's hand gripping his six-gun.*" Another screenplay, such as *Shakespeare in Love,* may simply name the setting, and whether it is an interior or an exterior, and whether the time is day or night. The technicalities of camera placement are left to the director and the cinematographer.

Unless you already know a great deal about camera placement, you will probably want to use the simpler method in your own screenplay. However, this does not alter the fact that descriptions of visuals will be as important in your screenplay as the dialogue will be. It may happen that at times, you describe several camera shots in a row without any dialogue at all, or with only one line of dialogue in a given shot.

## Practice Your Skills

### *Writing Camera Directions*

**Return to the shorter version of the dialogue that you wrote in the previous activity. Now divide the conversation into at least three separate camera shots. Write directions for each shot, using the simpler format shown in *Shakespeare in Love*.**

## Communicate Your Ideas

### SCREENPLAY

Using your **journal** notes, practice activity responses, and any prewriting techniques that you desire, conceptualize an idea for a movie scene. Use the suggestions on subjects, characters, setting, dialogue, and camera directions to help you create it. Write a first draft that includes both dialogue and action. Then, revise both for content, and for cinematic touches that occur to you. Make a final copy, using the same screenplay format used in *Shakespeare in Love,* for interested readers, classmates, friends, and relatives. Publication of a screenplay usually implies making it into a film; however, screenplays are also published in book form. **PORTFOLIO**

# Writing a Poem

Dig deeply into your feelings, and you may discover not a story waiting to be written, but a poem. Poems are usually more tightly structured than stories, and poems use words not only to express feelings, but also to "paint pictures" and produce "a kind of music." In this section you will be guided as you express your creativity through poetry.

**Poetry** is a form of writing that encourages the expression of feelings through sound, images, and other imaginative uses of language.

**Your Writer's Journal**

Freewrite whatever is in your mind right now. Then go over your freewriting and circle the words and phrases that seem to you to be most powerful, pleasing, or well-chosen. As you go on to create a poem in this section, consider using freewriting, and those circled words, as possible starting points.

## Finding Ideas for Poems

Poetry is not reserved for lofty or romantic subjects such as patriotism, the soaring of an eagle, or a great love. In fact, any subject can be poetic. W. D. Snodgrass wrote "Lobsters in the Window," and Pablo Neruda wrote "Ode to My Socks."

To find an idea for a poem, then, you need not look for an imaginative subject. Instead, look for an imaginative response to a subject by searching inside yourself. Probe your emotions and sensations in both ordinary and dramatic situations. For example, what does a traffic jam make you think of? How does it feel to sleep late on a weekend morning? What comes to mind when you look at a particular picture? What do you associate with the color orange? Concentrate on your impressions and sensations as you dig into your thoughts.

Filling out a chart might help you launch some ideas. Begin by listing some general subject areas and then brainstorm or list examples for each one. Use your **journal** as well as your memory as a source of examples. The following part of a chart may be used as a guide.

| IDEA CHART | |
|---|---|
| **EVENTS** | birthday, football touchdown, first moon landing |
| **SCENES** | streets after a rain, bus stop, surface of Venus |
| **SENSATIONS (SMELLS)** | fish frying, shampooed hair, air after a rainstorm |

Look over the ideas on your chart and start exploring the most promising ones. Use freewriting, brainstorming, clustering, questioning, and any other technique that will prod your imagination and encourage ideas and images to flow freely.

## PRACTICE YOUR SKILLS

### *Charting to Find Ideas for a Poem*

**Use item 1 and four others to create a chart like the one above. List at least ten examples for each subject. Keep your chart.**

1. some personal values
2. world events
3. busy scenes
4. peaceful scenes
5. sensations: smells
6. sensations: sounds
7. sensations: textures
8. sensations: tastes
9. emotions
10. hopes and dreams

### *Focusing to Find Ideas for a Poem*

**Write your responses to the questions on the next page. Focus on the sensations, emotions, images, and impressions that come to mind.**

1. What does a spider bring to mind?
2. Why does a hot shower feel good?
3. What do you associate with the color yellow?
4. What thoughts do you have about free speech?

## Using Sound Devices

Since poems are usually meant to be read aloud, poets use the sounds of words as well as their meanings to achieve an effect. The following chart shows the major sound devices you can use when you write a poem.

### SOUND DEVICES

**ONOMATOPOEIA** Use of words whose sounds suggest their meaning:

snap, howl, hiss, whine, creak, murmur

**ALLITERATION** Repetition of a consonant sound at the beginning of a series of words:

And in the **p**retty **p**ool the **p**ike stalks

—*Stevie Smith* "Pretty"

**CONSONANCE** Repetition of a consonant sound or sounds with different vowel sounds, usually in the middle or at the end of words:

And whe**re** the wat**er** had dri**pp**ed
**fr**om the ta**p**. . .

—*D. H. Lawrence,* "Snake"

**ASSONANCE** Repetition of a vowel sound within words:

And r**a**diant r**ai**ndrops c**ou**ching in cool
fl**ow**ers. . .

—*Rupert Brooke,* "The Great Lover"

**REPETITION** Repetition of a word or phrase:

**We are the hollow men**
**We are the stuffed men . . .**
Remember us—if at all—not as lost

Violent souls, but only
**As the hollow men**
**The stuffed men.**

—*T. S. Eliot,* "The Hollow Men"

**Rhyme** Repetition of accented syllables with the same vowel and consonant sounds:

I was angry with my **friend:**
I told my wrath, my wrath did **end.**
I was angry with my **foe:**
I told it not, my wrath did **grow.**

—*William Blake,* "A Poison Tree"

Before you compose a poem, you may want to compile a word-and-phrase list from which you can draw as you write. Begin by listing words and phrases associated with your subject. Then, for each item on your list, think of words and phrases associated with it by sound or by meaning. You can keep an eye and ear out for sound patterns by speaking words aloud as you work. Although you will not include all the listed items in your poem, the act of creating the list will help you focus your thoughts and identify sound patterns.

## Rhythm and Meter

A basic part of the sound of a poem is its **rhythm**—the beat created by the arrangement of accented and unaccented syllables. Sense the rhythm as you read the lines below, with different marks for accented and unaccented syllables.

Tíger, Tíger, búrning bríght
Ín the fórests óf the níght . . .

—*William Blake,* "The Tiger"

The rhythm of poetry is usually more regular than that of prose, shaping its effect and providing a musical quality. When the rhythm follows a strict pattern, as it does in Blake's lines above, it is called **meter.** The most common meter in English is a line of five accented syllables called **iambic pentameter** shown in the following example.

> ˘ / ˘ / ˘ / ˘ / ˘ / ˘
> A thing of beauty is a joy forever . . . .
>
> —*John Keats,* "Endymion"

Not all poems follow a strict meter. Some are written in **free verse,** with a freely moving rhythm that flows from the rhythm of the words. Sometimes the rhythm will emerge naturally as you write a poem; other times you will want to plan the pattern of syllables. Experiment with your subject. A single phrase or image may set the rhythm for an entire poem.

## Practice Your Skills

### *Developing Sound Devices for a Poem*

**Using item 1 and two others for ideas, find three subjects for a poem. For each subject develop word lists and sound devices as suggested above.**

**1.** values you do not admire
**2.** music
**3.** big moments in sports
**4.** someone you would like to meet
**5.** something you fear

## Using Figurative Language

Poetry should appeal to the mind's eye as well as to the ear. Poets use the following major devices to paint pictures with words.

## FIGURATIVE LANGUAGE

| | |
|---|---|
| **IMAGERY** | Use of concrete details to create a picture and appeal to the senses:<br><br>And now a gusty shower wraps<br>The grimy scraps<br>Of withered leaves about your feet . . .<br>—*T. S. Eliot,* "Preludes" |
| **SIMILE** | Comparison between unlike things, using *like* or *as:*<br><br>She walks in beauty like the night . . .<br>—*Lord Byron,* "She Walks in Beauty" |
| **METAPHOR** | Implied comparison between unlike things:<br><br>Life's but a walking shadow, a poor player<br>That struts and frets his hour upon<br>the stage . . .<br>—*William Shakespeare,* Macbeth |
| **PERSONIFICATION** | Giving human qualities to something nonhuman:<br><br>As Earth stirs in her winter sleep . . .<br>—*Robert Graves,* "She Tells Her Love While Half Asleep" |
| **HYPERBOLE** | Use of exaggeration or overstatement:<br><br>Our hands were firmly cemented . . .<br>—*John Donne,* "The Ecstasy" |
| **OXYMORON** | Use of opposite or contradictory terms, such as *joyful misery, living death, dark snow:*<br><br>Beautiful tyrant! fiend angelical!<br>—*William Shakespeare,* Romeo and Juliet |
| **SYMBOL** | Use of one thing to stand for another, as the sea journey mentioned below stands for death:<br><br>And may there be no moaning of the bar,[1]<br>When I put out to sea . . .<br>—*Alfred, Lord Tennyson,* "Crossing the Bar" |

[1] sandbar

Once you have chosen the subject of your poem, find related images, figures of speech, and symbols by closing your eyes and focusing on different aspects of your subject. Put all your senses to work as you dig into your imagination. If you want to take a few notes, try not to interrupt the flow of your thoughts and feelings too much. Then, after your mind has traveled for a while, brainstorm or freewrite. Promising ideas are bound to emerge.

## PRACTICE YOUR SKILLS

*Developing Figurative Language for Poems*

**Return to the sound devices you developed. Now use the techniques described above to explore figurative language for each of the three subjects. Save your notes.**

## Choosing a Form

Most poems have a pattern of sound and rhythm, plus a visual arrangement of words. These patterns help to hold the reader's attention and to strengthen the effect of the poem. The pattern of rhyme, rhythm, and lines determines the form of a poem. At times you may wait for the details of form to reveal themselves as you work. At other times you will decide on these elements in advance, especially if you want the form to help establish a particular mood or tone.

**Writing a Rhymed Poem** A rhymed poem usually has a tighter structure than an unrhymed poem does. You can think of rhymes in your head, experiment on paper, or use a rhyming dictionary, in which words are grouped by their endings.

The pattern of rhyme, or **rhyme scheme,** can be shown by letters of the alphabet, each letter standing for a different rhyme. Notice in the following two poems that the rhyme scheme does not dictate a particular meter. The first poem has four accents per line, for example, while the second poem, following, has five.

Had we but world enough, and **time,** *a*
This coyness lady were no **crime.** *a*
We would sit down, and think which **way** *b*
To walk, and pass our long love's **day.** *b*

*Andrew Marvell,* "To His Coy Mistress"

It is a beauteous evening, calm and **free,** *a*
The holy time is quiet as a **Nun** *b*
Breathless with adoration; the broad **sun** *b*
Is sinking down in its **tranquility.** *a*

*William Wordsworth,* "It is a Beauteous Evening, Calm and Free"

Lines with similar rhyme schemes and rhythms can be grouped into **stanzas,** as in the poem below, which has yet another rhyme scheme. As you read it, notice the **half rhymes,** which are words that have similar but not identical sounds (*plow/furrow, falling/stumbling*)

My father worked with a horse **plow,** *a*
His shoulders globed like a full sail **strung** *b*
Between the shafts and the **furrow.** *a*
The horses strained at his clicking **tongue. . .** *b*

I was a nuisance, tripping, **falling,** *c*
Yapping always. But t**oday** *d*
It is my father who keeps **stumbling** *c*
Behind me, and will not go **away**. *d*

*–Seamus Heaney,* "Follower"

You do not need to follow any of the rhyme schemes shown in this section or, in fact, any rhyme scheme at all. As the poet, you decide what rhyme scheme to use, if any. Simply try a few alternatives and then choose the one that works best for you.

**Writing Free Verse** **Free verse** is verse that does not have a strict meter. Instead, the rhythm flows freely from the natural beats of the spoken language. Lines and stanzas, if any, may vary in length. If there is rhyme, it is usually irregular, as in the following excerpt from the poem "Snake" by D. H. Lawrence.

## Snake

A snake came to my water trough
On a hot, hot day, and I in pajamas for the heat,
To drink there.

In the deep, strange-scented shade of the great dark
    carob tree
I came down the steps with my pitcher
And must wait, must stand and wait, for there he was
    at the trough before me.

He reached down from a fissure in the earth-wall in the
    gloom
And trailed his yellow-brown slackness soft-bellied
    down, over the edge of the stone trough
And rested his throat upon the stone bottom,
And where the water had dripped from the tap, in a
    small clearness,
He sipped with his straight mouth,
Softly drank through his straight gums, into his slack
    long body.
Silently.

*—D. H. Lawrence*

## Communicate Your Ideas

### POEMS

Write two poems on the same theme—one in rhyme and one in free verse. For ideas refer to your **journal,** your notes from Practice Your Skills activities, and the charts on pages C317 and C320. When you have finished your final drafts, read them aloud to some classmates or friends. Do your listeners prefer one poem over the other? Do you? Why?

**Time Out to Reflect**

You have learned several strategies and skills for effective creative writing. Next year, you may be in college, or working at a job, or in the military, or doing a combination of these. Which of these skills do you think you will be most useful for you and why? Do you expect that you will want to make creative writing part of your life in the future? If so, why, and if not, why not? If you do, what steps could you take to make it happen?

## An Interactive Poem

**P**oems once existed primarily on paper. Before that, poems existed only orally. In our time, poems exist in both those ways and in cyberspace. A poem on the screen, however, can acquire extra dimensions. The development of the World Wide Web has made poetry interactive. Hyperlinks may lead to any of the following:

- A biography of and interviews with the author
- Other works by the poet
- Explanations of difficult concepts, plus additional background material
- The author's portrait
- A recording of the author reading the poem
- A discussion group among readers

### Media Activity

Plan and create an interactive version either of Shakespeare's "Shall I Compare Thee to a Summer's Day" or of a poem you wrote for this chapter. Specify how you would use the interactive features described above—and add any other features you can imagine. After finishing your creation, discuss the following questions.

### Questions for Analyzing Interactive Poetry

- How much access to the Internet does the average American have?
- How might the audiences for printed poetry and interactive poetry be different or similar?
- If you were a poet, would you want your poem to be available online, or only on paper? Explain.
- What is the difference in impact between "Shall I Compare Thee to A Summer's Day" on paper and online?
- Can the extra features of online poetry affect a poem's meaning? If so, how, and is it a good thing?
- Do you think the existence of interactive media might change the way poets write? If so, how, and if not, why not?

## Process of Writing Stories, Plays, and Poems

Remember that you can move back and forth among the stages of the writing process. For example, during revising, you may want to return to the drafting stage to add details that have occurred to you while revising. The page numbers in parentheses refer to pages where you can get help with your writing.

### Writing a Short Story

#### PREWRITING

- Choose a conflict. *(pages C284–C285)*
- Sketch all the characters. *(page C287)*
- Choose a point of view. *(pages C288–C289)*
- Match the setting of your story to the action, mood, and characters' feelings. *(pages C290–C291)*
- Plan a plot, including a climax and a resolution. *(pages C291–C292)*
- Present the events in chronological order except for flashbacks. Then prepare a story outline. *(page C292)*

#### DRAFTING

- Write a beginning that introduces the setting, the main character, and conflict that engages the reader. *(pages C294–C295)*
- Use transitions, dialogue, and descriptive details. *(page C296)*
- Write an ending that ties the events together. *(pages C296–C297)*

#### REVISING

- Improve the plot and characterization. *(pages C297–C299)*
- Match your style to fit the theme, events, and characters. Then use the Evaluation Checklist for Revising. *(pages C300–C301)*

#### EDITING

- Use the Editing Checklists to correct errors in grammar, spelling, and mechanics. *(pages C46 and C304)*
- Pay special attention to punctuating, capitalizing, and indenting dialogue. *(pages C303–C304)*

#### PUBLISHING

- Prepare and share a final copy of your story. *(page C305)*

### Writing a Play or Screenplay

- Develop an idea for a dramatic conflict involving interesting characters in a specific stage setting. *(pages C308–C311)*
- Write dialogue that is appropriate for the characters. *(pages C311–C312)*
- Use stage directions in moderation to enhance readers' understanding of tones, gestures, and actions. *(pages C312–C313)*

### Writing a Poem

- Use sound devices and figurative language. *(pages C317–C321)*
- Write rhymed verse or free verse. *(pages C321–C323)*

# A Writer Writes

## A Short Story

**Purpose:** **to entertain with an adventure, a science-fiction story, or a mystery story**

**Audience:** **your classmates**

### Prewriting

When you select a piece of fiction to read, what type of story do you choose? Would you most likely choose a story of adventure, such as one that involved the exploration of an uncharted island? Perhaps, on the other hand, a science-fiction story or a good mystery novel would appeal to you more. Regardless of what type of story you would choose, you would find at the core of each story a protagonist who is confronted with a conflict—internal and/or external. For example, in the story "First Love," the narrator is faced with a conflict between escapist fantasy and childhood reality.

Prepare to write an adventure story, a science-fiction story, or a mystery story in which the conflict is about values. The negative value of greed, for instance, could be the focus of a story in any of the three genres. You could write a science-fiction story about a greedy scientist who tries to gain control of the resources on a wealthy planet in another galaxy. A mystery story could focus on a greedy but charming business person who cheats a partner to gain control of that partner's share of the company. An adventure story could be about a greed-driven archaeologist who desperately wants to locate and possess a famous lost treasure.

Once you have plenty of ideas and have selected a conflict or problem, choose a theme. Then briefly sketch the characters and setting, choose a point of view, and go on to

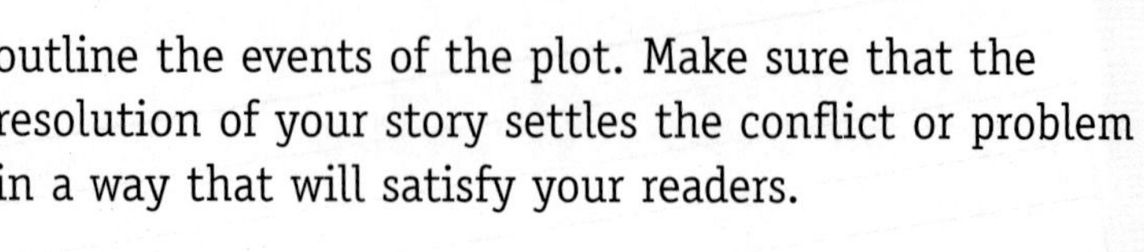
outline the events of the plot. Make sure that the resolution of your story settles the conflict or problem in a way that will satisfy your readers.

## Drafting

As you write your first draft, include descriptive words and figurative language to make your setting and characters come alive in the minds of the readers. Also add dialogue to lend realism to your story and to move the plot along. For example, mystery writers sometimes will supply clues in different statements that the characters make.

## Revising

In addition to the checklist on page C301, use the following questions as guides to your revision. Are the events in chronological order? Do all of the events lead to the climax of the story? Have you included sufficient details, figurative language, and sensory words to make your story clearly visible in the minds of your readers?

## Editing

Edit your short story, using the checklists on pages C46 and C304.

## Publishing

After you have finished editing, make a neat final copy and be prepared to read it to your classmates.

## Representing in Different Ways

**From Print . . .**

**. . . to Visuals**

Draw a storyboard for this scene from your aunt's film for children. Show at least three separate panels from Blinky's scene.

BIG TOP MAYHEM: Scene 65

Blinky the clown gets caught in a terrible windstorm. Tree limbs are falling down, and tumbleweeds and papers are scattering everywhere. Blinky is trying to walk home, but suddenly he loses his hat. He rushes to catch it, but the wind is too strong. He walks across a road, and just as he is about to catch the hat, a truck zooms by. Blinky's collar is caught on the side-view mirror of the truck. Blinky flies into the air, turns three mid-air somersaults, and lands in a large bucket of stewed tomatoes.

**From Visuals . . .**

**. . . to Print**

Thanks to your imaginative skills, your aunt has asked you to write a scene in story form for her newest film for children, *The Seal with Appeal*. She has given you the three storyboard panels shown above. Write the scene for your aunt, paying special attention to specific details and vivid sensory language.

- **Which strategies can be used for creating both written and visual representations? Which strategies apply to one, not both? Which type of representation is more effective?**
- **Draw a conclusion, and write briefly about the differences between written ideas and visual representations.**

## Writing in the Workplace

### *Humorous Poems for a Greeting Card*

You work at the How-R-U Greeting Card Company. Recently your boss noticed you have a knack for poetry, and she has transferred you from the janitorial department to the more lucrative position of writer! Your first assignment is to create a rhyming poem, from ten to twenty lines long, that expresses sympathy for someone's first speeding ticket.

**Write the poem for How-R-U's new series of cards for unusual occasions. Use rhyme in the poem, and include at least one instance of onomatopoeia. In addition, try to use a humorous tone for the poem.**

**What strategies did you use to develop rhymes and make your poem humorous?**

*You can find information on writing poems on pages C315–C324.*

## Writing for Oral Communication

### *Informal Bedtime Story*

The last time you babysat for your seven-year-old cousin Mervin, he was a complete terror! He dipped the dog's paws in ketchup, glued the pages of your biology book together, and refused to go to sleep until you told him a bedtime story. You have to babysit again tomorrow night. This time you will be ready for him. Your idea for a story involves a little boy named Mervin and all that befalls him on one dark night.

**Prepare the story you will tell to Mervin. Arrange the events chronologically, create tension, and build the story to an effective resolution to tie the events together.**

**What strategies did you use to tell an effective bedtime story to Mervin?**

*You can find information on writing stories on pages C284–C305.*

# Assess Your Learning

Sally Stanley was walking home from her job at the tire factory. She was exhausted from her day's work, and the weather was cold and rainy. Coming toward her, beside the bridge, was a young man with a bright and happy face, his nose in the air, his eyes sparkling. His clothes were new and fashionable, and he seemed to completely ignore Sally. Just as they were about to cross paths, Sally heard a cry of help. It was coming from the river below the bridge. As she looked down, she saw a pair of young boys in a canoe. They were heading quickly for the dangerous whitewater falls! Sally and the young man looked at each other. They knew they had to help.

▶ **Write a short story about what happens next in this scene. Include additional details and vivid descriptions about the scene and the characters involved. Use figurative language and sensory words. Be sure to choose an appropriate point of view, and to tie each step in the plot together coherently.**

*Before You Write* **Consider the following questions:**
What is the ***subject?***
What is the ***occasion?***
Who is the ***audience?***
What is the ***purpose?***

*After You Write* **Evaluate your work using the following criteria:**

- Have you used natural-sounding dialogue that fits the personality of the characters involved?
- Have you used descriptive details about appearance and behavior?
- Have you presented the events in chronological order? Are your ideas organized to ensure coherence and logical progression?
- Do the events in your story add tension and build to the climax?
- Does your resolution tie up the events in your story?
- Have you demonstrated control over grammatical elements, such as subject-verb agreement, pronoun-antecedent agreement, verb forms, and parallelism?

**Write briefly on how well you did. Point out your strengths and areas for improvement.**

CHAPTER 8

# Writing to Inform and Explain

Sometimes an essay or article describes a process, defines a word, explains a concept, or sets out information, teaching you something you did not know. Perhaps you have read a newspaper review of a recent play or film, or a magazine feature about cultural diversity. At a more immediate level you have probably had to answer essay questions or write brief reports for school. All of these are examples of informative writing.

The informative essay is one of the most frequently encountered forms of writing. Whenever you compare or contrast events or ideas, analyze people, places, and things, or explain something, you will use your informative writing skills. Informative writing will help you formulate and organize your thoughts and communicate your knowledge about an almost infinite range of subjects.

## *Reading with a Writer's Eye*

The selection you are about to read was written by Coretta Scott King in 1969, just two years after her husband, civil rights leader Martin Luther King, Jr., was slain by an assassin's bullet. Read through the passage to gain an understanding of the events King describes. Note how she imparts a sense of significance to the information.

FROM

# *My Life with* MARTIN LUTHER KING, JR.

***Coretta Scott King***

Of all the facets of segregation in Montgomery, the most degrading were the rules of the Montgomery City Bus Lines. This Northern-owned corporation outdid the South itself. Although seventy percent of its passengers were black, it treated them like cattle—worse than that, for nobody insults a cow. The first seats on all buses were reserved for whites. Even if they were unoccupied and the rear seats crowded, Negroes would have to stand at the back in case some whites might get aboard; and if the front seats happened to be occupied and more white people boarded the bus, black people seated in the rear were forced to get up and give them their seats. Furthermore—and I don't think Northerners ever realized this—Negroes had to pay their fares at the front of the bus, get off, and walk to the rear door to board again. Sometimes the bus would drive off without them after they had paid their fare. This would happen to elderly people or pregnant women, in bad weather or good, and was considered a great joke by drivers.

On December 1, 1955, Mrs. Rosa Parks, a forty-two-year-old seamstress whom my husband aptly described as "a charming person with a radiant personality," boarded a bus to go home after a long day working and shopping. The bus was crowded, and Mrs. Parks found a seat at the beginning of the Negro section. At the next stop more whites got on. The driver ordered Mrs. Parks to give her seat to a white man who boarded; this meant that she would have to stand all the way home. Rosa Parks was not in a revolutionary frame of mind. She had not planned to do what she did. Her cup had run over. As she said later, "I was just plain tired, and my feet hurt." So she sat there, refusing to get up. The driver called a policeman, who arrested her and took her to the courthouse. From there Mrs. Parks called E.D. Nixon, who came down and signed a bail bond for her.

Mr. Nixon was a fiery Alabamian. He was a Pullman porter who had been active in A. Philip Randolph's Brotherhood of Sleeping Car Porters and in civil-rights activities. Suddenly he also had had enough; suddenly, it seemed, almost every Negro in Montgomery had had enough. It was spontaneous combustion. Phones began ringing all over the Negro section of the city. The Women's Political Council suggested a one-day boycott of the buses as a protest. E.D. Nixon courageously agreed to organize it.

The first we knew about it was when Mr. Nixon called my husband early in the morning of Friday, December 2. He had already talked to Ralph Abernathy. After describing the incident, Mr. Nixon said, "We have taken this type of thing too long. I feel the time has come to boycott the buses. It's the only way to make the white folks see that we will not take this sort of thing any longer."

Martin agreed with him and offered the Dexter Avenue Church as a meeting place. After much telephoning, a meeting of black ministers and civic leaders was arranged for that evening. Martin said later that as he approached his church Friday evening, he was nervously wondering how many leaders would really turn up. To his delight, Martin found over forty people, representing every segment of Negro life, crowded into the large meeting room at Dexter. There were doctors, lawyers, businessmen, federal-government employees, union leaders, and a great many ministers.

. . . After a stormy session, one thing was clear: however much they differed on details, everyone was unanimously for a boycott. It was set for Monday, December 5. Committees were organized; all the ministers present promised to urge their congregations to take part. Several thousand leaflets were printed on the church mimeograph machine describing the reasons for the boycott and urging all Negroes not to ride buses "to work, to town, to school, or anyplace on Monday, December 5." Everyone was asked to come to a mass meeting at the Holt Street Baptist Church on Monday evening for further instructions. . . .

Saturday was a busy day for Martin and the other members of the committee. They hustled around town talking with other leaders, arranging with the Negro-owned taxi companies for special bulk fares and with the owners of private automobiles to get the people to and from work. I could do little to help because Yoki was only two weeks old, and my physician, Dr. W. D. Pettus, who was very careful, advised me to stay in for a month. However, I was kept busy answering the telephone, which rang continuously, and coordinating from that central point the many messages and arrangements.

Our greatest concern was how we were going to reach the fifty thousand black people of Montgomery, no matter how hard we worked. The white press, in an outraged exposé, spread the word for us in a way that would have been impossible with only our resources.

As it happened, a white woman found one of our leaflets, which her Negro maid had left in the kitchen. The irate woman immediately telephoned the newspapers to let the white community know what the blacks were up to. We laughed a lot about this, and Martin later said that we owed them a great debt.

On Sunday morning, from their pulpits, almost every Negro minister in town urged people to honor the boycott.

Martin came home late Sunday night and began to read the morning paper. The long articles about the proposed boycott accused the NAACP of planting Mrs. Parks on the bus—she had been a volunteer secretary for the Montgomery chapter—and likened the boycott to the tactics of the White Citizens' Councils. This upset Martin. That awesome conscience of his began to gnaw at him, and he wondered if he were doing the right thing. Alone in his study, he struggled with the question of whether the boycott method was basically unchristian. Certainly it could be used for unethical ends. But, as he said, "We are using it to give birth to freedom . . . and to urge men to comply with the law of the land. Our concern was not to put the bus company out of business, but to put justice in business." He recalled Thoreau's words, "We can no longer lend our cooperation to an evil system," and he thought, "He who accepts evil without protesting against it is really cooperating with it." Later Martin wrote, "From this moment on I conceived of our movement as an act of massive noncooperation. From then on I rarely used the word *boycott.*"

Serene after his inner struggle, Martin joined me in our sitting room. We wanted to get to bed early, but Yoki began crying and the telephone kept ringing. Between interruptions we sat together talking about the prospects for the success of the protest. We were both filled with doubt. Attempted boycotts had failed in Montgomery and other cities. Because of changing times and tempers, this one seemed to have a better chance, but it was still a slender hope. We finally decided that if the boycott was 60 percent effective we would be doing all right, and we would be satisfied to have made a good start.

A little after midnight we finally went to bed, but at five-thirty the next morning we were up and dressed again. The first bus was due at 6 o'clock at the bus stop just outside our house. We had coffee and toast in the kitchen; then I went into the living room to watch. Right on time, the bus came, headlights blazing through the December darkness, all lit up inside. I shouted, "Martin! Martin, come quickly!" He ran in and stood beside me, his face lit with excitement. There was not one person on that usually crowded bus!

We stood together waiting for the next bus. It was empty too, and this was the most heavily traveled line in the whole city. Bus after empty bus paused at the stop and moved on. We were so excited we could hardly speak coherently. Finally Martin said, "I'm going to take the car and see what's happening in other places in the city."

He picked up Ralph Abernathy, and they cruised together around the city. Martin told me about it when he got home. Everywhere it was the same. A few white people and maybe one or two blacks in otherwise empty buses. Martin and Ralph saw extraordinary sights—the sidewalks crowded with men and women trudging to work; the students of Alabama State College walking or thumbing rides; taxi cabs with people clustered in them. Some of our people rode mules; others went in horse-drawn buggies. But most of them were walking, some making a round trip of as much as twelve miles. Martin later wrote, "As I watched them I knew that there is nothing more majestic than the determined courage of individuals willing to suffer and sacrifice for their freedom and dignity."

# Thinking as a Writer

## Evaluating an Informative Essay

- From what point of view does Mrs. King present the information about the bus strike and its causes?
- What details of the narrative elicited the strongest response from you?
- What aspects of Mrs. King's explanation of the events most successfully emphasize their significance? Why?

## Reading for Emphasis

Oral Expression

- Read the essay aloud. Use your voice to emphasize the changes of tone. Then listen and evaluate your classmates as they take turns reading the essay. What features of this essay do you think make it especially suitable, or unsuitable, for reading aloud?

## Constructing a Visual Narrative

Viewing

- Compare the two photographs, one of Martin Luther King, Jr., in the early stages of the civil rights movement, the other of his memorial headstone. What particular details do you think best serve as commentary on the history and nature of the civil rights movement in the 1960s? What story do the pictures tell?

REV. MARTIN LUTHER KING, JR.
1929 — 1968
"Free at last. Free at last.
Thank God Almighty
I'm Free at last."

# The Power of Informative Writing

You have read the selection from Mrs. King's book, an example of writing that informs about a historical event. An informative essay can take many forms, but its main purpose is to set forth an explanation or to communicate information.

## Uses of Informative Writing

**The following are just a few of the uses of informative writing in our daily lives.**

- **Research scientists inform their colleagues** and the public of the latest discoveries in their fields.
- **Journalists inform the public** and provide commentary in newspapers and periodicals about current and past events.
- **Anthropologists explain the customs** of diverse cultures in professional journals and popular magazines.
- **Dot com companies provide online tutorials** on using the latest technology.
- **Investigative reporters expose corruption** at home and abroad.
- **Business analysts write annual reports** to inform board members and stockholders about the performance of their investments.
- **College applicants write of their accomplishments** and qualifications in essays accompanying college admission applications.

# Process of Writing an Informative Essay

Writing—both inside and outside school—is one way you can explore subjects and learn about your world. When your purpose is to explain or provide information about a subject, you will be writing an informative essay.

An **informative essay** presents information or offers an explanation.

## Prewriting

Writing Process

As you know by now, you do not begin an essay simply by composing an opening sentence. Instead, careful thinking and planning need to take place before you ever write that first sentence. This thinking and planning occurs in the first stage in the writing process—the prewriting stage. You begin this stage with the search for an idea and end it by shaping that idea into an organized plan for an essay. Your initial step in writing an informative essay, therefore, is to discover possible subjects by using prewriting strategies.

### Your Writer's Journal

In your journal compile a list of topics you know about that might be developed into an informative essay. Jot down notes about any subjects that interest you and about which you would like to be better informed. Perhaps you have a personal experience to relate or a special skill that you would like to teach to others. Perhaps you have seen or heard something that piqued your curiosity to learn more.

## Discovering Subjects

How can the seniors raise money to defray the cost of the senior class trip? What do birds do when it rains? What strategy do you use to get a good seat at a baseball game? Why was George Washington an effective President? How has popular music changed in the last five years? Possible subjects for an informative essay, such as these, are limited only by your own interests and knowledge. Once you begin to tap the vast store of information you carry around, your challenge will not be to find a subject to write about but to choose one from the great number available to you.

Countless ideas for subjects are inside your head right now. The task is to bring them to the surface by letting your mind relax or by asking yourself some probing questions. Start by using the strategies discussed in Chapter 1 on pages C10–C15: taking an inventory of your interests, freewriting, and using your **journal**. You can also skim books and magazines and afterward ask yourself questions about what you saw or read. Another idea is to look over your textbooks and class notes for possible topics.

## PRACTICE YOUR SKILLS

### *Discovering Ideas Through Questions*

**Answer each of the following questions as thoroughly as you can. Then put your answers in your writing folder for later use.**

1. What subjects do I enjoy talking about at school? at home? with friends?
2. What faraway places have I had the opportunity to visit? What nearby places?
3. What sports, musical, dramatic, or other activities do I enjoy?
4. What kind of advice do my friends ask me for? What do they consider me knowledgeable about?
5. What subjects outside myself do I think about when I am alone?
6. What kinds of problems have I solved?

### *Discovering Ideas Through Other Sources*

**Answer each question thoroughly. Then put your answers in your writing folder.**

1. What topics in history class have I found interesting?
2. What have I been reading about in other classes that interests me?
3. What magazine articles or television shows have caught my attention recently?
4. What people has the media been covering lately?
5. What lessons have I taken outside of school?

## Choosing and Limiting a Subject

The following guidelines will help you choose a subject from the many ideas you gather.

### Guidelines for Choosing a Subject

- Choose a subject that you would enjoy writing about.
- Choose a subject that you know enough about to develop adequately in a short essay.
- Choose a subject that your readers want to know about.

Your next step is to make sure that your subject is narrow enough to be covered adequately in a short essay. The following questions will help you limit your subject.

### Questions for Limiting a Subject

- What aspect of my subject do I want to explain?
- How can I narrow it even further?
- Who are my readers? What do they need to know to understand my subject?
- What insight can I draw from my subject?
- How might I express my main idea in one sentence?

Suppose you chose a subject you had read about in psychology class and had found fascinating: a boy who was discovered living in the wild in Aveyron, France, in the early 1800s. The answers to the five questions for limiting a subject might look like the following.

- I want to explain what happened to the wild boy after he was discovered.
- I can explain how the wild boy was educated.
- Because my readers probably have not heard of the wild boy, they will need some background information.
- Finding the wild boy gave scientists a chance to study how heredity and environment influence human development.
- Work with the wild boy has led to new ideas in education and psychology.

## Practice Your Skills

### *Limiting a Subject*

**Use the questions on page C342 to help you limit each subject below to one that is appropriate for a short informative essay.**

1. summer
2. baseball
3. household chores
4. earning money
5. the American Revolution

## Communicate Your Ideas

**PREWRITING** *Subject and Audience*

Use the answers you wrote for the practice activities above and on page C341 and your **journal** notes to list ten possible subjects for an informative essay. Then choose a subject and limit it. Save your work for later use.

SAVE YOUR WORK

## Gathering Information

Once you have limited your subject, you can begin to gather information that will help you explain it. Make use of observing, freewriting, brainstorming a list, clustering, and questioning. Choose whichever techniques seem to work best for your approach and subject. Use one or two or try them all. Go back and forth among them as different ideas occur to you. If you need more information, research your subject using the reference materials in your library or media center—magazines, newspapers, and other sources. Remember that your goal is to accumulate enough details to cover your subject most effectively. The specific types of details you select will usually indicate the method of development you should use. Your list may include any of the following types of details.

*You can learn about methods of development in informative writing on page C128.*

| TYPES OF DETAILS USED IN INFORMATIVE ESSAYS | | |
|---|---|---|
| facts | steps in a process | similarities/differences |
| examples | incidents | analogies |
| reasons | definitions | causes/effects |

The following notes are on the subject of the wild boy of Aveyron. They are not, however, arranged in any logical order.

**Model: List of Details**

**Limited Subject:** EDUCATION OF THE WILD BOY OF AVEYRON

FACTS AND EXAMPLES AS DETAILS

- doctor's name was Jean-Marc-Gaspard Itard
- François Truffaut made a movie about the boy
- Itard named the boy Victor
- Victor was found in France in 1800, age twelve
- had 23 scars on him
- couldn't talk; trotted instead of walked
- learned how to fetch water and say *milk*
- had a nice smile
- expressed only joy and sorrow at first

- Itard made sure the boy's needs were met before educating him
- Tarzan and Mowgli are fictional wild children
- insensitive to heat and cold and some sounds
- responded only to sounds related to foods
- hard to imagine how boy survived by himself
- Itard played games with him to develop thinking powers; games Victor was most interested in involved food
- could reach into boiling water and not express pain
- work with Victor helped Itard develop ideas about how to teach deaf people
- educator Maria Montessori was influenced by Itard's work

## Practice Your Skills

### *Listing Supporting Details*

**Use observing, freewriting, clustering, and/or questioning to develop five details for each of these subjects.**

1. the importance of teamwork in school sports
2. reasons for getting a high school diploma
3. the qualities of a good television show
4. the jobs of the future

## Communicate Your Ideas

**PREWRITING** *Supporting Details*

Using your limited subject, observe, brainstorm, cluster, question, and/or do research to develop details. Save your list of details.

Writing Is Thinking

## Analogies

An effective device for explaining unfamiliar ideas or processes in an informative essay is an analogy. An **analogy** is an extended comparison that uses a familiar object to explain something abstract or unfamiliar by pointing out a number of similarities between the two things. For example, suppose you want to explain the process of interviewing for a job by comparing interviewing for a job to advertising a new car. To think through the analogy, make a chart like the following. Begin by writing your idea for the analogy (interviewing for a job *is like* advertising a new car) at the top of the chart. Then list parallel processes on both sides of your chart.

ANALOGY CHART

| Interviewing for a Job | Advertising a New Car |
|---|---|
| Make experience and qualifications clear | Make features of car (comfort, reliability) apparent |
| Make best appearance by dressing neatly, combing hair, polishing shoes | Present product attractively by using good photography in beautiful surroundings |
| Emphasize what you can do for employer: do quality work, solve problems | Emphasize what new car can do for consumer: provide comfortable transportation, communicate an image |

### THINKING PRACTICE

**Choose one of the following analogies or make up your own. Then make a chart like the one above to help you draw parallels between the abstract concept and the familiar concept.**

1. success is like mountain climbing
2. fear is like a virus
3. friendship is like a mirror

## Developing a Working Thesis

No matter what information-gathering technique you use, the process of generating details will uncover a variety of information and ideas. At this point you need to pull together all the information you have gathered and identify a main idea that grows out of connections and patterns you see in the information. This main idea around which you will select and organize your details is called the **working thesis**. Later, as you develop your informative essay, you will refine your working thesis into a polished thesis statement.

### Steps for Developing a Working Thesis

- Review your prewriting notes and the questions you answered to limit your subject.
- Express your main idea.
- Look closely at your notes to see that your working thesis covers all of your information and ideas.

Using the steps above, you might develop the following working thesis about the wild boy of Aveyron.

WORKING THESIS — The methods Dr. Itard used to help the wild boy had an influence on education and psychology.

**Selecting Details** The methods you use to develop details are aimed at opening your mind. Not all the details that spill out, of course, will be usable. Once you have chosen a working thesis, go over your list of details and check off only those that directly fit within the thesis. These are the details that you will use in your essay. Given the working thesis above, you would *not* use the following details about the wild boy of Aveyron.

- François Truffaut made a movie about the boy
- Tarzan and Mowgli are fictional wild children
- hard to imagine how boy survived by himself

Irrelevant details such as these, no matter how interesting, can detract from the unity of your essay if you include them in the body. Hold them in reserve, however, for you may be able to use them to enliven your introduction or conclusion.

## Communicate Your Ideas

**PREWRITING** *Working Thesis*

Using the limited subject and the list of possible supporting details you have saved in your writing folder, develop a working thesis for your informative essay. Then select the details in your list that fit within your thesis. If you prefer to generate another thesis statement and list of supporting details, you may go back and do so. However, the working thesis you formulate here will be the foundation for the thesis statement you will compose in Drafting. Save your work for use later.

## Organizing and Outlining

The final step in prewriting involves the arranging of your ideas in a logical order. The thoughts that occurred to you as you generated details now need to be grouped into categories and arranged in an order that the reader can easily follow. Many writers use a two-step process to create an outline for their essay: (1) grouping supporting details into categories and (2) arranging those categories in a logical order with letters and numbers.

**Writing Tip**

Organize your notes in an outline that shows how you will cover the **main topics, subtopics, and supporting details** of your subject.

**Grouping Supporting Details into Categories** Scan your list of supporting details, asking yourself what each detail might have in common with the other details. Try to create three to five main categories into which most of your details will fit. Details that do not easily fit into one of your main categories may be usable in the introduction or conclusion of your essay. The following categories have been created from the notes about the wild boy of Aveyron.

**Model: Grouping Details**

**Itard's methods and successes in helping Victor**

- Itard made sure boy's needs were met before educating him
- Itard played games with him to develop thinking powers; games Victor most interested in involved food
- learned how to fetch water
- learned how to say *milk*

**How Itard's work influenced later educational practices**

- work with Victor helped Itard develop ideas about how to teach deaf people
- educator Maria Montessori was influenced by Itard's work

**Boy's state when found**

- had 23 scars on him
- trotted instead of walked
- had a nice smile
- expressed only joy and sorrow at first
- couldn't talk
- insensitive to heat and cold and some sounds
- could reach into boiling water and not express pain
- responded only to sounds related to foods

IN THE MEDIA

## Across the Media: News Coverage

Our understanding of the world around us is as complete or as limited as our sources of information. Different people can have widely divergent views about the same event if they are relying on different media for their information. Consider, for example, the coverage of a single event across the media.

If you read about the event in the **newspaper**, you will not have up-to-the minute results. You will have to rely on descriptive writing and black-and-white photos to provide you with a visual sense of the event. Your knowledge will consist primarily of highlights, selected quotes, and statistics. The event is frozen in time as a succession of great moments.

If you listen on the **radio,** you will have no visual connection with the event. You must rely on the descriptive powers of the commentators to bring the event to life before your mind's eye. Your imagination fills in the blanks. Unlike the newspaper, however, the radio may offer real-time coverage, periodically interrupted by advertisements.

The **Internet** combines advantages of the newspaper and radio, and adds the dimension of interactivity. E-mail or live discussions, links to related stories, and multimedia content are among the features offered by this medium.

The **television** viewer can follow coverage of the event. The viewer sees what the camera is focused on. The viewer also hears live commentary and learns about the background of the event through special features, interviews, etc. Commercials are a regular feature.

### Media Activity

Form four groups in your class. Choose a particular ongoing news event. Group leaders draw lots to see which group will follow the event in a particular medium. Discuss the event the next day, keeping the following questions in mind: What do the different media have in common? On what particular points did they differ? To what extent does one's choice of media dictate one's sense of reality?

**Arranging Categories in Logical Order** The categories you create when you group your supporting details are the main topics that you will use to support your thesis statement. Your next step is to arrange these topics in a logical order. If your essay presents steps in a process or uses an incident to explain something, **chronological order** is probably best. If your essay analyzes an object, **spatial order** might be the most logical. If your essay focuses on the similarities and differences between two items, the method of **comparison and contrast** would be the best. Otherwise you will probably want to use either **order of importance** or **developmental order,** the most common arrangements for informative essays.

The most logical organization for the main topics about the wild boy is developmental order. If a Roman numeral is assigned to each category, a simple outline for the body of this essay would appear as follows.

**MODEL: Simple Outline**

**I.** Boy's state when found
**II.** Itard's methods and successes in helping Victor
**III.** Itard's influence on later educational practices

Notice that the wording of the third main topic is different from the wording on page C349. The change was made so that the three main topics would be expressed in **parallel form.** The main topics and each group of subtopics in an outline should always be parallel expressions.

After your simple outline is complete, you continue the outlining process by arranging the items within each category in a logical order. These items, called **subtopics,** are assigned capital letters. As you build your outline, you may add new ideas as you think of them, provided there is a logical place for them in your outline.

The following is an appropriate outline for an informative essay about the wild boy of Aveyron. Notice the indentation of the topics.

**Model: Outline**

| | |
|---|---|
| Main Topic | **I.** Boy's state when found |
| Subtopics | **A.** Physical appearance |
| | **B.** Emotions |
| | **C.** Insensitivities |
| Main Topic | **II.** Itard's methods and successes in helping Victor |
| Subtopics | **A.** First step: meeting boy's needs |
| | **B.** Second step: developing boy's sensitivities |
| | **C.** Third step: playing thinking games |
| | **D.** Fourth step: teaching language and chores |
| Main Topic | **III.** Itard's influence on later educational practices |
| Subtopics | **A.** Idea of good learning environment |
| | **B.** Education for deaf |
| | **C.** Influence on Montessori |

Your final step in outlining is to add any necessary supporting points under the subtopics. These supporting points are assigned Arabic numerals. If your supporting points can be broken down even further, use lowercase letters to show the divisions.

The following pattern indicates the correct form for an outline, adding supporting points and details.

**Model: Outline Form**

**I.** (Main topic)
  **A.** (Subtopic)
    **1.** (Supporting point)
    **2.** (Supporting point)
      **a.** (Detail)
      **b.** (Detail)
  **B.** (Subtopic)
    **1.** (Supporting point)
    (etc.)

The following is the final outline for the essay on the wild boy of Aveyron.

**MODEL: Final Outline**

**I.** Boy's state when found
- **A.** Physical appearance
  - **1.** Scars
  - **2.** Method of walking
- **B.** Emotions
  - **1.** Smile
  - **2.** Expression of only joy or sorrow
- **C.** Insensitivities
  - **1.** Heat and cold
  - **2.** Certain sounds
    - **a.** Failure to take notice of speech
    - **b.** Ready notice of sounds relating to food

**II.** Itard's methods and successes in helping Victor
- **A.** First step: meeting boy's needs
- **B.** Second step: developing boy's sensitivities
- **C.** Third step: playing thinking games
- **D.** Fourth step: teaching civilized ways
  - **1.** Language
  - **2.** Chores

**III.** Itard's influence on later educational practices
- **A.** Idea of good learning environment
- **B.** Education for deaf and developmentally challenged
- **C.** Influence on Montessori

After you have finished a draft of your outline, use the checklist on the next page to verify its form.

### Questions for Checking an Outline

- Did you use Roman numerals for main topics?
- Did you use capital letters for subtopics?
- Did you use Arabic numerals for supporting points?
- If your supporting points are broken down, did you use lowercase letters?
- If you put subtopics under topics, do you have at least two?
- If you included supporting points under subtopics, do you have at least two?
- If you broke down your supporting points, do you have at least two items in the breakdown?
- Does your indentation follow the model of the final outline on page C353?
- Did you capitalize the first word of each entry?
- Are your main topics and each group of subtopics expressed in parallel forms?

## Practice Your Skills

### *Grouping Ideas into Categories*

**The following prewriting notes are on the subject of machines that play a role in classical music. Find three categories into which you can group all of the ideas–except one. Then list the ideas under the appropriate category. Save your work for later use.**

- spinning-wheel sound imitated in Richard Wagner's opera *The Flying Dutchman* (1843)
- George Antheil composed *Airplane* sonata for piano in 1922
- Arthur Honegger portrayed sound of express train in *Pacific 231* (1923)
- Richard Strauss imitated sound of telephone ring in his opera *Intermezzo* (1924)
- Mikhail Glinka wrote "Song of the 1846 Railways" (1846)

- Alban Berg imitated telephone sound in his opera *Lulu* (1936)
- George Antheil used two aircraft propellers as instruments in his *Ballet Mécanique* (1924)
- Gian-Carlo Menotti wrote opera called *The Telephone* (1947)

### *Outlining*

**Use the categories you created in the previous activity to prepare an outline. The outline should include three main topics, with at least two subtopics under each one. Organize the main topics and subtopics in a logical way. Save your work for later use.**

**Organizing Comparison and Contrast** A common type of informative essay is the comparison and contrast. In a **comparison** you explain how two subjects are similar. For example, you might give an idea about how a computer works by comparing it to an airport terminal. A **contrast,** on the other hand, emphasizes the differences rather than the similarities. For instance, you might explain how made-for-television movies are different from movies made for the theater. In a comparison and contrast essay, you will examine both the similarities and the differences between two subjects.

If the comparison and contrast method of development is appropriate for your essay, you can choose one of two patterns for organizing your information. In one pattern, called the **AABB pattern,** you include all that you have to say about subject *A* before you discuss subject *B*. You can discuss subject *A* in one paragraph and subject *B* in another paragraph, or you can explain both in the two halves of the same paragraph. In one section of the essay about Civil War generals Robert E. Lee and Ulysses S. Grant, the historian Bruce Catton uses this *AABB* pattern.

## Model: AABB Pattern of Organization

**(A) Lee** was tidewater Virginia, and in his background were family, culture, and tradition . . . the age of chivalry transplanted to a New World which was making its own legends and its own myths. **(A) He** embodied a way of life that had come down through the age of knighthood and the English country squire. . . . **(A) Lee** stood for the feeling that it was somehow of advantage to human society to have a pronounced inequality in the social structure. There should be a leisure class, backed by ownership of land; in turn, society itself should be keyed to the land as the chief source of wealth and influence. It would bring forth (according to this ideal) a class of men with a strong sense of obligation to the community; men who lived not to gain advantage for themselves, but to meet the solemn obligations which had been laid on them by the very fact that they were privileged.

**(B) Grant,** the son of a tanner on the Western frontier, was everything Lee was not. **(B) He** had come up the hard way and embodied nothing in particular except the eternal toughness and sinewy fiber of the men who grew up beyond the mountains. **(B) He** was one of a body of men who owed reverence and obeisance to no one, who were self-reliant to a fault, who cared hardly anything for the past but who had a sharp eye for the future. These frontier men . . . stood for democracy, not from any reasoned conclusion about the proper ordering of human society, but simply because they had grown up in the middle of democracy and knew how it worked. . . . No man was born to anything, except perhaps to a chance to show how far he could rise. Life was competition.

–*Bruce Catton,* "Grant and Lee: A Study in Contrasts"

The second way to organize a comparison and contrast essay is to use the **ABAB pattern.** In this pattern you point out one similarity or one difference between subject *A* and subject *B* and then go on to another similarity or difference. For instance, if you are contrasting travel by airplane and travel by car, you might start with one difference: the amount of time it takes to travel long distances. In a sentence or two, you would state that for long distances, travel by airplane is faster. Then you would go on to another difference: the expense. Later in his essay on Grant and Lee, Bruce Catton shifts to this *ABAB* pattern of organization.

**MODEL: ABAB Pattern of Organization**

> Yet it was not all contrast, after all. Different as they were—in background, in personality, in underlying aspiration—these two great soldiers had much in common. . . . Each man had, to begin with, the great virtue of utter tenacity and fidelity. **(A) Lee** hung on in the trenches at Petersburg after hope itself had died. **(B) Grant** fought his way down the Mississippi Valley in spite of acute personal discouragement and profound military handicaps. In each man there was an indomitable quality . . . the born fighter's refusal to give up as long as he can still remain on his feet and lift his two fists. Daring and resourcefulness they had, too; the ability to think faster and move faster than the enemy. These were the qualities which gave **(A) Lee** the dazzling campaigns of Second Manassas and Chancellorsville and won Vicksburg for **(B) Grant.**
>
> –*Bruce Catton,* "Grant and Lee: A Study in Contrasts"

## PRACTICE YOUR SKILLS

### *Organizing Comparison and Contrast*

**Choose one of the following pairs of items and make a list of their similarities and differences. If you need additional information, use encyclopedias and other reference materials in your library or media center. Then organize your information according to either the *ABAB* pattern or the *AABB* pattern.**

**1.** an office building and a beehive

**2.** movies made for television and movies made for the theater

**3.** the telephone and E-mail

**4.** a mountain and a goal in life

Communicate Your Ideas

PREWRITING *Outlining*

Following the model of an outline on page C353, use your list of supporting details from the activity on page C345 to prepare an outline for your informative essay. When you have completed your outline, review the questions on page C354. Then save your outline for later use.

## Drafting

Writing Process

With the use of your outline and other prewriting notes, you are ready to write your essay. During this drafting stage, you will transform the bits and pieces you have accumulated into complete sentences and paragraphs.

As you go about writing your first draft, you are likely to think of new ideas. You may incorporate them into your draft, as long as they relate to your main idea and help to clarify and develop it. Although this first draft does not have to be polished or neat, it should include all the parts of an essay: an introduction with a thesis statement, a body of supporting paragraphs, and a conclusion.

## Drafting the Thesis Statement

Even if your essay does not begin with your thesis, you should first refine your working thesis to keep your main idea in focus. The steps shown in the following chart will help you draft your thesis statement.

### Steps for Drafting Your Thesis

- Review your outline and revise your working thesis so that it covers all of your main topics.
- Avoid expressions that weaken your thesis, such as "In this paper I will . . ." or "This essay will be about . . ."

Review the prewriting notes and the outline on the wild boy of Aveyron on page C353. Then study the problems in the following thesis statements.

| | |
|---|---|
| WEAK THESIS STATEMENT | When he was first captured in 1800, the wild boy of Aveyron was very different from a normal child. (too narrow: does not cover boy's education and the influence of Itard's work) |
| WEAK THESIS STATEMENT | Wild children exist in both fiction and fact. (too general: does not even mention the wild boy of Aveyron) |
| WEAK THESIS STATEMENT | This essay will be about the wild boy of Aveyron. (focuses reader's attention on the essay instead of on the wild boy) |

In contrast, the thesis statement below is appropriately specific and covers all the supporting details.

| | |
|---|---|
| STRONG THESIS STATEMENT | Dr. Itard's methods in attempting to civilize the wild boy from Aveyron led to new developments in education and psychology that people take for granted today. |

## PRACTICE YOUR SKILLS

### *Refining Thesis Statements*

**Review the notes you made on machines in music. Write the following thesis statements, leaving a blank line after each one. Then, in each blank space, explain in one sentence what is wrong with the thesis statement. Use the models above as a guide.**

**1.** Airplanes and telephones have been celebrated in classical music.

**2.** In this essay I will show how composers have paid tribute to machines.

**3.** Composers often try to reflect in their music the social changes of the day.

**4.** This paper will be about music and machines.

**5.** George Antheil's *Airplane* sonata is a good example of how composers celebrate machines.

*Writing a Thesis Statement*

**Following the steps on page C358, write a thesis statement for an essay about machines and music. Be sure your thesis statement is appropriately specific and covers all of the main topics in the outline you wrote.**

*Communicate Your Ideas*

DRAFTING *Thesis Statement*

Review your working thesis and the outline you've saved. Refine the working thesis into a thesis statement that accurately reflects both the intent and the content of your planned informative essay. Keep the statement in your writing folder to use when you draft the introduction of your essay.

## Drafting the Introduction

The introduction is the place to state your subject and thesis and to set the tone for the entire essay. The tone may be direct, reflective, casual, bitter, comic, joyous.

The **tone** of the essay is the author's attitude toward his or her subject and audience.

On the next page are suggestions for some effective ways to open your essay.

### Strategies for Drafting an Introduction

- Begin with an incident that shows how you became interested in your subject.
- Begin by giving some background information.
- Begin with an example that catches the reader's attention.
- Establish the tone.

When you write your introduction, you may need to revise your thesis statement to make it work with the other sentences. Notice in the following introduction about the wild boy that the thesis statement has been reworked to fit smoothly into the introduction. Notice also that some of the original ideas that could not fit under any of the outline headings have been included in the introduction as part of the background information.

**Model: Introduction of an Informative Essay**

The idea of a child's growing up away from all other humans and being raised by animals has turned up again and again in popular tales. *Tarzan of the Apes,* a creation of Edgar Rice Burroughs, and Rudyard Kipling's Mowgli the wolf boy are two famous examples. Wild children turn up in fact as well as in fiction, although there is no evidence that any were raised by animals. One of the most interesting and famous factual cases is that of Victor, the wild boy of Aveyron, France. The doctor who worked with the boy after he was captured in the wild in 1800 was Jean-Marc Gaspard Itard. The young doctor's methods in trying to civilize the boy, whom he named Victor, led to new ideas in education and psychology—ideas that people take for granted today.

Refined Thesis Statement

## PRACTICE YOUR SKILLS

### *Identifying Introductions*

**Write *personal incident, background information,* or *attention-getting example* to indicate how each essay introduction begins.**

**1.** I remember, to start with, that day in Sacramento, in a California now nearly thirty years past, when I first entered a classroom—able to understand about fifty stray English words. The third of four children, I had been preceded by my older brother and sister to a neighborhood school. Neither of them, however, had revealed very much about their classroom experiences. They left each morning and returned each afternoon, always together, speaking Spanish as they climbed the five steps to the porch.

Their mysterious books, wrapped in brown shopping bag paper, remained on the table next to the door, closed firmly behind them.

–*Richard Rodriguez,* "Aria: A Memoir of a Bilingual Childhood"

**2.** With his 47-pound bow drawn taut, a carbon graphite arrow held close to his cheek and EEG wires flowing from his scalp to monitor his brain, Rick McKinney seemed to be gazing absently at the majesty of Pikes Peak towering above the U.S. Olympic Training Center in Colorado Springs. Suddenly, he released the arrow and hit a perfect bull's eye that stood 98.6 yards downrange. Dr. Daniel Landers, an exercise scientist from Arizona State University, looked up from his EEG monitor, smiled and nodded with approval. McKinney had really not been thinking during the shot; the left side of his brain had shown diminished electrical activity.

–*Lee Torrey,* "How Science Creates Winners"

**3.** For almost three-quarters of a century, James Van DerZee has with rare artistry compiled a sweeping photographic survey of a way of life among black people of eastern America, particularly Harlem, that is unique and irreplaceable. It is both an historical record of value and an achievement of disciplined and feeling art. Van DerZee is only now beginning to be recognized as one of the notable photographers of middle-class people of the country.

–*Clarissa K. Wittenberg,* Smithsonian

### *Drafting Introductions for Informative Essays*

**Write two different introductory paragraphs that include the following thesis. In the first introduction, provide background information; in the second, use a personal incident or an attention-getting example. You should revise the thesis statement as needed to fit each introduction.**

| | |
|---|---|
| THESIS STATEMENT | Parks come in a variety of sizes and offer a variety of attractions, from the neighborhood park to the sprawling national park. |

## *Communicate Your Ideas*

**DRAFTING** *Introduction*

Now you are ready to begin drafting your informative essay. Find the thesis statement and the outline you've been saving in your writing folder, and write an introduction that will make an effective lead-in to the body of your work. Use the strategies on page C361 as your guide. Don't be concerned if your introduction isn't exactly the way you want it because you can refine it as you go along. Save the introduction, as well as your prewriting notes, in your writing folder for later use.

## Drafting the Body

Use your outline to draft the body of your essay, moving from point to point in the same order as the outline. You may add new ideas that would improve your essay. Check, however, to make sure each new idea relates to the main idea expressed in your thesis statement.

As you write the body of your essay, you will also need to supply transitions to connect your thoughts within and between paragraphs. In each case, select the transition that will best direct your reader from thought to thought. Using transitions will help give your essay **coherence**, the quality that makes each sentence seem related to the one before. Following are some other ways you can achieve coherence.

*You can learn more about transitions and coherence on pages C38 and C110.*

### Strategies for Achieving Coherence

- Repeat a key word from an earlier sentence.
- Repeat an idea from an earlier sentence using new words.
- Use a pronoun in place of a word used earlier.

In the following draft, the outline on the wild boy of Aveyron on page C353 has been fleshed out into complete sentences and paragraphs. The transitions, which have been added, are in **bold** type. Keep in mind that this first draft must still undergo revising and editing.

**Model: Body of an Informative Essay**

From I in Outline

Itard and other scientists were interested in finding out how much of a human's development is inborn and how much is learned through civilization. Victor provided an opportunity to study this question, for when he was captured at the age of twelve, he was in an extremely uncivilized state. Twenty-three scars from burns, bites, and scratches covered his dirty body, and he trotted instead of walked. He had a pleasing smile, but he expressed only extremes of emotion: joy, especially when he was fed or taken on walks, and sorrow about not being free. He could not speak, and he appeared insensitive to heat and cold. He could reach into a pot of boiling water and pull out a potato. The only sounds of interest to him related to food. For Itard, working with Victor was a rare chance to study a human raised in isolation and to examine the influence of environment on human behavior.

From II in Outline

Itard's first step in educating Victor was attending to his needs and desires. He gave Victor the foods he liked (mainly vegetables), plenty of rest, privacy, and exercise. **Then** he began developing the boy's sensitivities, such as those of sight and hearing, for Itard believed that no attempt to teach him to talk would succeed unless he was first sensitive to sound. **Next** he tried to play games with Victor to stretch the boy's mental powers. He **soon** learned that only when food was involved did Victor pay any attention. To motivate Victor, Itard devised a game in which Victor would find a chestnut under one of three inverted cups. When he **finally** began teaching Victor to speak and read, **however**, Itard met with very little success. **After** years the only words Victor learned were *milk* and *Oh God,* the latter expression having been picked up by imitating his caretaker, Madame Guérin. Victor never learned to read. He did, **however,** learn some simple chores, including fetching water and sawing wood. He never became what most people would consider a normal person, although he did respond to the affectionate concern of those around him.

From III in Outline

Itard's methods, whatever their failings with Victor, opened new doors in education. **First,** the idea that a child can learn only after his or her needs are met showed the importance of a good learning environment. **In addition,** working with Victor enabled Itard to make discoveries about teaching deaf children to speak, and it helped him create a whole new field of study: teaching the developmentally challenged. **Finally,** Maria Montessori, a pioneer in educating very young children, was influenced by Itard's work with Victor.

## Practice Your Skills

### *Analyzing the Body of an Essay*

**Refer to the draft of the essay about Victor, the wild boy of Aveyron, on pages C364–C366 to answer the following questions.**

1. In the first supporting paragraph, the last sentence refers to an earlier idea. Where is that earlier idea expressed?
2. What transitions are used in the second supporting paragraph?
3. Find the sentence that begins *After years the only words* near the end of the second supporting paragraph. What key word appears in that sentence that is repeated in the next two sentences? What pronoun is repeated in the last two sentences of the paragraph?
4. In the third supporting paragraph, the words *whatever their failings with Victor* appear. To what earlier idea does the phrase refer?
5. What transitions are used in the third supporting paragraph?

## Communicate Your Ideas

**DRAFTING** *Body of an Essay*

Using your outline, thesis, and introduction, draft the body of your essay. As you write, use transitions to achieve coherence. Save your draft.

Now that you have written the first draft of your essay, how well do you think you understand the element of coherence? Has the process of writing a thesis statement, an outline, and a draft helped you to see how any thoughts are effectively linked? What difficulties are you trying to overcome? What skills might you still need to learn? Record your answers in the Learning Log section of your **journal.**

## Drafting the Conclusion

Like the introduction, the conclusion of an essay is usually more general than the supporting paragraphs in the body. In fact, the conclusion provides a good opportunity to express whatever insight your subject has inspired. One or a combination of the following may be an effective way to end an informative essay.

### Strategies for Concluding an Informative Essay

- Summarize the essay or restate the thesis in new words.
- Refer to ideas in the introduction to bring the essay full circle.
- State your personal reaction to the subject.
- Draw a conclusion from the details in the body of your work.
- Relate an incident supporting your thesis or conclusion.
- Ask a question that leaves the reader thinking.
- Appeal to the reader's emotions.

The closing to the essay about Victor on the next page draws a conclusion based on the supporting details in the body. The last sentence, often called a **clincher** because it fixes the message firmly in the reader's mind, provides a strong ending.

**MODEL: Conclusion of an Informative Essay**

After Itard stopped working with Victor, the French government paid for Victor's care for the rest of his life. He never fit into normal society. Itard concluded that the early years of human life are precious periods of learning; and if a child is deprived of a human environment during those years, full learning can never take place. Although scientists and psychologists are still debating the influences of heredity and environment, Itard drew his own conclusion. It is human society—civilization—that makes us what we are, and no amount of inborn humanity could make up for the loss of companionship that Victor endured in the wild.

CLINCHER

**Drafting a Title** To complete your first draft, you need to think of an appropriate title. You may take your title from words and phrases within the essay, or you may compose a headline-type phrase.

A good **title** suggests the main idea and makes your reader want to read on.

## PRACTICE YOUR SKILLS

*Analyzing a Concluding Paragraph*

**Use the entire draft of the essay about Victor on pages C361, C364–C366, and C368 to write answers to the following questions.**

1. Where in the essay besides the concluding paragraph is some form of the word *civilized* used?
2. To which sentence in the first supporting paragraph do the last two sentences of the conclusion refer?

3. Which names in the last sentence of the body are repeated in the first sentence of the conclusion?
4. What other key word in the last sentence of the body is repeated in the first sentence of the conclusion?
5. What information is offered in the concluding paragraph to reinforce the conclusion drawn?

### *Writing a Concluding Paragraph*

**Reread the introduction and body of the essay about Victor on pages C361 and C364–C366. Then write an alternative concluding paragraph. Make your paragraph appeal to the reader's emotions.**

### *Drafting Titles*

**Draft five possible titles for the essay about Victor. Use words or phrases from the essay for two of the titles and a headline style for the others.**

## Communicate Your Ideas

**DRAFTING** *Conclusion*

Reread your thesis statement and the draft of your essay. Think about the ideas you presented. Then draft a conclusion that presents your last thought on the subject and effectively ends your essay. Finally, experiment with possible titles. Save your conclusion and titles.

## Revising

Writing Process

In the revising stage, your aim is to improve your first draft—to make it clearer, smoother, livelier, and more readable. Always leave yourself time to put your essay away for a while before revising it. Distancing yourself from your work can clear your mind and help you think of new and better ways to express your meaning.

Sometimes you may need to write a second or third draft before you are satisfied with the effectiveness of your essay. Your main concern in the revising stage, of course, is your audience. Ask yourself over and over again, "Will my readers understand exactly what I mean?"

## Checking for Unity, Coherence, and Emphasis

In a unified informative essay, the paragraphs work together to develop a single thesis. The topic sentence of each supporting paragraph relates directly to the thesis, and each sentence within a paragraph relates directly to the topic sentence. As you revise, watch for and delete ideas that stray from the main point.

Also be on the alert for transitions that are needed to keep your work coherent. Look for ways to improve the organization and flow of ideas. Your writing should guide your reader along a logical path of thought.

As you revise, check for appropriate emphasis. **Emphasis** is the quality in essays that makes the most important points stand out clearly in the reader's mind. You can achieve the proper emphasis by devoting more space to the most important ideas, by using transitional words and phrases to indicate relative importance, and by repeating the most important points.

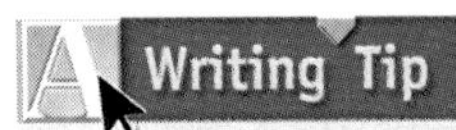


A good essay has **unity, coherence,** and **emphasis.**

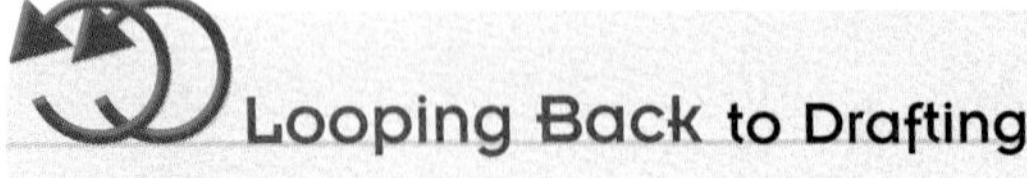


***Transitions***

Now that you are revising, take the time to study the transitions you used in your draft. Are they specific? Do they connect ideas *as precisely as possible?* Do they make your essay a unit, rather than a collection of unrelated paragraphs?

Because of the number and variety of points to be checked in the revision stage, you should read through your essay several times. An evaluation checklist—like the one that follows—can help you keep track of what you are looking for and what you have completed.

## Evaluation Checklist for Revising

**Checking Your Essay**

✓ Does the introduction set the tone and capture attention? *(pages C360–C361)*

✓ Does the thesis statement make your main idea clear? *(pages C358–C359)*

✓ Does your essay have unity? Does the topic sentence of each paragraph relate directly to the thesis statement? *(page C370)*

✓ Are the paragraphs arranged in a logical order? *(pages C364–C366)*

✓ Do transitions smoothly connect the paragraphs? *(page C370)*

✓ Did you use the techniques for achieving coherence between paragraphs? *(page C364)*

✓ Did you use transitions to show the importance of your ideas? *(page C370)*

✓ Did you devote the most space to the most important ideas? *(page C370)*

✓ Did you repeat key ideas to show their importance? *(page C370)*

✓ Do you have a strong concluding paragraph? *(pages C367–C368)*

✓ Did you add a title? *(page C368)*

**Checking Your Paragraphs**

✓ Does each paragraph have a topic sentence? *(page C101)*

✓ Is each paragraph unified and coherent? *(pages C107–C110)*

**Checking Your Sentences and Words**

✓ Are your sentences varied? *(pages C72–C79)*

✓ Are your sentences clear and concise? *(pages C66–C68)*

✓ Did you avoid faulty sentences? *(pages C79–C87)*

✓ Did you use specific words and sensory words? *(pages C60–C64)*

✓ Did you include figurative language?*(page C61)*

## Communicate Your Ideas

**REVISING** *Evaluation Checklist*

Use the evaluation checklist on the previous page to revise the essay you finished drafting. Save your revision. 

## Editing

Writing Process

In the editing stage you will produce an error-free manuscript. Your Personalized Editing Checklist will help you avoid the types of errors you are prone to make.

## Communicate Your Ideas

**EDITING**

Reread your essay one more time, checking for grammatical errors, errors of punctuation, and factual inaccuracies. Check information—such as numbers, dates, and the spellings of place names, names of institutions, and personal names—to make sure your information is accurate. 

## Publishing

Writing Process

Once you have revised and edited the final draft of your essay you are ready to share it with others.

## Communicate Your Ideas

**PUBLISHING**

After you write a final copy, ask an adult to read it and discuss your ideas with you. 

# Verbs

In her description of the Montgomery bus boycott, Coretta Scott King wrote the following sentence:

> [Martin] picked up Abernathy, and they cruised together around the city.

Partly because of her choice of the verbs *picked up* and *cruised,* the scene is particularly easy for readers to picture in their minds. The following line would have produced a fuzzy image.

> [Martin] got Ralph Abernathy, and they went together around the city.

## Tenses of Verbs

**Tense** expresses a particular time and makes the order of events clear to your readers. Following are examples of the six tenses.

| | |
|---|---|
| PRESENT | The empty bus **pauses** at the stop. |
| PAST | The empty bus **paused** at the stop a few minutes ago. |
| FUTURE | The empty bus **will pause** at the stop in an hour. |
| PRESENT PERFECT | The empty bus **has paused** at the stop many times. |
| PLUPERFECT | The empty bus **had never previously paused** at the stop. |
| FUTURE PERFECT | By noon, the empty bus **will already have paused** at the stop. |

## Shift in Tense

As you edit, correct any shifts in tense. If you began to write in the past tense, avoid unnecessary shifts into the present tense.

## Process of Writing an Informative Essay

Remember that the writing process is recursive—you can move back and forth among the stages of the process to achieve your purpose. For example, during editing, you may wish to return to the revising stage to add details that have occurred to you while editing. The page numbers in parentheses refer to pages where you can get help with your writing.

### PREWRITING

- Find ideas by asking yourself questions and by reading. *(page C341)*
- Choose a subject to develop into an essay from a list of possible subjects. *(page C342)*
- Limit your subject by asking questions about your subject and your audience. *(page C342)*
- Develop a list of supporting details. *(page C344)*
- Develop a working thesis based on the supporting details. *(page C347)*
- Organize your details into an outline. *(pages C348–C354)*

### DRAFTING

- Refine your thesis. *(pages C358–C359)*
- Draft an introduction that includes your thesis. *(pages C360–C361)*
- Use your outline to write a first draft of the body of the essay. *(pages C364–C366)*
- Use connecting devices to link your thoughts. *(page C364)*
- Draft a concluding paragraph. *(pages C367–C368)*
- Draft a title. *(page C368)*

### REVISING

- Use the Evaluation Checklist for Revising to revise your essay for structure, well-developed paragraphs, unity, coherence, emphasis, and varied and lively sentences and words. *(page C371)*

### EDITING

- Use the Editing Checklist to check your essay for errors in grammar, spelling, and mechanics. *(pages C46 and C374)*

### PUBLISHING

- Follow standard manuscript form and make a final copy of your work. Then publish it, using any of the ways listed on page C49.

# A Writer Writes

## A Comparison and Contrast Essay

**Purpose: to compare and contrast a particular aspect of race relations in current times with race relations in the 1960s**

**Audience: classmates**

### Prewriting

How have race relations changed since the Montgomery bus strike of 1963? Have they changed very much since the 1940s, when the world was still caught up in World War II? Find information in your library or media center—newspapers, books, and journals as well as audio and video clips that are available on the Internet. Talk to people who were teenagers during the 1960s. Ask questions about different areas such as schooling, work, recreation, and health. Then choose the one area that interests you the most or zero in on one significant difference or similarity in relations then and now. Limit your subject so that you can handle it effectively in a short essay.

To develop a working thesis, concentrate on the main similarities and/or differences you discovered. Group relevant details into categories and choose a pattern—either *AABB* or *ABAB*—for your comparison and contrast essay. Finally, use your categories as the basis of an outline.

### Drafting

After you refine your thesis statement to cover all of your ideas and details, draft your essay. Make sure that your introduction includes your thesis statement, captures your reader's interest, and sets the tone. For the body of your essay, draft a supporting paragraph for each main category of details. Then, after you draft a concluding paragraph, think of an interesting title for your essay.

## Revising

If you can put your draft away for a time, you will be able to revise it with fresh eyes. During your revision read through your essay several times, each time looking for a different item on the **Evaluation Checklist for Revising** on page C371. If possible, also get a friend's or family member's comments. Then make whatever changes or adjustments you think will make your essay more effective.

## Editing

When you are pleased with essay, edit it, using the checklists on pages C46 and C373.

## Publishing

After you prepare a neat, final copy, give your essay to your teacher, who will publish it in a classroom book called "Then and Now." You also may want to share your essay with anyone you interviewed during prewriting.

## Representing in Different Ways

**From Print . . .**

1000 East 72nd Street
New York, NY 10021
June 12, 2000

Dear Cassandra,

Now that I have lived in New York City for a month I finally understand how people can live in such an enormous city. Surprisingly, daily life is not much different from that in Smallton. For example, I do not have to walk far to the convenience store or to the video store because they are both just around the corner from where I am staying. The people who work in the stores are nice to me too, just like they are in Smallton. In fact, I see many of the same people when I walk to work every day. The only difference is that I do not have to stop to say hello and talk like I do every morning in Smallton.

Don't get me wrong. I miss Smallton! I miss breathing in the clean air each morning, and I miss the wide-open space that surrounds me as soon as I walk out of the center of town. On some mornings in New York all you can smell is the exhaust of buses and cars, and all you can see are cars and buildings.

I hope to see you soon.

Sincerely,

*Eliado*

**. . . to Visuals**

Using the information in the letter, create a Venn diagram that compares and contrasts Smallton and New York City.

**From Visuals . . .**

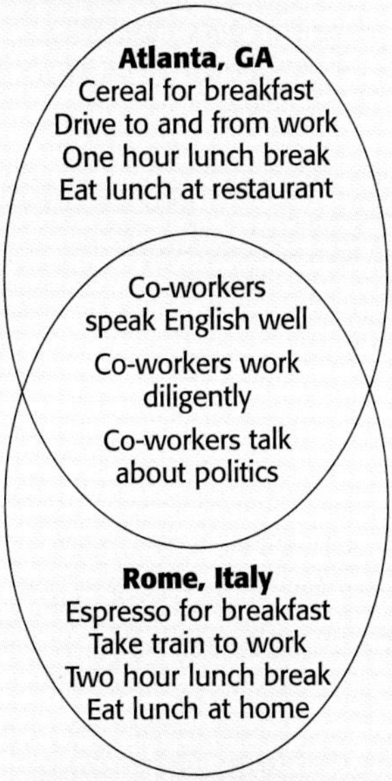

**Atlanta, GA**
Cereal for breakfast
Drive to and from work
One hour lunch break
Eat lunch at restaurant

Co-workers speak English well
Co-workers work diligently
Co-workers talk about politics

**Rome, Italy**
Espresso for breakfast
Take train to work
Two hour lunch break
Eat lunch at home

**. . . to Print**

Using the information in the Venn diagram, write a friendly letter to Eliado comparing and contrasting the experience of working in Atlanta, Georgia, with the experience of working in Rome, Italy.

- **Which strategies can be used for creating both written and visual representations? Which strategies apply to one, not both? Which type of representation is more effective?**
- **Draw a conclusion and write briefly about the differences between written ideas and visual representations.**

## Writing in Everyday LIfe

### *Informative Letter*

You live in a quaint, peaceful neighborhood in a small town. But then one day, Johnny Crash, the rock star, moves into the house next door. Unfortunately, his entourage also moves in. Johnny is so popular that there are swarms of fans camped outside on the street. He practices with his band on your front lawn until 2 A.M. and often leaves his drum set in your driveway.

**Write a letter to the rock star explaining some of the problems you have with his behavior. Inform him of how you think he should behave as a considerate neighbor. Organize your details in their order of importance and write with a serious tone.**

**What strategies did you use to inform the rock star about his neighborly behavior?**

*You can find information on writing letters on pages C580–C601.*

## Writing for Academic Areas

### *Informative E-mail*

As a scientist who specializes in animal behavior, you observe and record all activities of two chimpanzees, Frick and Frack. Your main task is to look for ways in which chimpanzees can mimic human behavior. So far you have been concentrating on facial expressions and have come to the conclusion that sometimes Frick and Frack appear to be laughing at you.

**Write an E-mail message to your colleague, Dr. Gibbon, informing him of your observations. Be sure to write a thesis statement that expresses the main idea clearly. Explain how chimps mimic humans with details that support your thesis statement.**

**What strategies did you use to inform Dr. Gibbon of the behavior you observed in chimpanzees?**

*You can find information on writing E-mail in* A Writer's Guide to Using the Internet, *pages C828–C833.*

# Assess Your Learning

Your history teacher, Dr. Melinda Megahertz, is also a computer technician and programmer who is developing a virtual reality device to make her lectures more exciting and interesting for her students. Once completed, the device will create animated holograms of famous figures and events in history. Dr. Megahertz has chosen you as a representative of the students to write a letter to the board of education requesting that it increases the funding for her project.

- **Write a letter to the board of education informing it of the educational benefits of using a virtual reality device to teach history in the classroom. Provide examples of which historical figures or events you would like to re-create.**
- **Develop a working thesis around which you can select and organize your details and then refine it into a polished thesis statement. Arrange your ideas in logical order. Decide whether the ideas should be organized in chronological order, spatial order, comparison and contrast order, order of importance, or developmental order.**

*Before You Write* **Consider the following questions:**
What is the ***subject?***
What is the ***occasion?***
Who is the ***audience?***
What is the ***purpose?***

*After You Write* **Evaluate your work using the following criteria:**

- Have you developed a working thesis around which you can select and organize your details?
- Have you refined your working thesis into a polished thesis statement?
- Does your letter include a strong introduction, body, and conclusion?
- Have you written in a voice and style appropriate to your audience and purpose?
- Does your introduction make your subject, purpose, tone, and thesis clear to readers?
- Does the body clearly support the thesis and lead to your conclusion?

**Write briefly on how well you did. Point out your strengths and areas for improvement.**

CHAPTER 9

# Writing to Persuade

You are probably tired of the glut of advertisements on radio, television, and the Internet. You may feel like the target of persuasive ads every time you read a magazine or pick up the newspaper. Yet you probably believe that some worthwhile topics such as homelessness or improving the environment should be discussed, and on those subjects you are willing to be convinced.

Writing that attempts to convince is persuasive. In persuasion, a writer takes a stand on an issue that he or she feels strongly about. Then, by offering compelling facts, by developing a logical argument, and by writing fluently and movingly, he or she urges the reader to agree. Whether or not the appeal is successful depends mostly on the writer's skill and the effectiveness of the argument. In this chapter you will study the tools of persuasion and will have a chance to convince readers that your opinion about an issue of importance to you is right.

## *Reading with a Writer's Eye*

The persuasive essay that follows offers the opinion of a college professor who has strong beliefs about the value of Internet research. What points does he make? Are they logical? As you read, follow his argument and note whether or not he presents it effectively. Decide if he has persuaded you to his point of view.

# NO COMPUTER CAN HOLD THE PAST

*Robert Darnton*

Does the Internet help college students learn? Enthusiasts proclaim that it has made a world of information available to any freshman with a computer. Skeptics warn that cyberspace is so full of junk that research in it will never amount to anything more than garbage collecting.

As a college teacher who has just started a program for publishing historical monographs on the Web, I concede that the skeptics have a case. But the problem with doing research on the Internet is not about garbage. It's that, by doing all their homework on the Internet, students may develop a misunderstanding of research itself and even of the subjects they are studying.

Historical research takes place in libraries and archives, but it is not a straightforward process of retrieving information. You may open a box of manuscripts and confront information in the form of letters or diaries or memos. But this raw material isn't raw at all. It's cooked. Every document embodies some rhetorical convention, argues for some hidden agenda, must be read between the lines and related to all the surrounding documents.

Moreover, most documents never make it into archives—they didn't 100 years ago and they don't today, when government agencies shred, erase, or discard most of the material they produce. And far from taking place primarily in governments, history happens to everyone.

Unfortunately for historians, the vast majority of humans have disappeared into the past, without leaving a trace of their existence. What remains amounts to nothing more than a tiny fragment of human experience, even though the components of that fragment could fill so many archival boxes that you couldn't get through a statistically significant sample of them if you read for centuries. How can you assemble a few pieces into a meaningful picture of the past?

The task seems daunting, yet our students arrive in class with the illusion that we've got history pretty well under control. It's in books, they think: hard facts bound between hard covers, and now we're making it all available online. How can we teach them that history is an interpretive science, not a body of facts; that it involves argument from evidence, not mere information; that it has no bottom line but is, by its very nature, bottomless?

To help students understand the nature of historical knowledge, we assign them research papers. Most of them will never open a box of manuscripts, but all of them can try to find a path of their own through printed sources scattered in a library. By studying texts and relating texts to one another, they can appreciate the tenuousness as well as the rigor involved in the attempt to make sense of the past. But instead of reading for meaning in books, many students search for information on the Internet.

Of course, the Internet can open up bibliographical pathways and can even provide digitized versions of primary sources. But no digitized text can duplicate the original—its handwriting or typography, its layout, its paper and all the paratextual clues to its meaning. We read the front page of a newspaper as if it were a map of yesterday's events. We gauge the importance of each article by the size of its headline, its position (lead story on the right, off-lead on the left, lighter fare below the fold) and by whatever photographs or sidebars may accompany it. If we merely read the article in isolation on a screen, we would miss the context that shapes its meaning.

Digitizers often dump texts onto the Internet without considering their quality as sources, and students often fail to read those texts critically. Instead, they scan them with search engines, locate key words, jump in at any point and cobble passages together by computerized cutting and pasting.

"Where do you find history?" I imagine asking the students of the future.

"On the Web," they answer.

"How do you get at it?"

"By surfing."

"What method will you use to write your paper?"

"Access, download, hyperlink and printout."

Such thoughts touch off Luddite[1] fantasies: smash all the computers and leave the Internet to drown in the ocean of its own junk. But that way madness lies, and my students have taught me that, if handled with care, the Internet can be an effective tool.

Last semester, I directed a student who was writing a research paper in Paris. After consulting me by E-mail, she followed the leads I gave her by logging on to French library catalogues. She located the relevant sources, read them, E-mailed drafts to me, rewrote extensively and got a well-earned A.

The Web can provide a way to publish research in fields where the monograph has become an endangered species, owing to the costs of publishing conventional books. The American Historical Association, with a grant from the Andrew W. Mellon Foundation, is sponsoring a program, Gutenberg-e, to publish dissertations—not by dumping them unedited on the Internet but by reworking them into electronic books of the highest quality with skilled editors at Columbia University Press.

Instead of turning our backs on cyberspace, we need to take control of it—to set standards, develop quality controls and direct traffic. Our students will learn to navigate the Internet successfully if we set up warning signals and teach them to obey: "Proceed with caution. Danger lies ahead."

---

[1] **Luddite:** One who is opposed to technological change.

## Thinking as a Writer

### Analyzing a Persuasive Appeal

- Did you find yourself violently disagreeing or passionately concurring with the writer's argument? Were you uninterested in or bored by the opinion expressed in the persuasive newspaper article? Analyze your response. Does your reaction say more about what the writer wrote or more about who you are and what your interests and beliefs are?
- Imagine you are a student in Professor Darnton's class. What single comment would you make to him about the effectiveness of his use of persuasion in the article? How do you think he would respond to what you say?

### Evaluating the Use of Visual Design

Viewing Study the opening screens of several information sites on the Internet. For example, you might look up the sites of the National Aeronautics and Space Administration (NASA), Mothers Against Drunk Driving (MADD), Greenpeace (the environmental protection group), your favorite music group or performer, or any others that interest you. (Remember, you don't need to know a precise Web address. You can simply enter the name of the organization or individual in the search box provided by any search engine.) From a quick visual scan, which sites make you feel most confident that the information provided will be objective and accurate? Did the visual design inspire your confidence or your skepticism regarding the objectivity and accuracy of the site?

### Formulating a Response to a Persuasive Argument

Oral Expression Work with a partner to find three sites on the Internet that provide more up-to-date and thorough information about any subject than print resources possibly could offer.

- Imagine you are presenting your findings to a group of students—after Professor Darnton gives a speech based on his article. How would you answer Professor Darnton's arguments?

# The Power of Persuasion

The selection you have just read is an example of a persuasive article. Persuasion, however, takes many forms and confronts the reader at several different levels of sophistication. It runs the gamut from the eloquent orations of the ancient Roman orator Cicero to a used car ad in a daily newspaper. Here are several other situations in which you may encounter persuasive appeals.

## Uses of Persuasion

- **The school debate team persuades the audience** that it is more important to spend limited public funds on libraries rather than on parks.
- **A local newspaper columnist writes an editorial** about the environmental dangers of clearing land to build malls and parking lots.
- **You convince a neighborhood business** to hire you as a part-time worker.
- **A doctor explains the results of physical exams and tests** to persuade a patient to follow a new course of treatment.
- **A critic writes a rave review** that convinces crowds that they should flock to the theater to see a new play or hear a new band.
- **A member of a homeowner's association writes a flyer** to persuade other members to vote for hiring a recycling firm.

# Refining Your Skills of Persuasion

Mark Twain once wrote, "It were not best that we should all think alike; it is difference of opinion that makes horse-races." Twain can rest assured that modern society will never lack for "horse-races," for there is probably no question on which everyone thinks alike. As a result, to obtain agreement on a certain issue, you sometimes must try to persuade people to accept the position you feel is best. One way to do so is to write a persuasive essay in which your purpose is to win readers over to your side of an issue or to motivate them to take a certain action.

A **persuasive essay** states an opinion and uses facts, examples, and reasons to convince readers to accept that opinion and/or take a specific action.

When you write essays for the purpose of persuading, you can draw on several types of writing, including **narrative writing** and **descriptive writing.** You will also be able to use different methods of **classification** to organize information you are using to support your opinions. Finally, you will find the skill of **evaluating** helpful in writing persuasion. "Writing Is Thinking" on page C410 will offer insights about evaluating.

*You can find more on narrative and descriptive writing on pages C114–C127. You can find more on classification of information on pages C128–C138.*

### Your Writer's Journal

What ideas stir your sense of fairness or provoke your moral sense? Make a list of the topics on which you have strong opinions—opinions that you would soundly defend if you had the chance. As you come across other topics, add them to your journal. For each one, mention the issue and your feelings about it. These simple journal notes will get you thinking about ideas to address in the persuasive writing you will do in this chapter.

A persuasive essay is like other essays in its structure but not its substance. The core of a persuasive essay lies in its arguments—the logical presentation of facts designed to move the reader to believe or act in a certain way. To analyze a persuasive essay it is necessary to analyze its arguments. This section will examine both the structure and the substance of the persuasive essay.

## Persuasive Essay Structure

Like other kinds of essays, a persuasive essay is composed of three basic parts—an introduction, a body of paragraphs, and a conclusion. The following chart shows the function of each of these three parts.

### Structure of a Persuasive Essay

- The **introduction** presents the issue and the writer's opinion on the issue, which is expressed in the thesis statement.
- The **body** of supporting paragraphs presents facts, reasons, statistics, incidents, examples, the testimony of experts, and other kinds of evidence to support the writer's opinion.
- The **conclusion** provides a strong summary or closing that drives home the writer's opinion.

Read the following persuasive essay in which the main parts are labeled. Notice how the writer presents the issue and his opinion in the introduction, supports his opinion in the body, and reinforces his main idea in the conclusion.

**Model: Persuasive Essay**

### *Controlling Alaska's Wolves*

**Introduction:** PRESENTS THESIS STATEMENT; LAYS OUT ISSUE

The plan to eliminate humanely some of Alaska's soaring number of wolves makes good sense. Those who would deny Alaska's right to control its burgeoning wolf population have failed to realize the ability of the wolf population to bounce back.

**First Body Paragraph:** GIVES EXAMPLES AND FACTS

At one time, up to six federal varmint hunters ranged the Territory, poisoning, trapping, and shooting wolves from the air. As a result, at statehood few wolves remained. Since then, Alaska has worked hard to bring its wolves back. It added the wolf to its big game trophy and fur animal lists, which brought it under protection of bag limits and other regulations. It has shown flexibility in adjusting these regulations in response to wolf population changes. It has banned hunting wolves from an airplane as a sport. Finally, it has supported wolf research to learn how the animal lives.

**Second Body Paragraph:** GIVES STATISTICS

The wolf, with its remarkable resilience, has responded dramatically. In fact, there are so many wolves in some areas they are destroying their own food supply. In Alaska, the wolf's diet varies regionally but is mainly moose, deer, and caribou. Such prey is scarce in parts of the state now. The Arctic caribou herd crashed from 240,000 in 1970 to 60,000 in 1976; wolves may be killing up to 12,000 annually. The Tanana Flats near Fairbanks once supported 6,000 to 12,000 moose; now the region contains only 3,000. In southeastern Alaska, deer herds thinned by severe winters have been kept at dangerously low levels by wolves. The wolves also starved, as deer became depleted.

**Third Body Paragraph:** CONCEDES THAT WOLVES ALONE ARE NOT TO BLAME

Besides severe winters, there are a number of other reasons behind these alarming trends, including hunting by humans. Game is the main food for many wilderness residents. Nevertheless, in specific areas, there is little doubt that wolves have decimated moose, caribou, and deer.

**Conclusion:** REINFORCES MAIN IDEA

For many years, Alaska's game managers have demonstrated good wolf management. Now, unless the state can control soaring wolf numbers in specific areas, by humane and strictly controlled means, Alaska stands to lose many more caribou, moose, and deer—and, ultimately, its wolves.

–*Jim Rearden,* National Wildlife

## Practice Your Skills

### *Analyzing a Persuasive Essay*

The following essay takes a different view of the plan to eliminate some of Alaska's wolves. Read it carefully and answer the questions that follow it. The paragraphs are numbered for easy reference.

### *Wolves as Scapegoats*

**(1)** The Alaska fish and game department has chosen the wolf as a scapegoat for its own disastrous mistakes in game management. In 1970 the Nelchina caribou herd numbered only 10,000 animals. Five years before, there had been 80,000. The same trend has been true of the Tanana moose herd. The great western Arctic caribou herd, which in 1972 contained 240,000 animals, numbered only 60,000 in 1977.

**(2)** Is this decimation of the western Arctic herd the wolf's doing? State game officials have declared that it is. However, they have no research to support that view. They do not even have a scientific count of how many wolves there are. Undaunted by what they do not know, they are determined to use aerial gunner teams to kill eight out of every ten western Arctic wolves. The caribou they want to defend, however, are the same ones they allowed hunters to kill without limits or closed seasons from 1959 until April of 1976. In 1976 alone, native hunters killed over 30,000 western Arctic caribou.

**(3)** In January of 1977, the fish and game department was caught trying to hush up the results of its own research on the Nelchina moose herd—research designed to demonstrate scientifically, once and for all, what effect wolves have on calf survival. The research showed no significant wolf impact. So, instead, the department released to the press totally unscientific data.

**(4)** One department official in Anchorage said in April of 1977 that if every wolf in Alaska were killed, the western Arctic caribou herd would still not be helped. He added that, because the natives in the area were paying so little attention to the new seasons and limits set by the state, nothing could save the herd.

**(5)** In the spring of 1977 one house of the Alaska legislature passed a bill to ban all cow and calf moose hunting. We can hope that the blame for wildlife crises will now be placed where it belongs—on the shoulders of the Alaska fish and game department.

*–James L. Pitts,* National Wildlife

1. What is the thesis statement of this essay?
2. What statistic in the introduction is also used in the opposing essay by Jim Rearden on pages C387-C388?
3. Which restates the main idea of paragraph 2?
   - **a.** Wolves are not responsible for the decimation of the western Arctic herd.
   - **b.** Game officials have insufficient evidence to blame wolves for the decimation of the western Arctic herd.
4. What statistic in paragraph 2 is omitted from Jim Rearden's opposing essay? What persuasive purpose does it serve here, in the essay by James L. Pitts?
5. One of Rearden's arguments is that the Alaska fish and game department has been doing a good job. How does Pitts counter that argument in paragraph 3?
6. To what authority does Pitts refer in paragraph 4?
7. Which restates the main idea of paragraph 4?
   - **a.** Immoderate hunting threatens caribou more than wolves do.
   - **b.** Even a department official believes that immoderate hunting threatens caribou more than wolves do.
8. Which word in the last sentence of paragraph 3 is used in the first sentence of paragraph 4 as a transition?
9. The last sentence of the essay restates an idea and adds a new emphasis. Write the earlier sentence to which it refers.
10. Explain in a paragraph which essay you found more persuasive.

# Political Campaign

There's a tight race for mayor in your city. The hot issue in the election is new development in the downtown area. Incumbent mayor Anita Rodriguez favors large-scale development, arguing that more businesses downtown will make more tax money available for social services. Her closest challenger, Sam Silver, a local business owner, believes a more moderate development makes sense. He's afraid an overdeveloped downtown will result in empty storefronts and traffic problems. The third candidate, Florence Channing, is a minister. She believes that a more run-down part of town should be redeveloped first to give residents in that community a share in the benefits of new development.

How will the candidates persuade enough people to vote for them so that they can carry through on the positions they have taken? Form a group to choose one of the candidates and plan a political media campaign.

## Steps for Planning a Political Campaign

- Which of your candidate's qualities do you want to highlight?
- What group of voters would be most likely to support your candidate?
- What campaign events do you want your candidate to take part in?
- What would be effective slogans and/or graphics to use on a campaign poster?
- Sketch out a newspaper ad including graphics and text.
- Write scripts for a 15-second radio ad and a 30-second television ad for your candidate. Decide what kinds of stations to play them on and explain your reasons.
- List three themes for your candidate to focus on in televised debates. What advice would you give about how to talk about the opponents? Why?

After each group has made its presentation, compare campaigns. What do they have in common? What was memorable about each? What kind of relationship was there between the candidate's position and his or her campaign slogan and other media products?

## Facts and Opinions

Every persuasive essay is composed of two types of statements: facts and opinions. The soundness of the essay hangs on the writer's awareness of the difference between the two; facts can be proven true while opinions cannot.

A **fact** is a statement that can be proved. An **opinion** is a judgment that cannot be proved.

One plus one equals two. That is a fact, for it can be demonstrated within your own experience. If you add one pencil or orange or shoe to another, you will always end up with two. Some facts, however, cannot be verified by you directly, as shown in the following example.

FACT During a solar eclipse, the moon's shadow covers the sun.

Even if you have witnessed a solar eclipse, you cannot state from your own experience that the moon's shadow was the cause. Astronomers, however, can establish the cause by using sophisticated observations and calculations. Therefore, statements by experts can be used to verify facts that lie outside your experience.

**Writing Tip**

Use your own experience and reliable authorities to verify **facts**.

Opinions can vary from person to person, and they can take the form of judgments, interpretations, predictions, or preferences. The following are some examples of opinions.

OPINIONS *Dick Tracy* was a better movie than *Batman*.

Lawmakers should reduce all speed limits to drastically lower the number of automobile accidents.

Alfred, Lord Tennyson is the most highly respected English poet.

Broccoli tastes better than spinach.

Robots will soon perform all manual labor tasks in our households.

Opinions, by definition, cannot be proved. Some, however, can at least be supported with convincing evidence. Opinions that can be backed up with facts are called **arguable propositions.**

An **arguable proposition** is an opinion that can be supported by factual evidence.

Arguable propositions, as their name implies, can be argued. Opinions that express only personal preferences, on the other hand, are not worth arguing, for there are no facts to support them.

| | |
|---|---|
| ARGUABLE PROPOSITION | The performers' waiting room should be painted green. (Experiments have provided evidence that green has a calming effect.) |
| PREFERENCE | Green is a prettier color than blue. (No facts are available to back up this statement.) |

Always remain alert to the distinction between fact and opinion and remember that opinions need to be supported by facts, not by other opinions. As a writer, be sure to back up every opinion with facts. As a reader, be on your guard for unsupported opinions and for opinions offered up as facts. Remember that only arguable propositions form a solid basis for a persuasive essay.

### *Identifying Arguable Propositions*

**Identify each statement as an *arguable proposition* or a *preference.***

**1.** Airplane rides are more exciting than train rides.

2. There should be more rigorous training for flight mechanics in order to improve airline safety.
3. Aircraft of the future will be controlled by computers.
4. An airplane takeoff is the most thrilling sight there is.
5. Air traffic controllers should have more frequent rest periods in order to perform more effectively.
6. Takeoff is the most exciting part of a flight.
7. Takeoff is one of the riskiest parts of a flight.
8. Passengers should pay careful attention to the safety instructions at the beginning of each flight.
9. Flying remains a relatively safe way to travel.
10. After a number of flights, flying loses its excitement and becomes monotonous.

### *Supporting Opinions with Facts*

**Write one fact that, if verified, you would accept as evidence to back up each of the following arguable propositions.**

| | |
|---|---|
| EXAMPLE | The guitar is one of the most versatile of musical instruments. |
| POSSIBLE ANSWER | The guitar is used in playing folk, classical, and rock music. |

1. Too much television watching can have a harmful effect on performance in school.
2. Raising fines can help to keep people from double parking.
3. Americans should consume more fruits and vegetables.
4. Electrical appliances should not be used near water.
5. New sources of energy should be developed.
6. On hot days joggers should run only in the morning.
7. Using a computer makes writing easier and more fun.
8. Police work has become increasingly dangerous.
9. Eva Ramirez is a better candidate than Nelson Gooden.
10. The minimum age for a driver's license should be eighteen.

### *Analyzing Persuasive Writing*

**In a newspaper or other publication, choose an editorial or some other piece of persuasive writing. List the opinions and facts that are found in the text. Then identify each opinion as either a *preference* or an *arguable proposition*. Finally, write a paragraph explaining the argument presented and expressing your opinion of its soundness, using the arguable propositions to support your analysis. Save your work for later use.**

## Reasoning

As you have seen, personal experience and the statements of experts can provide evidence for an opinion. However, facts by themselves do not form a solid argument. What do the facts mean? Why are they relevant? How do they fit together? Interpreting facts in these ways to construct an argument requires reasoning power, or logic.

**Logic** is clear, organized thinking that leads to a reasonable conclusion. To understand how logical thinking applies to persuasive writing, you must understand inductive reasoning and deductive reasoning.

**Inductive Reasoning and Generalizations** **Inductive reasoning** is a formal term for something that you do quite naturally, that is, use known facts to make a generalization. A **generalization** is a statement about a group of things based on observations about a few items in that group. If one or two encounters with roses have left you sneezing, you may conclude that roses make you sneeze. You draw a general conclusion from specific facts, or evidence.

**Writing Tip**

Use **inductive reasoning** to form a **generalization** based on known facts about particulars.

The following chain of thoughts about naval officers is another example of inductive reasoning.

| | |
|---|---|
| SPECIFIC FACT | A fleet admiral is the highest officer in the navy. |
| SPECIFIC FACT | A fleet admiral wears one large gold strip and four smaller gold stripes. |
| SPECIFIC FACT | An admiral is lower in rank than a fleet admiral. |
| SPECIFIC FACT | An admiral wears one large gold stripe and three smaller gold stripes. |
| GENERAL CONCLUSION | The rank of navy officers can probably be detected by the number of gold stripes on their uniforms. |

Notice the word *probably* in the general conclusion. Unless the stripes of every naval officer are examined, the conclusion cannot be stated with absolute certainty. The conclusions reached by the inductive method should always be qualified or limited in some way. A conclusion may be reasonable and sound, but it is not always a fact. It is always open to new evidence. Suppose, for example, you learned these new facts about the stripes on navy uniforms.

| | |
|---|---|
| NEW FACT | A commodore wears one two-inch gold stripe. |
| NEW FACT | An ensign wears one half-inch gold stripe. |
| NEW FACT | A commodore has a much higher rank than an ensign. |

The first conclusion equated rank with the number of gold stripes. However, if both a commodore and an ensign wear just one stripe, that conclusion cannot hold. The conclusion, however, can be revised to accommodate the new facts, as follows:

| | |
|---|---|
| REVISED CONCLUSION | The rank of navy officers can probably be detected by the number and size of the gold stripes on their uniforms. |

**Hasty Generalizations** Beware of **hasty generalizations**—generalizations that are too broad. If a poodle growls at you, you cannot conclude that all poodles are unfriendly. If your family does not like anchovies, you cannot conclude that no one likes anchovies.

| | |
|---|---|
| HASTY GENERALIZATION | No one ever likes anchovies. |
| SOUND GENERALIZATION | Some people do not like anchovies. |

The writer of the following paragraph attempts to use inductive reasoning but arrives at a conclusion too hastily.

**MODEL: Hasty Generalization**

If you dislike hot weather, you need to avoid not only the obvious places in the South and Southwest, but also a more surprising "hot spot" in the Northeast.

SPECIFIC FACTS

I have visited Boston three times, and every time I have been there the temperature has been 90 degrees or above. My first visit took place in May 1995. On the day I arrived, the mercury reached 95 degrees. I was there again in the summer of 1997 when the temperature hit 98 degrees. In late September 1999, I passed through Boston again, and even at that time of year, the temperature reached 91 degrees.

HASTY GENERALIZATION

Heat haters, beware! *Boston is one of the hottest cities in the nation.*

The writer bases the generalization on only three days over a four-year period. In addition, the writer fails to compare Boston's temperatures with those of other cities. The hasty generalization could have been avoided if the writer had followed the guidelines at the top of the next page.

### Avoiding Hasty Generalizations

- Examine a sufficient number of facts and examples.
- Be sure your examples are representative of the whole group.
- Check reliable authorities to confirm the generalization.
- Be able to explain any exceptions.
- Limit the generalization by using words like *some, many, most.*
- Avoid words like *all, complete, always, never, none.*

## PRACTICE YOUR SKILLS

### *Using Inductive Reasoning*

**Read each set of facts below. Then write a generalization based on the facts. Be sure to limit your generalization appropriately.**

| | |
|---|---|
| FACTS | Two weeks ago my new computer froze. On the day it froze, the weather was very hot and humid. Yesterday, on a hot and humid day, my computer froze again. |
| GENERALIZATION | High temperature and high humidity sometimes cause a computer to freeze. |

**1.** FACTS At my brother's college, my cousin's college, and my friend's college, more students major in business than in liberal arts.

**2.** FACTS *The Day the Earth Stood Still, E.T., and Close Encounters of the Third Kind* are all science fiction movies about visitors from outer space. All have remained popular.

**3.** FACTS When the Chicago White Sox meet the Toronto Blue Jays in Chicago, "The Star-spangled Banner" is played before "O Canada." When the Chicago White Sox meet the Toronto Blue Jays in Toronto, "O Canada" is played before "The Star-spangled Banner."

**4.** FACTS In winter, goats, sheep, and antelope leave the alpine zone of mountains for lower snow-free slopes. In winter squirrels and marmots in the alpine zone hibernate.

**Glittering Generalities** Careless thinking about general ideas can lead to another reasoning problem called **glittering generalities.** These are words and phrases most people associate with virtue and goodness that are used intentionally to trick people into feeling positively about a subject.

Here are some words that typically stir positive feelings in people.

| | | |
|---|---|---|
| DEMOCRACY | FAMILY | MOTHERHOOD |
| VALUES | MORAL | EDUCATION |

What one person means by any of these words, however, can be very different from what another person means. When one of these words is attached to a controversial idea, chances are the writer or speaker is trying to force you to evoke your positive attitude toward this idea.

For example, suppose a politician says, "This new law is a threat to the liberty we cherish." He or she presumes you value liberty and will oppose the new law rather than surrender your freedom.

When you recognize a glittering generality, slash through it by asking yourself these questions, recommended by the Institute for Propaganda Analysis.

- What does the virtue word really mean?
- Does the idea in question have any legitimate connection with the real meaning of the word?
- Is an idea that does not serve my best interests being "sold" to me merely by its being given a name that I like?
- Leaving the virtue word out of consideration, what are the merits of the idea itself?

## PRACTICE YOUR SKILLS

### *Anaylzing a Glittering Generality*

**Analyze the following glittering generality by writing answers to the four questions above.**

"Unrestricted Internet access in the schools threatens the very foundation of the American family."

**Deductive Reasoning** While induction moves from the particular to the general, deduction moves from the general to the particular. In **deductive reasoning,** you begin with a general statement and then apply it to a particular case. The following chain of thoughts illustrates the deductive process.

| | |
|---|---|
| GENERALIZATION | No mail is delivered on legal holidays. |
| PARTICULAR | Today is a legal holiday. |
| CONCLUSION | Therefore, no mail will be delivered today. |

**Writing Tip**

Use **deductive reasoning** to prove that what is true about a group (general) will be true about an individual member of that group (particular).

The steps in the deductive process can be expressed in a three-part statement called a **syllogism**. Each part of the syllogism has a name.

| | |
|---|---|
| MAJOR PREMISE | All members of the jazz band are seniors. |
| MINOR PREMISE | Kristin is a member of the jazz band. |
| CONCLUSION | Therefore, Kristin is a senior. |

The following diagram illustrates how the conclusion must follow from the premises.

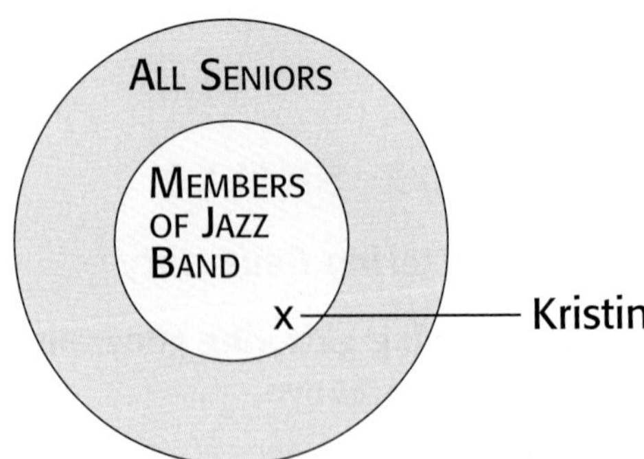

Since the smaller group is part of the larger group, and Kristin is in the smaller group, then she must also be in the larger group. As long as the premises are true, then the conclusion, like the one about Kristin, is also true, or **sound.** However, if either or both of the premises are false, then the conclusion is also false, or **unsound.**

In the following example, on the other hand, the conclusion is not logical even if both of the premises are true.

| | |
|---|---|
| MAJOR PREMISE | All members of the jazz band are seniors. |
| MINOR PREMISE | Kristin is a senior. |
| CONCLUSION | Therefore, Kristin is a member of the jazz band. |

The following diagram shows why the reasoning here is not logical.

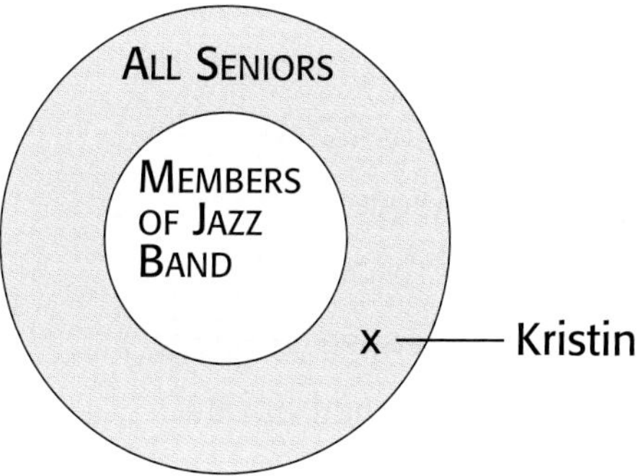


The fact that Kristin belongs to the larger group, seniors, does not guarantee that she belongs to the smaller group, the jazz band. The conclusion is illogical, or **invalid.**

A **syllogism** is *sound* if the premises are true. A syllogism is *valid* if the reasoning is logical.

## Practice Your Skills

### *Recognizing Flaws in Deductive Reasoning*

**Each syllogism below is unsound or invalid. Write *unsound* if the premises are not true. Write *invalid* if the reasoning is illogical.**

**1.** All late papers will be given failing grades.
Bill's paper was given a failing grade.
Therefore, Bill's paper was late.

**2.** All seniors are honor students.
Elena is a senior.
Therefore Elena is an honor student.

**3.** All southern states begin with the letter *M*.
Florida is a southern state.
Therefore, Florida begins with the letter *M*.

**4.** All four-legged animals are cows.
My cat is a four-legged animal.
Therefore, my cat is a cow.

**5.** All cats are four-legged animals.
My cow is a four-legged animal.
Therefore, my cow is a cat.

### *Using Deductive Reasoning*

**Study the following example of deductive reasoning. Then supply the logical conclusion for each of the following sets of premises.**

| | |
|---|---|
| Example | All city officials live within the city boundaries. Sal Savetti is a city official. |
| Answer | Therefore, Sal Savetti lives within the city boundaries. |

**1.** All Triple Crown winners have won the Kentucky Derby. Seattle Slew was a Triple Crown winner.

2. All bowling team members must have a minimum average of 175. Carlos is a bowling team member.
3. All of the fruit in this basket is either apples or oranges. This piece of fruit from the basket is not an apple.
4. All Marx brothers movies are comedies. *A Day at the Races* is a Marx brothers movie.
5. The seniors do not have to come to school this Thursday and Friday. Jonathan is a senior.

**Combining Inductive and Deductive Reasoning** The arguments in a persuasive essay are not neatly arranged in three-part syllogisms. Actual reasoning normally involves a back-and-forth process of induction and deduction. For example, a writer may gather evidence in order to draw a general conclusion (induction) and then use that conclusion as the premise of a syllogism (deduction).

| | |
|---|---|
| EVIDENCE | Scientific studies have shown that walking, running, and swimming benefit the heart and lungs. |
| CONCLUSION | Aerobic exercises benefit the body. |
| MAJOR PREMISE | Aerobic exercises benefit the body. |
| MINOR PREMISE | Dancing is an aerobic exercise. |
| CONCLUSION | Therefore, dancing benefits the body. |

One famous example of combining inductive and deductive reasoning is the Declaration of Independence. This document can be viewed as an essay that sought to persuade Great Britain and the rest of the world that the American colonies were justified in severing their ties with the British Crown. As you read the following excerpt from the Declaration of Independence, use the side labels to help you follow the reasoning.

## Declaration of Independence

We hold these truths to be self-evident, that all men are created equal, that they are endowed by their Creator with certain unalienable Rights, that among these are Life, Liberty and the pursuit of Happiness. That to secure these rights, Governments are instituted among Men, deriving their just powers from the consent of the governed. That whenever any form of Government becomes destructive of these ends, it is the Right of the People to alter or to abolish it, and to institute new Government. . . . Such has been the patient sufferance of these Colonies; and such is now the necessity which constrains them to alter their former Systems of Government. The history of the present King of Great Britain is a history of repeated injuries and usurpations, all having in direct object the establishment of an absolute Tyranny over these States. To prove this, let Facts be submitted to a candid world. . . .

MAJOR PREMISE OF SYLLOGISM

MINOR PREMISE OF SYLLOGISM

FACTS SUPPORTING MINOR PREMISE

He has refused his Assent to Laws, the most wholesome and necessary for the public good.

He has combined with others to subject us to a jurisdiction foreign to our constitution, and unacknowledged by our laws; giving his Assent to their Acts of pretended Legislation:

For quartering large bodies of armed troops among us:

For protecting them, by a mock Trial, from punishment for any Murders which they should commit on the Inhabitants of these States:

For cutting off our Trade with all parts of the world:

For imposing Taxes on us without our Consent:

For depriving us in many cases, of the benefits of Trial by Jury. . . .

In every stage of these Oppressions We Have Petitioned for Redress in the most humble terms:

Our repeated Petitions have been answered only by repeated injury. A Prince, whose character is thus marked by every act which may define a Tyrant, is unfit to be the ruler of a free people. . . . We, therefore, the Representatives of the United States of America, in General Congress, Assembled, appealing to the Supreme Judge of the world for the rectitude of our intentions, do, in the Name, and by Authority of the good People of these Colonies, solemnly publish and declare, That these United Colonies are, and of Right ought to be Free and Independent States. . . .

CONCLUSION OF SYLLOGISM

The Declaration of Independence is based on a deduction that can be expressed in the following syllogism.

| | |
|---|---|
| MAJOR PREMISE | When a government violates natural rights, the people have a right and duty to abolish it. |
| MINOR PREMISE | The British Crown violated the natural rights of the colonists. |
| CONCLUSION | Therefore, the colonists have a right and duty to break their ties with Great Britain. |

Inductive reasoning also plays its part. The minor premise—that Great Britain violated the colonists' rights—is a generalization based on specific facts presented about the behavior of the king.

## PRACTICE YOUR SKILLS

### *Analyzing Persuasive Writing*

**Continue the analysis of the selection you began on page C395. Write an additional paragraph that discusses inductive and deductive reasoning as well as the soundness of the reasoning and the conclusion.**

# Process of Writing a Persuasive Essay

As you prepare to write a persuasive essay of your own, always keep your purpose in sight. Your efforts at every stage are directed at finding a means of convincing the reader to think a certain way or to act a certain way. Clear, logical arguments and a strong, consistent approach to your position are your most effective tools.

## Prewriting

Writing Process

The prewriting stage is the most critical in the development of a persuasive essay. Take time to prepare and organize your arguments thoroughly before you write. The more carefully you think through your position, the more forcefully you will be able to present it. In the prewriting stage, you will choose your subject, develop your thesis, and gather and organize your evidence.

### Choosing a Subject

The world is full of opinions, but not every opinion makes a good subject for a persuasive essay. Only certain issues will stir your thoughts and your emotions. Furthermore, of the many opinions you hold, only some will be arguable propositions. Others, such as a liking for apples over pears, would be difficult to defend. Only an issue that you care about and that you can support makes an appropriate subject for a persuasive essay.

Try to be more aware of the controversial issues all around you—in the newspapers, on TV, in your school, and in your home. Notice matters about which you can say, "I think" or "I believe." Brainstorm or freewrite answers to questions such as "What do I care about?" When you have accumulated a list of possible subjects, use the following guidelines to help you choose among them.

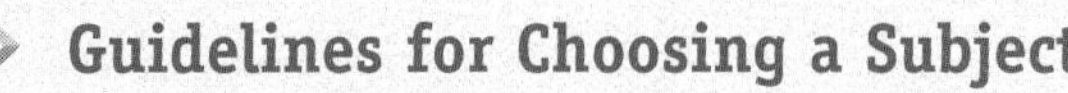

### Guidelines for Choosing a Subject

- Choose an issue that has at least two sides.
- Choose an issue that you feel strongly about.
- Choose an issue for which there is an audience whose belief or behavior you would like to influence.
- Choose an issue that has a position you can support with facts, examples, and reasons.

## Practice Your Skills

### *Brainstorming a Subject*

**Use brainstorming or freewriting to complete each of these statements. Keep your finished sentences in a folder, or perhaps in your journal, for later use.**

**1.** The things I care about at school are . . .

**2.** The things I worry about at school are . . .

**3.** The things that concern other people at school are . . .

**4.** Some things I would like to change at school are . . .

**5.** If I had a million dollars to give to the school system, I would want it used for . . .

## Communicate Your Ideas

**PREWRITING** *Subject and Audience*

Look back over the entries you made in your writer's **journal.** Select several that you feel strongly about and that would be good subjects for a persuasive essay about an educational issue. Your audience will be the local school board. Then with the help of the guidelines above, select your most appropriate subject. Save your work for later use. SAVE YOUR WORK

## Developing a Thesis Statement

Once you have selected a subject, you should develop a thesis statement. Often the statement will be a recommendation that includes a word such as *should*, *ought*, or *must*. Stay away from statements of fact or preference, for they do not make suitable thesis statements for a persuasive essay.

| | |
|---|---|
| FACT | In some areas wolves are near extinction. |
| PREFERENCE | I am horrified by the killing of wolves. |
| THESIS | Laws protecting wolves must be strengthened. |

After you write your thesis, ask yourself the following questions. If your thesis does not meet all of these guidelines, you should rethink your position or look for a more appropriate issue.

### Guidelines for Developing a Thesis Statement

- Can you state the thesis simply in one sentence?
- Is the statement either a judgment or a recommendation rather than a fact or a preference?
- Is the point of view debatable as you have expressed it? Can you think of any opposing arguments?

## PRACTICE YOUR SKILLS

### *Identifying Suitable and Unsuitable Thesis Statements*

**Write whether each statement is *suitable* or *unsuitable* for a persuasive essay and why.**

1. Despite its potential for education, television has developed into a negative influence.
2. Our society is becoming too dependent on computers.
3. We must learn to make better use of the sun for energy.
4. The incidence of violent crime in our nation is horrifying.
5. We must all learn to respect one another more.

## Communicate Your Ideas

**PREWRITING** *Thesis Statement*

Write a one-sentence thesis statement on the subject you chose for your persuasive essay. Keeping your audience in mind, follow the guidelines on the previous page. If your original subject does not follow the guidelines, revise your thesis so that it does, or choose another subject from your **journal.** Save your work for later use.

## Developing an Argument

Once you are satisfied with your thesis statement, you should gather and evaluate evidence to support it. First think about your audience. List arguments they might find convincing and then search for the appropriate evidence. You will want to find material that not only supports your position but also material that refutes it so that you can offer counterarguments. Your evidence will normally take the form of facts, examples, incidents, reasoning, and expert opinions. This needed information can be found in library reference material, books, magazines, newspapers, personal interviews, and your own experience. Once you have collected evidence and evaluated it, use the following guidelines to help you build an argument.

### Guidelines for Developing an Argument

- List all positions in your prewriting notes and be prepared to address the opposing views.
- To support your opinion, use facts and refer to well-respected experts and authorities who support your opinion.
- If the opposing view has a good point, admit it. *Conceding* a point in this way will strengthen your credibility.
- Use logical reasoning, both deductive and inductive, to pull your evidence together and draw conclusions from it.
- Express your arguments in polite and reasonable language.

Writing Is Thinking

## Evaluating Evidence

When you write to persuade, you make your argument convincing by presenting evidence that strongly supports your opinions. When you choose facts, examples, incidents, statistics, and expert opinions, you should use the skill of evaluating to judge each piece of evidence critically as to its strength in support of your position. To evaluate a piece of evidence, use the following criteria.

- Is evidence clearly related to the thesis and up to date?
- Is the source of the evidence reliable?
- Is the evidence unbiased and objective?

Suppose, for example, that you are arguing in favor of allowing seventeen-year-olds in your state to vote in primary elections. The following chart shows how you could evaluate evidence on this issue.

| EVIDENCE | EVALUATION |
|---|---|
| • Polls show that seventeen-year-olds are as knowledgeable as eighteen-year-olds. | • Supports thesis–explains logical reason to extend vote to seventeen-year-olds |
| • A low percentage of eighteen-year-olds turn out to vote. | • Does not support thesis–evidence focuses on eighteen-year-olds |
| • Seventeen-year-olds claim that such a law will encourage civic awareness. | • Does not support thesis–source of evidence may be biased and not objective |

### THINKING PRACTICE

**Choose one of the arguable propositions below or one based on an issue that is important to you. Think of relevant facts. Then make a chart like the one above to evaluate the evidence for your position.**

1. Leash laws should be strictly enforced in public parks.
2. Public libraries should be open longer hours.
3. Good personal grooming is essential to obtaining a job.

## Practice Your Skills

*Listing Pros and Cons*

**For each of the following thesis statements, list three facts, examples, incidents, or personal experiences that support the statement and three that oppose it. Save your notes in case you want to develop your own pros and cons later.**

1. A greater percentage of our tax money should go to improving the quality of education.
2. We should make our holidays less commercial.
3. We should live for the moment and not worry about the future.
4. Speed limits on all interstate highways should be raised to 75 miles per hour.
5. For many people a college education is the most important investment for the future.

When you are trying to sort out the parts of an argument, it may be useful to use a classmate as a sounding board. During prewriting (or at any appropriate stage of the writing process) read to your partner the points you want to make, and ask for feedback. Your classmate may see a flaw in reasoning that you missed, or may be able to suggest additional or alternate points to cover in the argument.

## Organizing an Argument

After you have gathered the information you need to build your argument, you should organize your ideas in a logical way. Many persuasive essays use order of importance or developmental order. Spatial order and chronological order, however, do not usually serve the persuasive purpose as well. Whatever organization you choose, however, you will need to use transitions like the following to guide the reader through your arguments.

*You may want to refer to the ways of organizing and connecting ideas on pages C32-C34.*

| TRANSITIONS SHOWING CONCESSION OR CONTRAST | | |
|---|---|---|
| while it is true that | nonetheless | despite |
| although | however | even though |
| admittedly | still | nevertheless |

## PRACTICE YOUR SKILLS

### *Organizing a Persuasive Argument*

**Choose one thesis from the "Listing Pros and Cons" activity on the previous page. Decide whether you want to argue *for* or *against* the thesis, and make an outline like the one below.**

1. Amend the thesis statement as necessary to express your view.
2. List the three supporting points from least to most important.
3. Assign each point a Roman numeral as in an outline.
4. Add at least two supporting points under each numeral.

Your outline should look like this.

**I.** (Least important point)
- **A.** (Supporting point)
- **B.** (Supporting point)

**II.** (More important point)
- **A.** (Supporting point)
- **B.** (Supporting point)

**III.** (Most important point)
- **A.** (Supporting point)
- **B.** (Supporting point)

## Communicate Your Ideas

**PREWRITING** *Outline and Graphic Organizer*

Develop an argument based on the thesis statement you generated. Then make an outline to arrange your points and supporting evidence from least to most important. Save your work for later use.

If you have been thorough in working through the steps of the prewriting stage, then the drafting stage should be essentially a matter of putting your prewriting notes together. Nevertheless, you may find as you write that some of your ideas need to be modified or that new ideas occur to you. Always remember that because you are beginning with a first draft, you will be able to review and rewrite.

Begin by writing your thesis, which you may want to refine. Then write an introduction that includes the thesis. Because your introduction will explain your subject and state your position, you must capture the reader's attention. Make the reader both aware of the importance of the subject and interested in what you have to say.

Next draft the body of the essay, devoting one or more paragraphs to each main topic in your outline. In addition to presenting your own supporting evidence, include counterarguments and concede points where appropriate. Also remember to add transitions to guide the reader. Finally, write a concluding paragraph that summarizes your argument and, if appropriate, urges the reader to take action.

### COMPUTER TIP

If you are in the process of drafting and discover that you need some specialized information or reference material, go to an online library for help. Many of the country's largest public and university libraries allow people to log in and download reference material as they need it. To access the collections of the New York Public Library, for instance, enter *New York Public Library* in the text field of your search engine. Double-click on the library name and you'll be invited to log on to **CATNYP**, the **CAT**alog of the **N**ew **Y**ork **P**ublic Library. Three pages of simple instructions give you searching tips for most of the collections the library owns.

## Persuasive Rhetoric

In general you will be more persuasive if the tone of your essay is calm and reasonable. Inflamed, emotional language, on the other hand, may only persuade your reader not to support your proposition.

| | |
|---|---|
| INFLAMED | Nasty, unruly dogs are terrorizing decent citizens. |
| REASONABLE | We need a leash law to discourage pet owners from allowing their animals to run free. |

If you choose your words carefully, however, you can make effective use of **persuasive rhetoric**—language with strong positive or negative connotations that appeals to the reader's emotions. When you use persuasive rhetoric, be sure to support statements with facts.

| | |
|---|---|
| PERSUASIVE RHETORIC | Tens of thousands of our precious young people are massacred and maimed each year by drunk drivers. |

## Practice Your Skills

### *Using Persuasive Rhetoric*

**Rewrite each sentence below using calm, persuasive rhetoric to replace inflammatory, emotionally charged words and expressions.**

1. The swindling scoundrels on the city council ought to be run out of town.
2. The airlines must be forced to inspect and repair their rattletraps to prevent millions of innocent travelers from being mangled and mutilated in fiery crashes.
3. The riffraff who foul our roadways and rivers should be forced to live in their own trash.
4. The only course open to us is to boot out those arrogant, insensitive clods before they run roughshod over the entire population.
5. Instead of gouging the poor for more and more rent, the slumlords must raze those vermin-ridden tenements and build decent housing.

## Communicate Your Ideas

**DRAFTING** *Persuasive Rhetoric*

Using your thesis statement and the outline you prepared earlier, write a draft of your essay. Be sure to use calm and reasonable persuasive rhetoric rather than inflammatory prose. Save your work for later use.

No matter how carefully you have prepared and drafted your essay it can still benefit from revising. You may need to bolster your opening, strengthen your arguments, refine your language, or add evidence or counterarguments. Review your essay several times, focusing on a different aspect each time. However, reserve at least one reading to check your logic, looking especially for the fallacies discussed below.

*You may wish to refer to the information on recognizing different forms of propaganda on pages C687–C690.*

## Eliminating Logical Fallacies

A **fallacy** is a flaw in reasoning like the hasty generalization and the faulty syllogism discussed on pages C397 and C400–C401. The following six fallacies also merit special attention, since they often surface in a poorly reasoned argument.

**Attacking the Person Instead of the Issue** This fallacy is often called *argumentum ad hominem,* which is Latin for "argument against the man." Writers who commit this fallacy target the character of their opponent instead of the real issue.

| | |
|---|---|
| Ad Hominem Fallacy | Senator Moreland has missed every important vote this year. How could his new bill have any merit? |
| Ad Hominem Fallacy | Sally Jones has never been late to work. She should be our mayor. |

Although Moreland's voting record may be irresponsible, his new bill may have merit. Promptness is not a mayor's most important quality.

**Either-Or/If-Then Fallacies** Writers guilty of these fallacies assume that there are only two sides to an issue; they ignore other viewpoints. Notice how the following issues are limited to two choices.

| | |
|---|---|
| EITHER-OR FALLACY | Either we stop using nuclear power for energy or we face certain disaster. |
| IF-THEN FALLACY | If you are against the new social center, then you are against the young people of our town. |

In the first example, "certain disaster" might be averted by better nuclear waste management. In the second example, the plans for the social center might be faulty. Between the two extreme positions on most issues lie a number of valid viewpoints.

**The Fallacy of Non Sequitur** In Latin, the words *non sequitur* mean "It does not follow." You have already seen some examples of conclusions that do not necessarily follow from the evidence. Most *non sequiturs* are the result of illogical deductive thinking.

| | |
|---|---|
| NON SEQUITURS | My sister liked this book; therefore, it must be good. |
| | John's car was more expensive than mine; he must be richer than I am. |

Like the fallacy of *either-or*, the *non sequitur* can neglect possible alternatives. Judgments about the quality of books vary greatly, and your sister's taste may not match your own. John may have gone into serious debt to buy an expensive car.

**Confusing Chronology with Cause and Effect** This fallacy assumes that whatever happens after an event was caused by that event.

| | |
|---|---|
| CAUSE-EFFECT | On my birthday I wished that I would win something. That week I won two concert tickets in a raffle. Wishing really works! |
| | The roof collapsed today because of yesterday's snowfall. |

In the first example, only coincidence relates the two events. In the second example, the snowfall may, indeed, have contributed to the collapse of the roof. The fallacy lies in assuming that the snow was the only cause, for if the roof had been sound, it probably could have withstood the snowfall. Such errors in reasoning often result from failing to consider more than one cause.

**False Analogies** An **analogy** is a comparison between two things that are alike in some significant ways. A **false analogy** attempts to compare two things that are not enough alike to be logically compared.

| | |
|---|---|
| FALSE ANALOGY | The phone company's discontinuation of my service was unfair, since even a criminal gets one phone call. |

There are no logical grounds for comparing the situation of a free citizen who has not paid his or her telephone bill and that of a person arrested for a crime.

**Begging the Question** A writer who "begs the question" builds an argument on an unproved assumption.

| | |
|---|---|
| BEGGING THE QUESTION | That unethical doctor should not be allowed to practice medicine. |
| | George Bernard Shaw was a great playwright because he wrote a number of superb plays. |

In the first example, the writer bases the conclusion—that the doctor should not be allowed to practice medicine—on the unproved assumption that the doctor is unethical. The second sentence provides an example of circular reasoning, which affords no proof. All the sentence says is that Shaw was a great playwright because he was a great playwright.

## Practice Your Skills

### *Identifying Fallacies*

**Write the letter for the fallacy committed in each statement.**

**A.** attacking the person instead of the issue

**B.** either-or/if-then

**C.** *non sequitur*

**D.** confusing chronology with cause and effect

**E.** false analogy

**F.** begging the question

1. Either you allow the hunting of wolves, or you end up with slaughtered farm animals.
2. The dog is barking; someone must have rung the doorbell.
3. The sun reappeared after the cave dwellers chanted a hymn during the eclipse. The chanting must have caused the sun to reappear.
4. I didn't hear Jennifer's speech, but I know I disagree with it. She's always so disorganized!
5. These unnecessary taxes are a burden on taxpayers.
6. Just as a car needs gasoline to keep running, a hospital needs volunteers.
7. If you don't clean your room, then you obviously do not care what people think about you.
8. The show was a flop; the actors must not have rehearsed enough.
9. Since I have been running regularly, my grades have improved. Running must make me smarter.
10. The shortsighted plan to cut the trees down will have unpleasant future consequences.

### *Correcting Fallacies*

**Rewrite the sentences above to eliminate the fallacy in each one. You need not suggest an alternative action in any of them as long you correct the fallacy with logical reasoning and different wording.**

## Looping Back to Prewriting

As you revise, you may find that your topic is compelling, your argument is solid, and your facts are verifiable; yet you seem to have overlooked an idea that you wanted to include. It is often helpful to refer to your **journal** and prewriting notes to monitor the development of your work. Tracing an idea back to its source and following it as it grows into an essay may reward you with a sense of surprise, of realization, and a wonderful new feeling of self-confidence.

## Communicate Your Ideas

**REVISING** *Fallacies*

Revise the draft of your persuasive essay, checking for unity, organization and coherence, calm persuasive rhetoric, and an orderly progression of ideas. Eliminate any fallacies that weaken your argument. Then check your conclusion. Does it follow from the introduction and the facts and examples you used in the body? Have you forcefully restated your thesis? Have you called upon your readers to act on the issue that you so eloquently presented? Have you committed any fallacies that you need to eliminate?

### Evaluation Checklist for Revising

**Checking Your Introduction**

✓ Does your thesis statement express your opinion clearly? *(page C408)*

✓ Does the introduction capture attention? *(page C387)*

✓ Are your emotional appeals, if any, sincere and restrained? *(page C414)*

**Checking Your Body Paragraphs**

✓ Does each paragraph have a topic sentence? *(page C100)*

✓ Is each paragraph unified and coherent? *(pages C107–C112)*

- ✓ Have you chosen an appropriate order for your arguments page and followed that ordering consistently? *(page C411)*
- ✓ Have you supported your main points? *(pages C392–C393)*
- ✓ Have you evaluated your evidence? *(page C410)*
- ✓ Have you considered counterarguments? *(page C409)*
- ✓ Did you concede a point if appropriate? *(page C411)*
- ✓ Did you avoid logical fallacies? *(pages C416–C418)*

**Checking Your Conclusion**

- ✓ Does your conclusion summarize the main points? *(page C387)*
- ✓ Do you restate your thesis forcefully?
- ✓ Have you asked your reader to take some action, if that was your purpose? *(page C413)*
- ✓ Are your emotional appeals, if any, sincere and restrained? *(page C414)*

**Checking Your Words and Sentences**

- ✓ Are your sentences varied and concise? *(pages C66–C79)*
- ✓ Did you avoid faulty sentences? *(pages C79–C88)*
- ✓ Did you use specific words with correct connotations? *(pages C60–C61)*

As you edit your persuasive essay, watch for spelling errors, such as the use of *right* for *write* or *capitol* for *capital*. If you are using a word-processing program, you can use the Spell Checking feature, but remember that it will not catch usage errors. Go back over quoted material to check on the spellings of the names of people and organizations. Then check your punctuation. As you work, refer to your Personalized Editing Checklist often to assure yourself that you have avoided—or corrected—the kinds of errors you have made before. Ask someone else to do a quick reading of your work. Finally, prepare the last draft of your essay following the models on pages C387-C388 and C404-C405.

## Communicate Your Ideas

### EDITING

As you carefully reread your persuasive essay looking for errors, refer to your Personalized Editing Checklist to ensure you are not repeating errors you have made in the past. The checklist on page C424 will also help you check your work. Ask a classmate or family member to help you catch any errors.

## Publishing

Writing Process

You might publish your persuasive essay by reading it aloud to your classmates, sharing it with your family, making a recording of it, or placing the printed version in a collection of essays written by the class. Whatever method you choose, keep a copy of the essay for yourself.

## Communicate Your Ideas

### PUBLISHING

Publish your persuasive essay in one of the following forms. You might send it to a local or regional newspaper, to a teen magazine, or to a magazine that deals specifically with the issue you wrote about. Reference books from your library or media center can explain how to go about submitting a manuscript to a magazine or to a publishing company. If your school has an Intranet you can save your essay as an HTML file and upload it as a Web page. Produce a final draft of your persuasive essay using standard manuscript form. Share it with your local school board. Place a copy of your essay in your portfolio.

# Quotations

Editing a persuasive essay—whether you researched other people's ideas to support your own, quoted a headline in a newspaper story, or referred to a body of writing or a work of art—will require a close look at mechanics. Here are a few items against which you might want to check your work.

## Capitalization

Capitalize the first word of a quotation even if it does not begin a sentence.

EXAMPLE It was Cicely Tyson who once remarked, "**C**hallenges make you discover things about yourself that you never really knew."

## Quotation Marks

Use quotation marks around the exact words of a person.

EXAMPLE **"**But the only way of discovering the limits of the possible is to venture a little way past them into the impossible,**"** said Arthur C. Clarke.

When you rephrase a quotation, do not enclose it in quotation marks.

EXAMPLE Arthur C. Clarke advised writers to venture into the impossible if they want to find the limits of the possible.

## Titles

The names of books, plays, newspapers, periodicals, works of art, long musical works, plays, and long poems are underlined in handwriting and typed in italic on a computer. The names of short stories, songs, chapter titles, articles, short essays, and short poems are enclosed in quotation marks.

EXAMPLE The article "Modern Life" in the Raleigh *News and Observer* caught my eye.

Homer's *Odyssey* offers great insights into the uses and abuses of power.

Margaret Atwood's "Gertrude Speaks" shows a cunning queen of Denmark.

## Commas

Use commas and quotation marks when interrupting quotations.

EXAMPLE "I believe more in the scissors**,**" said Truman Capote, "than I do in the pencil."

Use commas to set off a group of items or ideas.

EXAMPLE According to environmentalist Rachel Carson, the worst of our assaults on the environment is our contamination of air, earth, rivers, and sea with dangerous and even lethal materials.

## Ellipses

Use ellipsis points (. . .) to indicate that you have used only part of a quotation.

EXAMPLE According to Goethe, "One ought, everyday, to hear a song, read a fine poem, and **. . .** speak a few reasonable words."

### Editing Checklist

- ✔ Have you correctly used capitalization and quotation marks when directly quoting people or sources in your essay?
- ✔ Have you correctly used underlining and italics or quotation marks for titles of works?
- ✔ Have you correctly used commas and ellipses?

## Process of Writing a Persuasive Essay

Writing is like learning how to skate; you pick up a few skills at a time, and sometimes forget how to do one or two, but with practice you eventually learn all you need to know. There is always an opportunity to go back and polish your skills. The following list includes ideas and tips that may be useful as you write. The numbers in parentheses refer to pages where you can get help.

### PREWRITING

- Use brainstorming, freewriting, or clustering to identify subjects about which you have strong opinions. *(pages C406–C407)*
- Develop a thesis statement that states your opinion. Then collect the evidence needed to support it. *(pages C408–C409)*
- Use your own experiences and reliable authorities to verify facts. *(pages C392–C393)*
- Develop an argument by listing pros and cons, facts and examples, and counterarguments. *(pages C409–C411)*
- Construct an argument by using logical reasoning: inductive and/or deductive. *(pages C395–C403)*
- Avoid hasty generalizations, glittering generalities, unsound syllogisms, and invalid syllogisms. *(pages C397–C401)*

### DRAFTING

- Draft an introduction that presents the issue and states your opinion in the thesis statement. *(page C413)*
- Draft the body of the essay, presenting facts, reasons, statistics, incidents, examples, the testimony of experts, and other kinds of evidence to support your opinion. *(page C413)*
- Draft a conclusion that provides a summary and a strong closing that drives home your opinion. *(page C413)*

### REVISING

- Revise to eliminate logical fallacies—including false analogies and *non sequiturs*. *(pages C416–C420)*
- Use the Evaluation Checklist for Revising. *(page C420–C421)*

### EDITING

- Use the editing checklists to correct errors in grammar, spelling, usage and mechanics. *(pages C46 and C424)*

### PUBLISHING

- Follow standard manuscript form and make a neat final copy of your work. Then publish your essay in an appropriate form. *(page C422)*

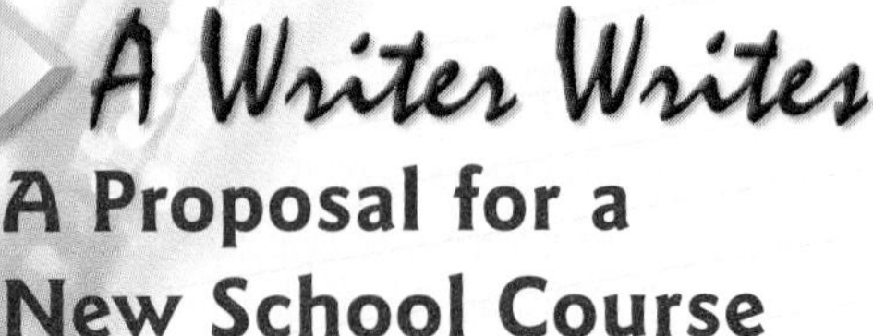

## A Proposal for a New School Course

**Purpose:** **to persuade your school administration to offer a specific new course**

**Audience:** **your school community**

### Prewriting

What subjects do you wish were offered at your school? Why? For example, would you like to learn how to be a wise shopper? Influence television programming? Buy stocks? Help the environment? Choose a career? Fix a car? Identify the stars? Speak Japanese? Prepare to write a letter to be printed in the school newspaper in which you present a favorable evaluation of a course of interest to you. Your letter will also be sent to the principal and other school officials. Your purpose will be to persuade school officials to offer the course.

To help you explore some subjects, brainstorm or free-write completions to the following sentences. Use your imagination to include subjects that are challenging and original.

1. If I could study anything I like, I would study . . .
2. It is important for young people today to understand . . .
3. After I graduate, I will need to know how to . . .

Speak to students at other schools and find out what different or unusual courses are offered in your area. Then explore in a library what courses are taught in other states and in other countries. After you review all your notes, list the subjects that interest you most. For each subject, jot down facts, examples, and reasons to support its being taught. For example, is it practical? Will it motivate students to do more? Will it help students cope in today's world? Is it something from which students can derive benefit throughout their lives?

Choose a subject that you can support effectively and write about enthusiastically.

Write a one-sentence thesis in the form of a recommendation that a certain subject should be offered at your school.

Speak to teachers and other students to find out their reactions to your recommendation. Then build an argument to support it, using the guidelines on page C409.

Organize your ideas in outline form based on order of importance or developmental order.

## Drafting

Draft your letter, keeping your audience and purpose in mind. Remember that you are addressing adults in a position of authority and choose your language, tone, and content accordingly. Feel free to make use of humor, persuasive language, and emotional appeals, but suit all of these to your audience and back them with facts.

## Revising

Try to read your letter to one or more adult listeners and ask for suggestions. Do your listeners find the letter persuasive? Can they spot any logical fallacies? Then use the **Evaluation Checklist for Revising** on pages C420–C421 to go over your work.

## Editing

Go over your letter for grammatical and mechanical errors, using the **Editing Checklists** on pages C46 and C424.

## Publishing

Copy your draft neatly in appropriate letter form and submit it to your school newspaper.

# Connection Collection

## Representing in Different Ways

***From Print . . .***

5150 Wacky Lane
Crazyville, KS 66033
January 23, 2001

The President of the United
States of America
The White House
1600 Pennsylvania Avenue
Washington, DC 20500-0001

Dear Mr. President:

In the past four months the percentage of Americans under the age of 21 who have reported thumb soreness has risen by 400 percent. In January, 2,500 cases were reported; in February, 4,250; in March, 6,500; in April, 10,000.

As executive director of National Union for Thumb Safety (NUTS), I believe that the increase in thumb injuries is a direct result of today's young people spending far too much time playing video games.

We at NUTS are intensely concerned about this phenomenon. The long-term implications of these thumb injuries are frightening indeed. Young people who injure their thumbs early in life may develop serious problems as they grow older. For example, individuals with improperly functioning thumbs may have difficulty giving the "thumbs-up" sign when they feel great.

We strongly urge you to support a new piece of legislation in the Congress that will make all video games illegal.

Sincerely,
*Thomas Thumb*
Thomas Thumb

***. . . to Visuals***

From the above text, create a line graph illustrating the increase in thumb injuries over the past six months.

*From Visuals . . .*

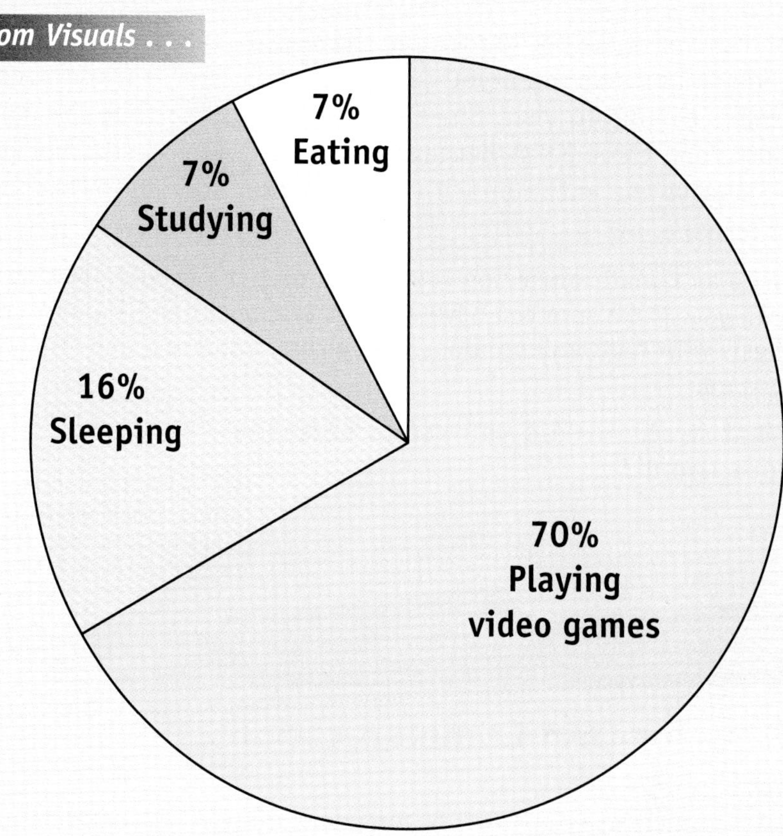


*. . . to Print*

The above chart represents the average day of a typical teenager in Crazyville, KS. Using the information from the chart, write a letter to the teenagers of Crazyville to convince them that such use of their time is unwise.

- **Which strategies can be used for creating both written and visual representations? Which strategies apply to one, not both? Which type of representation is more effective?**
- **Draw a conclusion and write briefly about the differences between written ideas and visual representations.**

## Writing in Everyday Life

### *Persuasive E-mail*

You and Oliver, your pet guinea pig, have just moved into a tiny one-room apartment when you receive a letter from a friend who says she is coming to visit. She mentions in passing that she plans to bring along three Saint Bernards, six cats, and Godzilla, her pet emu. She says the entire bunch is planning on staying for six weeks or more.

**Write an E-mail convincing your friend that she should not stay with you. Make sure you have a thesis statement and support your thesis with facts and opinions. Be sincere, unbiased, and straightforward.**

**What strategies did you use to persuade your friend?**

*You can find information on writing E-mail in* A Writer's Guide to Using the Internet, *pages C828–C833.*

## Writing for Oral Communication

### *Persuasive Speech*

The city council in your town is considering banning skateboarders from the city parks. You love skateboarding and are very upset about the prospect of the skateboarders being banned. The city council is holding a meeting on the future of skateboards in the park. You have decided to attend the meeting and speak on why you feel skateboarding should be allowed in city parks.

**Prepare a persuasive speech to be delivered to the city council supporting your contention that skateboarding should be allowed in city parks. Remember to acknowledge opposing views. Also remember to avoid making hasty generalizations and using false analogies.**

**What strategies did you use to persuade the city council?**

*You can find information on writing speeches on pages C672–C680.*

# Assess Your Learning

At the high school you attend a group of students who are upset by the performance of the soccer team has been circulating a petition to have the name of the team changed. The soccer team has been named the Lions for over thirty years, and you do not see any good reason for changing it, whether it wins or not. The group of dissatisfied students, however, wants the team name changed to the Weasels. You think this is an awful idea.

**Write a letter to the school board convincing them not to change the name of the soccer team. Remember to have a thesis statement and to support your thesis statement with reasons, facts, and examples. Also remember to avoid logical fallacies such as *ad hominem* attacks.**

*Before You Write* **Consider the following questions:**
What is the ***situation?***
What is the ***occasion?***
Who is the ***audience?***
What is the ***purpose?***

*After You Write* **Evaluate your work using the following criteria:**

- Do you have a thesis statement? What is it?
- Have you supported your thesis statement with facts, examples, and expert opinions?
- Have you acknowledged opposing viewpoints and conceded points?
- Have you used opinion words such as *good, better,* and *best* or *bad, worse,* and *worst*?
- Have you used transitions for persuasive writing such as *although* and *however* and *admittedly*? How effectively were these transitions used?
- Have you avoided *ad hominem* attacks?
- Have you avoided biased and emotionally charged words?

**Write briefly on how well you did. Point out your strengths and areas for improvement.**

CHAPTER 10

# Writing About Literature

When you read a book to entertain yourself on a long trip, see a play on a date, or attend a poetry reading, you most likely have a personal response to the work. You may find the book disappointingly dull, the play romantic, or the poetry hilarious. When you discuss, think, and write about literature, you consider the reasons behind your response. The dialogue in the book may be stilted and forced; the setting for the play may be the lush countryside of Italy; the imagery in the poems may be outrageously funny. Whether or not you realize it, you are analyzing the work—breaking it down and examining each part. You are also evaluating the work—determining its meaning and judging its value for you.

As you analyze and evaluate the short stories in this chapter, you will uncover many insights about literature.

## *Reading with a Writer's Eye*

Most people have heard an older relative or friend talk about "the good old days." For some, the past was a time when people were more respectful and businesses better served their customers. In John Galsworthy's "Quality," the narrator experiences such changes. Read the story for pleasure. Then reread it and consider how the narrator's experience relates to changes in quality you've heard about and observed for yourself.

# QUALITY

*John Galsworthy*

I knew him from the days of my extreme youth, because he made my father's boots; inhabiting with his elder brother two little shops let into one, in a small by-street—now no more, but then most fashionably placed in the West End.

That tenement had a certain quiet distinction; there was no sign upon its face that he made for any of the Royal Family—merely his own German name of Gessler Brothers; and in the window a few pairs of boots. I remember that it always troubled me to account for those unvarying boots in the window, for he made only what was ordered, reaching nothing down, and it seemed so inconceivable that what he made could ever have failed to fit. Had he bought them to put there? That, too, seemed inconceivable. He would never have tolerated in his house leather on which he had not worked himself. Besides, they were too beautiful—the pair of pumps, so inexpressibly slim, the patent leathers with cloth tops, making water come into one's mouth, the tall brown riding-boots with marvelous sooty glow, as if, though new, they had been worn a hundred years. Those pairs would only have been made by one who saw before him the Soul of Boot—so truly were they prototypes, incarnating the very spirit of all footwear. These thoughts, of course, came to me later, though even when I was promoted to him, at the age of perhaps fourteen, some inkling haunted me of the dignity of himself and brother. For to make boots—such boots as he made—seemed to me then, and still seems to me, mysterious and wonderful.

I remember well my shy remark, one day, while stretching out to him my youthful foot:

"Isn't it awfully hard to do, Mr. Gessler?"

And his answer, given with a sudden smile from out of the sardonic redness of his beard: "Id is an Ardt!"

Himself, he was a little as if made of leather, with his yellow crinkly face, and crinkly reddish hair and beard, and neat folds slanting down his cheeks to the corners of his mouth, and his guttural and one-toned voice; for leather is a sardonic substance, and stiff and slow of purpose. And that was the character of his face, save that his eyes, which were gray-blue, had in them the simple gravity of one secretly possessed by the Ideal. His elder brother was so very like him—though watery, paler in every way, with a great industry—that sometimes in early days I was not quite sure of him until the interview was over. Then I knew that it was he, if the words, "I will ask my brudder," had not been spoken, and that, if they had, it was the elder brother.

When one grew old and wild and ran up bills, one somehow never ran them up with Gessler Brothers. It would not have seemed becoming to go in there and stretch out one's foot to that blue iron-spectacled face, owing him for more than—say—two pairs, just the comfortable reassurance that one was still his client.

For it was not possible to go to him very often—his boots lasted terribly, having something beyond the temporary—some, as it were, essence of boot—stitched into them.

One went in, not as into most shops, in the mood of: "Please serve me, and let me go!" but restfully, as one enters a church; and, sitting on the single wooden chair, waited—for there was never anybody there. Soon—over the top edge of that sort of well—rather dark, and smelling soothingly of leather—which formed the shop, there would be seen his face, or that of his elder brother, peering down. A guttural sound, and the tip-tap of bast slippers beating the narrow wooden stairs, and he would stand before one without coat, a little bent, in leather apron, with sleeves turned back, blinking—as if awakened from some dream of boots, or like an owl surprised in daylight and annoyed at this interruption.

And I would say: "How do you do, Mr. Gessler? Could you make me a pair of Russia leather boots?"

Without a word he would leave me, retiring whence he came, or into the other portion of the shop, and I would continue to rest in the wooden chair, inhaling the incense of his trade. Soon he would come back, holding in his thin, veined hand a piece of gold-brown leather. With eyes fixed on it, he would remark: "What a beaudiful biece!" When I, too, had admired it, he would speak again. "When do you wand dem?" And I would answer: "Oh! As soon as conveniently can." And he would say: "Tomorrow fordnighd?" Or if he were his elder brother: "I will ask my brudder!"

Then I would murmur: "Thank you! Good-morning, Mr. Gessler." "Goot-morning!" he would reply, still looking at the leather in his hand. And as I moved to the door, I would hear the tip-tap of his bast slippers restoring him, up the stairs, to his dream of boots. But if it were some new kind of foot-gear that he had not yet made me, then indeed he would observe ceremony—divesting me of my boot and holding it long in his hand, looking at it with eyes at once critical and loving, as if recalling the glow with which he had created it, and rebuking the way in which one had disorganized this masterpiece. Then, placing my foot on a piece of paper, he would two or three times tickle the outer edges with a pencil and pass his nervous fingers over my toes, feeling himself into the heart of my requirements.

I cannot forget that day on which I had occasion to say to him: "Mr. Gessler, that last pair of town walking-boots creaked, you know."

He looked at me for a time without replying, as if expecting me to withdraw or qualify the statement, then said:

"Id shouldn't 'ave greaked."

"It did, I'm afraid."

"You goddem wed before dey found demselves?"

"I don't think so."

At that he lowered his eyes, as if hunting for memory of those boots, and I felt sorry I had mentioned this grave thing.

"Zend dem back!" he said; "I will look at dem."

A feeling of compassion for my creaking boots surged up in me, so well could I imagine the sorrowful long curiosity of regard which he would bend on them.

"Zome boods," he said slowly, "are bad from birdt. If I can do noding wid dem, I dake dem off your bill."

Once (once only) I went absent-mindedly into his shop, in a pair of boots bought in an emergency at some large firm's. He took my order without showing me any leather, and I could feel his eyes penetrating the inferior integument[1] of my foot. At last he said:

"Dose are nod my boods."

The tone was not one of anger, nor of sorrow, not even of contempt, but there was in it something quiet that froze the blood. He put his hand down and pressed a finger on the place where the left boot, endeavoring to be fashionable, was not quite comfortable.

"Id 'urds you dere," he said. "Dose big virms 'ave no self-respect. Drash!" And then, as if something had given way within him, he spoke long and bitterly. It was the only time I ever heard him discuss the conditions and hardships of his trade.

"Dey get id all," he said, "dey get id by adverdisement, nod by work. Dey dake id away from us, who lofe our boods. Id gomes to this—bresently I haf no work. Every year id gets less—you will see." And looking at his lined face I saw things I had never noticed before, bitter things and bitter struggle—and what a lot of gray hairs there seemed suddenly in his red beard!

As best I could, I explained the circumstances of the purchase of those ill-omened boots. But his face and voice made a so deep impression that during the next few minutes I ordered many pairs! Nemesis fell! They lasted more terribly than ever. And I was not able conscientiously to go to him for nearly two years.

---

[1] **integument:** Covering.

When at last I went I was surprised that outside one of the two little windows of his shop another name was painted, also that of a bootmaker—making, of course, for the Royal Family. The old familiar boots, no longer in dignified isolation, were huddled in the single window. Inside, the now contracted well of the one little shop was more scented and darker than ever. And it was longer than usual, too, before a face peered down, and the tip-tap of the bast slippers began. At last he stood before me, and, gazing through those rusty iron spectacles, said:

"Mr.—, isn'd id?"

"Ah! Mr. Gessler," I stammered, "but your boots are really *too* good, you know! See, these are quite decent still!" And I stretched out to him my foot. He looked at it.

"Yes," he said, "beople do nod wand good boods, id seems."

To get away from his reproachful eyes and voice I hastily remarked: "What have you done to your shop?"

He answered quietly: "Id was too exbensif. Do you wand some boods?"

I ordered three pairs, though I had only wanted two, and quickly left. I had, I know not quite what feeling of being part, in his mind, of a conspiracy against him; or not perhaps so much against him as against his idea of boot. One does not, I suppose, care to feel like that; for it was again many months before my next visit to his shop, paid I remember, with the feeling: "Oh! well, I can't leave the old boy—so here goes! Perhaps it'll be his elder brother!"

For his elder brother, I knew, had not character enough to reproach me, even dumbly.

And, to my relief, in the shop there did appear to be his elder brother, handling a piece of leather.

"Well, Mr. Gessler," I said, "how are you?"

He came close, and peered at me.

"I am breddy well," he said slowly; "but my elder brudder is dead."

And I saw that it was indeed himself—but how aged and wan! And never before had I heard him mention his brother. Much shocked, I murmured: "Oh! I am sorry!"

"Yes," he answered, "he was a good man, he made a good bood; but he is dead." And he touched the top of his head, where the hair had suddenly gone as thin as it had been on that of his poor brother, to indicate, I suppose, the cause of death. "He could nod ged over losing de oder shop. Do you wand any boods?" And he held up the leather in his hand: "Id's a beaudiful biece."

I ordered several pairs. It was very long before they came—but they were better than ever. One simply could not wear them out. And soon after that I went abroad.

It was over a year before I was again in London. And the first shop I went to was my old friend's. I had left a man of sixty, I came back to find one of seventy-five, pinched and worn and tremulous, who genuinely, this time, did not at first know me.

"Oh! Mr. Gessler," I said, sick at heart; "how splendid your boots are! See, I've been wearing this pair nearly all the time I've been abroad; and they're not half worn out, are they?"

He looked long at my boots—a pair of Russia leather, and his face seemed to regain its steadiness. Putting his hand on my instep, he said:

"Do dey vid you here? I 'ad drouble wid dat bair, I remember."

I assured him that they had fitted beautifully.

"Do you wand any boods?" he said. "I can make dem quickly; id is a slack dime."

I answered: "Please, please! I want boots all round—every kind!"

"I will make a vresh model. Your food must be bigger." And with utter slowness, he traced round my foot, and felt my toes, only once looking up to say:

"Did I dell you my brudder was dead?"

To watch him was quite painful, so feeble had he grown; I was glad to get away.

I had given those boots up, when one evening they came. Opening the parcel, I set the four pairs out in a row. Then one by one I tried them on. There was no doubt about it. In shape and fit, in finish and quality of leather, they were the best he had ever made me. And in the mouth of one of the town walking-boots I found his bill. The amount was the same as usual, but it gave me quite a shock. He had never before sent it in until quarter day. I flew downstairs and wrote a check, and posted it at once with my own hand.

A week later, passing the little street, I thought I would go in and tell him how splendidly the new boots fitted. But when I came to where his shop had been, his name was gone. Still there, in the window, were the slim pumps, the patent leathers with cloth tops, the sooty riding-boots.

I went in, very much disturbed. In the two little shops—again made in one—was a young man with an English face.

"Mr. Gessler in?" I said.

He gave me a strange, ingratiating look.

"No, sir," he said, "no. But we can attend to anything with pleasure. We've taken the shop over. You've seen our name, no doubt, next door. We make for some very good people."

"Yes, yes," I said, "but Mr. Gessler?"

"Oh!" he answered; "dead."

"Dead! But I only received these boots from him last Wednesday week."

"Ah!" he said; "a shockin' go. Poor old man starved 'imself."

"Good God!"

"Slow starvation, the doctor called it! You see he went to work in such a way! Would keep the shop on; wouldn't have a soul touch his boots except himself. When he got an order, it took him such a time. People won't wait. He lost everybody. And there he'd sit, goin' on and on—I will say that for him—not a man in London made a better boot! But look at the competition! He never advertised! Would 'ave the best leather, too, and do it all 'imself. Well, there it is. What could you expect with his ideas?"

"But starvation—!"

"That may be a bit flowery, as the sayin' is but I know myself he was sittin' over his boots day and night, to the very last. You see, I used to watch him. Never gave 'imself time to eat; never had a penny in the house. All went in rent and leather. How he lived so long I don't know. He regular let his fire go out. He was a character. But he made good boots."

"Yes," I said, "he made good boots."

# Thinking as a Writer

## Understanding the Writer's Purpose

- Why do you think John Galsworthy wrote "Quality"? What is he attempting to say about society's standards, or idea of quality?
- With your idea of Galsworthy's purpose in mind, write an alternate title for the short story. For example, if you think Galsworthy wants to emphasize that the old must always give way to the new, you might title the story "Hello to the New."

## Analyzing Visual Evidence of Change

Viewing

- Using evidence from the story and your own experiences and ideas, list the ways in which these two photographs show different ideas of quality and value.
- Which picture is closer to Galsworthy's concept of quality? Which is closer to your idea of value?

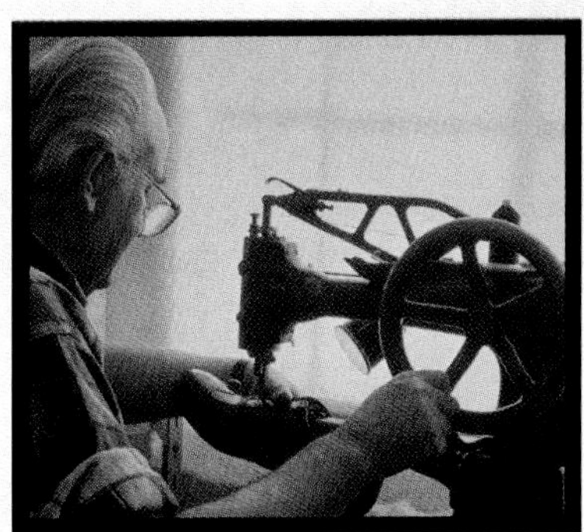

## Evaluating Character

Oral Expression

- Form groups of three or more and discuss how Mr. Gessler in "Quality" represents one set of values, while the young bootmaker at the end of the story represents another. What are the pros and cons for each?
- Work with a partner and play the roles of the old bootmaker and the young bootmaker. Debate one another, defending each character's set of values.

# The Power of Literary Analysis

In thinking about the author's purpose, analyzing visual evidence of change, and evaluating characters' viewpoints, you have begun thinking critically about a work of literature.

## Uses of Literary Analysis

**Here are some examples of how the skills of thinking, writing, and speaking about literature are used both in school and in life.**

- **Students read and analyze passages from works of literature** for college admissions tests, standardized tests, and class tests.
- **An innovative theater group decides to perform a well-known play as a musical.** They transform the dialogue into songs and include interpretive dance numbers to express certain scenes.
- **A group forms a club to read and discuss books** as well as to share experiences, and to socialize.
- **An Internet entertainment magazine previews one chapter of an author's upcoming memoir.** Readers are invited to chat online with the author about the experiences she relates in the book.
- **A critic for a literary magazine reviews the poetry he heard at a poetry reading.** He comments on the style, effectiveness, and technique of each poet, and recommend his favorite poems.

# Process of Writing a Literary Analysis

"To read without reflecting is like eating without digesting," declares Sir Francis Bacon in his essay "Of Studies." A work of literature that is read but not considered in a thoughtful manner is as ineffectual as a meal that is eaten but not digested. The story or play or poem fulfills its purpose when you, the reader, respond to the work—personalize, analyze, and evaluate it—and determine the significance of the work for yourself and for other readers. By writing about the works of literature in this chapter, you will master the process that allows you to digest literature. By learning how to write about literature, you will learn methods that help you better appreciate literary forms.

A **literary analysis** presents an interpretation of a work of literature and supports that interpretation with appropriate responses, details, quotations, and commentaries.

The structure of a literary analysis is shown in the following chart. As you will see, it has the same basic structure as other kinds of essays.

| STRUCTURE OF A LITERARY ANALYSIS | |
|---|---|
| **Title** | Identifies which aspect of the work the writer will focus on |
| **Introduction** | Names the author and the work<br>Contains a thesis statement expressing an interpretation of some aspect of the work |
| **Body** | Supports the thesis statement with responses, details from the work, quotations from respected sources, and commentary |
| **Conclusion** | Summarizes, clarifies, or adds an insight to the thesis statement |

**Your Writer's Journal**

For school and personal enjoyment, you have read many works of literature. Think of a story, a play, and a poem that stand out in your memory. In your journal, write down each of their titles. Draw some general conclusions about the works you find most meaningful and enjoyable. When you write a literary analysis in this chapter, you will be evaluating the works based partly on what you find most valuable. Your journal notes will give you a head start on deciding which works are most significant for you.

# Prewriting

**Writing Process**

The meaning of a literary work is not found on the pages alone. Part of its meaning is to be found in you—in the experiences and knowledge you bring to whatever you read.

In this way, reading is a two-way process. The author makes a statement and you respond. Because your background, knowledge, and personal experiences are unique, the meaning of a work will also be unique to you. To uncover that meaning, you need to look inside yourself as you read—to become aware of your reactions and the reasons for them.

## Responding from Personal Experience

When have you been affected by a story or poem? Perhaps you were moved by characters or situations that reminded you of your own life. Perhaps you were intrigued by strange, faraway worlds or disturbed by a conflict that was resolved in a way that you found disappointing or unreal.

Reading sets up a special relationship between you and the writer. A writer's words can leap off the page into your mind and memory, where they take on a meaning that is special to you. Your response will not always be positive, however; you may even feel annoyed, confused, or uninterested. Both negative and positive responses serve as starting points for expressing your ideas about a work of literature. Reading, as a result, becomes a richer experience.

The strategies below will help you identify feelings and memories that can enrich your reading. When you use these strategies, record your responses in your **journal**.

### Personal Response Strategies

1. Freewrite answers to the following questions:
   - **a.** Which character do you identify with most closely? Why? How do your feelings about that character change?
   - **b.** How do certain characters remind you of people you know?
   - **c.** Would you behave the same way as certain characters?
   - **d.** How are plot situations like or unlike situations in your life?
   - **e.** What feelings does the work evoke? How did it move you? Why?
2. Write a personal response statement that explains what the work means to you. Use any form that allows you to express your response comfortably.
3. In small discussion groups, share your reactions to the questions in item 1 above. Listen carefully to the reactions of others; compare and contrast them with your own. Be open to other points of view that may convince you of a new way to look at the work. Later, write freely about how and why the discussion affected your ideas.

## PRACTICE YOUR SKILLS

### *Responding from Personal Experience*

**Answer the following questions about John Galsworthy's "Quality," on pages C433–C440.**

1. Do see yourself in any character? Why or why not?
2. How would you feel if you were the narrator? How would you behave?
3. Which character reminds you of someone you know? How?
4. Do the events in the story remind you of anything in your own life? How was your experience similar? Different?

## Communicate Your Ideas

**PREWRITING** *Personal Response*

Read the excerpt from the story "First Love," by Vladimir Nabokov, on pages C281–C283. After you have read the story, use the questions in the Personal Response Strategies chart on the preceding page to freewrite a personal response to the story. Save your work for later use.

SAVE YOUR WORK

## Responding from Literary Knowledge

In a sense you already are a literary critic, for you usually approach a piece of literature with certain expectations. You base these expectations on your past experience and on your knowledge from reading other stories, poems, or plays.

When you respond to literature on the basis of your literary knowledge, you analyze the elements—the characteristics—of a literary work. The way you approach a work, of course, will depend on the type of work it is—fiction, poetry, or drama. Although each type has its own set of elements, there is much that overlaps. For example, plot is critical in fiction, but it is also important in drama and some poetry. Dialogue is basic to drama, but it also has a place in fiction and sometimes in poetry.

The following chart lists the main elements and their functions according to fiction, poetry, and drama. Since drama shares many of the same elements as fiction, the elements listed under drama pertain only to the reading of a dramatic work.

| ELEMENTS OF LITERATURE | |
|---|---|
| | **FICTION** |
| **Plot** | events that lead up to a **climax**, or high point, and resolve the central **conflict** or explain the outcome |
| **Setting** | when and where the story takes place |
| **Characters** | people in the story whose thoughts and actions move the events forward |

| | |
|---|---|
| **Dialogue** | conversations among characters that reveal personalities, actions, and **motivations** or reasons characters behave as they do |
| **Tone** | the author's attitude toward the events and the characters |
| **Mood** | the prevalent feeling or **atmosphere** in a piece of literature |
| **Irony** | the occurrence of the opposite of what is expected; can be verbal, dramatic, or situational |
| **Point of View** | the "voice" telling the story: first person (*I*) or third person (*she* or *he*) |
| **Theme** | the main idea or message of the story |

## POETRY

| | |
|---|---|
| **Persona** | the person whose "voice" is saying the poem |
| **Meter** | the pattern of stressed and unstressed syllables in each line |
| **Rhyme Scheme** | the pattern of rhymed sounds in a poem, or at the end of each line |
| **Sound Devices** | ways in which sounds are used to create certain effects, such as **onomatopoeia**<br>*You may wish to read more about sound devices on page C317.* |
| **Figures of Speech** | imaginative language, such as **similes** and **metaphors**<br>*You may wish to read more about figures of speech on pages C319–C321.* |
| **Imagery** | expressions that appeal to the senses |
| **Symbols** | objects or events that stand for other things |
| **Allusions** | references to persons or events in literature or in the past |
| **Shape** | the way a poem looks on the printed page, which may contribute to the poem's overall meaning |
| **Theme** | the overall feeling or underlying meaning of the poem |

| DRAMA | |
|---|---|
| **Setting** | the time and place of the action; lighting and the stage sets, as described in the stage directions |
| **Characters** | the people who participate in the action of the play |
| **Plot** | the story of the play divided into acts and scenes and developed through the characters' words and actions |
| **Theme** | the meaning of a play, revealed through the setting and the characters' words and actions |

**How Literary Elements Contribute to Meaning** Plot, character, dialogue, setting—these and other literary elements contribute to the meaning of a work. Therefore, when you analyze a work, you break it down into various elements. In poetry, for example, you would examine how the rhyme scheme, figures of speech, and certain other elements contribute to the meaning of a poem. The following groups of questions will help you to explore the meaning of a short story or a novel, a poem, or a play.

### Questions for Finding Meaning in Fiction

#### Plot

- What is the significance of each main event in the development of the plot? How does each event in the plot affect the main characters?
- Which details in the plot reveal the central conflict?
- What do the climax and the ending reveal about the theme?

#### Setting

- How does the setting contribute to the tone or mood of the story? How do details of the setting help define the characters?
- Which details of the setting are most important in the development of the plot? How do these details relate to the theme?

**Characters**

- How do the characters relate to their setting?
- How does each character contribute to the plot development?
- How are the characters revealed by their thoughts, actions, words, or others' actions toward them?
- How does the point of view of the story affect the characterizations?
- What does the point of view contribute to the theme?

**Theme**

- What passages and details in the story best express the main theme? What other story elements contribute to the meaning?
- How does the author communicate the theme through the development of setting, characters, and plot?
- Does this theme have meaning for you? What else have you read that has a similar theme?

## Questions for Finding Meaning in Poetry

- What is the poet's persona? How does the persona relate to the subject, mood, and theme of the poem?
- How does the meter affect the rhythm of the poem? How does that rhythm express the mood?
- How does the rhyme scheme affect the expression of thoughts and feelings?
- If the poet uses sound devices like alliteration and onomatopoeia, what sounds do you hear in the poem? What images do those sound devices create in your mind?
- What images do the figures of speech create? What feelings do those images suggest?
- How does the shape of the poem relate to the subject, mood, or theme?
- What effect does the poem have on you? How does the poem achieve its effect?
- What feeling, theme, or message does the poem express? What meaning does the poem have for you?

### Questions for Finding Meaning in Drama

- What details of setting and character do the stage directions emphasize? How do those details add to the impact of the play?
- What are the key relationships among the characters? How do those relationships reveal the central conflict? What changes in the relationships help resolve the conflict?
- How does the dialogue advance the plot? What plot developments occur with each change of act and scene?
- What subject and theme are treated in the play? What in the play has meaning for you?

**Evaluating a Literary Work** When you analyze a piece of literature, you make judgments about the work. You set standards for each element and judge how well those standards are met. To evaluate a work, you do not simply ask, "Is it good?" Instead, you use the standards for each literary element to break the question down into more specific questions, such as "Does the plot build to a high point?" and "Does the setting fit the story?" As you build your evaluating skills, you will gain an increased appreciation not only of the literature but also of the techniques that go into its creation. Because there are different standards of evaluation, you may find it helpful to know the following criteria by which great literature—a **classic**—is usually judged.

### Some Characteristics of Great Literature

- Explores great themes in human nature and the human experience that many people can identify with—such as growing up, family life, personal struggles, or war
- Expresses universal values—such as truth or hope—to which people from many different backgrounds and cultures can relate
- Conveys a timeless message that remains true for many generations of readers
- Presents vivid impressions of characters, settings, and situations that many generations of readers can treasure

If a literary work you are reading is not regarded as a classic, you can apply other standards of evaluation. For example, when you are making judgments about a work, use the questions below to help you evaluate it.

### Questions for Evaluating Literature

- How effectively does the writing achieve the purpose?
- How vividly and believably are the characters, settings, dialogue, actions, and feelings portrayed?
- In fiction, how well structured is the plot? Does it contain a satisfying resolution of the central conflict?
- How strongly did you react to the work?
- Did you identify with a character, situation, or feeling?
- Did the work evoke any memories or emotions?
- Did the work have meaning for you? Will you remember anything about it a year from now?

## Practice Your Skills

### *Responding from Literary Knowledge*

**Answer the following questions about "Quality" on pages C433–C440.**

1. What is the central conflict? What are the key events? How is the story finally resolved?
2. Describe the main setting. How does it create a suitable backdrop for the events? What does it add to the story?
3. Describe the tone. What is the author's approach to the events and characters?
4. Describe the mood of the story. How do the characters reflect the mood?
5. Describe the main character, Mr. Gessler. How does the narrator feel about him?
6. How would you describe the narrator? What is his impact on the story?

7. From what point of view is the story told? How might it have been different if told from a different point of view?
8. What is the underlying theme of the story?
9. How well does the author convey the theme through the characters and plot?
10. Do the characters, dialogue, and plot seem believable? How vividly are the setting and the feelings portrayed?
11. How do the different elements fit together? How do they convey meaning?
12. What is the meaning for you? Was your response to the story positive or negative? Why?

## Communicate Your Ideas

### PREWRITING *Literary Response*

In your **journal,** freewrite a literary response to "First Love." Using the list on pages C446–C447, identify the literary elements the writer uses to evoke your individual response. How does the setting or theme or plot or imagery influence how you interpret the story? Save your work for later use.

**Time Out to Reflect**

Now that you have explored your personal and literary responses to the story "Quality," take a moment to think about the thoughts and ideas that overlapped between the two. Understanding the connections will help you come up with a subject that you will be able to communicate clearly.

## Making Inferences

When you write about literature, you will find that there are a variety of elements about which to write. For example, from the story "Quality" you could focus on the motivation of the bootmaker, Mr. Gessler. But to figure out the bootmaker's motivation, you would have to make **inferences.** That is, you would have to make reasonable guesses about his motivation, basing your guesses on clues in the story.

A reliable method of making inferences is to recall and apply your own experience. Suppose you read in a story, "The man's bushy eyebrows gathered in a frown." In your own experience, you have seen people gather their eyebrows together in a frown. You can thus infer that the character is displeased.

The following chart shows how you can make inferences about the motivation of the bootmaker in "Quality."

### INFERENCE CHART

| Type of Clue | Clue |
|---|---|
| Description of the character | "Himself, he was a little as if made of leather, with his yellow crinkly face, and crinkly reddish hair and beard. . . ." |
| Statements about the character | ". . . he would stand before one without coat, a little bent . . . blinking–as if awakened from some dream of boots." |
| Character's own words | "Zome boots," he said slowly, "are bad from birdt. If I can do noding wid dem, I dake dem off you bill." |
| Other characters' words | "He was a character. But, he made good boots. . . ." |

**Inference:** Mr. Gessler was a bootmaker who was concerned with the art of making perfect boots, not with the business of selling boots.

### THINKING PRACTICE

**Make an inference chart like the one above to explain the motivation of the narrator in "Quality."**

## Choosing a Subject

By the time you have explored your personal and literary responses, you have not only become familiar with the work, but you have also accumulated some writing ideas. Your next task is to review your ideas and focus on ones that seem especially suitable as a subject for a literary analysis.

Unless you have been assigned a subject by your teacher, you will have a wide choice of possible subjects. To narrow the choice, first determine what subjects appeal to you personally. By asking yourself the following questions, you may be able to locate ideas that spark your interest.

### Questions for Choosing a Subject

- What parts of the work puzzle me? What would I like to understand better?
- What parts of the work do I find moving? Surprising? Disappointing? Why do they have that effect on me?
- What details or images made a strong impression on me? What do they contribute to the overall work?
- With which character do I most identify? Why?
- How do the characters differ from one another? What motivates each one?
- What does the work "say" to me? What message does it convey? What insight or understanding have I gained from it?
- What other works does this remind me of? How are the works similar? How are they different?

Since you probably have dealt with some of these questions in your previous responses, review your answers to the questions together with all your other notes. As you do, search for subjects that catch your interest. Be on the lookout especially for ideas that come up more than once. These are apt to be topics that strike a chord and that are probably worth exploring further.

A helpful procedure as you search for a topic is to synthesize, or combine, your personal and literary responses. First, zero in on some strong personal reaction.

For example, suppose that the story "Quality" brought to mind an older relative who frequently talks about how things were better in the past. This personal response to the story can provide the beginning of an essay subject. To make this idea for a subject more specific, you need to synthesize, or bring together, your personal response with your literary response to the story. To do so, think about the elements of the story that have to do with the change of values from past to present. Some elements from "Quality" related to this theme are as follows.

- Mr. Gessler carefully crafts each boot, showing his respect for bootmaking as an art. (characterization)
- Mr. Gessler looks as if he is made of leather. (symbolism)
- Mr. Gessler loses business because he doesn't advertise. (plot)
- Mr. Gessler's brother dies of disappointment over the loss of business. (plot)
- Mr. Gessler says, "beople do nod wand good boods, id seems." (dialogue)

The theme of changing of values is developed through several elements. Thus, your subject for this literary essay would be the effects of a change in society's values. To develop that subject, you would analyze how the change of values theme is dramatized through several elements of the story.

For a literary analysis—as for everything you write—you need to consider not only your own background and interests but also those of your audience. In this case you can assume you are writing for an audience familiar with the work, usually your classmates or teacher.

## Practice Your Skills

### *Choosing Subjects*

**For each of the elements shown below, think of a possible subject for a literary analysis on the story "Quality."**

| | |
|---|---|
| Example | theme |
| Possible Answer | what the story says about the changing view of quality |

**1.** character **2.** mood **3.** plot **4.** point of view **5.** tone

Communicate Your Ideas

**PREWRITING** *Subject*

As you prepare to write a literary analysis of the excerpt from "First Love," consider what the story has to say about the relationship between the narrator and Collette. Your essay will deal with what the story has to say about the theme of relationships, but the specific approach and focus will be up to you to decide. Begin your search for that focus by reviewing your personal and literary responses to the story and the Questions for Choosing a Subject on page C454. Then synthesize your two sets of responses to help direct you toward a subject for your literary analysis. Save your work in your folder for later use.

## Limiting a Subject

After you have chosen a subject, you will probably have to narrow its scope to one that you can handle adequately in an essay. The first step in limiting your subject is to decide on the approach you want to take. Do you want to focus on content by analyzing one or more elements of the work, or do you want to focus on the author's presentation, analyzing some aspect of the writing style or technique? Once you have decided on the approach you want to take, start limiting your subject.

Usually the more you qualify a subject, the narrower you make it. Begin, then, by turning a one-word subject into a phrase or a short phrase into a longer one. As you work, ask yourself, "What do I want to say about the subject?" Your answers will lead you to an appropriately limited subject. Another option may be to focus on the author's choice of material. What did the author bring to the material out of his or her own unique experience? Conversely, there may be some elements of your personal response to the work that will help you limit your subject.

The model on the following page is an abbreviated version of the steps the writer went through to narrow the subject of an essay on the story "Quality."

**MODEL: Limiting a Subject**

| | |
|---|---|
| TOO GENERAL | How the theme is carried out |
| ASK | What do I want to say about how the theme is carried out? |
| POSSIBLE ANSWER | The writer uses the failure and death of the old bootmaker to show how society's interest in real quality is declining. |
| LIMITED SUBJECT | The author uses the decline of the bootmaker to portray the decline of standards in society. |

## PRACTICE YOUR SKILLS

### *Limiting Subjects*

**Narrow each of the following broad subjects to a suitably limited subject for a literary analysis of the story "Quality."**

| | |
|---|---|
| EXAMPLE | setting |
| LIMITED SUBJECT | how the writer uses details about the shop to help portray the bootmaker |

**1.** honesty
**2.** the narrator
**3.** dialogue
**4.** the bootmaker
**5.** tone

## *Communicate Your Ideas*

**PREWRITING** *Limited Subject*

Limit the subject you chose for your essay about "First Love" by asking yourself, "What do I want to say about the subject?" Save your work for later use.

## Developing a Thesis

A literary analysis is based on a **thesis**, or proposition, that states your interpretation of some aspect of a piece of literature. Because you bring your own experiences and reactions to a work, your interpretation will most likely be different from the interpretation of another reviewer. Your task, therefore, is to defend your proposition by presenting evidence that will convince the reader that your interpretation is valid.

A literary analysis, then, is not just a collection of hasty and careless reactions to a work but rather a carefully reasoned set of arguments. All of your arguments, if they relate to and support the limited subject you have chosen, can be refined to a concise statement that states your interpretation clearly—i.e., your thesis.

Once you have limited your subject, you are well on the way toward stating your thesis. In fact, if your limited subject is clear and specific, all you may have to do is rephrase it as a sentence. If you need to narrow your thesis further, you can use a technique like the one used for your limited subject. Keep asking yourself, "What exactly do I want to say about the subject as it relates to this story?" until you arrive at a statement that you can defend convincingly.

The thesis you develop in the prewriting stage is a working thesis only. It should be clear and specific enough to guide your thoughts, but it can be revised and even rewritten as you move deeper into your process of writing. For an essay on the story "Quality," one writer moved from the limited subject to the thesis shown below.

**Model: Developing a Thesis**

| | |
|---|---|
| **Limited Subject** | How the author uses the decline of the bootmaker to help portray the decline of standards in society |
| **Thesis** | In the short story "Quality," John Galsworthy uses the decline of a skilled bootmaker to show the general decline of standards in society. |

IN THE MEDIA

## Media Texts: The Art of Parody

The process of defining your thesis statement is one way in which writing a literary analysis helps deepen your understanding of a creative work. Another technique for exploring a work of art is to create a **parody,** or spoof. Parodies are funny only if they capture the essence of the original.

In the classic 1957 Swedish film by Ingmar Bergman called *The Seventh Seal,* a dejected knight returns from the Crusades in search of life's meaning. Death arrives in the form of the Grim Reaper, but the knight stalls him with a game of chess. The movie is a dark, haunting mystery.

Thirty-four years later, the film *Bill and Ted's Bogus Journey* included a parody of *The Seventh Seal.* When Bill and Ted meet the "Reaper Dude," they challenge him to a game of Battleship™ and note that "he has a lot to learn about sportsmanship."

### Media Activity

Working with a partner, choose a well-known work of entertainment to parody. One way to make your choice is to think about memorable characters with memorable flaws. For example, Hamlet's memorable flaw, among others, is his inability to make decisions. A parody of Hamlet might be a scene in which he is *almost* ready to commit murder but he just can not make up his mind.

Another way to choose a subject for a parody is to think of someone with a very distinctive style and to imagine how that artist would present someone else's work. For example, what would a movie version of *Hamlet* look like if it were created by the people at Pixar (*Toy Story*) or directed by Spike Lee?

When you have chosen your subject, refer to A Writer's Guide to Electronic Publishing, pages C799–C809, to produce your audio or video parody. Invite friends and family to an evening at school for a showing of the parody and follow-up discussion.

## Communicate Your Ideas

**PREWRITING** *Thesis*

Use your limited subject to develop a thesis statement for your literary analysis about the short story "First Love." This thesis should state exactly what you want to say about the story. Save your thesis statement for later use.

## Gathering Evidence

As you read, you automatically gather details and fit them into a pattern in your mind, basing that pattern on your own store of memories and facts. It is this pattern that allows you to make sense of what you read and that helps you form an impression of a work. Thus, the first time you read "Quality," whether or not you were aware of it, you were already noting details that eventually led you to your thesis. Now you need to return to the story to collect those details and gather others that can back up your thesis. This time go through the story with your thesis in mind and systematically look for supporting material. Dialogue, description, events, thoughts—anything you find in the story can be used as evidence.

While your arguments should be based on the story, you may want to seek additional support from works such as literary histories, author biographies, and collections of reviews. For outside sources use recognized and respected experts only. Furthermore, credit each source in your essay and always use quotation marks when you quote a source directly. You can learn more about citing sources on pages C555–C565. The following steps will help you gather evidence for a literary analysis.

### Gathering Details for a Literary Analysis

- Scan the work, looking for quotations and other details that support your interpretation. Details can include events, descriptions, and any other ingredients of the work.
- Write each detail on a commentary card. If it is a quotation, indicate who said it and write the page number on which it

appears. If it is from a reference work, write the source. (In drama, note the act and scene; in poetry, the line number.)

- Add a note telling how the detail supports your interpretation.
- Use a separate card or piece of paper for each detail.

The following pages show some commentary cards for an essay on the story "Quality." The commentary cards appear on the right. On the left are the portions of the story from which the notes were made. The details were chosen by the writer to support the thesis that Galsworthy uses the physical decline of the bootmaker to show the decline of standards in society.

**Model: Gathering Evidence**

I knew him from the days of my extreme youth, because he made my father's boots; inhabiting with his elder brother two little shops let into one, in a small by-street—now no more, but then most fashionably placed in the West End.

1. Bootmaker combined two little shops into one. In early days the shop was "most fashionably placed" and "had a certain quiet distinction." (p. C433)
—Shows bootmaker was successful

"Id 'urds you dere," he said. "Dose big virms 'ave no self-respect. Drash!" And then, as if something had given way within him, he spoke long and bitterly. It was the only time I ever heard him discuss the conditions and hardships of his trade.

"Dey get id all," he said, "dey get id by adverdisement, nod by work. Dey dake id away from us, who lofe our boods. Id gomes to this—bresently I haf no work. Every year id gets less—you will see."

2.a. Bootmaker sees poor quality of other boots. Speaks bitterly about big firms taking business away from craftsmen—"Every year id gets less...."
—(bootmaker, p. C436)

2.b. Shows bootmaker bitter about changing standards and what's going to happen

And looking at his lined face I saw things I had never noticed before, bitter things and bitter struggle—and what a lot of gray hairs there seemed suddenly in his red beard!

3. Narrator sees bitterness and first signs of decline: "and what a lot of gray hairs there seemed suddenly in his red beard!" (p. C436)—Bitterness showing; physical decline starting; affects narrator.

As best I could, I explained the circumstances of the purchase of those ill-omened boots. But his face and voice made a so deep impression that during the next few minutes I ordered many pairs!

---

When at last I went I was surprised that outside one of the two little windows of his shop another name was painted, also that of a bootmaker —making, of course, for the Royal Family. The old familiar boots, no longer in dignified isolation, were huddled in the single window. Inside, the no contracted well of the one little shop was more scented and darker than ever.

4. Bootmaker had to give up half the shop to another, larger firm. (p. C437) —Decline in business.

---

It was over a year before I was again in London. And the first shop I went to was my old friend's. I had left a man of sixty, I came back to find one of seventy-five, pinched and worn and tremulous, who genuinely, this time, did not at first know me.

5. Next visit more than a year later. "I had left a man of sixty, I came back to find one of seventy-five, pinched and worn and tremulous...." (narrator, p. C438)—Had declined terribly.

---

"That may be a bit flowery, as the sayin' is, but I know myself he was sittin' over his boots day and night, to the very last. Never gave 'imself time to eat; never had a penny in the house. All went in rent and leather. How he lived so long I don't know. He regular let his fire go out."

6. "...he was sittin' over his boots day and night, to the very last...." (new owner, p. C440) —Bootmaker used last bit of energy to keep up his high standards.

Communicate Your Ideas

**PREWRITING** *Evidence*

Gather evidence from "First Love" on pages C281–C283 to support your working thesis. On a separate commentary card or piece of paper, write each detail, its page number, and a brief note explaining its importance. Save your work for later use.

## Organizing Details into an Outline

Once you have the details to support the thesis of your essay, you need to organize them. As the following chart illustrates, your method of organization will depend on the nature of your thesis.

**PRIMARY METHODS OF ORGANIZATION**

| Thesis | Method |
|---|---|
| changes in a character over time | chronological order (*page C110*) |
| similarities and differences between the characters or comparison of two different works | comparison and contrast: the *AABB* or the *ABAB* pattern of development (*page C464*) |
| analysis of a character's motivation or the significance of the setting | order of importance (*page C110*) |
| conclusions about the theme | developmental order (*page C110*) |

**Comparison and Contrast** Comparing and contrasting different characters, settings, or works is a common approach to writing a literary essay. When you compare and contrast, you examine both the similarities and differences between two works of literature.

In a comparison and contrast literary analysis, you can organize the details in several ways. In one pattern of organization, called **AABB** or **whole by whole**, you show how subjects are similar and different by discussing all the points about the first subject (A) and then all the points about the second subject (B). In the second pattern, called **ABAB** or **point by point** organization, you discuss each point and show how subjects are similar and different with regard to that point. When you are comparing and contrasting, experiment with these arrangements. Choose the one that helps you present your arguments in the most effective way.

*You may wish to read more about the comparison and contrast method of organization on pages C157–C158 and C355–C357.*

Suppose, for example, that you were comparing and contrasting Mr. Gessler and the young bootmaker in "Quality" based on their ideas of value and their success in business. You could arrange details according to either pattern of organization.

**METHODS OF ORGANIZATION IN COMPARISON AND CONTRAST**

| AABB PATTERN | ABAB PATTERN |
|---|---|
| Mr. Gessler (subject A)<br>  Ideas of Value (point 1)<br>  Success in Business (point 2) | Ideas of Value (point 1)<br>  Mr. Gessler (subject A)<br>  Young Bootmaker (subject B) |
| Young Bookmaker (subject B)<br>  Ideas of Value (point 1)<br>  Success in Business (point 2) | Success in Business (point 2)<br>  Mr. Gessler (subject A)<br>  Young Bootmaker (subject B) |

**Outlining** After choosing a method of organization, arrange your details in an outline you can use to guide your writing. The outline should be formal, with several levels of topics. The following formal outline was prepared for the body of a literary analysis about the short story "Quality." To suit the thesis about the decline of a bootmaker and the decline of standards in society, the writer arranged the ideas chronologically.

THESIS In the short story "Quality," John Galsworthy uses the decline of a skilled bootmaker to show the general decline of standards in society.

**Model: Outline**

| | |
|---|---|
| Main Topic: | **I.** Successful bootmaker |
| Subtopics | **A.** Combined two shops into one |
| | **B.** Located in fashionable neighborhood |
| | **C.** Considered bootmaking "an Ardt" |
| Main Topic: | **II.** First sign of decline |
| Subtopics | **A.** Narrator wearing low-quality boots |
| | **B.** Big firms taking business away |
| | **C.** Bootmaker beginning to age |
| Main Topic: | **III.** Two years later |
| Subtopics | **A.** Narrator's return to shop |
| | **B.** Shop's division |
| Main Topic: | **IV.** Aged bootmaker |
| Subtopics | **A.** Bootmaker's physical decline |
| | **B.** Brother's death |
| | **C.** Bootmaker's ideals |
| Main Topic: | **V.** Last encounter with bootmaker |
| Subtopics | **A.** Bootmaker shows extreme decline |
| | **B.** Narrator orders boots |
| | **C.** Bootmaker dies |

If you have taken notes on a story but have difficulty fitting those notes into an outline, mapping the story's meaning can be a helpful intermediate step. A **meaning map** plots a story's main events in sequence, along with other major elements such as setting and characters. Each element is linked to a statement about what that element contributes to the thesis about the story. This map can help make clear which topics to emphasize as major topics and which ones should be subtopics.

## Practice Your Skills

### *Organizing Ideas in a Meaning Map*

**Copy the meaning map on the following page and complete it for "Quality." Use the thesis (page C464) for the preceding model.**

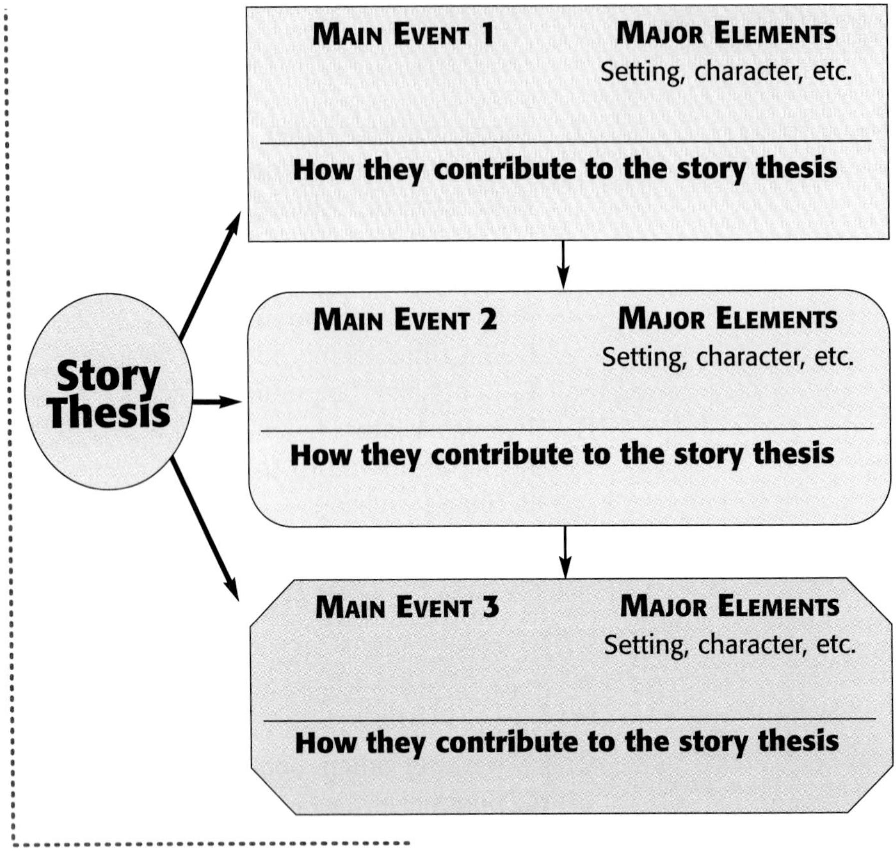

Main Event 1
Major Elements
Setting, character, etc.
How they contribute to the story thesis
Story Thesis
Main Event 2
Major Elements
Setting, character, etc.
How they contribute to the story thesis
Main Event 3
Major Elements
Setting, character, etc.
How they contribute to the story thesis

## *Communicate Your Ideas*

**PREWRITING** *Outline*

Review the notes you took about "First Love," and make a meaning map for the story. Group the major details into categories, or main topics, and decide on an appropriate order for the topics. Develop an outline for your analysis of the story. Save your work.

## Drafting

Writing Process

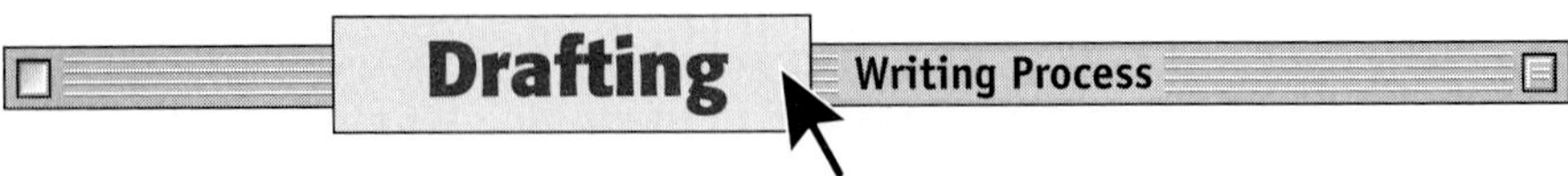

Now that you have organized your ideas into an outline, you should begin to draft your essay. Adjust your outline as needed to accommodate new ideas or new directions that come up as you write. You should also consult your notes so that you do not forget important details. Use the following guidelines to help you draft your essay.

### Guidelines for Drafting a Literary Analysis

- Do not retell the story. You can assume that your readers have read the work you are analyzing.
- Keep yourself and your feelings out of the essay. Use the third-person point of view and avoid *I*.
- Use the present tense to discuss the work. (For example, write, "The character **is** respected at first . . ." or "In the third stanza, the poet **speaks** about . . .")
- In the introduction, identify the title of the work and the author.
- Revise your thesis statement as needed and work it into the introduction as smoothly as possible.
- In the body of your essay, present your supporting details in a clearly organized form.
- Put each topic into its own paragraph. Use transitions to show how one detail relates to another.
- In the conclusion, draw together your details to reinforce the main idea of your essay. You may want to restate the thesis in a slightly different form.
- Throughout your essay, use direct quotations from the work to strengthen the points you want to make.
- Add a title that suggests the focus of your essay.

## Using Quotations

When you planned your essay, you took notes to use as evidence to support your thesis. These notes included descriptive details, lines of dialogue, narrative details, and other types of details. When you draft your essay, you should work this evidence into your essay as convincingly as possible. One way to do so is to quote directly from the work. Therefore, you should use quotations to support a point.

Use **direct quotations** from the work to support your points and provide evidence that strengthens your position.

You should not just drop the quotations randomly into your essay. Instead, work them smoothly into your writing and punctuate them correctly. The following guidelines will help you.

### Guidelines for Using Direct Quotations

- Always enclose direct quotations in quotation marks.
- Follow the examples below when writing quotations in different positions in the sentence. Notice that quotations in the middle or end of a sentence are not ordinarily capitalized.

| | |
|---|---|
| BEGINS SENTENCE | "**T**he old familiar boots, no longer in dignified isolation," were added to the pile of shoes in the window. |
| INTERPRETS SENTENCE | Noting their low quality, "**h**e spoke long and bitterly" about big firms.<br>The bootmaker is shockingly "**a**ged and wan," with thinning hair. |
| ENDS SENTENCE | The shop has "**a**n air of distinction." |

- Use ellipsis—a series of three dots (. . .)—to show that words have been left out of a quotation.

  His "hair had suddenly . . . gone wan and thin."

- If the quotation is two lines or longer, set it off by itself, without quotation marks. Indent on both sides and leave space above and below it.

  > I had left a man of sixty, I came back to find one of seventy-five, pinched and worn and tremulous, who genuinely, this time, did not at first know me (C438).

- After each quotation cite the page number of the source in parentheses. The citation should precede punctuation marks such as periods, commas, colons, and semicolons. For plays or long poems, also give the act and scene of the play or part of the poem, plus line numbers.

Below is a sample of a literary analysis. Since it has already been revised and edited, it is considerably more polished than your first draft will be. Nevertheless, you should use it as a model of what to aim for as you draft your own essay.

**MODEL: Literary Analysis**

TITLE: IDENTIFIES FOCUS

## A Double Decline in Quality

INTRODUCTION: IDENTIFIES AUTHOR AND TITLE

In "Quality" John Galsworthy tells the story of an aging bootmaker in a changing society. After spending his life making boots of the highest quality, Mr. Gessler cannot fit into a world that cares more about doing things quickly than well. Through the physical decline of the bootmaker, Galsworthy shows the decline of standards in society.

THESIS STATEMENT

FIRST BODY PARAGRAPH: DESCRIBES MR. GESSLER AS A RESPECTED BOOTMAKER

At the beginning of the story, Mr. Gessler is a respected craftsman. He is successful enough to have combined two little shops into one, which is "most fashionably placed" and has "a certain quiet distinction" (C433). The young narrator is impressed by the dignity of the bootmaker and the wonder of his craft. "For to make boots—such boots as he made—seemed to me then, and still seems to me, mysterious and wonderful" (C433). To Mr. Gessler bootmaking is "an Ardt" (C434), and he is completely devoted to that art. The joy of working with a beautiful piece of leather and shaping it into a perfect boot—that is his entire life.

SECOND BODY PARAGRAPH: USES SPECIFIC DETAILS TO SHOW SIGN OF DECLINE

For a while people appear to appreciate Mr. Gessler and the remarkable boots he creates. However, the first sign of decline comes when the narrator enters the shop wearing boots bought somewhere else. "Dose are nod my boods" (C436), the bootmaker recognizes immediately. Noting their low quality "he spoke long and bitterly" (C436) about big firms who use advertising, not quality, to take business away from real craftsmen. He predicted what was happening: "Id gomes to this—bresently I haf no work. Every year id gets less—you will see" (C436). As Mr. Gessler gives his bitter speech, the narrator notices "what a lot of gray hairs there seemed suddenly in his red beard" (C436). The bootmaker is beginning his decline, along with the standards he holds so high.

**THIRD BODY PARAGRAPH:** OFFERS DETAILS TO SHOW DECLINE

Two years later the narrator returns and is surprised to see that the shop has been divided. "And it was longer than usual, too, before a face peered down" and the bootmaker appeared (C437). Things are obviously getting worse, and "beople do nod wand good boods, id seems" (C437).

**FOURTH BODY PARAGRAPH:** SHOWS PROGRESSION OF DECLINE—AFFECTS BOOTMAKER PHYSICALLY

The decline continues. When the narrator visits the shop again many months later, he finds the bootmaker shockingly "aged and wan" (C438), and his "hair had suddenly gone . . . thin" (C438). Mr. Gessler has lost his brother and half his shop, and he is obviously falling apart physically. Still, he takes joy in a beautiful piece of leather and fashions boots that "were better than ever" (C438). The struggle to hold on to his ideals is aging him, but he is not giving them up.

**FIFTH BODY PARAGRAPH:** SETS OFF DIRECT QUOTATION TO EMPHASIZE DECLINE

It is more than a year before the narrator returns, and this time the bootmaker's decline is extreme.

> I had left a man of sixty, I came back to find one of seventy-five, pinched and worn and tremulous, who genuinely, this time, did not at first know me (C438).

The narrator orders boots and hurries away, for "To watch him was quite painful, so feeble had he grown" (C439). When the boots finally arrive, however, "they were the best he had ever made me" (C439). The bootmaker seems to have used up his last bit of energy, "sittin' over his boots day and night, to the very last" (C440), for then he died.

**CONCLUSION:** RESTATES THESIS

At the end of the story, the new young bootmaker explains that even though "not a man in London made a better boot" (C440), there is no place in the modern world for someone who does all his own work, who takes time to do a job right, who insists on the best leather, and who never advertises for customers. The old bootmaker himself knows he no longer fits in a changed world, and so he leaves it. Do his precious values die with him? Galsworthy seems to say that they do.

## Communicate Your Ideas

**DRAFTING** *Literary Analysis*

Use your outline and your notes to help you draft your literary analysis of "First Love." Incorporate quotations from the story smoothly into your own writing. Use the Guidelines for Writing Direct Quotations on pages C468–C649. When you use a quotation, remember to cite the page number in parentheses. Save your draft for later use. 

## Looping Back to Prewriting

### *Reworking Your Thesis*

After writing the first draft of your literary analysis, think about the main point you make in the analysis. Then reread the thesis you wrote and saved in your writing folder. You may find that although you began with a certain thesis, your draft has taken off in a different direction. If you find that your draft makes a different point than you first intended, you need to rewrite your thesis to reflect your new point.

## Revising

Rework your draft until you are reasonably satisfied with it. Then do not look at it for a day or two so that you can return to it with a critical eye. If possible, give your draft to another student to read and comment on in the meantime. Then use your classmate's suggestions and the checklist below to make your revisions.

### Evaluation Checklist for Revising

**Checking Your Essay**

✓ Do you have a strong introduction that identifies the author and the work you will discuss? *(page C467)*

✓ Does your introduction contain a clearly worded thesis? *(page C467)*

✓ Does the body of your essay provide ample details from the work to support your thesis? *(page C460)*

✓ Have you quoted from the work to strengthen your points? *(pages C467–C469)*

✓ Are your major points organized in a clear, appropriate way? *(pages C463–C464)*

✓ Does your conclusion synthesize the details in the body of the essay and reinforce the thesis statement? *(page C467)*

✓ As a whole, does your essay show unity and coherence? *(pages C194–C195)*

✓ Do you have an interesting appropriate title? *(pages C37 and C467)*

**Checking Your Paragraphs**

✓ Does each paragraph have a topic sentence? *(pages C100–C103)*

✓ Is each paragraph unified and coherent? *(pages C107–C110)*

**Checking Your Sentences and Words**

✓ Are your sentences varied and concise? *(pages C66–C79)*

✓ Are your words specific and lively? *(pages C60–C63)*

## Communicate Your Ideas

**REVISING** *Supporting Details*

Return to the draft of your literary analysis of "First Love." Exchange papers with a partner. How well do the details support the thesis? Use the **Evaluation Checklist for Revising** on the previous page and your partner's comments to revise your draft. Save your work for later use.

**Time Out to Reflect**

With the comments from your peer reviewer fresh in your mind, think back to responses to other essays you have written. Are your reviewers and teachers making similar remarks each time about your strengths and weaknesses? Record your findings, as well as any strategies for improving, in the Learning Log portion of your **journal.**

**COMPUTER TIP**

If you are revising on a computer, you can use the Save As function to save more than one version of your essay. Save your original draft with its own title. After revising your essay, click the Save As key and give the revised version a new name. If you find that some of the revisions you have made do not work as well as your original material, you still have a complete copy of your original draft.

## Editing

**Writing Process**

Although you probably began the writing process with the rules of grammar in mind, take time at this stage to edit your work for grammar, spelling, mechanics, and usage. Pay special attention to the participial phrases in your essay. Make sure you have used and punctuated them correctly.

The **Editing Workshop** on pages C475–476 will help you as you edit your literary analysis.

## Communicate Your Ideas

**EDITING** *Verbal Phrases*

Read aloud your revised literary analysis of "First Love" in order to hear whether your words and ideas flow smoothly. Listen for verbal phrases, and whenever you find one, look carefully to make sure you have punctuated it correctly. Listen for sentences that sound too short or abrupt. Consider combining short sentences using a verbal phrase. Then prepare a final draft in the form shown on pages C469–C471. Save your work for later use.

Publishing a literary analysis is a way to fulfill your writing purpose—to have readers read and reflect upon your work.

## Communicate Your Ideas

**PUBLISHING** *Literary Magazine*

Prepare a neat final copy of your literary analysis. Find out whether your school's literary magazine includes works of analysis, and, if so, submit yours for publication. Be sure to follow any guidelines the magazine has about presentation for submitted works. Save a copy of your literary analysis in your portfolio.

PORTFOLIO

# Verbal Phrases

At one point in "Quality," John Galsworthy writes, "Then, placing my foot on a piece of paper, he would two or three times tickle the outer edges with a pencil. . . ." In the sentence the group of words *placing my foot on a piece of paper* is called a **phrase** because it has no subject and verb. In particular, *placing my foot on a piece of paper* is a **verbal phrase** because it begins with a verb form called a verbal.

Verbal phrases can contribute much to your writing style. You can use them at the beginning of a sentence for variety in your sentence structure, and you can eliminate choppiness in your writing by using them to combine sentences. Because verbals begin with a verb form, they—by their very nature—also add a liveliness to your writing.

## Participial Phrases

A participial phrase is one kind of verbal phrase. A **participle** is a verb form that is used as an adjective to describe a noun or a pronoun. Present participles end in *–ing,* and past participles end in *–ed, –n, –t,* and *–en*. A participle plus its modifiers and complements forms a **participial phrase.** In the following examples, the participial phrases add a certain action or energy to the sentences. In addition, the participial phrase that comes at the beginning of the second example sentence creates sentence variety.

PARTICIPIAL PHRASE

I would continue to rest in the wooden chair, **inhaling the incense of his trade.**

**Placing my foot on a piece of paper,** he would two or three times tickle the outer edges with a pencil. . . .

## Punctuation with Participial Phrases

When a participial phrase comes at the beginning of a sentence—as in the second example above—it is separated from the rest of the sentence with a comma. You should also use commas to enclose a nonessential participial phrase. A **nonessential participial phrase** is one that can be removed from a sentence without changing the meaning of that sentence.

| | |
|---|---|
| NONESSENTIAL PARTICIPIAL PHRASE | Mr. Gessler, **showing his dislike for the store-bought boots,** treats the narrator coldly. (You could remove the participial phrase without changing the meaning of the sentence: *Mr. Gessler treats the narrator coldly.*) |
| ESSENTIAL PARTICIPIAL PHRASE | I could feel his eyes **penetrating the inferior integument of my foot.** (The participial phrase *penetrating the inferior integument of my foot* is essential because the idea is incomplete if it is removed.) |

## Combining Sentences by Using Participial Phrases

Your ability recognize participial phrases gives you the option of using them to combine short, choppy sentences to form more concise sentences. When you combine sentences, you are also able to show important relationships between two ideas.

| | |
|---|---|
| TWO SENTENCES | The narrator enters the shop. He is greeted by a new bootmaker. |
| COMBINED | **Entering the shop,** the narrator is greeted by a new bootmaker. |
| TWO SENTENCES | The narrator hears the news that Mr. Gessler is dead. The narrator is bewildered. |
| COMBINED | The narrator is bewildered, **hearing the news that Mr. Gessler is dead.** |

## Process of Writing a Literary Analysis

Remember that the writing process is recursive—you can move back and forth among the stages of the writing process to achieve your purpose. For example, during editing, you may wish to return to the revising stage to add details that have occurred to you while editing. The numbers in parentheses refer to pages where you can get help with your writing.

### PREWRITING

- Read the work carefully and respond to it from both personal experience and literary knowledge. *(pages C444–C451)*
- Choose and limit a subject for your essay by synthesizing your personal and literary responses. *(pages C454–C457)*
- Shape your limited subject into a thesis statement that will provide a focus as you write. *(page C458)*
- Scan the work, looking for details that will support your thesis statement. On separate note cards, write each detail, the page reference, and a note explaining its significance. *(pages C460–C462)*
- Decide on an appropriate order for your details and use it to organize them into an outline. *(pages C463–C465)*

### DRAFTING

- In the introduction identify the title of the work and the author. *(page C467)*
- Revise your thesis statement as needed and work it into the introduction as smoothly as possible. *(page C467)*
- In the body of your essay present your supporting details in a clearly organized form. *(page C467)*
- Put each subtopic into its own paragraph. Use transitions to show how one detail relates to another. *(page C467)*
- In the conclusion draw together your details to reinforce the main idea of your essay. You may want to restate the thesis in a slightly different form. *(page C467)*

### REVISING

- Use the Evaluation Checklist for Revising to help you revise your literary analysis. *(page C472)*

### EDITING

- Check your work for grammar, spelling, usage, and mechanics. Pay special attention to the punctuation of direct quotations. *(pages C468–C469)*

### PUBLISHING

- Follow standard manuscript form and prepare a neat final copy of your literary analysis. Then present it to an interested reader. *(page C474)*

# A Writer Writes

## A Literary Review

**Purpose: to analyze a short story, play, or poem**

**Audience: people who are familiar with the literary work, especially your classmates and teacher**

### Prewriting

You have most likely read and heard and seen reviews of movies. Critics generally recap the relevant plot points, without giving away any surprises. They also respond to the acting, dialogue, direction, and other cinematic elements and share a personal reaction to the film. Movie critics use a catchy system (stars or jalapeños) to rate a film and an unmistakable symbol (thumbs up or down) to recommend or express dislike for a film. With these typical features of a movie review in mind, prepare to write a review of a story, play, or poem to present to your class.

Select a work of literature with which you are familiar, perhaps one of the works you've read in school. Freewrite personal and literary responses to the work. What strikes you about the work? How does the writer, poet, or playwright evoke your response? The main point of your review will answer this question: Why should others experience or avoid this work?

### Drafting

The purpose of a review is to state an opinion about a work and to convince others, using evidence from the work, that their opinion would be similar to yours. Draft a review of your chosen work, keeping in mind the idea that you are writing a kind of script for an oral presentation. How can you concisely and effectively convey the gist of the work, the techniques the writer uses to produce and support the theme of the work, and the recommendation that others read or do not read the work for themselves?

## Revising

Read the draft of your review aloud. Using the **Evaluation Checklist for Revising** on page C472 and the following questions, revise your review.

- Is your thesis clearly and appropriately stated? Will your classmates know why you do or do not recommend the story, play, or poem?
- Do you have enough evidence to support your opinion?
- Will the review have an impact on the audience?

## Editing

Using the checklists as guides, search for errors in grammar, usage, mechanics, and spelling in your review. Again, read your review aloud. Listen for short, choppy sentences that could be improved by combining them.

## Publishing

Prepare a neat final copy of your review. Practice reading it in front of a mirror. If possible, memorize it so that you can make a more effective presentation to your class. Some good ways of keeping your presentation engaging are making eye contact with your audience, making sure your voice is audible to each audience member, and including video clips, posters, or slides in your presentation.

# Connection Collection

## Representing in Different Ways

*From Print . . .*

That summer the horses were always wet. It rained uncommonly, the southwest monsoon sweeping in. The shining horses stood out on the prairie, withers streaming, manes dripping, and one would suddenly start off, a fan of droplets coming off its shoulders like a cape. Ottaline and Aladdin wore slickers from morning coffee to goodnight yawn. Wauneta watched the television weather while she ironed shirts and sheets. Old Red called it drip and dribble, stayed in his room chewing tobacco, reading Zane Grey in large-print editions, his curved fingernail creasing the page under every line. On the Fourth of July they sat together on the porch watching a distant storm, pretending the thick, ruddy legs of lightning and thunder were fireworks.

—*Annie Proulx,* "The Bunchgrass Edge of the World"

*. . . to Visuals*

You have just read an excerpt from "The Bunchgrass Edge of the World," a short story by Annie Proulx. Your teacher wants you to find a particular simile from the story and illustrate it. Locate a simile from the above passage. Then find a photograph or painting from a magazine or Internet site that illustrates the simile.

## From Visuals . . .

## . . . to Print

Find the metaphor in the selection from Annie Proulx's short story, "The Bunchgrass Edge of the World" that is illustrated by the above photograph. How effective is the imagery and figurative language in the story? What personal response do you get from these images? Write a paragraph discussing Proulx's use of imagery and figurative language. Be sure to support your points with specific examples from the paragraph.

- **Which strategies can be used for creating both written and visual representations? Which strategies apply to one, not both? Which type of representation is more effective?**
- **Draw a conclusion and write briefly about the differences between written ideas and visual representations.**

## Writing in the Workplace

### *Analytical Memo*

Your boss at the Advertising Agency of White and Bank is in a rage! Your competitors at Wart and Blank Incorporated have come up with a new television commercial that everyone in the business is calling a masterpiece. Your boss cannot understand the reasons for its success and has asked you to write a memo to the entire staff of White and Bank about the commercial.

**Write a memo to your co-workers analyzing the commercial and explaining why it is a success. Choose a television commercial you think is especially effective. Pay close attention to any metaphors or allusions it might make. Examine its images and dialogue, relating them to the commercial's meaning. Explain to your audience why you feel the commercial is so successful.**

**What strategies did you use to analyze the commercial's success for your co-workers?**

*You can find information on writing memos on pages C645–C646.*

## Writing for Oral Communication

### *Radio Presentation*

WWHY-FM, a local radio station, sponsors a weekly "You are the Deejay" contest. To enter you must submit a playlist of five songs you will play if you are the lucky winner. You must also prepare an introduction to each song explaining why the songs are significant to you.

**Prepare a list of songs and a presentation you will give to WWHY. Think about five songs that hold meaning for you. For each song, write a personal response that shares how and why these songs affect you. Analyze the songs in the way you might analyze a poem. After you have prepared the speech you will submit on the tape, present it to your class members.**

**What strategies did you use to prepare an effective radio presentation for the station?**

*You can find information on oral presentations on pages C672–C680.*

# Assess Your Learning

The new principal at your high school, Dr. Hardy Science, recently addressed the school about his plans for reshaping the school. He is making plans to cut funding for the English and literature classes because he firmly believes that "reading poems, short stories, and plays is nothing but plain entertainment." You agree that reading literature is entertaining, but you strongly believe that literature serves a greater purpose as well. You think that the best way to explain this to Dr. Science is to write an essay for the school newspaper.

- **Find a short story, poem, or play that has special meaning to you. Responding from personal experience, write an essay for the school newspaper that explains how and why the short story, poem, or play has special meaning for you. Also explain what you have learned from the work.**
- **Be sure to include a strong introduction that identifies the author and the title of the work you will discuss. Narrow your subject and focus on a specific thesis and be sure to quote direct lines and images from the work. Discuss the work in present tense.**

*Before You Write* **Consider the following questions:**
What is the ***subject?***
What is the ***occasion?***
Who is the ***audience?***
What is the ***purpose?***

*After You Write* **Evaluate your work using the following criteria:**

- Do you have a strong introduction that identifies the author and the work you will discuss?
- Have you narrowed your subject and focused on a specific thesis for your analysis?
- Have you quoted direct lines and images from the work to support your points?
- Have you used present tense when discussing the work?
- Does your conclusion draw together your details to reinforce your main idea about the work?
- Have you revised the text of your introduction by deleting, combining, and rearranging the text?

**Write briefly on how well you did. Point out your strengths and areas for improvement.**

CHAPTER 11

# Summaries and Abstracts

The President of the United States does not have time to read newspapers and journals word for word. Instead, his staff provides him with summaries and abstracts that briefly give him the main facts about all the news and new information reported from the United States and around the world. A summary is a condensation of a longer piece of writing. An abstract, which is even briefer, sums up the thesis and essential information of an article so readers can decide at a glance whether to read the entire piece. This chapter will show you how these two forms of writing, summaries and abstracts, can save valuable time for busy people like the president—and you.

## *Reading with a Writer's Eye*

Read the abstract of the following essay to get a sense of the subject matter. Then read the essay itself, which describes and explains the geology of the San Andreas fault in California. After rereading the passage, think about the ways the author has made his technical subject interesting and intelligible to you, the reader. Then read the summary that follows the selection.

FROM

# ASSEMBLING CALIFORNIA

*John McPhee*

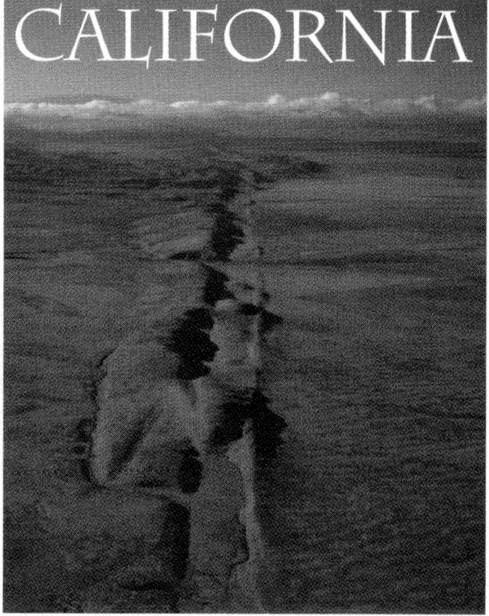

**ABSTRACT** The author presents a series of retrospective geological meditations about travels along the San Andreas fault. Scientific commentary is built around observations made at Mussel Rock, San Francisco, and the approach to the Sierra range. In *Annals of a Former World.* Farrar, Strauss and Giroux, 1998. Pages 432-36.

You go down through the Ocean View district of San Francisco to the first freeway exit after Daly City, where you describe, in effect, a hairpin turn to head north past a McDonald's to a dead end in a local dump. You leave your car and walk north on a high contour some hundreds of yards through deep grasses until a path to your left takes you down a steep slope a quarter of a mile to the ocean. You double back along the water, south to Mussel Rock.

Mussel Rock is a horse. As any geologist will tell you, a horse is a displaced rock mass that has been caught between the walls of a fault. This one appeared to have got away. It seemed to have strained successfully to jump out of the continent. Or so I thought the first time I was there. It loomed in fog. Green seas slammed against it and turned white. It was not a small rock. It was like a three-story building, standing in the Pacific, with brown pelicans on the roof. You could walk out on a ledge and look up through the fog at the pelicans. When you looked around and faced inland, you saw that you were at the base of a fifty-foot cliff, its lithology shattered beyond identification. A huge crack split the cliff from top to bottom and ran on out through the ledge and under the waves. After a five-hundred-mile northwesterly drift through southern and central California, this was where the San Andreas Fault intersected the sea.

I went to Mussel Rock that foggy afternoon in 1978 with the geologist Kenneth Deffeyes. I have returned a number of times since, alone or in the company of others. With regard to the lithosphere[1], it's a good place to sit and watch the plates move. It is a moment in geography that does your thinking for you. The San Andreas Fault, of course, is not a single strand. It is something like a wire rope, as much as half a mile wide, each strand the signature of one or many earthquakes. Mussel Rock is near the outboard edge of the zone. You cannot really say that on one side of the big crack is the North American Plate and on the other side is the Pacific Plate, but it's tempting to do so. Almost automatically, you stand with one foot on each side and imagine your stride lengthening—your right foot, say, riding backward toward Mexico, your left foot in motion toward Alaska. There's some truth in such a picture, but the actual plate boundary is not so sharply defined. Not only is the San Andreas of varying width in its complexity of strands, it is merely the senior fault in a large family of more or less parallel faults in an over-all swath at least fifty miles wide. Some of the faults are to the west and under the ocean; more are inland. Whether the plate boundary is five miles wide or fifty miles wide or extends all the way to central Utah is a matter that geologists currently debate. Nonetheless, there is granite under the sea off Mussel Rock that is evidently from the southern Sierra Nevada, has travelled three hundred miles along the San Andreas system, and continues to move northwest. As evidence of the motion of the plates, that granite will do.

For an extremely large percentage of the history of the world, there was no California. That is, according to present theory. I don't mean to suggest that California was underwater and has since come up. I mean to say that of the varied terranes and physiographic[2] provinces that we now call California nothing whatever was there.

---

[1]**lithosphere** (lĭth′ə sfîr) *n.:* 1. The solid part of the earth. 2. The rocky crust of the earth.
[2]**physiographic** (fĭz′ē ŏg rə fĭk) *adj.:* Pertaining to the natural features of the earth's surface, especially in its current aspects, including land formation, climate, currents and distribution of flora and fauna.

The continent ended far to the east, the continental shelf as well. Where California has come to be, there was only blue sea reaching down some miles to ocean-crustal rock, which was moving, as it does, into subduction zones to be consumed. Ocean floors with an aggregate area many times the size of the present Pacific were made at spreading centers, moved around the curve of the earth, and melted in trenches before there ever was so much as a kilogram of California. Then, a piece at a time—according to present theory—parts began to assemble. An island arc here, a piece of a continent there—a Japan at a time, a New Zealand, a Madagascar—came crunching in upon the continent and have thus far adhered. Baja is about to detach. A great deal more may go with it. Some parts of California arrived head-on, and others came sliding in on transform faults, in the manner of that great Sierra granite west of the San Andreas. In 1906, the jump of the great earthquake—the throw, the offset, the maximum amount of local displacement as one plate moved with respect to the other—was something like twenty feet. The dynamics that have pieced together the whole of California have consisted of tens of thousands of earthquakes as great as that—tens of thousands of examples of what people like to singularize as "the big one"—and many millions of earthquakes of lesser magnitude. In 1914, Andrew Lawson, writing the San Francisco Folio of the Geologic Atlas of the United States, wistfully said, "Most of the faults are the expression of energies that have been long spent and are not in any sense a menace. It is, moreover, barely possible that stresses in the San Andreas fault zone have been completely and permanently relieved by the fault movement of 1906." Andrew Lawson—who named the San Andreas Fault—was a structural geologist of the first order, whose theoretical conclusions were as revered in his time as others' are at present. For the next six decades in California, a growing population tended to imagine that the stresses were indeed gone—that the greatest of historic earthquakes (in this part of the fault) had relieved the pressure and settled the risk forever. In the nineteen-sixties, though, when the work of several scientists from various parts of the world coalesced to form the theory of plate tectonics, it became apparent—at least to geologists—that those twenty feet of 1906 were a minuscule part of a shifting global geometry. The twenty-odd lithospheric plates of which the rind of the earth consists are nearly all in continual motion; in these plate movements, earthquakes are the incremental steps. Fifty thousand major earthquakes will move something about a hundred miles. After there was nothing, earthquakes brought things from far parts of the world to fashion California.

Deffeyes and I had been working in Utah and Nevada, in the physiographic province of the Basin and Range. Now he was about to go east and home, and we wandered around San Francisco while waiting for his plane. Downtown, we walked by the Transamerica Building, with its wide base, its high sides narrowing to a point, and other buildings immensely tall and straight. Deffeyes said, "There are two earthquake-resistant structures—the pyramids and the redwoods. These guys are working both sides of the street." The skyscrapers were new, in 1978. In an earthquake, buildings of different height would have different sway periods, he noted. They would "creak and groan, skin to skin." The expansion joints in freeways attracted his eye. He said they might open up in an earthquake, causing roadways to fall. He called the freeways "disposable—Kleenexes good for one blow." He made these remarks in the shadowy space of Second Street and Stillman, under the elevated terminus of Interstate 80, the beginnings of the San Francisco Skyway, the two-level structure of the Embarcadero Freeway, and so many additional looping ramps and rights-of-way that Deffeyes referred to it all as the Spaghetti Bowl. He said it was resting on a bog that had once surrounded a tidal creek. The multiple roadways were held in the air by large steel Ts. Deffeyes said, "It's the engineer in a game against nature. In a great earthquake, the ground will turn to gray jello. Those Ts may uproot like tomato stakes. And that will seal everyone in town. Under the landfill, the preexisting mud in the old tidal channel will liquefy. You could wiggle your feet a bit and go up to your knees." In 1906, the shaking over the old tidal channel that is now under the freeways was second in intensity only to the San Andreas fault zone itself, seven miles away. "Los Angeles, someday, will be sealed in worse than this," he continued. "In the critical hours after a great earthquake, they will be cut off from help, food, water. Take one piece out of each freeway and they're through."

In a rented pickup, we had entered California the day before, climbing the staircase of fault blocks west of Reno that had led the Donner party to the crest of the mountains named for snow. In California was the prow of the North American Plate—in these latitudes, the sliding boundary. California was also among the freshest acquisitions of the continent. So radical and contemporary were the regional tectonics that the highest and the lowest points in the contiguous United States were within eighty miles of each other in California. As nowhere else along the fortieth parallel in North America, this was where the theory of plate tectonics was announcing its agenda.

Over the years, I would crisscross the country many times, revisiting people and places, yet the first morning with Deffeyes among the rocks of California retains a certain burnish, because it exemplified not only how abrupt the transition can be as you move from one physiographic province to another but also the jurisdictional differences in the world of the geologist. As we crossed the state line under a clear sky and ascended toward Truckee, we passed big masses of competent, blocky, beautiful rocks bright in their quartzes and feldspars and peppered with shining black mica. The ebullient Deffeyes said, "Come into the Sierra and commune with the granite."

# Summary

A trip by the author, John McPhee, to Mussel Rock on the Pacific coast of northern California, leads into a series of observations about the San Andreas fault and the geological origins of California. Mussel Rock marks where the northwestern end of the the San Andreas fault—a five hundred mile split in the earth's crust—intersects with the Pacific ocean.

The earth's surface comprises twenty shifting tectonic plates. California was created by the collision of such plates set in motion by hundreds of thousands of earthquakes over vast stretches of time. The split at Mussel Rock enables one to visualize the forces at work that created the distinctive topography of California. The split marks the separation of North American and Pacific plates of the lithosphere. At Mussel Rock those plates are only one foot apart. An underwater granite shelf on one side of the rift at Mussel Rock is evidence of the shifting of one plate all the way from Sierra Nevada, some 300 miles to the Southeast.

Geologist Andrew Lawson, who named the San Andreas fault, believed that the the "great" earthquake of 1906 marked the end of seismic disturbance in the area—a view that prevailed until the 1960s. Since then, geologists have maintained that this was but one of thousands of earthquakes of similar magnitude and that it was not likely to be the last.

Walking through San Francisco with the author, geologist Ken Deffeyes details the devastation that an earthquake would cause in the city. Freeways built upon an ancient tidal channel would collapse. Inhabitants would be unable to escape.

McPhee recalls the previous day when they had been at the other end of the fault, west of Reno, Nevada. There the movement of the North American plate, the "sliding boundary," accounts for the fact that the highest and lowest points in the contiguous United States are within eighty miles of one another. The travelers enter Nevada, where the granite of the Sierra— that on the coast had been underwater—looms overhead.

# Thinking as a Writer

## Comparing Summaries, Abstracts, and Originals

You have read an abstract, a summary, and the full text of an excerpt from the author's work.

- What points do the three versions have in common? How does the scope and content of each presentation vary?
- What uses might each version have? What sort of reader might find a summary or an abstract useful?
- What are the advantages of the abstract and the summary? What are the disadvantages?

## Adjusting the Content

Oral Expression

Take turns with a classmate telling of a trip you have taken that left a strong impression on you. First describe the trip in two or three sentences. Then, with as little detail as possible, relate the highlights of your trip in a two-minute summary. Finally, give a full version of your story, embellishing it with details.

## Viewing Icons as Summaries

The icons on a computer menu are designed to give you a sense of the underlying contents. In the picture below, the icon labeled *Utilities* is a visual summary of the many things your computer can do when you open that folder.

13 items, 2.5 GB available

| Name | Date Modified |
|---|---|
| Applications | Thu, Jul 1, 1999, 2:08 PM |
| System Folder | Fri, Jan 14, 2000, 5:09 PM |
| Utilities | Today, 3:55 PM |
| Disk First Aid | Wed, Jun 3, 1998, 2:00 PM |
| Drive Setup | Mon, Feb 23, 1998, 2:00 PM |
| Drive Setup Guide | Thu, Oct 23, 1997, 2:00 PM |

- Study the picture and jot down what you would expect to find if you clicked on each icon in the Utilities folder.
- Click on icons on your computer and see where they lead. Did the icons give an accurate picture of the contents?

# Developing Your Summarizing Skills

The summary, often called a *précis*, is a condensation of a longer piece of writing, covering only the main points of the original. Your main task when you write a summary is to restate the original ideas accurately and in your own words. Unlike an essay, a summary does not include personal comments, interpretations, or insights. Its purpose is to state clearly the most important ideas of a work by omitting the unnecessary details. The ideas are presented in the same order as in the original and with the same meaning. Writing a good summary takes some skill, then, for you must remain true to the original as you restate the main ideas and condense the details.

A **summary** is a concise condensation of a longer piece of writing, covering only the main points of the original.

## Analyzing a Summary

A summary enables you to record the essential contents of a long book or article for future reference. A summary should be thorough but brief. You can refer to a summary to refresh your memory and you can use it as a source for your own essay when writing about another author's ideas. Writing summaries is a way of thinking about what you have read. The following chart shows the essential features of a good summary.

### Features of a Summary

- usually no more than one-third the length of the original
- extracts the main ideas of the original, omitting all but vital details
- presents the main ideas in the same order as the original
- restates the main ideas of the original in the summary writer's own words

## PRACTICE YOUR SKILLS

### *Analyzing a Summary*

**Read both the original piece of writing and the summary that follows it. Then write answers to the numbered questions.**

ORIGINAL:

John Napier was a sixteenth-century Scottish mathematician whose neighbors feared he was a magician practicing the black arts. Fearful that Spain would invade the British Isles, he drew plans for all manner of strange defenses, from solar mirrors for burning ships at a distance to submarines and primitive tanks. However, his true fame rests on two great mathematical inventions: the decimal point and logarithms.

Today mathematicians take for granted these handy exponents of numbers that make it possible to multiply and divide by simple addition and subtraction. In Napier's day calculations were done laboriously in the old-fashioned way, and he fretted many hours over the time such arithmetic took. . . . In 1594, the thought struck Napier that all numbers could be written in exponential form, or as powers of a certain base number. For instance, 4 is $2^2$ and 8 is $2^3$. This alone is not startling, but Napier saw beyond it to a simple way of multiplying 4 times 8 without really multiplying. $2^2$ plus $2^3$ equaled $2^5$ in Napier's new arithmetic, and $2^5$ equals 32, the same as the product of 4 times 8. The same principle applies to exponents of all numbers, although there was a fantastic amount of work involved in computing these exponents extensively. In fact, it was not until 1614, twenty years after his revelation of the basic idea, that Napier published his logarithm tables. The result was something like the introduction of the electronic computer in our time. Logarithms drastically reduced the amount of work involved in mathematics and relieved scientists, particularly astronomers, from a great burden of mental drudgery.

—*Dan Halacy,* Charles Babbage: Father of the Computer

SUMMARY:

John Napier, an eccentric Scottish mathematician of the sixteenth century, invented the decimal point and logarithms. Napier was concerned about the time-consuming calculations needed to multiply and divide. In 1594, Napier realized that if numbers were expressed with exponents, the simpler tasks of addition and subtraction could be used instead of multiplication and division, with the same results. Twenty years of testing followed this discovery. When Napier finally published his logarithm tables in 1614, the time savings were similar to the efficiency offered by electronic computers in the present age.

1. Is the summary no longer than one-third the length of the original? To how many sentences is the first paragraph in the original reduced in the summary?
2. What two details about Napier from the first paragraph are omitted in the summary? What adjective in the summary sums up those omitted details?
3. The second paragraph in the original is reduced to how many sentences in the summary?
4. Is the specific example in the third paragraph of the original retained in the summary?
5. Are all the dates from the original in the summary?
6. Consider your answers to questions 2, 4, and 5. What is the difference between the details omitted in the summary and those retained?
7. What detail about the effect of the logarithm tables has been left out of the summary?
8. How are the main ideas ordered in the summary?

**Your Writer's Journal**

Reread the excerpt from "Assembling California." After you have finished, list his main ideas in order in your journal. Next to each idea, write a comment of your own.

# Process of Writing a Summary

For most types of writing, you begin with a main idea and then develop that idea by adding details. When writing a summary, however, you begin with a detailed composition and reduce it to its main ideas by omitting details. Before you write a summary, therefore, you need to understand the work thoroughly.

### Preparing to Write a Summary

- Read the original work to get the main idea.
- Read the work again, writing down unfamiliar words.
- Write a synonym or a simple definition for each word.
- Read the work a third time, writing down the main ideas in the order in which they are presented.
- Determine the length of the original. Count the words if the original is short; count the lines or pages if it is long.

To write a concise summary you should first learn how to identify the main ideas of a piece and how to restate them in your own words. During the prewriting stage you will practice these skills as you follow the steps for writing a formal summary.

## Recognizing Main Ideas

After you are certain you understand the selection, you can move on to distinguishing between main ideas and supporting ideas. To find the main ideas, ask, "Which idea is more general than all the others?" In many cases the sentence expressing the most general idea will be the topic sentence of a paragraph or the thesis statement of an essay or article. Sometimes, however, the main idea will be implied, not stated. In such cases, compose a statement of your own that expresses the main idea. Study these examples.

**MODEL: Main Idea Stated**

## Weight-Lifting Goals

Despite its apparent simplicity, or perhaps because of it, people have different ideas about what the sport of weight lifting should be. Some confine themselves to seeing how many pounds they can lift. Others feel that strength should be combined with speed. Still others think that what's most important is not what they lift but how their muscles look after they lift it.

—*William F. Allman,* "Weight Lifting: Inside the Pumphouse"

The main idea of the preceding paragraph is stated directly in the first sentence, or topic sentence. Now look for the implied main idea in the paragraph that follows.

**MODEL: Main Idea Implied**

## Teenagers and Gulls

An outsider might look at a group of teenagers standing in front of a school and see only a confused and apparently random grouping of individuals. This interpretation, however, would be misleading, just as misleading as it would be to describe a colony of herring gulls as a bunch of birds. The gullery is, in reality, a highly structured society with leaders and followers, defined territories, and a whole host of subtle but very powerful symbols that keep each gull in its place. It is the same with the teenagers standing in front of their school. Generally everybody in the group knows who the leaders are, and a careful observer might be able to spot the leaders by the particular confidence in the way that they walk or stand and by the way others in the group act toward them.

—*Daniel Cohen,* Human Nature, Animal Nature: The Biology of Human Behavior

In the preceding paragraph there is no stated idea that is more general than the others. The main idea is quite clear, nevertheless, and could be expressed as follows: *However random they may seem, certain groups of people, like certain groups of animals, are highly structured.* All the other sentences support this idea.

Find the **main idea** in a passage by identifying the most general statement or by expressing an **implied main idea** in your own words.

## PRACTICE YOUR SKILLS

### *Recognizing Main Ideas*

**Write the main idea of each paragraph that follows. If the main idea is implied, write your own sentence expressing the idea.**

**1.** Some of the most important movies to come from postwar Europe were the Neo-Realist films from Italy. These films show life as it is lived, not as film studios imagine it to be. They show the streets, the houses, the vital everyday people of a struggling world; they neglect glamour, fancy houses and clothes, and movie stars. They argue against poverty, unemployment, inadequate housing, and the moral chaos caused by the war; and they offer realistic approaches, if not solutions, to realistic problems. The postwar Neo-Realist movement was short-lived, but it contributed some film masterpieces and left a distinct influence on future film-making.

**2.** The producer works closely in the selection of actors and actresses, and he or she makes sure that the length of their contracts fits the overall shooting schedule. He or she goes over the shooting script (the screenplay broken down into shots, scenes, and locations) to plan indoor sound-stage settings and outdoor shooting locations. The locations must be scouted for such all-important variables as weather, geography, local facilities, transportation, and accessibility. The shooting schedule must be planned around another set of variables, which includes shooting "out of continuity" (in other words, a film in which the last scene might be shot before the first) and weather (when the script calls for sun, the schedule must be planned for a time of year when the sun is likely to shine). When the movie is completed, the producer is in charge of selling it to distributors, of planning advertising and publicity, and of other agreements, such as sales to television. If the film is successful at the box office, the producer takes a large share of the profits. If it wins awards, such as the Academy Award for the best picture, it is the producer, not the director, who receives it.

**3.** Movie photography is the responsibility of two people: the director of photography and the camera operator. The director of photography (also called the cinematographer) attends the story conference and plans the shots to be filmed in consultation with the director, writer, and other members of the unit. The camera operator is the person responsible for overseeing the lighting and operating the camera used in shooting the film. In many films the two roles are performed by the same person.

**4.** When Harrison Ford gets into a fight in *Raiders of the Lost Ark* (1981), the chances are that he is not in the fight at all but that a "double" is performing for him. Stunt performers act as doubles for actors and actresses when the action called for in the script is dangerous. Other stunt performers are experts at various sports or at driving fast cars or at falling off horses without getting hurt. Great skill is used in photographing these performers so that the audience sees their work but not their faces. When the film is edited, we are fooled into thinking that the stars of a picture are also excellent skiers or boxers or motorcyclists.

*Preceding Excerpts by Richard Meran Barsam,*
In the Dark: A Primer for the Movies

## Communicate Your Ideas

**PREWRITING** *Main Ideas*

Read "At Long Last, Another Sun with a Family of Planets," on pages C517–C519. Then list all the main ideas in the selection. Save your work for future use.

SAVE YOUR WORK

## Drafting

Writing Process

Once you understand all the main ideas of a selection, you are ready to write the first draft of your summary. The draft should include all the important ideas of the original, restated in your own words and presented in a shortened form.

## Condensing

Condensing means shortening the information in a passage. You can do this by eliminating repetitious ideas and other unnecessary details such as examples and descriptions. In addition you can combine ideas and reduce long phrases and clauses into shorter expressions. Study the following passage and its summary to see just how these techniques are applied. The sentences in both the original passage and the summary are numbered for easy reference.

**MODEL: Condensing**

### Mount Rushmore

ORIGINAL

**(1)** Rushmore got a great deal of free publicity in 1934 when the Hearst newspapers sponsored a contest for a six-hundred-word history to be carved on Mount Rushmore. **(2)** An inscription had been part of Gutzon Borglum's design for a long time. **(3)** At one point he had asked [President] Coolidge to write the inscription, but he and Coolidge disagreed over the wording, so nothing came of that. **(4)** Eight hundred thousand entries were submitted in the Hearst contest, and many cash prizes were given. **(5)** No entries were ever used because eventually Gutzon abandoned the inscription idea in favor of a great Hall of Records to be cut in the stone of the canyon behind the faces. **(6)** Gutzon felt that records carved or placed in a room in the mountain would last much longer than any identifying inscription on the surface of the mountain.

SUMMARY

**(1)** In 1934, the Hearst newspapers sponsored a contest for an inscription to be carved on Mount Rushmore, which had been part of artist Gutzon Borglum's original plan. **(2)** Eight hundred thousand people responded. **(3)** Although many won cash prizes, their inscriptions were abandoned when Borglum decided instead to create a Hall of Records, a room carved into the stone, which he felt would last longer than an outdoor inscription.

The following chart shows how the sentences from the original paragraph were condensed in the summary.

| ORIGINAL SENTENCE | | SUMMARY SENTENCE |
|---|---|---|
| 1 and 2 | → | 1 (main idea) |
| 3 | → | omitted (unnecessary detail) |
| 4 | → | 2 |
| 5 and 6 | → | 3 |

**Writing Tip**

**Condense** information by omitting repetition and unnecessary details and by combining ideas from two or more sentences into one sentence. Present the main ideas and the important supporting details in the same order as the original.

## Practice Your Skills

### *Condensing*

**Condense each of the following paragraphs to no more than two sentences.**

**(1)** Writers exclaim over the coast of Maine so often that their descriptions lose meaning. "Rugged," "rockbound," and "pineclad" generally fail to stir up any visions of this northeastern shore. Yet the Maine coast is all of them and much more, too. It is a splendid part of the country—shaped and hammered by vast natural forces, softened by forests, haunted by human history. People cannot visit these coves and harbors without falling hopelessly in love with the feeling of morning fog burning off under a warm sun, the scent of pine needles in the cool shade of the forest, the taste of wild blueberries, the muffled thunder of waves, the crisp hue of sunset on a cool evening. The best example of the 3,478-mile Maine coast (including the islands) is Acadia National Park, which became the first great park in the East.

**(2)** During the last Ice Age, this shoreline was pressed down by the huge weight of ice and snow. Glaciers scraped the rocky land, smoothed the hills, cracked loose rock away from parent ledges. The result is a sunken coast where what were once valleys are now sounds and inlets, where little granite islands jut from the ocean, where tumbled boulders clog the shore. Most of Maine is like this: Acadia typifies it. For here rise the heights of Mount Desert Island, the round-sculptured remnants of the pre-Ice Age mountain ridge. Its tallest summit is the highest point in the United States that overlooks the Atlantic, and one of the first to catch the rising sun's rays.

**(3)** A deep, narrow sound cuts Mount Desert Island almost in two: Somes Sound, the only true fjord on the New England coast. On either side the hills rise, covered with tough, stunted pine and spruce and rich with wild-flowers. Cadillac Mountain, 1,530 feet, marks the high point. Below it spreads Frenchman Bay and the old summer resort of Bar Harbor.

**(4)** The history of Mount Desert Island portrays a long struggle for ownership. Samuel de Champlain, a French explorer, discovered the island and named it L'Isle des Monts Deserts (the Isle of Bare Mountains). A French colony, later founded on the island, was taken over by English colonists from Virginia. Subsequently, the island was owned privately by several British and French aristocrats including Antoine de la Cadillac, who founded the city of Detroit, and Sir Francis Bernard, the last English governor of Massachusetts. After the Revolutionary War the land was sold to settlers in Maine. By 1900, Mount Desert Island was discovered by thousands of summer visitors.

**(5)** Acadia was donated to the Federal government by the summer residents (once called "rusticaters" by the locals) who, between them, owned most of Mount Desert Island. That's why the park boundaries are strangely uneven—they follow the property lines. Most of the 48-square-mile park lies on Mount Desert Island; some is across Frenchman Bay on the Schoodic Peninsula; some occupies part of the Isle au Haut, an offshore island southwest of Mount Desert. All these park lands contain choice elements of scenery. Fresh-water ponds and lakes gleam among the dark evergreens on Mount Desert. Trout, salmon, and bass flirt with the angler, while salt-water fishing invites visitors to brave the gray Atlantic in chartered vessels.

–*Paul Jensen,* National Parks

## Paraphrasing

Another valuable technique when summarizing material is **paraphrasing**—that is, using your own words to express the main ideas and essential details. One technique for paraphrasing information is to use synonyms to replace the original words. A second method is to vary the sentence structure of the original.

## Evaluating

When you plan a party, you do not invite everyone you know. Instead, you select people who know one another and who fit the occasion for the party. When you pack for a trip, you likewise do not take everything you own. Instead, you select only those things that will meet your needs on the trip. In each case you select items by **evaluating,** or judging, them according to a particular set of criteria, or standards. This is the procedure you should follow when you select ideas to include in a summary.

As you gain practice in writing summaries, you are likely to develop criteria of your own. The list below, however, will help you get started evaluating ideas. If you find you answer *yes* to one or more of the questions, you will probably want to include the idea in your summary.

### EVALUATING IDEAS TO INCLUDE IN A SUMMARY

**1.** Does the idea support the main thesis of the work?

**2.** Is the idea needed for the reader to understand the work? Does the thesis become unclear if the idea is omitted?

**3.** Does the idea provide new information, rather than repetitious information?

**4.** Is the idea necessary to the understanding of another idea, rather than just helpful or interesting as an example or anecdote?

**5.** Is the idea needed as a logical bridge connecting other ideas?

**6.** Summing up the work in your mind, do you find yourself including the idea?

### THINKING PRACTICE

**Use the criteria in the preceding chart to help you evaluate the main ideas you listed on page C499. Once you have evaluated each idea, put a check mark next to those ideas that you will include in your summary of "At Long Last, Another Sun with a Family of Planets." Then save your work for future use.**

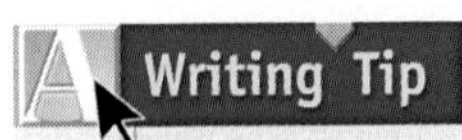


**Paraphrase,** or restate ideas in your own words, by using synonyms and varying the sentence structure of the original.

The following paraphrase shows you how the same ideas can be stated in different words.

**MODEL: Paraphrasing**

| | |
|---|---|
| ORIGINAL | Portuguese writer José Saramago was awarded the Nobel Prize for Literature in 1998 for imaginative, compassionate, and ironic parables. |
| PARAPHRASE | For the creative, sensitive and paradoxical stories he has given the world, Portuguese writer José Saramago was presented with the Nobel Prize for Literature in 1998. |

## PRACTICE YOUR SKILLS

*Paraphrasing*

**Read the following passage about the camel. Then paraphrase each sentence in the excerpt by using synonyms and by varying sentence structure. Look up unfamiliar words in a dictionary.**

**(1)** The camel has long had a reputation for being able to go for long periods of time without drinking any water. **(2)** Ancient writers believed that the camel had some mysterious internal water reservoir—a story that was told for so many centuries that it came to be believed. **(3)** No such reservoir, however, has ever been found. **(4)** Nevertheless, the camel is remarkably suited to getting along well on a minimum of water.

**(5)** Even in the Sahara's dry summer, when little natural food is available, camels can go for a week or more without water and for ten days without food. **(6)** Camels accomplish this feat by drawing on water from their body tissues and on water produced chemically as a breakdown product of fat. **(7)** The camel's hump contains up to 50 pounds of fat, which is accumulated when food and water are plentiful. **(8)** As the fat is used up to supply the camel's energy needs, about 1.1 pounds of water are produced for every pound of fat used up. **(9)** This is made possible because hydrogen is given off as a by-product in the breakdown of fat. **(10)** Oxygen from breathing is then combined with the hydrogen to produce water.

**(11)** With the help of this water-producing system, a camel can function well for a good many days, even when carrying a load. **(12)** When water is again available, the camel gulps down as much as 25 gallons at one time to compensate for the water lost during the period of deprivation.

—*William C. Vergara,* Science in the World Around Us

## Communicate Your Ideas

**DRAFTING** *Condensing and Paraphrasing*

Using your work from page C499 and page C503, write a first draft of a summary of "At Long Last, Another Sun with a Family of Planets." Use the techniques for condensing and paraphrasing. Save your work for future revision.

IN THE MEDIA

## Media Presentations

When you write summaries and abstracts, you condense your material to suit a special purpose. But media presentations are often condensed simply because there is not enough time to cover the story in detail. Some high-profile news events pre-empt regular programming, but for the most part news stories have to fit in whatever time is allotted for the newshour.

To make the stories fit, editors must cut back the information and resources they have. They may have only 30 seconds of air time to tell a story. They may have 10 minutes or more of video on the story, and 5 minutes of interviews. They simply have to cut what doesn't fit and try their best to present balanced coverage.

### Imagining What's Missing

As an exercise in judging the impact of editing on broadcast media, watch the evening news tonight. Have a stopwatch or clock nearby. When you see a story that interests you, note the time it begins. Listen closely to the story and take notes. At the end of the story, note the time and estimate how long the entire story lasted.

Now, use your imagination to ask yourself these questions: If there had been twice as long to air the story, what might have been included that was not? Would an additional person or two have been interviewed? What might they have said? Would those originally interviewed have added or clarified something that would have given a different slant to the story? What additional video clips might have been used? Write up your speculations in a paragraph.

## Abstracting

When you must make your way through vast seas of information, abstracts can serve as helpful guides. Whether you are looking for a good book to read for a research paper or whether you are simply making plans for the weekend, abstracts can save time and prevent wild-goose chases.

An **abstract** is a very condensed summary that communicates the essential content of a work in as few words as possible.

Abstracts appear in several formats and serve many purposes. A typical scientific or scholarly abstract tells the purpose of a study, the procedures of investigation, the findings, and the conclusions. Abstracts in various fields of study compile volumes of print and electronic information. Such **informative abstracts** seldom exceed 350 words, but contain enough detail for the reader to grasp the essential information without reading the full article.

You are probably more familiar with **indicative abstracts**, which give a general summary of an article, book, play, or movie in no more than two or three sentences. The entries that you find in annotated bibliographies such as the *Readers' Guide*, the content descriptions that appear in Internet search results, the synopses that appear in the table of contents of a journal, as well as the one or two line book and movie reviews of a newspaper or magazine are examples of indicative summaries. Both informative and indicative abstracts usually include the title, the author's name, a general statement of content, and publication information.

**Model: Abstracts**

*Purple Rain* (1984) A talented young musician struggles to succeed as a rival musician threatens to displace him, both professionally and romantically.

Spin Wheelright. *Thrasher Annals.* (June 1998) pages 23-34. Spin Wheelright tells of his skateboarding adventures and gives an eyewitness account of invention of the Ollie.

Read **abstracts** when compiling a list of sources to read for a research project.

## Revising

Writing Process

As you revise your summary, check for accuracy and conciseness. Reread the original to make sure you have represented the ideas accurately. Also try to reduce your summary to the fewest words possible. The following checklist will help you.

### Evaluation Checklist for Revising

- ✓ Compare your summary to the original. Are the ideas presented accurately? *(page C492)*
- ✓ Are the ideas in your summary presented in the same order as they appear in the original? *(page C492)*
- ✓ Is your summary no more than one-third the length of the original? If it is too long, condense your work further by using the strategies discussed on pages C499–C504.
- ✓ Did you use your own words and vary the sentence structure of the original? *(page C502)*
- ✓ Did you use transitions and other connecting devices to make your summary flow smoothly? *(pages C109–C110)*

## Practice Your Skills

### *Checking a Summary for Accuracy*

**Use the checklist on the preceding page to revise the following first draft of a summary. The original piece, which you will need to refer to as you revise, is on page C496.**

A group of teenagers in front of a school is as confused and random a group as a colony of herring gulls. Everybody in the group knows who the leaders are, and outsiders can spot the leaders by their confidence and the way others act toward them. Both are organized groups—with directors and followers, their own turf, and private signals.

### *Checking an Abstract for Accuracy*

**Refer to the same passage that you summarized above and write an abstract about it.**

## Communicate Your Ideas

**REVISING** *Accuracy of Summary*

Use the Evaluation Checklist for Revising on the previous page to revise the first draft of the summary you wrote of "At Long Last, Another Sun with a Family of Planets," for the activity on page C505. Save your work for later use.

In the editing stage you will tighten up your summary and abstract and check them both over to make sure that they communicate neither too much nor too little. It is important that you monitor your work for clarity, grammatical correctness, and logical consistency.

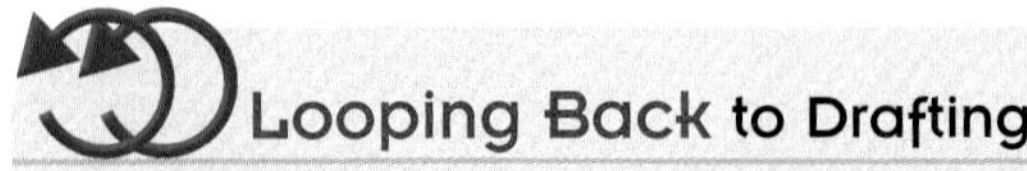

## Looping Back to Drafting

### *Recasting*

Rewrite the first draft of the summary you wrote of "At Long Last, Another Sun with a Family of Planets" as an abstract. Your first sentence may begin with either a stated or an implied subject.

## *Communicate Your Ideas*

### EDITING

Use the editing checklist on page C512 to edit the summary that you wrote of "At Long Last, Another Sun with a Family of Planets."

## Publishing

Writing Process

If you have followed the suggestions in this chapter's checklists and your summary is no more than one-third the length of the original, you have probably prepared a clear, accurate summary that is ready for publishing.

## *Communicate Your Ideas*

### PUBLISHING

Write a neat final copy of your summary. Then with your teacher's permission, meet in small discussion groups. Compare your summary with your classmates' summaries and analyze any major differences. Choose the one you think most accurately and concisely summarizes "At Long Last, Another Sun with a Family of Planets." PORTFOLIO

Prewriting Workshop
Drafting Workshop
Revising Workshop
**Editing Workshop**
Publishing Workshop

# Clauses

If there were no subordinate clauses in English, William C. Vergara's article about the camel on pages C504–C505 would have contained short, choppy sentences such as these that follow.

> The camel's hump contains up to 50 pounds of fat. The fat is accumulated when food and water are plentiful. The fat is used up to supply the camel's energy needs. About 1.1 pounds of water are produced for every pound of fat used up. Hydrogen is given off as a by-product in the breakdown of fat. Oxygen from breathing is then combined with the hydrogen to produce water.

A **subordinate clause** is a group of words that has a subject and verb but that cannot stand alone. With the underlined subordinate clauses, the sentences that Vergara actually wrote flow smoothly.

> The camel's hump contains up to 50 pounds of fat, which is accumulated when food and water are plentiful. As the fat is used up to supply the camel's energy needs, about 1.1 pounds of water are produced for every pound of fat used up. This is made possible because hydrogen is given off as a by-product in the breakdown of fat. Oxygen from breathing is then combined with the hydrogen to produce water.

**Adverb Clauses** One kind of subordinate clause—which begins with such words as *after, although, since,* and *when*—is an **adverb clause.** An adverb clause is used just like a single adverb or an adverb phrase, usually to modify a verb. In the following examples, the adverb clauses reduce unnecessary repetition and provide sentence variety.

| | |
|---|---|
| ADVERB CLAUSES | **As the fat is used up to supply the camel's energy needs,** about 1.1 pounds of water are produced for every pound of fat used up. |
| | This is made possible **because hydrogen is given off as a by-product in the break-down of fat.** |

**Punctuation with Adverb Clauses** Place a comma after an adverb clause that comes at the beginning of a sentence. Sometimes an adverb clause will interrupt the sentence. If it does, place a comma before and after the adverb clause.

| | |
|---|---|
| ADVERB CLAUSES | Even in the Sahara's dry summer, **when little natural food is available,** camels can go for a week or more without water and for ten days without food. |

**Combining Sentences with Adverb Clauses** By changing a sentence into an adverb clause and combining it with another sentence, you can express the relationship between two ideas, and eliminate unnecessary words.

| | |
|---|---|
| TWO SENTENCES | I read Vergara's article. I became interested in camels. |
| COMBINED | **After I read Vergara's article,** I became interested in camels. |

## Editing

When you edit a summary or abstract, check the form and punctuation of your clauses carefully.

### Editing Checklist

✓ Have you used subordinate clauses?

✓ Are all subordinate clauses punctuated correctly?

✓ Have sentences been combined with subordinate clauses to show the relationship between ideas?

## Process of Writing a Summary

As a student you will find it useful and even necessary to summarize information time and again, and you will find this to be even more so in many adult careers.

Refer to the following stages as you prepare written assignments throughout the year. Make them familiar enough to serve you lifelong.

### PREWRITING

- Read the original work once to understand the general idea. *(page C495)*
- Read the work a second time and make a list of unfamiliar words. *(page C495)*
- Look up each unfamiliar word and write a synonym for it or define it in your own words. *(page C495)*
- Read the work a third time, writing down the main ideas in the order in which they are presented. *(pages C495–C499)*
- Determine the length of the original work. Count words if the original is short; count lines or pages if it is long. *(page C495)*

### DRAFTING

- Present the main ideas and essential supporting ideas in the same order in which they appear in the original. *(pages C499–C500)*
- Condense the original to approximately one-third its length by
  - omitting repetition and unnecessary details. *(page C499)*
  - replacing long phrases and wordy clauses with short phrases or single words. *(pages C499–C500)*
  - combining ideas from several sentences into one concise sentence. *(pages C499–C500)*
- Restate ideas from the original in your own words by
  - using synonyms. *(pages C502–C505)*
  - varying sentence structure. *(pages C502–C505)*

### REVISING

- Use the **Evaluation Checklist for Revising** to check for accuracy and length. *(page C508)*

### EDITING

- Use the **Editing Checklists** to look for errors in grammar, usage, spelling, and mechanics. *(pages C46 and C512)*
- Use proofreading symbols to correct errors. *(page C47)*

### PUBLISHING

- Follow standard manuscript form and make a neat final copy of your work. Then find an appropriate way to share your work with others. *(pages C48–49 and C510)*

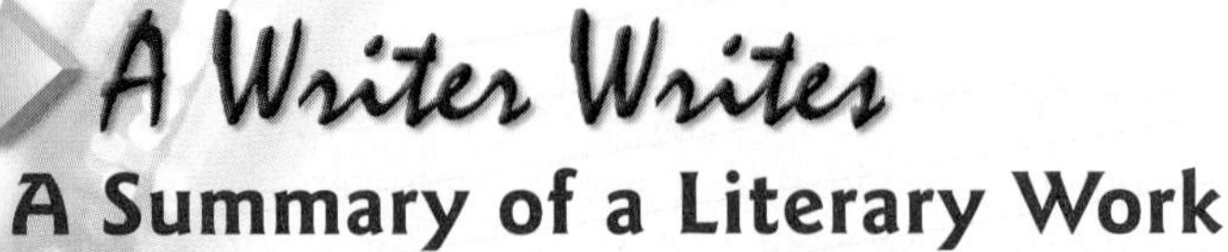


## A Summary of a Literary Work

**Purpose: to summarize a selection from your literature book and to write an abstract of the same selection as might appear in a literary journal**

**Audience: your teacher, fellow students, and other peers**

### Prewriting

Choose and reread thoughtfully a selection you have studied in your literature book. The selection may be an essay, a long narrative poem, a short story, or a short play. You might want to reread the piece a couple of times to make sure you understand the main thesis. Then complete the following prewriting tasks.

- Read the work again, listing any unfamiliar words. Look up each word and write a synonym for it or a definition in your own words.
- Read the work one more time, jotting down the main ideas in order. Evaluate the various ideas and details to determine which are basic to the main thesis of the selection. Be careful when you summarize an essay or other work that contains one or more stories or anecdotes as illustrations.
- Determine the approximate length of the work by counting the pages.

### Drafting

Begin to draft your summary by presenting the main ideas in order and condensing and paraphrasing the information. To condense the information, leave out minor details such as examples and descriptions. In addition, combine several sentences into one using phrases and clauses. Reduce the wordiness of the original by leaving out long expressions and unnecessary words. As you paraphrase the main ideas, use your own words by supplying synonyms for the original words and by varying the sentence structure.

## Revising Peer Conferencing

With your teacher's permission, discuss your summary with a partner. Compare the original selections to the summaries. Use the questions that follow to evaluate your partner's summary. Finally, use any insights you gained from your partner and the Evaluation Checklist for Revising on page C508 to finish the revision of your summary.

- Are all the important ideas of the original selection represented accurately in the summary?
- Are the ideas in the summary presented in the same order as in the original?
- Does the summary use concise language?

## Editing and Publishing

Edit your revised summary carefully, using the Editing Checklists on pages C46 and C512. To make corrections use the proofreading symbols on page C47. Then make a neat final copy to share with an interested reader. Along with other members of your class, you may want to read about and summarize the lives of some of the authors of the selections and collect your summaries into a classroom reference.

Finally, use your summary as a guide to write a concise abstract of your selection. You may want to look in literary journals in your library or on the Internet to get a feel for the way your selection's genre—short story, poem, essay, or drama—is usually treated in abstracts. Publish your abstract in a class literary journal. Consider writing abstracts of other works you have enjoyed and publishing them in the class literary journal, too.

CHAPTER 12

# Research Reports

By now, you have probably written your share of research reports. The research report is an important tool for gathering, organizing, and conveying information on any subject. When you read about a subject of personal interest or the results of the latest scientific investigations, you always learn something new. When you go a step further by analyzing and evaluating what you have read, you learn even more. When you write a research report of your own, incorporating what you have learned and contributing your thoughts, you make the information your own. This chapter will help you sharpen your investigative and analytical skills by providing step-by-step directions for writing the very best research reports that you can.

## *Reading with a Writer's Eye*

The following article from a 1999 issue of *The New York Times* online presents a startling astronomical discovery that may enable scientists to locate other solar systems like our own. Read the article until you understand the details of this discovery and its significance for research. Then, think about how you might investigate this topic, or a related scientific finding, for a research report of your own.

FROM

# At Long Last, ANOTHER SUN With a FAMILY of PLANETS

*John Noble Wilford*

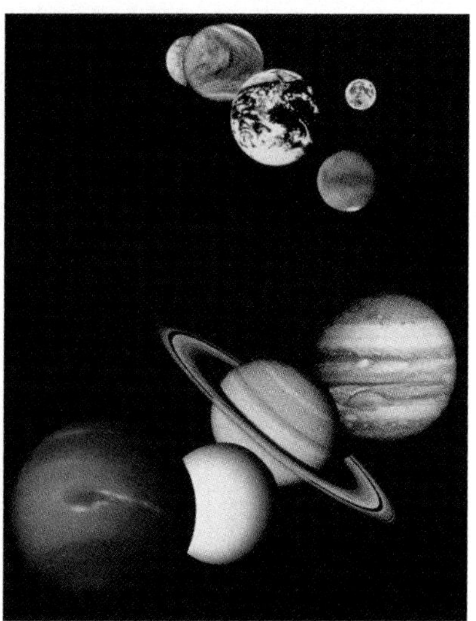

The solar system is not alone as an array of planets orbiting in the gravitational embrace of a shining star.

Laying to rest any lingering notion of the Sun's family being a singular phenomenon in the universe, astronomers announced [recently] the detection of three large planets around Upsilon Andromedae, a solar-type star 44 light-years away.

Solitary planets had been observed around several other stars in the last four years, but this is the first clear evidence showing another star accompanied by multiple planets in a stable system bearing some resemblance to the Sun's.

Two of the planets are several times more massive than Jupiter, the solar system's giant, which is 318 times heftier than Earth. The third planet, with at least three-quarters the Jovian mass, is so close to the star that it completes a full orbit—its year—every 4.6 Earth days. Astronomers said that they would not be surprised if they eventually find other, more distant objects around the star.

Other astronomers greeted the discovery with unbridled enthusiasm. They called it a major milestone in planetary science. Here, finally, was what they had eagerly been seeking: another planetary system to compare with their own. They expected further study of the Upsilon Andromedae system to challenge some theories of planet formation and evolution, and probably hatch new ones.

Of even greater philosophical as well as scientific importance, the discovery encouraged astronomers in their growing belief that the universe abounds in stars with planetary systems. This, in turn, increased the probability that some of them include habitable worlds, scientists said, though no such claim is being made for the newly discovered system.

"The single planets we found around other stars was a glorious discovery, but the architecture of other planetary systems had been missing," Dr. Geoffrey Marcy, a leader of the discovery team, said in an interview. "Here for the first time, we can see a kinship between these planets and our own solar system."

Dr. Alan P. Boss, a theorist of planetary systems at the Carnegie Institution of Washington, who must come to grips with the implications of the findings, said simply, "This is exciting stuff."

The discovery was made independently by two teams, one from San Francisco State University and the other from the Harvard-Smithsonian Center for Astrophysics in Cambridge, Massachusetts, and the National Center for Atmospheric Research in Boulder, Colorado. They joined in announcing the results at a news conference in San Francisco.

A full report, which has already been reviewed by more than a dozen independent astronomers, has been submitted for publication in The Astrophysical Journal.

"Having two completely independent sets of observations gives us confidence in this detection," said Dr. Debra Fischer, of the San Francisco team. And Marcy, the team leader and most prolific discoverer of extra-solar planets, said, "I would bet my house on it."

Although Upsilon Andromedae is a nearby bright star visible to the unaided eye, the three planets cannot be seen even with the most powerful telescopes. Astronomers infer their existence, orbits and minimum masses from years of careful study of their gravitational effects, characterized as reflex motions, on the host star. In their orbital courses, the planets tug first one way and then the other on the star, causing ever-so-slight changes in the star's velocity.

This observational technique has been responsible for the detection of 18 Jupiter-class extra-solar planets since 1995, when Swiss astronomers found the first planet around another normal star, 51 Pegasi.

Dr. Robert Noyes, a Harvard-Smithsonian astronomer, said the new observations should dispel any doubts that these objects are true planets.

"A nagging question was whether the massive bodies orbiting in apparent isolation around stars really are planets," Noyes said in a statement. "But now that we see three around the same star, it is hard to imagine anything else."

Dr. Douglas Lin, a theorist at the University of California at Santa Cruz who has sought to explain how such huge planets could exist so close to their stars, much closer than Jupiter is to the Sun, said the new detections should enable scientists to evaluate their various theories. They are struggling to understand if systems with several super-Jupiter planets, traveling eccentric orbits close to their stars, are more typical than the solar system, with its gaseous giant planets all traveling circular orbits at great distance from the Sun.

"This is a very, very important discovery," Lin said in an interview. "It tells us that planetary systems are quite ubiquitous, and some of them are quite stable. It also tells us that the existence of habitable planets is highly probable.". . .

After years of searching and speculation, both fanciful and educated, the discovery of multiple objects orbiting Upsilon Andromedae marked the beginning of the science of comparative planetary systems.

## Thinking as a Writer

### Evaluating Evidence and Intended Audience

- Read the previous article again closely. Then, determine the audience to which the evidence and findings are directed. (Keep in mind that the article may be written for more than one audience—for scientists as well as interested non-scientists.)
- Make two lists. One list should include evidence that you believe is directed at a scientific, scholarly audience. The other list should include evidence and findings that you feel are directed at a wider audience.
- Compare the two lists. Which has more items in it? What criteria did you use to categorize the evidence? If you were going to rewrite the article for only one audience or the other, what would you change? What other kinds of evidence would you include?

### Summarizing Scientific Data

Oral Expression

Many scientific reports contain what is known as an **abstract**—a one-paragraph summary of the most important findings in the report. The abstract is provided to give readers a quick and interesting introduction to the complete work.

- If you had to write a one-paragraph abstract for this article, what conclusions would you make? What would you say that would make someone want to read the entire report?
- With a partner, take turns reading your abstracts out loud. Evaluate each other for your presentation and delivery. Give each other constructive advice on ways to organize and revise these summaries.

### Comparing and Contrasting Visual Information

Viewing

- Referring to the illustrations on the following page, make a list of the similarities and differences between Earth's solar system and the system orbiting the star Upsilon Andromedae. What details from the diagram are also included in the article? If aspects of the illustrations are unclear, discuss how information presented in the article could be used to clarify the diagrams?

- Based upon the visual information available in the diagrams, what details would you add to the article to clarify the written descriptions?

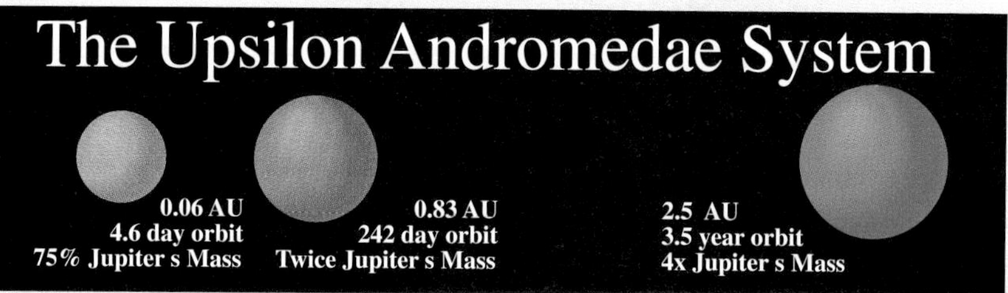


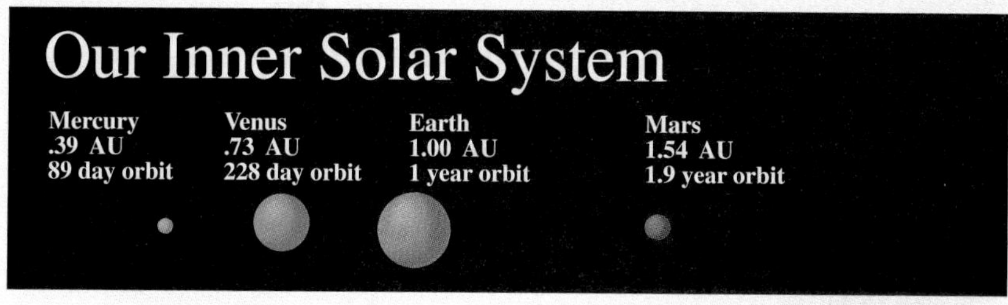

# The Power of Research Reports

Research reports are valuable means for communicating information not only in literature and the sciences, but also in your own daily life and in the lives of others. Here are some examples of situations in which research reports play important roles.

## Uses of Research Reports

**Here are just a few examples of the ways that research reports are used in everyday life.**

- **Librarians consult data from research reports,** in print and online, to determine the appropriate age groups for new reference texts.
- **Physicians use pharmacology studies** to determine whether a patient would benefit from a particular medication.
- **Mayors and city council members use land-use studies** to decide whether a new building can be constructed in a residential area.
- **College admissions officers review reports from standardized tests results,** personal essays, and high-school records to decide whether a student would be successful at their institution.
- **Attorneys review rulings in previous legal cases** and gather new evidence in order to argue their clients' cases effectively.

# Process of Writing a Research Report

"The greatest part of a writer's time is spent in reading in order to write," said Samuel Johnson, the 18th-century English author. "A man will turn over half a library to make one book." Rigorous data-gathering methods are the hallmark of a successful researcher, but extensive reading alone will not guarantee success. Equally important are the abilities to select the best material, discover the most important ideas, and organize them into a convincing research report.

A **research report** is an essay based on information drawn from books, periodicals, interviews, and media resources including Internet or other online sources.

When you write research reports, you draw on many different skills. For example, to find information in books, magazines, and electronic media, you exercise your reference and study skills. As you gather information and take notes, you use the skills of summarizing and paraphrasing. Finally, since the purpose of a research report is to convey information, you will use the skills of informative writing to help you present the information clearly and concisely.

### Your Writer's Journal

In your writer's journal, keep a list of ideas and topics that you are curious about. On the news, in a magazine article, or at a Web site you may learn about some recent scientific breakthroughs that you find particularly interesting. You may learn something in a class that you want to know more about. As you add to this list of ideas in your journal, identify the ones that you think would make a good subject for a research report. Make a note about where you might look for more information about your ideas or unanswered questions.

Your main goals in the prewriting stage of a research report are to choose your subject and then gather information about it. As you collect information, you will need a good system for organizing and keeping track of notes from different sources. Index cards, paper clips, rubber bands, and a folder with pockets will make your job easier.

## Discovering Research Subjects

Subjects for a research report can come from many sources. There are two fundamental places to look for ideas. One is inside you—your experiences and thoughts. The other is outside—the classes you take, the books you enjoy, the news stories you read, either in print or online. The following questions may help you generate ideas for an interesting subject.

## Practice Your Skills

### *Finding Ideas from Personal Experiences*

**Ask yourself the following questions and write answers to them.**

1. What dangerous situations have I found myself in? What could I tell others to help them avoid similar situations?
2. Who are my heroes? Why? What roles do heroes play today?
3. What careers interest me? What are some of the interesting aspects of these careers? What are some drawbacks?
4. What hobbies or other interests do I have? Who are the experts in these fields? What have they contributed?
5. What else would I like to know about computers or other kinds of technology?
6. How do I spend my leisure time? How do my friends spend their leisure time?

7. What places have I visited? What places would I like to visit? What places would I like to know as well as I know my own town?
8. What do I do well? What would I like to be able to do better?
9. How are the attitudes of my friends different from those of my parents? Why are they different?
10. What can I do to maintain my health and safety? What kinds of things should people know to prevent illness and injury?

### *Finding Ideas from Outside Sources*

**Ask yourself the following questions and write answers to them.**

1. What lessons in my classes would I like to know about on a deeper level?
2. Who are my favorite singers and musicians?
3. What readings have I enjoyed in English class this year?
4. What are some recent themes in movies today?
5. What political changes resulted from the last election?
6. What issues have I recently learned about from books, magazines, television, or radio shows?
7. What other classes or lessons do I take outside of school?
8. What have I learned lately from an older family member or friend?
9. What important events are happening in other parts of the world?
10. What newsworthy events happened recently?

## Choosing and Limiting a Research Subject

After you have explored your thoughts and experiences, use the following guidelines to help you choose one idea as a subject.

### Guidelines for Choosing a Research Subject

- Choose a subject you want to know more about.
- Choose a subject that will interest your audience.
- Choose a subject that can be adequately covered in a research report of about 2,000 words (or 7 typed pages).
- Choose a subject for which there is enough information from a variety of sources in the library or media center.

To see if sufficient information exists for your subject, check the computer catalog in the library or media center, as well as the *Readers' Guide to Periodical Literature*, either in print or online. If you cannot find at least two books, two magazine articles, and one online source for your subject, you should probably choose another one.

*You can learn more about using the* Readers' Guide *on pages C767–C770.*

**Limiting a Research Subject** When you are satisfied that you can find enough information, your next step is to limit your subject and give it a clear focus. The subject of black holes in space, for example, is broad enough to fill a whole book. Within that subject, though, are more specific subjects such as "how Albert Einstein's work predicted the possibility of black holes" or "how astronomers search for black holes," that are suitably limited.

One way to limit your subject is to ask yourself a series of "what about" questions. Each question helps you focus on a more specific aspect of the broader subject. The following model shows how to use "what about" questions to narrow down the broad subject of computers.

**Model: Limiting a Research Subject**

| | |
|---|---|
| BROAD SUBJECT | Computers |
| FIRST QUESTION | *What about* computers? |
| MORE LIMITED | how computers help people with disabilities |

| | |
|---|---|
| SECOND QUESTION | *What about* computers and people with disabilities? |
| MORE LIMITED | how computers help people with disabilities in language, vision, and motion |
| THIRD QUESTION | *What about* computers' helping with language, vision, and motion? |
| SUITABLY LIMITED | recent developments and successes in computers' helping people with disabilities in language, vision, and motion |

Continue your "what about" questions until your answer is a phrase. This statement will keep you focused as you work through the stages of the research and writing process.

**Limit** your subject by asking, "What about [the subject]?" until you can express the focus of your research report in a phrase or partial sentence.

One helpful way to limit a subject is by using a graphic organizer. In the following modified cluster, the broad subject appears in the middle, and the answers to your "what about" questions fill each area as you limit the subject even further.

How computers help people with disabilities

Recent developments and successes helping people with disabilities

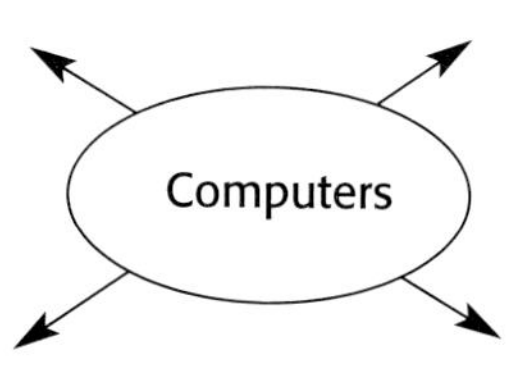


Helping people with language, vision, and motion disabilities

Recent developments helping people with language, vision, and motion disabilities

## Practice Your Skills

### *Evaluating a Research Subject*

**For each subject that follows, write *suitable* if the subject is narrow enough for a short research report, and *too broad* if it is not.**

1. the Japanese language
2. American Indian words that have become part of the English language
3. how the space shuttle serves business and research
4. baseball
5. physical fitness
6. what to do when you encounter potentially dangerous animals while hiking through the wilderness
7. Martin Luther King, Jr.
8. Poland
9. how engineers solved the problems in building the Brooklyn Bridge
10. the Ming dynasty

### *Limiting a Research Subject*

**For each subject above that is too broad, write a series of "what about" questions and answers until you arrive at a suitably limited subject. Use the model on pages C526–C527 as a guide and, if necessary, use a cluster diagram to organize your notes.**

## *Communicate Your Ideas*

**PREWRITING** *Research Subject*

Review your **journal** notes on a possible research subject. Identify those subjects that would be most appropriate for a report on recent scientific findings. You may want to review your answers to the questions on pages C524–C525 for some ideas, and you may want to review recent newspaper or magazine articles for other subject ideas. Once you have a list of at least five possible subjects, use the criteria on page C526 to help you select one subject. After you choose one, use a graphic organizer to limit it until your final choice is one that is focused and manageable. Save your work for later use. SAVE YOUR WORK

## Gathering Information

Once you have a suitably limited subject, your next step is to formulate a list of questions that your report should answer. If you have decided to write a report on current developments in how computers are helping people with disabilities, for example, your guide questions might include the following.

**MODEL: Guide Questions**

- Are there different kinds of computers for different disabilities?
- How do computers help people with language disabilities?
- How do they help people who have lost their ability to speak or have never been able to speak?
- In what ways do computers help people who are blind "see"? How do they help them read and write?
- How do computers help people who have limited mobility or are paralyzed? What tasks do they help them perform?
- What are the costs of this technology? What are the benefits?

After you have a list of five to ten questions, locating the appropriate library or media center resources will help you answer them. The following steps will guide you through the process of locating appropriate sources.

### Guidelines for Gathering Information

- Consult a general reference work such as an encyclopedia or handbook either in print or online to get an overview of your subject. Make note of any sources that are listed at the ends of relevant entries.
- In the library or media center, do a subject search in the online catalog for books on your subject, or check the subject cards in the card catalog.
- Consult the *Readers' Guide to Periodical Literature,* either in print or online, to find magazine articles on your subject.
- Use a search engine to do a keyword search on the Internet for Websites and other online resources for your subject. Note the exact addresses of sites that you think will be useful.
- For research on past events or federal policies, consult microfiche or microfilm databases to identify articles and government documents that may no longer be available in print.
- Be sure to use a variety of primary sources (firsthand accounts) and secondary sources (information about primary sources), to explore your subject in depth, especially if your subject is about an historic figure or event.
- Make a list of all the sources you find. For each one, record the author, title, copyright year, name and location of the publisher, and call number or Internet address, if there is one. If your source is a magazine or newspaper, record the name and date of the publication, the author, the title, and the location (section and page numbers) of the article.
- Assign each source a number to identify it in your notes.

As you begin to search for information about your subject, remember that not all sources you will find are equally reliable and credible. Depending on how you have limited your subject, many may not be useful for your research purpose. Before you use a source in your report, you need to evaluate it with some basic criteria in mind: All of your sources should be relevant to the topic and unbiased. The information should relate directly to your limited subject; the author should be a credible authority on the subject; the information should be current; and if the subject is debatable or controversial, your report should present a different points of view on the subject.

*For more information on evaluating online sources refer to pages C825–C827.*

**Writing Tip**

Be sure to evaluate your sources for credibility and relevance before using them in your report.

**Conducting an Interview** In some cases, you may need to do some original research to gather information that's not available in printed or online sources. If you know of one or more experts who can contribute valuable information to your report, make an appointment to interview them, either in person or by telephone. The following steps will help you prepare for an interview and conduct it productively.

### Steps for Conducting an Interview

- Prepare at least five specific questions to ask the person you are interviewing.
- Go to the interview with your questions in hand, either in a notebook, or on index cards. Take pencils, pens, and a note pad for taking notes. Bring a small tape recorder if you have one.
- If you are taking notes quickly, summarize the main ideas in your own words.
- Listen for important details and interesting phrases that you might be able to quote in your report. Be sure to write these quotes word for word and indicate them with opening and closing quotation marks.
- If you need extra time to write your notes, politely ask the interviewee to wait for a few moments while you finish writing.
- If you are recording the interview, be sure to take some notes in your own words at the same time, in case anything goes

wrong with the tape recorder. If you have time to record comments word for word, be sure to use quotation marks.

- Immediately after the interview, review your notes. Fill in any details that you may not have had time to write down.
- Thank the person for agreeing to the interview. Offer to share a copy of your finished report.

## PRACTICE YOUR SKILLS

### *Gathering Information*

**Using the resources in the library or media center, list five sources for three of the following subjects. At least two of your sources should be magazine articles, and one should be an online source. Be sure to include all the information named in the guidelines for gathering information on page C530.**

1. violence on television
2. pros and cons of nuclear power plants
3. improving public housing
4. new energy-efficient car designs
5. fighting air and water pollution

### *Conducting an Interview*

**Interview a classmate in preparation for a research report on the future plans of today's high school graduates. Follow the steps outlined in the Steps for Conducting an Interview on page C531 and above. After the interview is done, write a paragraph or two paraphrasing the conversation. Include some direct quotations in your paraphrase.**

*You may wish to review the information on paraphrasing on pages C502–C505.*

## Analyzing a Subject

Breaking something down into its various parts is usually the best way to understand it—whether it is a car, a story, or an idea. When you carry out the process systematically, you are **analyzing.** As you prepare to write a research report, stop to analyze your subject. Ask yourself how you can break it down into smaller parts. To open your mind and help you analyze the subject, try a cluster. Below, for example, is a cluster made by a student preparing a research report on computers.

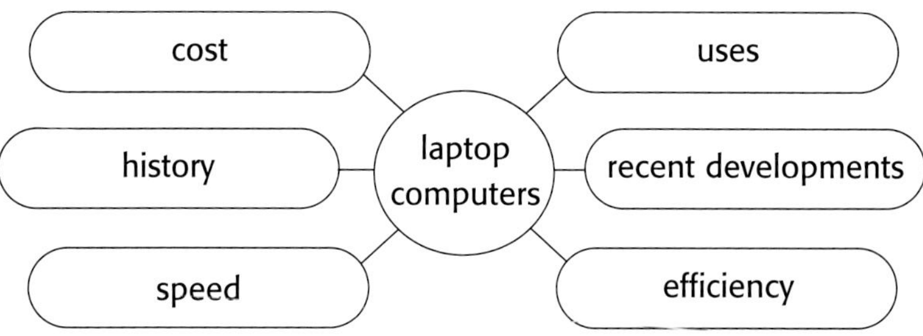


Once you have identified the major parts of a subject, you can use them to limit the subject and also point out specific directions for your research.

### THINKING PRACTICE

**Make a cluster to analyze the main parts of your research report, and use it to limit your subject and decide on specific aspects of your topic you should investigate**

## Evaluating Sources

An essential part of all research is making sure that your sources are current, accurate, and objective. If a book has an old publication date, for example, it may be missing critical new information. If the author is biased—has a strong leaning toward one viewpoint because of emotion or self-interest—then the book or article may have only information that supports the author's viewpoint. The following checklists will help you evaluate your sources.

### Checklist for Evaluating Books

- ✓ Check the table of contents and the index. Is there information on your limited subject in the book?
- ✓ What is the publication date? If the subject requires the most up-to-date information, such as recent medical findings, then avoid books that are more than a few years old.
- ✓ Who is the author? What are his or her credentials? You can find these by reading the book jacket or by reading about the author in a biographical reference work.
- ✓ Is there anything in the author's background that might suggest a biased viewpoint?

### Checklist for Evaluating Articles

- ✓ Does the article contain specific information on your limited subject?
- ✓ When was the article published? If your subject requires the most up-to-date information, then avoid publications that are more than a few years old.
- ✓ Who is the author? What are his or her credentials? You can find these in a note at the beginning or end of the article.
- ✓ Does the magazine or newspaper appeal to a special interest group that may have a biased viewpoint on your subject? For example, a magazine called *Conserving Energy* would probably try to persuade people to rely less on automobiles. A periodical called *Highways and Byways,* on the other hand, might try to boost tourism by encouraging people to use their automobiles for long trips.

### Checklist for Evaluating Internet Sources

- ✓ Start by identifying the top-level domain name. Is the site maintained by a for-profit company (.com) that might be trying to sell something? Is it an educational institution (.edu) which tends to be more reliable, or an independent organization (.org)? If it is an organization, is it one whose name you recognize or is it one that you have never heard of before?
- ✓ If the Website contains an article, is it signed? If it is not signed, you should be skeptical of its credibility. If you do not recognize the author's name, you can send a question to a newsgroup or listserver asking if anyone else knows something about this person. You can also do a Web search using the author's name as the keyword to get more information.
- ✓ Does it use reasonable and sufficient facts and examples to make its points? Is it free from obvious errors?
- ✓ Do the language and graphics avoid sensationalism?
- ✓ Has the site been recently updated? Is the information still current? Look for a date on the main Web page indicating the last time it was updated.
- ✓ Has it been evaluated by one of the Website ranking services, such as Lycos or Magellan? Did it receive a favorable rating?

After using the preceding checklists to evaluate books, articles, and online sources, use only those sources you can rely on for accuracy and objectivity. Five to ten good sources should supply you with enough information to build a strong research report.

## Practice Your Skills

*Evaluating Sources*

**Each of the following sources for a report on consumer safety suffers from one of the weaknesses listed below. Write the weakness that applies to each source.**

**A.** probably outdated **C.** lacks strong author credentials

**B.** probably biased **D.** does not relate to subject

1. "Unnecessary Safety Controls Will Raise Prices," article in *Toymaker's Trade,* written by Lara Scranton, director of public relations at Smile-a-While Toy Company, published in 1998.
2. "Consumer Price Index Holds Steady," article in *Today* magazine, written by Manuel Garcia, chief economist at Central State Bank, published in 1999.
3. *Consumer Rights and Safety,* book published in 1963, written by William Stepanian, researcher in the Office of Consumer Affairs in the state of Illinois.
4. "The Need for Warning Labels," article in *Your House* magazine, written in 1999 by Helene Mayer, a magazine writer who writes a regular column on fashion tips.
5. "Harmful Additives," pamphlet published in 1999 by Nature-Foods Industries, written by Kyle Gardner, Executive Vice President of Nature-Foods Industries.

## Communicate Your Ideas

**PREWRITING** *Sources*

Make a list of five to ten guide questions that will help you find more information about your limited topic. These are the questions that your report will answer. Then gather appropriate sources using the guidelines on page C530. Use the checklists on pages C534–C535 to evaluate each source you find. Eliminate any sources that do not fulfill the criteria or that you feel doubtful about. Keep your list of sources for later use.

## Taking Notes and Summarizing

The research guide questions you developed earlier will help you locate relevant information in each source. As you take notes on that information, keep the following guidelines in mind.

As you use each index card, write the identifying number of each source in the upper right-hand corner of the note card. Then, in the upper left-hand corner, write the topic of the note. In most cases that topic will correspond to one of your guide questions. On each card, include only notes that relate to a single topic. Then clip the cards from each source together. As you take notes, include only information that answers a guide question. However, as you acquire more information, you may want to revise your questions to be more specific or to cover different aspects of your subject.

**Writing Tip**

The goals of **note taking** are to summarize main points in your own words and record quotations that you might use in your research report.

The following paragraphs are from a *Forbes* magazine article. The source has been assigned the identifying number *10*. Read the excerpt and compare it with the sample note card that follows.

**Model: Taking Notes on a Source**

Past Cambridge University's King's College, where dozens of bicycles lean against time-blackened, 15th-century walls, a dim courtyard off Silver Street houses the Department of Applied Mathematics and Theoretical Physics.

There, in a cluttered, dank office, one of the true geniuses of 20th-century science quietly goes about his daily work of pondering the universe. He is Stephen Hawking, 45, the world's greatest theoretical physicist.

For more than 20 years this seminal thinker has suffered from amyotrophic lateral sclerosis, a progressively debilitating, ultimately fatal nerve disease that strips its victims of the ability to walk, talk, and eventually move even a finger. For a decade, Hawking has been wheelchair bound. Several years ago he lost his ability to speak altogether.

But Hawking keeps right on thinking and communicating from within his bodily prison, and for that both he and the world can thank the advances of computer technology and bionic medicine. At the office, Hawking writes and talks through an IBM personal computer equipped with a voice synthesizer and custom-designed communications software. Outside the university, he uses a battery-operated computer with a small, liquid crystal screen and a voice synthesizer that is mounted beneath the seat of his motorized wheelchair.

To start his desktop computer, Hawking moves his thumb (one of the few remaining activities he can perform) to press a button on a box that an assistant places in the palm of his hand. A menu of letters and words appears on the computer screen. Hawking presses another button to move his cursor to the desired words, which then slowly appear as complete sentences at the bottom of the screen. Another movement from his thumb sends the sentence to a built-in voice synthesizer, which generates speech. During a recent interview with *Forbes,* Hawking pressed on his box several times until the disembodied voice asked, "Can I have some tea?"

*—Richard C. Morais,* Forbes

**Sample Note Card**

topic

*Speech Loss* 10 — source number

—*Stephen Hawking, famous British physicist*

—*disease amyotrophic lateral sclerosis = limits talking and eventually all movement*

—*"But Hawking keeps right on thinking and communicating from within his bodily prison, and for that both he and the world can thank the advances of computer technology and bionic medicine."* — quotation

—*with thumbs move cursor to find letters and words on screen to form sentence* — paraphrase

—*with thumb pressers button and voice synthesizer "says" sentence*

*p. 142* — page number

## Practice Your Skills

### *Taking Notes*

**Take notes on the following excerpt about Stonehenge, the ancient arrangement of stones in England through which one can observe celestial activities. The excerpt is from pages 117–118 of the book *Stonehenge Decoded,* written by Gerald S. Hawkins and John B. White. Assume that the work has the identifying number *3.***

The Stonehenge sun-moon alignments were created and elaborated for two, possibly three, reasons: they made a calendar, particularly useful to tell the time for planting crops; they helped to create and maintain priestly power, by enabling the priest to call out the multitude to see the spectacular risings and settings of the sun and moon, most especially the midsummer sunrise over the heel stone[1] and the midwinter sunset through the great trilithon;[2] and possibly they served as an intellectual game.

To amplify a little on those three supposed reasons, let me state that it is well known that methods for determining the times of planting were of most vital concern to primitive peoples. Those times are hard to detect. One can't count backwards from the fine, warm days; one must use some other means. What better means could there be for following the seasons than observation of those most regular and predictable recurring objects, the heavenly bodies? Even in classic times there were still elaborate sets of instructions to help farmers to time their planting by celestial phenomena. Discussing the "deep question" of the "fit time and season of sowing corn," Pliny[3] declared, "this would be handled and considered upon with exceeding great care and regard; as depending for the most part on Astronomy . . . " Doubtless there are today farmers who time their planting by the sky.

---

[1] Large stone standing alone outside the circular structure and marked with a heel-shaped nick at the bottom.

[2] A trilithon is a grouping of three rocks in which two tall pillar rocks are connected at the top by a third that spans the distance between them.

[3] An ancient Roman writer.

As for the value of Stonehenge as a priestly power enhancer, it seems quite possible that the person who could call the people to see the god of day or night appear or disappear between those mighty arches and over that distant horizon would attract some of the aura of deity. Indeed, the whole people who possessed such a monument and temple must have felt lifted up.

The other possible reason for the astronomical ingenuity . . . of Stonehenge is, I must admit, my own invention. I think that those Stonehengers were true ancestors of ours. I think that the people who designed its various parts, and perhaps even some of the people who helped to build those parts, enjoyed the mental exercise above and beyond the call of duty. I think that when they had solved the problem of the alignments efficiently but unspectacularly, they couldn't let the matter rest. They had to set themselves more challenges, and try for more difficult, rewarding, and spectacular solutions, partly for the greater glory of their pre-Christian gods, but partly for the joy of humans, the thinking animals. I wonder if some day some authority will establish a connection between the spirit which animated the Stonehenge builders and that which inspired the creators of the Parthenon, and the Gothic cathedrals, and the first spacecraft to go to Mars.

## Communicate Your Ideas

**PREWRITING** *Source Notes*

Take out the sources you have evaluated for your research report and use your guide questions to take notes on each of them. Refer to the model note card on page C538 to help you with this process. Be sure to include all the indicated information to help you later in the writing process. When you have finished, clip your note cards together and save for later use.

## Developing a Working Thesis Statement

After you have finished taking notes, draft a **working thesis statement** that expresses the main idea of your report. The following working thesis statement is based on information gathered about computers helping people with disabilities.

*You may wish to review information on developing a thesis statement on pages C347–C348.*

**MODEL: Working Thesis Statement**

Computers are able to help people who have language problems, vision problems, and motion problems related to paralysis and loss of limb.

## PRACTICE YOUR SKILLS

### *Writing a Working Thesis Statement*

**Below are notes on automated sensors, which allow animated computers to sense objects around them. Write a working thesis statement that covers the information and then save your work.**

- Some animated computers are programmed to hear and respond to only one human voice giving commands.
- The sense of touch in some computers is controlled by receiving an electrical charge when it touches an object.
- Some computers can be programmed to respond to any human voice.
- The simplest form of computer sight is the ability to detect the presence or absence of light.
- In some hearing computers, a double-entry system is used. The first step is a voice command from its programmer; the second step is an additional command from the programmer.
- Some computers can control the amount of pressure they exert on an object through what is called force feedback.
- Some computers can "see" gradations of light and dark, not merely its presence or absence.
- Some computers use television cameras as a vision device.

- Some computers do not have to touch things to know they are nearby; proximity sensors tell them when they are near objects.

## Communicate Your Ideas

**PREWRITING** *Working Thesis Statement*

After reviewing the notes you made on your sources, formulate a working thesis statement that expresses the purpose and main idea of your research report. Save the statement for later use.

## Organizing Your Notes

Your working thesis statement and your guide questions are all you need to help you sort your note cards into categories. Notice, for example, that the following categories on the subject of computers helping people with disabilities are directly related to the questions that guided the research. Some questions have been left out, however, to control the length of the report.

**Model: Organizing Note Cards into Categories**

| | |
|---|---|
| Category 1 | How computers help those with language disabilities |
| Category 2 | How computers help those with vision-related problems |
| Category 3 | How computers help those with paralysis or loss of limb |
| Category 4 | Computer costs versus benefits |

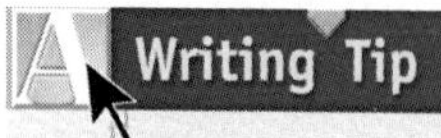


Group your notes into three or more main categories of information.

After you arrange your note cards by category, clip the cards in each group together. If some notes do not fit a category, put them into a separate group for possible use in your introduction or conclusion.

## PRACTICE YOUR SKILLS

*Creating Categories*

**Review the notes on automated sensors from your last practice exercise. List the three categories into which you can group the details and then, under each category, write the details that belong in that group. Save your work.**

## Outlining

Your final prewriting step is to organize your notes into an outline. As the basis for your outline, use the categories into which you grouped your notes. Then look over your notes to determine the overall organization of the details in the report. If your subject is a historical event, **chronological order** may be appropriate. If you intend to describe something, **spatial order** may be suitable. However, the two most common methods of organizing research reports are **order of importance** and **developmental order.**

*For more information about ordering information, you may want to review page C34.*

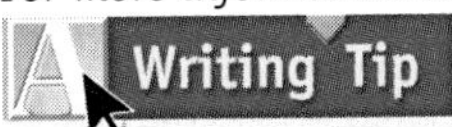


Plan the **outline** of your research report by deciding on a method of organization and by assigning your categories accordingly, using Roman numerals.

The following model is the beginning of the outline for the report on computers and people with disabilities. Notice the parallel phrasing.

**Model: Categories**

**I.** Computers helping people with language disabilities
**II.** Computers helping people with vision disabilities
**III.** Computers helping people with motion disabilities

The outline omits one category from the previous page—*Computer costs versus benefits*—because this material will be covered in the conclusion.

Once you have outlined your main topics, you can use the information on your note cards to add subtopics (listed with capital letters) and supporting points (listed with Arabic numerals). To check that the form of your outline is correct, refer to the checklist on page C352.

The following outline can serve as a model for your own outline. Each group of subtopics and details is phrased in parallel form.

**Model: Outline**

| | |
|---|---|
| Working Thesis Statement | Computers are able to help people who have language problems, vision problems, and motion problems related to paralysis and loss of limb. |
| Main Topic | **I.** Computers helping people with language disabilities |
| Subtopics | **A.** Program for children slow in speech development |
| | **B.** "Light talkers" for cerebral palsy victims |
| | **C.** Computer and speech synthesizer |
| | **II.** Computers helping people with vision disabilities |
| | **A.** "Seeing Eye" computers |
| | **B.** Reading machines |
| Supporting details | **1.** Convert print into vibrating rods |
| | **2.** Convert print into speech and Braille text |

3. Convert print into electronic impulses
4. Convert calculator operations into speech
5. Convert typed messages into speech

**III.** Computers helping people with motion disabilities

**A.** Wheelchairs with legs
**B.** Voice-operated computers
**C.** Eye-operated computers

1. ERICA
2. Sutter's Work

**D.** Work stations

## Practice Your Skills

### *Writing an Outline*

**Using your notes on creating a working thesis and creating categories, write an outline about automated sensors. Write your working thesis statement at the top of your report. Then, in your outline, show three main topics with at least three subtopics under each one. List the main topics with Roman numerals and the subtopics with capital letters.**

## Communicate Your Ideas

**REWRITING** *Outline*

Write an outline for your own research report. Begin by organizing your note cards into categories and arranging those categories. Then create an outline based on the categories you created. As you fill in subtopics and details from your notes, check the form of your outline. Save your work for later use.

COMPUTER TIP

Most word-processing software makes it easy to create an outline on the computer. Click on the **View** menu on the toolbar and choose **Outline.** Different heading styles are automatically assigned to each level of your outline. As you arrange and rearrange the headings and subheads, the program automatically applies the heading styles to them.

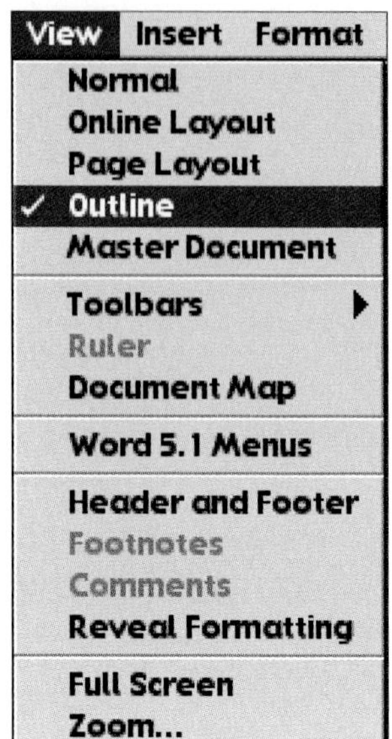


# Drafting

Writing Process

Once you have synthesized, or pulled together, your research to form an outline, you should use that outline as the basis of your first draft. As you draft, you want to flesh out your outline, adding an introduction and conclusion and working the results of your research into the flow of your report. You will begin by drafting a focused thesis statement.

## Writing the Thesis Statement

A clear, well-worded **thesis statement** expresses your main idea and serves as a guiding beacon to help you keep on track as you write your first draft. Therefore, before you start to write, evaluate your working thesis to ensure that it covers all the topics in your outline—and only those topics. You may have to try two or three times before your working thesis is focused. The following guidelines will help you revise your working thesis statement.

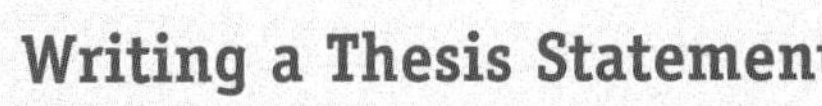

### Writing a Thesis Statement

- A thesis statement should make the main point of your research report clear to a reader.
- A thesis statement should be broad enough to cover all the main topics listed in your outline.
- A thesis statement should be narrow enough to cover only the topics listed in your outline.
- A thesis statement should fit smoothly into your introduction.

Suppose you are doing research on the subject of animals' natural camouflage and have come up with the following main topics.

I. Creatures with spots resembling eyes that appear threatening to would-be predators
II. Creatures with coloration that matches the environment
III. Creatures with coloration that changes with the seasons

You might then start with the following working thesis.

**MODEL: Working Thesis Statement**

> Many creatures find some protection from predators through coloration that blends into the environment.

The preceding thesis is too narrow because it fails to include the category of creatures with eyespots, whose camouflage does not blend into the environment but instead makes the creature appear threatening. A simple revision, however, can broaden the thesis.

**MODEL: Revised Thesis Statement**

> Many creatures adopt a disguise that helps protect them from predators.

## Practice Your Skills

### *Refining Thesis Statements*

**Rewrite each of the following numbered thesis statements so that it covers all the main topics in the accompanying outline (shown with Roman numerals).**

**1.** Many of Mexico's most important exports are foodstuffs.

I. Sugar

II. Cotton

III. Coffee

IV. Forestry products

**2.** The three climate zones of Mexico are determined by the various altitudes of the lands.

I. Tierra fria (cold lands), above 1,830 m (6,000 ft.)

II. Tierra templada (temperate lands), plateau region at 1,830 m

III. Tierra caliente (hot lands), coastal areas below 900 m (3,000 ft.)

IV. Shortage of rainfall in all climate zones except in some coastal areas

**3.** The Social Security System in Mexico is similar to that of the United States.

I. Benefits for accidents and disability

II. Retirement pensions

III. Differences

**4.** Mexico shows the influences of many different cultures.

I. Spanish influence on language

II. Spanish influence on customs

III. Survival of some ancient Indian languages and customs

**5.** The site of Mexico City is unusual.

I. Situated on former lake; land under buildings is sinking

II. Valley location makes waste disposal a problem

III. High altitude makes air pollution from cars a problem

**DRAFTING** *Revised Thesis Statement*

Using the guidelines for writing a thesis statement on pages C546–C547, revise the working thesis statement that you wrote at the top of your outline. Be sure that the thesis statement covers all the information you have gathered in your research. 

## Structuring the Research Report

With your thesis statement revised, you can move on to the remainder of your report. Below is a summary of the parts of a research report and their special purposes.

| THE STRUCTURE OF A RESEARCH REPORT | |
|---|---|
| **Title** | suggests the subject of the report |
| **Introduction** | captures attention<br>provides important and interesting background information<br>contains the thesis statement |
| **Body** | supports the thesis statement with information drawn from research<br>consists of a series of well-developed paragraphs |
| **Conclusion** | brings the report to a close by restating the thesis or giving fresh emphasis to ideas stated previously |
| **Citations** | credit appropriate sources of words, facts, and ideas |
| **Works Cited** | lists sources used in preparing the report<br>appears at the end of report |

Read the following model research report, noticing how each element fits into the whole structure. In addition, notice how research details are worked in and cited. When you write your own report, you will also incorporate words, ideas, and facts from your sources. Each time you use information from a source, write the title, author, and page number in parentheses directly after the detail. Since the following report has been revised and edited, you can use it as a model to work toward as you draft and redraft. As you read, notice how the paper follows both the **Structure of a Research Report** on page C549 and the outline on page C544.

**MODEL: Research Report**

TITLE

# *New Help for People with Disabilities*

INTRODUCTION

Computers have proved their usefulness in business, learning, and play. For much of the population, at work and at home, they have made ordinary tasks easier, faster, and often more fun. Computers, however, can do more than make already possible procedures more efficient. For many people with disabilities, computers can make the impossible possible by providing language for those who cannot speak, vision for those who cannot see, and movement for those who cannot move.

THESIS STATEMENT

BODY: MAIN TOPIC I

A computer program to help children with language disabilities communicate has been developed by Laura Meyers, a specialist in children's language development. As a child types on the keyboard, each letter, word, and sentence is displayed on the screen and "pronounced" by a voice synthesizer—a device that imitates the sound of a human voice. Meyers says, "The children see the thought printed. They hear it repeated, and it becomes psychologically real to them because they did it themselves" (Adelson 166). Once the computer has spoken for the children, they find it easier to speak for themselves.

BORROWED WORDS IN QUOTATION MARKS

The United Cerebral Palsy Association of Nassau County, New York, holds preschool classes in which children with cerebral palsy use "light talkers." They hit a switch that lights up a picture and sends a spoken message. If a child lights up the Cookie Monster, for example, the computer declares, "I'm hungry" (Cunningham 17). Older children use more complicated light talkers with many more pictures and messages.

Adults unable to speak as a result of disease or injury are also using speech synthesizers to communicate. A victim of the disease amyotrophic lateral sclerosis, the world-famous physicist Stephen Hawking is unable to talk or to move, except for his thumb. "But Hawking keeps right on thinking and communicating from within his bodily prison, and for that both he and the world can thank the advances of computer technology and bionic medicine" (Morais). Using his thumb on a keyboard, he selects words and letters and sends them to a voice synthesizer that speaks for him.

**BODY:**
MAIN TOPIC II

Computers are also opening new doors for the visually impaired. Scientists in the Mechanical Engineering and Applied Mechanics Mobile Robotics Lab at the University of Michigan have developed "GuideCane," an eight-pound cane with a motorized, steerable foot with ultrasonic sensors on all sides. The user can push a small joystick near the handle to tell the cane where they want to go, and the cane steers him or her in the correct direction around obstacles (Kaplan).

**BORROWED FACTS CITED WITH A NOTE**

Devices have also been developed to help people who are blind read. One reading machine converts printed characters into patterns of vibrating rods that can be "read" with the fingertips. Another more sophisticated machine converts a printed text into synthesized speech and also into Braille (Cattoche 59). A computer mouse, or pointer, has been adapted to carry electronic impulses that allow users who are blind to "read" the screen through their fingertips (Bronson 140). New York City's National Technology Center of the American Foundation for the Blind is working on advanced tools, such as talking scientific calculators (Cunningham 16). Finally, computers that use speech synthesizers to convert typed messages into "spoken" ones are extremely useful for students and workers who are blind, just as they are for people who are language-impaired.

**Body:** MAIN TOPIC III

Computers have come to the aid of people who are movement-impaired as well. "Even such familiar devices as wheelchairs are being souped up using microprocessors and sophisticated computer design" (Bronson 143). John Trimble at the Veterans Administration Hospital in Hines, Illinois, is working on a chair with movable legs controlled by a microprocessor. Mechanical devices work hand in hand with computers, even on the simplest level. A program at the University of Illinois produced a mechanical table that lowers a computer screen within the reach of a user who can move only one finger ("Engineers' Devices" 44).

In 1985, a football accident paralyzed Marc Buoniconti from the neck down. Four years later Marc was a college honors student, aided by a voice-operated computer that answered the phone, turned off lights, and performed other tasks (Rogers 66).

Even people who can neither move nor speak can begin to do things on their own. In August 1986, Jamie Mitchell, who was eighteen and had cerebral palsy, looked at a spot on a computer screen to signal that he wanted his back scratched —the first time he was able to communicate a wish. He used ERICA, the Eye-gaze Response Interface Computer Aid developed by Thomas Hutchinson, professor of biomedical engineering at the University of Virginia. "An infrared camera records light from the eye, and the computer indicates which portion of the screen the eye is focused on" (Albrecht 86). Dr. Lance Meagher, a victim of amyotrophic lateral sclerosis, cannot move, talk, or even breathe on his own. Yet one day he hopes "to fly solo around the world," thanks to Erich Sutter of San Francisco's Smith-Kettlewell Institute of Visual Sciences (Ward 30). Electrodes implanted in Meagher's skull pick up brain waves produced when his eyes focus on an object. By staring at a command on a computer screen, Meagher can make the computer carry out that command. Other systems are also being worked on to allow patients "to use their eyes as the sole means of communicating and controlling their environment" (Weiss).

"Robots may be the next logical partners for disabled workers" (Rogers 66). Work stations that combine computers with robot arms enable users to control lights, pick up books, even get things from the refrigerator. As a result, workers with disabilities can be fully productive. Schools, too, play a large role in integrating the disabled into the workplace. Denver Community College trains the visually impaired for programming and network administration jobs. Director Kevin Kellerman, who is himself blind, notes that the school has graduated more than 200 computer specialists. The training involves equipping students with adaptive technology, such as voice recognition software, which they can use on personal computers (York).

CONCLUSION

Although the costs of developing technological aids are enormous, the rewards are enormous too. Moreover, money that went into long-term care and hospitalization of those with disabilities, as well as lost wages and skills, can now be devoted to research into computer technology for people with disabilities. "This is the best chance we've had for those we have left behind to be allowed to catch up" (Rash 130).

**Works Cited**

Adelson, Suzanne. "Laura Meyers Creates Software That Talks Friendly to Help Disabled Kids Find Their Voices." People Weekly 4 Dec. 1989: 65–66.

Albrecht, Lelia. "With Thomas Hutchinson's Marvelous ERICA, a Flick of an Eye Brings Help to the Helpless." People Weekly 20 July 1987: 85–86.

Bronson, Gail. "In the Blink of an Eye," Forbes 23 Mar. 1987: 140+.

Cattoche, Robert J. Computers for the Disabled New York: Watts, 1986.

Cunningham, Ann Marie. "High-Tech Help." Technology Review Feb.-Mar. 1989: 16–17.

"Engineers' Devices Aid the Disabled." The New York Times 26 Feb. 1989, late ed., sec. 1: 43–44.

Kaplan, Karen. "High-Tech Tools Give Disabled the Senses of Accomplishment," Los Angeles Times 19 Jan. 1999, 20 Jan. 1999 <http://www.prodworks.conVIatimes 11899.html>

Morais, Richard C. "Genius Unbound." Forbes 23 Mar. 1987: 142.

Rash, Wayne, Jr. "A Helping Hand." Byte Dec. 1989: 129–30.

Rogers, Michael. "More Than Wheelchairs." Newsweek 24 Apr. 1989: 66–67

Ward, Darrell. E. "Gaze Control." Omni Dec. 1988: 30.

Weiss, Rick. "Disabled Communication: The Eyes Have It." Science News 20 Aug. 1988: 122.

York, Thomas. "Computer industry offers oppor tunities for disabled workers." CNN Interactive. 23 Sept. 1998, 25 Sept. 1998 <http://www.cnn.conVTECI-1/ computing/9809/25/jobopps.idg/>

## Using Transitions

Transitions help you achieve a smooth flow and a logical progression of ideas. Therefore, in your research report, use transitional words and phrases such *first, second, most important,* and *finally.* Other transitional devices are repeated key words or phrases from earlier sentences or paragraphs and pronouns used in place of nouns from earlier sentences.

*For a list of transitions and more information on using them refer to page C110.*

*Recognizing Transitions*

**Answer the following questions about the research report on computers and people with disabilities on pages C550–C554.**

1. What transitional word showing contrast prepares readers for the thesis statement?
2. What key word from the thesis statement is repeated in the first sentence of the second paragraph?
3. What transitional word leads into the fifth paragraph?
4. What transitional phrase in the sixth paragraph shows the relative sophistication of the vision aid that converts printed text into Braille?

## Using and Citing Sources

Because the words and ideas of authors are protected by copyrights, failure to give credit for borrowed words, ideas, and facts is a serious offense, called **plagiarism.** Therefore, give credit to the original authors for any borrowed material by providing parenthetical notes, footnotes, or endnotes. In addition, a list of works cited, which is similar to a bibliography, must appear at the end of your report.

**Using Sources** When you have worked hard to find appropriate sources and to obtain sound supporting material, you want to present it as effectively as possible. The following five techniques will help you work borrowed words and ideas smoothly into your writing, particularly when you write a research report.

### Tips for Using Sources

1. Use a quotation to finish a sentence you have started.

   EXAMPLE Other systems are also being worked on using patterns of eye movements to allow patients "to use their eyes as the sole means of communicating and controlling their environment" (Weiss).

2. Quote a whole sentence.

   EXAMPLE "This is the best chance we've had for those we have left behind to be allowed to catch up" (Rash 130).

3. Quote just a few words.

   EXAMPLE Yet one day he hopes "to fly solo around the world," thanks to Erich Sutter of San Francisco's Smith-Kettlewell Institute of Visual Sciences (Ward 30).

4. Paraphrase and summarize information from a source.
5. Quote five or more lines from your source. Start the quotation on a new line after skipping two lines and indenting ten spaces. Single-space the quoted lines. Do not use quotation marks for such an extended quotation. Use a colon in the sentence that introduces the quotation.

   EXAMPLE Stephen Hawking writes and talks by means of his computer and voice synthesizer:

   > A menu of letters and words appears on the computer screen. Hawking presses another button to move his cursor to the desired words, which then slowly appear as complete sentences at the bottom of the screen. Another movement from his thumb sends the sentence to a built-in voice synthesizer, which generates speech (Morais).

## PRACTICE YOUR SKILLS

### *Using Sources*

**Read the following article about continental drift and use it as a source to complete the assignment that follows.**

## *Catching the Drift*

The longer you wait to take that trip to Europe, the farther you'll have to go. Researchers at the National Aeronautics and Space Administration say that the continents of Europe and North America may be drifting apart at the rate of as much as two-thirds of an inch a year.

"Not only that," says Goddard Space Flight Center geophysicist David Smith, "but Peru moved two inches away from Hawaii in 1983, while Australia drifted two inches toward it." Smith and his colleagues have been collecting data from laser tracking stations located all over the world. The stations shoot a beam of laser light at a satellite as it flies overhead. The satellite is studded with hundreds of mirrors that are constructed in such a way that they reflect a light beam back at its source. By accurately calculating the orbit of the satellite and timing the laser beam's trip to the satellite and back, Smith and other geophysicists can map the positions of the tracking stations on the Earth to within nearly an inch. The scientists get similar results by clocking radio waves from space as they arrive at various points on Earth.

The research is the first direct measurement of the rate of continental drift. According to the theory of plate tectonics, already widely accepted among geologists on the basis of other geological evidence, the continents and ocean floors are not firmly rooted on the Earth but rather are part of large plates that "float" on the Earth's mantle. As the plates drift and slide into each other they are deformed, creating mountain ranges and deep sea trenches and causing earthquakes along the fault lines where the two plates meet. At one potential earthquake zone, California's San Andreas Fault, tracking stations on either side of the fault moved nearly three inches in one year.

*–Science '84*

**1.** Write a sentence about the drifts of Europe and North America. End your sentence with a quotation.

**2.** Write three sentences describing how the laser measurements are taken. One sentence should be a direct quotation.

3. Write a paragraph about continental drift and the theory of plate tectonics. Include an extended quotation of at least five lines. Be sure to indent and space the quoted lines correctly. Remember that quotation marks are not necessary.
4. Write a sentence about land's drifting toward and away from Hawaii, quoting just a few words from the source.
5. Write a paraphrase of the last sentence.

## *Communicate Your Ideas*

**DRAFTING** *First Draft*

Write a first draft of your research report. First, review your revised thesis statement, note cards, and outline. When drafting your introduction, rework your thesis statement so that it fits in smoothly. Then follow your outline to draft the body. At this point, do not worry about using the correct form for parenthetical citations. Instead, simply identify the source and page number fully enough so that you know which source you are using. After finishing the body, draft your conclusion, and save your work for later use.

**Citing Sources** The notes in a research report that show the original sources of borrowed words or ideas are called citations. There are three different types of citations.

| | |
|---|---|
| PARENTHETICAL CITATIONS | appear within parentheses directly following the borrowed material in the report itself |
| FOOTNOTES | appear at the bottom of the page |
| ENDNOTES | appear on a separate sheet at the end of the report, after the conclusion but before the works cited page or bibliography |

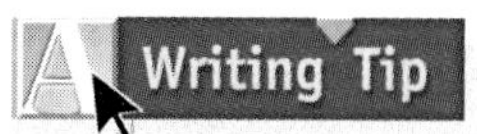


Cite the sources of information you include in your research report by using **parenthetical citations, footnotes,** or **endnotes.** Use only one type of citation throughout the report.

The following guidelines will help you determine which information in your report requires a citation.

### Tips for Citing Sources

- Cite the source of a direct quotation. Use direct quotations when the original wording makes the point more clearly.
- Cite the sources of ideas you gained from your research, even when you express the ideas in your own words.
- Cite the sources of figures and statistics that you use.
- Do not cite sources that are common knowledge.

**Using Parenthetical Citations** One way to cite a source in a research report is with a parenthetical citation, as shown in the model report. In a parenthetical citation, you give the reader just enough information in the report itself to identify the source. The reader then refers to the list of works cited at the end for more complete information about sources. The following information provides examples of the correct form for parenthetical citations.

| | |
|---|---|
| Books with a Single Author | Give author's last name and page reference: (Cattoche 46). |
| Books with Two or More Authors | Give both authors' names and a page reference: (Edwards and Barsett 23). |
| Article with Author Named | Give author's last name and a page reference if article is longer than a page: (Adelson 65). |
| Article with Author Unnamed | Give title or shortened form of title, article, and page reference if article is |

| | |
|---|---|
| | longer than a page: ("Engineers' Devices" 43). |
| ARTICLE FROM GENERAL REFERENCE WORK, AUTHOR UNNAMED | Give title or shortened form of title; no page number is needed if article is one page or if it is from an alphabetically arranged encyclopedia: ("Speech Synthesis"). |
| WORKS BY SAME AUTHOR | Give author's last name, title of work, and page reference: (Morais, "Genius Unbound" 142). |
| AUTHOR NAMED IN TEXT | Give only the page reference: (142). |
| ARTICLE FROM AN ONLINE DATABASE THAT COMES FROM A PRINT SOURCE | If the author is known, give the last name and a page or paragraph number. If the author is unnamed, give the title of the article (if brief) and a page or paragraph number. |
| ARTICLE FROM AN ONLINE DATABASE THAT HAS NO PRINT EQUIVALENT | Give name of the author, if available. If not available, give the name of the article or site, and the page or paragraph number. |
| ARTICLE FROM A CD-ROM | If the author is known, give the last name and a page number. If the author is unnamed, give the title of the article (if brief) and a page or paragraph number. |

You should place parenthetical citations as close as possible to the words or ideas being credited. In order to avoid interrupting the natural flow of the sentence, place the citations at the end of a phrase, a clause, or a sentence. The following guidelines will tell you specifically where to place the citation in relation to punctuation marks.

*See examples in the sample research report on pages C550–C554 and in the Tips for Citing Sources on page C559.*

### Correct Placement of Parenthetical Citations

- If the citation falls next to a comma or end mark, place the citation before the punctuation mark.
- If the citation accompanies a long quotation that is set off and indented, place the citation after the end mark.
- If the citation falls next to a closing quotation mark, place the citation after the quotation mark but before any end mark.

**Using Footnotes or Endnotes** The correct form for footnotes and endnotes is essentially the same. Both use a superscript, unlike parenthetical citations, which do not require one. A superscript is a number above the line in the text, to refer readers to the footnote or endnote with the same number. The superscript comes immediately after the borrowed material. In the final copy of your research report, individual footnotes are single-spaced (with a double space between each footnote), while endnotes are double-spaced.

**Model: Correct Form for Footnotes and Endnotes**

| | |
|---|---|
| General Reference Works | [1]George Epstein, "Computer," World Book Encyclopedia, 1990 ed. |
| Books With a Single Author | [2]Robert J. Cattoche, Computers for the Disabled (New York: Watts, 1986) 46. |
| Books With More Than One Author | [3]George Edwards, and Helen Bassett, Computers for the Visually Impaired (New York: Dover, 1999) 23. |
| Articles in Magazines | [4]Suzanne Adelson, "Laura Meyers Creates Software That Talks Friendly to Help Disabled Kids Find Their Voices," People Weekly 4 Dec. 1989: 65–66. |
| Articles in Newspapers | [5]"Engineers' Devices Aid the Disabled," The New York Times 26 Feb. 1989, late ed., sec. 1: 43–44. |

INTERVIEWS

[6]Dr. Michelle Harper, personal [or telephone] interview, 31 Aug. 1999.

ARTICLE FROM AN ONLINE DATABASE THAT COMES FROM A PRINT SOURCE

[7]Karen Kaplan, "High-Tech Tools Give Disabled the Senses of Accomplishment," Los Angeles Times, 19 Jan. 1999, 20 Jan. 1999 <http://www.prodworks.conVIatimes 11899.html>.

ARTICLE FROM AN ONLINE DATABASE THAT HAS NO PRINT EQUIVALENT

[8]Thomas York, "Computer industry offers opportunities for disabled workers." CNN Interactive, 23 Sept. 1998, 25 Sept. 1998 <http://www.cnn.conVTECI-1/computing/9809/25/jobopps.idg/>.

Notice in number 5 above that if the author of an article is not given, the footnote begins with the title of the article.

For repeated references, the author's last name and the page number are enough to refer to a work already cited in full. If you have cited more than one work by the author, include a shortened form of the title in the shortened footnote.

REPEATED REFERENCE

[1]Morais 142.
[2]Cattoche, Computers 61.

**List of Works Cited** All of the sources cited or mentioned in the report are listed in the works cited section.

A **works cited** page is an alphabetical listing of sources used in a research report. It appears at the end of the report.

The entries in a list of works cited differ from parenthetical citations, footnotes, and endnotes in four main ways. (1) The first line is not indented, but the following lines are. (2) The author's last name is listed first. (3) Periods are used in place of commas, and parentheses are deleted. (4) No specific page reference is necessary. The entries would be listed in alphabetical order—according to the first word of the entry—on one or more separate pages at the end of the research report. The entire works cited list should be double-spaced.

## Model: Correct Form for a List of Works Cited

| | |
|---|---|
| General Reference Works | Epstein, George. "Computer." World Book Encyclopedia. 1990 ed. |
| Books With A Single Author | Cattoche, Robert J. Computers for the Disabled. New York: Watts, 1986. |
| Books With More Than One Author | Edwards, George, and Helen Bassett. Computers for the Visually Impaired. New York: Dover, 1999. |
| Articles in Magazines | Adelson, Suzanne. "Laura Meyers Creates Software That Talks Friendly to Help Disabled Kids Find Their Voices." People Weekly 4 Dec. 1989: 65–66. |
| Articles in Newspapers | "Engineers' Devices Aid the Disabled." The New York Times 26 Feb. 1989, late ed., sec. 1: 43–44. |
| Article from an Online Database that Comes from a Print Source | Kaplan, Karen. "High-Tech Tools Give Disabled the Senses of Accomplishment," Los Angeles Times 19 Jan. 1999. 20 Jan. 1999 <http://www.prodworks.conVIatimes 11899.html>. |
| Article from an Online Database that Has No Print Equivalent | York, Thomas. "Computer industry offers opportunities for disabled workers." CNN Interactive. 23 Sept., 1998, 25 Sept. 1998 <http://www.cnn.conVTECI-1/computing/9809/25/jobopps.idg/>. |
| Interview | Harper, Michelle. Telephone interview. 31 Aug. 1999 |

In addition to or instead of a list of works cited, your teacher may ask you to include a **bibliography** or a list of works consulted.

These lists of sources include all of the sources that you used to research your subject, regardless of whether you cited them in the research report itself.

## Practice Your Skills

### *Citing Sources*

**Use the information in each item to write (1) a parenthetical citation and (2) a footnote. Follow the models on pages C561 and C562.**

**1.** Title of newspaper article: Engineers Fight the Mississippi's Sense of Direction
Location of article: Section IA, p. 36
Name and date of newspaper: Chicago Tribune; August 30, 1984

**2.** Title of book: Mighty Mississippi: Biography of a River
Publishing company: Ticknor and Fields
Author: Marquis W. Childs
Place and date of publication: New Haven; 1982
Page number: 72

**3.** Title of article in encyclopedia: Mississippi River
Edition of encyclopedia: 1980
Author of article: Johnson E. Fairchild
Name of encyclopedia: Collier's Encyclopedia

**4.** Name of magazine: National Geographic
Page number: 227
Author of magazine article: Douglas Lee
Title of article: Mississippi Delta: The Land of the River
Date of Magazine: August 1983

**5.** Author of magazine article: Susan Tiftt
Page number: 19
Name and date of magazine: Time. January 23, 1984
Title of article: Going with the Floe

*Preparing a Works Cited List*

**Use the information above to prepare a works cited list for a research report about the Mississippi River. Alphabetize the entries and follow the format shown on page C563.**

## Communicate Your Ideas

**DRAFTING** *List of Works Cited*

Prepare the list of works cited for your own research report. Place the entries in alphabetical order and follow the format on page C563. Then, using the examples on pages C559–C560, put your parenthetical citations in the correct form. If you need more information, refer to the *MLA Handbook of Writers of Research Papers* by Joseph Gibaldi and Walter S. Achtert. Save your work for later use.

## Revising

Writing Process

When you have finished the first draft of your report, if possible put it away for a day or so. Then come back to it with a fresh eye to find ways to improve it. Keep in mind as you reread the report that the writing process does not always move in a forward direction. Sometimes you must return to one of the earlier stages and do more work. For example, if you do not have all the information you need, you may have to return to your sources or look for additional sources. Ask yourself: Have I adequately covered all the main points in my outline? Have I consulted enough sources to write adequately on my subject? If not, consider returning to an earlier stage to do more work. The following guidelines will help you as you revise.

## Evaluation Checklist for Revising

**Checking Your Research Report**

✓ Does your introduction contain a well-worded thesis statement? *(pages C546–C547)*

✓ Does your research report support the thesis statement?

✓ Did you use transitional devices? *(pages C554–C555)*

✓ Did you use and cite sources correctly? *(pages C555–C565)*

✓ Does your report have unity, coherence, and emphasis? *(page C370)*

✓ Does your conclusion add a strong ending? *(page C367)*

✓ Does your report have a title?

**Checking Your Paragraphs**

✓ Does each paragraph have a topic sentence? *(page C101)*

✓ Is each paragraph unified and coherent? *(pages C107–C110)*

✓ Does one paragraph lead smoothly into the next? *(pages C554–C555)*

**Checking Your Sentences and Words**

✓ Are your sentences varied and concise? *(pages C68–C79)*

✓ Did you avoid faulty sentences? *(pages C79–C86)*

✓ Did you use specific words with appropriate connotations?

## Communicate Your Ideas

**REVISING** *Revised Draft*

Using the Evaluation Checklist for Revising above, revise the research report you've drafted. As you revise, you might find it helpful to have a writer's conference and share your work with another student whose judgment and opinions you respect. A person who reads it for the first time can often identify errors or suggest places for improvement that you have overlooked. Save your revised report for later use.

# Sentence Structure and Punctuation

When the findings from "At Long Last, Another Sun With a Family of Planets" were publicized in scientific journals and in the media, the information had to be accessible and interesting to different audiences. One way to make your writing consistently clear and interesting to your readers is to vary your sentence structure.

## Kinds of Sentence Structure

The four basic kinds of sentences—simple, compound, complex, and compound-complex—are classified by the number and kind of clauses within each sentence. A **simple sentence** consists of one independent clause that can stand alone as a sentence. A **compound sentence** consists of two or more independent clauses. A **complex sentence** consists of one independent clause and one or more subordinate clauses that have subjects and verbs but cannot stand alone as sentences. A **compound-complex sentence** consists of two or more independent clauses and one or more subordinate clauses. When you revise your writing, always check to see whether you have used a variety of sentences.

| | |
|---|---|
| Simple Sentence | They called it a major milestone in planetary science. |
| Compound Sentence | "The single planets we found around other stars was a glorious discovery, but the architecture of other planetary systems had been missing." |
| Complex Sentence | Dr. Robert Noyes, an astronomer, said the new observations should dispel any doubts that these objects are true planets. |

| | |
|---|---|
| COMPOUND-COMPLEX | Dr. Alan P. Boss, a theorist of planetary systems, who must come to grips with the implications of the findings, said simply, "This is exciting stuff." |

## Punctuation with Compound and Complex Sentences

The two independent clauses in a compound sentence can be joined by either a comma and a coordinating conjunction or by a semicolon.

| | |
|---|---|
| COMMA AND CONJUNCTION | "The single planets we found around the other stars was a glorious discovery, **but** the architecture of other planetary systems had been missing." |
| SEMICOLON | The third planet has at least three-quarters the mass of Jupiter**;** it completes a full orbit every 4.6 Earth days. |

## Capitalization and Punctuation of Titles

Apply the following rules to the works cited page in your research report.

- **Capitalize** the first word, the last word, and all important words in the titles of books, newspapers, magazines, and works of art.
- **Underline** or italicize the titles of long written or musical works that are published as a single unit.
- **Use quotation marks** to enclose the titles of chapters, articles, and stories.

### Editing Checklist

✔ Have different sentence structures been included to create variety?

✔ Are the sentences punctuated correctly?

✔ Are the titles written correctly?

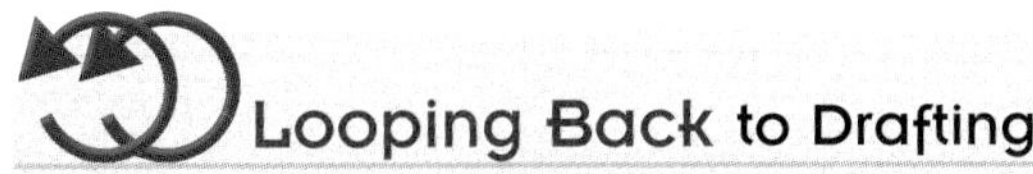


### *Order and Coherence*

Remember that the writing process is recursive—you often need to move back and forth among the stages of the process to achieve your writing purpose. As you edit your report, does the order of presentation still seem logical, coherent, and interesting? Sometimes, you may need to rearrange passages to make your report more clear. After making any necessary changes, reread the draft carefully to check for continuity and coherence.

The final version of your report should be a document that others can learn from and use as a reference. It may even be something that you want to submit for publication in a school newspaper or magazine. Therefore, your finished work should always be free of errors in spelling, punctuation, grammar, and mechanics that can detract from your ideas and weaken your presentation.

## Communicate Your Ideas

### EDITING

Using the guidelines in the **Editing Workshop** on pages C567–C568 and in the **Evaluation Checklist for Revising** on page C566 (as well as your personalized checklist), edit your report. Watch especially for words in which you've accidentally transposed letters or words that should be capitalized or lowercased. You may want to proofread your work using proofreading symbols to help you with this process. Save your work.

*You may want to review the list of proofreading symbols on page C47.*

## COMPUTER TIP

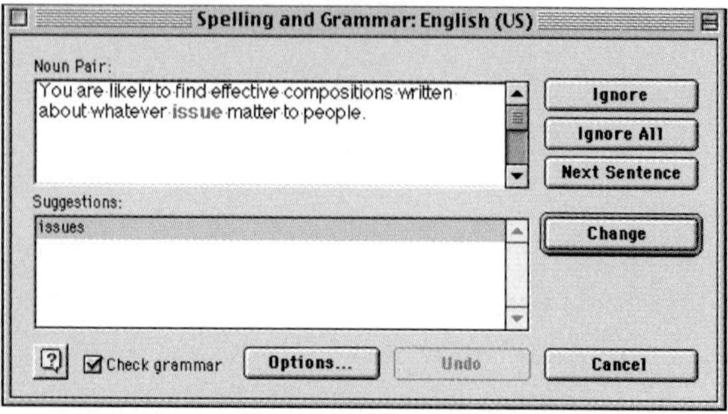


Always check your work for errors in spelling and grammar before saving the final version. The **Spelling and Grammar** feature found on the **Tools** menu of most word-processing programs can help you with this. Remember, a spell checker cannot check for proper usage if there is no spelling error. Always read your work carefully as you edit.

## Publishing

Writing Process

Always make a neat final copy of your report before sharing your work with others. You may want to submit it to a school, regional, or national publication, or a Website. If you prepared your research report on a computer, you might want to use its desktop publishing features to make a professional version of your work, complete with graphics and photos. Consider this possibility, as you choose the best way to present your research to the public.

## Communicate Your Ideas

### PUBLISHING

Make a neat final copy of your report before sharing your work with others. Use the guidelines for standard manuscript form shown on pages C49–C52 to prepare the final draft. You may want to post your report to a Website about your topic. Keep at least one copy of your finished report in your portfolio.

**PORTFOLIO**

*You can find more ideas for publishing your report on page C372, and more information about electronic publishing in* A Writer's Guide to Electronic Publishing, *pages C788–C813.*

## Documentary

The news media are bombarded with press releases every day. But what about the stories people *don't* want the press to know about? How do the hidden stories ever get told?

The answer lies in investigative journalism. Sometimes the investigations begin because of a rumor; sometimes they begin because someone calls reporters with a tip. Discovering answers to haunting questions is the basis of investigative work.

One way to stretch your research skills is to help create an investigative documentary. This is a video product that documents evidence previously unknown. Your project does not need to uncover a hidden ill of society or the wrong-doing of a public official—it should just present well-documented answers on a subject of genuine interest to you. The full procedures for planning, producing, and finishing a video are outlined in **A Writer's Guide to Electronic Publishing**, pages C799–C809. They require teamwork, so organize a team of at least six students.

Choosing the subject of your documentary is by far the most important task. Be sure the subject you choose:

- is one your group is genuinely interested in
- will hold the interest of your intended audience
- is feasible to document on film
- is feasible to research
- can be covered in no more than 15 minutes

When you have chosen a subject, write a few paragraphs to answer these questions:

- What idea will be communicated through the documentary?
- Who is the intended audience?
- What point of view will be used?
- What evidence will be collected?
- What effect is the documentary expected to have on the audience?

Develop a rough guide, or "treatment," for your documentary.

Finally, assign roles to your team members. These include the following at least:

- project leader/director
- production manager
- video engineer
- researchers/interviewers
- scriptwriters
- equipment manager
- sound recorders
- editors
- narrator(s)
- photographers
- location coordinator
- graphic artist (for titles)

Team members assigned to writing the script should think *pictures* first and then *audio*. They may want to work in a two-column format like the one shown below.

| **Video** | **Audio** |
|---|---|
| Sam stands at the bank of the river with the fertilizer plant clearly in the background over his left shoulder. He gestures toward the plant then looks down at the river water. | SAM: It is clear that the emissions from the fertilizer plant are largely responsible for the dead fish, the dying vegetation, and the stench that hangs over this once pleasant environment |

The scriptwriters should show the steps in the investigation itself, changing locations as needed, and summarize the results at the end.

When shooting begins, the director shapes the scenes while the equipment manager provides the lighting and other technical needs. Sound recordists and camera persons follow the director's lead. Remember to shoot more than you think you need, since much material is lost in the editing process. Work until you are satisfied that your scenes are in the best possible sequence, that you have used all the techniques of your visual medium to their best effect. Add music, if appropriate, any necessary voiceovers, and titles.

Before deciding you have a final cut, show a preview of your documentary and ask your audience to respond honestly. If necessary, re-edit to make the film more effective based on their reactions.

When you have finished, you might enjoy corresponding electronically with other student groups who have produced their first films. Inkspot.com, which calls itself "The Writer's Resource," offers discussions, bulletin boards, and opinion polls on many topics. You can find this site at <http://www.inkspot.com/forums/topics.html>.

## Process of Writing a Research Report

### PREWRITING

- After developing a list of possible subjects, choose one and limit it. *(pages C524–C529)*
- Make a list of questions to guide your research. *(page C529)*
- Gather information from books, magazines, newspapers, and interviews with experts. *(pages C529–C536)*
- Use note cards for taking notes and summarizing your sources. *(pages C536–C540)*
- Write a working thesis statement. *(page C541)*
- Organize your notes by finding categories. *(page C542)*
- Use your working thesis statement and note categories to outline the body of your research report. *(pages C543–C546)*

### DRAFTING

- Revise your working thesis statement as needed. *(pages C546–C547)*
- Write your first draft, including an introduction, body, and conclusion. *(pages C549–C555)*
- Avoid plagiarism by using and citing sources carefully. *(pages C555–C565)*
- Add a title. *(page C549)*

### REVISING

- Using the Evaluation Checklist for Revising, check your report for structure, well-developed paragraphs, unity, coherence, emphasis, and varied and lively sentences and words. *(page C566)*

### EDITING

- Using the Editing Checklist, check your grammar, spelling, punctuation, and mechanics. *(page C568)*
- Use proper manuscript form for footnotes, works cited, and for the bibliography. *(pages C561–C564)*

### PUBLISHING

- Make a neat and final copy of your report in standard manuscript form. Share your finished work with a classmate or other interested readers, either in print or online. *(page C570)*

**Time Out to Reflect**

Now that you have completed your research report, take a few minutes to stop and consider this project in relation to your past writing assignments. What did you consider the most challenging part of the assignment? Did this assignment give you a special feeling of accomplishment? How would you compare it to the other pieces you've written this year, or last year? What new skills have you learned while doing this assignment? What techniques might you be able to apply to your future writing, either in college or in the workplace? Record your answers to these questions in the Learning Log section of your **journal.**

# A Writer Writes

## An I-Search Report

**Purpose: to explain and inform**

**Audience: teachers and fellow students**

This is perhaps the most informal piece of writing you'll do this year. Its purpose is to explain how you went about learning something new—by doing research in the library or media center, and also by going out into the world and searching for original information on your own. I-Search reports are usually written in the first person, and their style tends to be less formal than a traditional research report. The research process itself may become part of the contents of the I-Search report.

### Prewriting

Begin by thinking about a topic you'd really like to know more about, not as an assignment for a class, but simply for your own personal interest and satisfaction. You may want to use the library or media center to explore some sources either in print or on line to generate ideas for a subject.

For your original research, you may want to seek out some "experts" who already know something about your chosen subject. In this case, an expert can be almost anyone in your area who knows a lot about the subject—a college professor, the best mechanic in town, the head chef of a popular restaurant, a local artist, or a news writer. If you do not know this person already, try contacting him or her by phone or e-mail first to arrange an appointment for an interview, either by phone or in-person. Even if your chosen experts can't help you, they may point you toward someone who will. Take notes or record what your specialists have to say.

### Drafting

Despite its informality, your report should still be organized in some logical way. Your introduction might begin by explaining

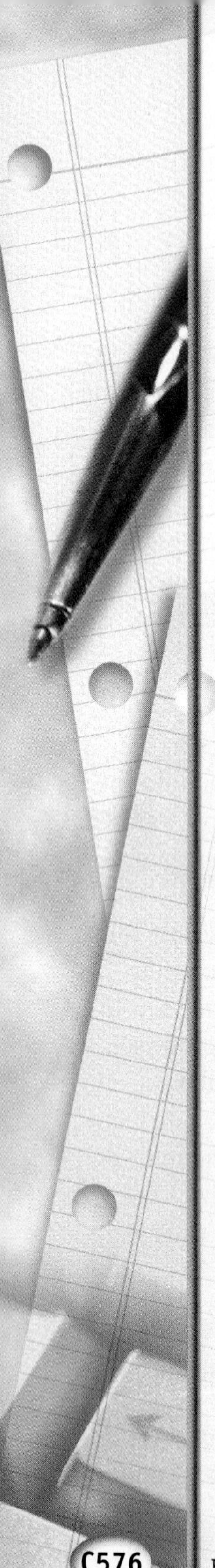

the reasons for your search and why the subject is important to you. The body of your report might tell the story of your search—how you found your sources as well as the experts you interviewed. In the conclusion, provide a list of the sources you've used, including the names of people who've helped you with information. These notes may be listed simply, but accurately, at the end of the report.

## Revising

Using the Evaluation Checklist for Revising on page C566, revise your work. Even though your style may be informal, aim at providing a simple, clear story of the investigation and its results. If other classmates are interested in the subject, share your report with them. They may be able to give you ideas for improving your work.

## Editing

Use the Editing Checklists on pages C46 and C568 to edit your report. Refer to the guidelines for proper manuscript form on pages C49–C52 for more help as you prepare a final draft.

## Publishing

Follow standard manuscript form to make a clean copy of your work. Then choose a method of publication to share your work with others. You may want to give copies to classmates or to the experts you interviewed. You may also consider submitting your report as an article to your school newspaper or to a Website having to do with your topic—perhaps one you discovered during your search.

*You can learn about other options for publishing your report on page C49, and more about electronic publishing in* A Writer's Guide to Electronic Publishing, *pages C788–C813.*

# Connection Collection

## Representing in Different Ways

### *From Print . . .*

### *. . . to Visuals*

From the information in the memo, design a desktop icon for each of the programs described. Make sure that your icon is easily recognizable and reflects the nature of the program it represents.

**Date:** 1/23/01
**To:** Marketing Department
**From:** Software Development
**Subject:** New products

This year Cyberblink Services plans to debut several new software products designed for the personal computer. Before we announce these programs publicly, we would like to describe them so you can design catchy desktop icons for our advertising campaign:

1. EMCSquare: This program determines the travel time between points on Earth in light years. It also provides maps, notifications of traffic conditions, and sight-seeing opportunities.
2. Edutainment!: Provides learning for adults in the form of an interactive sitcom.
3. Whoops!: A game that hides important files on your hard drive. It is like playing hide and seek on your computer!
4. Farmer: Grow a virtual beet. A science learning tool for all ages.

Thank you.

### *From Visuals . . .*

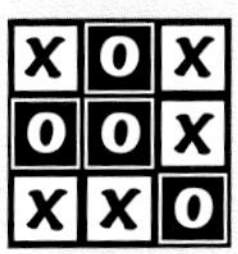

### *. . . to Print*

These four icons are being considered for Game Commander, a program that organizes game files on a personal computer. Analyze each of the icons and write a description of what kind of software program each icon suggests.

- **Which strategies can be used for creating both written and visual representations? Which strategies apply to one, not both? Which type of representation is more effective?**
- **Draw a conclusion and write briefly about the differences between written ideas and visual representations.**

## Writing in the Workplace

### *Informative Report*

You work as a talent manager, booking concerts for many successful musicians. It is up to you to convince the proprietor of the local concert hall that old-style boogie-woogie can attract a young audience and make a profit. You must convince him that the 1930s boogie-woogie piano style is a direct ancestor of rock and roll and that there is a market for this music.

**Research the history of boogie-woogie and its performers and write an informative report that will persuade the proprietor to book the concert. Remember to evaluate the accuracy of your research sources, and be sure to cite your sources properly. Be sure your report has unity and coherence.**

**What strategies did you use to write the report for the proprietor?**

*You can find information on writing reports in Chapter 12.*

## Writing for Oral Communication

### *Report for a Radio Broadcast*

You are a writer who has just published your 23rd book, *Beef Soup for the Inspired Soul,* which includes a chapter about interesting professions. You are going to be interviewed by phone for a morning radio talk show, and you need to prepare.

**Write a brief report on a career that you consider interesting. Use the method described in the I-Search section of this chapter to research the profession. Remember that you are promoting your book—you will need to capture the radio audience's attention quickly. Edit your report so that it takes no longer than two minutes to read and present orally. Then practice giving the speech to your classmates.**

**What strategies did you use to prepare your report for the talk show?**

*You can find information on writing reports in Chapter 12.*

# Assess Your Learning

You and your friends watch a lot of movies on videocassette and at the movie theater. You enjoy talking about them and sharing your reactions. Recently, a teacher at school suggested that you and your friends create a guide to help other moviegoers choose what films to see. You think this is a great idea—perhaps you could even start your own movie-review television show or publish your own film guide for teenagers!

- **Write a collection of at least four short film reviews. If possible, team up with a partner or group and make a larger collection of reviews. Provide creative titles for each film review. Then research your entries in magazines, newspapers, or on the Internet to list where to find the film, the principal cast, and the director. Next, write a summary of the film's plot. Finally, write a concise analysis of the film and state whether or not you recommend it. Establish a logical progression of ideas by organizing your information. Write your reviews for an audience of your peers.**

*Before You Write* **Consider the following questions:**
What is the ***subject?***
What is the ***occasion?***
Who is the ***audience?***
What is the ***purpose?***

*After You Write* **Evaluate your work using the following criteria:**

- Have you given your reviews titles that are both interesting and reflect the subject?
- Have you researched the entries in your book of reviews by using reliable sources of information?
- Which organizational strategies have you used (chronological, spatial, importance, or developmental)?
- Have you revised your movie reviews by deleting, combining, or rearranging the text?
- Have you organized your ideas in a manner that is easy to understand?
- Have you checked your work by proofreading it with a partner?

**Write briefly on how well you did. Point out your strengths and areas for improvement.**

CHAPTER 13

# Communication for Careers and College

As students pursuing higher education and as future employees seeking jobs, you will be required to communicate information and ideas in business letters, applications, résumés, and interviews. Students use business letters to request catalogs from various colleges or universities and to apply to them for admission. Job seekers use letters, résumés, and applications to present their qualifications to prospective employers.

In addition, you must learn to interview with college admissions officers and future employers. They will ask you questions to which you must learn to respond clearly and appropriately. In turn, you will want to ask effective and meaningful questions of them so that you can best learn about your own prospects as a student or employee.

Learning to use these forms will help shape you into a more effective communicator and ensure that you have skills to succeed.

## *Reading with a Writer's Eye*

The following is an excerpt from an article by a leading columnist, Jane Bryant Quinn, about how the Internet can help students make college choices. Read it once for understanding. As you read it again, notice how the writer organizes her ideas under boldfaced headings. Also notice that her ideas are expressed concisely and clearly. As you read, see how many of her specific suggestions might apply to your own search for college information.

# Internet Can Help Make an EDUCATED COLLEGE CHOICE

*Jane Bryant Quinn*

The college-search season is pretty much over for high school seniors. The mouse has been passed to juniors, whose turn it is to find a school.

Yes, the mouse. Every year, more students turn first to the Internet to see what the schools have to offer.

In a survey last year of 500 high-ability students, 78 percent had visited individual college Web sites, according to Art & Science Group, a college marketing consultant in Baltimore. That compares with 58 percent in 1997 and just 4 percent in 1996.

The colleges didn't expect the Internet hordes so soon. They're scrambling to put their best Web foot forward and deal with a rising tide of e-mailed questions and requests.

For students, the Web is a fast, free way to get a feel for different kinds of colleges and universities. You can reach beyond local and brand-name schools to find interesting places you might not otherwise have considered. Students now use the Web to:

## Take a college tour

Most schools offer on-line viewbooks, stocked with color photos of the campus at its best, or short recruiting videos. A few give video tours, where a camera follows a campus guide from place to place.

You might even find a 360-degree view of the campus, from various spots. Duke University's virtual tour provides 10 panoramic scenes.

Some schools sponsor a virtual open house. You join a live chat with students, faculty members and admissions officers.

This spring, the Cox School of Business at Southern Methodist University did two live video presentations. Prospective students heard about the curriculum, saw photos of the campus and business school, and could put questions to faculty and admissions officers.

Web tours provide a feel for faraway schools that might be too expensive to visit. And they narrow your choice among the schools within traveling range. For an on-line index of what's available, go to www.campustours.com.

Warning: If your modem is slow, clicking through Web tours will take a while. You might prefer the traditional viewbook, with photos in picture album form. You can usually order one on-line. . . .

* * *

## Gather data

You can check the school's list price, student-aid practices, student activities, classes taught in your field of interest and your odds of making the cut academically. To judge academics, look at the students' scores on the Scholastic Aptitude Tests.

On the Web, "students are looking for content, content, content, not the slick hyperbole-filled stuff that characterizes many viewbooks," says ASG's Rick Hesel. You can get straight information in the areas you want.

## Screen for schools

At some college-search sites, you can enter various criteria—location, size, cost, sports, major—and receive a list of schools to check. The most popular site: College-board.org. Some others: CollegeEdge.com, CollegeNET.com, CollegeView.com.

You'll receive different lists at different sites, depending on what's in their databases and whether they take payments from schools to be on display.

Payments aren't generally disclosed. But even paid sites expose you to schools you haven't heard of before, some of which might interest you.

## Schedule a visit

Some schools offer Preview Days, when prospective students come to campus, attend events and meet with professors. You can schedule your day on-line to avoid events that overlap.

But students are more reluctant to talk to admissions and financial-aid officers on-line, ASG reports. A majority would rather get on the phone with a person.

## Apply

Some schools provide on-line application forms. Starting in 1999, the business school at the Massachusetts Institute of Technology in Cambridge, Mass., outlawed paper applications.

Where they have a choice, however, even students who gather data on-line prefer to apply the traditional way, Hesel says. He's not sure why. Maybe they think that on-line applications won't be taken as seriously. Or they may want to enclose other things: artwork, music, videocassettes.

Helpful as the Web is, nothing beats a real visit to campus. But virtual tours help you find which school may suit you best.

## Thinking as a Writer

### Evaluating How the Article Works

- Imagine that writer Jane Bryant Quinn has asked you to give her some feedback on the effectiveness of her article. How does she grab the reader's attention early in the article? How effective is the way in which she organizes her ideas? What are some examples of specific facts and statistics she uses? Is there anything that you might have done differently if you had written a similar article?

### Presenting an Expert

Oral Expression

As you can see, Jane Bryant Quinn is well informed in the subject of using the Internet as a tool to explore colleges.

- Imagine that she is a guest speaker at your school, and you have been asked to introduce her. Write one or two paragraphs presenting Quinn, then read your presentation aloud to the class.

### Seeing for Yourself

Viewing

- Form a small group with one or two other students and talk about this viewbook page. Is this an example of the "slick hyperbole-filled stuff that characterizes many viewbooks"? How does it differ from what Quinn suggests you will find on the Internet? Give reasons for your answers.

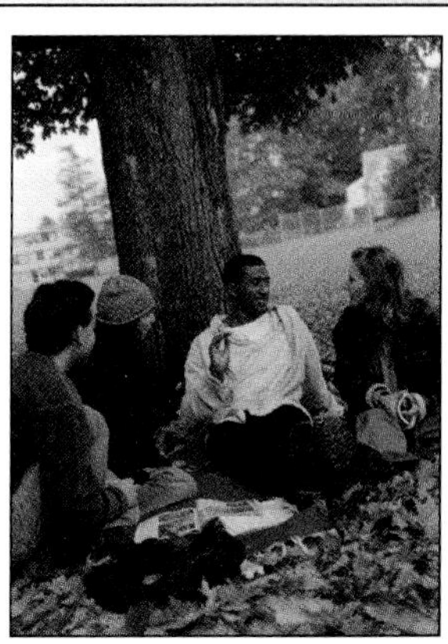

UNIVERSITY OF MAINE
2000–2001

*A Blend of Academics, Extracurricular Activities and Community Interaction Where...*

From lakes, streams, and a rocky coastline to forests and mountains, the state of Maine represents what life should be. In the heart of Vacationland, at the junction of two rivers—the Stillwater and the Penobscot—the University of Maine is situated on Marsh Island in Orono. Established in 1865 as Maine State College on the White and Goddard farms, UMaine is now the flagship of the University of Maine System and the land grant university and sea grant college of the state of Maine.

# Communication for Careers

A businessman named Thomas Fuller once wrote, "Boldness in business is the first, second, and third thing." In your written and oral communications—whether you are applying for college or for a job—boldness will serve you well.

Whatever career you decide to pursue, a letter or résumé will often be your first opportunity to communicate information about yourself, your experience, and your qualifications to a prospective employer. Your goal in writing the letter or résumé is to provide the employer with specific information about your background and experience, encouraging the employer to consider you for the position. Then, during the interview, your manner of communicating and the way you present yourself may be deciding factors in whether you are offered the job.

In this section, you will learn the correct form for business letters and résumés. In addition, you will practice strategies for interviewing for jobs. A **business letter** is a written communication intended to elicit a response. It is written and mailed to one person. A **résumé** is a written summary of your education, experience, and skills. In an **interview,** you'll be able to answer questions about your qualifications and ask questions about the job to which you are applying.

### Your Writer's Journal

In your journal, write a prediction about what you think you will be doing a year from now. Will you go to college? If so, where? What will you study? Will you get a job? If so, what will you do? Remember that imagining a thing is the first step to making it happen.

# Writing Business Letters

To get the best results, a business letter must express ideas in clear and polite language. In addition, a business letter must be in the correct form. Unlike personal letters, which may be written in informal English, business letters should be written in standard English. Following is a commonly used form for a business letter called the **modified block style**. The heading, closing, and signature are positioned at the right, and the paragraphs are indented. All sample letters in this chapter use the modified block style.

**Model: Modified Block Style**

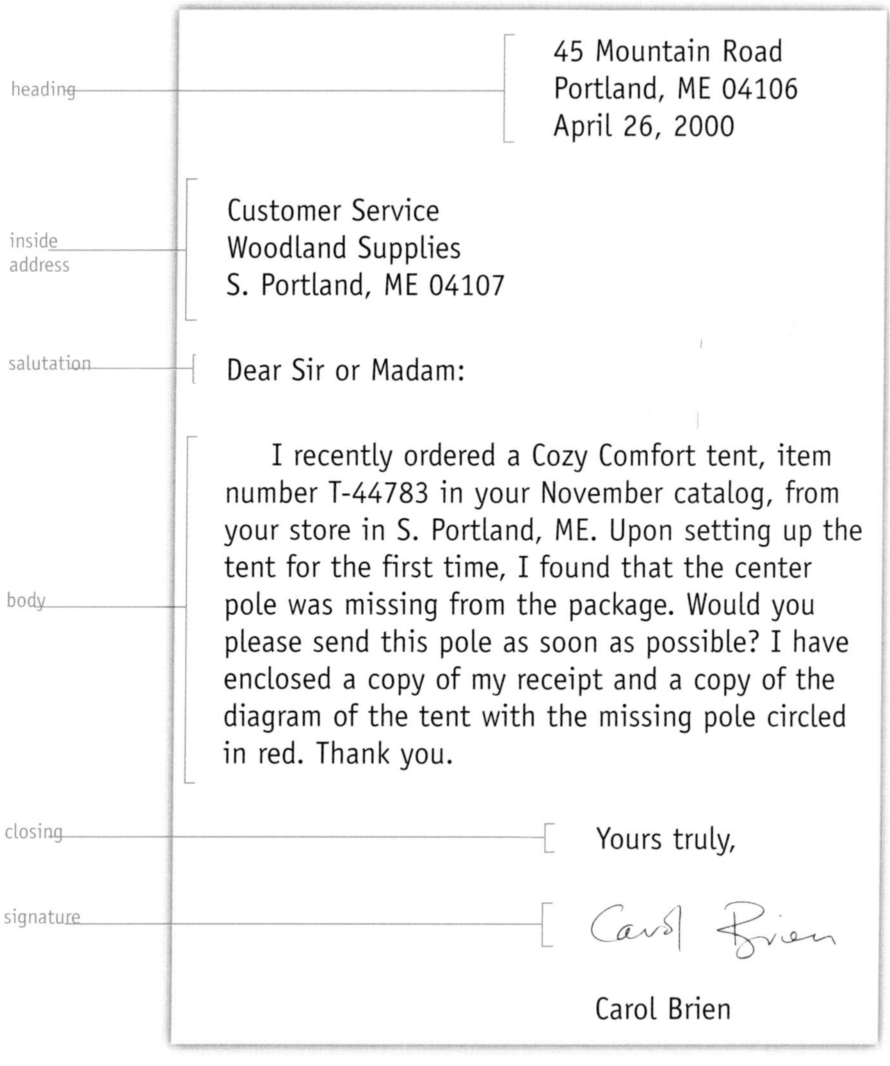


45 Mountain Road
Portland, ME 04106
April 26, 2000

Customer Service
Woodland Supplies
S. Portland, ME 04107

Dear Sir or Madam:

I recently ordered a Cozy Comfort tent, item number T-44783 in your November catalog, from your store in S. Portland, ME. Upon setting up the tent for the first time, I found that the center pole was missing from the package. Would you please send this pole as soon as possible? I have enclosed a copy of my receipt and a copy of the diagram of the tent with the missing pole circled in red. Thank you.

Yours truly,

Carol Brien

Carol Brien

All business letters have the same six parts: heading, inside address, salutation, body, closing, and signature.

### Parts of a Business Letter

**HEADING**

- Write your full address, including the ZIP code.
- Use the two-letter postal abbreviation for your state.
- Write the date.

**INSIDE ADDRESS**

- Write the receiver's address below the heading.
- Include the name of the person if you know it, using *Mr., Mrs., Ms., Dr.,* or some other title.
- If the person has a business title, write it on the next line.
- Use the two-letter postal abbreviation for the state.

**SALUTATION**

- Start one line below the inside address.
- Use *Sir or Madam* if you do not know the person's name. Otherwise, use the person's last name preceded by *Mr., Mrs., Ms.,* or some other title.
- Use a colon after the salutation.

**BODY**

- Start one line below the salutation.
- Double-space a single paragraph. For longer letters, single-space each paragraph, skipping a space between paragraphs.

**CLOSING**

- Start one line below the body.
- Line up the closing with the left-hand edge of the heading.
- Use a formal closing such as *Sincerely yours* or *Yours truly* followed by a comma.

**SIGNATURE**

- Type your full name four or five lines below the closing.
- Sign your full name in the space between the closing and your typed name.

## Business Envelopes

When writing a business letter, use the correct form for the envelope as shown in the following example.

**MODEL: Business Envelope**

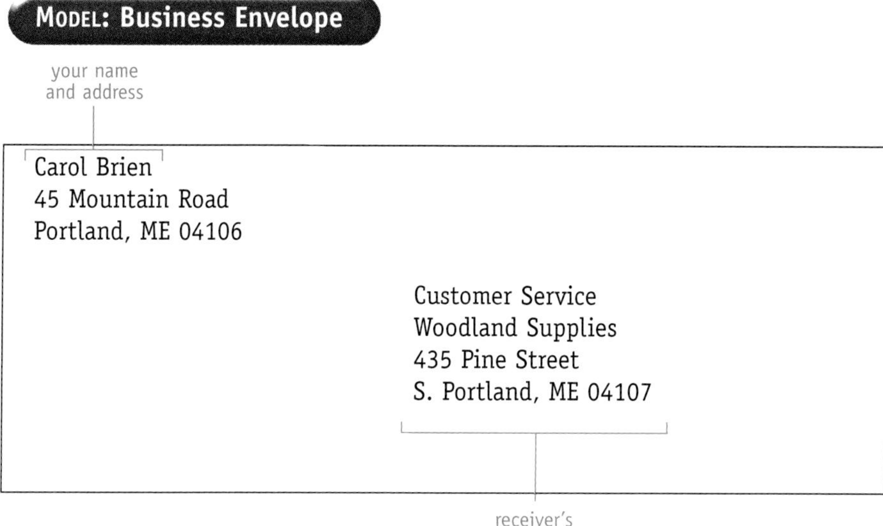

your name and address
Carol Brien
45 Mountain Road
Portland, ME 04106
Customer Service
Woodland Supplies
435 Pine Street
S. Portland, ME 04107
receiver's address


**COMPUTER TIP**

Many word-processing programs will automatically set up and print envelopes directly from your business letters. Check your software manual for specific instructions.

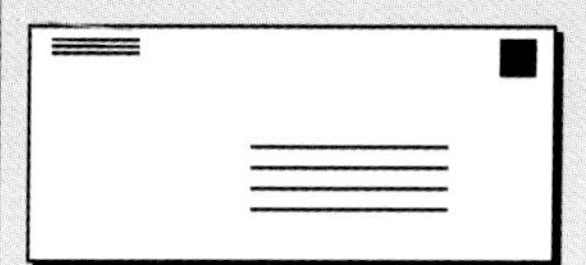

## Letters About Employment

When you apply for a job, you may write a letter to your potential employer. Your letter should state specifically the kind of job you desire and should also give information about your qualifications and experience. In addition, your letter should make a strong favorable impression by being grammatically correct and neat. Include the following information in a letter about employment.

| INFORMATION IN A LETTER ABOUT EMPLOYMENT | |
|---|---|
| **Position Sought** | In the first paragraph, state the job you are seeking and how you learned about the opening. |
| **Education** | Include both your age and your grade in school. Emphasize courses you have taken that apply directly to the job you are seeking. |
| **Experience** | State the kinds of work you have done. Although you may not have work experience that relates to the position open, any positions of responsibility you have held, paid or unpaid, are valuable work experiences. |
| **References** | Include at least two references, such as a teacher or a former employer, with either an address or a phone number for each. You should obtain permission in advance from the people you name as references. |
| **Request for an Interview** | In the last paragraph of your letter, ask for an interview. Indicate where and when you can be reached to make an appointment. |

In addition to using the correct format, apply the following tips as you prepare the final copy of your business letter.

### Tips for Neatness in a Business Letter

- Use white paper 8½- by 11-inches in size.
- Leave margins at least 1 inch wide.
- Type or word process whenever possible.
- If you type your letter, type your envelope.
- Fold your letter neatly in thirds to fit into a business-size envelope.

The following model illustrates an employment letter written by a student who is seeking employment as a management trainee at a place of business. In addition, it includes information about the position sought and the applicant's education and experience.

**MODEL: Employment Letter**

72 Helsey Avenue
Vineland, NJ 08360
May 4, 2000

Mr. William Coles
Optima Office Supplies
South Suburban Mall
Vineland, NJ 08360

Dear Mr. Coles:

I would like to apply for the management trainee position advertised in this morning's *Daily Express.* Next week I will graduate with honors from Bodes High School, where I have taken courses in retailing.

For the past three years, I have worked as a part-time salesclerk for the Monroe Computer Center in West Kilmer. Last summer I was a lifeguard at Lenape State Park.

Ms. Toni Armand, owner of the Monroe Computer Center, and Mr. Lance Dooley, staff coordinator at Lenape State Park, have agreed to supply references. Ms. Armand's business phone number is 663-3886; Mr. Dooley's is 947-2431.

I believe I am qualified for the position you have advertised. I would be pleased to come in for an interview at your convenience. My home telephone is 884-3887.

Very truly yours,

Michael Paci

Michael Paci

## Order Letters

Some catalogs and advertisements include an order blank. If none is available, use business-letter form to place an order. Be sure to include the order number, price, quantity, and size of the item you want. In addition, if you are sending a check or money order (never send cash), identify the amount enclosed in the letter.

**Model: Order Letter**

331 Gilgen Avenue N.E.
Missoula, MT 59801
June 30, 2000

Turquoise Treasures
8876 Tuscarawas Avenue
Black Eagle Mountain, MT 59414

Dear Sir or Madam:

Please send me the following items from your most recent catalog:

| | |
|---|---|
| 1 pair Star Teardrops Earrings, #44781, | $ 14.95 |
| 1 River of Dawn Necklace, #22801, | $ 18.95 |
| Shipping and handling | $ 3.00 |
| TOTAL | $ 36.90 |

A check for $36.90 is enclosed. Thank you.

Sincerely,
*Shirley Mason*
Shirley Mason

## Letters of Complaint

If a product or service fails to measure up to its promise, you can write a letter of complaint to try to remedy the problem. Most companies stand behind their goods and services and are willing to make suitable adjustments if there is a problem. If your letter is reasonable and polite, chances are it will bring the desired results. In the following example of a complaint letter, notice that the writer suggests a reasonable solution.

**MODEL: Letter of Complaint**

4544 Canyon Drive
Carson City, NV 89703
June 11, 2000

Adjustments
Keynote Stationers
435 Pine Street
Salt Lake City, UT 84133

Dear Sir or Madam:

In a letter dated May 15, I ordered several items from your catalog, including a Norman Rockwell poster. On June 9, I received the other merchandise in the mail, but the poster was not in the package.

Since I have paid in full for the poster, I request an explanation of the missing item as soon as possible. I am enclosing a copy of the packing slip, which shows that the poster was not included. If for some reason the poster is no longer available, please refund my money.

Thank you very much.

Sincerely,

Susan Lee

Susan Lee

## Writing a Résumé

A **résumé** is a careful summary of your work experience, education, and interests. The purpose of a résumé is to give a potential employer a brief but positive overview of your qualifications for a job. You will want to update your résumé whenever there is a significant change in your work or school experience.

Always accompany your résumé with a cover letter. The letter should use the correct form for a business letter. It should state the job you are applying for and summarize your qualifications for filling it. Your cover letter might end with a statement explaining how the employer can contact you further.

Organize your résumé according to categories of information. The following guidelines and model will help you write your own résumé.

### How to Write a Résumé

**General Form**

- Use one sheet of white 8½- by 11-inch paper.
- Use even margins and leave space between sections.
- Center your name, address, telephone number, and E-mail address at the top of the page.

**Work Experience**

- List your most recent job first.
- Include part-time, summer, and volunteer jobs you have done.
- For each job, include the dates you worked, your employer's name, your title, and your primary responsibilities.

**Education**

- List the name and address of each school and the years you attended.
- List any special courses you have taken that would help make you a valuable employee.

**Skills, Activities, Awards, Interests**

- List skills, such as word processing, computer literacy, or fluency in a foreign language, that may relate to the position you are applying for.
- List school or community activities in which you have participated, such as music lessons, volunteer work, or scouting.
- List awards or certificates of merit you have earned.
- Include any relevant hobbies or special interests.

**References**

- Give the names and addresses of people who have agreed to give you a recommendation, or write, "Available on request."
- As references, list one previous employer, one teacher or school administrator, and one adult friend. Choose people who can attest positively to your character and abilities. Be sure you obtain permission in advance from the people you list as references.

Here is an example of a résumé. Notice how it follows the preceding guidelines.

**Model: Résumé**

**Cynthia Klein**
21 Bluebonnet Lane
Odessa, TX 79766
(915) 426-7135
E-mail: cklein@myemail.com

| | |
|---|---|
| **Work Experience** | |
| 1999 to present | Alvis Dance Studio, 945 Main Street<br>Odessa, TX 79766<br>**Position:** Part-time dance instructor<br>**Responsibilities:** Teach ballet to children ages five to twelve |
| 1997 to 1999 | CRM Store, Ravenswood Mall<br>Odessa, TX 79766<br>**Position:** Cashier<br>**Responsibilities:** Rang up and bagged purchases at variety store |
| **Education** | |
| 1998 to present | Lone Star High School, Fassett Highway, Odessa, TX 79766<br>**Special Courses:** Fundamentals of Business, History of Dance, Modern Dance |
| 1996 to 1998 | Nimitz Middle School<br>350 Route 17, Odessa, TX 79766 |
| **Special Skills** | Speak Spanish<br>Can word process at 80 wpm |
| **Activities** | Tenth grade class president, Computer Club and Drama Club member |
| **Awards** | Odessa Fine Arts Achievement Award, 1999 |
| **Special Interests** | Dance, drama, computers |
| **References** | Available on request |

COMPUTER TIP

Use boldfacing, capitalization or different fonts to highlight certain parts of your résumé. Don't get too carried away, however. Make sure your résumé is clear and easy to read.

## Interviewing for Employment

When you apply for a job, the employer may ask you to come to a formal interview. The interview provides an opportunity for both you and the employer to learn more about whether you are well suited for the job—and vice versa. You will feel more confident during an interview if you take some time to prepare beforehand.

One way to prepare for an interview is to learn as much as possible about the employer's business. The more you know about what the employer does and how the business operates, the better able you will be to discuss the job and your qualifications for filling it. To obtain information about the business, you might talk with people you know who are employed there. In addition, many large companies publish annual reports, which may be available in the library or from the company itself. Information about companies may be available in business-oriented magazines or on the Internet.

The way you present yourself during an interview may determine whether the employer considers you further for the position. The following strategies will help you interview successfully.

### Strategies for Interviewing

- Prepare a list of questions that you would like to ask the person who interviews you. Ask questions about the job that display your interest in the business. See the chart on page C597 for specific suggestions.
- Be on time for the interview. If possible, show up a few minutes early in case you need to fill out any paperwork beforehand.
- Present a neat, clean appearance.
- Be polite to the interviewer.

- Make eye contact with the interviewer as you speak.
- Speak clearly and distinctly and use proper grammar.
- Answer all questions thoroughly and honestly.
- Thank the interviewer for his or her time when the interview is finished.
- Follow up the interview with a letter thanking the interviewer and expressing your interest in the position. Summarize the reasons that you think you are a good candidate for the job.

In most interviews, the interviewer wants you to "fill in" information that may be missing from your application, letter, or résumé. He or she also wants to get a feel for you as a person, how you speak, how you handle yourself in a conversation, and how clearly you can present information about yourself. Here are some questions you may be asked.

### Questions an Interviewer May Ask You

- How did you find out about this job opening?
- Why did you apply for this job?
- What previous experience and education do you think helps qualify you for this position?
- What activities do you enjoy in your leisure time?
- What do you study in school?
- Have you lived at your present address long? Where did you live before?
- What did you expect to earn at this job?
- How many hours can you work a week?
- Who can give you a good reference?
- When can you begin to work?
- Why do you want this job?
- What are your plans for the future?
- Do you have any questions before you leave?

Your answer to the last question should be "Yes." It is important to seem interested enough to ask some intelligent questions about the job for which you are applying. Remember, you need to discover if the job suits you as much as the interviewer needs to find out if you suit the job. Here are a few suggestions.

### Questions to Ask an Interviewer

- What exactly would my duties be?
- Where exactly would I work?
- Who would train me?
- Who would be my direct supervisor?
- How many hours a week would I be expected to work?
- Are the hours variable or always the same? If they are variable, who decides when I would work?
- How much does the job pay and how often are employees paid?
- Are there any benefits that come with this position, such as health insurance, sick pay, or employee discounts?
- Is there room for advancement in this job?
- When will you make a decision about whom you will hire?
- Is there any other information you need?

IN THE MEDIA

## Video Interview

One of the reasons video is so powerful a medium is that "seeing is believing." If you can see yourself on a video, you will have an accurate sense of how you come across. Any mannerisms or other traits you may want to either downplay or use more effectively in different situations will be easy to spot.

Work in groups of three. One person does the camera work. The other two role-play an interview for either work or college. Switch roles so that everyone has a turn at each role.

When you are in the role of the interviewer, you may want to ask questions like these:

- Why do you think you would be a good choice for a (student in this program) (employee in this job)?
- What are your strengths?
- What are your weaknesses?
- What accomplishment are you proudest of?
- What did you have the most trouble with in school?
- How would you describe the future you see for yourself?

After viewing the videotape, discuss with your other group members what you might improve on. Set yourself reasonable goals. (For example, your goal might be: "I will avoid saying *you know* and *like* because I see I say them way too often.")

## Retaping and Reevaluating

Repeat the process after about a week. Compare your first and second interviews. What was better in your second? What could you still improve on? Once again, set yourself reasonable goals.

# Writing Different Kinds of Letters

##  Letter About Employment

Write an employment letter for the following summer job, which has been posted in your school guidance office. Use your own address and today's date.

**POSITION AVAILABLE**

| | |
|---|---|
| **Job title:** | Landscape architect's assistant |
| **Place:** | Lawn & Leaf Landscaping Service, 151 Main Street, Pueblo, CO 81004 |
| **Duties:** | Assist with mowing, pruning, and landscaping tasks; operate mowers; plant and transplant shrubs, trees, and garden plants |
| **Hours:** | 8:00 A.M. to 5:00 P.M. Monday through Friday |
| **Salary:** | $7.00/hour |
| **Requirements:** | Person must be dependable, energetic, cooperative, and conscientious. |
| **Apply to:** | Mr. Paul Petrini |

##  Letter to Place an Order

Use the modified block style to write a letter ordering the following merchandise from a catalog. Unscramble the information below for the inside address and write it in the proper order. Use your own name and address and today's date.

| | |
|---|---|
| INSIDE ADDRESS | Order Department, Bart's Fly Shop, New York, New York, 555 East 55 Street, 10010 |

| | |
|---|---|
| MERCHANDISE | Six Catchem Rooster Tails, $2.95 each; three Gotcha Spinners, $2.95 each; one 500-yard reel of 30-pound test line, $10.99 |
| SHIPPING AND HANDLING | $5.00 |

## Letter of Complaint

Use the following information to write a letter of complaint. Unscramble the information in the inside address and write it in the proper order. Use your own name and address and today's date.

| | |
|---|---|
| INSIDE ADDRESS | Rutger's Music Store; Customer Service Department; Ramsey, New Jersey 07446; 465 Washington Street |
| SITUATION | You ordered several items from a music store, including a Patriot harmonica in the key of G, #471-12, for $15.00. When the rest of your order arrived, a harmonica in the key of C was included. |

## Interview Questions and Responses

Oral Expression

Pair up with another student to discuss a part-time job at a local bookstore that involves checking inventory, shelving new books, cashiering, helping customers, and record keeping. Using the lists above for suggestions, first draft five to ten questions that you want to ask. Then, spend about 15 minutes role-playing a mock job interview. When you are finished, spend some time discussing what you learned from this role-playing activity.

## Letter Requesting College Information

Find out the name and address of a college, university, or professional school near you. Consult a current college reference book in your library or guidance office to find the address or look for the college on the Internet. Draft a letter requesting a catalog and an application, following the model. Use your own name, address, and today's date.

## Letter Requesting an Interview

Find out the name and address of a college, university, or professional school near you. If possible, find out the name of the admission director using a college reference book or the Internet. Use the information to draft a letter requesting an interview, following the model above. Use your own name, address, and today's date.

**COMPUTER TIP**

Many colleges and universities provide on-line application forms. As you learned in Jane Bryant Quinn's essay, at least one university has even outlawed paper applications! Check the Websites of various schools for their policies regarding online applications.

# Communication for College

If you plan to continue your education after high school, there are two kinds of letters you should know how to write to colleges. The first is a brief request for information or a catalog from a college or professional school. If you want specific material, be sure to ask for it.

**MODEL: Request Letter for Information**

339 Wayland Street, Apt. 14-A
Lubbock, TX 79415
May 6, 2000

Director of Admissions
Grand Canyon College
Phoenix, AZ 85004

Dear Sir or Madam:

I am a senior at Lubbock High School in Lubbock, Texas. In the fall I plan to attend college with the intention of majoring in early childhood education. I would like to know if Grand Canyon College offers a degree in this field.

Please send me your current catalog, an application for admission, and any information on available scholarships.

Thank you very much.

Sincerely yours,

*Joseph Inman*

Joseph Inman

The second kind of letter you will write to a college is one requesting an interview. In your letter you should express your interest in the college, and suggest a convenient time for your visit to the campus or your meeting with an interviewer. You can probably find the name of the admissions director in a college reference book or on the Internet.

### Model: Letter Requesting a College Interview

945 Olaf Road
Rochester, MN 55906
May 2, 2000

Mr. Daniel J. Murray
Director of Admissions
Hamline University
St. Paul, MN 55104

Dear Mr. Murray:

Thank you very much for sending me the Hamline University catalog and the applications I requested. I would like to learn more about the university before I submit my application. Would it be possible to visit classes for one day during the week of April 7 through 11? I will be on vacation that week and can arrive any day you suggest. If possible, I would like to visit music theory and computer science classes since I hope to major in one of these disciplines.

In addition, I would like to arrange an interview with someone from your office. Please let me know a convenient date and time for my visit. I look forward to visiting Hamline University and learning more about it.

Sincerely yours,

George Chen

## Completing College Applications

Applications enable college admissions officers (and employers) to learn about your specific qualifications as a potential student. To give the admissions officer (or employer) a clear and accurate account of your experiences and accomplishments, it is important that you complete the application carefully and thoroughly. The following strategies may help you.

### Strategies for Completing College Applications

- Make one or two copies of each application to practice on, before you make your final copy.
- Read each application thoroughly, including all the directions, before you begin to answer any questions.
- Type or have someone else type your application or print neatly in dark blue or black ink.
- Make your responses to questions about work, travel, and awards as concise as possible.
- Do not be modest about your accomplishments but be selective. Stress your most important activities, those you have contributed the most to or learned the most from, instead of simply listing everything you have ever done.
- Make sure to answer every question. Do not leave any blanks. If a question asks about employment experiences and you have not had any, describe volunteer work you have done. If there are questions for which you have no answers, write "N/A" (not applicable).

Many colleges and universities use a common application for undergraduate admission. The common application makes it easier for those who are applying to several colleges at once and ensures that each school will receive the information it needs to review an applicant's qualifications. The first part of this application asks you to provide personal data. You need to read these factual questions carefully and answer them completely and accurately.

## COMMON APPLICATION

**PERSONAL DATA**

Legal name: ______ *Last/Family* ______ *First* ______ *Middle (complete)* ______ *Jr., etc.* ______ *Gender*

Prefer to be called: ______ (nickname) Former last name(s) if any: ______

Are you applying as a ❑ freshman or ❑ transfer student? For the term beginning: ______

Permanent home address: ______ *Number and Street*

______ *City or Town* ______ *State* ______ *Country* ______ *Zip Code +4 or Postal Code*

If different from the above, please give your mailing address for all admission correspondence:

Mailing address: ______ *Number and Street* Use from: ______ *Date* to ______ *Date*

______ *City or Town* ______ *State* ______ *Country* ______ *Zip Code +4 or Postal Code*

Phone at mailing address: ______ *Area Code* ______ *Number* Permanent home phone: ______ *Area Code* ______ *Number*

E-mail address: ______

Birthdate: ______ ❑ Citizenship: U.S./dual U.S. citizen. If dual, specify other citizenship: ______

❑ U.S.Permanent Resident visa. Citizen of ______ ❑ Other citizenship. Please specify country: ______

If you are not a U.S. citizen and live in the United States, how long have you been in the country? ______ Visa Type: ______

Possible area(s) of academic concentration/major: ______ or undecided

Special college or division if applicable: ______

Possible career or professional plans: ______ or undecided

Will you be a candidate for financial aid? ❑ Yes ❑ No If yes, the appropriate form(s) was/will be filed on: ______

**ACADEMIC HONORS**

Briefly describe any scholastic distinctions or honors you have won beginning with ninth grade:

______

______

______

______

**EXTRACURRICULAR, PERSONAL, AND VOLUNTEER ACTIVITIES (including summer)**

Please list your principal extracurricular, community, and family activites and hobbies in the order of their interest to you. Include specific events and/or major accomplishments such as musical instrument played, varsity letters earned, etc. Please (√) in the right column those activities you hope to pursue in college. To allow us to focus on the highlights of your activities, please complete this section even if you plan to attach a résumé.

| Activity | Grade level or post-secondary (PS) 9 | 10 | 11 | 12 | PS | Approximate time spent Hours per week | Weeks per year | Positions held, honors won, or letters earned | |
|---|---|---|---|---|---|---|---|---|---|
| | | | | | | | | | |
| | | | | | | | | | |

1999-2000 Name of Applicant ______ Social Security # ______ APP-1

**WORK EXPERIENCE**

List any job (including summer employment) you have held during the past three years.

| Specific nature of work | Employer | Approximate dates of employment | Approximate no. of hours spent per week |
|---|---|---|---|
| | | | |
| | | | |
| | | | |

In the space provided below or on a separate sheet if necessary, please describe which of these activities (extracurricular and personal activities or work experience) has had the most meaning for you, and why.

______________________________

______________________________

**PERSONAL STATEMENT**

This personal statement helps us become acquainted with you in ways different from courses, grades, test scores, and other objective data. It will demonstrate your ability to organize thoughts and express yourself. We are looking for an essay that will help us know you better as a person and as a student. Please write an essay (250-500 words) on a topic of your choice or on one of the options listed below. You may attach your essay on separate sheets (same size, please).

1) Evaluate a significant experience, achievement, or risk you have taken and its impact on you.
2) Discuss some issue of personal, local, national, or international concern and its importance to you.
3) Indicate a person who has had a significant influence on you, and describe that influence.
4) Describe a character in fiction, an historical figure, or a creative work (as in art, music, science, etc.) that has had an influence on you, and explain that influence.

**My signature below indicates that all information in my application is complete, factually correct, and honestly presented.**

Signature ______________________________ Date ______________

These colleges are committed to administer all educational policies and activities without discrimination on the basis of race, color, religion, national or ethnic origin, age, handicap, or sex. The admissions process at private undergraduate institutions is exempt from the federal regulation implementing Title IX of the Education Amendments of 1972.

1999-2000 Name of Applicant ______________________________ Social Security # __________ APP-1

## Writing Essays on College Applications

Many colleges request that you write an essay about a particular subject to be submitted with your application in order for them to become further acquainted with you. While the application gives you an opportunity to call attention to your important accomplishments and interests, the essay enables you to demonstrate how well you can organize your thoughts and express your ideas.

As you prepare an essay for a college application, apply the same strategies you use for writing a short composition or an essay for a classroom test. In addition, use the following guidelines.

### Guidelines for Writing a College-Application Essay

- Carefully read and interpret the directions, paying special attention to key words that will help you define your purpose and structure your essay.
- Note any requirements for the length of the essay. Some instructions may specify that you write a 250-word or a 500-word essay. Bear in mind that 250 words is about one and a half pages of typed, double-spaced material. A 500-word essay includes about three pages of typed, double-spaced material.
- Begin by brainstorming or freewriting to generate ideas about the topic. Then decide on your focus, write a thesis statement, and brainstorm supporting details.
- Organize your details in a modified outline.
- Draft your essay, being sure to include an introduction that states the main idea, supporting details organized in a logical order and connected by transitions, and a strong conclusion.
- Read your draft and look for ways to improve it. You might ask a teacher, parent, or friend to read your draft and make suggestions.
- Finally, word process or type your essay (unless the application specifically asks you to write by hand), using the form specified in the directions or standard manuscript form. (*pages C49–C52*)

## Interviewing for College Admission

Some colleges may request or require an interview. An interview gives a college admission officer an opportunity to evaluate you firsthand, and it also gives you an opportunity to learn more about the college by asking important questions. As you prepare for an interview, think about the questions you might be asked and the questions you want to ask.

### Questions an Interviewer May Ask

- How has high school been a worthwhile educational experience? How might it have been improved?
- What have been your best or favorite subjects in school? Which have given you the most difficulty or been your least favorite?
- How do you spend your time outside of school?
- What hobbies or sports do you especially enjoy?
- What was the last book you read that was not required reading in school? Did you enjoy it? Why or why not?
- Have you decided on a college major yet? If so, what will it be? Why did you choose it?
- How do you expect to benefit from your college experience?
- How do you imagine your living situation at college? What do you look forward to? What are your concerns?

### Questions to Ask at College Interviews

- How large are most freshman classes?
- As a freshman, will I have a faculty advisor? How many other advisees will this advisor have?
- At what point must a student decide on a major?
- Are there specific course requirements for freshmen?
- Are foreign or intercollegiate exchange programs offered?
- What is the average cost of the first year of college?
- What opportunities are there for part-time employment?
- What will be my choices of living situations?

## College Application Essay

Use the guidelines on page C607 to draft a 250-word essay on the following topic frequently used in college applications: "Which of your accomplishments are you most proud of and why?" With your teacher's permission, work with a partner to find ways to improve your draft.

## Interview Questions and Responses

Pair up with another student and designate yourselves "Interviewer" and "Applicant." Imagine that you are discussing your admission to a college or university. Using the lists on page C608 for suggestions, first draft five to ten questions that you want to ask. Then, spend about 15 minutes role-playing a mock job interview. If you are the interviewer, take notes about the candidate you are interviewing. If you are the applicant, practice giving responses that are brief, clear, and polite. When you are finished, spend some time discussing what you learned from this role-playing activity.

## Representing in Different Ways

### From Print . . .

Date: 4/22/00
To: Student Applicants
From: George Martínez, Artisan Design Group
Subject: Part-Time Design Position

Those of us here at Artisan Design Group are committed to excellence. We are also interested in supporting the creativity of young people. That is why we are currently looking for a part-time designer of high school age to work for our company. The applicant's first task will be to design a new logo for Artisan.

Before we look at résumés, we would first like to see sample logos. We are asking anyone interested in the job to submit a rough design of an Artisan logo. Do you have what it takes? Why not try? Send your submissions to our company address, and good luck!

Thanks.

### . . . to Visuals

The memo at the right appeared in the "job-market" bulletin board at your school. You think you would be perfect as a part-time student designer for Artisan. Create a logo for them that will attract Mr. Martínez's attention.

## From Visuals . . .

## . . . to Print

Congratulations! The logo you designed, as well as the design shown above, were the two finalists chosen by Mr. Martínez.
He has asked you to submit a résumé and a brief letter that explains why your logo should be chosen over the other. Based on the instructions in the chapter, create your résumé for him. Then compose a brief business letter that explains why your logo is better suited for Artisan.

- **Which strategies can be used for creating both written and visual representations? Which strategies apply to one, not both? Which type of representation is more effective?**
- **Draw a conclusion and write briefly about the differences between written ideas and visual representations.**

## Writing in Academic Areas

### *Essay for a College Application*

"What book has had the biggest influence on your life?" That is the question posed in the application materials for Brontosaur College, which you are hoping to attend next fall.

**Write a brief essay for the application review board for the college that will answer the question and give them a sense of your personality. The instructions specify a 300-word maximum length for the essay. Consider first which book you will choose and why. When you write the essay, remember to make your sentences clear, and your content full of specific details and supporting points.**

**What strategies did you use to win the attention of Brontosaur's application board?**

## Writing for Oral Communication

### *Informative Speech: Job Interviews*

You have recently been asked to be part of a statewide panel discussion called "Successful Interviews for Jobs and College." Your audience will be a group of other students of your age. Choose one of the following topics and prepare a five-minute speech.

- How to Dress for an Interview
- What Questions to Ask at an Interview
- How to Answer Questions Well
- How to Make a Good Overall Impression

**Begin by preparing note cards to guide your speech. Use the tips and information in this chapter as one resource. Practice the speech to make sure it is less than five minutes in length, and then present it to your classmates.**

**What strategies did you use to give an effective speech?**

*You can find information on speeches on pages C672–C682.*

# Assess Your Learning

For your spring holiday, you took a trip to Little River, Kansas, to visit your Aunt Deborah. Although you had a terrific time on your trip, the return home was terrible! You took a bus with Speed Demon Bus Lines, and you were not happy at all. The seats were torn, the bathroom was not working, and the driver played loud opera music during the entire seven-hour ride. In addition, you feel the $175.00 round-trip fare was too steep.

- **Write a complaint letter to Speed Demon Bus Lines. Their main offices are located at 375 Screeching Halt Road, Detroit, MI 47465. Use today's date and your own address, and supply an envelope for the letter.**
- **In your letter, include details about the trip to support your complaints. Even though you were not happy with the trip or the services of the bus line, make certain that your letter is reasonable and polite. Finally, suggest a reasonable solution to the problem.**

*Before You Write* **Consider the following questions:**
What is the ***subject?***
What is the ***occasion?***
Who is the ***audience?***
What is the ***purpose?***

*After You Write* **Evaluate your work using the following criteria:**

- Have you identified Speed Demon Bus Lines as your audience and developed your complaint letter with enough evidence to influence them?
- Does the complaint letter suggest a reasonable solution to the problem of your unfortunate bus trip?
- Have you organized the facts and opinions about the bus trip clearly?
- Have you followed the rules of structuring a business letter and envelope?
- Have you been reasonable and polite in the language of the letter?
- Does your complaint letter show accurate spelling and correct use of the conventions of punctuation and capitalization?

**Write briefly on how well you did. Point out your strengths and areas for improvement.**

CHAPTER 14

# Communication in the World of Work

Imagine you have asked an expert for an overview of today's economy so that you can decide how to invest the money you are saving for college. You get this reply:

> . . . we can tell you definitely there will be an easing up of the rate at which business has been easing off. Put another way, there will be a slowing up of the slowdown. By way of explanation, the slowing up of the slowdown is not as good as an upturn in the downturn. But it's a good deal better than either speeding up the slowdown or easing the downturn. I might suggest the climate's about right for an adjustment of this readjustment. (from *Doublespeak* by William Lutz)

People in a business setting are often tempted to inflate their language with impressive-sounding words but bloated language only wastes time and obscures the message. As with all writing the direct approach is usually the best. Regardless of your profession, you will need to communicate in writing with your employer, colleagues, or customers, and it will pay to be competent. This chapter will help you apply what you have learned about other kinds of writing in a business setting.

## *Reading with a Writer's Eye*

The following article from *Madison Magazine* imagines the workplace of the future. Read the piece once to discover the world as it might exist in the future. Then read the article again and look for the tools that the author used to communicate clearly and concisely.

# WELCOME TO THE FUTURE

***Melanie McManus***

*It's all comfy clothes and flex time, with day care, grocery stores, dry cleaners and fitness rooms at your fingertips. Why bother going home?*

Futurists say that 20 years from now, the traditional office will be anything but. The labor market will remain tight, and workers will still be faced with more demands than time allows. Among other things, that means employers will morph today's office space into an attractive, homey package flexible enough to serve the expanding needs of their workforce. This story takes a look at the bigger changes futurists say we'll all embrace—or endure, as the case may be.

### *Goodbye, cubicle?*

Tomorrow's offices will be set up as "neighborhoods," predicts Tim Erdman, president and CEO of Marshall Erdman & Associates Inc., a medical office design and construction company made famous by its trailblazing founder, Tim's late father, Marshall.

The centerpiece of tomorrow's office will be Main Street, Erdman says, with a "commons area" containing such things as a copier and reception services. A cafe, art gallery and other amenities will encourage people to congregate and relax there.

Branching off from Main Street will be the company's various departments, or "neighborhoods," where assigned work stations will be conspicuously absent. If you need to confer with people in marketing, you'll carry your laptop to the marketing neighborhood and work there. If you need to be alone, you'll plug in at one of the various neutral workstations scattered throughout the building.

"The average office is occupied only 30 percent of the time," says Erdman, quoting a figure from the book *The Demise of the Office* by Erik Veldhoen and Bart Piepers, which was first published in the Netherlands in 1995. "The rest of the time is spent in meetings or off-site," Erdman continues. "That's the reason behind these new offices." Whether there are formalized offices or not, many predict employers will be trying their hardest to encourage employee interaction, creativity, and even relaxation through their office design.

Laurel McManus, an interior designer with the Milwaukee-based architectural firm Kahler Slater, says companies spread over several floors are finding that set-up stymies critical communication between co-workers. More one-floor buildings are being constructed today, she says, and if several tiers are needed, escalators, not elevators, are being installed to move people between floors.

"People don't talk in elevators, but they do on escalators," notes McManus, who works out of Kahler Slater's Madison office.

Bland office designs of earlier generations have been giving way to more colors over the last decade or two, and office interior specialists say the offices of 2020 will be stunning in their broad array of colors and textures, and filled with work stations and furnishings of varying sizes and shapes. Why? With the advent of things like MTV and video games, we've become a very visual culture, says McManus.

"Besides," adds Vickie Wenzel, a principal at Insite Studio, a subsidiary of Rowley-Schlimgen office design, "you don't decorate your home all vanilla, so it doesn't make sense to do it in your office, where you live a lot of hours."

Bland office design also stifles the imagination—the last thing employers want to do, especially in the growing high-tech fields where inventiveness is highly valued. Ralph Kauten, president of the biotech firm PanVera Corp., hasn't chosen the interior colors yet for his new headquarters in Madison's University Research Park, but he is hard at work planning space for the traveling art shows he wants to bring through.

"We want a building that encourages creativity," Kauten says earnestly, "so people can say,

'Here's the work of a master in this particular art, and I'm here to be a master at my own art.'"

Wenzel reports that one of her clients hopes to foster creative brainstorming by constructing a "playroom" for employees, filled with comfy furniture, dry erase boards, laptop hookups and refreshments. The theory is that if workers can hang out in a comfortable spot, ideas will flow. Studies also indicate that if workers return to the space where an idea was launched, its development is much smoother.

Most business futurists say the pressure will be on for workers to go at it pretty hard, so they'll also need a place on-site to totally get away from it all—a difficult thing in today's pager/cell phone/e-mail society.

Local developer Derrick Van Mell of Van Mell Associates predicts more offices will contain "privacy zones," or areas off-limits to any form of communication.

### *The comforts of home*

Already, the lines between employees' private and professional lives are blurring. Many workers have home offices and faxes, and are increasingly connected to their work life via cell phones and pagers. With so much of the office being brought into the home, employers will reciprocate by bringing the home into the office.

When Auto Glass Specialists constructed a new headquarters building 18 months ago, president Bob Birkhauser says the company chose more luxurious amenities such as mahogany-trimmed work stations and high quality artwork to create a more homey feel. Zoned thermostat controls allow workers to regulate the temperature, and a new music system plays a combination of jazz, old rock and new rock in deference to the company's younger workforce.

"I'm confident our building acts as a recruiting tool," says Birkhauser.

The Madison Corporate Center at Highway 51 and Milwaukee Street goes a step further, recreating an entire neighborhood for its workers. Employees in the Center's first 40,000–square–foot building, developed by The Blettner Group Ltd., have a food court, day care center, health club, dentist, legal office, and bank all in the building with them. A second, 100,000-square-foot office building is currently under construction, and will be connected to the first structure via a skywalk.

"It's a twist on new urbanism," says Bob Blettner, chair and CEO of The Blettner Group. New urbanism in city planning tightly clusters homes in small neighborhoods containing such "staple" services as a bank, dry cleaner, and grocery store. Blettner has put that old-fashioned neighborhood right at the workplace. Employees "don't have to use their car to run errands and waste a lot of time," Blettner notes. "This hands people an hour and a half of free time every week. How can they get that anywhere else?"

In a similar set-up, The American Center, a sprawling 325-acre office park on Madison's far East Side, has a bank, credit union, child care center, and hotel on its campus; a health clinic is under construction; space is being pre-leased for a commercial services complex containing such businesses as a dry cleaner; and a fitness center is under consideration.

Dori Mowbray, an American Center marketing analyst, says employees find the amenities attractive and are clamoring for more. "We're seeking a restaurant, quick-stop gas station and a grocer," she says, "but we'll take whatever we can get."

Twenty years from now, employees may not even have to take their eyes from the computer monitor to access many of the new workplace perks. Janet Kraus is CEO of Circles, a national business concierge service she co-founded in 1997. Mainly used by large corporations, Circles performs everything on an employee's to-do list, from picking up the dry cleaning to sitting in your home waiting for the cable guy.

Why would an employer pay for someone to do your chores? To cultivate a dedicated workforce, for sure—but Kraus says savvy employers also realize workers will be more productive if they don't have to worry about their errands. It also serves as another corporate reward for people who take work home.

Employers increasingly want to pay back hard-working employees by letting them play at the office, too. PanVera's Kauten is installing sand volleyball courts outside his new building and will cement in a basketball hoop or two. He also chose what he considered to be the Research Park's choicest lot—one with a wooded area nearby so employees can relax in a backyard-type setting.

Stephen Kraus, a partner with the national market research firm Yankelovich Partners, says tomorrow's younger employees are definitely "going to want an environment that's fun." He already sees Gen-Xers playing roller hockey over the lunch hour, and notes that Intel has a sabbatical program that every five years gives employees an additional six weeks off to travel, to take classes or just relax and rejuvenate.

And forget about dressing up for work in 2020; it's casual all the way—and that's casual–casual, not business casual.

### Baby on board—next to the boardroom?

As our jobs increasingly encroach on our social lives, our social lives—namely our families—will become a major consideration for tomorrow's employers.

Already the pitter-patter of tiny feet can be heard around many offices, as employees' children are increasingly welcomed into the workplace. Vickie Wenzel of Insite Studio says an Appleton employer constructing a new facility is mapping out a special room filled with toys just for employees' kids if they need to come in with mom or dad. Fido, by the way, is welcome, too.

David Antonioni, chairman of UW-Madison's[1] Management School of Business and an organizational psychologist, says an East Coast company offers parenting classes to employees, partly as a perk, but also as an investment for itself. Moms and dads who expend a lot of energy parenting at home come to the office sapped; a parenting class should make employees more productive. And since workers sometimes use common parenting techniques to manage co-workers, the class should help with productivity as well.

Watch for taboos on office romances to be eased in the future, too, and family members will be

[1] University of Wisconsin at Madison.

encouraged to work at the same companies. "We sure believe in it," laughs Auto Glass' Birkhauser, who heads a family business. "We find it to be an enhancement. Employees think, 'There's something more for me at work than just doing my job.'"

Probably the one family perk all employees will demand of tomorrow's employers is flexibility–lots of it. With an ever-shrinking number of parents at home during the day, flex time to attend school conferences and plays, nurse a sick child, or care for an aging parent will be crucial. So crucial that Rolf Jensen, director of the Copenhagen Institute for Future Studies, the largest futurist think tank in Europe, predicts, "There will be no real work hours in 20 years. There will be results you need to accomplish, and projects that need to be finalized, but no fixed hours."

Yankelovich's Kraus calls this "week blending."

Your schedule is driven by you—your needs and desires—and there's no external calendar imposed on you," he says.

UW's Antonioni says expect more flexibility via job sharing, even with management positions, and the increased use of telecommuting. "People are starting to say, 'Work isn't my life,'" he says. "They want some balance."

"Workers are also yearning for an office environment that's truly like the one at home: warm, secure, loving people have a strong desire to go to work and experience a sense of trust and safety so they can just relax," says Antonioni. This desire will kick off the concept of the workplace as "spiritual," a place where employers foster a real sense of community by modeling a management-by-love style of behavior. Futurists are right, we'll have pretty cool offices in 20 years. We may even be able to work whenever, wherever and however we please. But on the flip side is this question: Are we winning or are we losing by not being able to drive home at the end of the day and leave it all behind?

# Thinking as a Writer

## Predicting Trends in Communication

In the article, Melanie McManus describes a vision of the workplace of the future. Such offices will be designed to encourage communication and comfort among other things, according to the author.

- Think about what you know about how offices look and feel today. What do you know about how communication takes place? What communication tools would you need to work in an office?
- How might you want the environment in an office to be in order to help you communicate more effectively? Write your ideas in a paragraph.

## Evaluating Different Kinds of Conversations

Oral Expression

The article notes that "people don't talk in elevators, but they do on escalators." It is true that the environment in which people find themselves shapes the kinds of conversations they have. Pair off with a classmate and improvise a conversation you might have with someone whom you do not know well in each of the following settings:

- Principal's office
- Doctor's office
- Friend's family room
- Escalator in multilevel movie theater

After your improvised chats, take a few minutes to talk about the differences in the conversations. How did the location change the kinds of things you discussed? How did the location change the way you discussed things—not only your style of speaking, but also the organization and presentation of what you said?

## Analyzing Visuals

Viewing Imagine that your job is to choose the artwork for an office of the future. You are trying to create a relaxed, cooperative feeling. Which of the following paintings would do the best job? Why? Discuss the sort of environment that would be better suited for the two pieces of art you chose not to display in this office setting.

Claude Oscar Monet. *Bridge over a Pool of Water Lilies,* 1899. Oil on canvas, 36 1/2 by 29 inches. The Metropolitan Museum of Art.

Georgia O'Keeffe. *Evening Star, III,* 1917. Watercolor on paper. 9 by 11 7/8 inches. The Museum of Modern Art.

Pablo Picasso. *Guernica,* 1937. Oil on canvas, 11 1/2 by 25 1/2 feet. Centro de Arte Reina Sofía, Madrid, Spain.

# Written Communication at Work

If you can write well, chances are very good that you will get a good job. Employers place a high premium on good writing skills, and for good reason. Business writing is often read in a hurried, deadline-driven environment, and important decisions are based on the ideas it expresses. More than other writing, business writing needs to achieve clarity almost instantly.

Good business writing achieves quick clarity by using the simplest, most direct ways to express ideas.

**Your Writer's Journal**

Imagine your ideal workplace of the future. Describe both the work itself and the environment in which you will be working. Ask yourself questions to fill in lots of details. For example, "If I look around my desk, what do I see? What do I see out the window? Am I even at a desk? Who is working near me? What will I need—in terms of tools, gadgets, and so on—to be relaxed, productive, and efficient?"

## Writing Reports

One of the most common forms of writing in the world of work is the report. There are many different kinds of reports, but each has the overall purpose of sharing key information.

### Writing Informational Reports

Without accurate information good decisions are impossible. Being able to research, interpret, and present information clearly will put you in demand in the world of work.

**Informational reports** present accurate information upon which business decisions may be based.

Writers of informational business reports try to give themselves as much time as possible to create their reports. During that period they go through a routine set of tasks. These are summarized in the chart below.

### Steps for Writing Informational Business Reports

1. Begin by answering three questions:
   - What specifically are the objectives of this report?
   - Who is my audience?
   - How much time can I realistically spend on this report?
2. Identify, evaluate, gather, and synthesize information from a wide variety of sources.
3. Prepare both written and graphic information. Maintain records of your information to ensure that it is current.
4. Convert information from one form to another if necessary for clarity (for example, change a written piece to a graphic, or vice versa).
5. Interpret information, and use technology to help organize and present information in a first draft of the report.
6. Evaluate your report against the objectives that you identified. Proofread the report for misspellings, correct grammar, and organization. Make any necessary revisions to be sure the report accomplishes its purposes.
7. Prepare the final report in a form which is impressive and clear, and whose presentation makes the desired impact on its audience.

The case study on the next page shows how an employee of a hospital traces these steps as he puts together an informational report.

## Expanding Physical Therapy — Case Study

Tony is in charge of the physical therapy unit at a community hospital in a small Midwestern town. His staff includes seven full-time therapists as well as an office clerk. Use of the hospital is increasing, and the board of trustees is considering a major fund-raising campaign to expand the facilities. To help the board make its decision, the head of the hospital has asked Tony to write an informational report on whether the hospital should expand its physical therapy unit. She needs the report in three months.

With his **objective, timeline,** and **audience** clear, Tony was ready to gather the necessary information. He began by collecting information on the existing department. He reviewed time sheets to find out how much overtime therapists had worked in the past year, and he interviewed each therapist.

Then he collected data about the community that might influence how many physical therapists were needed in the area that the hospital serviced. The hospital drew people from a region that included about 35,000 people. Within this region were four large retirement communities and three smaller ones. He spoke with physical therapists at similar-sized hospitals close to his to find out how busy they were. He collected reports on health data for the community from the state and federal governments, and census projections on population growth in the region.

As Tony gathered information, he **organized** it. Since he was working on a computer, he created a different set of files for his general notes, his statistical data, and his reports from interviews.

Finally, he began to **write** his report. Since he had been entering information into his computer as he went, he found it easy to cut and paste it into a word-processing program. He created charts as needed. He then proofread the report for spelling and grammatical errors.

When he finished the report, Tony printed out a copy for each board member, printing his chart in color to help make it easy to read. He put each report and accompanying chart in its own folder with a clear plastic cover. Tony was aware that a professional presentation would make a difference in how his hard work was received. When he was finished, Tony's report looked like this:

The physical therapy unit of Newburg Community Hospital (NCH) includes seven full-time therapists. This report presents information concerning whether that staff should be increased.

### Feasibility of Expansion of Physical Therapy Staff and Facility

#### The Need

NCH serves a community of 35,000 people. Nationally, the ratio of physical therapists to the general population is 1 to 3,500. Based on this ratio, our community is large enough to support 10 full-time physical therapists. Further, this region has a higher-than-average number of residents over the age of 65, people who are more likely to use physical therapy services.

#### Existing Resources

NCH employs seven full-time physical therapists. As the chart, "Hours of Overtime Worked by NCH Physical Therapists," shows, staff members worked about 1,000 hours of overtime last year. They report that they often feel rushed to complete appointments so they can squeeze in more patients.

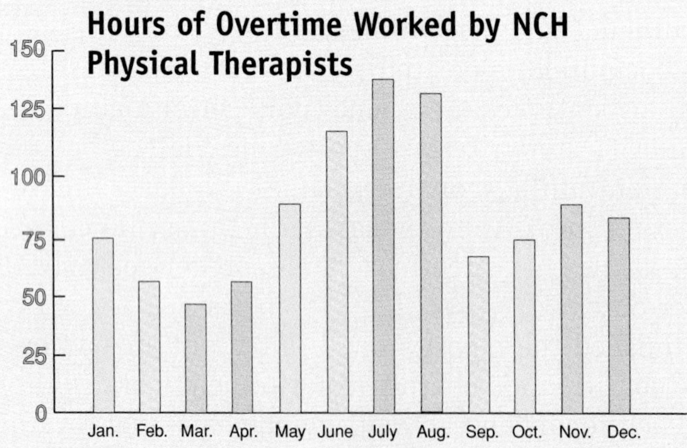

The four hospitals nearest to NCH are approximately 30 miles away, each in a different direction. Three of these, like NCH, are community-based hospitals. They all report that their physical therapy staffs are busy. To the east is the state university hospital. This is a large teaching hospital, one that has a large staff of physical therapists. In addition, there are approximately 20 physical therapists that work in retirement communities, for health clubs, or in private practice.

**Possibilities of Expansion**

The current physical therapy program uses most of the space available. Any significant expansion of the staff would require more space.

Tony's report was concise, easy-to-read, and to the point. It included the following features that good reports should have.

### Features of an Informational Business Report

- The purpose is plainly stated in the introduction.
- The scope is precisely outlined.
- The report suits the intended audience.
- Up-to-date and accurate information is presented in a logical way.
- Information is conveyed with graphics when they provide greater clarity than text.
- Headings and page layout simplify quick scanning.
- Ideas are expressed in as few words as possible. (*pages C66–C69*)
- The language is direct. (*page C60*)
- Errors in spelling, grammar, usage, and punctuation have been corrected.

### COMPUTER TIP

The careful use of type size and style can add to your report's "almost instant clarity." For example, you can show the relationship of ideas (which is more important, which is a sub-idea of another) by the size of the type. The heading for the main idea should use a larger-size type than the heading for subordinate points. Using boldface for headings will also help them "pop" so the reader can easily pick them up. The font style, typesize, and typeface are controlled in the Format menu of your word-processing screen or in the toolbar at the top of your screen.

## PRACTICE YOUR SKILLS

*Planning an Informational Business Report*

**You are a meteorologist employed by the state government. Several political leaders have noticed that student absenteeism, after dropping slowly for five years, has increased in each of the past four years. Several people blame the weather for the increase, although they disagree on whether the winters have been colder or warmer. You have been asked to analyze and evaluate the weather data to see if changes in weather have affected changes in school attendance.**

**Write a brief description of how you would draft this report. Refer to the steps on page C624 as a guide. State the objectives, audience, and scope for your report. Specify the types of sources you would consult for information. Describe at least one graphic that would improve your presentation.**

## Using Graphics

In an increasingly visual world, graphics are a necessary part of communication. They can take many forms. Some of the more common are tables, charts, graphs, illustrations, and maps. Whatever their type, they usually serve one of the following purposes.

### Purpose of Graphics

- To support an idea in the written text—to prove a point
- To clarify or simplify a complex relationship
- To emphasize an important idea
- To add drama to a presentation

The following examples may give you ideas for using graphics in your business writing.

**Charts** One common type of chart is the **organizational chart.** It shows in visual form the hierarchy, or levels of authority, of a business or other setting.

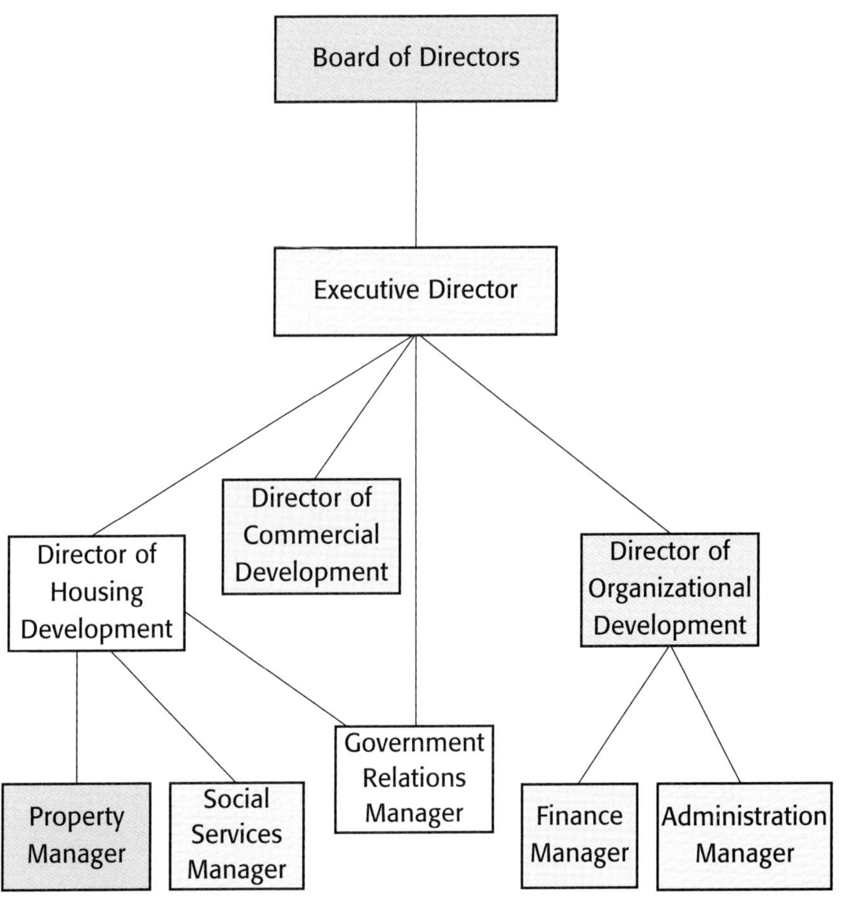

## Practice Your Skills

### *Creating an Organizational Chart*

**Create an organizational chart describing your school. You might include a school board, principal, teachers, parents, and students.**

The **flow chart** is widely used to show how a process works. The following flow chart shows how one magazine publisher goes about hiring a graphics designer.

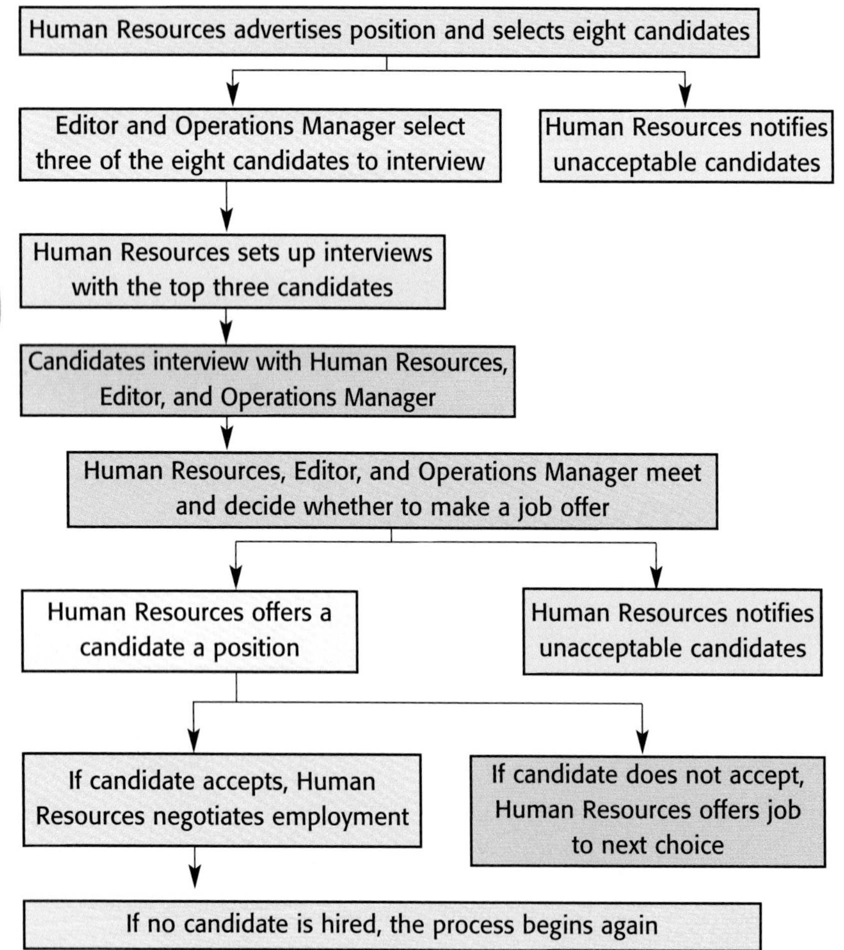
Hiring Procedure
Human Resources advertises position and selects eight candidates
Editor and Operations Manager select three of the eight candidates to interview
Human Resources notifies unacceptable candidates
Human Resources sets up interviews with the top three candidates
Candidates interview with Human Resources, Editor, and Operations Manager
Human Resources, Editor, and Operations Manager meet and decide whether to make a job offer
Human Resources offers a candidate a position
Human Resources notifies unacceptable candidates
If candidate accepts, Human Resources negotiates employment
If candidate does not accept, Human Resources offers job to next choice
If no candidate is hired, the process begins again

## Practice Your Skills

### *Creating a Flow Chart*

**Create a flow chart showing how you will make decisions about what to do after high school. Include the various options that you are considering and show whether each one leads to other decisions.**

A **pie chart** is often an effective way to show how a total amount breaks down into smaller categories, as in the following example of the different energy sources used in the United States. You can see at a glance that the two biggest sources are coal and natural gas.

Energy Sources In the United States

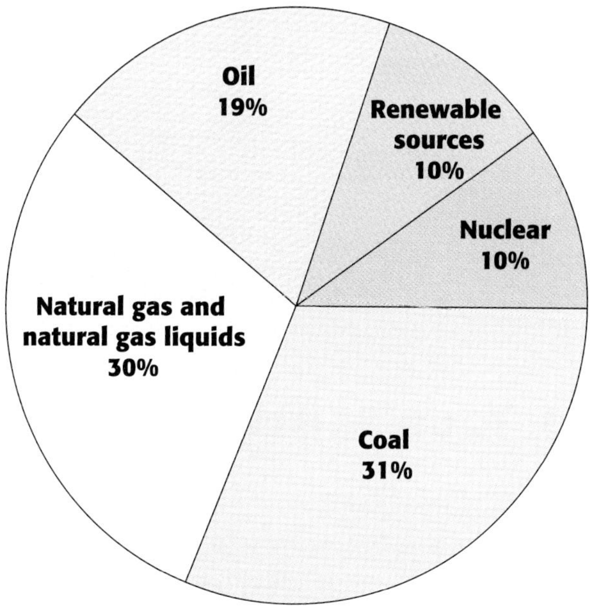


## Practice Your Skills

### *Creating a Pie Chart*

**Make a pie chart that shows how you use your time in a 24-hour period. Some of the categories you might use are attending school, doing homework, reading, eating, and sleeping. In your pie chart, the complete circle should equal 24 hours. Each slice should show how many hours you spend doing each activity.**

**Graphs** Graphs come in a variety of forms. The following examples show effective ways to use bar and line graphs.

**Bar graphs** are especially good at showing comparisons. The following bar graph displays how poultry consumption in the United States compares with that in other selected countries.

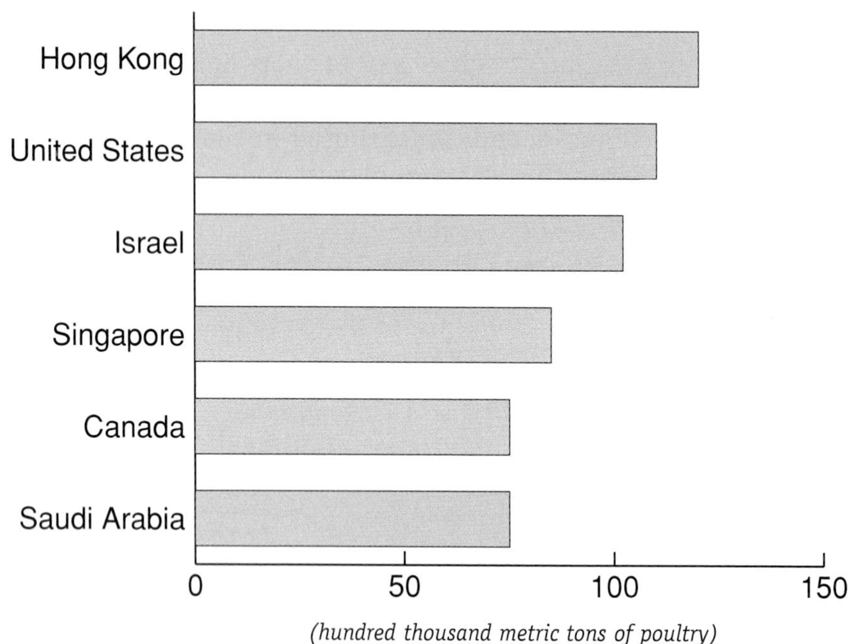


## PRACTICE YOUR SKILLS

### *Creating a Bar Graph*

**Make a bar graph that shows how much homework you have each day for a week. Decide whether to use minutes or hours as your unit of measure, and whether the bars should be horizontal or vertical. Label your graph carefully.**

**Line graphs** are effective at showing changes over time. The following line graph shows the changes in the number of new food products introduced in the United States over an eight-year period.

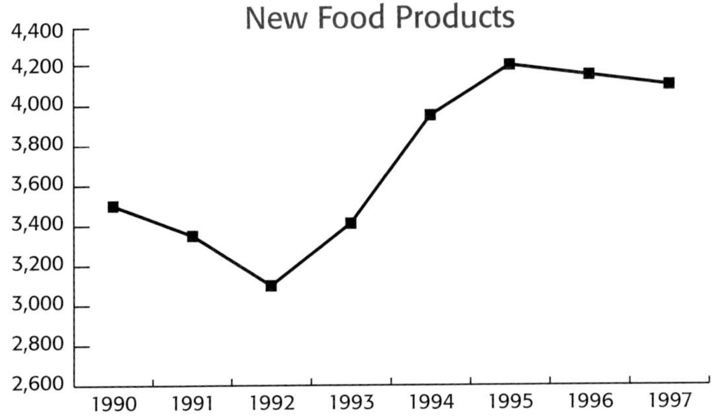


## PRACTICE YOUR SKILLS

*Creating a Line Graph*

**Make a line graph that shows how your level of happiness changes during a day. Use a scale of 0 to 10, with 10 being the happiest. For the other axis, use the hours of the day or time posts, such as "Alarm Rings," "Lunch," and "Band Practice."**

## Narrative Report

Another common type of business report is the **narrative.** Like its counterpart narrative writing, the business narrative's main purpose is to tell what happened.

A **narrative business report** tells what happened in a certain event or situation in a straightforward, factual way. It is used to report accidents and incidents as well as special events.

Many industries have regular conventions where both companies and customers come together. Typically, there is an exhibit room where the different companies in the industry set up booths and show their new products. They send representatives to staff the booths—that is, to be on duty when customers come by—and to be prepared to answer questions or take orders.

After staffing a booth at a convention, one employee wrote this narrative about the flow of visitors to the booth. Notice that the employee tries to estimate the number of people during each period of the day and to analyze this information.

**MODEL: Report on Booth Traffic**

Daniella and I staffed the company booth during the first day at the national convention. Traffic was heavy when the exhibit room opened at 8:00 A.M. It remained steady until about 10:00 A.M. In those two hours, we had approximately 100 visitors, a rate of 50 per hour. Many of the people we saw were current customers who wanted to see our new products.

Between 10:00 A.M. and 2:00 P.M., the number of visitors fell to about 20 per hour. Traffic at all booths seemed to slow down during this period. During these four hours, many people were attending the keynote speech and eating lunch.

Our biggest rush of visitors came between 4:00 P.M. and 5:00 P.M. In that hour alone, we had nearly 150 people stop by. The flow was heavy because many people were visiting the booth next to ours to meet the celebrity spokesperson for the company. Many of these people had almost no knowledge of our company and were pleased to find out that we exist. We had not anticipated the rush, and felt overwhelmed.

This report suggests two trends. First, the most important time for speaking with current customers and serious buyers is the beginning of the day. This is the best time for our key sales people to be available to greet people. Second, we should be prepared for a wave of casual visitors—who are potential new customers—when other booths have special events going on. For such events, we need more people and more brochures.

## Communicate Your Ideas

**DRAFTING** *Narrative Report*

Think of a time when you changed your mind about purchasing an item. Write a narrative account of your thoughts that would help a market research team. Factors you might include are price, display of product, and service. Save your work.

SAVE YOUR WORK

## The Language of Graphics

Although graphics can often convey facts and other kinds of information very efficiently, they may be even more powerful at conveying feelings, moods, and hidden messages. In fact, everywhere you turn you encounter a graphic image that someone—often a whole team of people—has worked very hard on to make sure it conveys the desired feeling and unspoken message. Two common examples of this type of graphic are visuals for advertisements and company logos. (Logos are the emblems or symbols companies use to identify themselves. The logos appear on company stationery and often in the company's ads.) The "secret" language these graphics use to communicate their message is the language of metaphor. Through this language, they imply that the actual subject (the product or company) they are representing has the same qualities as the subject of the visual.

Here's an example of how the process works. A housing developer is planning a new community of single-family houses for those with upper-middle-class income levels. It is to be located in a suburban area where there are many other new housing developments. The firm has done some market research and found that people in this income bracket who are attracted to this kind of real estate do not like the idea of living in a suburbia known for its strip malls and sameness of architecture. So the developer wants to make sure the name—and the logo that will be developed after the name is chosen—will suggest another, different kind of quality of life. After brainstorming and more market research, the firm decided on the name Prairie Grass for the community. They found people responded well to the idea it conveyed about being near nature and to a prairie metaphor.

The next step was to design a graphic that would represent the desired feeling. The following two logos were the finalists.

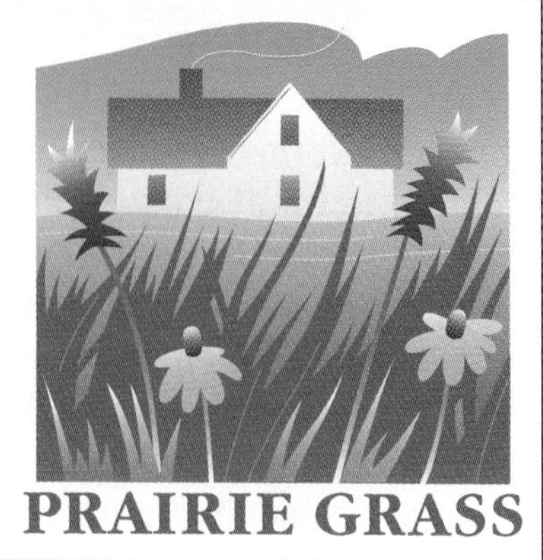


When the team met to make a final decision, they had these thoughts.

- They felt the first logo did a better job suggesting tranquility and nature. They felt the message was: "Living in Prairie Grass will be a peaceful experience, well away from the city's hustle and bustle, but not tacky."
- They felt the second logo suggested a little more convenience—although they would be living near nature, people would still have the convenience of being near human activity.
- They recalled that another concern of people was that the architecture not be too uniform, so they suggested adding a second house symbol in the second logo to show variety of shape.

The final modified logo, with the two houses, was finally selected because it conveyed all the key messages the firm's market research had found to be important.

## Media Activity

Find an interesting example of a company logo. Then think backward. Try to put yourself in the shoes of the team that developed that logo. What messages do you think they were trying to get across? How did they use metaphor to achieve their goal? Write a brief analysis as well as an evaluation of the logo's effectiveness.

## Progress Report

Do you know the song "Keep Your Eyes on the Prize"? It became widely known during the civil rights movement. Working to change the unfair laws was hard, tiring, and even dangerous at times. When the activists reminded themselves of the prize, the goal of equality, they could keep up their spirits and continue their hard work.

Even when the "prize" is far more modest, working toward goals is the best way to keep track of your work and move it along effectively. A good way to see how well you are achieving your goals is to write a progress report.

A **progress report** measures your performance against previously set goals and expectations.

The following report shows how one paralegal, an assistant in a law firm, monitored and evaluated her achievements. Her employer required progress reports every month.

**MODEL: Progress Report**

### Progress Report: July

During July I accomplished the following goals:

- I spent approximately 50 percent of my time researching legal cases relevant to the Grapevine Industries zoning case. I completed the search for relevant cases and have prepared summaries of half of them.
- I spent approximately 30 percent of my time preparing the documents on the interviews that members of our firm conducted in the Anderson disorderly conduct case. This concluded my work on this case.
- I spent approximately 20 percent of my time learning the new legal research software we purchased last month. After reading the documentation, I practiced using the program on the Grapevine case.

The one goal for the month that I did not accomplish was to conduct training sessions on the new software.

At the staff meeting on July 20, we decided to delay the training until next month.

During August, I expect to accomplish the following goals:

- I should complete the summaries of the cases in the Grapevine dispute by the second Friday of the month.
- I will prepare a written report of my Grapevine research and provide the lead attorneys with an oral summary of it.
- I will schedule and conduct the three training sessions on the new software. Each session will be approximately two hours long.

**Setting Effective Performance Goals** Carefully crafted goals are essential to both a good progress report and to the progress itself. Effective performance goals allow workers to assess themselves and measure the progress of a project. Successful workers set goals that are measurable, monitor their time accurately, and assess their progress.

**Measurable goals** are those that can be tested against a visible outcome—a specific quantity of work that will be completed by a certain time.

| | |
|---|---|
| MEASURABLE GOAL | I will send off two job applications by Tuesday. (If you sent two applications by Tuesday, you met your goal. The outcome is easy to measure.) |
| NONMEASURABLE GOAL | I will work on getting a job. (This goal cannot be measured. You have set yourself no time limit and you have not named a specific task related to getting a job.) |

It is important to set **achievable goals,** those with a realistic possibility of being accomplished. Setting unrealistic goals will only lead to failure. If you know, for example, that mixing the tape of your band's latest recording usually takes six to eight hours, don't promise it in two hours.

| | |
|---|---|
| ACHIEVABLE GOAL | This week I will make appointments at two recording companies to promote the band. |
| NONACHIEVABLE GOAL | This week I will visit every recording company in town. |

Only you will be able to know for sure what is achievable, given your workload. Effective goals should make you reach somewhat beyond your comfort zone, but unrealistic goals are wasteful.

## Communicate Your Ideas

**SETTING GOALS** *Progress Report*

What is your most pressing project right now? Write three measurable, achievable goals which you have to accomplish related to that project within the next week. At the end of the week write a progress report measuring your progress against the goals you set.

## Writing Proposals

Well-researched information presented in an easy-to-read report is the first step in building a sound business. But the real test of business creativity is how information is used. A proposal takes the business report one step further and recommends a course of action.

A **proposal** uses solid information and reasoning to recommend an action.

After Tony presented his informational report to the head of the hospital, she asked him to add his recommendation to it. Tony developed the following proposal.

**Model: Proposal**

**Analysis**

Three points stand out in the information.

1. The physical therapy staff of NCH is overworked. The amount of overtime worked by staff members, the shortness of appointments, and the tightness of the schedule all point to the need for more staff.
2. Our region is underserved. In the immediate town and surrounding rural area, many people go to the state university hospital for services that other people receive at NCH.
3. Future use will probably grow. The population in the region is increasing generally, and the elderly population is growing in particular.

**Recommendation**

All of the above points suggest that NCH should expand its physical therapy staff. I recommend that NCH hire one person immediately. I estimate from the statistics on overtime and the number of cases that our current patient load would more than pay for an additional therapist. Further, I recommend that we hire two more as soon as the facilities can be expanded.

Tony's proposal, especially alongside the original report, has all of the following features of a good proposal.

### Features of a Good Proposal

- The proposed actions are clearly stated.
- The information that supports the proposed actions is accurate and up-to-date.
- The ideas are well organized, often arranged in order of importance.
- The proposal includes a way to measure costs against the potential benefits.
- The proposal is addressed to the appropriate audience.
- The reader understands what he or she is called on to do.

## Communicate Your Ideas

**DRAFTING** *Proposal*

Tony's proposal is only one of many possible responses to the information he collected. Reread his original report. Then write a counterproposal that uses the same information but gives a different recommendation. You might consider proposals that do not include three full-time staff people or that use space in different ways. When you have finished, check your proposal against the qualities of good proposals listed above.

## Writing Procedures and Instructions

Procedures and instructions, widely used forms of business writing, have many features in common. *(You have already come across this kind of writing on pages C155–C156 when you practiced informative writing, specifically when you were asked to describe a process or write a set of instructions.)*

**Procedures** explain which steps are required to complete a job. **Instructions** explain how to complete the necessary steps.

A key difference between procedures and instructions is the scope of the task being described. Procedures often involve several different departments or a number of different employees. Instructions, on the other hand, are more focused. They involve smaller tasks that can be performed by one employee.

You have already seen an example of a procedure represented in a flow chart (*page C630*). Some procedures are so important, however, that they need to be described in writing. In fact, many companies provide a **procedures manual** to all employees to make sure everyone knows and follows the same procedures. The procedures are written so that even someone who has never performed a needed procedure before will be able to follow the guidelines easily.

The following model explains how employees are evaluated in one company.

**MODEL: Proposal**

**Employee Evaluation Procedure**

Each employee will be evaluated annually, usually in the month of the year in which he or she was hired. The purpose of evaluation is to help employees increase their value to the company, both by recognizing their strengths and by identifying areas for improvement.

**Step 1 Complete "Standard Evaluation Form"**

The employee and his or her supervisor will each fill out the "Standard Evaluation Form" independently. This form includes a section for numerical ratings and a section for open-ended written responses. This form is available from the Human Resources Office.

**Step 2 Submit Co-workers Names to the Human Resources Department**

The employee should submit to the Human Resources Department the names of ten individuals with whom he or she has worked in the past year. These individuals may be at any level of the company. The Human Resources Department will randomly select two of these individuals to complete the "Co-workers Evaluation Form." The Human Resources Office will not release the names of these individuals. It will send copies of the completed forms to both the employee and his or her supervisor.

**Step 3 Meet with Supervisor**

The employee and his or her supervisor will meet to review the evaluations each has completed, as well as those by the two co-workers. They should complete a "Final Evaluation Form," which consists of the numerical ratings section of the "Standard Evaluation Form." The two should reach an agreement, to within two points, of how to rate the employee on each item. They should also set goals for the coming year.

**Step 4 Carry Out Plans**

During the year the employee should strive to carry out the goals set in the annual review. The employee and his or her supervisor should review these goals periodically throughout the year.

For a routine task, written **instructions** are usually provided to employees. Often workers who are most familiar with the task prepare instructions for workers who are new to it. Supervisors sometimes write instructions to introduce a new technology or system to the workplace.

The following instructions tell employees how to request financial assistance for continuing education.

**MODEL: Instructions**

**Instructions for Receiving Continuing Education Money**

Syndergaard Industries will pay up to $1,000 per year per employee toward the costs of attending lectures, conferences, or courses that enhance an employee's professional skills. To apply for company support, please follow these procedures.

1. Write a brief description of the content of the lecture, conference, or course that you wish to attend, the cost of the program, and the benefit you expect to receive from it. This document should be no more than one page long.
2. Give the description to your supervisor and ask for his or her approval. If your supervisor approves, then he or she should sign it and return it to you.
3. Complete a check request form. On this form, indicate the amount requested, to whom the check should be written, and to whom it should be mailed.
4. Send the description, with your supervisor's signature, along with the check request to the Human Resources Department. Requests should be submitted one month before the program begins. The Human Resources Director may, at his or her option, approve payment for programs after they have been completed.
5. After one week, check with the Human Resources Department to see if they have written and mailed the check.

Well-written instructions and well-written procedures share the following features.

### Features of Good Procedures and Instructions

- They provide all the information necessary to complete a task or procedure.
- They clarify unfamiliar terms or items.
- They present the steps in their sequential order.
- They use numbering systems, when appropriate, to separate the various steps in the process.
- They use only the words necessary to describe the task.

# Practice Your Skills

*Writing Instructions*

**Write instructions for a process that you know well, but that others may not. For example, you might explain how to send an e-mail message, how to calculate an earned run average, or how to make salsa.**

## Writing Memos

The memo (short for *memorandum*) is the workhorse of the workplace. The simplicity of its form makes it the universal business communication.

A **memo** is a brief, somewhat informal communication that can serve a variety of purposes. Chiefly, it functions as an inter-office communication used among employees.

A memo is easy to spot. It typically begins with the same four headings (shown in **bold** in the following model).

**Model: Memo**

**To:** All members of Local 335
**From:** Al Levin, Shop Steward
**Date:** 2/17/00
**Subject:** Meeting on 3/15/00

Please plan to attend a meeting on 3/15/00 at 10:00 A.M. at the Civic Center, Room 118. The purpose is to inform you of some recent changes in the law regarding safety protection on the job.

Thank you.

**Business memos** are meant to be concise, usually no longer than a single page, but memos often contain complex information. The recipient probably hasn't much time to spend reading it. It is important organize the information so that its message is unambiguous.

### Common Purposes for Memos

- As reminders of meetings
- As transmittal sheets accompanying other materials
  The message in a transmittal memo would identify the materials being passed along (transmitted) and specify any requests for actions. For example:

  > Attached is my report on the need for physical therapists in our community. Please let me know if there is any additional information that you would like to have.

- As a written summary of a conversation, that will document any specific agreements

  > Thank you for the discussion about improving employee morale. We agreed that, as of 5/1/2000, the time clock will be replaced with the honor system.

- As a request

  > I would like to bring my ten-year-old daughter to work as part of the national Daughters at Work Day next Thursday, November 12. I would appreciate written approval of this request by November 6. Thank you.

- To transmit information about a project, either to fellow workers within a company or to a client or employee

As flexible as memos are, there are times when a phone call or face-to-face conversation is preferable. Everything you put into writing can be read by anyone, whether or not it is labeled "confidential." If you want to convey privileged information, use the phone, or meet with the person face-to-face. Also use the personal approach to resolve differences whenever possible. Human contact often promotes resolution.

**E-mail versus Paper Memos** More and more, employees are communicating with one another via e-mail rather than on paper. Memos sent via e-mail do not follow the same form as paper memos, partly because the *To, From,* and *Subject* are built into the e-mail format.

**MODEL: E-mail Memo**

| | |
|---|---|
| Subj: | Freelance work |
| Date: | 09/07/00 |
| To: | jtramer1311@isp.com (James Tramer) |
| From: | splough@mediawise.com (Suzanne Plough) |

Jim—Our staff met and gave the green light to your freelance work on our marketing project. I will be sending you a draft of the contract within a week. Welcome aboard!

E-mail also allows you to send the same message to many people, either by adding their e-mail addresses to the entry field or by adding them to a *CC:* (courtesy copy) field.

**Communicate Your Ideas**

**DRAFTING** *E-mail*

Using an e-mail program, compose a business-style e-mail, giving information for an upcoming school event. Include a description of the event, the time and place, and a brief reason for someone to attend.

## Nonwritten Communication at Work

Although technology offers an increasing number of options for telephone conveniences, the basic skills of speaking clearly, politely, and professionally on the phone have changed little. The skills used for telephone calls and other types of nonwritten communication remain essential for a successful career.

## Telephone Etiquette

Maybe you've heard the saying "You don't get a second chance to make a first impression." Often a customer's first impression of a company is formed in a telephone conversation. Here are some tips for ensuring that the impression is a good one.

### Tips for Professional Phone Calls

- Speak slowly and clearly. Keep the phone about one and a half inches from your mouth.
- Use a pleasant tone. Try smiling. Vary the pitch of your voice throughout the conversation.
- Listen carefully to the caller's points or questions.
- If you don't know an answer, say something like "That's a good question; let me try to find out for you."
- If the caller has a complaint, apologize for the problem and find some way to provide him or her satisfaction.
- Even if the caller is emotional, remain polite.
- Whenever possible, let the caller end the call. Say, "Thank you for calling," and replace the receiver gently when you hang up.
- Try to answer your calls by the second or third ring.
- Keep writing materials near the phone so you can take a message if you have to. Each message should include the name of the person called, the name and phone number of the caller, the time of the call, a brief summary of the message, and a good time to call back.

## Practice Your Skills

### *Telephone Role Play*

**Pair off with a classmate and role-play a business telephone call. Take turns being a slightly rude customer and an in-control, polite, and professional employee. Use your imagination to create the setting. Be prepared to role-play your call for the rest of the class.**

## Informal Meetings

As McManus points out in her article *(pages C615–620)*, employee interactions are so important that when future workplaces are designed there will be great care put into creating spaces that promote productive meetings. These spaces will no doubt try to encourage teamwork, for that is an essential part of the modern workplace.

The **team approach** helps companies achieve their goals by pointing everyone in the same direction.

Workplace teams have the following traits:

- All team members understand the goal.
- The structure is flexible enough for creative problem solving.
- Mutual respect provides team members with elevated spirit.
- Belonging to a team gives members a sense of identity.
- Team members learn from one another and develop a shared understanding.

When you meet informally with your co-workers, keeping your team attitude will help guide your behavior. Sometimes you may have to lead the way; other times you may have to follow another's lead. When you disagree, you need to express your thoughts respectfully and responsibly. Remember, the other members of your team are all working toward the same goal, and if your ideas are good, your fellow team members will recognize them as such.

## Formal Meetings

The team approach also works for formal meetings. The biggest differences between informal and formal meetings are the amount of structure and the presence of a designated leader.

The most important task as the leader of a meeting is to be well prepared.

### Leading a Meeting

- Carefully consider the purpose of the meeting. Decide what you want to accomplish, then outline an **agenda,** or order of topics, to ensure you achieve your purpose. When you are satisfied that you have listed all the necessary points, estimate the time needed to discuss each one. Include as your final item something like "Next Steps." This creates a call for action on the very issues that you will have just discussed.
- Send an advance copy of the agenda to all the people who are expected at the meeting. At the top, include a reminder of its scheduled time and place. You may invite people to propose changes to the agenda, but you, as leader, should retain the final authority so that the meeting does not become disorganized.
- When the meeting begins, plan to get the discussion started yourself, if necessary. As your co-workers begin participating, make sure that one or two voices do not take over. Call on people who do not volunteer to guarantee that all points of view are expressed. Listen to everyone respectfully, but feel free to politely ask those who are rambling to get to the point.
- Stick to your time schedule. Move the discussion from point to point even if you have not exhausted the topic.
- Wrap up the meeting with a brief summary of what it accomplished and a preview of next steps. Thank the participants.

## Participating in a Meeting

Meetings at which participants feel like members of a well-functioning team can be very stimulating—even fun. Try to develop a balance between asserting your carefully considered point of view and keeping an open mind to the good ideas of others. Successful participation in workplace meetings requires good listening skills and a genuine commitment to reaching your shared goal.

# On the Job: Videotape Editor

**Todd Roberts** thrives on the challenge of delivering breaking news on television.

## Background:

Television has always fascinated me. I grew up watching news on television with my family; we always talked about the events of the day.

## Education:

I studied electronics in high school and dabbled in the audiovisual department. Then I attended a technology institute, where I was in a two-year electronics technician's program. I've also studied graphic design, learning how to put graphics into video.

## Job Description:

I work closely with the writers and producers of the early morning show who send news footage for our 5:30 broadcast. I have to make sure that what is written will match up with the video. I work with the reporters, producers, and writers to determine what pictures to use in certain stories, what audio we would like to hear, so together it makes sense for the viewer.

## What Makes You Good at Your Job:

My strongest quality is my common sense. When a reporter is talkng about a fire, the fire scene needs to be shown—not a fire truck. I also have the ability to act quickly. Stories change until the minute we go on the air, and sometimes while we're on the air, we'll still be editing videotape and changing stories around.

## Job High:

We have deadlines that don't change. Stories have to be updated with the correct information and pictures. The most satisfaction comes from facing a deadline and making it. I also like that my job is not the same every day because the news changes.

## Job Low:

In the breaking news story, I see everything. Unfortunately in train and bus crashes, fires, and shootings, I see some ugly situations. I've cried when I've seen certain things, but you try to do that after the show airs and then move on.

## Advice to Students:

Gain experience any way you can. Don't be afraid to go to the small markets where you do everything. You shoot your own stories, you may be the reporter, you may be the editor, and you gain broad experience. You'll also get to find out what aspect of the field you like. Also, read books and newspapers, and know what's going on in the world.

### Tips for Participating Effectively in a Meeting

- Think through the issues raised by the meeting agenda ahead of time.
- Bring any useful information to the meeting to share with others.
- Respect the time constraints and speaks as succinctly as possible.
- Listen attentively to the ideas of others.
- Appreciate the diverse viewpoints that people from different backgrounds bring to a problem.
- Compromise when appropriate.

**Recording (Taking Notes or Minutes)** So that the good ideas (and any decisions, resolutions, or votes) can be put to use and widely understood, accurate records must be kept of all business meetings. If you are in charge of taking notes (called *minutes* if they are from a very formal meeting), consider using a tape recorder as a backup. You can then replay the tape should you find that you have missed something in your written notes.

Two skills are especially important in recording a meeting. One is careful listening *(pages C683–C690)*. The other is the ability to summarize (*pages C492–C495)*. Those skills, along with the following guidelines, will help you take reliable notes. Formal minutes sometimes require special guidelines, but these general points still apply.

### Guidelines for Recording a Meeting

- Be thorough.
- Write down word-for-word any formal decisions, votes, resolutions, and so forth.
- Record the name of each speaker as well as the ideas he or she puts forward.

- Use an icon (perhaps a star or a check) next to items that need action.
- Write up your final copy as soon after the meeting as possible so that the ideas are still fresh in your mind.
- Record only what happened. Do not add any of your own opinions or observations that were not actually expressed at the meeting.
- Distribute the notes to everyone who attended the meeting.

## Focus Groups

One specific kind of formal meeting is the focus group. Unlike the other kinds of meetings described previously, the **focus group** involves people outside the workplace. Their job is to evaluate products or services or test new ideas. In fact, many of the television shows you watch, jeans you wear, shampoos you use, and foods you eat reflect input from focus groups at which participants like you answered questions about their preferences and tastes.

### Guidelines for Focus Groups

**Planning**

- Identify the purpose of the focus group—what problem are you seeking to solve?
- Invite participants who are qualified to help you fulfill your purpose. For example, if you are testing a new line of junior-sized overalls, invite junior-sized teenagers.
- Arrange the logistics—the time, place, and the equipment needed. Focus groups should last about an hour and a half. If possible, arrange to have a tape recorder or video camera to record the event.
- Carefully craft the questions you will ask. Word the questions to avoid bias. Pose questions that are open-ended to promote further discussion.

- A few days before meeting, send a copy of the questions along with a reminder to each participant.

**Conducting the Meeting**

- Introduce yourself and anyone else present from your company. Thank everyone for coming. Review the purpose of the meeting, explain that it is being recorded, and ask all present (ideally six to ten people) to briefly introduce themselves.
- Ask each question. Follow the general guidelines of running a good meeting by making sure everyone participates. Keep your own comments brief.
- After all the questions, briefly summarize what has been said, thank everyone for coming, and close the meeting on time.

**Following Up**

- Having listened objectively to what the participants have said, process the data honestly, even if your favorite idea was unpopular.
- Share the results with the rest of your team and treat the outcome as one more piece of information to help you shape your business decision.

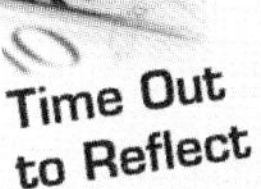

**Time Out to Reflect**

As you learn more about business communication, take a moment to think about how you can most effectively build on these skills. What are your goals for the future? Do you plan to attend college, or will you go directly to the world of work? Perhaps you have already had opportunities to use the kind of skills you are learning in this chapter. Focusing on the skills that you are most likely to need in the next few years can help you make effective use of this material.

## Practice Your Skills

### *Developing Focus Group Questions*

**Reread the proposal you wrote about physical therapists *(page C641)*. Imagine your boss has given her approval for you to test your ideas in a focus group. Copy the following onto a sheet of paper and complete the focus group form.**

FOCUS GROUP MEETING:

Date:

Time:

Place:

Purpose:

Kinds of participants:

Questions:

1. ____________________
2. ____________________
3. ____________________
4. ____________________
5. ____________________
6. ____________________

## Communicate Your Ideas

**REVISING** ***Proposal Based on Focus Group Response***

Tony conducted three focus groups to test his ideas on hiring new physical therapists. Here is a summary of the results.

- Group participants generally agreed that more staff was needed. Most people felt the physical therapy unit was "too busy." They thought that appointments were hard to get and that sometimes therapists tried to rush patients through their exercises.
- Several senior citizens who lived in a small community ten miles east of town said that they, or people they knew, went to the state university hospital instead of the community hospital for physical therapy. The university ran a bus each day to pick up people who lived in the community and worked or studied at the university. For the senior citizens, the convenience of easy transportation was more important than the extra time the trip took.
- Several parents said that daytime appointments were very difficult for them. They worked, their children attended school, and after-school activities were extensive. Some noted that local dentists had early-morning appointments specifically for students.

Write an analysis of these responses to make sure you understand them well. Then write a revised proposal that takes these ideas into account.

## A Writer Writes

# A Memo

**Purpose:** **to describe the growth needs of the physical therapy unit**

**Audience:** **the newly hired expansion coordinator**

## Prewriting

A thorough, thoughtful memo can be the most effective way to familiarize someone with a new situation.

Imagine that you are Tony and that the board of trustees has decided to expand the physical therapy unit at Newburg Community Hospital. The head of the hospital is hiring someone to supervise the expansion. This position will coordinate the activities of the realtor who will secure the raw space for the new clinic, the architect who will design it, and the search firm that will recruit the new staff therapists. The new coordinator, Devon Williams, needs all of the available information about the unit's needs for increased capacity.

Write a memo to Devon in which you describe the other physical therapy resources in your area, the additional capacity required in your clinic, and the concerns expressed by patients in your focus groups.

Before you begin writing, look at Tony's initial report and the two proposals you have written *(Communicate Your Ideas,* pages C641 and C657). Incorporate the results of the research and focus group findings into the memo. You may make your own recommendations based on this input, and be sure to include all the data your research has yielded. The expansion coordinator might need this information to refine your recommendations.

Begin by creating a rough outline, list, or freewriting draft—a "brain dump" of your ideas. Include any quotes and statistics you have collected from your research. Let your enthusiasm about the project guide you in this rough draft phase. Put all your ideas and notes on paper, and worry about organiziation later.

## Drafting

Organize your memo so that the most important information comes first, and so that the entire document is laid out in a clear fashion that is easy to understand. Organize your information in short sections with subheadings, bullets, numbers, boldface, underlining, and so forth, so it will be accessible at a glance. Allow the layout of the memo, the "geography," to be helpful in conveying your points.

Remember that the new coordinator will have many responsibilities and will appreciate information in an easily digestible format. Devon will need a short synopsis of facts that she can refer to as the project progresses, so a well-constructed format will continue to be useful.

## Revising

Put your memo away for a day or more. Then reread it with fresh eyes. Make sure the vocabulary is simple and direct. Refine your memo so that no unnecessary information is repeated and so that the document is as short as possible. Recheck the organization, subheadings, boldface, and so forth, to ensure the memo is easy to understand.

## Editing

Polish your article by checking your grammar, usage, spelling, and mechanics. Delete unnecessary words and make sure you have used simple and concise language. Be certain that you have maintained a polite and professional style.

## Publishing

Print out a final copy of the memo. Share it with a classmate who will pretend to be the new assistant manager.

# Connection Collection

## Representing in Different Ways

*From Print . . .*

*. . . to Visuals*

From the information in the letter, create a pyramid graph to organize the content of the letter according to the order of importance of the details. See the pyramid graph on the next page for an example.

12 Cannonball St.
Cycletown, NJ 00986
November 22, 2000

Mr. John Pumperwhiffle
Pedal Power Bicycles
Cycletown, NJ 00986

Dear Sir,

I am sorry to report that the bike I purchased from your store last week has all but crumbled beneath me. On a ride with my friend C. J. yesterday I attempted to jump over a very small river and landed on a rock. The frame of the bike broke in two and the handlebars came off in my hands. One of the pedals nearly hit C. J. in the head and I could not even find the bike seat.

Fortunately, we escaped unharmed, but the bike you sold me did not. I am dissatisfied with your product and I wish to receive a prompt refund of my money.

Thank you,

*Jennifer Bendebar*

Jennifer Bendebar

- **Which strategies can be used for creating both written and visual representations? Which strategies apply to one, not both? Which type of representation is more effective?**
- **Draw a conclusion and write briefly about the differences between written ideas and visual representations.**

*From Visuals . . .*

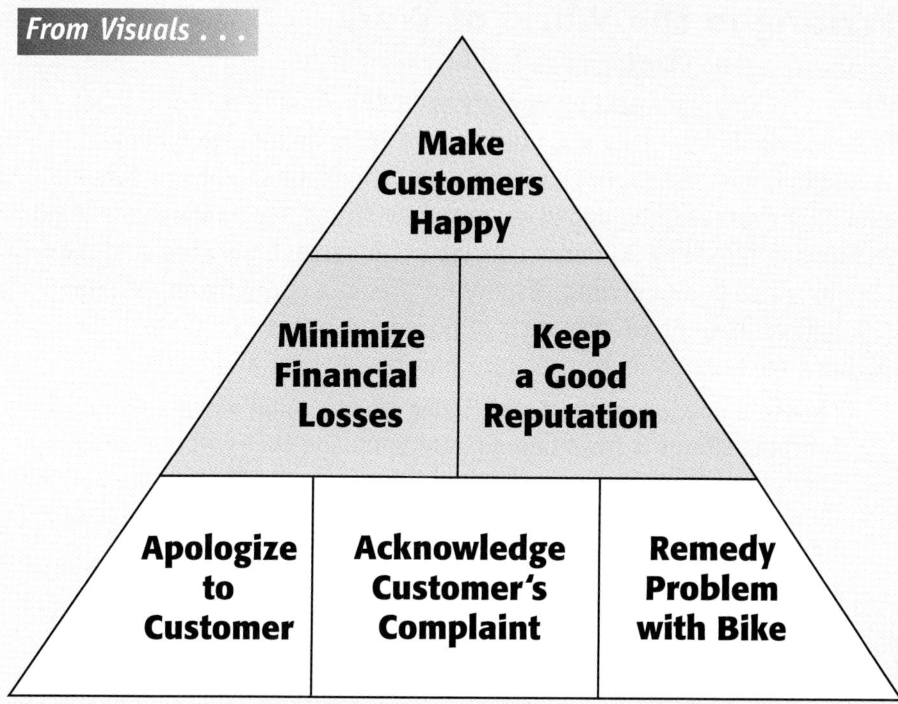


Handling Customer Complaints

*. . . to Print*

The pyramid graph above shows Peddle Power's policy on handling customer complaints. From the information in the graph, write a return business letter to Ms. Bendebar from Mr. Pumperwhiffle.

## Writing in the World of Work

### *Brochure for Students*

When you started working as curator of the Angelina Fossilfinder Museum of Natural History, you wanted it to be a place where students could see more than the usual dinosaur skeletons. Since then the museum has added several new wings and made some major improvements. Now students can visit the astronomy wing and planetarium, the geology wing displaying precious stones and minerals, the hall of ancient Greece with hundreds of artifacts, or the botanical gardens with its collection of rare plants, flowers, and birds.

**Choose a section of the Fossilfinder museum and write a short brochure about it for students. Use language that will encourage them to explore the area of science particular to that section of the museum. You may find information on the Internet, in an encyclopedia, or at your local natural history museum.**

**What strategies did you use to write your brochure?**

## Writing for Oral Communication

### *An Oral Proposal*

At work, you are constantly doing extra favors for your boss. He often asks you to use the company delivery van to run personal errands and to drive his kids to soccer practice. What you would really like to use the van for is to take a road trip to the beach with a group of your friends.

**Prepare and give an oral proposal to your boss regarding the use of the company van. Organize your proposal in a simple, economical way in order to express your ideas quickly and efficiently.**

**What strategies did you use to make your proposal efficient?**

# Assess Your Learning

Some of your young cousins have moved to your neighborhood and would like to open a glow-in-the-dark clothing store at the mall. They are unfamiliar with the world of retail clothing sales and would like you to inform them of some of the aspects of running a store. They have no idea how a sale is made or when their store will be most busy. Imagine that you have extensive sales experience. Think about the behaviour and trends you have seen when in clothing stores.

- **Write a business report to your cousins informing them of the typical elements of running a store.**
- **Avoid wordiness and jargon and use a direct approach. You may want to include a graph or chart to clearly synthesize your information.**

*Before You Write* **Consider the following questions:**
What is the ***subject?***
What is the ***occasion?***
Who is the ***audience?***
What is the ***purpose?***

*After You Write* **Evaluate your work using the following criteria:**

- Is your language simple and clear?
- Is your information accurate and presented in a logical way?
- Does your report suit its intended audience?
- Have you used conjunctions to connect ideas meaningfully?
- Is your scope clearly identified?
- Have you produced legible work that shows accurate spelling and correct use of the conventions of punctuation and capitalization?
- Are graphics used when they convey information more clearly than text?

**Write briefly on how well you did. Point out your strengths and areas for improvement.**

CHAPTER 15

# Speeches, Presentations, and Discussions

"Speech is civilization itself. The word, even the most contradictory word, preserves contact—it is silence which isolates." These words of the German writer Thomas Mann express the importance of spoken language. The goal of effective speaking is to communicate your thoughts and ideas to your audience in such a way that the members of the audience will be inspired, persuaded, entertained, or better informed about a subject. Speechmaking is one half of the communication process; listening and responding thoughtfully is the other half. Critical listening skills enable you to interpret and evaluate the speaker's message, whether you are attending a public lecture, holding a conversation with a friend, or working with a group to achieve a common goal. In this chapter you will learn both halves of the communication process.

## *Reading with a Writer's Eye*

The following is a commencement speech that Tom Brokaw delivered to College of Santa Fe students on May 15, 1999. Brokaw has been the anchor of the NBC Nightly News since 1983. Read his speech once to grasp his message. As you read it again, note how he puts words together to make his speech more effective.

# 50th Annual Commencement

## The College of Santa Fe
## Saturday, May 15, 1999

text of the commencement
address by Tom Brokaw

One hundred years ago another class of '99 was anticipating a new century, rich with the possibility of the new technologies - electricity, the auto-mobile, the first tentative steps toward flight. The men who controlled the railroads and steel and oil were amassing great fortunes and making America the new industrial and financial capital of the world. The labor leaders who aroused armies of workers to claim their fair share.

As it turns out, all of that exciting and empowering new technology was in its seminal stages, primitive, really, compared to what was to come - the splitting of the atom, jet travel and the space age, the mapping of the body's molecular structure, the expansive new universe of cyber-technology.

God, the possibilities for advancing the human condition and expanding the cosmos of intellectual understanding.

In fact, giant steps were taken, great leaps well beyond what the most prescient member of the class of 1899 could have anticipated.

The 20th century - what a triumph.

And what an ugly scar on the face of history.

Two world wars with millions of casualties, holocausts in the heart of Western civilization, in Southeast Asia and in Africa, killing millions more. An ideology designed to empower the masses became one of the most ruthless instruments of oppression. Rival nations pointed at each other terrible weapons capable of destroying life on Earth as we know it.

In the closing days of this momentous time, in the American culture, maniacal homicide committed by school boys shocked the nation into a dialogue of ill defined blame - while in Europe the most powerful political and military alliance on the globe made a clumsy attempt to neutralize a murderous tyrant and in the execution of that attempt, set off a refugee crisis of historic proportions.

The short lesson: technology is not enough, not even when it comes with a generous package of stock options, sabbaticals and leased time on a private plane.

The long lesson? It is not enough to wire the world if you short-circuit the soul. It is not enough to probe the hostile environments of distant galaxies if we fail to resolve the climate of mindless violence, ethnic and racial hate here in the bosom of Mother Earth. It is not enough to identify the gene that pre-determines the prospect of Alzheimer's disease if we go through the prime of life with a closed mind.

I am incapable of helping you advance your knowledge in the matters that brought you to this institution. Frankly, I still don't understand how the picture gets from where I work to your television set. I call it a miracle and leave it at that.

So I am all the more in awe of your capacity to change the gears on all the machinery of the world, broadly speaking.

But I have learned something of the political and social possibilities - and failings - of mankind in my 37 years as a journalist.

First, for all of its shocking and brutal stretches of oppression and extermination, the most powerful single idea of the 20th century is freedom. There is so much more political and individual freedom at the end of the 20th century than at the beginning and that is a tribute to the enduring and inherent instinct for self-determination, even in the darkest shadows of tyrannical control.

If we fail to first recognize then deal with these societal cancers in our system we will have squandered a priceless legacy left to us by what I have come to call THE GREATEST GENERATION. Some of them are here today, although they would not have you know it for they are characteristically modest. They prefer to let their lives and their sacrifices speak from them.

They are the men and women who came of age in the Great Depression when economic despair was on the land like a plague. There were great bands of migrant workers, drifting across the American landscape, looking for enough of a wage to get through the next day. In families youngsters quit school to go to work -- not to buy a car for themselves or a new video game. They quit to earn enough to help their family get through another week.

Then, just as the economic gloom was beginning to lift, World War. Two powerful and ruthless regimes, one east, the other west, were determined to choke off the idea of political freedom, political and ethnic pluralism - and to impose their twisted ideology on vast areas of the globe with brutal military might.

Here, the young men and women who had just been tested by the Great Depression were to be tested again - in the battlefields thousands of miles across the Atlantic or thousands of miles across the Pacific. In bitter European cold and the suffocating heat of the jungle. In the air and on the seas, they fought - often hand to hand - for more than three years, day in and day out. More than 12 million in uniform, millions more at home on the assembly lines, converting the American economy into a war machine overnight. Women went to work where only men had prevailed - in the cabs of trucks, in research labs, in ship building yards.

It was a tense, dangerous and vibrant time. The world was at stake - and at a time in their lives when their days should have been filled with the rewards of starting careers and families, their nights filled with love and innocent adventure, this generation was fighting for survival - theirs and the world's.

They prevailed through extraordinary acts of courage and heroism by ordinary people from the farms and the small towns, from the pavement of big cities, from the bucolic and privileged surroundings of great universities.

They saved the world. Nothing less.

Then, they came rushing home to go to college in record numbers, marry in record numbers, give us new art, breakthroughs in science and industry, expanded political freedoms and, always, a sense of the possible. They re-built their enemies and drew the line against a new form of oppression rising like a dark cloud out of Moscow.

They weren't perfect: they were to slow to recognize the equal place of women - and racial minorities, especially Black and Asian Americans. But those women and Black and Asian Americans were part of the tensile strength of this generation for they never gave up.

They all recognized that for all of the genius of the American political system and the framework of laws, beginning with the Constitution, the enduring strength of this immigrant nation has been its common ground, wide enough and strong enough to accommodate all races and beliefs.

Now great fault lines run through that common ground. We have allowed it to be so fractured we are in danger of becoming less than the sum of our parts. We have become the culture of cheap confrontation rather than resolution.

We have political leaders too eager to divide for their selfish aims rather than unify for the common good. And, yes, we have a mass media much too inclined to exploit those instincts. The quick hit has become a suitable substitute for thoughtful dialogue in both the political and journalistic arena.

In the business arena we celebrate the astonishing good fortune of those at the top without raising enough questions about the economic opportunity of those at the bottom.

I wonder, is this what the GREATEST GENERATION made all those sacrifices for? Did we win the war - then - and the Cold War later to lose our way?

Francis Fukuyama, the provocative student of social and historical trends, has given voice to the concerns of many, most recently in a long article in THE ATLANTIC MONTHLY. He concludes that in this post industrial information age the old conceit that social order has to come from a centralized, rational, bureaucratic hierarchy is outdated. Instead, he argues that in the 21st century societies and corporations will de-centralize and devolve power and rely on people to be self organizing, using the new tools of this age.

Social order norms have been disrupted by new technologies before. The shift from rural agrarian to urban industrial economies representing only the most recent example; the impact of freeways and jet travel; in establishing new living patterns.

So now, in this new age of spell-binding possibilities for communication, information retrieval, marketing and proselytizing we are undergoing another major shift in the norms of how society is organized for every day life, work and play.

It is wildly exciting to be on the frontier of such an empowering era.

But no piece of soft-ware, no server or search engine will offer you the irreplaceable rewards of a loving personal relationship, the strengths and comfort of a real community of shared values and common dreams, the moral underpinning of a life lived well, whatever the financial scorecard.

Nor will this new technology by itself make you more racially tolerant - more sensitive to the plight of the disenfranchised - more courageous to take a firm stand for what you know is right.

These are mere tools in your hands. Your hands are an extension not only of your mind but also of your heart and soul.

Taken altogether they're a powerful combination.

Use them well.

Take care of your Mother, Mother Earth.

Become color blind.

Hate hate.

Fight violence.

And take care of each other.

You have a whole new century to shape. I envy you, but I want to stand aside now because you have work to do.

# *Thinking as a Writer*

## Analyzing Language Techniques

Brokaw uses language to create vivid mental images.

- Consider the following statements from page C660.

> *It is not enough to wire the world if you short-circuit the soul. It is not enough to probe the hostile environments of distant galaxies if we fail to resolve the climate of mindless violence, ethnic and racial hatred here in the bosom of Mother Earth. . . . So I am all the more in awe of your capacity to change the gears on all the machinery of the world.*

- What metaphors does Brokaw use in these statements? Does the use of metaphor add to the impact of his speech? Explain. Find other uses of metaphors in this speech.

## Structuring Language for Oral Expression

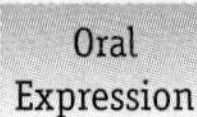


- Notice how Brokaw structures the last section of his speech (page C669).

> *These are mere tools in your hands. Your hands are an extension not only of your mind, but also of your heart and soul.*
>
> *Taken altogether they're a powerful combination.*
> *Use them well.*
> *Take care of your Mother, Mother Earth.*
> *Become color-blind.*
> *Hate hate.*
> *Fight violence.*
> *And take care of each other.*
> *You have a whole new century to shape. I envy you, but I want to stand aside now because you have work to do.*

- Read aloud the statements on the previous page. How does the language structure affect the way you read them? Now read aloud the sentences as if they were in a paragraph. What do you notice about the way you say them?

## Analyzing a Speaker's Attitude Toward His Subject

Viewing Tom Brokaw uses the history of the "Greatest Generation" to point out what he believes we have learned about the social possibilities—and failings—of human beings.

- What is his attitude toward his subject? Does this photograph of the raising of the flag at Iwo Jima reflect that attitude? Why or why not?

# Developing Public Speaking and Presentation Skills

You have already read an example of a speech written for a specific purpose. Brokaw's speech inspires young people to examine their lives. A common use of presenting a speech is both to inform and entertain.

## Preparing Your Speech

It is likely that there will be opportunities during your life when you will be called upon to prepare and deliver a speech. As a student you may have to speak to a class, a special-interest group, or a group of parents and teachers. In your career you may have to address formally a group of colleagues at a meeting or seminar or a group of townspeople at a local political rally.

### Knowing Your Audience and Purpose

Having your audience clearly in mind as you prepare your speech will help you deliver a speech that addresses the interests and concerns of your audience.

**Strategies for Considering Audience and Purpose**

- If possible, find out the interests of your audience. Decide how these interests are similar to or different from yours.
- Try to determine what your audience will already know about the subject you plan to discuss. Consider what your audience might expect to hear.
- Decide whether your purpose is to inform your audience, or to entertain them by expressing your thoughts and feelings, or by telling a story.

*You can learn more about the specific purposes for written and oral essays on pages C20–C22.*

Although most of the speeches you give in school will be to inform others about certain subjects, you may also be called upon to persuade or to entertain an audience. Most speeches have more than one purpose. For example, a speaker can inform while trying to persuade an audience to follow a particular course of action.

The following examples suggest three ways to limit the subject of traveling in a foreign country to suit your purpose.

**PURPOSES OF SPEECHES**

| Purpose of Speech | Example |
|---|---|
| to inform | explaining ways to travel cheaply |
| to persuade | convincing people to visit Mexico |
| to entertain | telling about the time you toured Washington, D.C. in one day |

## PRACTICE YOUR SKILLS

### *Determining a Subject That Relates to Audience and Purpose*

**1.** Write an example of a subject for a speech, the purpose of which is to inform.

**2.** Write an example of a subject for a speech, the purpose of which is to persuade.

**3.** Write an example of a subject for a speech, the purpose of which is to entertain.

**4.** Rewrite each example above to suit an audience of elementary school students, of your teachers, or of your classmates.

## Choosing and Limiting a Subject

After you decide on an interesting subject for your speech, it will be necessary to limit the subject so that you can cover it effectively in a given amount of time. As you choose and limit your subject, follow the strategies below.

### Strategies for Choosing and Limiting a Subject

- Choose a subject that interests you and is likely to interest your audience.
- Choose a subject that you know well or can research thoroughly.
- Limit the subject by choosing one aspect of a broader topic. For a 20-minute speech, for example, you could limit the subject "baseball greats" to "Babe Ruth: a great home-run hitter and pitcher."

## Practice Your Skills

### *Determining a Subject*

**For each of the following items, write a subject for a speech. Share your ideas with the class.**

1. personal experiences
2. experiences of others
3. current events or issues
4. past events or people
5. how to make something
6. how to do something
7. school-related subjects
8. jobs or professions
9. ideas for inventions
10. ideas about the future

### *Limiting a Subject*

**Limit each subject so that it would be suitable for a 20-minute speech.**

1. wildlife conservation
2. freedom and responsibility
3. Shakespeare's plays
4. in-line skating
5. careers in technology
6. Dr. Martin Luther King, Jr.
7. DNA
8. history of space travel
9. fashion movements
10. music trends

## Gathering and Organizing Information

To gather information for an informative speech, follow the same procedures you would for a written report. List everything you already know about the subject. Then consult several other good sources of information—including encyclopedia articles, books, and periodicals in the library or media center. You should also consider electronic sources of information such as the Internet or CD-ROM. In addition, you might interview people who are knowledgeable about your subject. When you are planning the interview, always make a list of the questions you want to ask.

*To learn more about writing an informative report, refer to pages C523–C574.*

**Taking Notes** Note taking is an important part of research. Note cards are the best way to record information from encyclopedias, periodicals, and books because the cards can be easily organized later. If you interview someone, you can take notes in modified outline form or use a microcassette to record your conversation. You should write down any words from the interview you intend to quote, put them in quotation marks, and get permission from the speaker to use the quotations. It is your ethical responsibility to see that your presentation contains accurate and truthful information.

**Collecting Audiovisual Materials** Audiovisual aids such as maps, pictures, slides, records, tapes, CD-ROMs, and multimedia slide presentations will add to the impact of your speech. Decide which of your main points to enhance with the use of audiovisual aids and gather or create these materials as you prepare your speech.

**COMPUTER TIP**

Following the guidelines of your school's Acceptable Use Policy, you can search the Internet for information that might help you make your points and capture the interest of your audience. Interesting Websites should be saved, or bookmarked as favorites. Bookmarks will enable you to return to the Website later. It is also a good idea to cut and paste the address, or URL, of a favorite site from your browser window into a word-processing file. If your presentation software allows you to create links to the World Wide Web, you will need this address.

### Strategies for Organizing a Speech

- Arrange your note cards by topics and subtopics.
- Use the cards to make a detailed outline of your speech and then draft an introduction and conclusion.
- To capture the interest of your audience, begin your speech with an anecdote, an unusual fact, a question, an interesting quotation, or some other attention-getting device.
- Present and advance a clear thesis in your introduction. *(pages C546–C549)*
- Support your message in the body of your speech with logical points, claims, and arguments.
- Use appropriate appeals to support your claims and arguments.
- Choose valid proofs from reliable sources to support your claims.

- Arrange your ideas in a logical order and think of the transitions you will use to connect the ideas. *(pages C549–C554)*
- When defending a point of view, use precise language and appropriate detail.
- Write a conclusion for your speech that summarizes your main idea and signals the audience that you have finished. *(pages C549–C550)*

## Practice Your Skills

*Gathering and Organizing Information*

**Choose and limit a subject for a 20-minute speech in which your purpose is to inform. Write what you know about the subject on note cards. Next visit the library or media center and find additional information for at least ten more note cards. Then organize your cards in the order in which you will present your information and write an outline of your speech. Gather any audiovisual aids and online resources you plan to use. Finally, draft a strong introduction and conclusion.**

## Practicing Your Speech

Although rehearsing your speech is important, in most cases you should not attempt to write it out or to memorize it. Instead, use your outline or convert your outline and note cards into cue cards. Cue cards include your main points along with key words, phrases, and quotations listed in the order you want to follow in your speech. While you are delivering your speech, your cue cards will help you to remember your important points and supporting details. The following strategies will help you when you practice your speech.

### Strategies for Practicing a Speech

- Practice in front of a long mirror so that you will be aware of your gestures, posture, and facial expressions.
- Practice looking at an imaginary audience as you practice your speech.
- Time your speech. Add or cut information if necessary. To time yourself, keep the following rule of thumb in mind: It takes about as much time to give a 20-minute speech as it does to read aloud slowly an 8-page report or essay typed double-space.
- Practice using cue cards and any audiovisual aids you plan to use.
- Practice microphone technique if you will be using a mike.
- Practice over a period of several days. Your confidence will grow each time you practice your speech, and as your confidence grows, your nervousness will decrease.

**COMPUTER TIP**

You can create a folder to contain text, sound, and image files for a multimedia slide presentation. Save any material that you have gathered from the Internet. You can copy and paste information from these files directly onto the slides of a multimedia presentation program.

You can revise your speech as you practice. Feel free to experiment with word choice and to add and delete information to clarify your main points. In addition, if you practice your speech with a classmate or a friend, the listener's comments will help you improve your speech before you deliver it.

## Practice Your Skills

*Practicing and Revising Your Speech*

**Prepare cue cards for the informative speech you developed on page C677. Ask a relative, friend, or classmate to listen to you as you practice the speech. Afterward, discuss your speech and revise it, using listeners' comments as a guide.**

## Delivering Your Speech

The time you spent researching your speech, organizing it, and practicing it will pay off when you get up in front of your audience to deliver it. Just before you begin, however, you can alleviate your nervousness by reminding yourself that you are now an expert who knows more about your subject than does anyone in your audience. Also keep in mind these strategies.

### Strategies for Delivering a Speech

- Have ready all the materials you need, such as your outline or cue cards and audiovisual aids or props.
- Make sure that your computer equipment is assembled and running properly.
- Wait until your audience is quiet and settled.
- Relax and breathe deeply before you begin to speak.
- Stand with good posture, your weight evenly divided between both feet. Avoid swaying back and forth.
- During your speech, make sure you talk to the audience, not to the particular visual on display.
- Look directly at the people in your audience, not over their heads. Try to make eye contact all around the audience.
- Speak slowly, clearly, and loudly enough to be heard. Adjust the pitch and tone of your voice to enhance communication of your message.
- Strive for good, clear diction.
- Be aware of using correct grammar and well-formed sentences with well chosen-words.
- Choose informal, standard, and technical language appropriate to the purpose, audience, occasion, and task.
- Use rhetorical strategies appropriate to the message, whether your purpose is to inform or to persuade.
- Emphasize your main points with gestures and facial expressions.
- Since your speech is not over until you have taken your seat, walk to your seat without making comments to the audience.

### COMPUTER TIP

Most presentation software programs enable you to run your slide show manually or automatically. Manual mode requires you to advance each slide with a remote control. For automatic advance, you set timings and the slides advance at intervals that you have predetermined. Practice working with the slide show before you give your presentation.

## Evaluating an Oral Presentation

Evaluating your own speech and accepting the comments of others about your speech will help you improve your performance on future speeches. When you listen to a speech, try to determine how well the speaker knows and covers the information. Also decide whether the speaker makes a good impression on the audience by speaking clearly, making eye contact, and choosing appropriate words. By providing and receiving effective and appropriate verbal and nonverbal feedback to the opinions and views of others, the evaluation process will help you and your classmates set goals for future presentations. The Oral Presentation Evaluation Form on the next page may be helpful.

## PRACTICE YOUR SKILLS

### *Delivering and Evaluating Your Speech*

**Present the speech you practiced and revised. Afterward, complete the Oral Presentation Evaluation Form for your speech at the same time that your classmates are evaluating it. In addition, complete an evaluation form for any speeches presented by your classmates. Share your comments with the speaker you evaluated and read the comments your classmates wrote about your speech. Use the listeners' suggestions to note ways that you can improve your future speeches.**

## ORAL PRESENTATION EVALUATION FORM

**Subject:**________________________________________

**Speaker:**_______________________________________

**Date:**__________________________________________

### Content

- Are the subject and purpose of your speech appropriate for the audience?
- Is the main point clear?
- Are there enough details and examples?
- Do all the ideas clearly relate to the subjects?
- Is the length appropriate (not too long nor too short)?

### Organization

- Does the speech begin with an interesting introduction?
- Do the ideas in the body follow a logical order?
- Are transitions used between ideas?
- Does the conclusion summarize the main points?

### Presentation

- Does the speaker choose appropriate words?
- Is the speech sufficiently loud and clear?
- Is the rate appropriate (not too fast nor too slow)?
- Does the speaker make eye contact with the audience?
- Does the speaker use gestures and pauses effectively?
- Are audiovisual aids or other props used effectively?
- Are cue cards or an outline used effectively?

**Comments** ____________________________________

________________________________________________

________________________________________________

________________________________________________

# The Art of the Interview

Although interviews are commonplace on television, their effectiveness varies greatly. Some interviewers listen to and pick up on answers their subjects give; others seem to have a set of questions that they follow no matter how their subject responds. Sometimes interviewers are limited by the time they have and leave interesting possibilities unexplored. Others seem unaware of the other possibilities.

## Media Activity

Evaluate the effectiveness of three television interviews from shows of your choice. Use the following standards, and be sure to give a specific explanation of why you think the interviewer did or did not meet that standard. Write a paragraph for each interview.

**Criteria For Evaluating Interviews**

The interviewer listens:

- critically
- empathetically
- appreciatively
- reflectively

Take turns interviewing a classmate about his or her plans for the future while a third student looks on and evaluates you with the same criteria as above. When all three have had a turn interviewing, compare your assessments of one another and set personal goals for improving your skills.

# Developing Your Critical Listening Skills

A good listener engages in critical, empathetic, reflective, and appreciative listening. Skillful listening requires that you pay close attention to what you hear. When listening for information or ideas, you must be able to evaluate critically and reflect upon what the speaker says. When listening to a persuasive speech it is important that you evaluate the speaker's evidence as well as the organization and logic of the argument. By recording the information in an organized way, you will be able to remember the information for future reference. You can also assess the emotional tone of the speech by putting yourself in the speaker's place. Empathetic listening, or listening with feeling, will help you recognize the misuse of illogical emotional appeals. Skills that you have practiced while learning how to prepare and present a speech will be invaluable to you as you work to develop your critical listening skills.

## Listening Appreciatively to Presentations and Performances

Sometimes you may find yourself listening to a reading or dramatic performance of a work of literature, an essay, or a report. Oral interpretation is the performance or expressive reading of a written work. The oral interpreter emphasizes the message through judicious use of voice and gesture.

Pauses, changes of volume, intonation, and pitch can be used to highlight important structural elements in the passage such as rhyme and imagery. As a listener you must judge how successfully the reader has matched his or her voice to the intentions and style of the work performed. The strategies on the next page will help you listen appreciatively to oral presentations and performances.

### Strategies for Listening Appreciatively

- Focus your attention on the message of the work being performed.
- Be alert to the expressive power of pause.
- Observe the use of gesture, voice, and facial expression to enhance the message.
- Listen for changes of volume, intonation, and pitch to emphasize important ideas.
- Listen for rhymes, repeated words, and sounds.
- Listen for rhetorical strategies and other expressive features of the language.
- Take time to reflect upon the message and try to experience with empathy the thoughts and feelings being expressed.

You can find many opportunities to practice your appreciative listening skills. Perhaps your local bookstore hosts readings of original works of prose and poetry by well-known authors. A nearby theater group might be performing a dramatic work that you have read for school, such as *Much Ado About Nothing*. You will get the most out of the experience by developing a listening strategy suited to the speaker's subject and purpose.

## Practice Your Skills

### *Listening to Presentations and Performances*

**Develop your own strategies for listening to and evaluating the following oral presentations. Identify what you would listen for in each case.**

**1.** an actor delivering a dramatic monologue from a play
**2.** a poet reading from a collection of poetry excerpts
**3.** an author reading selections from a novel
**4.** a public figure delivering a graduation speech

### *Interpreting for Performance*

**Choose a poem, short story, or dramatic scene to perform before the rest of the class. Instruct your classmates to take notes and analyze the effect of the following artistic elements in the performance of the literary texts.**

**1.** character development

**2.** rhyme

**3.** imagery

**4.** language

## Listening to Directions

Throughout a normal day, you will be given many sets of directions to follow, from how to do a homework assignment to how to get to a new shopping mall. Whatever kind of directions you hear, always listen carefully—from beginning to end. Do not assume you already know what the speaker is going to say before he or she finishes. In addition, follow the strategies below.

### Strategies for Listening to Directions

- Write down the directions as the speaker gives them.
- If any part of the directions is unclear, ask specific questions to help you understand.
- When you finish an assignment, review the directions once more to make sure you have followed them correctly.

## PRACTICE YOUR SKILLS

### *Following Directions*

**Ask someone you know, either a friend or a relative, to give you directions to an unfamiliar place in your area. Then see if you can accurately repeat or write the directions. Explain in your journal why you think the strategies you learned helped or did not help you to listen to directions more effectively.**

### *Evaluating the Effectiveness of Directions*

**To practice giving and following directions, think of a simple task that can be completed in the classroom, such as tying a complicated knot, or making a puppet out of a paper bag. Write step-by-step directions for completing the task. Read your directions to a classmate and ask the classmate to follow them using the guidelines on the previous page.**

## Listening for Information

Hearing becomes listening only when you are able to understand the information you have heard well enough to evaluate it and apply it. The strategies that follow should help you use listening skills effectively in order to learn new information.

### Strategies for Listening for Information

- Sit comfortably and stay alert. Try to focus attention on what the speaker is saying without being distracted by people and noises.
- Determine whether the speaker's purpose is to inform, to persuade, to entertain, or to express thoughts and feelings.
- Listen for verbal cues, to identify the speaker's main idea. Often, for example, a speaker emphasizes important points by using words such as *most important, also consider, remember that, first*, and *finally*.
- Watch for nonverbal clues, such as gestures, pauses, or changes in the speaking pace. Such clues often signal important points.
- Monitor the message for clarity and understanding.
- Determine the speaker's point of view about the subject. For example, what is the speaker's position? Is the speaker arguing for or against an issue?

- Take notes to organize your thoughts and to help you remember details. Your notes provide a basis for further discussion. You may also want to use your notes to outline the speech or write a summary of it. If the speech is a course lecture, notes will help you study for a test on the subject.
- Ask clear and relevant questions to clarify your understanding.
- Take time to reflect upon what you have heard.

*You can find information about taking notes pages C536–C540.*

## PRACTICE YOUR SKILLS

*Listening and Taking Notes*

**Ask a classmate to explain to a small group how to do something, such as using a digital camera. Compare the notes each person took. Try to determine why all members recorded certain points and not others.**

## Recognizing Propaganda

As you listen to the literal meanings of words, pay attention to any hidden purposes or motives behind those words. Also listen carefully for the speaker's point of view or bias. What is the intent of a commercial, an editorial, or political speech? **Propaganda** misrepresents or distorts information or presents opinions as if they were facts. Do not confuse propaganda with persuasion. In persuasion the speaker uses facts, evidence, and logical arguments to promote a viewpoint. In propaganda, on the other hand, the speaker uses emotional language, exaggeration, and sometimes even scare tactics to win people over.

## Confusion Between Fact and Opinion

A **fact** is a statement that can be proved, but an **opinion** is a personal feeling or judgment about a subject. When opinions are stated as facts, listeners can be confused or misled. Understanding the difference will help you be a more critical listener. You can avoid confusion by listening critically to distinguish between facts and opinions.

| | |
|---|---|
| FACT | My sister is on the varsity basketball team. |
| OPINION | Basketball players are the most talented athletes. |

## PRACTICE YOUR SKILLS

### *Distinguishing Between Fact and Opinion*

**Label each of the following statements *F* for fact or *O* for opinion.**

1. Shakespeare wrote most of his works during the 1600s.
2. Males are smarter than females in math, but females are smarter than males in English.
3. Acid rain will destroy all of our forests before Americans stop polluting the air.
4. Every senior in Mrs. Mason's English classes must write a research paper.
5. The senior year is the best year of high school.
6. Acid rain is destroying valuable forest land in the United States and Canada.
7. Shakespeare was the greatest playwright of all time.
8. Last year every senior—except two—bought a yearbook.
9. Last summer 68 percent of students took the new French exam.
10. Students who are not going to college should not have to write a research paper in Mrs. Mason's English class.

## Bandwagon Appeals

The **bandwagon appeal** tries to get you to do or think the same thing as everyone else. Often bandwagon appeals are used in advertising to make customers feel inadequate if they do not buy a certain product. These appeals are used in politics to make potential voters feel that they must support a particular candidate or risk being out of step with everyone else.

> Rosemary Filippo has the support of all our city workers. She has the support of the young, the middle-aged, and the seniors. Rosemary Filippo has the support of all the people! Doesn't she deserve your support too?

## Testimonials

A famous person's endorsement of a product is called a **testimonial**. A testimonial, however, can be misleading because it often suggests that because the famous person uses the product or endorses it, the product is so good that everyone else should also use it. A testimonial may suggest that using the product will give you the same success as the famous person endorsing it. The following testimonials are misleading for both of these reasons.

> Hi, Guys, I'm Jeff Strong. I hope you liked my last movie, *Muscle Head*. When I auditioned for the movie I made sure to wear my InvisiVision contact lenses. Glasses are a bother when I am doing all those actions shots. So get yourself some InvisiVision lenses if you want to be a star in your own neighborhood!
>
> I'm Dunk Hooper, basketball player of the year. I rely on more than sheer leaping power for my high-altitude hoopitorial acrobatics. I wear Hiptop Footflyers with the "energy booster" heel. Try Footflyers and you too will enjoy life above the rim.

## Unproved Generalizations

A **generalization** is a conclusion based on many facts and examples. A generalization is proved, however, if it is based on only one or two facts or examples. Unproved generalizations often contain words such as *always, never, all,* or *none*. Statements using words such as these can easily be disproved by finding just one exception.

| | |
|---|---|
| UNPROVED GENERALIZATION | Flowers at Blossom's Blossom are **always** the freshest you can buy. |
| ACCURATE GENERALIZATION | Flowers at Blossom's Blossom are **usually** the freshest you can buy. |

## PRACTICE YOUR SKILLS

### *Identifying Propaganda Techniques*

**Label each statement *B* for bandwagon, *T* for testimonial, or *U* for unproved generalization.**

**1.** Look down! What do you see? Everyone is wearing Prairie Rider cowboy boots. They are in, and you be out if you don't hurry to get your own pair of Prairie Riders!

**2.** If your car is sick, take it to Dr. Sharon at Sharon's Garage, where you always find the latest electronic equipment and the lowest prices in town.

**3.** Everyone—from Grandma to Junior—is eating Yummy-Oats for breakfast. Don't wait till morning; eat a bowl now. Don't miss out on this great taste-tingling experience!

**4.** Because I run, kick, and fall every Sunday on the soccer field, I always look forward to a good hot shower afterward and the soothing feeling of Chill-Out ointment. Got any tense, tired muscles like me? Relax them away with Chill-Out.

**5.** All of Dr. Johnson's patients look forward to their next appointment. Going to the dentist is always a happy time—no matter who you are!

# Participating in Group Discussions

One effective way to communicate ideas, exchange opinions, solve problems, and reach conclusions is through group discussions. Discussions may be informal and conversational, as in discussing what movie to see, or formal, as in contributing to a panel discussion or debate. In informal discussion groups, you express your views freely and share your ideas and experiences. In formal discussion groups, you usually present evidence—reasons or facts—to support a point of view. Group discussions serve a variety of practical purposes. As a part of the prewriting stage in the writing process, you may brainstorm in a group or have a round-table discussion. You may also use discussion skills to prepare a speech or an oral report or to study for a test. As part of a study group, you may discuss assigned readings, help your group to reach agreement on answers to questions, or prepare for a test. Use the strategies that follow to help you participate in group discussions.

### Strategies for Participating in Group Discussions

- Listen carefully and respond respectfully and appropriately to others' views.
- Ask questions to make sure you understand others' views or information.
- State or express your own ideas clearly. Present examples or evidence to support your ideas.
- Keep in mind that everyone in the group should have an equal opportunity to speak.
- Make sure your contributions to the discussion are constructive and relevant to the subject.
- Help your group to draw a conclusion or to reach a consensus.
- Give constructive comments in group discussions.
- Encourage group members by giving praise to valuable contributions.

# Directed Discussions

Sometimes the teacher will lead the discussion and make sure that it does not stray from the agenda. Sometimes a group appoints its own leader to focus the discussion and keep it on track. Such discussions are referred to as **directed discussions**. The leader, or moderator, of a directed discussion group has certain additional responsibilities. If you are chosen to lead a group discussion, use the following strategies for meeting these responsibilities.

### Strategies for Leading a Discussion

- Introduce the subject, question, or problem. With the group's help, state the purpose or goal of the discussion.
- If the subject or problem is complicated, divide it into manageable tasks and ask or assign group members to take responsibility for each task.
- Keep the discussion on track to help the group achieve its goal.
- Encourage everyone to participate.
- Make sure that everyone has an equal opportunity and equal time to speak.
- Keep a record of the group's main points and decisions, or assign this task to a group member.
- At the end of the discussion, summarize the main points and point out any conclusions or decisions the group reached.

## Practice Your Skills

### *Conducting a Directed Discussion*

**Form small groups and conduct a discussion on a topic having to do with careers of interest to the group members. Choose a leader and set a time limit for the discussion. Afterward assess your participation in the group.**

## Cooperative Learning

**Cooperative learning** means working together in a group to accomplish a specific purpose or goal. Your group might, for example, be assigned to report on South Africa for your history class. Every group member will have a specific task to do. One member might provide information on climate, and another might research the changes in the government. Still another student might prepare maps. Another might prepare materials for a multimedia slide presentation. After doing this individual work, the members of the group coordinate their efforts and prepare and present the final report. The individual is important in teamwork and every group member has a unique contribution to make. Remember, there is no *I* in *team*. The cooperative learning group is interactive—everybody, working together, will get the job done.

### Strategies for Cooperative Learning

- If you have been given a particular task, support your group by coming to the discussion prepared.
- Help your group to achieve its goal by taking your fair share of responsibility for the group's success.
- Cooperate in helping to resolve any conflict, solve any problem, reach a consensus, draw a conclusion, or make a decision.

## Practice Your Skills

### *Organizing a Cooperative Learning Project*

**Form a cooperative learning group with three to five other students to plan a presentation related to a current national issue. Decide together on a topic, choose a leader, and assign tasks. Allow adequate time to prepare and present it to the class. Finally, assess your own participation in the group according to the Strategies for Cooperative Learning.**

# A Speaker Speaks

## Oral Interpretation

**Purpose: to express yourself artistically through the reading of a narrative scene, a dramatic text, or a poem**

**Audience: your classmates and teachers**

As a performer, you must understand the meaning of a work before you can convincingly express it to an audience. The oral interpreter conveys the meaning through expressive use of voice and gesture. When acting a speech from a dramatic work, for example, you must be able to convince your audience, through effective use of voice and body language, that you *are* the character. When reciting verse, you can employ pauses, changes of volume, intonation, and pitch to emphasize important structural elements in the passage such as rhyme and imagery. Take advantage of the expressive power of punctuation and grammar. Aim for clear and convincing communication of meaning to your listeners.

### Preparing

Form a small group and choose either the sonnet scene from *Shakespeare in Love* or an excerpt from Nabokov's "First Love" to perform as a reading for your classmates. Sit in a circle and read through the text. Look up unfamiliar words. Analyze the content and discuss the ideas that you think are most important in the scene. Identify rhymes, repeated words and sounds, rhetorical devices, and other features of oral interpretation of literary works that you wish to stress.

Using the following questions as a starting point, analyze the scene for an understanding of

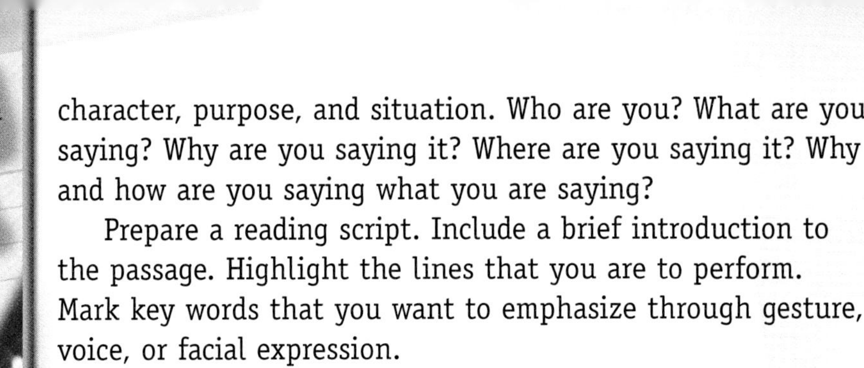

character, purpose, and situation. Who are you? What are you saying? Why are you saying it? Where are you saying it? Why and how are you saying what you are saying?

Prepare a reading script. Include a brief introduction to the passage. Highlight the lines that you are to perform. Mark key words that you want to emphasize through gesture, voice, or facial expression.

## Practicing

Rehearsing is revising. Every performance brings out different meanings. When rehearsing, emphasize different words each time you read your part, until you arrive at the interpretation that you think is best. If you are performing a scene from a play, listen to the other characters as they speak, and respond to them as though you were conducting a real conversation. Dramatic performance is a dynamic group effort. Share your work and build upon the work of others. Use the techniques that you have learned to assess your performance and that of your peers. Give praise where it is due and make constructive suggestions for improvement.

## Performing

Perform the reading for your classmates. When you have finished, ask them to critique your performance. Use their feedback to determine whether you successfully conveyed the meaning of the scene, poem, or narrative. Record your performance and send a copy of your tape to the local radio station. Give a performance at an elder-care center or at a day-care center for children. Share with members of your community the riches you have found in literature.

# Connection Collection

## Representing in Different Ways

**From Print . . .**

TO: a_sanchez@starlabs.com (Alexa Sanchez)
FROM: c_carpenter@starlabs.com (Carmen Carpenter)
SUBJECT: Taste Tests DATE: 09/07/00

Hello.

I conducted two taste tests with my students. They tried small sandwiches made with your peanut butter and two other brands. An impressive 70% of my students preferred your brand, while 22% liked Mega Chunk, and only 8% chose Nutty Spread. However, a month after you altered your "secret recipe" the results were different: 52% preferred your brand, 38% preferred Mega Chunk, and 10% picked Nutty Spread.

When asked to give their reasons, 16 students responded that the new taste was bland, while 14 said the texture was too thin, 8 said there were not enough peanuts, and 4 students were undecided. We hope you return to the old recipe!

Thank you.

**. . . to Visuals**

Based on the information in Ms. Carpenter's E-mail, create two bar graphs: first, to show the results of both taste tests; and second, to show the responses of students who changed their minds about Snappy's New Recipe.

**From Visuals . . .**

**. . . to Print**

Using the graph above, and Ms. Carpenter's results, prepare a speech for Snappy's President to persuade her to return to the old formula. Consider ways to make your arguments vivid and strong.

- **Which strategies can be used for creating both written and visual representations? Which strategies apply to one, not both? Which type of representation is more effective?**
- **Draw a conclusion, and write briefly about the differences between written ideas and visual representations.**

## Speaking in Everyday Life

### *Informal Speech*

This semester, you have agreed to be a teacher's aide for Ms. Sanchez and her fourth grade class. On your first day, the students are acting restless, so Ms. Sanchez asks you to speak to them about the differences between student life in high school and in grade school.

**Prepare a speech for the fourth graders. Be sure to make your introduction and conclusion lively and interesting and choose details that will hold the attention of the children. Remember to adjust your speaking to this audience of fourth graders. Keep your speech clear and concise so they will not be distracted from your subject.**

**What strategies did you use to talk to the young students about your experience of high school?**

*You can find information on giving informal speeches on pages(C672–C682).*

## Speaking in the Workplace

### *Business Speech*

You are one of the city's leading entrepreneurs in the pet store business. Known to many in the field as "Gills" McGillicuddy, you have devised ways to help pet fish live longer, healthier lives. Because of your recent success, you have the opportunity to move your pet store to a location on Knight Street, your city's fanciest shopping area. However, some of the local business owners are unenthusiastic about a pet store on Knight Street.

**Prepare an informal talk to give to the local shop owners during their next planning meeting. Try to persuade them that your store will be an asset to their businesses. Include personal stories, vivid details, and a graphic display to help support your argument.**

**What strategies did you use to persuade the shop owners of Knight Street?**

*You can find information on giving persuasive speeches on pages (C672–C682).*

## Speaking in Academic Areas

### *Environmental Speech*

As Pat Peppermill, one of the country's leading environmental scientists, you have terrific ideas on what citizens can do to keep our land and water resources from disappearing. This coming weekend, you will speak to a group of teenage students who live in both rural and urban areas.

**Prepare a speech to give to the students explaining how they can take actions to protect the environment. Brainstorm a list of different activities they can do to help. Remember that some students come from sprawling cities and others come from suburban communities and farms. Be sure your speech has a clear, concise introduction, a body, and a conclusion.**

**What strategies did you use to inform your audience about protecting our natural resources?**

*You can find information on giving environmental speeches on pages (C672–C682).*

## Speaking for Oral Communication

### *A Guided Tour*

Some wealthy tourists from Gooseland, a small inland island of Finland, have chosen your town for their annual holiday trip. Because of your excellent speaking skills and knowledge of local history, the local merchants have chosen you to prepare a speaking tour of your hometown to give to the visiting Gooselanders.

**Prepare a guided tour of the cultural and historical features of your hometown. Organize your ideas for clarity, conciseness, and logical flow. Think about graphic information you may want to include. Practice your spoken tour to strengthen your supporting details. Remember that the tourists from Gooseland are not native English speakers.**

**What strategies did you use to give a guided tour of your hometown to the visitors from Gooseland?**

*You can find information on writing informative speeches on pages (C672–C682).*

# Assess Your Learning

The principal of your school has asked a group of students to present short speeches entitled "Highlights of My High School Years." These speeches will be given to your classmates and faculty at an upcoming all-school assembly.

- **Choose and narrow a topic for the five-minute speech to be delivered to your audience.**
- **Prepare an outline for the speech, making sure your introduction grabs the assembly's attention. Prewrite and draft the body of your talk to fill it with supporting details that are concise and memorable. Brainstorm for possible graphics you could use to make your speech as clear and vivid as possible. Consider your audience in choosing highlights from your high school experiences. What details are unique to you as an individual student? Be sure to include anecdotes that are funny as well as nostalgic. What could you add that would enlighten the teachers about the life of a high school student?**

***Before You Write*** **Consider the following questions:**
What is the ***subject?***
What is the ***occasion?***
Who is the ***audience?***
What is the ***purpose?***

***After You Write*** **Evaluate your work using the following criteria:**

- Have you arranged notes logically in order to present pertinent information to your audience?
- Did you use a strong introduction, personal narratives, and specific examples to spark your listener's imagination?
- Have you provided sufficient evidence to support your points?
- Does your speech flow smoothly between ideas and make logical transitions?
- Have you included visual materials to help you keep the audience's attention?
- Does your conclusion summarize important points and leave the audience with a memorable sentence, phrase, or image?

**Write briefly on how well you did. Point out your strengths and areas for improvement.**

CHAPTER 16

# Vocabulary

Whether you go to college or take a job after high school graduation, you will constantly encounter unfamiliar words. Your vocabulary is something you can add to throughout your entire life; you will find that as you grow older and learn more and more words, the better able you will be to communicate effectively, both in school and on the job. Also, the deeper your understanding of words, the deeper your understanding of the world around you.

## *Reading with a Writer's Eye*

The English language has always been a malleable, adaptable creation; it absorbs cultural influences and is shaped by social events and technological developments. The following selection from *Wired Style: Principles of English Usage in the Digital Age* discusses the way technology and speed are pushing English into new, unanticipated areas.

# ANTICIPATE THE FUTURE

The Editors of *Wired*

Language moves in one predictable direction: forward. Writers may often be guided by a certain nostalgia—reading the classics, digging into the past to trace etymologies, plumbing *The Oxford English Dictionary* for layers of meaning. But technology is pushing us forward, toward the cultural and linguistic frontier. Techies invent terms daily; fresh slang sweeps through the online community within hours; new media shifts how we use words.

At *Wired* we keep our eyes trained on the future. We know the arc of language and strive to follow it. Whenever we're faced with a dicey style question, we try to anticipate the inevitable evolution of language, constantly asking ourselves: Where are style and usage headed? and Can we stay ahead of the trajectory?

Our mantra is not *How has it been?* but *How will it be?*

Which isn't to say the language we use lacks the richness of history. The phrase "brave new world" rolled from Shakespeare to Huxley, picking up steam along the way; it's used frequently in our pages as a metaphor for the perils of the digital age. One of our pet verbs—*grok*—cropped up in Robert A. Heinlein's *Stranger in a Strange Land*, reappeared in Tom Wolfe's *The Electric Kool-Aid Acid Test* and has become a fixture at *Wired* editorial meetings.

New terms spring constantly from new technologies. We embrace these neologisms enthusiastically. And *Wired's* tendency to close up words grows very much out of the science and technology worlds we write about. From computer commands like *whois* and onscreen nouns like *logon*, we have evolved this commandment: *When in doubt, close it up.* Words spelled solid—like *videogame* or *gameplay* or *homepage*—may seem odd at first, but the now-common *modem* offers a perfect example of how quickly words move from the strange to the familiar: Who even knows that the piece of hardware allowing computers to talk to each other was once called a *modulator/demodulator?*

Our style for *electronic mail* is another example of this principle. The magazine never observed the convention of abbreviating *electronic* with an uppercase E. Sure, it's C-ration, H-bomb, V-Chip–but *E-mail* didn't look right, and certainly no one styled it that way on the Net. We originally used a hyphen to underscore the trace of the word *electronic*, but as email caught on, and as more and more people started spending more and more time on the Net, *e-mail* became more and more anachronistic. An email query on how to style the word elicited these replies from *Wired* editors:

> *"Who doesn't type email in the heat of an electronic moment? But I still argue for hyphens when a single letter is pronounced as a syllable."*
>
> (Constance Hale)

> *"The lexical tides are flowing against us. I suspect email will become standard."*
>
> (Gary Wolf)

> *"It just seems like hyphens ultimately vanish; words are concatenated; it's the way of the world. Electronic mail became e-mail became email."*
>
> (Louis Rossetto)

The way of the net is just not a hyphenated way. Today we spell email solid. But what about *e-zine* and *emoney*? Read on.

*Save a keystroke* is another style commandment rooted in the way of the Net. As email and online writing continue to blossom, look for initial capital letters to go the way of hyphens. Terms we've let slip into lowercase include gopher, telnet, technopagan, and webmaster.

## desktop

> As a noun, it represents the physical space on top of a desk, or the virtual space on your computer screen where icons representing hard drives, files, and applications reside. As an adjective-as in **desktop computer**-it suggests an approximate size: bigger than a laptop, smaller than a desk.

### download

> To copy a document or application from a network or BBS to a personal computer. Usage has spread to the colloquial, where to download may simply mean to absorb.

### log on

> The verb must stay detached from the preposition—after all, would the verb survive in the past tense as logoned or logged-on? And the gerund would be a spelling train wreck: loggingon. Some change the preposition for **log in,** but that combo is not as common. The noun **logon** is collapsed into one word. It refers to the procedure to gain access to a network. When you are done, you execute a **logoff.** Also an adjective: *Some boards offer 20 minutes a day free logon time.*

### pixel

> The shortened form of "picture element," for the dots that make up an image or character on a computer or TV screen. The more pixels, the better the resolution.

### pulldown

> An adjective describing an interface device or "menu" you can pull down using a mouse or a keystroke.

### screenshot

> An image captured from or displayed on a computer screen. Also known as a **screengrab.**

### upload

> To transfer a file from a PC to a server—or onto the Net. As a noun, a synonym for those transmitted files.

### workstation

> High-end, expensive, powerful desktop machine. Preferred for graphics and usually networked. Historically Unix-based, though a PC with a powerful chip could qualify as a workstation. Others include Sun's SPARCstation, SGI's Indigo, and IBM's RS/6000.

## Thinking as a Writer

### Exploring the History of Words

Make a list of what the preceding selection indicates have been the contemporary forces influencing the English of today. Which of these influences was most impressive to you and why? How does the selection help you imagine the ways the English language might change in the future? Keep your list of observations for future reference.

### Observing Changes in Language

Oral Expression

- With a classmate, read aloud the excerpt from *Beowulf* below. The excerpt is a description of the funeral of Beowulf's father, Scyld. When you are finished looking at the original text, examine the translation for how much the spelling and vocabulary have changed from Old English to Modern English. Summarize what you observe and report your findings to the class.

> Tha gyt hie him asetton segen geldenne/
> heah ofer heafod, leton holm beran/,
> geafon on garsecg; him wæs geomor sefa,
> murnende mod. Men ne cunnon
> secgan to soethe, selerædende/,
> hæle eth under heofenum, hwa thæm hlæste
> onfeng.

- Here is the translation.

> Then besides they placed a golden banner
> high over his head, let the sea take him,
> have him into the ocean; their spirit was sad,
> mood mournful. Men could not
> say certainly, hall-counselors,
> warriors under the heavens, who received that load.

After reading, discuss with your classmate the similarities you observe in the language, and also what you observe that is dissimilar. Be specific, citing particular words and phrases as needed. Report your findings to the class.

# Understanding the Development of the English Language

##  Yesterday, Today, and Tomorrow

English—like Latin, Greek, and many other languages—goes back to a parent language called Indo-European. Although Indo-European was an unwritten prehistoric language, linguists have been able to reconstruct it to some extent. To do so, they have studied words that are similar in several different languages. The following example shows how English is closely connected to Dutch, German, Irish, Latin, and Greek.

| | | | | | |
|---|---|---|---|---|---|
| **English** | brother | **German** | bruder | **Latin** | frater |
| **Dutch** | broeder | **Irish** | brathair | **Greek** | phrater |

The English that people use today has gone through three principal stages, the first of which began about 1,500 years ago.

## Old English (450–1150)

You have already encountered some Old English with the passage from *Beowulf*. This earliest form of English was the language of three German tribes: the Angles, the Saxons, and the Jutes. These tribes invaded England and then settled there. They seem to have called their language *Englisc* (from *Engle*, "the Angles"). Although the language's vocabulary was extensive, only a small fraction of its words have survived. Among them, however, are some of the most common words in Modern English.

| WORDS FROM OLD ENGLISH | |
|---|---|
| **Familiar Objects** | horse, cow, meat, stone, earth, home |
| **Family Members** | father, mother, brother, sister, wife |
| **Pronouns** | I, you, he, she, we, they, who |

| | |
|---|---|
| **Numbers** | one, two, three, four, five, six, seven |
| **Articles** | a, an, the |
| **Prepositions** | in, out, at, by, under, around |

## Middle English (1150–1500)

In 1066, the Normans, who came from what is now northwestern France, invaded England under the command of William the Conqueror. This invasion, known as the Norman Conquest, had far-reaching effects on the language. For centuries afterward the rulers and the upper classes of England spoke French—the Normans' language—although religious and legal documents continued to be written in Latin. During this period, Old English, French, and Latin gradually became intermixed. Consequently, synonyms for many words came from all three languages. For example, *old* is from Old English, *ancient* is from French, and *venerable* is from Latin.

Geoffrey Chaucer wrote the famous *Canterbury Tales* in Middle English. In this passage one of the travellers, a monk, is telling the story of Holofernes, a powerful and cruel king.

**Model: Middle English**

### De Oloferno

Was nevere capitayn under a kyng
That regnes mo putte in subjeccioun,
Ne strenger was in feeld of alle thyng,
As in his tyme, ne gretter of renoun,
Ne moore pompous in heigh presumpcioun
Than Oloferne, Which Fortune ay kiste
So likerously, and ladde hym up and doun,
Til that his heed was of, er that he wiste.

Nat oonly that this world hadde hum in awe
For lesynge of richesse or libertee,
But he made every man reneyen his lawe.
"Nabugodonosor was god," seyde hee;
"Noon oother god sholde adoured bee."
Agayns his heeste no wight dar trespace

Save in Bethulia, a strong citee,
Where Eliachim a preest was of that place.

But taak kep of the deth of Oloferne;
Amydde his hoost he dronke lay a nyght,
Withinne his tente, large as is a berne,
And yet, for al his pompe and al his myght,
Judith, a womman, as he lay upright
Slepynge, his heed of smoot, and from his tente
Ful pryvely she stal from every wight,
And with his heed unto hir toun she wente.

–*Geoffrey Chaucer,* The Canterbury Tales

Here is the same passage, as translated over five hundred years later.

**Model: Modern English**

## Holofernes

Was never a captain under a king
That had more kingdoms thrown in subjection,
Nor stronger there was in fields of all things,
As in his time, nor greater of renown,
No one more pompous in high presumption,
Than Holofernes, whom Dame Fortune kissed
So lecherously, and led him up and down
Until his head was off before 'twas missed.

Not only did this world hold him in awe
For taking all its wealth and liberty,
But he made every man renounce old law.
"Nebuchadnezzar is your god," said he,
"And now no other god shall adored be."
Against his order no man dared trespass,
Save in Bethulia, a strong city,
Where Eliachim priest was of that place.

But from the death of Holofernes learn.
Amidst his host he lay drunk, on a night,

Within his tent, as large as is a barn,
And yet, for all his pomp and all his might,
Judith, a woman, as he lay upright,
Sleeping, smote off his head and from his tent
Stole secretly away from every sight,
And with his head to her own town she went.

–*Geoffrey Chaucer,* The Canterbury Tales

## Practice Your Skills

*Analyzing Language*

**With a partner, describe the differences you observe between Middle English and modern English in the two passages from The Canterbury Tales. Be specific, citing particular words and phrases as needed. Also, describe what similarities you see. Note that both the original and the translation conform to ten syllables per line, and that this attention to form helps clarify how certain words are pronounced. When it is your partner's turn to speak, listen carefully and attentively. Ask questions of your partner if you need clarification. Summarize what you have observed and report your findings to the class. Support your findings with specific examples.**

## Modern English (1500 to Present)

By 1500, the assimilation of the contributing languages that formed the basis of English was largely complete. William Shakespeare wrote his great works early in the Modern English period, and more than 200 years later the documents of the American Revolution were written in Modern English. Of course, changes have continued to occur in English since 1500, as more and more cultures contributed words and customs to the language. Today English is a rich, versatile language with choices and variants that are acceptable in different situations and different parts of the country.

Read aloud the opening soliloquy from the play *Richard III*, by William Shakespeare, as it appeared in 1597. Compare the language with Old or Middle English, and notice how much closer this passage is to the English that you are used to speaking.

## Model: Modern English

Now is the winter of our discontent,
Made glorious summer by this sonne of Yorke:
And all the cloudes that lowrd vpon our house,
In the deepe bosome of the Ocean buried.
Now are our browes bound with victorious wreathes,
Our bruised armes hung vp for monuments,
Our sterne alarmes changd to merry meetings,
Our dreadfull marches to delightfull measures.
Grim-visagde warre, hath smoothde his wrinkled front,
And now in steed of mounting barbed steedes,
To fright the soules of fearefull aduersaries
He capers nimbly in a Ladies chamber,
To the lasciuious pleasing of a loue.
But I that am not shapte for sportiue trickes,
Nor made to court an amorous looking glasse,
I that am rudely stampt and want loues maiesty,
To strut before a wanton ambling Nymph:
I that am curtaild of this faire proportion,
Cheated of feature by dissembling nature,
Deformd, vnfinisht, sent before my time
Into this breathing world fearce halfe made vp,
And that so lamely and vnfashionable,
That dogs barke at me as I halt by them:
Why I in this weake piping time of peace
Haue no delight to passe away the time,
Vnlesse to spie my shadow in the sunne,
And dscant on mine owne deformity.

–*William Shakespeare,* Richard III

## Practice Your Skills

*Analyzing Language*

**With a partner, cite specific examples of how Shakespeare's language in the soliliquy above is different from Old English and also how it is different from the English you speak today. Then cite specific examples of how it is linked to Old English and the English you speak. Summarize what you discover and report your findings to the class.**

## American English

Although most of the words in use in the United States today were brought to this country by English settlers, other cultural groups have also contributed—and continue to contribute—words to American English. For instance, the various Native American languages have had a significant influence on place names in the United States—*Omaha, Wichita,* and *Niagara,* for example. Some other English words that come from Native American languages are *succotash*, *raccoon*, and *opossum*.

In addition to Native Americans, many explorers, settlers, and visitors from other countries brought with them their own contributions to American English. For example, the words *Los Angeles* and *tornado* are Spanish, and *opera* and *spaghetti* are Italian. Here are more examples.

| | |
|---|---|
| **Spanish** | breeze, poncho, mustang, alligator, rodeo |
| **French** | cartoon, dentist, liberty, garage, parachute |
| **German** | hamster, nickel, zinc, noodle, waltz |
| **Dutch** | landscape, skipper, cookie, cruise, iceberg |
| **Italian** | zero, candy, magazine, pizza, stanza, opera |
| **African** | Gullah, banjo, banana, dashiki, okra |
| **Chinese** | tea, kowtow, chow, shanghai, typhoon |

The following two readings come from different periods in American history. As you read the selections look for differences and similarities in vocabulary and sentence structure. The first selection is from President George Washington's First Inaugural Address on April 30, 1789.

Fellow Citizens of the Senate and of the House of Representatives: Among the vicissitudes incident to life no event could have filled me with greater anxieties than that of which the notification was transmitted by your order, and received on the fourteenth day of the present month. On the one hand, I was summoned by my country, whose voice I can never hear but with veneration and love, from a retreat which I had chosen with the fondest predilection, and, in my flattering hopes, with an immutable decision, as the asylum of my declining years—a retreat which was rendered every day more necessary as well as more dear to me by the addition of habit to inclination, and of frequent interruptions in my health to the gradual waste committed on it by time. On the other hand, the magnitude and difficulty of the trust to which the voice of my country called me, being sufficient to awaken in the wisest and most experienced of her citizens a distrustful scrutiny into his qualifications, could not but overwhelm with despondence one who (inheriting inferior endowments from nature and unpracticed in the duties of civil administration) ought to be peculiarly conscious of his own deficiencies. In this conflict of emotions all I dare aver is that it has been my faithful study to collect my duty from a just appreciation of every circumstance by which it might be affected. All I dare hope is that if, in executing this task, I have been too much swayed by a grateful remembrance of former instances, or by an affectionate sensibility to this transcendent proof of the confidence of my fellow citizens, and have thence too little consulted my incapacity as well as disinclination for the weighty and untried cares before me, my error will be palliated by the motives which mislead me, and its consequences be judged by my country with some share of the partiality in which they originated.

–*George Washington,* First Inaugural Address

The second selection is President William Clinton's Second Inaugural Address, given on January 20, 1997.

My fellow citizens: At this last presidential inauguration of the twentieth century, let us lift our eyes toward the challenges that await us in the next century. It is our great good fortune that time and chance have put us not only on the edge of a new century, in a new millennium, but on the edge of a bright new prospect in human affairs, a moment that will define our course and our character for decades to come. We must keep our old democracy forever young. Guided by the ancient vision of a promised land, let us set our sights upon a land of new promise.

The promise of America was born in the eighteenth century out of the bold conviction that we are all created equal. It was extended and preserved in the nineteenth century, when our nation spread across the continent, saved the Union, and abolished the scourge of slavery.

Then, in turmoil and triumph, that promise exploded onto the world stage to make this the American century.

What a century it has been! America became the world's mightiest industrial power, saved the world from tyranny in two world wars and a long cold war, and time and again reached across the globe to millions who longed for the blessings of liberty.

Along the way, Americans produced the great middle class and security in old age, built unrivaled centers of learning and opened public schools to all, split the atom and explored the heavens, invented the computer and the microchip, and deepened the wellspring of justice by making a revolution in civil rights for African-Americans and all minorities and extending the circle of citizenship, opportunity, and dignity to women.

–*William Jefferson Clinton,* Second Inaugural Address

## Practice Your Skills

*Analyzing Language*

**With a partner, discuss the differences you observe between the words of President Washington and President Clinton. Draw conclusions about how English has changed based on your analysis of the similarities and differences between the two selections. Be specific, citing particular words and phrases to support your findings. Organize your ideas in writing to ensure coherence, logical progression, and support. Write a summary of what you observe and report your findings to the class.**

*Words with Unusual Origins*

Sometimes the names of characters in literature and mythology and the names of real people, places, and historical events become familiar English words. The word *quixotic,* meaning "idealistic to an impractical degree," derives from the name *Don Quixote,* the hero of the seventeeth-century novel *Don Quixote de la Mancha,* by Miguel de Cervantes. Some words have their origins in mythology: *cereal,* for example, comes from *Ceres,* the Roman goddess of the harvest and grain. The *diesel* engine is named for its inventor, Rudolf Diesel. Here are some other words with unusual origins.

| WORD | MEANING | ETYMOLOGY |
|---|---|---|
| malapropism | humorous misuse of a word | from *Mrs. Malaprop,* a character noted for mis-using words in Richard Sheridan's 1775 comedy, *The Rivals* |
| waterloo | decisive or final defeat or setback | from *Waterloo,* Belgium, the scene of Napoleon's defeat in 1815 |
| boycott | refrain from having any dealings with | from Charles *Boycott,* a land agent in Ireland who in 1897 was ostracized for refusing to reduce rents |

## English in the New Millennium

"Editors at *Wired* are constantly navigating the shifting verbal currents of the post-Gutenberg era. When does jargon end and a new vernacular begin? Where's the line between neologism and hype? What's the language of the global village? How can we keep pace with technology without getting bogged down in empty acronyms? How can we write about machines without losing a sense of humanity and poetry?" So writes editor Constance Hale in the introduction to *Wired Style*. No one can say with certainly what the English language will be like in the future. Perhaps it will not have changed very much, or perhaps the influence of new technologies and diverse cultures will make the English we use today as foreign to people in the future as Old English is to us today. One thing is certain to be true: the language will continue to change. As technology erases cultural and geographic borders, English will surely reflect the diversity of influences with which it comes in contact.

*Computer Language*

Many of the terms associated with computers are used because they are convenient and descriptive. As these words are used more freely, their new meanings become as significant as their original meanings. There are words that have taken on new meanings. For example, *virus* is no longer associated only with a living organism; it now has high-tech connotations. Other examples of words that have been transformed by the technology revolution are *portal, bug, browser, driver,* and *cookie*.

**Your Writer's Journal**

The more you read, the more your vocabulary will expand. Then as your vocabulary grows, your writing will also improve. One way to expand your vocabulary is to use your Writer's Journal to jot down unfamiliar words you encounter. Throughout the year, add to this list as you come across unfamiliar words. Then, when you are writing, look over the list and use any of the words that are suitable for your purpose.

# Understanding the Varieties of English

Although English has many different dialects (for example, the various southern, southwestern, New England, British and Australian dialects), none is so different that one group cannot understand another.

## American Dialects

Humorist and essayist Roy Blount, Jr., wrote of the differences between the northern dialect and southern dialect, "The language needs a second-person plural, and *y'all* is manifestly more precise, more mannerly and friendlier than *you people* or *y'uns*." As English has developed, so too have many different ways of speaking the language. These variations are called *dialects*. As Blount points out, dialects differ from one another in vocabulary, pronunciation, and even grammar.

## Standard American English

Using dialect in your fiction, poetry, or plays can help you create believable characters. For example, Sandra Cisneros's book *The House on Mango Street* is written in the inner-city dialect of a young girl. However, when writing an informative essay, it is best to use standard English. Standard English is the formal English taught in school and used in newspapers, scholarly works, and many books.

**Writing Tip**

Use **standard English** when writing for school and for a large general audience.

## Practice Your Skills

*Identifying Dialects*

**With your peers decide what type of dialect you speak. Provide examples of your vocabulary, pronunciation, and grammar that characterize your dialect. What culture has influenced your dialect? Compare and contrast your examples with standard English and with the dialects of other parts of the country (a southern dialect compared to a southwestern dialect, for example). Make a chart, index, or dictionary of words to introduce your regional dialect to people from other parts of the country.**

## Colloquialisms, Idioms, Slang, and Jargon

When you speak to your friends, you probably use **colloquialisms, slang, idioms,** and **jargon.** These informal types of language make oral communication a pleasure, but they are usually not appropriate for formal, written English.

| Informal Language | Definition | Example |
|---|---|---|
| **Colloquialism** | informal expressions used in conversation but usually not in writing | Cecil was <u>dog-tired</u> after running twenty laps around the track |
| **Idiom** | a phrase or expression that has a meaning different from the literal translation of the words | Mark was driving by the hardware store when a car <u>cut him off</u>. |
| **Slang** | colorful or exaggerated expressions and phrases that are used by a particular group | Hope missed the fiesta last night because she went to the <u>flicks</u> with Leonard. |

| | | |
|---|---|---|
| **Jargon** | a specialized vocabulary most often used in a technical, scientific, or professional field | Whatever cyber-punk hacked the mainframe has ultra-killer apps. |

**Idioms, colloquialisms, slang,** and **jargon** can make your fiction and poetry convincing and lively. They are not, however, appropriate for formal writing such as you will do in school and work.

## Clichés, Tired Words, Euphemisms, and Loaded Language

When expressing and explaining your thoughts and ideas, it is important to realize that certain common expressions have become so overused that they are no longer precise or vivid. Similarly, there are other expressions that are misleading. Using these words and expressions without being aware of it can weaken your writing.

| Type of Expression | Definition | Example |
|---|---|---|
| **Cliché** | a trite or overused expression | We invited everyone we knew to Michelle's birthday party, because you know what they say, "the more the merrier." |
| **Tired Words** | language that has been exhausted of strength or precision through overuse | I went surfing in Mexico last month and it was really fun. |

| | | |
|---|---|---|
| **Euphemism** | the substitution of a mild, indirect term for one considered blunt or offensive | When the old steam radiator began leaking water all over the floor, Neal called the facility engineer. |
| **Loaded Language** | words that are weighted with meaning or emotional importance | Many people will tell you that they have a natural-born right to watch television. |

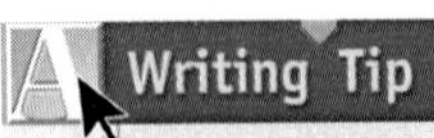

Avoid **clichés, tired language, euphemisms** and **loaded language**. Your writing will be more precise, vivid, and accurate.

## Practice Your Skills

*Identifying Language*

**Read the following sentences. Identify colloquialisms, idioms, slang, jargon, clichés, tired words, euphemisms, and loaded words.**

1. When Jason explained that I should purge my disk cache, reboot and rebuild my desktop, I nodded, but I really had no idea what he was talking about.
2. The reviewer gives movies four stars so often that nobody pays any attention to his reviews anymore.
3. It's a shame that Amy's car broke down, but that's the way the cookie crumbles.
4. Arturo sleeps like a log.
5. When Rose gets caught up in a book, she's oblivious to the noise around her.

6. The landlord had advertised an apartment with "city views," but we soon discovered our only view was of the air-shaft and a wall of bricks.
7. The destruction of the world's coral reefs was described by one environmentalist as "an insult to Mother Nature."
8. After the cashier rang up my purchase and wished me a nice day, I left the store.
9. Between midnight and one in the morning, the cops pulled over twelve cars.
10. When Senator McGalliard accused the president of being a hawk, the media blasted him for being a liberal.

## Denotation and Connotation

When you look up a word in the dictionary, you will find its **denotative** meaning. Some words, however, have an additional meaning based on how the word is emotionally perceived by the reader or listener. This is called the **connotative** meaning. For example, *photo* and *snapshot* have a similar denotative meaning. *Snapshot*, however, connotes (or suggests) something more casual than *photo*.

## Practice Your Skills

### *Identifying Denotations and Connotations*

**The following pairs of words all have similar denotative meanings. Describe their connotative differences.**

1. mirror, looking-glass
2. lanky, svelte
3. old, ancient
4. noodles, pasta

**Create five pairs of your own, using the dictionary as needed. Your pairs should all have similar denotative meanings but different connotative meanings. When you have completed your five pairs, share them with the class.**

## Television

**Y**ou have seen how computers have an influence on the English language. Another influence on English is the entertainment industry. In the following selection from the *Chicago Tribune*, Jonathan Storm discusses how vocabulary is shaped by popular television shows.

You unlock this door with the key of your remote control.

Behind it is a dimension of television that lies far above the pit of the mundane, at the summit of the craft. It is a fifth dimension, beyond that which is known to most TV writers and producers.

It is a dimension as seductive as a warm bath and as stimulating as a brisk shower, a dimension of sound and a dimension of sight, but most of all a dimension of mind.

This is the dimension of imagination. You're moving into the land of both shadow and substance, of emotion and ideas. You've just crossed over into—the Writing Zone.

Some TV shows just sound good, imbued by their authors with dialogue that creates a world we do not know that invites us in and compels us to get comfortable.

"Maybe it was a bar, where the perp that threw him out the window went looking for him."

"I am the master of my own domain."

"Just the facts, ma'am."

"D'oh!" "Woo-hoo" and "Don't have a cow, man."

Often, when the language is distinctive, the show becomes so popular that the writing enters the vernacular. Tom Hanks quotes Homer Simpson's "D'oh!" in "You've Got Mail," and many families use "Simpsons"-isms to communicate among themselves.

Sometimes, series with smaller audiences have writing that's just as distinctive as that of "NYPD Blue," "Seinfeld," "Dragnet" and Rod Serling's

"The Twilight Zone" (from which the beginning of this article was proudly adapted).

"School is a battlefield for your heart," Angela Chase observed in the first five minutes of "My So-Called Life." "Cafeteria is the embarrassment capital of the world. It's like a prison movie."

"Amy is a witch, and Michael is whatever the boy of witch is, plus being the poster child for yuck," complains the gorgeous, if interpersonally challenged, Cordelia to Buffy (The Vampire Slayer), about her friends.

"The world in which I'm confident is running right into the world in which I'm not," laments Dana Whitaker, queen bee of "Sports Night," but unlucky in love.

Nobody really talks like this, and that's the point. Some writers relish language, and they use it to create characters that really do exist in a different dimension from those in less compelling series.

## Media Activity

With a group of your peers, brainstorm in order to come up with at least five expressions from television shows. Consider TV comedies, dramas, game shows, talk shows, and even news shows. Your expressions should be comments that you have heard outside of TV, and they should not be examples that Storm has written about in his article. Share your examples with the class. After all the expressions have been shared, discuss the influence of television on your own speech.

### Questions for Analyzing Television Vocabulary

- What expressions do you use that come from television?
- How do you feel letting other people create language for you?
- What expressions have you ever coined?
- What goals do you have for your own vocabulary?

# Determining Word Meanings

Because learning and understanding new words is valuable to both your reading and your writing, the rest of this chapter will give you some ways to unlock the meanings of unfamiliar words.

## Context Clues

The **context** of a word is the sentence, surrounding words, or situation in which the word appears. Usually the context of a word gives clues to meaning rather than an actual definition.

| | |
|---|---|
| RESTATEMENT | The sun reached its *zenith*, **or highest point in the sky**, just as we began to eat lunch. (The word *or* introduces an appositive that defines the word *zenith*.) |
| EXAMPLE | *Symmetry* often contributes to the beauty of architecture, as it does, for example, **in the perfect proportions and balanced forms of the Taj Mahal**. (By using the well-known Taj Mahal as an example, the writer makes clear what is meant by *symmetry*.) |
| COMPARISON | A *prodigy* in music, she was **nearly the equal of Mozart, the composer who wrote a sonata at the age of eight.** (The comparison with Mozart shows that *prodigy* means "a highly talented child.") |
| CONTRAST | **Mark's customized purple jeep, with a gilt crown for a hood ornament**, is as *gaudy* as Mr. Foster's gray sedan is plain. (The contrast between Mark's car and Mr. Foster's car shows that gaudy means just the opposite of plain: "showy, garish, and possibly tasteless.") |

PARALLELISM — She was **determined**, he was **iron-willed**, and I was equally *resolute*. (The parallel sentence structure suggests that resolute is a synonym for determined and iron-willed.)

## PRACTICE YOUR SKILLS

### *Using Context Clues*

**Use context clues to help you choose the meaning for the underlined words. Consult the dictionary to check your answers.**

**1.** Congress passed a statute, or law, to provide for federal enforcement of the Constitutional amendment.

(A) request (B) written rule (C) sculptured likeness (D) book (E) statement

**2.** The king decided to abdicate, as King Edward VIII did when he gave up the throne of England in 1936.

(A) relinquish power (B) be crowned (C) control (D) marry (E) escape

**3.** Amity exists between Switzerland and its neighbors, in contrast to the ill will that exists between some other neighboring nations of the world.

(A) rivalry (B) hostility (C) borders (D) friendship (E) helplessness

**4.** Inquiring about his son's career, the man naturally took a paternal interest in the boy's success.

(A) brotherly (B) long-term (C) fatherly (D) excessive (E) mild

**5.** The recent political caucus, unlike those old-time small gatherings, was well reported by the press.

(A) defeat (B) meeting (C) campaign (D) dinner (E) platform

6. A referee should be completely <u>impartial</u>, favoring neither team.

(A) businesslike (B) enthusiastic (C) outspoken
(D) cordial (E) fair

7. This is a <u>facsimile</u>, or replica, of a five-hundred-dollar bill issued by the Confederate States of America.

(A) reproduction (B) variety (C) counterfeit
(D) bonanza (E) display

8. When the foreman was warned about his <u>laxity</u>, he changed overnight and became a complete perfectionist.

(A) extravagance (B) appearance (C) negligence
(D) ignorance (E) temper

9. Although the candidate failed to win a majority of votes in the primary, he did have a sizable <u>plurality</u> over the first runner-up.

(A) loss of votes (B) excess of votes (C) celebration
(D) concern (E) surprise

10. Among the other pleasant smells in the village was the <u>savory</u> odor of chili coming from a small café.

(A) appetizing (B) sturdy (C) flowery (D) gracious
(E) rural

11. In some countries military service is <u>compulsory</u>; in others it is voluntary.

(A) enjoyable (B) unnecessary (C) disagreeable
(D) required (E) illegal

12. He holds the <u>orthodox</u>, or customary, view of what the company should do to increase sales.

(A) modern (B) religious (C) thoughtful
(D) unpopular (E) traditional

13. Dr. Elroy tried to <u>ascertain</u> the cause of the illness, but he was never sure he was right.

(A) cure (B) destroy (C) treat (D) determine
(E) dismiss

**14.** The lake was <u>placid</u> after the storm, its surface as smooth as a tabletop.

(A) peaceful (B) transparent (C) choppy (D) muddy (E) cold

**15.** Every <u>recipient</u> of the humanitarian-of-the-year award gives an acceptance speech.

(A) promoter (B) loser (C) receiver (D) giver (E) producer

**16.** A handwritten note is not enough; you must have an <u>affidavit</u>, a signed and witnessed document.

(A) instruction (B) explanation (C) alibi (D) oral oath (E) sworn statement

**17.** Sally is so <u>meticulous</u> in her work that she rewrites a whole page to correct one small error.

(A) prompt (B) careful (C) excitable (D) remarkable (E) indifferent

**18.** Some board games require very little thought or intelligence, but chess is quite <u>cerebral</u>.

(A) simple (B) intellectually demanding (C) thrilling (D) socially impressive (E) ancient

**19.** It is almost as hard to <u>decipher</u> Mr. Cook's handwriting as it is to crack a tough foreign code.

(A) study (B) imitate (C) analyze (D) interpret (E) print

**20.** Emily Dickinson's <u>renown</u>, or fame, is based on a collection of short, brilliant poems.

(A) pseudonym (B) gentleness (C) technical mastery (D) obituary (E) honored status

### Your Writer's Journal

Choose eight words from the list you are compiling in your journal. Write a sentence for each word. Make sure the sentence gives a context clue to help you remember the meaning of the word.

# Prefixes, Suffixes, and Roots

Besides using the context of a word, you can use a word's structure, or parts, to find clues to its meaning. These word parts are prefixes, roots, and suffixes. A **root** is the part of a word that carries the basic meaning. A **prefix** is one or more syllables placed in front of the root to modify the meaning of the root or to form a new word. A **suffix** is one or more syllables placed after the root to affect its meaning and often to determine its part of speech.

The English language contains hundreds of roots, prefixes, and suffixes. With a knowledge of even a few examples of each kind of word part, you should be able to make reasonable guesses about the meanings of words that contain these parts. The following examples illustrate how the meaning of each word part contributes to the meaning of the word as a whole.

**WORD PARTS WITH LATIN ORIGINS**

| WORD | PREFIX | ROOT | SUFFIX |
|---|---|---|---|
| abrasive | ab- (away) | -rase- (erase) | -ive (toward action) |
| component | com- (together) | -pon- (put) | -ent (one that performs) |
| inaccessible | in- (not) | -access- (approach) | -ible (capable of) |

**WORD PARTS WITH GREEK ORIGINS**

| WORD | PREFIX | ROOT | SUFFIX |
|---|---|---|---|
| amorphous | a- (without) | -morph- (form) | -ous (quality of) |
| ejection | e- (out) | -ject- (throw) | -ion (act or process) |
| precedence | pre- (before) | -ced- (go) | -ence (act or process) |

As you can see, the meanings of prefixes, roots, and suffixes seldom give a complete definition of a word. Rather, they give clues to the meaning of a word. Following are dictionary definitions of the previous examples.

**abrasive:** tending to rub or wear away

**component:** simple part or element of a system

**inaccessible:** not capable of being approached

**amorphous:** having no definite form, shapeless

**ejection:** act of throwing out or off from within

**precedence:** act of going before

##  Prefixes

Many **prefixes** have clear and familiar meanings. The number prefixes, such as *mono-, bi-,* and *tri-,* are good examples. Other prefixes, however, have more than one meaning and spelling. The prefix *ad-,* for example, may mean "to" or "toward." It may be spelled *ad-* (adjacent), *ac-* (acquire), or *al-* (allure), depending on the first letter of the root to which it is attached. The following charts show common Latin and Greek prefixes.

| PREFIXES FROM LATIN | | |
|---|---|---|
| **PREFIX** | **MEANING** | **EXAMPLE** |
| ab-, a- | from, away, off | ab + errant: wandering away from the right or normal way |
| ad-, ac-, af-, ag-, al-, ap-, as-, at | to, toward | ad + jacent: nearby<br>ac + quire: get as one's own<br>al + lure: entice by charm<br>as + sure: make certain or safe |

| | | |
|---|---|---|
| ante- | forward, in front of, before | ante + chamber: outer room, such as a waiting room |
| bi- | two, occurring twice | bi + lingual: using two languages with equal skill |
| circum- | around, about | circum + navigate: travel completely around |
| com-, col-, con- | with, together | com + press: squeeze together<br>con + cur: happen together |
| contra- | opposite, against | contra + dict: resist or oppose in argument |
| de- | do the opposite of, remove | de + activate: make inactive or ineffective |
| dis- | opposite of, not | dis + assemble: take apart |
| ex- | out of, outside | ex + clude: shut out |
| in-, il-, im-, ir- | not, in, into | in + animate: not spirited<br>im + press: affect deeply |
| inter- | between, among | inter + stellar: among stars |
| intra-, intro- | within, during | intra + venous: within or entering by way of a vein |
| non- | not | non + committal: not giving a clear indication of attitude |
| ob- | against, in the way | ob + stacle: something that stands in the way |
| post- | after, behind | post + script: writing added after a complete work |
| pre- | earlier than, before | pre + determine: decide or establish in advance |
| re- | again, back | re + organize: arrange or systematize again |

| | | |
|---|---|---|
| retro- | backward, back, behind | retro + spect: review of past events |
| semi- | half of | semi + circle: half of a circle |
| sub- | beneath, under | sub + plot: secondary series of events in a literary work |
| super- | over and above, more than | super + human: exceeding normal human size, capability |
| trans- | across, beyond, through | trans + atlantic: extending across the Atlantic Ocean |
| ultra- | beyond in space, beyond limits of | ultra + violet: a violet beyond that which is visible in the spectrum |
| vice- | one who takes the place of | vice + principal: person who acts in place of the principal |

**PREFIXES FROM GREEK**

| PREFIX | MEANING | EXAMPLE |
|---|---|---|
| a-, an- | without, not | a + typical: not regular or usual |
| anti- | against | anti + pathy: dislike, distaste |
| cata-, cat-, cath- | down | cata + comb: underground passageway or tomb |
| dia-, di- | through, across | dia + gonal: extending from one edge of a solid figure to an opposite edge |
| dys- | difficult, impaired | dys + lexia: disturbance of the ability to read |

| | | |
|---|---|---|
| epi- | over, after, outer | epi + dermis: outer layer of skin |
| hemi- | half | hemi + sphere: half a sphere |
| hyper- | above, excessive | hyper + tension: abnormally high blood pressure |
| para- | beside, closely related to | para + phrase: restate a text in another form or in other words |
| peri- | all around, surrounding | peri + pheral: relating to the outward bounds of something |
| pro- | earlier than, in front of | pro + logue: introduction to a literary work |
| syn-, sym- | with, at the same time | syn + thesize: combine to from a new, complex product |

## Practice Your Skills

### *Combining Prefixes and Roots*

**Find the Latin or Greek prefix with the same meaning as the underlined word or words. Combine the prefix with the root and write the word.**

EXAMPLE between + cede = act as mediator in a dispute
ANSWER inter + cede = intercede

**1.** two + lingual = using two languages

**2.** back + active = extending to a prior time or to conditions that existed in the past

**3.** half of + circle = half of a circle

**4.** against + toxin = substance that counteracts poison

5. with + league = associate in a profession
6. opposite of + continue = cease to operate or use
7. not + fallible = perfect
8. before + bellum = existing prior to a war
9. around + ference = perimeter of a circle
10. excessive + active = excessively energetic
11. after + mortem = occurring after death
12. beside + graph = distinct division in written composition, often shown by indentation
13. again + generate = form or create again
14. down + clysm = momentous event marking demolition
15. remove + moralize = weaken the morale of

##  Suffixes

There are two kinds of **suffixes.** One kind, called an *inflectional suffix* (or grammatical suffix), serves a number of purposes. An **inflectional suffix** changes the number of nouns *(computer, computers)*, the possession of nouns *(woman, woman's)*, the degree of comparison for modifiers *(soft, softer, softest)*, and the form of verbs *(care, cared, caring)*. An inflectional suffix does not change the essential meaning of the word or its part of speech.

A second kind of suffix is the *derivational suffix,* which is more important than the inflectional suffix in vocabulary study. The **derivational suffix** changes the meaning and very often the part of speech of the word to which it is added. Look at the changes the derivational suffixes make when they are added to the verb *observe*.

| | |
|---|---|
| WITHOUT SUFFIX | observe (verb) |
| WITH *-ance* | observance (noun) |
| WITH *-able* | observable (adjective) |
| WITH *-ly* | observably (adverb, *-ly* added to the adjective form) |

Some suffixes form nouns, some form adjectives, some form verbs, and some form adverbs.

| SUFFIXES | | |
|---|---|---|
| **SUFFIX** | **MEANING** | **EXAMPLE** |
| -ance,<br>-ence | action, process, quality, state | exist + ence: state or fact of being |
| -ard,<br>-art | one that does to excess | bragg + ard: one who boasts excessively |
| -cy | action, state, quality | normal + cy: state of being average or regular |
| -dom | state, rank, or condition of | free + dom: state of having liberty or independence |
| -er,<br>-or | one who is, does, makes | retail +er: one who sells directly to customers |
| -ion | act, process, result, state | react + ion: act of responding |
| -ism | act, state, or characteristic of | critic + ism: act of evaluating |
| -ity | state, quality degree | moral + ity: doctrine or system of correct conduct |
| -ness | state, quality | brisk + ness: state of being keenly alert and lively |
| -ure | act, process, function | post + ure: position or bearing of the body |
| -able,<br>-ible | capable of, fit for, tending to | expend +able: capable of being consumed by use |
| -al | characterized by, relating to | tradition + al: relating to the handing down of customs |
| -en | belonging to, made of | earth + en: made of soil or clay |
| -ful | full of, having the qualities of | master + ful: having the skill of a qualified worker |

| | | |
|---|---|---|
| -ic | having the character of | hero + ic: being courageous and daring |
| -ish | characteristic of, inclined to | clown + ish: having characteristics of a clown |
| -less | not having | purpose + less: lacking goals |
| -ly | like in appearance, manner, or nature | friend + ly: of, relating to or befitting a friend |
| -ory | of, relating to, producing | transit +ory: of brief duration |
| -ous | full of, having the qualities of | clamor + ous: marked by a confused din or outcry |
| -some | characterized by action or quality | burden + some: characterized by being a heavy load to bear |
| -ate | act on, cause to become | captive + ate: influence by special charm |
| -en | cause to be or have | height + en: cause to have increased amount or degree of |
| -fy, -ify | make, form into, invest with | spec + ify: make clear and state explicitly |
| -ize | become like, cause to be | character + ize: cause to be a distinguishing trait of |

Some suffixes can form more than one part of speech. The suffix *-ate,* for example, can be used to form verbs *(activate)*, nouns *(candidate)*, and adjectives *(temperate)*.

### COMPUTER TIP

Most word-processing programs have a *search* or *find* feature. By using this feature you can look for words or parts of words in your document. If you look up a root, such as *script*, you may find dozens of words with that root.

## PRACTICE YOUR SKILLS

### *Adding Suffixes to Words*

**Write the suffix that has the same meaning as the underlined word or words. Then write the complete word.**

| | |
|---|---|
| EXAMPLE | category + cause to be = classify |
| ANSWER | category + ize = categorize |

1. zeal + full of = full of eagerness and enthusiasm
2. convention + characterized by = relating to established customs
3. survey + doer = one who measures tracts of land
4. complicate + act of = act of making complex or difficult
5. serf + state of = state of being in a servile class in the feudal system
6. amalgam + act on = merge into a single body
7. lag + one who does to excess = one who lingers too much
8. flavor + full of = full of pleasant taste
9. pleasure + capable of = capable of gratifying
10. daunt + not having = having no fear
11. material + cause to be = cause to come into existence
12. sheep + characteristic of = resembling a sheep in meekness
13. break + capable of = capable of being cracked or smashed
14. orate + one who does = one who delivers a formal, elaborate speech

15. angel + having the character of = having the goodness of an angel
16. enlight + cause to be = cause to receive knowledge
17. gull + capable of = capable of being easily deceived or cheated
18. tire + characterized by = characterized by being wearisome
19. malice + full of = full of spite and ill will
20. bounty + full of = characterized by providing abundantly

## Roots

The **root** of a word may be well known in English, or it may be less obvious, having come from Latin or Greek. Sometimes a root may stand alone, as in the word *self*. A root may be combined with a prefix *(retract)*, a suffix *(portable)*, or even another root *(autograph)*. The following charts show some common Latin and Greek roots that are the basic elements of many English words.

**LATIN ROOTS**

| ROOT | MEANING | EXAMPLES |
|---|---|---|
| -aqua-, -aqui- | water | aquarium, aqueous |
| -aud- | hear | audience, auditorium |
| -bene- | good, well | benefit, benevolence |
| -cred- | believe | credential, credit |
| -cid- | kill | germicidal, insecticide |
| -fid- | faith, trust | bona fide, infidel |
| -fract-,<br>-frag- | break | fraction, refract<br>fragile, fragment |
| -grat- | pleasing,<br>thankful | grateful, gratitude<br>gratuity |

| | | |
|---|---|---|
| -loqu- | speak | eloquent, colloquium |
| -mor-, -mort- | death | immortal, mortuary |
| -omni- | all, every | omniscient, omnivorous |
| -ped- | foot | pedestrian, centipede |
| -port- | carry | portable, import |
| -rupt- | break, burst | rupture, interrupt |
| -scrib-<br>-script- | write | describe, prescribe,<br>inscription, manuscript |
| -sequ- | follow | sequel, subsequent |
| -tort- | twist | distort, tortuous |
| -tract- | draw, pull | traction, retract |
| -vert-,<br>-vers- | turn | invert, subvert,<br>versatile, reverse |
| -vic-, vinc- | conquer | victory, convince,<br>invincible |
| -viv, -vit- | life, live | survive, vivacious |

**GREEK ROOTS**

| ROOT | MEANING | EXAMPLES |
|---|---|---|
| -anthrop- | man, human | anthropology |
| -arch- | rule | monarch, hierarchy |
| -auto- | self | autograph, automobile |
| -biblio- | book | bibliography |
| -bio-, -bi- | life | biology, antibiotic |
| -chrom- | color | chromatic,<br>monochromatic |
| -cosm- | world, order | cosmic, macrocosm |
| -geo- | earth, ground | geography, geology |

| -gram- | drawing, writing | grammatical, program |
|---|---|---|
| -graph- | write | graph, typography |
| -log-, -logy- | speech, reason, study, science | catalog, monologue, bacteriology |
| -micro- | small | microfilm, microwave |
| -mono- | one, single | monopoly, monograph |
| -morph- | form | amorphous |
| -neo- | new | neon, neoclassical |
| -path- | suffering | pathetic, apathy |
| -phon- | sound | phonetic, telephone |
| -pod- | foot | podiatrist, tripod |
| -poly- | many | monopoly, polytechnic |
| -psych- | mind | psychology, psychic |
| -tele- | far off | telescope, telegraph |
| -therm- | heat | thermal, thermometer |

## Practice Your Skills

### *Recognizing Latin and Greek Roots*

**Write the root of each of the following words. Then use the charts of prefixes, suffixes, and roots to help you write the word's definition. Use the dictionary to check your work.**

EXAMPLE audible
ANSWER aud—capable of being heard

**1.** disruption
**2.** subscription
**3.** gratify
**4.** convertible
**5.** graphic
**6.** colloquial
**7.** transport
**8.** convivial
**9.** infraction
**10.** sequential

### *Using Roots, Prefixes, and Suffixes*

**Using what you have learned in this chapter, write the letter of the phrase closest in meaning to the word in capital letters.**

**1.** MERITORIOUS
(A) without value (B) having worthy qualities
(C) wise

**2.** COMPATIBLE
(A) capable of getting along together (B) in the manner of a friend (C) well qualified

**3.** EMANCIPATE
(A) obey a king (B) cause to become free
(C) win great acclaim

**4.** POLYCHROMATIC
(A) science of color (B) metal alloy
(C) having many colors

**5.** ILLOGICAL
(A) between reason and knowledge (B) within reason
(C) not valid, or without skill in reasoning

**6.** TRANSITION
(A) secret underground passage (B) process of going across from one place to another (C) loss of credibility

**7.** BIPED
(A) able to walk backward (B) bicycle
(C) two-footed animal

**8.** RETROGRESS
(A) lack of progress (B) in need of repairs
(C) go backward

**9.** COMMUNICABLE
(A) capable of being transmitted (B) full of unnecessary information (C) condition of being infected

**10.** RECOIL
(A) jump forward suddenly (B) draw back
(C) lose sight of

## Your Writer's Journal

Choose ten words from your journal list. Divide the words into their constituent elements: prefix, root, suffix. Define each word part. Then determine the meaning of each word by using the charts in this chapter. Use the dictionary to check your work.

# Synonyms and Antonyms

Another way of expanding your vocabulary is to have a thorough understanding of synonyms and antonyms. A **synonym** is a word that has the same or nearly the same meaning as another word. An **antonym** is a word that has the opposite or nearly the opposite meaning as another word.

There are often several synonyms for a word. For instance, among the synonyms for the word *candor* are *sincerity* and *forthrightness*. Notice that these words have slightly different shades of meaning. Dictionary entries often explain the slight differences between synonyms. You have probably also used the specialized dictionary for synonyms called a *thesaurus*. Usually a thesaurus is indexed to help users find the synonyms they need.

## Practice Your Skills

### *Recognizing Synonyms*

**Decide which word is the best synonym of the word in capitals. Check your answers in a dictionary.**

**1.** ADAMANT
(A) skillful (B) unworthy (C) unyielding
(D) distressing (E) faithful

**2.** INDICT
(A) accuse (B) show (C) imprison
(D) warn (E) release

**3.** ULTIMATE
(A) preliminary (B) substitute (C) rewarding
(D) eventual (E) concealed

**4.** NOTORIOUS
(A) legal (B) fortunate (C) unfavorably known
(D) unfamiliar (E) industrious

**5.** BESTOW
(A) discard (B) give (C) restore
(D) darken (E) lackluster

**6.** PREDATORY
(A) entertaining (B) tragic (C) corrupt
(D) preying (E) lackluster

**7.** LATERAL
(A) potential (B) upward (C) sluggish
(D) afterward (E) related to the side

**8.** ARBITRATION
(A) authority (B) mystery (C) concern
(D) mediation (E) treatment

**9.** BEGUILE
(A) deceive (B) begin (C) explain
(D) reject (E) learn

**10.** ARABLE
(A) feathery (B) fashionable (C) tillable
(D) windy (E) livable

## *Recognizing Antonyms*

**Decide which word is the best antonym of the word in capitals. Check your answers in a dictionary.**

**1.** FEASIBLE
(A) faulty (B) impossible (C) impoverished
(D) fatigued (E) insecure

**2.** ACCENTUATE
(A) de-emphasize (B) protest (C) regulate
(D) disagree (E) relinquish

**3.** ERRONEOUS
(A) mistaken (B) possible (C) skillful
(D) tardy (E) correct

**4.** VULNERABLE
(A) unsusceptible (B) cheerful (C) greedy
(D) ridiculous (E) modest

**5.** EMANCIPATE
(A) forget (B) strengthen (C) disallow
(D) enslave (E) forget

**6.** CYNICAL
(A) soothing (B) stable (C) trustful
(D) square (E) charming

**7.** OBLIQUE
(A) brilliant (B) questionable (C) direct
(D) passive (E) painful

**8.** ALLEVIATE
(A) forget (B) associate (C) persuade
(D) improve (E) aggravate

**9.** HERETIC
(A) villain (B) conformist (C) saint
(D) traitor (E) critic

**10.** EQUILIBRIUM
(A) disapproval (B) observation (C) hope
(D) imbalance (E) high pitch

## Your Writer's Journal

Look back over an essay or other composition you wrote earlier this year. Choose one paragraph to rewrite. Before you rewrite the paragraph, find synonyms for five of the words in the paragraph. Experiment with several different word choices before you make your final decision. If possible, use some of the words from the list you've compiled in your journal.

## Analogies

You will come across **analogy** items on standardized tests. Analogy items require you to identify the relationships between given pairs of words. While many kinds of relationships are used in analogy items, synonyms and antonyms are the most frequent.

HUGE:GIGANTIC :: (A) liberate:imprison
(B) noise:clamor (C) mature:juvenile

To answer this test item, you must first identify the relationship between the two words in capital letters. Those words, *huge* and *gigantic*, are synonyms because they have similar meanings. The next step is to find the other pair of words with the same relationship. Only the words in answer choice *B* are also synonyms, *noise* and *clamor*. The other two answers are not correct because they are not synonyms. *Liberate* and *imprison* are antonyms, and so are the words *mature* and *juvenile*.

## Practice Your Skills

### *Understanding Analogies*

**Read the first pair of words and determine the relationship between them. Then write the letter of the pair of words that has the same relationship as the first pair. Write *synonym* or *antonym* to identify the relationship.**

**1.** INFINITE:LIMITLESS :: (A) disorganized:orderly
(B) inaccessible:available (C) placid:calm

**2.** PURGE:CLEANSE :: (A) ornate:plain
(B) privacy:seclusion (C) impartial:biased

**3.** MALICIOUS:KIND :: (A) gaudy:flashy
(B) harmony:discord (C) adage:proverb

**4.** AUSPICIOUS:FAVORABLE :: (A) saga:epic
(B) retreat:advance (C) savory:bland

**5.** LUSTROUS:DULL :: (A) gobble:devour
(B) faultless:perfect (C) infallible:unreliable

6. CRYPT:TOMB :: (A) covetous:desirous
(B) dictate:obey (C) fictitious:factual

7. ORTHODOX:UNCONVENTIONAL :: (A) lament:mourn
(B) trinket:ornament (C) acquire:forfeit

8. SECLUDED:EXPOSED :: (A) parched:wet
(B) paraphrase:reword (C) rousing:lively

9. OBSCURE:OBVIOUS :: (A) brave:dauntless
(B) decrease:maximize (C) famous:renowned

10. TOLERANT:LENIENT :: (A) jovial:merry
(B) inopportune:convenient (C) hollow:full

### Your Writer's Journal

As you study the analogies, be sure to add unfamiliar words to your journal. Have you been able to establish the relationship between every pair of words? If not, write those unexplained pairs of words in your journal. Use a dictionary or thesaurus to help you figure out each relationship.

## Practice Your Skills

### *Creating Your Own Analogies*

**Select ten words from your journal. Use a thesaurus or dictionary to come up with a synonym and antonym for each word. You will now have ten pairs of synonyms and ten pairs of antonyms. Use these pairs to create your own analogies. When you are finished, trade with a partner and answer each other's analogies.**

**Time Out to Reflect**

Look back at an essay you wrote early in the year. How would the vocabulary differ if you were writing the essay now? What vocabulary skills do you need to work on the most? Record your thoughts in the Learning Log section of your **journal.**

# A Writer Writes

## About Your Future Vocabulary

**Purpose: to prepare you for the vocabulary you will encounter in your area of interest after graduation**

**Audience: your peers in class and in the area of your interest**

### Prewriting

Decide on an interest that you expect to pursue in the coming year. For example, if you are going to college, what will be your major? If you are joining the workforce, what will be your job? If you are joining the military, in what area of the service do you intend to find yourself? When you have decided on your area of interest, freewrite about the vocabulary that is used in that area. Include examples of jargon, idioms, and slang that you already know; while you freewrite, speculate about what the origins of this vocabulary might be and try to generate ideas for how you could learn more.

Use the Internet to find out more about your area of interest. Keep notes about all the new vocabulary words that you encounter. Also note new uses of common words. Consult at least five Web pages while making your vocabulary list. Try to have a list of between thirty and fifty words and expressions that are used in your area of interest.

When you have your list, use the dictionary and the Internet to write clear, concise definitions. Use each word and expression in a sentence and provide context clues to the meaning. Also write down the origin and etymology of the words and expressions.

After you have researched and defined the words on your list, contact someone within your area of interest and see if that person can also define the words. Ask that person if he or she knows of any other words or expressions that should be added to your list.

## Drafting

Organize your text by writing an introduction in which you explain what your area of interest is and why it appeals to you. Then examine the vocabulary you have been studying. Provide examples of how the vocabulary is used, what it means, and what its origins are. Employ precise language to communicate your research and ideas clearly and concisely.

## Revising

With a partner, read your vocabulary text aloud. When it is your partner's turn to read, listen carefully. Has your partner organized the content well? Is he or she writing in a voice and style that is appropriate to the audience and purpose? Is he or she using effective transitions to achieve coherence and meaning? When you offer feedback, do so in a clear, concise manner.

As you revise, make sure that you are producing legible work that uses accurate spelling and demonstrates your control over grammatical elements.

## Editing

Use the checklist on page C46 to edit your vocabulary text for spelling, grammar, usage, and mechanics.

## Publishing

Consider the following ways to publish your work.

- Prepare a class dictionary using your new vocabulary. Discuss what similarities and differences there are in the way language is used in your classmates' areas of interest.
- Create a Website to post the words and phrases from your class and encourage other people to post vocabulary from their areas of interest.
- Update your resume using the vocabulary you have learned.

CHAPTER 17

# Reference Skills

It may impossible to know everything, but almost anything worth knowing can be found in your library or media center. Libraries contain, preserve, and provide access to knowledge that has survived since the advent of the written word. In the library or media center you can learn from the great teachers in all fields. However, when embarking on the glorious quest for knowledge, it is advisable to take a compass. Research skills are a precision instrument to help you find exactly what you seek. In the past, browsing a library catalogue was like taking a leisurely walk in the garden. Today it is more like space travel at a pace approaching the speed of light. The Internet enables you—in a split second—to call up information that used to take all day to find. In this chapter you will learn the research skills needed to find your way quickly, effortlessly, and directly to relevant information on almost any subject imaginable.

## *Reading with a Writer's Eye*

Read the following selection from both the writer's point of view and the researcher's point of view. As a researcher, think about the resources Steve Parker must have consulted. How did he find his facts and information? As a writer, think about how he has shaped the information to help you understand electricity. How does the writer make the subject comprehensible and interesting?

# A MYSTERIOUS FORCE

Steve Parker

*Since the beginning of the universe, there was electricity. Even when there was no life on our planet, more than 4 billion years ago, great bolts of lightning lit up the skies. Lightning is one of nature's most dramatic demonstrations of the energy form we call electricity. As life evolved, electricity became a vital part of the living world. It forms the basis of a nerve signal. Eyes receive light rays and turn them into tiny electric signals that pass along nerves into the brain and the rest of the body. Our whole awareness and ability to think and move depends on tiny electrical signals whizzing around the nerve pathways inside the brain. In the past two centuries, scientists have gradually begun to unravel the mysteries of electricity. Their advances were often linked to progress in other areas of science. Following this scientific research came exploitation. Inventors turned electrical energy into our servant.*

## Ideas about Electricity

In the early days of experiments with electricity, scientists had no batteries to make electricity. Instead, they made it themselves by rubbing certain materials together. Around 1600 William Gilbert suggested there were two kinds of electricity, based on the material used to do the rubbing, though he did not know why this was so. Glass rubbed with silk made vitreous electricity, and amber rubbed with fur made resinous electricity. His experiments showed that objects containing the same kind of electricity repelled each other, while those containing different kinds attracted each other. Benjamin Franklin also believed that there were two kinds of electricity. He proposed that electric charge was like "fluid" spreading itself through an object. It could jump to another object, making a spark.

## The Quest for Knowledge

During the 18th century many scientists experimented with electric charge in their laboratories. As yet, there were no practical uses for electricity; what interested scientists was the quest for knowledge. They observed how electric charge could be seen as sparks, and how it behaved differently with different substances. Since electricity was invisible, instruments were needed to detect and measure it. Initially, progress was haphazard. There was no way to make a sustained flow of electric charge—that came later from the battery. Startling new discoveries were made that are now taken for granted. For instance, in the 1720s the English scientist Stephen Gray (1666–1736) proposed that any object which touches an "electrified (charged) body will itself become electrified." Charge transferring from one substance to another one that touches it is a process called electrical conduction.

## Collecting Electric Charge

Today, charge-producing electrostatic generators are an unfamiliar sight, confined to museums and research laboratories. These machines were designed to produce large charges and extremely high voltages. Charge-storing devices are vital components found inside many electrical devices, from washing machines to personal stereos. There are many different types of condenser, yet they all use the same principle as the Leyden jar, which was the first electrical storage container. Condensers, sometimes called capacitors, are the only electric devices, other than batteries, that can store electrical energy. They are also used to separate alternating current (AC) from direct current (DC).

## Using Charges

The dust resting on a television screen is an example of electrostatic attraction. The glass surface of the screen becomes electrically charged while the television is on. It then attracts and holds any floating specks which happen to come near. This phenomenon of electrostatic forces, where there is attraction by unlike charges, and repulsion by like ones, is put to work in a variety of modern machines and processes. For instance, in the body-painting shop of a car manufacturer, tiny droplets of spray paint are all given the same electric charge. They repel each other and are attracted towards the car's body, and so settle on it as a more even coating. This is exactly the same principle as the charge that amber, when rubbed, produces to pick up feathers.

## *Thinking as a Writer*

### Evaluating Information

- How would you describe the author's work? Is it informative? Lacking in information? Explain your ideas, along with examples to support it.
- Write a list of at least five specific facts the author includes in the selection.
- In which reference materials might the author have found the information? List your ideas and explain the information the reference supplied.

### Discussing the Use of Reference Materials

Oral Expression

- With a small group of classmates discuss the methods you have used in the past to research a report. What do you like and dislike about doing research?
- Discuss the reference materials that you find the most helpful. Explain why.

### Using Visual Information Sources

Viewing

The following illustration is from the National Lightning Safety Institute's Website at http://www.lightningsafety.com.

- Using the information in this illustration, write a brief paragraph about lightning safety.
- Use the Website to get more information about lightning safety. How is the information presented? How is visual information used?

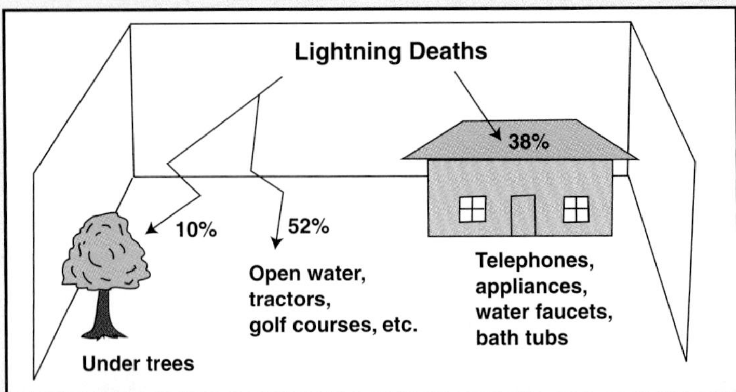

# Developing Your Researching Skills

In the excerpt from *Electricity*, you have seen how researching an article and becoming familiar with a topic enables you to write an interesting and well-crafted piece. With so many avenues of research to explore, applying your reference skills can be an enjoyable part of the writing process, and an exciting way to expand your knowledge about any subject imaginable.

When you are on you own a short time from now, where will you look for help when it comes time to buy a car, rent an apartment, or get a full-time job? A library or media center holds information that can help you handle many tasks throughout life. Now is a good time to become familiar with all of these resources.

**Your Writer's Journal**

Each time you see something that captures your interest, such as an article, a story, a poem, an advertisement, even a picture, save it in some way. Ideas can be found all around you—in family photos, the school newspaper, a flyer announcing a local event, a catalog in the mail. Record all your ideas in your writer's journal. Any and all of these entries could ultimately serve as jumping-off points for writing ideas.

## Using the Library or Media Center

The library is an unequaled resource for information and ideas. Books, magazines, newspapers, and pamphlets contain information on an almost limitless number of subjects. Most libraries also provide non-print materials, such as records, CDs, films, videos, cassettes, and computer software. Understanding the library's arrangement and the wide variety of resources available will help you efficiently locate the materials you need.

## Library or Media Center Arrangement

For many years the most popular system of organizing books was the **Dewey decimal system**. As library collections grew to include more than 30,000 titles, another system became necessary. As a result, the **Library of Congress system**, which can be used to classify millions of books, as developed. Today large libraries, such as those at colleges and universities, use the Library of Congress system.

**Dewey Decimal System** Most school libraries and media centers use the Dewey decimal system. In this system works of fiction, such as short stories and novels, are kept separate from nonfiction works. Works of fiction are arranged alphabetically by the authors' last names. These books can also be marked with the letters **F** or **Fic**. When searching for works of fiction, remember the following guidelines.

### Guidelines for Finding Fiction

- Two-part names are alphabetized by the first part of the name. (**De** Soto, **O**'Connor, **V**an Buren)
- Names beginning with **Mc** or **St.**, are alphabetized as if they began with **Mac** or **Saint**.
- Books by authors with the same last name are alphabetized by the authors' first names.
- Books by the same author are alphabetized by the first important word in the title.
- Numbers in titles are alphabetized as if they were written out. (40,000 = forty thousand)

In the Dewey decimal classification system, nonfiction books are assigned a number according to their subjects, as shown in the following chart.

| DEWEY DECIMAL SYSTEM | |
|---|---|
| 000–099 | General References |
| 100–199 | Philosophy and Psychology |
| 200–299 | Religion |
| 300–399 | Social Sciences (law, education, economics) |
| 400–499 | Languages |
| 500–599 | Natural Sciences (math, biology, chemistry) |
| 600–699 | Technology (medicine, inventions) |
| 700–799 | Arts (painting, music, theater) |
| 800–899 | Literature |
| 900–999 | Geography and History (including biography and travel) |

For each main subject area, there are ten smaller divisions. The following subdivisions show how the main subject *Literature* is classified by number.

| 800–899 LITERATURE | | | |
|---|---|---|---|
| 800–809 | General | 850–859 | Italian |
| 810–819 | American | 860–869 | Spanish |
| 820–829 | English | 870–879 | Latin |
| 830–839 | German | 880–889 | Greek |
| 840–849 | French | 890–899 | Other |

These subdivisions are divided further with the use of decimal points and other identifying symbols. The shelves are also marked with numbers so that books can be easily located.

The numbers identifying a book make up the **call number**. Every book has a different call number. In addition to the call number, some books carry a special label to show the section of the library in which they are shelved. Biographies, for example, are often marked with a **B** or **92** (a shortened form of 920 in the Dewey decimal system).

The following chart shows some other special labels.

| CATEGORIES | SPECIAL LABELS |
|---|---|
| Juvenile Books | J or X |
| Reference Works | R or REF |
| Records | REC |
| Audiocassettes | AC |

## Biographies and Autobiographies

Biographies and autobiographies are often in a section of their own. They are arranged in alphabetical order according to the name of the person they are about. Books about the same person are further arranged according to the author's last name.

### *Using the Dewey Decimal System*

**Using the list of classifications on page C753, write the subject numbers for each book. If the title is marked with an asterisk (*), also write the subdivision listed on page C753.**

EXAMPLE *Shakespeare's Imagery* *
ANSWER 800-899, 820–829

1. *This Chemical Age*
2. *Anglo-Saxon Riddles**
3. *Drawing Portraits*
4. *New Church Programs for the Aging*
5. *Basic Principles of Geometry*
6. *Twentieth-Century French Literature**
7. *The British Empire before the American Revolution*
8. *Guide to Philosophy**
9. *Greek Lyric Poetry**
10. *Principles of Political Economy*

**The Library of Congress System** This system differs from the Dewey decimal system in two main ways: it uses letters to identify subjects rather than numbers; and works of fiction and nonfiction are grouped together. The letters correspond to 20 main subject areas, rather than the 10 designated by the Dewey decimal system. The chart below outlines the 20 subject categories found in the Library of Congress system.

| LIBRARY OF CONGRESS SYSTEM | | | |
|---|---|---|---|
| **A** | General works | **M** | Music |
| **B** | Philosophy, religion | **N** | Fine Arts |
| **C** | Sciences of history | **P** | Language and literature |
| **D** | Non-American history and travel | **Q** | Science |
| **E** | American history | **R** | Medicine |
| **F** | U.S. local history | **S** | Agriculture |
| **G** | Geography, anthropology | **T** | Technology |
| **H** | Social sciences | **U** | Military science |
| **J** | Political science | **V** | Naval science |
| **L** | Education | **Z** | Library science |

These 20 main categories can be further divided by using a second letter. *QB*, for example, refers to the general category of science, with a focus on philosophy. Further subdivisions are made by using numbers and letters.

## Practice Your Skills

### *Using the Library of Congress System*

**Copy the book titles from the previous Practice Your Skills. Then, referring to the classification chart for the Library of Congress, write the first letter of the call number for each books.**

EXAMPLE *Shakespeare's Imagery*

ANSWER P

## Types of Card Catalogs

Most libraries or media centers have replaced their **traditional card catalogs** with online computer catalogs. Nevertheless, many still have both types of card catalogs. The traditional card catalog is a cabinet of drawers filled with cards arranged in alphabetical order. Each drawer is labeled to show what part of the alphabet it contains. All books, fiction and non-fiction, have title and author cards. Nonfiction books, however, also have subject cards and sometimes cross-reference cards that tell where additional information on the subject can be found. All catalog entries give the title, author, and call number of the book. Some may also give publication facts, indicate the book's page count, or show whether it contains illustrations or diagrams.

An **online catalog** is a computerized version of the card catalog, and it uses the same categories as the traditional card catalog. An online catalog, however, can locate information more quickly. Computer systems can vary from library to library, but generally the search methods are the same. You can search an online catalog by author, title, or subject. Authors' names are written last name first; for most titles, the words *A, An,* and *The* are skipped at the beginning of a title; and for subjects, enter the important words for each category.

On some systems, you can execute a keyword search, just as you would on an Internet search engine. A keyword search can sort through the library's collections by both title and subject headings simultaneously. The computer can tell you whether the book you seek is available or—if it has been has been checked out—when it is due back. By using the Web to search other library databases, the librarian can also tell you if the book is available elsewhere.

If your book is available, the computer displays an entry similar to that in the following example. Hypertext links enable you to move back and forth between sections of the catalog.

### ONLINE CATALOG RECORD

| | |
|---|---|
| **Call Num.** | D-18 5778 |
| **Author** | Miller, Arthur, 1915- |
| **Title** | The price; a play. |
| **Imprint** | New York: Harper & Row, c1989 |
| **Location** | Humanities-Gen Research |
| **Descript** | 116 p. 21 cm. |
| **Subject** | American drama -- 20th century. |

*To learn more about searching online see* Strategies for Using an Online Catalog *on pages C762–C763.*

## Catalog Entries

A card in the card catalog will tell you where to find a book, but it cannot tell you if the book has been checked out. If a book is not on the shelf where it should be, you will need to ask the media specialist to help you locate it. Although the card catalog is a more tedious research instrument, it is still useful. Both computerized and traditional systems provide the same information about a source, and both are equally precise. Most important, familiarity with the organization of the card catalog will make you a better online researcher.

The traditional card catalog contains cards for every book in the library. Most books have three cards in the card catalog: the **author card**, the **title card**, and the **subject card**. These cards are arranged either alphabetically or in separate file cabinets.

**Author Cards** The **author card** is often considered the main entry because it contains the most information. When you need a particular book by an author, look under the author's last name in the card catalog.

**Author Card**

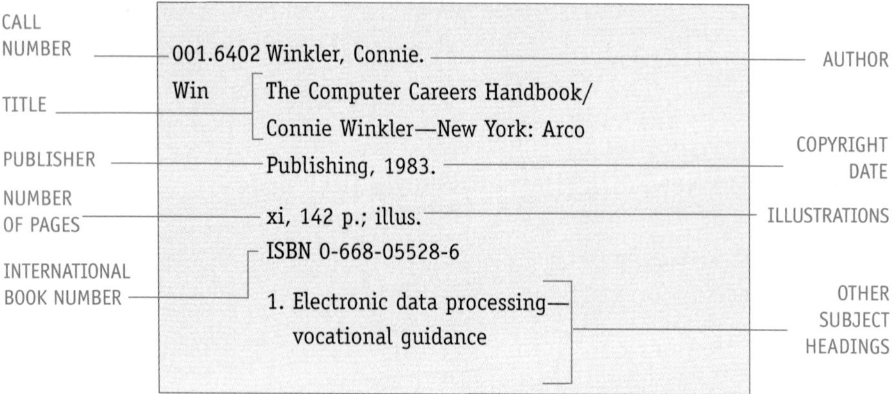


If you search for this author's name in an online catalog, you will probably get a list of several authors with the same last name. You might even get a list of several authors with the same first and last name. If the author wrote more than one book, you will see a full list of titles for that name. From that list, you can select the book you want, and you will see this information. The following entry is from an online search of the Library of Congress online catalog.

| | |
|---|---|
| LC Control Number: | 82018460 |
| Type of Material: | Book (Print, Microform, Electronic, etc.) |
| Personal Name: | Winkler, Connie. |
| Main Title: | The computer careers handbook/ Connie Winkler. |
| Published: | New York : Arco Publishing, 1983 |
| Description: | xvi, 142 p. : ill. ; 26 cm. |
| ISBN: | 0668055308 (pbk)<br>0668055286 (hard): |
| Subjects: | Electronic data processing—Vocational guidance |
| LC Classification: | QA76.25 .W56 1983 |
| Dewey Class No.: | 001.64/023 19 |
| Call Number: | QA76.25 .W56 1983 |

**Title Cards** **Title cards** list the title of the book at the top of the card. They are alphabetized by the first important word in the title.

**Title Card**

TITLE
CALL NUMBER
PUBLISHER
NUMBER OF PAGES
The Computer Careers Handbook
001.6402 Winkler, Connie.
WIN The Computer Careers Handbook/
Connie Winkler—New York:
Arco Publishing, 1983.
xi, 142 p.; illus.
ISBN 0-668-05528-6
AUTHOR
TITLE
COPYRIGHT DATE
ILLUSTRATIONS
INTERNATIONAL BOOK NUMBER



The following is what might appear if you ran an online title search for the same work. An online title search will lead you directly to a card that fully describes the book you want to find.

| | |
|---|---|
| LC CONTROL NUMBER: | 82018460 |
| TYPE OF MATERIAL: | Book (Print,Microform,Electronic, etc.) |
| PERSONAL NAME: | Winkler, Connie. |
| MAIN TITLE: | The computer careers handbook/ Connie Winkler. |
| PUBLISHED: | New York : Arco Publishing, 1983 |
| DESCRIPTION: | xii, 142 p. : ill. ; 26 cm. |
| ISBN: | 0668055308 (pbk.) : 0668055286 (hard): |
| SUBJECTS: | Electronic data processing—Vocational guidance |
| LC CLASSIFICATION: | QA76.25 .W56 1983 |
| DEWEY CLASS NO.: | 001.64/023 19 |
| CALL NUMBER: | QA76.25 .W56 1983 |

**Subject Cards** **Subject cards** are especially useful if you do not know the title or author of a specific book or if you do not have a specific book in mind. These cards are arranged alphabetically according to the first main word in the subject heading. Subject headings under history, however, are filed in chronological order.

**Subject Card**

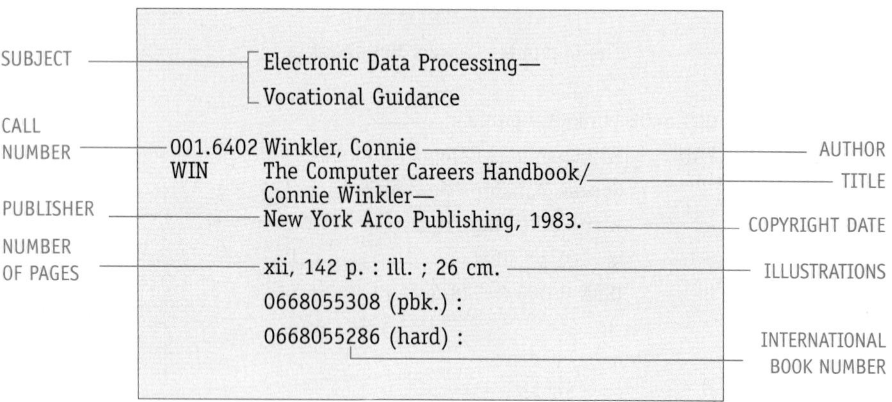


Online searches arrive at the same destination by different routes. An online subject search will lead you to the same entry produced by the title and author search.

| | |
|---|---|
| LC CONTROL NUMBER: | 82018460 |
| TYPE OF MATERIAL: | Book (Print, Microform, Electronic, etc.) |
| PERSONAL NAME: | Winkler, Connie. |
| MAIN TITLE: | The computer careers handbook/ Connie Winkler. |
| PUBLISHED: | New York : Arco Publishing, 1983 |
| DESCRIPTION: | xii, 142. : p ill.; 26cm. |
| ISBN: | 0668055308 (pbk.)<br>0668055286 (hard) |
| SUBJECTS: | Electronic data processing—Vocational guidance |
| LC CLASSIFICATION: | QA76.25 .W56 1983 |
| DEWEY CLASS NO.: | 001.64/023 19 |
| CALL NUMBER: | QA76.25 .W56 1983 |

Most card catalogs are alphabetized by word rather than letter by letter. For example, the entry *car safety* would come before the entry *Caracas*.

**Cross-Reference Cards** In addition to three cards for each book, the catalog contains "see" and "see also" cards. These are also called **cross reference** cards because they refer you to other listings in the catalog. A "see" card tells you that the subject you have looked up is under another heading. A "see also" card refers you to additional headings you could look up to find relevant titles about your subject.

Online versions of "see" and "see also" cards appear as text notes in the search results. When you enter a large category such as literature, the database will list in alphabetical order several subcategories. Cross-references appear when other search words are recommended. An online search under subject of *games* produces a list like the following, with cross reference cards to help you refine your search.

| | | |
|---|---|---|
| 1 | -- see also Amusements | 1 |
| 2 | -- see also Ball games | 1 |
| 3 | -- see also Bible games and puzzles | 1 |
| 4 | -- see also Bingo | 1 |
| 5 | -- see also Board games | 1 |
| 6 | -- see also Card games | 1 |
| 7 | -- see also Darts (Game) | 1 |
| 8 | -- see also Dice games | 1 |
| 9 | -- see also Dominoes | 1 |
| 10 | -- see also Dozens (Game) | 1 |
| 11 | -- see also Educational games | 1 |

If you are searching for a work that is part of a collection, an **analytic card** will help you find it. These cards are alphabetized according to the specific work you are seeking. They also, however, list all the other pieces contained within the collection.

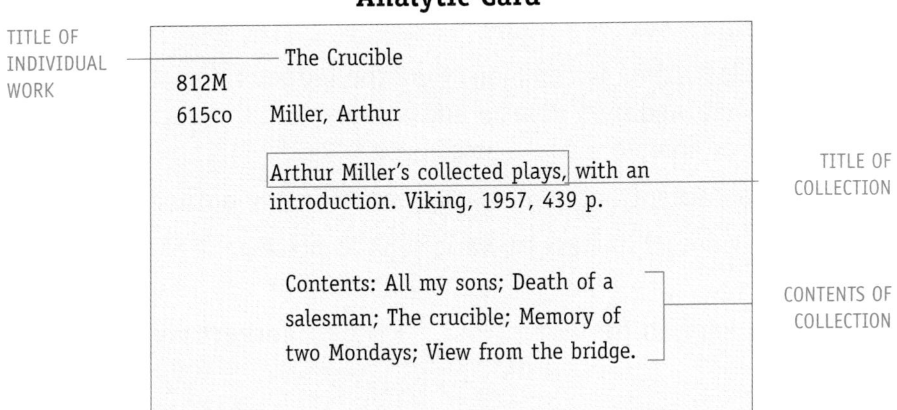

TITLE OF INDIVIDUAL WORK
The Crucible
812M
615co
Miller, Arthur
Arthur Miller's collected plays, with an introduction. Viking, 1957, 439 p.
TITLE OF COLLECTION
Contents: All my sons; Death of a salesman; The crucible; Memory of two Mondays; View from the bridge.
CONTENTS OF COLLECTION

## Strategies for Using a Traditional Card Catalog

- Think about the information you already have. Do you know the book's author? The title? The subject?
- Look for the book you want by finding the appropriate card.
- Read the card to determine if the book is likely to contain information that you need. Check the copyright to see how current the information is.
- In your notebook or journal, copy the call number, the title, and the name of the author (any information you don't already know), for each book you want to find.
- Use the call number, located on the book's spine to find each book. The first line of the call number tells you which section of the library or media center to look in. Then find each book on a library shelf by looking for its call number.

| | |
|---|---|
| F or FIC | fiction section |
| B or 92 | biography section |
| Dewey Number | nonfiction section |

## Strategies for Using an Online Catalog

- Think about what you already know that can limit your search. A title or author search will always give you more focused results than a subject search. If you are doing a subject search, find a way to limit the category, either by year or by subcategory.

**Searching by Author's Name**

- If the last name is common, type the author's complete last name followed by a comma and a space and the author's first initial or complete first name.
- Omit all accent and punctuation marks in the author's name.
- For compound names, try variations in placement of the parts:

**von karajan herbert** or **karajan herbert von**

**Searching by Title**

- If the title is long, type only the first few words. Omit capitalization, punctuation, accent marks, and articles.

  **bell for adano**

  **grapes of wrath**

  **plains trains and automobiles**

- If you are unsure of the correct form of a word, try variations such as:
  - spelling out or inserting spaces between initials and abbreviations,
  - entering numbers as words,
  - using an ampersand (&) for *and*, or
  - spelling hyphenated words as one or two words.

**Searching by Subject**

- Omit commas, parentheses, and capitalization.
- Broad categories can be divided into subcategories to make your search more specific.
- If you don't know the correct subject heading, find at least one source relevant to your topic by doing a title or keyword search. Use one or more of the subject headings listed there for additional searches.

**Searching by Keyword**

- Searching with a single word such as **Shakespeare** will find that word anywhere in the entry: in the title, author, subject, or descriptive notes.
- A phrase such as **space travel** finds entries containing the words **space** and **travel**. To search for space travel as a phrase, type **space and travel**, or **space adj travel** (adj = adjacent).
- An open search will look anywhere in the entry for your word. You can limit your keyword searches to specific search fields (either author, title, or subject) by checking the keyword menu and selecting the appropriate field.

## COMPUTER TIP

You can also limit your search by using the **Boolean** search terms (and, or, not).

**and** searches for several terms anywhere in the same entry

**or** searches for any or all of the terms in the same entry

**not** searches for the first term and will match the words only if the second word is NOT in the same entry

# PRACTICE YOUR SKILLS

## *Using the Card Catalog*

**Look at the catalog card below. Answer each question about it.**

| | |
|---|---|
| BW | Harlan, Louis R. |
| 2276 | |
| Ha | Booker T. Washington: the wizard of Tuskegee, 1901-1915 |
| | New York: Oxford Univ. Press, 1983. |
| | xiv 548p. |
| | ISBN 0-19-503202-0 |
| | 1. Washington, Booker T., 1856-1915 |
| | 2. Afro-Americans— Biography |
| | 3. Educators— United States —Biography |

1. Is this catalog card an author, subject, or title card?
2. Who is the author of this book?
3. What is the call number for this book?
4. How do you know that this book is a biography?
5. Who is the publisher?
6. Does this book contain illustrations?
7. Books about this subject are listed under what headings?
8. What is the book's copyright date?
9. What is the international book number for this book?
10. What do the letters *Ha* stand for in the call number?

### *Searching in Online Catalogs*

**Write the category you would use to search for each of the following items. Write what you would type into the computer catalog to search for each one.**

1. the life and times of Emilio Zapata
2. the books of Mark Twain
3. the skills of rollerblading
4. Sherlock Holmes stories
5. a history of writing
6. the castles of Germany
7. the poems of Nikki Giovanni
8. Mayan calendars
9. bicycling through France
10. falconry in India

## Parts of a Book

The first step in the research process is to find sources that can help you with your project. Once you find several sources, you need to spend some time looking through them to see if they have any information that you can use. Books have features that can make finding this information easier, if you know how to use the parts of a book effectively.

| INFORMATION IN PARTS OF A BOOK | |
|---|---|
| **Title Page** | shows the full title, author's name, publisher, place of publication |
| **Copyright Page** | gives the date of first publication and dates of any revised editions |
| **Table of Contents** | lists chapter or section titles in the book and their starting page numbers |
| **Introduction** | gives an overview of the author's ideas in each chapter and in relation to the work that other writers have done on the subject |
| **Appendix** | gives additional information on subjects in the book; charts, graphs, and maps are sometimes included here |

| | |
|---|---|
| **Glossary** | lists, in alphabetical order, difficult or technical words found in the book and their definitions |
| **Bibliography** | lists sources that the author used to write the book, including titles and copyright information for works on related topics |
| **Index** | lists topics that are mentioned in the book and gives the page numbers where these topics can be found |

## Practice Your Skills

### *Using Parts of a Book*

**Write the part of the book you would use to find each of the following items of information.**

**1.** a chart or graph with additional information
**2.** the name and location of the publisher
**3.** the title of a specific chapter
**4.** the name and publication information for a source used by the author
**5.** the year of publication
**6.** definition of a difficult or technical word
**7.** a specific topic or person mentioned in the book
**8.** the author's explanation of the book's contents

## Using Print and Nonprint Reference Materials

In most libraries and media centers, reference materials are kept in a separate room or area. Since these materials cannot be removed from the media center, a study area is usually provided. Following are some of the reference materials you may find most helpful in the reference section of your library or media center.

### Print and Electronic References

- general and specialized encyclopedias
- general and specialized dictionaries
- atlases, almanacs, and yearbooks
- specialized biographical and literary references
- online indexes to periodicals (including magazines, newspapers, and journals)
- CD-ROM versions of specialized encyclopedias, dictionaries, and almanacs
- microfilm and microfiche files of periodicals and government documents
- computer terminals with access to the Internet and World Wide Web
- audio recordings and video documentaries
- vertical file of print material

## Readers' Guide to Periodical Literature

Each year indexes help readers locate thousands of newspaper and magazine articles by naming the author, title, date, and periodical. Most indexes are arranged alphabetically by subject and author. The *Readers' Guide to Periodical Literature* is one of the most useful and popular indexes. It indexes articles, short stories, and poems published in more than 175 magazines. It is issued in paperback form once in February, July, and August and twice during all other months. The *Readers' Guide* can also be found in print form in the library stacks. Notice the numerous cross-references and abbreviations in the following excerpt.

COLLEGE EDUCATION

*See also*

Colleges and universities

**Costs**

*See also*

Scholarships and fellowships

State college tuition savings plans

Student aid

College daze. K. D. Smith. il *Money* v28 no11 p195-7 N 1999

Financing college 101. C. Tevis. il *Successful Farming* v97 no11 p66 O 1999

Your retirement or junior's tuition. D. M. Rankin. il *New Choices* v39 no9 p92+ N 1999

COLLEGE EDUCATION AND STATE

*See also*

Catholic colleges and universities—Laws and regulations

COLLEGE PROFESSORS AND INSTRUCTORS *See* College teachers

COLLEGE SCHOLARSHIPS *See* Scholarships and fellowships

COLLEGE STUDENT ACHIEVEMENTS *See* Student achievements

COLLEGE STUDENTS

**Admission**

*See* Colleges and universities—Admission

**Attitudes**

At the millennium, a student view [Columbia Journalism School students discuss 20th century journalism] il *Columbia Journalism Review* v38 no4 p57 N/D 1999

**Financial aid**

*See* Student aid

**Political activities**

*See also*

Student protests, demonstrations, etc.

**Protests, demonstrations, etc.**

*See* Student protests, demonstrations, etc.

**Psychology**

Smart enough to excel [address, September 9, 1999] C. Mariano. *Vital Speeches of the Day* v66 no2 p62-4 N 1 1999

COLLEGE TEACHERS

**Political activities**

Faculty protest proposed reform [Korea] M. Baker. il *Science* v285 no5427 p507 Jl 23 1999

COLLEGE TEACHERS AND STUDENTS

*See also*

Sexual harassment in education

COLLEGE TEACHING

*See also*

College teachers

The *Readers' Guide* online is organized like a computer catalog. Searches can be done by author, title, or subject, and for specific articles. If you entered the words *college education, value of* for a title search, a specific entry would appear. Once you select the entry, the following information will appear.

| | |
|---|---|
| NUMBER: | BRGA85037801 |
| AUTHOR: | Bellavance, Thomas E. |
| TITLE: | Measuring the value of a college education. address, May 11, 1985 |
| SOURCE: | Vital Speeches of the Day v. 51 (July 15 '85) p. 603-5 |
| STANDARD NO: | 0042-742X |
| DATE: | 1985 |
| RECORD TYPE: | art |
| CONTENTS: | feature article |
| ABSTRACT: | In an address to the Pocomoke (Maryland) High School Annual Honors Awards Dinner on May 11, the president of Salisbury State College discusses the worth of a college education. The importance of a college education is often discussed in vague platitudes. The measurable benefits—better job skills, higher earning potential, the road to middle-class status—are evident. The real value of a college education, however, is in learning to see and understand the complexity of life in all its forms. To an educated person, a simple tree can take on enormous significance, not only from a biological, physical, and even mathematical viewpoint, but in its poetic, cultural, and philosophical dimensions. The same analysis is even more critical when observing humans and human events. Ignorance thrives on simple |

answers; the educated mind has a wider view and more profound comprehension of life.

SUBJECT: College education, value of

Whether you search in print or online, once you know the name of the magazine or journal you want, you will still need to check the computer catalog to see if the library or media center has the specific periodical that you need.

## Practice Your Skills

### *Using the* Readers' Guide to Periodical Literature

**Using the *Readers' Guide* on page C768, write the answers to the following questions.**

1. What six subheadings are under the heading *College Students*?
2. Who wrote about financing for college?
3. Under what heading would there be articles about college scholarships and fellowships?
4. What are the titles of the three articles about college costs?
5. Which magazine published an article about a faculty protesting proposed reform?
6. Who is the author of the article "College Daze"?
7. What is the title of the article under the subhead *Attitudes*?
8. Name one subject referred to under *College Education.*
9. Under what other subject headings would articles about college students be found?
10. What is the article listed under the subheading *attitudes* about?

## Newspapers

The periodical reading room in the library or media center should have the most recent print issues of all its newspaper subscriptions. To save space, most media centers store older issues of newspapers as photographic reproductions on rolls or sheets of film. These materials are located in another part of the library or media center and can be viewed on special projectors.

*To learn more about using these archives, see* **Microforms** *on page C778.*

If a particular newspaper is available, a title search in the computer catalog will tell you where it is located—either in the reading room or on microform. Newspapers on photographic film are assigned call numbers that are listed in the computer catalog. A title search may also show you a hyperlink with an Internet address for the current newspaper's home page.

Most major newspapers now have Web sites and electronic databases where you can view current issues and search for archived articles. Online, you can also search databases that access the home pages of newspapers from every state in the U.S. and many countries around the world. Both of the sites below list hundreds of newspapers by location (country and state) and by subject (arts, business, trade journals, or college papers).

| | |
|---|---|
| The Internet Public Library | http://www.ipl.org/reading/news |
| Newspapers Online | http://www.newspapers.com |

An online news service can search the databases of hundreds of newspapers, periodicals, and other documents at the same time. Check with the media specialist to see if your media center subscribes to these news services.

| | |
|---|---|
| Lexis-Nexis | http://www.lexis-nexis.com/lncc |
| ProQuest | http://www.umi.com.au |

Remember: always read the guidelines at the home page for each newspaper or news service. Recent articles are usually available free of charge, but you may have to pay a fee to download and print an archived article.

## Encyclopedias

Encyclopedias provide basic information on just about every subject imaginable. The subjects are arranged in alphabetical order. Letters on the spines of each volume show which part of the alphabet that volume covers. A volume *Nel–O,* for example, would have information about the North Pole, the octopus, and the Olympic Games. Guide words at the top of each page show you at a glance which entries are on that page.

Some encyclopedias have a comprehensive index, either as a separate volume or at the back of the last volume. This index will help you find out quickly if your subject is covered, and under what headings. If it is not covered, it might suggest other subjects to look up. At the end of each encyclopedia article, you might also find a listing of additional topics to reference. For example, after the article on sky, one encyclopedia says, "*See also:* Astronomy, Horizon, and Light."

General encyclopedias include *Collier's Encyclopedia*, *Encyclopedia Britannica*, and *The New Columbia Encyclopedia*. Several general encyclopedias are also available on CD-ROM and online. These can be used to look up information just as you would with any other published encyclopedia.

| | |
|---|---|
| PRINT | *Collier's Encyclopedia*<br>*Encyclopedia Britannica*<br>*The New Columbia Encyclopedia* |
| CD-ROM | *Encarta Encyclopedia*<br>*The World Book Multimedia Encyclopedia*<br>*Compton's Interactive Encyclopedia* |
| ONLINE | http://www.encyclopedia.com |

**Specialized Encyclopedias** Specialized encyclopedias focus on a variety of specific subjects, from auto racing to weaving. Because they concentrate on a specific subject, these encyclopedias provide more in-depth information than general encyclopedias do. Some specialized encyclopedias include the *Encyclopedia of Chemistry* and *The Encyclopedia of Dance and Ballet*. These can also be found in the reference section of the library. Specialized encyclopedias online let you search for information by subject and connect to other Web sites on your topic through hyperlinks. The online *Encyclopedia Smithsonian*, for example, covers topics in physical sciences, social sciences, U.S., and natural history.

PRINT

*Encyclopedia of Mythology*
*Encyclopedia of Chemistry*
*The Encyclopedia of Dance and Ballet*
*The Baseball Encyclopedia*
*The Encyclopedia for American Facts and Dates*
*The International Encyclopedia of the Social Sciences*

ONLINE

*Encyclopedia Smithsonian*
http://www.si.edu/resource/faq/start.htm
The World eText Library
http://www.netlibrary.net/WorldReferenceE.html
*Includes: Arts and Leisure Encyclopedia, Techweb/Technology Encyclopedia, and the Britannica Internet Guide*

## Biographical References

Information about famous historical figures can be found in encyclopedias. To find information about contemporary personalities, you may need to use other biographical references. For example, *Who's Who, Who's Who in America*, and *Who's Who of American Women,* now published each year, have biographical sketches on people in popular culture that are not always found in an encyclopedia. Several online and CD-ROM resources, in particular, document the lives of women and African Americans in U.S. history, and some multimedia versions contains film clips and audio recordings of important historical events.

PRINT:

*Who's Who* and *Who's Who in America*
*Who's Who of American Women*
*Current Biography*
*Dictionary of American Biography*
*Dictionary of National Biography*

| | |
|---|---|
| | *Webster's Biographical Dictionary* |
| | *American Men and Women of Science* |
| MULTIMEDIA CD-ROM | *Her Heritage: A Biographical Encyclopedia of Famous American Women* |
| ONLINE | *Distinguished Women of Past and Present* |
| | http://www.netsrq.com |
| | *Encyclopedia Britannica Guide to Black History* |
| | http://www.blackhistory.eb.com |

## References About Language and Literature

The following reference works, which are usually shelved with the general works of the same type, provide information about language and literature.

| | |
|---|---|
| SPECIALIZED DICTIONARIES | *Webster's New Dictionary of Synonyms* |
| | *A Dictionary of Literary Terms* |
| SPECIALIZED ENCYCLOPEDIAS | *Cassell's Encyclopedia of World Literature* |
| | *Reader's Encyclopedia of American Literature* |
| | *Encyclopedia of World Literature in the 20th Century* |
| BIOGRAPHICAL REFERENCES | *Contemporary Authors* |
| | *British Authors of the Nineteenth Century* |
| | *American Authors 1600–1900* |
| | *Contemporary Poets of the English Language* |
| | *Black American Writers Past & Present* |

A handbook is another kind of literary reference work. A handbook explains literary terms, gives plot summaries, and describes characters.

A book of quotations can tell you the source of a particular quotation. In addition to printing the complete quotation, it will list other quotations about the same subject.

Indexes are useful references when you are looking for a specific poem, short story, or play. An index lists the books that contain the particular section you are looking for.

On CD-ROM, *The Columbia Granger's World of Poetry,* tells you where to find specific poems indexed by subject, title, and first line; and the *Gale Literary Index* contains information about authors and their major works.

| | |
|---|---|
| PRINT | *Bartlett's Familiar Quotations*<br>*The Oxford Dictionary of Quotations*<br>*The Oxford Companion to American Literature*<br>*The Oxford Companion to English Literature*<br>*The Reader's Encyclopedia*<br>*Granger's Index to Poetry*<br>*Ottemiller's Index to Plays in Collections*<br>*Short Story Index* |
| CD-ROM | *Gale's Quotations: Who Said What?*<br>*The Columbia Granger's World of Poetry*<br>*Gale Literary Index* |
| ONLINE | *Bartlett's Familiar Quotations*<br>http://www.bartleby.com/99 |

## PRACTICE YOUR SKILLS

### *Using Literary References*

**Write the name of one source listed above that you could use to answer each question.**

**1.** In what year did Leo Tolstoy write *War and Peace*?

**2.** Where could you find a short story called "Flowering Judas" by Katherine Anne Porter?

**3.** What American novelists were at work during the Civil War period?

**4.** Which poem begins, "The time you won your town the race"?

**5.** What does the term *picaresque* mean in literature?

## Atlases

Besides being a book of maps, an atlas usually contains information about the location of continents, countries, cities, mountains, lakes, and other geographical features and regions. Some atlases, however, also have information about population, climate, natural resources, industries, and transportation. Historical atlases show maps of the world during different moments in history. Some online resources from the United States Geological Survey incorporate satellite imagery to let you examine the geography of the United States by state and by region.

| | |
|---|---|
| PRINT: | *Goode's World Atlas*<br>*The Times Concise Atlas of the World*<br>*The World Book Atlas*<br>*Hammond Medallion World Atlas*<br>*Rand McNally International World Atlas*<br>*The National Geographic Atlas of the World*<br>*Rand McNally Atlas of World History* |
| ONLINE: | U.S. Geological Survey<br>**http://www.nationalatlas.gov/mapit.html** |

## Almanacs and Yearbooks

Almanacs are generally published each year and contain up-to-date facts and statistical information such as: population, weather, government, and business. Almanacs also provide historical facts and geographic information. *The Old Farmer's Almanac* provides weather and seasonal information.

| | |
|---|---|
| PRINT: | *Goode's World Atlas*<br>*Information Please Almanac*<br>*Guinness Book of World Records*<br>*World Almanac and Book of Facts*<br>*Collier's Yearbook* |
| ONLINE: | *The Old Farmer's Almanac*<br>**http://www.almanac.com** |

## Specialized Dictionaries

When you do research on a specialized subject, you often encounter a word that you do not recognize. You will find that specialized dictionaries can be very helpful. These dictionaries provide information about the vocabulary used in specific fields of study, like medicine, music, and computer science. Often, you can find online sources of dictionaries in several languages.

| | |
|---|---|
| PRINT: | *Harvard Dictionary of Music*<br>*Concise Dictionary of American History*<br>*Webster's New Geographical Dictionary*<br>*Dictionary of Science and Technology* |
| ONLINE: | English and foreign language dictionaries; and excerpts from *MLA Handbook for Writers of Research Papers*<br>http://www.dictionary.com.<br>*Strunk's Elements of Style.*<br>http://www.bartleby.com/141/index.html. |

## Books of Synonyms

A specialized dictionary, called a thesaurus, features synonyms (words with the same meanings) and antonyms (words with opposite meanings). This resource is especially helpful if you are looking for a specific word or if you want to vary your word usage and build your vocabulary.

| | |
|---|---|
| PRINT: | *Roget's Thesaurus in Dictionary Form*<br>*Webster's New Dictionary of Synonyms*<br>*Funk and Wagnall's Standard Handbook of Synonyms, Antonyms, & Prepositions* |
| ONLINE: | *Roget's Thesaurus*<br>http://www.thesaurus.com. |

## Practice Your Skills

### Using Specialized References

**Write one kind of reference work, other than a general encyclopedia, which would contain information about each of the following.**

1. newspaper articles about space shuttles
2. information about a senator's life
3. how ocean currents affect climate
4. pamphlet on obtaining a lifesaver's certificate
5. the meaning of the computer term *interface*
6. the highest mountain peak in the Himalayas
7. synonyms for the word *imagination*
8. pamphlets on windsurfing or board sailing
9. magazine articles about job opportunities in Alaska
10. college and university catalogs

## Other Reference Materials

Most libraries and media centers have a variety of printed materials that are not found in bound form. They also have other non-print resources such as audio recordings and video documentaries that contain information that cannot be conveyed in print form.

**Vertical Files** Libraries often store pamphlets, catalogs, and newspaper clippings alphabetically in a filing cabinet called the vertical file. Materials are stored in folders in file cabinets and arranged alphabetically by subject.

**Microforms** Many libraries and media centers save space by saving some documents and back issues of periodicals on **microfilm** and **microfiche**—photographic reproductions of printed material that are stored on rolls or sheets of film. References stored on microforms usually include past issues of newspapers, magazines, journals, and other periodicals; government documents from state and federal agencies; and original, historic records and papers.

These rolls and sheets of film are stored in filing cabinets in another part of the library or media center and can be viewed easily on special projectors. Newspapers, for example, are arranged in file drawers alphabetically by keywords in their titles. The holdings for each newspaper are then filed chronologically by date. For example, if you wanted to know what happened in Dallas, Texas on New Year's Day in the year you were born, you could go to the file cabinets and get the roll of film for the *Dallas Morning News* on that day in that year.

**Audio, Video, CD-ROM** Audiovisual materials and CD-ROMs are also available through your library or media center. Audiovisual materials may include recordings of interviews and speeches, and videotapes of documentaries and educational programs. CD-ROMs make it possible to include multimedia features like audio recordings and video clips along with text information. Many CD-ROMs also contain hyperlinks and working Internet software that allow you to connect to Websites with more information on each subject. The CD-ROM collection of your library or media center may include specialized references such as *Encarta* and *Compton's Encyclopedias* and specialized dictionaries such as the complete *Oxford English Dictionary*.

**Time Out to Reflect**

How do online references compare to some of the print resources you have used in terms of access, quality, and reliability? What new strategies have you learned that make researching easier? What notes would you make to help yourself do research in the future? Record your thoughts in the Learning Log section of your **journal**.

IN THE MEDIA

## Multiple Media Identities: Check Us Out Online

In addition to their primary medium, most large media corporations also have an extensive presence on the World Wide Web. The following are just a few examples.

| | |
|---|---|
| **Magazines** | |
| *Discover Magazine* | http://www.discover.com |
| *Time Magazine* | http://www.time.com |
| **Newspapers** | |
| *The Washington Post* | http://www.washingtonpost.com |
| *The New York Times* | http://www.nytimes.com |
| **Television Stations** | |
| The Discovery Channel | http://www.discovery.com |
| NBC | http://www.msnbc.com |
| PBS | http://www.pbs.org |
| **Radio** | |
| National Public Radio | http://www.npr.org |

### Analyzing Online Value

Each of the examples above would be worth using in research projects in its original medium. To find out what extra value, if any, the online presence adds, choose two of the references above and carefully research their websites. Write a paragraph for each one comparing the kinds of information available in the original and online versions and offering an opinion on the value of the Internet material.

# Developing Your Word-Search Skills

"Words are wise men's counters," noted the 17th century philosopher Thomas Hobbes, "—they do but reckon by them; but they are the money of fools." Such profitable wisdom begins with a knowledge and understanding of words. Whether you are a writer, speaker or reader, you should make the dictionary your faithful companion.

## Using the Dictionary

The dictionary is a valuable resource tool. As you read, the dictionary can help you define unfamiliar words. As you write, it can help you make accurate word choices. Whatever your purpose, the dictionary can usually provide the answers.

### Information in an Entry

All words listed in the dictionary are called entry words. Entry words are printed in heavy type and are broken into syllables to show how the word is divided. In addition to the entry word itself, the dictionary includes the part of speech of the word, other forms of the word, the meaning of the word, the history of the word, and often synonyms and antonyms. All of this information about each word is called a main entry. The following list shows different types of entry words and how they would be listed in the dictionary in alphabetical order.

| | |
|---|---|
| Single Word | mercy |
| Suffix | -mere |
| Prefix | meso- |
| Compound Word | mess kit |
| Abbreviation | Messrs. |

**Preferred and Variant Spellings** Some words have more than one correct spelling. The spelling most commonly used, called the **preferred spelling,** is the initial entry word in dark type. Less common spellings, called **variants**, usually follow the preferred spelling, as shown below.

PREFERRED SPELLING → **caddie** *also* caddy ← VARIANT SPELLING

## PRACTICE YOUR SKILLS

### *Finding Preferred Spellings*

**The words below have been spelled using the variant spelling. Look up each variant spelling in the dictionary. Write the preferred spelling.**

**1.** pilaff
**2.** cooky
**3.** sulphur
**4.** chlorophyl
**5.** dialog

**Division of Words into Syllables** Sometimes when you write an essay or report, you may need to divide a word at the end of a line with a hyphen. The dictionary shows the correct division of syllables for each entry word.

**re • sus • ci • tate** **ret • i • cence** **re • vers • i • ble**

**Pronunciation** Following the entry word is the **phonetic spelling** of the word, which shows you how to pronounce the word.

**in·au·gu·rate** (ĭn-ô′gyə-rāt′) *tr.v.* **-rat·ed, -rat·ing, -rates. 1.** To induct into office by a formal ceremony. **2.** To cause to begin, especially officially or formally: *inaugurate a new immigration policy.* See Synonyms at **begin. 3.** To open or begin use of formally with a ceremony; dedicate: *inaugurate a community center.* [Latin *inaugurāre, inaugurāt-* : *in-*, intensive pref.; see IN–[2] + *augurāre*, to augur (from *augur*, soothsayer; see **aug-** in Appendix).] **—in·au′gu·ra′tor** *n.*

A chart at the front of the dictionary contains a complete list of phonetic symbols. Most dictionaries also provide a partial pronunciation key at the bottom of every other page.

**PARTIAL PRONUNCIATION KEY**

| | | | | | | | |
|---|---|---|---|---|---|---|---|
| ă | **pa**t | ĭ | **pi**t | oi | b**oy** | th | **th**in |
| ā | **pay** | ī | **pie** | ou | **out** | *th* | **th**is |
| â | **care** | îr | **pier** | o͝o | **took** | hw | **wh**ich |
| ä | f**a**ther | ŏ | **po**t | o͞o | **boo**t | zh | vi**s**ion |
| ĕ | **pe**t | ō | **toe** | ŭ | **cu**t | ə | **a**bout, |
| ē | **be** | ô | **paw** | ûr | **ur**ge | | it**e**m |

♦ regionalism

Stress marks: ′ (primary), ′ (secondary), as in **dictionary** (dĭk′shə-nĕr′ĕ)



To find out how to pronounce the vowel sound in the last syllable of the word *inaugurate*, for example, find the symbol ā in the key. You can see that this *a* is pronounced like the *a* in *age*.

To distinguish vowel sounds, dictionaries place **diacritical marks** above them. *The American Heritage Dictionary*, for instance, shows two different ways to pronounce the letter *o*.

DIACRITICAL MARKS

ō as in g**o** ô as in **law**

All vowels can sometimes be pronounced *uh*. This sound is represented by the symbol **[ə]**, called a *schwa*. In the word *inaugurate*, for example, the third syllable contains the *schwa* sound.

SCHWA

ĭn-ô′gyə-rā t′

Phonetic spellings also show which syllables are stressed. A heavy accent mark, called the **primary stress**, shows which syllable receives the most emphasis. A **secondary stress** indicates a syllable that receives a lesser emphasis.

PRIMARY STRESS — SECONDARY STRESS

**ro · deo** (rō′dē-ō′)(rōdā′ō)

If a word can be pronounced in more than one way, the dictionary will show each pronunciation. The first one shown is the preferred pronunciation. In some dictionaries only those parts of an alternate pronunciation that differ are shown.

ALTERNATE PRONUNCIATIONS

**en · ve · lope** (ĕn ′ və -l ōp, ŏ′ )

Check the front of your dictionary to learn the phonetic symbols that are used.

## Practice Your Skills

### *Using a Pronunciation Key*

**The words in Column A show phonetic spellings. Match the spellings with the words in Column B. Refer to the pronunciation key on page C783 to help you.**

| Column A | Column B |
|---|---|
| **1.** fyo͞od′ l-ĭz′əm | **a.** pterodactyl |
| **2.** tĕr′ ə-dăk′ təl | **b.** pseudonym |
| **3.** so͞od′ n- ĭm′ | **c.** feudalism |
| **4.** sĭb′ ə-lənt | **d.** fustian |
| **5.** fŭs′ chən | **e.** sibilant |

**Parts-of-Speech Labels** Another helpful piece of information supplied by a dictionary is which part of speech the word is. The following abbreviations are found in a word entry that indicate the part of speech. Some words may be used in several ways. The most common usage of the word is usually listed first.

| PARTS-OF-SPEECH LABELS | | | | |
|---|---|---|---|---|
| | *n.* | noun | *v.* | verb |
| | *pron.* | pronoun | *prep.* | preposition |
| | *adj.* | adjective | *conj.* | conjunction |
| | *adv.* | adverb | *interj.* | interjection |

**Multiple Meanings** Many words have more than one meaning. Dictionaries will usually list the most common meaning first. Some dictionaries, however, may list meanings in historical order, showing the oldest meaning first.

Dictionaries also use labels to indicate differences in meaning. These are called **restrictive labels,** since they restrict the meaning of a word to a certain geographic area, a certain subject area, or a certain level of usage (informal, slang, etc.). Meanings also vary according to their parts of speech. The following is an excerpt from *The American Heritage Dictionary* entry that illustrates the various meanings of the word *quarter.*



**quar·ter** (kwôr′tər) *n.* *Abbr.* **q., qr., quar.** **1.** One of four equal parts. **2.** A coin equal to one fourth of the dollar of the United States and Canada. **3.** One fourth of an hour; 15 minutes. **4. a.** One fourth of a year; three months: *Sales were up in the second quarter.* **b.** An academic term lasting approximately three months. **5.** *Astronomy.* **a.** One fourth of the period of the moon's revolution around Earth. **b.** One of the four phases of the moon: *the first quarter; the third quarter.* **6.** *Sports.* One of four equal periods of playing time into which some games, such as football and basketball, are divided. **7.** One fourth of a yard; nine inches. **8.** One fourth of a mile; two furlongs. **9.** One fourth of a pound; four ounces. **10.** One fourth of a ton; 500 pounds. Used as a measure of grain. **11.** *Chiefly British.* A measure of grain equal to approximately eight bushels. **12. a.** One fourth of a hundredweight; 25 pounds. **b.** One fourth of a British hundredweight; 28 pounds. **13. a.** One of the four major divisions of the compass. **b.** One fourth of the distance between any two of the 32 divisions o... compa... One ... four majo... divisions of th... horizon ... min... fo... points ...

The last part of an entry is often a list of synonyms with an explanation of their different shades of meaning.

## Practice Your Skills

### *Recognizing Multiple Meanings*

**Use the dictionary entry for the word *quarter* shown on the previous page. Write the part of speech and number of the definition that suits the use of the word *quarter* in each sentence.**

1. The moon has shrunk visibly in this last quarter.
2. Would you lend me a quarter?
3. My grade in physics this quarter should be a B+, giving me an A- for the entire year.
4. Duncan Hooper won the basketball game by scoring twenty points in the final quarter.
5. Business for the Acme Shoe Company was brisk during the first quarter.

**Inflected Forms and Derived Words** **Inflections** are endings that change the form of the word but not its part of speech. Verbs, for example, can be inflected with the endings *-ed* or *-ing* to show a change from one principal part to another. Adjectives can be inflected with *-er* or *-est* to show degrees of comparison. Nouns can be inflected by adding *-s* or *-es* to make them plural. Dictionaries usually show these inflected forms only when they are formed irregularly.

**Derived words** are also formed by adding endings, but in such cases the part of speech of the word also changes. For example, adding the suffix *-ly* turns the adjective *hungry* into the adverb *hungrily*. Such derived words are listed at the end of a main entry.

**juic•y** (jo͞o′sē) *adj.* **-i•er, -i•est. 1.** Full of juice; succulent. **2.a.** Richly interesting: *a juicy mystery novel.* **b.** Racy; titillating: *a juicy bit of gossip.* **3.** Yielding profit; rewarding or gratifying: *a juicy raise; a juicy part in a play.* **—juic′i•ly** *adv.* **—juic′i•ness** *n.*

**Etymologies** The **etymology** of a word is an explanation of its origin and history. In an etymology, abbreviations are used to stand for the different languages from which a word has developed. Symbols are used to stand for such words as *derived from* (<) or *equal to* (=). A chart at the beginning of the dictionary lists all the abbreviations and symbols used in the etymology of a word. In the following etymology, the most recent source of the word is listed first.

> **pre·am·ble** (prē′ăm′bəl, prē-ăm′-) *n.* **1.** A preliminary statement, especially the introduction to a formal document that serves to explain its purpose. **2.** An introductory occurrence or fact; a preliminary. [Middle English, from Old French *preambule,* from Medieval Latin *preambulum,* from neuter of *praeambulus,* walking in front : *prae-,* pre- + *ambulāre,* to walk; see AMBULATE.] **—pre·am′bu·lar′y** (-byə-lĕr′ē) *adj.*



The etymology for the word *preamble* can be translated as follows: The word *preamble* comes from the Middle English, which came from the Old French *preambule*. *Preambule* came from the Medieval Latin word *praeambulum,* which was taken from the Late Latin word *praeambulus,* which meant "walking in front." *Praeambulus* was from the Latin prefix *prae,* meaning "in front," and *ambulare,* meaning "to walk."

## PRACTICE YOUR SKILLS

### *Tracing Word Origins*

**Use your dictionary to find the etymology of each word. Then choose one etymology and write its translation. (Use the example of *preamble* as a model.)**

1. bellicose
2. chromosome
3. forceps
4. geranium
5. guitar
6. hominy
7. menace
8. nightmare
9. philodendron
10. verdict

# A Writer's Guide to Electronic Publishing

Using the Internet, your local media center, plus E-mail and other research sources, you can gather an abundant amount of data to help you create a well-developed article or an up-to-date report. Once all your material is written and organized, the question you will want to ask yourself is, How can I publish my information?

Years ago, your options might have been limited to using text from a typewriter, photos and glue, construction paper and art materials. Today the world of electronic publishing has opened a world of options. Depending on the nature of your project, just some of the choices open to you include desktop publishing, audio and video recordings, and online publishing on the World Wide Web.

Each of these communication methods has unique advantages and drawbacks. Some media are more suitable to certain types of projects. For example, a visual topic, such as an article about bonsai trees, might be better expressed as a video. Reports with numerous facts, figures, and graphs might be better served in a document. An opinion poll in which many people are interviewed might lend itself well to an audio recording. And a subject that branches off into many different areas, such as a presentation about volunteer opportunities in your community, could be very effective as a Website.

Talk to your teacher to help you decide which publishing method is right for your project. Then let your imagination go and take advantage of all the creative possibilities electronic publishing has to offer.

# Desktop Publishing

The computer is a powerful tool that gives you the ability to create everything from party invitations and banners to newsletters and illustrated reports. Many software programs deliver word-processing and graphic arts capabilities that once belonged only to professional printers and designers. Armed with the knowledge of how to operate your software, you simply need to add some sound research and a healthy helping of creativity to create an exciting paper.

## Word-Processing Magic

The written word is the basis of almost every project. Using a standard word-processing program, such as Microsoft Word, makes all aspects of the writing process easier. Use a word-processing program to:

- create an outline;
- save multiple versions of your work;
- revise your manuscript;
- proof your spelling, grammar, and punctuation;
- produce a polished final draft document.

## Fascinating Fonts

Once your written material is revised and proofed, it's fun to experiment with type as a way to enhance the content of your written message. Different styles of type are called **fonts** or **typefaces**. Most word-processing programs feature more than 30 different choices. You'll find them listed in the Format menu under Font.

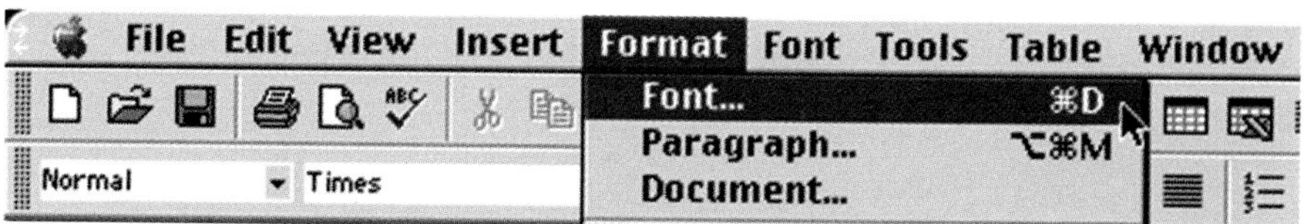

Or they may be located on the toolbar at the top left of your screen.

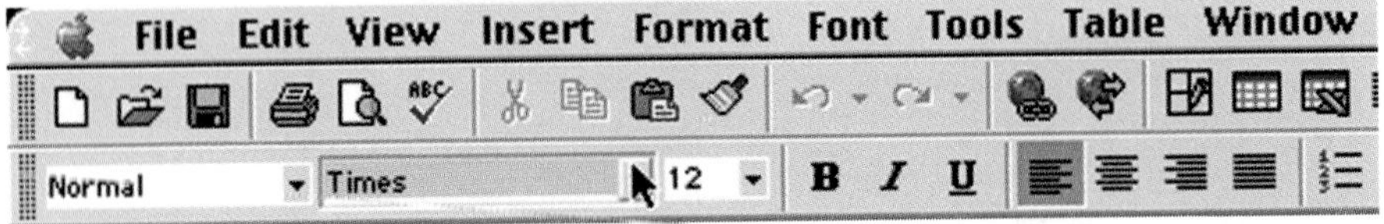


Although each typeface has its own distinguishing characteristics, most fonts fall into one of two categories: serif typefaces or sans serif typefaces. A serif is a small curve or line added to the end of some of the letter strokes. A typeface that includes these small added curves is called a **serif** typeface. A font without them is referred to as **sans serif,** or in other words, *without* serifs.

> Times New Roman is a serif typeface.
>
> Arial is a sans serif typeface.

In general, sans serif fonts have a sharp look and are better for shorter pieces of writing, such as headings and titles. Serif typefaces work well as body copy.

Of all the typefaces, whether serif or sans serif, which is best? In many cases, the answer depends on your project. Each font has a personality of its own and makes a different impression on the reader. For example:

> *This is French Script MT and might be fun to use in an invitation to a special birthday party.*
>
> **This is Playbill and would look great on a poster advertising a melodrama by the Theatre Club.**
>
> **This is Stencil and would be a great way to say "Top Secret" on a letter to a friend.**

As fun as they are, these three typefaces are probably inappropriate for a school report or term paper. Specialized fonts are great for unique projects (posters, invitations, and personal correspondence) but less appropriate for writing assignments for school or business.

Since most school writing is considered formal, good font choices include Times New Roman, Arial, Helvetica, or Bookman Antiqua. These type styles are fairly plain and straightforward. They allow the reader to focus on the meaning of your words instead of being distracted by the way they appear on the page.

One last word about fonts: With so many to choose from, you may be tempted to include a dozen or so in your document. Be careful! Text **printed** *in* multiple fonts *can* be extremely *confusing* **to read**. The whole idea of different typefaces is to enhance and clarify your message, not the other way around!

## A Sizeable Choice

Another way to add emphasis to your writing is to adjust the size of the type. Type size is measured in points. One inch is equal to 72 points. Therefore, 72-point type would have letters that measure one inch high. To change the point size of your type, open the Format menu and click Font.

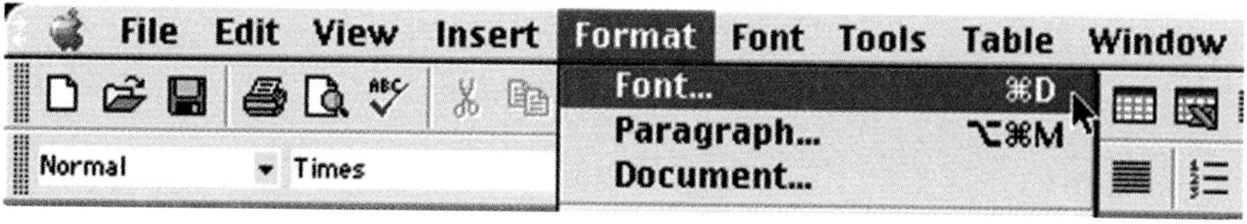


Or use the small number box on the toolbar at the top left side of your screen.

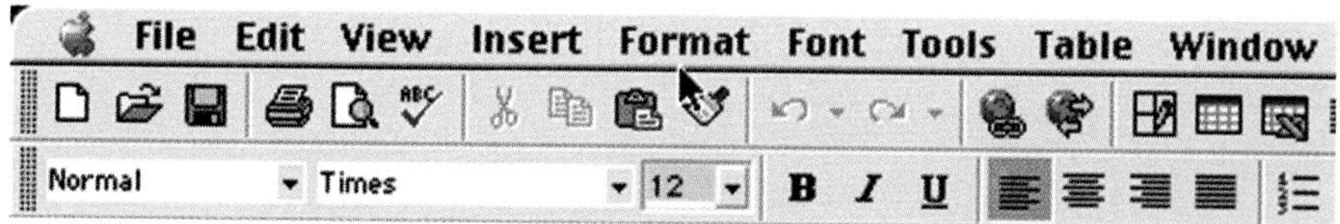


For most school and business writing projects, 10 or 12 points is the best size type for the main body copy of your text. However, it's very effective to change the type size for titles, headings, and subheadings to give the reader a clear understanding of how your information is organized. For example, look how the type in the subheading "A Sizeable Choice" is different from the rest of the type on this page, indicating the beginning of a new section.

Another way to add emphasis is to apply a style to the type, such as **bold,** *italics,* or underline. Styles are also found in the Format menu under Font.

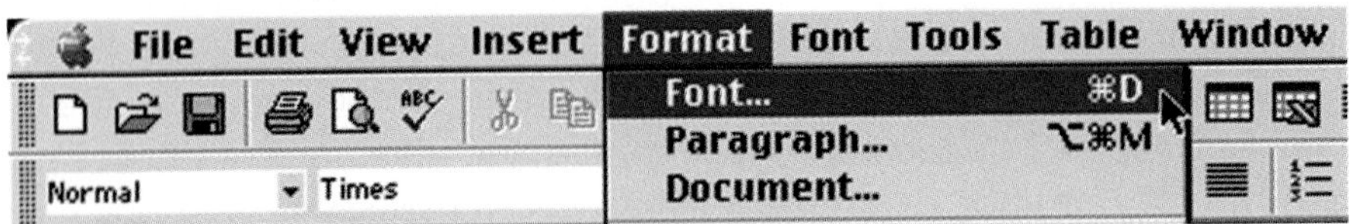


Or look for them in the top center section of the toolbar on your screen abbreviated as **B** for bold, *I* for italics, and U for underline.

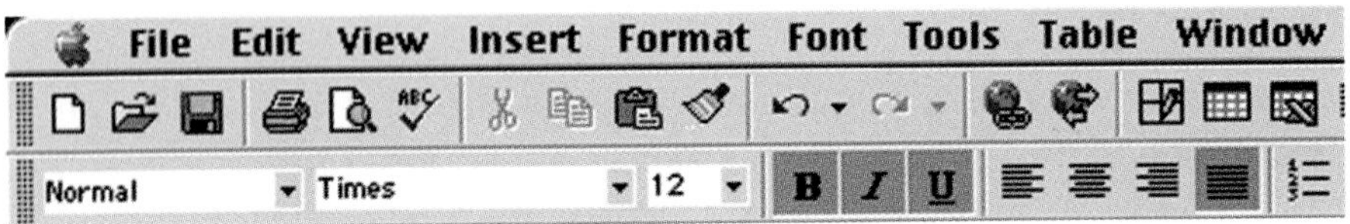


Here's one more suggestion—color. If you have access to a color printer, you may want to consider using colored type to set your heading apart from the rest of the body copy. Red, blue, or other dark colors work best. Avoid yellow or other light shades that might fade out and be difficult to read.

Like choosing fonts, the trick with applying type sizes, styles, and colors is to use them sparingly and consistently throughout your work. In other words, all the body copy should be in one style of type. All the headings should be in another, and so on. If you pepper your copy with too many fonts, type sizes, styles, and colors, your final product could end up looking more like a patchwork quilt than a polished report.

## Layout Help from Your Computer

One way to organize the information in your document is to use one of the preset page layouts provided by your word-processing program. All you have to do is write your document using capital letters for main headings, and uppercase and lowercase letters for subheadings. Set the headings apart from the body copy with returns. Then open the Format menu and click the Autoformat heading.

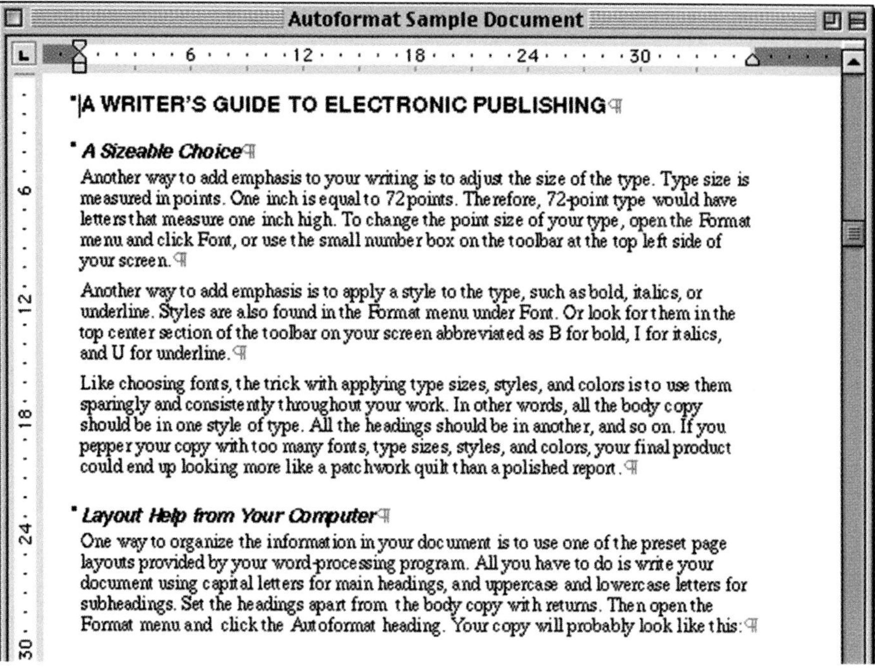
Autoformat Sample Document

A WRITER'S GUIDE TO ELECTRONIC PUBLISHING

*A Sizeable Choice*

Another way to add emphasis to your writing is to adjust the size of the type. Type size is measured in points. One inch is equal to 72 points. Therefore, 72-point type would have letters that measure one inch high. To change the point size of your type, open the Format menu and click Font, or use the small number box on the toolbar at the top left side of your screen.

Another way to add emphasis is to apply a style to the type, such as bold, italics, or underline. Styles are also found in the Format menu under Font. Or look for them in the top center section of the toolbar on your screen abbreviated as B for bold, I for italics, and U for underline.

Like choosing fonts, the trick with applying type sizes, styles, and colors is to use them sparingly and consistently throughout your work. In other words, all the body copy should be in one style of type. All the headings should be in another, and so on. If you pepper your copy with too many fonts, type sizes, styles, and colors, your final product could end up looking more like a patchwork quilt than a polished report.

*Layout Help from Your Computer*

One way to organize the information in your document is to use one of the preset page layouts provided by your word-processing program. All you have to do is write your document using capital letters for main headings, and uppercase and lowercase letters for subheadings. Set the headings apart from the body copy with returns. Then open the Format menu and click the Autoformat heading. Your copy will probably look like this:

This automatic, preset format is probably fine for most of the writing you do in school. You'll also find other options available in the File menu under Page Setup.

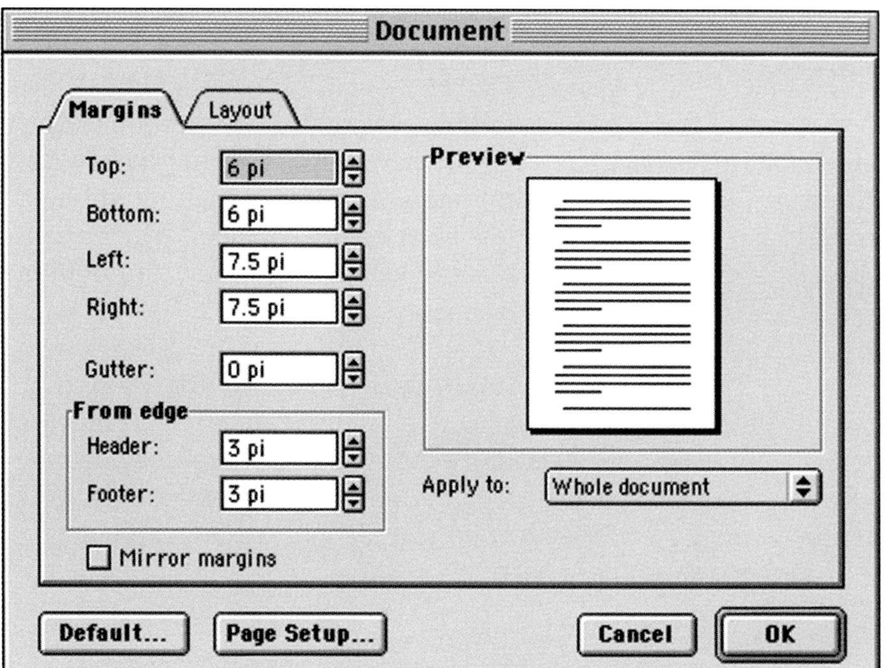

Here you can change the margins and add headers, footers, and page numbers. **Headers** and **footers** are descriptive titles that automatically appear at the top or bottom of each page without having to retype them each time. For example, you may wish to add the title of your project and the date as a header or footer to each page.

Header
Project Title Here¶
Date Here¶

## Let's Get Graphic

The old saying, "A picture is worth a thousand words" is particularly true when it comes to spicing up papers and reports. Desktop publishing programs (such as Adobe PhotoDeluxe Home Edition, Macromedia FreeHand, Microsoft PhotoDraw, and Microsoft PowerPoint) give you the ability to include photographs, illustrations, and charts in your work that can express your ideas more clearly and succinctly than words alone.

The key to using graphics effectively is to make sure each one conveys a message of importance. Don't use them just for decoration. Be sure they add something meaningful, or you'll actually detract from your written message.

**Drawings** Many paint and draw programs allow you to create or **import** (bring in from another program) an illustration into your document. Drawings can help illustrate concepts that are difficult to describe, such as mechanical parts or procedures. Cartoons can also add a nice touch. If you use them sparingly, they can lighten up an otherwise dry, technical report.

**Clip Art** Another kind of drawing is called **clip art.** These simple, black-and-white or color line pictures are often included in desktop publishing or word-processing programs. Pre-drawn clip art usually is not very good for illustrative purposes, but it does work well as graphic icons that can help guide your reader through various parts of a long report.

For example, suppose you are writing a report on the top arts programs in the United States. You might choose the following clip art for each of the sections.

When you introduce the section of your report that deals with music, you might use the music icon at the large size pictured above. Then, in the headers of all the following sections that deal with music, you might use a smaller version of the icon that looks like this:

Using clip art as icons in this manner lets your reader know at a glance which part of the report they are reading.

**Charts and Graphs** If your project, or part of your project, deals with comparing numbers and statistics, one of the best ways to communicate this information is by using charts and graphs. Programs such as Microsoft PowerPoint allow you to create bar graphs, pie charts, and line graphs that can communicate fractions, figures, and comparative measurements much more powerfully than written descriptions.

**Photographs** When you flip quickly through a book or a magazine, what catches your eye? Probably photographs. Most of us are naturally curious and want to see what we are reading about. Photos are the perfect companions to written work. With the widespread availability of digital cameras and scanners, adding photos to your project is an easy and effective way to enhance your content.

Using a digital camera or a scanner, you can load photos directly into your computer. Another option is to shoot photographs with a regular camera, but when you have them developed, specify that they be returned to you as "pictures on disc," which you can open on your computer screen.

Photographic images are stored as bits of data in an electronic file. Once you have the photos in your computer, you can use a graphics program such as Adobe PhotoDeluxe Home Edition to manipulate the images in a variety of ways and create amazing visual effects. You can crop elements out of the photo, add special filters and colors, combine elements of two different pictures into one—the possibilities are endless.

After you have inserted the edited photo into your document, be careful when you print out your final draft. Standard printers often don't reproduce photographs well. You may want to take your document on disc to a professional printing company and have it printed out on a high-resolution printer to make sure you get the best quality.

**Captions and Titles** While it's true that a single photo can say a great deal, some pictures still need a little explanation in order to have the strongest impact on your reader. Whenever you include an illustration or photograph in a document, also include a simple caption or title for each image.

Add captions in a slightly smaller type size than the body copy and preferably in a sans serif typeface. Use the caption to add information that isn't immediately apparent in the photo. If there are people in the picture, tell us who they are. If the photo features an odd-looking structure, tell us what it is. Be smart with your captions. Don't tell the reader the obvious. Give him or her a reason to read your caption.

For example, suppose you are doing a report about Mt. Everest and you include a dramatic photo of its snowy peak.

| | |
|---|---|
| WEAK CAPTION | The summit of Mt. Everest is very high and treacherous. |
| STRONG CAPTION | At its summit, Mt. Everest soars to 29,028 feet, making it the tallest mountain in the world. |

If you were preparing a travel brochure about Venice, Italy, to present to your class you might research Venice's history and points of interest. After preparing the text, you decide to include a few photos to convey to the reader the beauty of Venice. Which of the two photos conveys information to the reader that is insightful and interesting?

Flowers adorn this Venetian apartment's window.

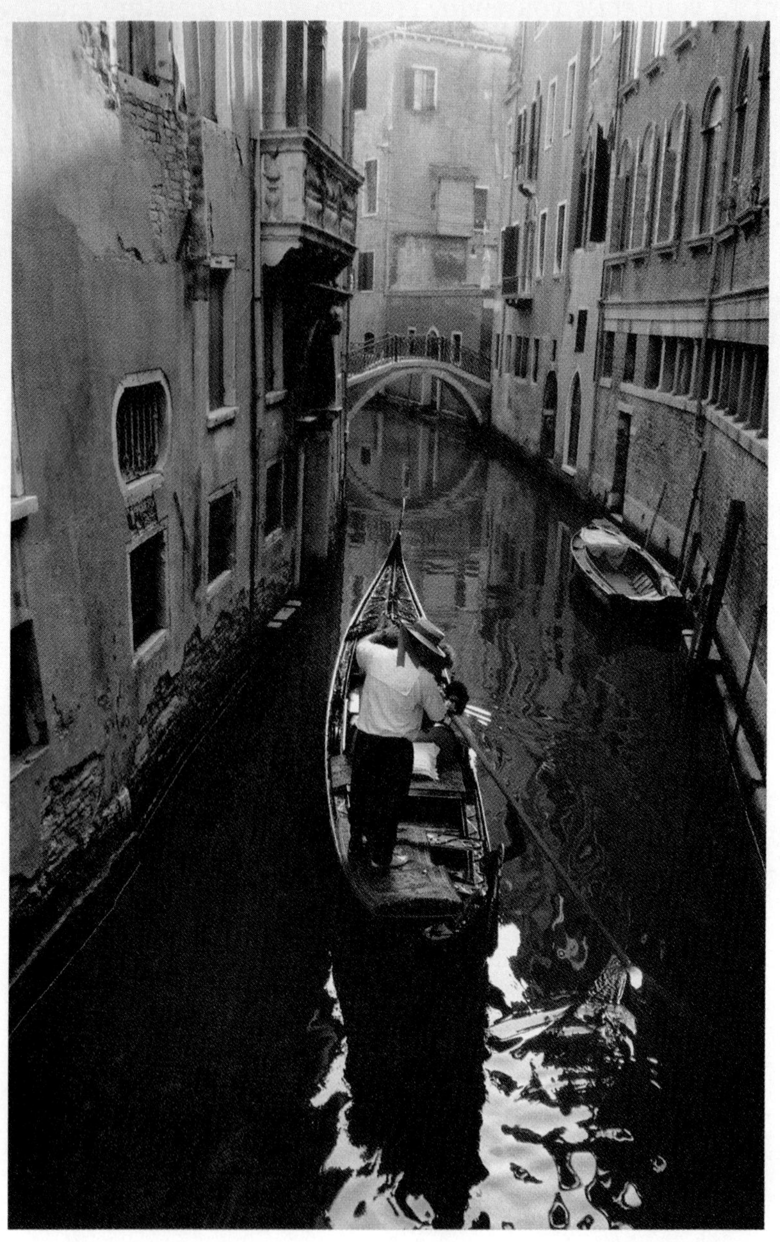

The lock gates, which were invented by Leonardo da Vinci in 1495, still control the water levels in Venice's canals today.

**Stand-Alone Graphics** Occasionally you may include well-known graphics or logos in a story or report. These graphics convey powerful messages on their own and don't require captions. Examples of these logos or symbols include:

# Nonprint Media—Audio and Video

The world we live in is becoming increasingly more multimedia-savvy. The power of the spoken word and the visual image is widely recognized for the impact it carries. Many businesses rely extensively on multimedia presentations to market their products or convey messages to consumers and employees. Exciting opportunities exist for people who can produce clear, concise messages in audio and visual formats.

## Pre-production—Put It on Paper First

Although the final presentation of your subject material may be an audiotape or a video, your project needs to begin on paper first. When you write down your ideas, you do four things.

- Organize your thoughts.
- Narrow your focus.
- Isolate the main messages.
- Identify possible production problems.

Grabbing a tape recorder or camcorder and then running off to record your project is a sure-fire way to create an unorganized mess. This helter-skelter collection of shots and sound bites probably takes hours longer to unravel and fix than if you had taken the time to plan your production in the first place. Resist the urge to jump right in! You'll be glad you did.

**Concept Outline** The first task in the writing process is a short, one-page document that describes the basic idea of the project. Ideally this should be three paragraphs—one paragraph each describing the beginning, the middle, and the end. Do not go forward until you have clearly identified these three important parts of your project.

**Brief** Next ask yourself, What is the purpose of this video or audiotape? Who is the audience? What is the result you hope to achieve when this group of people sees or hears your presentation? Do you want them to be informed about something? Motivated to do something? Emotionally moved in some way? Or excited about something? Write one to two pages that describe in detail the point of your project: how it will be used, who the intended audience is, and what you hope to achieve with the presentation.

**Treatment** The next phase of the writing process fleshes out the ideas you expressed in your outline and brief. The treatment is several pages long. It contains descriptions of the characters, dialogue, and settings, and describes the presentation scene by scene in order of how it will appear. Include in your treatment descriptions of the mood and the tone of your piece. Is it upbeat and whimsical, or dark and ominous? If your project is a video, set the stage by describing the overall look and feel of the production.

**Script** Once you've completed the first three steps, you are ready to go to script. The script is the blueprint for your production, similar to a blueprint for a house. Everything that is mentioned in the script is what will wind up in the audio recording or on the screen. Conversely anything that is left out of the script will likely be overlooked and omitted from the final production. So, write this document carefully.

For an audio recording, the script contains all narration, dialogue, music, and sound effects. For a videotape, it contains all of these elements plus descriptions of the characters, any sets, props, or costumes, plus all camera shots and movements, special visual effects, and onscreen titles or graphic elements. In short the audio script encompasses everything that is heard, and the video script covers everything that is seen and heard.

**Storyboard** Last, for video productions, it's also helpful to create storyboards—simple frame-by-frame sketches with explanatory notes jotted underneath—that paint a visual picture of what the video will look like from start to finish.

The final stages of pre-production include assembling all of the elements you will need before you begin recording your audiotape or shooting your video. Here's a general checklist.

### Pre-production Checklist

**Audiotape Tasks**

- ✓ Arrange for audio recording equipment
- ✓ Cast narrator/actors
- ✓ Find music (secure permission)
- ✓ Arrange for sound effects
- ✓ Set up recording schedule
- ✓ Coordinate all cast and crew
- ✓ Arrange for transportation if needed
- ✓ Rehearse all voice talent

**Videotape Tasks**

- ✓ Arrange for video equipment (including lighting and sound recording equipment)
- ✓ Cast narrator/host/actors
- ✓ Find music (secure permission)
- ✓ Arrange for sound/visual effects
- ✓ Set up shooting schedule
- ✓ Coordinate all cast and crew
- ✓ Arrange for transportation if needed
- ✓ Set up shooting locations (secure permission)
- ✓ Arrange for costumes, props, sets
- ✓ Arrange for make-up if needed
- ✓ Rehearse all on-camera talent

**Video Production Schedule** Tucked into the list of pre-production tasks is "Set up recording/shooting schedule." For videotaping, this means much more than just deciding what day and time you will begin shooting.

During the video production phase of your project, the idea is to shoot everything that your script calls for in the final production. Often the most efficient way to do this is what is called "out-of-sequence" filming. This means that, rather than shoot scenes sequentially (that is, in the order that they appear in the script), you shoot them in the order that is most convenient. Later you will edit them together in the correct order in post-production.

For example, your video might begin and end in the main character's office. Rather than shoot the first office scene, then move the cast and crew to the next location, then later at the end of the day return to the office, it might be easier to shoot both office scenes back-to-back. This will save a great deal of time and effort of moving people, lights, and props back and forth.

Lighting may be a factor in the order in which you shoot your scenes. For example, scenes 3, 4, and 7 may take place in the daytime, and scenes 1, 2, 5, and 6 may take place at night.

To accommodate all of these factors, you will need to plan your shooting schedule carefully. The difference between a smooth shoot day and chaos is a well thought-out shooting schedule.

Last, for video or audio recording, it's also a good idea to assemble your team for a pre-production meeting before you begin. This is your chance to read through the script together, go over time schedules, review responsibilities of each person involved, plus answer any questions or discuss potential problems *before* you begin rolling tape. Pre-production meetings are worth their weight in gold for reducing stress levels and headaches during production!

## Production—We're Rolling!

At last, you've completed all your preparation. Now it's time to roll tape!

**Audio Production** The better the recording equipment, the higher-quality sound recording you will be able to achieve. The most convenient format for student audio recording is the audiocassette—a high-quality tape in a plastic case that you simply drop inside your cassette recorder.

The forerunner of the audiocassette was reel-to-reel tape in which audiotape was threaded through a recording machine from one reel to another. This format is still used in some recording studios, although recording on CDs—compact discs—has become increasingly common.

Most professional recording facilities record on DAT—digital audiotape. DAT provides the cleanest, highest-quality sound of all, but the equipment is still quite expensive and limited usually to professional recording situations.

If you are using an audiocassette recorder, use an external microphone rather than the built-in microphone on the tape recorder for best results. To ensure the quality of your production, do the following:

- Select a high-quality, low-noise tape stock.
- Choose a quiet place to do your recording. Look for a quiet room with carpeting, soft furniture, and a door you can close firmly. Hang a sign outside the door that says, "Quiet Please—Recording in Progress" so you will not be disturbed in the middle of your session.
- Do a voice check before you begin recording so you know whether the sound level on the recorder is set correctly.
- Lay the script pages out side-by-side to eliminate the rustling sound of turning pages.
- If music is part of your production, cue up the correct cut and practice turning it on and fading the volume up and down at the appropriate parts. Do a sound check on the music volume before you start. Do the same with any sound effects.

**Video Production** As with audio recording, there are a number of different formats to choose from for video recording. Some of the more common ones include those listed on the following page.

### Video Recording Formats

| | |
|---|---|
| **VHS** | A full-sized tape machine that produces moderate quality video. The camera is large, heavy, and requires some skill to operate effectively. |
| **VHSC** | A compact version of the VHS model. The camera is easier to hold and use. You will need a special adapter to play the tape back on a standard VCR tape player. |
| **Super VHS** | A format that produces excellent picture and sound quality, but is very expensive to buy or rent. Super VHS cannot be played on a standard VCR tape machine. |
| **Super VHSC** | A compact version of Super VHS. |
| **Video 8** | A format sometimes referred to as a camcorder. The Video 8 shoots 8-millimeter videotape. It produces a good quality picture and hi-fi sound. With special cable attachments, you can play the tape back through your VCR or television. |
| **High 8** | A compact and lightweight format. High 8 is substantially more expensive than Video 8, but the quality of sound and picture is excellent. High 8 video can be played back on a TV or VCR using special cable attachments. |
| **Betacam** | A professional standard video that delivers top-quality sound and picture. Most news crews shoot Betacam video. Betacam tape can only be played back on a Betacam tape deck. |

Ideally you will have ironed out issues regarding shooting sequence when you wrote your production schedule back in the pre-production phase. This will leave you free during production to focus on your production values, your camera shots, and your actors' performances.

**Production value** is another way of saying how polished and professional your project turns out. There are many ways to increase the production value of your presentation. Some of the easiest include the following:

- Use a tripod to keep the camera steady. Nothing screams "Amateur!" louder than shaky, hand-held camera shots. If you can't get your hands on a tripod, lean against something sturdy, such as a tree or the side of a car, to keep your subjects from bouncing around in the frame.

- Use sufficient light. If your audience can't see what's happening, they will quickly lose interest in your show. The best way to light a subject is from one side at a 45-degree angle with the light shining in a downward direction. Supplement this with a slightly less powerful light from the other side and even from behind your subject to avoid unsightly shadows.
- Check your focus frequently. Don't wait until your entire production is nearly finished to check whether the shots are clear. Sometimes the manual focus on some cameras is more reliable than the auto-focus feature. Experiment with your camera using both methods *before* your shoot day to see which gives you the better result.
- Use an external microphone. The built-in microphone on the camera will only pick up sounds that are very close by. If you want to record sounds that are farther off, try using an external microphone that can plug into the video recorder. Poor sound quality can greatly diminish the production values of your video.

Next think about *how* you shoot your video. One way to keep your production lively and interesting is to vary your camera shots. The next time you watch a television show or movie, keep a little notepad handy. Every time you notice a different camera move or cut, make a hash mark on your notepad. At the end of 15 minutes, count the hash marks. You may be amazed to find out how many shots were used!

To hold the interest of your audience, use a variety of camera shots, angles, and moves. Check your local library or media center for good books on camera techniques that describe when and how to use various shots—from long shots to close-ups, from low angles to overhead shots. As a rule, every time you change camera shots, change your angle slightly as well. This way, when the shots are edited together, you can avoid accidentally putting two nearly identical shots side-by-side, which creates an unnerving jarring motion called a "jump cut."

Do some research on framing techniques as well to make sure you frame your subjects properly and avoid cutting people's heads off on the screen. Also, try to learn about ways to move the camera in order to keep your audience interested.

For example, three common but effective camera moves include panning, tracking, and zooming. **Panning** means moving the camera smoothly from one side of the scene to another. Panning works well in an establishing shot to help orient your audience to the setting where the action takes place.

**Tracking** means moving the camera from one place to another in a smooth action as well, but in tracking, the camera parallels the action, such as moving alongside a character as he or she walks down the street. It's called tracking because in professional filmmaking, the camera and the operator are rolled forward or backward on a small set of train tracks alongside the actor or actress.

**Zooming** means moving the camera forward or back, but zooming actually involves moving the lens, rather than the camera. By touching the zoom button, you can push in on a small detail that you would like to emphasize, or you can pull out to reveal something.

The important factor in any kind of camera move is to keep the action fluid and, in most cases, slow and steady. Also, use camera movement sparingly. You want to keep your audience eager and interested, not dizzy and sick!

Another good way to keep your presentation moving is to use frequent cuts. While the actual cuts will be done during post-production, you need to plan for them in production. Professional filmmakers use the word *coverage* for making sure they have ample choices for shots. You can create "coverage" for your production by planning shots such as the following:

### Kinds of Video Shots

| | |
|---|---|
| **establishing shot** | This shot sets up where the action of the story will take place. For example, if your story takes place inside an operating room, you might begin with an establishing shot of the outside of the hospital. |

| | |
|---|---|
| **reaction shot** | It's a good idea to get shots of all on-camera talent even if that person does not have any dialogue but is listening to, or reacting to, another character. This gives you the chance to break away from the character that is speaking to show how his or her words are affecting other people in the scene. |
| **cutaway shot** | The cutaway shot is a shot of something that is not included in the original scene, but is somehow related to it. Cutaways are used to connect two subjects. For example, the first shot may be of a person falling off a boat. The second shot could be a cutaway of a shark swimming deep below the water. |

If you are adventurous, you might also want to try some simple special effects. Dry ice can create smoke effects. You can also have your actors freeze; then stop the camera, remove an object from the set, and restart the camera. This technique will make objects seem to disappear as if by magic. Other effects can be achieved using false backdrops, colored lights, and filters. Just use your imagination!

## Post-production—The Magic of Editing

Without access to a sound mixing board, it's difficult to do post-production on audio recordings. However, there's a vast amount of creative control you can have over your video project in post-production using your camera and your VCR.

Once all of your videotaping is complete, it's time to create the **final cut**—that is, your choice of the shots you wish to keep and the shots you wish to discard. The idea, of course, is to keep only your very best shots in the final production. Be choosy and select the footage with only the best composition, lighting, focus, and performance to tell your story.

## Three Basic Editing Techniques

| | |
|---|---|
| **in-camera editing** | In this process you edit as you shoot. In other words, you need to shoot all your scenes in the correct sequence in the proper length that you want them to appear. This is the most difficult editing process because it leaves no margin for error. |
| **insert editing** | In insert editing you transfer all your footage to a new video. Then on your VCR you record over any scenes that you don't want with scenes that you do want in the final version. |
| **assemble editing** | This process involves electronically copying your shots from the original source tape in your camera onto a new blank tape, called the **edited master**, in the order that you want the shots to appear. This method provides the most creative control. |

In the best scenario, it's ideal to have three machines at your disposal—the camera, a recording VCR for transferring images, and a post-production machine or computer program for adding effects. These effects might include a dissolve from one shot to another instead of an abrupt cut. A **dissolve** is the soft fading of one shot into another. Dissolves are useful when you wish to give the impression that time has passed between two scenes. A long, slow dissolve that comes up from black into a shot, or from a shot down to black, is called a **fade** and is used to open or close a show.

In addition to assembling the program, post-production is the time to add titles to the opening of your program and credits to the end of the show. Computer programs, such as Adobe Premiere, can help you do this. Plus, some cameras are equipped to generate titles too. If you don't have any electronic means to produce titles, you can always mount your camera on a high tripod and focus it downward on well-lit pages of text and graphics placed on the floor. Then edit the text frames into the program.

Post-production is also the time to add voiceover narration and music. Voiceovers and background music should be recorded separately and then edited into the program on a separate sound track once the entire show is edited together. Video editing programs for your computer, such as Adobe Premiere, allow you to mix music and voices with your edited video. Some VCRs will allow you to add additional sound tracks as well.

# Publishing on the World Wide Web

The World Wide Web is an exciting part of the Internet where you can visit thousands of Websites, take part in online discussion groups, and communicate with other people all over the world via E-mail. You can also become a part of the exciting Web community by building and publishing a Website of your own.

## Scoping Out Your Site

There are no hard and fast rules on how to build a Website. However, the Web is a unique medium with distinctive features that make it different from any other form of communication. The Web offers:

- universal access to everyone;
- interactive communication;
- the ability to use photos, illustrations, animation, sound, and video;
- unlimited space;
- unlimited branching capabilities;
- the ability to link your site with other Websites.

If you are going to publish on the Web, it makes sense to take advantage of all of these features. In other words, it's possible to take any written composition, save it in a format that can be displayed in a Web browser, upload it to a server, and leave it at that. But how interesting is it to look at a solid page of text on your computer screen?

Just like planning a video, you need to plan your Website. Don't just throw text and graphics together up on a screen. The idea is to make your site interesting enough that visitors will want to stay, explore, and come back to your site again—and that takes thought and planning.

## Back to the Drawing Board

Again, you need to capture your thoughts and ideas on paper before you publish anything. Start with a one-page summary that states the purpose of your Website and the audience you hope to attract. Describe in a paragraph the look and feel you think your site will need in order to accomplish this purpose and hold your audience's attention.

Make a list of the content you plan to include in your Website. Don't forget to consider any graphics, animation, video, or sound you may want to include. Next go on a World Wide Web field trip.

Ask your friends and teachers for the URLs of their favorite Websites. Visit these sites. Click around and then ask yourself, Do I like this site? Why or why not? Determine which sites are visually appealing to you and why. Which sites are easy to navigate and why? Bookmark and print out the pages you like best, and write notes on your reactions.

On the other hand, which sites are boring and why? Print out a few of these pages too, and keep notes on how you feel about them. Chances are the sites you like best will have clean, easy-to-read layouts, be well written, contain visually stimulating graphic elements, and have intuitive **interfaces** that make it simple to find your way around.

One characteristic that will surely detract any Website's appeal is long, uninterrupted blocks of text. Scrolling through page after page of text is extremely boring. Plan to break up long passages of information into manageable sections. What will be the various sections of your site? Will there be separate sections for editorial content? News? Humor? Feedback? What sections will be updated periodically and how often?

Pick up your drawing pencil and make a few rough sketches. How do you envision the "home" page of your site? What will the icons and buttons look like? Then give careful thought to how the pages will connect to each other starting with the home page. Your plan for connecting the pages is called a **site map**.

Because the Web is an interactive medium, navigation is critical. Decide how users will get from one page to another. Will you put in a navigation bar across the top of the page or down the side? Will there be a top or home page at the beginning of each section?

Once you have planned the content, organized your material into sections, and designed your navigation system, you are ready to begin creating Web pages.

## Planning Your Pages

In order to turn text into Web pages, you need to translate the text into a special language that Web browsers can read. This language code is called HTML—HyperText Markup Language. There are three methods available:

- You can use the Save as HTML feature in the File menu of most word-processing programs.
- You can import your text into a Web-building software program and add the code yourself if you know how.
- You can use a software program such as Adobe PageMill that does the work for you. Web-building software programs are referred to as WYSIWYG (pronounced "Wiz-E-Wig"), which stands for "What You See Is What You Get."

Web-building software also allows you to create links to other Web pages using a simple process called **drag and drop.** Be sure to read the directions that come with your software package for complete instructions.

## Putting It All Together

Writing for the Web is different from writing for print. The Web is a fast medium. It's about experiences, not study time, so write accordingly. Keep your messages succinct and to the point. Use short, punchy sentences. Break up your copy with clever subheads. Try not to exceed 500 to 600 words in any single article on any one page.

Compose your Web copy on a standard word-processing program. This will give you access to your formatting tools and spell-check features. Following the directions of your Web-building software, you can then import the completed text into the software program for placement on your Web page.

Next you will want to lay out your Web page and flow the text around some interesting graphics. Be sure to include blank space on the page as well. Blank space lets your page "breathe" and makes for a much more inviting experience.

You can use a variety of images on your Website including charts, graphs, photographs, clip art, and original illustrations. Collect graphics for the Web in exactly the same way you would get graphics for any desktop publishing project—scan in images, use a digital camera, or create your own graphics using a graphics software program.

It's also possible to add audio files and video files (referred to as QuickTime Video) to your Website. These are fun and interesting additions. However, there are two drawbacks—audio and video files are very time-consuming to prepare and take a long time for the user to load. Also, audio quality can be quite good on the Net, but full-motion video is still not at the broadcast-quality level most people have come to expect.

As an alternative to video, consider animated graphics. Animated graphics are much easier to create using graphics software programs. These programs also allow you to compress the animations so that they load much faster than video files and still run smoothly on screen.

If you would like to learn more about adding audio and video features, as well as graphics, to your Web pages, visit http://msc.pangea.org/tutorials/www/cap_5-eng.htm. For more information about adding other multimedia features, check out Plug-ins for Browsers at http://www.seidata.com/~city/reference/plugins/.

## Going Live

Once all your pages are put together you are ready to go live on the World Wide Web, right? Not quite.

Before you upload your new Website, it's a good idea to test all your pages first, using common Web browsers such as Netscape's Navigator or Microsoft's Internet Explorer—browsers your visitors are likely to use. Open your pages on these browsers and look at them closely. Do the text and graphics appear the way you had designed them? Are all the page elements fitting neatly into the screen space, or do you need to tweak the copy or graphics a little to make them fit better?

Test all links on your page. Click on every page and be sure that it takes you to the site you originally intended. Click on all your navigation elements and buttons. Is everything working the way it's supposed to work? Make any corrections on your home or classroom computer before uploading your Website to a host server and going live to the world.

Your Web-building software program has built-in features that make uploading and adding files to your Website a snap. In fact, some of this software is even available free on the Internet and is easy to download right onto your home or classroom computer.

For more information on how to build and launch your own Website, check the Web. You'll find some great tips at http://www.hotwired.com/webmonkey/kids.

This site even features a guided lesson plan called "Webmonkey for Kids" with step-by-step directions on how to create your own site. It also has information about useful software programs that schools and other educational institutions can download free.

Here's one more shortcut to building a Website. If you or your school already has an Internet Service Provider (ISP), you may be entitled to a free Website as part of your service package. In fact, if you already have an E-mail address for correspondence, this address can be modified slightly and serve as the URL address of your Website. Call your ISP and ask about Website services included in your sign-up.

Last, beware of small errors that can occur during the transmission of your Website material to the Web. As soon as you have finished uploading your Website, open your browser, enter the URL address, and take your new site out for a test drive. Click on all your navigational buttons, links, animations, or any other multimedia features. Check to make sure all the pages are there and everything looks the way you planned it.

Does everything check out? Great. Now all you have to do is send an E-mail to everyone you know and invite each person to visit your brand new Website!

# A Writer's Guide to Using the Internet

The Internet is a global network of computers connected to one another with high-speed data lines and regular telephone lines. Anyone with a computer, a modem, and a telephone or cable line can be connected to it—including you!

The idea of the Internet began in 1969, when a government agency called ARPA (Advanced Research Projects Agency) connected the computers of four universities together. They called this connection the ARPANET. It was used primarily to exchange research and educational information between scientists and engineers.

Gradually people outside the scientific community began to realize the potential of this tool. By 1980, the U.S. Department of Defense had created an early version of the Internet. Soon most universities and government agencies were using it too.

Up to this point, the information was not organized in any way. Imagine a library with thousands of books and no card catalog! The next challenge was to find a way to locate and access information quickly and efficiently. Over the next few years, several different search tools were proposed. The names of these systems included Archie, Jughead, and Veronica. If you haven't already guessed, these program names were inspired by the *Archie* comics.

One of the best search systems developed, and today the most widely used, is the World Wide Web. The Web is a network of computers *within* the Internet. This network is capable of delivering multimedia content—images, audio, video, and animation as well as text. Like the Internet, it comes over the same communication lines into personal computers worldwide, including yours!

# How Does the Internet Work?

The Internet is comprised of literally thousands of networks all linked together around the globe. Each network consists of a group of computers that are connected to one another to exchange information. If one of these computers or networks fails, the information simply bypasses the disabled system and takes another route through a different network. This rerouting is why the Internet is so valuable to agencies such as the U.S. Department of Defense.

No one "owns" the Internet, nor is it managed in a central place. No agency regulates or censors the information on the Internet. Anyone can publish information on the Internet as he or she wishes.

In fact, the Internet offers such a vast wealth of information and experiences that sometimes it's described as the *Information Superhighway*. So how do you "get on" this highway? It's easy. Once you have a computer, a modem, and a telephone or cable line, all you need is a connection to the Internet.

## The Cyberspace Connection

A company called an Internet Service Provider (ISP) connects your computer to the Internet. Examples of ISPs that provide direct access are AT&T, Microsoft Network, Earthlink, MediaOne, and Netcom. You can also get on the Internet indirectly through companies such as America Online (AOL) and Prodigy.

ISPs charge a flat monthly fee for their service. Unlike the telephone company, once you pay the monthly ISP fee, there are no long-distance charges for sending or receiving information on the Internet—no matter where your information is coming from, or going to, around the world! Once you are connected to the Information Superhighway, all you have to do is learn how to navigate it.

## Alphabet Soup—Making Sense of All Those Letters!

Like physical highways, the Information Superhighway has road signs that help you find your way around. These road signs are expressed in a series of letters that can seem confusing at first. You've already seen several different abbreviations so far—ARPA, ISP, AOL. How do you make sense out of all these letters? Relax. It's not as complicated as it looks.

Each specific group of information on the World Wide Web is called a **Website** and has its own unique address. Think of it as a separate street address of a house in your neighborhood. This address is called the URL, which stands for Uniform Resource Locator. It's a kind of shorthand for where the information is located on the Web.

Here's a typical URL: **http://www.bkenglish.com.**

All addresses, or URLs, for the World Wide Web begin with **http://**. This stands for HyperText Transfer Protocol and is a programming description of how the information is exchanged.

The next three letters, **www,** let you know you are on the World Wide Web. The next part of the URL—**bkenglish**—is the name of the site you want to visit. And the last three letters, in this case **com**, indicate that this Website is sponsored by a **com**mercial company. Here are other common endings of URLs you will find:

- **org** is short for organization, as in http://www.ipl.org, which is the URL of the Website for the Internet Public Library.
- **edu** stands for education, as in the Web address for the Virtual Reference Desk of Purdue University, http://thorplus.lib.purdue.edu/reference/index.html, featuring online telephone books, dictionaries, and other reference guides.
- **gov** represents government-sponsored Websites, such as http://www.whitehouse.gov, the Website for the White House in Washington, D.C.

To get to a Website, you use an interface called a **browser.** Two popular browsers are Netscape Navigator and Microsoft Internet

Explorer. A browser is like a blank form where you fill in the information you are looking for. If you know the URL of the Website you want to explore, all you have to do is type it in the field marked Location, click Enter on your keyboard, and wait for the information to be delivered to your computer screen.

There are many other ways to find information on the Web. We'll talk more about these methods later in this guide.

## Basic Internet Terminology

Here are some of the most frequently used words you will hear associated with the Internet.

**address** The unique code given to information on the Internet. This may also refer to an E-mail address.

**bookmark** A tool that lets you store your favorite URL addresses, allowing you one-click access to your favorite Web pages without retyping the URL each time.

**browser** Application software that supplies a graphical interactive interface for searching, finding, viewing, and managing information on the Internet.

**chat** Real-time conferencing over the Internet.

**cookies** A general mechanism that some Websites use both to store and to retrieve information on the visitor's hard drive. Users have the option to refuse or accept cookies.

**cyberspace** The collective realm of computer-aided communication.

**download** The transfer of programs or data stored on a remote computer, usually from a server, to a storage device on your personal computer.

**E-mail** Electronic mail that can be sent all over the world from one computer to another. May also be short for Earth-mail because no paper (and no rainforest acreage) is involved.

**FAQ** The abbreviation for Frequently Asked Questions. This is usually a great resource to get information when visiting a new Website.

**flaming** Using mean or abusive language in cyberspace. Flaming is considered to be in extremely poor taste and may be reported to your ISP.

**FTP** The abbreviation for File Transfer Protocol. This is a method of transferring files to and from a computer connected to the Internet.

**home page** The start-up page of a Website.

**HTML** The abbreviation for HyperText Markup Language—a "tag" language used to create most Web pages, which your browser interprets to display those pages. Often the last set of letters found at the end of a Web address.

**http** The abbreviation for HyperText Transfer Protocol. This is how documents are transferred from the Website or server to the browsers of individual personal computers.

**ISP** The abbreviation for Internet Service Provider—a company that, for a fee, connects a user's computer to the Internet.

**keyword** A simplified term that serves as subject reference when doing a search.

**link** Short for Hyperlink. A link is a connection between one piece of information and another.

**Net** Short for Internet.

**netiquette** The responsible and considerate way for a user to conduct himself or herself on the Internet.

**network** A system of interconnected computers.

**online** To "be online" means to be connected to the Internet via a live modem connection.

**plug-in** Free application that can be downloaded off the Internet to enhance your browser's capabilities.

**real time** Information received and processed (or displayed) as it happens.

**search engine** A computer program that locates documents based on keywords that the user enters.

| | |
|---|---|
| **server** | A provider of resources, such as a file server. |
| **site** | A specific place on the Internet, usually a set of pages on the World Wide Web. |
| **spam** | Electronic junk mail. |
| **surf** | A casual reference to browsing on the Internet. To "surf the Web" means to spend time discovering and exploring new Websites. |
| **upload** | The transfer of programs or data from a storage device on your personal computer to another remote computer. |
| **URL** | The abbreviation for Universal Resource Locator. This is the address for an Internet resource, such as a World Wide Web page. Each Web page has its own unique URL. |
| **Website** | A page of information or a collection of pages that is being electronically published from one of the computers in the World Wide Web. |
| **WWW** | The abbreviation for the World Wide Web. A network of computers within the Internet capable of delivering multimedia content (images, audio, video, and animation) as well as text over communication lines into personal computers all over the globe. |

## Why Use the Internet?

By the end of the 1990s, the Internet had experienced incredible growth. An estimated 196 million people were using the Internet worldwide, spending an average of 8.8 hours a week online. By 2003, this number is estimated to increase to more than 500 million people who will be surfing the Web. Why? What does the Internet offer that makes so many people want to go online? And what are the advantages of using the Internet for writers in particular?

## The World at Your Fingertips

The Internet offers an amazing amount of knowledge and experiences at the touch of your computer keyboard. For writers it's a great way to get ideas and do in-depth research. You'll find thousands upon thousands of Websites offering a mind-boggling array of subjects. You can explore the Web as a way to jumpstart your creativity or tap into unlimited information.

The Internet also lets you communicate with experts that you might not otherwise have access to. Plus, you can connect with other people all over the world who have the same interests you do—maybe even find a new writing partner!

In short, the Internet is an invaluable tool for creating great writing. In the next section, we'll explore just some of the exciting advantages.

## Just an E Away

One of the most popular features of the Internet is electronic mail, or E-mail for short. Unlike traditional mail (nicknamed "snail mail" by tech-savvy people), E-mail messages are practically instantaneous. It's so convenient that, in 1999, 46 percent of Americans were sending or receiving E-mail every day.

E-mail is a fun and easy way to keep in touch with friends and relatives. You can send anything from a lengthy family newsletter to a quick question or "news flash." E-mail is also appropriate for formal correspondence, such as responding to a job opening and sending a résumé. In this case it's a good idea to follow up with hard copies in the traditional mail.

Have you ever teamed up with another student or a maybe a group of students in your class to work on a project together? With E-mail you can collaborate with other students in other states or even other countries! Many schools are taking advantage of E-mail to pair a class in say, San Jose, California, to work on a cooperative project with a class in New York City, or maybe one as far away as Sydney, Australia.

For writers, E-mail is an especially valuable tool. It's a great way to communicate with people who are experts in their fields. Many times, well-known authorities who are difficult to reach by phone or in person will respond to questions and requests for information via E-mail. E-mail comes in particularly handy when the person you would like to communicate with lives in another part of the world. It eliminates the expense of long-distance phone calls and awkward problems due to different time zones.

An easy way to locate experts in a particular area is to visit Websites about that subject. Many times these Websites will list an E-mail address where you can send questions.

Another way writers can use E-mail is to gather information and make contacts. E-mail queries can be sent out to many people in a single click by simply adding multiple addresses to the same message. For example, suppose you are writing a paper about raising exotic birds. With one click you can send out an E-mail to 30 friends and associates that asks, "Do you know anyone who has an exotic bird?" Chances are at least a few of the people you ask will have one or two contacts they can provide—and think how much faster corresponding by E-mail is than making 30 phone calls!

*You can learn more about sending E-mail on pages C828–C831.*

## Widening Your World

Your E-mail account also gives you access to **mailing lists**—discussion groups that use E-mail to exchange ideas. Subscribing to a mailing list is free and opens a floodgate of information about specific subjects that is sent directly to your E-mail box. There are hundreds of lists to choose from, with topics ranging from animal rights to Olympic volleyball. Join a mailing list about the subject you are currently writing about, and it will net you dozens of messages about your topic every day. (Don't worry—you can always *un*subscribe at any time from these lists!)

A similar way to get information and contacts about a particular topic is through the Users Network, called Usenet for short. Usenet is the world's largest discussion forum, providing people with common interests the opportunity to talk to one another in smaller groups called **newsgroups.**

Like mailing lists, there are thousands of newsgroups you can join. Instead of receiving information via E-mail, newsgroups post articles and information on their sites. Subscribing to a newsgroup is like subscribing to a magazine. By visiting the newsgroup site, you can select which articles you wish to read. You can also reply to articles and discuss them with other people in the newsgroup to gather more ideas.

*You can find out more about mailing lists and newsgroups on pages C832–C834.*

 One **cautionary note** when surfing the Web:

- No matter how tempting, do not give out your name, address, telephone number, or school name to any site that may ask for this information.
- If you are interested in getting on a mailing list or joining a newsgroup, check with your teacher and/or your parents first.

## Picture This

Whatever you write will probably have more impact if it's accompanied by some sort of visual. Many sites on the World Wide Web offer photos, illustrations, and clip art that can be downloaded and integrated into your work. Sometimes there are fees associated with this artwork, but many times it's free.

Another way to illustrate your writing is to take your own photos, turn them into electronic images, and integrate them into your work. One way to do this is to use a digital camera and download the images directly into your computer. If you don't have a digital camera, you can also take pictures using a regular camera. When you have the photos developed, ask the developer if you can have them returned to you either on disc or via E-mail.

Another option is to use a scanner, a device that looks somewhat like a copy machine. You place the photo on the glass, and the image is scanned into your computer.

Once you have an image in your computer, you can add it to a report or article in a number of ways—for example, on the cover page as a graphic or border design. There are even a number of photo-editing programs available that give you the ability to manipulate images in all sorts of creative ways.

Sometimes a graph or chart can help you illustrate your point more clearly than just text. Using a program such as Microsoft PowerPoint, you can create a myriad of graphs and tables that you can incorporate into your writing project for extra emphasis.

One of the best advantages of photos, charts, and artwork that are stored as electronic images is that you can also send them as E-mail attachments. Imagine—with a click of a button, you can:

- share photos of your last soccer game instantly with friends and relatives anywhere in the world.
- take your pen pals on a "virtual" tour of your home, school, or neighborhood.
- swap pictures and graphs with writing partners in other classrooms across the globe and double your resources.

## Online Help

You're working on a paper for your Shakespeare class. You come across the phrase, "Thou craven rough-hewn maggot-pie" in the text. Huh? Find out all about how to make sport of someone using Shakespearean language at The Shakespearean Insult Server at http://www.alabanza.com/kabacoff/Inter-Links/sgi/bard.cgi.

This is only one of hundreds of Websites that can help you with specific subjects you are probably studying right now. These sites cover a variety of topics in English, history, math, science, foreign languages, and more. Here's just a sample of some of the sites waiting to help you.

- How to Be a Web Hound! (http://www.mcli.dist.maricopa.edu/webhound/index.html)
- The Guide to Grammar and Writing (http://webster.commnet.edu/HP/pages/darling/grammar.htm)
- The Math Forum—featuring interesting math challenges and the whimsical "Ask Dr. Math" (http://forum.swarthmore.edu/students)
- MapQuest—type in your starting point and destination and get exact mileage and directions (http://www.mapquest.com)
- The Guide to Experimental Science Projects (http://www.isd77.k12.mn.us/resources/cf/SciProj Inter.html)

- The Human Languages Page—gateways to foreign-language resources on the Web (http://www.june29.com/HLP/)
- The Smithsonian Institution—featuring links to sites ranging from Aeronautics to Zoology (http://www.si.edu)
- The Perseus Project—*the* online resource for studying the ancient world (http://www.perseus.tufts.edu/)
- Education Index—a guide to useful educational Websites (http://www.educationindex.com/)
- Up Your Score—the underground guide to scoring well on the SAT (http://www.workmanweb.com/upyourscore/)
- My Homework Helpers/My Virtual Reference Desk (http://www.refdesk.com/homework.html)
- The Writing Center (http://researchpaper.com/writing.html)

The Internet also offers free programs and services that can be of use to writers. For example, sometimes valuable articles are available in a format called PDF, which stands for Portable Document Format. In order to view this kind of document, you must have software called the Adobe Acrobat Reader. You can download this software free of charge by visiting the Adobe Website at http://www.adobe.com.

## Fun and Games

Many people enjoy the fun side of the Internet's personality. A vast number of Websites offer news, entertainment, online games, and adventures in shopping (often referred to as **e-commerce)**.

While these areas may not seem to be related to writing, if the topic you are working on crosses into the realm of news or the entertainment industry, a gold mine of material awaits you. Then again, maybe a quick game is just what you need to shake off a touch of writer's block!

## Don't Believe Everything You Read

Wow, all this terrific information is just a click away. There's only one problem: Not all of it is credible or accurate.

When you check out a book from the library, a librarian or a committee of educators has already evaluated the book to make sure it's a reliable source of information, but remember, no one owns or regulates the Internet. Just because you read something online doesn't mean it's true. How can you tell the difference? Here are a few guidelines on how to evaluate an online source.

- **Play the name game**
  First, find out who publishes the site. Does the URL end in ".com" (which means it's a commercial company)? If so, is it a large, reputable company, or one you've never heard of that might just be trying to sell you something? An educational site in which the URL ends in ".edu," such as a college or university, might be a more reliable choice. Or a site sponsored by a well-known organization (with a URL that ends in ".org"), such as the American Red Cross (http://www.crossnet.org), would also probably be a credible source.
- **Scope it out**
  Click around the site and get a feel for what it's like. Is the design clean and appealing? Is it easy to navigate the site and find information? Are the sections clearly labeled? Does the site accept advertising? If you think the site seems disjointed or disorganized, or you just have a negative opinion of it, listen to your instincts and move on to another one.
- **Check the Source**
  Suppose you find an article on the Web that seems chock-full of great information. The next question you need to ask yourself is, "Who is the author? Is the person an acknowledged expert on the subject?" If you don't recognize the author's name, you can send a question to a newsgroup asking if anyone knows about the person. You can also do a search on the Web, using the author's name as the keyword, to get more information about him or her.

In some cases, an article won't list any author at all. If you don't find an author's name, be skeptical. A credible site clearly identifies its authors and usually lists the person's professional background and his or her credentials.

- **Is this old news?**
  If you are doing research on the Roman Empire, it's probably all right if the information wasn't posted yesterday. But if you're looking for information in quickly changing fields, such as science and politics, be sure to check the date of publication before you accept the data as true.
- **Ask around**
  Reliable Websites frequently provide E-mail addresses or links to authors and organizations connected to the content on the site. Send off a quick E-mail to one of these sources, tell them what you are writing, and ask them: Is this material accurate?

Perhaps the best way to find out if the information on any Website or the information in any article (signed or unsigned) is accurate is to check it against another source—and the best source is your local library or media center.

## Internet + Media Center = Information Powerhouse!

Although the Internet is a limitless treasure chest of information, remember that it's not catalogued, so it can be tricky to locate the information you need, and sometimes that information is not reliable. The library is a well-organized storehouse of knowledge, but it has finite resources. If you use the Internet in *conjunction* with your local media center, you will have everything you need to create well-researched articles, reports, and papers.

### Use the Internet to

- get great ideas for topics to write about.
- gather information about your topic from companies, colleges and universities, and professional organizations.
- connect with people who are recognized experts in your field of interest.
- connect with other people who are interested in the same subject and who can provide you with information or put you in touch with other sources.

### Use the Media Center to

- find additional sources of information either in print or online.
- get background information on your topic.
- cross-check the accuracy and credibility of online information and authors.

## I Don't Own a Computer

You can still access the Internet even if you don't have your own computer. Many schools have computer labs that are open after school and on weekends. Some schools will even allow students to use these labs whether or not they are enrolled at that particular school. Many libraries are also equipped with computers and Internet connections.

Consider taking a computer course after school or even attending a computer camp. You'll find information about these programs listed at the library, the YMCA, and in parenting magazines or maybe you have a friend or neighbor with a computer that you can use in exchange for a service you might provide, such as baby-sitting or yard work.

# How to Communicate on the Internet

E-mail, mailing lists, and newsgroups are all great ways of exchanging information with other people on the Internet. Here's how to use these useful forms of communication, step-by-step.

## Keep in Touch with E-mail

Any writer who has ever used E-mail in his or her work will agree that sending and receiving electronic messages is one of the most useful ways of gathering information and contacts for writing projects. It's fast, inexpensive, and fun!

Once you open your E-mail program, click on the command that says Compose Mail or New Message. This will open a new blank E-mail similar to the one pictured below. Next, fill in the blanks.

Type the person's E-mail address here. There is no central listing of E-mail addresses. If you don't have the person's address, the easiest way to get it is to call and ask the person for it. You can address an E-mail to one or several people, depending on the number of addresses you type in this space.

**CC** stands for *courtesy copy*. If you type additional E-mail addresses in this area, you can send a copy of the message to other people.

**BCC** stands for *blind courtesy copy*. By typing one or more E-mail addresses here, you can send a copy of the message to others without the original recipient knowing that other people have received the same message. Not all E-mail programs have this feature.

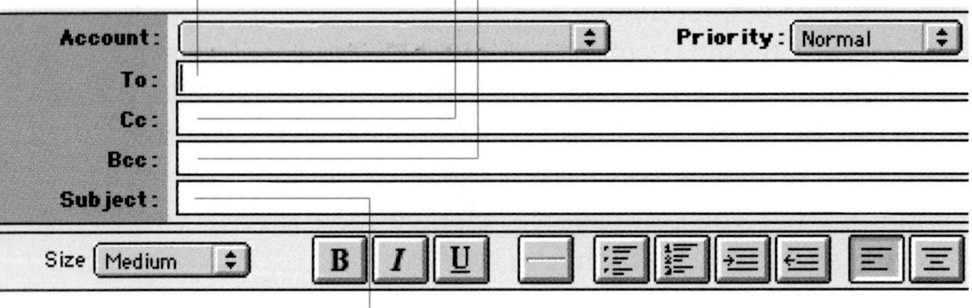


This is where you type your message.

This is called the subject line. Write a few brief words that best describe what your E-mail message is about.

## Say It with Style

Like regular letters, E-mail can assume different tones and styles depending on your purpose and audience. Usually informal E-mails, such as instant messages (IMs) to close friends, are light, brief, and to the point. In the case of more formal E-mails, such as a request for information from an expert or a museum, it's important to keep the following guidelines in mind.

- Make sure your message is clear and concise.
- Use proper grammar and punctuation.
- Check your spelling. (Some E-mail programs have their own spell-check function—use it!)
- Double-check the person's E-mail address to be sure you've typed it correctly.

Because E-mail is a fast medium designed for quick communication, E-mail users have developed a kind of shorthand that helps them write their messages even faster. Here are a few commonly used abbreviations that you may find in informal E-mail.

**COMMON E-MAIL ABBREVIATIONS**

| | | | |
|---|---|---|---|
| BRB | be right back | BTW | by the way |
| FYI | for your information | F2F | face-to-face |
| HAND | Have a nice day | J/K | just kidding |
| IMHO | in my humble opinion | IOW | in other words |
| LOL | laughing out loud | L8R | later |
| OIC | Oh, I see | ROFL | rolling on the floor laughing |
| WU | What's up? | | |

IMHO, TBC RTTR ETU, FWIW!
(*Translation:* In my humble opinion, the best conversations are those that are easiest to understand, for what it's worth!)

Are you sending the E-mail to a friend or relative? If so, would you like to add a touch of fun? Then you may want to explore **emoticons** (also know as "smileys")—little faces made out of keyboard symbols that you add to your messages to express how you feel about something.

| EMOTICONS | | | |
|---|---|---|---|
| :) | happy | :( | sad |
| :-D | laughing | :`-( | crying |
| ;-) | winking | :-} | smirking |
| :-0 | shocked | :-/ | skeptical |
| :-# | my lips are sealed | *<\|:-) | Santa Claus |
| :s | confused | :<> | bored |
| 8) | I'm wearing glasses | B) | I'm wearing sunglasses/shades |

## Attach a Little Something Extra

When you send E-mail, you can also send other information along with your message. These are called **attachments**. Depending on your E-mail program's capabilities, you can attach documents, photos, illustrations—even sound and video files. Click Attach, and then find and double-click on the document or file on your computer that you wish to send.

After you have composed your message and added any attachments you want to include, click the Send button. Presto! Your message arrives in the other person's mailbox seconds later, regardless of whether that person lives right next door or on the other side of the world. Because there is usually no charge to send E-mail, it's a great way to save money on postage and long-distance telephone calls.

## Follow Up

It's important to note that just because you have sent a message, you shouldn't automatically assume that the other person has received it. Internet Service Providers (ISPs) keep all messages that are sent until the recipient requests them. The person you sent your E-mail to might be away from his or her computer or may not check messages regularly.

Also, the Internet is still an imperfect science. From time to time, servers go down or other "hiccups" in electronic transmissions can occur, leaving your message stranded somewhere in cyberspace. If you don't get a reply in a reasonable amount of time, either resend your original E-mail message or call the person and let him or her know that your message is waiting.

## You've Got Mail

When someone sends *you* an E-mail message, you have several options:

| | |
|---|---|
| **Reply:** | Click Reply, and you can automatically send back a new message without having to retype the person's E-mail address. (Be sure you keep a copy of the sender's E-mail address in your Address Book for future use.) |
| **Forward:** | Suppose you receive a message that you would like to share with someone else. Click Forward, and you can send a copy of the message, plus include a few of your own comments, to another person. |
| **Print:** | In some instances you may need to have a paper copy of the E-mail message. For example, if someone E-mails you directions to a party, click Print to take a hard copy of the instructions with you. |
| **Store:** | Do you want to keep a message to refer to later? Some E-mail programs allow you to create folders to organize stored messages. |
| **Delete:** | You can discard a message you no longer need just by clicking Delete. It's a good idea to throw messages away regularly to keep them from accumulating in your mailbox. |

## Care to Chat?

Another way to communicate online is Internet Relay Chat (IRC), or "chat rooms" for short. Chat rooms focus on a large variety of topics, so it's possible you'll be able to find a chat room where people are discussing the subject you are writing about.

"Chat" is similar to talking on the telephone except that instead of speaking, the people in the chat room type their responses back and forth to each other. As soon as you type your comment, it immediately appears on the computer screen of every person involved in the "conversation." There are also more advanced forms of chat available on the Net, such as 3-D chat and voice chat.

To participate in a chat room, you'll need to invent a nickname for yourself. This name helps to identify who is speaking, yet allows you to remain anonymous. Everyone uses a made-up name in chat rooms (like Zorro, Twinkle, Madonna, or Elvis), so don't make the mistake of believing that people really are who their name says they are!

To get started, you will need a special program for your computer. Two sites that offer this program free of charge include mIRC program (http://huizen.dds.nl/~mirc/index.htm) and Global Chat (http://www.prospero.com/globalchat).

**One last word about chat rooms:** While they are a great way to meet and communicate with other people, the anonymous nature of a chat room can make people less inhibited than they might otherwise be in person. If you sense that one of the participants in your chat room is responding inappropriately, ask your parents or teacher to step in, or simply sign off.

## Join the Group

Mailing lists and newsgroups are larger discussion forums that can help you get even more information about a specific subject.

**Mailing Lists** To find a directory of available mailing lists, check out http://www.neosoft.com/internet/paml. If you find a mailing list that interests you and wish to subscribe to it, just send a message to the administrative address. You will start to receive messages from the mailing list within a few days.

Remember, mailing lists use E-mail to communicate, so be sure to check your E-mail often because once you subscribe to a list, it's possible to receive dozens of messages in a matter of days. In fact, it's a good idea to unsubscribe from mailing lists whenever you go on vacation. Otherwise, you might come home to a mailbox stuffed to overflowing with messages!

Another good idea is to read the messages in your new mailing list for a week or so before submitting a message of your own. This will give you a good idea of what has already been discussed so you can be considerate about resubmitting old information.

You can reply to a message any time you wish. However, it doesn't do anyone any good to respond by saying, "Yes, I agree." Get in the habit of replying to messages only when you have something important to add. Also, be sure to repeat the original question in your reply so that people understand which message you are responding to.

Be sure that you really want to belong to a mailing list before you subscribe. Unwanted E-mail can be a nuisance. Fortunately, if you change your mind, you can always unsubscribe to mailing lists at any time.

**Newsgroups** To join a newsgroup, check with your ISP. Service providers frequently list available topics under the heading "Newsgroups." Another way to find a newsgroup about a topic you want to research is to visit Deja News at http://www.dejanews.com on the World Wide Web.

Newsgroups are named with two or more words separated by a period. For example, there is a newsgroup named rec.sport.baseball.college. The first three letters—"rec"—define the main subject, in this case *recreation*. Each word that follows—*sport, baseball,* and *college*—narrows the scope of the subject to an increasingly specific area of interest.

As with mailing lists, you can always unsubscribe to newsgroups at any time.

## Mind Your Manners

As in any social setting, there are a few guidelines to follow when you are talking to people online—via E-mail, in a chat room, or in a newsgroup. This conduct is called **netiquette.** The following suggestions will help you be considerate of others in cyberspace.

### E-mail and Chat

- Never use harsh or insulting language. This is called **flaming** and is considered rude. A continuing argument in which derogatory are terms swapped back and forth is called a **flamewar**. Avoid this situation.

- Type your messages using uppercase and lowercase letters. WRITING IN ALL CAPITAL LETTERS IS DIFFICULT TO READ AND IS REFERRED TO AS "SHOUTING."
- Respect other people's ideas and work. Don't forward a message or attach documents written by someone else without first asking the author's permission.
- Don't send spam. **Spamming** refers to sending messages to entire lists of people in your E-mail address book, on mailing lists, or in newsgroups for the purpose of selling something.
- Respect other people's privacy. The Internet is an enormous public forum, so be careful what you write and post on the Internet that hundreds or thousands of people might see. Don't use E-mail to spread rumors or gossip.

### Newsgroups

- Read the articles in a newsgroup for 7 to 10 days before posting articles yourself. No one in a newsgroup wants to read the same article twice.
- Make sure the article you are posting is appropriate to the subject of the newsgroup.
- If you are going to post an article, be sure you express the title clearly in the subject heading so readers will know what the article is about.
- Read the FAQ (Frequently Asked Questions) so you can avoid repeating a question that has already been discussed.

## How to Do Research on the Internet

The Information Superhighway could be the best research partner you've ever had. It's fast, vast, and always available. But like any other highway, if you don't know your way around, it can also be confusing and frustrating. This is particularly true of the Internet because the sheer volume of information often can be intimidating.

In this section we'll explore ways to help you search the Web effectively. Be patient. It takes time to learn how to navigate the Net and zero in on the information you need. The best thing to do is practice early and often. Don't wait until the night before your term paper is due to learn how to do research on the Internet!

## Getting Started

Just as there are several different ways to get to your home or school, there are many different ways to arrive at the information you're looking for on the Internet.

**CD-ROM Encyclopedia** One way to begin is not on the Web at all. You might want to start your search by using a CD-ROM encyclopedia. These CD-ROMs start with an Internet directory. Click the topic that is closest to your subject. This will link you to a site that's likely to be a good starting point. From there, you can link to other resources suggested in the site.

**Search Page** Another good place to start is your browser's search page.

Netscape Center screenshot ©2000 Netscape Communications Corporation. Used with permission.

**Search Tools** There are several different free search services available that will help you find topics of interest by entering words and phrases that describe what you are searching for. Just some of these tools, sometimes referred to as **search engines,** include:

- AltaVista—http://www.altavista.com
- Excite—http://www.excite.com
- HotBot—http://www.hotbot.com
- InfoSeek—http://www.infoseek.com
- Lycos—http://www.lycos.com
- WebCrawler—http://www.webcrawler.com
- Yahoo!—http://www.yahoo.com

Search services usually list broad categories of subjects; they may also offer other features, such as "Random Links" or "Top 25 Sites," and customization options. Each one also has a search field. Type in a word or short phrase, called a **keyword**, that describes your area of interest. Then click Search or the Enter key on your keyboard. Seconds later a list of Websites known as "hits" will be displayed containing the word you specified in the search field. Scroll through the list and click the page you wish to view.

So far this sounds simple, doesn't it? The tricky part about doing a search on the Internet is that a single keyword may yield a hundred or more sites. Plus, you may find many topics you don't need. For example, suppose you are writing a science paper about the planet Saturn. If you type the word *Saturn* into the search field, you'll turn up some articles about the planet, but you'll also get articles about NASA's Saturn rockets and Saturn, the automobile company.

## Search Smart!

Listed below are a few pointers on how to narrow your search, save time, and search *smart* on the Net.

- The keyword or words that you enter have a lot to do with the accuracy of your search. Focus your search by adding the word *and* or the + sign followed by another descriptive word. For example, try Saturn again, but this time, add "Saturn + space." Adding a third word "Saturn + space + rings"—will narrow the field even more.

- On the other hand, you can limit unwanted results by specifying information that you do *not* want the search engine to find. If you type "dolphins not football," you will get Websites about the animal that lives in the ocean rather than the football team that lives in Miami.
- Specify geographical areas using the word *near* between keywords as in "islands near Florida." This lets you focus on specific regions.
- To broaden your search, add the word *or* between keywords; for example, "sailboats or catamarans."
- Help the search engine recognize familiar phrases by putting words that go together in quotes such as "Tom and Jerry" or "bacon and eggs."
- Sometimes the site you come up with is in the ballpark of what you are searching for, but it is not exactly what you need. Skim the text quickly anyway. It may give you ideas for more accurate keywords. There might also be links listed to other sites that are just the right resource you need.
- Try out different search engines. Each service uses slightly different methods of searching, so you may get different results using the same keywords.
- Check the spelling of the keywords you are using. A misspelled word can send a search engine in the wrong direction. Also, be careful how you use capital letters. If you capitalize the word *Gold*, some search services will only bring up articles that include the word with a capital *G*.

## Pick a Category

Another way to search for information is by using subject directories. Many of the search engines on the Web provide well-organized subject guides to a variety of handpicked Websites. On the next page, you can see what a sample subject-tree directory looks like on Yahoo under the topic "Food Safety."

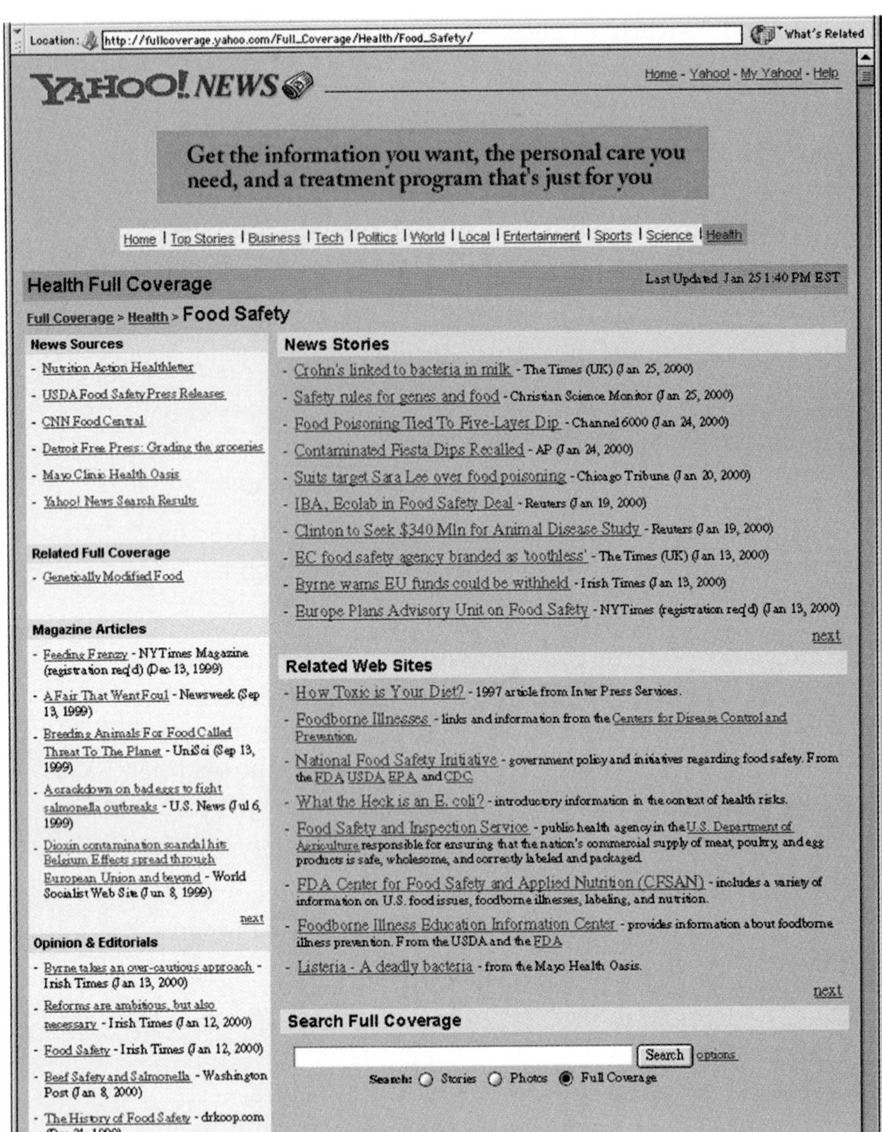




## Saving a Site for Later

You may want to keep a list handy of favorite Websites or sites you are currently using in a project. This will save you time because you can just click on the name of the site in your list and return to that page without having to retype the URL.

Different browsers have different names for this feature. For example, Netscape calls it a **bookmark**, while Microsoft's Internet Explorer calls it **favorites**.

## Searching Out a Subject

Suppose you are writing a paper about the unique role computer-generated special effects play in today's blockbuster motion pictures. Here's an idea of one way to research this topic.

- First, we'll select a search engine. We'll start with WebCrawler—at http://www.webcrawler.com. The first keywords we enter are "computer generated graphics." The search engine found these sites:

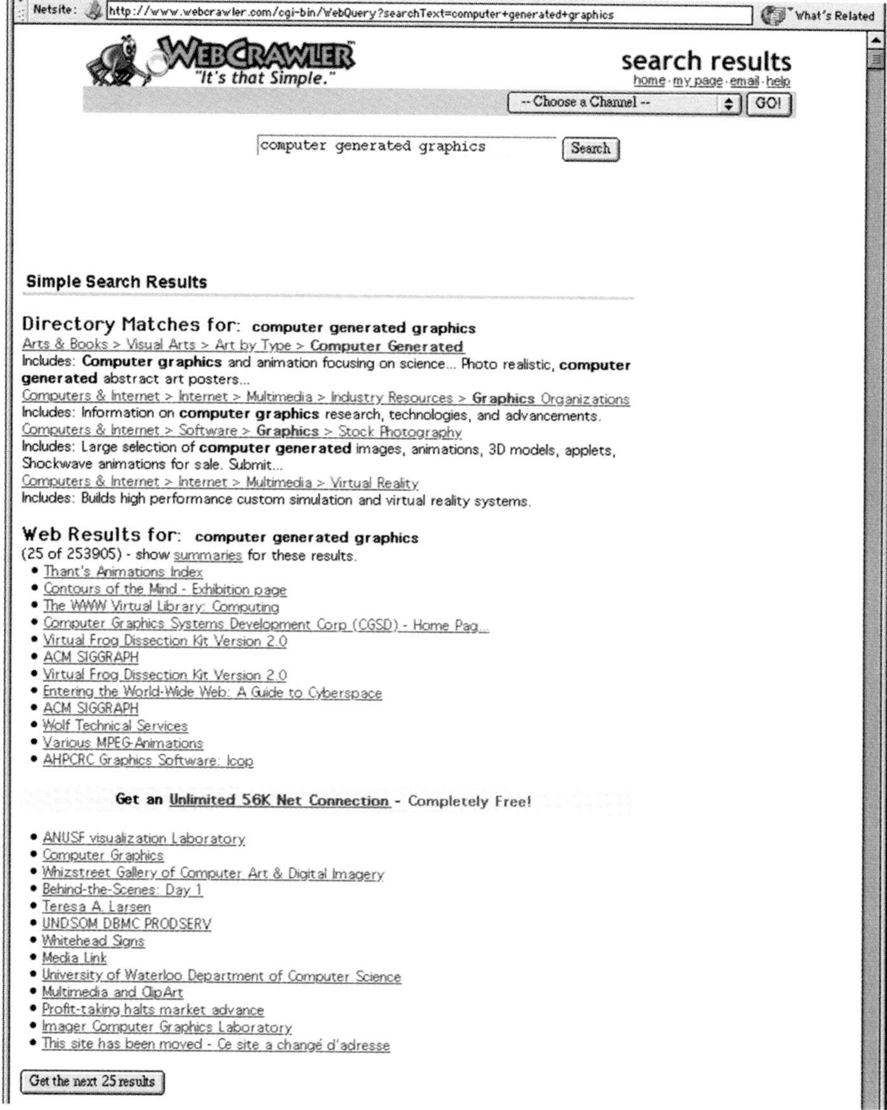

No good. Few sites on this list seem to mention special effects or computer graphics. Let's narrow the search. We'll try again, but this time we'll enter the keywords "computer generated effects + films." Now look at the list of topics:

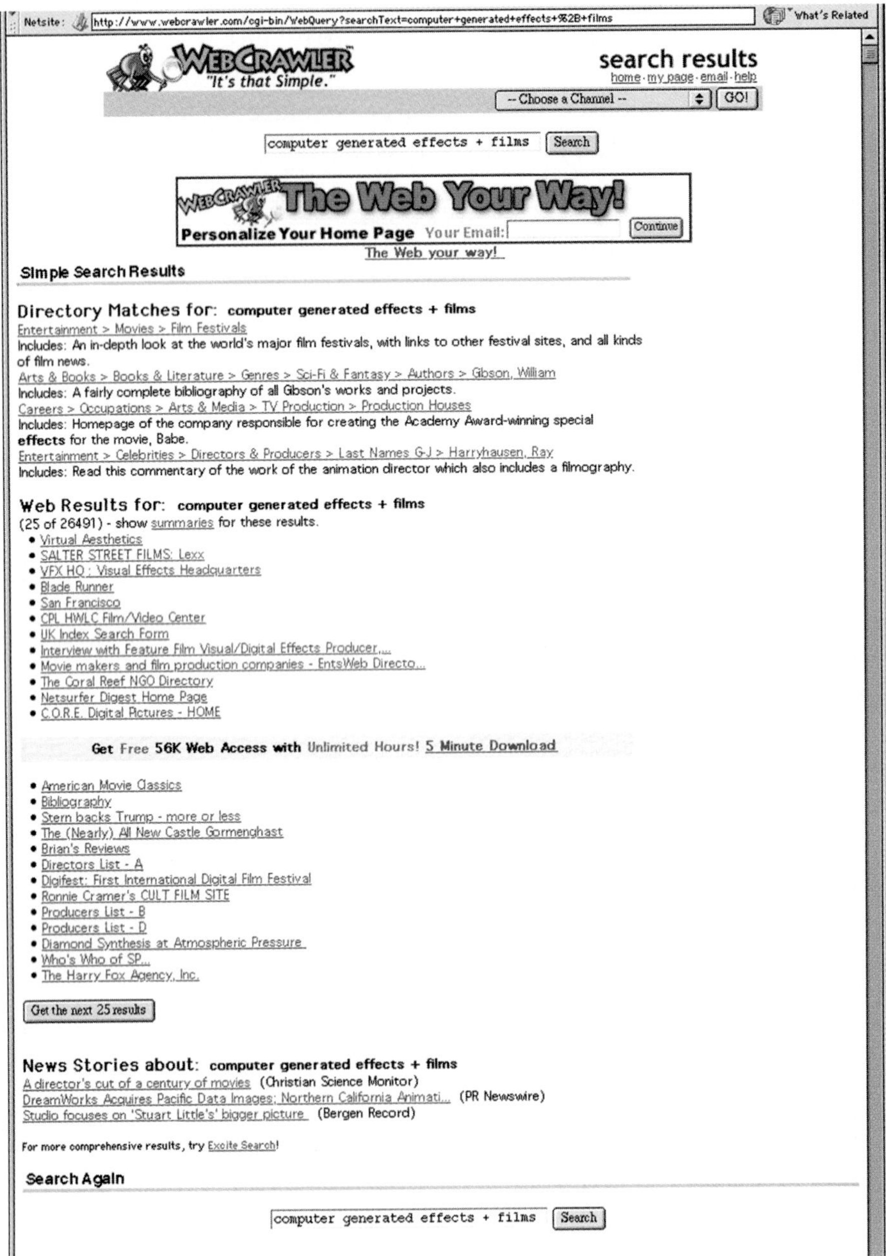

As you can see, there are many more choices to pick from. We'll click Visual Effects Headquarters Archive.

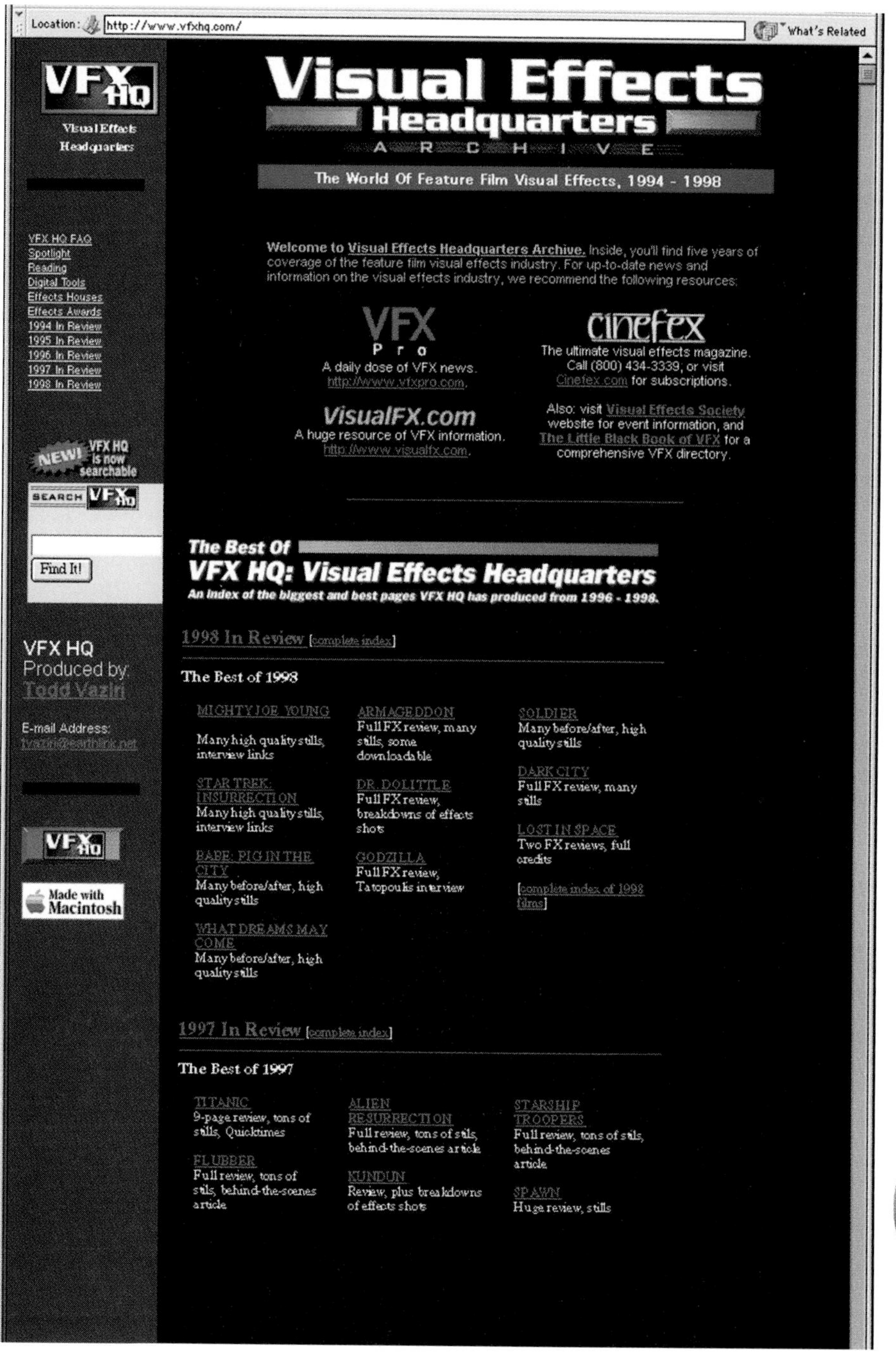


VFX HQ produced by Todd Vaziri . . . http://www.vfxhq.com . . . email tvaziri@earthlink.net.

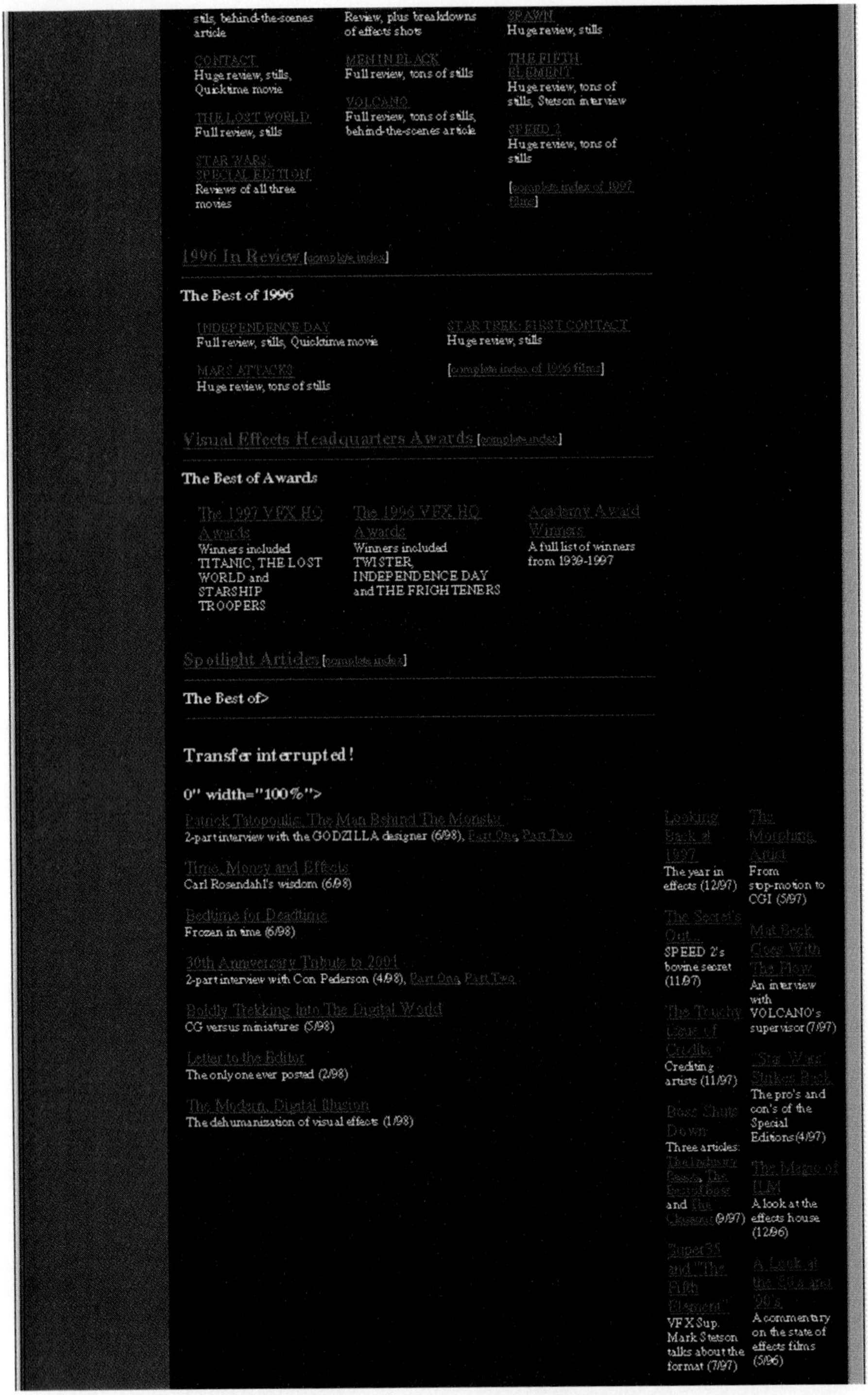

stills, behind-the-scenes article

CONTACT
Huge review, stills, Quicktime movie

THE LOST WORLD
Full review, stills

STAR WARS: SPECIAL EDITION
Reviews of all three movies

Review, plus breakdowns of effects shots

MEN IN BLACK
Full review, tons of stills

VOLCANO
Full review, tons of stills, behind-the-scenes article

SPAWN
Huge review, stills

THE FIFTH ELEMENT
Huge review, tons of stills, Stetson interview

SPEED 2
Huge review, tons of stills

[complete index of 1997 films]

## 1996 In Review [complete index]

**The Best of 1996**

INDEPENDENCE DAY
Full review, stills, Quicktime movie

MARS ATTACKS
Huge review, tons of stills

STAR TREK: FIRST CONTACT
Huge review, stills

[complete index of 1996 films]

## Visual Effects Headquarters Awards [complete index]

**The Best of Awards**

The 1997 VFX HQ Awards
Winners included TITANIC, THE LOST WORLD and STARSHIP TROOPERS

The 1996 VFX HQ Awards
Winners included TWISTER, INDEPENDENCE DAY and THE FRIGHTENERS

Academy Award Winners
A full list of winners from 1939-1997

## Spotlight Articles [complete index]

**The Best of>**

**Transfer interrupted!**

**0" width="100%">**

Patrick Tatopoulis: The Man Behind The Monster
2-part interview with the GODZILLA designer (6/98), Part One, Part Two

Time, Money and Effects
Carl Rosendahl's wisdom (6/98)

Bedtime for Deadtime
Frozen in time (6/98)

30th Anniversary Tribute to 2001
2-part interview with Con Pederson (4/98), Part One, Part Two

Boldly Trekking Into The Digital World
CG versus miniatures (5/98)

Letter to the Editor
The only one ever posted (2/98)

The Modern, Digital Illusion
The dehumanization of visual effects (1/98)

Looking Back at 1997
The year in effects (12/97)

The Secret's Out...
SPEED 2's bovine secret (11/97)

The Touchy Issue of Credits
Crediting artists (11/97)

Boss Shuts Down
Three articles: [illegible] and [illegible] (9/97)

Super35 and "The Fifth Element"
VFX Sup. Mark Stetson talks about the format (7/97)

The Morphing Artist
From stop-motion to CGI (5/97)

Mat Beck Goes With The Flow
An interview with VOLCANO's supervisor (7/97)

"Star Wars" Strikes Back
The pro's and con's of the Special Editions (4/97)

The Magic of ILM
A look at the effects house (12/96)

A Look at the 80's and 90's
A commentary on the state of effects films (5/96)

VFX HQ produced by Todd Vaziri . . . http://www.vfxhq.com . . . email tvaziri@earthlink.net.

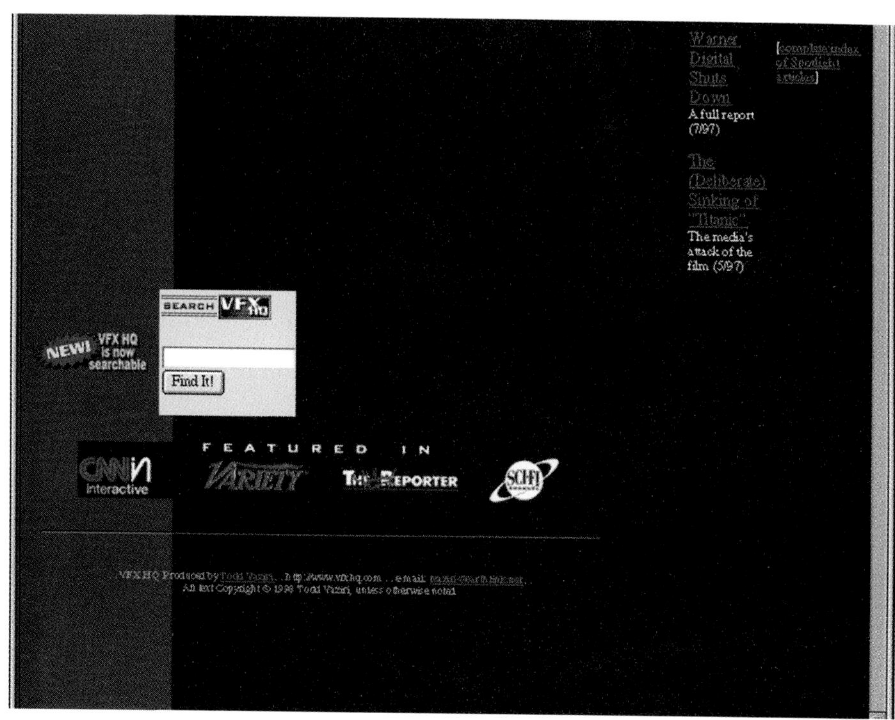


VFX HQ produced by Todd Vaziri . . . http://www.vfxhq.com . . . email tvaziri@earthlink.net.
All text Copyright ©Todd Vaziri, unless otherwise noted.

Wow—look at all these articles about computer-generated effects in well-known movies! Let's click "Babe, Pig in the City."

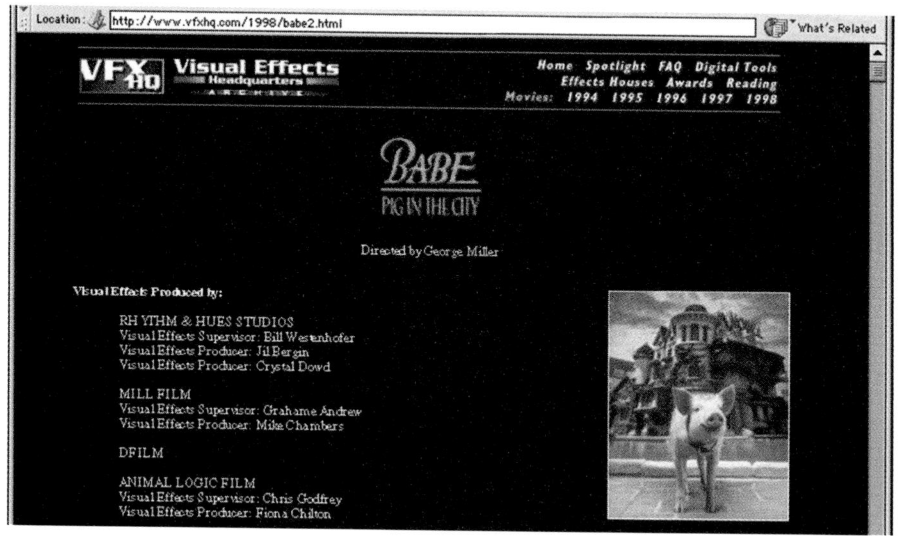


VFX HQ produced by Todd Vaziri . . . http://www.vfxhq.com . . . email tvaziri@earthlink.net.
All text Copyright ©Todd Vaziri, unless otherwise noted.

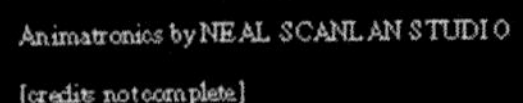
Animatronics by NEAL SCANLAN STUDIO

[credits not complete]

Even more talking animals are featured in BABE: PIG IN THE CITY, sequel to 1995's highly successful BABE. The original won an Academy Award for Best Visual Effects in 1995, and Mill Film, Rhythm & Hues, and Animal Logic contributed to the visual effects to the sequel.

These shots, accomplished by Rhythm & Hues Studios, feature real-life animals 'fitted' with digital prosthetics. The snouts of the animals were meticulously matchmoved in 3D, where a photorealistic mouth was animated and composited over the real mouth. In many cases, parts of the animals' real mouth (if not the entire mouth, snout, chin, etc.) had to be digitally erased.

**Official Web Site:** http://www.babeinthecity.com

Back to the 1998 Menu

Home Spotlight FAQ Digital Tools
Effects Houses Awards Reading
Movies: 1994 1995 1996 1997 1998

There's some interesting information here about how they made the animals appear to speak using computer effects. We might also want to incorporate some of these fun pictures of the talking pig into our finished project. Again, more interesting information about how computer-generated effects contributed to the making of the film. For now, let's click the Back button and return to the Visual Effects Headquarters Archive to check out another film—*Godzilla*.

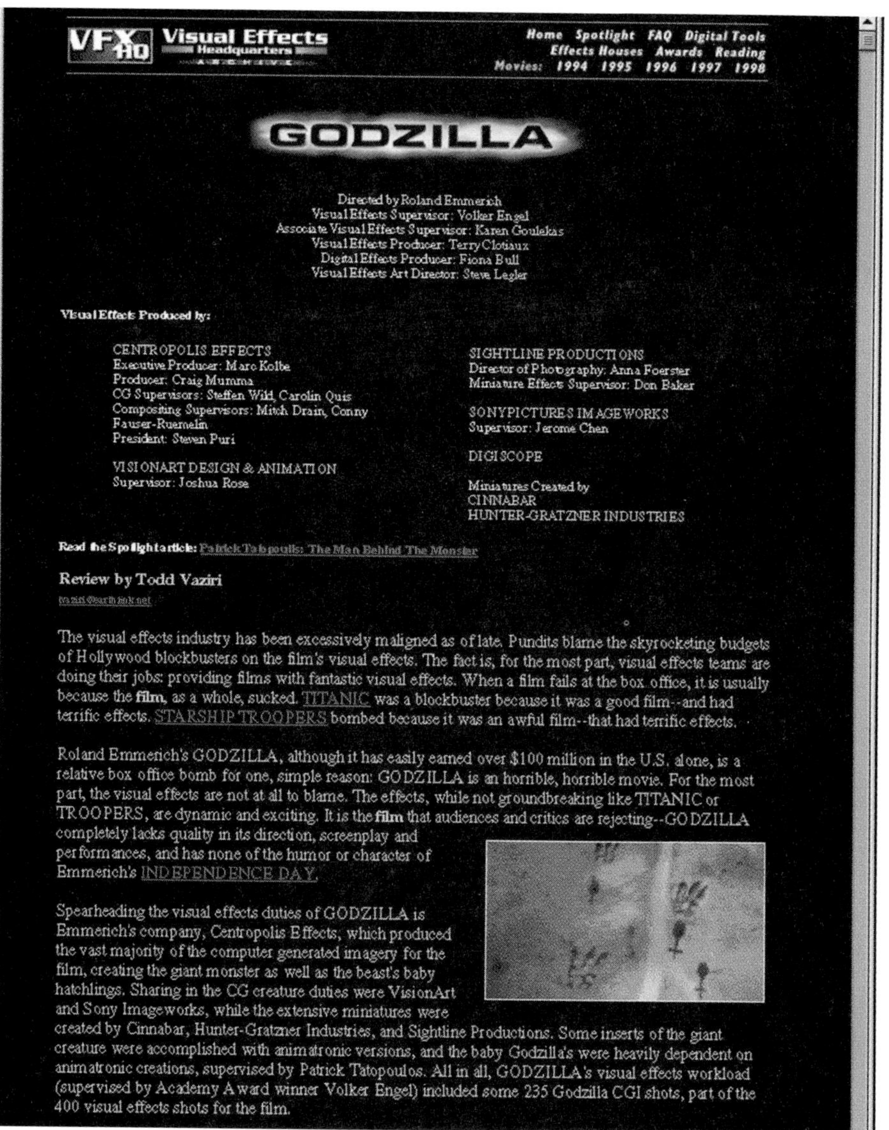

VFX HQ Visual Effects Headquarters Archive

Home Spotlight FAQ Digital Tools
Effects Houses Awards Reading
Movies: 1994 1995 1996 1997 1998

GODZILLA

Directed by Roland Emmerich
Visual Effects Supervisor: Volker Engel
Associate Visual Effects Supervisor: Karen Goulekas
Visual Effects Producer: Terry Clotiaux
Digital Effects Producer: Fiona Bull
Visual Effects Art Director: Steve Legler

**Visual Effects Produced by:**

CENTROPOLIS EFFECTS
Executive Producer: Marc Kolbe
Producer: Craig Mumma
CG Supervisors: Steffen Wild, Carolin Quis
Compositing Supervisors: Mitch Drain, Conny Fauser-Ruemelin
President: Steven Puri

VISIONART DESIGN & ANIMATION
Supervisor: Joshua Rose

SIGHTLINE PRODUCTIONS
Director of Photography: Anna Foerster
Miniature Effects Supervisor: Don Baker

SONY PICTURES IMAGEWORKS
Supervisor: Jerome Chen

DIGISCOPE

Miniatures Created by
CINNABAR
HUNTER-GRATZNER INDUSTRIES

**Read the Spotlight article:** Patrick Tatopoulis: The Man Behind The Monster

**Review by Todd Vaziri**

The visual effects industry has been excessively maligned as of late. Pundits blame the skyrocketing budgets of Hollywood blockbusters on the film's visual effects. The fact is, for the most part, visual effects teams are doing their jobs: providing films with fantastic visual effects. When a film fails at the box office, it is usually because the **film**, as a whole, sucked. TITANIC was a blockbuster because it was a good film--and had terrific effects. STARSHIP TROOPERS bombed because it was an awful film--that had terrific effects.

Roland Emmerich's GODZILLA, although it has easily earned over $100 million in the U.S. alone, is a relative box office bomb for one, simple reason: GODZILLA is an horrible, horrible movie. For the most part, the visual effects are not at all to blame. The effects, while not groundbreaking like TITANIC or TROOPERS, are dynamic and exciting. It is the **film** that audiences and critics are rejecting--GODZILLA completely lacks quality in its direction, screenplay and performances, and has none of the humor or character of Emmerich's INDEPENDENCE DAY.

Spearheading the visual effects duties of GODZILLA is Emmerich's company, Centropolis Effects, which produced the vast majority of the computer generated imagery for the film, creating the giant monster as well as the beast's baby hatchlings. Sharing in the CG creature duties were VisionArt and Sony Imageworks, while the extensive miniatures were created by Cinnabar, Hunter-Gratzner Industries, and Sightline Productions. Some inserts of the giant creature were accomplished with animatronic versions, and the baby Godzilla's were heavily dependent on animatronic creations, supervised by Patrick Tatopoulos. All in all, GODZILLA's visual effects workload (supervised by Academy Award winner Volker Engel) included some 235 Godzilla CGI shots, part of the 400 visual effects shots for the film.

VFX HQ produced by Todd Vaziri . . . http://www.vfxhq.com . . . email tvaziri@earthlink.net.

Much has been said and written about the incessant rain that obscures the giant creature in its New York setting. While the addition of rain to these night shots obscures some artifacts and allows artists to 'get away' with more, it also complicates the CG process, since the creature must appear to be rain-soaked in nearly every scene. Looking at the entire film, the most satisfying Godzilla shots are those where he is completely visible, in daylight, with the camera not moving. Godzilla's first appearance in a New York's harbor featured plenty of daylight (albiet overcast) shots of the giant monster--beginning with tight shots of his massive foot smashing cars, and ending with his dazzling confrontation with cameraman Hank Azaria, where Godzilla is fully revealed. Early shots of the sequence contained terrific matchmoving--the real camera and the CG camera were perfectly in synch--and the interaction between the CG creature and the real-life elements, like cars and people, was very convincing. Careful attention to shadows and extensive rotoscoping of foreground elements allowed these sequences to be successful, although the lack of motion blur on the creature frequently hurt CG shots.

The mutated lizard wanders its way through New York City. The CGI Godzilla was created by newly formed Centropolis Effects. Only a handful of shots of the title creature were completed with animatronic versions of the beast.

©1998 Tri-Star Pictures

The subsequent full-body shots of Godzilla confronting Azaria are brilliant, especially because of the kinetic camera movement. The director was able to use as many dollys and cranes as he wanted, and the CG and compositing teams were able to place the creature realistically within the scene. The best shot of the sequence is a terrific rotational camera move around Azaria as Godzilla approaches his position. Once again, lighting and rotoscoping of these shots make them successful.

Less successful is the design and texture of Godzilla. A monster movie's main creature needs to have character--something inherent to the design of the beast that lends an idea as to its character, its emotions, its desires. TROOPERS' bugs, JURASSIC PARK's dinosaurs, even T2's T-1000 all have some visual characteristics that give us a glimpse of what drives them. Godzilla looks like a man in a lizard suit, plainly and simply. This is not only due to the design, but the choreography and direction of the Godzilla sequences. There seems to be no rhyme or reason to his movements; the audience subsequently cares very little about this creature.

Not to be forgotten are some of the film's non-lizard effects shots. The very best of which is the fantastic helicopter shot of the beached tanker found on the Panamanian coast. From the POV of a hovering helicopter, the camera rotates around the massive liner, perched on the sandy shores of the beach. The shot is incredible--the CG boat is perfectly lit and matchmoved into the scene, even with the bouncy nature of the helicopter-shot background plate. The subsequent bluescreen shot of Matthew Broderick staring at the clawprint on the hull of the ship is less successful, due to the widly varying contrast levels of that shot, relative to the rest of the sequence.

"...the compositing of the creature into the backgrounds make these effects shots look like... well... effects shots."

Speaking of helicopters, they're all over GODZILLA. Flying overhead, helicopter POVs, even in the distant background, there are dozens upon dozens of shots involving the compositing of CG and model helicopters

VFX HQ produced by Todd Vaziri . . . http://www.vfxhq.com . . . email tvaziri@earthlink.net.

into background plates. The most convincing shots are those where the camera is on the ground, slightly drifting to follow the path of the choppers. The most obvious are those where the helicopters fly only a few feet away from the camera, in situations where no real camera could possibly photograph the action. Overall, textures and lighting of the helicopters are quite realistic.

As these choppers pursue Godzilla through the streets of New York, the camera weaves down city streets. The CG creature and (mainly) CG helicopters were composited into background plates of miniature cityscapes, and although these shots are exciting, they do not look photorealistic. The lights from buildings' windows are far too bright and have an unnatural glow, and the compositing of the creature into the backgrounds make these effects shots look like... well... effects shots. The miniatures for the film, overall, are quite fantastic--the best of which appear in daylight shots, where miniature buildings are destroyed right and left with the accurate appearance of scale.

As revealed by a massive panning shot of the Madison Square Garden interior, Godzilla has laid hundreds of eggs. The reveal shot, realized with extensive miniatures, looks muddy and blurry, while subsequent shots of the Garden interior are much more successful. (An earlier version of this review incorrectly stated that a matte painting was used for the reveal shot. VFX HQ regrets the error.) The hatchlings were executed with a combination of animatronic and CG techniques, and the visual differences between them is obvious. Many of the CG baby shots seemed rushed--lighting, animation and compositing are sometimes brilliant, integrating the raptors--ahem, lizards into their background plates, and at other times awful, as if the CG elements were cut and pasted into plates without concern to shadows, reflections, or color levels. There are a ton of baby Godzilla shots, and only half of them achieve the realistic integration of CG element and background plate as such films as JURASSIC PARK and STARSHIP TROOPERS.

> "It's too bad that director Emmerich and producer Dean Devlin couldn't have done a better job creating the non-effects shots."

The single best Godzilla sequence occurs after his 'resurrection'--his chase of our heroes, fleeing in a NYC cab, as Godzilla pursues them. Although one must suspend disbelief heavily for the sequence to work (as if big 'G' couldn't smash the cab with one swoop of his foot), the scene displays the best animation, lighting, and compositing of any other of the film. The Brooklyn Bridge sequence is perhaps more complicated than it has to be, with the bridge disintegrating around Godzilla, poles and supports flying all over the place. The eventual destruction of the beast isn't particularly interesting, with explosions obviously composited over and behind big 'G'.

The few effects' shortcomings aside, the effects teams did a terrific job on GODZILLA. It's just too bad that director Emmerich and producer Dean Devlin couldn't have done a better job creating the non-effects shots.

Check out **Cinefex 74**.
**Official Web Site:** http://www.godzilla.com
GODZILLA ©1998 Tri-Star Pictures

VFX HQ produced by Todd Vaziri . . . http://www.vfxhq.com . . . email tvaziri@earthlink.net.


One more time, let's go back to Visual Effects Headquarters Archive, but this time, we're going to scroll down to the bottom of the page. Here, they have links to more than a dozen articles about visual effects and the movie industry. Let's try "The Magic of ILM."

The Magic of ILM
By Todd Vaziri

If you've visited the Effects Houses section of the VFX HQ, you have seen over a dozen of the biggest names in visual effects. Every house listed creates great images for today's feature films. Although parity of the industry exists, there is a definitive leader of the pack: Lucas Digital's Industrial Light & Magic (ILM).

Effects technology has become much cheaper over the years, and the capital it takes to start a new company has slowly been shrinking. Software like Softimage is now available to the consumer market, and SGIs are becoming a bit more affordable. Also, the talent pool seems to be getting larger as universities train students on valuable animation software.

VFX HQ produced by Todd Vaziri . . . http://www.vfxhq.com . . . email tvaziri@earthlink.net.

Amidst all of the competition, ILM remains on top. They have the experience, the creativity, the tools, the history and the power to work on high profile shows and consistently perform well. The folks who built ILM pioneered the use of many techniques that are commonplace today. Think of how important CG imagery is in today's films. Where did feature film's use of CG begin? The most significant step in CG, in my opinion, was 1982's STAR TREK II: THE WRATH OF KHAN, whose dramatic Genesis simulation was an entirely computer generated sequence, the first of its kind. The group that worked on the sequence at ILM later separated from LucasArts and became a company called Pixar, whose TOY STORY represented yet another huge step in CG animation.

The Pixar example is just one of many arms of ILM's far-extending reach. Nearly every respected effects veteran is or was connected to ILM. The president of Sony Pictures Imageworks, Ken Ralston, spent almost two decades at ILM. Richard Edlund, who was integral to the effects of STAR WARS founded his own company, Boss Film Studios. Phil Tippett, the go-motion innovator, did the same and is currently running Tippett Studios. Digital Domain was founded by three men, all of which had serious relationships with ILM; James Cameron worked with ILM on THE ABYSS and T2, Stan Winston collaborated with them on JURASSIC PARK and T2, and Scott Ross was ILM's general manager.

The past ten years have been extraordinary for ILM in terms of the shows on which they've worked. (Never mind the fact that ILM provided effects for such blockbusters as E.T., RAIDERS OF THE LOST ARK, the STAR WARS trilogy, etc.) Since 1987, ILM has earned seven out of nine Academy Awards for visual effects. Just like other effects houses, ILM must prove its worth during the negotiations period--productions do not simply hand off their project to ILM blindly. Take TWISTER, for example. Director Jan DeBont and producer Steven Spielberg needed to be convinced that a CG tornado would work on film, or else the picture wouldn't have been made at all. The ILM test team was led by effects veteran Dennis Muren, and consisted of fx producer Kim Bromley, animator Dan Taylor, and CG artists Scott Frankel, Carol Hayden, Stewart Lew and Scott Frankel. The test was overwhelmingly successful--you may have even seen it. It was so fantastic, Warner Bros. attached it to the end of the teaser and trailer for the film.

The continuing power of ILM is also due to the snowball effect. ILM revolutionized effects in 1977, they get more high-profile, big-budget projects, ILM grows, the tools and resources expand, ILM gets more big-budget projects, ILM expands its talent, ILM gets another $80 million movie, etc.

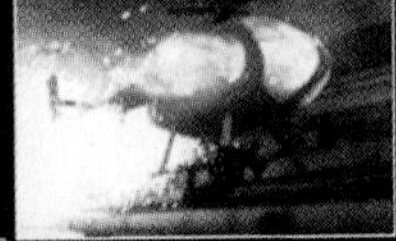

ILM has brought about effects revolutions; techniques such as the morph and CG creation and animation were used effectively in their shows. They successfully graduated from the optical world to the digital world. Just look at the compositing in MISSION: IMPOSSIBLE and TWISTER. It is impeccable.

High profile, risky projects are nothing new to ILM. No matter what imagery is presented before them in a screenplay--not even if the technology isn't available yet--the effects house comes through with stunning results. A mysterious water tentacle? "We can do that (THE ABYSS)." Fully computer generated dinosaurs? "We can do that (JURASSIC PARK)." A chase scene with a virtual helicopter, a virtual train and a virtual tunnel? "We can do that (MISSION: IMPOSSIBLE)." They are constantly given the impossible and achieve it.

Owner George Lucas has crafted the company into an image factory. Easily the largest of all the effects houses, ILM is sometimes criticized for its 'assembly line' attitude in creating visual effects. No matter how ILM runs its business, they are at the top of their game.

The effects industry should be very proud of itself right now. Fantastic images are being created by the big companies, like ILM and Digital Domain, as well as other companies like Boss Film and Rhythm & Hues. But ILM is the heart of the industry--they are the most consistent effects house in terms of quality and quantity of images. The company is synonymous with special effects because of its rich history and continually expanding resources and talent.

---

Back to the Spotlight Main Menu

VFX HQ produced by Todd Vaziri . . . http://www.vfxhq.com . . . email tvaziri@earthlink.net.



This article is more about the history of the company, ILM, than it is about how computer-generated effects are used in movies. Let's drill down a little farther. Inside this article is some hot type on *Star Wars*. The *Star Wars* movies introduced some amazing advances in computer-generated effects. This might be a good place to investigate.

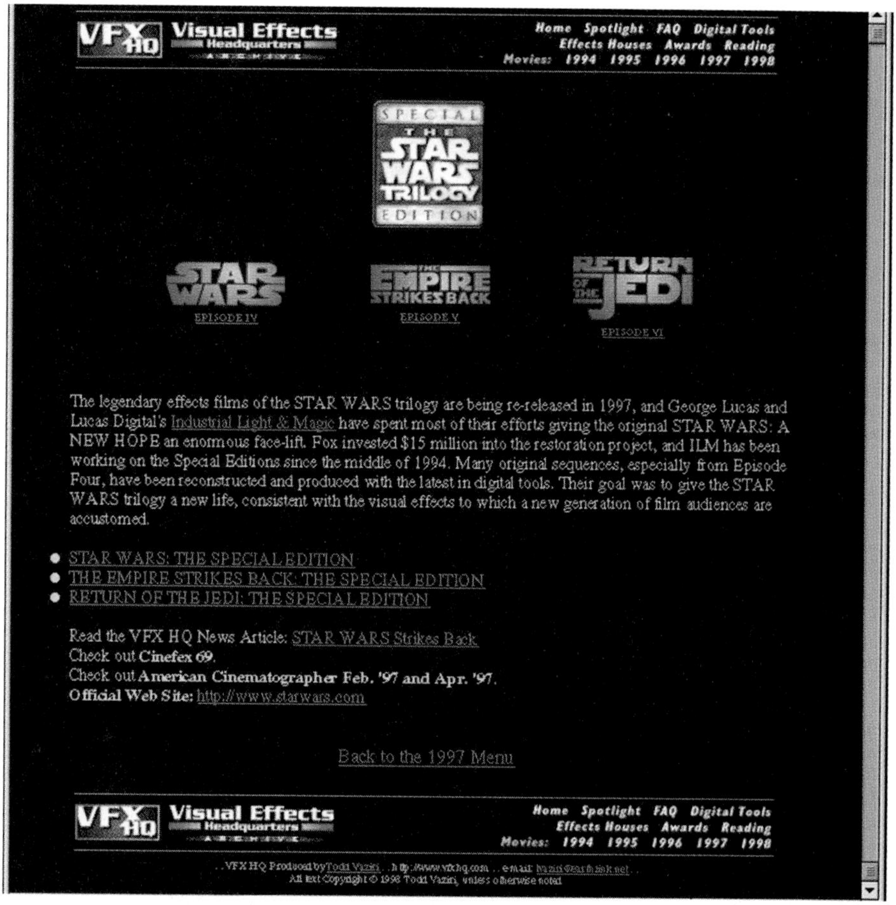

VFX HQ Visual Effects Headquarters
Home Spotlight FAQ Digital Tools
Effects Houses Awards Reading
Movies: 1994 1995 1996 1997 1998
SPECIAL THE STAR WARS TRILOGY EDITION
STAR WARS
EPISODE IV
THE EMPIRE STRIKES BACK
EPISODE V
RETURN OF THE JEDI
EPISODE VI
The legendary effects films of the STAR WARS trilogy are being re-released in 1997, and George Lucas and Lucas Digital's Industrial Light & Magic have spent most of their efforts giving the original STAR WARS: A NEW HOPE an enormous face-lift. Fox invested $15 million into the restoration project, and ILM has been working on the Special Editions since the middle of 1994. Many original sequences, especially from Episode Four, have been reconstructed and produced with the latest in digital tools. Their goal was to give the STAR WARS trilogy a new life, consistent with the visual effects to which a new generation of film audiences are accustomed.
STAR WARS: THE SPECIAL EDITION
THE EMPIRE STRIKES BACK: THE SPECIAL EDITION
RETURN OF THE JEDI: THE SPECIAL EDITION
Read the VFX HQ News Article: STAR WARS Strikes Back
Check out Cinefex 69.
Check out American Cinematographer Feb. '97 and Apr. '97.
Official Web Site: http://www.starwars.com
Back to the 1997 Menu
VFX HQ Visual Effects Headquarters
Home Spotlight FAQ Digital Tools
Effects Houses Awards Reading
Movies: 1994 1995 1996 1997 1998

VFX HQ produced by Todd Vaziri . . . http://www.vfxhq.com . . . email tvaziri@earthlink.net.
All text Copyright ©Todd Vaziri, unless otherwise noted.

Again, still no specific information. Let's keep drilling. We'll click "*Star Wars* Special Edition."

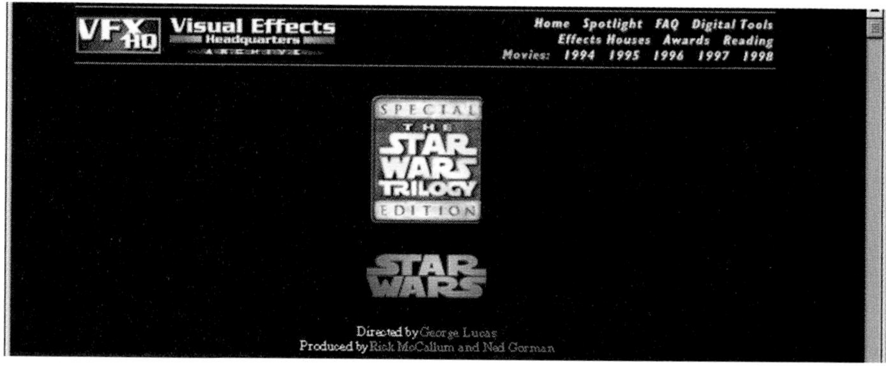

VFX HQ Visual Effects Headquarters
Home Spotlight FAQ Digital Tools
Effects Houses Awards Reading
Movies: 1994 1995 1996 1997 1998
SPECIAL THE STAR WARS TRILOGY EDITION
STAR WARS
Directed by George Lucas
Produced by Rick McCallum and Ned Gorman

VFX HQ produced by Todd Vaziri . . . http://www.vfxhq.com . . . email tvaziri@earthlink.net.
All text Copyright ©Todd Vaziri, unless otherwise noted.

INDUSTRIAL LIGHT & MAGIC
**Visual Effects Supervisors:** Dave Carson, John Knoll, Steven Williams, Bruce Nicholson and Alex Seiden
**Visual Effects Producer:** Tom Kennedy
**Visual Effects Consultant:** Dennis Muren
**CG Supervisors:** Joe Letteri and John Berton

The impetus of the STAR WARS project was the desire to restore of the classic film for its 20th Anniversary. Lucas and Fox jumped at the chance to re-release all three films in grand fashion, adding and enhancing certain visual effects shots.

Certain effects shots from the film have been completely replaced using digital technology, while others use original photography as plates for brand new background and foreground elements. With a few exceptions, the new and enhanced shots fit seamlessly into the classic sci-fi flick.

The first of the brand new shots is a gorgeous establishing shot of R2D2 on Tatooine, just before the Jawas capture him. The shot begins on a stunning Tatooine sky at dusk, and tilts down to the lonely droid navigating the Tatooine surface.

In addition to the new R2 establishing shot, two more new 'replacement' establishing shots were made for Obi-Wan's home and Luke's moisture farm. The 1977 Obi-Wan establishing shot was an odd, nondescript, low angle of Luke's speeder parked outside a hut. This new shot is very wide and beautiful, featuring a lot of great colors and textures of the Tatooine surface. A slight zoom was added to the shot--if the artists had created a dolly-in instead of a zoom, the shot wouldn't have fit into the film. If you look carefully at the original film, there are very few dynamic camera movements, like cranes and dollys. The other establishing shot is an extended wide shot of Luke's farm. Using the original 1977 shot, the artists shrunk the footage, and added more sky, more of the Jawa's cruiser and more of Luke's farm in this breathtaking shot.

An isolated shot of the new CG Dewback and CG Stormtrooper. The background plate is a new shot, photographed in Yuma, AZ. Notice the slight highlight added to the trooper's helmet, consistent with the filters used back in 1977 for Tatooine scenes.

A CG Stormtrooper dismounts from a CG Dewback in this enhanced shot. The animation of the Trooper getting off the beast is phenomenal.

The first shot of the search sequence features real Stormtroopers and the synthetic Dewback and trooper in the background, along with an Imperial craft zooming across the sky.

Searching for the C3PO and R2D2, Imperial Stormtroopers use Dewbacks to help in the search. Originally, the scene consisted of a single shot of a Stormtrooper on an unmoving Dewback far in the distance--then the camera pans left to two troopers in the foreground. The sequence is now three shots long, with two brand new shots using newly shot Stormtrooper footage in Yuma, Arizona (the original photography took place in Tunisia). The two brand new shots feature fully computer generated Dewbacks with CG Stormtroopers riding them. The CG models look great, and the compositing of these two shots have the same 'look' as the original 1977 photography. The last shot is the 1977 pan, but instead of the immobile Dewback in the distance, we now see fully mobile CG Dewbacks and Stormtroopers. The CG elements and plate photography are perfectly married together.

A great new tigher shot of the Jawa's land cruiser is included in the Special Edition, replacing a very long, wide shot of the same cruiser.

Many of Luke's landspeeder shots (around 6 in all) have been 'fixed'--the orange optical blur underneath the floating speeder from the 1977 version has been erased and a new shadow was created.

VFX HQ produced by Todd Vaziri . . . http://www.vfxhq.com . . . email tvaziri@earthlink.net.

The enhanced landspeeder shots (4 in all) add the illusion of the floating craft.

This enhanced shot features a man walking a Ronto (frame left) and the elimination of the orange distortion pattern underneath the floating landspeeder.

A speeder-bike nearly hits a Ronto as its Jawa riders get flung off the beast in this all-new shot from the Mos Eisley sequence.

Luke, Obi-Wan Kenobi and the two droids then venture off to Mos Eisley, Tatooine's bustling spaceport. The new Mos Eisley sequences feature both completely brand new shots as well as many brilliant enhanced shots.

The first is a brand new wide shot of the spaceport--the view that Obi-Wan and the gang sees as Kenobi calls it "a wretched hive of scum and villany." Spacecraft can be seen zooming in and out of the port, and the buildings look a lot more dense in this great establishing shot.

The landspeeder zooms over the camera into the city in another replacement shot. Instead of a blank sandy surface, many tiny creatures are seen hanging around the city--the Mos Eisley equivalent of pigeons. The design is very cute and the animation is really nice as the landspeeder zooms overhead, although it was quite apparent that the effect was accomplished in post-production. The contrast levels seemed a bit too high--the animals didn't seem as if they were actually in front of the camera.

The hero shot of the sequence appears next, as a completely new shot begins on two fighting droids, follows the landspeeder with a pan right, and cranes up, dozens of feet above the ground, allowing the audience to see the large, bustling city for the first time. The animation of the two droids (one a human-like droid and the other a floating probe droid) is fanatstic and quite funny. Numerous CG elements made up the shots, along with many digital matte paintings and miniatures. Although the shot technically and aesthetically brilliant, it simply does not fit into STAR WARS. The establishing crane shot is a standard in many films, but the 1977 version of STAR WARS had very little camera movement.

The hero shot of the sequence appears next, as a completely new shot begins on two fighting droids, follows the landspeeder with a pan right, and cranes up, dozens of feet above the ground, allowing the audience to see the large, bustling city for the first time. The animation of the two droids (one a human-like droid and the other a floating probe droid) is fanatstic and quite funny. Numerous CG elements made up the shots, along with many digital matte paintings and miniatures. Although the shot technically and aesthetically brilliant, it simply does not fit into STAR WARS. The establishing crane shot is a standard in many films, but the 1977 version of STAR WARS had very little camera movement.

Another five shots follow (some brand new, some enhanced), and many include new, thirty foot tall creatures, called Rontos. The animation and models of these CG models look fantastic, and compositing of these shots integrated them into the plate photography. If the Ronto's shape looks familiar, it should--it's actually a altered version of the CG model created for JURASSIC PARK's Brontosaurus, hence the name Ronto. In a few other shots outside the cantina, CG Rontos and Dewbacks, along with the floating Imperial droids are featured in the backgrounds of original 1977 photography. The match-moving and rotoscoping of these shots are **fantastic**--the shadows created for the floating droid are right on the money and are completely integrated into the 1977 shot.

The CG Stormtrooper makes another appearance in an enhanced shot--the Stormtrooper dismounts from the Dewback in some of the best humanoid CG animation I've ever seen.

VFX HQ produced by Todd Vaziri . . . http://www.vfxhq.com . . . email tvaziri@earthlink.net.

Jabba the Hutt makes a cameo in STAR WARS in this newly restored sequence.

One of the biggest new scenes is the restored conversation between Han Solo and Jabba the Hutt. Originally shot with a human actor as Jabba, CG Supervisor Joe Letteri and animator Steve "Spaz" Williams replaced him with a fully CG Jabba slug, as he appeared in RETURN OF THE JEDI. This Jabba can slithers and squirms his way to Han, and has a discussion with Solo in the 5 shot sequence. Small alterations to Harrison Ford's movements were made to accomplish a seamless (and sometimes very funny) encounter between the human and the CG creature. A new feature to the sequence is Boba Fett--an actor in costume performed in front of a bluescreen in order to integrate the bounty hunter into the sequence. One problem I have with the new Jabba sequence is Jabba's eyes. The bright orange eyes of the puppet Jabba in JEDI are realized in the new shots as glossy, desaturated bulbs. Also, Jabba is far too expressive in this chapter of the STAR WARS saga, which betrays the way Jabba appears in RETURN OF THE JEDI.

An exclusive side-by-side comparison of the 1977 production footage and the newly enhanced shot including a computer generated Jabba. Careful erasure of the original actor as well as extensive rotoscoping and animation of Solo add to the realism of the sequence.

As the Falcon takes off from Mos Eisley, one brand new shot shows a CG Falcon rising from Bay 94, and an enhanced wide shot of the Falcon zooming into the air features a new, dynamic aerial move. As the Falcon tries to escape the Death Star's tractor beam, new, accurate camera shake animation was added to the interior shots.

A new explosion was shot for Alderaan's destruction, and features a colorful shockwave, very similar to ILM's shockwave created for STAR TREK VI. The Death Star's explosion was enhanced with this shockwave, as well.

A terrific enhanced shot was created for Han Solo's furious attack on a group of Stormtroopers. In the original shot, eight Stormtroopers turn around and fire on Solo. In the hilarious enhanced shot, an entire legion of Stormtroopers appear in the background.

In this incredible composite, the Rebel base exterior has been enhanced, giving the huge structure a new, rougher exterior.

No new model photography was used for space sequences for the Special Edition of STAR WARS--all spacecraft were created as CG models. Textures were scanned directly off of the original miniature models created in the late '70's, however. CG representations of the Millennium Falcon, the X- and Y-Wing fighters, as well as TIE Fighters will appear onscreen.

Intending to keep the pacing of the original film intact, the effects artists crafted each new space shot (around 30) to be the same frame length as the original shot. The choreography of the shots in question was enhanced--the new CG craft afford the animators a greater range of movement than the motion-control shot models. Instead of a limited three dimensional space for which the camera and the model to interact (due to stage size, model and camera rigging, etc.), the virtual camera and virtual model have infinite possibilities in terms of distance and perspective. New, exciting dynamics have been created to **enhance** the sequences' drama, not alter them.

VFX HQ produced by Todd Vaziri . . . http://www.vfxhq.com . . . email tvaziri@earthlink.net.

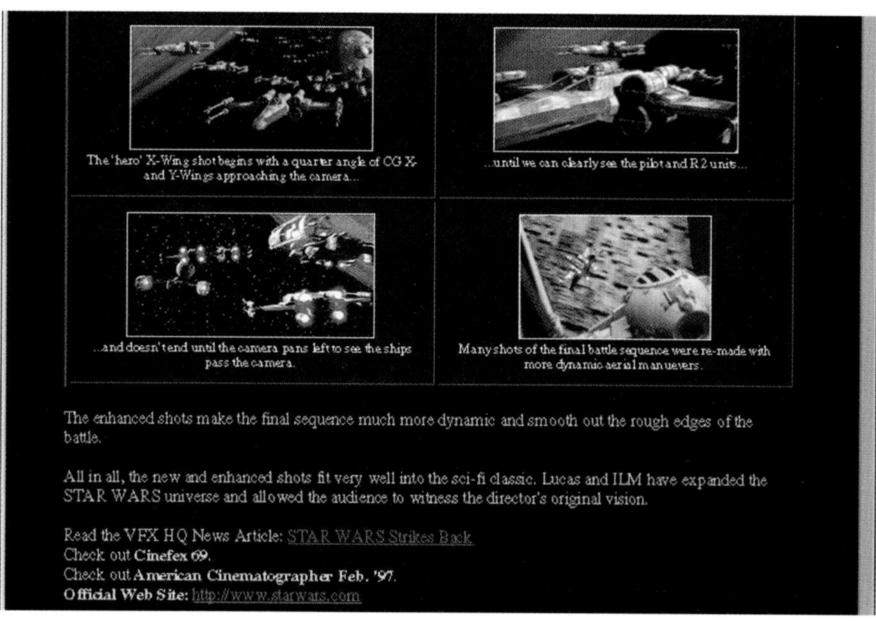

The 'hero' X-Wing shot begins with a quarter angle of CG X- and Y-Wings approaching the camera...
...until we can clearly see the pilot and R2 units...
...and doesn't end until the camera pans left to see the ships pass the camera.
Many shots of the final battle sequence were re-made with more dynamic aerial manuevers.
The enhanced shots make the final sequence much more dynamic and smooth out the rough edges of the battle.
All in all, the new and enhanced shots fit very well into the sci-fi classic. Lucas and ILM have expanded the STAR WARS universe and allowed the audience to witness the director's original vision.
Read the VFX HQ News Article: STAR WARS Strikes Back
Check out Cinefex 69.
Check out American Cinematographer Feb. '97.
Official Web Site: http://www.starwars.com


VFX HQ produced by Todd Vaziri . . . http://www.vfxhq.com . . . email tvaziri@earthlink.net.


Here's the payoff! This article talks about how several years after the original *Star Wars* film was completed, advanced computer-graphic effects enhanced the Special Edition version of the film.

The Visual Effects Headquarters Archive produced a wealth of articles for our project. We could spend much longer on this one site alone. For now, let's set a bookmark here and go back to the Webcrawler site listing one more time.

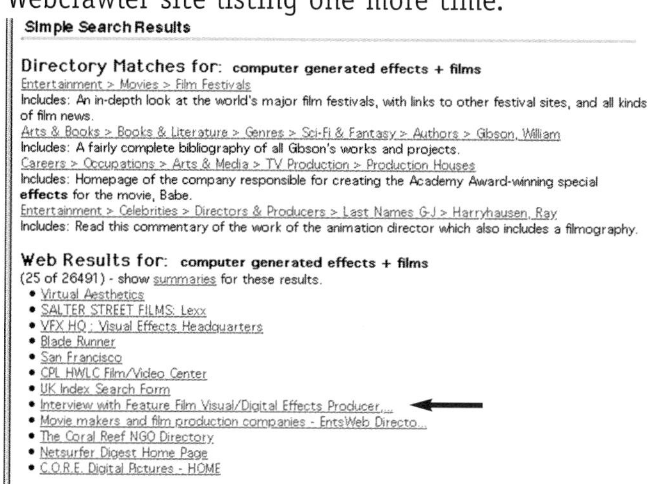
**Simple Search Results**

**Directory Matches for: computer generated effects + films**
Entertainment > Movies > Film Festivals
Includes: An in-depth look at the world's major film festivals, with links to other festival sites, and all kinds of film news.
Arts & Books > Books & Literature > Genres > Sci-Fi & Fantasy > Authors > Gibson, William
Includes: A fairly complete bibliography of all Gibson's works and projects.
Careers > Occupations > Arts & Media > TV Production > Production Houses
Includes: Homepage of the company responsible for creating the Academy Award-winning special **effects** for the movie, Babe.
Entertainment > Celebrities > Directors & Producers > Last Names G-J > Harryhausen, Ray
Includes: Read this commentary of the work of the animation director which also includes a filmography.

**Web Results for: computer generated effects + films**
(25 of 26491) - show summaries for these results.

- Virtual Aesthetics
- SALTER STREET FILMS: Lexx
- VFX HQ : Visual Effects Headquarters
- Blade Runner
- San Francisco
- CPL HWLC Film/Video Center
- UK Index Search Form
- Interview with Feature Film Visual/Digital Effects Producer,...
- Movie makers and film production companies - EntsWeb Directo...
- The Coral Reef NGO Directory
- Netsurfer Digest Home Page
- C.O.R.E. Digital Pictures - HOME

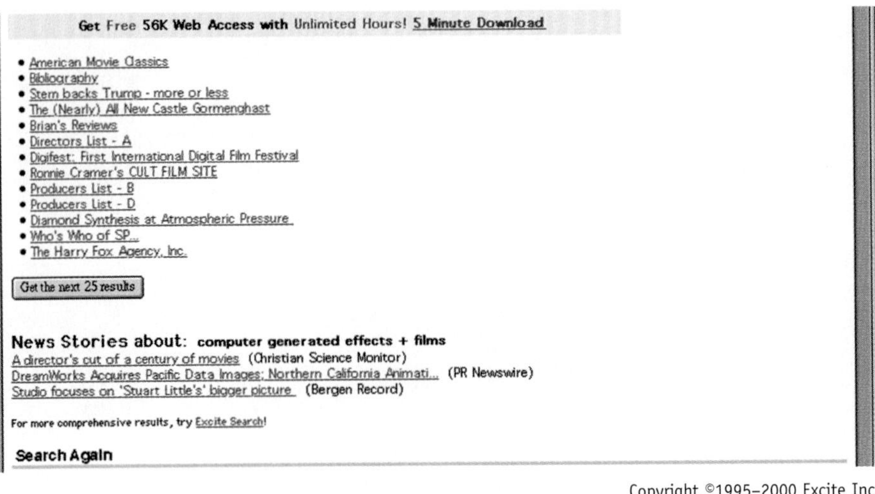
Get Free 56K Web Access with Unlimited Hours! 5 Minute Download

- American Movie Classics
- Bibliography
- Stern backs Trump - more or less
- The (Nearly) All New Castle Gormenghast
- Brian's Reviews
- Directors List - A
- Digifest: First International Digital Film Festival
- Ronnie Cramer's CULT FILM SITE
- Producers List - B
- Producers List - D
- Diamond Synthesis at Atmospheric Pressure
- Who's Who of SP...
- The Harry Fox Agency, Inc.

Get the next 25 results

**News Stories about: computer generated effects + films**

A director's cut of a century of movies (Christian Science Monitor)
DreamWorks Acquires Pacific Data Images; Northern California Animati... (PR Newswire)
Studio focuses on 'Stuart Little's' bigger picture (Bergen Record)

For more comprehensive results, try Excite Search!

Search Again



Here we find another article about computerized effects, but this one is from a producer's perspective.

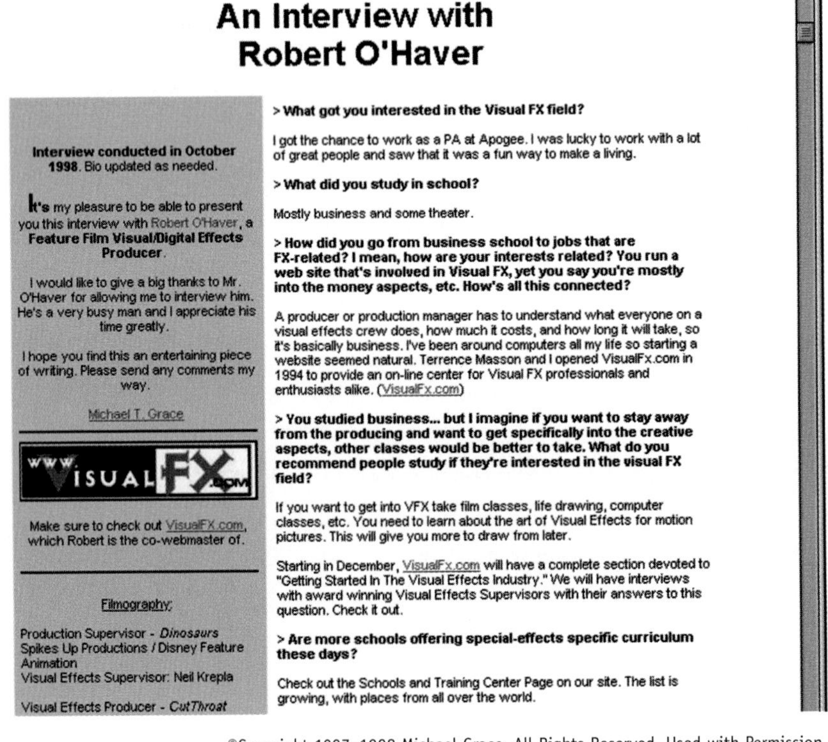
The Reel Site

# An Interview with Robert O'Haver

**Interview conducted in October 1998.** Bio updated as needed.

It's my pleasure to be able to present you this interview with Robert O'Haver, a **Feature Film Visual/Digital Effects Producer**.

I would like to give a big thanks to Mr. O'Haver for allowing me to interview him. He's a very busy man and I appreciate his time greatly.

I hope you find this an entertaining piece of writing. Please send any comments my way.

Michael T. Grace



Make sure to check out VisualFX.com, which Robert is the co-webmaster of.

Filmography:

Production Supervisor - *Dinosaurs*
Spikes Up Productions / Disney Feature Animation
Visual Effects Supervisor: Neil Krepla

Visual Effects Producer - *CutThroat*

**> What got you interested in the Visual FX field?**

I got the chance to work as a PA at Apogee. I was lucky to work with a lot of great people and saw that it was a fun way to make a living.

**> What did you study in school?**

Mostly business and some theater.

**> How did you go from business school to jobs that are FX-related? I mean, how are your interests related? You run a web site that's involved in Visual FX, yet you say you're mostly into the money aspects, etc. How's all this connected?**

A producer or production manager has to understand what everyone on a visual effects crew does, how much it costs, and how long it will take, so it's basically business. I've been around computers all my life so starting a website seemed natural. Terrence Masson and I opened VisualFx.com in 1994 to provide an on-line center for Visual FX professionals and enthusiasts alike. (VisualFx.com)

**> You studied business... but I imagine if you want to stay away from the producing and want to get specifically into the creative aspects, other classes would be better to take. What do you recommend people study if they're interested in the visual FX field?**

If you want to get into VFX take film classes, life drawing, computer classes, etc. You need to learn about the art of Visual Effects for motion pictures. This will give you more to draw from later.

Starting in December, VisualFx.com will have a complete section devoted to "Getting Started In The Visual Effects Industry." We will have interviews with award winning Visual Effects Supervisors with their answers to this question. Check it out.

**> Are more schools offering special-effects specific curriculum these days?**

Check out the Schools and Training Center Page on our site. The list is growing, with places from all over the world.

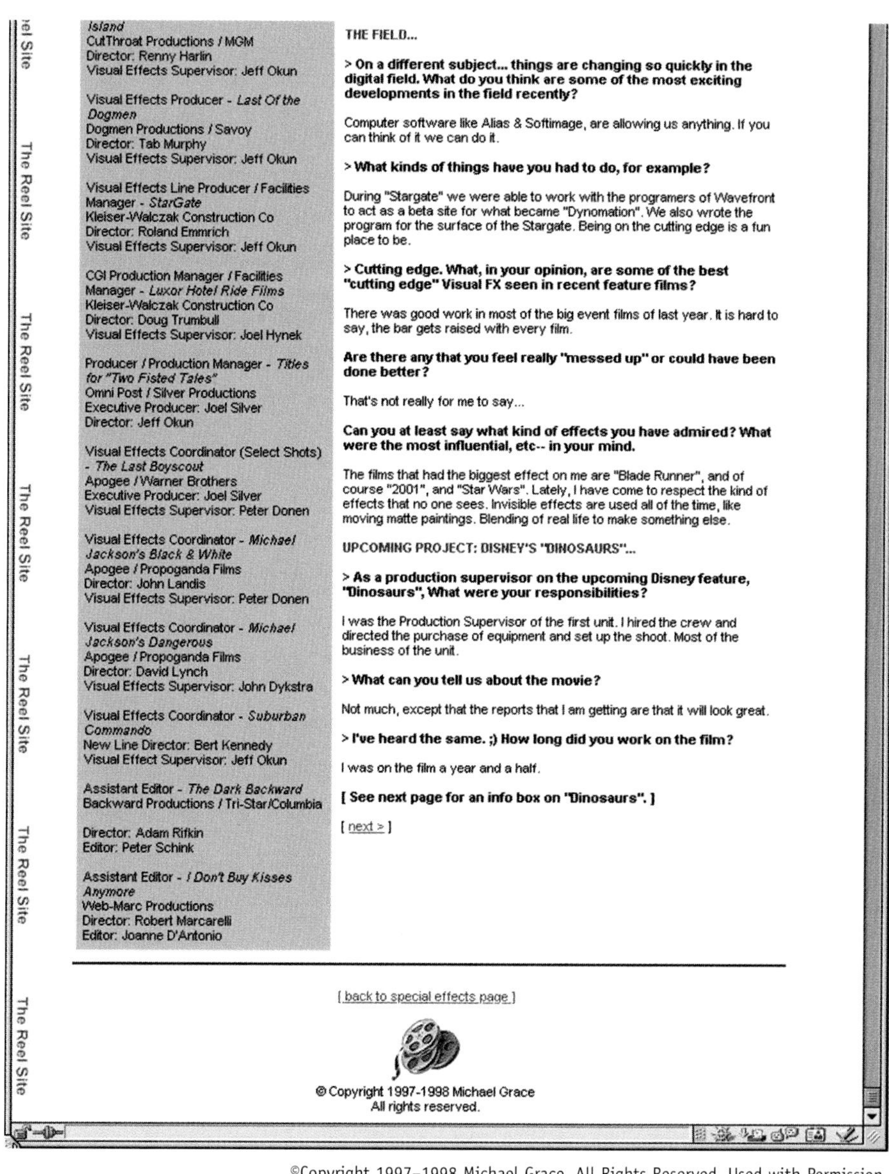

THE FIELD...

> On a different subject... things are changing so quickly in the digital field. What do you think are some of the most exciting developments in the field recently?

Computer software like Alias & Softimage, are allowing us anything. If you can think of it we can do it.

> What kinds of things have you had to do, for example?

During "Stargate" we were able to work with the programers of Wavefront to act as a beta site for what became "Dynomation". We also wrote the program for the surface of the Stargate. Being on the cutting edge is a fun place to be.

> Cutting edge. What, in your opinion, are some of the best "cutting edge" Visual FX seen in recent feature films?

There was good work in most of the big event films of last year. It is hard to say, the bar gets raised with every film.

Are there any that you feel really "messed up" or could have been done better?

That's not really for me to say...

Can you at least say what kind of effects you have admired? What were the most influential, etc-- in your mind.

The films that had the biggest effect on me are "Blade Runner", and of course "2001", and "Star Wars". Lately, I have come to respect the kind of effects that no one sees. Invisible effects are used all of the time, like moving matte paintings. Blending of real life to make something else.

UPCOMING PROJECT: DISNEY'S "DINOSAURS"...

> As a production supervisor on the upcoming Disney feature, "Dinosaurs", What were your responsibilities?

I was the Production Supervisor of the first unit. I hired the crew and directed the purchase of equipment and set up the shoot. Most of the business of the unit.

> What can you tell us about the movie?

Not much, except that the reports that I am getting are that it will look great.

> I've heard the same. ;) How long did you work on the film?

I was on the film a year and a half.

[ See next page for an info box on "Dinosaurs". ]

[ next > ]

*Island*
CutThroat Productions / MGM
Director: Renny Harlin
Visual Effects Supervisor: Jeff Okun

Visual Effects Producer - *Last Of the Dogmen*
Dogmen Productions / Savoy
Director: Tab Murphy
Visual Effects Supervisor: Jeff Okun

Visual Effects Line Producer / Facilities Manager - *StarGate*
Kleiser-Walczak Construction Co
Director: Roland Emmrich
Visual Effects Supervisor: Jeff Okun

CGI Production Manager / Facilities Manager - *Luxor Hotel Ride Films*
Kleiser-Walczak Construction Co
Director: Doug Trumbull
Visual Effects Supervisor: Joel Hynek

Producer / Production Manager - *Titles for "Two Fisted Tales"*
Omni Post / Silver Productions
Executive Producer: Joel Silver
Director: Jeff Okun

Visual Effects Coordinator (Select Shots) - *The Last Boyscout*
Apogee / Warner Brothers
Executive Producer: Joel Silver
Visual Effects Supervisor: Peter Donen

Visual Effects Coordinator - *Michael Jackson's Black & White*
Apogee / Propoganda Films
Director: John Landis
Visual Effects Supervisor: Peter Donen

Visual Effects Coordinator - *Michael Jackson's Dangerous*
Apogee / Propoganda Films
Director: David Lynch
Visual Effects Supervisor: John Dykstra

Visual Effects Coordinator - *Suburban Commando*
New Line Director: Bert Kennedy
Visual Effect Supervisor: Jeff Okun

Assistant Editor - *The Dark Backward*
Backward Productions / Tri-Star/Columbia

Director: Adam Rifkin
Editor: Peter Schink

Assistant Editor - *I Don't Buy Kisses Anymore*
Web-Marc Productions
Director: Robert Marcarelli
Editor: Joanne D'Antonio

[ back to special effects page ]







The keywords "computer generated effects + films" seemed to work well. Let's try our search again using the Lycos search engine this time. We'll also narrow our search even further by adding the word *visual,* so our keywords will be "computer generated visual effects + films." Here's the list the service retrieved.

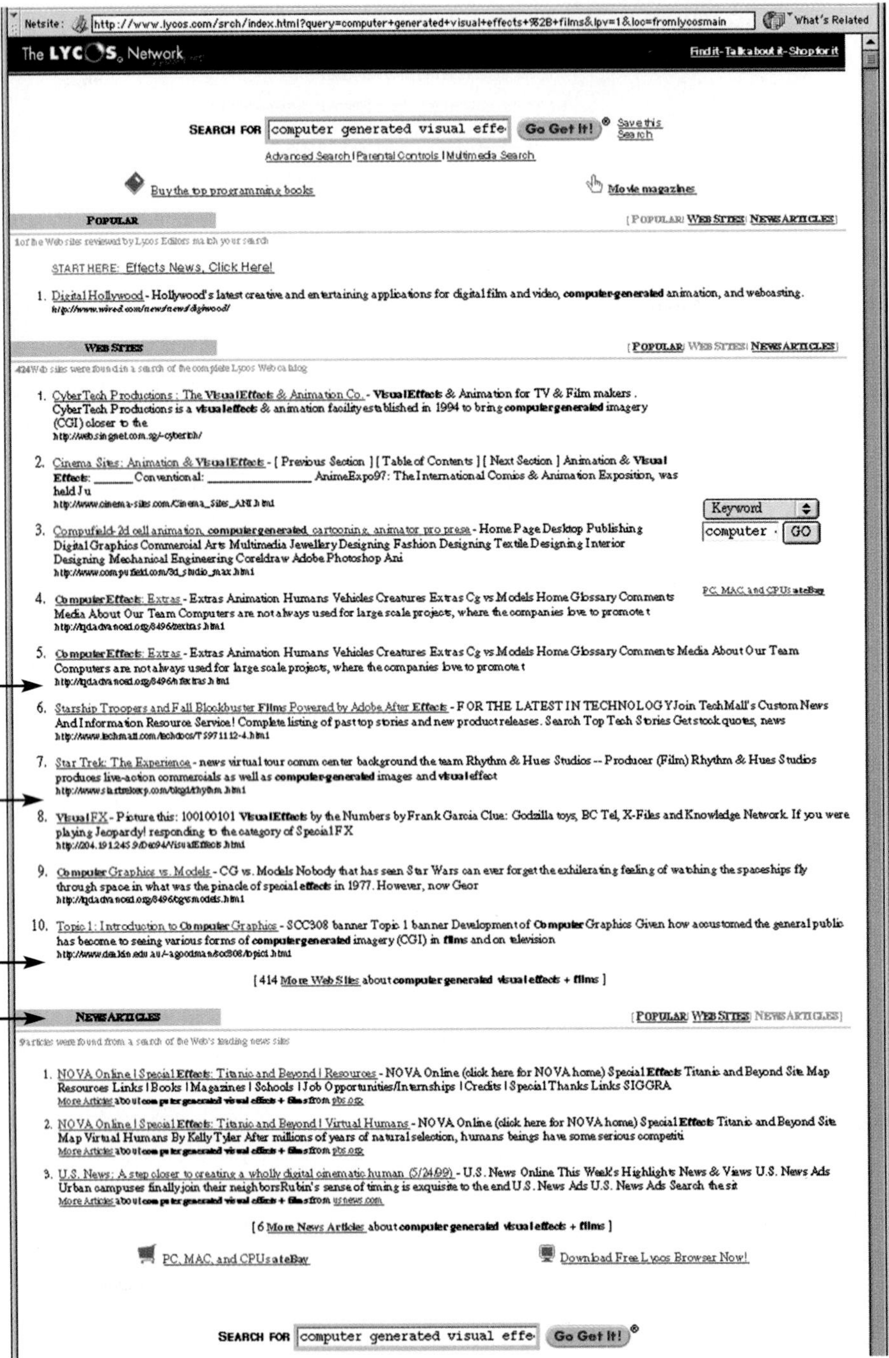




Again, we've found a great assortment of articles. Here are four that look interesting.

Location: http://library.thinkquest.org/3496/nfextras.html

EXTRAS

ANIMATION | HUMANS | VEHICLES | CREATURES | EXTRAS | CG/MODELS
HOME | GLOSSARY | COMMENTS | MEDIA | ABOUT

Computers are not always used for large scale projects, where the companies love to promote the advanced technology used in their films. Many of the jobs computers do are not so flashy. And lots of the time the studio would rather that you didn't realize there had been computers at work. And it's to these little things that we devote this page.

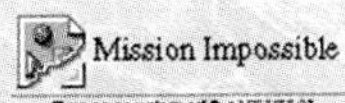

[Image courtesy of the VFXHQ]

**Rod Removal** - When puppets are used to fulfill a scene, they don't move by themselves. The puppeteers below manipulate the models by hand, and then computers are needed to digitally remove the rods. That way the puppets look alive, and the audience hopefully won't know the difference. Similarly, actors are sometimes required to "fly" in a frame. By hanging the actors, and then digitally removing the wires and compositing the actor into the shot, the character appears to fly. A prime example of this technique is the final action scene from Mission Impossible. Tom Cruise's character is propelled by an explosion to land on a speeding bullet train. The shot combines the best of 3d computer work with a small amount of extra help: the wires used to fly Cruise through the frame were removed by Industrial Light and Magic. Hopefully you'll suspend your belief in reality to think that Cruise actually flew through the air. Sorry if we spoiled the effect for you.

**Scenery** - For the "Avalon" scene in Dragonheart, the director needed a convincing castle that could have been the historic home of King Arthur and his Knights of the Round Table. The digital effects crew at Illusion Arts combined pictures of the coast of Catalina Island with a digital painting of a castle and computer generated mist. The waves crashing against the shores next to the castle were all computer anmiated as well. For interior shots of the castle, an existing castle in Eastern Europe was combined with computer generated columns and headstones for a more historic and gloomy yet significant look.
Twister had its own problems with the surroundings. As detailed in the Twister page, the crews had to shoot in different locations, Iowa and Oklahoma. This caused a problem, because the corn in Iowa was beginning to grow tassels. ILM had to remove the tassels to make the corn blend with the wheat from Oklahoma. ILM was also responsible for creating houses and barns for the tornados to rip apart.

[Image courtesy of the VFXHQ]

**Lighting** - When the *Twister* crew tried to film stormy weather in Oklahoma, they ran into lots of sunlight. The sky was easily corrected by having artists at ILM paint in series' of malicioius looking clouds. However, lighting on the ground was an entirely different problem. While the tornados could be modified to appear without the extra lighting, the rest of the surrounding area would still appear sunny. Several of the shots were simply darkened and the tornado applied to match that lighting.
*Dragonheart* also had a few lighting problems. When working in scenes invovling the dragon's heart, the director wanted a red glow to come from it. The light from the heart was entirely computer generated. Another problem stemmed from the lava in the dragon's cave. The light from the set just looked to fake. So the teams softened the light on the actors faces, adding a bit more of a glow to it, and also gave the rest of the surrounding area a soft glow.
Another spectacular example of lighting can be seen in Independence Day. When the alien ships are flying into position, computers were used to create made by the ships. These shadows crawl up buildings, flow across Central Park, and climb the Statue of Liberty as the ships move along.

**Lasers** - Another place that computers are used is to create those classic sci-fi stand-bys: laser blasts. In many cases, computers are used to animate a particle or cylinder moving very quickly from origin to target and blurred to create the effect of laser blasts. Other times the lasers a simply drawn in by hand using any number of programs.

**Missiles, Smoke** - When the planes in the movies launch their missiles, the missiles don't alwyas pack it. So, computers have to take over the job. *Independence Day* and True Lies both contain excellent examples of how well missiles can be rendered, along with the smoke trails behind them. Since everybody assumes it's real, the studios don't bother making a big deal out if it.

[Image courtesy of the VFXHQ]

**Titles** - Before you can watch a movie, you have to know which movie you're watching. And since the audience can get bored real fast if there's nothing interesting going on, the studios have come up with all kinds of fancy title sequences to amaze theater goers. One of the most recent and most spectacular titles came from *Twister*. 525 Post Productions was in charge of creating a title that would set the audience up for a film full of special effects. What they came up with was swirling debris, flying letters, explosions, and lots of wind. Using Discreet Logic's Flame, 525 started off with 20,000 images, combined those to create the final 1,300 images, and finished with 32 layers of computer generated imagery. While this is one of the most complex titles around, it gives you an idea of the fine details that go into making a title for a movie.

Extras are all the little things that people don't notice. The little details that every computer effects shot require are the major center of the extra bits. Even the smallest little items are special. In this summer's The Island of Dr. Moreau, Marlon Brando's costume didn't fit quite right. ILM was paid $50,000 to airbrush out the underwear that was peeking out the back. THATS called attention to the little things.

RELATED LINKS

Location: http://www.techmall.com/techdocs/TS971112-4.html
What's Related

TechMall
FOR THE LATEST IN TECHNOLOGY



Home

Tech Story Index
Complete listing of past top stories and new product releases.

Search Top Tech Stories

Search

Info Search
Get stock quotes, news, weather, find people and more with over 50 of the best web search tools!

Editor's Choice
The best of the Web... brought to you by the TechMall Surf Team.

Nuts & Bolts
HTML help, editorials, and survival tips for the Internet wilderness.

After Hours
Joke archive, a science trivia quiz, and more!

Submissions
Submit your press release information here!

Software
A technical guide to the web -- useful programs, links, and beyond.

## Top Tech Stories

### Starship Troopers and Fall Blockbuster Films Powered by Adobe After Effects Dazzle Audiences with Eye-Catching Content

After Effects Speeds Production Saving Filmmakers Time and Money

SAN JOSE, Calif., Nov. 12 -- The long-awaited "Starship Troopers" opened Friday with thousands of giant alien insects and human soldiers battling it out on faraway planets. Many special effects in this movie, and other forthcoming blockbuster films, were created with desktop computers using Adobe® After Effects®. Compositing and animation tools such as After Effects play increasingly important roles in major Hollywood films. After Effects enables filmmakers to dazzle audiences with more elaborate special effects and animations at a fraction of the time and cost of traditional post-production methods. Using After Effects, filmmakers can create content on both the Macintosh and Windows platform that has traditionally been produced using more expensive workstations.

Control, flexibility, time and cost savings make After Effects an industry leader in the compositing of moving imagery. After Effects combines resolution-independent compositing controls and sophisticated motion controls with advanced special effects capabilities. Its tight integration with industry standard products such as Adobe Photoshop® and Adobe Illustrator®, provides filmmakers with a complete design and compositing workflow solution.

In addition to "Starship Troopers," After Effects plays a leading role in other major upcoming films including "The Jackal" and "Lost In Space." Summer blockbuster films that used After Effects include "Men In Black," "Spawn," "Event Horizon" and "George of the Jungle."

After Effects Saves Filmmakers Time and Money

Starship Troopers

Using After Effects, production artists for "Starship Troopers" created visual excitement by transforming 20 Starship Troopers into 400, compositing thousands of alien bugs into live action scenes and adding environmental elements like shadows, muzzle flashes, squirting blood and flying dust to make the scenes look real.

"After Effects is much faster than traditional post-production methods and is one of the best compositing tools out there, on any platform, at any price," said Tippett Studios' Brennan Doyle, lead compositor for "Starship Troopers." "Our primary reason for using After Effects is that the viewer will never notice that we did our job in the first place. The best compositing is unseen. We can make 20 extras look like 400, or we can put a giant bug in a scene and make it look like it has always been there. That's what compositing is about."

The Jackal

"The Jackal" is somewhat of a landmark in digital visual effects work. There are over 100 digital effects shots in the movie and virtually all of them, including the high-voltage subway chase scene with the hero pursuing the Jackal, were composited using After Effects.

"The effects themselves are not the kind of shots which elicit gasps of wonder from the audience," said Richard Patterson, digital effects supervisor at Illusion Arts studio. "In fact, the measure of the success of the shots may well be how unaware the audience is that any kind of special effects were required to produce the scenes."

"Because of its ease-of-use and cost benefits, After Effects has enabled us to produce high-end special effects for major films," continues Patterson. "After Effects is a sophisticated compositing program with a user interface that makes sense. The program is extremely well designed, straightforward and user friendly."

Men In Black

The memorable dragonfly scene depicted in the first two minutes of the summer blockbuster "Men In Black" was composited entirely in After Effects.

"We create multi-million dollar sequences for pennies, and we are able to do so because of After Effects," said Joe Conti of Autumn Light Entertainment. "There was a tremendous amount of digital work done in 'Men and Black.' We created 3,600 frames of animation in a fraction of the time it would have taken using traditional post-production methods."

Spawn

Los Angeles-based Banned From the Ranch Entertainment (BFTR) used After Effects for the majority of their supernatural visual effects and graphics work on the movie "Spawn." After Effects was used in combination with MetaCreations' particle system plug-ins to generate elements -- from rolling storm clouds to animated fire -- and composite the final film-resolution shots.

"After Effects allowed us to dial up a wide variety of special effects, from light rays to particle systems, that would typically require a 3D package," said BFTR lead digital artist, Erich Ippen. "After Effects gave us the ability to do everything we wanted and more, with respect to compositing, at a fraction of the cost of other film compositing systems."

After Effects Improves Productivity

Lost In Space

The challenge of making spaceship data screens appear both real and futuristic for the forthcoming film "Lost In Space" was met with the help of After Effects. Using After Effects, a team of six generated graphics for on-set screens that were made to look like spaceship 'communicators' used to present navigational, engineering, weapons systems and life support information to the crew throughout the film.

"We found After Effects to be a vital piece of software for our production methods. Indeed, I cannot think of any other animation programs that could provide such intuitive yet powerful flexibility," said Richard Briscoe, freelancer for Bionics Productions, Ltd. "Both the timeline and motion path controls, as well as the filters, allow for an enormous range of possibilities. After Effects allows for the production of the highest quality material, with all the control one could wish for."

George of the Jungle

In "George of the Jungle," After Effects and Photoshop were used in combination exclusively for the film's matte painting work, bringing the mysterious Ape Mountain to life. Sophisticated composites of George's pet, Shep the elephant, were accomplished quickly utilizing After Effects.

"We knew from the outset that After Effects would be an integral part of 'George of the Jungle's visual effects," said Tim Landry. "Features such as the integration of Photoshop layers, offer effects options that are simply not available in any other compositing package."

Event Horizon

AMXdigital used After Effects in conjunction with Photoshop and Illustrator to design and produce computer screen graphics for the two spaceships in "Event Horizon." AMX developed a series of animated sequences displaying internal computer systems, ship's log, video consoles and communications devices for each of the space vessels. In total, 11,520 frames were generated for eight minutes of special effects.

According to Zoe Black, the producer on the project, "Going from basic animation to sophisticated project structure was easy and straightforward with After Effects. The software was also extremely stable and coped well with multiple animated layers."

About Adobe After Effects

With After Effects, users can combine unlimited layers of moving and still images, add any number of keyframes, animate and apply special effects to each layer and adjust layers until the composite looks and moves exactly as intended. After Effects gives users precise control over every aspect of the composite -- from sub-pixel positioning to controlling the shape and velocity of each animation path. After Effects is available on both the Macintosh and PC platforms, and offers sophisticated support for multiprocessing to take advantage of today's high-performance desktop systems.

About Adobe Systems Inc.

Based in San Jose, California, Adobe Systems Incorporated develops and supports products to help people express and use information in more imaginative and meaningful ways across print and electronic media. Founded in 1982, Adobe helped launch the desktop publishing revolution. Today, the company offers a market-leading line of application software and type products for creating and distributing visually rich communication materials; licenses its industry-standard technologies to major hardware manufacturers, software developers, and service providers; and offers integrated software solutions to businesses of all sizes. For more information, see Adobe's home page at http://www.adobe.com on the World Wide Web.



SOURCE Adobe Systems Inc.

*CONTACT: Press/Analyst Contact: Heidi White of Cunningham Communication, Inc., 650-858-3759, or hwhite@ccipr.com*

Location: http://library.thinkquest.org/3496/cgvsmodels.html What's Related

Nobody that has seen Star Wars can ever forget the exhilerating feeling of watching the spaceships fly through space in what was the pinacle of special effects in 1977. However, now George Lucas and Industrial Light and Magic are investing $10 million to recreate the Star Wars trilogy in special editions to be released in 1997. Almost all of the ships from the previous films will be replaced with computer generated vehicles. Which raises an interesting question: which works better? Hand-built models or computer graphics?

As in just about any effects shot, with models it's the details that count. Model builders, computer or otherwise, will spend hours working on the smallest items to bring the level of realism to the highest possible. After all, an audience will quickly get bored with an object if there isn't anything interesting to see after the first look. Details are a big part, and it's relatively easy to modify a hand-built model with a small piece from a battleship model, or other off-the-shelf set. However, computer graphics people can't do that. A little spray of paint for the model builder is several days of drawing textures and then applying them for the computer people. A quick dent in the plastic will translate into a couple hours of reworking the wireframe, and then rerendering the entire object. If it's one large, static model you're trying to build, a hand-built model will probably be the fastest, easiest and cheapest. But once you begin to grow beyond just the one model, the pros begin to move toward the computer's side.

When creating the large number of spaceships for his Star Wars films, Lucas had a couple of options to make the large space battles come to life. The first was much more time consuming: he could have the effects people build a different model for each craft. Or he could take a quicker and cheaper way, and take numerous shots of the same model, or a small number of models, and composite them together to make it appear as if there were a number of ships flying about. But there are problems with both of these approaches. To build a large number of models is expensive and takes time. But to shoot just a few models limits what the audience is seeing, and to pull off such an effect, the camera couldn't stay on one ship too long, or the viewers will realize it's the same ship over and over.

The problem is further complicated by lighting. To get a certain level of lighting on one ship is not a problem; just position a light and let the camera roll. But to get the lighting to fit the same on hundreds of ships is almost impossible. Small flaws quickly become amplified, and the shot becomes transparent. Computers can solve the lighting problem and the difficulty of creating numerous ships.

By taking the original model on the computer and replicating it several times, a graphics artist can make small changes on each of the wireframes to keep the ship from looking the same, and then combine the models into the same shot with a static light source. This ensures that all the models will have the same amount of shading, as if they were all being filmed at the same time.

Computer models also allow for a much greater degree of maneuverability. Rather than needing to reposition the wires and bars that keep a hand-built model in place, and then moving the camera to keep the shot right. With a computer model, moving the wireframe to fit the request is faster and easier. And rather than needing to set the camera on a robotic arm and move it past the model, often resulting in a blocky effect, a computer can simulate a path of motion for a ship and execute it numerous times without error or need for adjustment. Computer generated ships can also be manipulated to fit the constraints of gravity and centripital force. Mathematical models guarantee that a tight turn by a fighter plane will look as if the ship were turning in real life.

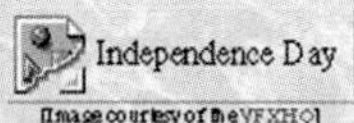

[Image courtesy of the VFXHQ]

Basically, models have one big plus working for them. There's nothing more impressive than a large pyrotechnic display to amaze the audience. As Independence Day demostrated, models still have a good grip on the explosion area. Small charges can be set and sequenced to obliterate a scale model of a structure. Explosions are one thing that computer artists haven't been able to emulate correctly. The small particles that explosions create have to be individually built and rendered. Mathematical models can create realistic flight paths for the debris, but a computer can't really work out the structural weaknesses of a building and pinpoint where the blast will break out the walls. And if any fire is required (it usually is), programmers have yet to render a realistic looking flame. Models are quite simply more realistic, faster and more cost effective when dealing with explosions.

For the most part, models and computer graphics each have their pros and cons. They work best when put together. A prime example is a certain shot from Twister. A oiltanker was scripted to fly down from the sky and then explode ahead of the character's truck. A CG rendered tanker was created to fly from the sky, and a large full scale model was built to drop in front of the truck and explode. A perfect combination of two technologies, the scene comes off flawlessly.

To conclude, each technique has it's own uses. Computers are quickly replacing what models used to do, but the models still have a position to fill. Until the next generation of computer artists works out the kinks in 3d rendering, we'll continue to see a small version of the White House exploding on screen, and we'll still be content.

RELATED LINKS

Location: http://www.deakin.edu.au/~agoodman/scc308/topic1.html

What's Related

# SCC308: Computer Graphics

# Introduction

## Development of Computer Graphics

Given how accustomed the general public has become to seeing various forms of *computer generated imagery* (CGI) in films and on television over the least few years, they might be forgiven for thinking that computer graphics was somehow 'invented' about a decade ago. In fact, the urge to display the output from computer programs in graphical form - originally on paper and then on a display screen - goes back to late 1950s. The beginnings of a commecial computer graphics industry lie in the late 1960s, based initially on the development of military applications, notably flight simulators. Throughout the 1960s and 1970s computer graphics was primarily used in research - as indeed, were most computers - and, to a lesser extent, in business. It is only in the last fifteen years that computer graphics has become 'mainstream', first in various parts of the mass entertainment industry (films, advertising, games and television) and then in home computer and entertainment systems.

### Goals of Computer graphics

As we shall see, various development 'threads' have come together to create the explosive growth in computer graphics that we have seen in recent years. We can define these by the continuing attempts to achieve greater levels of **INTERACTIVITY**, a greater degree of image **REALISM**, and **REAL-TIME** image generation. There has traditionally been some degree of mutual exclusivity between these goals: greater levels of realism mean more calculations, which means less possibility of real-time image creation; if images cannot be generated in real-time then the system cannot really be interactive. However, developments in hardware (and, to a lesser extent, improved algorithms) have taken us much closer to simultaneously achieving all three of these goals. High-end graphics workstations can generate high-quality, fully rendered images and are fast enough to allow the user to manipulate them 'on the fly'. This capability will almost certainly become commonplace in desktop systems within the next few years.

### The "Distinctiveness" of Computer Graphics

Although computer graphics is obviously in one sense just another branch of computer science - like databases, expert systems, parallel processing and so on - it can be argued that it exhibits some distinctive features that set it apart. The most significant of these are:

1. It provides a *dynamic environment* . From its earliest days computer graphics has been expected to provide real-time image support. No-one is going to be very interested in working with a flight simulator that takes thirty seconds to re-draw 'the screen' each time a pilot moves the controls; even less in a missile early-warning systems that takes five minutes to re-display a set of points (missiles!).
2. It provides an *interactive environment* . There are two kinds of interactivity of relevance here: the ability of the creater of graphic to work with the images in an easy and useful manner, and the ability of the 'consumer' of graphics (particulaly in the entertainment field) to control them smoothly and effortless and quickly.
3. It provides a *simulation environment* . One of the great strengths of computer graphics is that it can generate images of imaginary (and indeed impossible) worlds just as readily as it can produce representations of our 'real' world. Some of these worlds are mathematical abstractions, and 'exist' only as equations and their graphical representations.
4. It provides an environment for *visualising* large quantities of data. The most significant contribution that computer graphics has made in science has been the development of technqiues for visualising - seeing the structure of - huge amounts of data that are generated by modern data collection techniques.

### Computer Graphics "Operations"

Computer graphics has certain operations that are common to whatever field it is applied. In particular, the creation of 'realistic' images - of people, places or things - basically involves the following stages:

#### Modelling

In order to create images we need to define objects in some way; we may do this by using

- coordinates of the 'corners' of objects
- primitives (two-dimensional and three-dimensional geometric objects such as squares and circles, scubes and spheres)
- equations that define the two-dimensional and three-dimensional 'shape' of objects

Most objects also have *attributes* - such as colour, density, surface texture etc - which can be regarded as a 'property' of the object, or a consequence of the technique we use to generate (**render**) the image.

#### Storing

In most cases we will want to retain the scenes and images we create for future use, first in the computer memory (whilst they are being processed and manipulated) and later on disk, so that we can re-use them, or convert them to another form.

#### Manipulating

Central to the interactive process of computer graphics is the ability to changing the shape, position and characteristics of objects and images.

**Rendering**

Just as in the 'real world' we see things because of the physical interaction between light, objects and our visual system, so in computer graphics we need to 'create' a picture by applying an algorithmic version of the physics of the real world to create the artificial image. This is what in computer graphics is called the **rendering** process.

**Viewing**

Once a scene made up of objects (static or dynamic) has been rendered it must be able to be displayed, from various viewpoints, on various devices (screen printer, film ...) - otherwise, how can we see it?

### Interactive vs Non-interactive graphics

Until relatively recently the most significant distinction between different graphics systems was their level of *interactivity* . This was basically a 'binary' division: a small number of specialised systems were designed to work interactively, but most images were generated using some form of offline operation, mainly by using batch processing techniques. Now, with the development of a broad market for graphics systems and the consequent R&D into improved graphics hardware, most graphics are created dynamically and interactively. The exceptions are fully-rendered images on desktop systems (which are still too slow for this to be done in anything approaching real-time), and production-quality animation.

### Major application areas

- **Business graphics.** Much of the 'profit' in computer graphics comes from the use of relatively low-quality (and simple) charts and diagrams in business presentations. Consequently, much effort has been expended on the development of hardware (overhead display panels, film recorders) and software (charting and presentation graphics systems) to support this area.
- **Computer-aided design.** Computer aided-design (CAD) - and its linked technology, computer-aided manufacturing (CAM) - has been a mainstay of computer graphics on mainframes and workstations since the mid 1960s. Indeed, much of the development of surface and solid modelling technqiues were carried otu to enable the creation of more sophisticated software for designing automobiles and airplanes. In the 1980s CAD became a staple of the small business and home environment with the development of PC-based CAD systems - led by AutoCAD - that offered most of the functionality of workstation systems, running somewhat more slowly, but at far lower costs. Today 'low-end' two-dimensional CAD systems offer the functionality of workstation systems of fifteen years ago, and high-end three-dimensional systems support high-quality modelling and interactive 'walkthroughs'. Specialised modelling software is routinely used to design mechanical components, from simple gears to entire machines.
- **Data plotting and visualisation.** Computer graphics has always found a ready place among the tools available to scientists and engineers for plotting and analysing their data. In recent years new techniques for 'seeing' the structure of massive data sets - such as those generated by remote probes, or by medical imaging systems - have made data visualisation one of the fastest-growing areas of graphics technology.
- **Image processing.** The same circumstances referred to in the previous point also apply to the evolution of image processing techniques. The impetus for these have come in particular from the need to develop new ways of extracting detailed information from 'noisy' images, such as those transmitted over vast distances from space probes.
- **Animation.** If there is one area of computer graphics that has grabbed public attention in recent times it has been computer animation. So common has the use of computers in animation become that most people are hardly aware of how often they actually see compuer-aided animation. Most animation from major production studios like Disney use computer naimation to supplement conventional techniques; hundreds of production houses artound the world turn out thousands of adverts which are partially or totally computer-animated. Occasionally a particular film - like *Jurassic Park* , *The Mask* or *Toy Story* - will be publicly linked with computer animation; but many other feature films use subtle image processing and editing techniques to create images that are uneconomic or impossible by other means.
- **'Art'.** Just as no two people can seem to agree on what is art, so no two people in computer graphics can seem to define the difference between images created 'functionally' (to illustrate, educate or entertain) and those created 'artistically'. Nevertheless, there are clearly a growing number of people - many with backgrounds in the 'traditional' artistic fields like painting and sculpture - who are turning to the computer as a creative tool.
- **Electronic Publishing.** The 'revolution' in publishing that many people have argued is taking place with the establishment of electronic - rather that the paper-based systems of the last six hundred years - is firmly based on the ability of users to create, with computer graphics software, artwork that matches - and in many exceeds - that of traditional drawing, drafting and illustration techniques.

### Evolution of Computer Graphics

The following table summarises a personal view of some of the key developments in computer graphics over the last thirty years:

| Date | Development | People - organisations - institutions |
|---|---|---|
| 1951 | WHIRLWIND | The Whirlwind project, under the direction of *Jay Forrester* , was the US missile early-warning system of the late 1950s. Central to this system were large-format vector display screens that displayed the crticial data in high resolution, and that could be updated continually. |
| 1950's | "Computer Art" | The earliest attempts to use computer displays in a 'non-functional' way were made by James Whitney Sr. in the late 1950s when he generated 'visual feedback loops' by pointing a camera at the the display screen and using the image as input to the system to generate abstract patterns. |
| 1962 | Sketchpad | At the start of the 1960s a doctorate student at MIT, *Ivan Sutherland* , created what we today would call a graphics workstation, complete with display system, input device (lightpen) and interactive engineering design software. The system - called *Sketchpad* - was the forerunner of all modern graphics systems. |

Albert Goodman, November 1998. Used with permission.

| | | |
|---|---|---|
| 1964- | 'Photorealism' at the University of Utah | Many of the techniques that are at the heart of 'realistic' c.g.i. were developed at Utah in the late 1960s and early 1970s. Key figures - all of whom went on to make other contributions to the growth of computer graphics - include *Ivan Sutherland*, *David Evans*, *Edwin Catmull* and *James Blinn* |
| 1969 | Evans & Sutherland | In the late 1960s *Ivan Sutherland* and *David Evans* set up what was effectively the first commercial c.g. company when they formed Evans & Sutherland. The company remains at the forefront of simulation systems, particularly flight simulators. |
| 1974-77 | Animation at NYIT | In the early 1970s *Edwin Catmull* set up a computer graphics laboratory at the New York Institute of Technology with two aims: to develop computer-based animation systems that would be produce output of sufficient quality to be attractive to the film industry, and to involve artists in the animation process. The most important artist to work in the laboratory - and whose work had the most influence on the development of computer animation - was probably *Ed Emshwiller*. |
| 1982 | *TRON*<br>*Star Trek* (Genesis effect) | Although the NYIT1aboratory largely failed in its first aim, two films released in 1982 had long-term impact on the development of computer graphics. Whilst c.g.i. was used throughout *Tron* - and proved quite cost-effective to produce - its impact was lessened by its 'non-realism' and realtively low technical quality.<br>On the other hand, the short section of c.g.i in *Star Trek* from Lucasfilm's computer graphics division (which would later split into Industrial Light and Magic, and Pixar) would have a profound effect, introducing as it did several key technical effects (such as particle systems and caustics) that would become an essential part of the 'armoury' of computer animators. |
| 1982 | Ray Tracing |  Although new techniques for defining the appearance of objects had been developed, by the early 1980s there was still no rendering technique that had any real approximation to the physical processes by which 'real' things are seen. The development of the ray tracing method by *Turner Whitted* changed this, and today this is one of the most widely-used rendering methods. It is especially good at rendering reflections, refractions and shadows. |
| 1983 | Fractals |  One of the key limitations of modelling 'natural' scenes was that most conventional geometric systems could not generate the key components of natural-looking landscape - such as mountains, trees and clouds. The application of fractal systems to these areas by *Loren Carpenter* and others radically extended the range of 'scenes' that could be effectively modelled and rendered. |
| 1985 | Radiosity | The attraction of ray tracing was somewhat offset by its slowness, and by its emphasis on reflections and 'shininess'. In order to render more realistically the 'softer' world around us - particularly that of lighted interiors - *Don Greenberg* and his colleagues at Cornell University developed the *radiosity* rendering process, based on physical principles established by lighting engineers. |
| 1986 | Renderman | In order to smoothly link animation and rendering, and to allow animators to create scenes without needing to program them, a group at Pixar - led by *Pat Hanrahan* - created an extensible 'procedural language' for controlling the animation/rendering process. |

| 1988 | *Tin Toy* | Having set up Pixar to continue his aim of integrating animation into the 'mainstream', *Edwin Catmull* hired the 'traditonal' animator *John Lassiter*, whose emphasis on character and story were quite different from the 'technology-driven' approach of most other computer animators. As well as commercial work, Lassiter produced a series of successful short films, culminating in *Tin Toy* : the first completely computer-animated film to win the Academy Award for animation. |
|---|---|---|
| 1989 | *The Abyss* | One of the strongest advocates of the utility of c.g.i. in films has been the director *James Cameron* ; in a series of films - starting with *The Abyss* and including *Aliens* and *The Terminator* - he used *Industrial Light and Magic* to create effects that were central to both the visual astyle and narrative structure of the films. |
| 1995 | *Toy Story* | The release of Pixar's *Toy Story* is significant for two reasons: it is the first full-length, wholly computer-generated, feature film, and it was backed financially by the Disney Corporation (for whom the film's director, John Lassiter used to work) - the 'home' of conventional film animation. Computer animation has clearly become "mainstream". |

Contents Re-read Next

[Contents] [Re-read] [Next topic]

*Last modified 3 rd November 1998*

Albert Goodman, November 1998. Used with permission.

Obviously we could go on and on. The important thing to remember is to use your imagination plus a little deductive reasoning. Just imagine you are a cyberspace detective sniffing out clues on a case!

When doing research on the Internet, never give out your name, address, telephone number, or school name without checking with your teacher and/or your parents. Although most sites are safe, a few sites may not use the information in the way they say they are going to use it.

# LANGUAGE

CHAPTER 1

# The Parts of Speech

### *Directions*

**Write the letter of the term that correctly identifies the underlined word in each sentence.**

EXAMPLE **1.** What is realism in a literary <u>work</u>?

**1** **A** noun
**B** pronoun
**C** verb
**D** adverb

ANSWER **1 A**

1. Realistic writing emphasizes accuracy <u>of</u> detail.
2. Realism generally concerns <u>itself</u> with common people.
3. A realistic novel <u>is</u> neither moralistic nor preachy.
4. Realism became <u>trendy</u> in the nineteenth century.
5. It may have started <u>earlier</u> with the writings of Defoe and Fielding.
6. In <u>America</u>, Howells and James were important realists.
7. French realists include Flaubert <u>and</u> Balzac.
8. An outgrowth of realism was the <u>naturalism</u> of Zola and Dreiser.
9. Naturalists <u>believed</u> in social and economic determinism.
10. Their subjects primarily come from the <u>lowest</u> depths of society.

1 **A** adjective
**B** adverb
**C** preposition
**D** noun

2 **A** noun
**B** pronoun
**C** verb
**D** adverb

3 **A** preposition
**B** pronoun
**C** verb
**D** adverb

4 **A** adjective
**B** adverb
**C** preposition
**D** noun

5 **A** adjective
**B** adverb
**C** preposition
**D** noun

6 **A** adjective
**B** adverb
**C** preposition
**D** proper noun

7 **A** conjunction
**B** interjection
**C** preposition
**D** adjective

8 **A** adjective
**B** adverb
**C** preposition
**D** noun

9 **A** noun
**B** pronoun
**C** verb
**D** adverb

10 **A** conjunction
**B** interjection
**C** preposition
**D** adjective

Andy Warhol.
*Moonwalk,* 1987.
Screenprint, 38 by 38 inches.
Courtesy of Ronald Feldman Fine Arts, New York.

**Describe** What historic event is portrayed in this famous print by Andy Warhol? What colors does the artist use?

**Analyze** How has the artist used a few key figures to symbolize an event?

**Interpret** Suppose a poet were to write about this particular historic event, man's first landing on the moon. How might he or she use a few key words—such as colors and/or symbols—to signify the entire episode?

**Judge** Do you think art or writing works better to capture the significance of historic events? Explain your answer.

At the end of this chapter, you will use the artwork to stimulate ideas for writing.

# Nouns and Pronouns

Nouns and pronouns are two of the eight parts of speech. The grammatical elements covered in this chapter include all eight parts of speech. Remember, though, that the part of speech of a word can vary depending upon its use in a sentence.

Understanding the function of grammatical elements can help you as a writer. If you know, for example, when a word is a noun and when a word is a verb, then you can diagnose a problem such as incorrect agreement between a subject and a verb as you edit your work.

| THE EIGHT PARTS OF SPEECH | |
|---|---|
| **noun** (names) | **adverb** (describes, limits) |
| **pronoun** (replaces) | **preposition** (relates) |
| **verb** (states action or being) | **conjunction** (connects) |
| **adjective** (describes, limits) | **interjection** (expresses strong feeling) |

## Nouns

A **noun** is the name of a person, place, thing, or idea.

There are more nouns in our language than any other part of speech. Nouns can be classified in several ways.

### Concrete and Abstract Nouns

A **concrete noun** names a person or an object that can actually be seen, touched, tasted, heard, or smelled. An **abstract noun** names qualities, conditions, and ideas that cannot be perceived through the senses.

| CONCRETE AND ABSTRACT NOUNS | |
|---|---|
| **Concrete Nouns** | table, feather, lemon, salt, bells, roses |
| **Abstract Nouns** | courage, joy, friendship, loyalty, freedom |

## Common and Proper Nouns

A **common noun** names any person, place, or thing. Always beginning with a capital letter, a **proper noun** names a particular person, place, or thing.

| COMMON AND PROPER NOUNS | |
|---|---|
| **Common Nouns** | quarterback, state, city |
| **Proper Nouns** | Sam Levin, New Jersey, Houston |

Some proper nouns, such as *Sam Levin* and *New Jersey*, include more than one word; but they are still considered one noun. *Sam Levin* is one person, and *New Jersey* is one state.

*You can learn about capitalizing proper nouns on pages L399–L409.*

## Compound Nouns

A **compound noun** is made up of more than one word. Since a compound noun can be written as one word, written as a hyphenated word, or written as two or more separate words, it is always best to check a dictionary for the correct, up-to-date form.

| COMPOUND NOUNS | |
|---|---|
| **One Word** | peacemaker, falsehood |
| **Hyphenated Words** | sister-in-law, hobby-horse |
| **Two Words** | life jacket, city hall |

*You can learn about spelling the plural forms of compound nouns on page L557.*

## Collective Nouns

A **collective noun** names a group of people or things. Following are some collective nouns.

| COMMON COLLECTIVE NOUNS | | | |
|---|---|---|---|
| band | congregation | flock | nation |
| class | crew | gang | orchestra |
| committee | crowd | herd | swarm |
| colony | family | league | team |

Some nouns are more colorful and convey meaning more vividly than other nouns. For instance, a noun such as ***building*** is a general term, but ***skyscraper***, ***Sears Tower***, ***factory***, and ***hut*** are more specific and lively. In your writing, whether formal or informal, use the most precise nouns possible.

*You can learn about spelling plural nouns on pages L552–L560. You can learn about possessive nouns on pages L471–L473.*

## Practice Your Skills

Check Your Understanding

***Identifying Nouns***

General Interest

**Write the nouns in the following paragraphs.** A date should be considered a noun.

The Eiffel Tower is perhaps the most familiar human-made landmark on Earth. It was designed for the Paris Exposition in 1889. The tower can now accommodate 10,000 visitors annually. Some people, however, go there for publicity, not for enjoyment. A man once climbed 363 steps on stilts, and a stuntman came down on a unicycle.

The tower is repainted every seven years, requiring thousands of gallons of paint. As a part of one cleanup, nearly 1,000 tons of rust and dirt were shaved off. This kind of effort signifies the tremendous pride the city takes in its famous structure—even if only a very small percentage of its visitors are Parisians.

### Connect to the Writing Process: Drafting
***Using Specific Nouns***

**For each general noun below, write at least two specific, lively alternatives. Then write sentences using 10 of your new and improved word choices.**

**1.** visitor
**2.** car
**3.** store
**4.** driver
**5.** hat
**6.** bag
**7.** building
**8.** picture
**9.** money
**10.** happiness
**11.** fruit
**12.** furniture

### Connect to the Writing Process: Editing
***Capitalizing Proper Nouns***

**Write each proper noun in the paragraph. Capitalize any proper nouns that are not capitalized.**

Distinctive geographical features serve as landmarks across the united states. Each year Carlsbad Caverns attracts crowds of sightseers to new mexico. In Arizona, tourists flock to view the grand canyon. Popular for its beaches, florida lures tourists to its swamps and bayous as well. A famous geyser named old faithful draws nature enthusiasts to yellowstone national park. Avid downhill skiers throng the snowy slopes of colorado. Vacationers to Hawaii enjoy waterfalls and volcanoes. Carved into mount rushmore are the faces of four presidents: george washington, thomas jefferson, abraham lincoln, and theodore roosevelt. Landmarks in America celebrate our nation's natural and historical heritage.

## Communicate Your Ideas

### APPLY TO WRITING

**Descriptive Paragraphs: *Nouns***

Just as the Eiffel Tower is a Paris landmark, structures such as the Gateway Arch in St. Louis, Missouri, and the Golden Gate Bridge in San Francisco, California, are landmarks in those cities. You are a travel writer, and you have received an assignment to write about a landmark of your own choosing. Write two paragraphs describing a landmark you have seen, whether it is in your hometown or across the world. Make your descriptions as specific and interesting as possible by using a variety of nouns: concrete nouns, abstract nouns, common nouns, proper nouns, compound nouns, and collective nouns. Be prepared to identify the nouns you used.

## Pronouns

A **pronoun** is a word that takes the place of one or more nouns.

The word the pronoun replaces or refers to is called its **antecedent**. The antecedent of a pronoun can be in the same sentence or in another sentence. In the following examples, an arrow has been drawn from each pronoun to its antecedent.

Stephen wore **his** new jacket to study hall.

Rob and Beth are at the library. **They** have **their** exams tomorrow.

Occasionally the antecedent will follow the pronoun.

"That homework is **mine**," Heather said.

*You can learn more about pronouns and their antecedents on pages L267–L273.*

## Personal Pronouns

Personal pronouns, the most commonly used type of pronoun, are divided into the following groups.

| PERSONAL PRONOUNS | |
|---|---|
| **FIRST PERSON** | (the person speaking) |
| SINGULAR | I, me, my, mine |
| PLURAL | we, us, our, ours |
| **SECOND PERSON** | (the person spoken to) |
| SINGULAR | you, your, yours |
| PLURAL | you, your, yours |
| **THIRD PERSON** | (the person or thing spoken about) |
| SINGULAR | he, him, his, she, her, hers, it, its |
| PLURAL | they, them, their, theirs |

| | |
|---|---|
| FIRST PERSON | **We** want to publish a study guide. |
| SECOND PERSON | Did **you** ever find **your** article? |
| THIRD PERSON | **He** told **them** to call **him** if **they** needed more study advice. |

## Reflexive and Intensive Pronouns

Reflexive and intensive pronouns are formed by adding *–self* or *–selves* to personal pronouns.

| REFLEXIVE AND INTENSIVE PRONOUNS | |
|---|---|
| **Singular** | myself, yourself, himself, herself, itself |
| **Plural** | ourselves, yourselves, themselves |

A **reflexive pronoun** refers to the noun or pronoun that is the subject of the sentence. It is an essential part of the sentence. An **intensive pronoun** is included in a sentence to add emphasis—or intensity—to a noun or another pronoun. Because an intensive pronoun is not a necessary part of a sentence, it can be removed without affecting the meaning of the sentence.

Reflexive Pronoun Rob taught **himself** to speak French.

(*Himself* cannot be removed from the sentence without changing the meaning.)

Intensive Pronoun Rob **himself** volunteered to help.

(*Himself* can be removed from the sentence. *Rob volunteered to help.*)

## Practice Your Skills

Check Your Understanding

### *Identifying Personal Pronouns and Their Antecedents*

Contemporary Life

**Write the personal, reflexive, or intensive pronoun(s) in each sentence. Then beside each one, write its antecedent.**

**1.** Roberto lost his essay test in the subway when he was going home.

**2.** "Is this essay yours?" Megan asked Roberto the next day.

3. Roberto was relieved that Megan had found his test, and he thanked her for returning it.
4. Megan told herself that she could do better on the next essay test.
5. Roberto told Megan, "I myself have developed a study technique that I could share with you."
6. "An essay test is not as difficult if I write a practice answer ahead of time," Roberto said.
7. "We should study together for the next test," Megan told Roberto.
8. "I will set up a study group with you and Roger," Roberto said to Megan.
9. "When I helped Roger study for the last test, he made excellent progress for himself," Roberto continued modestly.
10. Megan was glad that she could study with Roberto and Roger, and she was certain that her grades would improve with her hard work.

Connect to the Writing Process: Revising

***Replacing Nouns with Pronouns***

**Rewrite the following paragraph, replacing repetitious nouns with pronouns.**

Bill always waits as long as Bill can before Bill studies for a test. On the night before a test, Bill calls several friends and asks the friends if the friends will lend Bill the friends' notes. Bill sometimes does not attend the classes, so Bill is missing notes from several lectures. Usually Bill can find some sympathetic friends. Are the friends doing Bill a favor by lending Bill the friends' notes? Would you lend Bill your notes?

## Indefinite Pronouns

**Indefinite pronouns** often refer to unnamed persons or things and usually do not have specific antecedents.

| COMMON INDEFINITE PRONOUNS | |
|---|---|
| **SINGULAR** | another, anybody, anyone, anything, each, either, everybody, everyone, everything, much, neither, nobody, no one, one, somebody, someone, something |
| **PLURAL** | both, few, many, others, several |
| **SINGULAR/PLURAL** | all, any, most, none, some |

**Few** attended the meeting.
**Most** of the teachers did **something** to help **everybody** who failed the midterm.

*You can learn about indefinite pronouns functioning as antecedents on pages L270–L273.*

## Demonstrative Pronouns

A **demonstrative pronoun** is used to point out a specific person, place, or object in the same sentence or in another sentence.

| DEMONSTRATIVE PRONOUNS | |
|---|---|
| **SINGULAR** | this (points out an object close by)<br>that (points out an object in the distance) |
| **PLURAL** | these (points out objects close by)<br>those (points out objects in the distance) |

**This** is the perfect place for a rest.
Of all the books, **these** were the best.

## Interrogative Pronouns

An **interrogative pronoun** is used to ask a question.

| INTERROGATIVE PRONOUNS | | | | |
|---|---|---|---|---|
| what | whom | which | whose | who |

**Which** is the best class on filmmaking?
**Who** wrote that screenplay?
**Whose** is better?

### Connect to Speaking and Writing

In casual conversation, you often can use a single pronoun to express your thoughts without causing confusion.

Your friend says, "You'll never guess what I just did!"
You respond, **"What?"**

Your brother asks, "Which boots are yours?"
You answer, **"Those."**

A classmate asks, "Who can join that study group?"
You tell her, **"Anyone."**

*Relative pronouns are another kind of pronoun. They are used to introduce adjective clauses. You can learn about relative pronouns on pages L148–L152.*

## Practice Your Skills

Check Your Understanding
***Identifying Pronouns***

Contemporary Life **Write each pronoun in the following sentences. Beside each pronoun, write what type it is.**

**1.** Who is going to lead our study group this week?
**2.** Few attended last week's session.
**3.** We have to do something to increase involvement.
**4.** These should generate a definite interest.

5. I will post some of the fliers near the lockers.
6. Which of the boxes do you want Krista to take?
7. Tell her to take those.
8. Whose is this?
9. That is Tyrell's drawing, and this is Lee's photograph.
10. Either could win an award.

## Communicate Your Ideas

### APPLY TO WRITING

**Speech:** ***Nouns and Pronouns***

Attributed to Tamura Suio. *Ladies' Pastimes in Spring and Autumn*, 18th century. On handscroll, ink and color on paper, 12⅜ by 96$\frac{1}{16}$ inches. The New York Public Library.

You have volunteered to talk to a fifth grade class about a painting, and you have chosen *Ladies' Pastimes in Spring and Autumn*. Write an informal speech that you could give, discussing any aspect of the painting that appeals to you. One idea is to explain what each group of women is doing and then relate these activities to modern careers. After you have written your speech, underline each noun and circle each pronoun.

# Verbs

**A verb is a word that expresses action or a state of being.**

A verb is an essential part of a sentence because it tells what the subject does, is, or has.

## Action Verbs

**An action verb tells what action a subject is performing.**

Action verbs can show several types of action.

| ACTION VERBS | |
|---|---|
| **PHYSICAL ACTION** | drive, march, soar, sing, talk, paint |
| **MENTAL ACTION** | believe, think, dream, imagine, wish |
| **OWNERSHIP** | have, own, possess, keep, control |

**CONNECT TO SPEAKING AND WRITING**

Many action verbs can be used alone to create a one-word action command. These commands can be particularly effective in grabbing a listener's attention.

A drill sergeant tells a soldier: **"March!"**
Your older brother tells you: **"Move!"**
A teacher tells her student: **"Think."**

### Transitive and Intransitive Verbs

An action verb is **transitive** if it has an object. You can find an object by asking the question *What?* or *Whom?* after the verb. An action verb is **intransitive** if it has no object.

| | |
|---|---|
| TRANSITIVE | I **found** a new restaurant. (*Found* what?) |
| INTRANSITIVE | We **met** there Friday. (*Met* what or whom?) |

Some action verbs may be either transitive or intransitive.

| | |
|---|---|
| TRANSITIVE | She **writes** restaurant reviews in her spare time. |
| INTRANSITIVE | She often **writes** to me. |

*You can learn more about the objects of transitive verbs on pages L72-L75.*

## PRACTICE YOUR SKILLS

### Check Your Understanding
*Identifying Transitive and Intransitive Verbs*

Science Topic **Write each action verb. Then label each one *transitive* or *intransitive*.**

1. Rings on the scales of some fish show the age of the fish.
2. The electric eel throws a charge of 600 volts.
3. Rays live on the ocean bottom.
4. The Nile catfish swims upside down.
5. Minnows have teeth in their throat.
6. The female marine catfish hatches her eggs in her mouth.
7. The trout belongs to the salmon family.
8. The flounder changes its color.
9. Some fish thrive in underground streams and caves.
10. Sharks, despite their reputation, rarely attack humans.

### Connect to the Writing Process: Drafting
*Writing Sentences*

**Use each word to write sentences about a science class. If the verb is a transitive verb, draw an arrow to its object.**

11. speak
12. write
13. copy
14. walk
15. study
16. carry
17. find
18. have
19. lock
20. paint

## Verb Phrases

A **verb phrase** is a main verb plus one or more helping verbs.

Another name for **helping verb** is **auxiliary verb.**

| COMMON HELPING VERBS | |
|---|---|
| **be** | am, is, are, was, were, be, being, been |
| **have** | has, have, had |
| **do** | do, does, did |
| **OTHERS** | may, might, must, can, could, shall, should, will, would |

In the following examples, the helping verbs are in **bold** type, and the verb phrase is underlined.

Jeff **has been** bringing our food promptly.
You **should have been** notified of the reservations.

A verb phrase is often interrupted by contractions or other words.

Marvin **will** soon **apply** for that job.
**Have** you always **taken** the server's suggestions?
I **do**n't **want** any dessert.

### CONNECT TO SPEAKING AND WRITING

You probably use many contractions in your everyday conversations. When you are writing, though, you need to consider whether contractions are appropriate. The use of contractions depends on your purpose and audience. If you are writing a letter to a friend, contractions are appropriate. If you are writing a research report, you probably should avoid using contractions.

*You can learn more about contractions on pages L479–L480.*

*Throughout the rest of this book, the term* verb *will refer to the whole verb phrase.*

## Practice Your Skills

Check Your Understanding

### *Identifying Verbs*

Social Science **Write the verb in each sentence. Include all helping verbs.**

**1.** Sushi comes from Japan.

**2.** Some sushi is carefully rolled in a wrapper of very thin, edible seaweed.

**3.** Sushi consists of raw fish, raw shellfish, and cooked rice.

**4.** The Japanese have been making sushi for more than a thousand years.

**5.** Sushi was originally made with salt as a preservative.

**6.** The fish and salt were aged over several weeks or months.

**7.** Nowadays, chefs often prepare sushi without the preservative.

**8.** The sushi is immediately served to the customer.

**9.** The preparation and display of sushi can be considered an elegant art form.

**10.** The sushi chef does consider all details of color, texture, and taste.

Connect to the Writing Process: Revising

### *Writing Sentences with Verb Phrases*

Each of the sentences below contains a verb phrase. Rewrite the sentence, adding an interrupter so that the meaning of the sentence changes. Underline the verb.

**11.** I have liked that Mexican restaurant.

**12.** We can give our order to the server.

**13.** Our order was sent to the kitchen.

**14.** The server has returned with our water.

**15.** The dish for the chips and salsa has been empty.

Communicate Your Ideas

APPLY TO WRITING

**Instructions: *Verbs***

A nearby restaurant has announced a search for a new dish for the "Local Favorites" section of its menu. You have decided to enter one of your favorite dishes. You must write clear, simple, step-by-step instructions for preparing the food. Use precise, colorful verbs. For example, instead of *mix*, you might write *whisk* or *whip*. After you write your instructions, underline each verb.

## Linking Verbs

A **linking verb** links the subject with another word in the sentence. The other word either renames or describes the subject.

A linking verb serves as a bridge between the subject and another word in the sentence.

History **is** my favorite subject. (*Subject* renames *history*.)

This election **has been** exceptionally competitive. (*Competitive* describes the subject *election*.)

The most common linking verbs are the various forms of *be*.

| COMMON FORMS OF *BE* | | |
|---|---|---|
| be | can be | has been |
| is | could be | had been |
| am | should be | could have been |
| are | would be | should have been |
| was | may be | would have been |
| were | might be | might have been |
| shall be | must be | must have been |
| will be | have been | |

Diane **may be** our new class president.

These votes **should have been** anonymous.

The forms of *be* are not always linking verbs. Only a verb that links the subject with another word in the sentence that renames or describes the subject can be a linking verb. In the following examples, the verbs simply make a statement or describe a state of being.

Her running mate **is** here.
She **was** in Memphis on Tuesday.
The campaign buttons **could be** in the box.
They **must have been** there all the time.

Forms of *be* are not the only linking verbs. The verbs in the following box may also be used as linking verbs.

| ADDITIONAL LINKING VERBS | | |
|---|---|---|
| appear | look | sound |
| become | remain | stay |
| feel | seem | taste |
| grow | smell | turn |

Jonathan **became** my campaign manager.
(*Manager* renames the subject *Jonathan*.)

The campaign posters **look** very professional.
(*Professional* describes the subject *posters*.)

Most of the additional linking verbs listed in the box can be linking verbs in some sentences and action verbs in other sentences.

| | |
|---|---|
| LINKING VERB | The governor **appeared** weary.<br>(*Weary* describes the subject *governor*.) |
| ACTION VERB | The bodyguard **appeared** beside him.<br>(No word describes the subject *bodyguard*.) |

*Subject complements complete the meaning of linking verbs.* *You can learn more about subject complements on pages L77–L81.*

## PRACTICE YOUR SKILLS

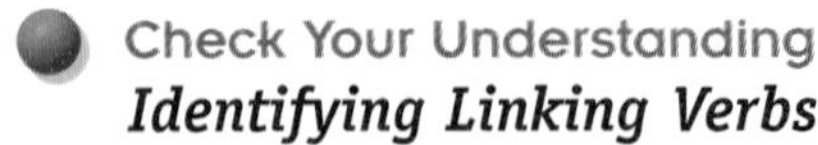

Check Your Understanding

### *Identifying Linking Verbs*

History Topic **Write each linking verb. If a sentence does not have a linking verb, write *none*.**

1. During the Civil War, Abraham Lincoln was the president of the United States.
2. Lincoln was assassinated while in a theater.
3. Other leaders have been targets for assassins also.
4. Dr. Martin Luther King, Jr., was shot on April 4, 1968.
5. James Earl Ray grew old in prison for that crime.
6. President John F. Kennedy appeared in Texas in November 1963.
7. His assassination seemed a conspiracy to some people.
8. President Ronald Reagan nearly became the victim of John Hinckley.
9. Reagan was whisked away to a hospital and survived.
10. Hinckley had been insane at the time of the crime.

Connect to the Writing Process: Drafting

*Writing Sentences*

**Write two sentences for each verb. In the first sentence, use the word as an action verb. In the second sentence, use the word as a linking verb.**

**11.** become
**12.** look
**13.** seem
**14.** felt
**15.** appeared
**16.** remains

## Communicate Your Ideas

### APPLY TO WRITING

**Writer's Craft:** ***Analyzing the Use of Verbs***

Writers usually choose vivid action verbs so that readers can experience what is happening. In "Araby," James Joyce tells the story of a young man hopelessly in love who goes to a fair to find a gift for a young woman. This passage describes what the young man sees when he arrives. Read the passage and then follow the instructions.

> Nearly all the stalls were closed and the greater part of the hall was in darkness. I recognized a silence like that which pervades a church after a service. I walked into the center of the bazaar timidly. A few people were gathered about the stalls which were still open. Before a curtain, over which the words *Café Chantant* were written in colored lamps, two men were counting money on a salver. I listened to the fall of the coins.
>
> —*James Joyce,* "Araby"

- List all the verbs in the passage.
- How many of the verbs are forms of *be* or verb phrases with *be*?
- Does the use of *be* make the passage more vivid or less vivid? Why do you think Joyce chose to use these verbs? Explain your answer.

# Adjectives and Adverbs

An adjective and an adverb have similar functions in a sentence. They both modify or describe other parts of speech. Adjectives and adverbs improve the style of sentences by adding vividness and exactness.

## Adjectives

An **adjective** is a word that modifies a noun or a pronoun.

An adjective answers one of the following questions about a noun or a pronoun.

| ADJECTIVES | | |
|---|---|---|
| **What Kind?** | **fresh** ideas | **plaid** shirt |
| **Which One(s)?** | **red** curtain | **those** few |
| **How Many?** | **six** actors | **many** pages |
| **How Much?** | **extensive** role | **much** publicity |

An adjective may come in one of three places.

| | |
|---|---|
| Before a Noun or a Pronoun | The **young, eager** playwright wrote a script about Homer. |
| After a Noun or a Pronoun | The playwright, **young** and **eager**, wrote a script about Homer. |
| After a Linking Verb | The playwright of the script about Homer was **young** and **eager**. |

*You can learn about adjectives that follow linking verbs on pages L78–L81.*

### PUNCTUATION WITH TWO ADJECTIVES

Sometimes you will write two adjectives before or after the noun or pronoun they describe. If those adjectives are not connected by a conjunction—such as *and* or *or*—you might need to put a comma between them.

To decide if a comma belongs, read the adjectives and add the word *and* between them.

- If the adjectives make sense, put a comma in to replace *and*.
- If the adjectives do not make sense with the word *and* between them, do not add a comma.

| | |
|---|---|
| **COMMA NEEDED** | I read a realistic, scary book. (*Realistic* and *scary book* reads well.) |
| **NO COMMA NEEDED** | It was an unusual mystery story. (*Unusual* and *mystery story* does not read well.) |

*You can learn more about using commas to separate adjectives before a noun on pages L438–L441.*

CONNECT TO WRITER'S CRAFT

A talented writer chooses adjectives that are fresh, vivid, and specific. For example, a ***good*** steak expresses a general idea, but a ***succulent*** steak expresses a more specific, vivid idea. A football player's ***strong*** muscles are one thing, but ***Herculean*** muscles are another.

## Proper Adjectives

Because a **proper adjective** is formed from a proper noun, it begins with a capital letter.

### PROPER ADJECTIVES

| | |
|---|---|
| **Roman** emperor | **Greek** cuisine |
| **Hawaiian** island | **Shakespearean** play |

*You can learn more about capitalizing proper adjectives on pages L409–L411.*

## Compound Adjectives

A **compound adjective** is made up of more than one word. Since a compound adjective may be one word, a hyphenated word, or two or more separate words, you may need to check a dictionary for the correct form.

| COMPOUND ADJECTIVES | |
|---|---|
| **seaworthy** vessel | **spellbound** audience |
| **long-term** project | **high school** play |

## Articles

The words *a, an,* and *the* form a special group of adjectives called **articles.** The article *a* comes before words starting with a consonant sound, and *an* comes before words starting with a vowel sound.

| ARTICLES | | |
|---|---|---|
| **a** comedy | **an** understanding | **the** apple |
| **a** harp | **an** hour | **the** ball |

*You will not be asked to list articles in the exercises in this book.*

## Practice Your Skills

Check Your Understanding
***Identifying Adjectives***

Literature Topic **Write each adjective. Then write the word the adjective modifies.**

1. Homer was a famous Greek poet.
2. He told the great story of the Trojan War.
3. Homer also recounted the fantastic adventures of Odysseus in *The Odyssey*.
4. The larger-than-life man lived in a seaside city.
5. An important philosopher of ancient times was Plato.

6. Even today, ambitious scholars choose the study of Platonic philosophy.
7. One of Plato's well-known works is *The Republic*.
8. A Roman writer, Ovid, composed the long poem, *Metamorphoses*.
9. *Metamorphoses* includes the romantic story of the handsome Pyramus and the beautiful Thisbe.
10. Nick Bottom and Francis Flute are characters in a Shakespearean play.
11. Bottom and Flute play Pyramus and Thisbe in a hilarious production of Ovid's story.
12. Sappho, a Greek poet, wrote beautiful poems about love, marriage, and friendship.

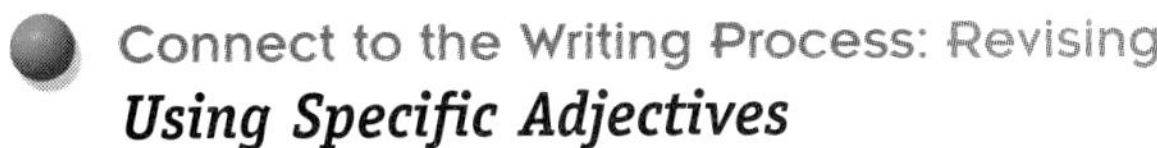


***Using Specific Adjectives***

Work with another student. Ask your partner to look around the room and describe ten things that he or she sees. Write down each description. Then, working together, revise each so that it contains vivid and specific adjectives.

## Other Parts of Speech Used as Adjectives

Sometimes a word will be used as a noun in one sentence and as an adjective in another sentence.

| | NOUNS USED AS ADJECTIVES |
|---|---|
| **Nouns** | flower, glass, refrigerator |
| **Adjectives** | **flower** garden, **glass** vase, **refrigerator** door |

Also, the same word may be a pronoun in one sentence and an adjective in another sentence. The words in the box on the following page are adjectives when they come before a noun and modify that noun. They are pronouns when they stand alone.

| WORDS USED AS ADJECTIVES OR PRONOUNS | | | |
|---|---|---|---|
| **Demonstrative** | **Interrogative** | **Indefinite** | |
| this | what | all | many |
| these | which | another | more |
| that | | any | most |
| those | | both | neither |
| | | each | other |
| | | either | several |
| | | few | some |

ADJECTIVE **These** scripts must be yours.
PRONOUN **These** must be yours.

ADJECTIVE **Each** actor was given a new costume.
PRONOUN **Each** of the actors was given a new costume.

The possessive pronouns *my*, *your*, *his*, *her*, *its*, *our*, and *their* are sometimes called **pronominal adjectives** because they answer the adjective question *Which one(s)?*

*Throughout this book, these words will be considered pronouns.*

## PRACTICE YOUR SKILLS

Check Your Understanding
***Identifying Adjectives***

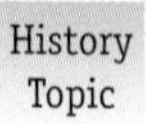


**Write the adjectives in the following paragraph.**

According to the ancient Greeks, eyes could reveal a personality. The Greeks compared the eyes of people to the eyes of various animals. Then they attributed the personality traits of those animals to people. Lion eyes, for example, are almond-like. In a person they signified a sense of fairness, a sense of justice, and leadership skills. Monkey eyes are small in relation to the face, but they have large irises. The Greeks thought that people with these eyes were unpredictable and shy. Elephant eyes are long and narrow with several folds of skin on the upper and lower eyelids. People with elephant eyes, it was believed, could handle difficult problems and solve them in a thoughtful, methodical manner. This unusual list of eye types also included the eyes of sheep, horses, wolves, hogs, snakes, and fish.

### Connect to the Writing Process: Drafting

### *Writing Sentences*

**Write two sentences for each word. In the first sentence, use the word as an adjective. In the second sentence, use the word as a noun or a pronoun. Above the word, label it *adjective*, *noun*, or *pronoun*.**

1. these
2. other
3. baseball
4. porch
5. book
6. science
7. both
8. all
9. stone
10. wool

## APPLY TO WRITING

### Analysis: *Adjectives*

Georges Rouault. *The Old King,* 1871–1958. Oil on canvas, 30¼ by 21¼ inches. The Carnegie Museum of Art, Pittsburgh, Patrons Art Fund, 40.1.

Study Georges Rouault's painting *The Old King*. Look at the expression on the king's face. Are those flowers in his hands? Observe the colors the painter chose to use. Now imagine that this king is Oedipus, and he has blinded himself after discovering the horrible truth that he has killed his father. Write an essay describing the emotions and thoughts you think this king must be experiencing. Express your ideas vividly and precisely by using specific adjectives. Share your essay with your classmates.

# Adverbs

An **adverb** is a word that modifies a verb, an adjective, or another adverb.

Although many adverbs end in *–ly*, some do not. Common adverbs that do not end in *–ly* are listed in the box.

| COMMON ADVERBS | | | |
|---|---|---|---|
| afterward | fast | now | soon |
| again | hard | nowhere | still |
| almost | here | often | straight |
| alone | just | outside | then |
| already | late | perhaps | there |
| also | long | quite | today |
| always | low | rather | tomorrow |
| away | more | seldom | too |
| down | near | so | very |
| even | never | sometimes | well |
| ever | next | somewhat | yesterday |
| far | not (n't) | somewhere | yet |

## Adverbs That Modify Verbs

Adverbs answer the questions *Where? When? How?* and *To what extent?* Notice in the following examples that adverbs that modify verbs modify the whole verb phrase.

WHERE? Enrique went **outside**.

WHEN? Donna will be swimming **tomorrow**.

HOW? The divers have been competing **fiercely**.

Be careful not to confuse an adverb that ends in *–ly* with an adjective that ends in *–ly*.

| | |
|---|---|
| ADVERB | Enrique meets **weekly** with his team. (When?) |
| ADJECTIVE | The **weekly** meeting is a time to plan strategy. (What kind?) |

CONNECT TO SPEAKING AND WRITING

Sometimes when you are performing an action, another person will use a single adverb to tell you how to do it.

You are carelessly stacking china dishes, and your mother says, ***"Carefully."***

You are driving rapidly through a school zone, and your passenger reminds you, ***"Slowly."***

You are slowly picking up your clothes, and your dad says, ***"Quickly!"***

## Adverbs That Modify Adjectives and Other Adverbs

When adverbs modify adjectives or other adverbs, they usually answer the question *To what extent?* Notice in the following examples that the adverbs that modify the adjectives and the other adverbs come before that word.

| | |
|---|---|
| MODIFYING AN ADJECTIVE | This swimsuit is **too** loose. |
| | The **extremely** hot sand burned the soles of his feet. |
| MODIFYING AN ADVERB | Sammy moves through the water **very** quickly. |
| | She **almost** always spends the day collecting shells. |

*You can learn about using adjectives and adverbs to show degrees of comparison on pages L327–L345.*

# PRACTICE YOUR SKILLS

Check Your Understanding
***Identifying Adverbs***

Contemporary Life

**Write the adverbs from the sentences below. Then beside each adverb, write the word the adverb modifies.**

**1.** Enrique always keeps the members of the swim team in stitches.

**2.** Yesterday he solemnly asked someone for directions in a fake language.

**3.** The person listened courteously to him and then walked rapidly in the opposite direction.

**4.** Another time, he impulsively popped popcorn without the lid on the pan.

**5.** Popcorn flew crazily around the kitchen, and the dog ran around in circles.

**6.** When Enrique drove too fast, he irritably paid the fine in pennies.

**7.** Last week Enrique secretly started an odd rumor about himself.

**8.** The rumor evolved radically before it eventually came back to him.

**9.** He was bored in math class today and carefully wrote his work in Roman numerals.

**10.** Occasionally he dresses his little brother and cheerfully sends him to preschool with his clothes on backward.

Connect to the Writing Process: Drafting
***Using Adverbs to Modify Adjectives and Other Adverbs***

**Write a sentence for each adjective and adverb below. Then add an adverb to modify each adjective and adverb.**

**11.** clearly
**12.** fast
**13.** loud
**14.** loudly
**15.** well
**16.** slowly
**17.** badly
**18.** thin
**19.** warmly
**20.** neat

## Nouns Used as Adverbs

The same word may be used as a noun in one sentence and as an adverb in another sentence.

| | |
|---|---|
| NOUN | The **outdoors** is the best location for the reptile habitat. |
| ADVERB | We will move the reptile habitat **outdoors**. (Where?) |
| NOUN | **Tomorrow** is the day for the lizards' release. |
| ADVERB | I will release the lizards **tomorrow**. (When?) |

## PRACTICE YOUR SKILLS

Check Your Understanding

### *Identifying Adverbs*

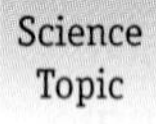

Science Topic

**Write the adverbs from the sentences below. Then beside each one, write the word or words each adverb modifies.**

**1.** Southwest deserts appear totally empty of life.

**2.** Many animals, birds, and insects survive very well in this barren land.

**3.** An unusually hardy inhabitant of these bleak areas is one type of lizard.

**4.** This lizard can swiftly skim along the sandy surface and can easily burrow into the sand.

**5.** You have probably watched swimmers at the ocean or a lake on a hot summer day.

**6.** These bathers often run quickly to the water, dive in, and then disappear beneath the surface.

**7.** In the same way, this lizard runs very fast, dives into the sand, and disappears without a trace.

**8.** During the course of this swift run, the lizard may actually fly for a few seconds.

9. The body of the lizard is perfectly suited for this incredible stunt.
10. During the dive a group of scales cleverly protects the eyes of the lizard.

Connect to the Writing Process: Drafting

### *Using Adverbs and Nouns to Write Sentences*

**Write two sentences for each word. In the first sentence, use the word as a noun. In the second sentence, use the word as an adverb.**

11. yesterday
12. downstairs
13. there
14. downtown
15. afternoon
16. more
17. later
18. tomorrow
19. well
20. outside

## Communicate Your Ideas

### APPLY TO WRITING

**News Story:** ***Adverbs***

Imagine that you are a reporter for your local newspaper. You have been asked to cover a high school competition for the readers of the newspaper. You may choose any competition you wish—for example, cheerleading, soccer, football, dance team, tennis, quiz team, or any other. Be sure you use adverbs as you explain the action of the contest.

 Mixed Practice

Contemporary Life

**Divide your paper into two columns. In the first column, write the adverbs and the word each adverb modifies. In the second column, write the adjectives and the word each adjective modifies.**

1. Yesterday I went to an unusual water park.
2. In a huge tank, baby dolphins swam peacefully.
3. The older dolphins and their trainers performed daily water shows indoors.
4. I most enjoyed the activities available outside.
5. A few visitors can swim with the dolphins.
6. I was incredibly pleased about this unusual opportunity.
7. The trainers carefully gave me several instructions.
8. There was a trainer beside me constantly.
9. I quickly became friends with a large, happy dolphin. I swam playfully beside him for an hour.

# Other Parts of Speech

Prepositions, conjunctions, and interjections are the three remaining parts of speech.

## Prepositions

A **preposition** shows the relationship between a noun or a pronoun and another word in the sentence.

In the following examples, the words in **bold** type are prepositions. Notice how the different prepositions change the relationship between the plant and the table.

The plant **on** the table is a geranium.
The plant **beside** the table is a geranium.
The plant **near** the table is a geranium.

Following is a list of common prepositions. Prepositions of two or more words are called **compound prepositions**.

| COMMON PREPOSITIONS | | | | |
|---|---|---|---|---|
| aboard | before | down | off | till |
| about | behind | during | on | to |
| above | below | except | onto | toward |
| across | beneath | for | opposite | under |
| after | beside | from | out | underneath |
| against | besides | in | outside | until |
| along | between | inside | over | up |
| among | beyond | into | past | upon |
| around | but (“except”) | like | since | with |
| as | by | near | through | within |
| at | concerning | of | throughout | without |

| COMPOUND PREPOSITIONS | | |
|---|---|---|
| according to | by means of | instead of |
| ahead of | in addition to | in view of |
| apart from | in back of | next to |
| aside from | in front of | on account of |
| as of | in place of | out of |
| because of | in spite of | prior to |

A preposition is always part of a group of words called a **prepositional phrase**. A prepositional phrase begins with a preposition and ends with a noun or a pronoun called the **object of a preposition.** One or more modifiers may come between the preposition and its object. The prepositional phrases in the following examples are in **bold** type.

> **During history class** we watched a film **about carrier pigeons**.
>
> **On account of the war**, pigeons carried mail **throughout the country**.

## Preposition or Adverb?

The same word may be a preposition in one sentence and an adverb in another sentence. A word is a preposition if it is part of a prepositional phrase. An adverb stands alone.

| | |
|---|---|
| Preposition | I saw the pigeon ***outside*** *the window*. |
| Adverb | I saw the pigeon **outside**. |
| Preposition | Professor Reilly speaks well ***before*** *an audience*. |
| Adverb | Have you heard this lecture **before**? |

*You can learn more about prepositional phrases on pages L97–L103.*

## Practice Your Skills

### Check Your Understanding
*Identifying Prepositional Phrases*

History Topic **Write the prepositional phrases in the following paragraph.** (There are 20 prepositional phrases.)

In a sense the French were the originators of airmail service. During the siege of Paris in the Franco-Prussian War of the 1870s, mail was sent from the capital by balloon, along with hundreds of homing pigeons. Return letters were photo-reduced on thin film, which held an average of 2,500 letters. Then pigeons delivered the letters to the capital. Approximately 300 pigeons carrying the mail were dispatched. Some of these got past the Prussian pigeon snipers. In Paris the messages were enlarged on a projection screen, copied by clerks, and delivered to addresses within the city.

### Connect to the Writing Process: Drafting
*Writing Sentences with Prepositions and Adverbs*

**Write two sentences about mail for each word. In the first sentence, use the word as a preposition. In the second sentence, use the word as an adverb.**

1. around
2. below
3. near
4. by
5. down
6. up

## Communicate Your Ideas

### APPLY TO WRITING

**Web Site Sample Page: *Prepositional Phrases***

You are a Website developer, and you are writing a proposal to the marketing director of a company that specializes in historical memorabilia. You decide to end your proposal by writing a sample page about the era of history that interests you most. For your sample page, write a short summary about your chosen time period. Use prepositional phrases to make your sample page as specific and vivid as possible.

# Conjunctions

A **conjunction** connects words or groups of words.

**Coordinating conjunctions** are single connecting words, and **correlative conjunctions** are pairs of connecting words.

| CONJUNCTIONS | | | | |
|---|---|---|---|---|
| **Coordinating** | | | **Correlative** | |
| and | nor | yet | both/and | not only/but also |
| but | or | | either/or | whether/or |
| for | so | | neither/nor | |

Following are some uses of a conjunction.

**Neither** *Marty* **nor** *Lana* has a credit card. (connects nouns)
**Either** *write* her a check **or** *pay* cash. (connects verbs)
That dollar bill is *old* **and** *dirty*. (connects adjectives)
*I can't pay the balance,* **for** *I don't have the money.* (connects sentences)

*Subordinating conjunctions are used to introduce adverb clauses. You can learn about subordinating conjunctions on pages L142–L143.*

## Connect to Speaking and Writing

In casual conversation, your listener may prompt you to finish a thought by stating an appropriate conjunction for you to use.

> You say, "I went to the airport yesterday."
> Your friend does not understand why you're telling him this, so he says, **"And . . ."**
> You are prompted to finish the thought. "I went to the airport yesterday **and** applied for a job."

## Practice Your Skills

Check Your Understanding

### *Identifying Conjunctions*

General Interest **Write and label the coordinating and correlative conjunctions in the following paragraphs.**

Visitors to the Bureau of Engraving and Printing in Washington can buy 150 dollars' worth of United States currency for 75 cents, but there is a catch. The money is real, but it has been shredded. Every day the bureau shreds not only new, misprinted currency but also stamps and other items that are not fit for circulation. Anyone can take home some souvenir money, for in the bureau's visitor center, machines automatically dispense 75-cent packets of shredded currency.

Each of the twelve Federal Reserve district banks is also authorized to dispose of unusable currency whether it be old, soiled, or worn. Residents of Los Angeles can either drop by the district bank or request a delivery. For the sum of 83 dollars, the branch will deliver an entire day's output—up to 5,550 pounds—to your door if you live closer than the nearest dump. Some of this currency later appears in novelty stores in one form or another.

Connect to the Writing Process: Revising

***Using Conjunctions***

**Revise the following paragraphs to make them less repetitive and choppy. Use coordinating and correlative conjunctions to join words, phrases, and sentences.**

Every year criminals think they have discovered a foolproof way to counterfeit money. They use color copiers. They use scanners. They use high-quality printers. They scrutinize watermarks. They scrutinize paper quality. They scrutinize tiny markings. In 1997, more than 135 million dollars in counterfeit U.S. currency appeared worldwide. Three-fourths of it was discovered. Three-fourths of it was confiscated before it was circulated.

The United States government is well versed in detecting counterfeit money. It issued the first paper currency in 1861. Fewer than five years later, one-third of all notes in circulation were counterfeit. It created the Secret Service in 1865. Its sole mission was to quell the usage of fake currency. It is part of the U.S. Department of Treasury. It has developed new security features such as inks that change color when viewed from different angles. It has developed new security features such as fine-line printing patterns that are hard for printers and scanners to duplicate.

## Communicate Your Ideas

### APPLY TO WRITING

**Journal Entry:** ***Conjunctions***

If you received a million dollars as an unexpected legacy, what would you do with the money? Brainstorm a list of possibilities. Then arrange the items in that list from most important to least important. Finally, write a journal entry explaining what you would do with the money and why you would use it this way. Underline each conjunction you use.

# Interjections

An **interjection** is a word that expresses strong feeling or emotion.

Fear, anger, surprise, and happiness are just some of the emotions expressed by interjections. A comma or an exclamation point always separates an interjection from the rest of the sentence, depending on whether strong or mild feeling is being expressed.

> **Wow!** This price is unreasonable.
> **Yes,** I will lend you money.

## PRACTICE YOUR SKILLS

Check Your Understanding

***Identifying Interjections***

Contemporary Life

**Write the interjections in the sentences below. If there is no interjection, write *none*.**

1. Help! I've been robbed.
2. Whew! It could have been worse.
3. The thief wanted my cash but not my credit cards!
4. No, I did not see his face well enough to identify him if I saw him again.

5. Stop! Don't touch my arm there.
6. The thief hit my arm to make me let go of the cash I was holding.
7. Yes, I was standing in line to pay for my candy and gasoline.
8. Oh! I remember a distinctive ring he wore.
9. Come back!
10. Well, I can sketch the ring as I remember it, and I think you'll be able to use the information to catch the thief.

Connect to the Writing Process: Revising

***Adding Interjections***

You can change the intensity of each sentence below by adding an interjection to it. Write each sentence, adding a correctly punctuated interjection.

11. That was my favorite ring.
12. I have to get it back.
13. Wait a minute.
14. I see something shiny on the floor.
15. The thief must have dropped it as he ran away.

## Communicate Your Ideas

### APPLY TO WRITING

Letter: ***Prepositions, Conjunctions, and Interjections***

Your guidance counselor has invited each student in your class to write her an informal letter describing the ideal job fair. She is interested in your ideas and reactions to different careers, pay rates, work environments, and so on. Take this opportunity to influence what type of job fair you and the other students are provided, and write an expressive letter describing your ideas, opinions, and feelings. Be prepared to identify each preposition, conjunction, and interjection.

# Parts of Speech Review

A chameleon can change its color to blend with its surroundings. Many words in English are like chameleons. They can become different parts of speech, depending on how they are used in different sentences.

| | |
|---|---|
| NOUN | The **last** of the books has arrived. |
| VERB | The rare book sale will **last** two more days. |
| ADJECTIVE | The **last** book to sell was by George Eliot. |
| ADVERB | Her signed edition of *Silas Marner* sold **last.** |

To determine what part of speech a word is, read the sentence carefully. Then ask yourself, *What is each word doing in this sentence?* The following summary of the eight parts of speech will help you determine how a word is used in a sentence.

| | |
|---|---|
| NOUN | Is the word naming a person, place, thing, or idea?<br>The **friendship** between **Silas Marner** and his **neighbor** lasted for many **years**. |
| PRONOUN | Is the word taking the place of a noun?<br>**Everything they** said about **him** was true. |
| VERB | Is the word either showing action or linking the subject with another word in the sentence?<br>I **read** the book. It **was** fascinating. |
| ADJECTIVE | Is the word modifying a noun or a pronoun? Does it answer the question *What kind? Which one(s)? How many?* or *How much?*<br>**That large stone** fireplace was very **cozy**. |
| ADVERB | Is the word modifying a verb, an adjective, or an adverb? Does it answer the question *How? When? Where*? or *To what extent?*<br>Baby Eppie was **rather** curious and found Marner's fireplace **very quickly**. |

| | |
|---|---|
| PREPOSITION | Is the word showing a relationship between a noun or a pronoun and another word in the sentence? Is it part of a phrase?<br>***By means of*** *her determination*, Molly carried Eppie ***through*** *the snowstorm*. |
| CONJUNCTION | Is the word connecting words or groups of words?<br>Molly was **either** unconscious **or** dead, **for** she lay motionless in the snow. |
| INTERJECTION | Is the word expressing strong feeling?<br>**Wow!** Godfrey Cass is really selfish. |

## PRACTICE YOUR SKILLS

Check Your Understanding

***Identifying Parts of Speech***

**Write each underlined word in the following paragraph. Beside each one write its part of speech, using these abbreviations.**

| | |
|---|---|
| noun = *n.* | adverb = *adv.* |
| pronoun = *pron.* | preposition = *prep.* |
| verb = *v.* | conjunction = *conj.* |
| adjective = *adj.* | interjection = *interj.* |

*Adam Bede*, considered a masterpiece by some, was written by George Eliot and published in 1859. Today this book is still one of the most widely read Victorian novels. Eliot's purpose in telling this story was to show her readers what ordinary life was like. What does that mean? Well, the setting is not any more colorful or the characters any more heroic than readers of her day were likely to find in their own experience.

Connect to the Writing Process: Drafting

### *Writing Sentences Using Parts of Speech*

**Write two sentences for each word. In the first sentence, use the word as one part of speech. In the second sentence, use the word as a different part of speech.**

1. today
2. few
3. iron
4. advance
5. line
6. shower
7. well
8. either
9. fast
10. each

## Mixed Practice

Contemporary Life

**Write the underlined word in each sentence. Then beside each word, write its part of speech.**

1. Where is the party invitation?
2. Both girls had seen it on the counter.
3. Jack said to come over this afternoon.
4. Well, that's a surprise!
5. Turn off that loud music.
6. At what time did you arrive?
7. The rest of my friends are not here yet.
8. Will they party all night?
9. Oh! I forgot the paper cups.
10. Is this well water?
11. What is that?
12. You should rest now.
13. Don't sing too loudly.
14. This is your seat.
15. Both of the twins are here.

CheckPoint

## Determining Parts of Speech

**Write each underlined word. Then beside each word, write its part of speech using the following abbreviations.**

noun = *n.* pronoun = *pron.* verb = *v.*
adjective = *adj.* adverb = *adv.* preposition = *prep.*
conjunction = *conj.*

Aldous Huxley is primarily remembered today as the author of the frightening science-fiction novel *Brave New World.* Huxley began his career as a student of medicine. Temporarily blinded by a disease that affected his eyes, he was unable to practice medicine. His essays and novels, however, reflect his very strong interest in science. Huxley's novels include *Eyeless in Gaza* and *After Many a Summer Dies the Swan.* The lead character in *After Many a Summer Dies the Swan* is a man obsessed with rejuvenation. He discovers that the man who first experimented with rejuvenation is now a 200-year-old ape! *Brave New World* is a treatise that studies the effects of scientific progress run amok. Humans, created in bottles, are trained to be passive. The title, of course, is a phrase from Shakespeare's *The Tempest.*

Huxley himself came from a long line of intellectuals. His grandfather Thomas Huxley, a follower of Charles Darwin, was a famous lecturer and essayist. His great-uncle Matthew Arnold was a great English poet and critic. His brother Julian was a popular science writer, and his half-brother Andrew won the Nobel Prize for physiology in 1963, the same year that Huxley died.

## Determining Parts of Speech

**Write the underlined word in each sentence. Then, beside each word, write its part of speech using the following abbreviations.**

| | | |
|---|---|---|
| noun = *n.* | pronoun = *pron.* | verb = *v.* |
| adjective = *adj.* | adverb = *adv.* | preposition = *prep.* |
| conjunction = *conj.* | interjection = *interj.* | |

1. He walked out.
2. These are delicious.
3. He writes very well.
4. Jane has a new cat.
5. He leaves at ten.
6. Did you see my hat?
7. We can tomatoes.
8. Finish your banana split.
9. Fill the car with gas.
10. Both children slept well.
11. The gas heater warmed us.
12. Cat fur makes me itch.
13. I like these songs.
14. The leaves are turning red.
15. My! You are quite funny.
16. The dog went out the door.
17. May I have both?
18. Well! That was rude.
19. Recycle that can.
20. Split some logs for the fire.

## Understanding Parts of Speech

**Write five sentences that use the following words as the different parts of speech. Then underline each word and label its use in the sentence.**

1. some—pronoun, adjective
2. alarm—verb, noun
3. either—pronoun, adjective, conjunction
4. down—adverb, preposition, adjective
5. chilled—verb, adjective

## Using Parts of Speech

**Write a paragraph in which you use each of the eight parts of speech at least once. Write about one of the following topics or one of your choice: someone whose actions you admire or an author whose work you enjoy. Then underline and label one use of each part of speech.**

# Language and *Self-Expression*

Andy Warhol was a founder of the Pop Art movement of the 1960s, a movement that made art out of the icons of popular culture. In this print Warhol took a famous photograph of a moonwalk and made it his own, silkscreening it onto canvas and transforming the colors and rhythms of the photograph.

In this work two key figures, an astronaut and an American flag, are shown on the surface of the moon. These figures are all you need to conjure up this historic event. Think of a recent significant event in local or world history. Boil down the event to two or three key images. Then use those images to write an unrhymed poem that captures the event in words. As you write, think about precise nouns, verbs, and adjectives you might use to make your images come alive for a reader.

**Prewriting** Choose an event in recent history. Quickwrite two or three adjective-noun pairs that seem to be key images related to the event. Some examples from the moonwalk might be *white uniform, horizontal flag, rough surface.*

**Drafting** Include your adjective-noun pairs as you describe the key images in your unrhymed poem.

**Revising** Reread your poem or have a classmate critique it. Replace dull, ordinary nouns, verbs, and adjectives with vivid, precise ones.

**Editing** Review your poem, looking for errors in grammar, capitalization, punctuation, and spelling. Make any corrections that are necessary.

**Publishing** Prepare a final copy of your poem. Then publish it in a notebook of poems by your classmates. Take the time to read your classmates' poems. As a class, discuss the power of a few words to portray the essence of an event.

## The Parts of Speech

### A **noun** is the name of a person, place, thing, or idea.

A **common noun** names any person, place, or thing. *(page L6)*
A **proper noun** names a particular person, place, or thing. *(page L6)*

### A **pronoun** is a word that takes the place of one or more nouns.

A **reflexive pronoun** is formed by adding *–self* or *–selves* to personal pronouns. *(page L11)*
An **intensive pronoun** is included to add emphasis or intensity. *(page L11)*
An **indefinite pronoun** often refers to unnamed persons or things. *(page L13)*
A **demonstrative pronoun** points out a specific person, place, or thing. *(page L13)*
An **interrogative pronoun** is used to ask a question. *(page L14)*

### A **verb** is a word that expresses action or a state of being.

An action verb is **transitive** if it has an object. *(page L16)*
An action verb is **intransitive** if it has no object. *(page L16)*

### An **adjective** is a word that modifies a noun or pronoun.

The words *a, an,* and *the* form a special group of adjectives called **articles**. *(page L26)*

### An **adverb** is a word that modifies a verb, an adjective, or another adverb.

### A **preposition** is always part of a group of words called a **prepositional phrase**.

### A **conjunction** connects words or groups of words.

### An **interjection** is a word that expresses strong feeling or emotion.

### *Directions*

**Write the letter of the term that correctly identifies the underlined word in each sentence.**

EXAMPLE **1.** My mother <u>introduced</u> me to the work of the Brontë sisters.

**1** **A** noun
**B** pronoun
**C** verb
**D** adverb

ANSWER **1 C**

**1.** The Brontë <u>family</u> produced three novelists: Emily, Charlotte, and Anne.

**2.** Charlotte worked as a teacher and governess, <u>but</u> she wrote verse on the side.

**3.** In 1845, she discovered that <u>her</u> sisters Emily and Anne also wrote poetry.

**4.** The sisters collected their <u>poems</u> in a volume, using the pseudonyms Currer, Ellis, and Acton Bell.

**5.** Neither the poems nor Charlotte's first novel <u>was</u> successful.

**6.** However, in 1847, Charlotte's book *Jane Eyre* became very <u>popular</u>.

**7.** *Wuthering Heights,* Emily's one novel, is considered the Brontës' <u>best</u> work.

**8.** <u>My</u>, it is a passionate and inspired work of fiction!

**9.** Anne, the youngest Brontë, is the <u>least</u> famous of the sisters.

**10.** She published two novels <u>before</u> her death in 1849.

1. **A** adjective
   **B** adverb
   **C** preposition
   **D** noun

2. **A** adjective
   **B** adverb
   **C** preposition
   **D** conjunction

3. **A** adjective
   **B** adverb
   **C** pronoun
   **D** noun

4. **A** noun
   **B** pronoun
   **C** verb
   **D** adverb

5. **A** noun
   **B** pronoun
   **C** verb
   **D** adverb

6. **A** conjunction
   **B** interjection
   **C** preposition
   **D** adjective

7. **A** adjective
   **B** adverb
   **C** preposition
   **D** noun

8. **A** conjunction
   **B** interjection
   **C** preposition
   **D** adjective

9. **A** noun
   **B** pronoun
   **C** verb
   **D** adverb

10. **A** conjunction
    **B** interjection
    **C** preposition
    **D** adjective

CHAPTER 2

# The Sentence Base

## Pretest

### Directions

**Write the letter of the term that correctly identifies the underlined word or words in each sentence.**

EXAMPLE **1.** *The New Yorker* was founded by Harold Ross.

**1** **A** simple subject
**B** simple predicate
**C** complete subject
**D** complete predicate

ANSWER **1** **B**

**1.** Among the early contributors to the magazine were Dorothy Parker and E. B. White.
**2.** *The New Yorker* specializes in short fiction, essays, and cartoons.
**3.** After Harold Ross's death, William Shawn became the editor.
**4.** The magazine sometimes carries entire books in installments.
**5.** You should look at a copy someday.
**6.** Ogden Nash and S. J. Perelman contributed to the magazine's reputation for humor.
**7.** Nash wrote light satirical verse and served as an editor for many years.
**8.** His collections of verse include *Everyone But Thee and Me* and *Bed Riddance*.
**9.** East Coast intellectuals were targets of Nash's wit.
**10.** Perelman often used dreadful puns in his satires.

1 **A** simple subject
**B** simple predicate
**C** complete subject
**D** complete predicate

2 **A** simple subject
**B** simple predicate
**C** complete subject
**D** complete predicate

3 **A** simple subject
**B** simple predicate
**C** compound subject
**D** complete predicate

4 **A** simple subject
**B** simple predicate
**C** complete subject
**D** complete predicate

5 **A** simple subject
**B** simple predicate
**C** complete subject
**D** complete predicate

6 **A** compound subject
**B** compound verb
**C** compound direct object
**D** compound predicate nominative

7 **A** compound subject
**B** compound verb
**C** compound direct object
**D** compound predicate nominative

8 **A** compound subject
**B** compound verb
**C** compound direct object
**D** compound predicate nominative

9 **A** direct object
**B** indirect object
**C** predicate nominative
**D** predicate adjective

10 **A** direct object
**B** indirect object
**C** predicate nominative
**D** predicate adjective

Chuck Jones. *Love Is in the Hare,* 1998.
Limited edition giclée, 20 by 15 inches. © Warner Bros.

**Describe** Who is the focus of this caricature? How does the title suggest that this artwork is meant to be humorous?

**Analyze** How does the cartoonist use exaggeration in the caricature?

**Interpret** Exaggeration is a technique also used by writers in tall tales and satires. If you were to describe Bugs Bunny in words, how would you express the ridiculous aspects of his appearance and character?

**Judge** If you wanted to satirize someone, do you think it would be more effective to do so in the form of a cartoon or in writing? Why do you think so?

At the end of this chapter, you will use the artwork to stimulate ideas for writing.

# Subjects and Predicates

A well-constructed house has a foundation, which basically holds all the other parts of the house together. Like a house a sentence must also have a foundation. The foundation, or base, of a sentence is composed of a subject, a predicate (verb), and sometimes a complement. All other words in the sentence are added to this foundation.

A **sentence** is a group of words that expresses a complete thought.

A group of words that does not express a complete thought is called a **fragment**. In many cases a group of words is a fragment because it does not have a subject or a predicate.

| Fragment | Sentence |
|---|---|
| Under the briefcase. | The script is under the briefcase. |
| The characters. | The characters seem real. |
| Designing the set. | Mike is designing the set. |
| Auditioned for the part. | She auditioned for the part. |

To express a complete thought, a group of words must have both a subject and a predicate.

A **subject** names the person, place, thing, or idea the sentence is about.

The **predicate** tells something about the subject.

| Complete Subject | Complete Predicate |
|---|---|
| My aunt from Alabama | is performing in *Hamlet.* |
| The box on the counter | contains costumes for the actors. |
| The audience | clapped for ten minutes today. |
| The final cast member | took a bow. |

*You can learn more about sentence fragments later in this chapter on pages L68–L71.*

## Simple Subjects and Predicates

A **simple subject** is the main word in the complete subject.

A **simple predicate**, or **verb**, is the main word or phrase in the complete predicate.

Each complete subject and predicate can be narrowed down to a single word or phrase. In the following examples, the simple subjects and the verbs are in **bold** type.

complete subject | complete predicate

The narrow wooden **stage curved** to the right.

complete subject | complete predicate

Two **reviews** recently **appeared** in the *Chronicle*.

complete subject | complete predicate

The **New Globe** in Acton **is raising** money for new seats.

In the last example, *New Globe* is a single proper noun; therefore, both words make up the simple subject. Notice also that the verb phrase *is raising* is considered the verb of the sentence.

Throughout the rest of this book, the term *subject* will refer to a simple subject, and the term *verb* will refer to a simple predicate, which may be a single verb or a verb phrase.

*You can learn more about using verbs on pages L16–L23 and about subject-verb agreement on pages L289–L317.*

### CONNECT TO SPEAKING AND WRITING

Anyone—even a three-year-old—can express ideas using a few random words. However, you will express yourself much more precisely and persuasively if you have mastered the basic sentence. You will argue more effectively, describe more vividly, and entertain more creatively. People will pay more attention to what you say because you say it with skillfully formed sentences. By understanding the two main parts of a sentence, the subject and the verb, you will be able to create these powerful sentences.

## Finding Subjects and Verbs

To find the subject of an action verb, ask yourself *Who?* or *What?* before the verb. The answer to either question will be the subject of the sentence. In the following examples, each subject is underlined once, and each verb is underlined twice.

> Mandy has taken drama classes for two years. (The action verb is *has taken*. Who has taken? The subject is *Mandy*.)
>
> His performance is improving rapidly. (The action verb is *is improving*. What is improving? The subject is *performance*.)

To find the subject of a linking verb, ask yourself, *About whom or what is the statement being made?* When you have answered that question, you will have identified the subject.

> My brother is a stagehand at a dinner theater. (The linking verb is *is*. About whom is the statement being made? The subject is *brother*.)
>
> The stage curtains feel exceptionally heavy. (The linking verb is *feel*. About what is the statement being made? The subject is *curtains*.)

*You can learn more about linking verbs on pages L20–L23.*

When you look for a subject and a verb, it is often helpful to eliminate all modifiers and all prepositional phrases from the sentence. Remember: *A subject is never part of a prepositional phrase.*

> ~~Numerous~~ masterpieces ~~by Shakespeare~~ are performed ~~throughout England~~. (*Masterpieces* is the subject; *are performed* is the verb.)
>
> ~~His~~ plays can ~~still~~ be seen ~~at the reconstructed Globe Theatre in London~~. (*Plays* is the subject; *can be seen* is the verb.)

*You can learn more about modifiers on pages L107–L111 and L120–L122 and prepositional phrases on pages L97–L103.*

# PRACTICE YOUR SKILLS

## Check Your Understanding
### *Identifying Subjects and Verbs*

Literature Topic **Write the subject and the verb in each sentence.**

**1.** William Shakespeare lived from 1564 to 1616.
**2.** At his death this famous playwright left a most unusual will.
**3.** Considerable real-estate holdings in and near Stratford went to his two daughters, Susanna and Judith.
**4.** Shakespeare did, however, make some curious bequests.
**5.** The following line from his will is still confusing many historians.
**6.** "I give unto my Wiffe my 2nd-best bed with the furniture."
**7.** He apparently had just scribbled these words into the will as an additional note.
**8.** His will never mentions his plays.
**9.** This omission has raised serious doubts in some historians' minds.
**10.** The writer of this will may not have been the author of the Elizabethan dramas.

## Connect to the Writing Process: Drafting
### *Writing Simple Subjects and Verbs*

**Add subjects or verbs to the following words to create complete sentences. If you are given a verb, add a simple subject. If you are given a subject, add a verb.**

**11.** auditioned for the role of Duncan, King of Scotland.
**12.** For the next three weekends, tryouts.
**13.** painted the wooden props.
**14.** will practice each night.
**15.** The flamboyant drama teacher.
**16.** Everyone's favorite actor.

17. wants her own room with a star on the door.
18. had never read *The Tragedy of Macbeth*.
19. Seth Ramsey.
20. said she will write a letter of recommendation for him.

## Communicate Your Ideas

### APPLY TO WRITING

**Play Scene: *Subjects and Verbs***

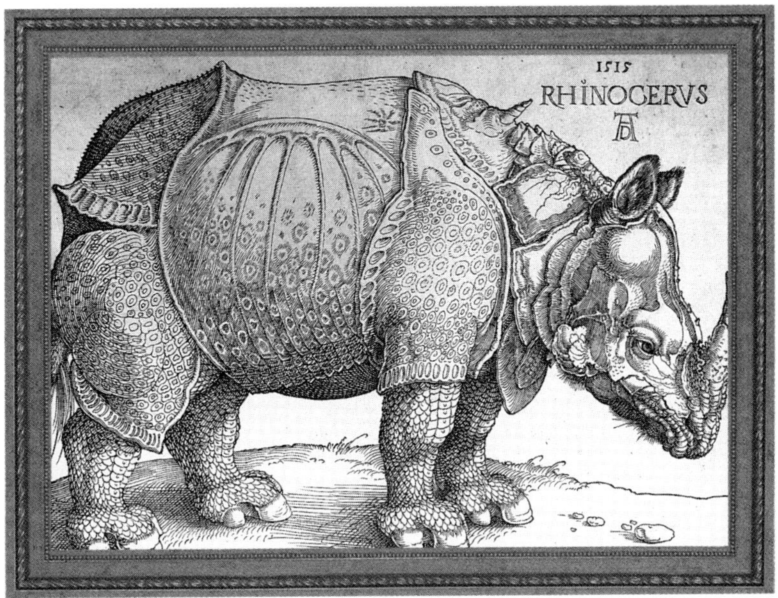


Albrecht Dürer. *Rhinoceros,* 1515.
Woodcut, 9¼ by 11¾ inches. Prints Collection, New York Public Library.

A writer's choice of verbs determines how clearly the reader pictures the action. In *Macbeth*, Macbeth says that he would rather face an "arm'd rhinoceros" than the ghost that is in front of him. In Shakespeare's time, *armed* meant that one not only carried weapons but also was covered with armor—much like the thick-skinned rhinoceros armed with a sharp horn.

Which do you think would be scarier for Macbeth to confront, a rhinoceros or a ghost? Study Dürer's drawing

*Rhinoceros*, and assume that this rhinoceros, rather than the ghost, appears to Macbeth. Write an action scene in which Macbeth is faced with this rhinoceros. Be prepared to identify the subjects and verbs in your scene.

## Different Positions of Subjects

When a sentence is in its **natural order**, the subject comes before the verb. For various reasons a sentence may also be written in **inverted order**, with the verb or part of the verb phrase coming before the subject. Subjects in sentences in inverted order are sometimes difficult to find.

**Questions** are often phrased in inverted order. To find the subject and the verb in a question, turn the question around to make a statement.

| | |
|---|---|
| QUESTION | Have you seen my model of the inner ear? |
| STATEMENT | You have seen my model of the inner ear. |

***There* and *here*** begin sentences that are in inverted order. To find the subject and the verb, place the words in the sentence in their natural order. Sometimes the word *there* or *here* must be dropped before the sentence can be put in its natural order.

| | |
|---|---|
| INVERTED ORDER | Here is your inner-ear model. |
| NATURAL ORDER | Your inner-ear model is here. |
| INVERTED ORDER | There will be a test given on the ear. |
| NATURAL ORDER | A test will be given on the ear. (Drop *there*.) |

**Emphasis and variety** are other reasons for inverted sentences. To create emphasis or variety, you may sometimes deliberately write a sentence in inverted order. To determine the subject and the verb, put the sentence in its natural order.

| | |
|---|---|
| INVERTED ORDER | Throughout the body are innumerable muscle fibers. |
| NATURAL ORDER | Innumerable muscle fibers are throughout the body. |
| INVERTED ORDER | Across the gym lay the muscle-building equipment. |
| NATURAL ORDER | The muscle-building equipment lay across the gym. |

**Understood *You*** is the subject of most commands and requests. Although *you* seldom appears in such sentences, it is still understood to be there. In the following examples, *you* is the understood subject of each sentence.

Smell this fragrant lotion!
(*You* is the understood subject.)

Cathy, breathe deeply.
(*You* is the understood subject even though the person receiving the command is named.)

*You can learn more about subject-verb agreement and inverted order on pages L303–L305.*

## PRACTICE YOUR SKILLS

Check Your Understanding

### *Identifying Subjects and Verbs in Inverted Order*

Science Topic

**Write the subject and the verb in each sentence. If the subject is an understood *you*, write *you* in parentheses.**

1. Listen to this fascinating information!
2. Within the skull is the average three-pound human brain.
3. Here is the detailed diagram of the respiratory system.
4. Have you studied the respiratory system yet?

5. There are millions of tiny air sacs in the lungs.
6. Think of this fact at your next mealtime.
7. On the table in the food is your supply of vitamins and minerals.
8. There are 9,000 taste buds on a person's tongue.
9. With increased age comes an inability to hear fewer high-pitched sounds.
10. How does the circulatory system transport 680,000 gallons of blood a year?

Connect to the Writing Process: Drafting
*Writing Sentences in Inverted Order*

**11.–18. Write two sentences for each type of inverted order sentence: *Questions, There and Here, Emphasis or Variety,* and *Understood You.* Then underline the subjects and circle the verbs.**

Communicate Your Ideas

APPLY TO WRITING

Expository Essay: *Inverted Sentences*

Choose one system of the body, such as the respiratory system, the circulatory system, or the central nervous system, and write a short expository essay about some aspect of it for your science teacher. (You may first want to do some research.) The main point of your essay should be the remarkable functions that a system has. Incorporate some inverted sentences to give your essay variety and interest.

## Compound Subjects and Verbs

A **compound subject** is two or more subjects in one sentence that have the same verb and are joined by a conjunction.

A sentence can have more than one subject and more than one verb. You can ask yourself the same questions to find compound subjects and verbs as you did to find simple subjects and verbs.

> The rings and bracelets disappeared suddenly.
> Maria, Barry, and Martin searched for the jewels.

A **compound verb** is two or more verbs that have the same subject and are joined by a conjunction.

> You can join the treasure hunt or stay in the cabin.
> This map will assist our search and will guarantee success.

A sentence can have both a compound subject and a compound verb.

> Paul and his sister had the jewelry and buried it deeply.
>
> Maria and Barry received a treasure map and immediately organized a search party.

*You can find out more about conjunctions on pages L40–L43. You can learn about subject-verb agreement with compound subjects on pages L298–L301.*

## PRACTICE YOUR SKILLS

Check Your Understanding

***Identifying Compound Subjects and Verbs***

General Interest **Write the subjects and the verbs in the following sentences.**

**1.** Gold and silver in the *Atocha*'s hold lay on the bottom of the sea and tempted treasure hunters for centuries.

**2.** In 1622, the ship was bound for Spain but sank in the waters off the Florida coast during a hurricane.

**3.** Because of a second hurricane, other vessels could not rescue the *Atocha*'s treasure.

**4.** The position of the ship either was not recorded or was forgotten.

**5.** Eventually ocean currents covered the ship with sand and hid it from searchers.

6. The legend of the *Atocha* and the promise of great wealth brought many treasure hunters to Florida.
7. Mel Fisher and his family joined the others and became full-time treasure hunters.
8. Mel had once run a chicken farm and then had operated a diving shop.
9. He not only had some original ideas about the possible location of the ship but also used clever techniques in the search.
10. Both Mel and his family continued their search in the face of many hardships and much scorn.

Connect to the Writing Process: Prewriting
***Brainstorming for Ideas***

**Read the following paragraph to find out what eventually happened to the *Atocha*'s treasure. Write each subject and each verb. Using these subjects and verbs for ideas, brainstorm and list additional subjects and verbs that relate to treasure-hunting. Be sure to include plenty of compound subjects and verbs.**

Critics constantly laughed at the efforts of the Fishers. Finally, in June 1975, Fisher's crew found a cannon from the *Atocha* and silenced the critics. The joy of the Fisher party was intense yet brief. On the night of July 18, 1975, Fisher's son, his daughter-in-law, and another diver drowned. Neither Mel nor his wife stopped their work. The tragedies would then have been meaningless. They continued and salvaged more and more objects. They could not keep all of the treasure. The state of Florida claimed a portion of the treasure and held much of it for a long period of time.

## Communicate Your Ideas

### APPLY TO WRITING

**Newspaper Story: *Subjects and Verbs***

Using the lists of subjects and verbs you wrote for the preceding exercise, write a newspaper story of a treasure found years after being lost and forgotten. Be sure to use compound subjects and compound verbs in some of your sentences.

Mixed Practice

Contemporary Life

**Make two columns. Label one column *Subjects* and the other *Verbs*. Then write the subjects and verbs in each sentence under the appropriate heading.**

1. Jamaica is a lush, green island in the Caribbean Sea.
2. There is sparkling clear water surrounding this popular vacation destination.
3. Deep-sea divers and eager swimmers rent boats and buy snorkeling equipment for water recreation.
4. Have you seen the beautiful coral reefs off the coast of Jamaica?
5. Just below the calm surface of the sea grows living coral.
6. Wear a scuba mask for the best view of the coral.
7. Trisha, Jerry, and Ling saw a baby octopus and accidentally frightened it away.
8. Tomorrow I will windsurf, shop, and sunbathe until nightfall.
9. Here are the picture postcards and small souvenirs from our shopping trip.
10. In the early morning hours, enjoy your breakfast and then meet me at the beach for a swim.

# Sentence Fragments

A sentence fragment is not a sentence at all. It is an incomplete thought that usually leaves the reader confused with unanswered questions.

A **sentence fragment** is a group of words that does not express a complete thought.

To communicate clearly and completely when you write, be sure to check your work for sentence fragments like the following.

**Fragments due to incomplete thoughts** are a common kind of fragment. A fragment that expresses an incomplete thought is often missing a subject or a verb.

| | |
|---|---|
| FRAGMENT | Applied to five different colleges. |
| CORRECTED | Jackie applied to five different colleges. (*Jackie* is the subject.) |
| FRAGMENT | All of my friends in homeroom. |
| CORRECTED | All of my friends in homeroom graduated. (*Graduated* is the verb.) |

**Fragments due to incorrect punctuation** are another kind of fragment. If you place a period between the parts of a compound verb, you create a fragment. Likewise, if you place a period before a list of items, you create a fragment.

| | |
|---|---|
| FRAGMENT | Martin rewrote his application essay five times. And made it stronger each time. |
| CORRECTED | Martin rewrote his application essay five times and made it stronger each time. (*Rewrote* and *made* are a compound verb.) |
| FRAGMENT | Sarah consulted many sources for advice. Books, teachers, relatives, and friends. |
| CORRECTED | Sarah consulted many sources for advice: books, teachers, relatives, and friends. (A colon precedes the list of sources.) |

*You can find out about other kinds of sentence fragments on pages L123–L125 and L164–L166.*

## Ways to Correct Sentence Fragments

You can correct a fragment in one of two ways. You can add words to it to make a complete sentence, or you can attach it to the sentence next to it. Sometimes when you attach a fragment to a sentence next to it, you may have to add or drop words.

| | |
|---|---|
| FRAGMENT | Asked her guidance counselor for direction. |
| ADD WORDS | Katia asked her guidance counselor for direction.<br>(Who asked for advice? Words are added to complete the sentence.) |
| FRAGMENT FOLLOWING A SENTENCE | Leon wanted an academic scholarship. Studied diligently all year. |
| ATTACH TO PREVIOUS SENTENCE | Leon wanted an academic scholarship and studied diligently all year.<br>(The conjunction *and* is added to connect the fragment to the sentence before it.) |
| FRAGMENT PRECEDING A SENTENCE | Good grades, social skills, and academic potential. These are all important to the application committee. |
| ATTACH TO FOLLOWING SENTENCE | Good grades, social skills, and academic potential are all important to the application committee.<br>(*Grades*, *skills*, and *potential* form a compound subject for the verb *are*.) |

## Connect to Writer's Craft

Writers of fiction use sentence fragments to make written dialogue sound more realistic. They know that in daily life, few people speak in complete sentences all the time. Poets often use fragments to focus readers' attention on the thought or idea expressed by the fragment rather than on a complete thought. All formal writing, however, requires complete sentences. An essay, business report, or formal letter free of sentence fragments is the sign of an educated writer.

## Practice Your Skills

Check Your Understanding

***Identifying Sentence Fragments***

Contemporary Life

**Write *F* if the item is a sentence fragment and *S* if it is a sentence. Then correct each sentence fragment.**

1. The most important preparation for college admission. Begins long before you fill out the application.
2. Do homework and take thorough notes. In every class.
3. Most college freshmen. They wish they had taken high school more seriously.
4. Don't forget the value of exercise and sleep.
5. Community involvement.
6. Verbal, math, and analytical skills. Tested by standardized tests.
7. Many smart people. Afflicted by test anxiety.
8. Become familiar with the SAT and ACT formats. And take a few practice tests beforehand.
9. Many tips and facts about tests and applications. Freely available from guidance counselors and college admissions offices.
10. Your best plan is simple. Study, practice, and plan.

Connect to the Writing Process: Revising

*Sentence Fragments*

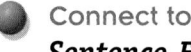

**Read the following advice on writing college admission essays. Then rewrite the paragraph, correcting each sentence fragment you find.**

Two important things. They will help you write a strong college admission essay. First, one or several admissions officers. Dedicated, overworked, experienced. Will read your essay. Sentence fragments, poor grammar, and spelling errors. These will destine an essay for the rejection stack. Second, each reader will look for a connection with you through the essay. You can make this connection. By keeping the focus of the essay on the most important topic—you. For example, if you are writing about "An Event That Changed My Life," which do you think is a better statement: "My parents divorced when I was ten. And they spent the next seven years fighting over the house, the furniture, and me" or "I was ten when my parents divorced. And I quickly learned. Responsibility, self-discipline, and dedication"? Is the better sentence. Focuses on the positive qualities in you. Will help make you a successful college student.

## Communicate Your Ideas

### APPLY TO WRITING

**College Admission Essay:** ***Complete Sentences***

The Director of Admissions of your choice of colleges has requested that you send a writing sample. Write a short college admission essay about an event that changed your life. Then team up with a writing partner to check for sentence fragments in your and your partner's writing. Help each other correct any fragments you find because you want to impress the Director!

# Complements

Sometimes a sentence needs more than a subject and a verb to sound complete. Such a sentence also needs a completer, or complement. None of the following sentences, for example, would be complete without the complements in **bold** type.

> Todd wrapped the **gift**.
> Dan gave **me flowers**.
> Kate has become an **expert** on customs.
> The stores are **open**.

There are five kinds of complements. Direct objects, indirect objects, and objective complements complete the meaning of action verbs. Predicate nominatives and predicate adjectives, which are called subject complements, complete the meaning of linking verbs.

## Direct Objects and Indirect Objects

**A direct object is a noun or a pronoun that receives the action of the verb.**

To find a direct object, ask yourself *What?* or *Whom?* after an action verb. Notice in the third example below that a direct object can be compound.

> d.o.
> Leo removed the **packages** from his briefcase. (Leo removed what? *Packages* is the direct object.)
>
> d.o.
> I drove **Heather** to the airport. (I drove whom? *Heather* is the direct object.)
>
> d.o. d.o.
> Heather will visit **associates** and **clients** in Japan. (Heather will visit whom? *Associates* and *clients* make up the compound direct object.)

Each part of a compound action verb can have its own direct object.

> d.o. d.o.
>
> Heather focused her **camera** and snapped the **picture**.
>
> (*Camera* is the direct object of *focused*, and *picture* is the direct object of *snapped*.)

*You can learn more about action verbs and transitive verbs on pages L16–L17.*

An **indirect object** is a noun or a pronoun that answers the question *To or for whom?* or *To or for what?* after an action verb.

If a sentence has a direct object, the same sentence may also have an indirect object. To find an indirect object, first find the direct object by asking *What?* or *Whom?* after the action verb. Then ask *To or for whom?* or *To or for what?* after the direct object. An indirect object always comes before a direct object in a sentence.

> i.o. d.o.
>
> I bought **Paul** a new catcher's mitt.
>
> (*Mitt* is the direct object of the verb *bought*. I bought a mitt for whom? *Paul* is the indirect object. Notice that the indirect object comes before the direct object.)
>
> i.o. d.o.
>
> The students gave **Mr. Beacon** tokens of appreciation.
>
> (*Tokens* is the direct object of the verb *gave*. The students gave tokens to whom? *Mr. Beacon* is the indirect object.)

An indirect object may be compound.

> i.o. i.o. d.o.
>
> Sashina Chi is teaching **Lee** and **Kelly** Japanese.
>
> (*Japanese* is the direct object of the verb *is teaching*. Sashina Chi is teaching Japanese to whom? *Lee* and *Kelly* make up the compound indirect object.)

Remember that neither a direct object nor an indirect object is ever part of a prepositional phrase.

i.o. d.o.

We gave **Roger** an album for his birthday.

(*Roger* is the indirect object. It comes before the direct object *album* and is not part of a prepositional phrase.)

d.o.

We gave an album to Roger for his birthday.

(In this sentence *Roger* is not the indirect object because it follows the direct object *album* and is the object of the preposition *to*.)

*You can learn more about prepositional phrases on pages L97–L103.*

## PRACTICE YOUR SKILLS

Check Your Understanding

### *Identifying Direct and Indirect Objects*

Contemporary Life

**Write the direct and indirect objects in the following sentences. Then beside each one state whether it is a *direct object* (d.o.) or an *indirect object* (i.o.).**

1. My Japanese friend Keiko shipped me a collection of herbal teas.
2. Last month I gave her a tea service for her birthday.
3. Later Keiko recommended a book about gifts to me.
4. I read the book with great interest.
5. I learned several facts about gift customs in Japanese culture.
6. During the year-end gift-giving season, called *O-seibo*, employers treat employees and clients lavishly.
7. Department stores stock special sections of appropriate gift items and wrappings.
8. Friends, relatives, students, and teachers surprise others with gourmet candy, cookies, and other treats.

**9.** They sometimes send overseas friends souvenir stamps, small pins, or fancy soaps.

**10.** Visitors to Japan should learn the customs about gifts.

## Objective Complements

An **objective complement** is a noun or an adjective that renames or describes the direct object.

To find an objective complement, first find the direct object. Then ask the question *What?* after the direct object. An objective complement will always follow the direct object. Notice the compound objective complement in the third example.

> Chin-yau declared the gift **perfect.** (*Gift* is the direct object. Chin-yau declared the gift what? *Perfect* is the objective complement. It follows the direct object and describes it.)
>
> The Chinese consider red a joyful **color** for gift wrap. (*Red* is the direct object. The Chinese consider red what? *Color* is the objective complement. It follows the direct object and renames it.)
>
> The award made Ming **happy** and **proud.** (*Ming* is the direct object. The award made Ming what? The words *happy* and *proud* make up the compound objective complement. These words follow the direct object and describe it.)

### Check Your Understanding
### *Identifying Complements*

General Interest

**Write the complements in the following sentences. Beside each one, write whether it is a *direct object* (d.o.), *indirect object* (i.o.), or *objective complement* (o.c.).**

**1.** The right bouquet will make the recipient happy and appreciative.

**2.** The Spanish consider chrysanthemums a flower of sadness.

3. This flower forms floral arrangements for funerals.
4. Don't give your girlfriend a chrysanthemum arrangement in Spain.
5. In France yellow flowers symbolize infidelity.
6. Mexicans use yellow flowers in their "Day of the Dead" events.
7. In either country, give loved ones bouquets of flowers in a different color.
8. The Japanese comfort the ill with flowers and use flowers at times of death.
9. The Japanese also give a future spouse flowers during courtship.
10. Like the Spanish, the Japanese use yellow chrysanthemums for funerals.

Connect to the Writing Process: Prewriting

***Freewriting for Ideas***

You are a member of the committee that organizes activities for International Student Celebration Week. You will not only advise the committee on international gift etiquette, but you will write a feature article on the topic for a small booklet the committee will distribute. To develop ideas for your article, freewrite for ten minutes on anything that comes to mind regarding gifts and etiquette. Then underline and label the complements: *direct object* (d.o.), *indirect object* (i.o.), and *objective complement* (o.c.).

## Communicate Your Ideas

### APPLY TO WRITING

**Informative Article: *Complements***

Using the ideas you developed in your freewriting activity, write an informative article on gifts and etiquette. Your audience will be students at your school who participate in festivities during International Student Celebration

Week. You may want to plan a trip to the library or a search session on the Internet to gather interesting facts for your article. Use direct and indirect objects and objective complements to make your writing accurate and engaging. Be prepared to identify them.

##  Subject Complements

Two kinds of complements, called **subject complements**, complete the meaning of linking verbs.

A **predicate nominative** is a noun or a pronoun that follows a linking verb and identifies, renames, or explains the subject.

To find a predicate nominative, first find the subject and the linking verb. Then find the noun or the pronoun that follows the verb and identifies, renames, or explains the subject. Notice in the second example that a predicate nominative can be compound.

p.n.
Bart will become an art **teacher**. (*teacher* = *Bart*)

p.n. p.n.
The winners of the art scholarships are **Bryan** and **Julie**. (*Bryan* and *Julie* = *winners*)

p.n.
David was a visiting art **scholar**. (*scholar* = *David*)

Like other complements, a predicate nominative is never part of a prepositional phrase.

p.n.
Pamela is **one** of the artists at the Colorado Artists' Colony. (*One* is the predicate nominative. *Artists* is the object of the preposition *of*.)

p.n.
Jeff and Luis were a **couple** of the sculptors there. (*Couple* is the predicate nominative. *Sculptors* is the object of the preposition *of*.)

## Connect to Speaking and Writing

Often when someone asks you a question beginning with *Who is*, he or she wants a predicate nominative for an answer.

"Who is that man?"
"He is the **photographer**."

"Who is your favorite cartoonist?"
"Scott Adams is my favorite **cartoonist.**" 

The other subject complement is a predicate adjective.

**A predicate adjective is an adjective that follows a linking verb and modifies the subject.**

To find a predicate adjective, first find the subject and the linking verb. Then find an adjective that follows the verb and modifies, or describes, the subject. Notice in the third example that a predicate adjective can be compound.

p.a.
That painting was **impressionistic**. (*Impressionistic* describes the subject: *the impressionistic painting*.)

p.a.
The colors were **vivid**. (*Vivid* describes the subject: *the vivid colors.*)

p.a. p.a.
The paints looked **dry** and **lumpy.** (*Dry* and *lumpy* describe the subject: *dry, lumpy paints*.)

Remember that a predicate adjective follows a linking verb and modifies, or describes, the subject. Do not confuse a predicate adjective with a regular adjective.

| | |
|---|---|
| Predicate Adjective | Carlos is **brilliant.** (*Brilliant* describes the subject *Carlos*.) |
| Regular Adjective | Carlos is a **brilliant** sculptor. (*Brilliant* describes the word *sculptor*.) |

*You can review lists of linking verbs on page L21.*

CONNECT TO SPEAKING AND WRITING

Now that you've studied subjects, verbs, and complements, you may notice something about newspaper headlines. Usually the headline is not a complete sentence. Instead, it contains the simple subject, the main verb, and perhaps the complement. Consider these examples:

**Murderer Declared Insane** (subject-verb-complement)
**Philanthropist Donates Millions** (subject-verb-complement)
**Election Results Disappointing** (subject-verb)
**Hurricane Approaching!** (subject-verb)

## PRACTICE YOUR SKILLS

Check Your Understanding

### *Identifying Subject Complements*

Art Topic

**Write the subject complement in each sentence. Beside it, label it *p.n.* for predicate nominative or *p.a.* for predicate adjective.**

**1.** Shelby has become a cartoonist.

**2.** My favorite colors have always been blue and purple.

**3.** *Hue* is another word for *color* or *shade*.

**4.** The silver sequins felt too brittle and fragile.

**5.** My brother is a senior at the Savannah College of Art and Design in Georgia.

**6.** The art museum in my hometown has grown old and drafty.

**7.** After graduation my sister became a graphic artist for a local publisher.

**8.** Woodcarving is a forgotten art form.

**9.** This color scheme seems progressive.

**10.** The foreground appears bright, and the background seems shadowy.

Connect to the Writing Process: Drafting

### *Using Subject Complements*

**Complete each sentence by adding a predicate nominative or adjective. Then write five sentences of your own to continue discussing the ideas. Use at least one compound predicate nominative and one compound predicate adjective. Label the predicate nominatives and adjectives in all 10 sentences.**

**11.** The colors in the mural seemed ■.

**12.** Across the room, the mural artist was ■.

**13.** Her favorite subject is obviously ■.

**14.** The exhibition room felt ■.

**15.** The award-winners are ■.

## Communicate Your Ideas

### APPLY TO WRITING

**Oral Report: *Complements***

William Wegman. *Cinderella,* 1992.
Unique Polacolor ER photograph, 20 by 24 inches. © William Wegman. From the book *Cinderella*. Hyperion Books for Children, New York, New York, 1993.

Write a short oral presentation about William Wegman's photograph *Cinderella*. Describe the artwork for your classmates and express your opinions about it. Also, use the five types of complements to add detail and clarity to your opinions.

Mixed Practice

Literature Topic

**Write each complement. Then label each one using the following abbreviations:**

direct object = *d.o.*
indirect object = *i.o.*
objective complement = *o.c.*
predicate nominative = *p.n.*
predicate adjective = *p.a.*

1. Mr. Williams gave the class a list of fiction genres.
2. I consider the western a boring category of fiction.
3. I read approximately three mystery novels every month.
4. Two best-selling mystery novelists are Patricia Cornwell and Sue Grafton.
5. The category of science fiction is amazing and exciting.
6. My friend declared Toni Morrison her favorite author of all time.
7. Many bookstores devote special shelves, large posters, and special sales to popular books.
8. Several of my classmates are eager readers and devoted fans of Larry McMurtry's intricate novels about the Southwest.
9. Well-informed bookstore employees show patrons the current favorites in each section of the store.
10. Regular customers often buy themselves a new book and a cup of coffee on the weekend.

# Sentence Patterns

## Using Sentence Patterns

Each sentence you write seems unique—like the patterns and shapes of snowflakes. Looking more closely at the sentences you write, however, you will see that each falls into one of six basic sentence patterns. You can vary your writing style by expanding these basic sentence patterns. They can be expanded by adding modifiers, appositives, prepositional phrases, and verbal phrases. Any of these patterns can also be expanded by making the subject, the verb, or any of the complements compound. In this way you create many variations within a particular pattern itself.

**Pattern 1: S-V** (subject-verb)

S V
Cattle graze.

S V
Cattle belonging to Matt always graze in the far pasture.

**Pattern 2: S-V-O** (subject-verb-direct object)

S V O
Girls swam laps.

S V O
The girls on the swim team effortlessly swam many laps.

**Pattern 3: S-V-I-O** (subject-verb-indirect object-direct object)

S V I O
Todd sent me tickets.

S V I O
Todd unexpectedly sent me tickets to the Ice Capades.

**Pattern 4: S-V-N** (subject-verb-predicate nominative)

S V N
Campers are hikers.

S V N
Many campers in this group are enthusiastic hikers.

**Pattern 5: S-V-A** (subject-verb-predicate adjective)

S V A
Spectators grew restless.

S V A
The eager spectators suddenly grew very restless.

**Pattern 6: S-V-O-C** (subject-verb-direct object-objective complement)

S V O C
Everyone considers Roy trustworthy.

S V O C
Everyone in my school considers Roy absolutely trustworthy.

## PRACTICE YOUR SKILLS

### *Check Your Understanding*

**Write the sentence pattern for each of the five following sentences.**

1. Freshly cut hay always smells clean and sweet.
2. Many historians consider Harriet Tubman a major personality in United States history.
3. The coach of the field hockey team gave each member a certificate of achievement.
4. Fallen meteors have been discovered by scientists in various parts of the world.
5. The correct answer to the question is the last one.

### *Writing an Expository Paragraph*

Have you ever wondered how food is canned or how the ancient Egyptians built the pyramids? Brainstorm for a list of *How?* questions you would like answered and then choose one question. Research the answer on the Internet or in reference books at school or in the media center. Take notes on the information you find that will answer your question and then organize your details in a logical order. Write a topic sentence for your paragraph. Then write the first draft of an expository paragraph that answers the *How?* question you chose. As you revise and edit your paragraph, make certain it includes a variety of sentence patterns. Then write a final copy.

## Diagraming the Sentence Base

A **diagram** is a picture of words. By placing the words of a sentence in a diagram, you can often see the relationship between the parts of a sentence more clearly.

**Subjects and Verbs** All diagrams begin with a baseline. The subject and the verb go on the baseline but are separated by a vertical line. Capital letters are included in a diagram, but punctuation is not. Notice in the second diagram that compound subjects and verbs are placed on parallel lines. The conjunction joining the subjects or the verbs is placed on a broken line between them.

He is working.

He | is working

Lupe and Carl both sang and danced.

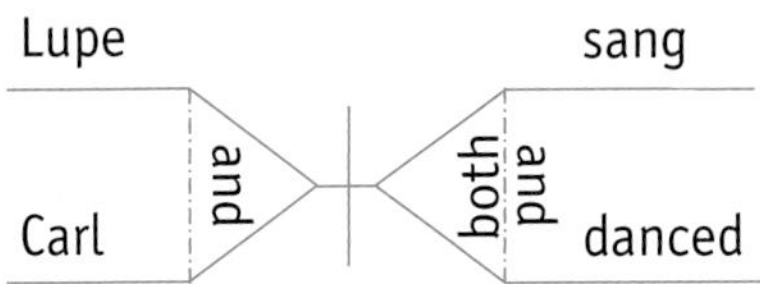


**Inverted Order and Understood Subjects** An inverted sentence is diagramed like a sentence in natural order. The understood subject *you* is diagramed in the subject position with parentheses around it.

Have you eaten?

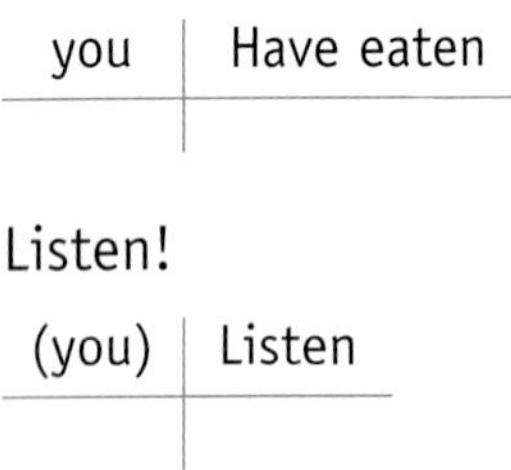


Listen!

**Adjectives and Adverbs** Adjectives and adverbs are connected by a slanted line to the words they modify. Notice that a conjunction joining two modifiers is placed on a broken line between them. Notice, too, how an adverb that describes another adverb is written parallel to the word it modifies.

Her small but valuable diamond sparkles quite brilliantly.

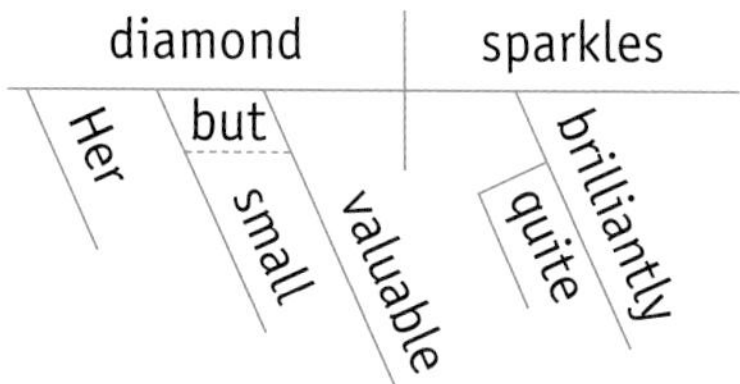


***Note:*** Possessive pronouns, such as *Her* in the example above, are diagramed like adjectives.

## Complements

All complements except the indirect object are diagramed on the baseline with the subject and the verb.

**Direct Objects** A short vertical line separates a direct object from the verb. Notice in the second example that the parts of a compound direct object are placed on parallel lines. The conjunction is placed on a broken line.

I have already seen that movie.

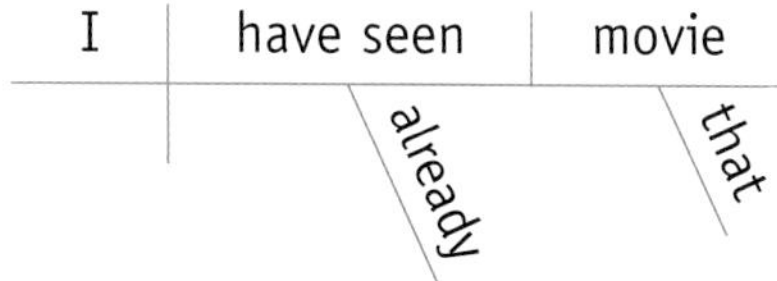


Buy four oranges and six bananas.

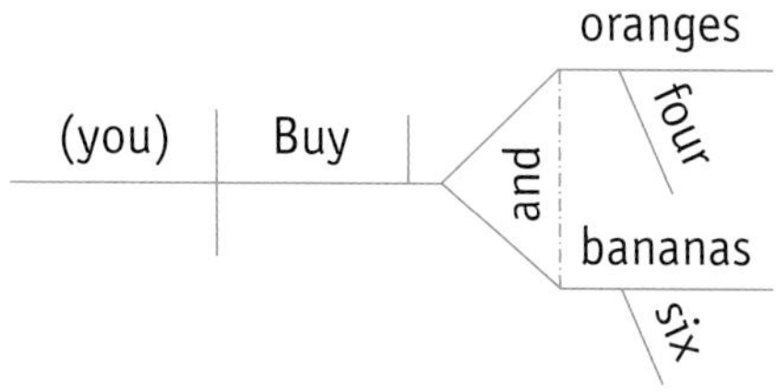

**Indirect Objects** An indirect object is diagramed on a horizontal line that is connected to the verb by a slanted line. Notice in the second example that the parts of a compound indirect object are diagramed on horizontal parallel lines. The conjunction is placed on a broken line between them.

Send them an invitation.

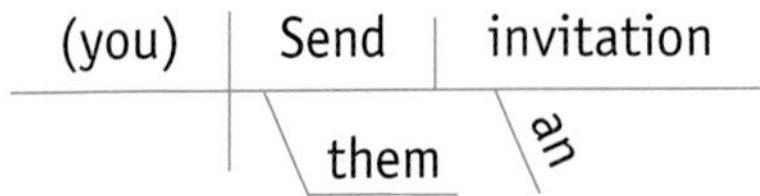


Aunt May bought David and me identical sweaters.

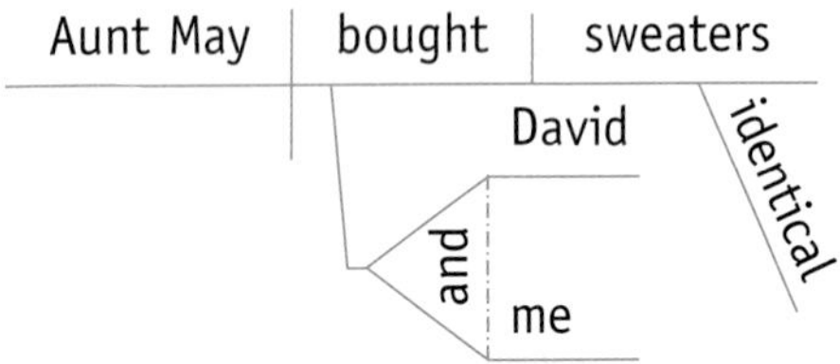


**Objective Complements** Since an objective complement renames or describes the direct object, it is placed to the right of the direct object on the baseline. A slanted line that points toward the direct object separates the two complements. Notice in the second example that a compound objective complement is placed on horizontal parallel lines. The conjunction is placed on a broken line between them.

We named our dog King.

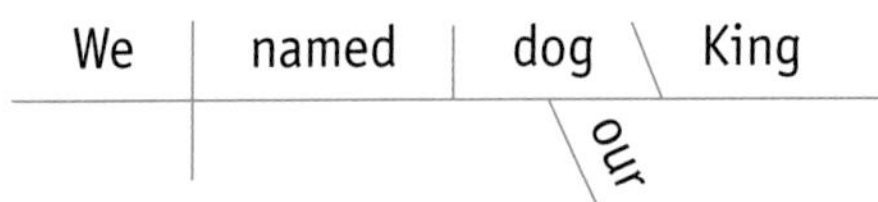


Mom will paint the kitchen yellow or green.

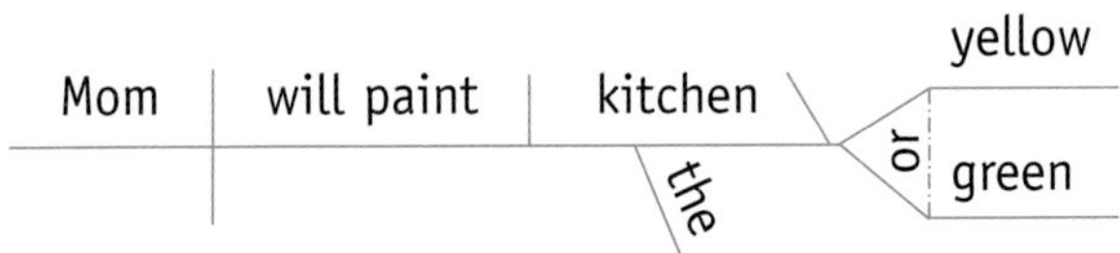


**Subject Complements** A predicate nominative and a predicate adjective are diagramed in exactly the same way. They are placed on the baseline after the verb. A slanted line that points back toward the subject separates a subject complement from the verb. Notice in the second example that a compound subject complement is placed on horizontal parallel lines. The conjunction is placed on a broken line between them.

This camera was a birthday present.

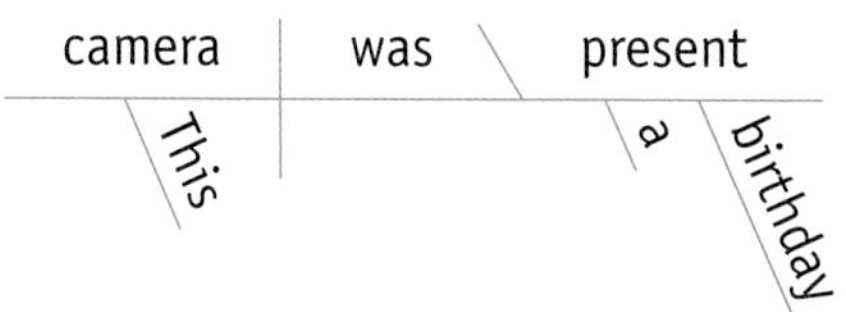


This lecture was not only interesting but also informative.

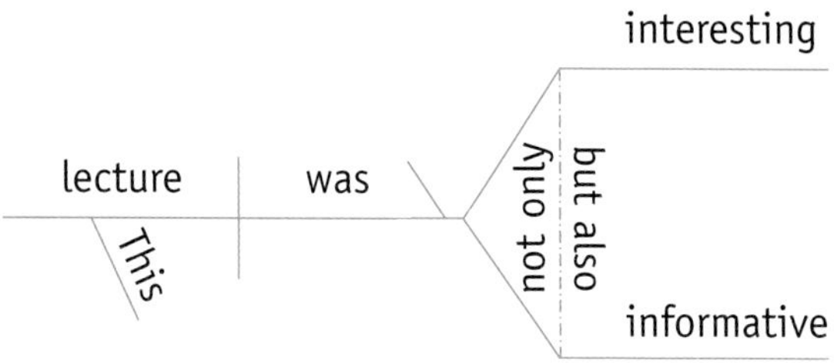


## PRACTICE YOUR SKILLS

### *Diagraming Sentences*

**Diagram the following sentences or copy them. If you copy them, draw one line under each subject and two lines under each verb. Then label each complement using the following abbreviations.**

direct object = *d.o.*
indirect object = *i.o.*
objective complement = *o.c.*
predicate nominative = *p.n.*
predicate adjective = *p.a.*

**1.** Would you be an astronaut?

**2.** The first American astronauts were Abe and Miss Baker.

**3.** These very brave astronauts were monkeys!

**4.** They gave scientists important information.

**5.** Space travel could be safe and reliable.

**6.** The space shuttle has been a really huge success.

**7.** NASA named the first shuttle *Columbia*.

**8.** Shuttles quite often carry many astronauts and large cargo.

**9.** Astronauts now successfully repair satellites.

**10.** Tell us more.

## CheckPoint

# Finding Subjects and Verbs

**Write the subjects and verbs in the following sentences. If the subject is an understood *you,* write *you* in parentheses.**

1. The giant tortoise of the Galápagos Islands may weigh as much as 500 pounds and may live up to 150 years.
2. Here are the balloons and streamers for Leah's birthday party.
3. Did you contact the Better Business Bureau about the problem with your new television set?
4. Most people remember Paul Revere's patriotism but forget his work as a silversmith and engraver.
5. Over the horizon that August day sailed the ships of Columbus's small fleet.
6. Revise your report carefully.
7. There are many inlets and bays along the coast of Nova Scotia.
8. There are more than 200 CDs of classical and popular music in the cabinet.
9. Have you seen the exciting new computers on sale?
10. Brad, take these shirts back to the store for a refund.
11. There is no living descendant of William Shakespeare.
12. Hasn't he answered your letter yet?
13. American Indians do not pay taxes on their land.
14. John Adams, John Quincy Adams, John F. Kennedy, and George Bush were all born in Norfolk County, Massachusetts.
15. Slowly over the mountaintops rose the brilliant morning sun.

## Finding Complements

**Write each complement. Then label each one, using the following abbreviations:**

direct object = *d.o.*
indirect object = *i.o.*
objective complement = *o.c.*
predicate nominative = *p.n.*
predicate adjective = *p.a.*

**1.** The Puritans considered buttons a sign of vanity.
**2.** At first the old trunk in the basement appeared empty.
**3.** Michelle showed Mom a copy of the yearbook.
**4.** Many early American settlers found the Indians friendly and helpful.
**5.** In Williamsburg, Virginia, we visited several old shops.
**6.** Their grandfather clock is quite old and very valuable.
**7.** James Monroe was the fourth president from Virginia.
**8.** Tell Alma and James that funny story about your uncle.
**9.** From the top of Mount Irazu in Costa Rica, a person can see the Atlantic Ocean and the Pacific Ocean.
**10.** Centuries ago a collection of books was a sign of wealth.

## Using the Sentence Base

**Write five sentences that follow the directions below. (The sentences may come in any order.) Write about this topic or a topic of your choice: a trip back in time to a historic event.**

**Write a sentence that . . .**

**1.** includes a direct object.
**2.** includes an indirect object.
**3.** includes a predicate nominative.
**4.** includes a predicate adjective.
**5.** includes an object complement.

**Underline each subject once, each verb twice, and label each complement.**

# Language and *Self-Expression*

Chuck Jones brought characters such as Bugs Bunny, Elmer Fudd, Roadrunner, and Porky Pig to life. He has won three Academy Awards for his animated films, and his artwork has been shown at museums worldwide.

Jones uses exaggeration and word play to add humor to his cartoons. The disproportionate cheeks, feet, and teeth on Bugs Bunny and his friend add to the amusing quality of their appearance. The title of the artwork includes a pun that involves the substitution of *hare* for *air.*

Let this cartoon inspire you to write your own humorous sketch. Choose a person who is in the news or a character from history. Write a character sketch that exaggerates that person's features and actions for humorous effect. If possible, title your character sketch with a phrase that includes a play on words.

**Prewriting** Choose a famous person whom you would like to lampoon in a character sketch. Quickwrite a list of phrases and images that come to mind when you think about that person's appearance and actions.

**Drafting** Use your list to draft a character sketch. Begin by introducing the character. Add details that exaggerate the person's appearance and actions. Try to give your character sketch a title that includes a play on words.

**Revising** Reread your character sketch critically, analyzing its flow and clarity. Cut and add details as needed. Vary your sentence patterns to add interest to your writing.

**Editing** Review your paragraph, looking for errors in grammar, capitalization, punctuation, and spelling. Make any corrections that are necessary.

**Publishing** Prepare a final copy of your character sketch. You might try to publish your paragraph in your school newspaper or magazine.

# Another Look

## The Sentence

A **sentence** is a group of words that expresses a complete thought.

A **sentence fragment** is a group of words that does not express a complete thought.

## Subjects and Predicates

A **subject** names the person, place, thing, or idea the sentence is about. *(page L57)*

A **simple subject** is the main word in the complete subject. *(page L58)*

A **predicate** tells something about the subject. *(page L57)*

A **simple predicate**, or **verb**, is the main word or phrase in the complete predicate. *(page L58)*

A **compound subject** is two or more subjects in one sentence that have the same verb and are joined by a conjunction. *(page L64)*

A **compound verb** is two or more verbs that have the same subject and are joined by a conjunction. *(page L65)*

## Other Information About Subjects and Predicates

Recognizing inverted order *(page L62)*

Recognizing understood *you* *(page L63)*

## Complements

A **direct object** is a noun or a pronoun that receives the action of the verb. *(page L72)*

An **indirect object** answers the questions *To or for whom?* or *To or for what?* after an action verb. *(page L73)*

An **objective complement** is a noun or an adjective that renames or describes the direct object. *(page L75)*

A **predicate nominative** is a noun or a pronoun that follows a linking verb and identifies, renames, or explains the subject. *(page L77)*

A **predicate adjective** is an adjective that follows a linking verb and modifies the subject. *(page L78)*

## Directions

**Write the letter of the term that correctly identifies the underlined word or words in each sentence.**

EXAMPLE **1.** Before 1914, Carl Sandburg was an unknown poet.

**1** **A** simple subject
**B** simple predicate
**C** complete subject
**D** complete predicate

ANSWER **1** **B**

1. The now famous Carl Sandburg was born in 1878 in Galesburg, Illinois.
2. Sandburg served as a soldier during the Spanish-American War.
3. His political beliefs would influence his poetry.
4. Have you read any of his early work?
5. Many of his poems reveal a vision of democracy.
6. Industrial America and American workers are a recurrent theme.
7. Besides free verse, Sandburg also wrote biographies and books for children.
8. Sandburg's biography of Lincoln is a remarkable study and a powerful memorial to that great president.
9. *The American Songbag* is a collection of almost 300 folk songs.
10. Sandburg recorded several of the songs himself.

1 **A** simple subject
**B** simple predicate
**C** complete subject
**D** complete predicate

2 **A** simple subject
**B** simple predicate
**C** complete subject
**D** complete predicate

3 **A** simple subject
**B** simple predicate
**C** complete subject
**D** complete predicate

4 **A** simple subject
**B** simple predicate
**C** complete subject
**D** complete predicate

5 **A** simple subject
**B** simple predicate
**C** complete subject
**D** complete predicate

6 **A** compound subject
**B** compound verb
**C** compound direct object
**D** compound predicate nominative

7 **A** compound subject
**B** compound verb
**C** compound direct object
**D** compound predicate nominative

8 **A** compound subject
**B** compound verb
**C** compound direct object
**D** compound predicate nominative

9 **A** direct object
**B** indirect object
**C** predicate nominative
**D** predicate adjective

10 **A** direct object
**B** indirect object
**C** predicate nominative
**D** predicate adjective

CHAPTER 3

# Phrases

### *Directions*

**Write the letter of the term that correctly identifies the underlined phrase in each sentence.**

EXAMPLE **1.** In the 1970s, Maya Angelou and Toni Morrison had their first fame as writers.

**1** **A** prepositional
**B** participial
**C** gerund
**D** infinitive

ANSWER **1** **A**

**1.** Growing up in Arkansas, Maya Angelou knew sorrow and hardship from a young age.
**2.** Maya Angelou's autobiographical work, *I Know Why the Caged Bird Sings*, appeared in 1970.
**3.** Triumphing over adversity is a recurring theme in her work.
**4.** It is evident in her collection of poetry, *And Still I Rise*.
**5.** Distilling the female and black experience, Angelou writes sensitive, hopeful poetry and prose.
**6.** She prefers raising up to casting down.
**7.** Her optimism has appealed to critics and presidents alike.
**8.** Toni Morrison, an editor and novelist, published three important novels in quick succession.
**9.** *The Bluest Eye, Sula,* and *Song of Solomon* owe some of their color to folklore and myth.
**10.** The experience of black women is Morrison's focus.

1 **A** prepositional
**B** participial
**C** gerund
**D** infinitive

2 **A** prepositional
**B** participial
**C** appositive
**D** gerund

3 **A** prepositional
**B** participial
**C** gerund
**D** infinitive

4 **A** prepositional
**B** participial
**C** appositive
**D** gerund

5 **A** prepositional
**B** participial
**C** gerund
**D** infinitive

6 **A** prepositional
**B** participial
**C** appositive
**D** gerund

7 **A** prepositional
**B** participial
**C** gerund
**D** infinitive

8 **A** prepositional
**B** participial
**C** appositive
**D** gerund

9 **A** prepositional
**B** participial
**C** gerund
**D** infinitive

10 **A** prepositional
**B** participial
**C** appositive
**D** gerund

Andy Goldsworthy. *Sand Brought to an Edge to Catch the Light,* August, 1991. Shore of Lake Michigan. ©Andy Goldsworthy. Photograph courtesy of the artist.

**Describe** What are three adjectives you might use to describe this artwork?

**Analyze** This artist creates art by manipulating landscapes and natural objects. How does he connect the natural and human-made worlds in his art?

**Interpret** How do writers you know get across the message that commonplace objects in nature have a peculiar beauty? Can you think of any examples?

**Judge** Unlike a painted landscape or a written poem, this artwork's life was fleeting. If you wished to convey this artist's message in a more permanent way, how might you do it?

At the end of this chapter, you will use the artwork as a visual aid for writing.

# Prepositional Phrases

The subject, the verb, and sometimes a complement are the foundation of a sentence. Once you are familiar with the basic structure of a sentence, you can build on it. In a way, you become an architect. Instead of adding rooms, however, you are adding grammatical elements, such as phrases. The rooms in a house have specific purposes, and their different shapes and sizes make the house interesting and unique.

Similarly, different phrases have different purposes. Some phrases are used to expand or to qualify an idea, while others are used to show relationships between ideas. Using different kinds of phrases will make your writing more varied and more interesting.

A **phrase** is a group of related words that functions as a single part of speech. A phrase does not have a subject or a verb.

In this chapter you will first review prepositional phrases and appositive phrases. Then you will review the three kinds of verbal phrases: participial, gerund, and infinitive. Finally, you will review misplaced and dangling modifiers and phrase fragments.

A **prepositional phrase** is a group of words that begins with a preposition and ends with a noun or pronoun called the **object of the preposition**. The prepositional phrases in the following sentences are in **bold** type.

**Before midnight** the athlete **from Canton** withdrew **from the competition**.

**In spite of the weather forecast**, all teams are proceeding **with their plans for the outdoor events**.

Prepositional phrases are used like single adjectives and adverbs to modify other words in a sentence.

*You can find a list of prepositions on page L37.*

## Adjective Phrases

**An adjective phrase is a prepositional phrase used to modify a noun or a pronoun.**

The following examples show how an adjective phrase works exactly like a single adjective.

| | |
|---|---|
| SINGLE ADJECTIVE | Did you see **that** score? (*That* tells which score.) |
| ADJECTIVE PHRASE | Did you see the score **on the scoreboard**? (*On the scoreboard* also tells which score.) |

A single adjective and an adjective phrase answer the same questions: *Which one(s)*? and *What kind?*

| | |
|---|---|
| WHICH ONE(S)? | The runner **in the first lane** is Morgan. |
| WHAT KIND? | I like athletic events **with music**. |

An adjective phrase usually follows the word it modifies. That word may be the object of a preposition of another prepositional phrase.

Thousands ***of* athletes *of* the highest skill** become Olympic competitors.

All ***of* the winners *of* the medals *for* first place** have arrived.

Two adjective phrases occasionally will modify the same noun or pronoun.

Pick up those programs ***of* events *on* the counter.**

## Adverb Phrases

**An adverb phrase is a prepositional phrase used to modify a verb, an adjective, or an adverb.**

An adverb phrase works exactly like a single adverb. Notice in the following examples that an adverb phrase, like a single adverb, modifies the whole verb phrase.

| | |
|---|---|
| SINGLE ADVERB | The discus throwers will compete **soon.** (*Soon* tells when the discus throwers will compete.) |
| ADVERB PHRASE | The discus throwers will compete **on Friday**. (*On Friday* also tells when the discus throwers will compete.) |

A single adverb and an adverb phrase answer the same question: *Where? When? How? To what extent?* or *To what degree?* An adverb phrase also answers the question *Why?*

| | |
|---|---|
| WHERE? | I left my sneakers **in my locker**. |
| WHEN? | The practice lasted **until ten o'clock**. |
| HOW? | I performed the move **according to his instructions**. |
| WHY? | **Because of the heavy traffic**, we missed the opening ceremony. |

### CONNECT TO WRITER'S CRAFT

Writers use prepositional phrases to add clarity to their writing and to enhance the images in their audience's minds. Sports writers, for example, could not write effective articles without using prepositional phrases to identify the types and locations of games and players. Many questions in a reader's mind will be answered by the prepositional phrases the writer uses.

> ***Which*** baseball player? The player **in left field** caught the fly ball.
>
> ***To what extent*** did the team practice? The team practiced **until eleven o'clock**.
>
> ***Where*** did the team play? The team played **at Fenway Park in Boston**.

Two or more adverb phrases may modify one verb.

**For the game days,** all the flags were flying **above the stadium.**

**Over the weekend** I put my medals **into the cabinet.**

Although most adverb phrases modify a verb, some modify adjectives and adverbs.

| | |
|---|---|
| Modifying an Adjective | Coach Margo is kind **to everyone**. |
| Modifying an Adverb | My team arrived late **in the afternoon**. |

**PUNCTUATION WITH ADVERB PHRASES**

- Do not place a comma after a short introductory adverb phrase unless it is a date or is needed for clarity.
- Place a comma after an adverb phrase of four or more words or after several introductory phrases.

| | |
|---|---|
| **No Comma** | **From my seat** I can see the finish line. |
| **Comma** | **From my seat at the edge of the track**, I can see the finish line. |

## Connect to Speaking and Writing

When you are speaking, you pause for various lengths of time so your listeners can better understand you. When you are writing, you use punctuation to indicate these pauses. Since the reader does not have the benefit of listening to you, he or she must rely on your placement of commas to understand your meaning. Sometimes, using a comma is advisable though not required. Compare the following sentences.

Behind Peggy Sue sat and watched the competition.
Behind Peggy, Sue sat and watched the competition.

Without the comma, it is easy to misread the sentence. 

# Practice Your Skills

## Check Your Understanding

### *Recognizing Prepositional Phrases as Modifiers*

Sports Topic

**Write the prepositional phrases in the following sentences. Then beside each phrase, write the word it modifies.**

**1.** The first champion of the modern Olympic Games was James Brendan Connolly.

**2.** In 1896, when he was a 27-year-old undergraduate at Harvard, he read about the revival of the ancient Greek games.

**3.** At that time Connolly was the triple-jump champion of the United States.

**4.** Connolly left school and went to Athens in March.

**5.** Ten American athletes and one trainer spent 16½ days on a ship to Naples and another day on a train to Athens.

**6.** On the following day, the Olympics began with the triple jump.

**7.** Before his turn Connolly surveyed the mark of the leader on the ground and threw his cap beyond it.

**8.** He then jumped beyond his cap and became the first champion of the modern Olympics.

**9.** He later became a journalist and the author of 25 novels.

**10.** Connolly died in 1957 at age 88.

## Check Your Understanding

### *Identifying Uses of Prepositional Phrases*

General Interest

**Write the prepositional phrases in the following sentences. Then beside each phrase, label it *adjective* or *adverb*.**

**11.** In 1936, Jesse Owens, a famous track star, beat a horse in the hundred-yard race.

**12.** During the following year, an Olympic hurdler named Forest Towns beat a horse in the hundred-yard hurdles.

**13.** Micki King, a gold-medal winner in the 1972 Olympics, became a diving coach at the U.S. Air Force Academy.

**14.** Award-winning gymnast Cathy Rigby had a lung ailment during her youth.

**15.** For six years Hugh Daily played baseball for several major-league teams.

**16.** As a pitcher he held a long-standing record of 19 strikeouts in a single game.

**17.** Hugh Daily was a man with only one arm.

**18.** Fourteen-year-old Nadia Comaneci had seven perfect scores in gymnastics at the Montreal Olympics.

**19.** She scored the first perfect 10 in the history of Olympic gymnastics.

Connect to the Writing Process: Revising

### *Using Prepositional Phrases*

**Make the following sentences more exact by adding an adverb phrase to each one. Use a comma where needed.**

**20.** Stan could see every gymnastic event.

**21.** Sarah could see only the backs of people's heads.

**22.** The competitors stretched and practiced.

**23.** The events would begin in ten minutes.

**24.** The gymnasts exited the floor and waited in an outer hall.

**25.** Mary Lou Retton stood ready to narrate the events for television cameras.

**26.** The judges entered.

**27.** The gymnasts entered.

**28.** They marched slowly and prepared to perform.

**29.** The music began to play.

**30.** The first gymnast stepped forward.

## Communicate Your Ideas

### APPLY TO WRITING

**Writer's Craft:** ***Analyzing the Use of Prepositional Phrases***

Read several sports articles from a newspaper and choose one to use in this exercise. Read the article carefully and then follow these instructions:

- Write each prepositional phrase and then beside it, write the word it modifies.
- Read the article *without* the prepositional phrases. What do you think of this version? What images or ideas are lost when the prepositional phrases are not included?
- Write a paragraph describing in detail the images and ideas that came to your mind as you read the article. Then review your writing and underline each prepositional phrase you have used. Label each one *adjective* or *adverb*.

Mixed Practice

General Interest **Write the prepositional phrase or phrases in each sentence and label them *adjective* or *adverb*.**

1. Some youngsters under the age of four are learning gymnastics skills.
2. Parents take these children to the gym each week.
3. They jump on the trampoline.
4. On the low balance beam, they walk carefully.
5. Their instructors encourage them with words of praise.
6. Somersaults are a common sight on the gym floor.
7. The older siblings of these young children are often found on the high bars.
8. They gather momentum and swing from one bar to the next.

# Appositives and Appositive Phrases

An **appositive** is a noun or a pronoun that identifies or explains another noun or pronoun in the sentence.

An appositive usually follows the word or words it identifies or explains.

My friend **Bart** is working at an art gallery.

The museum houses an exhibit of sculptures by the French artist **Auguste Rodin.**

I enjoyed my favorite hobby, **sketching**.

Most often an appositive is used with modifiers to form an **appositive phrase**. Notice in the second example that one or more prepositional phrases may be part of an appositive phrase.

Chicago, **the Windy City of the Midwest**, is home to the Art Institute of Chicago.

I just bought *Twentieth-Century Painting and Sculpture*, **a pictorial of art at The Art Institute of Chicago**.

**PUNCTUATION WITH APPOSITIVES AND APPOSITIVE PHRASES**

If an appositive contains information essential to the meaning of a sentence, no punctuation is needed.

- Information is essential if it identifies a person, place, or thing.

If an appositive or an appositive phrase contains nonessential information, a comma or commas should be used to separate it from the rest of the sentence.

- Information is nonessential if it can be removed without changing the basic meaning of the sentence. An appositive that follows a proper noun is usually nonessential.

| | |
|---|---|
| **Essential** | The famous artist **Manet** was born in 1832. (No commas are used because *Manet* is needed to identify which artist.) |
| **Nonessential** | Manet, **a famous French artist**, was born in 1832. (Commas are used because the appositive could be removed from the sentence: Manet was born in 1832.) |

## Practice Your Skills

Check Your Understanding

### *Identifying Appositives and Appositive Phrases*

Art Topic **Write each appositive or appositive phrase.**

1. Georgia O'Keeffe, an American abstract painter, was famous for her paintings of the desert region of the Southwest.
2. The painting *Sunflowers* is one of van Gogh's most recognized masterpieces.
3. Claude Monet, one of the most well-known impressionist painters, had undergone operations for cataracts when he painted *The Japanese Bridge* from around 1923 to 1925.
4. John William Waterhouse painted a picture of the ill-fated woman in Tennyson's poem *The Lady of Shallott.*
5. The Victorian artist William Holman Hunt also painted a scene from *The Lady of Shallott.*
6. Alexandra Nechita, a painter in the abstract cubist style, published a book of her work at age ten.
7. This book, *Outside the Lines*, includes her popular painting *Variation on the Lion King*.
8. The 1995 Caldecott Award–winning artist, Trina Schart Hyman, received the award for illustrating *Saint George and the Dragon.*

9. The French artist Eugène Delacroix painted a battle scene, *Combat Between the Giaour and Hassan*, after becoming inspired by Lord Byron's poem "The Giaour."
10. Byron's poem is about a Venetian man who sets out to avenge his mistress's murder by Hassan, a Turk.

Connect to the Writing Process: Editing

***Using Commas with Appositive Phrases***

**Write each sentence, punctuating the appositives or appositive phrases correctly. If a sentence is correct, write *C*.**

11. Theodor Seuss Geisel Dr. Seuss was born in 1904 in Springfield, Massachusetts.
12. Dr. Seuss a writer and cartoonist is famous for his rhyming children's books.
13. *And to Think That I Saw It on Mulberry Street* the first of his children's books was published in 1937.
14. *The Cat in the Hat* one of his most famous books was published in 1957.
15. *The Cat in the Hat* a story with only 237 different words was based on a word list for first-grade readers.

## Communicate Your Ideas

### APPLY TO WRITING

**Biographical Oral Report: *Appositive Phrases***

Prepare to give a five-minute oral report to your classmates. Choose an artist whose life interests you and look up biographical information on this person. Read the material and take notes. Then write the first draft of a report that summarizes the artist's life. Remember to put the information into your own words. Also, devote special effort to creating smooth and effective sentences by using appositives and appositive phrases. Be sure you punctuate appositive phrases correctly.

# Verbals and Verbal Phrases

Verbals are part of your everyday speech. If you have ever apologized for your *unmade* bed or told someone that you would be ready *to leave* at six o'clock, you have used verbals. A **verbal** is a verb form that is used not as a verb, but as a noun, an adjective, or an adverb. Because verbals are verb forms, they are usually lively words that add action and vitality to your writing. The three kinds of verbals are participles, gerunds, and infinitives.

## Participles and Participial Phrases

**A participle is a verb form that is used as an adjective.**

Used like an adjective, a participle modifies a noun or a pronoun and answers the adjective question *Which one(s)?* or *What kind?* The participles in the examples are in **bold** type. An arrow points to the word each participle modifies.

> The **rising** sun was reflected on the **frosted** glass of the mayor's limousine.
>
> **Broken** campaign promises are sometimes the downfall of an **elected** official.

There are two kinds of participles: a present participle and a past participle. A **present participle** ends in *–ing*, while a **past participle** has a regular ending of *–ed* or an irregular ending of *–n*, *–t*, or *–en*.

| PARTICIPLES | |
|---|---|
| **Present Participles** | spinning, shrinking, ringing, winning |
| **Past Participles** | buried, defeated, worn, bent, stolen |

Be careful not to confuse a participle, which is used as an adjective, with the main verb of a sentence. A participle will have one or more helping verbs if it is used as a verb.

| | |
|---|---|
| PARTICIPLE | The governor's **reserved** seats are in the sixth row of the mezzanine. |
| VERB | We **have reserved** four seats for the senator's speech. |
| PARTICIPLE | The **broken** clock on the mantel in the living room belonged to President Johnson. |
| VERB | During the voter registration, a small table **was broken**. |

## Participial Phrases

Because a participle is a verb form, it may have modifiers and complements. Together these words form a participial phrase.

A **participial phrase** is a participle with its modifiers and complements—all working together as an adjective.

The following examples show three variations of a participial phrase. As you can see, a participle may be followed by an adverb, a prepositional phrase, or a complement.

| | |
|---|---|
| PARTICIPLE WITH AN ADVERB | **Ordered early**, the campaign posters were ready for the rally. |
| PARTICIPLE WITH A PREPOSITIONAL PHRASE | Our mayor, **speaking to the senior class**, described her path to success. |
| PARTICIPLE WITH A COMPLEMENT | Who is that political aide **raising his right hand**? |

The present participle *having* is sometimes followed by a past participle.

***Having met* the senator in person**, I was surprised at how tall she was.

Sometimes an adverb that modifies a participle may come before the participle. The adverb in this position is still part of the participial phrase.

> The post-election ball is a grand event ***usually* involving bands and caterers.**
>
> ***Never* having entertained at such a function,** the members of the chorus were nervous.

### PUNCTUATION WITH PARTICIPIAL PHRASES

Always place a comma after an introductory participial phrase.

**Arriving at the White House,** I registered for the tour.

Participial phrases that come in the middle or at the end of a sentence may or may not need commas.

- If the information in a phrase is essential to identify the noun or the pronoun it describes, no comma is needed.
- If the information is nonessential, a comma is needed to separate it from the rest of the sentence. A phrase is nonessential if it contains information that can be removed from the sentence without changing the basic meaning. A phrase that follows a proper noun is usually nonessential.

| | |
|---|---|
| **Essential** | The FBI agent **guarding the limousine** is Jason Jackson.<br>(No commas are used because the phrase is needed to identify which agent.) |
| **Nonessential** | Jason Jackson, **guarding the limousine**, has twelve years of experience with the FBI.<br>(Commas are used because the phrase can be removed, and the meaning is still clear: Jason Jackson has twelve years of experience with the FBI.) |

## Practice Your Skills

### Check Your Understanding
*Recognizing Participial Phrases as Modifiers*

Government Topic **Write each participial phrase. Then beside each one, write the word or words it modifies.**

1. Winning the confidence of many voters, women have become the mayors of several large cities in the United States.
2. One report identifies some of the women elected in recent years.
3. Jane Byrne of Chicago captured the office held by Mayor Richard J. Daley for 21 years until his death.
4. Isabelle Cannon, having won the support of young people, became the mayor of Raleigh in a major upset.
5. Having complained unsuccessfully about a dangerous intersection, Janet Gray Hayes ran for mayor of San Jose.
6. Gaining prominence in a nonpartisan campaign, she went on to win the election.
7. Demonstrating her leadership abilities, Mayor Margaret Hance of Phoenix won a second term.
8. Mayor Carole McClellan of Austin, gathering 79 percent of the vote, also won a second term.
9. Effectively governing San Francisco, Dianne Feinstein became nationally prominent.
10. All of these remarkable women led the way for other women entering politics.

### Connect to the Writing Process: Editing
*Using Commas with Participial Phrases*

**Write each sentence, adding or deleting commas if necessary. If a sentence is already correct, then write *C*.**

11. The candidates, running for Town Council, will hold a debate in the town hall.
12. Arriving early I took a seat up front.

13. That is my sister, passing out campaign buttons.

14. Spoken with sincerity, the candidate's words stirred the voters.

15. Kathleen Sullivan elected to the School Committee by a wide margin instituted many changes.

16. Having lived in the district her entire life, she had some practical ideas.

17. Ms. Sullivan convinced of the value of school uniforms rallied the other board members to her point of view.

18. Less convinced some parents and many students objected to the notion of a mandatory dress code.

Connect to the Writing Process: Drafting

***Distinguishing Between Verbs and Participles***

Work with a writing partner. Together, form a list of five verbs that you associate with the activities of government or politics. Then each of you write two sentences for each word. The first sentence should use the word as a verb. The second sentence should use the word as a participle in a participial phrase. Use punctuation where needed. Compare your sentences.

## Communicate Your Ideas

### APPLY TO WRITING

**Opinion Essay:** ***Participles and Participial Phrases***

Prepare for a class summit on politics. You will have an opportunity to speak your mind on any political issue you choose. You can review the sentences you wrote above to get ideas and to "break the blank page barrier." Write the first draft of your opinion essay to get as many ideas on paper as possible. Then review your writing, looking for opportunities to use participial phrases to help clarify your ideas and to create sentence variety. Finally, prepare the final copy.

# Gerunds and Gerund Phrases

A **gerund** is a verb form used as a noun.

Because a gerund ends in *–ing*, it looks like a present participle. A gerund, however, is used as a noun. The gerunds in the following examples are in **bold** type.

> **Dating** brings out the creativity in some people. (subject)
>
> Kyle and Sasha enjoy **rollerblading**. (direct object)

## Gerund Phrases

Like other verbals, a gerund may be combined with modifiers and complements to form a phrase.

A **gerund phrase** is a gerund with its modifiers and complements—all working together as a noun.

A gerund or a gerund phrase may be used in all the ways in which a noun may be used. A gerund may be followed by an adverb, a prepositional phrase, or a complement.

| | |
|---|---|
| Subject | **Playing tennis** is an enjoyable date. |
| Direct Object | I like **riding on roller coasters**. |
| Indirect Object | My brother gave **writing a love poem** his full attention last Saturday. |
| Object of a Preposition | We drove to the pizza parlor across town without **making a single stop**. |
| Predicate Nominative | Her most enjoyable date was **riding a two-person bicycle**. |
| Appositive | Heather's weekend plan, **applying for jobs for date money**, is admirable. |

The possessive form of a noun or a pronoun comes before a gerund and is considered part of the gerund phrase.

> What do you think of **Eric's asking Cindy for a date**?
>
> **Her asking Todd out** was surprising.

*You can learn more about possessive nouns and pronouns on pages L471–L475.*

## Practice Your Skills

### Check Your Understanding
### *Identifying Gerund Phrases*

Contemporary Life **Write each gerund phrase. Then underline each gerund.**

**1.** We can get good seats for the movie by buying our tickets early.

**2.** Buying snacks at the concession stand takes time and a great deal of money.

**3.** I couldn't understand her refusing the buttery popcorn and soda.

**4.** My creative cousin is capable of planning some very unusual dates.

**5.** His idea last Saturday was renting a large moving van for the day.

**6.** Decorating the van's interior like a four-star restaurant was his morning activity.

**7.** After shopping carefully for ingredients, he cooked a gourmet meal.

**8.** His date was thrilled with his creating this enjoyable dinner experience.

**9.** Going to a local bookstore was my most recent memorable date.

**10.** Our afternoon activity, listening to the children's story hour, was different and fun.

### Check Your Understanding
## *Determining the Uses of Gerund Phrases*

Contemporary Life **Write each gerund phrase. Then label the use of each one, using the following abbreviations.**

| | |
|---|---|
| subject = *subj.* | object of a preposition = *o.p.* |
| direct object = *d.o.* | predicate nominative = *p.n.* |
| indirect object = *i.o.* | appositive = *appos.* |

**11.** Dancing by the lake is Julie's idea of the perfect evening.

**12.** Jackie's spontaneous nature welcomes jumping puddles in the rain.

**13.** Last month Mike surprised his girlfriend by taking her to a fruit orchard.

**14.** His idea, picking fruit together, was a success.

**15.** One date I'll never forget was test-driving a new car together.

**16.** For a sweet evening, give baking cinnamon rolls a try.

**17.** Two of my friends succeeded in running a marathon together.

**18.** My bright idea, pretending to be an artist at the beach, was hilarious.

### Connect to the Writing Process: Prewriting
## *Distinguishing Between Gerunds and Participles*

Work with a writing partner to brainstorm at least ten gerunds and participles. Use word association to generate words, beginning with the word *dating*. Write down the first *–ing* gerund or participle you think of, and then your writing partner will write down the first *–ing* word that comes to mind. Continue until your combined list totals ten words. Then each of you choose five words and write two sentences for each word. The first sentence should use the word as a gerund. The second sentence should use the word as a participle. Use punctuation where needed. Compare your sentences.

Communicate Your Ideas

### APPLY TO WRITING

**Guidebook: *Gerunds and Gerund Phrases***

Your class will write a handbook of dating tips and ideas that will be useful to anyone who is interested in dating. Each student will write one entry for this handbook. Use your prewriting from the preceding exercise to start your first draft. Write a first draft, devoting extra care to using gerunds and gerund phrases. Edit your writing for errors in spelling, punctuation, and grammar. Then prepare the final copy.

## Infinitives and Infinitive Phrases

An **infinitive** is a verb form that usually begins with *to*. It is used as a noun, an adjective, or an adverb.

Infinitives do not look like the other verbals because they usually begin with the word *to*. An infinitive has several forms. The infinitives of *change*, for example, are *to change*, *to be changing*, *to have changed*, *to be changed*, and *to have been changed*. The infinitives in the following examples are in **bold** type.

Pat wanted **to win.** (noun, direct object)

She couldn't think of a story **to write.** (adjective)

The unexpected ideas from Jill were nice **to receive.** (adverb)

Do not confuse a prepositional phrase that begins with *to* with an infinitive. A prepositional phrase ends with a noun or a pronoun; an infinitive ends with a verb form.

| | |
|---|---|
| Prepositional Phrase | Give the book **to me**. |
| Infinitive | When is it time **to read**? |

## Infinitive Phrases

An infinitive may be combined with modifiers and complements to form an infinitive phrase.

An **infinitive phrase** is an infinitive with its modifiers and complements—all working together as a noun, an adjective, or an adverb.

The following examples show how an infinitive phrase may be used as a noun, an adjective, or an adverb. Notice that like other verbals, an infinitive phrase may also take several forms. An infinitive, for example, may be followed by an adverb, a complement, or a prepositional phrase.

| | |
|---|---|
| Noun | **To write well** requires patience. (subject)<br>I tried **to buy two rare books.** (direct object) |
| Adjective | These are the fables **to read for tomorrow.** |
| Adverb | We printed the story **to create public awareness.** |

Occasionally the word *to* is dropped when an infinitive phrase follows such verbs as *help, dare, feel, make, let, need, see,* or *watch*. It is, nevertheless, understood to be in the sentence.

We helped **collect** (to collect) **picture books for the preschool.**

Unlike other verbal phrases, an infinitive phrase can have a subject. An infinitive phrase with a subject is called an **infinitive clause.**

d.o.

Everyone expected **Pat to win the storytelling contest.**

(*Pat* is the subject of *to win*. The whole infinitive clause is the direct object of *everyone expected. Everyone expected* what?)

d.o.

We asked **her to distribute the awards.**

(*Her* is the subject of *to distribute*. The subject of an infinitive clause is in the objective case. The whole infinitive clause is the direct object of *we asked*.)

## Practice Your Skills

### Check Your Understanding
***Identifying Infinitive Phrases***

Literature Topic **Write each infinitive or infinitive phrase.**

**1.** To be brave from a distance is easy. —*Aesop*

**2.** Aesop created fables to teach people lessons.

**3.** The ant wanted to store food.

**4.** The grasshopper was the one to play all summer.

**5.** The shepherd boy promised to tend sheep.

**6.** He cried "Wolf!" to get a little excitement.

**7.** However, there really was a wolf to fear.

**8.** Later the wolf came to eat the sheep.

**9.** The shepherd boy tried to get help, but no one believed him.

**10.** A runaway slave named Androcles helped pull a thorn from a lion's paw.

### Check Your Understanding
***Determining the Uses of Infinitive Phrases***

Literature Topic **Write the infinitive or infinitive phrases in the following sentences. Then label how each one is used: *noun*, *adjective*, or *adverb*.**

**11.** The fables to read are by Aesop and other Greek storytellers.

**12.** To credit Aesop with writing all Greek fables has been the tendency.

13. Legend says that Aesop was freed from slavery to become a diplomat for King Croesus.

14. To starve a free man is better than being a fat slave. —*Aesop*

15. A young wife wants her husband to look more like herself.

16. She plucks out his gray hairs each night to create a younger appearance.

17. The second wife to pluck hairs from the man's head is older.

18. This wife decides to remove all the brown strands.

19. As a result, each wife helped make the husband bald.

20. To bend with the wind is the Reed's wise choice in "The Tree and the Reed."

Connect to the Writing Process: Drafting

***Writing Sentences with Infinitive Phrases***

**Write sentences that follow the directions below.**

21. Use an infinitive phrase as a subject.

22. Use an infinitive phrase as a direct object.

23. Use an infinitive phrase as an adjective.

24. Use an infinitive phrase as an adverb.

25. Use two infinitive phrases.

## Communicate Your Ideas

### APPLY TO WRITING

**Fable:** ***Infinitives and Infinitive Phrases***

If possible, read several fables by Aesop to get ideas for writing a fable of your own for middle-schoolers. You'll notice that in fables the animals talk and think as people, and the story always teaches a lesson or moral. Also, fables are usually only 150 to 200 words long. When you write your fable, use infinitive phrases to add variety and interest. Be prepared to identify how you used infinitive phrases—as *subject, direct object, adjective,* or *adverb*.

Mixed Practice

General Interest **Write the verbal phrases in the following sentences. Then label each one *participial, gerund,* or *infinitive*.**

**1.** Born in New York in 1856, Louise Blanchard Bethune is considered the first woman architect.

**2.** After designing many buildings, she became the first woman to gain membership in the American Institute of Architects.

**3.** The first American woman to receive the Nobel Peace Prize was Jane Addams.

**4.** In 1931, she was recognized for establishing a center for social reform in Chicago.

**5.** The first woman to be pictured on a United States coin in circulation was suffragist Susan B. Anthony.

**6.** Treasury officials had first considered picturing only a representative female figure such as Miss Liberty.

**7.** Anthony, appearing later on a one-dollar coin, was selected over Jane Addams and Eleanor Roosevelt.

**8.** Long before Sarah Walker became the first African American woman millionaire, she supported herself by taking in laundry.

**9.** In 1905, after eighteen years as a launderer, she decided to create a line of hair products especially for African American women.

**10.** Working at home, she formulated shampoos and oils.

**11.** Concerned for other African American women, Walker created many college scholarships.

# Misplaced and Dangling Modifiers

The meaning of a sentence sometimes gets confused because a modifier is placed too far away from the word it describes. When that happens, the modifier appears to describe some other word. Such modifiers are called **misplaced modifiers**. Remember to place phrases used as modifiers as close as possible to the word or words they describe.

| | |
|---|---|
| MISPLACED | Rob will answer this ad for a gardener **in the *Globe***. |
| CORRECT | Rob will answer this ad **in the *Globe*** for a gardener. |
| MISPLACED | I found the seedlings **looking through a catalog**. |
| CORRECT | **Looking through a catalog**, I found the seedlings. |

Another problem sometimes arises when a phrase that is being used as a modifier does not have a word to describe in the sentence. This kind of phrase is called a **dangling modifier**.

| | |
|---|---|
| DANGLING | **To be a good park ranger**, knowledge of animals is needed.<br>(*Knowledge* cannot be a good park ranger.) |
| CORRECT | **To be a good park ranger**, you need knowledge of animals. |
| DANGLING | **Filling the bird feeder**, birds will be attracted to your yard.<br>(*Birds* cannot fill the bird feeder.) |
| CORRECT | **Filling the bird feeder**, you will attract birds to your yard. |

## Practice Your Skills

Check Your Understanding

***Recognizing Misplaced and Dangling Modifiers***

Contemporary Life

**Write the misplaced or dangling modifier in each sentence. If a sentence is correct, write *C*.**

**1.** Walking through the nature preserve, we saw many interesting sights.

**2.** Rummaging through the trash can, we saw the raccoon.

**3.** I found the raccoon family picking up litter.

**4.** I followed Lisa as she ran around the pond on my bike.

**5.** Booming in the distance, I was startled by the thunder.

**6.** Enjoying the sound of the rain, he fell asleep.

**7.** Trotting through the forest, Kate's ears detected a babbling brook.

**8.** My little brother wanted to play with the baby frogs wearing shorts in the pond.

**9.** Roaring loudly, Juan took a picture of the lion.

**10.** Rowing steadily, the canoe was brought to the dock.

**11.** Jenny stood on a rock trying to get a good view of the baby birds.

**12.** Having eaten the food, the dish was empty.

**13.** Following the posted rules, we did not attempt to feed any of the animals.

**14.** Bending over, we could see the tall giraffe.

**15.** Walking around the preserve, the many kinds of plants were amazing.

Connect to the Writing Process: Revising

***Correcting Misplaced and Dangling Modifiers***

**16.–27. Correct each of the misplaced and dangling modifiers in the previous exercise. Either place the phrase closer to the word it modifies, or add words and change the sentence so the phrase has a noun or a pronoun to modify. Use punctuation where needed.**

## Communicate Your Ideas

### APPLY TO WRITING

**Description: *Modifiers***

Alma Gunter, *Dinner on Grounds,* 1979–1980.
Acrylic on canvas, 24 by 18 inches. African American Museum, Dallas, Texas.

You are spending the afternoon with a friend who is blind, and she asks you to describe a painting to her. Study the painting *Dinner on Grounds*, and then write a description that would make your friend feel as though she were taking part in this scene. Along with describing what you see, describe the other senses—touch, taste, hearing, and smell. Use plenty of modifiers to help make these sensory experiences come alive. Finally, edit for dangling and misplaced modifiers before preparing your final copy.

## Phrase Fragments

Since a phrase is a group of words that does not have a subject and a verb, it can never express a complete thought. As a result, when a phrase is written as if it were a sentence, it becomes a **phrase fragment.**

To correct a phrase fragment, add a group of words that contains a subject, a verb, or both; or like the following examples in **bold** type, attach a phrase fragment to a related sentence.

| | |
|---|---|
| PREPOSITIONAL PHRASE FRAGMENT | After 1945, many new words and expressions came into our language. **Such as *baby-sit, cutback, rat race*, and *soap opera*.** |
| CORRECTED | After 1945, many new words and expressions, such as *baby-sit, cutback, rat race,* and *soap opera*, came into our language. |
| APPOSITIVE PHRASE FRAGMENT | Alice Walker wrote *The Color Purple*. **The 1983 Pulitzer Prize–winning novel.** |
| CORRECTED | Alice Walker wrote *The Color Purple*, the 1983 Pulitzer Prize–winning novel. |
| PARTICIPIAL PHRASE FRAGMENT | O. Henry produced a story a week for the *World*. **Living in New York City.** |
| CORRECTED | Living in New York City, O. Henry produced a story a week for the *World*. |
| GERUND PHRASE FRAGMENT | **Winning the Nobel Prize in literature.** This is the dream of many authors. |
| CORRECTED | Winning the Nobel Prize in literature is the dream of many authors. |

| | |
|---|---|
| Infinitive Phrase Fragment | **To provide facts about authors, works of literature, and literary terms.** This is the primary purpose of a literary encyclopedia. |
| Corrected | To provide facts about authors, works of literature, and literary terms is the primary purpose of a literary encyclopedia. |

*You can find information about other types of fragments on pages L68–L71 and L164–L166.*

### Connect to Writer's Craft

If you are like most writers, your first drafts probably contain fragments. That is because writers are primarily thinking about subject matter, not accuracy or style. After you have written your first draft, however, you should always edit your work to make sure all your sentences are complete.

## Practice Your Skills

Check Your Understanding

***Recognizing Phrase Fragments***

Literature Topic

**Write the phrase fragments in the following paragraph. Then label the use of each one *prepositional, appositive, participial, gerund,* or *infinitive*.**

Admired as a great writer. Mark Twain was also an inventor. To make millions on his ideas. This was Twain's hope. Twain predicted innovations such as microfilm, data storage and retrieval, and television. He had great ideas, but he was not a good businessman. He lost $300,000, for example. On an automatic typesetting machine. It had moving parts, but it seldom worked. Numbering 18,000. Twain did make a small profit on one of his ventures. Mark Twain's Self-Pasting Scrapbook. Finally, having lost a fortune. Twain had to earn a living by writing.

Connect to the Writing Process: Revising
*Correcting Phrase Fragments*

**Revise the above paragraph on Mark Twain by correcting the phrase fragments. Either add a group of words that contains a subject or a verb or attach the phrase fragment to a related sentence.**

## Communicate Your Ideas

### APPLY TO WRITING

**Summary:** ***Complete Sentences***

You have adopted a pen pal in a retirement home, and you want to include some entertaining information in your next letter to this person. Skim the table of contents of a current almanac or other book of interesting information. (You might also search the Internet.) Find a topic particularly interesting to you, read it, and take notes. Then write the first draft of a paragraph that summarizes the topic you chose. Remember to put the information into your own words. After you have revised your summary, edit it, correcting any phrase fragments, and prepare the final copy.

## Diagraming Phrases

The way a phrase is used in a sentence determines how and where the phrase is diagramed.

**Prepositional Phrases** An adjective or an adverb phrase is connected to the word it modifies. The preposition is placed on a connecting slanted line. The object of a preposition is placed on a horizontal line that is attached to the slanted line. The following example includes two adjective phrases and one adverb phrase. Notice that an adjective phrase can modify the object of the preposition of another phrase.

The assignment for Mr. Marshard's class in English literature must be completed by tomorrow.

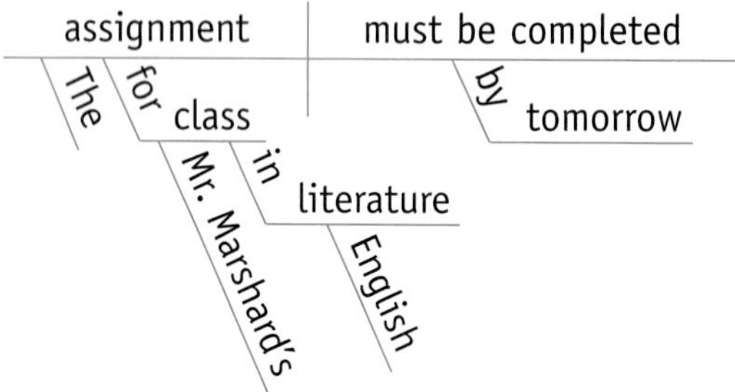


An adverb phrase that modifies an adjective or an adverb needs an additional horizontal line that is connected to the word modified.

The two trophies stood close to each other on the mantel.

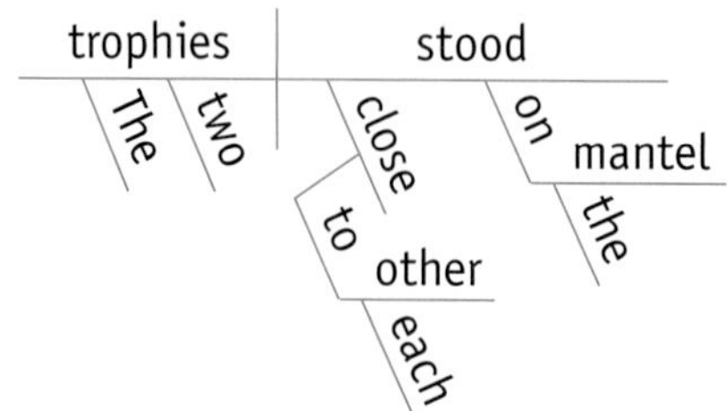

**Appositives and Appositive Phrases** An appositive is diagramed in parentheses next to the word it identifies or explains. Its modifiers are placed directly underneath it.

The appetizer, egg rolls with hot mustard, arrived before a huge meal of several Chinese dishes.

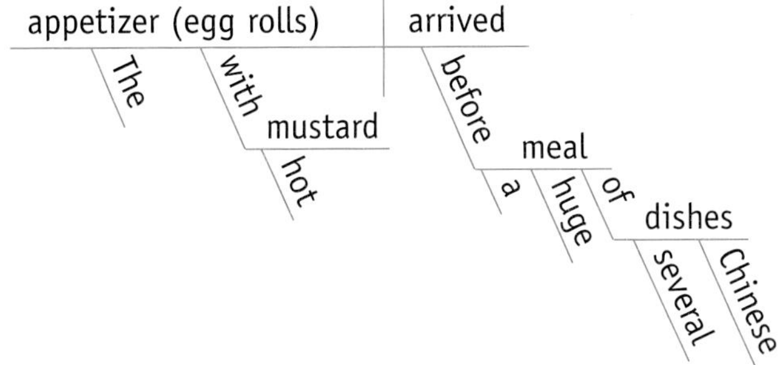


**Participial Phrases** Like an adjective, a participle is always diagramed under the word it modifies. The participle, however, is written in a curve. In the first example below, the participial phrase modifies *Marcy*, the subject of the sentence. In the second example, the participial phrase modifies the direct object *tree*.

Seeing the time on the kitchen clock, Marcy rushed out the door.

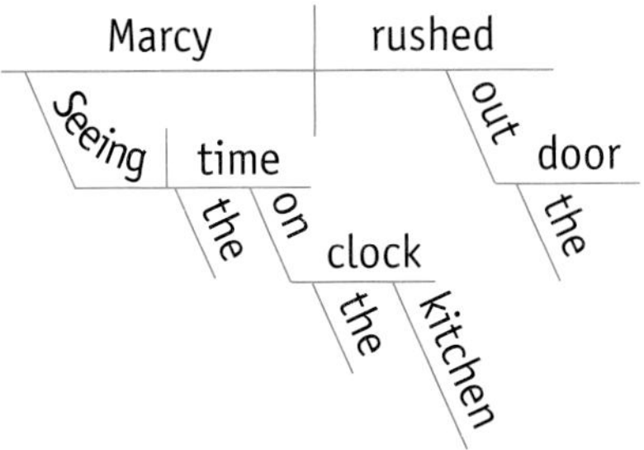


I transplanted the maple tree growing in our backyard.

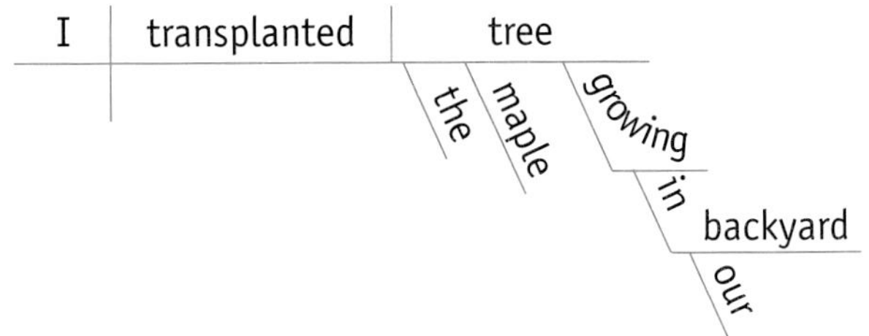

**Gerund Phrases** A gerund phrase is diagramed in any position in which a noun is diagramed. In the next diagram, the gerund phrase is used as a direct object. In the diagram after that, a gerund phrase is used as a subject, and another gerund phrase is used as the object of a preposition. Notice that an adverb, a prepositional phrase, and a complement may be part of a gerund phrase.

During my summer vacation, I enjoy sitting quietly by the lake.

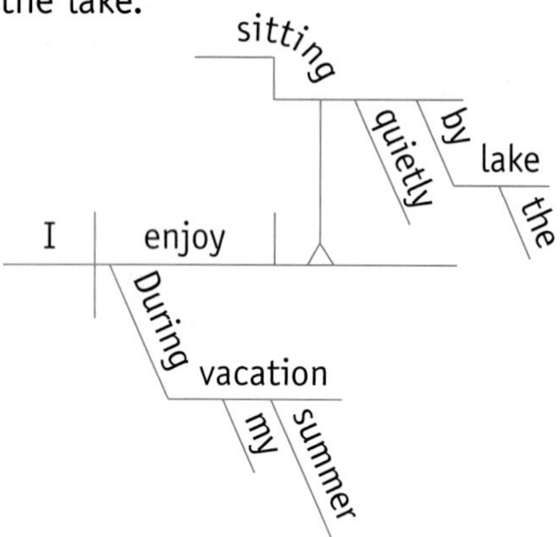


Studying hard is a sure way of guaranteeing a good grade.

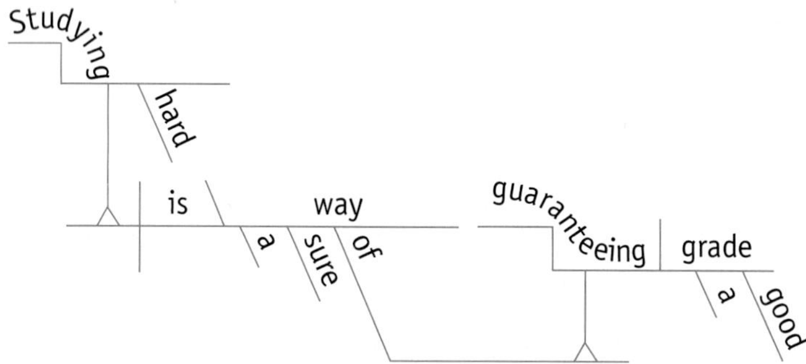


**Infinitive Phrases** Because an infinitive phrase may be used as a noun, an adjective, or an adverb, it is diagramed in several ways. In the following example, one infinitive phrase is used as an adjective and one is used as a predicate nominative. In the example after that, the infinitive phrase is used as a direct object. Notice that these infinitive phrases all have complements.

The only way to have a friend is to be one. —*Emerson*

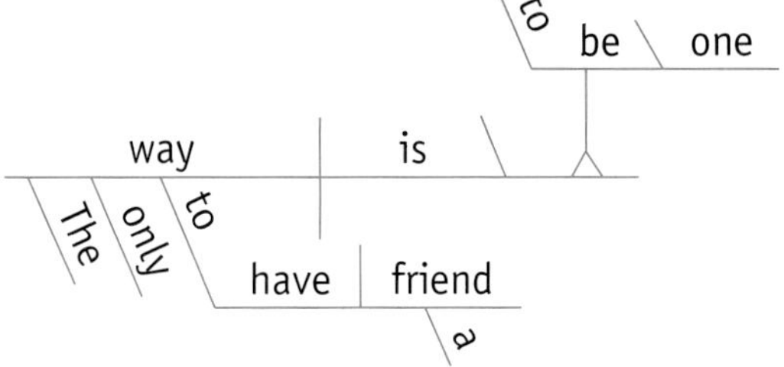


If the *to* of an infinitive is omitted from the sentence, it is diagramed in parentheses.

Do you dare interview the mayor?

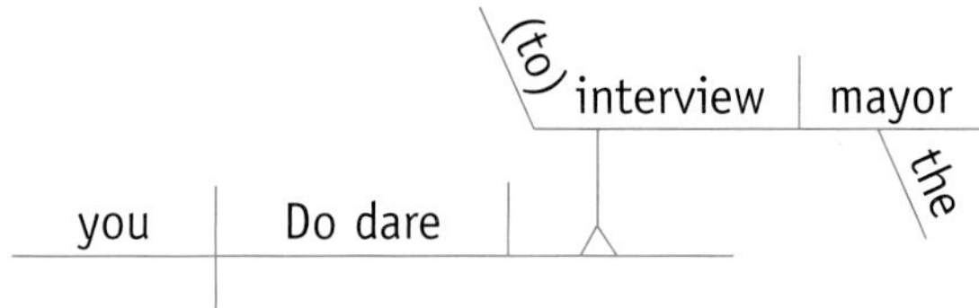


## PRACTICE YOUR SKILLS

*Diagraming Phrases*

**Diagram the following sentences or copy them. If you copy them, draw one line under each subject and two lines under each verb. Then put parentheses around each phrase and label each one *prepositional, appositive, participial, gerund,* or *infinitive.***

1. I like to visit my relatives in Tennessee.
2. We always go to Opryland in Nashville.
3. Buddy, the first dog for the blind, was trained in Nashville.
4. Born in Tennessee, Davy Crockett became a national legend.
5. You can visit his home by taking a tour through the mountains.
6. I liked learning about the real Davy Crockett.
7. Arriving in Memphis, we went to Graceland, the home of Elvis Presley.
8. To visit his home was my idea.
9. We saw his gold records hanging on the walls.
10. The best way to travel through Tennessee is by car.

## CheckPoint

### Identifying Phrases

**Write the phrases in the following sentences. Then label each one *prepositional, appositive, participial, gerund,* or *infinitive*.**

1. Seaweed sometimes grows to 200 feet in length.
2. At the end of February, Jonathan decided to send in his application.
3. Transporting pollen is the worker bees' job.
4. Meteors, known as shooting stars, may be seen on almost any clear night.
5. Both Cervantes and Shakespeare, two enormously important writers, died on April 23, 1616.
6. Scoring five runs immediately, the Red Sox took command of the game.
7. I enjoy swimming laps every morning.
8. An old game, played since ancient times, is marbles.
9. Do you want to frame your diploma?
10. Running the bases clockwise was the custom during baseball's early years.
11. Joan, my oldest aunt, was an Olympic swimmer and a distance runner.
12. The club's secretary handed me the minutes, typed neatly on bond paper.
13. Dan's father enjoys restoring antique cars.
14. The President, planning an important Cabinet appointment, studied the list of possible candidates.
15. In some places in the world, people actually train geese to tend sheep.

## Identifying Phrases

**Write each phrase in the following paragraph. Then label each phrase *prepositional, appositive, participial, gerund,* or *infinitive.***

### *Early Will*

Little is known about the early life of William Shakespeare, the playwright. There are, however, many legends like these. Abandoning his family to pursue a more carefree life, Shakespeare became a soldier, lawyer, or teacher. Joining an acting troupe, Shakespeare left his home in Stratford-upon-Avon and went to London. Shakespeare, having stolen Sir Thomas Lucy's deer, left his birthplace to avoid prosecution. Little or no proof exists, though, to support these legends.

## Using Phrases

**Write five sentences that follow the directions below. (The sentences may come in any order.) Write about one of the following topics or a topic of your choice: why you enjoy speaking up in class or why you fear public speaking.**

**Write a sentence that . . .**

1. includes at least two prepositional phrases.
2. includes an appositive phrase.
3. includes an introductory participial phrase.
4. includes a gerund phrase.
5. includes an infinitive phrase.

**Underline and label each phrase. Then check for correct punctuation in each sentence.**

# Language and *Self-Expression*

**B**ritish sculptor Andy Goldsworthy has created sculptures out of ice, grass, twigs, and sand—among other natural objects. He has worked in places as varied as the shores of Lake Michigan, where this artwork was created, and the North Pole.

Imagine the public reaction to this artwork. Suppose you were a journalist reporting on the artwork's creation and unveiling. Write a newspaper article explaining how the work was made, what the public thought about it, and how you yourself reacted when you saw it for the first time. Your article might include "interviews" with the artist, invited guests, and passersby. Vary your sentences as you write by including phrases of all sorts in different positions within the sentence.

**Prewriting** Jot down ideas that answer these questions about the artwork: *Who? What? When? Where? How? Why?* As you reread your notes, use the information you included to come up with a lead for your story.

**Drafting** Begin with a lead that introduces the artwork. Add details that answer the questions you responded to in Prewriting. If you wish, include "quotes" from people you "interviewed" for the article.

**Revising** Reread your article, focusing on the flow of ideas and sentence variety. Find places where you might add phrases to clarify details or move phrases to vary sentence construction.

**Editing** Check your article for errors in grammar, capitalization, punctuation, and spelling. Make any needed corrections.

**Publishing** Prepare a final copy of your article by typing it up on a computer and printing it. Exchange articles with students in your class and discuss how different writers recorded the same event.

# Another Look

A **phrase** is a group of related words that functions as a single part of speech. A phrase does not have a subject and a verb.

## Prepositional Phrases

An **adjective phrase** is a prepositional phrase that is used to modify a noun or pronoun. *(page L98)*

An **adverb phrase** is a prepositional phrase that is used to modify a verb, an adjective, or an adverb. *(page L98)*

## Appositives and Appositive Phrases

An **appositive** is a noun or pronoun that identifies or explains another noun or pronoun in the sentence. *(page L104)*

An **appositive phrase** is a group of words that contains an appositive and its modifiers. *(page L104)*

## Verbals and Verbal Phrases

A **participle** is a verb form that is used as an adjective. *(page L107)*

A **participial phrase** is a participle with its modifiers and complements—all working together as an adjective. *(page L108)*

A **gerund** is a verb form that is used as a noun. *(page L112)*

A **gerund phrase** is a gerund with its modifiers and complements—all working together as a noun. *(page L112)*

An **infinitive** is a verb form that usually begins with *to*. It is used as a noun, an adjective, or an adverb. *(page L115)*

An **infinitive phrase** is an infinitive with its modifiers and complements—all working together as a noun, an adjective, or an adverb. *(page L116)*

## Other Information About Phrases

Punctuating adverb phrases *(page L100)*
Punctuating appositives and appositive phrases *(page L104)*
Punctuating participial phrases *(page L109)*
Recognizing misplaced modifiers *(page L120)*
Recognizing dangling modifiers *(page L120)*
Avoiding phrase fragments *(page L123)*

### *Directions*

**Write the letter of the term that correctly identifies the underlined phrase in each sentence.**

EXAMPLE **1.** Eugene O'Neill is surely one of our most brilliant playwrights.

**1** **A** prepositional
**B** participial
**C** gerund
**D** infinitive

ANSWER **1** **A**

1. Eugene O'Neill grew up in a theatrical family.
2. Both of his parents, James and Ella, were actors.
3. O'Neill worked as a merchant seaman before tuberculosis forced him to rest and educate himself.
4. Writing twelve one-act plays and two longer works kept him busy for two years.
5. Falling into three main phases, O'Neill's work grew stronger during his life.
6. His early plays feature sailors and their dreams of a better life.
7. *Beyond the Horizon* and *Anna Christie* are his most important plays written before 1921.
8. Both plays won the Pulitzer Prize, an award from the trustees of Columbia University.
9. *The Emperor Jones,* considered America's first expressionist play, owes a lot to Swedish playwright August Strindberg.
10. It marks the beginning of a more experimental phase.

**1** **A** prepositional
**B** participial
**C** gerund
**D** infinitive

**2** **A** prepositional
**B** participial
**C** appositive
**D** gerund

**3** **A** prepositional
**B** participial
**C** gerund
**D** infinitive

**4** **A** prepositional
**B** participial
**C** appositive
**D** gerund

**5** **A** prepositional
**B** participial
**C** gerund
**D** infinitive

**6** **A** prepositional
**B** participial
**C** appositive
**D** gerund

**7** **A** prepositional
**B** participial
**C** gerund
**D** infinitive

**8** **A** prepositional
**B** participial
**C** appositive
**D** gerund

**9** **A** prepositional
**B** participial
**C** gerund
**D** infinitive

**10** **A** prepositional
**B** participial
**C** appositive
**D** gerund

CHAPTER 4

# Clauses

### Directions

**Write the letter of the term that correctly identifies each sentence or underlined part of a sentence.**

EXAMPLE **1.** Aesop may have been a Phrygian slave.

**1** **A** simple sentence
**B** compound sentence
**C** complex sentence
**D** compound-complex sentence

ANSWER **1** **A**

**1.** Aesop, who lived from 620 to 560 B.C., was a writer of fables.
**2.** We can infer from Aristotle's descriptions that Aesop was a freed slave, but little else is known about him.
**3.** Some scholars doubt that he ever lived.
**4.** His fables exist, however, and fortunately they have been passed down to us.
**5.** Some fables attributed to Aesop appear on Egyptian papyri dated 1000 years before his birth.
**6.** <u>What we know as *Aesop's Fables*</u> certainly includes tales from older sources.
**7.** The translators <u>who collected the fables</u> added other stories they knew.
**8.** <u>Some stories may have originated in Asia</u>, and others may come from Africa.
**9.** Do you know <u>what a fable is</u>?
**10.** A fable is a story <u>that illustrates a moral</u>.

1
A simple sentence
B compound sentence
C complex sentence
D compound-complex sentence

2
A simple sentence
B compound sentence
C complex sentence
D compound-complex sentence

3
A simple sentence
B compound sentence
C complex sentence
D compound-complex sentence

4
A simple sentence
B compound sentence
C complex sentence
D compound-complex sentence

5
A simple sentence
B compound sentence
C complex sentence
D compound-complex sentence

6
A independent clause
B adverb clause
C adjective clause
D noun clause

7
A independent clause
B adverb clause
C adjective clause
D noun clause

8
A independent clause
B adverb clause
C adjective clause
D noun clause

9
A independent clause
B adverb clause
C adjective clause
D noun clause

10
A independent clause
B adverb clause
C adjective clause
D noun clause

Leo and Diane Dillon. Illustration from *Why Mosquitoes Buzz in People's Ears,* by Verna Aardema. Watercolor, pastel, and ink.

**Describe** What animals are visible in this watercolor? Describe the patterns and shapes you see.

**Analyze** In what way do you think this illustration is suitable as an accompaniment to an African folk tale?

**Interpret** How do you think the painting shows the character of each animal? How might a folk tale use description to do the same thing?

**Judge** When this folktale was told originally, only the teller's words conveyed the imagery and characterization. How can illustrations help a reader better understand a story?

At the end of this chapter, you will use the artwork to stimulate ideas for writing.

# Independent and Subordinate Clauses

You could paint a landscape with just one color, but it would be a dull, unrealistic picture when you finished. You could also write only simple sentences in essays, reports, and letters. People would certainly understand what you wrote. Like the picture painted all in one color, however, your written work would be a dull, unrealistic representation of ordinary speech.

You can add color and interest to your writing by varying the structure of your sentences. One way to do this is to include various combinations of clauses within your sentences.

A **clause** is a group of words that has a subject and a verb.

This chapter will cover independent clauses and subordinate clauses and show you how a subordinate clause can be used as an adverb, an adjective, or a noun. This chapter will also show you how clauses form different kinds of sentences.

An **independent** (or **main**) **clause** can usually stand alone as a sentence because it expresses a complete thought.

When an independent clause stands alone, it is called a sentence. When it appears in a sentence with another clause, it is called a clause. In the following examples, each subject is underlined once, and each verb is underlined twice. Notice that each independent clause can stand alone as a separate sentence.

independent clause — independent clause

Greg waited a long time, but his new saddle never arrived.

independent clause — independent clause

Greg waited a long time. His new saddle never arrived.

A **subordinate** (or **dependent**) **clause** cannot stand alone as a sentence because it does not express a complete thought.

A subordinate clause has a subject and a verb; nevertheless, it does not express a complete thought. It can never stand alone as a sentence. A subordinate clause is dependent upon an independent clause to complete its meaning.

subordinate clause | independent clause

When we attended the rodeo, we sat in the bleachers.

independent clause | subordinate clause

We found some red paint that matches the barn.

independent clause | subordinate clause

Nobody at the livestock show knew that you were a newcomer.

## PRACTICE YOUR SKILLS

### Check Your Understanding

***Distinguishing Between Independent and Subordinate Clauses***

Contemporary Life

**Label each underlined clause *I* for independent or *S* for subordinate.**

1. We had an enjoyable weekend when we spent two days on Lloyd's farm.
2. Before the sun came up, we had eaten a huge breakfast.
3. Jeremy helped milk several cows, and Tamara spread grain for the chickens.
4. I slowly drove the tractor to the barn, but Steven attached the tractor's trailer.
5. After we loaded the trailer with bales of hay, we hauled the load into the pasture.
6. I wasn't afraid of the cows until one of them lumbered toward me.

# Uses of Subordinate Clauses

Like a phrase, a subordinate clause can be used in a sentence as an adverb, an adjective, or a noun. Keep in mind, however, the basic difference between a clause and a phrase. A clause has a subject and a verb; a phrase does not.

## Adverb Clauses

An **adverb clause** is a subordinate clause that is used as an adverb to modify a verb, an adjective, or an adverb.

An adverb clause is used just like a single adverb or an adverb phrase. In the following examples, the single adverb, the adverb phrase, and the adverb clause all modify the verb *arrived*.

| | |
|---|---|
| Single Adverb | The hockey team arrived **early**. |
| Adverb Phrase | The hockey team arrived **at five o'clock**. |
| Adverb Clause | The hockey team arrived **before the rink opened**. |

In addition to the questions *How? When? Where? How much?* and *To what extent?*, adverb clauses also answer *Under what condition?* and *Why?* Although most adverb clauses modify verbs, some modify adjectives and adverbs.

| | |
|---|---|
| Modifying a Verb | **After the snow stopped**, we organized a snowball war. (The clause answers *When?*) |
| Modifying an Adjective | Some ice sports are faster **than others are**. (The clause answers *How much?*) |

| | |
|---|---|
| MODIFYING AN ADVERB | The snow was piled higher **than I had ever seen before.** (The clause answers *To what extent?*) |

## Subordinating Conjunctions

An adverb clause usually begins with a **subordinating conjunction.** Notice in the following list such words as *after, before, since,* and *until;* these words can also be used as prepositions. Notice also that subordinating conjunctions can be more than one word, such as *even though*.

| COMMON SUBORDINATING CONJUNCTIONS | | |
|---|---|---|
| after | because | though |
| although | before | unless |
| as | even though | until |
| as far as | if | when |
| as if | in order that | whenever |
| as long as | since | where |
| as soon as | so that | wherever |
| as though | than | while |

An adverb clause that describes a verb modifies the whole verb phrase.

You may watch the team's photo session **as long as you are quiet.**

**When you get your hockey equipment**, you must call me.

The goalie, **after he blocked the puck,** was lying on the ice.

### PUNCTUATION WITH ADVERB CLAUSES

Always place a comma after an adverb clause that comes at the beginning of a sentence.

> **Since the country roads were icy,** I drove at a slow and safe speed.

When an adverb clause interrupts an independent clause, place a comma before it and after it.

> The crowd**, after they had enjoyed the exciting game,** applauded the winners.

When an adverb clause follows an independent clause, no comma is needed.

> We hurried out of the arena **before the parking lot became congested.**

### CONNECT TO WRITER'S CRAFT

You can improve your writing by using subordinating conjunctions to show a clear relationship between two ideas.

> I worked all summer. I did not get the athletic scholarship.
>
> I worked all summer **because** I did not get the athletic scholarship.
>
> The MVP is a skilled ball player. He is not a skilled speaker.
>
> **Although** the MVP is a skilled ball player, he is not a skilled speaker.

If you do not clarify the relationship between ideas, your reader must guess at the connection and may guess incorrectly!

## Practice Your Skills

Check Your Understanding

### *Recognizing Adverb Clauses as Modifiers*

Contemporary Life

**Write each adverb clause. Then beside it write the word or words the adverb clause modifies.**

**1.** When a thunderstorm strikes on a hot day, hail may fall.

**2.** We sloshed through puddles after the storm ended.

**3.** We went back inside so that we could find our umbrellas.

**4.** After the snowstorm ended, we shoveled the walk and the driveway.

**5.** As soon as you build the snowman, call me.

**6.** We left for the ice-skating lesson later than we had planned.

**7.** We can share the snowboard if each of us pays half.

**8.** Put the snow chains on your tires after you read the directions.

**9.** Because Cheryl wanted skis, she worked at the sports store until she saved enough money.

**10.** Before she skied down the steep hill, she watched the more experienced skiers.

Connect to the Writing Process: Editing

### *Punctuating Adverb Clauses*

Contemporary Life

**Write the following sentences, adding a comma or commas where needed. If no comma is needed, write *C* for correct.**

**11.** When the thunderstorm began we ran for shelter.

**12.** We stayed beneath the trees as long as the rain continued.

**13.** All day long the downhill skiing champion walked as though she had injured her leg.

**14.** Because Judy practiced faithfully she did well in the figure skating competition.

**15.** John after he completed his bachelor's degree in architecture started an ice arena design company.

**16.** He worked on a design for an Olympic-sized ice arena until he was satisfied with every detail.

**17.** Even though we were cold we played hockey on the frozen lake for an hour.

**18.** The mayor of Denver left after he had cut the ribbon at the opening of the new ski resort.

**19.** I placed a padded cover over my car so that the hail could not damage the paint.

**20.** Even though I had taken this precaution the hail dented the bumper.

## Elliptical Clauses

Words in an adverb clause are sometimes omitted to streamline a sentence and to prevent unnecessary repetition. Even though the words are omitted, they are still understood to be there. An adverb clause in which words are missing is called an **elliptical clause.** Notice in the following examples that the elliptical clauses begin with *than* or *as* and are missing only the verb.

Alvin visits the zoo more often **than I.** (The completed elliptical clause reads "than I *do*.")

A hippopotamus may weigh as much **as a medium-sized truck.** (The completed elliptical clause reads "as a medium-sized truck *weighs*.")

Sometimes the subject and the verb, or just part of the verb phrase, may be omitted in an elliptical clause.

I collected more donations to the wildlife fund this weekend **than last weekend.** (The completed elliptical clause reads "than *I collected* last weekend.")

**When sighted**, the zebra had already begun to run. (The completed elliptical clause reads "When *it was* sighted.")

*You can learn more about using the correct case of a pronoun in an elliptical clause on pages L148–L152.*

### Connect to Writer's Craft

You may more easily remember what an elliptical clause is if you are familiar with using the mark of punctuation called the **ellipses**. An ellipses is a series of three dots that indicate where the writer has omitted words, usually in a quotation. Just as an **elliptical clause** omits words that the reader understands to be there, an ellipses indicates an omission of words that the reader understands to be in the original.

## Practice Your Skills

### Check Your Understanding
***Recognizing Elliptical Clauses***

Science Topic **Write each elliptical clause and then complete it.**

1. At five and a half feet tall, the black rhinoceros is as tall as many people.
2. The white rhinoceros stands about six inches shorter than the black rhino.
3. Most rhinoceroses are taller than the hippopotamus.
4. The hippopotamus weighs the same as the rhinoceros.
5. When told that the rhinoceros is not a meat-eater, many people are surprised.
6. While searching for leaves, twigs, and fruits for food, a rhinoceros stirs up insects from the grass.
7. Egrets, while riding on the backs of rhinoceroses, eat these insects.
8. The white rhino is more sociable than the black rhino.
9. Although timid, the white rhino will defend itself when threatened.
10. There are thousands fewer rhinoceroses in Africa today than a decade ago.

### Connect to the Writing Process: Prewriting
***Freewriting Using Adverb Clauses***

Many species of animals and plants become extinct every year, and usually the cause for extinction is a human cause. Here is a list of a few of the animals that are endangered:

| | |
|---|---|
| black rhinoceros | brown pelican |
| gorilla | California condor |
| Amazon River dolphin | Peruvian penguin |
| Asian elephant | king salmon |
| Hawaiian monk seal | Florida manatee |
| short-tailed albatross | woodland caribou |
| Idaho spring snail | Wyoming toad |
| Kirtland's warbler | pallid sturgeon |

For ten minutes freewrite about endangered species. Write your thoughts, feelings, questions, and ideas. If you run out of ideas, look over the list of subordinating conjunctions on page L142, and write the first clause that comes to mind.

## Communicate Your Ideas

### APPLY TO WRITING

**Informative Report:** ***Adverb Clauses***

Write a brief report informing your classmates and teacher about an endangered species. To begin, use your freewriting from the above exercise. A trip to a library or a search session on the Internet will help you find additional facts. You may also be able to talk to personnel at a local zoo or an environmental group. After studying several strong sources, write your report, making sure to use a variety of adverb clauses and elliptical clauses to form informative, varied sentences.

## Adjective Clauses

An **adjective clause** is a subordinate clause that is used as an adjective to modify a noun or a pronoun.

An adjective clause is used as a single adjective or an adjective phrase. In the following examples, the single adjective, the adjective phrase, and the adjective clause all modify *fire*.

| | |
|---|---|
| SINGLE ADJECTIVE | The **intense** fire destroyed the building. |
| ADJECTIVE PHRASE | The fire **with billowing flames and thick smoke** destroyed the building. |
| ADJECTIVE CLAUSE | The fire, **which raged out of control**, destroyed the building. |

Like a single adjective, an adjective clause answers the question *Which one(s)?* or *What kind?*

| | |
|---|---|
| WHICH ONE(S)? | The firefighters **who volunteered their time last night** became heroes. |
| WHAT KIND? | They saved a historic building **that was constructed of valuable hardwoods**. |

### Relative Pronouns

A relative pronoun usually begins an adjective clause. A **relative pronoun** relates an adjective clause to its antecedent. The relative adverbs *where* and *when* also introduce adjective clauses.

| RELATIVE PRONOUNS | | | | |
|---|---|---|---|---|
| who | whom | whose | which | that |

Lakeview's firefighters, **who sponsor a fundraiser each summer**, have not raised enough money for new hoses.

Charles Daly moved here from Miami, **where he had worked as a mechanic at a fire station.**

The relative pronoun *that* is sometimes omitted from an adjective clause; nevertheless, it is still understood to be in the clause.

Playing with matches is something **everyone should avoid.** (***That*** *everyone should avoid* is the complete adjective clause.)

## Practice Your Skills

Check Your Understanding

### *Recognizing Adjective Clauses as Modifiers*

General Interest **Write each adjective clause. Then beside it write the word it modifies.**

1. Firefighting is a dangerous job that requires a commitment to public service.
2. Fire hoses, which carry 2,000 gallons of water per minute, will test the user's strength and dexterity.
3. Fire hydrants, where firefighters access critical water supplies, must never be blocked by parked cars.
4. Firefighters, who often carry unconscious people down stairs, must develop strong muscles.
5. Their coworkers, whom they trust with their lives every day, often become close friends for many years.
6. Did you hear about the conference that will update us on firefighting technology?
7. These conferences, workshops, and seminars are events every firefighter should attend.
8. Jerry, whose high school diploma hangs on the wall, passed the firefighter's examination.
9. Some colleges offer fire science programs, which attract many firefighters who are already on the job.

**Functions of a Relative Pronoun** A relative pronoun functions in several ways in a sentence. It usually introduces an adjective clause and refers to another noun or pronoun in the sentence. A relative pronoun also has a function within the adjective clause itself. It can be used as a subject, direct object, or object of a preposition. A relative pronoun can also show possession.

| | |
|---|---|
| SUBJECT | Robert Frost, **who read a poem at President Kennedy's inauguration**, lived from 1874 to 1963. (*Who* is the subject of *read*.) |
| DIRECT OBJECT | The poems **you like** were written by Emily Dickinson. (The understood relative pronoun *that* is the direct object of *like: you like that . . . .*) |
| OBJECT OF A PREPOSITION | The volume **in which I found Frost's biography** is quite interesting. (*Which* is the object of the preposition *in*.) |
| POSSESSION | Carl Sandburg is an American poet **whose father emigrated from Sweden**. (*Whose* shows possession of *father*.) |

**PUNCTUATION WITH ADJECTIVE CLAUSES**

No punctuation is used with an adjective clause that contains information essential to identify a person, place, or thing in the sentence.

A comma or commas, however, should set off an adjective clause that is nonessential.

- A clause is nonessential if it can be removed from the sentence without changing the basic meaning of the sentence.
- An adjective clause is usually nonessential if it modifies a proper noun.

The relative pronoun *that* usually begins an essential clause, and *which* often begins a nonessential clause.

| | |
|---|---|
| **ESSENTIAL** | The author **who was Poet Laureate of the United States from 1993–1994** was Rita Dove. (No commas are used because the clause is needed to identify which author.) |
| **NONESSENTIAL** | Rita Dove, **who was Poet Laureate of the United States from 1993 to 1994**, received the Heinz Award in the Arts and Humanities in 1996. (Commas are used because the clause can be removed from the sentence.) |

## PRACTICE YOUR SKILLS

Check Your Understanding

***Determining the Function of a Relative Pronoun***

Literature Topic

**Write each adjective clause. Then label the use of each relative pronoun, using the following abbreviations. If an adjective clause begins with an understood *that*, write *(that)* and then write how *that* is used.**

| | |
|---|---|
| subject = *subj.* | object of a preposition = *o.p.* |
| direct object = *d.o.* | possession = *poss.* |

**1.** Robert Frost, whose poetry was awarded the Pulitzer Prize, first published his poems at age thirty-eight.

**2.** The poet who dressed entirely in white is Emily Dickinson.

**3.** The poem from which I get my inspiration is "The Road Not Taken" by Frost.

**4.** The poem you memorized has only six lines.

**5.** The lines "The fog comes / on little cat feet," which comprise the poem's first stanza, create a vivid image in my mind.

**6.** Carl Sandburg, who wrote this short poem, lived from 1878 to 1967.

7. The African American poet about whom I wrote my essay is Rita Dove.
8. The recordings of her poetry that I heard were on the Internet.
9. Wallace Stevens, who wrote "The Emperor of Ice Cream," dropped out of Harvard and then later went to law school.
10. The students whose essays are the most interesting are the students who felt a true connection with the poets they studied.

Connect to the Writing Process: Editing

## *Punctuating Adjective Clauses*

Literature Topic **Write the sentences, adding commas where needed. If no commas are needed, write *C* for correct.**

11. Emily Dickinson who lived in Amherst, Massachusetts was considered a recluse later in life.
12. This intelligent woman whose poems fascinate millions of readers often gave sweets to neighborhood children.
13. The poet would tie the treats to a string that she lowered from her window.
14. Adults who visited in the parlor almost never saw Emily there.
15. The poems which she wrote all her life are about nature, religion, and personal emotions.
16. The person to whom she turned for advice was Thomas Wentworth Higginson who was a literary critic.
17. Her poems which do not have titles are numbered for purposes of organization.
18. Mabel Todd who lived near the Dickinsons became friends with Emily.
19. The friendship the two women shared was established through notes, poems, and flowers.
20. Todd met Dickinson face-to-face on only one occasion which was Emily Dickinson's funeral!

## Communicate Your Ideas

### APPLY TO WRITING

**Writer's Craft:** ***Analyzing the Use of Adjective Clauses***

As you have learned, an adjective clause usually is next to the word it modifies. However, poets often rearrange thoughts to create particular effects. In each stanza in this poem are two adjective clauses that modify the same word. Read the poem and then follow the instructions below.

Who is the East?
The Yellow Man
Who may be Purple if He can
That carries in the Sun.

Who is the West?
The Purple Man
Who may be Yellow if He can
That lets Him out again.

*—Emily Dickinson*

- Write each adjective clause. Beside it, write the word it modifies.
- How do the adjective clauses make the poet's description more vivid?
- For the reader, what is the overall effect of Dickinson's use of these adjective clauses?

## Misplaced Modifiers

To avoid confusion, place an adjective clause as near as possible to the word it describes. Like a phrase, a clause placed too far away from the word it modifies can cause confusion and is called a **misplaced modifier.**

| | |
|---|---|
| MISPLACED | Tim discovered a park near his new house that included a pond and walking trail. |
| CORRECT | Near his new house, Tim discovered a park **that included a pond and walking trail.** |
| MISPLACED | Dennis ran to take the meat off the grill, which was burned to a crisp. |
| CORRECT | Dennis ran to take the meat, **which was burned to a crisp**, off the grill. |

*You can learn more about misplaced and dangling modifiers on pages L120–L122.*

## PRACTICE YOUR SKILLS

Check Your Understanding

### *Identifying Misplaced Modifiers*

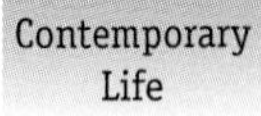

Contemporary Life

**Write *MM* for misplaced modifier if the underlined modifier is used incorrectly in the sentence. If the modifier is used correctly, write *C*.**

1. Monique packed a picnic basket full of tasty food that was made of straw.
2. Monique's best friend loaded the car with blankets, sunscreen, and a volleyball who was also going on the picnic.
3. I showed the lawn chairs to the girls that I had just bought.
4. My neighbor offered to drive us in his car whom I had invited on the picnic.
5. The car belongs to my neighbor, which has the convertible top.
6. The trunk of the car could barely contain all of our picnic supplies, which was the size of a suitcase.
7. We spread a cloth over the table that had a red-and-white checkered pattern.

8. Some ducks, which were cute and fluffy, begged for food.
9. Ed and I tossed a large disk across the grassy clearing that was made of black plastic.
10. We feasted on food that was tasty and enjoyed each other's company.

Connect to the Writing Process: Revising
***Correcting Misplaced Modifiers***

**11.–18. Rewrite the incorrect sentences from the preceding exercise, correcting each misplaced modifier. Use a comma or commas where needed.**

## Noun Clauses

A **noun clause** is a subordinate clause that is used as a noun.

A noun clause is used in the same ways a single noun can be used. The examples show some of the uses.

| | |
|---|---|
| SUBJECT | **What Jenny planned** was a river cruise. |
| DIRECT OBJECT | Julian knows **that the current is swift.** |
| INDIRECT OBJECT | Give **whoever arrives** a life jacket. |
| OBJECT OF A PREPOSITION | People are often surprised by **what they find on the river bottom.** |
| PREDICATE NOMINATIVE | A challenging trip down the rapids is **what I want right now.** |

The following list contains words that often introduce a noun clause. Remember, though, that *who, whom, whose, which*, and *that* can also be used as relative pronouns to introduce adjective clauses.

| COMMON INTRODUCTORY WORDS FOR NOUN CLAUSES | | | | |
|---|---|---|---|---|
| how | what | where | who | whomever |
| if | whatever | whether | whoever | whose |
| that | when | which | whom | why |

CONNECT TO SPEAKING AND WRITING

It would be impossible to communicate some ideas without using noun clauses—just try it! Suppose you tell the editor of the yearbook staff, "Send **whomever** this brochure." You have spoken in a complete sentence, yet vital information is missing.

Send **whoever paid ten dollars** this brochure.
Send **whoever is on the committee** this brochure.

Noun clauses add clarity and variety to your writing and speaking, whether that communication be a personal letter, a set of instructions, or a business report.

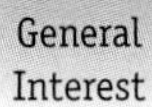

## PRACTICE YOUR SKILLS

Check Your Understanding
***Identifying Noun Clauses***

General Interest **Write the noun clause in each sentence.**

1. How people live in other countries interests many people.
2. A trip to the ancient monuments of Egypt is what the historians requested.
3. That the tour included the Nile River and Alexandria was pleasing news.
4. The tour guide gave the best seats to whoever arrived first.
5. Did you know that the Nile is the longest river in the world?

6. The tour guide said that the Amazon River in Brazil is the second longest river.
7. Give whomever you wish a list of the longest rivers in each country.
8. Does anyone in class know how a stream becomes a river?
9. Tell me whatever you know.
10. Where the Rio Grande flows is the border between Texas and Mexico.

### Check Your Understanding
## *Determining the Uses of Noun Clauses*

Science Topic **Write each noun clause. Then label the use of each one, using the following abbreviations.**

subject = *subj.*
direct object = *d.o.*
indirect object = *i.o.*
object of a preposition = *o.p.*
predicate nominative = *p.n.*

11. Did you know that heart disease kills people every day?
12. How people can learn about heart health interests me.
13. That a cardiologist can implant donor or artificial hearts is impressive.
14. Nutritionists tell whoever will listen facts about the heart.
15. People are often surprised by what they learn from these experts.
16. Few have heard that every 20 seconds a person in the United States suffers a heart attack.
17. Healthful foods and an exercise program are what people need.
18. That walking is good exercise is well documented in medical journals.
19. A sedentary lifestyle is what people should avoid.
20. Good eating habits can be taught to whoever is willing to learn.

Connect to the Writing Process: Drafting

### *Using Noun Clauses in Sentences*

**Use each noun clause in a complete sentence. Then write how you used the noun clause, using the following abbreviations.**

subject = *subj.*
direct object = *d.o.*
indirect object = *i.o.*
object of a preposition = *o.p.*
predicate nominative = *p.n.*

**21.** why exercise is essential

**22.** whoever is interested

**23.** that medical school is worth the time and money

**24.** what they learn during these years

**25.** whoever registers for a cholesterol test

**26.** where she will be doing her internship

**27.** if I can get loans for tuition payments

**28.** how the application process works

**29.** whomever you admire

**30.** that a medical degree is yours for life

## Communicate Your Ideas

### APPLY TO WRITING

**Career Profile: *Noun Clauses***

You and your classmates will create a catalog of career profiles that will assist students in choosing and planning their careers. First, choose a career for your profile. Interview people in your chosen career to find out the required education, the years of schooling involved, typical job duties, the average pay rate, and any other information that will help students decide whether this career is what they want. Write a draft of the profile. Use noun clauses to make your writing clear and specific. Then edit your work for grammar, spelling, and punctuation, and write your final draft.

## Mixed Practice

Science Topic

**Write the subordinate clauses in the following sentences. Then label the use of each one, using the following abbreviations.**

adverb = *adv.* noun = *n.*
adjective = *adj.*

**1.** When the earth, moon, and sun are in line, an eclipse occurs.

**2.** What most people associate with Saturn are the rings around the planet.

**3.** Our science teacher, Mrs. Jeffries, told us that Mercury is the planet closest to the sun.

**4.** The planet that is furthest from the sun is Pluto.

**5.** As I built my model of the solar system, I consulted at least three reference books.

**6.** A thick dictionary with diagrams and charts is what helped me the most.

**7.** Although the sun shone brightly, the weather forecasters maintained that the weekend would be rainy.

**8.** A planetarium, which contains a working model of the solar system, offers students a chance to see the planets in motion.

**9.** Mars is the planet that is notable for its red color.

**10.** I became more interested in the solar system when I learned that Mars is both a planet and the name of the Roman god of war.

# Kinds of Sentence Structure

A sentence can be simple, compound, complex, or compound-complex, depending on the number and the kind of clauses in it.

**A simple sentence consists of one independent clause.**

World War II airplanes fascinate me.

A simple sentence can have a compound subject, a compound verb, or both. In the examples below, the subject is underlined once and the verb is underlined twice.

Balloons and blimps can carry passengers.

The airplane and the tank crashed and burned.

**A compound sentence consists of two or more independent clauses.**

A compound sentence should be composed of only closely related independent clauses joined by a coordinating conjunction such as *and, but, for, nor, or, so,* or *yet*.

independent clause — independent clause

I ran to the airport terminal, but I missed my plane.

independent clause — independent clause — independent clause

The pilot has arrived, the flight attendants are checking tickets, and the passengers may now board.

*You can learn about punctuating a compound sentence on pages L441–L442.*

**A complex sentence consists of one independent clause and one or more subordinate clauses.**

A complex sentence consists of one independent clause and one or more subordinate clauses that are connected by a subordinating conjunction such as *because, that,* or *if*.

independent clause — subordinate clause

We bought a vacation package that included airfare.

independent clause — subordinate clause

We flew to Florida because we had tickets to a theme park

subordinate clause

that was ready to open.

*You can find a list of subordinating conjunctions on page L142. You can learn about punctuating complex sentences on pages L143 and L150–L151.*

A **compound-complex sentence** consists of two or more independent clauses and one or more subordinate clauses.

Conjunctions and punctuation in compound-complex sentences are used in the same way as they are used in compound sentences and in complex sentences.

independent clause — independent clause — subordinate clause

I have dreamed of becoming a pilot, but I have not taken flying lessons because I am saving the necessary money.

CONNECT TO WRITER'S CRAFT

A paragraph with all simple sentences becomes dull and monotonous to read. On the other hand, a paragraph with all complex or compound-complex sentences can be confusing. A paragraph that includes a combination of different kinds of sentences is by far the most interesting. Notice the combination of the different kinds of sentences in the following paragraph.

> The plane began its descent to the airport. Passengers looked out the windows, but all they could see was whiteness. The plane bumped through the turbulent air. When the plane was almost over the runway, it finally broke free of the clouds. After landing the plane safely, the pilot turned off the seat-belt sign.

## Practice Your Skills

Check Your Understanding

### *Classifying Sentences*

Science Topic **Label each sentence *simple, compound, complex,* or *compound-complex*.**

1. In 1984, Byron Lichtenberg, who is a biomedical engineer, became a member of a spacecraft crew.
2. Lichtenberg discovered that dealing with zero gravity was difficult.
3. The other two astronauts were able to control their movements, but at first Lichtenberg kept bouncing off the walls.
4. Lichtenberg found that eating was not easy either.
5. He ate with only a spoon because he had to hold onto his food with his other hand.
6. Once he tried to make a sandwich, but this task was much harder than he had expected.
7. The beef and cheese floated around, but then he clamped them together with the bread.
8. Peanuts were the most fun to eat.
9. When Lichtenberg tried to pour them down his throat, they escaped and floated around the cabin.
10. Eventually he chased them down like a cat and mouse.

Connect to the Writing Process: Revising

### *Combining Sentences*

**Combine the first five pairs of sentences into compound sentences. Then combine the next three pairs into complex sentences. Combine the last two pairs into compound-complex sentences.**

11. Mythology associates the winged horse Pegasus with lightning. The modern era associates Pegasus with poetic inspiration.
12. An airplane has wings like a bird. They do not flap like a bird's wings.

**13.** Wings are associated with Christian angels. They have also been associated with spirits and demons of ancient cultures.

**14.** Wings can symbolize physical flight above the earth. They can represent rising high above earthly cares and concerns.

**15.** Fairies are seen as dainty creatures. They are drawn with the wings of butterflies and dragonflies.

**16.** Wings work in pairs. One is not enough for successful flight.

**17.** Humans do not have wings. They must fly in spacecraft and aircraft.

**18.** The Wright brothers made their first flight in 1903. Flying developed relatively quickly.

**19.** The afternoon was clear and sunny. I felt like flying a kite. I had made the kite from a special kit.

**20.** I tried to fly the kite in a park. I could not keep it in the air. The kite string kept tangling in the sycamore trees.

## Communicate Your Ideas

### APPLY TO WRITING

**Plan of Action:** ***Kinds of Sentence Structure***

For high school graduation, you are given a voucher for a free airline ticket to a destination of your choice. You must write down a tentative itinerary to leave with family members before you go. Write a plan of action for this trip. Describe where you are going, where you'll stay, and what you plan to do. In addition to simple sentences, make sure you use compound sentences, complex sentences, and compound-complex sentences to vary your writing. Be prepared to identify each kind of sentence.

## Clause Fragments

Even though a subordinate clause has both a subject and a verb, it does not express a complete thought. Therefore, it cannot stand alone as a sentence. When it stands alone, a **clause fragment** results. To correct a clause fragment, add or change words to express a complete thought or attach the clause to a related sentence.

| | |
|---|---|
| ADVERB CLAUSE FRAGMENT | **Whenever I have the opportunity.** I enjoy learning about animals. |
| CORRECTED | Whenever I have the opportunity, I enjoy learning about animals. |
| NOUN CLAUSE FRAGMENT | **That a cow has four stomachs called the rumen, reticulum, omasum, and abomasum.** I know. |
| CORRECTED | I know that a cow has four stomachs called the rumen, reticulum, omasum, and abomasum. |
| ADJECTIVE CLAUSE FRAGMENT | At the workshop she visited booths. **That featured veterinary information.** |
| CORRECTED | At the workshop she visited booths that featured veterinary information. |

*You can learn about other kinds of sentence fragments on pages L68–L71 and L123–L125.*

### CONNECT TO SPEAKING AND WRITING

When someone asks you a question that begins with the word *why,* you probably begin your answer with the word *because.*

> Why did you visit the career fair? **Because** I wanted to learn more about job opportunities.

Sentences that begin with *because* are often fragments. While acceptable in conversation, they should be avoided in writing. 

## Practice Your Skills

Check Your Understanding

*Identifying Clause Fragments*

Science Topic **Write *S* if the word group is a sentence. Write *F* if the word group is a clause fragment.**

**1.** Ruminants are animals that chew their cud.

**2.** As soon as I heard about them.

**3.** Because I had never seen a moose up close.

**4.** That the oryx has long, pointed horns that point upward.

**5.** Whoever drew the picture of the kudu's long spiral horns.

**6.** I liked the chamois, whose soft skin is sometimes used as a "chamois cloth."

**7.** That I would never use a real leather chamois cloth again.

**8.** Until you know the difference between a bison and a musk ox.

**9.** So that I could also see the striped-backed duikers.

**10.** When I saw the gazelles.

**11.** After she saw the picture of a unicorn.

**12.** Does the Loch Ness monster really exist?

**13.** Before the American bald eagle was taken from the endangered list.

**14.** The alligator that made its home in the swamp.

**15.** Despite the differences between an alligator and a crocodile, many people cannot tell them apart.

Connect to the Writing Process: Revising

*Correcting Clause Fragments*

**16.–26. Correct each clause fragment you identified in the preceding exercise by either adding or changing words to express a complete thought.**

Communicate Your Ideas

## APPLY TO WRITING

**Description:** ***Complete Sentences***

You have created a Website in honor of your beloved pet. You have already scanned in a photograph of Fluffy/Spike/Fishy, and now you must write an engaging description of him/her. Write a paragraph describing what makes your pet so lovable or cute or interesting. If you don't have a pet, write about a pet you used to have or make one up. Use a variety of clauses, but make sure you don't have any fragments.

# Run-on Sentences

A **run-on sentence** is two or more sentences that are written as one sentence and are separated by a comma or no mark of punctuation at all.

Run-on sentences result either from writing too fast or from the mistaken idea that very long sentences sound more scholarly. A run-on sentence is usually written in either of the following two ways.

| | |
|---|---|
| WITH A COMMA | Horticulturists grow beautiful plants, they often organize garden shows for interested audiences. |
| WITH NO PUNCTUATION | In the winter some trees lose their leaves others do not. |

## Ways to Correct Run-on Sentences

A run-on sentence can be corrected in several ways. (1) It can be written as two separate sentences. (2) It can be written as a compound sentence with a comma and a conjunction or with a semicolon. (3) It can be written as a complex sentence by changing one part of the run-on sentence into a subordinate clause.

| | |
|---|---|
| RUN-ON SENTENCE | This botanical garden covers over four acres, it is the second largest in the state. |
| SEPARATE SENTENCES | This botanical garden covers over four acres**.** It is the second largest in the state. |
| COMPOUND SENTENCE | This botanical garden covers over four acres, **and** it is the second largest in the state. (with a comma and a conjunction) |

This botanical garden covers over four acres; it is the second largest in the state.
(with a semicolon)

COMPLEX SENTENCE

This botanical garden, **which covers over four acres,** is the second largest in the state.
(adjective clause)

**Since this botanical garden covers over four acres,** it is the second largest in the state.
(adverb clause)

## PRACTICE YOUR SKILLS

### Check Your Understanding
### *Identifying Run-on Sentences*

Science Topic

**Label each group of words as *RO* for run-on or *S* for sentence.**

**1.** Many plants have poisonous leaves or fruits, these cause skin irritation or sickness.

**2.** The belladonna has a beautiful name and poisonous berries, it is also called deadly nightshade.

**3.** Holly, commonly used for holiday decoration, has poisonous leaves and berries.

**4.** Another seasonal flower, the lily of the valley, has berries too these should not be eaten by anyone either.

**5.** Many people love rhubarb pie, they do not know that rhubarb leaves should not be eaten.

**6.** Like most people, I cannot touch poison ivy, it gives me a rash.

**7.** Digitalis is a plant used in some medicines the leaves are poisonous when eaten.

**8.** As a child I learned not to touch the nettle, I learned the hard way.

**9.** Children and pets don't know the dangers of poisonous plants, some will innocently eat them and become sick or die.

**10.** English ivy foliage is not poisonous, but the berries are.

Connect to the Writing Process: Editing

*Correcting Run-on Sentences*

**11.–18. Rewrite the run-on sentences you identified in the preceding exercise as separate sentences, compound sentences, or complex sentences. Use conjunctions and punctuation as needed.**

## Communicate Your Ideas

### APPLY TO WRITING

**Personal Narrative:** ***Complete Sentences***

As you finish high school and prepare for graduation, you may find yourself remembering certain events in your senior year with emotions such as happiness, regret, humor, or anger. Write a personal narrative about one of these memories for your Senior Scrapbook. Use different kinds of sentences for variety. Remember that run-on sentences usually occur when you are focused on getting ideas down on paper in a first draft. Therefore, be sure to edit your work for run-on sentences and then prepare a final copy.

## Diagraming Sentences

Each clause—whether independent or subordinate—is diagramed on a separate baseline like a simple sentence.

**Compound Sentences** Each independent clause is diagramed like a simple sentence. The clauses are joined at the verbs with a broken line on which the conjunction is written.

The cafeteria food is good, but I still take my lunch.

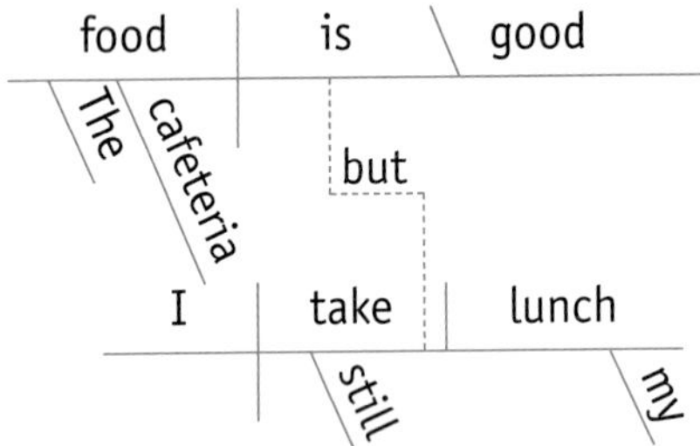


**Complex Sentences** An adverb or an adjective clause in a complex sentence is diagramed beneath the independent clause it modifies. The following diagram contains an adverb clause. The subordinating conjunction goes on a broken line that connects the verb in the adverb clause to the modified verb, adverb, or adjective in the independent clause.

Before I begin my article, I must do more research.

I | must do | research
more
Before
I | begin | article
my

The relative pronoun in an adjective clause is connected by a broken line to the noun or the pronoun the clause modifies.

We recently bought a clock that chimes on the hour.

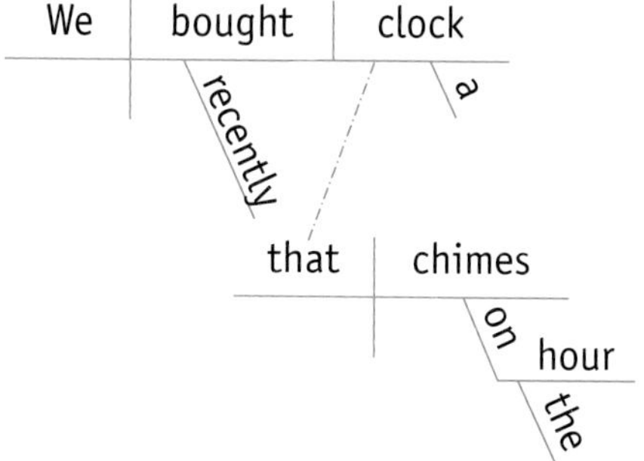


A noun clause is diagramed on a pedestal in the same position as a single noun with the same function, such as a direct object.

Tell us what you want for your birthday.

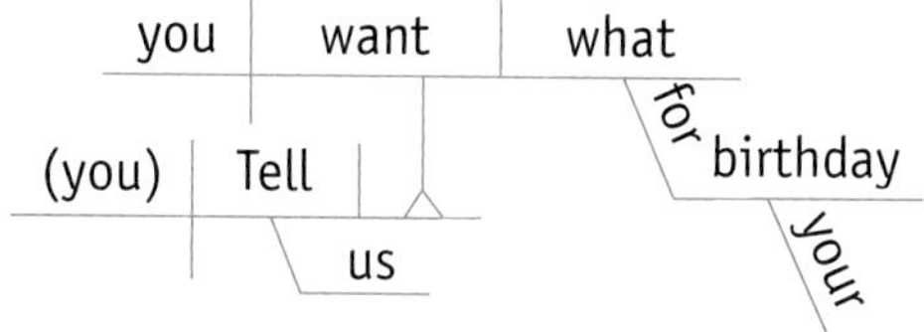


**Compound-Complex Sentences** To diagram these sentences, apply rules for diagraming compound and complex sentences.

## Practice Your Skills

### *Diagraming Sentences*

**Diagram the following sentences or copy them. If you copy them, draw one line under each subject and two lines under each verb. Then put parentheses around each subordinate clause and label each one *adverb, adjective,* or *noun.***

1. An earthquake begins when underground rocks move.
2. This movement creates waves of energy which travel up to the surface.
3. Because earthquakes often cause severe damage, architects now can build earthquake-proof buildings.
4. Thousands of earthquakes occur during a year, but only a few are large ones.
5. What scientists still cannot do is predict earthquakes.

CheckPoint

## Identifying Clauses

**Write each subordinate clause. Then label each one *adverb, adjective,* or *noun.***

1. Although many tornadoes occur throughout the United States, they are quite rare west of the Rockies.
2. Several champion ice-hockey teams have come from Canada, where ice-skating is a very popular sport.
3. I heard that trucks can no longer travel on Grove Street.
4. Wrap that meat in foil before you put it into the freezer.
5. Since I will have a test in Spanish, I went to the language lab.
6. The microphone that he used had a cord attached to it.
7. If you take a trip to Mount Vernon, you will be taken back two centuries into the past.
8. Parachutists often fall a considerable distance before they pull the cord that opens the parachute.
9. Someone once said that an egotist is a person who is "me-deep" in conversation.
10. My mother, who seemed happy and relieved, reported that she had found a new apartment for us.
11. Don ran when he saw a huge bull approaching him.
12. Whoever is qualified for the job will have an interview.
13. Early schoolhouses were always red because red paint was the cheapest paint available.
14. The oldest fossils date back to a time when seas covered large areas that have long since become dry land.
15. Since I wasn't there, I honestly don't know what happened.

## Classifying Sentences

**Label each sentence *simple, compound, complex,* or *compound-complex.***

1. John Paul Jones moved to America to avoid a trial that involved his handling of a mutiny.
2. Although he was born in Scotland, he became a hero of the American Revolution.
3. He battled British ships off the coast of North America.
4. His most famous victory occurred in 1779 aboard the *Bonhomme Richard.*
5. His ship was badly damaged, but Jones refused to give up.
6. He was urged to surrender, but he called out, "Sir, I have not yet begun to fight," words that have gone down in history.
7. Jones was only in his early 30s when he captured the British warships *Drake* and *Serapis.*
8. After the war American shipping became vulnerable to attacks by pirates.
9. Thomas Jefferson suggested that John Paul Jones could destroy the pirates.
10. He mentioned this in a letter to James Monroe, but nothing came of it.

## Using Sentence Structure

**Write five sentences that follow the directions below. (The sentences may come in any order.) Write about an unrecognized hero or a topic of your choice.**

1. Write a simple sentence.
2. Write a complex sentence with an introductory adverb clause.
3. Write a complex sentence with an adjective clause.
4. Write a compound sentence.
5. Write a complex sentence with a noun clause.

**Label each sentence and check its punctuation.**

# Language and *Self-Expression*

Leo and Diane Dillon attended New York City's Parsons School of Design and School of Visual Arts. They have collaborated on many picture books for children. The illustrations for this one, Verna Aardema's retelling of *Why Mosquitoes Buzz in People's Ears,* won the Caldecott Medal in 1976.

Folktales of this kind are designed to explain natural phenomena. They might tell, for example, "How the Leopard Got His Spots" or "Why the Elephant Has a Trunk." Think of a natural occurrence among animals that you could "explain" through a folktale. Write a tale that features animals who talk and interact. Use your knowledge of clauses to add interest to your writing.

**Prewriting** Begin with your title. Then outline your story, working backward as shown here:

Why Mosquitoes Buzz in People's Ears

I.
II.
III.
IV. Today, mosquitoes buzz in people's ears.

**Drafting** Refer to your outline as you draft your folktale. Begin with a paragraph that introduces your main characters and setting. Continue with the problem that is to be solved. End with a solution that "explains" the phenomenon mentioned in your title.

**Revising** Read your folktale critically, looking for ideas that do not flow smoothly or that seem extraneous. Cut and add material as needed.

**Editing** Review your folktale, looking for errors in grammar, capitalization, punctuation, and spelling. Make any corrections that are necessary.

**Publishing** Prepare and illustrate a final copy of your folktale. Publish it by sharing it with your class.

# Another Look

A **clause** is a group of words that has a subject and a verb.

## Types of Clauses

An **independent (or main) clause** can usually stand alone as a sentence because it expresses a complete thought. *(page L139)*

A **subordinate (or dependent) clause** cannot stand alone as a sentence, because it does not express a complete thought. *(page L139)*

## Uses of Subordinate Clauses

An **adverb clause** is a subordinate clause that is used like an adverb to modify a verb, an adjective, or an adverb. *(page L141)*

An adverb clause usually begins with a **subordinating conjunction.** *(page L142)*

An **adjective clause** is a subordinate clause that is used like an adjective to modify a noun or pronoun. *(page L148)*

An adjective clause usually begins with a **relative pronoun.** *(page L148)*

A **noun clause** is a subordinate clause that is used as a noun. *(page L155)*

## Kinds of Sentence Structure

A **simple sentence** consists of one independent clause. *(page L160)*

A **compound sentence** consists of two or more independent clauses. *(page L160)*

A **complex sentence** consists of one independent clause and one or more subordinate clauses. *(page L160)*

A **compound-complex sentence** consists of two or more independent clauses and one or more subordinate clauses. *(page L161)*

## Other Information About Clauses

Punctuating adverb clauses *(page L143)*

Punctuating adjective clauses *(page L150)*

Recognizing elliptical clauses *(page L145)*

Avoiding misplaced modifiers *(page L153)*

Avoiding clause fragments *(page L164)*

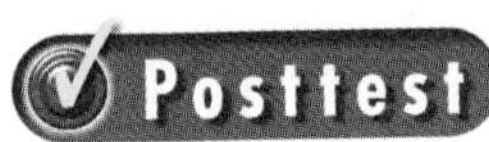

## Directions

**Write the letter of the term that correctly identifies each sentence or underlined part of a sentence.**

EXAMPLE **1.** *Stream of consciousness* refers to the free flow of thoughts through a character's mind.

**1** **A** simple sentence
**B** compound sentence
**C** complex sentence
**D** compound-complex sentence

ANSWER **1** **A**

**1.** James Joyce was a great master of stream of consciousness.

**2.** Joyce, however, owed much to a French novelist who had used the technique much earlier.

**3.** Edouard Dujardin experimented with the technique in 1887 when he published *The Laurels Are Cut Down*.

**4.** His novel is rarely read today, but it influenced many writers.

**5.** Dujardin defined his *interior monologue* as "an unspoken discourse without a hearer present. . . ."

**6.** Some critics distinguish interior monologue from stream of consciousness; they feel that there is a clear difference.

**7.** Although both include a character's thoughts and feelings, interior monologue indicates nothing in the way of a narrator.

**8.** Joyce used both in *Ulysses,* which is one of his finest works.

**9.** If you read Virginia Woolf's work, you will see many examples of stream-of-consciousness writing.

**10.** *To the Lighthouse* alternates between the thoughts of Mr. Ramsay, whose mind works rationally and dispassionately, and those of his wife, a creative, intuitive person.

1 **A** simple sentence
**B** compound sentence
**C** complex sentence
**D** compound-complex sentence

2 **A** simple sentence
**B** compound sentence
**C** complex sentence
**D** compound-complex sentence

3 **A** simple sentence
**B** compound sentence
**C** complex sentence
**D** compound-complex sentence

4 **A** simple sentence
**B** compound sentence
**C** complex sentence
**D** compound-complex sentence

5 **A** simple sentence
**B** compound sentence
**C** complex sentence
**D** compound-complex sentence

6 **A** independent clause
**B** adverb clause
**C** adjective clause
**D** noun clause

7 **A** independent clause
**B** adverb clause
**C** adjective clause
**D** noun clause

8 **A** independent clause
**B** adverb clause
**C** adjective clause
**D** noun clause

9 **A** independent clause
**B** adverb clause
**C** adjective clause
**D** noun clause

10 **A** independent clause
**B** adverb clause
**C** adjective clause
**D** noun clause

CHAPTER 5

# Using Verbs

### Directions

**Read the passage and choose the word or group of words that belongs in each underlined space. Write the letter of the correct answer.**

EXAMPLE **1.** Modern dance __(1)__ its origins in ancient sacred and ceremonial dance.

**1 A** will have
**B** have
**C** have been
**D** has

ANSWER **1 D**

In prehistoric times, dancing __(1)__ an early form of artistic expression. Along the shores of the Mediterranean Sea, decorative carvings found in Egyptian tombs __(2)__ that dances __(3)__ during funerals and parades as well as in religious rituals. Dancing always __(4)__ an important part in Greek celebrations. The Romans, too, __(5)__ ceremonial dancing to Italy from Greece, still use it in theatrical performances.

During the Middle Ages dance continued __(6)__ an important role in both courtly and village life. The peasants especially __(7)__ performing sword dances, Maypole dances, chain dances, and circle dances. Change, however, __(8)__ in the air. Professional performances __(9)__ as *balletti* originated in the Renaissance and within a few years __(10)__ over all of Europe.

1 **A** have been
**B** were
**C** was
**D** will be

2 **A** reveal
**B** revealed
**C** are revealing
**D** do reveal

3 **A** will have been performed
**B** have been performed
**C** perform
**D** were performed

4 **A** has played
**B** have played
**C** is played
**D** were played

5 **A** have brought
**B** having brought
**C** bringing
**D** had brought

6 **A** played
**B** to play
**C** did play
**D** having been played

7 **A** have enjoyed
**B** will enjoy
**C** enjoy
**D** enjoyed

8 **A** were
**B** is
**C** was
**D** has been

9 **A** known
**B** were known
**C** knew
**D** having been known

10 **A** sweep
**B** swept
**C** had swept
**D** sweeping

Pierre-Auguste Renoir. *Le Moulin de la Galette,* 1876.
Oil on canvas, 68 by 51 inches. Musée d'Orsay, Paris.

| | |
|---|---|
| **Describe** | What is happening in the foreground of the painting? What is happening in the middle ground and background? |
| **Analyze** | At what time of day does the action in the painting take place? How do you know? What do you think the woman bending over in the center foreground is doing? How do the people respond to her? What do you think the light splotches in the painting mean? |
| **Interpret** | If you wrote art reviews for a newspaper, what would you report about Renoir's technique? What headline might you write for a review? |
| **Judge** | Would you prefer to see a photo of this scene, read a review of the painting, or study the painting? Why? |

At the end of this chapter, you will use the artwork to stimulate ideas for writing.

# The Principal Parts of Verbs

This is the first chapter on usage. The next three chapters will show you how to use pronouns correctly, how to make a verb agree with its subject, and how to determine which form of a modifier to use. These chapters on using the grammar that you have learned are extremely important. Knowing grammar without knowing proper usage is like buying a new car and leaving it parked in the driveway because you never learned to drive!

This first chapter covers verbs. Why should you know what a verb is? If you know which word in a sentence is a verb, you can consciously substitute a specific, colorful verb for a dull, general one. Once you have chosen a particular verb, however, you must know which form of that verb to use. In this chapter you will learn to use the correct forms of verbs.

The four basic forms of a verb are called its principal parts. The six tenses of a verb are formed from these principal parts.

The **principal parts** of a verb are the present, the present participle, the past, and the past participle.

Notice that helping verbs are needed with the present participle and the past participle when they are used as the main verb of the sentence.

| | |
|---|---|
| PRESENT | I usually **eat** lunch after drama class. |
| PRESENT PARTICIPLE | I ***am*** **eating** lunch earlier this week. |
| PAST | I **ate** lunch an hour ago. |
| PAST PARTICIPLE | I ***have*** already **eaten** lunch. |

## Regular and Irregular Verbs

Verbs are sometimes classified in two categories: regular verbs and irregular verbs. How a verb forms its past and past participle will determine how it is classified.

A **regular verb** forms its past and past participle by adding *–ed* or *–d* to the present.

An **irregular verb** does not form its past and past participle by adding *–ed* or *–d* to the present.

## Regular Verbs

Most verbs are classified as regular verbs because they form their past and past participle in the same way—by adding *-ed* or *-d* to the present. Following are the four principal parts of the regular verbs *talk, use, equip,* and *commit*. Notice that the present participle is formed by adding *-ing* to the present form, and as the rule says, the past participle is formed by adding *-ed* or *-d* to the present form.

| REGULAR VERBS | | | |
|---|---|---|---|
| **Present** | **Present Participle** | **Past** | **Past Participle** |
| talk | (is) talking | talked | (have) talked |
| use | (is) using | used | (have) used |
| equip | (is) equipping | equipped | (have) equipped |
| commit | (is) committing | committed | (have) committed |

When endings such as *-ing* and *-ed* are added to some verbs like *use, equip,* and *commit,* the spelling changes. If you are unsure of the spelling of a verb form, look it up in the dictionary.

**CONNECT TO SPEAKING AND WRITING**

Some verb forms are easier to write than to say. Be careful not to drop the *–ed* or *–d* from such frequently used verb forms as *asked, helped, looked, seemed, supposed, talked, used,* and *walked* when you are speaking, especially in formal situations.

| | |
|---|---|
| INCORRECT | This was **suppose** to be an ancient pottery exhibit. |
| CORRECT | This was **supposed** to be an ancient pottery exhibit. |

## Practice Your Skills

Check Your Understanding

### *Determining the Principal Parts of Regular Verbs*

Art Topic

**Write each verb form. Beside it, label its principal part: *present, present participle, past,* or *past participle*. (Do not include any helping verbs.)**

1. I sketched too many portraits.
2. Thelma is running for Art Club president.
3. I have committed to summer art classes.
4. I like watercolors.
5. Trish is mixing tempera paints.
6. She has searched for the perfect still life.
7. Tonya and Kyle are arranging fruit in a stained glass bowl.
8. The fruit looks beautiful.
9. Everyone else painted fruit yesterday.
10. I have signed up for a class in stained glass.
11. Louis C. Tiffany greatly impacted the Art Nouveau movement with his stained glass.
12. He started his career as a landscape artist.
13. Tiffany experimented with color and texture.
14. He incorporated beautiful images of nature in glass.
15. Studio artists have sketched patterns for each product.

## Irregular Verbs

Some common verbs are classified as irregular because they form their past and past participle in different ways and do not add *–ed* or *–d* to the present. The irregular verbs have been divided into groups according to the way they form their past and past participle.

Remember that *is* is not part of the present participle and *have* is not part of the past participle. They have been added to the following lists of irregular verbs, however, to remind you that all present and past participles must have a form of one of these helping verbs when they are used as a verb in a sentence.

**Group 1** These irregular verbs have the same form for the present, the past, and the past participle.

| PRESENT | PRESENT PART. | PAST | PAST PART. |
|---|---|---|---|
| burst | (is) bursting | burst | (have) burst |
| cost | (is) costing | cost | (have) cost |
| hit | (is) hitting | hit | (have) hit |
| hurt | (is) hurting | hurt | (have) hurt |
| let | (is) letting | let | (have) let |
| put | (is) putting | put | (have) put |

**Group 2** These irregular verbs have the same form for the past and the past participle.

| PRESENT | PRESENT PART. | PAST | PAST PART. |
|---|---|---|---|
| bring | (is) bringing | brought | (have) brought |
| buy | (is) buying | bought | (have) bought |
| catch | (is) catching | caught | (have) caught |
| feel | (is) feeling | felt | (have) felt |
| find | (is) finding | found | (have) found |
| get | (is) getting | got | (have) got or gotten |
| hold | (is) holding | held | (have) held |
| keep | (is) keeping | kept | (have) kept |
| lead | (is) leading | led | (have) led |
| leave | (is) leaving | left | (have) left |
| lose | (is) losing | lost | (have) lost |
| make | (is) making | made | (have) made |
| say | (is) saying | said | (have) said |
| sell | (is) selling | sold | (have) sold |
| send | (is) sending | sent | (have) sent |
| teach | (is) teaching | taught | (have) taught |
| tell | (is) telling | told | (have) told |
| win | (is) winning | won | (have) won |

## Practice Your Skills

### Check Your Understanding
*Using the Correct Verb Form*

History Topic **Write the past or the past participle of each underlined verb.**

1. In 1836, the Mexican General Santa Anna lead his army to the Alamo.
2. He had bring with him an army of thousands.
3. He find fewer than 200 Texas soldiers at the mission.
4. These volunteer freedom fighters had put their lives at risk for their beliefs.
5. After 13 days of battle, every soldier in the Alamo had lose his life.
6. Despite the bloodshed, they had make history.
7. Santa Anna had win the battle but at great cost.
8. One of Santa Anna's colonials say they couldn't afford many more "victories" like the Alamo.
9. The next month Santa Anna was catch at the Battle of San Jacinto.
10. Santa Anna had tell everyone he was "the Napoleon of the West."

### Check Your Understanding
*Determining the Principal Parts of Irregular Verbs*

**Make four columns on your paper. Label them *Present, Present Participle, Past,* and *Past Participle*. Then write the four principal parts of the following verbs.**

11. buy
12. keep
13. let
14. put
15. hurt
16. tell
17. sell
18. get
19. teach
20. leave

Connect to the Writing Process: Editing

***Correcting Verb Forms***

**Rewrite the following paragraph, correcting the verb forms.** (You will correct 8 forms in all.)

Francis Scott Key, author of "The Star-Spangled Banner," hold a degree from St. John's College. He make his living as a lawyer. In 1814, he finded himself aboard a British ship within sight of the British attack on Fort McHenry in Baltimore. He had leaved Fort McHenry but could clearly see the bombs. Many bursted in the air above, and others hitted the fort. Key felt such strong emotions about the battle that he wrote "The Star-Spangled Banner." After the war, he get a job as United States District Attorney. In 1843, he contracted pleurisy, which costed him his life.

Connect to the Writing Process: Drafting

***Using Verb Forms in Sentences***

**Write sentences about a career you would like to have. Follow each direction.**

1. Use the past participle of *find,* and name your career.
2. Ask about it using the past participle of *make*.
3. Write a command using the present tense of *leave.*
4. Include a description using the past participle of *said*.
5. Write a command using the present tense of *lead*.
6. Use the past participle of *sent* in a sentence.
7. Exclaim using the present participle of *catch*.
8. Include the present tense of *put* in a command.
9. Use the past participle of *kept* in a sentence.
10. Use the present participle of *bring* in a sentence.

**Group 3** These irregular verbs form the past participle by adding *–n* to the past.

| PRESENT | PRESENT PART. | PAST | PAST PART. |
|---|---|---|---|
| break | (is) breaking | broke | (have) broken |
| choose | (is) choosing | chose | (have) chosen |
| freeze | (is) freezing | froze | (have) frozen |
| speak | (is) speaking | spoke | (have) spoken |
| steal | (is) stealing | stole | (have) stolen |

**Group 4** These irregular verbs form the past participle by adding *–n* to the present.

| PRESENT | PRESENT PART. | PAST | PAST PART. |
|---|---|---|---|
| blow | (is) blowing | blew | (have) blown |
| draw | (is) drawing | drew | (have) drawn |
| drive | (is) driving | drove | (have) driven |
| give | (is) giving | gave | (have) given |
| grow | (is) growing | grew | (have) grown |
| know | (is) knowing | knew | (have) known |
| see | (is) seeing | saw | (have) seen |
| take | (is) taking | took | (have) taken |
| throw | (is) throwing | threw | (have) thrown |

## Practice Your Skills

Check Your Understanding

### *Using the Correct Verb Form*

Contemporary Life **Write the past or the past participle of each underlined verb.**

**1.** Willis has <u>throw</u> three balls through the hoop.

**2.** Brian <u>steal</u> two bases during the sixth inning.

**3.** Every day at camp, we <u>take</u> polo lessons.

**4.** Last night we <u>see</u> the team's most exciting game ever.

**5.** Mom <u>drive</u> us home after the game.

6. Chris asked if we had choose a captain yet.
7. Last fall I break my arm playing softball.
8. My arm has grow stronger with the help of exercise.
9. Tori know how to play softball before she came to camp.
10. A strong, cold wind blow down the goals last night.
11. The canoes in the water nearly freeze in the ice storm.
12. I thought I had speak to you about the canoes.
13. The counselors had take the canoes to a boathouse.
14. Mia give her old tennis racket to her young camper.
15. Our team draw a poster for our counselor.

## Check Your Understanding
### *Determining the Correct Verb Form*

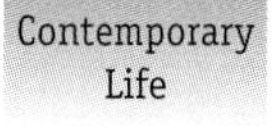


**Write the correct form of each underlined verb. If the verb is correct, write *C*.** Remember that all the action took place the previous summer.

16. I buy a bonsai tree at Bao's Bonsai Garden last summer.
17. I had see this quaint little nursery before.
18. I had take the opportunity and had speak to Bao.
19. I could not forget about owning a beautiful bonsai.
20. Monday, I get up early and make my way to Bao's store.
21. I choose a tiny, perfect tree.
22. Bao give me a tree-care guide.
23. She say most people have never grow a bonsai before.
24. She had draw pictures of how to trim the tree's roots.
25. Also, she had make a chart of pruning and watering schedules for the tree.
26. I know I would need fertilizer and other supplies.
27. I take a basket and then choose pruning shears and a wide, flat pot for the tree I had buy.
28. I feel satisfied with my new purchases.
29. I leave the store a happy customer.
30. I have faithfully take care of my miniature tree.

Connect to the Writing Process: Editing

### *Using Verb Forms*

**Rewrite the following paragraph, changing the present-tense verbs to the past tense and the past-tense verbs to the past participle.** (You will change 21 verb forms in all.)

June bursts into the room and makes an announcement. She says she had saw a kit for a window-sill herb garden. She had drove to the farmer's market and had sold some fresh vegetables she had grew in her large garden. Afterwards, she grows interested in the other booths. She takes a stroll down the aisles. She finds the herb kit and knows she wants it. It costs only a few dollars, and so she gives the seller her money. She puts her new purchase in the trunk and then finds her car keys in her large bag. She feels happy about the herb-garden project. She takes the shortcut across the pasture and drives quickly home.

June takes the kit into her garage. She breaks its seal. She found a calendar schedule for the garden in the directions.

**Group 5** These irregular verbs form the past and the past participle by changing a vowel.

| PRESENT | PRESENT PART. | PAST | PAST PART. |
|---|---|---|---|
| begin | (is) beginning | began | (have) begun |
| drink | (is) drinking | drank | (have) drunk |
| ring | (is) ringing | rang | (have) rung |
| shrink | (is) shrinking | shrank | (have) shrunk |
| sing | (is) singing | sang | (have) sung |
| sink | (is) sinking | sank | (have) sunk |
| swim | (is) swimming | swam | (have) swum |

**Group 6** These irregular verbs form the past and the past participle in other ways.

| PRESENT | PRESENT PART. | PAST | PAST PART. |
|---|---|---|---|
| come | (is) coming | came | (have) come |
| do | (is) doing | did | (have) done |
| eat | (is) eating | ate | (have) eaten |
| fall | (is) falling | fell | (have) fallen |
| go | (is) going | went | (have) gone |
| ride | (is) riding | rode | (have) ridden |
| run | (is) running | ran | (have) run |
| tear | (is) tearing | tore | (have) torn |
| wear | (is) wearing | wore | (have) worn |
| write | (is) writing | wrote | (have) written |

### Connect to Speaking and Writing

If you've been around young children much, you know they have difficulty using irregular verbs. They are apt to say proudly, "I **putted** my toys away" or to complain loudly, "She **drinked** my juice." You can help children learn the correct form by rephrasing their statements: "Good! You **put** your toys away," or "She **drank** your juice?"

## Practice Your Skills

Check Your Understanding

***Using the Correct Verb Form***

General Interest **Write the past or the past participle of each underlined verb.**

1. Thousands of people go to the rodeo.
2. Many come from far away.
3. They wear their best boots and a new hat.
4. Cowboys had begin practicing for the bull rides long ago.
5. These daring men and women had fall many times.

6. Some had even tear ligaments or muscles.
7. Nevertheless, they had come to the rodeo ready to ride.
8. In another show talented vocalists sing country songs.
9. I ate and drink until I thought my waistband shrink.
10. I enjoyed what Rachel do.
11. She ride her pony and ring the starting bell for the race.
12. She had write to the rodeo organizers ahead of time.
13. Also, she had go to fill out an application.
14. She got the job and begin work on the first rodeo day.
15. I had accidentally sink my trailer in the mud and could not bring my pony.

Check Your Understanding

### *Supplying the Correct Verb Form*

Contemporary Life

**Complete each pair of sentences by supplying the past or the past participle of the verb in parentheses at the beginning of the sentence.**

16. (begin) The school play ___ 15 minutes ago. It should have ___ a half hour ago.
17. (do) Have you ___ your homework? I ___ mine at school.
18. (run) Matthew ___ for Student Council president last year. He should have ___ again this year.
19. (drink) We ___ some ice water after cheerleading practice. We should never have ___ it fast.
20. (go) Have you ___ to a pep rally yet? Yes, I ___ to one Friday.
21. (write) I ___ my essay last night. Have you ___ yours?
22. (swim) Kelly ___ the fastest today. I have ___ faster than her many times.
23. (sing) Have you ever ___ in school choir before? Once I ___ a solo in our chorus concert.
24. (eat) I just ___ lunch in the cafeteria. Have you ___ yet?
25. (ride) The basketball team ___ to the last game in the new bus. They had ___ in rusty old buses all season.

Connect to the Writing Process: Editing

*Correcting Verb Forms*

**Rewrite the following paragraphs, using past and past participle verb forms.** (You will change 23 verb forms in all.)

Brandy comes to my school last month. Before, she had went to another school. I speak to her before homeroom because I know what it's like to be new. I find Brandy knows sign language. She teaches me some before class. I see her again at lunch and get up from my seat. She sees me and comes over. She had already ate her lunch, but she drinks a soda while I eat. We write down ideas for a sign language club. By the end of lunch period, we had make much progress.

Later we send a copy of our plans to the class president. He chooses to support our idea. He speaks to the student council, and they draw up a plan for the club. Brandy and I go to several planning sessions. We also begin telling other students about the sign language club. The club has became my favorite school activity.

## Communicate Your Ideas

### APPLY TO WRITING

**Persuasive Letter:** ***Verb Forms***

A new student is transferring to your homeroom, and you want to convince him or her to join your favorite school activity. Using past and past participle verb forms, write a letter to the new student, describing what your group has done this year. Try to convince him or her to join.

## Six Problem Verbs

Some verbs present problems, not because they are regular or irregular, but because their meanings are easily confused. Always make sure, therefore, that you have chosen the verb that correctly expresses what you want to say or write.

### *lie* and *lay*

*Lie* means "to rest or recline." *Lie* is never followed by a direct object. *Lay* means "to put or set (something) down." *Lay* is usually followed by a direct object.

*You can learn more about direct objects on pages L72–L77.*

| PRESENT | PRESENT PART. | PAST | PAST PART. |
|---|---|---|---|
| lie | (is) lying | lay | (have) lain |
| lay | (is) laying | laid | (have) laid |

LIE Her party dresses **lie** on the floor of the guest bedroom.

They are **lying** in a heap now.

They **lay** there last weekend, too.

They **have lain** in the guest bedroom for weeks.

LAY **Lay** the servers' aprons on the table.
(You lay what? *Aprons* is the direct object.)
Harry **is laying** the aprons on the table.
Shoshana **laid** the aprons on the table last night.
Usually **I have laid** the aprons on the table.

**CONNECT TO SPEAKING AND WRITING**

When ***lie*** means "to tell a falsehood," the principal parts are *lie, is lying, lied,* and *(have) lied.* Be sure to include enough information to make the meaning clear because some of the principal parts are the same as those for *to lie,* meaning "to rest or recline."

CONFUSING Jesse never ***lies*** about.
CORRECT Jesse never ***lies*** about his chores. 

***rise* and *raise*** *Rise* means "to move upward" or "to get up." *Rise* is never followed by a direct object. *Raise* means "to lift (something) up," "to increase," or "to grow something." *Raise* is usually followed by a direct object.

| PRESENT | PRESENT PART. | PAST | PAST PART. |
|---|---|---|---|
| rise | (is) rising | rose | (have) risen |
| raise | (is) raising | raised | (have) raised |

RISE **Rise** early for the breakfast shift.
Marianne **is rising** early for her new job.
Marianne **rose** at sunrise yesterday.
She **has risen** early for several weeks.

RAISE **Raise** the cattle for the restaurant supplier.
(You raise what? *Cattle* is the direct object.)
He **is raising** the cattle for beef.
He **raised** cattle for the beef suppliers.
He **has raised** cattle for two decades.

***sit* and *set*** *Sit* means "to rest in an upright position." *Sit* is never followed by a direct object. *Set* means "to put or place (something)." *Set* is usually followed by a direct object.

| PRESENT | PRESENT PART. | PAST | PAST PART. |
|---|---|---|---|
| sit | (is) sitting | sat | (have) sat |
| set | (is) setting | set | (have) set |

SIT **Sit** near me at the awards banquet.
She **is sitting** at the head table.
She **sat** there near Tim.
She **has** never **sat** near Tim before tonight.

SET **Set** the awards on the podium.
(You set what? *Awards* is the direct object.)
He **is setting** the awards on the podium.
He **set** the awards on the podium this morning.
He **has set** the awards on the podium every year.

*You can learn more about other confusing verbs on pages L352–L387.*

## Practice Your Skills

### Check Your Understanding
### *Using the Correct Verb Form*

Contemporary Life

**Write the correct verb form from the choices provided.**

1. (lie/lay) I will ▢ on the sofa for a rest before the party.
2. (sitting/setting) Why are you ▢ on the sofa?
3. (sat/set) Charlie has ▢ the record for hosting the most parties in a summer.
4. (rise/raise) Tell Jane she must ▢ funds to buy the cake.
5. (lain/laid) You have ▢ on that sofa for too long.
6. (sit/set) Perry, will you ▢ the fine china on the table?
7. (lying/laying) Shelly is ▢ a napkin across her lap.
8. (rising/raising) I am ▢ to the challenge of entertaining.
9. (sat/set) That shy girl has ▢ in the corner all evening.
10. (rise/raise) If you want to play charades, ▢ your hand.

### Connect to the Writing Process: Editing
### *Correcting Verb Form*

Contemporary Life

**Write each sentence, correcting the verb form. If the verb form is correct, write *C*.**

11. Sherm's father has rose enough money for a restaurant.
12. At the opening gala, I will set next to Keisha.
13. She is laying her clothes out for the gala, now.
14. Keisha's mother has sat a cool glass of water on the side table for me.
15. Prices at restaurants are rising.
16. I lie my nice jacket over the chair.
17. The waiter is sitting the dessert tray on the table.
18. Let's raise and go get dessert.
19. You shouldn't leave your purse laying there.
20. Don't forget where we are sitting.

Communicate Your Ideas

## APPLY TO WRITING

### News Article: *Problem Verbs*

You are a journalist who covers the social events in a small town. Write a news article that describes the latest social news, whether it be a wedding, fund raiser, park dedication, restaurant opening, or some other community event. Use each of the following problem verbs at least once: *lie, lay, rise, raise, sit, set.*

Mixed Practice

Sports Topic

**Write the past or the past participle of each verb in parentheses.**

1. For over seven decades, the Harlem Globetrotters have (bring) an unusual dimension to basketball.
2. In 1926, the Globetrotters (begin) as a serious team.
3. They (play) some of their first games in the Savoy Ballroom in Chicago.
4. When the dance hall (fall) on hard times, the team (go) on the road.
5. Since that time the Globetrotters have never (leave) the touring circuit.
6. Abe Saperstein, who (form) the first team, always (choose) the best players he could find.
7. As a result, his team eventually (get) so good that no one (want) to play them.
8. That's when Saperstein (make) an important decision.
9. He (break) from tradition and (add) comedy routines.
10. Ever since, the Globetrotters have (be) as famous for their humor as for their basketball skills.

# Verb Tense

Knowing the four principal parts of a verb, you can easily form the six tenses: the present, past, future, present perfect, past perfect, and future perfect.

The time expressed by a verb is called the **tense** of a verb.

In the following examples, the six tenses of *drive* are used to express action at different times.

| | |
|---|---|
| PRESENT | Bart **drives** Tad to school. |
| PAST | Bart **drove** Tad to school yesterday. |
| FUTURE | Bart **will drive** Tad to school tomorrow. |
| PRESENT PERFECT | Bart **has driven** Tad to school all month. |
| PAST PERFECT | Bart **had** never **driven** Tad to school before February. |
| FUTURE PERFECT | By May, Bart **will have driven** Tad to school for four months. |

## Uses of the Tenses

The six basic tenses—three simple tenses and three perfect tenses—and their various forms have particular uses. Clearly communicating your ideas will sometimes depend upon knowing the distinctions among these tenses. As you review the various uses, remember that all of the tenses are formed from the four principal parts of a verb and the helping verbs *have, has, had, will,* and *shall*.

**Present tense** is the first of the three simple tenses. It is used mainly to express (1) an action that is going on now, (2) an action that happens regularly, or (3) an action that is usually constant or the same. To form the present tense, use the present form (the first principal part of the verb) or add *–s* or *–es* to the present form.

| | |
|---|---|
| PRESENT TENSE | **Look** at this scuba suit. (current action) |
| | I **dig** for treasure each weekend. (regular action) |
| | Geology class **interests** me. (constant action) |

Occasionally you will also use the present tense in two other ways. Use the **historical present tense** when you want to relate a past action as if it were happening in the present. Also, when you write about literature, you can use the present tense.

| | |
|---|---|
| HISTORY | Christopher Columbus **encourages** his sailors daily. |
| LITERATURE | In *Beowulf*, the poet **tells** of Grendel's underwater lair. |

**Past tense** is used to express an action that already took place or was completed in the past. To form the past tense of a regular verb, add *–ed* or *–d* to the present form. To form the past of an irregular verb, check a dictionary for the past form or look for it on pages L183–L190.

| | |
|---|---|
| PAST TENSE | I **organized** the artifacts last week.<br>I **wrote** about my findings. |

**Future tense** is used to express an action that will take place in the future. To form the future tense, use the helping verb *shall* or *will* with the present form. In formal English, *shall* is used with *I* and *we*, and *will* is used with *you, he, she, it,* or *they*. In informal speech, however, *shall* and *will* are used interchangeably with *I* and *we*—except *shall* is still always used with *I* and *we* for questions.

| | |
|---|---|
| FUTURE TENSE | I **shall organize** the artifacts tomorrow.<br>Leonore **will write** about the shipwreck. |

*You can learn more about* shall *and* will *on page L378.*

Another way to express a future action is to use a present-tense verb with an adverb or group of words that indicate a future time.

| | |
|---|---|
| FUTURE ACTION | Leonore **presents** her report to the committee tomorrow. |

**Present perfect tense** is the first of three perfect tenses. It has two uses: (1) to express an action that was completed at some indefinite time in the past and (2) to express an action that started in the past and is still going on. To form the present perfect tense, add *has* or *have* to the past participle.

| | |
|---|---|
| PRESENT PERFECT TENSE | I **have organized** several boxes of artifacts. |
| | (action completed over an indefinite time) |
| | She **has written** the reports for more than five years. |
| | (action that is still going on) |

**Past perfect tense** expresses an action that took place before some other action. To form the past perfect tense, add *had* to the past participle.

| | |
|---|---|
| PAST PERFECT TENSE | I **had organized** the artifacts before I read the instructions. |
| | Leonore **had written** the report by the time I arrived. |

**Future perfect tense** expresses an action that will take place before another future action or time. To form the future perfect tense, add *shall have* or *will have* to the past participle.

| | |
|---|---|
| FUTURE PERFECT TENSE | **I shall have organized** fifty artifacts by tonight. |
| | By next semester, Leonore **will have written** six reports. |

## Verb Conjugation

A **conjugation** lists all the singular and plural forms of a verb in its various tenses. A conjugation of the irregular verb *eat* follows.

**CONJUGATION OF *EAT***

**FOUR PRINCIPAL PARTS:** eat, eating, ate, eaten

**SIMPLE TENSES**

**Present**

| SINGULAR | PLURAL |
|---|---|
| I eat | we eat |
| you eat | you eat |
| he, she, it eats | they eat |

**Past**

| SINGULAR | PLURAL |
|---|---|
| I ate | we ate |
| you ate | you ate |
| he, she, it ate | they ate |

**Future**

| SINGULAR | PLURAL |
|---|---|
| I shall/will eat | we shall/will eat |
| you will eat | you will eat |
| he, she, it will eat | they will eat |

**PERFECT TENSES**

**Present Perfect**

| SINGULAR | PLURAL |
|---|---|
| I have eaten | we have eaten |
| you have eaten | you have eaten |
| he, she, it has eaten | they have eaten |

**Past Perfect**

| SINGULAR | PLURAL |
|---|---|
| I had eaten | we had eaten |
| you had eaten | you had eaten |
| he, she, it had eaten | they had eaten |

**Future Perfect**

| **Singular** | **Plural** |
| --- | --- |
| I shall/will have eaten | we shall/will have eaten |
| you will have eaten | you will have eaten |
| he, she, it will have eaten | they will have eaten |

*The present participle is used to conjugate only the progressive forms of a verb. You can learn more about the progressive forms of verbs on pages L212–L213.*

Since the principal parts of the verb *be* are highly irregular, the conjugation of that verb is very different from other irregular verbs.

**CONJUGATION OF *BE***

**Four Principal Parts:** am, being, was, been

**Simple Tenses**

**Present**

| **Singular** | **Plural** |
| --- | --- |
| I am | we are |
| you are | you are |
| he, she, it is | they are |

**Past**

| **Singular** | **Plural** |
| --- | --- |
| I was | we were |
| you were | you were |
| he, she, it was | they were |

**Future**

| **Singular** | **Plural** |
| --- | --- |
| I shall/will be | we shall/will be |
| you will be | you will be |
| he, she, it will be | they will be |

**Perfect Tenses**

**Present Perfect**

| **Singular** | **Plural** |
| --- | --- |
| I have been | we have been |
| you have been | you have been |
| he, she, it has been | they have been |

| Past Perfect | |
|---|---|
| **SINGULAR** | **PLURAL** |
| I had been | we had been |
| you had been | you had been |
| he, she, it had been | they had been |

| Future Perfect | |
|---|---|
| **SINGULAR** | **PLURAL** |
| I shall/will have been | we shall/will have been |
| you will have been | you will have been |
| he, she, it will have been | they will have been |

### CONNECT TO SPEAKING AND WRITING

While most people develop an "ear" for proper verb conjugation, people in some careers use their knowledge of verb conjugation on a daily basis. These careers include language teacher, spokesperson, linguist, journalist, speech writer, translator, editor, copy editor, fiction writer, and proofreader. You can probably think of other careers as well.

## PRACTICE YOUR SKILLS

Check Your Understanding

***Identifying Verb Tenses***

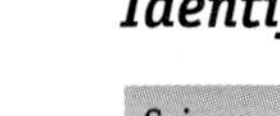


**Write the tense of each underlined verb.**

1. An underwater archaeologist studies shipwrecks and artifacts from watery graves.
2. Archaeologists have found underwater treasures such as jewels, precious metals, and even medical instruments.
3. Radioactive material in the Garigiano River made underwater searches there dangerous.
4. Many students of archaeology will have completed an archaeological dig by graduation.
5. Students will learn about certain underwater worms.

6. These worms eat the wooden parts of a shipwreck.
7. Bodies of water with less salt have provided wooden artifacts in the best condition.
8. Riverbeds and lake bottoms in Europe hold much of the world's riches.
9. After World War II, divers found ammunition beneath old battle sites.
10. The United States government had passed a law about archaeological findings.
11. Underwater archaeologists cannot steal or destroy their discoveries.
12. Officials will monitor the dive teams and their projects.
13. Many fields of science incorporate underwater archaeology.
14. Biologists, geologists, and chemists have studied underwater excavations.
15. Students everywhere will have learned valuable information about past civilizations from these digs.

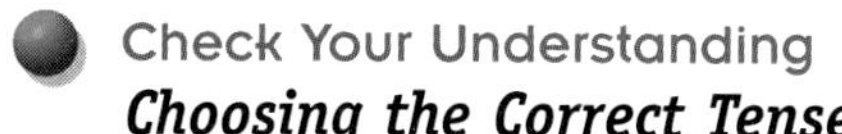

### Check Your Understanding
### *Choosing the Correct Tense*

General Interest

**Write the correct form of the verb in parentheses. Beside it, identify its tense using the following abbreviations:**

| | |
|---|---|
| present = *pres.* | present perfect = *pres. p.* |
| past = *past* | past perfect = *past p.* |
| future = *fut.* | future perfect = *fut. p.* |

16. In a few years, I (shall train/have trained) as a forensic pathologist in the state medical examiner's office.
17. By then I (will have achieved/achieved) the same career goals as my role model, Aunt Maya.
18. In college Maya (studies/studied) forensic anthropology.
19. This science (applied/applies) physical anthropology to the legal process.
20. She (has become/became) an expert in her field over the past five years.

**21.** A forensic pathologist (helped/helps) solve murders.

**22.** Now Maya (took/has taken) a job as forensic pathologist.

**23.** I often (ask/had asked) her questions about her job.

**24.** She once (determines/determined) the age and gender of a victim by studying the bones.

**25.** I (have asked/ask) Maya for a letter of recommendation for my college application.

Connect to the Writing Process: Drafting

***Writing Answers to Questions***

**Write an answer to each question. Then underline the verb you used and identify its tense.**

**26.** Did Mr. Lewis finish college last year?

**27.** Will you choose a career in education?

**28.** Why did Bettina attend the study-skills workshop?

**29.** Will this topic work for a college admissions essay?

**30.** Have you done your student teaching yet?

**31.** Where will you take the teacher-certification test?

**32.** Which friend will be your college roommate?

**33.** Did I pass the English test?

**34.** Will you be my lab partner?

**35.** When had you written that history report?

## Communicate Your Ideas

### APPLY TO WRITING

**Thank-You Note: *Verb Tenses***

Write a thank-you note to a teacher or coach who has made an impact on you. If the person taught you in a previous year, write in past tense. If she or he currently teaches you, write in present tense. Include a description of a time in the past when the teacher was especially helpful. Also include a description of how the knowledge you gained will help you in the future. After you complete your note, check that you used the correct verb tenses.

 Mixed Practice

Social Studies

**Write each verb and label its tense using the following abbreviations:**

| | |
|---|---|
| present = *pres.* | present perfect = *pres. p.* |
| past = *past* | past perfect = *past p.* |
| future = *fut.* | future perfect = *fut. p.* |

**1.** After this week I will have learned about several cultural holidays.

**2.** I look forward to next May.

**3.** I had heard about Cinco de Mayo before this week.

**4.** Some friends excitedly described this Mexican holiday.

**5.** Now I have learned more information about the Cinco de Mayo celebration.

**6.** Spanish speakers will translate the name as Fifth of May.

**7.** On this date in 1862, a Mexican army defeated a French army at the Battle of Puebla.

**8.** The French eventually occupied Mexico after all.

**9.** Nevertheless, this battle has become a symbol of Mexican unity and pride.

**10.** By the early 1800s, Mexico had faced another enemy.

**11.** Mexico won its independence from Spain in 1810.

**12.** This holiday is *Diez y Seis de Septiembre* (Sixteenth of September).

**13.** Mexican-American communities throughout the United States have celebrated both of these holidays for many years.

**14.** The festivities include parades, *mariachi* music, dancing, and feasting.

**15.** By year's end, my friends and I shall have enjoyed all of these activities.

## Problems Using Tenses

Knowing the tenses of verbs and their uses will eliminate most of the verb errors you may have been making. There are, however, a few special problems you should keep in mind when you edit your writing.

**The tense of the verbs you use depends on the meaning you want to express.**

### Past Tenses

If you want to express two past events that happened at the same time, use the past tense for both. Sometimes, however, you will want to tell about an action that happened before another action in the past. In such a situation, use the past perfect to express the action that happened first.

| | |
|---|---|
| PAST/PAST | When the author **arrived** (past), we **cheered** (past). |
| | (Both events happened at the same time.) |
| PAST/ PAST PERFECT | I **wrote** (past) the play after I **had gone** (past perfect) to Broadway. |
| | (I went to Broadway before I wrote the play.) |

#### Connect to Speaking and Writing

A common error in speaking is to use the words *would have* in a clause starting with *if* when that clause expresses the earlier of two past actions. You should instead use the past perfect tense to express the earlier action.

| | |
|---|---|
| INCORRECT | If John **would have studied**, he might have passed the literature test. |
| CORRECT | If John **had studied**, he might have passed the literature test. |
| | (The past perfect shows that studying would have come before passing the test.)  |

## Present and Past Tenses

To express an exact meaning, occasionally you will have to use a combination of present and past tense verbs.

PRESENT/PAST — Kelly **knows** (present) that I **borrowed** (past) her book yesterday.
(*Knows* is in the present tense because it describes action that is happening now, but *borrowed* is in the past tense because it happened at a definite time in the past.)

PAST/PRESENT PERFECT — Ever since I **discovered** (past) *Wuthering Heights*, I **have read** (present perfect) that book every night.
(*Discovered* is in the past tense because it occurred at a definite time in the past, but *have read* is in the present perfect because it started in the past and is still going on.)

Check Your Understanding
***Identifying Combinations of Tenses***

Literature Topic **Write the tense of each underlined verb.** Be prepared to explain why the tense is correct.

present = *pres.* present perfect = *pres. p.*
past = *past* past perfect = *past p.*
future = *fut.* future perfect = *fut. p.*

**1.** I went to class and I received a copy of *Canterbury Tales.*
**2.** I smiled because I had heard of the tales before.
**3.** I hope we read "The Pardoner's Tale."
**4.** My classmates discovered that Geoffrey Chaucer had written the tales in verse form.
**5.** Chaucer began *Canterbury Tales* after he had penned *Troilus and Criseide*.

## Past Participles

Like verbs, participles have present and past tenses to express specific time.

| PARTICIPLES OF *EAT* | |
|---|---|
| **PRESENT PARTICIPLE** | eating |
| **PAST PARTICIPLE** | eaten |

Use *having* with a past participle in a participial phrase to show that one action was completed before another one.

INCORRECT **Applying** for the job, she waited for the manager's phone call.
(The use of *applying*, the present participle, implies illogically that she was still applying while she waited for the phone call.)

CORRECT **Having applied** for the job, she waited for the manager's phone call.
(The use of *having* with the past participle *applied* shows that she applied for the job *before* she waited for the phone call.)

*You can learn more about participial phrases on pages L108–L111.*

## Present and Perfect Infinitives

Like participles, infinitives also have different forms.

| INFINITIVES OF *EAT* | |
|---|---|
| **PRESENT INFINITIVE** | to eat |
| **PERFECT INFINITIVE** | to have eaten |

To express an action that takes place *after* another action, use the present infinitive, but to express an action that takes place *before* another action, use the perfect infinitive.

| | |
|---|---|
| PRESENT INFINITIVE | For a year I waited **to apply** for a job on the school newspaper. |
| | (The applying came *after* the waiting.) |
| PERFECT INFINITIVE | I feel very happy **to have applied** for a job in journalism. |
| | (The applying came *before* the feeling of happiness.) |

*You can learn more about infinitives on pages L115–L119.*

## PRACTICE YOUR SKILLS

Check Your Understanding

***Identifying Correct Tenses of Participles and Infinitives***

Art Topic **If the tense of the underlined participle or infinitive is incorrect, write *I*. If the sentence is correct, write *C*.**

**1.** I feel happy to view Leonardo Da Vinci's *Mona Lisa*.

**2.** He feels confident to write to the Duke of Milan.

**3.** Having explained his credentials as designer, inventor, and artist, he was hired.

**4.** For months he strove to have honored the Duke's father with the consignment of a great sculpture.

**5.** Having drawn the sculpture, Da Vinci sought materials.

**6.** Da Vinci is pleased to design a colossal horse.

**7.** Creating the design, he named it *Il Cavallo,* meaning "The Horse" in Italian.

**8.** Designing the statue, Da Vinci soon built a clay model.

**9.** Having attacked Milan, French forces threatened the safety of everyone.

**10.** French archers are jubilant to have destroyed the clay model with arrows.

**11.** Sacrificing the bronze for the war, the dream ended.

**12.** The rest of his life, da Vinci waited rebuilding it.

**13.** He feels sad to have missed his opportunity.

**14.** Having read about *Il Cavallo*, Charles Dent pursued Da Vinci's dream.

**15.** Having founded an organization, he raised funds.

**16.** The organization feels confident to hire the artist, Nina Akamu.

**17.** Having completed the design, Akamu cast the statue.

**18.** Having required 15 tons of bronze, it stood 24 feet tall.

**19.** The people of Milan are happy to have received *Il Cavallo*.

**20.** Shipping the horse 500 years late, Da Vinci's dream and Charles Dent's dream came true.

Connect to the Writing Process: Editing

### *Correcting the Tenses of Participles and Infinitives*

**21.–30. Rewrite the incorrect sentences in the preceding exercise, correcting the tenses of the participles and infinitives.**

Connect to the Writing Process: Editing

### *Correcting Tenses*

Each sentence in the paragraphs contains an improper shift in tense. Write each sentence, using the correct tense. (You will correct tenses 9 times in all.)

Yesterday I went to an art exhibit, and I have enjoyed it very much. Having heard of the Art Guys, I want to see some of their work. I have never seen so many unusual sculptures and displays before, and I will want to tell you about one of them.

The artists had designed one room to be entertaining people. When I walked into the room, I hear jets flying overhead. As I looked up, I am noticing that they had hung televisions pointing straight down from the ceiling. Each television was playing a video of jets that had been flying in the sky.

I am glad to go to the exhibit. I intended to return soon.

## Communicate Your Ideas

### APPLY TO WRITING

**Description:** ***Verb Tenses***

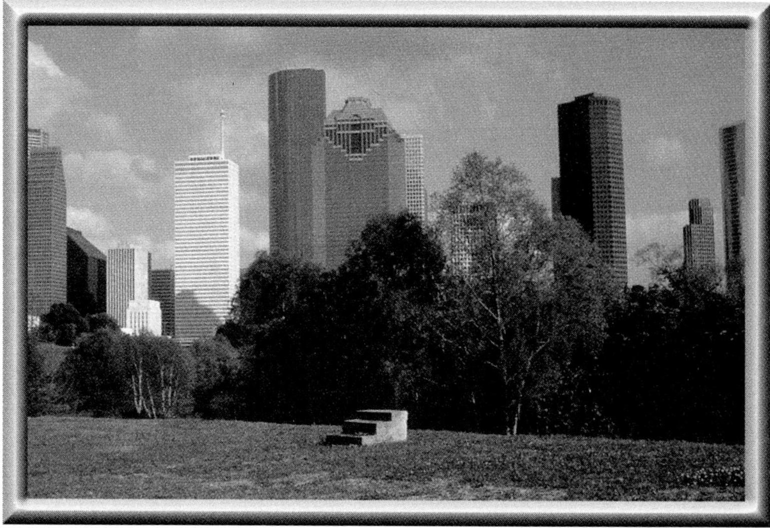

The Art Guys. *Phantom Neighborhood,* 1990.
Concrete steps, varying dimensions.

You are in Buffalo Bayou Park in Houston, Texas, and you see the mysterious steps shown in this photo. A passing tourist asks you why they are there. Write an explanation for this tourist. Describe the past, present, and future purpose of the steps. Try to incorporate all the verb tenses you have been studying. Then edit your work for improper shifts in tense.

## Progressive and Emphatic Verb Forms

In addition to the six basic tenses, every verb has six progressive forms and an emphatic form for the present and past tenses.

### Progressive Forms

The **progressive forms** are used to express continuing or ongoing action. To write the progressive forms, add a present or perfect tense of the verb *be* to the present participle. Notice in the following examples that all of the progressive forms end in *–ing*.

| | |
|---|---|
| Present Progressive | I am eating. |
| Past Progressive | I was eating. |
| Future Progressive | I will (shall) be eating. |
| Present Perfect Progressive | I have been eating. |
| Past Perfect Progressive | I had been eating. |
| Future Perfect Progressive | I will (shall) have been eating. |

The **present progressive** form shows an ongoing action that is taking place now.

I **am playing** volleyball now.

Occasionally the present progressive can also show action in the future when the sentence contains an adverb or a phrase that indicates the future—such as *tomorrow* or *next month*.

I **am playing** volleyball after school tomorrow.

The **past progressive** form shows an ongoing action that took place in the past.

I **was playing** volleyball when the rain began.

The **future progressive** form shows an ongoing action that will take place in the future.

I **will be playing** volleyball when you have your party.

The **present perfect progressive** form shows an ongoing action that is continuing in the present.

> I **have been playing** volleyball for the past two and a half years.

The **past perfect progressive** form shows an ongoing action in the past that was interrupted by another past action.

> I **had been playing** volleyball when Coach Williams asked me to play basketball instead.

The **future perfect progressive** form shows a future ongoing action that will have taken place by a stated future time.

> By next summer I **will have been playing** volleyball for over three years.

## Emphatic Forms

The **emphatic forms** of the present and past tenses of verbs are mainly used to show emphasis or force. To write the present emphatic, add *do* or *does* to the present tense of a verb. To write the past emphatic, add *did* to the present tense.

| | |
|---|---|
| PRESENT | I **eat** lunch every day at twelve o'clock. |
| PRESENT EMPHATIC | I **do eat** lunch every day at twelve o'clock. |
| PAST | I **ate** lunch yesterday. |
| PAST EMPHATIC | I **did eat** lunch yesterday. |

The emphatic forms are also used in some questions and negative statements.

| | |
|---|---|
| QUESTIONS | **Do** you **eat** lunch every day? |
| NEGATIVE STATEMENT | I **did** not **eat** lunch Monday. |

### Connect to Writer's Craft

Do you remember *Green Eggs and Ham* by Dr. Seuss? You probably never realized that one of the things that makes the story fun to listen to is the emphatic verb forms.

> **Do** you **like** green eggs and ham?
> I **do** not **like** them, Sam-I-am. I **do** not **like** green eggs and ham.
>
> I **do** not **like** them in a house. I **do** not **like** them with a mouse. I **do** not **like** them here or there. I **do** not **like** them anywhere.
>
> –*Dr. Seuss,* Green Eggs and Ham 

## Practice Your Skills

### Check Your Understanding

***Identifying Progressive and Emphatic Forms***

Contemporary Life

**Write the progressive or emphatic form in each sentence. Beside it write *P* for *progressive* or *E* for *emphatic.***

1. Did you go to the swim meet?
2. I will be buying season tickets tomorrow.
3. I have been saving my money all month.
4. Coach Chang didn't know about the new uniforms.
5. He will have been looking for the old uniforms for two hours.
6. He does look frantic.
7. I am going to the football game.
8. I shall be sitting at the fifty yard line.
9. I had been running track until I sprained my ankle.
10. I didn't have a sports bandage for my ankle.
11. Stephanie is jogging tomorrow afternoon.
12. She does love that activity.

13. She will have been jogging for one hour by dark.

14. Jon has been timing her laps.

15. Marcos will be lifting weights two days a week.

16. I did lift weights this morning.

17. Sarah is meeting Cleo at the gym this afternoon.

18. Do you like to lift weights?

19. Sarah was stretching when the music started.

20. By July Pablo will have been biking for one year.

21. He does ride five miles every day.

22. Conrad will be training with Pablo next month.

23. They have been planning a bike tour.

24. Next summer they will have graduated from college.

25. They will be touring the United States afterward.

Connect to the Writing Process: Drafting

*Using Emphatic Verbs*

**26.–30. Brainstorm for five ideas that you emphatically agree or disagree with. Write an emphatic statement expressing each of these ideas. Underline the emphatic form of the verb in each statement.**

## Communicate Your Ideas

### APPLY TO WRITING

**Opinion Essay:** ***Progressive and Emphatic Forms***

Choose one of the emphatic statements you wrote in the above exercise. Write an opinion piece to share with your classmates. State your opinion on the topic, and describe an event that helped you develop this opinion. Use progressive and emphatic verb forms to express your ideas. Be prepared to identify the two verb forms.

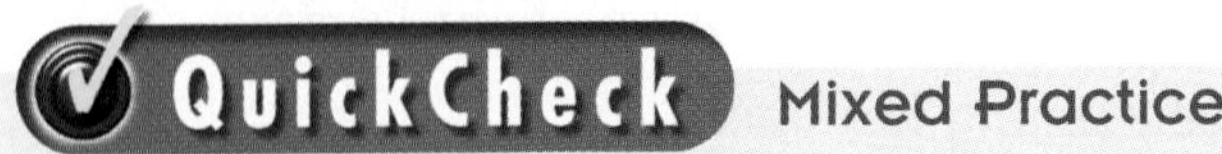


Mixed Practice

General Interest **Write the tense of each underlined verb.**

1. In health class we are learning about vegetarian diets.
2. I have always wanted to learn about this topic.
3. In college Ms. Summers had taken a nutrition class.
4. Afterward she designed a lesson plan on vegetarian diets.
5. The class was taking careful notes.
6. We will be planning a vegetarian banquet for our class on Friday.
7. *Vegans*, or strict vegetarians, do not consume meat or animal products of any kind.
8. By the end of the school year, Ms. Summers will have been following a vegan diet for ten years.
9. I am not feeling comfortable with the vegan diet.
10. *Lactovegetarians* always have eaten milk, cheese, and other dairy products.
11. Lactovegetarians don't eat meats, poultry, or eggs.
12. My friend Kandie resolved to be a lactovegetarian.
13. By the end of class, she had changed her mind.
14. An *ovolactovegetarian* will eat eggs and dairy products.
15. An ovolactovegetarian does not eat meats or poultry.
16. Having learned about vegetarian diets, I plan to be a part-time vegetarian.
17. I have been analyzing my diet.
18. I felt I had been consuming too much red meat.
19. I will design my meals around fruits and vegetables.
20. In addition to these fruits and vegetables, I am planning to eat meat once or twice a week.

# Active and Passive Voice

All verbs have tense, but some action verbs also have voice. Transitive verbs can be in the active voice or the passive voice.

The **active voice** indicates that the subject is performing the action.

The **passive voice** indicates that the action of the verb is being performed upon the subject.

Notice in the following examples that the verb in the active voice has a direct object, making it a transitive verb. However, the verb in the passive voice does not have a direct object.

| | d.o. |
|---|---|
| ACTIVE VOICE | Horace **found** a silver dollar. |
| PASSIVE VOICE | A silver dollar **was found** by Horace. |
| | (no direct object) |
| | d.o. |
| ACTIVE VOICE | Marie **sent** the money by courier. |
| PASSIVE VOICE | The money **was sent** by courier. |
| | (no direct object) |

*You can learn about transitive verbs on pages L16–L17.*

Changing a verb from the active voice to the passive voice, you automatically turn the direct object into the subject. In the previous example, *money* was the direct object when the verb was active, but it became the subject when the verb became passive. Notice also that verbs in the passive voice consist of some form of the verb *be* plus a past participle—such as *was found* and *was sent*.

In addition to a direct object, some transitive verbs can also have an indirect object. When such a verb and its objects are changed to the passive voice, either of the two objects can become the subject of the sentence. The other object remains an object and is called a **retained object.**

| | |
|---|---|
| Active Voice | The judges gave each **winner** (i.o.) fifty **dollars** (d.o.). |
| Passive Voice | Each winner was given fifty **dollars** (r.o.) by the judges. |
| Passive Voice | Fifty dollars was given each **winner** (r.o.) by the judges. |

## Practice Your Skills

Check Your Understanding

### *Identifying Active and Passive Voice*

General Interest **Write the verb in each sentence. Then label each one *A* for *active* or *P* for *passive*.**

1. The early American colonists used currencies from several different countries.
2. America once issued a five-cent bill.
3. The first Continental coin was designed by Benjamin Franklin.
4. The dies for that coin were engraved by Abel Buell.
5. Tobacco was used as money in Virginia and Maryland.
6. Martha Washington may have donated several of her silver forks and spoons for the minting of a series of half dimes.
7. The buffalo nickel was designed by James Earle Fraser, a famous sculptor.
8. Fraser's model for the nickel had been borrowed from the Bronx Zoo.
9. Nickels contain mostly copper.
10. The average United States dollar bill has a life span of less than one year.

## Use of Voice in Writing

Because verbs in the active voice are more forceful and have greater impact than verbs in the passive voice, you should use the active voice as much as possible. The passive voice, however, should be used in the following situations: (1) when the doer of the action is unknown or unimportant and (2) when you want to emphasize the receiver of the action or to emphasize the results.

The extra tickets **were sold** at a profit.

(doer unknown or unimportant)

The crumbling currency **was made** during the Civil War.

(emphasis on the results)

### Connect to Speaking and Writing

Newspaper headlines must convey in a few words what the article's main focus is. The writers use active or passive voice, depending on what they want to highlight. When you read the active-voice headline **"Workers Strike at Factory,"** you know that the article will focus on the workers. However, when you read the passive-voice headline **"Factory Is Closed by Strike,"** you know the article will focus on the factory.

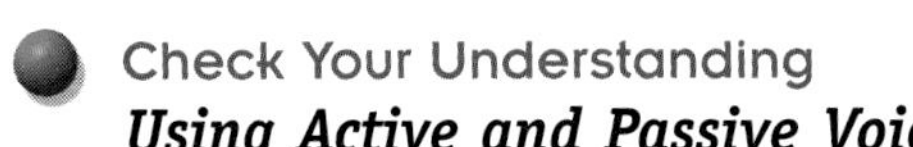


Check Your Understanding

***Using Active and Passive Voices***

Literature Topic **Write the verb in each sentence. Then label each one *A* for *active* or *P* for *passive*.**

1. An interesting novel was given to my class by our literature teacher.
2. *Robinson Crusoe* was written by Daniel Defoe.
3. In the story, Robinson Crusoe is shipwrecked on an island.

4. Later, the character Friday befriends Crusoe.
5. This novel was published in 1719.
6. It is judged by scholars to be one of the first English novels ever written.
7. Before this time period, stories were written in verse form by authors.
8. Defoe was born in London in 1660.
9. His father named him Daniel Foe.
10. Around 1695, the name was changed to Defoe by Daniel.

Connect to the Writing Process: Revising

***Using Active and Passive Voice***

**11.–18. Rewrite the passive-voice sentences in the preceding exercise, changing the passive voice to the active voice if appropriate. If a sentence is better in the passive voice, write *C*.**

Connect to the Writing Process: Drafting

***Using Active and Passive Voice in Sentences***

**Write sentences that follow the directions below.**

19. In an active-voice statement, name a book you have read.
20. Write a passive-voice statement that tells the name of the author.
21. Write a passive-voice statement that tells when the book was published.
22. Use an active-voice statement to describe the main character.
23. Write a passive-voice statement that describes the setting.
24. Write an active-voice statement that states the conflict.
25. Identify the solution in a passive-voice statement.
26. Write an active-voice statement that tells your opinion of the book.

## Communicate Your Ideas

### APPLY TO WRITING

**Writer's Craft:** ***Analyzing the Use of Voice***

In *Robinson Crusoe*, Defoe shows Crusoe fighting for his life in the water after the shipwreck. Read the following passage, and then follow the instructions.

> The wave that came upon me again, buried me at once 20 or 30 foot deep in its own body; and I could feel my self carried with a mighty force and swiftness towards the shore a very great way; but I held my breath, and assisted my self to swim still forward with all my might. I was ready to burst with holding my breath, when, as I felt my self rising up, so to my immediate relief, I found my head and hands shoot out above the surface of the water; and tho' it was not two seconds of time that I could keep my self so, yet it relieved me greatly, gave me breath and new courage. I was covered again with water a good while, but not so long but I held it out;...
>
> –*Daniel Defoe,* Robinson Crusoe

- Write each verb and label it *active*, *passive*, or *linking*.
- Now look at the verbs in active voice. What is the effect of expressing these actions in active voice instead of passive voice?
- What is performing the action of the verb in passive voice?
- What is the effect on the reader of using passive voice to express the action?

# Mood

The mood of a verb is the way in which the verb expresses an idea. In English there are three moods: indicative, imperative, and subjunctive.

The **indicative mood** is used to state a fact or to ask a question.

The **imperative mood** is used to give a command or to make a request.

Since the indicative mood is used to state facts or ask questions, it is used most often in both writing and speaking.

| | |
|---|---|
| INDICATIVE | A national park **makes** a good vacation spot.<br>What **makes** camping so much fun? |
| IMPERATIVE | **Look** at this brochure on Yellowstone National Park. **Consider** a trip to Mesa Verde. |

The **subjunctive mood** is used to express (1) a condition contrary to fact, which begins with words such as *if*, *as if*, or *as though*, (2) a wish, and (3) a command or a request after the word *that*.

| | |
|---|---|
| CONTRARY TO FACT | If I **were** you, I'd pack a water bottle.<br>(I am not you.)<br>If Karla **were** here, she could go with us.<br>(She is not here.) |
| A WISH | I wish I **were** a better skier.<br>I wish that **were** our flight. |
| COMMAND/ REQUEST BEGINNING WITH *THAT* | I demand *that* we **be** given a better camp site.<br>(If not in the subjunctive mood, the subject and verb would be *we are given.*) |

She ordered *that* nobody **hike** without proper boots.

(If not in the subjunctive mood, the subject and verb would be *nobody hikes.*)

In English, the subjunctive verb forms differ from the indicative forms in only two situations.

The **present subjunctive** uses the base form of the verb for all persons and numbers, including the third-person singular, but indicative verbs use the –*s* form.

| | |
|---|---|
| INDICATIVE | My camp fire **is** small. |
| SUBJUNCTIVE | The park ranger suggested that all fires **be** small. |

In the present subjunctive, the verb *to be* is always *be*.

He recommended that all canoe trips **be** in the afternoon.

The **past subjunctive** form of the verb *to be* is *were* for all persons and numbers.

If my grandfather **were** here, he would enjoy the horseback riding.

Although the subjunctive mood is not used much today, it still shows up in a number of idiomatic expressions such as the following.

| | |
|---|---|
| SUBJUNCTIVE EXPRESSIONS | **Be** that as it may, . . .<br>Far **be** it from me to . . . |

CONNECT TO SPEAKING AND WRITING

The subjunctive voice is a persuasive tool. It can be used to soften a suggestion or strengthen a command.

I wish I were going to the park.
I demand that she take me to the park. 

## Practice Your Skills

### Check Your Understanding
### *Using the Subjunctive Mood*

General Interest **Write the correct form of the verb in parentheses.**

**1.** I wish I (was, were) brave enough to ski the steep slopes.

**2.** Tom talks as if he (was, were) the hike leader.

**3.** I wish Earl (was, were) here.

**4.** If I (was, were) you, I'd wear a life jacket.

**5.** I suggest that you (be, are) at the dock in an hour.

**6.** Lisa wished she (was, were) at the beach right now.

**7.** Marnie requested that he (be, is) in the boat.

**8.** After ten minutes in the sun, my skin felt as though it (was, were) already burned.

**9.** Cheryl asked that we (be, are) ready at noon.

**10.** If Todd (was, were) here, he would want to surf.

### Connect to the Writing Process: Revising
### *Using Subjunctive and Indicative Mood in Sentences*

**Write each sentence using either the subjunctive or the indicative mood of the verb form. Then write *S* for *subjunctive* or *I* for *indicative*.**

**11.** Yosemite National Park (be) a national treasure.

**12.** If I (be) you, I'd hike up Bridalveil Falls.

**13.** I wish I (be) a mountain climber.

**14.** I demand that we (allow) to climb El Capitan.

**15.** If I (be) you, I would not climb El Capitan.

**16.** That mountain (be) 7,569 feet high.

**17.** I wish I (rappel) up its flat face.

**18.** The ranger requested that we all (be) in before dark.

**19.** Far (be) it from me to disagree with you.

**20.** The Merced River (flow) through Yosemite Valley.

21. The terrain (offer) meadows and steep mountains.

22. Yosemite Falls (drop) 1,430 feet into the valley.

23. I expect that we (give) a beautiful campsite.

24. Mirror Lake (reflect) the beautiful mountains.

25. Chipmunks (scamper) along the mountain trails.

***Writing Sentences***

**Write sentences that follow the directions below.**

26. Include an indicative-mood verb that makes a statement.

27. Include an indicative-mood verb that asks a question.

28. Include a verb in the imperative mood.

29. Include a subjunctive-mood verb that is used to express an idea contrary to fact.

30. Include a subjunctive-mood verb that is used to express a wish.

31. Include a subjunctive-mood verb that is used to make a request.

## Communicate Your Ideas

### APPLY TO WRITING

**Campaign Speech:** ***Voice and Mood***

You have been nominated to run for Student Advisor to the Principal. Write a campaign speech describing what you would do for your fellow students if you were elected. What kinds of issues would you raise with the principal if you were to talk with him or her? What do you wish were different at your school? Use the subjunctive mood to express these thoughts.

## CheckPoint

# Using the Correct Verb Form

**Write the past or past participle of each verb in parentheses.**

1. We (speak) to her before she (drive) to New York.
2. I should have (know) his name because we both (grow) up in Park Ridge.
3. She (write) to the manufacturer after the boat had (sink) for the second time.
4. Grandmother (make) two blueberry pies and (take) them to the fair.
5. I (begin) thinking about entering the race because I have (ride) bicycles for ten years.
6. He has (begin) a letter that he should have (write) months ago.
7. Yesterday I (rise) about 6:00 A.M. and (run) around the reservoir.
8. Since I have (hear) his opinion many times, I have (give) the matter a great deal of thought.
9. Paolo has just (catch) the baseball and has (throw) it to first.
10. After I (do) most of my homework, I (go) for a walk.

# Correcting Verb Tenses

**Write the correct form of any incorrect verb in each sentence.**

1. Ever since 1787, the bald eagle was America's national bird.
2. If that dog was mine, I would take better care of him.
3. Mike just realized that he left his books in Leroy's car.
4. Since the senator has been reelected, Pam is happy to work on her campaign.
5. Because Karen sleep late, she missed the bus again.

6. Since I was young, I was afraid of bees.
7. As the buzzers sounded, the quarterback has thrown a pass into the end zone.
8. I wish I was already graduated from high school.
9. Raymond noticed that he saw the same red car pass by our house twice.
10. Dad knows I have worked hard yesterday.

## Determining Active and Passive Voice

**Write the verb in each sentence and label it *active* or *passive*. Then rewrite any sentence in the passive voice that should be in the active voice.**

1. Because of the severe ice storm, the school was closed for the day.
2. An interesting experiment was performed by us in chemistry.
3. In 1863, Lincoln made Thanksgiving a national holiday.
4. Great interest in space exploration has been shown by the United States.
5. The SATs were taken by many seniors on Saturday.

## Writing Sentences

**Write five sentences that follow the directions below.**

1. Write a sentence with a perfect participle and a verb in the future tense.
2. Write a sentence in the subjunctive mood.
3. Write an imperative sentence. Use one verb in the present tense along with an infinitive.
4. Write a sentence with one verb in the passive voice and another in the active voice.
5. Write a sentence using both the verb *rise* and the verb *sit* in the past tense.

# Language and *Self-Expression*

**A**uguste Renoir was one of the leaders of the Impressionist school of painting. The Impressionists were interested in showing the play of light and shadow that often defined the subjects they painted. Since light changes so quickly, an Impressionist painting actually portrays a subject as it appears only at one particular moment.

The play of light and shadow affects lives as well. You may have heard these expressions–somewhat changeable depending on the subject–"She lights up my life" and "A shadow passed over my heart." Write a brief essay about the way that light and/or shadow (literally or figuratively) affects your life. Be sure to use verbs correctly as you write.

**Prewriting** Brainstorm moments of special happiness and deep sadness you have experienced. List them briefly.

**Drafting** Choose one example of happiness and one of sadness. Then write a thesis statement for your essay. Write your first paragraph about your moment of happiness. Concentrate on the feeling of light, or elation, that made the moment glow. Then write a paragraph on your moment of sadness. Focus on the darkness or heaviness cast by the shadow. End your essay by reflecting on the two experiences.

**Revising** Reread your draft. Do the sentences flow naturally from one to the next? Do they all relate to your two "light and shadow" experiences?

**Editing** Review your work, this time concentrating on grammar, mechanics, and especially usage. Be sure your verb tenses are correct. Check your spelling as well.

**Publishing** Make a clean copy of your essay. Publish your work by joining a classmate and taking turns reading to each other.

A **regular verb** forms its past and past participle by adding *–ed* or *–d* to the present.

An **irregular verb** does not form its past and past participle by adding *–ed* or *–d* to the present.

**Tense** is the time expressed by a verb.

The three **simple tenses** are present, past, and future. *(pages L197–L199)*
The three **perfect tenses** are present perfect, past perfect, and future perfect. *(page L199)*

## Voice

The **active voice** indicates that the subject is performing the action. *(page L217)*
The **passive voice** indicates that the action of the verb is being performed upon the subject. *(page L217)*

## Mood

The **indicative mood** is used to state a fact or to ask a question. *(page L222)*
The **imperative mood** is used to give a command or to make a request. *(page L222)*
The **subjunctive mood** is used to express a condition contrary to fact that begins with words such as *if, as if,* or *as though;* a wish; and a command or a request after the word *that.* *(page L222)*

## Other Information About the Use of Verbs

Using the problem verbs *lie, lay; sit, set;* and *rise, raise* *(pages L193–L196)*
Conjugating an irregular verb *(page L200)*
Conjugating the verb *be* *(page L201)*
Using present and past participles *(page L208)*
Using present and perfect infinitives *(pages L208–L209)*
Using progressive and emphatic verb forms *(pages L212–L216)*

### Directions

**Read the passage and choose the word or group of words that belongs in each underlined space. Write the letter of the correct answer.**

**EXAMPLE** **1.** Colleges and universities __(1)__ people for many kinds of professional careers.

**1** **A** prepare
**B** had prepared
**C** will have been preparing
**D** prepares

**ANSWER** **1** **A**

Did you know that modern universities __(1)__ from schools that originated in Europe during the Middle Ages? Such schools __(2)__ their name from the Latin word *universitas,* meaning "a group of people assembled for a common purpose." In early English schools, colleges __(3)__ within universities to provide living quarters and dining rooms for various groups of students. Such students __(4)__ members of a college and a university at the same time. Today, however, both colleges and universities __(5)__ teaching institutions.

My friend Paul __(6)__ to attend a small liberal-arts college. However, I __(7)__ a university with several colleges, or branches, each offering course work in a different discipline. Freshmen and sophomores must take certain basic courses before __(8)__ on a major field of interest. If it __(9)__ not for this regulation, students might choose majors that are not suited to them. __(10)__ for two years to select a major, for example, my sister Tawnee knew she really wanted to major in chemistry even though she had also been interested in physics and engineering.

**1** **A** develop
**B** will have developed
**C** developed
**D** develops

**2** **A** took
**B** has taken
**C** taking
**D** were taking

**3** **A** form
**B** have been formed
**C** will be formed
**D** were formed

**4** **A** were becoming
**B** have become
**C** become
**D** became

**5** **A** were
**B** are
**C** will be
**D** was

**6** **A** choose
**B** chosen
**C** were chosen
**D** chose

**7** **A** have selected
**B** will have selected
**C** selecting
**D** to select

**8** **A** decide
**B** decided
**C** deciding
**D** having been decided

**9** **A** was
**B** were
**C** have been
**D** is

**10** **A** Waiting
**B** To wait
**C** Having waited
**D** Waited

# Using Pronouns

## Pretest

### *Directions*

**Read the passage and choose the pronoun that belongs in each underlined space. Write the letter of the correct answer.**

EXAMPLE **1.** Wilbur Wright once said, "Since we were children, Orville and __(1)__ have always done things together."

**1** **A** me
**B** I
**C** us
**D** my

ANSWER **1** **B**

__(1)__ are Wilbur and Orville Wright? As everyone knows, these men from Dayton, Ohio, became famous when __(2)__ invented __(3)__ most famous invention, the airplane. Before 1900, most people could not even imagine __(4)__ flying through the air like a bird! Of course, it took two extraordinary individuals to create such an inconceivable machine. Each of the brothers brought __(5)__ own unique talents and qualities to the collaboration. Wilbur, __(6)__ few knew well because of his quietness, was the visionary of the two. __(7)__ was the one __(8)__ first dreamed of flying. Orville, on the other hand, was more mechanically minded than __(9)__ . It was also Orville's enthusiasm that carried __(10)__ throughout the long years preceding their first flight at Kitty Hawk, North Carolina.

**1** **A** Who
**B** Whom
**C** Whose
**D** Whomever

**2** **A** them
**B** they
**C** theirs
**D** their

**3** **A** them
**B** they
**C** theirs
**D** their

**4** **A** them
**B** they
**C** theirs
**D** their

**5** **A** his
**B** his or her
**C** their
**D** theirs

**6** **A** whoever
**B** whomever
**C** who
**D** whom

**7** **A** He
**B** Him
**C** His
**D** Their

**8** **A** who
**B** whom
**C** whose
**D** whoever

**9** **A** he
**B** him
**C** their
**D** them

**10** **A** they
**B** them
**C** their
**D** he

Glenna Goodacre. *Vietnam Women's Memorial,* 1993.
Bronze cast, height 92 inches. National Mall, Washington, D.C.

**Describe** Identify the figures in the sculpture. What is the central character doing? Are the figures depicted realistically or impressionistically?

**Analyze** What expression do you see on the face of the woman? What bond do you think is there between the soldier and the woman looking down at him? Give reasons for your answer.

**Interpret** Who do you think would come closer to the real spirit of the sculpture, a writer of fiction or a writer of nonfiction? Why?

**Judge** Would you rather read a newspaper article about the scene or study the sculpture? Why?

At the end of this chapter, you will use the sculpture as a visual aid for writing.

# The Cases of Personal Pronouns

As a child you learned that the colors of traffic lights are signals to motorists and pedestrians. You also learned another set of signals. You learned, for example, that you should use the pronoun *he* in one situation, *him* in another situation and *his* in still another situation.

*He, him,* and *his* send out different signals because they indicate the case of a pronoun. A pronoun has a different form and a different function for each case. When you use a particular form of a pronoun, therefore, you are signaling to a reader or a listener how that pronoun is being used in a sentence. (Nouns change form only in the possessive case. For example, *girl* becomes *girl's* in the possessive case.)

**Case** is the form of a noun or a pronoun that indicates its use in a sentence.

English has three cases: the nominative case, the objective case, and the possessive case. Many pronouns change form for each of the cases. Notice, though, that *you* and *it* are the same in both the nominative and the objective cases.

| NOMINATIVE CASE | |
|---|---|
| (Used for subjects and predicate nominatives) | |
| **Singular** | I, you, he, she, it |
| **Plural** | we, you, they |

| OBJECTIVE CASE | |
|---|---|
| (Used for direct objects, indirect objects, objects of prepositions, and objects of verbals) | |
| **Singular** | me, you, him, her, it |
| **Plural** | us, you, them |

| POSSESSIVE CASE | |
|---|---|
| (Used to show ownership or possession) | |
| **Singular** | my, mine, your, yours, his, her, hers, its |
| **Plural** | our, ours, your, yours, their, theirs |

## The Nominative Case

*I, you, he, she, it, we,* and *they* are the personal pronouns in the nominative case.

The **nominative case** is used for subjects and predicate nominatives.

### Pronouns as Subjects

A pronoun can be used as a subject of an independent clause or a dependent clause.

| | |
|---|---|
| Independent Clause | **We** applied for jobs in the campus bookstore. |
| Dependent Clause | As soon as **he** had filled out the application, the boss hired him. |

The case of a pronoun that is part of a compound subject is sometimes not as obvious as a single-subject pronoun. That is why it is important to double-check any pronoun in a compound subject to make sure that it is in the nominative case. To do this, say the nominative and the objective pronouns separately—to find out which one is correct.

Jason and (he, him) cashed the paychecks.
**He** cashed the paychecks.
**Him** cashed the paychecks.

The nominative case *he* is the correct form to use.

Jason and **he** cashed the paychecks.

This method of checking for the correct case also works if both subjects are pronouns.

He and (she, her) worked at the campus bookstore.
**She** worked at the campus bookstore.
**Her** worked at the campus bookstore.

The nominative case *she* is the correct form to use.

He and **she** worked at the campus bookstore.

## Pronouns as Predicate Nominatives

A predicate nominative follows a linking verb and identifies, renames, or explains the subject.

That was **I** who won the scholarship.

The preceding example probably sounds extremely formal—or even incorrect—to you. However, while *That was me* or *It's me* is common usage in conversation, it should be avoided in written work.

It was **she.** That is **he.** The winners are **they.**

To decide whether the pronoun in a compound predicate nominative is in the correct case, turn the sentence around to make the predicate nominative the subject. Then say the nominative and the objective pronouns separately to find out which one is correct.

The finalists for the essay award are Ben and (she, her).
Ben and (she, her) are the finalists for the essay award.
**She** is a finalist.
**Her** is a finalist.
The finalists for the essay award are Ben and **she.**

Sometimes the wording of a sentence becomes awkward when pronouns or compound pronouns are used as predicate nominatives. You can avoid this awkwardness by turning the sentence around.

| | |
|---|---|
| AWKWARD | The financial aid officer is **she.** |
| TURNED AROUND | **She** is the financial aid officer. |
| AWKWARD | The financial aid recipients are Di and **he.** |
| TURNED AROUND | Di and **he** are the financial aid recipients. |

*You can learn more about predicate nominatives on pages L77–L81. Also, you can find lists of common linking verbs on page L21.*

## Nominative Case Pronouns Followed by Appositives

An **appositive** is a noun or a pronoun that renames or identifies another noun or pronoun in the sentence. Occasionally when *we* is used as a subject or a predicate nominative, a noun or a pronoun functions as the appositive of *we.* The noun appositive that follows *we* never affects the case of *we.* The best way to check whether you have used the correct pronoun is to drop the appositive mentally from the sentence.

**We** *language specialists* thoroughly enjoy our jobs.
(We thoroughly enjoy our jobs.)

The newest college students on campus are **we** *freshmen.*
(The newest college students on campus are we.)

CONNECT TO SPEAKING AND WRITING

An appositive is an excellent tool for clarifying information for the reader or listener.

| | |
|---|---|
| VAGUE | We completed our applications. |
| MORE SPECIFIC | We students completed our applications. |

## Nominative Case Pronouns as Appositives

An appositive is in the same case as the noun or pronoun to which it refers. Occasionally a pronoun itself will be part of an appositive to a subject or a predicate nominative. Then the pronoun should be in the nominative case.

The exchange students, *Yuri* and ***he***, work in the language lab.

*Yuri* and *he* are appositives to the subject *students.* Since the subject is in the nominative case, an appositive to the subject is also in the nominative case.

## Practice Your Skills

Check Your Understanding

***Using Pronouns in the Nominative Case***

Contemporary Life

**Write the correct form of the pronoun in parentheses.**

**1.** The students concerned about the cost of college are (we, us) seniors.

**2.** Several financial aid advisors, Victor and (they, them), spoke to us.

**3.** Todd and (him, he) described the best ideas.

**4.** Neither Ava nor (me, I) is worried about college fees.

**5.** Of all our classmates, (her, she) and (I, me) are the ones who immediately took the advisors' suggestions.

**6.** It was (me, I) who learned about college work-study.

**7.** It was (she, her) who got the application forms.

**8.** The recipients of grant money are Ava and (I, me).

**9.** Maddy and (he, him) will apply for athletic scholarships.

**10.** The champions of our track meet are (them, they).

**11.** It wasn't (me, I) who applied for an academic scholarship at the university.

12. Suzanne believes that both (she, her) and Jake will be awarded scholarships.

13. The valedictorian and salutatorian of our class are (them, they).

14. (We, Us) students from lower-income families applied for need-based financial aid.

15. Trisha said that (her, she) and Tyrone would apply for guaranteed student loans.

16. The twins, Angela and (she, her), have already applied for loans.

17. The persons responsible for paying back the loans are (them, they).

18. The students awarded scholarships by the English department are Miguel and (her, she).

19. The recipient of the journalism scholarship is either Jenny or (he, him).

20. The graduates ready for our freshman year in college are (we, us) financial aid applicants.

### Connect to the Writing Process: Editing
### *Using the Nominative Case*

**If an underlined pronoun is in the wrong case, write it correctly. If it is in the correct case, write C.**

21. Mom said that Monica and him would get summer jobs.
22. The new burger chefs are Ben and her.
23. We workers are saving our money for college.
24. Last summer, Juan and him saved enough for tuition.
25. Gloria and me will live in the dorms to save money.
26. The people awarded the internships are Holly and she.
27. Their parents and them are visiting the campus soon.
28. The students who most appreciate their education are us workers.
29. Two friends, Amy and him, pay their own expenses.
30. The new lab assistants are her and me.

Connect to the Writing Process: Drafting

*Writing Sentences*

**Write a sentence for each of the following groups of words. Use one group as a compound subject, one as a compound predicate nominative, and one as a compound appositive. Then label each one.**

**31.** you and I **32.** he and she **33.** Julio and they

## Communicate Your Ideas

### APPLY TO WRITING

**Plan of Action:** ***Nominative Case Pronouns***

Look at the picture of the student working. She might be saving money to help pay for her college education.

How do you plan to pay for your college expenses? Write a plan of action that you can share with other seniors. Include details such as where you want to work and how you will balance work and school, what forms of financial aid you will apply for, and what you will do to cut down on expenses. Remember to use nominative case pronouns correctly.

Contemporary Life **If an underlined pronoun is in the wrong case, write it correctly. If it is in the correct case, write C.**

1. Me and him went to the zoo last weekend.
2. The tour guides are them.
3. Us animal lovers never tire of observing the zoo's inhabitants.
4. The ticket-takers, Arnold and she, are in our high-school biology class.
5. Them and us sometimes help feed the lambs in the petting zoo.
6. It was me who noticed the new reptile exhibit.
7. The reptile caretakers, Lynn and her, told us about the heat lamps.
8. Lynn said, "The luckiest employees here are we snake handlers!"
9. Petra and him watched the poison arrow frogs.
10. This frog sweats poison when he senses danger.
11. They, the frogs, live in South America.
12. One of this frog's enemies is us humans.
13. My friend Jeremy and him enjoy visiting the lions.
14. Monique and her, two of my good friends, found us by the orangutans.
15. We students watched the orangutans eat fruit.

## The Objective Case

*Me, you, him, her, it, us,* and *them* are the personal pronouns in the objective case.

The **objective case** is used for direct objects, indirect objects, objects of prepositions, and objects of verbals.

## Pronouns as Direct and Indirect Objects

A pronoun that is used as a direct object will follow an action verb and answer the question *Whom?* A pronoun that is used as an indirect object will answer the question *To whom?* or *For whom?* after the direct object.

DIRECT OBJECTS — Dad will drive **us** to work.
The optician will assist **her** now.

INDIRECT OBJECTS — i.o. d.o.
The cashier gave **me** a receipt.

i.o. d.o.
Give **him** those eyeglass frames.

To check for the correct case of a compound direct object, say the nominative and the objective case pronouns separately.

Jason saw the Dyers and (they, them) at the optical store.
Jason saw **they** at the optical store.
Jason saw **them** at the optical store.

The objective case *them* is the correct form to use.

Jason saw the Dyers and **them** at the optical store.

Compound indirect objects can be checked in the same way.

i.o. i.o d.o.
Fred gave Beth and (I, me) new sunglasses.
Fred gave **I** new sunglasses.
Fred gave **me** new sunglasses.

The objective case *me* is the correct form to use.

i.o. i.o d.o.
Fred gave Beth and **me** new sunglasses.

*You can learn more about direct objects and indirect objects on pages L72–L77.*

## Pronouns as Objects of Prepositions

A prepositional phrase begins with a preposition and ends with a noun or a pronoun called the **object of a preposition.** As the following examples show, a pronoun that is used as an object of a preposition is in the objective case.

> You can ride to work with **us.**
> (*With us* is the prepositional phrase.)
>
> Is this lab coat for **me?**
> (*For me* is the prepositional phrase.)
>
> The patient gave his insurance card to **you.**
> (*To you* is the prepositional phrase.)

You can check to see that a pronoun in a compound object of a preposition is in the objective case by saying the nominative and objective case pronouns separately.

> The ophthalmologist wrote prescriptions for David and (she, her).
>
> The ophthalmologist wrote prescriptions for **she**.
>
> The ophthalmologist wrote prescriptions for **her**.

The objective case *her* is the correct form to use.

> The ophthalmologist wrote prescriptions for David and **her**.

You might have noticed that sometimes people will use nominative case pronouns after the preposition *between* in an effort to sound formal or correct. However, all pronouns used as objects of a preposition should be in the objective case.

> INCORRECT The sales agreement was *between* ***he*** *and* ***I.***
> CORRECT The sales agreement was *between* ***him*** *and* ***me.***

*You can learn more about objects of prepositions on page L97. Also, you can find a list of common prepositions on pages L37–L38.*

## Practice Your Skills

### Check Your Understanding

*Using Pronouns as Objects*

Contemporary Life

**Write the correct form of the pronoun in parentheses. Then write how the pronoun is used, using the following abbreviations.**

direct object = *d.o.* indirect object = *i.o.*
object of a preposition = *o.p.*

1. Like you and (I, me), Yvonne is looking for a job.
2. The manager hired Tim and (I, me) as opticians.
3. Dad called Megan and (he, him) to tell them about our jobs as interns.
4. We should talk to Rebecca and (she, her), our coworkers.
5. For four hours I waited on Mr. Stuart and (they, them), my best customers.
6. Give the customer and (we, us) copies of the receipt.
7. Between you and (I, me), I plan to become the assistant manager.
8. Mrs. Samuelson will pay (they, them) or (we, us) fifteen dollars to repair her antique spectacles.
9. Would you like to go to the training seminar with Tom and (we, us)?
10. Why did you disagree with the experienced lens cutter and (he, him)?
11. Ask Janice or (she, her) about the schedule.
12. You should clean these ground lenses for the Kents and (they, them).
13. Ms. Randolph gave Alma and (I, me) a large tip.
14. We will notify Andrea or (she, her) when your eyeglasses are ready.
15. After school yesterday Neal showed (he, him) and (she, her) the new sunglasses I sold him.

16. No employees work on Sunday except Jacqueline and (he, him).
17. Please bring Brent Morgan and (she, her) some eyeglass frames to try on.
18. This break room is for the receptionist and (we, us).
19. Danielle will meet Scott and (they, them) after work.
20. Leave your key to the store with Heather or (she, her).

## Pronouns as Objects of Verbals

Because participles, gerunds, and infinitives are verb forms, they can take objects. The direct object of a verbal is in the objective case.

| | |
|---|---|
| PARTICIPIAL PHRASE | *Seeing* ***her*** *in the restaurant,* Jeff asks the tennis star for her autograph. (The phrase is *seeing her in the restaurant. Her* is the object of the participle *seeing.*) |
| GERUND PHRASE | I don't recall *seeing* ***him*** *at practice.* (The phrase is *seeing him at practice. Him* is the object of the gerund *seeing.*) |
| INFINITIVE PHRASE | I want *to watch* ***them*** *soon,* but I am very busy. (The phrase is *to watch them soon. Them* is the object of the infinitive *to watch.*) |

A pronoun in a compound object of a verbal can be checked by saying the nominative and objective case pronouns separately.

I hope to see Bill and (she, her) at the game.
I hope to see **she** at the game.
I hope to see **her** at the game.
I hope to see Bill and **her** at the game.

*You can learn more about verbals on pages L107–L119.*

## Objective Case Pronouns Followed by Appositives

An appositive of *us* does not affect the case of *us*. To check whether you have used the correct pronoun, mentally drop the appositive from the sentence.

> Give **us** *fans* those season tickets.
> (Give *us* those season tickets. *Us* is used as an indirect object, and *fans* is the appositive.)

## Objective Case Pronouns as Appositives

Occasionally a pronoun itself is part of an appositive to a direct object, an indirect object, or an object of a preposition. Then the pronoun should be in the objective case.

> d.o.
> We found two volunteers, *Gladys* and **him,** to work at the refreshment stand.
> (*Gladys* and *him* are the appositives to the direct object *volunteers.* Since a direct object is in the objective case, an appositive to the direct object is also in the objective case.)

## PRACTICE YOUR SKILLS

Check Your Understanding

### *Using Objective Case Pronouns*

Contemporary Life

**Write the correct form of the pronoun in parentheses.**

1. Making (he, him) the shortstop was a wise decision.
2. The principal asked (we, us) athletes for our opinion on the new gymnasium.
3. Finding (he, him) in the weight room, the coach helped the bodybuilder.

4. Be sure to tell Carrie and (she, her) about the basketball game after school.
5. At the awards ceremony, the coach gave special recognition to two athletes, Pedro and (he, him).
6. It was a great disappointment to (we, us) fans when Mason struck out.
7. Alex tried in vain to find Sarah and (he, him) in the crowded stadium.
8. I don't recall seeing Nat and (they, them) at the soccer game last week.
9. They interviewed two of my favorite baseball players, Mark and (he, him), for the evening newscast.
10. Watching Liz and (they, them) on the field, Mom was very proud.
11. We asked several baseball players, Andy and (they, them), to help out with Little League.
12. I remember helping Terrence and (she, her) learn to spike a volleyball.
13. I don't want to coach Sammy and (they, them) in the drizzling rain.
14. Meeting the pro wrestler and (him, he) in person was a memorable event.
15. Giving the boys and (she, her) our tickets, we went back home.
16. We asked the coach to give (we, us) runners some time to warm up.
17. I found two alumni, Troy and (him, he), to speak at the sports banquet.
18. Coach Hernandez tried not to mislead the captain and (they, them) about their chances of winning.
19. When we got to P.E. class we begged, "Give (us, we) hard workers a day off!"
20. During homeroom the principal announced the Mr. and Ms. Fitness winners, Alex and (she, her).

## Connect to the Writing Process: Editing
### *Using Objective Case Pronouns*

**If an underlined pronoun is in the wrong case, write it correctly. If it is in the correct case, write *C*.**

**21.** Please save seats for <u>he</u> and Sharon.

**22.** Will you show Marcia and <u>I</u> your canoe over the holiday weekend?

**23.** Dad had warned you and <u>she</u> about that thin ice!

**24.** The assistant coach explained the plays to <u>we</u> quarterbacks.

**25.** Will Roger be able to drive <u>us</u> home after the game?

**26.** We saw the performances of the two finalists, Pat and <u>he</u>.

**27.** He should never have taken <u>her</u> and the dog rafting.

**28.** We saw Dad watching our cousin and <u>they</u> on the balance beams.

**29.** Mom sent Harold and <u>I</u> to summer basketball camp.

**30.** Be sure to call <u>we</u> parents when you get to the ball park.

## Connect to the Writing Process: Drafting
### *Writing Sentences*

**Write sentences that follow the instructions.**

**31.** Use *it* as a direct object.

**32.** Use *us* as a direct object followed by an appositive.

**33.** Use *her* as an indirect object.

**34.** Use *Beth and him* as an object of a preposition.

**35.** Use *me* in a participial phrase as the object of a verbal.

**36.** Use *you* in a gerund phrase as the object of a gerund.

**37.** Use *them* in an infinitive phrase as the object of an infinitive.

**38.** Use *Luke and her* as an appositive.

## Communicate Your Ideas

### APPLY TO WRITING

**Descriptive Account:** ***Objective Case Pronouns***

Study the photograph of two ethnic Albanian refugees who fled Kosovo in 1999. Imagine that you are either the man or the child in this photo. You have been violently driven out of your home and out of your country, and as you sit on a bus with other refugees, a reporter snaps your picture. The reporter then asks you to tell him what has happened to you and how it has made you feel.

Create an account of events and write a description for the reporter. You may want to look up newspaper articles about Kosovo's Albanian refugees to get ideas and factual information. In your account, use objective case pronouns in the various ways you have learned in this section. Then work with a writing partner to edit mistakes in pronoun usage. Finally, write the revised copy.

Mixed Practice

Contemporary Life

**Write each underlined pronoun that is incorrectly used; beside it, write the correct objective case pronoun.**

1. Taking they to the counter, I paid for the guitar picks with my allowance.
2. Dad bought new CDs by our favorite rock group for Leslie and I.
3. Photographing she and he during their concert is my job.
4. The ticket agents sold we country-western fans discount tickets.
5. I wanted to invite the new band members, Steve and they, to the party.
6. Mr. Vernon trained Valerie and he on the cello.
7. I forgot to wish the drummers, she and Emily, good luck on their audition.
8. After telling my brother and they about my new baby grand piano, I invited them over to see it.
9. I laughed when Peter said, "Take we groupies backstage!"
10. We asked two people, he and Kathy, to take turns driving the tour bus.

## The Possessive Case

*My, mine, your, yours, his, her, hers, its, our, ours, their,* and *theirs* are the personal pronouns in the possessive case.

The **possessive case** is used to show ownership or possession.

Possessive case pronouns are most often used before a noun or by themselves.

| | |
|---|---|
| BEFORE A NOUN | This is **my** poem. |
| BY THEMSELVES | These are **mine**, but which are **his**? |

Be careful not to confuse certain possessive pronouns with contractions. A personal pronoun in the possessive case never includes an apostrophe. *Its, your, their,* and *theirs* are possessive pronouns. However, *it's, you're, they're,* and *there's* are contractions.

CONNECT TO SPEAKING AND WRITING

Context clues help a listener determine whether a speaker is using a possessive pronoun or a contraction.

| | |
|---|---|
| POSSESSIVE PRONOUN | **Their** poems are in the class binder. |
| CONTRACTION | **They're** proud of the original poems. |

## Possessive Pronouns with Gerunds

As you may recall, a gerund is a verb form ending in *–ing* that is used in all the ways a noun is used. If a pronoun comes directly in front of a gerund, it should be in the possessive case—in just the same way a possessive pronoun would come in front of a regular noun.

gerund

We were pleased at ***his*** *writing the story.*
(The whole gerund phrase is *his writing the story*. It is used as an object of the preposition *at*. Since *writing* is a gerund, it is preceded by a possessive pronoun: *his writing*.)

gerund

A big surprise was ***their*** *publishing his story.*
(The whole gerund phrase is *their publishing his story*. It is used as a predicate nominative. Since *publishing* is a gerund, it is preceded by a possessive pronoun: *their publishing*.)

A common error is to put a nominative or objective case pronoun before a gerund—instead of a possessive case pronoun.

| | |
|---|---|
| INCORRECT | We were pleased at **him** writing the story. |
| INCORRECT | A big surprise was **they** publishing his story. |

Another possible error is confusing a gerund with a participle because both are verb forms that end in *-ing*. However, since a participle is used as an adjective, it would never be preceded by a possessive pronoun.

| | |
|---|---|
| GERUND | The children enjoyed ***our*** *reading to them*. (The gerund phrase is the direct object. The children enjoyed what? *Our reading to them*. Since *reading* is a gerund, it is preceded by a possessive pronoun.) |
| PARTICIPLE | We baby-sat the children and watched ***them*** *reading to one another*. (*Them* is a direct object in this sentence. We watched whom? *Them*. Since *them* is a direct object, it is in the objective case. The participial phrase is used as an adjective to describe *them*.) |

*You can learn more about gerunds on pages L112–L115. You can find out more about participles on pages L107–L111.*

## PRACTICE YOUR SKILLS

Check Your Understanding

***Using Pronouns in the Possessive Case***

Contemporary Life **Write the correct pronoun in parentheses.**

**1.** (Theirs, There's) is the remodeled bookstore on Pier 21.

**2.** We were surprised at (them, their) buying the building.

**3.** (Him, His) renovating it was a smart business move.

4. This shelf and (its, it's) hardware are covered in rust.
5. Is there any chance of (you, your) getting a job at the Recycled Books and More store?
6. That shipment of used books must be (ours, our's).
7. Dan was surprised at (me, my) knowing so much about bookbinding.
8. I hadn't heard about (him, his) getting hired as assistant manager.
9. We all appreciated (you, your) explaining the employee insurance benefits to us.
10. My parents are pleased at (me, my) learning the bookstore business.
11. The idea of buying used textbooks for the store was (hers, her's).
12. (Him, His) stocking the shelves with the recycled textbooks was my suggestion.
13. The job of buying used CDs for the music section is (their's, theirs).
14. (Her, She) finding the true crime section of the store took five minutes.
15. These paperbacks are (your's, yours), but the hardbacks are mine.
16. We were grateful for (they're, their) bringing in old grocery bags for their book purchases.
17. During (our, ours) first week of business, we made a nice profit.
18. (His, Him) cleaning the entire Recycled Books and More store each night saves money on janitorial services.
19. Another money-saving service was (my, mine) painting the walls.
20. We are all so happy about (them, their) making a success of the store.
21. I donated (my, mine) box of mystery books.
22. Jeanne spent (her, hers) morning sorting books.
23. We listened to (you, your) return policies.

**24.** (Your, You're) knowledge about books is awesome.

**25.** (Her, She) shopping at garage sales is a good idea.

Connect to the Writing Process: Revising

### *Using Possessive Pronouns*

**Write each sentence, replacing the possessive nouns with possessive pronouns.**

**26.** The National Book Foundation awards the National Book Award each year for The National Book Foundation's choice of best fiction in the United States.

**27.** In 1951, William Faulkner won the National Book Award for William Faulkner's *The Collected Stories.*

**28.** Alice Walker won the National Book Award in 1983 for Alice Walker's novel *The Color Purple.*

**29.** Authors in the British Commonwealth of Nations are eligible to win the British Commonwealth of Nations' Booker Prize for the authors' full-length novels.

**30.** In 1992, Michael Ondaatje and Barry Unsworth were each awarded the Booker Prize for Michael Ondaatje's and Barry Unsworth's novels *The English Patient* and *Sacred Hunger.*

**31.** Ondaatje later agreed to let Ondaatje's novel be made into a film that received much critical acclaim and several Academy Award nominations.

**32.** Since Nobel Prizes are awarded internationally, writers in any country may be given the award for the writers' literary work.

**33.** An author who receives the Nobel Prize in literature receives the award for the author's entire body of work up to that point.

**34.** Authors who receive the Pulitzer Prize in literature are given the honor for the authors' novels about American life, even though they may have written other books.

**35.** Joseph Pulitzer established the Pulitzer Prize through Joseph Pulitzer's endowment to Columbia University.

## Communicate Your Ideas

### APPLY TO WRITING

**Poetry: *Possessive Pronouns***

Read the following lines taken from Li Po's "Ballad of Ch'ang-Kan" and then follow the instructions below.

> My hair barely covered my forehead then.
> My play was plucking flowers by the gate.
> You would come on your bamboo horse,
> Riding circles round my bench, and pitching
> green plums.
> Growing up together here, in Ch'ang-kan.
> Two little ones; no thought of what would come.
> At fourteen I became your wife,
> Blushing and timid, unable to smile,
> Bowing my head, face to dark wall.
> You called a thousand times, without one answer.
> At fifteen I made up my face,
> And swore that our dust and ashes should be one. . . .
>
> –*Li Po*, "Ballad of Ch'ang-Kan"

- List the possessive pronouns in the order in which they are used.
- Referring to your list, notice that the choice of possessive pronouns changes from the beginning of the poem to the end. What does the progression tell you about the speaker's attitude toward her listener?
- Next to every pronoun on your list, write a possessive noun that might replace that possessive pronoun within the poem. Read aloud the poem using the possessive nouns.
- What would happen if the poet had used possessive nouns instead of possessive pronouns? How would possessive nouns change your response to the poem?

Mixed Practice

General Interest

**Write each pronoun that is in the wrong case. Then write it correctly. If a sentence is correct, write *C*.**

1. Mr. Ayers, the librarian, showed Alicia and I some books about holidays.
2. Them will be enjoyable to read.
3. I listened to Mr. Ayers and she discussing Kwanzaa.
4. Tell we listeners about the seven principles of Kwanzaa.
5. Him and me are planning a Kwanzaa celebration.
6. Notifying them of the plans will take time.
7. The sets for the Christmas play were painted by two people, Carmen and I.
8. In the car, dressed in red and green, were Ben and her.
9. Everyone was glad to hear of me joining the choir.
10. We latke lovers will serve crispy latkes to our guests during Hanukkah.
11. Kyle and them enjoy the eight days of Hanukkah.
12. Is there any chance of you lending me your extra silver menorah?
13. He found two teachers, Mr. Kendall and she, who will chaperone the Holiday Dazzle Dance.
14. Ask the food committee, Sue and he, about traditional holiday foods.
15. The best dancers in the class are Beverly and him.
16. For the slow dance, Tiffany played the violin with the other instrumentalists, John and they.
17. Taking him by the hand, Lauren led him onto the dance floor.
18. This winter vacation will give we guys a chance to work on restoring Oliver's 1934 Buick.
19. Give your ticket to Ted, Maya, or he.
20. Please find us something to eat.

# Pronoun Problems

Has anyone at the other end of the telephone ever said to you, "Whom may I say is calling"? The next time you hear that expression, you will know that the speaker has just made a pronoun error. This section will cover the cases of the pronouns *who* and *whoever,* pronouns in comparisons, and reflexive and intensive pronouns.

## Who or Whom?

**The correct case of *who* is determined by how the pronoun is used in a question or a clause.**

Like personal pronouns, the pronouns *who* and *whoever* change their forms—depending upon how they are used within a sentence.

| | WHO AND WHOEVER |
|---|---|
| **Nominative Case** | who, whoever |
| **Objective Case** | whom, whomever |
| **Possessive Case** | whose |

*Who* and *whoever* and their related pronouns are used in questions and in subordinate clauses.

**In questions** *who* and *whoever* and their related pronouns are frequently used. The case you should use depends upon how the pronoun is used.

| | |
|---|---|
| Nominative Case | **Who** volunteered for Meals on Wheels? (subject) |
| Objective Case | **Whom** did you assist at the shelter? (direct object) |
| | To **whom** did you donate the shoes? (object of the preposition *to*) |

When deciding which case to use, turn a question around to its natural order.

| | |
|---|---|
| QUESTION | **Whom** did you assist? |
| NATURAL ORDER | You did assist **whom**. |

CONNECT TO SPEAKING AND WRITING

In casual conversation you might hear people say, "**Who** did you invite?" instead of "**Whom** did you invite?" This informal usage is accepted in most casual settings; however, in your formal written work, you should use *whom.*

**In clauses** forms of *who* and *whoever* and their related pronouns are also used. The case you use depends, once again, upon how the pronoun is used in an adjective or noun clause. The following examples show how forms of *who* are used in adjective clauses.

| | |
|---|---|
| NOMINATIVE CASE | Eva is a girl **who enjoys helping others.** (*Who* is the subject of *enjoys.*) |
| OBJECTIVE CASE | Mr. Jenkins is the man **whom the community theater group consulted.** (*Whom* is the direct object of *consulted.* The theater group consulted whom.) |
| | Peg is the health aide **from whom I learned about candystripers.** (*Whom* is the object of the preposition *from. From* is part of the clause.) |

The following examples show how forms of *who* and *whoever* are used in noun clauses.

| | |
|---|---|
| NOMINATIVE CASE | **Whoever collects clothing for the charity drive** will receive a free lunch. (*Whoever* is the subject of *collects.*) |
| | Jerry didn't know **who the new volunteer was.** (*Who* is a predicate nominative. The volunteer was who.) |

| | |
|---|---|
| Objective Case | Invite **whomever you want.** (*Whomever* is the direct object of *want*. You want whomever.) |
| | At the soup kitchen, Ray gives help to **whomever he sees.** (The entire clause is the object of the preposition *to*. *Whomever* is the direct object of *sees*.) |

Sometimes an interrupting expression such as *I believe, we know, do you suppose,* and *I hope* appears in a question or a clause. Mentally drop this expression to avoid any confusion.

**Who** *do you suppose* will win the fundraiser raffle? (Who will win the fundraiser raffle? *Who* is the subject of *will win.*)

Otis, **who** *I think* is a volunteer at the YMCA, is a senior. (Otis, who is a volunteer at the YMCA, is a senior. *Who* is the subject of *is.*)

*You can learn more about adjective and noun clauses on pages L148–L159.*

## Practice Your Skills

Check Your Understanding

***Using* Who *and Its Related Pronouns***

Contemporary Life **Write each form of *who* or *whom* that is used incorrectly. If a sentence is correct, write *C*.**

1. Whom may I say is volunteering for the campus cleanup on Saturday?
2. I met Roth, who is a community service director.
3. Tell whoever you see about the neighborhood playground project.
4. Did they say whom the sponsors of Paint the Playground Day are?
5. With who did you work at the park?

6. Who did you nominate as volunteer of the year?
7. Do you know who the event director is?
8. The school board will give 50 dollars to whomever organizes a school-improvement event.
9. With whom did you travel recently to the Volunteer America conference?
10. Mr. Davis is the social worker who we know from the homeless shelter.
11. Aaron usually likes whoever he works for.
12. From who should we request a new supply of the drug education materials?
13. It was Marshall whom we all agree did the most to establish the free art school for kids.
14. Whom did he think should join our active environmentalist group?
15. Do you know whom the director of the YMCA is?

Connect to the Writing Process: Editing

### *Using Forms of* Who *and* Whom

**16.–27. Rewrite the incorrect sentences in the preceding exercise, using the correct form of *who* or *whom*. Then, using the following abbreviations, write how each pronoun is used.**

| | |
|---|---|
| subject = *subj.* | predicate nominative = *p.n.* |
| direct object = *d.o.* | object of a preposition = *o.p.* |

Connect to the Writing Process: Drafting

### *Writing Sentences with* Who *and* Whom

**Write sentences that follow the instructions, using the correct forms of *who* and *whom*.**

28. as a subject
29. as a direct object
30. in a question
31. as the object of a preposition
32. to introduce an adjective clause
33. to begin a noun clause

## Pronouns in Comparisons

Pronouns are often used in comparisons. A problem sometimes arises when a comparison is made but not said or written out completely. The result is an elliptical clause.

An **elliptical clause** is a subordinate clause that begins with *than* or *as.*

Although words are omitted from an elliptical clause, they are still understood to be in the clause.

Mr. Lee coached Eric more **than I.**
Mr. Lee coached Eric more **than me.**

Depending upon what meaning is intended, both of the preceding examples are correct.

Mr. Lee coached Eric more **than I coached Eric.**

(*I* is correct because it is the subject of *coached.*)

Mr. Lee coached Eric more **than he coached me.**

(*Me* is correct because it is the direct object of *coached.*)

In an elliptical clause, use the form of the pronoun you would use if the clause were completed.

To decide which pronoun to use in an elliptical clause, mentally complete the clause. Then choose the form of the pronoun that expresses the meaning you want.

An elliptical clause, however, can sometimes correctly express only one meaning.

Do you think David Greene shoots hoops as well as (I, me)?

Do you think David Greene shoots hoops as well **as I shoot hoops?**

*You can learn more about elliptical clauses on pages L145–L147.*

## Practice Your Skills

Check Your Understanding

### *Using Pronouns in Elliptical Clauses*

Contemporary Life **Write each pronoun that is used incorrectly in an elliptical clause. If a sentence is correct, write *C*.**

**1.** Amy ran more laps than me.

**2.** In the tryouts I think Susannah did better than her.

**3.** When coaching Little League, Barry has more patience than him.

**4.** Andrea is as experienced a gymnast as me.

**5.** Martha likes the softball uniforms more than us.

**6.** At the track meet, Anna earned more ribbons than me.

**7.** Coach Ferguson trained that player better than ~~he~~.

**8.** Ben is not as tall as her, but he runs much faster.

**9.** My sister was always better in sports than me.

**10.** Mary cheered for Doug more than him.

Connect to the Writing Process: Editing

### *Using Pronouns in Comparisons*

**11.–20. Referring to the preceding sentences, complete each elliptical clause, using the correct pronoun. If a clause can be completed two ways, write them both.**

Connect to the Writing Process: Drafting

### *Using Elliptical Clauses in Sentences*

**Write sentences that follow the instructions. Then underline the elliptical clause in each sentence.**

**21.** Write a comparison that includes *than I.*

**22.** Write a comparison that includes *than they.*

**23.** Write a comparison that ends with *as he.*

**24.** Write a comparison that ends with *as they.*

**25.** Write a comparison that ends with *than she.*

## Reflexive and Intensive Pronouns

Because reflexive and intensive pronouns end in *–self* or *–selves,* they are easy to recognize. These pronouns are often used for emphasis.

| REFLEXIVE AND INTENSIVE PRONOUNS | |
|---|---|
| **SINGULAR** | myself, yourself, himself, herself, itself |
| **PLURAL** | ourselves, yourself, themselves |

**Reflexive pronouns** always refer back to a previous noun or pronoun in the sentence.

REFLEXIVE PRONOUNS

Tiffany voted for **herself**.

They saw **themselves** as rivals.

**Intensive pronouns** are used to emphasize a noun or another pronoun in the sentence.

INTENSIVE PRONOUNS

Ben **himself** was elected homecoming king.

They **themselves** decorated the gym.

Never use reflexive or intensive pronouns by themselves. They always have to have an antecedent in the same sentence.

INCORRECT — Laura and **myself** are the only candidates. (*Myself* has no antecedent in the sentence.)

CORRECT — Laura and **I** are the only delegates.

### CONNECT TO SPEAKING AND WRITING

In daily conversation, you may hear *theirself* used as a reflexive or intensive pronoun. For example, a friend may say, "When they laughed in class, they couldn't help theirself." *Theirself,* however, is not a word; you should always use *themselves* instead. Similarly, you would never say, "He cut *hisself.*" Instead, you would say "He cut *himself.*"

## Practice Your Skills

### Check Your Understanding
*Using Reflexive and Intensive Pronouns*

Contemporary Life

**Write the reflexive and intensive pronouns in the following sentences. Then write *I* if the pronoun is incorrect and *C* if the pronoun is correct.**

**1.** The nominees for homecoming queen are Amber Stockton and myself.

**2.** I can see myself in the crown already.

**3.** I noticed themselves in the top row of the bleachers.

**4.** The football team and ourselves marched onto the field.

**5.** The quarterback bought hisself a new tux.

**6.** The former homecoming queen will perform the crowning herself.

**7.** When last year's homecoming king arrived, the announcer said, "Himself is here."

**8.** I myself did not see himself.

**9.** The band of my corsage had tangled itself on my ring.

**10.** The girls in the court admired theirself in the mirrors.

### Connect to the Writing Process: Editing
*Replacing Reflexive and Intensive Pronouns*

**11.–17. Write the pronoun that correctly replaces the incorrect pronoun in each sentence in the preceding exercise.**

### Connect to the Writing Process: Drafting
*Using Reflexive and Intensive Pronouns in Sentences*

**Write sentences that follow the instructions.**

**18.** Include *myself* in a compound subject.

**19.** Use *herself* to emphasize a noun.

**20.** Use *himself* to refer back to a noun.

**21.** Use *themselves* to emphasize another pronoun.

**22.** Include *yourself* with an antecedent.

## Communicate Your Ideas

### APPLY TO WRITING

**Friendly Letter: *Pronouns***

One of your friends is in the hospital, and you want to cheer him or her up. Write an amusing letter, describing your recent school experiences. (Feel free to embellish them.) Use the pronouns you studied in this section: the *who/whom* pronouns, pronouns in comparisons, and reflexive and intensive pronouns. Edit your letter for mistakes in pronoun usage, and then write the final copy.

### Mixed Practice

Contemporary Life

**Write each pronoun that is used incorrectly. Then write it correctly. If a sentence is correct, write *C*.**

1. I answered the telephone by saying, "Whom may I say is calling?"
2. A salesperson asked to speak to whomever was "the lady of the house."
3. If they could hear theirself talk, salespeople wouldn't say things like that.
4. This is the kind of telemarketer whom I believe should be banned.
5. Maria and I have spoken to more salespeople than her.
6. Do you think she is more sympathetic to pushy salespeople than I?
7. Whom do you think buys useless junk?
8. Wayne, who everyone knows is too trusting, buys whatever a salesperson shows I22.
9. No one has more encyclopedias than him.
10. Maria and myself use the encyclopedias at school.

# Pronouns and Their Antecedents

A pronoun's **antecedent** is the word that the pronoun refers to or replaces. A pronoun and its antecedent must agree in number and gender since they both are referring to the same person, place, or thing.

**Number** is the term used to indicate whether a noun or a pronoun is singular (one) or plural (more than one). **Gender** is the term used to indicate whether a noun or a pronoun is masculine, feminine, or neuter.

| | GENDER | | |
|---|---|---|---|
| **Masculine** | he | him | his |
| **Feminine** | she | her | hers |
| **Neuter** | it | its | |

To make a pronoun agree with its antecedent, first find the antecedent. Then determine its number and gender. Making a pronoun agree with a single-word antecedent usually is not a problem.

**Nancy** must plant **her** vegetable garden soon.
(*Nancy* is singular and feminine; therefore, *her* is correct because it also is singular and feminine.)

**Members** of the landscape team presented **their** ideas at a special meeting.
(*Members* is plural; therefore, *their* is plural.)

If the antecedent of a pronoun is more than one word, you need to remember two rules.

If two or more singular antecedents are joined by *or, nor, either/or,* or *neither/nor,* use a singular pronoun to refer to them.

All the conjunctions listed in this rule indicate a choice—one *or* the other. In the following example, Harold *or* Cliff gave me his shovel—not both of them. As a result the pronoun must be singular.

Either Harold or Cliff gave me **his** shovel.

When one antecedent is singular and the other is plural, the pronoun agrees with the closer antecedent.

Neither Sue nor the other two gardeners planted **their** begonias in the proper soil.

Neither my brothers nor my father brought **his** rake.

If two or more singular antecedents are joined by *and* or *both/and,* use a plural pronoun to refer to them.

The conjunctions *and* and *both/and* indicate more than one. In the following example, both Greta and Mavis—two people—planted their spring flowers too early. Because the antecedent is plural, the plural pronoun must be used.

Both Greta and Mavis planted **their** spring flowers too early.

The gender of most antecedents is obvious. *Harold* and *Cliff* are masculine; *Greta* and *Mavis* are feminine. The gender of some antecedents, however, is not as obvious. Standard English solves the agreement problem in such cases by using the phrase *his or her* to refer to antecedents of unknown gender.

Each horticulturist should photograph **his or her** prize roses.

Overusing *his or her* in a short passage can make writing sound awkward. You can often avoid this problem by rewriting such sentences, using plural forms.

All horticulturists should photograph **their** prize roses.

*You can learn more about pronouns and antecedents on pages L9–L15.*

## Practice Your Skills

### Check Your Understanding

***Making Pronouns Agree with Their Antecedents***

General Interest **Write the pronoun that correctly completes each sentence.**

1. Every American should know what ▒ state flower is.
2. Texans see ▒ state flower, the bluebonnet, bloom in March and April.
3. Both Florida and Delaware have fruit blossoms as ▒ state flowers.
4. Florida claims the orange blossom as ▒ flower, and Delaware claims the peach blossom.
5. Each member of the Women's Garden Club in Rhode Island makes sure that ▒ grows the state flower, the violet, in ▒ garden.
6. In Nevada some residents are allergic to ▒ state flower, sagebrush.
7. Iris and Lily know that ▒ mothers named ▒ after Tennessee's and Utah's flowers.
8. Maine residents know that the pine cone is ▒ state flower.
9. Either Jonah or Carl left ▒ picture of the North Carolina dogwood on the table.
10. Neither my aunts nor my uncle realized that ▒ home state, Alaska, has the forget-me-not as ▒ flower.
11. School children in Kansas can easily draw ▒ state flower, the sunflower.
12. Both Nebraska and Kentucky have adopted goldenrod as ▒ flower.
13. Hawaii's foliage is as lush and exotic as ▒ state flower, the red hibiscus.
14. An Oklahoma native decorates ▒ home at Christmas time with the state flower, the mistletoe.
15. The men on the road crew in Wyoming decided that ▒ would not mow down the Indian paintbrush.

Connect to the Writing Process: Editing

### *Making Pronouns and Antecedents Agree*

**Rewrite the paragraphs, correcting errors in pronoun and antecedent agreement.**

A gardener should test their soil to see if they should add fertilizer or compost. A local garden center should have testing kits on their shelves. If the gardener's soil is too alkaline or acidic, they can buy additives to mix into them. Smart gardeners develop soil that crumbles easily in its hands. Sometimes they have to add sand, clay, or compost to create rich soil. Both my neighbor, Mrs. Kent, and I turn ~~their~~ soil with a shovel and mix in other soil types.

I learned that soil which sticks together when you press it probably has too much clay in them. Clumpy, sticky clay packs too tightly around a plant's roots, and they cannot drain properly. Conversely, a loose and sandy soil loses his nutrients and the plants can't get what it will need to thrive. Loam is the best kind of soil because she is not too sticky or sandy. Either leaves or manure will provide their nutrients to any soil you mix them into. A gardening center stocks bags of compost and fertilizer on their shelves.

## Indefinite Pronouns as Antecedents

Based on their number, the common indefinite pronouns have been divided into the following three groups.

| COMMON INDEFINITE PRONOUNS | |
|---|---|
| **SINGULAR** | anybody, anyone, each, either, everybody, everyone, neither, nobody, no one, one, somebody, someone |
| **PLURAL** | both, few, many, several |
| **SINGULAR/PLURAL** | all, any, most, none, some |

A personal pronoun must be singular if its antecedent is one of the singular indefinite pronouns.

**Each** of the girls is bathing **her** puppy.

A personal pronoun must be plural if its antecedent is one of the plural indefinite pronouns.

**Both** of the brothers donated **their** time to the humane society.

If the antecedent of a personal pronoun is one of the singular/plural indefinite pronouns, the personal pronoun agrees in number and gender with the object of the preposition that follows the indefinite pronoun.

**Some** of the dog *food* has ants in **it**. (singular)

**Some** of the cat *owners* have declawed **their** pets. (plural)

Sometimes the gender of a singular indefinite pronoun is not indicated by other words in the sentence. Standard English solves this problem by using *his or her* to refer to antecedents of unknown gender. You can also rewrite the sentence, using the plural form.

**Each** of the riders must register **his or her** horse by Monday.

**All** of the riders must register **their** horses by Monday.

## Practice Your Skills

### Check Your Understanding
### *Making Pronouns Agree*

Science Topic **Write the pronoun that correctly completes each sentence.**

1. Neither of the squirrels has had ■ dinner of sunflower seeds and strawberries.
2. All of the parakeets had green feathers on ■ wings.
3. Both of my parrots recently learned to say ■ names.
4. Most of the lizards sat cozily beneath ■ heat lamps.
5. Each of the Siamese fighting fish must have ■ own bowl in which to swim.
6. If any of these shells will work, put ■ in the hermit crab's case.
7. Several of my cats have torn apart ■ cat toys.
8. One of the boys said that ■ would groom my poodle.
9. Most of the floor of the rabbits' cage had alfalfa on ■.
10. Either of the women should place broccoli in ■ turtle's food dish.
11. Each hamster sleeps in ■ corner during the day.
12. Most of the cages have wheels in ■.
13. Each of the water bottles has vitamins in ■.
14. Some of the guinea pigs ate ■ carrots.
15. Neither the finches nor the parakeets built ■ nests.

### Connect to the Writing Process: Prewriting
### *Using Pronouns and Antecedents*

You have just learned that a product you use nearly every day (shampoo, lipstick, allergy medication, etc.) is tested on animals. Take five minutes to list your opinions, questions, and ideas about product-testing on animals. Use pronouns and antecedents in your statements and check for agreement in number and gender.

## Communicate Your Ideas

### APPLY TO WRITING

**Persuasive Essay: *Pronouns and Antecedents***

Refer to the prewriting you generated in the preceding exercise, and write a persuasive essay about testing products on animals. Convince your classmates to see the issue as you do. For example, do you believe testing on animals is never okay? Is it acceptable when developing life-saving medicine but unacceptable when developing a new kind of mascara? Use specific examples to illustrate your opinions. Check for pronoun and antecedent agreement before you write your final copy.

### Mixed Practice

Contemporary Life

**Write a pronoun that correctly completes each sentence.**

1. Participants in the auto show should bring ▒ vehicles to the lot by Saturday.
2. All of my sisters received cars on ▒ sixteenth birthdays.
3. Both Ray and Otis forgot ▒ keys today.
4. Most of these abandoned vehicles will never be claimed by ▒ owners.
5. Somebody who owns the red convertible has left ▒ car unlocked.
6. Some of the girls are riding to the game with ▒ friends.
7. Many of the boys in shop class have already rebuilt ▒ carburetors.
8. Susan and Julie asked ▒ father for a ride to the library.
9. Neither of my brothers could find ▒ spare tire.
10. Several of my friends drive ▒ cars to school every day.

# Unclear, Missing, or Confusing Antecedents

Not only does a pronoun have to agree in number and gender with its antecedent, but that antecedent must also be very clear. If an antecedent is hard to determine or if it is missing entirely, then your writing will become confusing or even misleading. As a result, as part of your editing, you should look for unclear, missing, or confusing antecedents.

**Every personal pronoun should clearly refer to a specific antecedent.**

## Unclear Antecedents

Although words such as *it, they, this,* and *that* might vaguely refer to antecedents within a piece of writing, you still should substitute specific antecedents to avoid any confusion or misunderstanding.

| | |
|---|---|
| UNCLEAR | Chuck is a tour guide, but none of his friends chose **it** as a career.<br>(The antecedent of *it* is not clear. The context of the sentence only suggests that the pronoun *it* refers to guiding tours as a profession.) |
| CLEAR | Chuck is a tour guide, but none of his friends chose **guiding tours** as a career. |
| UNCLEAR | The recreation director pulled the bell cords, and **they** rang out loudly.<br>(Although the antecedent of *they* is not clear, the context of the sentence suggests that the antecedent is *bells*.) |
| CLEAR | The recreation director pulled the bell cords, and the **bells** rang out loudly. |

UNCLEAR — I spent the summer at a horse ranch. **This** convinced me I wanted to become a veterinarian.
(*This* has no clear antecedent, but it suggests the experience of being at the horse ranch.)

CLEAR — I spent the summer at a horse ranch. **This experience** convinced me I wanted to become a veterinarian.

You may have noticed that sometimes the pronoun *you* is incorrectly used in a sentence because *you* does not refer to the person being spoken to. In many cases, the *you* is actually referring to the person who is speaking. As a result, the pronoun *you* does not have a clear antecedent either.

UNCLEAR — I work at the YMCA recreation center because **you** can be outdoors all summer.

CLEAR — I work at the YMCA recreation center because **I** can be outdoors all summer.

## Missing Antecedents

Occasionally pronouns are written without any antecedents at all. To correct this kind of mistake, you most often have to rewrite the sentence and replace the pronoun with a noun.

MISSING — In the book **it** shows how to re-string a guitar.
(The antecedent of *it* is missing.)

CLEAR — The **book** shows how to re-string a guitar.

MISSING — In the spring **they** are offering public recitals at the music academy.
(The antecedent of *they* is missing.)

CLEAR — In the spring **the music academy** is offering public recitals.

## Confusing Antecedents

The problem with some other pronouns is that they have more than one possible antecedent. As a result, readers can easily confuse the sentence's meaning. To correct this mistake, you must rewrite the sentence and replace the pronoun with a specific noun.

| | |
|---|---|
| CONFUSING | As Paulo was showing Mike the boat, **he** fell into the water. (Who fell in, Paulo or Mike?) |
| CLEAR | As Paulo was showing Mike the boat, **Mike** fell into the water. |
| CONFUSING | Rita had oars in both hands, but now **they** have disappeared. (What disappeared, the oars or her hands?) |
| CLEAR | Rita had oars in both hands, but now **the oars** have disappeared. |

## PRACTICE YOUR SKILLS

Check Your Understanding

***Identifying Unclear, Missing, and Confusing Antecedents***

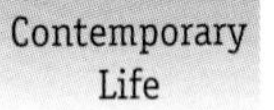

Contemporary Life **Write *I* if the sentence contains a pronoun-antecedent error and *C* if the sentence is correct.**

1. When Jane told Shawna about the new jet skis, she was very excited.
2. After my father and grandfather stowed the gear, he said, "All aboard!"
3. The Virgin Islands are our destination, and you can snorkel there.
4. I could hardly see the jellyfish and stingray underwater because it was cloudy.
5. Later I told Michelle and Marla about our trip, and they said it sounded enjoyable.

6. Wearing flippers on both feet, Geoffrey jumped into the water and then they fell off.
7. I packed a sun hat and tanning lotion, and it spilled inside my bag.
8. I asked Erica or Joanne to lend me a towel, and they both offered me one.
9. After I took the fish off the hooks, I threw them into the water.
10. When the boat hit the rock, it was a disaster.

Connect to the Writing Process: Revising

### *Correcting Antecedent Problems*

**11.–18. Rewrite the sentences from the preceding exercise, correcting unclear, missing, or confusing antecedents.**

Connect to the Writing Process: Revising

### *Correcting Unclear, Missing, and Confusing Antecedents*

**Rewrite the paragraphs, using clear pronouns and antecedents.**

I bought a large supply of oil paints, knowing I would enjoy it. On the flyer it said beginners were welcome. Later, when I saw the colors in my paintings, I decided I didn't like them. I had seen Minnie and Leo mixing reds and blues, so I copied them. In the directions it had said to experiment with color, but I don't like it when you feel completely lost when you're doing a new project.

I tried to create an impressionist painting of flowers in vases, but they looked like cartoon creatures from outer space. This taught me new respect for Renoír, Monet, and other painters of impressionist works. They make it look easy, but it is actually difficult.

Despite my trouble with paints and brushwork, it was not completely disappointing. If I hold a simple pen in my hand, it serves me well. When I showed my pen-and-ink sketches to Minnie and Leo, they were sitting by the windows. They admired my sketches, and that encouraged me to create more.

## Communicate Your Ideas

### APPLY TO WRITING

**Fantasy:** ***Antecedents***

Study the photograph and think, "adventure."

Create a fantasy adventure involving you and your best friend. First write freely, creating an imaginary world of strange surroundings and bizarre creatures. (For ideas, think of science-fiction movies like *Star Wars* or fantasy stories like *Gulliver's Travels.*) Next, write some action scenes: How did you and your friend get to this peculiar place? What is your first obstacle? How do you overcome it?

Now write the first draft. Use pronouns and antecedents carefully. Include vivid details and references to the senses when describing the land and its inhabitants. Then edit your story and check for unclear, missing, or confusing antecedents; make corrections. Write a final copy and read your story to a friend.

Mixed Practice

Contemporary Life

**Rewrite each sentence, correcting unclear, missing, or confusing antecedents.**

1. On the map of South Padre Island, it shows where the best swimming areas are.
2. Clark and Billy bought hamburgers for the swimmers and then ate them.
3. When my friends and I tossed cheese puffs to the seagulls, they flew through the air.
4. It says "No Diving" on the sign at the end of the dock.
5. Shari and Shane do not want sunburns, so they used plenty of sunblock.
6. In the morning I watched the sun rise over the water. That stayed in my mind all day.
7. We placed our tent and ice chest near the sand dunes, and later they were gone.
8. Hunter swam just beneath the water's surface with a plastic shark fin on his back. This backfired when I kicked him with my sharp toenails.
9. I had no idea that when you throw a foam cup into the campfire, it melts.
10. As the surfboard skimmed the water, it reflected the bright sun.

CheckPoint

## Using Pronouns in the Correct Case

**Write the correct form of the pronoun in parentheses.**

1. Mrs. Winters asked my friend Raymond to mow the lawn (himself, herself).
2. (Who, Whom) do you think will win the award for best singer?
3. Roy knows more about both folk music and country music than (she, her).
4. Was it Ken or (she, her) who saved that man's life at the beach yesterday?
5. Daniel, (who, whom) the coach promoted from junior varsity, has become one of Reading's best players.
6. The mayor promised three seniors, Carla, Al, and (he, him), summer jobs at City Hall.
7. Is Spencer older than (she, her)?
8. Show your pass to (whoever, whomever) is at the entrance to the estate.
9. Three of (we, us) boys volunteered to help load the moving van for Mr. Rodriguez.
10. Both Mom and Dad were surprised at (me, my) offering to clean the garage.
11. (Who, Whom) did you visit in Albany?
12. Neither the blue jay nor the sparrow abandoned (its, their) nest during the storm.
13. The only ones in the store were Kim and (he, him).
14. Both Lynn and Donna brought (her, their) umbrellas to the baseball game.
15. When am I going to ride in (your, you're) new car?

## Editing for Pronoun Problems

**Find at least one error in each sentence below. Write the sentences correctly.**

1. With who are you going to the senior prom?
2. Daniel talks to Beth more than she talks to he.
3. Whom do you suppose will replace Mrs. Bennett?
4. E-mailing Antoine probably would be much easier than phoning himself.
5. Our friend Barbara asked whom the man in the blue seersucker suit was.

## Making Pronouns Agree with Antecedents

**Write the pronoun that correctly completes each sentence.**

1. All the girls on the softball team packed ■ gear into the minivan.
2. Every duck in the pond had a piece of bread in ■ beak.
3. Neither Jeremiah nor Vincenzo submitted ■ history report on time.
4. One of the girls must have sold ■ bicycle.
5. Dogs perspire through ■ paw pads.

## Writing Sentences

**Write five sentences that follow the directions below.**

1. Write a sentence using a form of the word *you* preceding a gerund.
2. Write a sentence with two pronouns in an appositive that agrees with the subject.
3. Write a sentence that correctly uses the word *whomever.*
4. Write a sentence that includes an elliptical clause.
5. Write a sentence using a form of *we* followed by an appositive.

# Language and *Self-Expression*

Glenna Goodacre was deeply impressed by the suffering, the heroism, and the kindness shown by members of the armed forces during the Vietnam War. She was especially proud of the work done by women both as officers and as medical and support personnel.

Sometimes a realistic sculpture can evoke emotional responses that paintings and photographs cannot quite summon. Walking around a sculpture, touching the tears on a face, or tracing the folds in a shirt brings out the reality and raw emotional appeal of its subject. Think about the people portrayed in this sculpture and imagine their hope and their sorrow. Write a paragraph that describes both the sculpture and your feelings about it.

**Prewriting** Brainstorm or use a word web to list objects and emotions associated with war. For example, you may use objects evident in the sculpture. Choose the ones that affect you most deeply. Then list your choices in some logical order, such as from the top to the bottom of the sculpture, or from the left to the right.

**Drafting** Write your description and your feelings in the order in which you listed them in the prewriting activity. Conclude your description by giving your feelings about the sculpture as a whole.

**Revising** Read your paragraph as a critic would read it, searching for elements that are spatially incorrect or that do not fit together smoothly. Add transitions, rearrange ideas, and build toward a single effect.

**Editing** Read your work again, this time looking for errors in grammar, spelling, and usage. Check that all of the pronouns you used are correct.

**Publishing** Make a clean copy of your paragraph. If you wish, photocopy the picture of the sculpture and enlarge it to show the details you focused on.

# Another Look

**Case** is the form of a noun or a pronoun that indicates its use in a sentence.

## Cases of Personal Pronouns

The **nominative case** is used for subjects and predicate nominatives. *(page L236)*

The **objective case** is used for direct objects, indirect objects, objects of prepositions, and objects of verbals. *(page L242)*

The **possessive case** is used to show ownership or possession. *(page L251)*

## Who and Whom

The correct case of *who* is determined by how the pronoun is used in a question or a clause. *(page L258)*

## Pronouns in Comparisons

An **elliptical clause** is a subordinate clause that begins with *than* or *as*. *(page L262)*

## Reflexive and Intensive Pronouns

Both reflexive and intensive pronouns end in *–self* or *–selves*. *(page L264)*

A **reflexive pronoun** always refers to a previous noun or pronoun in a sentence. *(page L264)*

An **intensive pronoun** emphasizes a noun or another pronoun in a sentence. *(page L264)*

## Pronouns and Their Antecedents

If two or more singular antecedents are joined by *or, nor, either/or,* or *neither/nor,* use a **singular** pronoun to refer to them. *(page L267)*

If two or more singular antecedents are joined by *and* or *both/and,* use a **plural** pronoun to refer to them. *(page L268)*

Every personal pronoun should clearly refer to a specific antecedent. *(page L274)*

## Other Information About the Use of Pronouns

Using indefinite pronouns as antecedents *(pages L270–L273)*

Avoiding unclear, missing, or confusing antecedents *(pages L274–L279)*

### *Directions*

**Read the passage and choose the pronoun that belongs in each underlined space. Write the letter of the correct answer.**

EXAMPLE **1.** Walt Disney's wife once said, "I didn't want Walt to make a feature film, but he didn't listen to __(1)__."

**1** **A** I
**B** me
**C** my
**D** mine

ANSWER **1** **B**

Most young people today have seen __(1)__ fair share of full-length animated movies, such as *The Lion King* or *A Bug's Life*. In fact, you probably remember __(2)__ seeing movies such as *Cinderella* and *Toy Story* when you were younger. However, before 1937, a full-length cartoon feature had never been made. It was Walt Disney, of course, __(3)__ produced the first one, *Snow White and the Seven Dwarfs*.

Back then, no one thought __(4)__ idea would succeed. For example, Walt's brother and business partner Roy O. Disney, who was more conservative than __(5)__, feared financial ruin. Nevertheless, Walt was confident that __(6)__ watched it would love it, and Walt wanted to show __(7)__ and everyone else that he was right.

For three years each of the animators worked hard on __(8)__ drawings of Snow White. Walt gave __(9)__ high standards to follow, but all of the difficult work eventually paid off. When the movie ended its first showing, the members of the audience rose from __(10)__ seats and cheered wildly.

**1** **A** they
**B** them
**C** their
**D** theirs

**2** **A** you
**B** your
**C** yours
**D** their

**3** **A** who
**B** whom
**C** whoever
**D** whoever

**4** **A** he
**B** him
**C** his
**D** himself

**5** **A** he
**B** him
**C** his
**D** their

**6** **A** who
**B** whoever
**C** whom
**D** whoever

**7** **A** he
**B** his
**C** him
**D** their

**8** **A** their
**B** theirs
**C** his
**D** him

**9** **A** him
**B** his
**C** they
**D** them

**10** **A** they
**B** them
**C** their
**D** theirs

# Subject and Verb Agreement

Pretest

### *Directions*

**Write the letter of the best way to write the underlined verb(s) in each sentence. If the underlined part contains no error, write *D*.**

EXAMPLE **1.** Hurricanes arises in warm water and travel across the ocean.

**1 A** arised
**B** arise
**C** arose
**D** No error

ANSWER **1 B**

**1.** Storm trackers track hurricanes and map their locations.
**2.** The data compiled by storm trackers are both extensive and important.
**3.** Each year a few storms was defined as *major hurricanes*.
**4.** Hurricanes in the eastern U.S. has caused great damage.
**5.** Each of the hurricanes seem worse than the one before.
**6.** One hundred miles inland are a common distance for a storm to travel.
**7.** Both of these storms is very dangerous.
**8.** An area struck by either of these storms often suffer great damage.
**9.** Neither storms nor other bad weather are avoided by a move to another state.
**10.** The media inform us that storms occur everywhere.

**1** **A** maps
**B** is mapping
**C** has mapped
**D** No error

**2** **A** is
**B** has proven
**C** was proven
**D** No error

**3** **A** has been defined
**B** are defined
**C** were defined
**D** No error

**4** **A** was caused
**B** is causing
**C** have caused
**D** No error

**5** **A** seems
**B** have seemed
**C** do seem
**D** No error

**6** **A** is
**B** seem
**C** were
**D** No error

**7** **A** seems
**B** are
**C** be
**D** No error

**8** **A** suffers
**B** has suffered
**C** suffering
**D** No error

**9** **A** were avoided
**B** be avoided
**C** is avoided
**D** No error

**10** **A** has informed
**B** was informing
**C** informing
**D** No error

Painter of Micali. *Hydria with Running Figures,* date unknown. Museo Gregoriano Etrusco, Rome.

**Describe** What is depicted in this Etruscan vase painting inspired by Greek black-figured art? What are the figures wearing? What technique does the artist use to create a sense of movement?

**Analyze** Notice the vase has two handles. What do you think the vase was used for? Do you think it had more of a functional or decorative use?

**Interpret** Would you consider the painting on the vase great art? Why or why not?

**Judge** What advantage might the artwork—and the vase itself—have over a written description of the scene? Suppose the image were unavailable and all you had was a description. Who do you think would do the best job of describing it—a novelist, a writer of nonfiction prose, or a poet? Why?

At the end of this chapter, you will use the artwork as a visual aid for writing.

# Agreement of Subjects and Verbs

How many times have you seen the "perfect" pair of jeans, tried them on, and then discovered to your great disappointment that they were either too loose or too short? "Perfect" as they are, you cannot wear them because they do not fit. In a way, subjects and verbs are like people and jeans. Some fit together; others do not. When words do fit together, they are said to be in **agreement.** This chapter will review the different types of subjects and verbs. Then it will show you which agree and which do not.

## A verb must agree with its subject in number.

**Number** determines whether a word is singular (one) or plural (more than one). A subject and a verb agree when they have the same number.

To understand agreement, you must know the singular and plural forms of nouns, pronouns, and verbs. The plurals of most nouns are formed by adding *–s* or *–es* to the singular form. Some nouns, however, form their plurals irregularly. For example, *children* is the plural of *child.* Certain pronouns also form their plurals by changing form.

| NOUNS | | PRONOUNS | |
|---|---|---|---|
| **Singular** | **Plural** | **Singular** | **Plural** |
| lion | lions | I | we |
| fox | foxes | you | you |
| goose | geese | he, she, it | they |

Verbs also have singular and plural forms, but only present tense verbs change endings. The third-person singular of present tense verbs ends in *–s* or *–es.* However, most plural forms of present tense verbs do not end in *–s* or *–es.* Notice that *I* and *you* take the plural form of the verb.

| | |
|---|---|
| THIRD PERSON SINGULAR | (He, She, It) **sits.** |
| OTHERS | (I, You, We, They) **sit.** |

In the following box are the singular and the plural forms of the irregular verbs *be, have,* and *do* in the present tense. Notice that *be* also has irregular forms for both the singular and the plural in the past tense.

| PRESENT TENSE | PAST TENSE |
|---|---|
| **Singular** | **Singular** |
| I **am, have, do** | I **was** |
| you **are, have, do** | you **were** |
| he, she, it **is, has, does** | he, she, it **was** |
| **Plural** | **Plural** |
| we **are, have, do** | we **were** |
| you **are, have, do** | you **were** |
| they **are, have, do** | they **were** |

Since a subject and a verb both have number, they must agree in a sentence.

**A singular subject takes a singular verb.**

**A plural subject takes a plural verb.**

| | |
|---|---|
| The lion pounces. | The lions pounce. |
| The fox hides. | The foxes hide. |
| The goose flies. | The geese fly. |
| It is a hawk. | They are hawks. |

*Be, have,* and *do* are often used as helping verbs. When they are, they must agree in number with the subject.

**The first helping verb must agree in number with its subject.**

Pamela **is** studying primates in science class.

The baby gorillas **were** found in the jungle.

The birds **have** flown away.

Mark **does** have a pet cockatoo.

*You can learn more about regular and irregular verbs on pages L181–L192.*

CONNECT TO WRITER'S CRAFT

Mark Twain is one writer who is known for breaking rules of grammar in the dialogue of his characters. For example, Huckleberry Finn tells the reader that when "Mr. Mark Twain" wrote *Tom Sawyer,*

"There was things which he stretched, but mainly he told the truth."

You probably noticed that the correct grammar is "There *were* things that he stretched." Twain's misuse of subject and verb agreement is one aspect of **local color writing.** With this type of writing, authors write sentences exactly as the people in a particular region would speak them.

## PRACTICE YOUR SKILLS

Check Your Understanding

***Making Subjects and Verbs Agree***

Science Topic **Write the correct form of the verb in parentheses.**

**1.** Alex (is, are) a 22-year-old gray parrot.

**2.** Trainers (talks, talk) to Alex every day.

**3.** Irene Pepperberg (train, trains) Alex to speak and reason.

**4.** The teacher (hold, holds) a tray of wood, plastic, and wool items.

5. She (asks, ask) Alex, "How many wood?"
6. Alex (respond, responds) with the correct number of wooden objects.
7. As a reward, Irene (gives, give) a wooden object to Alex to play with.
8. Sometimes Alex (want, wants) a treat instead of a toy.
9. On these occasions, the parrot (say, says), "Wanna nut."
10. Some scientists (believes, believe) that gray parrots (rival, rivals) dolphins and apes in intelligence.

Connect to the Writing Process: Editing

***Correcting Subject and Verb Agreement***

**Edit the sentences in the following paragraphs for subject-verb agreement. If a subject and verb do not agree in number, write the sentence correctly.**

Koko were born in 1971. She are a black gorilla, and she weigh about 280 pounds. Her handlers has taught her to understand over 2,000 words of American Sign Language. The teachers shows Koko how to form the words, or they molds Koko's hands into the proper shape. The techniques is very similar to teaching sign language to a human. Koko speak to people using over 1,000 signs. Koko's gorilla friend Michael also have learned some sign language—over 500 signs. Sometimes, the two gorillas communicates with each other in this way.

Koko were able to name her own pet kitten, whom she called All Ball. Her favorite color are red, and her favorite toys is rubber alligators. She love to watch *Wild Kingdom* on television, and she also like films about children and animals, such as *Free Willy*. Koko's caregivers at the Gorilla Foundation has noticed that the gorilla's favorite book are *The Three Little Kittens*.

Also, a computer company were able to make a special computer for Koko. When she touch icons on the screen, the computer "speak" the word the icon represent. Koko also recognize the letters in her own name. Fans has wanted to send E-mail to Koko, but the gorilla's computer are not online.

## Interrupting Words

Often a subject and a verb are side by side in a sentence. When they are, agreement between them is usually easy to recognize. Many times, however, a phrase or a clause modifying the subject separates it from the verb. In such sentences a mistake in agreement may occur. The error that might happen is to make the verb agree with the word closest to it—rather than with its subject. To avoid making this mistake in agreement, first find the subject and then make the verb agree with it.

**The agreement of a verb with its subject is not changed by any interrupting words.**

Notice in each of the following examples that the subject and the verb agree in number—regardless of any interrupting words.

| | |
|---|---|
| Prepositional Phrase | The games on the computer **were** installed yesterday afternoon. (The plural helping verb *were* agrees with the plural subject *games,* even though the singular noun *computer* is closer to the verb.) |

| | |
|---|---|
| PARTICIPIAL PHRASE | The monitor, covered with notes, is mine. (*Is* agrees with *monitor,* not *notes.*) |
| NEGATIVE STATEMENTS | The program architects, not their manager, design the project. (*Design* agrees with *architects,* not *manager.*) |
| ADJECTIVE CLAUSES | Computer programs that compose music are a form of artificial intelligence. (*Are* agrees with *programs,* not *music.*) |

A compound preposition—such as *in addition to, as well as, along with,* and *together with*—will often interrupt a subject and a verb. Make sure the verb always agrees with the subject, not the object of the compound preposition.

Gail, together with her sisters, **is** starting a computer software company.
(*Is* agrees with *Gail,* not *sisters.*)

The boys, as well as my uncle, **are** installing the satellite dish.
(*Are* agrees with *boys,* not *uncle.*)

## PRACTICE YOUR SKILLS

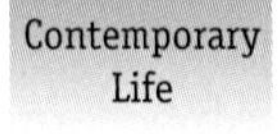

Check Your Understanding

***Making Interrupted Subjects and Verbs Agree***

Contemporary Life

**Write the subject in each sentence. Next to each subject, write the form of the verb in parentheses that agrees with it.**

**1.** Many students at the science fair (was, were) honored for their technological creations.

**2.** The inventions, arranged on a table, (includes, include) telephones, speakers, and other electronics.

**3.** The cost of each project (averages, average) one hundred dollars.

4. Tyrone Purdy, unlike other students, (has, have) a parent who is a scientist.
5. Dr. Purdy, so helpful to us students, (hands, hand) out the awards while a photographer takes pictures.
6. The telephone that "speaks" the names of callers (is, are) my favorite invention.
7. The pager-on-a-necklace, including ports for phone jacks and printers, (wins, win) an award as well.
8. The underwater fisher's camera, not the musical earrings, (was, were) the first-place winner.
9. The lucky students who won first, second, and third place (was, were) given scholarships for college.
10. The second-place winner, as well as several other participants, (plan, plans) to attend M.I.T.

Connect to the Writing Process: Editing

### *Using Subject and Verb Agreement*

**Write each verb that does not agree with its subject. Beside the verb, write its correct form.**

Scientists who work at universities and laboratories regularly invents amazing items. Their expensive inventions, often funded by grants, introduces creative applications for technology. Scientists at the Massachusetts Institute of Technology Media Lab was able to create "intelligent clothes." For example, a television reporter, together with journalists of all kinds, are now able to stay ahead of the competition by wearing gloves! The reporter wear a glove equipped with a video camera in the palm. A pair of special glasses show the image being recorded.

These scientists at M.I.T. has created other wearable technology. People who travel to a foreign country has the option of wearing a translation vest. These vests, not a foreign language dictionary, is what will translate the tourists' speech. A speaker, wearing the vest, talk normally. Microphones built into the vest records the spoken words, and speakers at shoulder level relays the translation.

Also, pool players can wear smart caps. The camera on the hat analyze the position of the balls. Then the special software, which is loaded in these caps, identify the easiest shot. Special eyeglasses (like the reporter's glasses) shows the pool player how to line up winning shots.

## Communicate Your Ideas

### APPLY TO WRITING

**Description:** ***Subject and Verb Agreement***

Your class is planning a Science Fair of the Future, and the theme is "wearable hardware." As a sample exhibit idea, you are shown the photograph on the preceding page of a pair of shoes that converts the wearer's steps into music. Wearing them, you could create your own dance music or analyze your jogging stride.

Write a description of your own idea for a "wearable hardware" creation. Describe what its purpose is, how it works, and where a person will wear it. Edit your writing for agreement between subjects and verbs. Make any necessary corrections, and then write the final copy.

Mixed Practice

General Interest

**Write the subject in each sentence. Then write the form of the underlined verb that agrees with the subject. If the verb is correct, write C.**

**1.** This lawn, covered with weeds, need Rodney's attention and expertise.

**2.** Rodney, one of my neighbors, own a lawn care and landscaping business.

**3.** His customers is impressed by his knowledge and skill.

**4.** Rodney have told me how he learned the business.

**5.** Informative books, not luck, explains his success.

**6.** In their high school, students who have money buys clothes and CDs.

**7.** Rodney, as well as his brothers, was not able to buy these things.

**8.** The books in the library was the key to their small business success.

**9.** The brothers, immersed in study, was able to learn lawn care and irrigation techniques.

**10.** Now, their accounts in the bank hold plenty of money for what the brothers need or want.

# Common Agreement Problems

When you edit your writing, look for the following common agreement problems.

## Compound Subjects

When you make two or more subjects agree with a verb, you should remember two rules.

**When subjects are joined by *or, nor, either/or*, or *neither/nor,* the verb agrees with the closer subject.**

> Either Joe or Lola buys vegetables at the Vine Street Farmers' Market.
> (*Buys* agrees with the closer subject *Lola*.)
>
> A ladybug or an earthworm is a helpful creature for a vegetable garden.
> (*Is* agrees with the closer subject *earthworm*.)

The same rule applies when one subject is singular and the other subject is plural.

> Neither the trowel nor our shovels were in sight.
> (*Were* agrees with the closer subject *shovels*—even though *trowel* is singular.)

When compound subjects are joined by other conjunctions, however, a different rule applies.

**When subjects are joined by *and* or *both/and,* the verb is plural.**

These conjunctions always indicate more than one. Since more than one is plural, the verb must be plural also.

The mulch and the fertilizer are in the barn.
(Two items—the *mulch* and the *fertilizer*—are in the barn. The verb must be plural to agree with both of them.)

Both the rakes and that wheelbarrow **were** left in the rain.
(Even though *wheelbarrow* is singular, the verb is still plural because the wheelbarrow and the rakes—together—were left in the rain.)

The second rule has certain exceptions. Two subjects joined by *and* occasionally refer to only one person or one thing. In such a case, the verb must be singular.

Fruit and cheese is my mom's favorite dessert.
(*Fruit and cheese* is considered one item.)

Strawberries and cream is also very good.
(*Strawberries and cream* is considered one item.)

Another exception involves the words *every* and *each*. If one of these words comes before a compound subject that is joined by *and*, each subject is considered separately. As a result, the verb must be singular to agree with a singular subject.

Every barn and fence receives a fresh coat of paint.

Each pond and creek brims with rainwater.

CONNECT TO WRITER'S CRAFT

If you take a look at the next sales circular that arrives in your mailbox, you will see how subject and verb agreement can make the difference between your getting a good buy or not.

Lawn Mower or Rototiller, Only $449.99!
Lawn Mower and Rototiller, Only $449.99!

In both instances, the ad omitted the verb—*is* in the first ad, *are* in the second—but you should be able to supply the verb that agrees with the subject.

## Practice Your Skills

### Check Your Understanding
### *Making Verbs Agree with Compound Subjects*

Horticulture Topic

**Write the correct form of the verb in parentheses.**

1. Wheat and corn (grows, grow) well in Washington.
2. For some reason neither snails nor slugs (crawl, crawls) over crushed eggshells.
3. Each flower garden and vegetable plot (was, were) sprinkled with eggshells.
4. Either chicken wire or a wooden fence (form, forms) a good garden enclosure.
5. On a busy farm, every man, woman, and child (is, are) given duties.
6. Bacon and eggs (are, is) many farmers' favorite breakfast food.
7. Neither chemical fertilizers nor chemical pesticides (is, are) used in organic gardens.
8. Every horticulturist and gardener (know, knows) that lavender repels insects in the garden and moths in the closet.
9. Peanuts or potatoes (grow, grows) on many of Oklahoma's farms.
10. Both cantaloupe and spinach (flourishes, flourish) in southwest Texas along the border of Mexico.

### Connect to the Writing Process: Revising
### *Making Compound Subjects and Verbs Agree*

**Write each sentence, replacing each subject with a compound subject. Use a variety of joining words, such as *either/or, both/and,* and *or.* Then change the verb form if necessary, making it agree with the compound subject.**

11. Fruit is on sale at the market.
12. Each stump was cleared from the new garden plot.
13. Jelly is the peanut farmer's favorite sandwich.

14. Grapefruit is commonly grown in Florida.
15. The flowerpots are in the shed.
16. Every morning is a good time to water the bean patch.
17. The blackbird was not afraid of the scarecrow.
18. The squirrel was able to get into my garden despite the chain link fence.
19. Water is necessary for every plant's survival.
20. Each cherry was picked with care.

## Indefinite Pronouns as Subjects

**A verb must agree in number with an indefinite pronoun used as a subject.**

The indefinite pronouns in the following chart have been grouped according to number.

| COMMON INDEFINITE PRONOUNS | |
|---|---|
| **SINGULAR** | another, anybody, anyone, anything, each, either, everybody, everyone, everything, much, neither, nobody, no one, one, somebody, someone, something |
| **PLURAL** | both, few, many, others, several |
| **SINGULAR/PLURAL** | all, any, most, none, some |

A singular verb agrees with a singular indefinite pronoun, and a plural verb agrees with a plural indefinite pronoun.

SINGULAR One of my golf balls is muddy.

PLURAL Many of my golf balls are muddy.

The number of an indefinite pronoun in the singular/plural group is determined by the object of the prepositional phrase that follows it.

| | |
|---|---|
| SINGULAR | Some of the equipment is on sale. |
| OR PLURAL | Most of the barbells are on sale. |

## PRACTICE YOUR SKILLS

### Check Your Understanding
### *Making Verbs Agree with Indefinite Pronoun Subjects*

Contemporary Life **Write the subject in each sentence. Next to it, write the form of the verb in parentheses that agrees with the subject.**

**1.** All of the players (has, have) received their letters.
**2.** Everybody at the pep rally (are, is) wearing the school colors, green and gold.
**3.** Both of the teams (wear, wears) green jerseys.
**4.** Most of the opposing team (have, has) the flu.
**5.** Neither of those footballs (is, are) mine.
**6.** Some of the basketball fans (has, have) arrived.
**7.** Others (plans, plan) to be here soon.
**8.** Everyone, including the band, (was, were) thirsty during halftime.
**9.** Any of the game plan (is, are) open to revision.
**10.** Another of my teammates (has, have) become severely dehydrated.
**11.** Several of the rackets (was, were) damaged.
**12.** All of the field (is, are) artificial grass.
**13.** Something left in one of these gymnasium lockers (smell, smells) horrible.
**14.** Each of those skates (needs, need) new blades.

15. Anything (is, are) possible with a team this dedicated.
16. Some of the court (was, were) being resurfaced.
17. Many of those helmets (fits, fit) too tightly.
18. One of my sisters (has, have) just made the track team.
19. None of my baseball bats (is, are) aluminum.
20. Few of the cracked hockey masks (gives, give) the players much protection.

Connect to the Writing Process: Revising

*Making Verbs and Indefinite Pronouns Agree*

**Rewrite each sentence twice. First, add a prepositional phrase with a plural object. Second, add a prepositional phrase with a singular object.** Be sure to check that all subjects and verbs agree.

21. Some have finished the marathon.
22. Any are welcome.
23. None is accused of cheating.
24. Most train all day.
25. All is in the locker.

## Subjects in Inverted Order

A sentence is said to be in **inverted order** when the verb or part of the verb phrase comes before the subject. Even though a verb may precede a subject, it still must agree with the subject in number.

The subject and the verb of an inverted sentence must agree in number.

There are several types of inverted sentences. When you are looking for the subject in an inverted sentence, turn the sentence around to its natural order. To have the sentence make sense, you must occasionally drop *here* or *there* when putting the sentence into its natural order.

| | |
|---|---|
| INVERTED ORDER | In the valley is a babbling brook. (A babbling *brook is* in the valley.) |
| QUESTION | Was the mountain visible in the fog? (The *mountain was* visible in the fog.) |
| SENTENCES BEGINNING WITH *HERE* OR *THERE* | Here are the hiking trails. (The hiking *trails are* here.) |
| | There is a waterfall on the edge of the cliff. (Drop *there.* A *waterfall is* on the edge of the cliff.) |

*You can learn more about sentences written in inverted order on pages 62–64.*

# PRACTICE YOUR SKILLS

Check Your Understanding

***Making Subjects and Verbs in Inverted Order Agree***

Geography Topic

**Write the subject in each sentence. Next to it write the form of the verb in parentheses that agrees with the subject.**

1. Along the Tennessee-North Carolina border (run, runs) a mountain range.
2. (Has, Have) you ever heard anyone talk about the Great Smoky Mountains?
3. There (is, are) a park called Great Smoky Mountain National Park on the highest peak.
4. (Do, Does) they know that the Great Basin between the Sierra Nevada and Wasatch Range in the western United States has no outlet to the sea?
5. Here (is, are) colorful, current maps of the five Great Lakes: Superior, Michigan, Huron, Erie, and Ontario.
6. (Were, Was) souvenir shops selling pieces of the Berlin Wall after it was brought down?

7. Across western Australia (stretches, stretch) the sands of the Great Sandy Desert.
8. (Is, Are) the tour scheduled to visit the Greater Antilles, a group of islands in the West Indies?
9. There (is, are) a seaport called Great Yarmouth on the eastern coast of England in Norfolk.
10. Off the northeast coast of Australia (lies, lie) the Great Barrier Reef, a coral reef 1,250 miles long.

Connect to the Writing Process: Prewriting
***Brainstorming: Sentences in Inverted Order***

Referring to the preceding exercise, choose one of the geographical locations that interests you. Using sentences in inverted order, write down your thoughts and questions about this place. For example, you might write, "In the Great Smoky Mountains is a great hiking trail" or "Where is Australia located?" Then save your sentences for the following activity.

## Communicate Your Ideas

### APPLY TO WRITING

**Oral Presentation:** ***Common Agreement Problems***

Using the prewriting you generated in the preceding exercise, write an oral presentation for your classmates. Answer the questions you have about the location, explain where the place is in relation to the United States, and describe other information that your classmates would find interesting. You will probably need to use reference sources such as maps and encyclopedias to gather information. When you finish, be sure to edit your presentation for agreement between subjects and verbs, paying special attention to compound subjects, indefinite pronouns as subjects, and subjects in inverted order.

## QuickCheck Mixed Practice

Literature Topic **Write each sentence, using the correct present tense form of the verb in parentheses.**

1. (is) Both Sherlock Holmes and Dr. Watson ■ characters in a popular series of mystery stories.
2. (read) Many of the world's mystery fans ■ these stories by Arthur Conan Doyle.
3. (investigate) Throughout London and the surrounding countryside, Holmes ■ murders and thefts.
4. (is) There ■ cases such as the murderous "speckled band" and the disappearance of a horse called Silver Blaze.
5. (find) Across a windowsill, Hilton Cubitt ■ drawings of little stick-figure men.
6. (is) Neither Hilton nor the police ■ able to solve the mystery of the dancing men.
7. (is) All of the "dancing" hieroglyphics ■ interpreted by Holmes.
8. (chop) Someone ■ off a man's thumb in the story, "The Engineer's Thumb."
9. (is) "Where ■ we to find the photograph?" Holmes asks in "A Scandal in Bohemia."
10. (solve) No one ■ the mystery of the Musgrave Ritual until Holmes steps in.
11. (appear) The villain Colonel Moran ■ in "The Adventure of the Empty House."
12. (include) Some of Sherlock Holmes' talents ■ boxing and swordsmanship.
13. (analyze) Three characteristics Holmes ■ about suspects are nails, sleeves, and stride.
14. (Do) ■ Holmes know a great deal about chemistry?
15. (is) There ■ cases in which Holmes depends on his great knowledge of literature.

# Other Agreement Problems

There are several other situations in which agreement between a subject and a verb may present a problem.

## Collective Nouns

You may recall that a **collective noun** names a group of people or things. A collective noun may be either singular or plural—depending on how it is used in a sentence.

| COMMON COLLECTIVE NOUNS | | | |
|---|---|---|---|
| band | congregation | flock | orchestra |
| class | crew | gang | swarm |
| committee | crowd | herd | team |
| colony | family | league | tribe |

**Use a singular verb with a collective-noun subject that is treated as a unit. Use a plural verb with a collective-noun subject that is treated as individual parts.**

The class **is** presently holding elections.
(The class is working together as a whole unit in this sentence. As a result, the verb is singular.)

The class **are** casting their ballots today.
(The members of the class are acting independently—each one casting a ballot. As a result, the verb is plural.)

### CONNECT TO SPEAKING AND WRITING

In informal language, collective nouns are often used with singular verbs. It sounds awkward to use plural verbs. Therefore when you discuss a collective noun as separate parts, practice using plural verbs to master agreement.

The band **are** voting for a new Drum Major. 

## Words Expressing Amounts or Times

Subjects that express amounts, measurements, weights, or times usually are considered to be a single unit. However, they often have plural forms.

**A subject that expresses an amount, a measurement, a weight, or a time is usually considered singular and takes a singular verb.**

| | |
|---|---|
| QUANTITY | **Ten dollars** is the amount of my campaign contribution. (one amount of money) |
| | **Five miles** is the distance from my house to City Hall. (one unit of distance) |
| | **Two pounds** is the weight of this box of campaign buttons. (one unit of weight) |
| TIME | **Six months is** needed to prepare the candidates. (one period of time) |
| | **Thirty minutes** is how long the legislator spoke. (one period of time) |

If an amount, measurement, weight, or time is treated in its individual parts, then the verb must be plural.

**Two pounds** of pencils **were** lost.

**Ten dollars** were in the treasurer's hand.

**Six months have** passed since the election.

When the subject is a fraction or a percent, the verb agrees with the object of the prepositional phrase that follows the subject.

| | |
|---|---|
| SINGULAR | **One third** of my salary goes to taxes. |
| PLURAL | **One fourth** of the seniors are old enough to vote. |

## *The Number of, A Number of*

Although these expressions are very similar, one expression takes a singular verb and one takes a plural verb.

Use a singular verb with *the number of* and a plural verb with *a number of.*

**The number of** students touring the White House is surprising. (singular)

**A number of** high school students intend to go into city government. (plural)

CONNECT TO WRITER'S CRAFT

Be sure to choose the correct expression for your writing purpose. **A number of tourists visit yearly** focuses on the action of the **tourists**. **The number of tourists escalates yearly** focuses on the action of the **number**.

## Singular Nouns That Have Plural Forms

Even though a word ends in *–s,* it may not take a plural verb. Some nouns are plural in form but singular in meaning because they name a single thing—one area of knowledge or one type of disease, for example.

| SINGULAR NOUNS WITH PLURAL FORMS | | | |
|---|---|---|---|
| civics | economics | gymnastics | mathematics |
| measles | molasses | mumps | news |
| physics | social studies | the United States | |

Use a singular verb with certain subjects that are plural in form but singular in meaning.

Civics is the study of citizens' rights and responsibilities.

The local news covers the mayor's weekly activities.

A second group of similar nouns are usually plural, as their form indicates. A third group can be either singular or plural—depending on how they are used in a sentence. If you are confused about a particular noun, it sometimes helps to check the dictionary.

| | SIMILAR NOUNS |
|---|---|
| **Usually Plural** | barracks, data, eyeglasses, media, pliers, scissors, shears, slacks, thanks, trousers |
| **Singular/Plural** | acoustics, athletics, headquarters, ethics, politics, tactics |

Your eyeglasses **were** found in the courtroom. (plural)

The headquarters for the United Nations **is** located in New York City. (singular—an administrative center)

The headquarters **are** located on the outskirts of the town. (plural—a group of buildings)

Notice that if the word *pair* precedes a word that is usually plural, the verb is nevertheless singular because the verb then agrees with the singular noun *pair*.

| | |
|---|---|
| Singular | That pair of scissors is dull. |
| Plural | Those scissors are dull. |

**Connect to Speaking and Writing**

Although *data* and *media* are both plural nouns, many people use them as singular nouns in informal speech. However, in your formal speaking and writing, it is best to use *data* and *media* as plural nouns; their singular forms are *datum* and *medium*.

| | |
|---|---|
| Singular | My favorite medium of communication is the newspaper. |
| Plural | Various media are radio, television, and print. |
| Singular | This datum is not the result I expected. |
| Plural | The data I collected are accurate. |

## PRACTICE YOUR SKILLS

### Check Your Understanding
### *Making Subjects and Verbs Agree*

General Interest **Write the correct form of the verb in parentheses.**

**1.** A large number of the candidates (is, are) female.

**2.** Campaigning for school government (takes, take) up most of my sister's spare time.

**3.** Two thirds of the people in town (does, do) not vote.

**4.** Ten minutes (was, were) not a long wait to vote.

**5.** Sixty percent of the student body (has, have) voted in student government elections.

**6.** Three miles (is, are) the distance from here to the governor's mansion.

**7.** The jury (was, were) in complete disagreement throughout the deliberations.

**8.** The headquarters for Steve's campaign for class president (is, are) the corner pizza parlor.

**9.** The city government news (is, are) broadcast at five o'clock.

**10.** Almost three fourths of the apples in the basket (was, were) used in pies at the mayor's reception dinner.

### Connect to the Writing Process: Editing
### *Correcting Subject and Verb Agreement Problems*

**Write the subject and the correct verb form. If a sentence is correct, write *C*.**

**11.** A swarm of reporters want to question the politician.

**12.** "Mumps are preventable with a vaccine," said the new county health commissioner.

**13.** Approximately four dollars was paid for each nominee's campaign poster.

**14.** The number of candidates for Student Council is surprisingly large.

15. The committee was arguing about the details of the voting procedure.
16. A group of students from the twelfth grade are ready to vote.
17. That pair of red suspenders look good on the senator.
18. Economics are Kevin's major at the University of Florida in Gainesville.
19. The media are distorting the candidate's remarks.
20. A number of students is planning for political careers.

## *Doesn't* or *Don't?*

*Doesn't* and *don't* are contractions. When checking for agreement with a subject, say the two words of a contraction separately. Also keep in mind which contractions are singular and which are plural.

| CONTRACTIONS | |
|---|---|
| SINGULAR | doesn't, hasn't, isn't, wasn't |
| PLURAL | don't, haven't, aren't, weren't |

The verb part of a contraction must agree in number with the subject.

This cold weather **does**n't bother me at all.
These rainstorms **do**n't alter my plans.

## Subjects with Linking Verbs

A predicate nominative follows a linking verb and identifies, renames, or explains the subject. Occasionally, however, a subject and its predicate nominative will not have the same number. The verb, nevertheless, agrees with the subject.

A verb agrees with the subject of a sentence, not with the predicate nominative.

Hail is small pieces of ice in a thunderstorm.
(The singular verb *is* agrees with the singular subject *hail*—even though the predicate nominative *pieces* is plural.)

Small pieces of ice in a thunderstorm are hail.
(*Are* agrees with the plural subject *pieces*—not with the singular predicate nominative *hail.*)

CONNECT TO SPEAKING AND WRITING

When writing, avoid creating sentences in which the subject and the predicate nominative do not agree in number.

| | |
|---|---|
| INCORRECT | Hailstones are a small **piece** of ice. |
| CORRECT | Hailstones are small **pieces** of ice.  |

*You can find lists of linking verbs on page L21.*

## Titles

Some titles may seem plural because they are composed of several words. A title, nevertheless, is the name of only one book, poem, play, work of art, country, or the like. As a result, a title is singular and takes a singular verb. Most multiword names of businesses and organizations are also considered singular.

**A title is singular and takes a singular verb.**

| | |
|---|---|
| BOOK | *Great Expectations* is a novel by Charles Dickens. |
| POEM | "The Planters" is a poem by Margaret Atwood. |
| PLAY | *Death of a Salesman* is my favorite play. |
| WORK OF ART | *Midsummer* is an oil painting by Albert Joseph Moore. |

| | |
|---|---|
| COUNTRY | The Netherlands is an interesting vacation destination. |
| COMPANY | Barrett's Book Barn **is** having a sale on mystery novels. |

## PRACTICE YOUR SKILLS

Check Your Understanding

***Making Subjects and Verbs Agree***

General Interest **Write the correct form of the verb in parentheses.**

**1.** Snowy ski slopes (is, are) a great attraction in Colorado.

**2.** He (doesn't, don't) know the way through the fog.

**3.** *The Iceman Cometh,* a play with four acts, (is, are) Eugene O'Neill's most celebrated work.

**4.** These rain boots (is, are) the perfect gift.

**5.** Ick! The snow (feel, feels) slushy and grainy.

**6.** (Doesn't, Don't) the weather bureau issue tornado warnings?

**7.** A tornado spinning across fields (look, looks) violent.

**8.** *Human Figure with Two Birds* (was, were) created from scrap wood, black paper, emery paper, and oil paints by Max Ernst.

**9.** Car Havens (is, are) the store for snow tires.

**10.** (Doesn't, Don't) daylight saving time start tonight?

Connect to the Writing Process: Drafting

***Writing Sentences in Which Subjects and Verbs Agree***

**Write sentences, following the directions indicated.** Be sure that the subject and verb agree.

**11.** Use *doesn't.*

**12.** Use *don't.*

**13.** Use a linking verb.

**14.** Use the title of a book.

**15.** Use the title of a company.

**16.** Use the title of a poem.

## *Who, Which,* and *That*

*Who, which,* and *that* are often used as relative pronouns to begin an adjective clause. When one of these words is the subject of the clause, the number of its verb will depend upon the number of the pronoun's antecedent.

**In an adjective clause in which the relative pronoun *who, which,* or *that* is used as the subject, the verb agrees with the antecedent of the relative pronoun.**

Bobby read a nonfiction **book** that was a thousand pages long.
(The antecedent of *that* is *book.* Since *book* is singular, *was* is also singular.)

Find the titles of three **books** that deal with space exploration.
(The antecedent of *that* is *books.* Since *books* is plural, *deal* is also plural.)

If an adjective clause is preceded by the expression *one of,* the verb in the clause is usually plural.

Alfred, Lord Tennyson is *one of* the **poets** who **were** appointed poet laureate of England.
(The antecedent of *who* is *poets,* not *one.*)

*You can learn more about adjective clauses on pages L148–L153.*

## Practice Your Skills

Check Your Understanding

***Making Verbs Agree with Relative Pronouns***

Literature Topic **Write the correct form of the verb in parentheses.**

**1.** Did you see the film that (was, were) adapted from Charlotte Brontë's *Jane Eyre?*

**2.** Jane Eyre and Mr. Rochester, who (is, are) the primary characters, grow to love each other.

**3.** A mysterious, ghostlike woman, who (is, are) locked in the attic, sets Jane's room afire.

**4.** *Wide Sargasso Sea,* which (were, was) written by Jean Rhys, creates a story for this mysterious woman.

**5.** *Shirley* is one of the novels that (was, were) written by Charlotte Brontë.

**6.** This author had two sisters who (was, were) writers.

**7.** *Wuthering Heights* is the novel that (was, were) published under Emily Brontë's pen name, Ellis Bell.

**8.** This is a story that (contain, contains) love and hate, riches and poverty, curses and ghosts.

**9.** The poems that the sisters wrote (was, were) published as *Poems by Currer, Ellis,* and *Acton Bell.*

**10.** Anne Brontë's novel *The Tenant of Wildfell Hall,* which (is, are) one of her two novels, was published in 1848.

### Connect to the Writing Process: Editing
### *Using Subject and Verb Agreement*

**Write the correct form of the verb in parentheses.**

**11.** (is) Miss Marple and Hercule Poirot, who ■ Agatha Christie's most famous creations, both solve crimes.

**12.** (is) These fictional characters, which ■ beloved by many, are featured in separate mystery series.

**13.** (discover) Jane Marple is an old woman who ■ murders and other crimes in unexpected places.

**14.** (is) *The Murder at the Vicarage,* which ■ her first adventure, chronicles a murder investigation.

**15.** (occur) The victim of the murder that ■ at the vicarage is the unlikable Colonel Protheroe.

**16.** (live) Two suspects are the vicar and his wife, who ■ in the vicarage.

**17.** (emerge) Other suspects who ■ are the victim's wife, Mrs. Protheroe, and her lover, Lawrence Redding.

**18.** (has) Miss Marple discovers seven people who ■ a motive for the murder.

**19.** (elude) The identity of the murderer, which ■ the police, is revealed by the demure Miss Marple.

**20.** (feature) A number of short stories ■ Miss Marple.

## Communicate Your Ideas

### APPLY TO WRITING

**Character Essay: *Subject and Verb Agreement***

You have decided to write a detective story for a mystery magazine. Write a letter to your literary agent, K. B. Anderson, asking if she thinks your detective is marketable. Describe your detective. What are his or her quirks? What types of mysteries does he or she solve? Where does he or she live? Pay attention to making subjects and verbs agree.

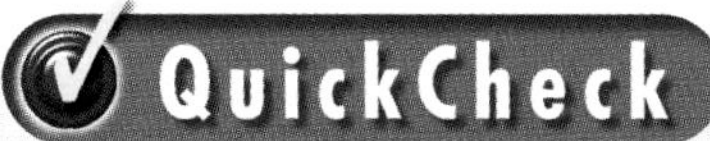

Mixed Practice

Science Topic

**Write the verbs that do not agree with their subjects. Then write those verbs correctly.**

What does you know about trees? Do you know that the leaves on a tree has several functions? One of these functions are to make food for the tree. Carbon dioxide from the air is taken in by the leaves. Water and minerals from the soil is taken in by the roots. The chlorophyll in leaves absorbs energy from the sun and then change the carbon dioxide and water into glucose, food.

Leaves also give off enormous quantities of water. Some of the water that flow from the roots to the leaves are used to make food. Most of the rest of the water in leaves evaporate through tiny holes on the surface of the leaves.

## CheckPoint

# Correcting Errors with Modifiers

**Write the correct form of each verb in parentheses.**

1. New Orleans—with its ornate grillwork, marvelous food, and fascinating history—(attracts, attract) many tourists from around the world.
2. One of my presents (was, were) a gift certificate from the huge video store on Madison Avenue.
3. (Was, Were) many world records broken in the 1984 Olympics in Los Angeles?
4. Both the hockey team and the baseball team (has, have) won state championships this year.
5. Mathematics (is, are) a special kind of language.
6. (Is, Are) ten dollars too much for that thin paperback book?
7. My uncle, not my cousins, (was, were) visiting at the end of August.
8. A grouping of millions of stars (is, are) called a galaxy.
9. Ham and eggs (makes, make) a hearty breakfast for our family.
10. In the basket (was, were) two apples, a pear, and a bunch of grapes.
11. (Doesn't, Don't) Richard play on the varsity basketball team anymore?
12. There (is, are) more than 19 species of buzzards.
13. Neither the center nor the guard (knows, know) that play well.
14. A gift and a card (was, were) on the table.
15. All of today's newspaper (is, are) wet.

## Correcting Errors with Subject-Verb Agreement

**Write the following sentences, correcting each mistake. If a sentence is correct, write *C* after the number.**

1. Either a bookcase or some shelves is needed.
2. Two-thirds of the students has voted.
3. Has all the applicants been interviewed?
4. This week there have been several warm days.
5. Don't the movie start at 5:30?
6. Neither of these reports has any footnotes.
7. Barry's voice and acting ability is exceptional.
8. The number of boys who have jobs are growing.
9. Most of those cantaloupes are too soft.
10. Sam, along with members of his family, are here.
11. Both Kansas and Missouri has a Kansas City.
12. Pancakes and sausage are my favorite breakfast.
13. None of those buses stops at the mall.
14. Everyone, including the musicians, were lined up for the final curtain call.
15. Throughout the West is the ruins of once prosperous mining towns.

## Writing Sentences

**Write five sentences that follow the directions below.**

1. Write a sentence in which the subject is a number of miles.
2. Write a sentence with a collective noun as a subject. Write the sentence so that the members of the group act independently.
3. Write a question that begins with *doesn't* or *don't*.
4. Write a sentence in which the subject and the verb are separated by a participial phrase.
5. Write a sentence that contains a subordinate clause beginning with *that*. Make the subject in the independent clause singular.

# Language and *Self-Expression*

Painter of Micali. *Hydria with Running Figures,* date unknown. Museo Gregoriano Etrusco, Rome.

Artist unknown, Greek. *Women Gathering Fruit,* ca. 5th century B.C. Red-figured cup. Musée Vivenel, Compiègne, France.

Archaeologists consider red-figure pottery, such as the artwork pictured on the right, the product of a more advanced Greek culture than that of the black-figure period. In what ways might a culture advance enough for the differences to be reflected in its art? Write a short essay using both pieces to compare and contrast the different periods to which they belong.

**Prewriting** Make a two-column list of the differences you see in the artworks. If a graphic organizer would be a greater help, use a Venn Diagram.

**Drafting** Begin the first paragraph with a topic sentence stating that you will both compare and contrast the two works. Include the similarities if you mentioned comparison first. Then begin your second paragraph with a transitional expression to lead into your contrasts. End your essay with a concluding statement.

**Revising** Reread your work, several times if necessary. Be sure your sentences flow.

**Editing** Be sure that all your subjects and verbs agree. Also check grammar, spelling, and mechanics.

**Publishing** Once all corrections have been made, write or print out a clean copy of your essay. You might publish it by sharing it with your class.

## Agreement of Subjects and Verbs

A verb must agree with its subject in number. *(page L289)*

A singular subject takes a singular verb. *(page L290)*

A plural subject takes a plural verb. *(page L290)*

The first helping verb must agree in number with its subject. *(page L290)*

The agreement of a verb with its subject is not changed by any interrupting words. *(page L293)*

## Common Agreement Problems

When subjects are joined by *or, nor, either/or,* or *neither/nor,* the verb agrees with the closer subject. *(page L298)*

When subjects are joined by *and* or *both/and,* the verb is plural. *(page L298)*

A verb must agree in number with an indefinite pronoun used as a subject. *(page L301)*

The subject and the verb of an inverted sentence must agree in number. *(page L303)*

## Other Agreement Problems

Use a singular verb with a collective-noun subject that is thought of as a unit. Use a plural verb with a collective-noun subject that is treated as individual parts. *(page L307)*

A subject that expresses an amount, a measurement, a weight, or a time is usually considered singular and takes a singular verb. *(page L308)*

Use a singular verb with *the number of* and a plural verb with *a number of.* *(page L309)*

Use a singular verb with certain subjects that are plural in form but singular in meaning. *(page L309)*

The verb part of a contraction must agree in number with the subject. *(page L312)*

A verb agrees with the subject of a sentence, not with the predicate nominative. *(page L312)*

A title is singular and takes a singular verb. *(page L313)*

In an adjective clause in which the relative pronoun *who, which,* or *that* is used as the subject, the verb agrees with the antecedent of the relative pronoun. *(page L315)*

### *Directions*

**Write the letter of the best way to write the underlined verb(s) in each sentence. If the underlined part contains no error, write *D*.**

EXAMPLE **1.** Some of the detergent was spilled on the floor.

**1** **A** were spilled
**B** have been spilled
**C** are spilled
**D** No error

ANSWER **1** **D**

**1.** There are some traffic signs that is understood in all countries.

**2.** Two fifths of Dad's salary go into the family savings account every month.

**3.** The number of honor students are growing year by year at our school.

**4.** Neither my brother nor his friends wants to dance.

**5.** Amy, not her friends, supports my position on this issue.

**6.** Long grain white rice, along with cheese and pine nuts, are my favorite side dish.

**7.** Has the audience been seated?

**8.** Some of the dishes in the dining room cabinet has been broken.

**9.** The orchestra has put away all their equipment.

**10.** A number of students in this class has consistently appeared on the honor roll.

1 **A** was understood
**B** has been understood
**C** are understood
**D** No error

2 **A** have gone
**B** goes
**C** were going
**D** No error

3 **A** were growing
**B** is growing
**C** have been growing
**D** No error

4 **A** want
**B** has wanted
**C** does want
**D** No error

5 **A** support
**B** have supported
**C** were supporting
**D** No error

6 **A** were
**B** have
**C** is
**D** No error

7 **A** Have been seated?
**B** Were seated?
**C** Were being seated?
**D** No error

8 **A** have been broken
**B** was broken
**C** be broken
**D** No error

9 **A** was putting
**B** is putting
**C** have put
**D** No error

10 **A** is appearing
**B** have appeared
**C** was appearing
**D** No error

CHAPTER 8

# Using Adjectives and Adverbs

### *Directions*

**Read the passage and choose the word or group of words that belongs in each numbered, underlined space. Write the letter of the correct answer.**

EXAMPLE **1.** You __(1)__ to be a weather forecaster to predict weather.

**1** **A** don't never have
**B** don't have
**C** don't hardle have
**D** don't scarcely have

ANSWER **1** **B**

In 1803, Luke Howard, an English scientist, devised the basic system of cloud classification. This system of ten kinds of clouds still works __(1)__ even today. In fact, for over 200 years, his cloud classification system remains better than __(2)__ system. The __(3)__ clouds are nimbostratus clouds, which are called rain clouds. They are often __(4)__ than other clouds, and they __(5)__ exceed even a mile up into the sky. Because these clouds often produce rain or snow, they look __(6)__ to people with outdoor plans. __(7)__ threatening are stratus clouds. The rain in these clouds is always less than __(8)__ clouds. Stratus clouds are __(9)__ because they only produce drizzle or mist. The __(10)__ clouds of all, of course, are the cumulus clouds, which are called fair-weather clouds.

1 **A** well
**B** good
**C** better
**D** best

2 **A** any
**B** a
**C** any other
**D** this

3 **A** closer and most familiar
**B** closest and more familiar
**C** closer and more familiar
**D** closest and most familiar

4 **A** darker
**B** most darker
**C** more darker
**D** more darkerer

5 **A** don't never
**B** don't ever
**C** don't hardly
**D** don't barely

6 **A** bad
**B** badly
**C** more bad
**D** more badly

7 **A** Little
**B** Less
**C** Lesser
**D** Least

8 **A** other
**B** in other
**C** the rain in other
**D** the rain in

9 **A** nice
**B** nicer
**C** more nicer
**D** most nicest

10 **A** most best
**B** best
**C** bestest
**D** most better

Vincent van Gogh. *Enclosed Field with Rising Sun,* 1889.
Oil on canvas, 27⅔ by 35⅓ inches. Private collection.

**Describe** What kinds of lines does van Gogh use to depict the vegetation in the field? What kinds does he use for the sun and its rays? What do you see in the upper right of the canvas, just beyond the field's enclosure?

**Analyze** Even though van Gogh is more an impressionist than a realist painter, how are the lines in his painting true-to-life? In what ways are the colors he uses realistic?

**Interpret** What kind of order would a writer use to describe this painting? Why? If you were writing a description, where would you begin and end?

**Judge** How is this painting different from a photograph of the same field? Which would give you more detail? Which would offer you more emotion? If you had a choice, which would you prefer to depict this scene? Why?

At the end of this chapter, you will use the artwork to stimulate ideas for writing.

# Comparison of Adjectives and Adverbs

Everyone has preferences. You may feel, for example, that meat loaf tastes *good* and spaghetti tastes *better;* but a thick, juicy steak tastes the *best* of all. Adjectives and adverbs have more than one form to express such preferences. This chapter will review the different forms of comparison, as well as some problems you might have with making comparisons.

The three forms that most adjectives and adverbs take to show the degrees of comparison are the positive, the comparative, and the superlative.

## Most modifiers show the degree of comparison by changing form.

The basic form of an adjective or an adverb is the **positive degree.** It is used when no comparison is being made—when you simply are making a statement about a person or a thing.

| | |
|---|---|
| Adjective | This route to the track meet is **quick**. |
| Adverb | Brad can run **fast**. |

When two people, things, or actions are being compared, the **comparative degree** is used. Notice that *–er* has been added to *quick* and *fast.*

| | |
|---|---|
| Adjective | Of the two routes to the track meet, this one is **quicker**. |
| Adverb | Of the two runners, Brad can run **faster**. |

When more than two people, things, or actions are being compared, the **superlative degree** is used. Notice that *–est* has been added to *quick* and *fast.*

| | |
|---|---|
| Adjective | Of the three routes to the track meet, this one is **quickest**. |
| Adverb | Of all the runners in the race, Brad can run **fastest**. |

*You can learn more about adjectives and adverbs on pages L24–L36.*

## Regular and Irregular Comparison

Most adjectives and adverbs form their comparative and superlative degrees in the same way, following a few simple rules. A few modifiers, however, form their comparative and superlative degrees irregularly.

### Regular Comparison

The comparative and superlative forms of most adjectives and adverbs are determined by the number of syllables in them.

**Add *–er* to form the comparative degree and *–est* to form the superlative degree of one-syllable modifiers.**

**ONE-SYLLABLE MODIFIERS**

| Positive | Comparative | Superlative |
|---|---|---|
| young | younger | youngest |
| hot | hotter | hottest |
| soon | sooner | soonest |
| green | greener | greenest |

You probably have noticed that a spelling change sometimes occurs when an ending is added to a modifier. If you are not sure how to form the comparative or superlative degree of a modifier, check the dictionary.

Most two-syllable words form their comparative degree by adding *–er* and their superlative degree by adding *–est*. Some of these words, however, use *more* and *most* because the words would sound awkward—or be impossible to pronounce—if *–er* or *–est* were added. You would never say, for example, "carefuler" or "famouser." *More* and *most* are also used with all adverbs that end in *–ly*.

**Use *–er* or *more* to form the comparative degree and *–est* or *most* to form the superlative degree of two-syllable modifiers.**

| TWO-SYLLABLE MODIFIERS | | |
|---|---|---|
| **Positive** | **Comparative** | **Superlative** |
| graceful | more graceful | most graceful |
| early | earlier | earliest |
| slowly | more slowly | most slowly |

Use *more* to form the comparative degree and *most* to form the superlative degree of modifiers with three or more syllables.

| MODIFIERS WITH THREE OR MORE SYLLABLES | | |
|---|---|---|
| **Positive** | **Comparative** | **Superlative** |
| dangerous | more dangerous | most dangerous |
| rapidly | more rapidly | most rapidly |
| furious | more furious | most furious |

*Less* and *least* are used to form negative comparisons.

| NEGATIVE COMPARISONS | | |
|---|---|---|
| **Positive** | **Comparative** | **Superlative** |
| tasty | less tasty | least tasty |
| steadily | less steadily | least steadily |

## Irregular Comparison

A few adjectives and adverbs change form completely for the comparative and superlative degrees.

| IRREGULAR MODIFIERS | | |
|---|---|---|
| **Positive** | **Comparative** | **Superlative** |
| bad/badly/ill | worse | worst |
| good/well | better | best |
| little | less | least |
| many/much | more | most |

The endings *–er* and *–est* should never be added to the comparative and superlative forms of the irregular modifiers on the preceding page. For example, you should never use "worser" as the comparative form of *bad*.

## PRACTICE YOUR SKILLS

Check Your Understanding
### *Forming the Comparison of Modifiers*

**Write each modifier. Beside it, write its comparative and superlative forms.**

**1.** weak
**2.** hurriedly
**3.** good
**4.** horrible
**5.** busy
**6.** light
**7.** different
**8.** bad
**9.** great
**10.** unsafe
**11.** little
**12.** quickly
**13.** clever
**14.** many
**15.** swift

Check Your Understanding
### *Using the Correct Form of Comparison*

Contemporary Life

**Write the correct form of the modifier in parentheses.**

**16.** Of the three boys, Colin devised the (better, best) game plan.
**17.** Rita's, not Amy's, kite flew (higher, highest).
**18.** Jan swam across the pool (more, most) rapidly than Ty.
**19.** Which sport do you like (better, best): football, basketball, or tennis?
**20.** Which has the (more, most) photogenic mascot, our high school or theirs?
**21.** Of your two friends who play soccer, which one is (more, most) athletic?
**22.** Which city has the (larger, largest) sports arena: Dallas or San Francisco?
**23.** Since there are two acceptable candidates for team captain, the coach has to choose the (better, best) one.

**24.** I don't know which I like (less, least), running laps or doing push-ups.

**25.** Alex is the (louder, loudest) of all the fans.

### Connect to the Writing Process: Editing
### *Using Comparisons*

**Write each incorrect modifier. Beside it, write the correct form.**

On October 17, 1989, baseball fans attended what would become their more memorable game ever. On this fateful day, over 62,000 fans packed Candlestick Park for the third game of the World Series. As the game wore on, the fans became most excited, stomping their feet and doing the wave. At 5:04 P.M., a Richter-magnitude 7.1 earthquake struck. At first, fans did not suspect anything dangerouser than the bleachers' shaking from stomping feet. Then they realized that an event most life-threatening than rumbling bleachers had occurred: an earthquake had shaken the entire San Francisco Bay area. This 20-second earthquake was the baddest quake in years. Its shocks reached San Francisco from the epicenter, 60 miles to the south. Six years earlier, in 1983, Candlestick Park had been examined and then reinforced to a more high level of structural integrity. The 1989 Loma Prieta Earthquake, therefore, did not cause extensiver damage to the ballpark than could be repaired in about a week. Ten days after the earthquake, the World Series continued in Candlestick Park.

Connect to the Writing Process: Prewriting
***Brainstorming Comparisons***

Consider the sports featured in the following photographs or a sport you like more. Brainstorm a list of comparisons explaining why this sport is superior. Use regular and irregular comparisons.

## *Communicate Your Ideas*

### APPLY TO WRITING

**Persuasive Essay:** ***Regular and Irregular Comparisons***

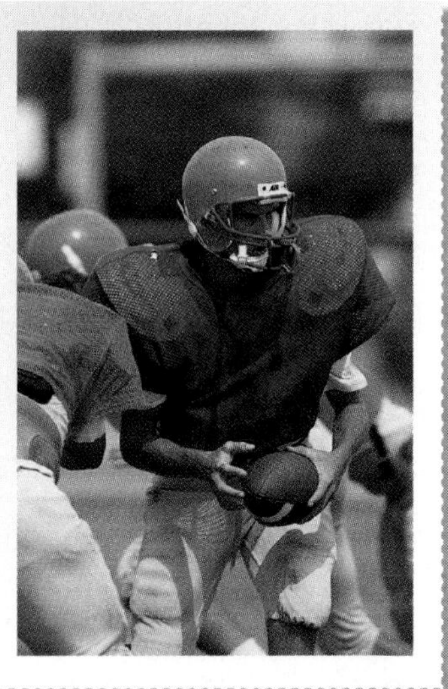

A graduate of your school has donated $5,000 to the athletic department. Your principal has announced an essay contest, and the winner will determine how the $5,000 is used.

Write a persuasive essay describing why your chosen sport is more deserving of the money than any other. Referring to the list you brainstormed, write the first draft. Include facts, examples, and details to support your major points. Then after you revise your essay, edit it, correcting any errors in regular and irregular comparisons.

Mixed Practice

General Interest

**Write the correct form of the modifier in parentheses.**

**1.** Which is (longer, longest), a yard or a meter?

**2.** Which one—George, Thomas, or Ken—ran (faster, fastest) in the 100-meter dash?

**3.** Since there were two liters of juice in the refrigerator, I drank the (older, oldest) one first.

**4.** Leroy's essay on the metric system was (more, most) informative than Maria's.

**5.** Who do you think is the (heavier, heaviest) person, the 50-kilo Lewis or the 50-pound James?

**6.** Which is (shorter, shortest): the centimeter, the millimeter, or the inch?

**7.** I think the inch is the (more, most) useful unit of measure.

**8.** Which costs (less, least), the ruler or the yardstick?

**9.** Of the centipede and the millipede, which has (more, most) legs?

**10.** The races include the one-kilometer, the two-kilometer, and the five-kilometer; I think the two-kilometer race would be (better, best) for you.

**11.** Jesse Owens jumped (farther, farthest) than Luz Long of Germany, a total of 26¾ feet, to win an Olympic gold medal for long jump in 1936.

**12.** Owens ran the 200-meter dash (faster, fastest) than all other runners to win gold again.

**13.** Kenny Brack averaged 153.176 mph per lap as the (better, best) of all drivers in the Indy 500 in 1999.

**14.** The track at Indianapolis is a 2½ mile oval on which the curves are (more, most) dangerous than the straight-away lengths.

**15.** Do you think a race-car driver is (less, least) fit than a long-distance runner?

# Problems with Comparisons

When you edit your work, look for the following problems that can result when adjectives and adverbs are used with comparisons.

## Double Comparisons

Use only one method of forming the comparative and superlative degrees at a time. Using both methods simultaneously results in a **double comparison**.

Do not use both *–er* and *more* to form the comparative degree, or both *–est* and *most* to form the superlative degree of modifiers.

| | |
|---|---|
| DOUBLE COMPARISON | That snake is **more longer** than this one. |
| CORRECT | That snake is **longer** than this one. |
| DOUBLE COMPARISON | This is the **most loudest** parrot. |
| CORRECT | This is the **loudest** parrot. |

## Illogical Comparisons

When you write a comparison, be sure you compare two or more similar things. When you compare different things, the comparison becomes illogical.

Compare only items of a similar kind.

| | |
|---|---|
| ILLOGICAL COMPARISON | A dachshund's **legs** are shorter than most other **dogs.**<br>(*Legs* are being compared with *dogs.*) |
| LOGICAL COMPARISON | A dachshund's **legs** are shorter than other dogs' **legs.**<br>(*Legs* are now being compared with *legs.*) |

| | |
|---|---|
| LOGICAL COMPARISON | A dachshund's **legs** are shorter than most other **dogs'.** (With the possessive *dogs', legs* is understood; therefore, *legs* are being compared with *legs*.) |
| LOGICAL COMPARISON | A dachshund's **legs** are shorter than **those** of other dogs. (The demonstrative pronoun *those* takes the place of *legs;* therefore, *legs* are being compared with *legs.*) |
| ILLOGICAL COMPARISON | Roy's **puppy** looked different from the **picture.** (*Puppy* is being compared with a picture.) |
| LOGICAL COMPARISON | Roy's **puppy** looked different from the **puppy** in the picture. (Now Roy's *puppy* is being compared with a *puppy* in a picture.) |

*You can learn about using an apostrophe with possessives on pages L471–L479.*

## *Other* and *Else* in Comparisons

Very often, one or more people or things will be compared with other people or things in the same group. When you make such a comparison, however, be sure you do not appear to compare a person or a thing with itself.

Add *other* or *else* when comparing a member of a group with the rest of the group.

| | |
|---|---|
| INCORRECT | In today's show Greased Lightning has won more awards than any horse. (Since Greased Lightning is a horse in the show, it is being compared with itself.) |
| CORRECT | In today's show Greased Lightning has won more awards than any **other** horse. (*Greased Lightning* is now being compared only with the *other* horses.) |

| | |
|---|---|
| Incorrect | The pet store manager, Mandy, knows more about fish than anyone in the store. (Since Mandy is in the store, she is being compared with herself.) |
| Correct | The pet store manager, Mandy, knows more about fish than anyone **else** in the store. (*Mandy* is now being compared only with the *other* people in the store.) |

### Connect to Speaking and Writing

The next time you listen to advertisements on the radio or television, notice the misleading manner in which many product "comparisons" are made. For example, some advertisers will give you the first half of a comparison but not the second half.

> Our pizza is Number One because it has more toppings. (It has more toppings than what?)

When you hear or read an advertisement that only partially completes a comparison, finish the comparison and then decide for yourself if the product is a superior one!

## Practice Your Skills

Check Your Understanding

***Identifying Mistakes with Comparisons***

General Interest **Using the following abbreviations, write the type of each mistake. If a sentence is correct, write *C.***

double comparison = *d.c.* illogical comparison = *i.c.*
needs *other* or *else* in comparison = *o.e.*

**1.** Fifi jumps higher and farther than any dog in the show.

**2.** A properly fed animal will perform more better than one indulged with unhealthy snacks.

3. Nathan has more pets than anyone on the obedience school staff.
4. Though not the prettiest canines, pit bulls are perhaps more popular watchdogs than any dog.
5. I think a rabbit's fur is more softer than even a cat's fur.
6. The beauty of this stray mutt is greater than the purebred Great Dane.
7. Andrew is fairer than any other judge on the regional cat show panel.
8. The African elephant probably has larger eyes than any animal in the world.
9. This dog-walkers' club is the most wonderful idea of the summer!
10. Chu is kinder to animals than anyone in his family.

Connect to the Writing Process: Editing
*Correcting Mistakes with Comparisons*

**11.–18. Write the incorrect sentences in the preceding exercise, correcting the mistakes in the use of comparisons.**

Connect to the Writing Process: Drafting
*Drafting: Writing Comparisons*

**Write a sentence that includes a comparison for each direction.**

19. Compare one owl to several owls.
20. Compare your two favorite animals.
21. Use *other* in a comparison.
22. Include *else* in a comparison.
23. Write a product ad for a pet product.
24. Compare a famous animal to other animals of the same species.
25. Compare two different kinds of fish.
26. Write an ad for a pet you would like to sell.

Communicate Your Ideas

## APPLY TO WRITING

### Evaluation: *Comparisons*

Henri Rousseau. *Tropical Storm with a Tiger (Surprise)*, 1891.
Oil on canvas, 51⅛ by 31³⁄₁₆ inches. National Gallery, London.

Wang Yani. *Little Monkeys and Mummy*, 1980.
Ink and pigment on paper, 15 by 21 inches.

You are a judge in an art contest, and you must decide which one of these works of art deserves first place. Write your evaluation of the two paintings for the awards committee. Compare strengths and weaknesses in use of color, use of space, originality, meaningfulness of content, and any other elements you choose to evaluate. After writing the first draft, edit your work for mistakes in using comparisons. Then write the final copy.

## QuickCheck Mixed Practice

Art Topic **Write each sentence, correcting the mistakes in comparisons. If a sentence is correct, write *C*.**

**1.** Primary colors like blue and red are more purer than secondary colors like purple and orange.

**2.** Yellow and green can be seen more readily by the human eye than any colors.

**3.** Isn't hot pink much more brighter than pastel pink?

**4.** These greens and yellows are more cheerful than black and silver.

**5.** Yellow, red, and orange hues are the most brightest colors of all.

**6.** That double rainbow was more vivid than any rainbow I have seen.

**7.** Does a rainbow exhibit more colors than a sunset?

**8.** Yellow is more analogous to yellow-green than to orange.

**9.** Colors that are opposite each other on the color wheel are more complementary than those next to each other.

**10.** Except for water, the sky contains more hues of blue and white than any part of nature.

**11.** Turquoise is the most universal color for people to wear.

**12.** Which is paler: orange, peach, or rust?

**13.** Purple is more quicker associated with royalty than red.

**14.** Blend white with any color to soften it.

**15.** A prism is a better tool than anything for refracting white light into the colors of a rainbow.

# Problems with Modifiers

You should be aware of the following usage problems with adjectives and adverbs.

## Adjective or Adverb?

Although adjectives and adverbs are both modifiers, they are very different in many other ways. You learned in the grammar section of this book that an adjective describes a noun or pronoun. You also learned that an adjective usually comes before the noun or pronoun it describes, or it follows a linking verb. Adjectives are usually easy for you to recognize because they answer the following questions.

| | |
|---|---|
| WHICH ONE? | That recipe is **easy.** |
| WHAT KIND? | This lemonade tastes **sweet.** |
| HOW MANY? | I have **three** cookies. |
| HOW MUCH? | I need **more** butter for this frosting. |

Remember that some verbs—such as *feel, smell,* and *taste*—can be either linking verbs or action verbs. When they are used as linking verbs, they are often followed by an adjective.

| | |
|---|---|
| LINKING VERB | The milk **smelled** sour.<br>(*Smelled* links *milk* and *sour*—sour milk.) |
| ACTION VERB | I **smelled** the milk.<br>(*Smelled* is used as an action verb.) |

If you are not sure whether a verb is being used as a linking verb or as an action verb, substitute the verb *is.* If the sentence makes sense, the verb is a linking verb. If it does not make sense, the verb is an action verb.

*You can find a list of common linking verbs and a list of additional linking verbs on page L21.*

Like adjectives, adverbs are modifiers. Adverbs describe verbs, adjectives, and other adverbs. Because adverbs can be placed almost anywhere in a sentence, ask the following questions to find them.

| | |
|---|---|
| WHERE? | Place the carved roast **here.** |
| WHEN? | **Yesterday** I made butterscotch pudding. |
| HOW? | **Briskly** whisk the eggs. |
| TO WHAT EXTENT? | Please don't stir the muffin batter **too long.** |
| | I'll have another of those **wonderfully** tasty crab puffs! |

Because so many adverbs end in *–ly,* they are usually easy to recognize. Remember, however, that a few adjectives—such as *early* and *lively*—also end in *–ly.*

| | |
|---|---|
| ADVERB | He cooks breakfast **daily.**<br>(*Daily* tells when he cooks breakfast.) |
| ADJECTIVE | His **daily** ritual includes a healthful breakfast.<br>(*Daily* tells what kind of ritual it is.) |

You may have noticed that a few words—such as *first, hard, high, late,* and *long*—do not change form whether they are used as an adjective or an adverb.

| | |
|---|---|
| ADVERB | Eat **first** and then wash the pans.<br>(*First* tells when you should eat.) |
| ADJECTIVE | His **first** omelet was a success.<br>(*First* tells which omelet was successful.) |

## *Good* or *Well?*

*Good* is always an adjective. *Well* is usually used as an adverb. *Well* is used as an adjective, however, when it means "in good health" or "satisfactory."

| | |
|---|---|
| ADJECTIVE | Sally is a **good** cook. |
| ADVERB | Sally cooks **well.** |
| ADJECTIVE | Sally doesn't feel **well** today. (in good health) |

## *Bad* or *Badly?*

*Bad* is an adjective and often follows a linking verb. *Badly* is used as an adverb.

| | |
|---|---|
| ADJECTIVE | This egg smells **bad.** |
| ADVERB | Oh! I've **badly** jammed the garbage disposal. |

CONNECT TO SPEAKING AND WRITING

In casual conversation, it is acceptable to use *bad* or *badly* after the verb *feel*. In formal writing, however, always use *bad* as an adjective and *badly* as an adverb.

| | |
|---|---|
| IN WRITING | I feel **bad** about taking the last cookie. |
| IN CONVERSATION | I feel **badly** about taking the last cookie. |

## Double Negatives

Some words are considered negatives. In most sentences two negatives, called a **double negative**, should not be used together.

Avoid using a double negative.

| COMMON NEGATIVES | |
|---|---|
| but (meaning "only") | none |
| barely | no one |
| hardly | not (and its contraction *n't*) |
| neither | nothing |
| never | only |
| no | scarcely |

| | |
|---|---|
| DOUBLE NEGATIVE | Sue does**n't** have **no** choice in this meal. |
| CORRECT | Sue does**n't** have any choice in this meal. |
| DOUBLE NEGATIVE | There is**n't hardly** any reason to eat now. |
| CORRECT | There is**n't** any reason to eat now. |
| CORRECT | There is **hardly** any reason to eat now. |

## PRACTICE YOUR SKILLS

Check Your Understanding

***Identifying Mistakes in the Use of Modifiers***

Contemporary Life

**Using the following abbreviations, write the type of each mistake. If a sentence is correct, write *C*.**

adjective or adverb = *a. a.* — *good* or *well* = *g. w.*
*bad* or *badly* = *b. b.* — double negative = *d. n.*

**1.** Everyone did good on the home economics final exam.
**2.** Jeff looked hungry at the feast the class cooked.
**3.** Liza did quite well in baking crab puffs.
**4.** No one knew nothing about making chocolate mousse.
**5.** Those who arrived to class early got the best utensils.
**6.** "The early bird gets the worm!" shouted Shelly, grabbing the best of the three mixers.
**7.** Don't feel bad if your first piecrust is a little tough.
**8.** That marmalade tastes bitterly.
**9.** There ain't no reason why you can't help wash dishes.
**10.** That fish casserole smells rather strongly.
**11.** I don't have hardly any sugar left.
**12.** Gareth felt bad about burning the cinnamon rolls.
**13.** Because of Don's confusing directions, we could not hardly make a successful soufflé.
**14.** Don't you think this frosted cake looks well?
**15.** After eating your cooking, I don't feel good.

**16.** We had not worked hardly a minute before someone broke a pie plate.

**17.** Mix the butter, sugar, and eggs together very well.

**18.** When Julie said she didn't want no dessert, I said I didn't want none neither.

**19.** My stomach never hurt as bad as it did when I ate that bad egg.

**20.** How good did you sterilize that surface where the poultry had lain?

Connect to the Writing Process: Editing
***Correcting Mistakes in Comparisons***

**21.–34. Write the incorrect sentences in the preceding exercise, correcting each mistake in comparisons.**

CONNECT TO WRITER'S CRAFT

Inexperienced writers often use comparisons that have become clichés through overuse. Similes such as "black as night," "flat as a pancake," and "thin as a rail" have been used so often that they no longer create any special image in a reader's mind. As you develop your writing skills, practice writing comparisons that are fresh, surprising, and vivid. The extra thought is worth the results!

## Communicate Your Ideas

### APPLY TO WRITING

**Description: *Similes***

From the list of trite similes on the following page, choose one that you often read or hear. (If you know of a different simile you'd rather use, that is fine.) Think of a new way to write this simile. Then write a description for your classmates, explaining how the two things in your new comparison are similar. Edit your writing, making sure you have used the correct forms of any adjectives and adverbs.

- quick as a wink
- soft as a baby's breath
- sharp as a tack
- slow as molasses
- green as grass
- pure as the driven snow

Mixed Practice

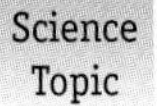

Science Topic

**Write the following paragraphs, correcting each error in the use of comparisons.**

Venus has been called Earth's twin. Second in distance from the sun, Venus comes more nearer to Earth than any planet. Venus's diameter, density, mass, and gravity are all close to Earth. Venus's year is about three fifths as long as Earth's. Venus's rotation, however, is from east to west, while Earth and most planets rotate from west to east.

Venus is masked by dense clouds. Astronomers knew hardly nothing about Venus's atmosphere and surface until radar and unpiloted spacecraft penetrated the clouds. Despite Venus's clouds, the surface gets much more hotter than Earth. The temperature on Venus can reach 460°C.

Because Venus is more closer to the sun than Earth is, you can see it only when you face in the general direction of the sun. During most of the daytime, the sun shines too vivid to allow you to see Venus. When Venus is east of the sun, however, the sun sets before it. Then Venus can be seen clear in the twilight of the western sky.

## CheckPoint

### Correcting Errors with Modifiers

**Write the following sentences, correcting each error. If a sentence is correct, write *C* after the number.**

1. We couldn't go swimming this morning because there wasn't no lifeguard on duty.
2. Which tastes worse, that bitter cough medicine or warm milk?
3. Today I feel the bestest I have felt in over a week.
4. Why haven't you never learned to swim?
5. After her argument with her brother Michael, Marsha felt badly.
6. Rich can paint both figures and landscapes better than anyone I know.
7. How was China's early civilization different from Egypt?
8. Avery's sweater and pants match well.
9. Next week I won't have ~~no~~ time to work at the Brewsters' music shop.
10. I think Yori's acting ability is better than Jason.
11. Which would you like best, a cruise or an overland trip to Alaska?
12. Steven Mitchell is the most wittiest reporter on the school newspaper.
13. The cheetah is different from members of the cat family because it can't hide its claws.
14. That shirt comes in blue, green, or yellow; I think blue would look better on you.
15. The fog is so thick this morning that I couldn't see nothing.

## Editing for Correct Use of Modifiers

**Read the following paragraphs. Then find and write the eight errors in the use of adjectives or adverbs. Beside each error write the correct form.**

Mercury is the planet most nearest the sun. Its diameter is about one-third that of Earth. Because of its smaller size, Mercury's gravity is also much weaker than Earth. One hundred kilograms on Earth, for example, would weigh only about 37 kilograms on Mercury.

Scientists knew hardly nothing about the surface of Mercury until *Mariner 10,* an unpiloted spacecraft, made flyby observations in 1974 and 1975. The photographs it took of Mercury turned out good. They showed that Mercury's surface was similar to the moon. Mercury's rocky landscape is marked by broad plains, a few large ringed basins, and highlands studded with more smaller craters. The plains were formed by lava. The basins and most of the craters were formed when rock masses from space collided forceful with Mercury. The most largest basin has a diameter of 1,300 kilometers and is ringed by mountains 2 kilometers high.

## Writing Sentences

**Write five sentences that follow the directions below.**

1. Write a sentence using the superlative degree of *good* and the comparative degree of *little.*
2. Write a sentence using the word *taste* first as an action verb and then as a linking verb.
3. Write a sentence using both *bad* and *badly.*
4. Write a sentence about a river, lake, or ocean. Use a positive adverb and a comparative adjective.
5. Write a sentence using *well* as an adjective.

# Language and *Self-Expression*

**V**incent van Gogh was a man with a passion for art and the natural world. When he looked at landscapes, he saw a kind of raw beauty which he translated into heavy brushstrokes of bright, clear colors.

Each of us sees the natural world from a different point of view. Imagine that you are studying a landscape you saw some time ago, perhaps as a child. Write a paragraph about the scene, but not about what you *see.* Instead, explain *how it made you feel.*

**Prewriting** Think about the landscape. Make a two-column list, one column for the actual things you saw—buildings, trees, people—and another for the emotions you felt when you observed them.

**Drafting** Begin with a sentence that puts you at the center of your view. Then "look" at individual people and objects and explain how you reacted to them, individually or together. Use your list to guide you. End the paragraph by summing up the experience with a single, clear emotion.

**Revising** Study your paragraph. Be sure the description moves from the view to the way you felt when you observed it. Check your adjectives and adverbs. Are they vivid? Do they express what you really remember?

**Editing** Read your work again. This time, look for errors in spelling, mechanics, and usage. Have you used the appropriate forms of adjectives and adverbs?

**Publishing** Make a clean copy of your paragraph. If you wish, share your work with a classmate or with the members of a small group. Keep in mind that your family, too, might be interested in your work--especially if they were present at the scene you remember.

Most modifiers show **degrees of comparison** by changing form.

## Regular and Irregular Comparisons

Add *–er* to form the **comparative degree** and *–est* to form the **superlative degree** of one-syllable modifiers. *(page L328)*

Use *–er* or *more* to form the **comparative degree** and *–est* or *most* to form the **superlative degree** of two-syllable modifiers. *(page L328)*

Add *more* to form the **comparative degree** and *most* to form the **superlative degree** of modifiers with three or more syllables. *(page L329)*

## Double, Illogical, and Other Comparisons

Do not use both *–er* and *more* to form the comparative degree, or both *–est* and *most* to form the superlative degree. *(page L334)*

Compare only items of a similar kind. *(page L334)*

Add *other* or *else* when comparing a member of a group with the rest of the group. *(page L335)*

Avoid using a double negative. *(page L342)*

## Special Cases

*Good* is always an adjective. *Well* is usually used as an adverb. *Well* is used as an adjective only when it means "in good health" or "satisfactory." *(pages L341–L342)*

*Bad* is an adjective and often follows a linking verb. *Badly* is an adverb. *(page L342)*

## Other Information About the Comparison of Modifiers

Using irregular modifiers *(page L329)*
Distinguishing between adjectives and adverbs *(pages L340–L341)*
Avoiding double negatives *(page L342)*

### Directions

**Read the passage and choose the word or group of words that belongs in each numbered, underlined space. Write the letter of the correct answer.**

**Example** **1.** The funnel of a tornado is one of the __(1)__ sights ever!

**1** **A** scarier
**B** most scariest
**C** scariest
**D** more scarier

**Answer** **1** **C**

Weather forecasters are __(1)__ today than they were even 25 years ago. __(2)__ have a hard time understanding why. Because of satellites and other technological advances, forecasters have __(3)__ information available to them than their predecessors did. Nevertheless, their predictions of violent storms like tornadoes remain __(4)__. Tornadoes, by far, are more destructive than __(5)__ storm on Earth! They are __(6)__ on the plain states than __(7)__ in the U.S. In 1925, one of the __(8)__ tornadoes of all times killed 700 people in only three and a half hours! Tornadoes cause so much destruction because their winds are stronger __(9)__ storms! Listen __(10)__ to this advice: If a tornado is approaching, go to a cellar or a closet far away from the outside walls of your house!

1 **A** more smarter
**B** smarter
**C** smartest
**D** most smarter

2 **A** No one scarcely would
**B** No one hardly would
**C** No one wouldn't
**D** No one would

3 **A** more
**B** most
**C** morer
**D** much

4 **A** badly
**B** more badly
**C** bad
**D** more badder

5 **A** any
**B** a
**C** any other
**D** this

6 **A** more common
**B** more commoner
**C** most common
**D** most commoner

7 **A** anywhere
**B** anywhere else
**C** everywhere
**D** nowhere

8 **A** bad
**B** badly
**C** worse
**D** worst

9 **A** than other
**B** than those of other
**C** than all other
**D** than most

10 **A** good
**B** better
**C** well
**D** most well

# A Writer's Glossary of Usage

Part of the growing process is learning that some behavior is appropriate and some is not. Everyone quickly learns as a child, for example, that throwing food on the floor is definitely not acceptable or appropriate behavior.

As children grow older, most learning becomes more complicated. No longer is everything either good or bad, right or wrong. Some behavior is appropriate in some situations but inappropriate in others. Using your fingers, for example, to eat fried chicken may be appropriate behavior at home, but it may become inappropriate at a fancy restaurant.

Different expressions of the English language are somewhat like certain types of behavior; they may be appropriate with one audience but not with another. Using contractions in your conversations, for example, is standard and acceptable, but using contractions in a research paper is not appropriate.

Professor Higgins in *My Fair Lady* prided himself on his ability to name the towns where people were born by analyzing their dialects. **Dialect** is a regional variety of language that includes grammar, vocabulary, and pronunciation. Like the English, Americans have different dialects. The accents and expressions of people from parts of Texas, for example, are quite different from the accents and expressions of people from parts of Massachusetts. In spite of these variations in dialect, though, people from Texas and people from Massachusetts can easily understand and communicate with each other.

The place of your birth, however, is not the only influence on the way you speak. Your ethnic and educational backgrounds, as well as other factors, also contribute to the particular way you speak. All of these combined factors add a richness and a vibrant diversity to the English language. These factors have also created the need for different levels of expression. Traditionally these levels are recognized as standard and nonstandard English.

**Standard English** is used in public by almost all professional people—such as writers, television and radio personalities, government officials, and other notable figures. Standard English uses all the rules and conventions of usage that are accepted most widely by English-speaking people throughout the world. (They are the same rules and conventions that are taught in this text.) The use of standard English varies, nevertheless, in formal and informal situations.

**Formal English,** which follows the conventional rules of grammar, usage, and mechanics, is the standard for all written work. It is used mainly in such written work as formal reports, essays, scholarly writings, research papers, and business letters. Formal English may include some words that are not normally used in everyday conversation and frequently may employ long sentences with complex structures. To maintain a formal tone of writing, most writers avoid contractions, colloquialisms, and certain other common verbal expressions. The following example of formal English is an excerpt from one of Carson McCullers' essays.

> Whether in the pastoral joys of country life or in the labyrinthine city, we Americans are always seeking. We wander, question. But the answer waits in each separate heart—the answer of our own identity and the way by which we can master loneliness and feel that at last we belong.
>
> —*Carson McCullers,* The Mortgaged Heart

**Informal English** does not mean "inferior English." Just like formal English, informal English follows the rules and the conventions of standard English; however, it follows them less rigidly. It includes some words and expressions, such as contractions, that would sound out of place in formal writing. English-speaking people around the world generally use informal English in their everyday conversation. It is also used in magazines, newspapers, advertising, and much of the fiction that is written today. The following example of informal English is a diary entry that was written by Admiral Byrd during one of his expeditions to Antarctica.

> Something—I don't know what—is getting me down. I've been strangely irritable all day, and since supper I have been depressed. . . . This would not seem important if I could only put my finger on the trouble, but I can't find any single thing to account for the mood. Yet it has been there; and tonight, for the first time, I must admit that the problem of keeping my mind on an even keel is a serious one.
>
> *–Richard Byrd,* Alone

**Nonstandard English,** which is suitable in certain instances, incorporates the many variations produced by regional dialects, slang, and colloquial expressions. However, it should be used in limited situations and only if the use of standard English, as set forth in the preceding section, is not required. Since nonstandard English lacks uniformity from one section of the country to the next and from year to year, you should always use standard English when you write. Some fiction authors use nonstandard English, however, to recreate the conversation of people from a particular locale or time period. This, for example, was Eudora Welty's purpose when she wrote the following passage.

> "This is what come to me to do," she said. "I going to the store and buy my child a little windmill they sells, made out of paper. He going to find it hard to believe there such a thing in the world. I'll march myself back where he waiting, holding it straight up in this hand."
>
> *–Eudora Welty,* "The Worn Path"

Some of the entries in the following glossary of usage make reference to standard and nonstandard English, the terms discussed in the previous section. Since the glossary has been arranged alphabetically, you can use it easily.

**a, an** Use *a* before a word beginning with a consonant sound. Use *an* before a word beginning with a vowel sound. Always keep in mind that this rule applies to sounds, not letters. For example, *an hour ago* is correct because the *h* is silent.

He finished painting **a** home on our block.
Then he asked for **an** honest evaluation of his work.

**accept, except** *Accept* is a verb that means "to receive with consent." *Except* is usually a preposition that means "but" or "other than." *Acceptance* and *exception* are the noun forms.

The players will **accept** all the new rules **except** one.

**adapt, adopt** Both of these words are verbs. *Adapt* means "to adjust." *Adopt* means "to take as your own." *Adaption*, *adaptation*, and *adoption* are the noun forms.

We can **adapt** to our new environment if we **adopt** some new habits.

**advice, advise** *Advice* is a noun that means "a recommendation." *Advise* is a verb that means "to recommend."

What **advice** would you give to a freshman?
I would **advise** any freshman to get involved in school activities.

**affect, effect** *Affect* is a verb that means "to influence" or "to act upon." *Effect* is usually a noun that means "a result" or "an influence." As a verb, *effect* means "to accomplish" or "to produce."

Eastern Kansas was seriously **affected** by the storm.
The **effects** of the storm cost the state millions of dollars.
The fear of mud slides **effected** detours.

**ain't** This contraction is nonstandard and should be avoided in your writing.

| | |
|---|---|
| NONSTANDARD | This **ain't** her first choice. |
| FORMAL | This **is not** her first choice. |
| INFORMAL | This **isn't** her first choice. |

**all ready, already** *All ready* means "completely ready." *Already* means "previously."

> Are the children **all ready** to go?
> Yes, they have **already** changed their clothes.

**all together, altogether** *All together* means "in a group." *Altogether* means "wholly" or "thoroughly."

> The members of our group were **all together** at the concert.
> The concert was **altogether** enjoyable.

**allusion, illusion** Both of these words are nouns. An *allusion* is "an implied or indirect reference; a hint." An *illusion* is "something that deceives or misleads."

> During the showing of the film, I noticed many biblical and mythological **allusions.**
>
> I also learned that movement in motion pictures is created by an optical **illusion.**

**a lot** These two words are often written as one word. There is no such word as "alot." *A lot* should be avoided in formal writing. (Do not confuse *a lot* with *allot*, which is a verb that means "to distribute by shares.")

| | |
|---|---|
| INFORMAL | Do you miss them **a lot?** |
| FORMAL | Do you miss them **very much?** |
| | I hope they will **allot** the chores equally. |

**among, between** Both of these words are prepositions. *Among* is used when referring to three or more people or things. *Between* is usually used when referring to two people or things.

> The senator moved **among** the people in the crowd.
> He divided his time **between** shaking hands and speaking.

**amount, number** *Amount* refers to a quantity. *Number* refers to things that can be counted.

> A small **number** of students raised a large **amount** of money for the athletic program.

# Practice Your Skills

## Check Your Understanding

### *Finding the Correct Word*

Literature Topic

**Write the word in parentheses that correctly (formally) completes each sentence.**

**1.** The (affect, effect) of the recent Globe Theater restoration has been to heighten interest (a lot, considerably) in this (all ready, already) well-known Elizabethan theater.

**2.** The Globe, which opened in 1599, was also known as "The Wooden O," (a, an) (allusion, illusion) to its shape.

**3.** A view of the building from above gives the spectator the (allusion, illusion) of a large "O."

**4.** Built to accommodate a large (amount, number) of people, the Globe could hold approximately three thousand people (all together, altogether).

**5.** William Shakespeare was (among, between) the five actors who (all together, altogether) owned half interest in the theater.

**6.** Although the exact (amount, number) of performances (ain't, isn't) known, Shakespeare's plays were often enacted at the Globe.

**7.** In 1613, the (affect, effect) of a malfunctioning cannon during a performance was the burning down of the theater.

**8.** Acting on good (advice, advise), the owners rebuilt the Globe in the same fashion (accept, except) for a tiled roof instead of a thatched one.

**9.** By 1642, however, the strict religious beliefs (adapted, adopted) by the Puritans had (all ready, already) adversely (affected, effected) the success of the Globe.

**10.** It, along with great (amounts, numbers) of theaters in England, was closed (all together, altogether) because of Puritan opposition to drama.

Connect to the Writing Process: Revising

***Recognizing Correct Usage***

**Rewrite the following paragraphs, changing the words that are used incorrectly.**

Adoption to the theatrical conventions of the Elizabethan era had a affect on the design of the Globe. For example, the adoption of an trapdoor in the center of the stage provided for the entrance and exit into "Hell." Two pillars, located among the two sides of the stage held up "Heaven." At the rear of the stage was a gallery that was already if needed for musicians or for a balcony scene. The stage itself extended out about thirty feet all together into the courtyard. Since the yard was an open area, the weather sometimes effected performances.

In this area there were a lot of spectators who were called groundlings. To be admitted, groundlings paid the amount of one penny. They stood through an entire performance and could move around accept when it was too crowded. Although often disruptive, the conduct of the groundlings was altogether accepted by the actors for economic reasons. The people who sat among the seven galleries upstairs had to pay the number of two pence for their seats.

**any more, anymore** Do not use *any more* for *anymore*. *Any more* refers to quantity. The adverb *anymore* means "from now on" or "at present."

Is there **any more** lettuce in the garden?
No, I don't raise lettuce **anymore.**

**anywhere, everywhere, nowhere, somewhere** Do not add *s* to any of these words.

| | |
|---|---|
| NONSTANDARD | Melanie wants to travel **everywheres.** |
| STANDARD | Melanie wants to travel **everywhere.** |

**as far as** This expression is sometimes confused with "all the farther," which is nonstandard English.

| | |
|---|---|
| NONSTANDARD | Is a mile **all the farther** you can walk? |
| STANDARD | Is a mile **as far as** you can walk? |

**at** Do not use *at* after where.

| | |
|---|---|
| NONSTANDARD | Let me know **where** the keys are **at.** |
| STANDARD | Let me know **where** the keys are. |

**a while, awhile** *A while* is an expression made up of an article and a noun. It must be used after the prepositions *for* and *in*. *Awhile* is an adverb and is not used after a preposition.

You won't get your test results for **a while.**
I think you should wait **awhile** before calling again.

**bad, badly** *Bad* is an adjective and often follows a linking verb. *Badly* is used as an adverb and often follows an action verb. In the first two examples, *felt* is a linking verb.

| | |
|---|---|
| NONSTANDARD | My sister felt **badly** about missing us. |
| STANDARD | My sister felt **bad** about missing us. |
| STANDARD | She was so upset that she burned the dinner **badly.** |

*You can learn more about using adjectives and adverbs on pages L24–L36 and pages L327–L345.*

**because** Do not use *because* after *the reason*. Use one or the other.

| | |
|---|---|
| NONSTANDARD | **The reason** he joined the exercise class was **because** he wanted to feel more energetic. |

| | |
|---|---|
| STANDARD | He joined the exercise class **because he** wanted to feel more energetic. |
| STANDARD | **The reason** he joined the exercise class was **that** he wanted to feel more energetic. |

**being as, being that** These expressions should be replaced with *because* or *since*.

| | |
|---|---|
| NONSTANDARD | **Being as** it rained on Saturday, I didn't run. |
| STANDARD | **Since** it rained on Saturday, I didn't run. |

**beside, besides** *Beside* is always a preposition that means "by the side of." As a preposition, *besides* means "in addition to." As an adverb, *besides* means "also" or "moreover."

Sit **beside** me at the PTA meeting. (by the side of)

**Besides** meeting the teachers, we also will tour the new facilities. (in addition to)

The school has a swimming pool, tennis courts, and an indoor track **besides.** (also)

**both** Never use *the* before *both*.

| | |
|---|---|
| NONSTANDARD | We saw **the both** of you at the mall. |
| STANDARD | We saw **both** of you at the mall. |

**both, each** *Both* refers to two persons or objects together, but *each* refers to an individual person or object.

**Both** office buildings were designed by the same architect; however, **each** building is quite different.

**bring, take** *Bring* indicates motion toward the speaker. *Take* indicates motion away from the speaker.

**Bring** me a stamp and then **take** this letter to the mailbox.

## Practice Your Skills

### Check Your Understanding
***Finding the Correct Word***

Contemporary Life **Write the word in parentheses that correctly completes each sentence.**

1. (Beside, Besides) the preliminary audition, those trying out for a high school musical usually have to attend a callback audition.
2. Although (both, each) of them are essential to the casting process, (both, each) has a different procedure.
3. (Both, The both) require student performance but with certain important differences.
4. For example, when going to the preliminary audition, students usually may (bring, take) their own music or may use a selection from the musical.
5. At the callback audition, students do not have a choice (any more, anymore), (being as, since) the musical theater team decides which selections it wishes to hear each student perform.
6. Similarly, for (a while, awhile), students have the option to read for any part they choose; however, at the callback, no matter how (bad, badly) they may want a particular role, the choice may not be theirs.
7. Even if permitted to read their favorite part, students may be asked to read dialogue from several other parts (beside, besides).
8. In the preliminary, to prevent students from feeling (bad, badly), they usually perform only in front of the drama director, choreographer, and musical director.
9. At callback, other students who are waiting to audition again are (everywhere, everywheres) while an individual is auditioning.
10. After (a while, awhile) students get used to having others (beside, besides) them while they're performing, thus helping to prevent the actors from having (any more, anymore) stage fright.

Connect to the Writing Process: Revising

***Recognizing Correct Usage***

**Rewrite the following paragraphs, changing the words that are used incorrectly.**

A musical theater team would assure you that nowheres is teamwork required any more than in a musical production. Collaboration begins with the drama director, choreographer, and musical director being that they must model cooperative behavior for their students. Even though they bring individual expertise to the production, together they take responsibility for evaluating, casting, encouraging, and critiquing the performers. After a while, students begin to understand how bad teamwork is needed to coordinate the details.

In many high schools, the students go all the farther promoting ticket sales, distributing posters, and coordinating costumes. Many productions even have two student stage managers, the both of whom share responsibilities. In other words, although both are involved with the smooth operation of every scene, each stage manager has particular duties. For example, one might instruct a performer where to stand at while the other might place props besides a piece of scenery. Beside being stage managers, students often operate both the lighting and sound equipment. Ultimately, the reason a production is successful is because each person contributes to the whole.

## Communicate Your Ideas

### APPLY TO WRITING

**Explanatory Writing: *Correct Usage***

The concept of collaboration, working together to create a desired result, may be applied in many subject areas. You have probably worked together at one time or another in your classes to produce a collaborative assignment. Some students prefer working together while others prefer doing independent work. Compose an original paragraph explaining your personal preference concerning collaborative assignments. In your explanation include at least five of the following words.

- *advice/advise*
- *affect/effect*
- *all together/altogether*
- *among/between*
- *both/each*

**can, may** *Can* expresses ability. *May* expresses possibility or permission.

> **Can** you see the third line of the eye chart?
> **May** I try one more time?

**can't help but** In this expression use a gerund instead of *but*.

> NONSTANDARD I **can't help but** notice your new haircut.
> STANDARD I **can't help** noticing your new haircut.

**capital, capitol** A *capital* is the chief city of a state. Also, names are written with *capital* letters, people invest *capital*, and a person can receive *capital* punishment. A *capitol* is the building in which the legislature meets.

> The name of the **capital** of Florida is written in **capital** letters on the **capitol** building in Tallahassee.

**coarse, course** *Coarse* is an adjective that means "loose or rough in texture" or "crude and unrefined." *Course* is a noun that means "a way of acting or proceeding" or "a path, road, or route." Also, people play golf on a *course*; an appetizer is one *course* of a meal; and students take *courses* in school. *Course* is also the word used in the parenthetical expression *of course*.

Many people heard his **coarse** remarks after the tennis match.
What **course** of action would you take to stop his behavior?

**continual, continuous** Both of these words are adjectives. *Continual* means "frequently repeated." *Continuous* means "uninterrupted."

The **continual** bolts of lightning frightened me.
The rain was **continuous** for over ten hours.

**different from** Use this form instead of *different than*. *Different than*, however, can be used informally when it is followed by a clause.

| | |
|---|---|
| INFORMAL | My sweater is **different than** the one Gram knitted for Maureen. |
| FORMAL | My sweater is **different from** the one Gram knitted for Maureen. |
| STANDARD | Her jacket is **different from** mine, also. |

**discover, invent** Both of these words are verbs. *Discover* means "to find or get knowledge of for the first time." *Invent* means "to create or produce for the first time." Something that is discovered has always existed but it was unknown. Something that is invented has never existed before. The noun forms of these words are *discovery* and *invention*.

I learned that Isaac Newton **discovered** the law of gravity and that Benjamin Franklin **invented** bifocal glasses.

**doesn't, don't** *Doesn't* is singular and should be used only with singular nouns and the personal pronouns *he, she,* and *it*. *Don't* is plural and should be used with plural nouns and the personal pronouns *I, you, we,* and *they*.

| | |
|---|---|
| NONSTANDARD | He **don't** need any help. |
| STANDARD | He **doesn't** need any help. |
| NONSTANDARD | An apple a day **don't** keep the doctor away. |
| STANDARD | An apple a day **doesn't** keep the doctor away. |

**done** *Done* is the past participle of the verb *do*. So, when *done* is used as a verb, it must be used with one or more helping verbs.

| | |
|---|---|
| NONSTANDARD | Eli **done** exactly what the doctor told him. |
| STANDARD | Eli **has done** exactly what the doctor told him. |

**double negative** Words such as *hardly, never, no, not* and *nobody* are considered negatives. Do not use two negatives to express one negative meaning.

| | |
|---|---|
| NONSTANDARD | He does**n't hardly** have any spare time. |
| STANDARD | He does**n't** have any spare time. |
| STANDARD | He **never** has any spare time. |

*You can learn more about the use of negatives on pages L342–L343.*

**emigrate, immigrate** Both of these words are verbs. *Emigrate* means "to leave a country to settle elsewhere." *Immigrate* means "to enter a foreign country to live there." A person emigrates *from* a country and immigrates *to* another country. *Emigrant* and *immigrant* are the noun forms.

Kin Fujii **emigrated** from Japan ten years ago.
Did he **immigrate** to this country for economic reasons?

**etc.** *Etc.* is an abbreviation for a Latin phrase, *et cetera,* that means "and other things." Never use the word *and* with *etc.* If you do, what you are really saying is "and and other things." It is best, however, not to use this abbreviation at all in formal writing.

| | |
|---|---|
| INFORMAL | For the salad we need grapes, oranges, **etc.** |
| FORMAL | For the salad we need grapes, oranges, **and other fruits.** |

**farther, further** *Farther* refers to distance. *Further* means "additional" or "to a greater degree or extent."

> How much **farther** will we travel tonight?
> The tour guide will give us **further** instructions shortly.

**fewer, less** *Fewer* is plural and refers to things that can be counted. *Less* is singular and refers to quantities and qualities that cannot be counted.

> I scored **fewer** points in basketball this year than last year.
> You should place **less** importance on the mistakes you make.

**former, latter** *Former* is the first of two people or things. *Latter* is the second of two people or things. (Use *first* and *last* when referring to three or more.)

> For the main course, we had a choice of roast beef or pork chops. We learned that the portions for the **former** would be larger than the portions for the **latter.**

## Practice Your Skills

Check Your Understanding

***Finding the Correct Word***

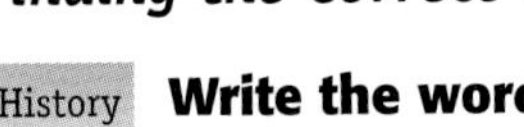

History Topic **Write the word in parentheses that correctly completes each sentence.**

**1.** One of the most dramatic occurrences of the Great Depression (can, may) be the Dust Bowl.

**2.** The (former, latter) affected the entire nation; the (former, latter) affected only the Great Plains states.

**3.** During the 1930s, no (fewer, less) than a million people were uprooted from their land and charted their (coarse, course) to California.

**4.** The combination of fear and hope they experienced (doesn't, don't) seem a great deal (different from, different than) that felt by the (emigrants, immigrants) to America at the turn of the 19th century.

5. Of (coarse, course), the exodus to California was a result of a (continual, continuous) drought that plagued the Great Plains.
6. Unknowingly, many farmers (done, had done) irreversible damage to the land by uprooting the natural sod that provided drought protection for the soil.
7. The drought gave rise to (farther, further) problems as enormous quantities of dust swirled across the plains forcing the farmers (farther, further) away from home.
8. The name "Okie" was (discovered, invented) to describe the migrating people even though many came from other states besides Oklahoma.
9. Today we (can hardly, can't hardly) imagine the endless line of homeless people traveling away from the plains in search of a new life.
10. Many (discovered, invented) that the stories of abundant jobs had been (discovered, invented) by wealthy landowners looking for cheap labor.

Connect to the Writing Process: Revising

### *Recognizing Correct Usage*

**Rewrite the following paragraphs, changing the words that are used incorrectly.**

Born in Salinas, California, John Steinbeck had an opportunity to discover the continuous plight of migrant workers. By living among them, he gained farther knowledge of them and their working conditions. He had done his research thoroughly; from those experiences, he discovered the characters for several of his works. Some critics considered his characters to be course and common. Others, however, felt Steinbeck had special empathy for the lonely, the mistreated, the poor, and others who suffered.

Readers can't help but recognize this continuous theme in works such as *Tortilla Flat, Of Mice and Men,* and *The Grapes of Wrath.*

No other account of the Dust Bowl migration has had more impact than John Steinbeck's *The Grapes of Wrath.* Although some consider this work a social protest, it can more accurately be described as a work of art. In 1940, the film version of the novel was well received even though the ending was different than the novel's. Steinbeck received no less than the Pulitzer Prize for this novel in the same year. Its artistic value hasn't never decreased; in fact, it has increased over the years. His literary acclaim spread farther when he received the Nobel Prize for his life's work in 1962.

**good, well** *Good* is an adjective and often follows a linking verb. *Well* is an adverb and often follows an action verb. However, when *well* means "in good health" or "satisfactory," it is used as an adjective.

Do you feel **good** this morning? (adjective)
Yes, I work **well** in the morning. (adverb)
Pat doesn't feel **well.** ("in good health")

*You can learn more about using adjectives and adverbs on pages L327–L345.*

**had of** Do not use *of* after *had.*

| | |
|---|---|
| NONSTANDARD | I would have taken my umbrella if I **had of** listened to the weather forecast. |
| STANDARD | I would have taken my umbrella if I **had** listened to the weather forecast. |

**have, of** Never substitute *of* for the verb *have*. When speaking, many people make a contraction of *have*. For example, someone might say, "We should've left sooner." Because *'ve* sounds like *of*, *of* is often incorrectly substituted for *have*.

| | |
|---|---|
| NONSTANDARD | You should **of** roasted the potatoes. |
| STANDARD | You should **have** roasted the potatoes. |

**hear, here** *Hear* is a verb that means "to perceive by listening." *Here* is an adverb that means "in this place."

If you stand over **here**, can you **hear** the phone ring?

**hole, whole** *Hole* is an opening in something. *Whole* means "complete or entire."

The **whole** time I watched the **hole,** no animal went in.

**imply, infer** Both of these words are verbs. *Imply* means "to suggest" or "to hint." *Infer* means "to draw a conclusion by reasoning or from evidence." A speaker implies; a listener infers. *Implication* and *inference* are the noun forms.

Grandmother **implied** that she might be visiting soon.
We **inferred** from what she said that she was excited.

**in, into** Use *into* when you want to express motion from one place to another.

The mixture **in** the bowl should be put **into** the blender.

**irregardless** Do not substitute this word for *regardless*.

| | |
|---|---|
| NONSTANDARD | **Irregardless** of anything you say, I still think he was telling the truth. |
| STANDARD | **Regardless** of anything you say, I still think he was telling the truth. |

CONNECT TO SPEAKING AND WRITING

Both the prefix *ir–* and the ending *–less* are negative. Since the use of a double negative should not be used to express one negative meaning, *irregardless* should not be used in speaking or writing.

**its, it's** *Its* is a possessive pronoun. *It's* is a contraction for *it is.*

The committee will announce **its** findings on Friday.
**It's** going to be a controversial report.

**kind, sort, type** These words are singular and should be preceded by *this* or *that. Kinds, sorts,* and *types* are plural and should be preceded by *these* or *those.*

Joan likes **that type** of book bag.
Joan likes **those types** of book bags.

**kind of, sort of** Never substitute these expressions for *rather* or *somewhat* in formal writing.

| | |
|---|---|
| NONSTANDARD | Calculus was **sort of** difficult for me. |
| STANDARD | Calculus was **rather** difficult for me. |

CONNECT TO SPEAKING AND WRITING

Practice using the words *rather* and *somewhat* during informal conversations. Practicing their use will help you to use them correctly when you write formally.

**knew, new** *Knew,* the past tense of the verb *know,* means "was acquainted with." *New* is an adjective that means "recently made" or "just found."

We **knew** all along that a **new** gym would be built.

**learn, teach** Both of these words are verbs. *Learn* means "to acquire knowledge." *Teach* means "to instruct."

| | |
|---|---|
| NONSTANDARD | Who **learned** you how to water-ski? |
| STANDARD | Who **taught** you how to water-ski? |
| STANDARD | I **learned** how to water-ski from my sister. |

**leave, let** Both of these words are verbs. *Leave* means "to depart." *Let* means "to allow" or "to permit."

| | |
|---|---|
| NONSTANDARD | **Leave** me fix dinner before the game. |
| STANDARD | **Let** me fix dinner before the game. |
| STANDARD | I want to **leave** early to get a good seat. |

## PRACTICE YOUR SKILLS

### Check Your Understanding

***Finding the Correct Word***

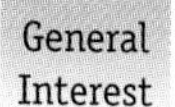


**Write the word in parentheses that correctly completes each sentence.**

1. Environmental issues, ranging from ocean pollution to a (hole, whole) in the ozone layer, plague the (hole, whole) world.
2. As our population grows, these (type, types) of issues will increase.
3. We (hear, here) horror stories every day about companies that pollute (irregardless, regardless) of environmental regulations.
4. (Its, It's) not unusual to have specials on TV that warn us about the damaging (implications, inferences) of air and water pollution.
5. (Its, It's) importance is (kind of, rather) difficult to (learn, teach) the public.
6. From the indifference displayed by many, we can only (imply, infer) that some people don't care about (learning, teaching).
7. Community projects, such as going (in, into) the streams to remove trash, (let, leave) us have an opportunity to help.
8. Promoting recognition (in, into) the community of environmentally safe products works (good, well).
9. More (knew, new) and innovative approaches are needed to make people feel (good, well) about their involvement.
10. We could (have, of) made more rapid progress if we had known how to increase public support.

Connect to the Writing Process: Drafting

***Practicing Usage***

**Answer each question using the correct form of the appropriate word in parentheses.**

**11.** How did you find out about the library at your school? (learn, teach)

**12.** Were you already acquainted with the different options for foreign language clubs? (new, knew)

**13.** Which subject interests you? (sort of, somewhat)

**14.** Is journalism an option at your school? (hear, here)

**15.** Who allowed your class to attend the workshop? (leave, let)

Connect to the Writing Process: Revising

***Recognizing Correct Usage***

**Rewrite the following paragraph, changing the words that are used incorrectly.**

One woman who new well how to raise public awareness was writer and scientist Rachel Carson. She is a well example of how it's possible to combine our interests with our learning to produce results. Drawn to nature as a child, she later wrote about it's wonders and also managed to learn a hole generation about environmental dangers. Also, she put a hole in the accepted theory in the 1920s that science was a profession kind of ill-suited for women. Irregardless of her gender, she earned a master's degree in zoology from Johns Hopkins University and went in the field of aquatic biology. With *The Sea Around Us*, she opened up a new world to the reading public. However, from the inferences in *The Silent Spring* about the harmful effects of pesticides, the public implied the threat to our environment.

## Communicate Your Ideas

### APPLY TO WRITING

#### Analysis of a Photograph

Rachel Carson's love of nature led her to write *The Sea Around Us*. This photograph of the California coastline illustrates the power and beauty of the sea. Imagine that you are seated on the shore and want to preserve the memory of the moment. Using at least six of the following words, describe the photograph in detail and explain what you think the photographer wanted to accomplish.

- *can/may*
- *continual/continuous*
- *farther/further*
- *hole/whole*
- *kind/sort/type*
- *learn/teach*

**lie, lay** *Lie* means "to rest or recline." *Lie* is never followed by a direct object. Its principal parts are *lie, lying, lay,* and *lain*. *Lay* means "to put or set (something) down." *Lay* is usually followed by a direct object. Its principal parts are *lay, laying, laid,* and *laid*.

Don't **lie** down now.
The workers will **lay** the new carpet in your room.

*You can learn more about using the verbs* lie *and* lay *on pages L193–L196.*

**like, as** *Like* can be used as a preposition to introduce a prepositional phrase. *As* is usually a subordinating conjunction that introduces an adverb clause. Although *like* is sometimes used informally as a conjunction, it should be avoided in formal situations.

| | |
|---|---|
| INFORMAL | The room is perfect just **like** it is. (clause) |
| FORMAL | The room is perfect just **as** it is. |
| FORMAL | The wallpaper is gray-striped **like** mine. (prepositional phrase) |

**loose, lose** *Loose* is usually an adjective that means "not tight." *Lose* is a verb that means "to misplace" or "not to have any longer."

Your tooth is very **loose**.
I hope you don't **lose** it before class pictures are taken.

**may be, maybe** *May be* is a form of the verb *be*. *Maybe* is an adverb that means "perhaps."

The chance of a lifetime **may be** in this envelope.
**Maybe** we have won the expense-paid vacation to Greece.

**most, almost** *Most* is a noun, a pronoun, or an adjective that modifies a noun or a pronoun. *Almost*, which means "nearly," is an adverb. Do not substitute *most* for *almost*.

| | |
|---|---|
| NONSTANDARD | Did you type **most** all of your term paper? |
| STANDARD | Did you type **almost** all of your term paper? |
| STANDARD | I spent **most** of the weekend on the computer. |

**nor, or** Use *neither* with *nor* and *either* with *or*.

**Neither** Fred **nor** Jane is coming to the party.
They are going to **either** the movies **or** the concert.

**of** Prepositions such as *inside, outside,* and *off* should not be followed by *of*.

| | |
|---|---|
| NONSTANDARD | The ball rolled **off of** the chair. |
| STANDARD | The ball rolled **off** the chair. |

**ought** Never use *have* or *had* with *ought.*

| | |
|---|---|
| NONSTANDARD | Ben **hadn't ought** to drive so fast. |
| STANDARD | Ben **ought not** to drive so fast. |

**passed, past** *Passed* is the past tense of the verb *pass*. As a noun *past* means "a time gone by." As an adjective *past* means "just gone" or "elapsed." As a preposition *past* means "beyond."

In the **past** she always **passed** her courses with *A's*.
(*past* as a noun)

For the **past** several mornings, I have walked **past** the park on my way to school.
(*past* as an adjective and then as a preposition)

**precede, proceed** Both of these words are verbs. *Precede* means "to be, go, or come ahead of something else." *Proceed* means "to move along a course," "to advance," or "to continue after a pause or an interruption."

One guide will **precede** our group down the mountain.
**Proceed** down the steep mountain with great caution.

**principal, principle** As an adjective *principal* means "main" or "chief." As a noun *principal* means "the head of a school" or "a leader." *Principle* is a noun that is synonymous with *law, truth, doctrine,* or *code of conduct.*

The **principal** reason he stayed in school was because of the advice given by the **principal** at Atlantic High.

Roberto decided to stick by the **principles** his parents had instilled in him.

**respectfully, respectively** *Respectfully* is related to the noun *respect,* which means "high regard or esteem." *Respectively* means "in the order given."

**Respectfully**, the guide inquired about my destination.
I replied that it would be London and Paris, **respectively**.

**rise, raise** *Rise* means "to move upward" or "to get up." *Rise* is never followed by a direct object. Its principal parts are *rise, rising, rose,* and *risen*. *Raise* means "to lift up," "to increase," or "to grow something." *Raise* is usually followed by a direct object. Its principal parts are *raise, raising, raised,* and *raised*.

> The spectators always **rise** when the judge enters the courtroom.
>
> They wondered if the attorney would **raise** the same issue that he brought up yesterday.

*You can learn more about using the verbs* rise *and* raise *on pages L194–L196.*

## PRACTICE YOUR SKILLS

Check Your Understanding

### *Finding the Correct Word*

Literature Topic

**Write the word in parentheses that correctly completes each sentence.**

**1.** (Almost, Most) all people agree that poetry (may be, maybe) described in a variety of ways.

**2.** Neither poets (nor, or) readers of poetry agree on how it (had ought, ought) to be defined.

**3.** Words, of (coarse, course), are the (principal, principle) components of poetry.

**4.** This fact (raises, rises) the question as to why one poem isn't basically (as, like) another.

**5.** However, in the usage and pattern of those words (lays, lies) the uniqueness of each poem.

**6.** In the (passed, past) some argued that a poem (ain't, isn't) true poetry unless it (passed, past) certain criteria—namely, the use of elevated language.

**7.** In the late 1800s, Walt Whitman (preceded, proceeded) to use the language of the common people.

**8.** The (loose, lose) style of Whitman's poetry, known as free verse, did not cause it to (loose, lose) a rhythmical quality.

9. His style (lay, laid) to rest the idea that poetry could not move (outside, outside of) the fixed forms of tradition.
10. Whitman has been (respectfully, respectively) praised as the "poet of the common man" and the "father of modern poetry."

Connect to the Writing Process: Revising
***Recognizing Correct Usage***

**Rewrite the following paragraphs, changing the words that are used incorrectly.**

Sonnets, revered in the passed, continue to be a principal part of poetry. The names of two major forms, Petrarchan and Shakespearean, proceed from their extensive use by Petrarch and Shakespeare. These are known also as either the Italian sonnet or the English sonnet, respectfully. Although each contains fourteen lines, they loose their similarity in most other elements.

Ballads, another fixed form, are based in principal on songs that tell a story; they may be one of the oldest forms of poetry. Proceeding the others, the first stanza typically ought to present the characters and the problem; the rest of the stanzas proceed to solve the dilemma presented by the first.

In contrast, the intent of the five-line limerick, whose name comes from a city in Ireland, is to amuse. May be the varied forms of poems ensure that poetry doesn't ever loose its universal appeal.

**says, said** Do not use *says*, the present tense of the verb *say*, when you should use the past tense, *said*.

| | |
|---|---|
| NONSTANDARD | Then she **says**, "I want to go with you." |
| STANDARD | Then she **said**, "I want to go with you." |

**–self, –selves** A reflexive or an intensive pronoun that ends in *–self* or *–selves* should not be used as a subject. (Never use "hisself" or "theirselves.")

| | |
|---|---|
| NONSTANDARD | Ken and **myself** were chosen. |
| STANDARD | Ken and **I** were chosen. |
| NONSTANDARD | They made **theirselves** sandwiches. |
| STANDARD | They made **themselves** sandwiches. |

**shall, will** Formal English uses *shall* with first-person pronouns and *will* with second- and third-person pronouns. Today, however, *shall* and *will* are used interchangeably with *I* and *we*, except that *shall* is usually still used with first-person pronouns for questions.

**Shall** I meet you at the mall?
**Will** you meet me at the mall?

**sit, set** *Sit* means "to rest in an upright position." *Sit* is never followed by a direct object. Its principal parts are *sit, sitting, sat,* and *sat*. *Set* means "to put or place (something)." *Set* is usually followed by a direct object. Its principal parts are *set, setting, set* and *set.*

**Sit** down and rest for a while.
I'll **set** the dishes on the shelf.

*You can learn more about using the verbs* sit *and* set *on pages L194–L196.*

**some, somewhat** *Some* is either a pronoun or an adjective that modifies a noun or a pronoun. *Somewhat* is an adverb.

| | |
|---|---|
| NONSTANDARD | School enrollment has declined **some.** |
| STANDARD | School enrollment has declined **somewhat.** |

**than, then** *Than* is usually a subordinating conjunction and is used for comparisons. *Then* is an adverb that means "at that time" or "next."

> I didn't think I would finish sooner **than** you.
> Finish your homework and **then** call me.

**that, which, who** These words are often used as relative pronouns to introduce adjective clauses. *That* refers to animals and things and usually begins an essential clause. *Which* refers to animals and things. *Who* refers to people.

> The ad **that** was posted on the board sounds interesting.
> That ad, **which** also runs on radio, will attract many people.
> Anyone **who** responds to the ad may fill out an application.

**their, there, they're** *Their* is a possessive pronoun. *There* is usually an adverb, and sometimes it will begin an inverted sentence. *They're* is a contraction for *they are*.

> **Their** car is parked over **there**, ready for the trip.
> **They're** leaving for Mobile tomorrow.

**theirs, there's** *Theirs* is a possessive pronoun. *There's* is a contraction for *there is*.

> **There's** an easy solution to my problem, but what about **theirs?**

**them, those** Never use *them* as a subject or an adjective.

| | |
|---|---|
| NONSTANDARD | **Them** are from whose garden? (subject) |
| STANDARD | **Those** are from whose garden? |
| NONSTANDARD | Rachel grew **them** tomatoes. (adjective) |
| STANDARD | Rachel grew **those** tomatoes. |

**this here, that there** Avoid using *here* and *there* in addition to *this* and *that*.

| | |
|---|---|
| NONSTANDARD | **That there** sunset looks beautiful. |
| STANDARD | **That** sunset looks beautiful. |
| NONSTANDARD | **This here** saddle is mine. |
| STANDARD | **This** saddle is mine. |

**this, that, these, those** *This* and *that* are singular and should modify singular nouns. *These* and *those* are plural and should modify plural nouns.

| | |
|---|---|
| NONSTANDARD | Does the Sport Shop sell **those** kind of bats? |
| STANDARD | Does the Sport Shop sell **that** kind of bat? |

**threw, through** *Threw* is the past tense of the verb *throw*. *Through* is a preposition that means "in one side and out the other."

I hope no one **threw** Sunday's newspaper away.
Look **through** the stack of papers on the table.

## PRACTICE YOUR SKILLS

Check Your Understanding
***Finding the Correct Word***

Sports Topic **Write the word in parentheses that correctly completes each sentence.**

**1.** It would be classified as an understatement if someone (said, says) that interest in soccer had increased (some, somewhat) in the United States.

**2.** In fact, most (shall, will) agree the sport has gone (threw, through) an amazing transformation.

**3.** Actually soccer has increased in popularity more (than, then) any other sport.

**4.** (This, This here) transformation began taking place in the 1950s; before (than, then), it was simply known as the favorite sport of Europe and South America.

**5.** The 1994 World Cup held in the United States (set, sit) in motion a nationwide interest.

6. At the matches, fans (threw, through) (theirselves, themselves) energetically into the excitement.
7. (These sort of, This sort of) excitement spilled over to playgrounds, recreation centers, and schools.
8. Many spectators (setting, sitting) in the stands had to learn the rules of soccer.
9. (These, These sort of) rules are actually much simpler (than, then) rules for American football.
10. (Shall, Will) we some day find that soccer has become the national sport of the United States?

Connecting to the Writing Process: Revising
***Recognizing Correct Usage***

**Rewrite the sentences below, changing the words that are used incorrectly. Write a brief explanation for each change.**

11. There has been a growing trend for U.S. schools to include soccer in they're athletic programs.
12. Their often set up to include teams for both young men and women there.
13. Theirs is an enviable task because theirs such an increased interest in this country.
14. Soccer is a game which requires stamina from its players, that must train rigorously.
15. Agility, that is another needed skill, poses a challenge for those which aspire to be competent soccer players.

**to, too, two** *To* is a preposition. *To* also begins an infinitive. *Too* is an adverb that modifies an adjective or another adverb. *Two* is a number.

> **Two** more people are **too** many **to** take in our car.
> We hurried **to** the picnic area before it got **too** crowded.

**try to** Use *try to* instead of *try and*, which is nonstandard.

| | |
|---|---|
| NONSTANDARD | Please **try and** be there on time. |
| STANDARD | Please **try to** be there on time. |

**use to, used to** Be sure to add the *–d* to *use.*

| | |
|---|---|
| NONSTANDARD | I **use to** paint with watercolors. |
| STANDARD | I **used to** paint with watercolors. |

**way, ways** Do not substitute *ways* for *way* when referring to a distance.

| | |
|---|---|
| NONSTANDARD | Aren't you a long **ways** from home? |
| STANDARD | Aren't you a long **way** from home? |

**weak, week** *Weak* is an adjective that means "not strong" or "likely to break." *Week* is a noun that means "a time period of seven days."

For the first **week** after your surgery, you'll feel quite **weak**.

**what** Do not substitute *what* for *that.*

| | |
|---|---|
| NONSTANDARD | The car **what** you bought was too expensive. |
| STANDARD | The car **that** you bought was too expensive. |

**when, where** Do not use *when* or *where* directly after a linking verb in a definition.

| | |
|---|---|
| NONSTANDARD | In the North, October is **when** you should plant tulip bulbs. |
| STANDARD | In the North, October is the **month when** you should plant tulip bulbs. |
| NONSTANDARD | The Hall of Mirrors is **where** the Treaty of Versailles was signed. |
| STANDARD | The Hall of Mirrors is the **room where** the Treaty of Versailles was signed. |
| NONSTANDARD | A harvest is **when** the farmers bring in their crops. |
| STANDARD | A harvest is **the time when** the farmers bring in their crops. |

**where** Do not substitute *where* for *that.*

| | |
|---|---|
| NONSTANDARD | I read **where** bowling is the number one participant sport in the United States. |
| STANDARD | I read **that** bowling is the number one participant sport in the United States. |

**who, whom** *Who*, a pronoun in the nominative case, is used either as a subject or a predicate nominative. *Whom*, a pronoun in the objective case, is used mainly as a direct object, an indirect object, or an object of a preposition.

**Who** is waving at you?
(subject)

It is Howard, **whom** I have known all my life.
(direct object of the verb *have known* in the adjective clause)

To **whom** will you give permission to drive?
(object of the preposition *to*)

CONNECT TO WRITER'S CRAFT

Except when using nonstandard English for special effect, professional writers use standard English even in the titles of their works. Notice the correct usage of *who* in the nominative case and *whom* in the objective case in the following titles.

*For **Whom** the Bell Tolls* by Ernest Hemingway
*The Man **Who** Came to Dinner* by Moss Hart

**whose, who's** *Whose* is a possessive pronoun. *Who's* is a contraction for *who is*.

**Whose** suitcase is that?
It belongs to the man **who's** walking this way.

**your, you're** *Your* is a possessive pronoun. *You're* is a contraction for *you are*.

**You're** sure you put **your** baseball glove in the car?

## Practice Your Skills

### Check Your Understanding
### *Finding the Correct Word*

Contemporary Life

**Write the word in parentheses that correctly completes each sentence.**

1. (Your, You're) senior year is one of the most important and memorable ones, (to, too, two).
2. Many (who, whom) previously thought they had a long (way, ways) to go before graduation realize that the time is rapidly approaching.
3. It is essential that you (try and, try to) keep a focus on the goals (that, what) you have set.
4. (Your, You're) certain (to, too, two) discover that all decisions about (your, you're) future need careful consideration.
5. (Whose, Who's) qualified to help with college or career decisions should determine (whose, who) help you seek.
6. If you should find yourself (weak, week) in a certain subject, find out (who, whom) can provide tutoring.
7. When in doubt, remember that (to, too, two) excellent sources from (who, whom) you can seek advice are your parents and guidance counselors.
8. If you are (use to, used to) letting decisions slide, (try and, try to) practice self-discipline.
9. Every (weak, week) that you procrastinate could affect your career.
10. (Too, To, Two) much depends on what (your, you're) planning for the future.
11. (Who, Whom) should you contact about touring a local college campus?
12. Confirm (that, what) the college-prep classes you took are transferable for credit.
13. Enjoy (your, you're) last year of school; the senior activities are fun, (to, two, too).

**14.** (Try to, Try and) save (your, you're) graduation programs, pictures, and memorabilia for a class scrapbook.

**15.** A class reunion is (where, the event at which) you could share your scrapbook with old friends.

**16.** You will not believe how (bad, badly) you will want to see your classmates after ten years.

**17.** At the reunion, (anywhere, anywheres) you look will be a familiar face.

**18.** Look carefully for your homecoming king and queen, because (the both, both) of them will have changed a great deal.

Connecting to the Writing Process: Revising

### *Recognizing Correct Usage*

**Rewrite the following paragraph, changing the words that are used incorrectly.**

Be sure to participate in senior activities leading up too you're graduation; they're two special to miss. The memories what you accumulate will last a lifetime. One event, the junior-senior prom, is where the junior class honors graduating seniors. The king and queen are the couple who juniors and seniors recognize symbolically at the dance. The academic awards program is designed to try to give recognition to those who are deserving. The yearbook signing is when seniors write final messages to one another. You're sure to have teachers, too, who wish to add congratulatory notes. This informal party, usually held the last weak of school, is a special memory before the formal activities of graduation actually begin.

## Communicate Your Ideas

### APPLY TO WRITING

**Personal Response: *Correct Usage***

The following words of George Will, a *Washington Post* columnist, are an excerpt from his column and the advice he offered his daughter's graduating class. Examine this excerpt and then read the instructions on the following page.

Well, we live and learn. Indeed, the happiest people live to learn. They live for the delightful astonishments that never stop coming to those who never stop learning.

So, said the columnist to the Class of '99: Go through life with, figuratively speaking, a crick in your neck from looking back at the path by which humanity got to today. It is a path littered with true stories that astonish. Understand that happiness is a talent, one that immunizes you against being bored. Boredom is sinful because, as a character says in a Saul Bellow novel, "Boredom is the shriek of unused capacities."

—*George Will,* "Will's Way"

Using any ten of the glossary words from *lie/lay* through *your/you're*, write a personal response to George Will's commencement advice. Underline the words you chose, checking that you used the correct form.

Mixed Practice

Contemporary Life

**Write the word in parentheses that correctly completes each sentence.**

1. While the rituals of (passed, past) high school graduations may have changed (some, somewhat), the excitement and solemnity of the occasion have not.
2. The importance of graduation is reflected in the (amount, number) of preparations made during the (preceding, proceeding) (weak, week).
3. The salutatorian and valedictorian usually make (farther, further) revisions to (their, they're) speeches.
4. A proper fit of the mortarboard is essential; if (it's, its) (to, too, two) (loose, lose), you might (loose, lose) it.
5. (To, Too, Two) achieve the full (affect, effect) and ensure that it fits (good, well), try on the robe, also.
6. Graduation practices are held to (learn, teach) graduates how to walk (all together, altogether) in the processional march.
7. At practice the coordinator (can, may) even (raise, rise) the issue of when and how to (raise, rise) at the proper time.
8. The coordinator also (learns, teaches) you how to properly adjust the tassel after receiving (you're, your) diploma.
9. Special instructions that (lay, lie) out important details are available (beside, besides) the stage.
10. As these preparations (infer, imply), the (hole, whole) ceremony is carefully planned.

CHAPTER 9

# Capital Letters

### *Directions*

**Read the passage and decide which word or words should be capitalized in each underlined part. Write the letter of the correct answer. If the underlined part contains no error, write *D*.**

EXAMPLE The south pole is an icy continent called antarctica. (1)

1 **A** Continent, Antarctica
**B** Icy
**C** South Pole, Antarctica
**D** No error

ANSWER 1 **C**

On the continent of Antarctica, the sun shines for half a year (1). I don't know if i could endure the other six months of darkness, although (2) the experience would be interesting. human populations do not live in Antarctica (3), but penguins and seals do. Can you picture yourself writing letters that begin, "dear mom, Here I am (4) on a giant glacier far from civilization (5)"?

**1** **A** Sun
**B** Continent
**C** Year
**D** No error

**2** **A** I
**B** Although
**C** Darkness
**D** No error

**3** **A** Populations
**B** Human
**C** Human, Populations
**D** No error

**4** **A** Dear
**B** Mom
**C** Dear Mom,
**D** No error

**5** **A** Giant
**B** Glacier
**C** Civilization
**D** No error

James Rosenquist. *Telephone Explosion*, 1983.
Oil on canvas, 78 by 66 inches. Courtesy of SBC Communications Inc. ©James Rosenquist/Licensed by VAGA, New York, NY.

**Describe** List specific objects you recognize in this painting.

**Analyze** What area of the painting do you notice first? Why do you think this area attracts your attention first?

**Interpret** What do you think the artist, James Rosenquist, is saying with this painting?

**Judge** If you could change one aspect of this painting, what would it be? How would your modification change the painting's message?

At the end of this chapter, you will use the artwork to stimulate ideas for writing.

# Capitalization

Until the advent of printing in the fifteenth century, words were written in all capital letters, and no punctuation was used. When scribes wrote, they ran words TOGETHERLIKETHIS.

Fortunately along with the printing press came specific uses for capitalization and the introduction of punctuation. As a result, not only could people read faster, but they could also understand more easily what they read. The correct use of capitalization and punctuation will add clarity to your writing and prevent any misunderstanding of your meaning.

When lowercase letters were first introduced, capital letters were used only in special situations. Today, however, a capital letter marks the beginning of certain constructions and emphasizes the importance of certain words. This chapter will review the uses of capitalization.

## First Words and the Pronoun *I*

Capitalization is used to draw attention to the beginning of a sentence, a direct quotation, and a line of poetry. The pronoun *I* is always capitalized, regardless of its position in a sentence or line of poetry.

### Sentences and Poetry

Capital letters draw a reader's attention to the beginning of a sentence or of a new line of poetry.

**Capitalize the first word of a sentence and of a line of poetry.**

SENTENCE **T**eenagers in our community have become increasingly involved in poetry readings.

POETRY

The panther is like a leopard,
Except it hasn't been peppered.
Should you behold a panther crouch,
Prepare to say Ouch.
Better yet, if called by a panther,
Don't anther.

*—Ogden Nash*

When only two or three lines of poetry are quoted, they can be written with a slash ( / ) between each line. Each new line after a slash begins with a capital letter.

"God in His wisdom made the fly / And then forgot to tell us why."

*—Ogden Nash*

Capitalize the first word when a direct quotation is used.

Marvin asked, "**D**o you understand this essay by Orwell?"

*You can learn more about capitalization in direct quotations on pages L506–L507.*

Some poets, especially modern poets, deliberately misuse or eliminate capital letters. If you are quoting a poem in your writing, copy it exactly as the poet has written it. Emily Dickinson, for example, sometimes capitalized common nouns for emphasis or to make them seem like people with feelings and actions.

The **S**ky is low—the **C**louds are mean,
. . .
A **N**arrow **W**ind complains all **D**ay
. . .

William Carlos Williams, on the other hand, wrote entire poems without using a single capital letter.

so much depends
upon

a red wheel
barrow

glazed with rain
water

beside the white
chickens

—"The Red Wheelbarrow"

These unusual ways of using capitalization contribute to the beauty and meaning of the poems. When you quote poetry in your writing, duplicate the author's capitalization, even if it "breaks the rules."

## Parts of a Letter

The first word in a salutation, or greeting of a letter, and the first word in the closing of a letter are capitalized.

**Capitalize the first word in the greeting and the first word in the closing of a letter.**

| PARTS OF A LETTER | | |
|---|---|---|
| **Greetings** | **D**ear Sir or Madam: | **A**ttention Subscriber: |
| | **T**o Whom It May Concern: | **M**y dearest Jimmy, |
| **Closings** | **S**incerely yours, | **B**est regards, |
| | **Y**our friend, | **C**ordially, |

### Connect to Writer's Craft

In some informal letters, people write a word in all capital letters to show emphasis—especially in E-mail messages, where many browsers do not permit formatting such as italics and boldface.

> You will NOT believe what I did at school today.
>
> I can't think of ANY way to make my presentation more creative.

## Outlines

Capital letters draw the reader's attention to the beginning of each heading in an outline.

**Capitalize the first word of each item in an outline and the letters that begin major subsections of the outline.**

I. **A**rgument for a student bookstore-café
  **A.** **E**ncourages reading for relaxation
  **B.** **P**rovides space for poetry readings
  **C.** **P**rovides school supplies and snacks

## Formal Resolutions

Some formal resolutions are constructed as clauses instead of sentences; nevertheless, the first word of the resolution is usually capitalized.

**Capitalize the first word in a formal resolution that follows the word *Resolved.***

*Resolved:* **T**hat this school should build a bookstore-café for the use of all students.

## Some Formal Statements

Formal statements are sometimes introduced with phrases ending in colons, such as *The decision is this:* and *The question was this:*. In these situations, the formal statement usually begins with a capital letter.

**Capitalize the first word of a formal statement that follows a colon.**

> The question was this: **C**ould we afford to pay a speaker as prestigious as Maya Angelou?
>
> The committee issued the following statement: **D**onations to the guest speaker's fund are needed.

*You can learn more about using colons on pages L491–L495.*

## The Pronoun *I*

The pronoun *I* is always capitalized, no matter its position in a sentence or a line of poetry.

**Capitalize the pronoun *I*, both alone and in contractions.**

> **I**'m sure **I** saw her in English class.
> **I** don't know if **I**'ll want to read my poem aloud.

*The first word of a direct quotation is also capitalized. You can learn more about capitalization with quotations on pages L506–L507.*

### CONNECT TO WRITER'S CRAFT

When writing a narrative in first-person, such as an autobiography, use the pronoun *I* sparingly unless you are striving for self-emphasis.

| | |
|---|---|
| SELF-EMPHASIS | **I** write poetry, **I** critique books, and **I** teach literature classes. |
| SUBJECT EMPHASIS | **I** write poetry, critique books, and teach literature classes. |

## Practice Your Skills

### Check Your Understanding

***Using Capitalization with First Words and* I**

Literature Topic

**Choose the item in each pair that is capitalized correctly. Then write the letter of each correct item.**

**1. a.** I sign all my letters "yours sincerely."

**b.** I sign all my letters "Yours sincerely."

**2. a.** Resolved: That the first day of spring be Poetry Day at our school.

**b.** Resolved: that the first day of spring be Poetry Day at our school.

**3. a.** I. Ideas for Poetry Day
A. Guest poet
B. Public reading
C. Contest

**b.** I. Ideas for Poetry Day
A. guest poet
B. public reading
C. contest

**4. a.** For Cynthia's birthday I'm getting her *Sonnets from the Portuguese* by Elizabeth Barrett Browning.

**b.** For Cynthia's birthday i'm getting her *Sonnets from the Portuguese* by Elizabeth Barrett Browning.

**5. a.** We have been assigned to write to an author whose work we enjoy. perhaps I will write to John Fowles.

**b.** We have been assigned to write to an author whose work we enjoy. Perhaps I will write to John Fowles.

**6. a.** Should I begin this letter with "Dear Sir" or "Dear Mr. Fowles"?

**b.** Should I begin this letter with "Dear sir" or "Dear Mr. Fowles"?

**7. a.** The question is this: can you read this entire novel by midterm?

**b.** The question is this: Can you read this entire novel by midterm?

**8. a.** "'beauty is truth, truth beauty,'—that is all
ye know on earth, and all ye need to know."
—*John Keats*

**b.** "'Beauty is truth, truth beauty,'—that is all
Ye know on earth, and all ye need to know."
—*John Keats*

**9. a.** Who wrote these lines: "That's my last Duchess painted on the wall, / looking as if she were alive. . . . "?

**b.** Who wrote these lines: "That's my last Duchess painted on the wall, / Looking as if she were alive. . . . "?

**10. a.** Now that i've studied Robert Browning, I know he wrote "My Last Duchess."

**b.** Now that I've studied Robert Browning, I know he wrote "My Last Duchess."

Connect to the Writing Process: Editing

### *Using Capitalization*

**Write each item using correct capitalization.**

**11.** T. S. Eliot's character J. Alfred Prufrock says, "I should have been a pair of ragged claws / scuttling across the floors of silent seas."

**12.** II. The early life of George Orwell
A. born in India
B. birth name Eric Blair
C. private school in England

**13.** in "Shooting an Elephant" Orwell writes, "in Moulmein, in Lower Burma, I was hated by large numbers of people—the only time in my life that I have been important enough for this to happen to me."

**14.** the narrator in O'Brien's "Sister Imelda" makes the following statement: "in our deepest moments, we say the most inadequate things."

**15.** this summer I'm going to read *Fahrenheit 451* by Ray Bradbury and then try to write my own futuristic short story.

**16.** Byron wrote the following to his publisher:

"Sept 15th. 1817
dear sir—
i enclose a sheet for correction if ever you get to another edition . . . ."

**17.** Resolved: that "Mutability" by Shelley be the official poem of the senior class.

**18.** In *Heart of Darkness,* Conrad writes: "no, it is impossible; it is impossible to convey the life-sensation of any given epoch of one's existence—that which makes its truth, its meaning—its subtle and penetrating essence. it is impossible. we live, as we dream—alone. . . ."

## Communicate Your Ideas

### APPLY TO WRITING

**Analyzing Poetry: *Capitalization***

Study the use of capitalization in this poem. Then answer the items that follow.

The Bustle in a House
    The Morning after Death
Is solemnest of industries
Enacted upon Earth,—

The sweeping up the Heart
And putting Love away
We shall not want to use again
Until Eternity.

*–Emily Dickinson*

- List all the words that Dickinson capitalizes.
- What rule of capitalization does Dickinson follow correctly?
- What words are capitalized that normally would not be? How does this affect the reader?

- Try writing the poem without the unusual capitalization, and then read it. What words do you skim over now that you previously noticed because of capitalization?

## Proper Nouns

Beginning a noun with a capital letter tells a reader that it is a **proper noun**—that it names a particular person, place, or thing.

### Capitalize proper nouns and their abbreviations.

Proper nouns may be divided into the following groups.

**Names of particular persons and animals** should be capitalized. Also capitalize the initials that stand for people's names.

| NAMES | |
|---|---|
| **PERSONS** | **J**ames, **J**ocelyn **W**eiss, **A**llison **R**. **F**errara |
| **ANIMALS** | **R**ex, **F**elix, **S**pot, **D**ancer, **T**hunderbolt |

Surnames that begin with *De, Mc, Mac, O',* or *St.* usually contain two capital letters. However, since such names do vary, it is always best to ask individuals how their names are spelled and capitalized.

| NAMES WITH TWO CAPITAL LETTERS | | | | |
|---|---|---|---|---|
| **D**e**J**ong | **M**c**G**uire | **M**ac**I**nnis | **O**'**H**ara | **S**t. **J**ames |

Capitalize a descriptive name, title, or nickname that is used as a proper noun or as part of a proper noun.

| DESCRIPTIVE NAMES | | |
|---|---|---|
| **C**alamity **J**ane | **H**onest **A**be | the **C**ornhusker **S**tate |

Capitalize abbreviations that follow a person's name.

Stephanie Wong, **M.D.**, will be tonight's guest speaker.

Capitalize common nouns that are clearly personified.

> "O Memory! thou fond deceiver."
>
> *—Oliver Goldsmith*

**Geographical names,** including the names of particular places, bodies of water, and celestial bodies should be capitalized.

| GEOGRAPHICAL NAMES | |
|---|---|
| STREETS, HIGHWAYS | **T**remont **S**treet (**S**t.), **M**eridian **T**urnpike (**T**pk.), **R**oute (**R**t.) 77, **M**ontgomery **F**reeway (**F**rwy.), **I**nterstate **H**ighway 35 (**I**-35), **C**harleton **B**oulevard (**B**lvd.), **S**unshine **H**ighway (**H**wy.), **M**ichigan **A**venue (**A**ve.), **T**hirty-second **S**treet (The second part of a hyphenated numbered street is not capitalized.) |
| CITIES, STATES | **R**apid **C**ity, **S**outh **D**akota (**SD**); **T**erre **H**aute, **I**ndiana (**IN**); **W**ashington, **D.C.** |
| TOWNSHIPS, COUNTIES, PARISHES | **P**ottsville **T**ownship, **B**roward **C**ounty, **N**ew **H**ope **P**arish |
| COUNTRIES | **S**audi **A**rabia, **T**hailand, **I**reland, **C**anada |
| SECTIONS OF A COUNTRY | the **N**orthwest, **N**ew **E**ngland, the **S**outh, the **S**un **B**elt (Words that are used as sections of the country are often preceded by *the.* Compass directions do not begin with a capital letter: *Go east on Route 23.*) |
| CONTINENTS | **S**outh **A**merica, **A**frica, **A**ustralia |
| WORLD REGIONS | **N**orthern **H**emisphere, **S**outh **P**ole, the **F**ar **E**ast |
| ISLANDS | **L**ong **I**sland, the **P**hilippine **I**slands |

| | |
|---|---|
| Mountains | Mount (**Mt.**) **H**ood, the **A**llegheny **M**ountains (**Mts.**), the **W**hite **M**ountains |
| Parks | **B**ryce **C**anyon **N**ational **P**ark |
| Bodies of Water | **P**acific **O**cean, **S**outh **C**hina **S**ea, **P**ersian **G**ulf, **M**errimack **R**iver, **C**edar **L**ake |
| Stars | **S**irius, **N**ova **H**ercules, **N**orth **S**tar |
| Constellations | **B**ig **D**ipper, **U**rsa **M**inor, **O**rion |
| Planets | **V**enus, **N**eptune, **S**aturn, **E**arth (Do not capitalize *sun* or *moon.* Also do not capitalize *earth* preceded by *the.*) |

*You can learn more about proper nouns on pages L6–L9.*

Words such as *street, mountain, river, island,* and *county* are capitalized only when they are part of a proper noun.

Which **l**ake is larger, **L**ake **S**uperior or **L**ake **M**ichigan?
Which **c**ounty is central, **T**ravis **C**ounty or **R**andall **C**ounty?

## Practice Your Skills

### *Using Capital Letters*

Geography Topic **Write the following items, using capital letters where needed.**

1. the columbia river
2. jackson park
3. the milky way
4. fifty-third st.
5. a trip to the southwest
6. the city of louisville
7. the earth and mars
8. mountains in the east
9. the gulf of suez
10. madrid, spain
11. north on hayes highway
12. his horse dusty
13. alfred moses, jr.
14. the state of ohio
15. lake victoria
16. the bluegrass state
17. newport news, va
18. a country in africa

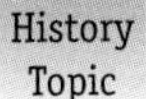

Check Your Understanding

***Using Capital Letters***

History Topic **Correctly write each word that should be capitalized.**

**19.** Woodrow Wilson, born in staunton, va, had a pet ram named old ike.

**20.** William J. Clinton and his family moved into the White House with their pet cat named socks.

**21.** Before they were known as the rocky mountains, they were called the stony mountains.

**22.** The first woman to swim the english channel in both directions was Florence Chadwick of california.

**23.** Old North Church-Christ Church, built in 1723, is the oldest church in boston.

**24.** It is the place where the signal lantern for the midnight ride of paul revere was hung.

**25.** Henry wadsworth longfellow wrote a poem about the famous ride.

**26.** The capital of texas was changed 15 times before austin was finally chosen.

**27.** mt. st. helens, a volcano in the state of Washington, erupted in 1980.

**28.** Address your letter to the President of the United States, 1600 pennsylvania ave., washington, dc 20500-0001.

Connect to the Writing Process: Drafting

***Writing Sentences with Proper Nouns***

**Use each of the following items in a sentence, correctly capitalizing each word that should be capitalized. Correct any words that are incorrectly capitalized.**

**29.** the nile river

**30.** a trip to the united kingdom

**31.** a Cruise to nassau in the caribbean

**32.** a Dog named cimarron lee

**33.** at the corner of citrus ave. and Thirty-First st.

**34.** ursa major, a Constellation

**35.** a party in central park

## Communicate Your Ideas

### APPLY TO WRITING

**Invitation:** ***Proper Nouns***

Write an invitation to a famous novelist or poet. Explain that your school district is planning a Reader's Theater and would like for him or her personally to read original poetry or excerpts. Determine the theme of the Reader's Theater for the writer. Then ask him or her to contact you. Also, provide directions to your school from the nearest airport. Include major highways, cities and towns, and states. When you finish, edit your invitation for mistakes in capitalization, and then write the final copy.

**Names of groups,** including the names of organizations, businesses, institutions, government bodies, political parties, and teams, should be capitalized.

| NAMES OF GROUPS | |
|---|---|
| **ORGANIZATIONS** | the **A**merican **R**ed **C**ross, the **B**oy **S**couts of **A**merica, the **A**ir **N**ational **G**uard |
| **BUSINESSES** | **F**ly **N**ow **A**irlines, **T**he **G**old and **S**ilver **C**ompany, **H**awthorne's **G**reenery, **T**aft **S&L** |
| **INSTITUTIONS** | **H**awthorne **H**igh **S**chool, **L**akeview **H**ospital, the **U**niversity (**U**niv.) of **P**ennsylvania, **N**ew **Y**ork **U**niversity (**NYU**)<br>(Words such as *school, hospital,* and *university* are not capitalized unless they are part of a proper noun.) |

| | |
|---|---|
| **Government Bodies or Agencies** | the **U**nited **S**tates **S**upreme **C**ourt, **C**ongress, the **S**enate, the **V**eterans **A**dministration, the **H**ouse of **C**ommons, **P**arliament, **NASA** |
| **Political Parties** | the **D**emocratic party, a **R**epublican |
| **Teams** | the **B**oston **B**ruins, the **S**eattle **S**eahawks, the **H**ouston **R**ockets, the **A**mes **L**ittle **L**eague |

**Specific time periods, events, and documents,** including the days of the week, months of the year, civil holidays, and special events are capitalized. Also capitalize the names of historical events, periods, and documents.

| **TIME PERIODS, EVENTS, AND DOCUMENTS** | |
|---|---|
| **Days, Months** | **T**uesday (**T**ues.), **W**ednesday (**W**ed.), **F**ebruary (**F**eb.), **D**ecember (**D**ec.) (Do not capitalize the seasons of the year—such as **s**ummer and **w**inter—unless they are part of a proper noun: **B**rooks **S**ummer **F**air.) |
| **Holidays** | **M**emorial **D**ay, **T**hanksgiving, **P**resident's **D**ay |
| **Special Events** | the **O**range **B**owl **P**arade, the **O**lympics, the **B**oston **M**arathon |
| **Historical Events** | the **T**rojan **W**ar, the **B**oston **T**ea **P**arty, the **L**ouisiana **P**urchase, **D**-**D**ay |
| **Time Periods** | the **M**iddle **A**ges, the **A**ge of **R**eason, the **G**reat **D**epression, **R**econstruction |
| **Time Abbreviations** | **A.M./P.M., B.C./A.D.** |
| **Documents** | the **T**ruman **D**octrine, the **T**reaty of **P**aris, the **F**irst **A**mendment, the **C**ivil **R**ights **A**ct |

Prepositions are not usually capitalized in proper nouns.

**Names of nationalities, races, languages, and religions,** including religious holidays and references, are capitalized.

| NATIONALITIES, RACES, LANGUAGES, AND RELIGIONS | |
|---|---|
| NATIONALITIES AND RACES | **C**hinese, **M**exican, **N**orwegian, **C**anadian, **I**rish, **D**utch, **P**ortugese, **C**aucasian, **A**sian, **A**frican, **C**herokee |
| LANGUAGES AND COMPUTER LANGUAGES | **S**panish, **G**reek, **R**ussian, **L**atin, **A**rabic, **C**++, **H**yper **T**ext **M**arkup **L**anguage (**HTML**), **C**obol, **J**ava |
| RELIGIONS | **R**oman **C**atholism, **J**udaism, **L**utheranism, **I**slam |
| RELIGIOUS HOLIDAYS AND REFERENCES | **P**urim, **K**wanzaa, **C**hristmas, **R**amadan, the **B**ible, the **N**ew **T**estament, the **T**orah, the **K**oran, **B**uddha, **G**od (Do not capitalize *god* when it refers to a polytheistic god.) |

CONNECT TO WRITER'S CRAFT

You may have noticed that some writers capitalize the pronouns *he* and *him* when referring to God. Other writers do not capitalize these pronouns.

God told Pharaoh to let **H**is people go.
God told Pharaoh to let **h**is people go.

Also, religious writers sometimes capitalize *thy, thine,* and *thou* (archaic words for *your, yours,* and *you*) when they use pronouns in direct address to God. Whatever decision you make regarding capitalization of such pronouns, you should be consistent.

**Other proper nouns** should also be capitalized.

| OTHER PROPER NOUNS | |
|---|---|
| AWARDS | the **N**obel **P**rize, the **D**avis **C**up |
| BRAND NAMES | a **T**rifect computer, **P**eaches soap (The product itself is not capitalized.) |

| | |
|---|---|
| **Structures, Memorials, Monuments** | **G**olden **G**ate **B**ridge, **S**ears **T**ower, **V**ietnam **M**emorial, **W**ashington **M**onument, **M**ount **R**ushmore |
| **Ships, Trains, Aircraft, Spacecraft** | ***SS M**innow, **O**rient **E**xpress, **S**pirit of **S**t. **L**ouis, **A**pollo 13, **C**hallenger* |
| **Technological Terms** | **I**nternet, **W**eb, **W**orld **W**ide **W**eb, **W**ebsite, **W**eb page, **W**eb art |
| **Names of Courses** | **C**hemistry II, **D**rafting I, **D**rawing 101 |

Unnumbered courses such as *history, science,* and *art* are not capitalized. Language courses such as *Spanish* and *English,* however, are always capitalized (even when unnumbered) because the name of a language is always capitalized. Also, do not capitalize class names such as *freshman* or *senior* unless they are part of a proper noun: ***S**enior **C**lass **P**icnic.*

Check Your Understanding

***Capitalizing Proper Nouns***

General Interest **Write the following items, using capital letters only where needed.**

1. math and spanish
2. the eiffel tower in paris
3. turkey on thanksgiving
4. dec.
5. the stone age
6. computer sciences corp.
7. the god zeus
8. computer book on java
9. harvard college
10. spring and summer
11. the supreme court
12. friday
13. allah, the islamic name of god
14. a jewish rabbi
15. website on the internet
16. a.m.
17. wise eyes sunglasses
18. political science 1302
19. new york police department
20. argus architects, inc.

## Check Your Understanding
### *Using Capital Letters*

General Interest **Correctly write each word that should begin with a capital letter.**

**21.** Edith Wharton won a pulitzer prize for her fiction.

**22.** John Adams was a member of the federalist party.

**23.** Dolley Madison was voted a seat in the house of representatives on january 9, 1844.

**24.** When my sister graduated from purdue university, she got a job with a computer company.

**25.** Did you visit mount vernon, george washington's home?

**26.** Ty Cobb of the detroit tigers made 4,191 base hits during his career.

**27.** Last year, when I was a junior, I enjoyed french, creative writing, art II, and mechanical drawing.

**28.** J. R. Andrews was captain of the *derwent,* which sailed between sydney and london in the 1880s and 1890s.

**29.** Stephanie Louise Kwolek, a scientist, was inducted into the national inventors hall of fame on july 22, 1995.

**30.** Do you think any inventor will ever be as well known as Thomas alva Edison?

## Connect to the Writing Process: Editing
### *Capitalizing Proper Nouns*

**Rewrite the following sentences, capitalizing the proper nouns and using lowercase for words that are incorrectly capitalized.**

**31.** A famous tourist attraction in italy is the Leaning Tower of pisa.

**32.** This Tower continues to lean each year.

**33.** The Cathedral of notre dame is a very famous Cathedral in Paris, france.

**34.** It is located on the Île de la Cité, a small Island of the Seine river.

**35.** The phrase *Notre dame* means "our lady" in french.

## Communicate Your Ideas

### APPLY TO WRITING

**Autobiography: *Proper Nouns***

Why is it important to learn about one's cultural heritage? Write your own autobiography to present orally to your class. Describe an aspect of your cultural heritage that has contributed to who you are, whether for good or for bad. Use correct capitalization when writing names, time periods, events, languages, and so on. Edit your use of capitalization carefully before writing the final copy.

Mixed Practice

General Interest **Correctly write each word that should begin with a capital letter.**

1. In an average year, santa fe, new mexico, receives 17 more inches of snow than fairbanks, alaska.
2. The first college for women, which opened in 1834, was wheaton college in norton, massachusetts.
3. andrew jackson fought in the revolutionary war when he was only thirteen years old.
4. the largest natural history museum in the world is the american museum of natural history.
5. The closest planet to the sun, mercury, is about one third the size of earth.
6. John glenn's space capsule, *friendship 7,* was picked up by the recovery ship *noah.*
7. The people of philadelphia first celebrated the fourth of july a year after the declaration of independence had been adopted by the continental congress.
8. In 1888 in new york, george eastman invented a box camera that held rolled film.

**9.** The philadelphia eagles started playing in the national football league in 1933.

**10.** The last state to join the union before alaska and hawaii was arizona, which was admitted on valentine's day in 1912.

**11.** Charles Lindbergh flew the *spirit of st. louis* solo from the U.S. to Paris in May, 1927.

**12.** Gold was discovered by accident at sutter's mill in California on January 24, 1848.

**13.** The statue of liberty was a gift from the french to celebrate the first centennial of independence in the U.S.

**14.** The *titanic* sank on April 14, 1912.

**15.** Toni Morrison won the 1993 nobel prize in literature for her six visionary and poetic novels.

## Proper Adjectives

Because proper adjectives are formed from proper nouns, they should be capitalized—as proper nouns are.

**Capitalize most proper adjectives.**

| PROPER NOUNS AND ADJECTIVES | |
|---|---|
| **Proper Nouns** | **S**pain, **I**daho |
| **Proper Adjectives** | **S**panish rice, **I**daho potatoes |

When adjectives are formed from the words that refer to the compass directions, such as *east,* no capital letters are used.

The wind was blowing from an **e**asterly direction.

Some proper adjectives derived from proper nouns are so familiar that they are no longer capitalized.

| COMMONPLACE PROPER ADJECTIVES | | |
|---|---|---|
| **c**hina plates | **p**asteurized milk | **q**uixotic vision |

When a proper adjective is part of a hyphenated adjective, capitalize only the part that is a proper adjective. Sometimes, however, both parts of a hyphenated adjective are proper adjectives.

| HYPHENATED PROPER ADJECTIVES | |
|---|---|
| all-**A**merican team | trans-**S**iberian journey |
| **I**ndo-**E**uropean languages | **A**frican-**A**merican literature |

## PRACTICE YOUR SKILLS

### Check Your Understanding
***Capitalizing Proper Adjectives***

Sports Topic **Correctly write each word that should begin with a capital letter. If a sentence is correct, write *C*.**

1. The olympic Athletes first competed in Greece.
2. Also popular were the Isthmian Games, which were held near the Isthmus of Corinth.
3. Baseball is often called the all-american game.
4. Nemesio Guillot began cuban baseball in 1866.
5. Guillot taught his fellow Cubans to play the game after learning it from Americans in the U.S.
6. American soccer is equivalent to the latin-american game of football.
7. In 1959, Rong Guotuan won a gold medal in table tennis, becoming the first athlete in chinese history to be a world champion.

8. Some activities we enjoy today—swimming, equestrian sports, rowing—were also popular ancient egyptian sports.

9. Cricket, tennis, and kabaddi (a combination of wrestling and rugby) are popular indian athletic activities.

10. A relatively cold climate encourages canadian youngsters to play ice hockey.

Connect to the Writing Process: Drafting

### *Writing Sentences: Using Proper Adjectives*

**Use each of the following proper nouns as a proper adjective in a sentence, capitalizing the adjective correctly.**

11. hawaii
12. italy
13. freud
14. democrat
15. shakespeare
16. trans-europe
17. victoria
18. texas
19. spain
20. hippocrates (hint: doctors' oath)

Connect to the Writing Process: Editing

### *Capitalizing Proper Nouns and Adjectives*

**Write each sentence, capitalizing the nouns and adjectives correctly. If a sentence is correct, write *C*.**

21. A republican senator spoke at assembly today.
22. The friday afternoon traffic near my school is heavy.
23. "An anglophile loves all things english," said my english teacher, Miss Gilbert.
24. Should I use roman numerals or arabic numerals?
25. I received a french dictionary for graduation.
26. Our class is going to hike in the appalachian mountains.
27. The history teacher showed us pre-columbian artifacts.
28. She also told us that the first non-indian visitor to arizona arrived in 1539.
29. In french class I learned that many of the numerous french-speaking people in canada live in quebec.
30. I plan to sign up for History 101 and beginning German.

# Titles

Capital letters signal the importance of titles of persons and works of art.

**Capitalize the titles of persons and works of art.**

## Titles with Names of People

Capitalize a title showing office, rank, or profession when it comes before a person's name.

| | |
|---|---|
| BEFORE A NAME | Is **J**udge Abraham Goodell in his chambers this morning? |
| USED ALONE | Who was the **j**udge at the recent grand larceny trial? |
| BEFORE A NAME | I worked on **S**enator Sheridan Ames's re-election campaign. |
| USED ALONE | The **s**enator from our district is running for re-election. |

Do not capitalize the prefix *ex–* or the suffix *–elect* when either is connected to a title.

The patriotic parade honored **e**x-Senator Hillmann and Governor-**e**lect Baray.

## Titles Used Alone

Capitalize a title that is used alone when it is substituted for a person's name in direct address or when it is used as a name. The titles for the current United States President and Vice President, for the Chief Justice, and for the Queen of England are almost always capitalized when they are being substituted for the person's name.

| | |
|---|---|
| USED AS A NAME | How is the patient in room 114 this evening, **D**octor? |
| NOT USED AS A NAME | The **d**octor will speak to you before she leaves. |
| HIGH GOVERNMENT OFFICIAL | The **P**resident and the **V**ice **P**resident will attend the summit meeting next month. |

Remember that *president* and *vice president* are capitalized when they stand alone only if they refer to the *current* president and vice president.

Was John F. Kennedy the youngest **p**resident ever to hold office?

## Titles Showing Family Relationships

Capitalize a title showing a family relationship when it comes before a person's name, when it is used as a name, or when it is substituted for a person's name.

| | |
|---|---|
| BEFORE A NAME | When did **U**ncle Ron and **A**unt Mary leave? |
| USED AS A NAME | Please tell **M**om that she has a visitor. |
| DIRECT ADDRESS | I'll help you paint the porch, **D**ad. |

Titles showing family relationships should not be capitalized when they are preceded by a possessive noun or pronoun—unless they are considered part of a person's name.

| | |
|---|---|
| NO CAPITAL | My **a**unt lives in California.<br>Aaron is taking Phil's **s**ister to the prom. |
| CAPITAL | When does your **U**ncle Ralph get home from work?<br>(*Uncle* is considered part of Ralph's name.) |

## Titles of Written Works and Other Works of Art

Capitalize the first word, the last word, and all important words that are used in the following titles: books, stories, poems, newspapers and newspaper articles, magazines and magazine articles, movies, plays, television series, musical songs and compositions, and works of art. Short prepositions, coordinating conjunctions, and articles should not be capitalized unless they are the first or last words in a title.

| | TITLES OF WORKS |
|---|---|
| BOOKS AND PARTS OF BOOKS | *Pride and Prejudice, Dictionary of Desktop Publishing,* Chapter 11, Vol. V, No. 4, Part IV |
| SHORT STORIES | "Odor of Chrysanthemums" |
| POEMS | "The Road Not Taken" |
| NEWSPAPERS AND NEWSPAPER ARTICLES | the *Chicago Tribune* (The word *the* before the title of a newspaper is usually not capitalized.), "New City Park Opens," "A Day in the Life of Our Mayor" |
| MAGAZINES AND MAGAZINE ARTICLES | *Discover Magazine, Newsweek,* "Ten Colleges Every Senior Should Know About" |
| MOVIES | *Men in Black, Gone with the Wind* |
| PLAYS | *Hamlet, The Importance of Being Earnest* |
| TELEVISION SERIES | *Dawson's Creek, Dateline, Tom and Jerry* |
| MUSICAL SONGS AND COMPOSITIONS | "Amazing Grace," "The Star-Spangled Banner," "Violin Concerto in E Minor" |
| WORKS OF ART | *Water Lilies* (painting by Claude Monet), *Sleeping Muse* (sculpture by Constantin Brancusi), *McPherson's Woods* (photograph by Matthew Brady) |

*You can learn about punctuating titles on pages L501–L504.*

## Practice Your Skills

### Check Your Understanding
*Capitalizing Titles*

Contemporary Life

**Correctly write each word that should begin with a capital letter. If an item is correct, write *C*.**

**1.** justice ruth bader ginsburg

**2.** *I never saw another butterfly,* a play by Celeste Raspunti

**3.** my science professor

**4.** *uncle tom's cabin,* a novel by Harriet Beecher Stowe

**5.** my best friend's uncle sam

**6.** *felicity,* a series on television

**7.** *the thinker,* a sculpture by Auguste Rodin

**8.** the *albuquerque journal*

**9.** "the forgotten city," a poem by William Carlos Williams

**10.** ex-speaker of the house of representatives

**11.** *tv guide*

**12.** "what a wonderful world," a song by Louis Armstrong

**13.** *Blizzard of one,* poetry by Mark Strand

**14.** *teen sports illustrated*

**15.** Will you lend me five dollars, dad?

**16.** the *lincoln statue* by Vinnie Reams

**17.** "the dog and the wolf," a fable by Aesop

**18.** *a tale of two cities,* a book by Charles Dickens

**19.** dr. martin luther king, jr.

**20.** "dance of the sugar plum fairy," from the ballet *the nutcracker suite*

**21.** my grandfather harry's farm

**22.** Former president carter is active in public service.

**23.** The doctor sent Lena to the hospital.

**24.** *Muhammed Ali: The World's Greatest Champion,* a biography by John Tessitore

**25.** *much ado about nothing,* a play by William Shakespeare

Communicate Your Ideas

## APPLY TO WRITING

### Descriptive Newspaper Article: *Capitalization*

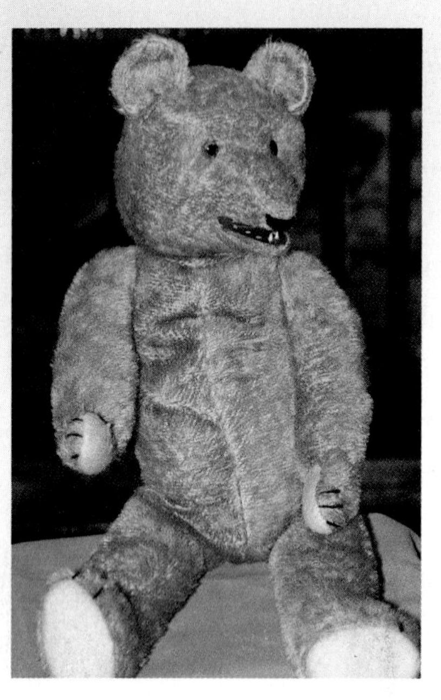

This is a photo of the Laughing Roosevelt Bear, which was crafted in 1907 to display President Roosevelt's toothy grin. The advertisement for the bear read, "The Laughing Teddy Bear laughs and shows his teeth at critics."

Choose a current public figure with a title—in politics, law, medicine, education, for example—and then choose a "mascot" for this person (like the teddy bear for Teddy Roosevelt). Write a newspaper article describing this public figure and his or her distinctive characteristics, and then describe how the animal or toy mirrors these characteristics. Be sure to give your article a title.

Edit your writing for correct capitalization of proper nouns, proper adjectives, and titles. Then write the final copy. If possible, find or draw a picture of the mascot to accompany your article.

Mixed Practice

General Interest

**Correctly write each word that should begin with a capital letter. Then answer each question, if you can!**

**1.** was alan b. shepard, jr., or john glenn the first american to orbit the earth?

**2.** was it the pilgrims or the puritans who landed at plymouth rock in 1620?

**3.** which is the most westerly state in the u.s., alaska or hawaii?

**4.** who is the author of *great expectations,* a novel written during queen victoria's reign in england?

**5.** in what country were the first olympic games held?

**6.** was william mckinley or theodore roosevelt the first president elected in the twentieth century?

**7.** who was the first american president elected in the twenty-first century?

**8.** what was the name of dorothy's dog in *the wizard of oz?*

**9.** is the geyser old faithful in wyoming or nevada?

**10.** "i want to hold your hand" was the first american number-one single of what british group?

**11.** did world war II end in 1942 or 1945?

**12.** is the cy young award given in baseball or football?

**13.** is sacramento or los angeles the capital of california?

**14.** general lee surrendered to general grant at the appomattox court house. in what state did this occur?

**15.** did clark kent work for the *metropolis journal* or the *daily planet?*

**16.** what was the russian equivalent of the u.s. central intelligence agency?

**17.** is the lincoln memorial or the washington monument the tallest structure in washington, d.c.?

**18.** is the astrodome in chicago or houston?

CheckPoint

## Using Capital Letters Correctly

**Correctly write each word that should begin with a capital letter.**

1. dalia's address is 43 thirty-third street, kokomo, indiana.
2. school usually starts on the wednesday after labor day.
3. the mediterranean sea is one of the most polluted seas on earth.
4. mount desert island, off the coast of maine, was discovered in 1604 by champlain, a french explorer.
5. have you any tickets for the chicago white sox game on saturday?
6. when i was a junior, my favorite course was biology, but this year i like english best.
7. the oscar weighs 7 pounds and is 10 inches high.
8. minnesota is called the land of 10,000 lakes, but it actually contains more than 11,000 lakes.
9. there really was a molly pitcher, but her real name was mary hayes mccauley.
10. during the battle of monmouth, she carried water in a pitcher to thirsty american soldiers.
11. when my parents went to canada last summer, they visited the small nova scotian town where mother was born.
12. have you ever read elizabeth jennings's poem "in memory of anyone unknown to me"?
13. last month the vice president represented the president on a tour of the far east.
14. the *andrea doria* collided with a swedish ship off the coast of nantucket in 1956.
15. i enjoy watching the television series *masterpiece theatre*.

## Editing for the Correct Use of Capital Letters

**Correctly write each word that should begin with a capital letter. Do not include words that are already capitalized.**

How did the state of idaho get its name? Some believe it is a shoshoni indian word meaning "gem of the mountains." The idaho state historical society, though, insists that the state's name does not have any meaning. It was first coined by a mining lobbyist in 1860 as a good name for a new territory in the pikes peak mining country. However, just before congress voted in washington, d.c., the hoax was discovered. That territory was then named colorado. The word *idaho*, nevertheless, kept popping up in the pacific northwest. For example, a steamboat that carried prospectors up and down the columbia river was named the *idaho*. As a result, three years later the name was again suggested to congress; but this time it was accepted.

## Writing Sentences

**At the library find a fact that pertains to each of the following topics. Each fact should include a proper noun, a proper adjective, or a title.**

**Write a sentence that includes . . .**

1. a fact about a famous bridge.
2. a fact about a holiday.
3. a fact about a state capital.
4. a fact about an English poet.
5. a fact about basketball.

# Language and *Self-Expression*

If you created a work of art focused on a method of communication, what would that method be? Would you choose the telephone, as Rosenquist did? An E-mail message? Face-to-face conversation? Think about the rules that are often placed on communication: "Don't pass notes in class," or "Don't talk too long on the phone."

Write a description of your personal view of communication, particularly communication between friends. Explain what method is most effective for you and why that is so. Explain the message you would express if you created artwork similar to Rosenquist's.

**Prewriting** List ways that you communicate with friends, and write friends' names beside the way in which you most often communicate with them. Draw a star next to the category that you use most.

**Drafting** Focusing on the category with the star by it, write several paragraphs on communication from your perspective. Use the other categories for comparison or contrast. You might mention restrictions that are sometimes or always placed on you, such as phone or computer privileges at home. Your conclusion could sum up the overall message you would want to show in a work of art.

**Revising** Check your writing for the clear progression of ideas. For example, make sure that you introduce and explain a concept before you describe how that concept should be changed.

**Editing** Check for correct use of capital letters as well as spelling and grammar.

**Publishing** Write a final copy and give it to your teacher. Then choose one of the friends you listed in your prewriting. Share your paper with that friend.

## Capitalizing First Words and the Pronoun *I*

Capitalize the first word of a sentence and of a line of poetry. *(pages L391–L393)*

Capitalize the first word in the greeting and the first word in the closing of a letter. *(page L393)*

Capitalize the first word of each item in an outline and the letters that begin major subsections of the outline. *(page L394)*

Capitalize the first word in a formal resolution that follows the word *Resolved*. *(page L394)*

Capitalize the first word of a formal statement that follows a colon. *(page L395)*

Capitalize the pronoun *I*, both alone and in contractions. *(page L395)*

## Capitalizing Proper Nouns

Capitalize proper nouns and their abbreviations. *(pages L399–L409)*

Capitalize names of particular persons and animals. *(pages L399–L400)*

Capitalize geographical names, including the names of particular places, bodies of water, and celestial bodies. *(pages L400–L401)*

Capitalize names of groups. *(pages L403–L404)*

Capitalize specific time periods, events, and documents. *(page L404)*

Capitalize names of nationalities, races, languages, and religions. *(page L405)*

## Capitalizing Proper Adjectives

Capitalize most proper adjectives. *(pages L409–L410)*

## Capitalizing Titles

Capitalize the titles of persons and works of art. *(pages L412–L414)*

Capitalize a title showing office, rank, or profession when it comes before a person's name. *(page L412)*

Capitalize a title that is used alone when it is substituted for a person's name in direct address or when it is used as a name. *(page L412)*

Capitalize the first word, the last word, and all important words that are used in the following titles: books, stories, poems, newspapers and newspaper articles, magazines and magazine articles, movies, plays, television series, and musical songs and compositions. *(page L414)*

### Directions

**Read the passage and decide which word or words should be capitalized in each underlined part. Write the letter of the correct answer. If the underlined part contains no error, write *D*.**

EXAMPLE Samuel <u>f. b. Morse lived in the nineteenth century, and he invented the telegraph</u>.
(1)

1 **A** F. B.
**B** Nineteenth Century
**C** Telegraph
**D** No error

ANSWER 1 **A**

The term "<u>morse code" refers to the method of communication</u> (1) using dots, dashes, and spaces to represent letters and numbers. <u>in electrical telegraphy, this code</u> (2) consists of short and long pulses; the code can be translated to short and long flashes of light, too. The <u>telegraph, invented in the u.s. in the 1830s by morse, uses electrical telegraphy</u> (3). Similarly, <u>ships can use bright lights to flash messages across long distances</u> (4) when radio communications are down. Many people know the <u>code for the distress call, sos</u> (5).

**1** **A** Morse Code

**B** Morse

**C** Method, Communication

**D** No error

**2** **A** Electrical Telegraphy

**B** In, Code

**C** In

**D** No error

**3** **A** U.S., Morse

**B** Telegraph, U.S.

**C** Electrical Telegraphy

**D** No error

**4** **A** Ships

**B** Long Distances

**C** Bright Lights

**D** No error

**5** **A** SOS

**B** Distress Call, SOS

**C** Distress Call

**D** No error

# End Marks and Commas

Pretest

*Directions*

**Read the passage and choose the mark of punctuation that belongs in each underlined space. Write the letter of the correct answer.**

EXAMPLE The Hercules beetle___(1)___ which is a type of scarab beetle, grows up to eight inches long.

**1** **A** period
**B** question mark
**C** exclamation point
**D** comma

ANSWER **1 D**

Wow___(1)___ Look over there by the tree at that huge beetle. It must be a Hercules beetle___(2)___ Did you know that a Hercules beetle has a horn that grows up to four inches long___(3)___ My science teacher, Dr___(4)___ Carpenter, told us these facts. Only the male beetle, not the female___(5)___ has this horn. Look at this picture of the beetle on the Internet___(6)___ Scarab beetles, which include the Hercules beetle, are found worldwide___(7)___ Other members of the scarab family are June bugs, Japanese beetles, rhinoceros beetles___(8)___ and dung beetles. Don't these beetles usually have a brilliantly colored body___(9)___ The female Hercules beetle has a layer of red hairs ___(10)___ and the Japanese beetle is a shiny green and brown.

1 A period
B question mark
C exclamation point
D comma

2 A period
B question mark
C exclamation point
D comma

3 A period
B question mark
C exclamation point
D comma

4 A period
B question mark
C exclamation point
D comma

5 A period
B question mark
C exclamation point
D comma

6 A period
B question mark
C exclamation point
D comma

7 A period
B question mark
C exclamation point
D comma

8 A period
B question mark
C exclamation point
D comma

9 A period
B question mark
C exclamation point
D comma

10 A period
B question mark
C exclamation point
D comma

Artist unknown, Egyptian.
*Head of Queen Tiy*,
ca. 1391–1353 B.C.
Yew wood with silver and glass, height 3½ inches. Ägyptisches Museum und Papyrussammlung, Berlin.

**Describe** Describe the artistic elements—including line, color, shape, value, and texture—that the sculptor used.

**Analyze** What aspect of this sculpture seems to be its central focus? Why does this aspect attract your attention?

**Interpret** What do you think this sculpture says about the personality or character of Queen Tiy?

**Judge** What do you think is the difference in effect between a sculpture of the head only and a sculpture of the complete human figure?

At the end of this chapter, you will use the artwork to stimulate ideas for writing.

## Kinds of Sentences and End Marks

A sentence has one of four different functions. It can make a statement, give a command, ask a question, or express strong feeling. Depending on its function, a sentence may be declarative, imperative, interrogative, or exclamatory. The end mark you use with a particular sentence is determined by the function of that sentence.

The first function of a sentence is to make a statement or to express an opinion. Most sentences fall into this category.

A **declarative sentence** makes a statement or expresses an opinion and ends with a period.

The following examples are both declarative sentences, even though the second example contains an indirect question.

Dinosaurs have fascinated people for many years.

I am not sure when dinosaurs lived.
(The direct question would be *When did dinosaurs live?*)

The second function of a sentence is to give directions, make requests, or give commands. Generally *you* is the understood subject of these sentences.

An **imperative sentence** gives a direction, makes a request, or gives a command. It ends with a period or an exclamation point.

If a command is given in a normal tone of voice, it is followed by a period when written. If it expresses strong feeling, it is followed by an exclamation point.

Use this map to get to Dinosaur, Colorado.
(normal tone of voice)

Don't play that silly dinosaur videotape again!
(emotional tone of voice)

Occasionally an imperative sentence is stated as a question, but no reply is expected. Since the purpose of the sentence remains the same—to make a request—the sentence is followed by a period or by an exclamation point.

Will you please hand me that book on dinosaur extinction**.**

The third function of a sentence is to ask a question—whether it is completely or incompletely expressed.

An **interrogative sentence** asks a question and ends with a question mark.

Have you seen the dinosaur display**?**

Where**?** Did I pass it**?**

CONNECT TO WRITER'S CRAFT

Watch for interrogative sentences in advertising—both in print and on television. A company will draw you in by asking you a question. Most people feel obligated to answer a question, and so they pay attention to the ad. For example, a magazine page is covered with photos of individual potato chips, and at the top you read, "Can you tell which chip is the fat-free chip?" For a moment, you're tempted to try to answer the question—and the chip company wins your attention!

The fourth function of a sentence is to express strong feeling, such as excitement or anger. Avoid overusing this type of sentence, for it can very quickly lose its impact.

An **exclamatory sentence** expresses strong feeling or emotion and ends with an exclamation point.

I think I've found a fossil**!**

An interjection, such as *wow* or *oh,* may also be followed by an exclamation point.

Ouch**!** This cat has teeth like a tiger's.

*You can learn more about punctuation with interjections on pages L43–L44.*

## Connect to Writer's Craft

Fiction writers are especially attentive to their use of end marks when they write dialogue. End marks help give the conversation dynamics—a sense of action—by conveying the speaker's emotions and attitudes quickly through punctuation. Consider the emotions related by the following lines:

> **"Stop,"** he said.
> **"Stop!"** he said.

Simply by looking at end marks, you can tell that the first speaker feels thoughtful and is in no particular hurry, while the second speaker feels a sense of urgent danger or excitement.

## Practice Your Skills

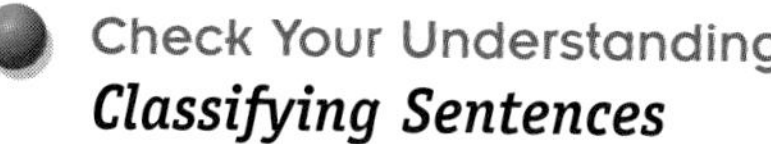

### Check Your Understanding
*Classifying Sentences*

General Interest

**Using the following abbreviations, label each sentence.** (Since none of the sentences end with punctuation marks, you will need to label each sentence according to its meaning.)

| | |
|---|---|
| declarative = *d.* | imperative = *imp.* |
| interrogative = *int.* | exclamatory = *ex.* |

**1.** Paleontologists study life from the geological past
**2.** Did you know that fossilized footprints tell us about dinosaurs' habits of movement
**3.** Will you look at this cast of a footprint
**4.** Wow, look at the size of it
**5.** Read the next chapter in your geology textbook
**6.** What caused the dinosaur extinction at the Cretaceous/Tertiary boundary
**7.** Everything from asteroids to volcanoes has been blamed
**8.** I wonder what it was like to watch dinosaurs roam
**9.** What an exciting time it must have been
**10.** Dinosaur bones have been discovered in Colorado

Connect to the Writing Process: Editing

***Punctuating Sentences***

**11.–20. Rewrite the sentences in the preceding exercise, adding the correct end punctuation.**

Connect to the Writing Process: Editing

***Using End Marks***

Notice that periods are the only end punctuation used in this E-mail message. Rewrite those sentences that are incorrectly punctuated, replacing periods with question marks and exclamation points where needed.

Alex,

You won't believe what I just found. You know how I'm supposed to be writing that report in science class. I found the perfect place to get all my information. It is this great dinosaur web site that has dozens of links to dinosaur information. Reliable information. A few of the links are broken, but most of them are up to date. You can look at photos of fossils and bones and then print them out. The webmaster calls himself "Virtual Geologist," and he will answer any questions you send him.

Aren't you and your family going camping somewhere this summer. You will want to follow the link to Dinosaur National Monument. This is a park on the border of Colorado and Utah where you can inspect dinosaur bones up close. Maybe your family will take me along. That would be great.

See you later,

Matt

## Communicate Your Ideas

### APPLY TO WRITING

**Writer's Craft:** ***Analyzing the Use of End Marks***

As you read the following passage, notice the kinds of sentences and end marks the author uses. Then answer the questions that follow.

> In the store, Thorne held the radio close to his cheek. "Okay," he said. "Sarah? Listen carefully. Get in the car, and do exactly what I tell you."
>
> "Okay fine," she said. "But tell me first. Is Levine there?"
>
> "He's here."
>
> The radio clicked. She said, "Ask him if there's any danger from a green dinosaur that's about four feet tall and has a domed forehead."
>
> Levine nodded. "Tell her yes. They're called pachycephalosaurs."
>
> "He says yes," Thorne said. "They're pachycephalosomethings, and you should be careful. Why?"
>
> "Because there's fifty of them, all around the car."
>
> —*Michael Crichton,* The Lost World

- List the kinds of sentences the author uses in this passage.
- Why do you think the author uses such a variety of sentence types within such a short passage?
- Which sentence do you think would work well with an exclamation point? Why?
- What tone of voice do you think Sarah might be using? Why?
- What kind of sentence do you think should follow this excerpt of dialogue? What would its purpose be?

##  Other Uses of Periods

Periods have several uses—in addition to ending a sentence.

### With Abbreviations

Using abbreviations is a good way to write faster when you are taking notes, but they should usually be avoided in formal writing, such as in essays and research papers.

**Use a period after most abbreviations.**

The following list contains some abbreviations that are acceptable in formal writing. Use the dictionary to check the spelling and punctuation of other abbreviations.

| ABBREVIATIONS | | | | | |
|---|---|---|---|---|---|
| Titles with Names | Mr.<br>Lt. | Ms.<br>Col. | Mrs.<br>Prof. | Rev.<br>Gov. | Dr.<br>Sr. |
| Initials for Names | A. E. Housman<br>Samuel T. Coleridge | | | J. R. R. Tolkien | |
| Times with Numbers | A.M. | P.M. | B.C. | A.D. | |
| Addresses | Ave.<br>Rd. | St.<br>Dr. | Blvd.<br>Ct. | Rt.<br>P.O. Box | Dept. |
| Organizations and Companies | Co. | Inc. | Corp. | Assoc. | |

Some organizations and companies are known by abbreviations that stand for their full names. The majority of these abbreviations do not use periods. A few other common abbreviations also do not include periods.

| ABBREVIATIONS WITHOUT PERIODS | |
|---|---|
| FBI = Federal Bureau of Investigation | km = kilometer |
| USAF = United States Air Force | mph = miles per hour |
| ISP = Internet Service Provider | |

If a statement ends with an abbreviation, only one period is needed at the end of the sentence. If an interrogative or an exclamatory sentence ends with an abbreviation, both a period and a question mark, or a period and an exclamation point, are needed.

> The graduation ceremony begins at 7:00 P.M.
> Does the graduation ceremony begin at 7:00 P.M.?

Today, almost everyone uses the post office's two-letter state abbreviations that do not include periods. You usually can find a list of these state abbreviations at the front of most telephone books. The following list includes a few examples.

| STATE ABBREVIATIONS | | |
|---|---|---|
| AK = Alaska | MD = Maryland | OR = Oregon |
| CA = California | MO = Missouri | TX = Texas |
| CO = Colorado | NJ = New Jersey | UT = Utah |
| HI = Hawaii | OK = Oklahoma | VT = Vermont |

## With Outlines

Periods are used in outlines to help mark each major and minor division.

**Use a period after each number or letter that shows a division in an outline.**

I. Popular entertainment awards on television
  A. MZTV Music Awards
    1. New Group
    2. Female Solo Artist
  B. Vision Fashion Awards
    1. Fall Collection
    2. Designer
II. Film industry awards
  A. Drama
    1. Original Screenplay
    2. Adapted Screenplay
  B. Comedy

## PRACTICE YOUR SKILLS

Check Your Understanding

***Using Abbreviations***

**Write each item, using proper abbreviations. Include periods where needed.** If you are unsure of the spelling or the punctuation of an abbreviation, look it up in the dictionary.

1. George Bush, Senior
2. New Jersey
3. Carlson Lumber Company
4. September
5. Captain Ahab
6. III Conclusion
7. Park Avenue
8. et cetera
9. a liter of milk
10. 1 pound
11. cash on delivery
12. *Anno Domini* 450

Connect to the Writing Process: Editing

***Using Abbreviations and End Marks***

**Write each sentence, abbreviating the underlined items and using end marks correctly.**

13. For the ribbon-cutting ceremony, we bought a 100-foot red ribbon
14. My friends and I were honored by Governor Richmond for cleaning up the old playground at 1300 Elm Avenue
15. At exactly 2:00 *post meridiem,* I will announce the contest winners
16. My sister will receive her Bachelor of Arts degree from the university this May
17. Have you applied for a summer intern position with the Department of Parks and Recreation in Boston, Massachusetts
18. I just passed my driver's test at the Department of Motor Vehicles
19. The City Builders Association gave the Green Builder Award to the Adobe Habitats, Incorporated
20. Lieutenant Raymond Leon Mason, Junior, received the Purple Heart

Communicate Your Ideas

## APPLY TO WRITING

### Outline of a Five-Year Plan: *End Marks*

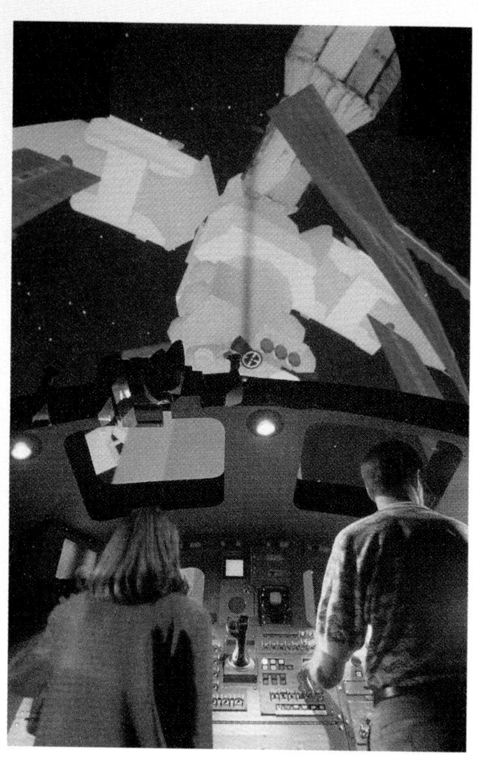

Consider the photograph. What steps do you think these people might have taken to build a foundation for an occupation in the space industry?

What do you want your life to be like five years from now? Write a statement that tells what you want to be doing in five years. Then make an outline of your five-year plan that shows how you intend to get there. In your outline, name the degrees, schools, companies, job titles, and so on that will be necessary to achieve your goal. Use abbreviations and proper end marks and double-check your work for accuracy.

# Commas

Although there may seem to be many comma rules, commas have basically only two purposes: to separate and to enclose items.

## Commas That Separate

If commas did not separate certain items from each other, all writing would be subject to constant misunderstanding. There is a difference, for example, between *pineapple juice and cheese* and *pineapple, juice, and cheese*. The following specific situations are places in which commas should be used to separate items.

### Items in a Series

A **series** is three or more similar items listed in consecutive order. Words, phrases, clauses, or short sentences that are written as a series are separated by commas.

Use commas to separate items in a series.

| | |
|---|---|
| WORDS | Dinner, movies, and parties are popular date ideas. (nouns) |
| | We joked, laughed, and talked all evening. (verbs) |
| PHRASES | I searched for his phone number in my notebook, on my desk, in my book bag, and throughout my house. |
| DEPENDENT CLAUSES | We aren't sure who should drive, where we should go, or how late we should stay out. |
| SHORT SENTENCES | The curtain fell, a brief silence followed, and then we applauded loudly. |

When a conjunction connects the last two items in a series, a comma is optional. It is always best, however, to include the comma before the conjunction in order to eliminate any possible confusion or misunderstanding.

CONFUSING My boyfriend makes delicious pea**,** chicken**,** tomato and onion soups.
(Does he make tomato soup or tomato and onion soup?)

CLEAR My boyfriend makes delicious pea**,** chicken**,** tomato**,** and onion soups.
(The last comma makes the meaning clear.)

If conjunctions connect all the items in a series, no commas are needed unless they make the sentence clearer.

This dance is fast **and** difficult **and** fun!

Some expressions, such as *needle and thread,* are thought of as a single item. If one of these pairs of words appears in a series, it should be considered one item.

For our picnic we packed yogurt**,** fruit and cheese**,** and oatmeal cookies.

Did you remember the chicken**,** bread**,** and ice cream and cake?

### Use commas after the words *first, second,* and so on when they introduce items in a series.

Josh's surprise party should include three key things: **first,** a live band; **second,** his favorite food; and **third,** all his close friends.

Notice that when the items in a series have internal commas, commas within the items themselves such as in the preceding example, the items are then separated by semicolons to avoid any confusion.

*You can learn more about semicolons on pages L484–L491.*

CONNECT TO WRITER'S CRAFT

You have probably noticed that newspaper headlines are usually very short—not even a sentence. When headline writers need to write longer headlines, they use commas to join ideas. This usage of commas is similar to using commas to join items in a series. With a headline, however, the "series" may be only two items long.

This headline has a two-item "series" of verbs:

Expos Shell Shane Reynolds**,** Withstand Astros' Barrage

This headline has a two item "series" of subjects:

Braves**,** Tom Glavine Blow Away Padres 

## Adjectives Before a Noun

A conjunction sometimes connects two adjectives before a noun. When the conjunction is omitted, a comma is often used instead.

A busy**,** enjoyable evening awaits us.

**Use a comma sometimes to separate two adjectives that directly precede a noun and that are not joined by a conjunction.**

There is a test you can use to decide whether a comma should be placed between two such adjectives. Read the sentence inserting *and* between the adjectives. If the sentence sounds natural, a comma is needed.

| | |
|---|---|
| Comma Needed | I'll wear my old**,** comfortable boots to the dance. (*Old and comfortable* sounds natural. When a comma is needed, you can also reverse the adjectives: *comfortable and old.*) |
| Comma Not Needed | I'll wear my new black boots to the dance. (*New and black* does not sound natural, nor could you reverse the adjectives to read *black and new.*) |

Usually no comma is needed after a number or after an adjective that refers to size, shape, or age. For example, no commas are needed in the following expressions.

| ADJECTIVE EXPRESSIONS | |
|---|---|
| four square boxes | a large Mexican hat |

*You can learn how to use commas with direct quotations on pages L508–L509.*

## PRACTICE YOUR SKILLS

Check Your Understanding

***Using Commas to Separate***

Contemporary Life

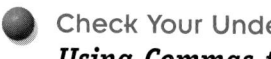

**Write each series or each pair of adjectives, adding a comma or commas where needed. If commas in a sentence are used correctly, write *C*.**

**1.** Owen and Daisy ate a dinner of rice beef and cheese enchiladas and salad.

**2.** I wore a red white and blue shirt to Stan's Fourth of July picnic.

**3.** Before picking up Marcia, Danny washed and waxed the car and vacuumed the floor mats.

**4.** For our first date, we didn't know whether to see a movie go to the park or eat dinner.

**5.** The local dinner theater production of *An Ideal Husband* was a brilliant date idea.

**6.** Stacey's prom dress was made of red satin and tulle and lace.

**7.** Stacey and Eric shared a sleek white limousine with Clark and Tabitha.

**8.** "I have no idea where they went what they are doing or when they'll be back," said Stacey's younger sister Janelle.

**9.** Shawn and Kelly rode the horses down the hill around the lake and through the trees.

**10.** The food is planned, the date is set, and the invitations are in the mail.

### Connect to the Writing Process: Drafting
### *Using Commas That Separate*

**Use each of the following items in a sentence. Add commas and semicolons where needed.**

**11.** peanut butter and jelly ham and cheese or egg salad

**12.** June July and August

**13.** fresh crisp apples and fresh tossed salad

**14.** large and roomy and bright

**15.** swam boated and sunbathed

**16.** first a committee to plan it second a caterer to supply food and third flyers to attract attention

**17.** in the car in the cafeteria or in the classroom

**18.** five lavender roses two white carnations and a tall crystal vase

**19.** chocolate chip peanut butter or cinnamon sugar

**20.** some cake and ice cream

**21.** mashed potatoes and gravy and turkey and stuffing

**22.** cool refreshing lemonade

**23.** mustard catsup and salt and pepper

**24.** chairs tablecloths and tables

**25.** plates napkins and forks

### Connect to the Writing Process: Editing
### *Using Commas That Separate*

**Write the following recipe. Insert commas where needed.**

*Crunchy Nutty Granola Cereal*

| | |
|---|---|
| *14 oz. oats not instant* | *1/3 cup peanuts chopped fine* |
| *1/2 cup dark brown sugar* | *1 stick (1/4 lb.) butter* |
| *1/2 cup cracked wheat* | *1 tsp. vanilla* |
| *1/4 cup bran oat or wheat* | *1/2 cup honey* |
| *1/2 cup raisins* | *1 cup 7-grain cereal* |
| *1/4 cup wheat germ* | |

Combine oats brown sugar cracked wheat bran raisins wheat germ and peanuts. Set aside. Melt butter. Stir together the butter vanilla and honey. Pour over cereal mixture stir until well moistened and add the 7-grain cereal. Mix well. Then spread mixture onto two cookie sheets. Bake at 325°, stirring frequently, until lightly browned, about 10–15 minutes.

Communicate Your Ideas

### APPLY TO WRITING

**Recipes:** ***Commas That Separate***

Your class is selling a *Senior Favorites Cookbook* as a fundraiser. Write the recipe for a dish you enjoy making—pizza with the works, maybe, or nine-layer dip. Follow the format of the recipe you edited in the preceding exercise. Write a list of ingredients with any necessary adjectives and then write the instructions. Edit your recipe for commas and end marks.

## Compound Sentences

The independent clauses in a compound sentence can be combined in several ways. One way is to join them with a comma and one of the coordinating conjunctions—*and, but, or, nor, for, so,* or *yet.*

Use a comma to separate the independent clauses of a compound sentence if the clauses are joined by a coordinating conjunction.

My sister has caught two fish**, but** I haven't caught any.

Friday is Sandy's birthday**, and** I will give her a hermit crab.

She wants a horse**, yet** she's scared to ride one.

No comma is needed in a very short compound sentence—unless the conjunction *yet* or *for* separates the independent clauses.

| | |
|---|---|
| No Comma | The car backfired **and** Buster barked. |
| Comma | Tiger hissed**, for** I'd startled her. |

Do not confuse a sentence that has one subject and a compound verb with a compound sentence that has two sets of subjects and verbs. A comma is not placed between the parts of a compound verb when there is only one subject.

| | |
|---|---|
| Compound Sentence | I feed the cows each evening**,** and John milks them each morning. (comma needed) |
| Compound Verb | I worked last night and couldn't feed the cows. (no comma needed) |

*A semicolon, or a semicolon and a transitional word, can also be used between independent clauses that are not separated by a conjunction.* *You can learn more about punctuation with clauses on pages 167–169.*

## Practice Your Skills

Check Your Understanding

### *Using Commas with Compound Sentences*

Science Topic

**Write *I* if commas are used incorrectly in a sentence. Write *C* if commas are used correctly.**

**1.** Wild pigs will eat almost anything but they won't overeat.

**2.** Give the dog some water or he'll dehydrate.

**3.** The gestation period for an elephant is 21 months and the newborn weighs 90 kilograms.

**4.** A hippo spends most of its time in water yet grazes for grass on land at night.

**5.** The cheetah can reach speeds up to 60 miles per hour, and maintain it for nearly half a mile.

**6.** The silkworm isn't a worm, but is actually a caterpillar.

7. Frogs breathe through their lungs as well as through their skins.
8. At first glance the desert may seem to lack life but it actually is alive with many plants and animals.
9. Cod can lay up to five million eggs at one time, but very few of the eggs hatch and mature.
10. The giant panda is a relative of the raccoon, but can weigh up to 300 pounds.
11. The horseshoe crab is a prehistoric creature, and it has blue blood.
12. Monarch caterpillars eat milkweed so they have a bitter taste that makes birds spit them out.
13. An adult manatee can eat up to 108 pounds of vegetation daily for they are herbivores.
14. The snail has two pairs of tentacles, but it has only one pair of eyes on the longer tentacles.
15. The trilobite cannot be found today for it has been extinct for 245 million years.

Connect to the Writing Process: Editing
### *Using Commas with Compounds*

**16.–25. Rewrite the incorrect sentences from the preceding exercise, adding or deleting commas as needed.**

Connect to the Writing Process: Drafting
### *Commas with Compound Sentences*

**Create compound sentences out of these simple sentences by adding a comma, a coordinating conjunction, and an additional independent clause.** (You may add the additional clause either to the beginning or end of the given sentence.)

26. I want a pet.
27. Marshall washed and groomed the poodle.
28. Sparky barked.
29. Black Beauty whinnied and pranced.
30. The catnip spilled onto the floor.

## Introductory Elements

A comma is needed to separate certain introductory words, phrases, and clauses from the rest of the sentence.

### Use a comma after certain introductory elements.

| | |
|---|---|
| WORDS | **Yes,** that is my calculator.<br>(*No, now, oh, well,* and *why* are other introductory words that are set off by commas—unless they contribute to the meaning of a sentence: Yes *was her answer.*) |
| PREPOSITIONAL PHRASE | **Throughout the entire math class,** Jessie coughed and sneezed.<br>(A comma comes after a prepositional phrase of four or more words.) |
| PARTICIPIAL PHRASE | **Hunting for my protractor,** I found a long-lost pair of gloves. |
| INFINITIVE PHRASE USED AS AN ADVERB | **To help Ellen,** I showed her how to find a cube root.<br>(A comma does not follow an infinitive phrase that is used as the subject of a sentence: *To pass the math test was my only concern.*) |
| ADVERB CLAUSE | **Before they left,** they figured out the amount for a 20 percent tip. |

Notice in the following examples that the punctuation of shorter phrases varies. Also never place a comma after a phrase or phrases followed by a verb.

| | |
|---|---|
| OTHER | **In June 1999,** 320 students applied for math scholarships.<br>(A comma follows a phrase that ends with a date or number.) |

**Up above,** the compass lay forgotten on the shelf.

(A comma is used to avoid confusion.)

**Across the board** was the longest equation I've ever seen.

(No comma is used because the verb follows the introductory phrase.)

## Practice Your Skills

Check Your Understanding

***Using Commas with Introductory Elements***

Mathematics Topic

**Write the introductory elements that should be followed by a comma. If a sentence is correct, write *C* after the number.**

**1.** Living in France in the early 1600s René Descartes applied algebraic concepts to geometry.

**2.** Nowadays we call Descartes's mathematical ideas Cartesian geometry.

**3.** From Euclid of Alexandria we get Euclidean geometry.

**4.** Called the leading mathematician of antiquity Euclid explained geometry concepts in *The Elements*.

**5.** To explain the parallel axiom Euclid said only one line can be drawn through a point parallel to a given line.

**6.** After leaving Samos around 532 B.C., the Greek Pythagoras lived in Italy.

**7.** A thousand years earlier the Babylonians had known about the theorem we call Pythagoras's theorem.

**8.** To prove the theorem was a challenge reserved for Pythagoras.

**9.** In 1750 Maria Gaëtana Agnesi held the chair of mathematics at the University of Bologna.

**10.** Noted for her work in differential calculus Agnesi was the first woman to occupy a chair of mathematics.

Connect to the Writing Process: Drafting

***Using Commas with Introductory Elements***

**Write sentences using each of these introductory elements. Use commas where needed.**

**11.** the word *no*

**12.** a prepositional phrase of four or more words

**13.** the prepositional phrase *within a week*

**14.** a prepositional phrase followed by a verb

**15.** a participial phrase

**16.** an infinitive phrase used as an adverb

**17.** an adverb clause

**18.** the phrase *long ago*

**19.** the phrase *in the year 2000*

**20.** the word *unfortunately*

Connect to the Writing Process: Editing

***Using Commas with Introductory Elements***

**Write the following paragraph, inserting commas after introductory elements where needed.**

Consisting of a frame with beads on vertical wires the abacus is an ancient arithmetic calculator. Used in China even today the abacus can be found in shops and classrooms. To tally bills quickly a merchant can use an abacus. To teach arithmetic to children a teacher can use an abacus to show, rather than tell, how addition and subtraction work. Oh this handy instrument needs neither batteries nor solar power. For more information you can search for tutorials on the Internet.

##  Commonly Used Commas

Commas are probably used most often to separate the items in a date or an address, but they are also used in letters.

### With Dates and Addresses

Use commas to separate the elements in dates and addresses.

Notice in the following examples that a comma is also used to separate the last item in a date or the last item in an address from the rest of the sentence.

> On Monday**,** October 12**,** 1999**,** we founded the Community Music Network.

Send your résumé to Ms. Faye Buscone, Meals on Wheels, 520 Johnson Street, Madison, Wisconsin 53703, before June 30.
(No comma is placed between the state and the zip code.)

If items in an address are joined by a preposition, no comma is needed to separate them.

A homeless shelter has opened at 45 Jackson Boulevard in Tacoma, Washington.

No comma is needed when just the month and the year are given.

Project Youth Horizons will reach its ten-year anniversary in July 2005.

## In Letters

Commas are used in the salutation of many letters and in the closing of all letters.

**Use a comma after the salutation of a friendly letter and after the closing of all letters.**

| SALUTATIONS AND CLOSINGS | | |
|---|---|---|
| **Salutations** | Dear David, | Dear Grandmother, |
| **Closings** | Sincerely yours, | Love, |

### Connect to Writer's Craft

E-mail messages are a modern form of letters, and they usually follow the same rules of punctuation as written letters do. However, since some people exchange E-mail messages with friends or co-workers practically all day long, they tend to use very informal salutations and closings. A message might begin "David," or "Hi," instead of "Dear David," but it still uses the comma. Likewise, the closing may be "Later," instead of "Sincerely yours," but the comma is still used to mark the signing off.

Often the use of too many commas is as confusing as not using enough commas. Use commas only where a rule indicates they are needed. In other words, use commas only where they make the meaning of your writing clear.

## Practice Your Skills

Check Your Understanding

***Commonly Used Commas***

General Interest **Write *a* or *b* to indicate the sentence that uses commas correctly.**

**1. a.** You can write to me at the Columbia Children's Refuge, Box 1254, Columbia, Missouri, 65201, after September 1.

**b.** You can write to me at the Columbia Children's Refuge, Box 1254, Columbia, Missouri 65201, after September 1.

**2. a.** Dear Professor Tucker,
You are invited to attend the ninth annual International Food Fair on February 9 2001.

**b.** Dear Professor Tucker,
You are invited to attend the ninth annual International Food Fair on February 9, 2001.

**3. a.** In 1844 George Williams founded the first YMCA.

**b.** In 1844, George Williams founded the first YMCA.

**4. a.** On March 30, 1937, Franklin Roosevelt established the Okefenokee Swamp as a national wildlife refuge.

**b.** On March 30 1937, Franklin Roosevelt established the Okefenokee Swamp as a national wildlife refuge.

**5. a.** Write to Student Study Support (SSS), 843 Woodcove Avenue, Pittsburgh, Pennsylvania 15216 for free study guides.

**b.** Write to Student Study Support (SSS), 843 Woodcove Avenue, Pittsburgh, Pennsylvania 15216, for free study guides.

Connect to the Writing Process: Drafting

### *Writing Sentences with Commas*

**Write a sentence for each of the following directions. Use commas correctly in each.**

6. Include today's date.
7. Tell when you will graduate.
8. Include the complete address of a company for which you would like to work.
9. Tell your school's name and complete address.
10. Tell the name and date of your favorite holiday.
11. Include the address of a local charity.
12. Write the name of an organization to which you belong and its address, including city and state.
13. Include the date on which you were born.

Connect to the Writing Process: Editing

### *Using Commas*

**Rewrite the following friendly letter, inserting commas where needed.**

Dear Friends

Thank you for your hard work on Saturday June 9. The Park Cleanup Day for Triple Oak Park 247 Oak Avenue was a success. I want to invite all of you to the first Park Play Day this Saturday June 16. A picnic and team events will be held in Triple Oak Park from noon to 5:00 P.M. Please let me know if you'll be there. Write me at 203 W. 15th St. Durant OK 74701 by Wednesday.

Best regards

Tiffany

## APPLY TO WRITING

### Informal Letters: *Commas*

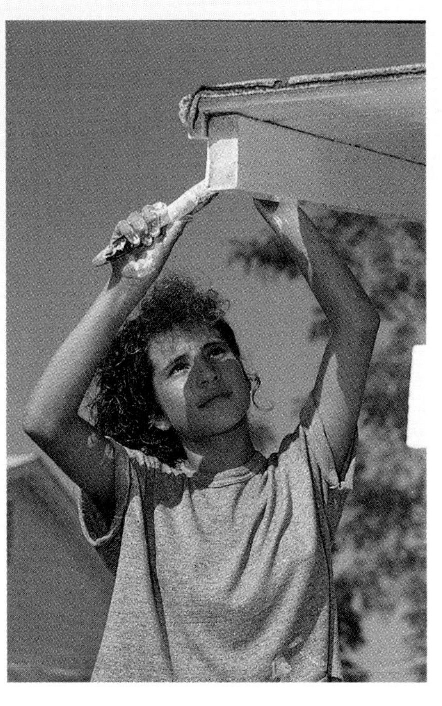

This photograph is on the cover of a brochure from the college you plan to attend. At this college one community-service project per semester is required for your chosen degree program. Write a letter to your friend Erin, who is already at the college. Describe your plans for your first project. Will it be in entertainment? service? education? sports? You might want to ask Erin about some of the community-service projects she has done. As you write your letter, use commas carefully with compound sentences, introductory elements, dates, addresses, and the salutation and closing. After editing your letter, write the final copy.

## QuickCheck Mixed Practice

History Topic **Write each sentence, adding a comma or commas where needed. If a sentence is correct, write *C*.**

**1.** Among the inventions of Thomas Edison are the light switch an electric pen and the microphone.

**2.** The parking meter was invented in Oklahoma City and was the brainstorm of Carlton Magee.

**3.** To pay off a debt Walter Hunt invented the safety pin.

**4.** Margaret E. Knight patented an improved paper machine and invented a machine for cutting out shoes.

**5.** James Watt was not the inventor of the first steam engine but he did improve the steam engine in 1769.

**6.** After Humphrey O'Sullivan had walked all day on the hot hard pavements of Boston he invented the rubber heel.

**7.** Joseph Friedman invented the first flexible plastic straw.

**8.** Amanda Theodosia Jones invented the vacuum process of preserving food and tried to establish a factory that would use her process.

**9.** To improve methods of farming Englishman Thomas Coke invented a new method of crop rotation during the 1700s.

**10.** Leonardo da Vinci designed a flying machine and Benjamin Franklin invented bifocals.

**11.** On June 22 1882 the U.S. Patent Office granted a patent for a propeller-driven rocking chair.

**12.** Until the envelope was invented in 1839 people folded their letters and sealed them with wax.

**13.** According to the United States Patent Office records a man named Chester Greenwood held patents on earmuffs and many other items.

**14.** Fixing a tricycle John Dunlop accidentally invented an inflatable tire.

**15.** Patented by George B. Hansburg the Pogo stick became an American fad during the 1920s.

**16.** When Sybilla Masters succeeded in inventing a machine that reduced corn into meal food preparation methods were greatly improved.

**17.** King Camp Gillette patented the safety razor in the year 1904.

**18.** Before the twentieth century engine-propelled air travel was not possible.

**19.** Whitcomb L. Judson patented an early form of the zipper in 1893.

**20.** Lee De Forest invented a vacuum tube in 1907 and this device helped develop electronic equipment.

## Commas That Enclose

Some sentences contain expressions that interrupt the flow of a sentence. These expressions usually supply additional information that is not necessary for understanding the main idea of a sentence.

If one of these interrupting expressions comes in the middle of a sentence, use two commas to enclose the expression—to set it off from the rest of the sentence. If an interrupting expression comes at the beginning or at the end of a sentence, use only one comma.

### Direct Address

Any name, title, or other word that is used to address someone directly is set off by commas. These interrupting expressions are called nouns of **direct address.**

Use commas to set off nouns of direct address.

**Kenneth,** what did you do with my new book?
Hurry**, Mandy,** or we'll miss Anne Rice's autograph session.
What is your favorite poem**, Maria?**

## Parenthetical Expressions

These expressions add meaning but are only incidental to the main idea of the sentence.

**Use commas to set off parenthetical expressions.**

The following is a list of common parenthetical expressions.

| COMMON PARENTHETICAL EXPRESSIONS | | |
|---|---|---|
| after all | however | moreover |
| at any rate | I believe (guess, hope, know, think) | nevertheless |
| by the way | in fact | of course |
| consequently | in my opinion | on the contrary |
| for example | | on the other hand |
| for instance | | therefore |

**By the way,** did you read Tony's new story?

Your essay**, of course,** was beautifully written.

We will proceed as planned**, nevertheless**.

Commas are used to set off the expressions in the preceding box *only* if the expressions interrupt the flow of a sentence. If the words are an essential part of the sentence, do not use commas.

| | |
|---|---|
| COMMAS | **On the other hand,** we did enjoy the author's book exhibit. |
| NO COMMAS | Wear that glove **on the other hand**. (*On the other hand* is necessary to the meaning of the sentence.) |
| COMMAS | I noticed**, however,** that the boy never paid for the book. |
| NO COMMAS | Our book club will wait in line for **however** long it takes! (*However* is part of a phrase that is necessary to the meaning of the sentence.) |

Expressions other than those listed in the box can also be parenthetical if they interrupt the flow of the sentence.

> Novels**, like movies,** can change your view of life.

Contrasting expressions, which often begin with *not, but, but not,* or *though not,* are also considered parenthetical expressions.

> Peggy**, not Angela,** will recite a poem at graduation.
>
> The actor**, though not well known,** will star in the play.

Occasionally an adverb clause will also interrupt a sentence.

> His novel sales**, if they hit nine million today,** will set a national record.

Many of the words listed in the box of common parenthetical expressions can also be used to join two independent clauses. When they do so, they are preceded by a semicolon and followed by a comma.

> I searched the library for hours**; nevertheless,** I could not find the information.
>
> I had to invite Professor Dinny to my first book signing**; after all,** she had inspired me to write.

*To learn more about joining two independent clauses, see pages L167–L169.*
*Parentheses and dashes are also used to set off parenthetical expressions.* *To learn more, see pages L528–L530.*

## Appositives

An appositive with its modifiers renames, identifies, or explains a noun or a pronoun in the sentence.

Use commas to set off most appositives and their modifiers.

> Mr. James**, my English teacher,** attended Ohio State.
>
> I read Harper Lee's only novel**, *To Kill a Mockingbird*.**

An appositive is occasionally preceded by the word *or, particularly, notably,* or *especially*. Some appositives that are introduced by *such as* are also set off by commas.

> Many students**, especially freshmen,** have entered the story contest.
>
> Use visual aids**, such as photos of the author.**

An appositive is not set off by commas if it identifies a person or a thing by telling which one or ones. Often these appositives are names and have no modifiers.

> The verb ***write*** is an irregular verb. (Which verb?)
>
> My cousin **Lucy** is writing a screenplay. (Which cousin?)

When adjectives, titles, and degrees are in the appositive position, they are also set off by commas.

| | |
|---|---|
| ADJECTIVES | The limerick**, short and funny,** is Wanda's. |
| TITLES | Frank Moore**, Sr.,** is a book editor. |
| DEGREES | Alicia Ray**, Ph.D.,** teaches Shakespeare. |

## PRACTICE YOUR SKILLS

Check Your Understanding

***Using Commas with Interrupters***

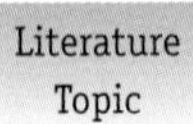


**Write the word or words in each sentence that should be enclosed in commas. If a sentence does not need any additional commas, write *C*.**

**1.** William Carlos Williams M.D. was a noted poet.

**2.** Uriah Heep the villain in Charles Dickens's *David Copperfield* was the focus of my English composition.

**3.** The great playwright Lillian Hellman was born in 1905.

**4.** Lydia have you met Toni Morrison author of *Beloved?*

**5.** The poet Shel Silverstein died I believe in May 1999.

6. He wrote my favorite story *The Giving Tree.*
7. *Apocalypse Now* Francis Ford Coppola's controversial film on the Vietnam War was based on Conrad's novel *Heart of Darkness.*
8. Epic poetry long and complex usually contains references to mythological gods, battles, and heroes.
9. I recommend poems by authors such as Edna St. Vincent Millay and Robert Frost.
10. Our book club selection for this month by the way is *House of Sand and Fog* by Andre Dubus III.

### Connect to the Writing Process: Drafting
### *Writing Sentences with Interrupters*

**Write sentences using interrupters, as directed. Use commas where needed.**

11. Use a friend's name in direct address.
12. Use a parenthetical expression.
13. Use an appositive.
14. Use an appositive preceded by *such as* or *particularly.*
15. Use the contrasting expression *but not today.*
16. Use the expression *after all* to interrupt the flow of a sentence.
17. Use the expression *after all* in a way that does not interrupt the flow of a sentence.
18. Use a title or degree following a name.
19. Use an adverb clause to interrupt a sentence.
20. Use *however* to connect two independent clauses.

### Connect to the Writing Process: Editing
### *Editing Commas with Interrupters*

**Rewrite each sentence, using the interrupter in parentheses. Use commas where needed.**

21. Edmund Spenser wrote *The Faerie Queene.* (not William Shakespeare)

**22.** Coleridge considered his friend the greatest poet since Milton. (Wordsworth)

**23.** John Locke is well-known for his essays. (like Jonathan Swift)

**24.** "A Modest Proposal" is Swift's best known essay. (I believe)

**25.** Many readers didn't realize Swift was being satirical. (not literal)

**26.** Modernist writers were very experimental in their writing style. (especially Joyce and Fitzgerald)

**27.** Many modernist novels do not have "happily ever after" endings. (for example)

**28.** Stephen Crane is another author who did not believe in happy endings. (if I remember correctly)

**29.** Oliver Sacks wrote *The Man Who Mistook His Wife for a Hat.* (M.D.)

**30.** Sack's book was made into a movie of the same name. *(Awakenings)*

## Nonessential Elements

Like other interrupters you have just reviewed, some participial phrases and some clauses are not needed to make the meaning of a sentence clear or complete. When a phrase or a clause is not needed to complete the meaning of a sentence, commas are used to enclose it.

### Use commas to set off a nonessential participial phrase or a nonessential adjective clause.

A participial phrase or an adjective clause is nonessential (nonrestrictive) if it supplies extra, unnecessary information. To decide whether a phrase or a clause is nonessential, read the sentence without it. If the phrase or the clause could be removed without changing the basic meaning of the sentence, it is nonessential. A phrase or a clause that modifies a proper noun is almost always nonessential.

| | |
|---|---|
| NONESSENTIAL PARTICIPIAL PHRASE | Birds' nests**, made from grass and twigs,** were visible in the trees. (*Birds' nests were visible in the trees.*) |
| NONESSENTIAL ADJECTIVE PHRASE | A dog**, which is my favorite kind of pet,** is more loyal than a cat. (*A dog is more loyal than a cat.*) |

An essential (restrictive) phrase or clause identifies a person or a thing by answering the question *Which one?* Therefore, no commas are used. If an essential phrase or clause is removed from a sentence, the meaning of the sentence will be unclear or incomplete. (An adjective clause that begins with *that* is usually essential.)

| | |
|---|---|
| ESSENTIAL PARTICIPIAL PHRASE | The horse **named Prince** should be removed from the show. (*The horse should be removed from the show.* The phrase is needed to identify which of many horses should be removed from the show.) |
| ESSENTIAL ADJECTIVE CLAUSE | The parakeets **that you wanted** were already sold. (*The parakeets were already sold.* The clause is needed to identify which parakeets were already sold.) |

## PRACTICE YOUR SKILLS

Check Your Understanding

### *Using Commas with Nonessential Elements*

Science Topic

**Find each interrupter and state whether it is *essential (E)* or *nonessential (N)*.** (Note that the commas that should enclose nonessential elements are not present.)

**1.** The lizard called the gecko can grow a new tail.

**2.** The carrier pigeon which was once a common message carrier is now extinct.

**3.** Ralph Winters fishing in Beaver Brook caught a trout.

4. Scientists who classify insects are called entomologists.
5. We watched the geese flying south.
6. A tarantula's bite which is not usually fatal still causes a great deal of pain.
7. The ostrich which is the largest of all birds can outrun a horse.
8. The exoskeleton of an insect is made of chitin which is lighter and far more flexible than bone.
9. The dog that has a black tongue is the chow chow.
10. The underwater enemy threatening the sea otter is the killer whale.

### Connect to the Writing Process: Editing
***Using Commas with Nonessential Elements***

**11.–15. Write each sentence in the preceding exercise that has a nonessential element, adding a comma or commas where needed.**

### Connect to the Writing Process: Revising
***Adding Phrases to Sentences***

**Rewrite each sentence twice. First, add a nonessential phrase or clause to the sentence. Second, add an essential phrase or clause. Use commas where needed.**

16. The dog is next door.
17. The mouse is trapped.
18. Giraffes are majestic.
19. My pet snake got loose.

## Communicate Your Ideas

### APPLY TO WRITING

**Opinion Essay:** ***Commas That Enclose***

What animal do you think is the most beautiful animal in existence? Prepare an opinion essay for your classmates. Describe the animal and then explain your opinion. Be sure to use essential and nonessential elements correctly.

## QuickCheck Mixed Practice

Science Topic **Write the following paragraphs, adding commas where needed.** (You will add 21 commas in all.)

Elizabeth Blackwell was the first woman to earn a medical degree but she had to travel a long hard road to get that degree. Even though 29 medical schools had refused to admit her she persisted. After three years of private study Blackwell was finally accepted to the Medical Institute of Geneva New York. The director doubtful and concerned passed her application on to the students for their approval. Thinking it was a joke everyone agreed to admit her. When Blackwell arrived however she was greeted with shock and anger. She was ridiculed ignored refused lodging and barred from some classroom activities.

Graduating at the head of her class on January 23 1849 Blackwell continued her studies in London and Paris. She finally returned to New York City and there she opened a hospital in 1853. Called the New York Infirmary for Women and Children it was staffed by women. With the help of Emily her younger sister Blackwell added a medical college for women to the site in 1868.

As a pioneer in medicine Blackwell opened the door for women in the medical field. She required that female students work harder than male students to establish themselves in the medical community. Because of her courage many women comfortably practice medicine today.

CheckPoint

## Using Commas Correctly

**Write each sentence, adding a comma or commas where needed. If a sentence needs no commas, write *C*.**

**1.** Among the heroes of the American Revolution was a gallant young Frenchman who risked his life and fortune.

**2.** Lafayette was born in Chavaniac France on September 6 1757.

**3.** Although at the age of nineteen he was both a French army captain and a popular nobleman he wasn't satisfied with life.

**4.** When the American colonies declared their independence from England France's ancient foe Lafayette sailed for America.

**5.** He offered his enthusiastic heartfelt services to Congress which rewarded him with the rank of major general.

**6.** Lafayette served under Washington who became his friend.

**7.** Lafayette who proved to be a good officer was slightly wounded in 1777 in his first battle the Battle of Brandywine.

**8.** His great achievement for the colonies was a treaty of alliance that he persuaded the French government to sign in 1778.

**9.** When he returned to France after the surrender of Cornwallis at Yorktown he joined the French Revolution.

**10.** He served as commander-in-chief of the National Guard which was organized to safeguard the revolution.

**11.** Lafayette however became disenchanted with the revolution.

**12.** He was proclaimed a traitor and was forced to flee to Belgium where he was imprisoned by the Austrians.

**13.** After five years in exile Lafayette was freed by Napoleon.

**14.** His life continued uneventfully until 1830 when he played a leading role in the overthrow of Charles X.

**15.** Although Lafayette's actions cost him his fortune they won for him the respect of Americans and the French alike.

## Kinds of Sentences and End Marks

**Write each sentence and its appropriate end mark. Then label each one *D* for declarative, *IM* for imperative, *IN* for interrogative, or *E* for exclamatory.**

1. Scientists estimate that about 100 acres of the remaining tropical rain forests are being cleared every minute
2. How big is an acre
3. In your mind, picture a football field minus the end zones
4. Now picture 100 of these football fields
5. That's how much of the remaining rain forests are being destroyed every single minute
6. Tropical rain forests are found in only seven percent of the world, but they play a vital part in sustaining many life forms
7. Why are rain forests so important
8. The trees provide huge amounts of the earth's oxygen, and the forests are great sources for many needed medicines
9. Of course, the rainforests are also the homes of many endangered species of animals and insects
10. Find out what you can do to stop the destruction of these vital rain forests

## Writing Sentences

**Write five sentences that follow the directions below. Write about one of the following topics or a topic of your choice: an interesting person from history or an environmental issue such as the rainforests.**

**Write a sentence that . . .**

1. includes a series of nouns.
2. includes two adjectives before a noun.
3. includes an introductory participial phrase.
4. includes an introductory adverbial phrase.
5. includes an appositive.

# Language and *Self-Expression*

**D**o you think a person's character can be seen in his or her face? Consider the sculpture of Queen Tiy's head. Tiy was an Egyptian queen in the 14th century B.C. She participated actively in state affairs and public ceremonies along with her husband, King Amenhotep III. Later she was an adviser to her son, King Amenhotep IV. Looking at her face, can you imagine her performing these royal duties?

In your mind, picture the face of someone in a leadership position that affects you—maybe a school official, a parent, or a coach. Then write a description of how this person's face does or does not reflect his or her true character. For example, do the person's eyes look determined, and does that person show determination in achieving goals?

**Prewriting** List the facial features and accessories (eyeglasses, jewelry, hats) of your chosen subject. Beside each one, describe the character trait it conveys to you. For example, a baseball cap on a coach makes a different impression than a baseball cap on a mayor.

**Drafting** Write a character sketch that is three or four paragraphs in length. Describe how your subject's features and accessories imply particular character traits. Your conclusion could state whether these impressions are truly present in the person's character.

**Revising** Check your writing for organization. For example, you might group the "accessories" ideas in a single paragraph.

**Editing** Check your writing for correct spelling and grammar as well as for correct use of end punctuation and commas.

**Publishing** Write a final copy and submit it to your teacher. If you think the subject of your paper would enjoy reading the character sketch, share a copy with that person as well.

# Another Look

A **declarative sentence** makes a statement or expresses an opinion and ends with a **period** (.).

An **imperative sentence** gives a direction, makes a request, or gives a command. It ends with a **period** or an **exclamation point** (. or !).

An **interrogative sentence** asks a question and ends with a **question mark** (?).

An **exclamatory sentence** expresses strong feeling or emotion and ends with an **exclamation point** (!).

## Using Periods

Use a period after most abbreviations. *(pages L432–L433)*
Use a period after each number or letter that shows a division in an outline. *(page L433)*

## Using Commas

Use commas to separate items in a series. *(pages L436–L437)*
Use commas after the words *first, second,* and so on when they introduce items in a series. *(page L437)*
Use a comma sometimes to separate two adjectives that directly precede a noun and that are not joined by a conjunction. *(pages L438–L439)*
Use a comma to separate the independent clauses of a compound sentence if the clauses are joined by a coordinating conjunction. *(pages L441–L442)*
Use a comma after certain introductory elements. *(pages L444–L445)*
Use commas to separate the elements in dates and addresses. *(pages L447–L448)*
Use a comma after the salutation of a friendly letter and after the closing of all letters. *(page L448)*
Use commas to set off nouns of direct address. *(page L453)*
Use commas to set off parenthetical expressions. *(pages L454–L455)*
Use commas to set off most appositives and their modifiers. *(pages L455–L456)*
Use commas to set off a nonessential participial phrase or a nonessential adjective clause. *(pages L458–L459)*

*Directions*

**Read the passage and write the letter of the answer that correctly punctuates each underlined part. If the underlined part contains no error, write *D*.**

EXAMPLE Keller listen (1) to these facts about sugar.

1 **A** Keller listen,
**B** Keller, listen,
**C** Keller, listen
**D** No error

ANSWER 1 **C**

Many people including teenagers are (1) unaware of the amount of sugar they consume. Foods like candy, soda, and maple syrup may contain more sugar than you think. For example suppose (2) you drink a twelve-ounce can of soda (3) You have drunk the equivalent of ten teaspoons of sugar. Are you surprised (4) If you are not surprised by that fact perhaps (5) this one will surprise you. Foods such as muffins, salad dressings, (6) yogurt and cheese spread (7) may have added sugar. Wow (8) Who would have guessed this (9) Nutritionists suggest a simple response to sugar. If you are in good health, eat it in moderation (10) If you are overweight, eat sugar sparingly.

1 **A** people, including teenagers, are
  **B** people including teenagers, are
  **C** people, including teenagers are
  **D** No error

2 **A** For example suppose,
  **B** For example! suppose
  **C** For example, suppose
  **D** No error

3 **A** soda,
  **B** soda.
  **C** soda?
  **D** No error

4 **A** surprised!
  **B** surprised?
  **C** surprised.
  **D** No error

5 **A** fact, perhaps
  **B** fact, perhaps,
  **C** fact. perhaps
  **D** No error

6 **A** muffins, salad dressings
  **B** muffins, salad, dressings,
  **C** muffins salad dressings
  **D** No error

7 **A** yogurt and cheese, spread
  **B** yogurt, and cheese spread
  **C** yogurt and cheese spread,
  **D** No error

8 **A** Wow,
  **B** Wow!
  **C** Wow.
  **D** No error

9 **A** this?
  **B** this!
  **C** this.
  **D** No error

10 **A** moderation!
  **B** moderation?
  **C** moderation.
  **D** No error

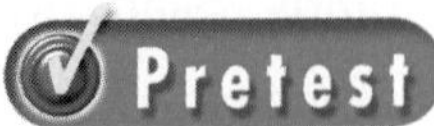

CHAPTER 11

# Other Punctuation

## Pretest

### *Directions*

**Each underlined part in the passage lacks one type of punctuation. Write the letter of the answer with the punctuation that correctly completes the underlined part.**

EXAMPLE — Are you a vegetarian? Abdul asked me. (1)

1 A Colon
  B Italics
  C Quotation marks
  D Dashes

ANSWER 1 C

Variety and creativity these (1) are the elements that make a vegetarian diet appealing. Many people and I include myself (2) think a dinner of only vegetables would be boring. Go to a Japanese or Thai restaurant and notice this restaurants use (3) of flavorings in vegetable dishes. You might taste the following spices garlic, cayenne pepper, and ginger (4). Youll get plenty of ideas (5) for your own vegetarian cuisine.

1 **A** Dash
**B** Apostrophe
**C** Hyphen
**D** Brackets

2 **A** Apostrophe
**B** Parentheses
**C** Italics
**D** Semicolon

3 **A** Colon
**B** Semicolon
**C** Dashes
**D** Apostrophe

4 **A** Colon
**B** Italics
**C** Parentheses
**D** Quotation marks

5 **A** Brackets
**B** Italics
**C** Apostrophe
**D** Hyphen

René Magritte. *The Mysteries of the Horizon*, 1955.
Oil on canvas, 19½ by 25⅓ inches. Private collection.

**Describe** What images has Magritte used in this painting? Describe the elements of color and space.

**Analyze** Find examples of unity or harmony through repetition of shapes, colors, and images.

**Interpret** Choose one of the images in the painting. What do you think this image symbolizes? How do you think it contributes to the overall mood or message of the painting?

**Judge** Which word better describes this painting: *realistic* or *surrealistic*? Why?

At the end of this chapter, you will use the artwork to stimulate ideas for writing.

# Apostrophes

Although end marks and commas are the punctuation marks most commonly used, all marks of punctuation are important. This chapter will cover punctuation marks other than end marks and commas. One such punctuation mark is the apostrophe.

You probably use apostrophes with contractions every time you write, but the apostrophe has another important and very common use. It is used with nouns and some pronouns to show possession.

## Apostrophes to Show Possession

By using apostrophes, you can indicate that nouns and some pronouns show possession.

### Possessive Forms of Nouns

The possessive of a singular noun is formed differently than the possessive of a plural noun.

**Add *'s* to form the possessive of a singular noun.**

To form the possessive of a singular noun, write the noun without adding or omitting any letters. Then add *'s* at the end.

friend + **'s** = friend**'s** This is my friend**'s** cabin.
cabin + **'s** = cabin**'s** The cabin**'s** walls need paint.

Singular compound nouns and the names of most businesses and organizations form their possessives in the way other singular nouns do.

Her mother-in-law**'s** lakeside barbecue is tomorrow.
I will order the ribs from Maher**'s** Meat Market.

To form the possessive of a plural noun, write the plural form of the word without making any changes. Then look at the ending of the plural noun. The ending will determine the way you will form the possessive.

### Add only an apostrophe to form the possessive of a plural noun that ends in *s.*

If the plural noun ends in *s,* add only an apostrophe.

| | |
|---|---|
| girls + **'** = girls**'** | The girls**'** rowing team has won! |
| Nelsons + **'** = Nelsons**'** | The Nelsons**'** raft seats two. |

### Add *'s* to form the possessive of a plural noun that does not end in *s.*

If a plural noun does not end in *s,* add *'s* to form the possessive—just as you would to a singular noun that does not end in *s.*

| | |
|---|---|
| men + **'s** = men**'s** | Where are the men**'s** hiking boots? |
| cacti + **'s** = cacti**'s** | The cacti**'s** blossoms are pink. |

Do not confuse a plural possessive with the simple plural form of a noun.

| | |
|---|---|
| POSSESSIVE | Marty is the **twins'** rowing coach. |
| PLURAL | Marty coaches the **twins**. |

## PRACTICE YOUR SKILLS

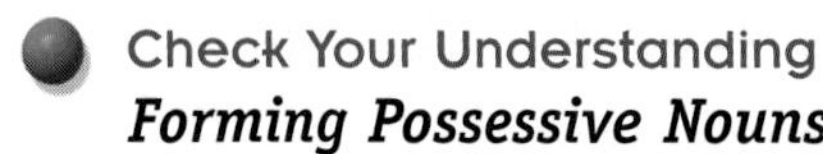

Check Your Understanding

***Forming Possessive Nouns***

**Write the possessive form of each noun.**

**1.** mother
**2.** sister-in-law
**3.** Karen
**4.** Palmers
**5.** editor-in-chief
**6.** oxen
**7.** women
**8.** city
**9.** geese
**10.** world
**11.** beaches
**12.** officers
**13.** birch
**14.** children
**15.** babies

## Check Your Understanding
### *Using Possessive Nouns*

Contemporary Life **Write the correct possessive noun in parentheses.**

**16.** The two (boys', boy's) canoe was bright orange.

**17.** (Terrys', Terry's) backpack is waterproof.

**18.** The primitive campsite is at (Papa Bear's Campground, Papa Bear Campground's).

**19.** Do you want my life jacket or (Suzys', Suzy's)?

**20.** This life (jackets', jacket's) strap is broken.

**21.** Hmm. All the life (jackets', jacket's) straps are broken.

**22.** Why don't we rent new life jackets from those (women's, womens') supply booth?

**23.** Look! I see the (McKlintocks', McKlintock's) camper!

**24.** Later I want to visit the (horse's, horses') stables.

**25.** Your (brother's-in-law, brother-in-law's) trail map is too old to be useful.

## Connect to the Writing Process: Editing
### *Using Apostrophes*

**Correctly write each word that needs an apostrophe or an apostrophe and an *s.***

**26.** A hunter jacket is usually made of camouflage fabric.

**27.** Who has November hunting itinerary?

**28.** All the tent metal poles are in good condition.

**29.** The poles construction is of aluminum.

**30.** How long will your father-in-law hunting trip last?

**31.** We appreciated the other men offer of firewood.

**32.** Charlies Market on the Highway 52 will buy our venison.

**33.** Is that bag of corn Paul?

**34.** He brought it for the deer feeding trough.

**35.** Mr. Wong four-wheel-drive vehicle saved us from being stuck in that mud hole.

## Possessive Forms of Pronouns

Personal pronouns and the pronoun *who* show possession by changing form, not by adding an apostrophe.

**The possessive forms of personal pronouns and the pronoun *who* do not use apostrophes.**

This is **his** yearbook, but **whose** is that?

None of the following possessive pronouns include apostrophes.

| POSSESSIVE PRONOUNS | | | |
|---|---|---|---|
| my, mine | his | its | their, theirs |
| your, yours | her, hers | our, ours | |

Do not confuse a contraction with a possessive pronoun. A possessive pronoun does not include an apostrophe, but a contraction does. *Its, your, their,* and *theirs* are possessive pronouns. *It's, you're, they're,* and *there's* are contractions.

*You can learn more about possessive pronouns on pages L236 and L251–L257.*

An indefinite pronoun forms its possessive in the same way a singular noun does—by adding *'s.*

No one**'s** yearbook is signed yet.

Did you ask for anyone**'s** signature?

*You can find a list of common indefinite pronouns on page L301.*

CONNECT TO WRITER'S CRAFT

Writers often use mnemonic phrases to help them remember the spelling of difficult words. The following sentence, for example, might help someone remember the spelling of the possessive pronoun *theirs*: "The ***heirs*** in ***theirs*** did not inherit an apostrophe."

## Practice Your Skills

### Check Your Understanding
***Using Possessive Pronouns***

Contemporary Life

**Write the correct form of each possessive pronoun in parentheses.**

**1.** (You're, Your) research papers are due on Friday.

**2.** (Everyone's, Everyones') speeches should be given by Tuesday.

**3.** I think this ruler is missing (it's, its) markings.

**4.** (Who's, Whose) is this sketch?

**5.** (There's, Theirs) is the classroom with the purple walls.

**6.** This new globe is (hers, her's).

**7.** (Your's, Yours) arrived first thing this morning.

**8.** (Someone's, Someones') jacket was left in the bleachers.

**9.** (Their, They're) report cards should be put over there.

**10.** (Her, Her's) photograph won a prize.

### Connect to the Writing Process: Editing
***Using Possessive Pronouns***

**Rewrite any incorrectly written possessive pronouns. If all of the pronouns in a sentence are written correctly, write *C*.**

**11.** The responsibility for sales of the yearbook is our's.

**12.** Soliciting advertising, however, is you're responsibility.

**13.** Theirs is a difficult job.

**14.** They must judge hundreds of amateur photos on each ones' merits.

**15.** That colorful photo of Mark spiking a volleyball is mine.

**16.** Who will design the cover is anybodies' guess.

**17.** The cover design I like best is your's.

**18.** All of the yearbook members can design there own page of highlights.

**19.** Somebodys' page design will win a prize of $100.

**20.** We want this year's book to have its own unique look.

## Apostrophes to Show Joint or Separate Ownership

In written work apostrophes can signal either joint or separate ownership. One apostrophe is used to show joint ownership. Two or more apostrophes are used to show separate ownership.

**Add 's to only the last word to show joint ownership.**

**Add 's to each word to show separate ownership.**

In the following example, the audiobook belongs to Paul and Craig. Since both people own the audiobook, an apostrophe is added to the second name only.

Paul and Craig**'s** audiobook has been returned.

If one of the words in a phrase showing joint ownership is a possessive pronoun, the noun must also show possession.

Paul**'s** and **his** audiobook has been returned.

In the following example, Paul and Craig own separate audiobooks; therefore, an apostrophe is added to each name.

Paul**'s** and Craig**'s** audiobooks have been returned.

## Apostrophes with Nouns Expressing Times or Amounts

When you use a noun that expresses time or amount as an adjective, write it in the possessive form.

**Use an apostrophe with the possessive form of a noun that expresses time or amount.**

She lost a week**'s** time by reading the wrong book.
I spent nine dollar**s'** worth of quarters on the new book.

Other words that express time include *minute, hour, day, month,* and *year.*

## Practice Your Skills

### Check Your Understanding
*Using Apostrophes Correctly*

Literature Topic **Write the correct possessive form of the noun or pronoun in parentheses.**

1. My grandparents always read ■ fairy tales to me. (the Grimm brothers and Andersen)
2. *Middlemarch* by George Eliot might be several ■ worth of reading. (month)
3. There is an interesting article about *Treasure Island* in ■ paper. (Sunday)
4. *Jude the Obscure* is one of ■ favorite novels. (LuAnn and her)
5. One of that ■ bestsellers is *A Night Without Armor* by Jewel. (year)
6. ■ novels are often made into movies. (Michael Crichton and Tom Clancy)
7. ■ joint publication is *Lyrical Ballads.* (Coleridge and Wordsworth)
8. ■ poems fill the volume with beautiful imagery. (Coleridge and Wordsworth)
9. ■ poems are always in anthologies of English literature. (Wordsworth and him)
10. You should have seen my hilarious portrayal of Puck in *A* ■ *Dream!* (*Midsummer Night*)

### Connect to the Writing Process: Editing
*Using Possessive Nouns and Pronouns*

**Rewrite any incorrectly written possessive noun or pronoun. If all possessive forms in a sentence are written correctly, write *C*.**

11. This weeks assignment is to write a poem.
12. Brandy and Kristen's poems will both serve as examples.
13. Kristen's and her works have been published frequently.
14. The first-place winner and the second-place winner's poems will be considered for publication.

15. The newspaper editor and English teacher's decisions are final.
16. She will have several hour's worth of reading to do.
17. Stan's and mine poems are both candidates for prizes.
18. Give me a days time to prepare my acceptance speech.
19. Becca or Nancy's poem will probably win third place.
20. Becca's and Nancy's poems are too somber for my taste.

## Communicate Your Ideas

### APPLY TO WRITING

**Opinion Statement: *Apostrophes***

One of your best friends has asked you to share an apartment after high school graduation. Your friend wants both of you to write a statement of ownership regarding food, furniture, dishes, and so on. What will belong to you jointly, and what will you possess individually? What will be your rights in using one another's personal possessions and food? Write a fair statement of ownership, using apostrophes to show possession. Edit for mistakes in punctuation and then write the final copy.

### Mixed Practice

Contemporary Life

**Correctly write each word that should be in possessive form.**

1. Alfred applied for the cashier position at the corner gas station.
2. The manager and assistant-manager impressions of him were favorable.
3. He begins his shift by breaking open two dollars worth of nickels, fifty cents worth of pennies, and other rolled coins.

4. His job also includes keeping the women and men restrooms stocked with paper towels and soap.
5. The employees uniform is a lime-green smock.
6. Everyone distaste for the color is apparent.
7. Alfred and Paul decision to ask for new uniforms was applauded by the staff.
8. Paul and his jobs were never in jeopardy.
9. The rest of the employees of Conroys Gas 'N Go supported the young mens request.
10. The new smocks color is black.
11. The Conroy family station hosted an anniversary celebration.
12. Each customer took a minute time to sign up for free prizes such as tune-ups and oil changes.

## Other Uses of Apostrophes

In addition to showing possession, apostrophes have several other uses.

### Apostrophes with Contractions

An apostrophe is substituted for letters omitted in a contraction.

**Use an apostrophe in a contraction to show where one or more letters have been omitted.**

| CONTRACTIONS | | |
|---|---|---|
| are n~~o~~t = aren't | that ~~i~~s = that's | I ~~wi~~ll = I'll |
| we ~~ha~~ve = we've | let ~~u~~s = let's | o~~f~~ ~~the~~ clock = o'clock |

The only contraction in which any letters are changed or added is the contraction for *will not,* which is *won't.*

## Practice Your Skills

### Check Your Understanding
***Writing Contractions***

**Write the contraction for each pair of words.**

**1.** do not
**2.** I have
**3.** did not
**4.** let us
**5.** we will
**6.** who is
**7.** they are
**8.** will not
**9.** I am
**10.** is not
**11.** were not
**12.** it is
**13.** you are
**14.** has not
**15.** I would
**16.** there is
**17.** does not
**18.** are not
**19.** we have
**20.** have not

### Connect to the Writing Process: Editing
***Using Contractions***

**Write the words in each sentence that may be replaced with a contraction. Then write the contraction. Some sentences contain more than one possible contraction.**

**21.** I cannot see the race track from here.
**22.** They are about to start the race.
**23.** We will move to better seats.
**24.** The race will begin at three of the clock sharp.
**25.** There will be a chance to meet the winners afterward.
**26.** They will accept their trophies and then mingle with the crowd.
**27.** I will be sure to get my picture taken next to the champion horse.
**28.** I have always wanted a horse of my own, but I am not sure I would know how to ride in a race.
**29.** Let us talk later about how we will buy a horse together and who is going to build the stables in his backyard!
**30.** I have not had this much fun in weeks, and I will not miss a minute of this race!

## Apostrophes with Certain Plurals

To prevent confusion, certain items form their plurals by adding *'s*.

**Add *'s* to form the plural of lowercase letters, some capital letters, and some words used as words.**

> Are these letters *s***'s** or *e***'s**?
> Should *O***'s** be round or oval?

The plurals of most other letters, symbols, numerals, and words used as words can be formed by adding an *s*.

> The Beatles led the British invasion in the 1960**s**.
> Entrepreneurs see $**s** when they recognize a popular fad.

### CONNECT TO WRITER'S CRAFT

Some writers prefer to add *'s*, instead of just *s*, to form the plural of all letters, symbols, numerals, and words used as words. This might lend a look of consistency in poetry, for example. When writing formally, however, follow the preceding rules.

| | |
|---|---|
| INFORMAL: | I choose my *2***'s** and my *3***'s**<br>And add them where I please. |
| FORMAL: | The children were divided into groups of *2***s** and *3***s**. |

## Apostrophes with Certain Dates

An apostrophe is also used when numbers are dropped from a date.

**Use an apostrophe to show that numbers are omitted in a date.**

> We bought this personal computer in **'**01. (2001)
> Our old PC was manufactured in **'**92. (1992)

## Practice Your Skills

Check Your Understanding

### *Using Apostrophes*

Contemporary Life

**Write each underlined item in its plural form, and shorten all dates to a two-digit form (such as '85).**

1. The binary numbering system used by computers consists of *0* and *1*.
2. When I write quick E-mails, I use & for *and*.
3. How many @ are in an E-mail address?
4. I've had my E-mail account since the late 1990.
5. In 1998, I changed my ISP.
6. You can separate parts of your message with a row of *.
7. Despite my worries, my computer changed from 1999 to 2000 easily.
8. I remember the concern about whether PC would be Y2K-compliant.
9. I stayed up so late playing a game over the Internet that now I need to get some *z*.
10. How many *w* are usually found in a typical Website address?

Connect to the Writing Process: Drafting

### *Writing Sentences*

**Write a sentence that follows each direction, using apostrophes and plural forms correctly.**

11. Use the two-digit form of the year you were born.
12. Use the two-digit form of the year you will graduate from high school.
13. Use the plural form of the dollar sign.
14. Use the four-digit form of the year that you began school.
15. Use the plural form of the letter *X*.

## Communicate Your Ideas

### APPLY TO WRITING

**Technical E-mail: *Apostrophes***

You bought a "refurbished" laptop computer, and many of the keyboard keys seem faulty. They type a different letter or symbol than the one printed on the key. Write an E-mail to the technical support division of Global PCs. Describe the keys that aren't working, give the date you purchased the computer, and state how many number *5*s are on your proof of purchase seal. Use plurals of all letters, symbols, and words used as words.

Mixed Practice

Contemporary Life

**Rewrite each incorrectly written letter or word. If a sentence is correct, write *C*.**

**1.** A student's life is very busy.
**2.** Diego's composition was well written, was'nt it?
**3.** The freshmen and seniors lockers were just painted.
**4.** The Queen of Englands coronation picture is hanging in my homeroom.
**5.** Teenager's interests in most areas have changed over the past fifty years.
**6.** There's their neighbor, waiting at the bus stop.
**7.** Gorman' advertisement in this mornings' *Herald* offers a discount for graduating seniors.
**8.** The Raidens' son got two *A*'s on his report card, and their daughter got three on her's.
**9.** Well need Dad's permission to go on the class trip next week.
**10.** Aren't there three *ms* in *commencement?*

# Semicolons and Colons

By using the semicolon (;) and the colon (:), you can create sentence variety in your writing.

##  Semicolons

**Use a semicolon between the clauses of a compound sentence when they are not joined by a conjunction.**

Two independent clauses not properly joined result in a **run-on sentence**. A run-on sentence can be corrected in several ways. One way to correct a run-on sentence is to join the clauses with a coordinating conjunction and a comma.

| | |
|---|---|
| RUN-ON | The goldfish is my pet the cat is my mom's. |
| CORRECTED | The goldfish is my pet**, and** the cat is my mom's. |

The clauses in a compound sentence can be joined by a semicolon when there is no conjunction.

A goldfish is a great pet**;** it demands only food and water from its caretaker.

A cat requires a little time**;** it needs to be pampered by whoever owns it.

The earthworm has no lungs**;** it breathes through its skin.

Only closely related clauses should be joined by a semicolon. Ideas not closely related belong in separate sentences.

| | |
|---|---|
| NOT CLOSELY RELATED | Ferrets make wonderful pets**;** everyone should have a pet. |
| CLOSELY RELATED | Ferrets make wonderful pets**;** they are friendly and use a litter box just as cats do. |

*You can learn more about correcting run-on sentences on pages L167–L169.*

## Semicolons with Conjunctive Adverbs and Transitional Words

The clauses in a compound sentence can also be joined by a semicolon and certain conjunctive adverbs or transitional words.

Use a semicolon between the clauses in a compound sentence when they are joined by certain conjunctive adverbs or transitional words.

He told me the dog was friendly**; however,** it barked ferociously at me.

The kitten's markings could inspire a name**; for example,** you could call her Stripes.

Notice in the previous examples that the conjunctive adverb *however* and the transitional words *for example* are preceded by a semicolon and followed by a comma.

The following are lists of common conjunctive adverbs and transitional words.

| COMMON CONJUNCTIVE ADVERBS | | |
|---|---|---|
| accordingly | furthermore | otherwise |
| also | hence | similarly |
| besides | however | still |
| consequently | instead | therefore |
| finally | nevertheless | thus |

| COMMON TRANSITIONAL WORDS | | |
|---|---|---|
| as a result | in addition | in other words |
| for example | in fact | on the other hand |

Some of the conjunctive adverbs and transitional words listed in the box can also be used as parenthetical expressions within a single clause.

| | |
|---|---|
| Joining Clauses | A katydid looks much like a harmless green grasshopper**; consequently,** people are surprised when it bites them. (A semicolon comes before the transitional word, and a comma follows it.) |
| Within Clauses | The grasshopper**, however,** doesn't bite. (A comma comes before and after the conjunctive adverb.) |

*You can learn more about parenthetical expressions on pages L454–L455.*

## Practice Your Skills

Check Your Understanding
***Using Semicolons and Commas***

Science Topic

**Write *I* if the sentence does not use semicolons and commas correctly. Write *C* if the sentence is correct.**

1. Plankton floats at the ocean's surface other sea animals rely on it for food.
2. The bivalve mollusk has two shells hinged together, similarly oysters and mussels have hinged shells.
3. Oysters are prized for the pearls they produce; as a result oyster beds are cultivated as "pearl farms."
4. The sponge is a plantlike animal, and it grows only in an underwater habitat.
5. Jellyfish are stunningly beautiful on the other hand; their sting is stunningly painful.
6. Coral looks like porous rock; however, it is a skeleton secreted by living marine polyps.
7. Polyps such as the sea anemone live individually, others live in colonies and form coral reefs.
8. The octopus has a smooth body with a mouth on the underside furthermore it has eight arms covered with suckers.

9. The ten-armed squid is often used as fish bait; consequently; "squidding" means to fish for squid or to fish with squid as bait.

10. A sea horse's head and neck resemble those of a horse, it swims with its head held upright like a horse's, and its tail curled beneath.

Connect to the Writing Process: Editing
***Using Semicolons and Commas***

**11.–18. Rewrite the incorrect sentences from the preceding exercise, using semicolons and commas where needed.**

## Semicolons to Avoid Confusion

To make your meaning clear, you may have to substitute a semicolon for a comma.

Use a semicolon instead of a comma in certain situations to avoid possible confusion.

A semicolon is used instead of a comma between the clauses of a compound sentence if there are commas within a clause.

> Military uniforms are often blue**,** gray**,** or black**;** but those are not the only colors used.
> (Normally, a comma comes before a conjunction separating the clauses in a compound sentence.)

Semicolons are also used instead of commas between items in a series if the items themselves contain commas.

> The President's schedule includes stops in London, England**;** Paris, France**;** Florence, Italy**;** Geneva, Switzerland**;** and New Delhi, India.
> (Normally, commas separate the items in a series.)

*You can learn more about using commas on pages L436–L461.*

## Practice Your Skills

### Check Your Understanding
### *Using Semicolons*

History Topic **Write each word that should be followed by a semicolon and then add the semicolon.** You may need to replace a comma or commas with semicolons.

1. Armistice Day is November 11 it is the anniversary of the cease-fire of World War I in 1918, which occurred during the eleventh day of the eleventh month at eleven o'clock.
2. The site of the 1898 Klondike gold rush wasn't Alaska in fact, it was the Yukon Territory of Canada.
3. Pocahontas's real name was said to be Matoak *Pocahontas* was a family name.
4. I want to write my research paper on General Douglas MacArthur, General George S. Patton, or General Robert E. Lee but I can't decide which general interests me the most.
5. Robert E. Lee's personal home was made into Arlington National Cemetery during the Civil War therefore, he never went home again.
6. The French and Indian War was 1754–1763 the American Revolutionary War was 1775–1783.
7. Reenactments of battles of the Civil War (1861–1865) will be performed on Saturday, June 8 Sunday, June 9 and Monday, June 10.
8. Alaska was bought from Russia in 1867 for 2.5 cents per acre however, it was not admitted into the union as a state until 1959.
9. Hawaii also was admitted as a state in 1959 it consists of several islands, has its capital in Honolulu, and is 6,424 square miles.
10. The Great Wall of China is more than just stone and mortar in fact, it has over 10,000 watchtowers, hundreds of passes, a rich historical value, and strong cultural influence.

## Check Your Understanding
### *Using Semicolons and Commas*

Geography Topic **Write each word that should be followed by a semicolon or comma and then add the semicolon or comma.**

**11.** The Sahara covers an area of about 3,500,000 square miles Europe covers about 4,100,000 square miles.

**12.** Florida is not the southernmost state in the United States Hawaii is farther south.

**13.** I have lived in Detroit Michigan Lincoln Nebraska and Ames Iowa.

**14.** Some people call Texas the biggest state in the union on the contrary Alaska is the biggest state.

**15.** Death Valley contains the lowest point in the Western Hemisphere this point is 282 feet below sea level.

**16.** Death Valley is not confined to one state it stretches across parts of Eastern California and Southern Nevada.

**17.** Popular European vacation destinations include Paris, France Rome, Italy and London, England however some tourists visit other destinations such as Brussels, Belgium.

**18.** Unmapped areas of the world include jungles in Papua New Guinea submerged caves in Wakulla Springs, Florida and areas of the Nahanni National Park in Canada.

**19.** The map of the world in other words is not complete.

**20.** The United States contains many parks and natural wonders furthermore you don't need a passport to see them.

**21.** Carlsbad Caverns National Park in New Mexico for example, has one of the world's largest underground chambers and the nation's deepest limestone cave.

**22.** Mauna Loa in Hawaii is one of the world's largest volcanoes it measures 9,842 yards from the seafloor.

**23.** Indonesia and Japan rank first and second as nations with active volcanoes the United States ranks third.

**24.** The giant sequoia is the largest tree on our planet in fact its height often exceeds 300 feet.

Connect to the Writing Process: Editing

### *Using Semicolons and Commas*

**Write the following paragraphs, adding semicolons and commas where needed.**

The Bermuda Triangle is a mysterious, triangle-shaped area of the North Atlantic Ocean it is located off the coast of Florida. Many ships, planes, and people have disappeared without a trace in this triangle in fact some say there is a powerful vortex beneath the water. Despite numerous accounts of disappearances within the Bermuda Triangle, the U.S. Board of Geographic Names does not record "Bermuda Triangle" as an official name moreover it does not maintain an official file on the area.

The Department of the Navy however acknowledges that there is an area of water where unexplained disappearances occur. The Navy maintains a Website at *http://www.history.navy.mil* called the *Bermuda Triangle Fact Sheet*. Follow the link for the "Frequently Asked Questions" page and then the "Bermuda Triangle" page. The FAQ sheet specifies the triangle's three corners as Miami, Florida San Juan, Puerto Rico and the island of Bermuda furthermore the sheet mentions Coast Guard searches for missing people and ships in that area. A group of five U.S. Navy Avenger Torpedo Bombers for example left Ft. Lauderdale, Florida, on a training mission and never returned. The flight lieutenant's compass failed while over the triangle he is reported to have sent a message before the planes disappeared forever. One of the rescue planes searching for the five planes also disappeared.

## Colons

Colons are used with lists, independent clauses, long quotations, and in certain conventional situations.

### Colons with Lists

A colon is used most often to introduce a list of items that will follow in a sentence.

**Use a colon before most lists of items, especially when a list comes after an expression such as *the following.***

When I think of California, I think of the following**:** beaches, sunshine, and surfing.

My favorite beaches are these**:** Huntington Beach, Malibu Beach, and Redondo Beach.

A colon, however, does not follow a verb or a preposition.

| | |
|---|---|
| No Colon | Ocean water **includes** salt, seaweed, and jellyfish. |
| Colon | Ocean water includes the following**:** salt, seaweed, and jellyfish. |
| No Colon | Salt is used **for** making glass, building roads, and tanning leather. |
| Colon | Salt is used in the following processes**:** making glass, building roads, and tanning leather. |

*Remember that commas usually separate items in a series. You can learn more about items in a series on* *pages L436–L441.*

## Colons with Certain Independent Clauses

Use a colon between independent clauses when the second clause explains or restates the first.

We learned why sodas sell so well**:** the United States consumes more soft drinks than any country but Mexico.

We now know why she named her new soft drink Key West Cola**:** she lives in Key West, Florida.

## Colons with Long, Formal Quotations and Formal Statements or Propositions

Use a colon to introduce a long, formal quotation or a formal statement or proposition.

Maimonides, the wise Jewish philosopher who lived from 1135 to 1204, wrote this advice**:** "Do not consider it proof just because it is written in books, for a liar who will deceive with his tongue will not hesitate to do the same with his pen."

The issue before the committee was this**:** It is necessary that more students be recruited to participate in next month's Trivia Scavenger Trek.
(The formal statement begins with a capital letter.)

*You can learn more about long quotations on page L516.*

## Colons with Conventional Situations

Use a colon in certain conventional situations.

| CONVENTIONAL SITUATIONS | |
|---|---|
| **Between Hours and Minutes** | 6**:**30 P.M. |
| **Between Biblical Chapters and Verses** | Psalms 46**:**10 |

| | |
|---|---|
| **Between Periodical Volumes and Pages** | *Futura* 16**:**3–8<br>Scientific American 9.4**:**32–44<br>(In this example, *4* is the issue number; the colon and page numbers follow it.) |
| **After Salutations in Business Letters** | Dear Sir or Madam**:** |
| **Between Titles and Subtitles** | *Star Wars***:** *The Phantom Menace* (movie); "Americans and Weight**:** Not a Trivial Matter" (article); *The Chieftains***:** *Tears of Stone* (recording) |

### Connect to Writer's Craft

More and more employers are giving job applicants the option of submitting cover letters and résumés through E-mail. Most people attach their résumé as a file attachment, but they do write out the cover letter as an E-mail message. These E-mail letters should follow the same rules for punctuating salutations and closings as typed letters; that is, use a colon after your salutation and a comma after your closing.

## Practice Your Skills

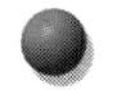

Check Your Understanding

### *Using Colons*

General Interest **Write each word or number that should be followed by a colon and add the colon.**

1. Answer this question How much U.S. trivia do you know?
2. Four women are represented in the U.S. Capitol's Statuary Hall Frances Willard, Maria Sanford, Florence Rena Sabin, and Esther Hobart Morris.
3. The following words are all twentieth-century creations *beautician, highbrow,* and *superhighway.*
4. Theodore Roosevelt stated "The only man who never makes a mistake is the man who never does anything."

5. I had a revelation on my eighteenth birthday I was now old enough to vote.
6. The President's State of the Union address should begin by 7 15 P.M. and be over by 8 30 P.M.
7. Our travel itinerary includes Carlsbad Caverns and the following state capitals Phoenix, Little Rock, and Austin.
8. We learned a valuable lesson Don't travel through the Southwest during the hot summer months.
9. At Bill Clinton's 1997 Presidential Inauguration, his Bible was opened to Isaiah 58 12.
10. John F. Kennedy once said "Ask not what your country can do for you but what you can do for your country."

Connect to the Writing Process: Editing
***Using Colons***

**Write each sentence, adding colons where appropriate. If a sentence is correct, write *C*.**

11. The assignment is this Write a paper about U.S. trivia or culture.
12. I'll expect your finished papers on Friday by 2 00 sharp.
13. You can get help with your research from the librarian, a tutor, or me.
14. Other research paper ideas are these life on an American farm, five American poets, and Native American culture.
15. The principal is making the following announcement Students who submit their research papers for publication in the school newsletter must do so by 2 45 on Wednesday.

## Communicate Your Ideas

### APPLY TO WRITING

**Expository Paragraph: *Semicolons and Colons***

Your history class is creating its own game of American Trivia, and each student must submit one trivia fact and an explanation of the fact. Brainstorm for trivia you know and choose one fact to write about. Write a paragraph explaining the trivia. For example, if your trivia fact is that New York is famous for its pizza, describe why New York pizza is special. Use semicolons and colons to form interesting sentences. Edit your paragraph for correct use of punctuation and then write the final copy. Finally, give your paragraph a title that includes a subtitle.

Mixed Practice

Health Topic **Write the following sentences, adding semicolons, colons, and commas where needed.**

1. The average adult uses 1,300 to 1,600 calories a day a child uses an average of 2,400 calories.
2. The Surgeon General has issued the following warning Smoking by pregnant women may result in fetal injury, premature birth, and low birth weight.
3. Bones are vital to the circulatory system they produce blood cells within their marrow.
4. The brain has these three parts the cerebrum, the cerebellum, and the cerebral cortex.
5. I knew that the heart, liver, and kidneys are organs I did not realize that skin is an organ.
6. The skin is in fact the body's largest organ.
7. The blood bank's plea is this Donate blood today.
8. Babies don't develop the cells necessary to see in color until they are six to eight months old therefore everyone is color-blind at birth.
9. A meal eaten at 6 00 P.M. is in some part of the digestive system until 6 00–9 00 A.M. the following day.
10. The guest speaker gave an impassioned plea "While you're still young, develop the healthy habit of exercising for 20–45 minutes several days a week—it could save your life."

# Italics (Underlining)

As you know, when words are printed in italics, they slant to the right *like this*. When you are using a computer, highlight what you want italicized and then press *Ctrl-I* for italics or look for the command for italics under *Format*. When you write, you can use underlining as a substitute for italics.

| | |
|---|---|
| ITALICS | Have you read *Dubliners* by James Joyce? |
| UNDERLINING | Have you read <u>Dubliners</u> by James Joyce? |

## Italicize (underline) letters, numbers, and words used as words. Also underline foreign words that are not generally used in English.

| | |
|---|---|
| LETTERS, NUMBERS | When you write your compositions, your capital *Q*'s look like *2*s. (Only the *Q* and the *2* are italicized—not the *'s* or *s*.) |
| WORDS, PHRASES | In Shakespeare's time the word <u>gentle</u> meant "noble." |
| | In the same era the phrase <u>for sooth</u> meant "for truth." |
| FOREIGN WORDS | In Hebrew *shalom* means "peace." |

## Italicize (underline) the titles of long written works or musical compositions that are published as a single unit. Also underline the titles of paintings and sculptures and the names of vehicles.

Long works include books, periodicals, newspapers, full-length plays, and very long poems. Long musical compositions include operas, symphonies, ballets, and albums. Vehicles include airplanes, ships, trains, and spacecraft. Titles of movies and radio and TV series should also be italicized (underlined).

| | |
|---|---|
| BOOKS | George Eliot wrote *Silas Marner.*<br>May I use your Dictionary of Symbolism? |
| MAGAZINES | I subscribe to *Poets & Writers.*<br>I also subscribe to Poetry Horizons. |
| NEWSPAPERS | I enjoy the movie reviews in the *Philadelphia Bulletin.*<br><br>Ari reads the comics in the Chicago Tribune. (*The* is generally not considered part of the title of a newspaper or a magazine.) |
| PLAYS AND MOVIES | Henrik Ibsen's plays *Hedda Gabler* and *A Doll's House* were written in the late 1800s.<br><br>The movie named A Doll's House after Ibsen's play stars Jane Fonda. |
| TELEVISION SERIES | The series *Biography* on A&E featured Vincent van Gogh.<br><br>Star Trek: The Next Generation included quotations of Shakespeare and references to his plays. |
| LONG MUSICAL COMPOSITIONS | Wolfgang Amadeus Mozart composed the opera *Don Giovanni* in Italian.<br><br>Mozart composed The Magic Flute in German. |
| WORKS OF ART | *Story Cloth,* embroidered by Yang Fang Nhu, is fiber art.<br><br>Listening is an oil on cardboard by Gabriele Münter. |
| NAMES OF VEHICLES | The *Gudgeon* was the first submarine to circle the earth.<br><br>Charles Lindbergh flew the Spirit of St. Louis. |

*You can learn more about the capitalization of titles on pages L412–L417.*

## Connect to Speaking and Writing

As computers become more common in households, many students are using word processing programs to write compositions. These programs allow you to use italics and other special text formatting that typewriting and handwriting do not offer. Remember, though, that italics *replace* underlining—use one or the other. You would not, for example, write *Romeo and Juliet*. Instead, you'd write *Romeo and Juliet.* Also, be sure to use one method—underlining or italics—consistently throughout your paper; that is, do not write Romeo and Juliet in one paragraph and *Romeo and Juliet* in another paragraph.

## Practice Your Skills

Check Your Understanding

***Using Italics (Underlining)***

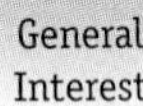

General Interest **Write and underline each letter, word, or group of words that should be italicized.**

1. Often The Learning Channel will air a series called Great Books.
2. Kaddara, an opera produced in 1921, is about Eskimos.
3. Charles Schulz, who created the character Charlie Brown, was once a cartoonist for a well-known magazine, the Saturday Evening Post.
4. The character Snoopy in You're a Good Man Charlie Brown would be a fun part to act.
5. Leonardo da Vinci's painting The Last Supper is considered one of the great art treasures of the world.
6. Why does my English teacher always say I must mind my p's and q's?
7. Biblioteca is Spanish for "library."
8. The name White House was given to the presidential residence by Theodore Roosevelt.
9. The Wall Street Journal offers reports on businesses and the stock market.

**10.** I read a travelogue on the Queen Elizabeth 2 in Travel Magazine.

**11.** Children on the Beach is a painting by American Impressionist Mary Cassatt.

**12.** Do you subscribe to Photomedia Magazine?

**13.** Of all Dickens's books that I have read, I enjoyed Oliver Twist the most.

**14.** The Sunday editions of major newspapers (like the Chicago Tribune) have a section on Life and Arts.

**15.** The term First Lady was not widely used until a comedy about Dolley Madison, called The First Lady in the Land, opened in New York in 1911.

Connect to the Writing Process: Editing

### *Using Italics (Underlining)*

**Write the following paragraph, adding italics (underlining) as needed.**

My goal is to manage a large bookstore that carries books, music, and periodicals. I would devote funds to a magnificent young adult section with plenty of bestsellers like The Giver by Lois Lowry and The Outsiders by S. E. Hinton. I would feature weekly displays of magazines such as Discover and Writer's Digest and carry major newspapers, including USA Today, the Chicago Tribune, and the Miami Herald. The overhead speaker system would play music from the store's music section. Handel's Messiah would be a good choice during the holidays. Posters of colorful, classical art such as A Sunday on La Grande Jatte by Georges Seurat would adorn the walls of the classical music section. The science and technology section would feature books about

Liberty Bell 7 (the second manned spacecraft) and other overlooked spacecraft. A bookstore with this much variety would require me to dot every i and cross every t, but I could do it.

## Communicate Your Ideas

### APPLY TO WRITING

**Descriptive Web Page:** ***Italics (Underlining)***

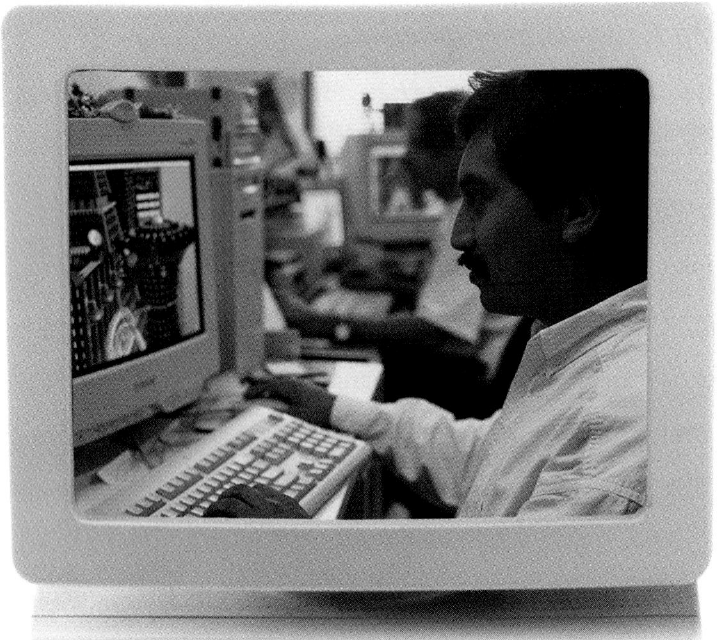

The man in this photograph is an advertising executive who is searching for Websites that will tell him about high school students' interests. Write a descriptive Web page with this man in mind as your audience. Describe your interests in books, magazines, newspapers, plays, movies, television, music, and art. Mention a favorite in each category, using italics (underlining) correctly.

# Quotation Marks and Ellipsis Points

Knowing how to use quotation marks correctly when you write fiction is important because conversations cannot be written without them. Authors often use conversation, or **dialogue**, to reveal important information about the characters and to add realism to fiction.

Quotation marks are also essential in research papers. If you omit or incorrectly use quotation marks in a research paper, you may, unwittingly, be plagiarizing someone else's words. Quotation marks show that the words you are writing are not your own—that they belong to someone else.

One of the most important things to remember about quotation marks is that they come in pairs. They are placed at the beginning and at the end of uninterrupted quotations and certain titles.

## Quotation Marks with Titles

**Use quotation marks to enclose the titles of chapters, articles, stories, one-act plays, short poems, and songs.**

The titles of long works of art and publications are italicized (underlined). These long works, however, are usually composed of smaller parts. A newspaper has articles, for example, and a book can include chapters, short stories, short plays, or poems. When the titles of these smaller parts are written, they should be enclosed in quotation marks.

Quotation marks are also placed around the titles of essays, compositions, episodes from TV series, and movements from long musical compositions.

| | |
|---|---|
| CHAPTERS IN A BOOK | "I Observe" is my favorite chapter in *David Copperfield* by Charles Dickens. |

| | |
|---|---|
| Poems | Yesterday we read Robert Browning's poem "My Star" in our anthology *English Literature.* |
| Articles in Magazines or Newspapers | "Facing the Future" was an informative article in *Time.* |
| | For homework please read "The Life of a Small-Town Writer" in the local newspaper. |
| Television Episodes | Tonight's episode of *The Simpsons* is "Lisa the Iconoclast." |
| Songs | I often listen to "Candle in the Wind" on Elton John's album *Goodbye Yellow Brick Road.* |

## Practice Your Skills

Check Your Understanding

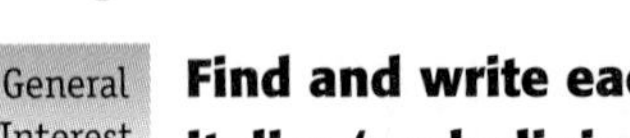

### *Using Quotation Marks with Titles*

General Interest **Find and write each title, adding quotation marks or italics (underlining) where needed.**

**1.** I'm using Automation on the Line, an illustrated article in the Detroit News, in my research paper.

**2.** The drama class presented the one-act play The Happy Journey to Trenton and Camden by Thornton Wilder.

**3.** The band played Yankee Doodle as we marched by.

**4.** You can find the short story The Bear in the book The Works of William Faulkner.

**5.** The Elizabethan Stage was the title of my essay.

**6.** Are we supposed to read Keats's poem To Autumn or Shelley's poem To a Skylark for class tomorrow?

**7.** In film class I learned that As Time Goes By is the famous song in the movie Casablanca.

**8.** In music class we're learning Cloudburst, the last movement from Grofé's Grand Canyon Suite.

**9.** Have you read the chapter The Turning Point in our textbook The History of the World?

**10.** As soon as I passed my driver's test, I read the article Buying a Used Car.

Connect to the Writing Process: Prewriting
***Brainstorming Using Quotation Marks***

**List the titles of all the printed and recorded materials you have read or listened to in the past week.** If you read a poem in an anthology, for example, you would list the anthology's title and the poem's title. Use quotation marks and italics (underlining) correctly.

## Communicate Your Ideas

### APPLY TO WRITING

**Compare and Contrast:** ***Quotation Marks with Titles***

Use the ideas you developed in the preceding exercise to write a comparison-contrast essay. From your list of titles, choose two items to work with—a song and a story, for example. Write an essay that compares and contrasts the two items. For instance, the song and the story may both tell a love story, but in different ways. Be sure to state complete titles and use quotation marks and underlining correctly. Edit the essay and then write the final copy.

Mixed Practice

General Interest **Write each title, adding quotation marks or italics (underlining) where needed.**

**1.** I enjoyed the story The Necklace by Guy de Maupassant.

**2.** It is in Fiction: A Longman Pocket Anthology, just after The Cask of Amontillado by Poe.

3. Have you read Alfred Noyes's tragic poem The Highwayman?
4. Loreena McKennitt set The Highwayman to music on her album The Book of Secrets.
5. The last episode of this TV show was called Graduation.
6. There is an article called Fairy Tale or Marketing Ploy? in Hollywood Weekly; it's about celebrity weddings.
7. I've read up to the chapter A Wedding Night in The Hunchback of Notre Dame.
8. Wasn't Roy Orbison's performance of Oh, Pretty Woman used in the movie Pretty Woman?
9. I read the chapter entitled Elements of the Novel.
10. I found a great article called How to Write a Poem.
11. The poem When the Frost Is on the Pumpkin by James Whitcomb Riley paints a picture of fall in the Midwest.
12. I'll analyze the chapter News from Lake Wobegon Days by Garrison Keillor.
13. Songs from the Princess by Alfred Lord Tennyson is included in the collection Victorian Poetry and Poetics.
14. Michael Crawford sang The Music of the Night in the London production of The Phantom of the Opera.

## Quotation Marks with Direct Quotations

Use quotation marks to enclose a person's exact words.

Quotation marks are placed around a **direct quotation**—the exact words of a person. They are not placed around an **indirect quotation**—a paraphrase of someone's words.

| | |
|---|---|
| Direct Quotation | Bill said, "I'm almost ready." |
| Indirect Quotation | Bill said that he was almost ready. (The word *that* often signals an indirect quotation.) |

A one-sentence direct quotation can be placed before or after a speaker tag, and it can also be interrupted by a speaker tag. In all three cases, quotation marks enclose only the person's exact words. Notice in the third sentence in the following examples that two sets of quotation marks are needed because quotation marks enclose only a person's exact words, not the speaker tag.

| | |
|---|---|
| BEFORE | **"**The game was very suspenseful,**"** he said. |
| AFTER | He said, **"**The game was very suspenseful.**"** |
| INTERRUPTED | **"**The game,**"** he said, **"**was very suspenseful.**"** |

Only one set of quotation marks is needed to enclose any number of quoted sentences—unless they are interrupted by a speaker tag.

> He said, **"**The game was very suspenseful. We were tied in the last inning. Then Will hit a home run.**"**

## PRACTICE YOUR SKILLS

Check Your Understanding

***Using Quotation Marks with Direct Quotations***

Contemporary Life

**Write *I* if quotation marks are used incorrectly. Write *C* if quotation marks are used correctly.**

**1.** "The volleyballs are low on air, Coach Mabry said."

**2.** "I'm not sure," I said, "where the air pump is."

**3.** Someone said "that the pump is in the supply closet."

**4.** The crowd chanted, "Two, four, six, eight! "Whom do we appreciate? The Rockets!

**5.** Did you say that you're going to resign as team captain?

**6.** I certainly did not say that, "Mark protested."

**7.** I replied, "Go ask Tyler. He heard it too."

**8.** "The new gym, our principal promised, will be everything we've hoped for."

**9.** "The builders said that the gym is nearly finished."

**10.** "Do fifty push-ups and no cheating, the coach commanded." "Then run ten laps around the track."

**11.** I can hardly breathe, puffed Taylor.

**12.** Chris added, "I prefer running laps over doing push-ups."

**13.** Raquel asked, "What's next?"

**14.** "I'd like," Suzanne suggested, "to practice my relay.

**15.** "Finish warming up! Coach shouted. You haven't even begun to work!"

Connect to the Writing Process: Editing
***Using Quotation Marks with Direct Quotations***

**16.–25. Rewrite the incorrect sentences from the preceding exercise, using quotation marks correctly. In this exercise place a comma or an end mark that follows a quotation *inside* the closing quotation marks.**

## Capital Letters with Direct Quotations

A capital letter begins a quoted sentence—just as it begins a regular sentence.

Begin each sentence of a direct quotation with a capital letter.

"**H**appiness is a long Saturday with nothing to do," Priscilla said.

**P**riscilla said, "**H**appiness is a long Saturday with nothing to do."
(Two capital letters are needed: one for the first word of the sentence and one for the first word of the quotation.)

"**H**appiness," Priscilla said, "is a long Saturday with nothing to do."
(*Is* does not begin with a capital letter because it is in the middle of the quotation.)

"**H**appiness is a long Saturday with nothing to do," Priscilla said. "**T**hat is the best antidote to stress I can give you."
(*That* is capitalized because it starts a new sentence.)

## Practice Your Skills

Check Your Understanding

*Using Capital Letters with Direct Quotations*

General Interest

**Write *I* if the sentence does not use capital letters and quotation marks correctly. Write *C* if it is correct.**

1. “the happy do not believe in miracles,” Goethe stated.
2. “Happiness is not a state to arrive at, but a manner of traveling,” Commented Margaret Runbeck.
3. “Those who won our independence . . . believed liberty to be the secret of happiness and courage to be the secret of liberty,” declared Justice Louis D. Brandeis.
4. “When one is happy, there is no time to be fatigued. being happy engrosses the whole attention, E. F. Benson said.”
5. Don Marquis mused, “Happiness is the interval between periods of unhappiness.”
6. “When a happy moment, complete and rounded as a pearl, falls into the tossing ocean of life,” Agnes Repplier said, “it is never wholly lost.”
7. Happiness is not being pained in body or troubled in mind, commented Thomas Jefferson.
8. C. P. Snow said, “the pursuit of happiness is a most ridiculous phrase. If you pursue it, you’ll never find it.”
9. William Lyon Phelps mused, “If happiness truly consisted in physical ease and freedom from care, then the happiest individual, I think, Would be an American cow.”
10. “happiness is not a matter of events. it depends upon the tides of the mind,” Alice Meynell once said.

Connect to the Writing Process: Editing

*Using Capital Letters with Direct Quotations*

**11.–17. Write each incorrect sentence from the preceding exercise, adding capital letters and quotation marks where needed. In this exercise place a comma or an end mark that follows a quotation *inside* the closing quotation marks.**

## Commas with Direct Quotations

A comma is used to separate a direct quotation from a speaker tag.

**Use a comma to separate a direct quotation from a speaker tag. Place the comma inside the closing quotation marks.**

Notice in the following examples that when the speaker tag follows the quotation, the comma goes *inside* the closing quotation marks.

> "You should enter the story contest**,**" she said.
> (The comma goes *inside* the closing quotation marks.)
>
> She said**,** "You should enter the story contest."
> (The comma follows the speaker tag.)
>
> "You should**,**" she said**,** "enter the story contest."
> (Two commas are needed to separate the speaker tag from the parts of an interrupted quotation. The first comma goes *inside* the closing quotation marks.)

## Practice Your Skills

### Check Your Understanding
### *Using Commas with Direct Quotations*

Literature Topic

**Write *I* if the sentence uses commas, capital letters, or quotation marks incorrectly. Write *C* if the sentence is correct.**

**1.** Agatha Christie said, "The best time for planning a book is while you're doing the dishes."

**2.** "I see but one rule: to be clear", wrote Stendhal. "If I am not clear, all my world crumbles to nothing."

**3.** Aristotle once said "The greatest thing in style is to have a command of metaphor."

**4.** "A book ought to be an ice pick" wrote Kafka, "to break up the frozen sea within us."

**5.** "Regarding writing," Guy de Maupassant advises "get black on white."

6. Isaac Bashevis Singer commented, “A story to me means a plot where there is some surprise . . . because that is how life is—full of surprises.”
7. “One writes to make a home for oneself,” Says Alfred Kazin, on paper, in time and in others’ minds.”
8. Fitzgerald wrote, “You don’t write because you want to say something; you write because you’ve got something to say.”
9. “When you’re writing, you’re trying to find out something which you don’t know”, James Baldwin commented.
10. Baldwin went on to explain “The whole language of writing for me is finding out what you don’t want to know, what you don’t want to find out. But something forces you to anyway.”

Connect to the Writing Process: Editing
***Punctuating Direct Quotations***

**11.–17. Rewrite the incorrect sentences from the preceding exercise, adding commas, capital letters, and quotation marks where needed.**

## End Marks with Direct Quotations

A period marks the end of a statement or an opinion, and it also marks the end of a quoted statement or opinion.

Place a period inside the closing quotation marks when the end of the quotation comes at the end of the sentence.

He said, “I think I’ll order lasagna**.**”
(The period goes *inside* the closing quotation marks.)

“I think I’ll order lasagna,” he said**.**
(The period follows the speaker tag, and a comma separates the quotation from the speaker tag.)

“I think,” he said, “I’ll order lasagna**.**”
(The period goes *inside* the closing quotation marks.)

If a quotation asks a question or shows strong feeling, the question mark or the exclamation point goes *inside* the closing quotation marks. Notice that the question mark goes *inside* the closing quotation marks in the three examples that follow.

> She asked, "Where did you pick the apples**?**"
> "Where did you pick the apples**?**" she asked.
> "Where," she asked, "did you pick the apples**?**"

The exclamation point also goes *inside* the closing quotation marks in the following three examples.

> He exclaimed, "It is time for dessert**!**"
> "It is time for dessert**!**" he exclaimed.
> "It is," he exclaimed, "time for dessert**!**"

A quotation of two or more sentences can include various end marks.

> "Did you see the cooking exhibit**?**" Laura asked.
> "I accidentally knocked over the wok**!**"

Question marks and exclamation points are placed inside the closing quotation marks when they are part of the quotation. Occasionally a question or an exclamatory statement will include a direct quotation. In such cases the end mark goes *outside* the closing quotation marks. Notice in the following examples that the end marks for the quotations themselves are omitted. Only one end mark is used at the end of a quotation.

> Did Nancy say, "The Chinese food has arrived"**?**
> (The whole sentence—not the quotation—is the question.)
>
> I couldn't believe it when Ben said, "They forgot our eggrolls"**!**
> (The whole sentence—not the quotation—is exclamatory.)

Semicolons and colons go *outside* closing quotation marks.

> My dad specifically said, "No parties while I'm gone"**;** therefore, I'll plan the pizza party for this weekend.
>
> The following are today's "savory selections"**:** baked beans, creamed corn, and mini-sausages.

## Practice Your Skills

### Check Your Understanding
### *Using End Marks and Commas with Direct Quotations*

Contemporary Life

**Write *I* if end marks and commas are used incorrectly. Write *C* if the sentence is correct.**

1. "Where is the saltshaker," Cindy asked.
2. I shouted "Don't touch that—it's hot"
3. "Those fresh tomatoes were delicious," Megan said. "Did you grow them yourself?"
4. Who said "Taste this unusual fruit."
5. "Wow" exclaimed Andie "Are these luscious brownies made from scratch"
6. "First you blend the dry ingredients," explained my mom. "Then you add the milk."
7. I asked "Should we use buttermilk or whole milk"
8. Did I actually hear you say, "I promise to wash all the dishes after dinner"?
9. "Yeast" she said "is what makes the dough rise".
10. He walked through the kitchen shouting "Brownies! Brownies! Who wants a brownie"
11. Do you think we use chocolate chips? asked Megan, I think we use cocoa.
12. I'm sure Mom said, "Use baking powder for your rising agent," so we don't need the yeast.
13. Max called out, "Make some ham and cheese sandwiches, too!"
14. Did Bart say, The Pattersons have arrived?"
15. "Is the food ready? Emily asked, I'm starving?"

### Connect to the Writing Process: Editing
### *Using End Marks and Commas with Direct Quotations*

**16.–25. Rewrite the incorrect sentences from the preceding exercise, using end marks and commas as needed.**

## Communicate Your Ideas

### APPLY TO WRITING

**Interviews: *Direct Quotations***

You are writing an article for the school newspaper, and you need several direct quotations to make the article come alive. Working with a classmate, interview him or her about a topic of your choice. (Possible topics include a student's right to privacy, what to do if your best friend deserts you, and key ingredients to a successful date.) Write down your interviewee's statements exactly, using quotation marks and end marks correctly. Your classmate can then interview you for his or her article.

Working alone now, write a short article that incorporates some of the direct quotations from your interview. Edit for correct use of all punctuation and then write the final copy.

### QuickCheck Mixed Practice

Literature Topic

**Rewrite each sentence, adding capital letters, quotation marks, and other punctuation marks where needed.**

**1.** the applause of a single human being is of great consequence Samuel Johnson said

**2.** the most beautiful adventures explained Robert Louis Stevenson are not those we go to seek

**3.** we need to restore the full meaning of the old word *duty* Pearl Buck remarked it is the other side of *rights*

**4.** Joseph Conrad stated an ideal is often but a flaming vision of reality

**5.** make up your mind to act decisively and take the consequences no good is ever done in this world by hesitation Thomas Huxley warned

6. Janet Erskine Stuart said to aim at the best and to remain essentially ourselves are one and the same thing
7. welcome everything that comes to you André Gide advised but do not long for anything else
8. can anything be sadder than work left unfinished Christina Rossetti asked yes, work never begun
9. did the poet W. B. Yeats say good conversation unrolls itself like the dawn
10. when people talk, listen completely stated Ernest Hemingway most people never listen

## Other Uses of Quotation Marks

In long quotations in reports and in conversations in stories, quotation marks require special applications.

### Unusual Uses of Words

Quotation marks can draw attention to a word that is used in an unusual way.

**Use quotation marks to enclose slang words, technical terms, and other unusual uses of words.**

| | |
|---|---|
| SLANG | "Surfing channels" and "surfing the Net" are slang expressions for watching TV and browsing the Internet. |
| TECHNICAL TERMS | A computer "crash" is a system failure. You will probably need to "reboot" your computer. |
| OTHERS | He plays so many computer games that I call him a "game-oholic." (invented word) |
| | Please don't "help" me anymore. You crashed my system! (irony/sarcasm) |

## Dictionary Definitions

When you write a dictionary definition within a piece of writing, you must include both italics (underlining) and quotation marks.

**When writing a word and its definition in a sentence, italicize (underline) the word but use quotation marks to enclose the definition.**

| | |
|---|---|
| DEFINITIONS OF WORDS | The word *mouse* can mean either "a computer input device" or "a small, furry rodent." |

CONNECT TO WRITER'S CRAFT

Writers often include definitions in their materials to clarify the meaning of words or phrases that might not be familiar to the reader. Technical terms, such as those related to the computer, are evolving at a phenomenal rate, and their definitions might be difficult to find in a standard dictionary.

## Dialogue

When you write **dialogue**—conversation between two or more people—begin a new paragraph each time the speaker changes. A new paragraph clearly indicates who is speaking.

> "Class," said Ms. Spoffard, turning from the board with a smile. "Who would like to help design the official Website for our school?"
>
> "I'll help," said Stephen, who had already designed his own site.
>
> "Excellent!" said Ms. Spoffard. "Who else?"
>
> "I volunteer David," said Alma, smiling brightly. She added, "He already works part time as a Webmaster."

In the preceding example, notice that actions or descriptions of the speakers are sometimes included within the same paragraph in which each one speaks.

If the speaker's sentences form more than one paragraph, begin each paragraph with a quotation mark, but place a closing quotation mark at the end of the last paragraph only.

> Ms. Spoffard said, "Let me begin by telling you what the major sections of the Website will be.
>
> "First, we need an attractive home page, where people can find basic information and links to other pages.
>
> "Next, we need pages on each major aspect of our school, including sports, clubs, social activities, and even the week's cafeteria menu.
>
> "Finally, we need a map of the school."
>
> The students sat silently, taking notes.
>
> "May I design the map?" Jordan asked. "I have a few ideas to share."
>
> "We need a floor plan of the actual structure," continued Ms. Spoffard, "that the viewer could surf through.
>
> "In addition, we need realistic details which will require an observant team."

### Connect to Writer's Craft

Some experimental writers deliberately omit quotation marks from dialogue or place more than one speaker's words in the same paragraph. James Joyce, for example, uses dashes to indicate the beginning of a speaker's words.

> Then he asked:
> —Are you good at riddles?
> Stephen answered:
> —Not very good.
> Then he said:
> —Can you answer me this one? Why is the county of Kildare like the leg of a fellow's breeches?
>
> *—James Joyce,* A Portrait of the Artist as a Young Man

Remember, though, that your writing will be understood more easily when you follow standard rules of punctuation. Always use correct punctuation with formal writing for school and business.

## Long Passages

When you quote five or more typed lines in a research paper, quotation marks are not necessary. Instead, begin on a new line and indent the quoted passage ten spaces along the left margin; the right margin remains even with the rest of the paper. This format is called a "blocked quote." After the blocked quote, begin your next sentence in the paper on a new line. Add text at the original margin width and continue in this format until you wish to add another quote.

> In his book *Editing Your Newsletter,* Mark Beach explains that with illustrations, you can have too much of a good thing:
>
> > Clip art was developed for display ads, not editorial matter. When using clip art in a newsletter, keep your objectives clear. Novice editors tend to use too many illustrations and to place them poorly. Even some experienced designers think readers like lots of drawings scattered at random.
>
> Beach urges newsletter editors to use clip art sparingly.

Another way to quote a long passage is to set it off from the rest of the text by indenting both left and right margins. If you are using a computer, you also could set the passage in a smaller type size. When you use this method of quoting a long passage, no quotation marks are needed.

**CONNECT TO SPEAKING AND WRITING**

As you have learned, there is more than one way to format a long quoted passage. When you write a research paper, therefore, be sure to consult your teacher's guidelines or the style handbook that your class uses to learn what format you should use. Then follow that format consistently.

*You can learn more about using colons with formal quotations and with formal statements and propositions on page L492. You can learn about citing sources on pages L540–L543.*

## Quotations Within Quotations

If a title or a quotation is included within another quotation, a distinction must be made between the two sets of quotation marks. To avoid any confusion, use single quotation marks to enclose a quotation or certain titles within a quotation.

> "Is the chapter 'Graphics and E-mail' a long one?" Li asked.
> Lou said, "I heard him say, 'The answers are on page 101.'"
> Lou asked, "Did he say, 'The answers are on page 101'?"

Notice in the second example above that the closing single quotation mark and the closing double quotation marks come together. The period is inside both of them.

## PRACTICE YOUR SKILLS

Check Your Understanding

***Using Quotation Marks***

Technology Topic

**Write *I* if quotation marks are used incorrectly. Write *C* if the sentence is correct.**

**1.** A "mouse potato' is someone who sits at the computer all day.

**2.** "Faith asked, Did someone say, Reboot all the computers now?"

**3.** You say you're working, but your work looks like personal E-mails.

**4.** A "computer virus" or "computer bug" causes a program to malfunction.

**5.** You probably remember hearing the news hype about the 'millenium bug.'

**6.** The word *click* "means to press a button on the mouse."

**7.** Does netiquette mean etiquette for the Internet?

**8.** The computer lab monitor said, "Print the warning that begins, 'Software piracy will be prosecuted.'"

**9.** A chatroom is a location on the Internet where you exchange written dialogue with other computer users.

10. When your computer is connected to the Internet, you are "on line."
11. "I heard Garrett say, 'The Internet is a technical highway of computerized information."
12. The word *E-mail* means 'electronic mail.'
13. The links on a Web page might include pictures or underlined text on which you would click to jump to another Web page.
14. Jason likes to "surf the net."
15. Have you contacted your "server" about better access to the Internet?

Connect to the Writing Process: Editing
*Using Quotation Marks*

**16.–25. Rewrite each incorrect sentence from the preceding exercise, using quotation marks correctly.**

Connect to the Writing Process: Drafting
*Writing Quotations Using Quotation Marks*

**26.–35. Write ten quotations of statements people have made to you in the past two days. Include at least two quotations within quotations. Use quotation marks where needed.**

## Communicate Your Ideas

### APPLY TO WRITING

**Dialogue:** ***Quotation Marks***

You are writing "A Typical Day in My Senior Year" for your Senior Scrapbook. Write a conversation in which you speak to a friend, teacher, or other acquaintance. (To begin, you may want to use one of the statements from the preceding exercise.) Punctuate and indent the dialogue following the rules you have learned.

Mixed Practice

Literature Topic

**Correctly rewrite the following dialogue between Ebenezer Scrooge and Bob Cratchit. Add punctuation and indentation as needed.**

Hallo growled Scrooge in his accustomed voice as near as he could feign it. What do you mean by coming here at this time of day? I am very sorry, sir said Bob. I am behind my time . . . . Yes. I think you are. Step this way, sir, if you please It's only once a year, sir pleaded Bob, appearing from the tank. It shall not be repeated. I was making rather merry yesterday, sir. Now, I'll tell you what, my friend said Scrooge. I am not going to tolerate this sort of thing any longer. Therefore . . . I am about to raise your salary!

—*Charles Dickens,* A Christmas Carol

## Ellipsis Points

Most often ellipsis points ( . . . ) are used with quotations to show that part of a complete quotation has been dropped.

**Use ellipsis points to indicate any omission in a quoted passage or a pause in a written passage.**

| | |
|---|---|
| QUOTED PASSAGE | "With malice toward none . . . let us strive on to finish the work we are in . . . ." Abraham Lincoln<br>(Notice that part of the quotation is omitted at the end of the statement; the three ellipsis points are followed by a period.) |
| WRITTEN PASSAGE | "Well . . . I don't know who won the election," said the ballot-counter. |

## Practice Your Skills

### Check Your Understanding
*Using Ellipsis Points*

Government Topic

**Write the following paragraphs, omitting the underlined portions and inserting ellipsis points as needed.**

Four score and seven years ago our fathers brought forth on this continent, a new nation, conceived in Liberty, and dedicated to the proposition that all men are created equal.

Now we are engaged in a great civil war, testing whether that nation, or any nation so conceived and so dedicated, can long endure. We are met on a great battle-field of that war. We have come to dedicate a portion of that field, as a final resting place for those who here gave their lives that that nation might live. It is altogether fitting and proper that we should do this.

—*Abraham Lincoln,* "The Gettysburg Address"

### Connect to the Writing Process: Revising
*Using Ellipsis Points*

**Write a shortened version of this paragraph, using ellipsis points to indicate where you omit words.**

The other day, one of the gentlemen from Georgia, an eloquent man, and a man of learning, so far as I can judge, not being learned myself, came down upon us astonishingly. He spoke in what the Baltimore American calls the "scathing and withering style." At the end of his second severe flash I was struck blind, and found myself feeling with my fingers for an assurance of my continued physical existence. A little of the bone was left, and I gradually revived. He eulogized Mr. Clay in high and beautiful terms, and then declared that we had deserted all our principles, and had turned Henry Clay out, like an old horse, to root. This is terribly severe. It cannot be answered by argument; at least, I cannot so answer it. I merely wish to ask the gentleman if the Whigs are the only party he can think of, who sometimes turn old horses out to root. Is not a certain Martin Van Buren an old horse, which your own party have turned out to root? and is he not rooting a little to your discomfort about now?

*–Abraham Lincoln*
(from a speech in the House of Representatives)

## Communicate Your Ideas

### APPLY TO WRITING

**Pauses in Written Dialogue: *Ellipsis Points***

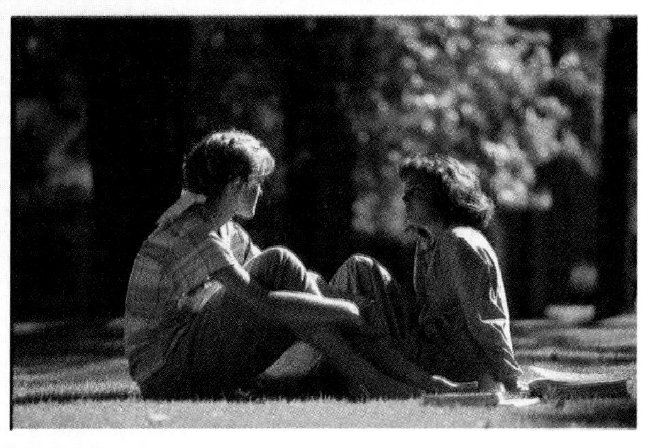

You have a serious issue to discuss with a friend, and you're not sure what to say. For example, the issue might be her unkindness toward you or your deep appreciation of his friendship. Write a "practice dialogue" to this friend; express your thoughts in writing as though you were actually speaking. Use ellipsis points to show where you would pause, either to think or to wait for a response to an idea or question. Check your work carefully for correct usage of ellipsis points, and then write the final copy.

# Other Marks of Punctuation

Hyphens, dashes, parentheses, and brackets are the other marks of punctuation covered in this section.

## Hyphens

A hyphen ( - ) has several uses besides its most common use, dividing a word at the end of a line.

**Hyphens with Divided Words** When you write a research paper or a composition, you should—wherever possible—avoid dividing a word at the end of a line.

Use a hyphen to divide a word at the end of a line.

If you must divide a word, use the following guidelines.

**GUIDELINES FOR DIVIDING WORDS**

1. **Divide words only between syllables.**
   hu-morous or humor-ous
2. **Never divide a one-syllable word.**

| laugh | brought | save | lead |
|---|---|---|---|

3. **Never separate a one-letter syllable from the rest of the word.**

| Do Not Break | a-dore | e-mit | i-ris |
|---|---|---|---|

4. **Hyphenate after two letters at the end of a line, but do not carry a two-letter word ending to the next line.**

| Break | be-lieve | re-call | in-vite |
|---|---|---|---|
| Do Not Break | tight-en | shov-el | over-ly |

5. **Usually divide words containing double consonants between the double consonants.**

| shim-mer | oc-cur | ship-ping | stag-ger |
|---|---|---|---|

6. **Divide hyphenated words only after the hyphens.**
   spur-of-the-moment father-in-law self-confident
7. **Do not divide a proper noun or a proper adjective.**
   Olivero Yonkers Himalayan Polish

*If you do not know how to hyphenate certain words, you can always look in a dictionary to find out where they can be divided between syllables.*

## Practice Your Skills

### Check Your Understanding
### *Using Hyphens to Divide Words*

**Write each word, using a hyphen or hyphens to show where the word can be divided at the end of a line. If a word should not be divided, write *no.***

**1.** educate
**2.** squeeze
**3.** follow
**4.** event
**5.** holiday
**6.** governor
**7.** octave
**8.** permit
**9.** planet
**10.** traitor
**11.** puzzle
**12.** immune
**13.** dress
**14.** Nigerian
**15.** tuition
**16.** decent
**17.** Reggie
**18.** method
**19.** carefully
**20.** respect

### Connect to the Writing Process: Editing
### *Editing for Hyphens that Divide Words*

Some of the following words have been divided incorrectly. Rewrite each word, using a hyphen or hyphens to show where the word can be divided. If a word is correct, write *C*.

**21.** pepp-er
**22.** tab-le
**23.** thre-ad
**24.** bask-etball
**25.** sweat-er
**26.** yes-terday
**27.** Lin-coln
**28.** a-void
**29.** envelo-pe
**30.** mer-ry-go-round
**31.** tele-vision
**32.** John-son
**33.** ampli-fier
**34.** tab-let
**35.** ba-tter

**Hyphens with Certain Numbers** Hyphens are needed when you write out certain numbers.

**Use a hyphen when writing out the numbers *twenty-one* through *ninety-nine*.**

> Seventy-four new math textbooks were shipped to us today.
> Since we ordered eighty-nine, we are missing fifteen.

**Hyphens with Some Compound Nouns and Adjectives** Some compound nouns and adjectives need one or more hyphens.

**Use one or more hyphens to separate the parts of some compound nouns and adjectives. Also use one or more hyphens between words that make up a compound adjective located before a noun.**

| HYPHENATED COMPOUND WORDS | |
|---|---|
| COMPOUND NOUNS | sister-in-law, flare-up, secretary-general |
| COMPOUND ADJECTIVES | skin-deep, long-term, run-of-the-mill |

A hyphen is used only when a compound adjective comes before a noun—not when it follows a linking verb and comes after the noun it describes.

| | |
|---|---|
| ADJECTIVE BEFORE A NOUN | This is a well-written paper on Pythagoras. |
| ADJECTIVE AFTER A NOUN | This paper on Pythagoras is well written. |

A hyphen is used only when a fraction is used as an adjective—not when it is used as a noun.

| | |
|---|---|
| FRACTION USED AS AN ADJECTIVE | A **one-fourth** minority of the students knows Pythagoras's theorem. |
| FRACTION USED AS A NOUN | **Three fourths** of the students had never heard of Pythagoras. |

Never use a hyphen between an adjective and an adverb ending in *–ly*.

That **fairly difficult** geometry test yielded no low scores. (no hyphen)

### Hyphens with Certain Prefixes

Several prefixes and one suffix are always separated from their root words by a hyphen.

Use a hyphen after the prefixes *ex-*, *self-*, and *all-* and before the suffix *-elect.*

A hyphen is used with all prefixes before most proper nouns or proper adjectives.

| HYPHENS WITH PREFIXES AND SUFFIXES | | | |
|---|---|---|---|
| ex-champion | self-control | all-around | mayor-elect |
| mid-Atlantic | pre-Columbian | pro-American | |

## PRACTICE YOUR SKILLS

Check Your Understanding

***Using Hyphens***

General Interest **Correctly write each word that should be hyphenated. If no word in the sentence needs a hyphen, write *C.***

**1.** Is Maya Nenno the write in candidate for class president?

**2.** The ex mayor of Morrisville teaches trigonometry at the University of Nebraska.

**3.** I still must work twenty five more equations.

**4.** Fifty six bushels of corn were picked today.

**5.** Have you heard of this mathematician from the mid Victorian era?

**6.** The metal used in the sculpture is one fourth copper.

**7.** This report includes up to date statistics.

**8.** Jamie is self confident about lecturing in math class.

9. These terrifyingly written word problems are difficult to answer!
10. I request your all out effort in helping me find biographies of famous mathematicians.

Connect to the Writing Process: Editing
*Using Hyphens*

**Some of the hyphens in these sentences are used incorrectly; others are missing. Correctly write each word that should be hyphenated. If a sentence is correct, write *C*.**

11. Thirty nine seniors are enrolled in honors math.
12. A three-fourths majority voted to host a free math clinic for the nearby junior high.
13. We expect only one-half of those who signed up actually to attend the clinic.
14. The student assistants at the math clinic must be self motivated-workers.
15. The day's program is all encompassing, including beginning and advanced skills.
16. This all encompassing format should meet the needs of every student.
17. We expect the entire day's worth of sessions to be an all around success.
18. In addition, we know that approximately two thirds of these students who participate will enter our high school next year.
19. These freshmen to be will already have a head start in math skills covered in our clinic.
20. We want our schools—all of them—to be seen as math-friendly environments.

**Hyphens to Avoid Confusion** Without a hyphen, some words would be difficult to read.

Use a hyphen to prevent confusion or awkwardness.

re-edit, anti-irritant, re-elect
(prevents awkwardness of two identical vowels)

co-operator
(prevents confusion with the word *cooperator*)

re-sign the contract
(prevents confusion with the word *resign*)

## Practice Your Skills

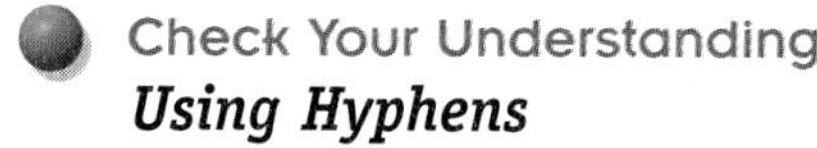

Check Your Understanding
***Using Hyphens***

Contemporary Life **Correctly write each word that should be hyphenated. If a sentence is correct, write C.**

1. I would like to reexamine those photographs.
2. At least one half of these photographs are of historical buildings in town.
3. Many of the buildings are of pre World War II construction.
4. We should repetition the town hall to hang these photos in the lobby.
5. A three fourths portion of the wall space is now covered in tattered travel posters.
6. These quality photographs would create a much improved look.
7. If the photo display is long term, perhaps it will attract customers to your gallery.
8. After all, the run of the mill citizen goes inside the town hall only occasionally.
9. The photos should be displayed long enough to be seen by at least one half of the townspeople.
10. Twenty to twenty five photographs should be sufficient for the display.

## Dashes, Parentheses, and Brackets

A dash (—) or (--), parentheses **( )**, and brackets **[ ]** are used to separate certain words or phrases from the rest of a sentence. Do not overuse these marks of punctuation and do not substitute them for other marks of punctuation such as commas or colons.

### Dashes

Like a comma, a dash is used to separate words or expressions. A **dash**, however, indicates a greater separation than a comma does. Dashes should be used in the following situations.

**Use dashes to set off an abrupt change in thought.**

Several students—there were five—applied for the job.
I've misplaced the book—oh, I see you have it.

Use dashes to set off an appositive that is introduced by words such as *that is, for example,* or *for instance.*

If an item is lost—for example, a book or a tape—pay the fee.

Sam's job—that is, assistant librarian—is interesting.

**Use dashes to set off a parenthetical expression or an appositive that includes commas. Also use dashes to call special attention to a phrase.**

Let's find a novel—mystery or historical—for you.
You can return the novel to me Monday or Wednesday—or Friday, for that matter—right after school.

**Use dashes to set off a phrase or a clause that summarizes or emphasizes what has preceded it.**

June 6, 7, and 8—these are the dates of the book auction.
A book and a T-shirt—I received these gifts for my birthday.

CONNECT TO SPEAKING AND WRITING

When you write a dash, remember that it is twice as long as a hyphen. If you are using a typewriter, use two hyphens to make a dash. If you are using a computer, you can use the special symbols menu to insert a dash (—), or you can type two hyphens to make a dash (--). Some word processing programs will automatically convert two hyphens into one dash.

## Parentheses

**Parentheses** separate from the rest of the sentence additional information that is not necessary to the meaning of the sentence. Definitions and dates, for example, are sometimes enclosed by parentheses. When using parentheses, remember to use pairs.

**Use parentheses to enclose information that is not related closely to the meaning in a sentence.**

To decide whether you should use parentheses, read the sentence without the parenthetical material. If the meaning and structure of the sentence are not changed, then add parentheses. Keep in mind that parenthetical additions to sentences slow readers down and interrupt their train of thought. As a result, you should always limit the amount of parenthetical material that you add to any one piece of writing.

Dylan Thomas **(**1914–1953**)** read his own poetry brilliantly.

Samuel Clemens did not invent the name Mark Twain **(**which means "a depth of 2 fathoms, or 12 feet"**)**.

**Use parentheses to identify a source of information such as a reference to an author or a page number.**

"Arthur Conan Doyle realized he could make more money writing mystery stories than practicing ophthalmology" **(**Garrett 22**)**.

When the closing parentheses come at the end of a sentence, the end mark usually goes outside of the parentheses. However, occasionally the end mark goes inside the parentheses if the end mark actually belongs with the parenthetical material.

> Many people enjoy Doyle's mystery stories. **(**I'm not one of them, though.**)**

## Brackets

When you write a research paper that includes quoted passages, you may need to use brackets.

**Use brackets to enclose an explanation within quoted material that is not part of the quotation.**

> Richard Ellman wrote, "He **[**W. B. Yeats**]** displayed and interpreted the direction in which poetry was to go."

The following summary may help you decide when to use certain kinds of punctuation.

**PUNCTUATING PARENTHETICAL INFORMATION**

Parenthetical (nonessential) information is always set off from the rest of the sentence by special punctuation. Depending on how important the parenthetical material is, use one of the following marks of punctuation.

- Use commas to enclose information that is loosely related to the rest of the sentence yet is nonessential. This method is the most common.
- Use parentheses to enclose information that is not essential to the meaning of the sentence but that adds an interesting point.
- Use dashes to signal a break in the train of thought.
- Use brackets to enclose your own words inserted into a quotation.

## Practice Your Skills

### Check Your Understanding
***Using Dashes, Parentheses, and Brackets***

Literature Topic

**Write *I* if the sentence is punctuated incorrectly. Write *C* if it is punctuated correctly.**

**1.** The Victorian poet, Alfred Lord Tennyson, 1809–1892 wrote *In Memoriam* over a period of seventeen years.

**2.** "Mariana," "Ulysses," and "Maud" all these are poems by Tennyson.

**3.** A number of Victorian authors—for example, Charles Dickens, Wilkie Collins, and Arthur Conan Doyle—wrote mystery stories.

**4.** At Dickens's death he died in 1870 his novel *The Mystery of Edwin Drood* was unfinished.

**5.** One of the most interesting characters was what was her name? Her Royal Highness the Princess Puffer.

**6.** Conan Doyle had interesting friends—for instance, the magician Harry Houdini.

**7.** Houdini [then known as "Ehrich, The Prince of the Air"] began his career in show business as a trapeze artist and contortionist.

**8.** "A Scandal in Bohemia" begins, "To Sherlock Holmes, she (Irene Adler) is always *the* woman."

**9.** I cannot—I repeat, cannot—find my copy of *The Moonstone* by Wilkie Collins.

**10.** Collins's *The Woman in White* was an instant sensation —published in 1860—that inspired a perfume and a dance.

### Connect to the Writing Process: Editing
***Using Dashes, Parentheses, and Brackets***

**11.–18. Rewrite the incorrect sentences from the preceding exercise, using commas, dashes, parentheses, and brackets correctly.**

## Communicate Your Ideas

### APPLY TO WRITING

**Narratives: *All Punctuation***

To help you make plans for the future, your school counselor has asked you to write a scene showing what you would like to be doing twenty years from now. Write freely, exploring ideas for action and dialogue. Then create a scene that places you twenty years in the future. Limit your narrative to a single location and add only one or two other characters. Include realistic dialogue to help the characterization come alive and use appropriate marks to set off parenthetical information. As you edit your narrative, check for the correct use of all punctuation.

Mixed Practice

General Interest **Write the following sentences, inserting hyphens, parentheses, dashes, and brackets as needed.**

**1.** Running, swimming, and riding these are good forms of exercise.

**2.** Because Mr. Pearson values sports, I think we should reelect him to the school board.

**3.** I think you are how shall I say it too short to be good at basketball.

**4.** The dates for some of this year's competitions football, tennis, and track have already been set.

**5.** Who was it that said, "He Tom Landry was the greatest football coach of all time"?

**6.** Let me tell you something and this is just between you and me.

**7.** I already know who the head coach to be is.

**8.** We need to add forty eight chairs that's four dozen.

9. Sasha she's our head cheerleader broke her leg.

10. A number of cheerleaders for instance, Terry, Holly, and Keisha have already asked to take Sasha's place.

Mixed Practice

Language Topic **Write the following paragraphs, adding any punctuation marks and capital letters that are needed.**

There arent any hard and fast statistics nevertheless the expression OK is probably the most widely used American expression in the world. For example, during World War II, there was a special international soccer match. One team was composed of members from the following four countries Poland, Czechoslovakia, Denmark, and Norway. The team had serious difficulties because of the language differences. Finally one of Polands players shouted, OK! Feeling confident that everyone finally understood the same thing, the team members went on to win the game.

Despite its international acceptance, the expression OK is really an all American expression. It first appeared in print in 1839 in a Boston newspaper, the Morning Post. A year later President Martin Van Buren he was born in Kinderhook, New York ran for a second term of office. He was called Old Kinderhook by his backers. The initials of his nickname were then used during the campaign. Later OK came into wide use as a catchword meaning all is right.

CheckPoint

## Using Correct Punctuation

**Write each sentence, adding punctuation where needed.**

1. The conservation department puts rainbow trout into the streams the lakes are stocked with salmon, herring, pickerel, and perch.
2. The prop committee still hasnt found the following items a straw hat, a wicker chair, and a large desk.
3. Everyones enthusiasm at the pep rally encouraged the players on Newtons all star team.
4. In the code the 2s stood for es.
5. The Eighteenth Amendment the prohibition amendment was not ratified by Connecticut and Rhode Island.
6. Most insects have no eyelids thus, their eyes are always open.
7. Six, forty, and ten these are the three correct answers.
8. Its time to apply for the dogs new license.
9. We have our choice of pink, aqua, or lavender unfortunately, we dont know which color would be best for the room.
10. A tree snake appears to fly through the air however it merely glides on air currents.
11. We couldnt possibly be at your house by 7 30.
12. Shiny metals for example, tin and copper turn into black powders when finely ground aluminum is an exception.
13. Gregor Mendel 1822–1884 was the Austrian botanist who developed the basic laws of heredity.
14. Bobs and Teds scores in their last bowling game were the best theyve ever had.
15. Only two copies of the works of the Greek sculptor Myron have survived one of those is the sculpture Discus Thrower.

## Punctuating Direct Quotations

**Write each sentence correctly, adding end marks, commas, and quotations marks where needed.**

1. Ogden Nash mused, I marvel that such small ribs as these can cage such vast desire to please
2. A dog's ideal is a life of active uselessness stated William Phelps
3. If dogs could talk Karel Capek said perhaps we would find it as hard to get along with them as we do with people.
4. A dog is a lion on his own street states a Hindu proverb
5. When did a dog ever turn up his nose at a smell asked C. E. Montague
6. I have always thought of a dog lover quipped James Thurber as a dog that was in love with another dog
7. Bertrand Wilberforce said Dogs are evidently intended to be our companions, protectors, and in many ways, our examples
8. Alexander Pope once said Histories are more full of examples of the fidelity of dogs than of friends
9. Money will buy a pretty dog, but it won't buy the wag of its tail commented Josh Billings
10. Outside of a dog, a man's best friend is a book inside of a dog, it is very dark cracked Groucho Marx

## Writing Sentences

**Write five sentences that follow the directions below.**

**Write a sentence that . . .**

1. includes the possessive form of the nouns *cousins* and *six months*.
2. includes the joint ownership of something.
3. includes a series of dates, including month, day, and year.
4. includes a colon at the beginning of a list.
5. includes a dash or pair of dashes.

# Language and *Self-Expression*

René Magritte once said, "The mind loves the unknown. It loves images whose meaning is unknown, since the meaning of the mind itself is unknown." How does Magritte use this idea in *The Mysteries of the Horizon*?

Does the painting remind you of mysterious mental images of your own? Can you imagine images like these coming to you in your sleep? If you painted the images from one of your dreams, would you use artistic elements in the way Magritte has? Why or why not? Write an essay answering these questions.

**Prewriting** Freewrite for ten minutes, answering the above questions. Don't worry about grammar, punctuation, or spelling at this point; rather, focus on getting as many ideas as you can onto paper.

**Drafting** Use your freewriting to create a first draft, perhaps devoting a separate paragraph to each question. The topic sentence for each paragraph could be a one-sentence answer to the question, and the body of the paragraph could explain in more detail.

**Revising** Make sure your paragraphs include specific references to artistic elements such as line, color, shape, and value. These descriptions will help your reader envision your ideas.

**Editing** Check your paper for errors in spelling and capitalization. Be sure you have used punctuation such as italics, apostrophes, and semicolons correctly.

**Publishing** Write a final copy for your English teacher. You could also use a copy of your paper to begin your own "dream journal," complete with descriptions and sketches.

# Another Look

## Using Apostrophes

Add *'s* to form the possessive of a singular noun. *(page L471)*

Add only an apostrophe to form the possessive of a plural noun that ends in *s*. *(page L472)*

Add *'s* to form the possessive of a plural noun that does not end in *s*. *(page L472)*

Add *'s* to only the last word to show joint ownership. *(page L476)*

Add *'s* to each word to show separate ownership. *(page L476)*

## Using Semicolons and Colons

Use a semicolon between the clauses of a compound sentence when they are not joined by a conjunction. *(page L484)*

Use a semicolon between the clauses in a compound sentence when they are joined by certain transitional words. *(pages L485–L486)*

Use a colon before most lists of items. *(page L491)*

Use a colon between independent clauses when the second clause explains or restates the first. *(page L492)*

## Italics (Underlining), Quotation Marks and Ellipsis Points

Italicize letters, numbers, and words used as words. *(page L496)*

Italicize certain titles. *(pages L496–L497)*

Use quotation marks to enclose certain titles. *(pages L501–L502)*

Use quotation marks to enclose a person's exact words. *(pages L504–L505)*

Use ellipsis points to indicate any omission in a quoted passage or a pause in a written passage. *(page L519)*

## Using Other Marks of Punctuation

Use a hyphen to divide a word at the end of a line. *(pages L522–L523)*

Use a hyphen when writing out certain numbers. *(page L524)*

Use dashes to set off an abrupt change in thought. *(page L528)*

Use parentheses to enclose information that is not related closely to the meaning in a sentence. *(page L529)*

### *Directions*

**Each underlined part in the passage may lack one type of punctuation. Write the letter of the answer with the punctuation that correctly completes the underlined part. If the underlined part contains no error, write *D*.**

EXAMPLE René Magritte the artist we studied in class yesterday was a master of Surrealist painting.
**(1)**

**1** **A** Italics
**B** Quotation marks
**C** Dashes
**D** No error

ANSWER **1** **C**

René Magritte 1898–1967 was **(1)** a Belgian artist who established a reputation as a talented artist in the Surrealist style. Horror, comedy, and mystery these are some **(2)** of the moods he created in his paintings. If you study a number of his paintings, you'll notice certain symbols are repeated throughout many of them the female **(3)** torso, the bowler hat, the castle, and others. Although Magrittes work is famous today **(4)**, he had to work earnestly for his success. His humble beginnings included nonglamorous jobs such as designing wallpaper **(5)** and sketching advertisements.

**1** **A** Parentheses
**B** Quotation marks
**C** Italics
**D** No error

**2** **A** Italics
**B** Parentheses
**C** Dash
**D** No error

**3** **A** Hyphen
**B** Semicolon
**C** Colon
**D** No error

**4** **A** Semicolon
**B** Dash
**C** Apostrophe
**D** No error

**5** **A** Semicolon
**B** Colon
**C** Dash
**D** No error

# A Writer's Guide to Citing Sources

Whenever you write a research paper, you need to know how to use citations. **Citations** in a research paper direct readers to the original sources of borrowed words or ideas. The following guidelines will help you determine when to cite a source of information.

**CITING SOURCES**

- Cite the source of a direct quotation. Use direct quotations only when the author's wording makes the point better than you could in your own words.
- Cite the source of any paraphrased fact or idea that your readers might otherwise assume is your own.
- Do not cite facts or ideas that are considered to be common knowledge.

You can document your sources using parenthetical citations, footnotes, or endnotes. **Parenthetical citations** briefly identify the source in parentheses. **Footnotes** are numbered notes at the bottom, or foot, of a page. The numbers correspond to numbers that appear in the text immediately after borrowed material. **Endnotes** are also notes that correspond to numbers in the text; however, endnotes appear on a separate page at the end of the paper.

The style of citation is often determined by your subject matter. Standards are set by professional organizations, such as the Modern Language Association (MLA) in the language arts or the American Psychological Association (APA) in the social sciences. Scholars of history and the humanities often refer to *The Chicago Manual of Style* (CMS) for guidelines. These styles of citation vary slightly.

For most literary research papers, you will use the MLA style of parenthetical citations. The examples on the following page should help you use parenthetical citations.

| | |
|---|---|
| Books with a Single Author | Give author's last name and a page reference: (Nostbakken 66). |
| Books with Two or More Authors | Give all authors' last names and a page reference: (Fujita and Pronko 220). |
| Article with Author Named | Give author's last name and a page reference: (Alleva 17).<br>Omit the page reference if the article is a single page: (Greenlaw). |
| Article with Author Unnamed | Give a shortened form of the title (unless full title is already short) and a page reference: ("Seminarian" 36–37).<br>Omit the page reference if the article is a single page: ("Playful"). |
| Article in a Reference Work; Author Unnamed | Give title (full or shortened). No page reference is necessary if the article is a single page from an encyclopedia arranged alphabetically: ("Sonnet"). |
| Author Named in Text | Give only the page reference from the text being cited: (56). |

If you are citing a different page from the work you have most recently cited in the paragraph, you do not need to include the author's name (or the title) again. List only a page reference.

You should keep parenthetical citations close to the words or ideas being credited without interrupting the flow of the sentence. Place them at the end of a phrase, clause, or sentence. Refer to the following guidelines for help in placing a citation.

**PLACEMENT OF PARENTHETICAL CITATIONS**

- If the citation falls next to a comma or end punctuation, place the citation before the punctuation mark.
- If the citation accompanies a long quotation (three or more lines) that is indented and single-spaced, place the citation after the end punctuation.
- If the citation falls next to a closing quotation mark, place it after the quotation mark but before the end punctuation.

The CMS cites sources with footnotes or endnotes. For either type of note, you mark any borrowed material with a number raised halfway above the line of a text—a **superscript**. The number refers the reader to citation information with the same number located either at the foot of the page, a footnote, or at the end of the paper but before the works cited page, an endnote. The following examples will help you write footnotes or endnotes.

| | |
|---|---|
| BOOKS WITH A SINGLE AUTHOR | [1] Faith Nostbakken, Understanding Macbeth: A Student Casebook to Issues, Sources, and Historical Documents (Westport: Greenwood Press, 1997) 99. |
| BOOKS WITH MORE THAN ONE AUTHOR | [2] Minoru Fujita and Leonard Pronko, eds., Shakespeare East and West (New York: St. Martin's Press, 1996) 220. |
| GENERAL REFERENCE WORKS | [3] Paul A. Jorgensen, "Macbeth," Encyclopedia Americana, 1999 ed.<br>[4] "Sonnet," World Book Encyclopedia, 1998 ed. |
| ARTICLES IN MAGAZINES | [5] Lavinia Greenlaw, "Shakespeare in Love: The Love Poetry of William Shakespeare," New Statesman 7 June 1999: 56. |
| ARTICLES IN NEWSPAPERS | [6] Eileen Blumenthal, "That Power-Mad Couple Seems So Familiar," New York Times, 1 Mar. 1998, sec. 2: 5. |
| INTERVIEWS | [7] Stephanie Smith, telephone interview, 25 Sept. 1999. |

Use an abbreviated footnote for a work you have already cited by including the author's last name (or the title if there is no author) and the page reference. If you have cited more than one work by the same author, also include the title (full or shortened).

| | |
|---|---|
| REPEATED REFERENCES | [1] Nostbakken 3.<br>[2] Blumenthal, "That Power-Mad Couple," 5. |

A **works-cited page** is a complete listing of all the sources you have cited in a research paper. You should compile a works-cited page in addition to whatever parenthetical citations, footnotes, or endnotes appear in your paper. The works-cited page is alphabetized by the author's last name or by title (if no author is given). It should appear on a separate page at the end of the paper.

Refer to the following examples for help formatting a works-cited page, but note the differences in formatting between a works-cited page and footnotes and endnotes.

| | |
|---|---|
| General Reference Works | Jorgensen, Paul A. "Macbeth." Encyclopedia Americana. 1999 ed.<br>"Sonnet." World Book Encyclopedia. 1998 ed. |
| Books with a Single Author | Nostbakken, Faith. Understanding Macbeth: A Student Casebook to Issues, Sources, and Historical Documents. Westport: Greenwood Press, 1997. |
| Books with More Than One Author | Fujita, Minoru, and Leonard Pronko. Shakespeare East and West. New York: St. Martin's Press, 1996. |
| Articles in Magazines | Greenlaw, Lavinia. "Shakespeare in Love: The Love Poetry of William Shakespeare." New Statesman 7 June 1999: 56. |
| Articles in Newspapers | Blumenthal, Eileen. "That Power-Mad Couple Seems So Familiar." New York Times. 1 Mar. 1998, sec. 2: 5. |
| Interviews | Smith, Stephanie. Telephone interview. 25 Sept. 1999. |
| CD-ROM | Discovering Shakespeare. CD-ROM. Dedham: Bride Media International, Inc., 1998. |
| Article from an Online Database with a Print Version | Siemens, R.G. "Disparate Structures, Electronic and Otherwise: Conceptions of Textual Organisation [sic] in the Electronic Medium, with Reference to Electronic Editions of Shakespeare and the Internet." Early Modern Literary Studies Jan. 1998: 29 pars. 20 Sept. 1999 <http://www.shu.ac.uk/emls/03-3/siemshak.html>. |
| Online Material with No Print Version | The Complete Works of William Shakespeare. Ed. Jeremy Hilton. 20 Sept. 1999 <http://www-tech.mit.edu/Shakespeare/works.html>. |

CHAPTER 12

# Spelling Correctly

### Directions

**Read the passage. Write the letter of the answer that correctly respells each underlined word. If the word is correct, write *D*.**

EXAMPLE British poetry is part of our curiculum. **(1)**

**1** **A** curicculum
**B** corriculum
**C** curriculum
**D** No error

ANSWER **1 C**

We recentally **(1)** read a poem by John Keats called "Ode to a Nightingale." This melencholy **(2)** poem expresses the poet's emoteons **(3)** as he listens to the bird's song. He remarks that the bird is imortal **(4)** and that the same song he hears was heard by ancient emporers **(5)**. The poet speaks of the numbness **(6)** he feels at the tyrany **(7)** of time. His heartache contrasts with the happyness **(8)** of the bird's melody. He speaks of flying to the bird on the invisable **(9)** wings of poetry. In dispair **(10)**, he wonders whether he is awake or dreaming.

1 **A** recently
**B** recenttly
**C** reccently
**D** No error

2 **A** melancoly
**B** melancholy
**C** melancholly
**D** No error

3 **A** emoteions
**B** emotions
**C** emottions
**D** No error

4 **A** imortle
**B** inmortal
**C** immortal
**D** No error

5 **A** emperors
**B** empirers
**C** emporrers
**D** No error

6 **A** numness
**B** nummness
**C** numbeness
**D** No error

7 **A** tirrany
**B** tiranny
**C** tyranny
**D** No error

8 **A** happiness
**B** hapiness
**C** happynes
**D** No error

9 **A** invizable
**B** invissable
**C** invisible
**D** No error

10 **A** despair
**B** dispare
**C** despare
**D** No error

# Strategies for Learning to Spell

Learning to spell involves a variety of senses. You use your senses of hearing, sight, and touch to spell a word correctly. Here is a five-step strategy that many people have used successfully as they learned to spell unfamiliar words.

### 1 Auditory

**Say the word aloud. Answer these questions.**

- Where have I heard or read this word before?
- What was the context in which I heard or read the word?

### 2 Visual

**Look at the word. Answer these questions.**

- Does this word divide into parts? Is it a compound word? Does it have a prefix or a suffix?
- Does this word look like any other word I know? Could it be part of a word family I would recognize?

### 3 Auditory

**Spell the word to yourself. Answer these questions.**

- How is each sound spelled?
- Are there any surprises? Does the word follow spelling rules I know, or does it break the rules?

### 4 Visual/Kinesthetic

**Write the word as you look at it. Answer these questions.**

- Have I written the word clearly?
- Are my letters formed correctly?

### 5 Visual/Kinesthetic

**Cover up the word. Visualize it. Write it. Answer this question.**

- Did I write the word correctly?

**If the answer is no, return to step 1.**

# Spelling Strategies

Being a good speller is an ongoing process. As you read and build your vocabulary, you also increase the number of words whose spellings you will want to master. The strategies in this chapter will help you spell new words as well as familiar words.

STRATEGY **Use a dictionary.** If you're not sure how to spell a word, or if a word you've written doesn't "look right," check the word in a dictionary. If you don't want to stop and check a word while you are writing, that is okay. Instead, circle the word and look it up when you finish.

STRATEGY **Proofread your writing carefully.** Read your paper one word at a time, looking only for spelling errors. Also, watch for words you're not sure you spelled correctly. If you are working on a computer, you can use the spell checker.

Check Your Understanding

*Recognizing Misspelled Words*

**Identify the misspelled word in each set. Then write the word correctly.**

| | (a) | (b) | (c) |
|---|---|---|---|
| **1.** | occurrence | neice | stretch |
| **2.** | fiery | drought | arial |
| **3.** | condemn | weight | interupt |
| **4.** | courtesy | milage | regrettable |
| **5.** | assistence | biscuit | carriage |
| **6.** | immigrant | fasinate | pitiful |
| **7.** | business | bargain | campain |
| **8.** | ilustrate | seize | reference |
| **9.** | chord | luxury | napsack |
| **10.** | analyze | ordinery | cooperate |

**STRATEGY** **Be sure you are pronouncing words correctly.** "Swallowing" syllables or adding extra syllables can cause you to misspell a word.

## PRACTICE YOUR SKILLS

### Check Your Understanding
***Pronouncing Words***

Oral Expression **Practice saying each syllable in the following words to help you spell the words correctly.**

1. am•big•u•ous
2. si•mul•ta•ne•ous
3. phe•nom•e•non
4. ca•tas•tro•phe
5. bank•rupt•cy
6. li•ai•son
7. a•non•y•mous
8. fo•li•age
9. pop•u•lar•i•ty
10. sim•i•le

**STRATEGY** **Make up mnemonic devices.** A sentence like "**Ants** have many descend**ants**" can help you remember that *descendant* ends with *ant*. "There are a pair 'a' **ll**'s in **parallel"** can help you remember where the double *l*'s belong in *parallel.*

**STRATEGY** **Keep a spelling journal.** Use it to record the words that you've had trouble spelling. Here are some suggestions for organizing your spelling journal.

- Write the word correctly.
- Write the word again, underlining or circling the part of the word that gave you trouble.
- Write a tip that will help you remember how to spell the word in the future.

| | | |
|---|---|---|
| *colossal* | *co<u>loss</u>al* | *Colossal has two <u>o</u>'s, two <u>l</u>'s, and two <u>s</u>'s, but only the <u>s</u>'s are side by side.* |

# Spelling Generalizations

Spelling generalizations are rules that apply to many different words. Knowing a few spelling generalizations can help you spell many different words correctly. The information that follows can help you decide when to use certain letter patterns, how to form plurals, and how to add prefixes and suffixes.

## Spelling Patterns

Probably the most well-known spelling generalization is the "*i* before *e,* except after *c*" pattern. Another familiar generalization covers spelling the "seed" sound at the end of words.

### Words with *ie* and *ei*

When the vowel sound is long *e,* write *ei* after *c* and *ie* after other consonant letters.

| ***IE* AND *EI*** | | | | |
|---|---|---|---|---|
| **Examples** | **cei**ling | re**cei**ve | de**cei**ve | de**cei**t |
| | f**ie**ld | ch**ie**f | bel**ie**ve | ach**ie**ve |
| **Exceptions** | s**ei**ze | **ei**ther | n**ei**ther | l**ei**sure |
| | w**ei**rd | prot**ei**n | | |

When the sound is long *a* or any vowel sound other than long *e,* write *ei.*

| **VOWEL SOUNDS OTHER THAN LONG *E*** | | | | |
|---|---|---|---|---|
| **Examples** | w**ei**gh | n**ei**ghbor | fr**ei**ght | r**ei**gn |
| | h**ei**ght | h**ei**r | forf**ei**t | h**ei**fer |
| **Exceptions** | v**ie**w | fr**ie**nd | misch**ie**f | anc**ie**nt |
| | s**ie**ve | f**ie**rce | t**ie** | p**ie**r |

The generalizations do not apply if the *i* and *e* are in different syllables.

| *IE* AND *EI* IN DIFFERENT SYLLABLES | | | |
|---|---|---|---|
| be•ing | de•ice | re•imburse | re•iterate |
| pi•ety | fi•esta | di•et | sci•ence |

## Words with *–sede, –ceed,* and *–cede*

The syllable that sounds like "seed" can be spelled *–sede, –ceed,* or *–cede.*

| *–SEDE, –CEED,* AND *–CEDE* | | | |
|---|---|---|---|
| –SEDE (ONLY ONE WORD) | super**sede** | | |
| –CEED (ONLY THREE WORDS) | ex**ceed** | pro**ceed** | suc**ceed** |
| –CEDE (ALL OTHERS) | ac**cede** | con**cede** | pre**cede** |

*There is no* –seed *ending except in words derived from the noun* seed, *such as* reseed, *which means "to sow again."*

## PRACTICE YOUR SKILLS

Check Your Understanding

### *Using Spelling Patterns*

**Write each word, adding *ie* or *ei*. If you are unsure about a spelling, check the dictionary.**

| | | |
|---|---|---|
| **1.** br ■ f | **8.** perc ■ ve | **15.** conc ■ t |
| **2.** for ■ gn | **9.** w ■ gh | **16.** dec ■ ve |
| **3.** th ■ r | **10.** y ■ ld | **17.** n ■ ther |
| **4.** n ■ ce | **11.** s ■ ge | **18.** med ■ val |
| **5.** rec ■ pt | **12.** hyg ■ ne | **19.** rel ■ ve |
| **6.** p ■ ce | **13.** s ■ zure | **20.** counterf ■ t |
| **7.** l ■ sure | **14.** rec ■ ve | |

**Write each word, adding *–sede, –ceed,* or *–cede.***

**21.** re

**22.** con

**23.** ex

**24.** inter

**25.** super

**26.** pro

**27.** se

**28.** ac

**29.** suc

**30.** pre

### Connect to the Writing Process: Editing

### *Using Spelling Patterns*

History Topic **Read this article, paying particular attention to the underlined words. Decide whether they are spelled correctly. Then rewrite those that are misspelled.**

Today much is known about the culture of ancent Egypt. Two centuries of study have yeilded a wealth of information about the religious beliefs and practices of anceint Egypt. At the beginning of the nineteenth century, Egyptian civilization was veiled in mystery. Jean-François Champollion was the first scholar to work in this field. He is veiwed as the founder of Egyptology.

Champollion worked with the Rosetta Stone to piece together the principles of heiroglyphics. The Rosetta Stone, which was discovered by Napoleon's troops near Alexandria, had been inscribed by priests of Ptolemy V. On it, the same text appears in hieroglyphic, demotic, and Greek. Using the stone, Champollion proceded to compare the Egyptian text to the Greek text and succeded in figuring out the key to hieroglyphics. For the study of ancient Egypt, this was an excedingly important acheivement.

# Plurals

There are a number of useful generalizations that will help you spell the plural of most nouns.

## Regular Nouns

To form the plural of most nouns, add *s.*

To form the plural of nouns ending in *s, ch, sh, x,* or *z,* add *es.*

| | | | | | |
|---|---|---|---|---|---|
| | | **MOST NOUNS** | | | |
| **SINGULAR** | geologist | frog | bicycle | rose | |
| **PLURAL** | geologist**s** | frog**s** | bicycle**s** | rose**s** | |
| | | ***S, CH, SH, X,* AND *Z*** | | | |
| **SINGULAR** | mo**ss** | bea**ch** | wi**sh** | ta**x** | walt**z** |
| **PLURAL** | moss**es** | beach**es** | wish**es** | tax**es** | waltz**es** |

Word Alert

The following related plurals are alike, except one ends in *s* and the other in *es.* Form the plurals carefully, because their meanings differ.

**cloths**—[plural noun] pieces of fabric with specific uses; often part of a compound word: *tablecloths, dustcloths, washcloths*

There are cleaning **cloths** in the broom closet.

**clothes**—[plural noun] garments or apparel, usually made of cloth

Everyone wore formal **clothes** to the prom.

## Nouns Ending with *y*

Add *s* to form the plural of a noun ending with a vowel and *y.*

| | | | | |
|---|---|---|---|---|
| | | **VOWELS AND *Y*** | | |
| **SINGULAR** | ess**ay** | journ**ey** | all**oy** | monk**ey** |
| **PLURAL** | essay**s** | journey**s** | alloy**s** | monkey**s** |

Change the *y* to *i* and add *es* to a noun ending in a consonant and *y*.

| CONSONANTS AND Y | | | | |
|---|---|---|---|---|
| **SINGULAR** | ene**my** | falla**cy** | catego**ry** | supp**ly** |
| **PLURAL** | enem**ies** | falla**cies** | categor**ies** | suppl**ies** |
| **EXCEPTIONS** | For proper nouns ending with *y,* just add *s.* | | | |
| | Jeremy | Avery | Nancy | |
| | Jeremy**s** | Avery**s** | Nancy**s** | |

## PRACTICE YOUR SKILLS

### Check Your Understanding
### *Forming Plurals*

**Write the plural form of each noun.**

**1.** fantasy
**2.** editor
**3.** latch
**4.** thistle
**5.** tragedy
**6.** fox
**7.** alley
**8.** phrase
**9.** hoax
**10.** reply
**11.** casualty
**12.** holiday
**13.** ally
**14.** railway
**15.** class
**16.** bench
**17.** six
**18.** sketch
**19.** melee
**20.** blueberry

### Connect to the Writing Process: Editing
### *Spelling Plural Nouns*

General Interest **Edit this paragraph, changing the underlined nouns from singular to plural.**

The names people give their <u>baby</u> go in and out of fashion. This is true of names given to both <u>sex</u>, but <u>switch</u> in popularity are particularly common for very old names given to <u>boy</u>. Consider Henry. The name Henry has been around for <u>century</u>. It means "one who rules the home and estate (amassed <u>property</u>)." History is full of famous <u>Henry</u>. There were eight <u>monarch</u> of England named Henry and six

Holy Roman emperor. Other recent historical personality include Henry Ford and Henry Kissinger. But for a while, during the middle decade of the twentieth century, the name Henry was not very popular. There were many Gary and Barry, but not very many Henry. Today family are once again naming their baby Henry. How many Henry do you know?

## Nouns Ending with *o*

Add *s* to form the plural of a noun ending with a vowel and *o.*

| VOWELS AND *O* | | | | |
|---|---|---|---|---|
| **SINGULAR** | stud**io** | rat**io** | ster**eo** | kangar**oo** |
| **PLURAL** | studio**s** | ratio**s** | stereo**s** | kangaroo**s** |

Add *es* to form the plural of many nouns that end with a consonant and *o.*

| CONSONANTS AND *O* | | | | |
|---|---|---|---|---|
| **SINGULAR** | toma**to** | torpe**do** | he**ro** | ec**ho** |
| **PLURAL** | tomato**es** | torpedo**es** | hero**es** | echo**es** |

Add *s* to form the plural of musical terms, proper nouns, and some other nouns that end in *o.*

| MUSICAL TERMS, FOODS, ETC. | | | | |
|---|---|---|---|---|
| **SINGULAR** | piccol**o** | tangel**o** | tac**o** | Pocon**o** |
| **PLURAL** | piccolo**s** | tangelo**s** | taco**s** | Pocono**s** |

When dictionaries give two forms for the plurals of some nouns ending in a consonant and *o,* the first form is the preferred one.

| PREFERRED FORMS | | | |
|---|---|---|---|
| **Singular** | tornado | zero | mosquito |
| **Plural** | tornadoes or tornados | zeros or zeroes | mosquitoes or mosquitos |

## Nouns Ending in *f* or *fe*

To form the plural of some nouns ending in *f* or *fe,* just add *s.*

| *F* OR *FE* | | | | | |
|---|---|---|---|---|---|
| **Singular** | chef | staff | roof | waif | giraffe |
| **Plural** | chefs | staffs | roofs | waifs | giraffes |

For some nouns ending in *f* or *fe,* change the *f* to *v* and add *es* or *s.*

| *F* OR *FE* TO *V* | | | | | |
|---|---|---|---|---|---|
| **Singular** | shelf | leaf | hoof | wife | knife |
| **Plural** | shelves | leaves | hooves | wives | knives |

When unsure which rule applies, consult a dictionary to find out the correct plural form of a word that ends with *f* or *fe.*

## Practice Your Skills

Check Your Understanding

***Forming Plurals***

**Write the plural form of each of these nouns. Check a dictionary to be sure you've formed the plural correctly.**

1. half
2. cello
3. tomato
4. burrito
5. sheriff
6. placebo
7. scenario
8. soprano
9. pimento
10. ratio
11. belief
12. banjo
13. silo
14. wharf
15. stereo
16. gulf
17. proof
18. self
19. folio
20. radio

### Connect to the Writing Process: Editing
***Spelling Plural Nouns***

Music Topic **Rewrite this paragraph, correcting any spelling errors.**

Of all the stringed instruments, the violin is the most versatile. It is unusual to see violas and celloes in a country music group, and you will rarely see banjoes and guitars in the symphony orchestra. Violins, however, have dual lifes. Going by the name of "fiddles," they do themselfs proud, playing with folk or bluegrass comboes. As violins, they are the principal voices in symphonies, sonatas, and concertoes. Alone, they can play soloes. With a cello and a viola, they can play trios. They are almost as versatile and popular as pianoes, and they are much more portable!

## Plurals of Numbers, Letters, Symbols, and Words Used as Words

To form the plurals of most numerals, letters, symbols, and words used as words, add an *s.* However, to prevent confusion, it is best to use an apostrophe and *s* with lowercase letters, some capital letters, and some words used as words.

EXAMPLES The *7***s** in this column should be *4***s.**
Interest rates were high in the 1980**s.**
Ampersands (*&***s**) replace the *and***s** in some company names.

EXCEPTIONS If *e***'s** are closed at the top, they look like *i***'s.**
(Without the apostrophe, *i's* become *is.*)
*A***'s** are easy letters to write. (*A's* become *As.*)

*Some writers prefer to add 's to form the plural of all numerals, letters, symbols, and words used as words.*

## Other Plural Forms

Irregular plurals are not formed by adding *s* or *es.*

| IRREGULAR PLURALS | | | | |
|---|---|---|---|---|
| **SINGULAR** | child | woman | tooth | mouse |
| **PLURAL** | child**ren** | wom**e**n | **teeth** | m**ice** |

For some nouns, the singular and the plural forms are the same.

| SAME SINGULAR AND PLURAL | | | | |
|---|---|---|---|---|
| sheep | moose | corps | scissors | Chinese |
| salmon | trout | species | series | Swiss |

## Compound Nouns

The plurals of most compound nouns are formed in the same way other plural nouns are formed.

| MOST COMPOUND NOUNS | | | |
|---|---|---|---|
| **SINGULAR** | stepchild | eyetooth | bookshelf |
| **PLURAL** | step**children** | eye**teeth** | book**shelves** |

In compound words in which one part of the compound word modifies the other, make the word that is modified the plural.

| SELF-MODIFYING COMPOUNDS | | | |
|---|---|---|---|
| **SINGULAR** | musk-ox | son-in-law | runner-up |
| **PLURAL** | musk-**oxen** | **sons**-in-law | **runners**-up |

## Foreign Plurals

The plurals of some foreign words are formed as they are in their original language. For some foreign words, there are two ways to form the plural.

| FOREIGN WORDS | | | | |
|---|---|---|---|---|
| **SINGULAR** | alg**a** | alumn**us** | bacteri**um** | ellips**is** |
| **PLURAL** | alg**ae** | alumn**i** | bacteri**a** | ellips**es** |
| **SINGULAR** | formul**a** | ind**ex** | hippopotam**us** | |
| **PLURAL** | formul**as** or formul**ae** | index**es** or indi**ces** | hippopotamus**es** or hippopotam**i** | |

Check a dictionary when writing the plural of foreign words. When two forms are given, the first one is preferred.

Listen and watch for foreign words that are becoming more commonly used. If you use them in your writing, be sure to form the plurals correctly.

**chapeau**—[noun, plural *chapeaux*, French] a hat

Brett put his **chapeaux** on the shelf.

**cravat**—[noun, plural *cravats*, French] a scarf or a tie

He bought two **cravats** in the shirt department.

## PRACTICE YOUR SKILLS

Check Your Understanding

***Forming Plurals***

**Write the plural form for each item. If you are not sure about the correct form, check a dictionary.**

**1.** memorandum
**2.** genus
**3.** stylus
**4.** thesis
**5.** nucleus
**6.** *but*
**7.** 8
**8.** 1890
**9.** dormouse
**10.** grandchild
**11.** die
**12.** ?
**13.** goose
**14.** goldfinch
**15.** tempo

### Connect to the Writing Process: Editing

***Forming Plurals***

Contemporary Life

**Decide if the underlined plurals in these paragraphs are formed correctly. Check a dictionary if you're not certain. If any of the underlined plurals are incorrectly formed, write the correct forms.**

Everyone knows something about dude ranches, where tenderfoots go to pretend they are cowpokes. Probably fewer people have heard of tourist farms because there hasn't been much publicity in the mediums yet. Tourist farms are one of the vacation phenomenons of the late 1990s. These farms offer city-dwellers who spend their workdays in offices the opportunity to experience life as their forefathers (and foremothers) might have in the 1890's. Parents and their childs spend their vacations on working farms, not as bystanders or looker-ons, but as farmhands. They plow fields and plant crops. They feed the poultries and collect the eggs. They milk the dairy cattles. They pick fruits from orchards. They learn the importance of windmills and other farm apparatus to traditional farms. If the windmills do not turn, the guests will help figure out how to pump water for the sheeps and other farm animals. Familys might spend mornings picking buckets of blackberrys, which later become pies, jellys, and jams. Farms may not be ideal vacation spots for couch potatoes or sticks-in-the-mud, but for people looking for relief from stress, farms can be ideal.

## Communicate Your Ideas

### APPLY TO WRITING

**Travel Brochure: *Plurals***

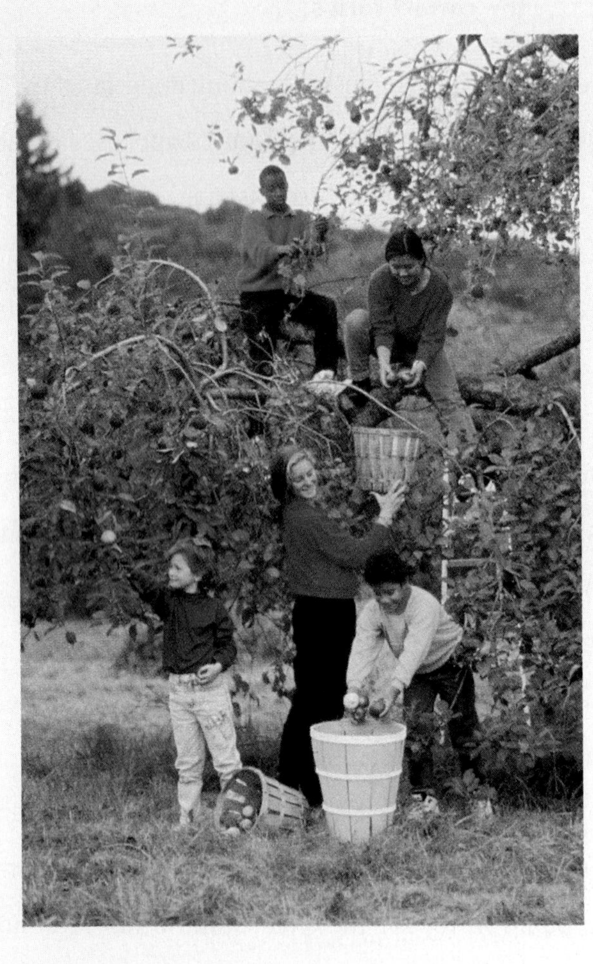

Imagine that this picture is an illustration for an advertising brochure for a vacation farm. You are an ad writer, and it is your job to write the copy for the brochure. Write one or two paragraphs that tell about the fun folks can have if they spend their vacations on farms. Use at least ten plural nouns in your brochure copy.

# Spelling Numbers

When you are writing, you may be unsure whether you should write a number as a numeral or in words. The following generalizations can help you decide.

## Numerals or Number Words

**Spell out numbers that can be written in one or two words. Use numerals for other numbers. Always spell out a number that begins a sentence.**

Our journey lasted **fifteen** days.

We traveled **3220** miles, from Portland, Maine, to Portland, Oregon.

**Three hundred eighty-seven miles** was the farthest we traveled in one day.

Be consistent. When you have many numbers in a passage, use numerals for them all.

We traveled an average of **230** miles a day, but one day we went **387** miles and another day we traveled only **95** miles.

## Ordinal Numbers

**Always spell out numbers used to tell the order.**

On the **first** day, we got a very late start.
By the **tenth** day, we were getting tired of traveling.

Use ordinal words to represent the names of streets numbered first through tenth. For street names greater than tenth, use ordinal figures: numbers ending in *st, nd, rd,* and *th*.

Fifth Avenue    44th Street    33rd Street

## Other Uses of Numerals

Use numerals in dates, addresses, times of day, and statistics and for numbers that identify.

| USES OF NUMERALS | | | |
|---|---|---|---|
| **Dates** | September **9, 2001** | A.D. **1066** | **500** B.C. |
| **Addresses** | **220** West End Avenue<br>Hudson, OH **43210-2104** | | |
| **Time** | **9:45** A.M. | **7:15** P.M. | |
| | (If you use *o'clock,* then write the hour: **six** o'clock) | | |
| **Statistics** | **90** degrees<br>**51** percent | **16** ounces<br>**47** points | |
| **Numbers that Identify** | Route **66**<br>Box **549** | Channel **11**<br>pages **11–17** | Room **213** |

## Practice Your Skills

Check Your Understanding

***Spelling Numbers***

General Interest **If the underlined number is written correctly, write C. If it is written incorrectly, rewrite it correctly.**

**1.** Grandma received 80 birthday cards on her eightieth birthday.

**2.** On the 17th of July, the hottest day of the summer, the temperature soared to a humid ninety-nine degrees.

**3.** Our 1st dog weighed 47 pounds, but the new puppy will weigh about 80 pounds when it is grown.

**4.** It's almost 5 o'clock, and in 60 minutes, 12 people will walk through that door, expecting dinner.

**5.** The drawing on page thirty-nine shows the Great Pyramid of Khufu, which was built in twenty-six eighty B.C. and is one of the Seven Wonders of the Ancient World.

**6.** A sonnet is 14 lines of iambic pentameter; each line has 10 beats and every 2nd beat is emphasized.

7. The final score was ninety-five to ninety-three, and Channel Three is showing game highlights at 11 o'clock.
8. Phillis Wheatley, the 1st published African American poet, was kidnapped from Africa when she was 7; she published her first book of poems when she was 17.
9. In 1803, the United States purchased eight hundred twenty-eight thousand square miles of land from France at a cost of about four cents an acre.
10. For 36 seasons, the Major League record for home runs was 61, but Negro League player Josh Gibson, who died in 1947, had a season record of 89 homers.

Connect to the Writing Process: Editing

***Writing Numbers***

Geography Topic

**Rewrite this paragraph, correcting any mistakes in writing numbers.**

Of the 48 contiguous United States, Minnesota is the state located farthest north. Minnesota covers a total of eighty-four thousand four hundred two square miles, and 4,567,267 people lived there in 1990, making Minnesota the 12th largest in size and 20th in population.

8 percent of all Minnesotans live in Minneapolis, the state's largest city. With a population of three hundred sixty-eight thousand three hundred eighty-three, Minneapolis ranks 42nd among the country's 50 largest cities. Minneapolis ranks much higher when it comes to quality of life. 6,000 acres of the city are devoted to parks, and a total of 5.5 square miles are covered by water. There are one hundred fifty-three parks in the city's park system, and there are 12 lakes within the city limits.

# Prefixes and Suffixes

A **prefix** is one or more syllables placed in front of a base word to form a new word. The base word's spelling does not change.

| PREFIXES | |
|---|---|
| **anti** + toxin = **anti**toxin | **re** + enact = **re**enact |
| **re** + introduce = **re**introduce | **over** + rule = **over**rule |
| **pre** + suppose = **pre**suppose | **in** + animate = **in**animate |

*When the prefix* re– *is followed by a word that begins with* e, *some writers prefer to hyphenate the word:* re + enact = re-enact.

Word Alert

The prefix *anti–* and the prefix *ante–* sound alike, but don't confuse them. Their meanings are quite different.

**anti**—[prefix] adds the meaning "against" or "opposite"

Many college students were part of the **anti-war** movement of the 1960s.
Raising interest rates is an **anti-inflation** strategy.
Vitamin K is a common **antitoxin**.

**ante**—[prefix] adds the meaning "before" or "prior"

In architecture, ***antebellum*** means before the Civil War and *prewar* means before World War II.
Many buildings in Boston **antedate** the Revolutionary War.

A **suffix** is one or more syllables added at the end of a base word to change its part of speech and possibly also its meaning.

## Suffixes *–ness* and *–ly*

The suffixes *–ness* and *–ly* are added to most base words without any spelling changes.

| ***–NESS*** **AND** ***–LY*** | |
|---|---|
| even + **ness** = even**ness** | usual + **ly** = usual**ly** |
| great + **ness** = great**ness** | friend + **ly** = friend**ly** |

### Words Ending in *e*

Drop the final *e* in the base word when adding a suffix that begins with a vowel.

| SUFFIXES WITH VOWELS | |
|---|---|
| imagine + **ary** = imagin**ary** | note + **able** = not**able** |
| refuse + **al** = refus**al** | destine + **y** = destin**y** |

Keep the final *e* when the suffix begins with a consonant.

| SUFFIXES WITH CONSONANTS | | |
|---|---|---|
| EXAMPLES | excite + **ment** = excite**ment** | |
| | grace + **ful** = grace**ful** | |
| EXCEPTIONS | judge + **ment** = judg**ment** | awe + **ful** = aw**ful** |
| | true + **ly** = tru**ly** | mile + **age** = mile**age** |

When the base word ends with *ce* or *ge*, the final *e* must stay to retain the soft sound of the consonant. In some base words ending with *ce*, *e* is changed to *i* before adding a suffix that begins with a vowel.

| *CE* OR *GE* | |
|---|---|
| change + **able** = change**able** | courage + **ous** = courage**ous** |
| notice + **able** = notice**able** | grace + **ous** = grac**ious** |

Word Alert

Pronounce the difference between *re′fuse* and *refuse′* by stressing the correct syllable. If you add a suffix to *refuse′* and mispronounce it, the word will not make sense.

**refuse′**—[verb] to express unwillingness to believe or to participate

I **refuse′** to watch the news coverage.

**re′fuse**—[noun] trash or garbage

The disaster left **re′fuse** throughout the city.

**refuse′** + **al** = **refus′al**

I accept your **refus′al** to watch.

## Practice Your Skills

Check Your Understanding
### *Adding Prefixes and Suffixes*

**Combine these base words and prefixes or suffixes. Remember to make any necessary spelling changes.**

1. dis + appear
2. re + elect
3. nerve + ous
4. imitate + ion
5. ir + regular
6. use + able
7. im + mobile + ity
8. under + rate
9. space + ous
10. store + age
11. argue + ment
12. manage + able
13. outrage + ous
14. grieve + ous
15. final + ly
16. true + ly
17. co + operate
18. race + al
19. style + ish
20. arrange + ment

Connect to the Writing Process: Editing
### *Spelling Words with Prefixes and Suffixes*

General Interest **Locate the words in this paragraph that have prefixes or suffixes, and rewrite correctly those that are misspelled.**

The nineteenth century saw the establishment of many utopian communities. Often founded in lovly locations, these communities were based on a combineation of socialism and religious commitment. "From each according to his gifts to each according to his needs" is a statment of the harmony and fairness these communities truely struggled to attain. Each member worked for the benefit and betterment of all members. Unfortuneately, self-interest is more natureal to humankind than concern for communal good. Too often selfishness and self-involvment stood in opposetion to the achievment of true community. As a result, many utopian communities ultimatly failed.

## Words Ending with *y*

Keep the *y* when adding a suffix to words that end in a vowel and *y.* Change *y* to *i* when adding a suffix to words that end in a consonant and *y.*

| SUFFIXES WITH *Y* | | |
|---|---|---|
| **Examples** | employ + **able** = employ**able**<br>pay + **ment** = pay**ment**<br>ally + **ance** = all**iance**<br>merry + **ly** = merr**ily** | |
| **Exceptions** | rely + **ing** = rely**ing**<br>hobby + **ist** = hobby**ist** | day + **ly** = da**ily**<br>shy + **ness** = shy**ness** |

## Doubling the Final Consonant

Double the final consonant when adding a suffix that begins with a vowel if the base word satisfies both these conditions: (1) It has only one syllable or is stressed on the final syllable and (2) It ends in one consonant preceded by one vowel.

| DOUBLE CONSONANTS | |
|---|---|
| **One-Syllable Words** | hop + ing = ho**pp**ing<br>wet + est = we**tt**est<br>fog + y = fo**gg**y |
| **Final Syllable Stressed** | upset + ing = upse**tt**ing<br>permit + ed = permi**tt**ed<br>rebel + ion = rebe**ll**ion |

**Word Alert** Don't confuse *personal* and *personnel*. *Personnel* is the French word for *personal,* but in English it has a special meaning.

**personal**—[adjective] specific to a certain person; done in person; involving human beings

> This store is my **personal** favorite.
> Customers receive **personal** attention.
> The management values **personal** relationships.

**personnel**—[noun] people employed by a business establishment

> The store's **personnel** are well trained and courteous.

## Words Ending with *c*

When adding a suffix that begins with *e, i,* or *y* to a word that ends with a vowel and *c,* do not double the final *c.* Instead add the letter *k* after the *c* to retain the hard *c* sound.

| FINAL *C* | |
|---|---|
| picnic + **ing** = picni**ck**ing | colic + **y** = coli**ck**y |

## PRACTICE YOUR SKILLS

Check Your Understanding

***Adding Suffixes***

**Combine these base words and suffixes. Remember to make any necessary spelling changes.**

**1.** lobby + ist
**2.** deny + al
**3.** vary + ance
**4.** study + ing
**5.** permit + ed
**6.** transmit + al
**7.** compel + ed
**8.** regret + able
**9.** politic + ing
**10.** worry + some
**11.** deter + ent
**12.** occur + ence
**13.** rely + able
**14.** shellac + ed
**15.** thirty + ish
**16.** person + al
**17.** panic + y
**18.** apply + ance
**19.** mimic + ed
**20.** profit + able

## Connect to the Writing Process: Editing

### *Adding Suffixes*

General Interest **Read these paragraphs, looking for words with suffixes that are spelled incorrectly. Write each word correctly.**

Many people experience recuring dreams. These dreams sometimes reveal things about the dreamer's personallity. Some people's recurring dreams are undenyably their very own. They are unique and unlike any other. Other people have dreams that are shared, with some personnal varyation, by many people.

A common recurring dream is the one in which the dreamer must take the final exam in a course she either didn't know or forgot she was registerred for. This can be a very upseting dream, and the dreamer is often panicing when he or she wakes up. Experts say that this dream is typickally experienced by people who are worried—sometimes excessively—about doing well.

Another dream that is reported frequentely to experts includes the action of jumping or flying. The dreamer often is comforted by the upward movement. Experts say that this dream usualy reveals a subconscious acknowledegment of the ability to overcome obstacles or to move beyond challenging situations. Those who have recuring dreams of this kind are sincerly appreciatetive of the positive explanation.

## Communicate Your Ideas

### APPLY TO WRITING

**Narrative: *Suffixes***

Write a story about a recurring dream similar to either one described on page L569. Create a character who might have such a dream. Describe what happens in the dream and what the character does—in the dream and upon waking. Use five of the following words with suffixes in your writing.

- *panic + y*
- *regret + able*
- *scary + est*
- *early + est*
- *enjoy + able*
- *compel + ed*
- *excel + ence*
- *deny + ing*
- *refuse + al*
- *prepare + ation*

### QuickCheck Mixed Practice

**Add the prefix or suffix to each of these base words, and write the new word.**

**1.** admit + ance
**2.** lazy + ness
**3.** day + ly
**4.** argue + ment
**5.** un + notice + able
**6.** repel + ing
**7.** hobby + ist
**8.** acknowledge + ment
**9.** buoy + ancy
**10.** re + place + able
**11.** courage + ous
**12.** lonely + ness
**13.** face + al
**14.** frolic + ing
**15.** picnic + er
**16.** mis + spell
**17.** infer + ed
**18.** il + logical
**19.** even + ness
**20.** study + ous

## WORDS TO MASTER

Make it your goal to learn to spell these fifty words this year. Use them in your writing, and practice writing them until spelling them correctly comes automatically.

a**cc**o**mm**odate
adole**sc**en**ce**
alle**gia**nce
anon**y**mous
a**tm**o**sph**ere
bib**lio**graphy
bi**zarre**
b**ou**l**e**vard
cam**ou**flage
**ca**ri**ca**ture
comple**x**ion
con**scie**n**ti**ous
cu**rr**iculum
d**e**sp**air**
dile**mm**a
dile**tt**an**te**
enviro**nm**ent
esp**io**nage
fi**ss**ion
fu**l**fi**ll**
**gu**arantee
ha**r**a**ss**ment
h**y**pocr**isy**
ini**tia**tive
interfe**rence**
lar**ynx**
main**ten**ance
man**eu**ver
mel**anch**o**ly**
mis**chie**vous
n**ai**ve
obso**lete**
or**ch**estra
para**ll**e**l**ism
p**er**ceive
**phy**sician
pla**gia**rism
**psych**ology
rem**i**n**isc**ent
r**e**nd**ez**vou**s**
spe**ci**men
strat**e**gic
s**y**mbo**l**ic
sy**mm**etrical
th**eo**retical
thes**au**rus
t**y**ra**nn**y
unscr**upu**lous
ve**hi**cle
vill**ain**

## CheckPoint

# Spelling Words Correctly

**Write the letter preceding the misspelled word in each group. Then write the word, spelling it correctly.**

**1.** (A) proceed (B) sharing (C) stereos
(D) acurracy (E) rendezvous

**2.** (A) deceive (B) occurred (C) managable
(D) eyeglasses (E) forgettable

**3.** (A) piece (B) excede (C) feign
(D) fifes (E) echoes

**4.** (A) thesaurus (B) usualy (C) descendant
(D) gauge (E) notaries public

**5.** (A) rarity (B) chefs (C) alloys
(D) rein (E) rehersal

**6.** (A) apparant (B) concede (C) referral
(D) patios (E) outrageous

**7.** (A) releive (B) seize (C) veil
(D) wives (E) thesis

**8.** (A) leisure (B) overrule (C) alumnuses
(D) obedient (E) bizarre

**9.** (A) changeable (B) disimilar (C) loneliness
(D) mosquito (E) bushes

**10.** (A) recurence (B) license (C) overture
(D) sieve (E) neither

# Another Look

## Spelling Patterns *(pages 549–551)*

When the vowel sound is long *e*, write *ei* after *c* and *ie* after other consonant letters. When the sound is long *a* or any vowel sound other than long *e*, write *ei*. The generalizations do not apply if the *i* and *e* are in different syllables.

The syllable that sounds like "seed" can be spelled *sede*, *ceed*, or *cede*.

## Plurals *(pages 552–560)*

To form the plural of nouns ending in *s, ch, sh, x,* or *z,* add *es*.

Change the *y* to *i* and add *es* to a noun ending in a consonant and *y*.

Add *es* to form the plural of many nouns that end with a consonant and *o*. For some nouns ending in *f* or *fe*, change the *f* to *v* and add *es* or *s*.

In compound words in which one part of the compound modifies the other, make the word that is modified the plural.

## Spelling Numbers *(pages 561–563)*

Spell out numbers that can be written in one or two words. Always spell out a number that is used to tell the order or that begins a sentence.

Use numerals in dates, addresses, times of day, and statistics and for numbers that identify.

## Prefixes and Suffixes *(pages 564–570)*

Drop the final *e* in the base word when adding a suffix that begins with a vowel. Keep the final *e* when the suffix begins with a consonant.

When the base word ends in *ce* or *ge*, the final *e* must stay in order to retain the soft sound of the consonant. In some base words ending in *ce, e* is changed to *i* before adding a suffix that begins with a vowel. Change *y* to *i* when adding a suffix to words that end in a consonant and *y*.

Double the final consonant when you add a suffix that begins with a vowel if the base word satisfies both these conditions: (1) It has only one syllable or is stressed on the final syllable and (2) It ends in one consonant preceded by one vowel.

When you add a suffix that begins with *e* or *i* to a word that ends with a vowel and *c*, do not double the final *c*. Instead add the letter *k* after the *c* to retain the hard *c* sound.

### *Directions*

**Read the passage. Write the letter of the answer that correctly respells each underlined word. If the word is correct, write *D*.**

EXAMPLE This is a <u>remarkable</u> book about a young boy.
**(1)**

**1 A** remarkeable
**B** remarkible
**C** remmarkable
**D** No error

ANSWER **1 D**

The *Catcher in the Rye* is an <u>extreamly</u> **(1)** popular book about <u>adolesence</u> **(2)** and coming of age. The hero, Holden Caulfield, runs away from his prep school as Christmas <u>vacation</u> **(3)** begins. On the <u>bulavards</u> **(4)** of New York, he finds himself involved in a <u>serie</u> **(5)** of adventures.

Holden is a <u>fascinateing</u> **(6)** character, at once both worldly and <u>niave</u> **(7)**. His <u>disatisfaction</u> **(8)** with the adult world around him is evident as he rails against <u>hypocracy</u> **(9)** and dishonesty. Holden's feelings are <u>remaniscent</u> **(10)** of the teenage rebellions that took place in the 1960s.

1 **A** extremally
**B** extremely
**C** exstreamly
**D** No error

2 **A** adolescence
**B** adolecense
**C** adolesense
**D** No error

3 **A** vacasion
**B** vaccasion
**C** vacateon
**D** No error

4 **A** boulevards
**B** bullavards
**C** boulavards
**D** No error

5 **A** series
**B** serieses
**C** seria
**D** No error

6 **A** fastenating
**B** fascinating
**C** fascanating
**D** No error

7 **A** nyive
**B** naiv
**C** naive
**D** No error

8 **A** disatissfaction
**B** dissatisfaction
**C** dissatisfashion
**D** No error

9 **A** hippocracy
**B** hypocrasy
**C** hypocrisy
**D** No error

10 **A** reminiscent
**B** remeniscent
**C** reminicent
**D** No error

# A Study Guide for Academic Success

Success in school is often measured by how well you perform on tests, both in your daily classes and in standardized testing situations. Developing good study skills and test-taking strategies, therefore, may be your key to success as a student.

There are a number of effective methods you can use when studying for tests. Many of these may seem simple—just using common sense—as they are outlined in this chapter. However, if you employ the strategies suggested in the following pages, you will develop the skills you need to tackle specific types of problems that occur regularly on tests.

The end result, however, is not simply a higher grade for a class or better scores on exams. Your ability to decipher the main idea of a reading passage or correct errors within a text enhances your ability to discriminate between accurate, well-written texts and those that are incorrect, biased or ambiguously written. You will rely on these skills throughout your life.

# Learning Study Skills

Tests are designed to evaluate how much you know about certain subjects. How well you do on these tests, however, often reflects how effectively you study and prepare assignments on a daily basis. How effective are your study habits?

**Strategies for Effective Studying**

- Choose an area that is well lighted and free from distractions.
- Equip your study area with everything you need for reading and writing, including, if possible, a dictionary, a thesaurus, and other print and non-print reference tools.
- Keep a notebook for recording assignments and due dates.
- Allow plenty of time. Begin your assignments early.

## Adjusting Reading Rate to Purpose

Whenever you read, it is important to understand your purpose for reading the material. Reading a story for entertainment requires different kinds of reading strategies than reading a textbook to learn important information. Reading textbooks requires an organized approach that enables you to focus your attention and achieve your purpose. The following strategies can help you read textbook material more effectively.

### Scanning

**Scanning** is reading to get a general impression and to prepare for learning about a subject. Scan a chapter or section by reading the title, headings, subheadings, picture captions, words and phrases in boldface and italics, parenthetical and appositive phrases, information set off by dashes, and any focus questions to determine quickly what the reading is about and what questions to keep in mind as you read.

## Skimming

After scanning a chapter, section, or article, skim the introduction, the topic sentence and summary sentence of each paragraph, and the conclusion. **Skimming** is reading to identify quickly the purpose, thesis, main ideas, and supporting ideas.

## Close Reading

After skimming a selection to learn the main ideas, read it more slowly to learn the details. **Close reading** is for locating specific information, following the logic of an argument, or comprehending the meaning or significance of information.

## Taking Notes

Note-taking is an important skill for helping you remember what you have read in a textbook or heard in class. Three methods for taking notes are the informal outline, the graphic organizer, and the summary.

In an **informal outline**, words and phrases are used to record main ideas and important details. When you study for an objective test, such as a multiple-choice test, an informal outline will help you easily see and review the important facts and details.

In a **graphic organizer,** words and phrases are arranged in a visual pattern to indicate main ideas and supporting details, among many other possibilities. A graphic organizer, or a cognitive map, is an excellent tool to use for studying information for an objective test, for an open-ended assessment, or for writing an essay. The visual organizer allows you, instantly, to see important information and its relationship to other ideas.

In a **summary**, sentences are used to express important ideas in your own words. Writing summaries is useful in preparing for an essay test because you must think about the information, see relationships among ideas, and draw conclusions.

In the following passage from a textbook, the essential information is underlined.

## Model: Essential Information

Thomas Hardy had two distinct literary careers, the first as a novelist and the second as a poet. His deepening pessimism in *Jude the Obscure,* coupled with the public burning of the book by an Anglican bishop, turned him away from novel writing and toward poetry.

Until the age of fifty-eight, Hardy was known only as a novelist. Among his best-known novels are *The Return of the Native* and *The Mayor of Casterbridge.* These novels show Hardy's pervasive gloominess, yet his rustic characters also reveal an underlying sense of humor. Hardy considered himself a meliorist, one who believes that things tend to improve.

For the last 30 years of his life, Hardy wrote nothing but poetry. His great epic drama, *The Dynasts,* is less well known than his shorter poems, such as "The Man He Killed," "Channel Firing," and "In Time of 'The Breaking of Nations.'" These poems tend to be sad and pessimistic, like his novels, but they also suggest the heroic dignity of humanity's struggle.

**Thomas Hardy**

INFORMAL OUTLINE:

1. Until age fifty-eight—known only as a novelist
   - **a.** Novels show gloominess but also humor
   - **b.** Meliorism—belief things tend to improve
2. Last 30 years of life—wrote only poetry
   - **a.** Short poems most familiar
   - **b.** Display sadness and pessimism
   - **c.** Reveal heroic dignity of human beings

GRAPHIC ORGANIZER:

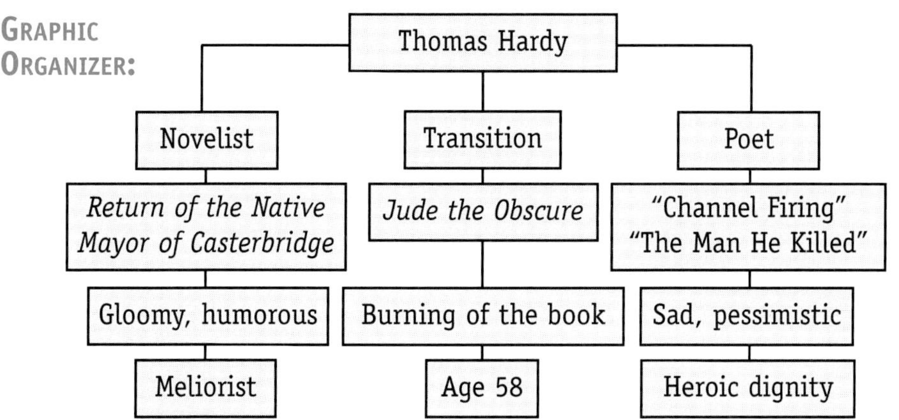

**SUMMARY:**

**Thomas Hardy**

Hardy had two different writing careers. He was a novelist until age fifty-eight and a poet thereafter. His most well-known novels are gloomy but show an underlying humor. Hardy believed that things tend to improve. His short poems, for which he is best known, display sadness and pessimism but also reveal humans' heroic dignity.

## Strategies for Taking Notes

- Label your notes with the title and page numbers of the chapter or section, or the topic and date of the class.
- Record only the main ideas and important details.
- Use the titles, subtitles, and words in special type or color to help you select the most important information.
- Use your own words; do not copy word for word.
- Use as few words as possible.

### Modified Outline

- Use words and phrases.
- Use main ideas for headings.
- List any supporting details under each heading.

### Graphic Organizer

- Use a logical visual representation.
- Use words or phrases.
- Place main ideas and supporting details to show relationships.

### Summary

- Write complete sentences, using your own words.
- Show the relationship among ideas, being careful to use only the facts stated in the textbook or class.
- Include only essential information.
- Organize ideas logically.

## Preparing Subject-Area Assignments

Using the strategies you have learned for reading textbooks, taking notes, and preparing for tests can be valuable when doing assignments in any subject area; using those study aids specific to various subject areas can be of special help. Mathematics and science texts often list important rules, formulas, charts, graphs, equations, or models. Consequently, you may spend much of your study time in these areas applying rules and practicing your analytical and computational skills along with problem-solving strategies. History materials, on the other hand, often emphasize such skills as analyzing and interpreting maps, charts, graphs, chronologies, time lines, documents, and statistical data, which you will use in preparing assignments. Use the following study tips to help you prepare assignments for whatever subject area you are studying.

### Tips for Preparing Subject-Area Assignments

- Carefully read all directions.
- Adjust your reading rate to suit your purpose.
- Take notes from both readings and classes. Use the technique of highlighting to help you remember important information, such as names, dates, terms, or facts.
- Be organized. For example, you will find it helpful to keep your reading notes and class notes on the same topic together in your notebook or journal.
- Keep a separate list of vocabulary words, key terms and concepts, or rules and equations for review.
- Keep a running list of questions that arise as you read, listen, or review. Seek answers promptly. If there is anything you do not understand, get help.
- Participate in study groups, following the principles of cooperative learning.
- In preparing for tests, leave ample time for study. Focus on anticipating and answering the questions you will be asked by your teacher. Ask for clarification of concepts.
- Practice applying what you have learned using the specialized learning aids and skills for the particular subject area in which you are working.

# Taking Standardized Tests

A standardized test assesses your abilities, skill, progress, and achievement. One section of the test assesses your understanding of the meaning of words and the way they are used in sentences. Questions within this section are often analogy questions, which assess your ability to understand word relationships; and sentence-completion questions, which require you to use the context to complete a sentence.

Standardized tests also include reading comprehension sections and writing assignments. Your skills are often checked with objective questions about grammar, usage, and mechanics as well as with open-ended questions and time-limited essays.

The best way to prepare for taking a standardized test, as for any other kind of test, is to work conscientiously on class work all along. Reading widely and becoming familiar with the standard testing formats is also good preparation.

### Strategies for Taking Standardized Tests

- Read the test directions carefully. Answer sample questions to be sure you understand what the test requires.
- Relax. Concentrate on doing the best you can.
- Preview the whole test by quickly skimming. This will give you an overview of the kinds of questions on the test.
- Plan your time carefully, allotting a certain amount of time to each part of the test.
- Answer first the questions you find easiest. Skip those you find too hard, coming back to them if you have enough time.
- Read all choices before you answer. If you are not sure of an answer, eliminate choices that are obviously wrong. Making an educated guess is usually wise, but check the test directions to find out if you will be penalized for guessing.
- If you have time, check your answers. Look for omissions and careless errors on your answer sheet.

## Analogies

Analogy questions assess your skill at seeing word relationships. Your first step is to decide how the words in capital letters are related. In the analogy HAND : FINGER, for example, the relationship is whole-to-part. The hand (whole) includes the finger (part). Your next step is to find the pair of words among the choices that shows the same relationship. The word order must be exactly the same in the answer as it is in the question. Determine the correct answer in the following analogy.

HAND : FINGER ::
(A) author : story (B) top : bottom (C) state : city
(D) handle : mug (E) joke : laughter

(The answer is *(C) state : city* because it contains the only whole-to-part relationship among the choices.)

Sometimes analogies are written in sentence form.

*Decipher* is to *decode* as *proclaim* is to ▪.
(A) influence (B) acknowledge (C) announce
(D) annoy (E) encode

(The first two italicized words are synonyms. Therefore, the correct answer is *announce,* a synonym for *proclaim.*)

Knowing some common types of analogies, such as those in the following chart, will help you figure out word relationships.

**COMMON TYPES OF ANALOGIES**

| Analogy | Example |
|---|---|
| word : synonym | evade : escape |
| word : antonym | feasible : impossible |
| part : whole | caboose : train |
| cause : effect | exercise : fitness |
| worker : tool | mason : trowel |
| worker : product | publisher : magazine |
| item : category | lobster : crustacean |
| item : purpose | bus : transport |

## Practice Your Skills

### Check Your Understanding
*Recognizing Analogies*

**Write the relationship using the preceding list of analogy types. Then write the letter of the word pair that has the same relationship as the word pair in capital letters.**

**1.** VERTEBRATE : MAMMAL ::
(A) crustacean : snake (B) money : bank
(C) fog : precipitation (D) element : copper
(E) silver : ore

**2.** INSPECT : EXAMINE ::
(A) condemn : encourage (B) cease : begin
(C) attempt : try (D) lead : inspire
(E) inform : confuse

**3.** TRIVIAL : IMPORTANT ::
(A) windy : wet (B) patron : client
(C) lazy : tired (D) complete : finished
(E) stale : fresh

**4.** EAVES : ROOF ::
(A) road : driver (B) forest : tree
(C) steps : staircase (D) germ : bacteria
(E) pen : ink

**5.** BRUSH : PAINTER ::
(A) sports : competitor (B) jeweler : gem
(C) stonecutter : chisel (D) shirt : price
(E) bowl : chef

### Check Your Understanding
*Completing Analogies*

**Use the chart on page L583 to determine the relationship of each analogy; then complete the analogy by writing the letter of the word that best completes the analogy.**

6. *Purpose* is to *intention* as *surplus* is to ▢.
(A) excess (B) equipment (C) storage
(D) discussion (E) determination

7. *Heat* is to *expansion* as *wind* is to ▢.
(A) erosion (B) donation (C) dismissal
(D) breeze (E) temperature

8. *Talent* is to *achievement* as *genius* is to ▢.
(A) innovation (B) prodigy (C) failure
(D) shrewdness (E) underachievement

9. *House* is to *frame* as *body* is to ▢.
(A) skin (B) torso (C) joint
(D) skeleton (E) brain

10. *Merge* is to *separate* as *flippant* is to ▢.
(A) swimming (B) unbalanced (C) talkative
(D) thrown (E) respectful

## Sentence-Completion Tests

Sentence-completion questions assess your ability to use the context to complete a sentence. These questions ask you to figure out what word or words make the most sense in the blanks of a sentence. Although the sentences cover a wide variety of subjects, they do not require that you have a prior knowledge of those subjects. By using key words, you should be able to determine the answers from the context alone.

First read the following sentence from beginning to end. Then choose the most appropriate word to complete the sentence.

> Because you failed to meet the April 30 deadline and have since refused to say when or whether you will complete the work, we are forced to ▢ our contract with you.
> (A) honor (B) discuss (C) terminate
> (D) negotiate (E) extend

(The answer is *(C) terminate.* The rest of the sentence clearly suggests that the contract has not been honored and that the time for negotiating has passed. The other choices do not make sense in the context of the sentence.)

Sentence-completion questions sometimes have two blanks in the same sentence. Find the correct answer in this example.

Despite ■ to the contrary, the detective was ■ that Mrs. Arnold had mislaid her jewels.

(A) suspicions . . . pleased (B) evidence . . . convinced
(C) feelings . . . certain (D) confessions . . . depressed
(E) furor . . . surprised

(The answer is *(B) evidence . . . convinced.* The key words that help you determine this are *contrary* and *mislaid. Feelings . . . certain* contains a contradiction, while the other choices do not make sense in the context of the sentence.)

When you answer an item like this, read the sentence to yourself with the words in place to be sure it makes sense.

Check Your Understanding

***Completing Sentences***

**Write the letter of the word or words that best complete each of the following sentences.**

**1.** Since we had to meet at the station at exactly 2:35 P.M., we decided to ■ our watches.

(A) synchronize (B) ignore (C) wind
(D) consider (E) hide

**2.** An economist stated that the ■ of foreign currency could stimulate the small country's economy.

(A) influx (B) suppression (C) study
(D) suitability (E) lack

**3.** The giraffe is ▒, feeding only on plants.

(A) quadruped (B) hoofed (C) herbivorous
(D) huge (E) endangered

**4.** Her acceptance speech was so long that we can print only an ▒ of it in the newspaper.

(A) extension (B) array (C) excerpt
(D) overture (E) understatement

**5.** As a young man, the actor was slim and lithe; but as the years passed, he became a ▒ character actor.

(A) loose-limbed (B) portly (C) well-paid
(D) forgotten (E) lackluster

Check Your Understanding

## *Completing Sentences with Two Blanks*

**Write the letter of the pair of words that best completes each of the following sentences.**

**6.** The detective claimed that the suspect, in his ▒ to leave the scene, ▒ left a laundry ticket behind.

(A) aversion . . . randomly (B) haste . . . inadvertently
(C) anger . . . purposely (D) decision . . . foolishly
(E) plot . . . absentmindedly

**7.** Great Britain, with its long coastline and ▒ ports, is one of the leading ▒ nations in the world.

(A) many . . . agricultural (B) outstanding . . . industrial
(C) excellent . . . nautical (D) crowded . . . financial
(E) overabundant . . . debtor

**8.** When the ▒ was cut to 18 players, Phil was retained despite his ▒ playing.

(A) team . . . superb (B) choice . . . exuberant
(C) staff . . . improved (D) roster . . . inconsistent
(E) management . . . unsatisfactory

**9.** After a lengthy discussion, the ■ of the group was that our ■ affairs should be handled by an accountant.

(A) disagreement . . . legal (B) intent . . . basic
(C) equality . . . fund-raising (D) vote . . . important
(E) consensus . . . budgetary

**10.** We agreed that any ■ who could play both Juliet and Lady Macbeth had to be very ■.

(A) woman . . . elderly (B) performer . . . tricky
(C) actress . . . versatile (D) stagehand . . . flexible
(E) amateur . . . professional

## Reading Comprehension Tests

Reading comprehension tests assess your ability to understand and analyze written passages. The information you need to answer the questions may be either directly stated or implied in the passage. You must study, analyze, and interpret a passage in order to answer the questions. The following strategies can help you answer such questions.

### Strategies for Answering Comprehension Questions

- Begin by skimming the questions that follow the passage.
- Read the passage carefully and closely. Notice the main ideas, organization, style, and key words.
- Study all possible answers. Avoid choosing one answer the moment you think it is a reasonable choice.
- Use only the information in the passage when you answer the questions. Do not rely on your own knowledge or ideas on this kind of test.

Most reading comprehension questions will ask you to interpret or evaluate one or more of the following characteristics of a written passage.

- **Main idea** At least one question will usually focus on the central idea of the passage. Remember that the main idea of a passage covers all sections of that passage, not just one section or paragraph.
- **Supporting details** Questions about supporting details test your ability to identify the statements in the passage that back up the main idea.
- **Implied meanings** In some passages not all information is directly stated. Some questions ask you to interpret information that the author has merely implied.
- **Tone** Questions on tone require that you interpret or analyze the author's attitude toward his or her subjects.

## Practice Your Skills

### Check Your Understanding

*Reading Comprehension Passage*

**Read the passage and answer the questions that follow.**

A pebble begins as part of a large rock and often ends up as part of a larger rock. As rocks erode, break away, become fragments, and are transported by water, they become pebbles. Pebbles are generally rounded and smooth, some more so than others. If the rounding and smoothing proceed far enough, the pebbles become gravel or sand. Although pebbles, gravel, and sand all exist independently, they can also form the basis of new rocks.

Pebbles of any size can be bonded together to form either a breccia or a conglomerate. Some rock fragments travel only a short distance by stream or river, and thus retain the sharp, angular features of the fragments produced by the original fracturing. If consolidation occurs at this point, the result is a breccia. A *breccia* is a rock formed by the natural cementing together of sharp, unrounded fragments into a fine-grained matrix.

As the traveling distance of the original eroded rock increases, rounding continues. The bonded rock that is made is called a *conglomerate.* Many of the pebbles in a conglomerate, unlike those in a breccia, will not have derived from rocks in the immediate vicinity. Some will have been transported long distances, perhaps moved along a seacoast by the action of tides. One famous deposit is in Devon, England. The pebbles in this conglomerate are thought to have come from the rock of the mountains in Brittany, France, and to have been washed to England by the tides.

**1.** The best title for the passage is

(A) Rocks, Wind, and Waves.
(B) What Is a Conglomerate?
(C) A Brief Look at Geology.
(D) The Life Cycle of Pebbles.
(E) Pebbles at Budleigh Salterton.

**2.** Breccia contains sharp, angular pebbles because

(A) there was no water to transport the pebbles.
(B) the water molded the pebbles into that shape.
(C) the pebbles did not go far in a stream or river.
(D) some pebbles are too hard to round off.
(E) cementing made the pebbles sharp.

**3.** The writer's attitude toward the subject of pebbles is

(A) impassioned.
(B) skeptical.
(C) friendly.
(D) pessimistic.
(E) objective.

## The Double Passage

Some tests may also ask you to read two passages together and then answer questions about each passage individually and about similarities and differences between the two. The questions about the individual passages are typically just like single-passage questions. The questions about both passages ask you to compare and contrast such issues as viewpoints, tones, and implied meanings. A short introduction that precedes the passages may help you anticipate the ways in which the passages are similar and different.

On these tests, both reading passages are presented first, followed by questions about Passage 1 and then questions about Passage 2. Then come the comparison questions. You may find it helpful to read Passage 1 first and immediately answer the questions related to that passage before you read Passage 2. When you have finished the Passage 1 questions, you can return to read the second passage and answer the remaining questions.

## Practice Your Skills

Check Your Understanding

***Reading for Comprehension with Double Passages***

The following passages present two views of heroes and heroism. The first passage is from the introduction of a popular book about heroes and heroines in our time. The second is from a book on mythology by Edith Hamilton. Read each passage and answer the questions that follow.

**Passage 1**

In a simple society such as the Greeks' of three thousand years ago, the heroes' world was straightforward and uncomplicated. It was, in the words of Joseph Campbell, a world of "monomyths": it had single goals, definite and clear purposes. The heroes and heroines of that society spoke for and perpetuated humankind's goals and purposes. In more complicated societies, such as our own, heroes and heroines wear many faces because of their numerous responses to the varied needs of individuals, groups of people, and national purposes.

As a society's needs become more complicated, so too do the heroes and heroines; as people become more sophisticated, the heroes and heroines become less modeled on the conventional demigods of the past, less clear-cut and obvious. In a swiftly moving society like America today, heroes and heroines undergo rapid transformation. They frequently develop in ways and for purposes that are not immediately apparent. Twentieth-century American heroes and heroines, existing in a highly technological society and driven by the electronics of mass communication, change quickly. They are often hailed as heroic today and forgotten tomorrow. But though they may disappear rapidly, they serve useful and needed purposes while they endure. So we continue to create heroes and heroines because they can concentrate the power of the people—of a nation—and serve as the driving force for the movement and development of individuals and society.

**Passage 2**

The world of Norse mythology is a strange world. Asgard, the home of the gods, is unlike any other heaven men have dreamed of. No radiancy of joy is in it, no assurance of bliss. It is a grave and solemn place, over which hangs the threat of an inevitable doom. The gods know that a day will come when they will be destroyed. Sometime they will meet their enemies and go down beneath them to defeat and death. Asgard will fall in ruins. The cause the forces of good are fighting to defend against the forces of evil is hopeless. Nevertheless, the gods will fight for it to the end.

Necessarily the same is true of humanity. If the gods are finally helpless before evil, men and women must be more so. This is the conception of life which underlies the Norse religion, as somber a conception as the mind of man has ever given birth to. The only sustaining support possible for the human spirit, the one pure unsullied good man can hope to attain, is heroism; and heroism depends on lost causes. The hero can prove what he is only by dying. The power of good is shown not by triumphantly conquering evil, but by continuing to resist evil while facing certain defeat.

**1.** According to the author of Passage 1, which of the following factors best explains why heroes in Greek society differ from heroes of today?

(A) lack of monomyths

(B) mass communication

(C) technological advancements

(D) simple versus complicated societies

(E) development of nations

**2.** In relation to paragraph 1 in Passage 1, the purpose of paragraph 2 is mainly to

(A) define heroes.

(B) trace the development of heroes through the centuries.

(C) contrast contemporary heroes with ancient heroes.

(D) elaborate the point made in sentence 1.

(E) illustrate the concept of monomyth.

**3.** According to the author of Passage 2, heroism in Norse mythology is achieved by

(A) overcoming the forces of evil.

(B) triumphing over death.

(C) fighting to the death against forces of evil.

(D) accomplishing great deeds.

(E) mastering godlike powers.

**4.** According to the author of Passage 2, which describes mythology's sphere of influence in Norse culture?

(A) spiritual (B) social (C) political

(D) intellectual (E) artistic

**5.** Which of the following ideas from Passage 1 holds true for the idea of heroism as described in Passage 2?

(A) Heroes undergo rapid transformation.

(B) Heroes may disappear rapidly.

(C) Heroes are not clear-cut and obvious.

(D) Heroes can concentrate the power of a people.

(E) Heroes are varied to reflect cultural diversity.

## Tests of Standard Written English

An objective test of standard written English assesses your knowledge of writing skills. The test contains passages or sentences with underlined words, phrases, or punctuation. The underlined parts may contain errors in grammar, usage, mechanics, vocabulary, and spelling. You must find each error or, on some tests, identify the best way to revise a faulty sentence or passage.

### Error Recognition

This kind of question tests grammar, usage, capitalization, punctuation, word choice, and spelling. As a rule, each item consists of a sentence with five underlined parts. Four of these underlined parts suggest possible errors in the sentence. The fifth indicates that there is no error. No sentence has more than one error. Read the following sentence carefully and identify the error, if there is one.

> The Pacific Ocean (A) is 36,198 feet deep in the Mariana's Trench, (B) even deeper then (C) Mount Everest or the mountain K2 is (D) high.
>
> (The answer is *C*. Standard usage requires *than* rather than *then* in this sentence.)

Sometimes you will find a sentence that contains no error. Be careful, however, before you choose *E* as the answer. The errors included in this kind of test are often common errors that are hard to notice.

Remember, however, that everything not underlined is presumed to be correct. You can often use the correct parts to help identify the error in the sentence.

## PRACTICE YOUR SKILLS

Check Your Understanding

*Recognizing Errors in Writing*

**Write the letter of the underlined word or punctuation mark that is incorrect. If the sentence contains no error write *E*.**

**(1)** The Reverend (A) William Spooner, who's (B) last name became a common noun, had (C) an (D) unusual quirk of speech. **(2)** Spooners' (A) quirk was to (B) transpose the initial sounds of two (C) or more (D) words. **(3)** There (A) are (B) a great many examples of his (C) odd, (D) humorous mistakes. **(4)** When Spooner spoke, (A) "a well-oiled bicycle," (B) for example, would come out as (C) "a well-boiled icicle". (D) **(5)** Spooner was an experienced, knowledgeable (A) teacher who (B) his (C) students liked and respected. (D) **(6)** If you was (A) to ask most of his students, they (B) would say (C) he was (D) unforgettable. **(7)** After all, (A) how could anyone (B) forget a man who said, "Let me sew you to your sheet," when he intends (C) to show you to your seat? (D) **(8)** Everyone who (A) knew Reverend Spooner had (B) their (C) own story to tell about him. (D) **(9)** Still, as time went by, the old man's (A) long service at New College, (B) Oxford, (C) was all but forgotten. (D) **(10)** Spoonerisms, however, are remembered to this day, (A) and are (B) the classic examples used (C) in all dictionary definitions of the word based on his (D) name.

## Sentence Correction

These questions assess your ability to recognize appropriate phrasing. Instead of locating an error, you must select the best way to write a sentence. In this kind of question, part of the sentence is underlined. Following the sentence are five different ways of writing the underlined part. The first way shown, *(A)*, is the same as the underlined part. The other four ways present alternatives. The choices may involve questions of grammar, usage, capitalization, punctuation, or diction. Your answer must not change the meaning of the sentence.

We all agreed that the guest lecturer was well informed, articulate, and he had a nice personality.

(A) he had a nice personality.
(B) he had a pleasant personality.
(C) a nice personality.
(D) likeable.
(E) nice personality wise.

(The answer is *(D)*. The problem with the original sentence, as well as with choices *(B)* and *(C)*, is lack of parallelism. Choice *(E)* is parallel but contains an awkward construction. Notice that *(D)* includes a new adjective, *likeable,* although *personable* would have been satisfactory.)

## Practice Your Skills

### Check Your Understanding

***Correcting Sentences***

**Write the letter of the correct or best way of phrasing the underlined part of each sentence.**

**1.** "Fair is foul, wrote Shakespeare, and foul is fair."

(A) foul, wrote Shakespeare, and
(B) foul, "wrote Shakespeare, "and
(C) foul", wrote Shakespeare, "and
(D) foul," wrote Shakespeare, "and
(E) foul," wrote Shakespeare, and

2. Each of us in the audience hopes to learn your views on the bond issue.
   (A) of us in the audience hopes
   (B) of we in the audience hopes
   (C) of us in the audience hope
   (D) of we in the audience hope
   (E) member of the audience hope
3. The prince, along with all his supporters, were observed coming toward the village.
   (A) his supporters, were observed coming toward
   (B) his supporters were observed, coming toward
   (C) his supporters, was observed coming toward
   (D) his supporters, was observed, coming toward
   (E) his' supporters, was observed coming toward
4. Was it Jacqueline who said, Its not too late to get a collar for your puppy?
   (A) Its not too late to get a collar for your puppy?
   (B) "Its not to late to get a collar for your puppy"?
   (C) "It's not too late to get a collar for you're puppy?"
   (D) It's not to late to get a collar for your puppy.
   (E) "It's not too late to get a collar for your puppy"?
5. The alarm should of begun ringing by now.
   (A) alarm should of begun
   (B) alarm, it should of begun
   (C) alarm should have begun
   (D) alarm should have began
   (E) alarm should of began

## Revision-in-Context

Another type of question you may encounter on a standardized test is revision-in-context. You will be asked to read a brief essay, one that represents an early draft of a student's work. In the questions that follow the essay, you will be asked to choose the best revision of a sentence, group of sentences, or the essay as a whole and to demonstrate your understanding of the writer's intention.

## Practice Your Skills

### Check Your Understanding

### *Correcting Sentences*

**Carefully read the passage and answer the questions that follow.**

**(1)** Recently, a questionnaire was developed that asked people to give their opinions. **(2)** What they were to give their opinions about was the value of leisure time. **(3)** Most people said that their favorite pastime was watching television. **(4)** Commenting on the quality of the shows, however, the programs were not very satisfying. **(5)** Most people felt that their time would be better spent if they pursued physical activities such as sports and athletics. **(6)** They felt such activities would make a noticeable change in the way they felt. **(7)** Unfortunately, they also felt there was little likelihood that they would take up exercise on a regular basis. **(8)** Many people, it seems, are willing to settle for so-so pastimes despite the fact that they know other pastimes might enhance the quality of their lives.

**1.** In relation to the rest of the passage, which of the following best describes the writer's intention in sentence (8)?

(A) to restate the opening sentence

(B) to draw a conclusion

(C) to provide examples

(D) to contrast active versus passive pastimes

(E) to offer contradictory evidence

**2.** Which of the following is the best revision of the underlined portion of sentence (4) below?

Commenting on the quality of the shows, however, the programs were not very satisfying.

(A) , however; the programs were not very satisfying.
(B) however the viewers reported that the programs were not very satisfying.
(C) , however, the viewers reported that the programs were not very satisfying.
(D) ; however, the programs were not very satisfying.
(E) , however, the viewers reported that, the shows were not very satisfying.

**3.** Which of the following is the best way to combine sentences (1) and (2)?

(A) Recently, a questionnaire was developed that asked people to give their opinions, and what they were asked to give their opinions about was the value of leisure time.
(B) Recently, a questionnaire was developed that asked people to give their opinions on the value of leisure time.
(C) Recently, people were asked to give their opinions of leisure time.
(D) Recently, a questionnaire was developed, it asked people to give their opinions on the value of leisure time.
(E) A recent questionnaire developed to ask people to give their opinions on the value of leisure time.

## Taking Essay Tests

The main difference between a classroom writing assignment and an essay test is time. Since you have a limited amount of time on a test, you must organize and express your ideas quickly, clearly, and logically.

## Kinds of Essay Questions

Before you begin to write your answers on an essay test, plan the amount of time you should spend on each part of the test. (The time you spend should be in proportion to the number of points allotted to each part.) Then when it comes time to begin your first question, look for key words, such as those listed in the following box. Such key words will tell you precisely what kind of question you are being asked to answer.

| KINDS OF ESSAY QUESTIONS | |
|---|---|
| **ANALYZE** | Separate into parts and examine each part. |
| **COMPARE** | Point out similarities. |
| **CONTRAST** | Point out differences. |
| **DEFINE** | Clarify meaning. |
| **DISCUSS** | Examine in detail. |
| **EVALUATE** | Give your opinion. |
| **EXPLAIN** | Tell how, what, or why. |
| **ILLUSTRATE** | Give examples. |
| **SUMMARIZE** | Briefly review main points. |
| **TRACE** | Show development or progress. |

As you read the instructions, jot down everything that is required in your answer, or underline key words and circle instructions. For instance, the key words are underlined and the instructions are circled in the following example.

> When Francisco Pizarro first landed in 1531 on the coast of what is now Ecuador, the Inca Empire was larger than any European city of the time. Nevertheless, within only several years, the Spanish were able to destroy this mighty empire. Analyze three possible reasons for the rapid collapse of the Inca Empire. Include specific details to support each point.

## Practice Your Skills

Check Your Understanding

*Interpreting Essay Test Questions*

**Write the key word in each question. Then write one sentence that explains what the question is asking you to do.**

1. Explain how carbon-14 is used to date objects.
2. Contrast an ode and an elegy.
3. Briefly summarize the plot of *Silas Marner,* a novel by George Eliot.
4. Trace the development of a tornado.
5. In your own words, define m*arket economy*.
6. How does the working of a gasoline engine compare with that of an electric engine?
7. In his *Dictionary of the English Language,* Samuel Johnson defines youth as "The part of life succeeding to childhood and adolescence; the time from fourteen to twenty-eight." Do you agree? Discuss Johnson's definition.
8. Briefly evaluate the scientific contributions of lasers.

## Writing an Effective Essay Answer

Since the procedures for writing an essay test are basically the same as those for a typical writing assignment, you should recall and apply all that you have learned about the process of writing an essay. However, because your time will be restricted in a test situation, you must do some extra preplanning.

You should first decide how much time you will work on each question and how much time you will spend on each step in the writing of each answer. A general guideline is to allow two minutes of planning and one minute of revising and editing for every five minutes of writing. As you calculate according to this timetable, plan to give more time to the essay answers worth the most points.

Knowing what you are going to write—and in what order you are going to write it—is essential before you begin to write your essay answer. Your first step, therefore, should be to organize your answer by writing a plan in the form of a simple informal outline or a graphic organizer. Study the following example.

**Reasons for the Collapse of the Inca Empire**

INFORMAL OUTLINE:

(thesis statement)

**1.** Reason 1: weapons

**2.** Reason 2: transportation

**3.** Reason 3: internal war

(conclusion)

GRAPHIC ORGANIZER:

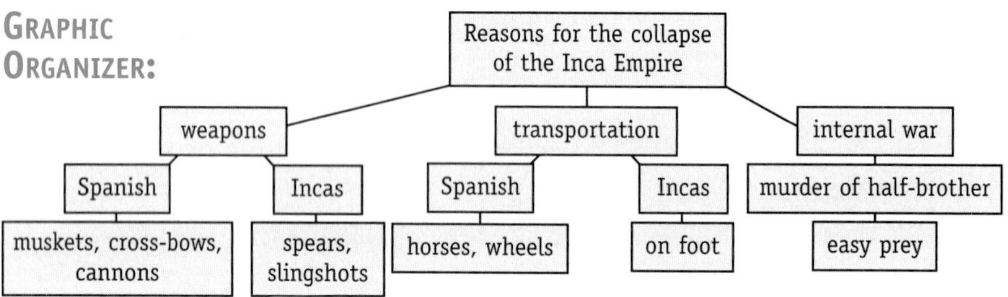


Your next step is to write a thesis statement that states the main idea of your essay and covers all of your major supporting ideas. A helpful hint when writing an essay answer is to reword the test question itself—if possible—into a thesis statement.

ESSAY QUESTION: When Francisco Pizarro first landed in 1531 on the coast of what is now Ecuador, the Inca Empire was larger than any European city at the time. Nevertheless, within only several years, the Spanish were able to destroy this mighty empire. Analyze three reasons for the rapid collapse of the Inca Empire.

THESIS STATEMENT: Although the Inca Empire was larger than any European city in 1531, the Spanish were able to destroy this mighty empire for three reasons.

As you write your essay answer, keep the following strategies in mind.

### Strategies for Writing an Essay Answer

- Begin with a thesis statement that states the main idea of your essay and covers all of your major supporting ideas.
- Follow the order of your plan, writing at least one paragraph for each main point.
- Provide adequate support for each main point—using specific facts, examples, and/or other supporting details.
- Make certain the essay contains a logical progression of ideas.
- End with a strong concluding statement that summarizes, or brings closure, to the main idea of the essay.
- Be certain the essay has an overall sense of unity.
- Communicate your ideas clearly and effectively.
- Write legibly, using standard English.

**Model: Essay Test Answer**

THESIS STATEMENT

Although the Inca Empire was larger than any European city in 1531, the Spanish were able to destroy this mighty empire for three reasons. Perhaps the most obvious reason was the discrepancy in the weapons that the Spanish and the Incas used. Having no knowledge of iron, the Incas fought mainly with bronze-edged spears and slingshots. The Spanish returned such attacks with muskets, crossbows, and full-sized cannons.

The Spanish were able to transport themselves, their cannons, and their supplies into the interior of the Inca Empire because they not only had horses, but they also had the use of the wheel.

Even though they had built a sophisticated system of roads, the Incas traveled only on foot. They did not have horses, and they could only carry, not pull, things since the wheel was unknown to them.

When Pizarro entered the empire, Atahuallpa had successfully captured the throne from his half-brother. Realizing the threat from the Spanish, Atahuallpa had his half-brother killed. However, shortly afterward the Spanish killed Atahuallpa himself. As a result the Incas, greatly divided and lacking a strong leader, became easy prey for the Spanish. At the time the combination of these

**CONCLUSION:** three factors was too much for the Incas. Could the course of history have a taken a different turn, however, if someone like Pizarro had come only 20 or 30 years later?

## Revising

Writing Process

Always leave yourself a few minutes to revise your essay answer. As you revise your work, ask yourself these questions.

- Did you thoroughly follow the instructions?
- Did you begin with a thesis statement?
- Did you include supporting details and examples?
- Did you use transitions to connect ideas and examples?
- Did you have a logical progression of ideas?
- Did you end with a strong concluding statement that summarized your essay?
- Did you create a sense of unity?
- Did you communicate your ideas clearly and effectively?

## Editing — Writing Process

Once you have made any necessary revisions, quickly read your essay for any mistakes in spelling, usage, or punctuation. To keep your paper as neat as possible, use proofreading symbols to make any corrections. If time permits, look for the following problems:

- lack of agreement between subjects and verbs *(pages L289–L317)*
- lack of agreement of pronouns and antecedents, especially indefinite pronouns *(pages L267–L273)*
- tense shift problems *(page C373)*
- incorrect verb inflections *(pages L181–L192)*
- incorrect form of adjectives and adverbs in the comparative and superlative forms *(pages L327–L333)*
- incorrect capitalization of proper nouns and proper adjectives *(pages L399–L411)*
- incorrect use of commas *(pages L436–L460)*
- incorrect use of apostrophes *(pages L471–L483)*
- incorrect divisions of words at the end of a line *(pages L522–L523)*

## Communicate Your Ideas

### APPLY TO WRITING

**Drafting: *Essay Test Question***

Select any subject area, including English, and write an essay question that is likely to be included on an upcoming test. Answer the question by following the strategies on pages L601–L602. First prepare a brief outline or graphic organizer and a thesis statement. Then draft your answer. Finally, revise and edit your essay answer.

## Timed Writing

The more you practice writing within a limited time period, the more confident you will feel as you enter a test situation in which you must complete a timed writing assignment.

Time limits can vary from 20 to 60 to 90 minutes depending upon the purpose and complexity of the task. Following the steps in the writing process, you might organize your time for a 20-minute essay in this way:

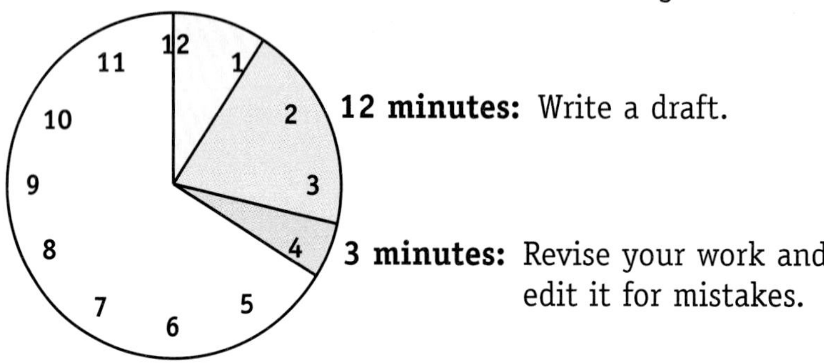
**5 minutes:** Brainstorm and organize ideas.
**12 minutes:** Write a draft.
**3 minutes:** Revise your work and edit it for mistakes.
12
1
2
3
4
5
6
7
8
9
10
11

### Communicate Your Ideas

#### APPLY TO WRITING

**Prewriting, Drafting, Revising, Editing: *Timed Writing***

Give yourself 20 minutes to answer the following:

- Keeping yourself informed of national and world news is an important task. Compare and contrast the strengths and weaknesses of television news programs and newspapers. Give specific examples from your own experiences.

Plan time for every step of the writing process, set a timer, and begin your answer.

# GLOSSARY

## A

**Abstract** summary of points of writing, presented in skeletal form.

**Abstract noun** word that names a quality, a condition, or an idea.

**Action verb** word that tells what action a subject is performing.

**Active voice** the voice a verb is in when it expresses that the subject is performing the action.

**Adjective** word that modifies a noun or a pronoun.

**Adjective clause** subordinate clause that is used like an adjective to modify a noun or a pronoun.

**Adjective phrase** prepositional phrase that is used to modify a noun or a pronoun.

**Adverb** word that modifies a verb, an adjective, or another adverb.

**Adverb clause** subordinate clause that is used like an adverb to modify a verb, an adjective, or an adverb.

**Adverb phrase** prepositional phrase that is used like an adverb to modify a verb, an adjective, or an adverb.

**Alliteration** repetition of a consonant sound at the beginning of a series of words.

**Allusion** reference to persons or events in the past or in literature.

**Analogies** logical relationships between pairs of words.

**Antecedent** word or group of words that a pronoun replaces or refers to.

**Antonym** word that means the opposite of another word.

**Appositive** noun or a pronoun that identifies or explains another noun or pronoun in a sentence.

**Assonance** repetition of a vowel sound within words.

## B

**Body** one or more paragraphs comprised of details, facts, and examples that support the main idea.

**Brainstorming** prewriting technique of writing down everything that comes to mind about a subject.

## C

**Case** form of a noun or a pronoun that indicates its use in a sentence. In English there are three cases: the nominative case, the objective case, and the possessive case.

**Cause and effect** method of development in which details are grouped according to what happens and why it happens.

**Characterization** variety of techniques used by writers to show the personality of a character.

**Chronological order** the order in which events occur.

**Citation** note that directs reader to the original source.

**Classification** method of development in which details are grouped into categories.

**Clause** group of words that has a subject and a predicate and is used as part of a sentence.

**Cliché** overused expression that is no longer fresh or interesting to the reader.

**Clustering** a visual form of brainstorming that is a technique used for developing supporting details.

**Coherence** logical and smooth flow of ideas connected with clear transitions.

**Common noun** names any person, place, or thing.

**Comparative degree** modification of an adjective or adverb used when two people, things, or actions are compared.

**Comparison and contrast** method of development in which the writer examines similarities and differences between two subjects.

**Complement** word that completes the meaning of an action verb.

**Complete predicate** all the words that tell what the subject is doing or that tell something about the subject.

**Complete subject** all the words used to identify the person, place, thing, or idea that the sentence is about.

**Complex sentence** one independent clause and one or more subordinate clauses.

**Compound adjective** adjective made up of more than one word.

**Compound-complex sentence** two or more independent clauses and one or more subordinate clauses.

**Compound noun** word made up of two smaller words that can be separated, hyphenated, or combined.

**Compound sentence** two or more independent clauses in one sentence.

**Compound subject** two or more subjects in one sentence that have the same verb and are joined by a conjunction.

**Compound verb** two or more verbs that have the same subject and are joined by a conjunction.

**Concluding sentence** a strong ending to a paragraph that summarizes the major points, refers to the main idea, or adds an insight.

**Conclusion** paragraph that completes an essay and reinforces its main idea.

**Conflict** struggle between opposing forces around which the action of a work of literature revolves.

**Conjunction** word that joins together sentences, clauses, phrases, or other words.

**Connotation** the meaning that comes from attitudes attached to a word.

**Consonance** repetition of a consonant sound, usually in the middle or at the end of words.

**Context clue** clue to a word's meaning provided by the sentence or passage in which the word is used.

**Coordinating conjunction** single connecting word used to join words or groups of words.

**Correlative conjunction** pairs of conjunctions used to connect compound subjects, compound verbs, and compound sentences.

## D

**Dangling modifier** phrase that has nothing to describe in a sentence.

**Declarative sentence** statement or expression of an opinion that ends with a period.

**Demonstrative pronoun** word that substitutes for a noun and points out a person or a thing.

**Denotation** the literal meaning of a word.

**Descriptive writing** writing that creates a vivid picture of a person, an object, or a scene by stimulating the reader's senses.

**Developmental order** information that is organized so that one idea grows out of the preceding idea.

**Dewey decimal system** system by which nonfiction books are arranged on shelves in numerical order according to ten general subject categories.

**Dialect** regional variation of a language distinguished by distinctive pronunciation and some differences in word meanings.

**Dialogue** conversation between two or more persons.

**Direct object** noun or a pronoun that receives the action of a verb.

**Direct quotation** passage, sentence or words written or spoken exactly as a person wrote or said them.

**Drafting** stage of the writing process in which the writer draws together ideas on paper.

## E

**Editing** stage of the writing process in which the writer polishes his or her work by correcting errors in grammar, usage, mechanics, and spelling.

**Elaboration** addition of explanatory or descriptive information to an essay, such as supporting facts, details, and examples.

**Electronic publishing** various ways to present information through the use of technology. It includes desktop publishing (creating printed documents on a computer), audio and video recordings, and online publishing (creating a Website).

**Elliptical clause** subordinate clause in which words are omitted but understood to be there.

**E-mail** electronic mail that can be sent all over the world from one computer to another.

**Essential phrase or clause** group of words essential to the meaning of a sentence and is therefore not set off with commas.

**Etymology** a word's history from its earliest recorded use to its present use.

**Exclamatory sentence** expression of strong feeling that ends with an exclamation point.

**Expository writing** writing that explains or informs with facts and examples or gives directions.

## F

**Fact** statement that can be proved.

**Fiction** prose works of literature, such as short stories and novels, that are partly or totally imaginary.

**Figurative language** imaginative, nonliteral use of language.

**Formal English** conventional rules of grammar, usage, and mechanics.

**Free verse** verse without meter or a regular, patterned beat.

**Freewriting** prewriting technique of writing freely about ideas as they come to mind.

## G

**Gerund** verb form ending in *–ing* that is used as a noun.

**Gerund phrase** a gerund with its modifiers and complements working together as a noun.

**Glittering generality** words and phrases most people associate with virtue and goodness.

## H

**Helping verb** auxiliary verb that helps to make up a verb phrase.

**Hyperbole** use of exaggeration or overstatement.

## I

**Imagery** use of concrete details to create a picture or appeal to senses other than sight.

**Imperative mood** verb form used to give a command or to make a request.

**Imperative sentence** a direction, a request, or a command that ends with either a period or an exclamation point.

**Indefinite pronoun** word that substitutes for a noun and refers to an unnamed person or thing.

**Independent clause** group of words that can stand alone as a sentence because it expresses a complete thought.

**Indicative mood** verb form used to state a fact or to ask a question.

**Indirect object** noun or a pronoun that answers the question *to or from whom?* or *to or for what?* after an action verb.

**Infinitive** verb form that usually begins with *to* and is used as a noun, an adjective, or an adverb.

**Inquiring** prewriting technique in which the writer asks questions such as *Who? What? Where? Why?* and *When?*

**Intensive pronoun** word that adds emphasis to a noun or another pronoun in the sentence

**Interjection** word that expresses strong feeling.

**Internet** a worldwide network of computers (see also *Basic Internet Terminology in a Writer's Guide to Using the Internet*).

**Interrogative pronoun** word used to ask a question.

**Interrogative sentence** a question; a sentence that ends with a question mark.

**Intransitive verb** an action verb that does not have an object.

**Introduction** paragraph that introduces a subject, states or implies a purpose, and presents a main idea.

**Inverted order** condition when the subject follows the verb or part of the verb phrase.

**Irregular verb** does not form its past and past participle by adding *–ed* or *–d* to the present.

## L

**Linking verb** links the subject with another word in the sentence. This other word either renames or describes the subject.

**Literary analysis** interpretation of a work of literature supported by appropriate responses, details, quotations, and commentaries.

## M

**Metaphor** figure of speech that compares by saying that one thing *is* another.

**Meter** the rhythm of a specific beat of stressed and unstressed syllables found in many poems.

**Misplaced modifier** phrase or a clause that is placed too far away from the word it modifies, thus creating an unclear sentence.

**Mood** overall atmosphere or feeling created by a work of literature.

## N

**Narrative writing** writing that tells a real or an imaginary story.

**Nonessential phrase or clause** group of words that is not essential to the meaning of a sentence and is therefore set off with commas.

**Nonfiction** prose writing that contains facts about real people and real events.

**Noun** a word that names a person, a place, a thing, or an idea. A common noun gives a general name. A proper noun names a specific person, place, or thing and always begins with a capital letter. A collective noun names a group of people or things.

**Noun clause** subordinate clause that is used like a noun.

## O

**Objective complement** noun or an adjective that renames or describes the direct object.

**Occasion** motivation for composing; the factor that prompts the writer to decide on process for communication.

**Onomatopoeia** use of words whose sounds suggest their meaning.

**Opinion** belief or judgment that cannot be proved.

**Oral interpretation** performance or expressive reading of a literary work.

**Order of importance** order in which supporting evidence is arranged from least to most or (most to least) important.

**Outline** information about a subject into main topics and subtopics.

## P

**Paraphrase** restatement of an original work in one's own words.

**Parenthetical citation** source and page number (in parentheses) within a sentence in which the source of information must be credited.

**Participial phrase** participle with its modifiers and complements—all working together as an adjective.

**Participle** verb form that is used as an adjective.

**Passive voice** the voice a verb is in when it expresses that the action is being performed upon its subject.

**Peer conference** a meeting with one's peers, such as other students, to share ideas and offer suggestions for revision.

**Personal pronoun** type of pronoun that can be categorized into one of three groups, dependent on the speaker's position: first person, second person, and third person.

**Personal writing** writing that expresses the writer's personal point of view on a subject drawn from the writer's own experience.

**Personification** comparison in which human qualities are given to an animal, an object, or an idea.

**Persuasive writing** writing that states an opinion and uses facts, examples, and reasons to convince readers.

**Phrase** group of related words that functions as a single part of speech and does not have a subject and a verb.

**Phrase fragment** phrase written as if it were a complete sentence.

**Play** a composition written for dramatic performance on the stage.

**Plot** sequence of events leading to the outcome or point of the story.

**Point of view** vantage point from which a writer tells a story or describes a subject.

**Portfolio** collection of work representing various types of writing and the progress made on them.

**Positive degree** adjective or adverb used when no comparison is being made.

**Possessive pronoun** pronoun used to show ownership or possession.

**Predicate adjective** adjective that follows a linking verb and modifies the subject.

**Predicate nominative** noun or a pronoun that follows a linking verb and identifies, renames, or explains the subject.

**Prefix** one or more syllables placed in front of a root or base word to modify the meaning of the root or base word or to form a new word.

**Preposition** word that shows the relationship between a noun or a pronoun and another word in the sentence.

**Prepositional phrase** group of words that begins with a preposition, ends with a noun or a pronoun, and is used as an adjective or an adverb.

**Prewriting** invention stage in the writing process in which the writer plans for drafting based on the subject, occasion, audience, and purpose for writing.

**Principal parts of a verb** the *present*, the *past*, and the *past participle*. The principal parts help form the tenses of verbs.

**Pronoun** word that takes the place of one or more nouns.

**Proofreading** carefully rereading and making corrections in grammar, usage, spelling, and mechanics in a piece of writing.

**Propaganda** effort to persuade by distorting and misrepresenting information or by disguising opinions as facts.

**Protagonist** principal character in a story.

**Publishing** stage of a writer's process in which the writer may choose to share the work with an audience or make the work "public."

**Purpose** reason for writing or for speaking.

## R

**Reflexive pronoun** pronoun formed by adding *–self* or *–selves* to a personal pronoun and is used to reflect back to another noun or pronoun.

**Regular verb** verb that forms its past and past participle by adding *-ed* to the present.

**Relative pronoun** pronoun that relates an adjective clause to the modified noun or pronoun.

**Repetition** repeat of a word or phrase for poetic effect.

**Research paper** a composition of three or more paragraphs that uses information from books, magazines, and other sources.

**Résumé** summary of a person's work experience, education, and interests.

**Revising** stage of a writer's process in which the writer rethinks what is written and reworks it to increase its clarity, smoothness, and power.

**Rhyme scheme** regular pattern of rhyming in a poem.

**Root** part of a word that carries the basic meaning.

**Run-on sentence** two or more sentences that are written together and are separated by a comma or have no mark of punctuation at all.

## S

**Sensory details** details that appeal to one of the five senses: seeing, hearing, touching, tasting, and smelling.

**Sentence fragment** a group of words that does not express a complete thought.

**Sequential order** the order in which details are arranged according to when they take place or where they are done.

**Setting** environment (location and time) of a story.

**Short story** short work of narrative fiction.

**Simile** figure of speech comparing two unlike objects using the words *like* and *as*.

**Simple predicate** main word or phrase in the complete predicate.

**Simple sentence** one independent clause.

**Simple subject** main word in a complete subject.

**Sound devices** ways to use sounds in poetry to achieve certain effects.

**Spatial order** order in which details are arranged, according to their location.

**Speech** oral composition presented by a speaker to an audience.

**Standard English** conventions of usage accepted most widely by English-speaking people throughout the world.

**Style** visual or verbal expression that is distinctive to an artist or writer.

**Subject** word or group of words that names the person, place, thing, or idea the sentence is about.

**Subjunctive mood** words such as *if, as if*, or *as though* or that are used to express a condition contrary to fact or to express a wish.

**Subordinate clause** group of words that cannot stand alone because it does not express a complete thought.

**Subordinating conjunction** single connecting word used in a complex sentence to introduce an adverb clause.

**Suffix** one or more syllables placed after a root or base word to change the word's part of speech and possibly its meaning.

**Summary** information written in a condensed, concise form, touching only on the main ideas.

**Superlative degree** modification of an adjective or adverb used when more than two people, things, or actions are compared.

**Supporting sentences** specific details, facts, examples, or reasons that explain or prove a topic sentence.

**Symbol** object, an event, or a character that stands for a universal idea or quality.

**Synonym** word that has nearly the same meaning as another word.

## T

**Tense** form a verb takes to show time. The six tenses are the present, past, future, present perfect, past perfect, and future perfect.

**Theme** underlying idea, message, or meaning of a work of literature.

**Thesis statement** statement of the main idea that makes the writing purpose clear.

**Tone** writer's attitude toward the subject and audience of a composition (may also be referred to as the writer's *voice*).

**Topic sentence** statement of the main idea of the paragraph.

**Transitions** words and phrases that show how ideas are related.

**Transitive verb** action verb that passes the action from a doer to a receiver.

## U

**Understood subject** unstated subject that is understood.

**Unity** combination or ordering of parts in a composition so that all the sentences or paragraphs work together as a whole to support one main idea.

## V

**Verb** word that expresses action or state of being

**Verbal** verb form used as some other part of speech.

**Verb phrase** main verb plus one or more helping verbs.

**Voice** particular sound and rhythm of language that the writer uses; writer's attitude toward the subject of a composition (may also be referred to as *tone*).

## W

**World Wide Web** a network of computers within the Internet, capable of delivering multimedia content and text over communication lines into personal computers all over the globe.

**Working thesis** statement that expresses the possible main idea of a composition or research report.

**Works cited page** alphabetical listing of sources cited in a research paper.

**Writing process** recursive series of stages a writer proceeds through when developing ideas and discovering the best way to express them.

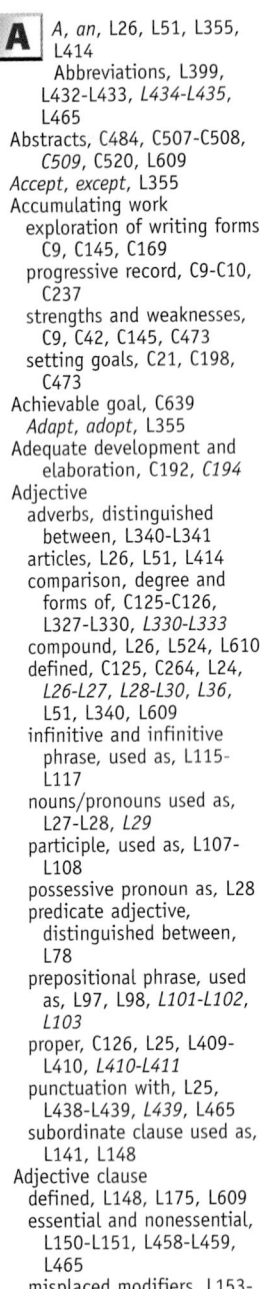

*Note: Italic page numbers indicate skill sets.*

*Note: Italic page numbers indicate skill sets.*

*Note: Italic page numbers indicate skill sets.*

*Note: Italic page numbers indicate skill sets.*

*Note: Italic page numbers indicate skill sets.*

*Note: Italic page numbers indicate skill sets.*

*Note: Italic page numbers indicate skill sets.*

*Note: Italic page numbers indicate skill sets.*

INDEX

*Note: Italic page numbers indicate skill sets.*

INDEX

*Note: Italic page numbers indicate skill sets.*

*Note: Italic page numbers indicate skill sets.*

*Note: Italic page numbers indicate skill sets.*

*Note: Italic page numbers indicate skill sets.*

*Note: Italic page numbers indicate skill sets.*

*Note: Italic page numbers indicate skill sets.*

*Note: Italic page numbers indicate skill sets.*

*Note: Italic page numbers indicate skill sets.*

*Note: Italic page numbers indicate skill sets.*

INDEX

*Note: Italic page numbers indicate skill sets.*

*Note: Italic page numbers indicate skill sets.*

INDEX

*Note: Italic page numbers indicate skill sets.*

*Note: Italic page numbers indicate skill sets.*

*Note: Italic page numbers indicate skill sets.*

Barrett Kendall Publishing has made every effort to trace the ownership of all copyrighted selections in this book and to make full acknowledgment of their use. Grateful acknowledgment is made to the following authors, publishers, agents, and individuals for their permission to reprint copyrighted material.

**Composition**

**C3:** Reprinted by permission of the publisher from *One Writer's Beginnings* by Eudora Welty, Cambridge, Mass.: Harvard University Press, Copyright © 1983, 1984 by Eudora Welty. **C55, C93:** Copyright © 1989 by the New York Times Co. Reprinted by permission. **C95:** "Tuxedo Junction" by P. Dee Boersma. © P. Dee Boersma. Reprinted by permission. **C171:** Excerpt from "Shakespeare's Sister" in *A Room of One's Own* by Virginia Woolf, copyright 1929 by Harcourt, Inc. and renewed 1957 by Leonard Woolf, reprinted by permission of the publisher. **C179:** Copyright © 1987 by the New York Times Co. Reprinted by permission. **C182:** From "Notes of a Translator's Son," from *I Tell You Now: Autobiographical Essays by Native American Writers,* University of Nebraska Press. **C183:** "On Holidays and How to Make Them Work" from *Sacred Cows and Other Edibles* by Nikki Giovanni. Copyright © 1988 by Nikki Giovanni. Reprinted by permission of HarperCollins Publishers, Inc., William Morrow. **C184:** From *How to do Things Right* by L. Rust Hills. Reprinted by permission of David R. Godine, Publisher, Inc. Copyright © 1993 by L. Rust Hills. **C186:** "Notes of a Biology-Watcher: Computers." Copyright © 1973 Massachusetts Medical Society. All rights reserved. Adapted with permission, 2001. **C187, C197:** From *Thinking Out Loud* by Anna Quindlen. Copyright © 1993 by Anna Quindlen. Reprinted by permission of Random House, Inc. **C190:** Special permission granted, *Career World®,* copyright 1999, published by Weekly Reader Corporation. All rights reserved. **C209:** "The Concert" by Gary Soto. Text copyright © 1986 by Gary Soto. Used with permission of the author and BookStop Literary Agency. All rights reserved. **C245:** Originally published in *The New Yorker.* Reprinted by permission of International Creative Management, Inc. Copyright © 1995 Chang-rae Lee. **C281:** By permission of Random House, Inc. **C306:** *Shakespeare in Love: A Screen Play,* by Marc Norman and Tom Stoppard. Hyperion/Miramax Books. **C317:** Scattered excerpt from "The Hollow Men" in *Collected Poems 1909–1962* by T.S. Eliot, copyright 1936 by Harcourt, Inc. copyright © 1964, 1963 by T.S. Eliot, reprinted by permission of the publisher. **C317, C323:** "Snake", from *The Complete Poems of D.H. Lawrence* by D.H. Lawrence, edited by V. de Sola Pinto & F.W. Roberts, copyright © 1964, 1971 by Angelo Ravagli and C.M. Weekley, Executors of the Estate of Frieda Lawrence Ravagli. Used by permission of Viking Penguin, a division of Penguin Putnam Inc. **C320:** "She Tells Her Love While Half Asleep" from *Collected Poems,* by Robert Graves. © 1975 by Robert Graves. Reprinted by permission of Oxford University Press, Inc. and A.P. Watt Ltd., on behalf of the executors of the Estate of Robert Graves. **C322:** Excerpt from "Follower" from *Opened Ground: Selected Poems 1966–1996* by Seamus Heaney. Copyright © 1998 by Seamus Heaney. Reprinted by permission of Farrar, Straus and Giroux, LLC. **C333:** From *My Life with Martin Luther King, Jr.,* by Coretta Scott King, Henry Holt, 1993. **C356, C357:** "Grant and Lee: A Study in Contrasts," from *The American Story,* Earl Schneck Miers, editor. Reprinted by permission of the U.S. Capitol Historical Society. **C381:** Copyright © 1999 by the New York Times Co. Reprinted by permission. **C387:** Copyright 1977 by the National Wildlife Federation. Reprinted with permission from *National Wildlife* magazine's August/September 1977 issue. **C389:** Copyright 1977 by the National Wildlife Federation. Reprinted with permission from *National Wildlife* magazine's August/September 1977 issue. **C433:** Reprinted with the permission of Scribner, a division of Simon & Schuster, from *The Inn of Tranquility* by John Galsworthy. Copyright © 1912 by Charles Scribner's Sons, renewed 1940 by Ada Galsworthy. **C485:** "Assembling California" from *Annals of the Former World,* by John McPhee. Farrar, Straus and Giroux. **C493:** *Charles Babbage: Father of the Computer,* by Dan Halacy. Macmillan Publishing. **C497, C498:** From *In the Dark: A Primer for the Movies* by Richard Meran Barsam. **C501, C502:** From *National Parks* by Paul Jensen. **C517:** Copyright © 1999 by the New York Times Co. Reprinted by permission. **C581:** © 1999, The Washington Post Writers Group. Reprinted with permission. **C583:** By permission of the University of Maine. **C665:** Commencement Speech at Mount Holyoke College. © Anna Quindlen. **C701:** *Wired Style: Principles of English Usage in the Digital Age,* from the Editors of *Wired,* Edited by Constance Hale. **C720:** The *Chicago Tribune,* Section 1, Saturday, September 11, 1999. **C747:** Taken from *Eyewitness Books: Electricity* by Steve Parker. Copyright © 1992 Dorling Kindersley Limited. Reprinted by permission of Dorling Kindersley Publishing, Inc.

**Language**

**L153:** Reprinted by permission of the publishers and the Trustees of Amherst College from *The Poems of Emily Dickinson,* Ralph W. Franklin ed., Cambridge, Mass. The Belknap Press of Harvard University Press, copyright © 1998 by the President and Fellows of Harvard College. Copyright 1951, 1955, 1979 by the President and Fellows of Harvard College. **L214:** From *Green Eggs and Ham* by Dr. Seuss. TM and copyright © 1960 and renewed 1988 by Dr. Seuss Enterprises, L.P. Reprinted by permission of Random House, Inc. **L256:** By permission of J.P. Seaton. **L386:** © 1999, The Washington Post Writers Group. Reprinted with permission. **L392:** Reprinted by permission of the publishers and the Trustees of Amherst College from *The Poems of Emily Dickinson,* Ralph W. Franklin ed., Cambridge, Mass. The Belknap Press of Harvard University Press, copyright © 1998 by the President and Fellows of Harvard College. Copyright 1951, 1955, 1979 by the President and Fellows of Harvard College. **L392:** From *I Wouldn't Have Missed It: Selected Poems by Ogden Nash.* Copyright 1940 by Ogden Nash. First appeared in *Saturday Evening Post.* By permission of Little, Brown and Company, Inc. **L393:** By William Carlos Williams, from *Collected Poems: 1909-1939,* Volume I. Copyright © 1938 by New Directions Publishing Corp. Reprinted by permission of New Directions Publishing Corp. **L397:** From *The Poems of John Keats,* edited by Jack Stillinger. Copyright © 1978, 1982 by the President and Fellows of Harvard College. Reprinted by permission of The Belknap Press of Harvard University Press. **L397:** From *The Love Song of J. Alfred Prufrock,* by T.S. Eliot. From *Collected Poems 1909–1962,* by T.S. Eliot. © 1936, 1963, 1964 by Harcourt. **L398:** Reprinted by permission of the publishers and the

Trustees of Amherst College from *The Poems of Emily Dickinson,* Ralph W. Franklin ed., Cambridge, Mass. The Belknap Press of Harvard University Press, copyright © 1998 by the President and Fellows of Harvard College. Copyright 1951, 1955, 1979 by the President and Fellows of Harvard College. **L398:** From *Byron's Letters and Journals,* Volume V, edited by Leslie A. Marchand. Editorial matter copyright © 1976 by Leslie A. Marchand. Byron copyright material © 1976 by John Murray. Reprinted by permission of The Belknap Press of Harvard University Press. **L591:** "Introduction" from *Contemporary Heroes and Heroines* by Ray Brown. © 1990 Gale Research, Inc.

**PHOTO CREDITS**

Key: (t) top, (c) center, (b) bottom, (l) left, (r) right.

**Composition**

**C6:** © Marji McNeely/Stock Connection/PNI. **C26:** © Lindsay Hebberd/Corbis. **C91:** © Charles E. Burchfield Foundation, courtesy of Kennedy Galleries, NY. **C95, C98:** © Phillip Colla. **C171:** © Hulton-Deutsch Collection/Corbis. **C176: (t)** © Hulton Getty/Liason Agency; **(l)** Dana White/PhotoEdit/PNI. **C196:** © Mike Kelly. **C211:** © Latin Focus. **C246:** © Earl & Nazima Kowa/Corbis. **C333:** © Archive Photos/PictureQuest. **C338: (l)** © Bettmann/Corbis; **(r)** © Flip Schulke/Corbis. **C441: (l)** © Miro Vintoniv/PictureQuest; **(r)** © Tony Stone Images. **C481:** © Jim Zuckerman/Corbis. **C485:** © Phil Degginger/Bruce Coleman/PictureQuest. **C622: (t)** The Metropolitan Museum of Art. H.O. Havemeyer Collection. Bequest of Mrs. H.O. Havemeyer, 1929. 29.100.113. Photograph © 1996 The Metropolitan Museum of Art; **(c)** The Museum of Modern Art, New York. Mr. and Mrs. Donald B. Staus Fund. Photograph © 1996 The Museum of Modern Art, New York. © 2001 The Georgia O'Keeffe Foundation/Artists Rights Society (ARS), New York; **(b)** © 2000 Estate of Pablo Picasso/Artists Rights Society (ARS), New York. Photograph by Giraudon/Art Resource, New York. **C665:** Robin Platzer/Liason Agency. **C671:** Corbis.

**Language**

**L4, L50:** Courtesy of Ronald Feldman Fine Arts, New York. © 2001 Andy Warhol Foundation for the Visual Arts/ARS, New York. Photograph by D. James Dee. **L15:** Spencer Collection, The New York Public Library. Astor, Lenox and Tilden Foundations. **L20:** Noriyuki Yoshida/SuperStock. **L30:** © 1997 Artists Rights Society (ARS), New York/ADAGP, Paris. **L56, L90:** Courtesy of Linda Jones Enterprises. **L560:** Richard Hutchings/PhotoEdit. **L61:** Print Collection Miriam and Ira D. Wallach Division of Art, Prints and Photographs, New York Public Library, Astor, Lenox and Tilden Foundations. **L96, L132:** © Andy Goldsworthy. Photograph courtesy of the artist. **L122:** Billy R. Allen Folk Art Collection. African American Museum, Dallas, Texas. Gift of Mr. and Mrs. Robert Decherd. **L138, L174:** From *Why Mosquitoes Buzz in People's Ears* by Verna Aardema, pictures by Leo and Diane Dillon, pictures copyright © 1975 by Leo and Diane Dillon. Used by permission of Dial Books for Young Readers, a division of Penguin Putnam Inc. **L180, L228:** Musée d'Orsay, Paris/SuperStock. **L211:** Art Guys Worldwide Photos. **L234, L282:** © 1993 Vietnam Women's Memorial Project, Inc. Photo by Gregory Staley, courtesy of Goodacre Studio, Santa Fe. **L241:** Jeffrey Sylvester/FPG International. **L250:** AP/Wide World Photos. **L 278:** Vladimir Pcholkin/FPG International. **L288, L320:** Scala/Art Resource, NY. **L296:** © Sam Ogden. **L320:** Erich Lessing/Art Resource, NY. **L326, L348:** Private collection/SuperStock. **L332:** Bob Daemmrich/Stock Boston. **L332:** Bob Daemmrich/Stock Boston. **L338:** Artwork © Wang Shiqiang. Courtesy of Byron Preiss Visual Publications/New China Pictures. **L338:** Trustees, National Gallery, London. Photograph © SuperStock. **L373:** Steve Vidler/SuperStock. **L386:** Mitch Kezar/Tony Stone Images. **L416:** Courtesy of Barbara Baldwin's Antiques. **L426, L464:** Ägyptisches Museum und Papyrussammlung, © BPK, Berlin, 1998. Photo by M. Büsing. **L435:** Chris Salvo/FPG International. **L446:** G & V Chapman/The Image Bank. **L451:** © Bob Daemmrich. **L470, L536:** Christie's Images/SuperStock. © 2001 C. Herscovici, Brussels/Artists Rights Society (ARS), New York. **L500:** Barrett Kendall photo by Andrew Yates. **L521:** George Glod/SuperStock.

## Proofreading Symbols

| Symbol | Meaning | Example |
|---|---|---|
| ∧ | insert | We completed an journey. (went on, eventful) |
| ∧, | insert comma | Meg enjoys hiking, skiing and skating. |
| ⊙ | insert period | Gary took the bus to Atlanta |
| ℊ | delete | Refer back to your notes. |
| ¶ | new paragraph | ¶ Finally Balboa saw the Pacific. |
| no ¶ | no paragraph | no ¶ The dachsund trotted away. |
| . . . . | let it stand | I appreciated her sincere honesty. |
| # | add space | She will be allright in a moment. |
| ⁀‿ | close up | The airplane waited on the run way. |
| ∩∪ | transpose | They only have two dollars left. |
| ≡ | capital letter | We later moved to the south. |
| / | lowercase letter | His favorite subject was Science. |
| (sp) | spell out | I ate 2 oranges |
| " " | insert quotes | I hope you can join us, said my brother. |
| = | insert hyphen | I attended a school related event. |
| ' | insert apostrophe | The ravenous dog ate the cats food. |
| ○ | move copy | I usually on Fridays go to the movies. |